2020

3-2-1 CODE IT!

Michelle A. Green
MPS, RHIA, FAHIMA, CPC

CENGAGE

Australia • Brazil • Mexico • Singapore • United Kingdom • United States

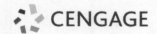

3-2-1 Code It!: 2020, 8th edition
Michelle A. Green

SVP, Higher Education & Skills Product:
Erin Joyner

Product Director: Matthew Seeley

Senior Product Manager: Stephen G. Smith

Product Assistant: Dallas Wilkes

Director, Learning Design: Rebecca von Gillern

Senior Manager, Learning Design:
Leigh Hefferon

Learning Designer: Kaitlin Schlicht

Marketing Director: Sean H. Chamberland

Marketing Manager: Jon athan Sheehan

Director, Content Creation: Juliet Steiner

Content Creation Manager: Stacey Lamodi

Senior Content Manager: Kara A. DiCaterino

Digital Delivery Lead: Lisa Christopher

Art Director: Angela Sheehan

Text Designer: Angela Sheehan

Cover Designer: Angela Sheehan

Cover and Interior Design Images:
© iStockPhoto.com/traffic_analyzer

The 2020 versions of CPT, HCPCS Level II, ICD-10-CM, and ICD-10-PCS were used in preparation of this product.

CPT publications are published by the American Medical Association and CPT is a registered trademark of the American medical Association. The American Medical Association is not affiliated with Cengage and has not sponsored, endorsed, or licensed this publication.

For product information and technology assistance, contact us at
Cengage Customer & Sales Support, 1-800-354-9706
or support.cengage.com.

For permission to use material from this text or product, submit all requests online at **www.cengage.com/permissions.**

Library of Congress Control Number: 2019919724

ISBN: 978-0-357-36264-8

Cengage
200 Pier 4 Boulevard
Boston, MA 02210
USA

Cengage is a leading provider of customized learning solutions with employees residing in nearly 40 different countries and sales in more than 125 countries around the world. Find your local representative at **www.cengage.com.**

Cengage products are represented in Canada by Nelson Education, Ltd.

To learn more about Cengage platforms and services, register or access your online learning solution, or purchase materials for your course, visit **www.cengage.com.**

Notice to the Reader

Publisher does not warrant or guarantee any of the products described herein or perform any independent analysis in connection with any of the product information contained herein. Publisher does not assume, and expressly disclaims, any obligation to obtain and include information other than that provided to it by the manufacturer. The reader is expressly warned to consider and adopt all safety precautions that might be indicated by the activities described herein and to avoid all potential hazards. By following the instructions contained herein, the reader willingly assumes all risks in connection with such instructions. The publisher makes no representations or warranties of any kind, including but not limited to, the warranties of fitness for particular purpose or merchantability, nor are any such representations implied with respect to the material set forth herein, and the publisher takes no responsibility with respect to such material. The publisher shall not be liable for any special, consequential, or exemplary damages resulting, in whole or part, from the readers' use of, or reliance upon, this material.

Printed at CLDPC, USA, 12-19

TABLE OF CONTENTS

List of Tables viii
Preface ix
About the Author xvii
Reviewers xviii
Acknowledgments xix
How to Use This Text xx

Part I: Coding Overview 1

Chapter 1: Overview of Coding 2
Career as a Coder 4
   Training .4
   Credentials 5
   Employment Opportunities 6
   Other Professions Related to
   Coding .6
Professional Associations 7
Coding Systems and Coding
Processes 8
   Coding Systems 9
   Medical Coding Process 11
   Computer-Assisted Coding 19
Other Classification Systems,
Databases, and Nomenclatures . .21
   Alternative Billing Codes (ABC
   Codes) .22
   Clinical Care Classification (CCC)
   System .22
   Current Dental Terminology (CDT) .22
   Diagnostic and Statistical Manual of
   Mental Disorders (DSM) 23
   Health Insurance Prospective
   Payment System
   (HIPPS) Rate Codes 23
   International Classification of
   Diseases for Oncology,
   Third Edition (ICD-O-3) 24
   International Classification of
   Functioning,
   Disability and Health (ICF) 27
   Logical Observation Identifiers
   Names and Codes (LOINC) 27
   National Drug Codes (NDC) 27
   RxNorm .27
   Systematized Nomenclature of
   Medicine Clinical Terms (SNOMED
   CT) 28
   Unified Medical Language System
   (UMLS) .29
Documentation as Basis for
Coding 30
   Medical Necessity 31
   Patient Record Formats 31
Health Data Collection 33

Reporting Hospital Data 34
Reporting Physician Office Data . . .34

Part II: ICD-10-CM and ICD-10-PCS Coding Systems 43

Chapter 2: Introduction to ICD-10-CM and ICD-10-PCS Coding 44
Overview of ICD-10-CM and ICD-10-
PCS 45
   ICD-10-CM and ICD-10-PCS (ICD-10-
   CM/PCS) 46
   Coding Manuals, Encoders, and
   Computer-Assisted Coding 47
   Format and Structure of
   ICD-10-CM 48
   Updating ICD-10-CM and ICD-10-
   PCS 48
   Mandatory Reporting of ICD-10-CM
   Codes .51
ICD-10-CM Index to Diseases and
Injuries .53
   Main Terms, Subterms, and
   Qualifiers 55
   Basic Steps for Using the
   ICD-10-CM Index to Diseases
   and Injuries 56
ICD-10-CM Tabular List of Diseases
and Injuries 58
ICD-10-CM Official Guidelines for
Coding and Reporting 60
   General ICD-10-CM Diagnosis
   Coding Guidelines 62
ICD-10-PCS Index and Tables 72
   Development of ICD-10-PCS 72
   Structure of ICD-10-PCS Codes . .73
   Format of ICD-10-PCS Coding
   Manual .74
   Build-a-Code Using ICD-10-PCS . .75
ICD-9-CM Legacy Coding
System 77
   General Equivalence Mappings
   (GEMs) .77

Chapter 3: ICD-10-CM and ICD-10-PCS Coding Conventions 84
Format and Typeface 85
Eponyms 87
Abbreviations 88
Punctuation 89
Boxed Notes 90
Tables 91
Includes Notes 93

Excludes1 and Excludes2
Notes 94
Inclusion Terms 95
Other, Other Specified, and
Unspecified Codes 97
Etiology and Manifestation
Rules 97
And 99
Due To 100
In 101
With 102
Cross-References 103
Code Assignment and Clinical
Criteria 104

Chapter 4: Chapter-Specific Coding Guidelines: ICD-10-CM Chapters 1–10 113
ICD-10-CM Chapter-Specific
Diagnosis Coding Guidelines . . .115
ICD-10-CM Chapter 1: Certain
Infectious and Parasitic
Diseases (A00–B99) 116
ICD-10-CM Chapter 2:
Neoplasms (C00–D49) 125
   Primary and Secondary
   Malignancies 127
   Anatomical Site Is Not
   Documented 128
   Inoperable Primary Site with
   Metastasis 129
   Reexcision of Tumors 129
   Morphology of Neoplasms 129
ICD-10-CM Chapter 3: Diseases
of the Blood and Blood-Forming
Organs and Certain Disorders
Involving the Immune Mechanism
(D50–D89) 135
ICD-10-CM Chapter 4: Endocrine,
Nutritional, and Metabolic Diseases
(E00–E89) 137
ICD-10-CM Chapter 5:
Mental, Behavioral, and
Neurodevelopmental Disorders
(F01–F99) 140
ICD-10-CM Chapter 6: Diseases of
the Nervous System
(G00–G99) 142
ICD-10-CM Chapter 7: Diseases of
the Eye and Adnexa (H00–H59) . .144
ICD-10-CM Chapter 8: Diseases of
the Ear and Mastoid Process
(H60–H95) 146
ICD-10-CM Chapter 9: Diseases of
the Circulatory System
(I00–I99) 147

ICD-10-CM Chapter 10: Diseases of the Respiratory System (J00–J99)...................151

Chapter 5: Chapter-Specific Coding Guidelines: ICD-10-CM Chapters 11–21   156

ICD-10-CM Chapter 11: Diseases of the Digestive System (K00–K95)...................157

ICD-10-CM Chapter 12: Diseases of the Skin and Subcutaneous Tissue (L00–L99)...................158

ICD-10-CM Chapter 13: Diseases of the Musculoskeletal System and Connective Tissue (M00–M99)..161

ICD-10-CM Chapter 14: Diseases of the Genitourinary System (N00–N99)...................163

ICD-10-CM Chapter 15: Pregnancy, Childbirth, and the Puerperium (O00–O9A)...................164

Obstetrical Discharges.........165

ICD-10-CM Chapter 16: Certain Conditions Originating in the Perinatal Period (P00–P96).....171

ICD-10-CM Chapter 17: Congenital Malformations, Deformations, and Chromosomal Abnormalities (Q00–Q99)...................174

ICD-10-CM Chapter 18: Symptoms, Signs, and Abnormal Clinical and Laboratory Findings, Not Elsewhere Classified (R00–R99).........175

ICD-10-CM Chapter 19: Injury, Poisoning, and Certain Other Consequences of External Causes (S00–T88)...................178

Fractures.....................178

Burns.......................179

Adverse Effects, Poisonings, Underdosings, and Toxic Effects.....................179

Chapter 20: External Causes of Morbidity (V00–Y99)..........189

Chapter 21: Factors Influencing Health Status and Contact with Health Services (Z00–Z99).....194

Reporting Z Codes............194

Chapter 6: ICD-10-CM and ICD-10-PCS Hospital Inpatient Coding   209

Acute Care Facilities (Hospitals)..................210

Inpatient Diagnosis Coding Guidelines....................213

Admitting Diagnosis............213

Principal Diagnosis............213

Other (Additional) Diagnoses with Documentation That Supports Reporting....................219

Inpatient Procedure Coding Guidelines................. 222

Principal Procedure and Significant Other Procedures............222

ICD-10-PCS Procedure Coding. 224

ICD-10-PCS Index..............224

ICD-10-PCS Tables.............226

Structure of ICD-10-PCS Codes..229

ICD-10-PCS Values.............229

ICD-10-PCS Coding Conventions..................230

Medical and Surgical Section Coding Guidelines............231

Obstetrics Section Coding Guidelines..................244

Placement Section............245

Administration Section.........245

Measurement and Monitoring Section....................246

Extracorporeal or Systemic Assistance and Performance Section....................246

Extracorporeal or Systemic Therapies Section...........246

Osteopathic Section..........246

Other Procedures Section.......246

Chiropractic Section..........247

Imaging Section...............247

Nuclear Medicine Section......247

Radiation Therapy Section......247

Physical Rehabilitation and Diagnostic Audiology Section...248

Mental Health Section.........248

Substance Abuse Treatment Section....................249

New Technology...............249

Coding Inpatient Diagnoses and Procedures..............251

Chapter 7: ICD-10-CM Outpatient and Physician Office Coding   265

Outpatient Care............. 266

Primary Care Services.........267

Hospital Outpatient Services.....267

Outpatient Diagnostic Coding and Reporting Guidelines.....272

Selection of First-Listed Condition..................272

Codes from A00.0 Through T88.9, Z00–Z99..................273

Accurate Reporting of ICD-10-CM Diagnosis Codes.............273

Codes That Describe Signs and Symptoms..................273

Encounters for Circumstances Other Than a Disease or Injury.......273

Level of Detail in Coding........273

ICD-10-CM Code for the Diagnosis, Condition, Problem, or Other Reason for Encounter/Visit.....................274

Uncertain Diagnoses..........274

Chronic Diseases.............275

Code All Documented Conditions That Coexist................275

Patients Receiving Diagnostic Services Only.................276

Patients Receiving Therapeutic Services Only................276

Patients Receiving Preoperative Evaluations Only............276

Ambulatory Surgery (or Outpatient Surgery)....................277

Routine Outpatient Prenatal Visits 277

Encounters for General Medical Examinations with Abnormal Findings.......277

Encounters for Routine Health Screenings..................277

Part III: Health Care Procedure Coding System (HCPCS) Level II Coding System   293

Chapter 8: HCPCS Level II Coding System   294

Overview of HCPCS.......... 295

HCPCS Level I................295

HCPCS Level II................295

HCPCS Level II Codes......... 296

Responsibility for HCPCS Level II Codes....................297

Types of HCPCS Level II Codes ..297

General Guidelines for Modifier Use.....................300

Modifiers Added to Surgical Procedures.................302

Modifiers Added to Radiology Services.................303

Reporting HCPCS Level II Modifiers.................303

Assigning HCPCS Level II Codes...................... 305

HCPCS Level II Index..........306

HCPCS Level II Code Sections...307

Determining Payer Responsibility...............312

Patient Record Documentation..313

Part IV: Current Procedural Terminology (CPT) Coding System   323

Chapter 9: Introduction to CPT Coding   324

History of CPT.............. 325

Overview of CPT............. 326

CPT Categories...............327

Organization of CPT......... 328

CPT Category I Codes.........328

CPT Category II Codes.........329

CPT Category III Codes.........329

CPT Code Number Format......330

CPT Index................. 330

Boldfaced Type 331
Italicized Type. 331
Cross-Reference Term. 332
Single Codes and Code Ranges . .332
Inferred Words 332
CPT Appendices **333**
CPT Symbols. **334**
**CPT Sections, Subsections,
Categories, and Subcategories** .**337**
CPT Guidelines 339
Notes 339
Descriptive Qualifiers. 340
CPT Modifiers **341**
**National Correct Coding
Initiative (NCCI).** **351**
Unbundling CPT Codes 353

**Chapter 10: CPT Evaluation
and Management   360**
**Overview of Evaluation and
Management Section** **361**
Place of Service (POS). 362
Type of Service (TOS) 362
**Evaluation and Management
Section Guidelines** **364**
Classification of E/M Services. . . .364
Definitions of Commonly Used
Terms. .365
Unlisted Service 367
Special Report 367
Clinical Examples. 367
**Evaluation and Management
Levels of Service.** **368**
Key Components 369
Contributory Components 377
**Evaluation and Management
Categories and Subcategories** **382**
Office or Other Outpatient
Services 382
Hospital Observation Services . . .384
Hospital Inpatient Services 387
Consultations 390
Emergency Department
Services. 393
Critical Care Services 395
Nursing Facility Services 397
Domiciliary, Rest Home (e.g.,
Boarding Home), or Custodial
Care Services 399
Domiciliary, Rest Home (e.g.,
Assisted Living Facility), or Home
Care Plan Oversight Services. . .399
Home Services 399
Prolonged Services 400
Case Management Services 403
Care Plan Oversight Services 403
Preventive Medicine Services 403
Non-Face-to-Face Services 404
Special Evaluation and Management
Services. 405
Newborn Care Services. 405
Delivery/Birthing Room Attendance
and Resuscitation Services 405

Inpatient Neonatal Intensive Care
Services and Pediatric and Neonatal
Critical Care Services 405
Cognitive Assessment and
Care Plan Services 406
Care Management Services 406
Psychiatric Collaborative Care
Management Services 407
Transitional Care Management
Services. 407
Advance Care Planning 407
General Behavioral Health Integration
Care Management. 408
Other Evaluation and Management
Services. 408

Chapter 11: CPT Anesthesia 418
Anesthesia Terminology **419**
Types of Anesthesia. 419
**Overview of Anesthesia
Section** **422**
Monitored Anesthesia Care
(MAC) 423
**Anesthesia Section
Guidelines** **425**
Reporting Codes for Monitoring or
Providing Other Services 427
Intra-Arterial Lines 429
Drug Administration Codes 430
Anesthesia Modifiers 430
Time Reporting. 432
Anesthesia Services 435
Supplied Materials 436
Separate or Multiple Procedures. .436
Unlisted Service or Procedure. . . .436
Special Report 436
Qualifying Circumstances 436
Anesthesia Subsections **439**
Head. 439
Neck 440
Thorax (Chest Wall and Shoulder
Girdle) .440
Intrathoracic 441
Spine and Spinal Cord. 441
Upper Abdomen. 441
Lower Abdomen. 443
Perineum 444
Pelvis (Except Hip) 444
Upper Leg (Except Knee). 444
Knee and Popliteal Area 445
Lower Leg (Below Knee, Includes
Ankle and Foot) 445
Shoulder and Axilla 445
Upper Arm and Elbow 445
Forearm, Wrist, and Hand 445
Radiological Procedures 446
Burn Excisions or Debridement. . .447
Obstetric. 447
Other Procedures. 447

Chapter 12: CPT Surgery I   457
Overview of Surgery Section . . **458**
Organization of Surgery Section . .460
Surgery Guidelines **463**

Services .463
CPT Surgical Package Definition. .464
Follow-Up Care for Diagnostic
Procedures 467
Follow-Up Care for Therapeutic
Surgical Procedures 468
Supplied Materials 468
Reporting More Than One
Procedure/Service 468
Separate Procedure. 469
Unlisted Service or Procedure. . . .470
Special Report 470
Imaging Guidance 470
Surgical Destruction 470
General Subsection **472**
**Integumentary System
Subsection** **472**
Skin, Subcutaneous and Accessory
Structures 473
Nails 478
Pilonidal Cyst 479
Introduction 480
Repair (Closure) 481
Destruction. 490
Breast. 492

Chapter 13: CPT Surgery II   501
**Musculoskeletal System
Subsection** **502**
Musculoskeletal System Notes . . .503
General. .507
Head. 511
Neck (Soft Tissues) and Thorax . .513
Back and Flank 514
Spine (Vertebral Column). 515
Abdomen. 520
Shoulder. 520
Humerus (Upper Arm) and Elbow .521
Forearm and Wrist 521
Hand and Fingers. 521
Pelvis and Hip Joint 522
Femur (Thigh Region) and Knee
Joint 522
Leg (Tibia and Fibula) and Ankle
Joint. 524
Foot and Toes 524
Application of Casts and
Strapping. 525
Endoscopy/Arthroscopy 526
**Respiratory System
Subsection** **528**
Nose. 529
Accessory Sinuses 532
Larynx. 534
Trachea and Bronchi 536
Lungs and Pleura 539

Chapter 14: CPT Surgery III 548
**Cardiovascular System
Subsection** **549**
Cardiovascular System Notes 550
Heart and Pericardium. 554
Arteries and Veins 569

Hemic and Lymphatic Systems Subsection **582**
Spleen .583
General. 584
Transplantation and Post-Transplantation Cellular Infusions 585
Lymph Nodes and Lymphatic Channels 585

Chapter 15: CPT Surgery IV   593

Mediastinum and Diaphragm Subsection **594**

Digestive System Subsection . . **596**
Lips. 598
Vestibule of Mouth 600
Tongue and Floor of Mouth 600
Dentoalveolar Structures. 600
Palate and Uvula 600
Salivary Gland and Ducts 601
Pharynx, Adenoids, and Tonsils . .602
Esophagus 603
Stomach .607
Intestines (Except Rectum) 609
Meckel's Diverticulum and the Mesentery 612
Appendix 613
Colon and Rectum 613
Anus 615
Liver 617
Biliary Tract 617
Pancreas 618
Abdomen, Peritoneum, and Omentum 619

Urinary System Subsection **621**
Kidney 623
Ureter 625
Bladder .626
Urethra .630

Chapter 16: CPT Surgery V   639

Male Genital System Subsection **641**

Reproductive System Procedures Subsection **645**

Intersex Surgery Subsection **645**

Female Genital System Subsection **646**

Maternity Care and Delivery Subsection **652**
Antepartum Services 652
Delivery Services 653
Postpartum Care 655
Delivery After Previous Cesarean Delivery 655
Abortion .656

Endocrine System Subsection . **656**
Thyroid Gland 657
Parathyroid, Thymus, Adrenal Glands, Pancreas, and Carotid Body 657

Nervous System Subsection . . . **658**
Skull, Meninges, and Brain 659

Spine and Spinal Cord 662
Endoscopic Decompression of Neural Elements and/or Excision of Herniated Intervertebral Discs . .664
Extracranial Nerves, Peripheral Nerves, and Autonomic Nervous System 668

Eye and Ocular Adnexa Subsection **671**
Eyeball .672
Anterior Segment 673
Posterior Segment 674
Ocular Adnexa 675
Conjunctiva 675

Auditory System Subsection . . .**677**
External Ear 678
Middle Ear 679
Inner Ear 679
Temporal Bone, Middle Fossa Approach 679

Operating Microscope Subsection **680**

Chapter 17: CPT Radiology   693

Radiology Terminology **694**
Planes of View 695
Positioning and Radiographic Projection 696
Radiology Procedures 696

Overview of Radiology Section . **698**
Professional Versus Technical Components 698
Use of Modifiers with Radiology Codes 700
Complete Procedure 700
Evaluation and Management (E/M) Services 701

Radiology Section Guidelines . . .**702**
Subject Listings 702
Separate Procedures 702
Unlisted Procedures 702
Special Report 702
Supervision and Interpretation, Imaging Guidance 702
Administration of Contrast Material(s) 703
Written Report 704

Radiology Subsections **705**
Diagnostic Radiology (Diagnostic Imaging). 705
Diagnostic Ultrasound 713
Radiologic Guidance 716
Breast, Mammography 717
Bone/Joint Studies 718
Radiation Oncology 719
Nuclear Medicine 727

Chapter 18: CPT Pathology and Laboratory   737

Overview of Pathology and Laboratory Section **738**
Specimens 739
Professional and Technical Components 739

Pathology and Laboratory Section Tables .741

Pathology and Laboratory Section Guidelines **742**
Services in Pathology and Laboratory 742
Separate or Multiple Procedures. . 742
Unlisted Service or Procedure. . . .743
Special Report 743
Modifier -51 and Modifier -91 743

Pathology and Laboratory Subsections **744**
Organ or Disease-Oriented Panels 744
Drug Assay and Therapeutic Drug Assays 745
Evocative/Suppression Testing . . .746
Consultations (Clinical Pathology). 746
Urinalysis 747
Molecular Pathology 748
Genomic Sequencing Procedures and Other Molecular Multianalyte Assays 748
Multianalyte Assays with Algorithmic Analyses. 749
Chemistry. 749
Hematology and Coagulation 749
Immunology 751
Transfusion Medicine 752
Microbiology 752
Anatomic Pathology 753
Cytopathology 753
Cytogenetic Studies 754
Surgical Pathology 755
In Vivo (e.g., Transcutaneous) Laboratory Procedures 756
Other Procedures. 757
Reproductive Medicine Procedures 757
Proprietary Laboratory Analyses. .758

Chapter 19: CPT Medicine   765

Overview of Medicine Section . .**766**

Medicine Section Guidelines . . .**766**
Add-On Codes 767
Separate Procedures 767
Unlisted Service or Procedure. . . .767
Special Report 767
Imaging Guidance 768
Supplied Materials 768

Medicine Subsections **768**
Immune Globulins, Serum or Recombinant Products 769
Immunization Administration for Vaccines/Toxoids 770
Vaccines, Toxoids 770
Psychiatry. 771
Biofeedback 773
Dialysis .773
Gastroenterology 776
Ophthalmology. 777
Special Otorhinolaryngologic Services. 778
Cardiovascular 779

Noninvasive Vascular Diagnostic
  Studies. .785
Pulmonary 786
Allergy and Clinical Immunology . .786
Endocrinology 787
Neurology and Neuromuscular
  Procedures 788
Medical Genetics and Genetic
  Counseling Services 791
Central Nervous System
  Assessments/Tests (e.g.,
  Neuro-Cognitive, Mental Status,
  Speech Testing). 791
Health Behavior Assessment and
  Intervention 792
Hydration, Therapeutic, Prophylactic,
  Diagnostic Injections and
  Infusions, and Chemotherapy and
  Other Highly Complex Drug or
  Highly Complex Biologic Agent
  Administration 792
Photodynamic Therapy 795
Special Dermatological
  Procedures 796
Physical Medicine and
  Rehabilitation. 796
Medical Nutrition Therapy 796
Acupuncture. 797
Osteopathic Manipulative
  Treatment. 797
Chiropractic Manipulative
  Treatment. 797

Education and Training for Patient
  Self-Management 798
Non-Face-to-Face Nonphysician
  Services. 798
Special Services, Procedures, and
  Reports .798
Qualifying Circumstances for
  Anesthesia. 799
Moderate (Conscious) Sedation . .799
Other Services and Procedures . .800
Home Health Procedures/
  Services. 800
Medication Therapy Management
  Services. 800

Part V: Insurance and Reimbursement Overview   807

Chapter 20: Insurance and Reimbursement   808

Third-Party Payers 811
  Health Insurance Marketplace. . . .815
  Types of Third-Party Payers 817
Health Care Reimbursement
Systems. 823
  Prospective Payment Systems, Fee
  Schedules, and Exclusions. 823

Case-Mix Analysis, Severity of Illness
  (SI), and Intensity of Services
  (IS) Systems. 837
Physician Documentation for Medical
  Necessity of Medicare Part A
  Hospital Inpatient Admissions . .839
Critical Pathways 840
Revenue Cycle Management. 840
Impact of HIPAA on
Reimbursement. 846
  Health Care Access, Portability, and
  Renewability 846
  Preventing Health Care Fraud and
  Abuse. 846
  Administrative Simplification 855
  Privacy and Security Rules 860
  Medical Liability Reform 861

Appendix I: E/M CodeBuilder   867
Bibliography   872
Glossary   873
Index   894

LIST OF TABLES

Table 1-1 Professional Associations

Table 1-2 Internet-Based Discussion Boards (Listservs)

Table 2-1 ICD-10-CM Index to Diseases and Injuries

Table 2-2 ICD-10-CM Tabular List of Diseases and Injuries

Table 2-3 Value Assigned to Each Character in a 7-Character ICD-10-PCS Code

Table 4-1 Portion of Chapter-Specific Coding Guidelines Table of Contents from *ICD-10-CM Official Guidelines for Coding and Reporting*

Table 4-2 Organisms

Table 6-1 Medical and Surgical Section Root Operations and Definitions

Table 7-1 Medical Specialties

Table 7-2 Freestanding, Hospital-Based, and Hospital-Owned Ambulatory Facilities

Table 8-1 Categories of HCPCS Level II Temporary Codes

Table 9-1 CPT Modifiers in a Quick View Format

Table 9-2 Organization of CPT Modifiers According to Reporting Similarity

Table 9-3 Partial Listing of National Correct Coding Initiative (NCCI) Edits

Table 10-1 History Elements, Definitions, and Examples

Table 10-2 Physical Examination Elements and Examples

Table 10-3 Complexity of Medical Decision Making

Table 10-4 Critical Care Services: Total Duration of Critical Care and Codes

Table 10-5 Prolonged Services Without Direct Patient Contact: Total Duration of Services and Codes

Table 10-6 Psychiatric Collaborative Care Management Services: Total Duration of Care and Codes

Table 11-1 Sample Portion of Anesthesia Base Unit Values

Table 11-2 Sample Portion of Modifying Units and Relative Values

Table 11-3 Sample Portion of Locality-Specific Anesthesia Conversion Factors

Table 11-4 Sample Coding Rules Associated with Head Subsection Anesthesia Codes

Table 11-5 Sample Coding Rules Associated with Neck Subsection Anesthesia Codes

Table 11-6 Sample Coding Rules Associated with Thorax (Chest Wall and Shoulder Girdle) Subsection Anesthesia Codes

Table 11-7 Sample Coding Rules Associated with Intrathoracic Subsection Anesthesia Codes

Table 11-8 Sample Coding Rules Associated with Spine and Spinal Cord Subsection Anesthesia Codes

Table 11-9 Sample Coding Rules Associated with Upper Abdomen Subsection Anesthesia Codes

Table 11-10 Sample Coding Rules Associated with Lower Abdomen Subsection Anesthesia Codes

Table 11-11 Sample Coding Rules Associated with Perineum Subsection Anesthesia Codes

Table 11-12 Sample Coding Rules Associated with Radiological Procedures Subsection Anesthesia Codes

Table 11-13 Sample Coding Rule Associated with Burn Excisions or Debridement Subsection Anesthesia Codes

Table 11-14 Sample Coding Rule Associated with Obstetric Subsection Anesthesia Codes

Table 11-15 Sample Coding Rules Associated with Other Procedures Subsection Anesthesia Codes

Table 12-1 Subheadings Typically Organized Below CPT Surgery Subsections

Table 12-2 Integumentary Procedures and Definitions

Table 12-3 Medical Terms for Adjacent Tissue Transfer/Rearrangement, Flap, and Graft Procedures

Table 12-4 Adjacent Tissue Transfer or Tissue Rearrangement Methods and Definitions

Table 12-5 Types of Codes for Tissue Rearrangement, Free Skin Grafts, and Flaps

Table 13-1 Types of Fractures, Joint Injuries, and Fracture Treatment

Table 14-1 Coding Central Venous Access Catheters and Devices

Table 17-1 Type of Radiologic Guidance and the Purpose of Each

Table 19-1 Gastroenterology Procedures and Services

Table 20-1 Claims and Coding Systems According to Type of Health Care Setting

Table 20-2 Prospective Payment Systems and Fee Schedules, Year Implemented, and Prospective Rate Type

Table 20-3 Sample Hospice Payment System Rates

Table 20-4 National Correct Coding Initiative (NCCI) Terms and Definitions

Introduction

Accurate coding is crucial to the successful operation of any health care facility or provider's office because reported codes determine the amount of reimbursement received. The annual (and sometimes more frequent) revision of coding guidelines and payer requirements serve to challenge coders. Those responsible for assigning and reporting codes in any health care setting require thorough instruction in the use of the ICD-10-CM, ICD-10-PCS, CPT, and HCPCS level II coding systems. Students who are completing formal coursework as part of an academic program and experienced coders who are already employed in the health care field will find that *3-2-1 Code It!* provides the required information in a clear and comprehensive manner.

Due to the comprehensive nature of the *3-2-1 Code It!* textbook, instructors may choose to cover its content in more than one course.

- Chapters 1 through 7 could be taught in an ICD-10-CM and ICD-10-PCS coding course.
- Chapters 8 through 19 could be taught in a CPT and HCPCS level II coding course.
- Chapter 20 could be included as required reading in an insurance and reimbursement course, either as an introductory or summary chapter.

Instructors for medical assistant (MA) and medical office administration (MOA) programs may choose to cover the following chapters only in their coding course(s):

- Chapters 2 through 5, and 8 in an ICD-10-CM, and HCPCS level II coding course (ICD-10-PCS is not used for outpatient or physician office coding.)
- Chapters 9 through 10, selected sections of 12 through 16, and 17 through 19 in a CPT coding course

 NOTE:

Your academic program's community of interest (e.g., employers of graduates) will determine which sections of Chapters 12 through 16 (CPT Surgery) should be covered in your CPT coding course. Likewise, if your graduates obtain employment assigning and submitting CPT Anesthesia codes, your course should include Chapter 11. If your graduates do not assign radiology or pathology/laboratory codes during their employment, Chapters 17 and 18 can be excluded from your CPT coding course.

Instructors can refer to the Instructor's Manual for sample course syllabi that organize textbook content into one or two courses. For example, the syllabus for a one-semester course includes content from *3-2-1 Code It!* appropriate for an introductory course.

The *3-2-1 Code It!* text requires users to have access to paper-based coding manuals (ICD-10-CM, ICD-10-PCS, HCPCS level II, and CPT) because they are used as references when coding rules are explained and for completing exercises and reviews in each chapter.

 NOTE:

Dental codes (D codes) are copyrighted by the American Dental Association. Purchase of a separate Current Dental Terminology (CDT) coding manual is required to assign dental codes.

The intended use of *3-2-1 Code It!* is for:

- Academic programs in coding and reimbursement, health information management, medical assisting, medical office administration, and so on

- In-service education programs in health care facilities (e.g., physicians' offices, hospitals, nursing facilities, home health agencies, hospices), health insurance companies, quality improvement organizations, and so on
- Individuals who want to use it for self-instruction to learn how to code or to update their coding skills
- Health care professionals who need a comprehensive coding reference to assist them in accurately assigning codes

It is recommended that students complete the following course work before they begin and/or during the same time they are learning concepts presented in *3-2-1 Code It!*:

- Essentials of health information management
- Medical terminology
- Anatomy and physiology
- Essentials of pharmacology
- Human diseases/pathophysiology

The text was designed and revised to support core learning objectives for the medical coder. Chapter objectives, content, and assessments are all aligned to ensure students learn and practice the concepts and skills they'll need on the job. Student learning is supported through chapter outlines and measurable objectives identified at the beginning of each chapter, as well as chapter headings and assessments that map to those chapter outlines and objectives.

Special attention was focused on selecting appropriate Bloom's taxonomy levels for each chapter along with mapping assessment items (e.g., exercises, exam questions) to each objective. In addition, the *Workbook to Accompany 3-2-1 Code It!* contains assignments that map to higher Bloom's taxonomy levels to provide students with more advanced activity-based learning experiences such as computer-assisted coding analysis, assignment of APCs and DRGs, and assigning codes to actual patient records.

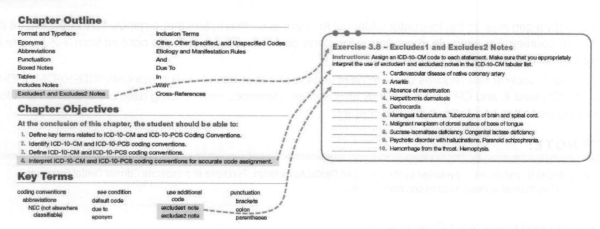

Organization of This Textbook

This textbook is organized into 20 chapters and one appendix.

NOTE:

Content about long-term care, home health care, and hospice coding is located at the textbook's Student Companion Site at http://login.cengage.com.

- Chapter 1 includes an overview of coding systems used to report inpatient and outpatient diagnoses and procedures and services to health plans. It also focuses on coding career opportunities in health care, the importance of joining professional organizations and obtaining coding credentials, the impact of networking with other coding professionals, and the development of opportunities for career advancement. Computer-assisted coding (CAC) is also covered.

  ○ The *Workbook to Accompany 3-2-1 Code It!* Chapter 1 contains high level Bloom's taxonomy assignments about validating ICD-10-CM/PCS codes, computer-assisted coding, face validity of data management reports, physician query process, determining medical necessity, and SNOMED CT.

- Chapters 2 and 3 cover general ICD-10-CM/PCS coding concepts, an overview about coding guidelines, including ICD-10-CM general coding guidelines, and provide coding practice. Chapters 4 and 5 cover ICD-10-CM chapter-specific coding guidelines and provide coding practice.

  ○ The *Workbook to Accompany 3-2-1 Code It!* Chapters 2 through 5 contain high level Bloom's taxonomy assignments about the ICD-10-CM index and tabular list, ICD-10-CM official guidelines for coding and reporting, ICD-10-PCS index and tables, ICD-10-CM/PCS coding conventions, and general equivalence mappings (GEMs), ICD-10-CM and ICD-10-PCS coding conventions, and ICD-10-CM disease coding.

- Chapter 6 is specific to inpatient coding concepts (and not typically covered by academic programs that focus on outpatient and physician coding), and Chapter 7 is specific to outpatient coding concepts. Inpatient coding concepts apply to acute care hospitals, and the chapters include ICD-10-CM and ICD-10-PCS official coding guidelines. Outpatient coding concepts covered include the physicians' office, and hospital emergency and outpatient departments. ICD-10-CM/PCS chapters are sequenced before HCPCS level II and CPT chapters in this textbook because diagnosis codes are reported to justify the medical necessity of procedures and/or services provided.

  ○ The *Workbook to Accompany 3-2-1 Code It!* contains high level Bloom's taxonomy assignments about the hospital inpatient physician query process, ICD-10-PCS procedure coding, selecting/coding principal and other (additional) diagnoses and procedures, and hospital inpatient cases for coding practice.

- Chapter 8 covers the HCPCS level II national coding system, which was developed by the Centers for Medicare & Medicaid Services.

  ○ The *Workbook to Accompany 3-2-1 Code It!* contains high level Bloom's taxonomy assignments about using the HPCS level II index, assigning modifiers, assigning codes, and additional coding practice.

- Chapters 9 through 19 cover CPT coding concepts. Each CPT section has its own chapter, except for the Surgery section, which requires five separate chapters.

  ○ The *Workbook to Accompany 3-2-1 Code It!* contains high level Bloom's taxonomy assignments about the CPT index, appendices, symbols, modifiers, E/M levels of service, assigning E/M codes, determining anesthesia service payments, anesthesia modifiers, assigning anesthesia codes, coding from operative reports, coding from radiology reports, coding from pathology and laboratory reports, coding from medicine reports. All of the related workbook chapters contain a significant number of coding practice assignments.

- Chapter 20 contains a detailed discussion of insurance and reimbursement concepts. (For comprehensive coverage of third-party payers and reimbursement methodologies, refer to Cengage's *Understanding Health Insurance: A Guide to Billing and Reimbursement*, by Michelle A. Green.)

  ○ The *Workbook to Accompany 3-2-1 Code It!* contains high level Bloom's taxonomy assignments about the chargemaster review process, interpreting a remittance advice, interpreting a Medicare fee-for-service payment error report, ambulatory payment classifications, interpreting diagnosis-related groups decision trees, and assigning diagnosis-related groups.

- Appendix I contains the E/M CodeBuilder, which can also be downloaded from the Student Companion Site at **http://login.cengage.com** and printed for use with Chapter 10 cases to select evaluation and management (E/M) service codes.

Features of the Textbook

Each textbook chapter contains the following elements:

- List of chapter headings
- Chapter learning objectives
- Key terms
- Introduction
- Exercises
- Internet links
- Summary
- Review

Textbook features include:

- Learning objectives and key terms located at the beginning of each chapter to help organize the material
- Boldfaced terms throughout each chapter to assist students in learning the technical vocabulary associated with coding systems
- Coding tips and notes that highlight important concepts presented in each chapter
- Exercises after each chapter section that reinforce content presented
- Multiple choice and coding practice reviews that allow for mastery of coding concepts

New to This Edition

- Chapter 4 was split into two new chapters to better organize the ICD-10-CM chapter-specific coding guidelines, and content about ICD-10-CM official guidelines for coding and reporting, including general coding guidelines, was relocated to Chapter 2.

- Chapters 5 through 19 were renumbered as chapters 6 through 20 (because Chapter 5 is now entitled ICD-10-CM Chapter-Specific Coding Guidelines: ICD-10-CM Chapters 11–21).

- The textbook and its ancillaries have been updated to include the latest ICD-10-CM, ICD-10-PCS, CPT, and HCPCS level II code sets, conventions, and guidelines.

- Textbook and workbook coding assignments, examples, exercises, and reviews have been updated to include the most recent ICD-10-CM, ICD-10-PCS, CPT, and HCPCS level II codes.

- Answer keys have been updated in the *Instructor's Manual to Accompany 3-2-1 Code It!*, which is located at the Instructor Companion Site (**http://login.cengage.com**).

- Chapter 1 includes updated content about professional associations, professional credentials, and computer-assisted coding (CAC).

- Chapter 2 was revised to update ICD-10-CM and ICD-10-PCS content. Content about the ICD-10-CM official guidelines for coding and reporting was relocated from Chapter 4, and its content has been updated.

- Chapter 3 includes updated content about coding conventions in ICD-10-CM and ICD-10-PCS, and examples allow educators and students to compare the use of conventions in the classification systems. Examples, exercises, and the chapter review have also been updated.

- Chapter 4 contains chapter-specific coding guidelines for ICD-10-CM chapters 1 through 10 only, and new Chapter 5 contains chapter-specific coding guidelines for ICD-10-CM Chapters 11–21 only. The reason for this is because the original Chapter 4 (in the previous edition) was too lengthy. In addition, content about ICD-10-CM official guidelines for coding and reporting was relocated to Chapter 2. Examples, exercises, and chapter reviews have been updated in both chapters.

- Chapter 6 includes updated content about inpatient ICD-10-CM diagnosis coding guidelines and inpatient ICD-10-PCS procedure coding guidelines. Examples, exercises, and the chapter review were also updated.

- Chapter 7 contains updated content about outpatient ICD-10-CM diagnosis coding guidelines. Examples, exercises, and the chapter review have also been updated.

- Chapter 8 contains updated content about HCPCS level II coding. Examples, exercises, and the chapter review have also been updated.

- Chapter 9 contains updated introductory content about CPT coding. Examples, exercises, and the chapter review have also been updated.

- Chapter 10 contains updated content about CPT's evaluation and management (E/M) section. Examples, exercises, and the chapter review have also been updated.

- Chapter 11 contains updated content about CPT's Anesthesia section. Examples, exercises, and the chapter review have also been updated.

- Chapters 12 through 16 contain updated content about CPT's Surgery section. Examples, exercises, and the chapter review have also been updated.

- Chapter 17 contains updated content about CPT's Radiology section. Examples, exercises, and the chapter review have also been updated.

- Chapter 18 contains updated content about CPT's Pathology and Laboratory section. Examples, exercises, and the chapter review have also been updated.

- Chapter 19 contains updated content about CPT's Medicine section. Examples, exercises, and the chapter review have also been updated.

- Chapter 20 contains updated content about insurance and reimbursement. Examples, exercises, and the chapter review have also been updated.

- Appendix I contains an E/M CodeBuilder (also available on the Student Companion Site), which can be used with Chapter 10 to assign evaluation and management codes.

Supplements

The following supplements accompany this text:

- Instructor Companion Site at http://login.cengage.com
- Student Workbook

- Student Companion Site at http://login.cengage.com
- MindTap at http://login.cengage.com

Instructor Companion Site

Spend less time planning and more time teaching with Cengage's Instructor Companion Site to Accompany *3-2-1 Code It!*: 2020. As an instructor, you will have access to all of your resources online, anywhere and at any time. All instructor resources can be accessed by going to http://login.cengage.com to create a unique user login. Contact your sales representative for more information. Online instructor resources at the Instructor Companion Site are password-protected and include the following:

- The Instructor's Manual consists of seven sections:
  - Section I—Instructor's Resources
  - Section II—Answer Keys to Textbook Chapter Exercises and Reviews
  - Section III—Answer Keys to Workbook Assignments and Reviews
  - Section IV—Answer Keys to Coding Patient Records (Workbook Appendices A–D)
  - Section V—Answer Key to Mock Certified Professional Coder (CPC) Certification Examination (Workbook Appendix E)
  - Section VI—Answer Key to Mock Certified Coding Specialist—Physician (CCS-P) Certification Examination (Workbook Appendix F)
  - Section VII—Answer Key to Mock Certified Coding Specialist (CCS) Certification Examination (Workbook Appendix G)
- *Cengage Learning Testing Powered by Cognero*, a flexible, online system that allows you to author, edit, and manage test bank content from multiple Cengage Learning solutions; you can also create multiple test versions in an instant, and deliver tests from your learning management system (LMS), classroom, or elsewhere.
- Customizable instructor support slide presentations in PowerPoint® format focus on the most important points for each chapter.
- Conversion grids, map *3-2-1 Code It!: 2020* to the seventh edition and to competing texts to make adapting your course to *3-2-1 Code It!* a snap.
- Access to all free student supplements, including additional textbook content.

Student Workbook

(ISBN: 978-0-357-36266-2)

The workbook follows the chapter organization of the text and contains higher-level Bloom's taxonomy assignments (that comply with academic program accreditation organization requirements, such as CAHIIM competencies), such as computer-assisted coding, assigning APCs and DRGs, and coding numerous diagnosis/procedure statements and case studies so that students can practice coding. Each assignment contains a list of objectives, an overview of content relating to the assignment, and instructions for completing the assignment. The last assignment in each workbook chapter contains review questions in multiple-choice format to emulate credentialing exam questions. The workbook also contains actual patient records and mock CPC, CCS-P, and CCS certification examinations.

Student Companion Site

Additional textbook resources for students and instructors can be found online at http://login.cengage.com.

All resources located on the Student Companion Site to accompany *3-2-1 Code It!* are free to textbook users. Student resources include:

- Revisions to textbook and workbook due to coding changes as they become available
- E/M Codebuilder (also found in Appendix I of the textbook)
- Tutorials for how to code patient records (to assist in coding patient records found in Appendices A–D of the workbook)
- Extra content about related coding topics, including long-term care, home health care, and hospice coding

MindTap

(ISBNs: 2-Year Instant Access Code: 978-0-357-36271-6

   2-Year Printed Access Code: 978-0-357-36272-3

   4-Year Instant Access Code: 978-0-357-36273-0

   4-Year Printed Access Code: 978-0-357-36274-7

Green's *3-2-1 Code It!*: 2020 on MindTap is the first of its kind in an entirely new category: the Personal Learning Experience (PLE). This personalized program of digital products and services uses interactivity and customization to engage students, while offering instructors a wide range of choice in content, platforms, devices, and learning tools. MindTap is device agnostic, meaning that it will work with any platform or learning management system and will be accessible anytime, anywhere: on desktops, laptops, tablets, mobile phones, and other Internet-enabled devices.

 NOTE:

The numbering of textbook review case studies matches MindTap™ numbering.

This MindTap includes:

- An interactive eBook with highlighting, note-taking (integrated with Evernote), and more
- Flashcards for practicing chapter terms
- Computer-graded activities and exercises
  - Self-check and application activities, integrated with the eBook
  - Case studies with videos
- Easy submission tools for instructor-graded exercises
- Medical Coding Trainer software for a real-world interactive coding experience
- Computer-assisted coding (CAC) cases

Optum360™ EncoderPro.com

Enhance your course with Cengage learning materials and an online coding tool from Optum360®. *EncoderPro.com Expert* is an online coding and reference tool designed to enhance your coding capabilities.

- Using online coding tools can help by saving you time and money;
- Increasing accuracy, reducing denials, and ensuring you receive complete reimbursement; and
- Reducing required storage space and paper.

Features of EncoderPro.com Expert include:

- ICD-10-CM/PCS, HCPCS level II, and CPT code content search
- ICD-10 mapping tools
- Coders' Desk Reference
- Complete code history
- Local Coverage Determinations (LCDs) and Medicare Pub. 100 access
- Medicare CCI edits
- Modifier crosswalk
- Enhanced compliance editor

- Enhanced LCD/NCD policy searching
- Cross-coder relationships from seven coding and billing specialty reference books

To make the switch and start saving on coding materials with Cengage and Optum360®, contact your Cengage Learning Consultant today at cengage.com/repfinder.

A Note About CPT Coding Manual Editions

Every attempt is made to make the material within this textbook and its ancillary products (e.g., Workbook, Instructor's Manual) as current as possible by updating to CPT 2020 just prior to publication.

Michelle A. Green, MPS, RHIA, FAHIMA, CPC, has been a college professor since 1984. She taught traditional classroom-based courses until 2000 at Alfred State College, when she transitioned all of the health information management and coding courses to an Internet-based format. In 2016, she began teaching for the health information management program at Mount Wachusett Community College, Gardner, Massachusetts. In 2017, she also began teaching for the health information technology program at Mohawk Valley Community College, Utica, New York. Prior to 1984, she worked as a director of health information management at two acute care hospitals in Florida's Tampa Bay area. Both positions required her to assign codes to inpatient cases. Upon becoming employed as a college professor, she routinely spent the semester breaks coding for a number of health care facilities so that she could further develop her inpatient and outpatient coding skills.

REVIEWERS

Content Reviewers

Dr. Lisa L. Campbell, PhD, RHIA, CDIP, CCS, CCS-P, CPC, COC
Associate Professor
DeVry University
Matteson, IL

Monica Carmichael, MHSA, MHRM, CPC
Director of Business Management and
    International Trade
Miller-Motte Technical College
North Charleston, NC

Melanie Grant, CPC, CPMA
HIT Instructor
Central New Mexico Community College
Albuquerque, NM

Judy Hurtt
Instructor, East Central Community College
Decatur, MS

Natunya D. Johnson Ed.S, MBA, CCA
Department Chair of Business and Office Technology
Holmes Community College
Ridgeland, MS

Patricia King, MA, BS, RHIA
Online HIM Faculty
Sullivan University
Louisville, KY

Roseanna J McGinn
Director Health Information Technology
University of New Mexico, Gallup
Gallup, NM

Cheryl A Miller MBA/HCM
Assistant Professor/Program Director
Westmoreland County Community College
Youngwood, PA

Merline Minott, MSHI, RHIT
Instructor/Director of HIM
Savannah Technical College
Savannah, GA

Donna Sue M. Shellman EdS, CPC
Program Coordinator, Medical Programs & Instructor,
    Office Systems Technology
Gaston College
Dallas, NC

Michelle Wellman-Miller, CPC, CEDC, COSC, CEMC
Instructor Coordinator
C-TEC of Licking County
Newark, OH

Technical Reviewer

Marsha Diamond, CCS, CPC, COC, CPMA
Instructor
City College
Altamonte Springs, Florida

and

Manager
Coding Compliance, Physician/Outpatient Services
Medical Audit Resource Services, Inc.
Orlando, Florida

Lisa Riggs, CPC, CPC-I, AAS
Senior Curriculum and Instructional Design Specialist
Ultimate Medical Academy
Tampa, FL

ACKNOWLEDGMENTS

In memory of my son, Eric, who always kept me "on task" by asking, "How much did you get finished in the chapter today, Mom?" Thank you for truly understanding my need to pursue my passion for teaching and writing. You always proudly introduced me as your mom, the teacher and writer. You remain forever in my heart, Eric. A special thank you to my brother, Dave Bartholomew, for his encouragement and help. You are my rock!

To my students, located throughout the world! You always ask me the toughest coding questions, and you also make me want to find the answers. You are truly critical thinkers!

To my technical reviewer, Marsha Diamond, thank you for your incredible attention to detail!

To Kaitlin Schlicht, Instructional Designer, for her invaluable support, patience, and guidance!

To Stephen Smith, Product Team Manager, for patiently listening to all of my concerns about the revision process!

To the incomparable Kara DiCaterino, Senior Content Manager, what can I say? You are simply the best!

To my mom, Alice B. Bartholomew, for her support and assistance. Between writing real-life case studies for my textbooks and having originally helped me select a health care career, your guidance is appreciated beyond words.

Special appreciation is expressed to Optum360 Publishing Group for granting permission to reprint selected images, tables, and pages from:

- *Coder's Desk Reference for Diagnoses*
- *Coders Desk Reference for Procedures*
- *Coding & Payment Guide for Anesthesia Services*
- *EncoderPro.com*
- *HCPCS Level II Professional*
- *ICD-10-CM Professional*
- *ICD-10-PCS Professional*

Michelle A. Green, MPS, RHIA, FAHIMA, CPC

Feedback

Contact the author at michelle.ann.green@gmail.com with questions, suggestions, or comments about the text or its supplements. Please realize that the publisher (www.cengage.com) authorizes the release of the Instructor's Manual (with coding answers) to educators only. The publisher also posts an AAPC CEU exam on the Student Companion Site.

xix

HOW TO USE THIS TEXT

Chapter Outline and Key Terms

The **Chapter Outline** organizes the chapter material at a glance. The **Key Terms** list represents new vocabulary in each chapter. Each term is highlighted in color in the chapter, where it is also defined and used in context. A complete definition of each term appears in the Glossary at the end of the textbook.

Objectives

The **Objectives** list the outcomes expected of the learner after a careful study of the chapter. Read the objectives before reading the chapter content. When you complete the chapter, read the objectives again to see if you can say for each one, "Yes, I know that." If you cannot say this about an objective, go back to the appropriate content and reread. These outcomes are critical to a successful career as an insurance specialist.

Chapter Outline

Career as a Coder
Professional Associations
Coding Systems and Processes
Other Classification Systems, Databases, and Nomenclatures
Documentation as Basis for Coding
Health Data Collection

Chapter Objectives

At the conclusion of this chapter, the student should be able to:

1. Define key terms related to the overview of coding.
2. Summarize the training, job responsibilities, and career path for a coder.
3. Differentiate among types of professional associations for coders, health insurance specialists, and medical assistants.
4. Summarize coding systems and processes.
5. Identify other classification systems and databases.
6. Identify how documentation serves as the basis for assigning codes.
7. Describe health data collection for the purpose of reporting hospital and physician office data.

Key Terms

application service provider (ASP)
Assessment (A)
assumption coding
automated case abstracting software
classification system
clearinghouse
CMS-1450
CMS-1500
code
coder
demographic data
concurrent coding
continuity of care
Current Procedural Terminology (CPT)
database
discharge note
documentation
document imaging
downcoding
electronic health record (EHR)

Introduction

There are two related classifications of diseases with similar titles. The *International Classification of Diseases (ICD)* is published by the World Health Organization (WHO) and is used to classify mortality (death) data from death certificates. WHO published the tenth revision of ICD in 1994 with a new name, *International Statistical Classification of Diseases and Related Health Problems*, and reorganized its 3-digit categories. (Although the name of the publication was changed, the familiar abbreviation ICD was kept.)

The *International Classification of Diseases, Tenth Revision, Clinical Modification* (ICD-10-CM) was developed in the United States and is used to code and classify morbidity (disease) data from inpatient and outpatient records, including physician office records. ICD-10-CM is a closed classification system that is used in the United States to classify diagnoses, which means that ICD-10-CM provides just one place to classify each condition.

All health care settings use ICD-10-CM to report diagnoses. The *International Classification of Diseases, Tenth Revision, Procedure Classification System* (ICD-10-PCS) is used to code and classify procedure data from hospital inpatient records only. (ICD-10-CM and ICD-10-PCS are abbreviated as ICD-10-CM/PCS.)

ICD-10-CM and ICD-10-PCS Official Guidelines for Coding and Reporting are used as a companion to ICD-10-CM and ICD-10-PCS, respectively, to ensure accurate coding. This chapter includes an overview about official guidelines for coding and reporting along with details about general ICD-10-CM diagnosis coding guidelines. (ICD-10-CM coding conventions are covered in Chapter 3. ICD-10-CM chapter-specific diagnosis coding guidelines are covered in Chapters 4 and 5. ICD-10-PCS coding guidelines are covered in more detail in Chapter 6.)

 NOTE:

Provider offices and health care facilities (e.g., hospitals) use ICD-10-CM to code diagnoses. Hospitals use ICD-10-PCS to code inpatient procedures. (Provider offices and outpatient health care settings use CPT and HCPCS level II to code procedures and services.) ICD-10-CM and ICD-10-PCS are abbreviated as ICD-10-CM/PCS.

⚠ HIPAA Alert!

The HIPAA regulations for electronic transactions require providers and third-party payers, including Medicare administrative contractors (MACs), to adhere to the *Official Guidelines for Coding and Reporting*. Thus, a violation of the coding guidelines is technically a HIPAA violation. Because some third-party payers and MACs do not appear to be aware of (or understand) this HIPAA provision, to obtain appropriate reimbursement for submitted ICD-10-CM (and ICD-10-PCS) codes, you may need to point out specific provisions in the regulation that reference the coding guidelines. For example, the Z51 (Encounter for other aftercare and medical care) codes in ICD-10-CM can be reported as a first-listed code for outpatient care. If third-party payers and MACs deny claims that report Z51 codes contact the regional CMS office or HIPAA enforcement office (located at CMS) for resolution.

Introduction

The **Introduction** provides a brief overview about major topics covered in the chapter. The introduction (and the objectives) provides a framework for your study of the content.

Notes

Notes appear throughout the text and serve to bring important points to your attention. The notes clarify content, refer you to reference material, provide more background for selected topics, or emphasize exceptions to rules.

HIPAA Alerts

The **HIPAA Alert** feature highlights issues related to the privacy and security of personal health information.

Coding Tips

The **Coding Tips** feature provides recommendations and hints for selecting codes and for the correct use of the coding manuals.

 Coding Tip

Make sure you read CPT code descriptions carefully. When the code description states "with or without" another procedure, that other procedure is not reported separately if it is performed (e.g., 57240, anterior colporrhaphy, repair of cystocele with or without repair of urethrocele, including cystourethroscopy, when performed).

Examples

Examples appear throughout the text to promote understanding of presented concepts.

EXAMPLE 1: ICD-10-CM TABULAR LIST OF DISEASES AND INJURIES—INCLUSION TERMS: The following inclusion terms are located in the Tabular List of Diseases and Injuries for diagnosis code M54.5, Low back pain:

- Loin pain
- Lumbago NOS

Exercises

Exercises reinforce chapter content.

Exercise 2.3 – ICD-10-CM Tabular List of Diseases and Injuries

Instructions: Complete each statement.

1. The ICD-10-CM _____ of Diseases and Injuries arranges codes and descriptions in alphanumerical order, and it contains 21 chapters that classify diseases and injuries.
2. The last chapter of ICD-10-CM tabular list codes that are reported for patient encounters when a circumstance other than disease or injury is documented (located in Table 2-1) are called Factors Influencing Health Status and Contact with Health Services or _____ codes.
3. I10 is an example of a _____ code, which has no further subdivisions.
4. Subcategory codes that require additional characters are _____ if the 4th, 5th, 6th, and/or 7th character(s) are absent.
5. The 5th and 6th characters of "x" in code O40.1xx0 are called _____ .

Summary

The **Summary** at the end of each chapter recaps the key points of the chapter. The summary also serves as a review aid when preparing for tests.

Summary

The *International Classification of Diseases, 10th Revision, Clinical Modification* (ICD-10-CM) and the *International Classification of Diseases, 10th Revision, Procedure Coding System* (ICD-10-PCS), abbreviated as ICD-10-CM/PCS, replaced ICD-9-CM effective October 2015. ICD-10-CM is a clinical modification of the World Health Organization's *International Classification of Diseases, Ninth Revision* (ICD-9). ICD-10-CM/PCS includes many more codes and applies to more users than ICD-9-CM because it is designed to collect data on every type of health care encounter (e.g., inpatient, outpatient, hospice, home health care, and long-term care). The ICD-10-CM Tabular List of Diseases and Injuries contains 21 chapters. It is a sequential list of codes contained within chapters based on body system or condition, and codes are then organized within major topic headings, categories, subcategories, and codes. ICD-10-CM disease and injury codes consist of three characters, but most are followed by a decimal point and between one and four additional characters. ICD-10-CM Index to Diseases and Injuries entries are organized according to main terms, subterms, second qualifiers, third qualifiers, and fourth qualifiers.

ICD-10-PCS is a procedure classification system developed by the Centers for Medicare & Medicaid Services (CMS) for use in the United States for inpatient hospital settings *only*. It uses a multiaxial 7-character alphanumeric code structure (e.g., 047K04Z) that provides a unique code for all substantially different procedures. It also allows new procedures to be easily incorporated as new codes. ICD-10-PCS contains more than 87,000 seven-character alphanumeric procedure codes.

Internet Links

ICD-10-CM/PCS updates: Go to *www.cms.gov*, click on the Medicare link, click on the ICD-10 link under Coding, and scroll down to click on this year's ICD-10-CM or ICD-10-PCS link.

JustCoding News free e-newsletter: Go to *www.justcoding.com*, and click on the eNewsletter Signup link at the top of the page.

Review

Matching – ICD-10-CM

Instructions: Match the format in Column 2 with each line of the ICD-10-CM Index to Diseases and Injuries entries in Column 1.

ICD-10-CM Index to Diseases and Injuries	Format
_____ 1. `Abnormal, abnormality, abnormalities` (*see*	a. 2nd qualifier
_____ 2. *also* Anomaly)	b. 3rd qualifier
_____ 3. `chromosome, chromosomal Q99.9`	c. Continuation line
_____ 4. `sex Q99.8`	d. Main term
_____ 5. `female phenotype Q97.9`	e. Subterm

Internet Links

Internet Links are provided to encourage you to expand your knowledge at various state and federal government agency, commercial, and organization sites.

Review

Each chapter **Review** includes multiple-choice questions and coding practice cases that will test your understanding of chapter content and critical thinking ability.

NOTES

Coding Overview

1: Overview of Coding, 2

CHAPTER 1

Overview of Coding

Chapter Outline

Career as a Coder

Professional Associations

Coding Systems and Processes

Other Classification Systems, Databases, and
    Nomenclatures

Documentation as Basis for Coding

Health Data Collection

Chapter Objectives

At the conclusion of this chapter, the student should be able to:

1. Define key terms related to the overview of coding.
2. Summarize the training, job responsibilities, and career path for a coder.
3. Differentiate among types of professional associations for coders, health insurance specialists, and medical assistants.
4. Summarize coding systems and processes.
5. Identify other classification systems and databases.
6. Identify how documentation serves as the basis for assigning codes.
7. Describe health data collection for the purpose of reporting hospital and physician office data.

Key Terms

application service
    provider (ASP)

Assessment (A)

assumption coding

automated case
    abstracting software

automated record

Centers for Medicare
    & Medicaid Services
    (CMS)

claims examiner

classification system

clearinghouse

CMS-1450

CMS-1500

code

coder

coding

coding system

computer-assisted
    coding (CAC)

concurrent coding

continuity of care

*Current Procedural
    Terminology* (CPT)

database

demographic data

*Diagnostic and Statistical
    Manual of Mental
    Disorders* (DSM)

diagnostic/management
    plan

discharge note

documentation

document imaging

downcoding

electronic health record
    (EHR)

electronic medical
    record (EMR)

encoding

evidence-based coding

evidence-verification coding

HCPCS level II

HCPCS national codes

health care clearinghouse

Healthcare Common Procedure Coding System (HCPCS)

health care provider

health data collection

Health Insurance Portability and Accountability Act of 1996 (HIPAA)

health insurance specialist

health plan

hospitalist

hybrid record

indexed

initial plan

integrated record

International Classification of Diseases for Oncology, Third Edition (ICD-O-3)

International Classification of Diseases, Ninth Revision, Clinical Modification (ICD-9-CM)

International Classification of Diseases, Tenth Revision, Clinical Modification (ICD-10-CM)

International Classification of Diseases, Tenth Revision, Clinical Modification/Procedure Coding System (ICD-10-CM/PCS)

International Classification of Diseases, Tenth Revision, Procedure Coding System (ICD-10-PCS)

International Classification of Functioning, Disability and Health (ICF)

internship

internship supervisor

jamming

listserv

Logical Observation Identifiers Names and Codes (LOINC)

manual record

medical assistant

medical coding process

medical management software

medical necessity

medical nomenclature

medical record

National Drug Codes (NDC)

Objective (O)

online discussion board

overcoding

patient education plan

patient record

physician query process

Plan (P)

problem list

problem-oriented record (POR)

progress notes

provider

resident physician

RxNorm

scanner

sectionalized record

source-oriented record (SOR)

specialty coders

Subjective (S)

Systematized Nomenclature of Medicine Clinical Terms (SNOMED CT)

teaching hospital

teaching physician

therapeutic plan

third-party administrator (TPA)

third-party payer

transfer note

UB-04

unbundling

Unified Medical Language System (UMLS)

upcoding

Introduction

This chapter focuses on coding career opportunities in health care, the importance of joining professional associations and obtaining coding credentials, the impact of networking with other coding professionals, and the development of opportunities for career advancement. It also provides a coding overview that explains clinical documentation improvement, the physician query process, and the use of computer-assisted coding (CAC) and encoder software. Documentation as a basis for coding includes patient record formats and the importance of establishing medical necessity. Health data collection covers the reporting of hospital and physician office data using abstracting software, medical practice management software, and CMS-1500 and UB-04 claims.

 NOTE:

This chapter does *not* require the use of ICD-10-CM, ICD-10-PCS, CPT, or HCPCS level II coding manuals. However, later chapters in this textbook do require them (because learning how to code is easier when you use paper-based coding manuals). Students should also learn how to use encoder and computer-assisted coding (CAC) software.

NOTE:

The following additional content is located on the Student Companion Site at http://login.cengage.com:
- *Documentation Requirements for Teaching Physicians 2012*
- History of Medical Classification and Coding Systems
- Alternate Health Care Coding Systems

Career as a Coder

A **coder** acquires a working knowledge of coding systems (e.g., CPT, HCPCS level II, ICD-10-CM, ICD-10-PCS), coding conventions and guidelines, government regulations, and third-party payer requirements to ensure that all diagnoses (conditions), services (e.g., office visits), and procedures (e.g., surgery, x-rays) documented in patient records are coded accurately for reimbursement, research, and statistical purposes. Excellent interpersonal skills are required of coders because they communicate with providers about documentation and compliance issues related to the appropriate assignment of diagnosis and procedure/service codes.

NOTE:

Although graduates of medical assistant and medical office administration programs typically do not become employed as full-time coders, they often are responsible for the coding function in a physician's office or medical clinic. This chapter provides the following resources for students pursuing any health-related academic program that includes coding as a job function:
- Professional associations that offer coding and other certification exams
- Internet-based discussion boards that cover coding and other topics
- Impact of HIPAA federal legislation on coding and reimbursement
- Coding references and other resources that facilitate accurate coding
- Physician query process as a way to prevent assumption coding
- Manual and automated patient record formats and health data collection

Training

Training methods for those interested in pursuing a coding career include college-based programs that contain coursework in medical terminology, anatomy and physiology, health information management, pathophysiology, pharmacology, ICD-10-CM, ICD-10-PCS, HCPCS level II, and CPT coding, and reimbursement methodologies. Many college programs also require students to complete a nonpaid internship (e.g., 120 hours) at a health care facility. Professional associations (e.g., the American Health Information Management Association) offer noncredit-based coding training, usually as distance learning (e.g., Internet-based), and some health care facilities develop internal programs to retrain health professionals (e.g., nurses) who are interested in a career change.

NOTE:

Pharmacology plays a significant role in accurate and complete coding. Coders review the medication administration record (MAR) to locate medications administered that impact diagnosis coding. For example, upon review of the MAR the coder notices that the patient received a course of Librium (chlordiazepoxide) during inpatient hospitalization. Librium is classified as an antianxiety medication, but it can be also used to counteract alcohol withdrawal symptoms. If the latter is the reason that the patient received the Librium (based on physician documentation), the coder can assign an appropriate alcohol dependence diagnosis code as well as alcohol detoxification procedure codes.

Coding Internship

The coding **internship** benefits the student and the facility that accepts the student for placement. Students receive on-the-job experience prior to graduation, and the internship assists them in obtaining permanent employment. Facilities benefit from the opportunity to participate in and improve the formal education process. Quite often, students who complete professional practice experiences (or internships) are later employed by the facility at which they completed the internship.

The **internship supervisor** is the person to whom the student reports at the site. Students are often required to submit a professional résumé to the internship supervisor and to schedule an interview prior to being accepted for placement. While this experience can be intimidating, it is excellent practice for the interview process that the student will undergo prior to obtaining permanent employment. Students should research the résumé writing and interview technique services available from the college's career services office. This office will review résumés and will provide interview tips. (Some even videotape mock interviews for students.)

 NOTE:

> Breach of patient confidentiality can result in termination from the internship site, failure of the internship course, and even possible suspension and/or expulsion from your academic program. Make sure you check out your academic program's requirements regarding this issue.

The internship is on-the-job training even though it is nonpaid, and students should expect to provide proof of immunizations (available from a physician) and possibly undergo a preemployment physical examination and participate in facility-wide and department-specific orientations. In addition, because of the focus on privacy and security of patient information, the facility will likely require students to sign a nondisclosure agreement (to protect patient confidentiality), which is kept on file at the college and by the professional practice site.

During the internship, students are expected to report to work on time. Students who cannot attend the internship on a particular day (or who arrive late) should contact their internship supervisor and program faculty. Students are also required to make up any lost time. Because the internship is a simulated job experience, students are to be well groomed and should dress professionally. Students should show interest in all aspects of the experience, develop good working relationships with coworkers, and react appropriately to criticism and direction. If any concerns arise during the internship, students should discuss them with their internship supervisor and/or program faculty.

Credentials

The American Health Information Management Association (AHIMA) and the AAPC (previously called the American Academy of Professional Coders) offer certification in coding. Credentials available from AHIMA include the following:

- Certified Coding Associate (CCA)
- Certified Coding Specialist (CCS)
- Certified Coding Specialist—Physician-based (CCS-P)

The AAPC offers the following core coding certification exams:

- Certified Professional Coder (CPC)
- Certified Inpatient Coder (CIC)
- Certified Outpatient Coder (COC)
- Certified Risk Adjustment Coder (CRC)

The AAPC also offers specialty certifications in response to a demand for **specialty coders** who have obtained advanced training in medical specialties and who are skilled in compliance and reimbursement areas, such as the Certified Ambulatory Surgical Center Coder (CASCC) credential.

The American Medical Billing Association (AMBA) offers the Certified Medical Reimbursement Specialist (CMRS) exam, which recognizes the competency of members who have met high standards of proficiency. According to AMBA, Certified Medical Reimbursement Specialists (CMRS) are skilled in facilitating the claims reimbursement process from the time a service is rendered by a health care provider until the balance is paid. The CMRS is knowledgeable in ICD, CPT, and HCPCS level II coding; medical terminology; insurance claims and billing; appeals and denials; fraud and abuse; Health Insurance Portability and Accountability Act (HIPAA) regulations; Office of Inspector General (OIG) compliance; information and Internet technology; and reimbursement methodologies.

The type of setting in which you seek employment will indicate which credential(s) you should pursue. Inpatient and/or outpatient coders obtain CCS and/or CIC certification, and physician office coders choose the CCS-P and/or CPC credential. Outpatient coders also have the option of selecting the COC credential. Insurance specialists who work for health care facilities and third-party payers obtain the CCS-P. Those who have not met requirements for field experience as a coder can seek apprentice-level certification as a CCA. (Once certified, professional associations require maintenance of the credential through continuing education [CE] recertification per two-year cycle.)

Employment Opportunities

Coders can obtain employment in a variety of settings, including clinics, consulting firms, government agencies, hospitals, insurance companies, nursing facilities, home health agencies, hospice organizations, and physicians' offices. Coders also have the opportunity to work at home for employers who partner with an Internet-based **application service provider (ASP)**, which is a third-party entity that manages and distributes software-based services and solutions to customers across a *wide area network (WAN)* (computers that are far apart and are connected via the Internet) from a central data center.

Other Professions Related to Coding

One profession that is closely related to a coder is that of a **health insurance specialist** (or **claims examiner**). When employed by third-party payers, these specialists review health-related claims to determine whether the costs are reasonable and medically necessary based on the patient's diagnosis. This process involves verification of the claim against third-party payer guidelines to authorize appropriate payment or to refer the claim to an investigator for a more thorough review.

Another profession that is closely related to a coder is the **medical assistant**. When employed by a provider, this person performs administrative and clinical tasks to keep the office and clinic running smoothly. Medical assistants who specialize in administrative aspects of the profession answer telephones, greet patients, update and file patient medical records, complete insurance claims, process correspondence, schedule appointments, arrange for hospital admission and laboratory services, and manage billing and bookkeeping.

When employed by a physician's office, health insurance specialists and medical assistants perform medical billing, coding, record keeping, and other medical office administrative duties. Health insurance specialists (or claims examiners) and medical assistants receive formal training in college-based programs or at vocational schools. They also receive on-the-job training.

- Health insurance specialists (or claims examiners) often become certified as a Certified Professional Biller (CPB) (through the AAPC).
- The health insurance specialist also has the option of becoming credentialed by the Medical Association of Billers (MAB) as a Certified Medical Billing Specialist (CMBS).
- Medical assistants often become credentialed as a Certified Medical Assistant (CMA) through the American Association of Medical Assistants (AAMA) or as a Registered Medical Assistant (RMA) through the American Medical Technologists (AMT).

Health insurance specialists (or claims examiners) and medical assistants obtain employment in clinics, health care clearinghouses, health care facility billing departments, insurance companies, and physicians' offices and with third-party administrators (TPAs). When employed by clearinghouses, insurance companies, or TPAs, they often have the opportunity to work at home, where they process and verify health care claims using an Internet-based application service provider (ASP).

Exercise 1.1 – Career as a Coder

Instructions: Match the description with its career. Answers may be assigned more than once.

_____ 1. Answers telephones, greets patients, and updates and files patient medical records

_____ 2. Communicates with providers about documentation and compliance issues related to code assignment

_____ 3. Reviews claims for third-party payers to determine whether costs are reasonable and medically necessary

_____ 4. Schedules hospital admission and laboratory services

_____ 5. Verifies claims against third-party payer guidelines to authorize appropriate payments

a. Coder

b. Health insurance specialist

c. Medical assistant

Professional Associations

Students are often able to join a professional association (Table 1-1) for a reduced membership fee and receive most of the same benefits as active members (who pay much more!). Benefits of joining a professional association include the following:

- Eligibility for scholarships and grants
- Opportunity to network with members (internship and job placement)
- Free publications (e.g., professional journals)
- Reduced certification exam fees
- Website access for members only

Attending professional association conferences and meetings provides opportunities to network with professionals. Another way to network is to join an **online discussion board** (or **listserv**) (Table 1-2), which is an Internet-based or email discussion forum that covers a variety of topics and issues.

TABLE 1-1 Professional Associations

Career	Professional Association
Coder	AAPC (previously called the American Academy of Professional Coders)
	American Health Information Management Association (AHIMA)
Health Insurance Specialist	Alliance of Claims Assistance Professionals (ACAP)
	American Medical Billing Association (AMBA)
	Medical Association of Billers (MAB)
Medical Assistant	American Association of Medical Assistants (AAMA)
	American Medical Technologists (AMT)

TABLE 1-2 Internet-Based Discussion Boards (Listservs)

Discussion Board	Website
AHIMA Engage	AHIMA members can log in at **www.ahima.org**.
Billing-Coding forum	Go to **www.billing-coding.com**, hover over More Resources, and select Forums from the pop-up menu.
Medicare Part B	Go to **www.partbnews.com**, hover over Communities, and select Forum from the pop-up menu.

Exercise 1.2 – Professional Associations

Instructions: Match the professional association with the type of professional. Answers may be assigned more than once.

_____ 1. AAMA   **a.** Coder

_____ 2. AAPC   **b.** Health insurance specialist

_____ 3. ACAP   **c.** Medical assistant

_____ 4. AHIMA

_____ 5. AMT

Coding Systems and Coding Processes

Coding systems and medical nomenclatures are used by health care facilities, health care providers, and third-party payers to collect, store, and process data for a variety of purposes (e.g., health care reimbursement). A **coding system** (or **classification system**) organizes a medical nomenclature according to similar conditions, diseases, procedures, and services, and it contains codes for each (e.g., ICD-10-CM arranges these elements into appropriate chapters and sections). A **medical nomenclature** includes clinical terminologies and clinical vocabularies that are used by health care providers to document patient care. _Clinical terminologies_ include designations, expressions, symbols, and terms used in the field of medicine, such as "pupils equal, round, and reactive to light," commonly abbreviated as PERRL in a patient's physical examination report. _Clinical vocabularies_ include clinical phrases or words along with their meanings, such as "myocardial infarction," which is defined as the sudden deprivation of blood flow to heart muscle due to coronary artery blockage resulting in tissue damage (necrosis) and commonly called a "heart attack." A **code** includes numeric and alphanumeric characters that are reported to health plans for health care reimbursement, to external agencies (e.g., state departments of health) for data collection, and internally (acute care hospital) for education and research. **Coding** is the assignment of codes to diagnoses, services, and procedures based on patient record documentation.

 NOTE:

You are already familiar with a well-known coding system called the United States Postal Service ZIP Code system, which classifies addresses as numbers (e.g., 12345-9876).

Coding Systems

- The *International Classification of Diseases, Ninth Revision, Clinical Modification* (ICD-9-CM) was adopted in 1979 to classify diagnoses (Volumes 1 and 2) and procedures (Volume 3). The *International Classification of Diseases, Tenth Revision, Clinical Modification* (ICD-10-CM) (and ICD-10-PCS) replaced ICD-9-CM on October 1, 2015, to classify all diagnoses.

- The *International Classification of Diseases, Tenth Revision, Procedure Coding System* (ICD-10-PCS) was developed by the National Center for Health Statistics (NCHS) to classify inpatient procedures and services, and it was implemented on October 1, 2015 (replacing Volume 3 of ICD-9-CM).

 NOTE:

International Classification of Diseases, Tenth Revision, Clinical Modification/Procedure Coding System (ICD-10-CM/PCS) is the shortened name the Centers for Medicare & Medicaid Services uses to identify both classification systems.

- The *Current Procedural Terminology* (CPT) was originally published by the American Medical Association (AMA) in 1966. Subsequent editions were published about every five years until the late 1980s, when the AMA began publishing annual revisions. CPT classifies procedures and services, and it is used by physicians and outpatient health care settings (e.g., the hospital ambulatory surgery department) to assign CPT codes for reporting procedures and services on health insurance claims. CPT is considered level I of the Healthcare Common Procedure Coding System (HCPCS).

- The **Healthcare Common Procedure Coding System (HCPCS)** also includes level II (national) codes, called **HCPCS level II** (or **HCPCS national codes**), which are managed by the **Centers for Medicare & Medicaid Services (CMS)**, an administrative agency in the federal Department of Health & Human Services (DHHS). HCPCS level II classifies medical equipment, injectable drugs, transportation services, and other services not classified in CPT. Physicians and ambulatory care settings use HCPCS level II to report procedures and services.

 NOTE:

HCPCS level III local codes were discontinued in 2004. They had been managed by Medicare carriers and fiscal intermediaries (FIs). You might come across their legendary use in health care facility or insurance company databases. Some payers still use them.

The **Health Insurance Portability and Accountability Act of 1996 (HIPAA)** is federal legislation that amended the Internal Revenue Code of 1986 to:

- improve portability and continuity of health insurance coverage in the group and individual markets;
- combat waste, fraud, and abuse in health insurance and health care delivery;
- promote the use of medical savings accounts;
- improve access to long-term care services and coverage;
- simplify the administration of health insurance by creating unique identifiers for providers, health plans, employers, and individuals;
- create standards for electronic health information transactions; and
- create privacy and security standards for health information.

To facilitate the creation of standards for electronic health information transactions, HIPAA requires two types of code sets to be adopted for the purpose of encoding data elements (e.g., procedure and service codes). **Encoding** is the process of standardizing data by assigning alphanumeric values (codes or numbers) to text and collecting other information (e.g., gender).

Large code sets encode:

- diseases, injuries, impairments, and other health-related problems and their manifestations;
- causes of injury, disease, impairment, or other health-related problems;
- actions taken to prevent, diagnose, treat, or manage diseases, injuries, and impairments; and
- substances, equipment, supplies, or other items used to perform these actions.

EXAMPLE: The diagnosis of *essential hypertension* is assigned ICD-10-CM code I10.

Small code sets encode:

- race/ethnicity;
- type of facility; and
- type of unit.

EXAMPLE: A patient's gender is assigned a 1 if male, a 2 if female, or a 3 if undetermined.

HIPAA also requires specific code sets to be adopted for use by clearinghouses, health plans, and providers, as follows:

- *International Classification of Diseases, Tenth Revision, Clinical Modification* and *Procedure Coding System* (ICD-10-CM/PCS)
- *Current Procedural Terminology* (CPT)
- HCPCS level II (national codes)
- *Current Dental Terminology* (CDT)
- *National Drug Codes* (NDC)

A **clearinghouse** (or **health care clearinghouse**) is a public or private entity (e.g., billing service) that processes or facilitates the processing of health information and claims from a nonstandard to a standard format. A **health plan** (or **third-party payer**) (e.g., Blue Cross/Blue Shield, a commercial insurance company) is an insurance company that establishes a contract to reimburse health care facilities and patients for procedures and services provided. A **provider** (or **health care provider**) is a physician or another health care professional (e.g., a nurse practitioner or physician assistant) who performs procedures or provides services to patients. Adopting HIPAA's standard code sets has improved data quality and simplified claims submission for health care providers who routinely deal with multiple third-party payers. The code sets have also simplified claims processing for health plans. Health plans that do not accept standard code sets are required to modify their systems to accept all valid codes or to contract with a health care clearinghouse that does accept standard code sets.

 NOTE:

A health care clearinghouse is not a **third-party administrator (TPA)**, which is an entity that processes health care claims and performs related business functions for a health plan. The TPA might contract with a health care clearinghouse to standardize data for claims processing.

Coding References

Professional organizations that are recognized as national authorities on CPT, HCPCS level II, ICD-10-CM, and ICD-10-PCS coding publish references and resources that are invaluable to coders. To ensure the development of excellent coding skills, make sure you become familiar with and use the following references and resources:

- *AHA Coding Clinic for ICD-10-CM and ICD-10-PCS,* and *AHA Coding Clinic for HCPCS*, quarterly newsletters published by the American Hospital Association and recognized by the CMS as official coding resources
- *Conditions of Participation* (CoP) and *Conditions for Coverage* (CfC), Medicare regulations published by CMS

NOTE:

- Official coding policy is published in the AHA *Coding Clinic for ICD-10-CM and ICD-10-PCS,* AHA *Coding Clinic for HCPCS,* and AMA *CPT Assistant,* and as National Correct Coding Initiative (NCCI) edits.
- The AAPC and AHIMA publish coding newsletters, journals, and so on, but such publications do not contain official coding policy.

- *CPT Assistant*, monthly newsletter published by the AMA and recognized by CMS as official coding resource
- *National Correct Coding Initiative* (NCCI), code edit pairs that cannot be used in the same claim (developed by CMS and published by the federal government's National Technical Information Service [NTIS])
- Compliance program guidance documents, guidelines published by the DHHS OIG
- *ICD-10-CM Official Guidelines for Coding and Reporting*, guidelines provided by CMS and NCHS to be used as a companion document to the official version of the ICD-10-CM
- *ICD-10-PCS Official Guidelines for Coding and Reporting*, guidelines provided by CMS and NCHS to be used as a companion document to the official version of ICD-10-PCS
- *Outpatient Code Editor with Ambulatory Payment Classification* (OCE/APC), software developed by CMS, distributed by NTIS, and used by hospitals to edit outpatient claims to help identify possible CPT/HCPCS level II coding errors and assign Ambulatory Payment Classifications (APCs) that are used to generate reimbursement

Incorporating the use of the above references and resources assists coders in avoiding the following abusive and fraudulent (dishonest and illegal) coding practices, depending on intent. (Abuse involves mistakenly submitting incorrect codes, and fraud involves intentionally submitting incorrect codes to increase reimbursement.)

- **Unbundling**: Reporting multiple codes to increase reimbursement when a single combination code should be reported.
- **Upcoding**: Reporting codes that are not supported by documentation in the patient record for the purpose of increasing reimbursement.
- **Overcoding**: Reporting codes for signs and symptoms in addition to the established diagnosis code.
- **Jamming**: Routinely assigning an unspecified ICD-10-CM disease code instead of reviewing the coding manual to select the appropriate code.
- **Downcoding**: Routinely assigning lower-level CPT codes as a convenience instead of reviewing patient record documentation and the coding manual to determine the proper code to be reported.

Medical Coding Process

The **medical coding process** requires the review of patient record documentation to identify diagnoses, procedures, and services for the purpose of assigning ICD-10-CM, ICD-10-PCS, HCPCS level II, and/or CPT codes. Each health care covered entity (e.g., hospital, medical clinic, physician office) implements a unique medical coding process, which requires adherence to the following:

- Code of ethics
- Steps to accurate coding
- Coding quality
- Avoid assumption coding
- Physician query process
- Clinical Documentation Improvement Program
- Coding compliance program

Code of Ethics

Professional associations establish a *code of ethics* to help members understand how to differentiate between "right" and "wrong" and apply that understanding to decision making. The AAPC publishes a code of ethics, and AHIMA publishes standards of ethical coding; both serve as guidelines for ethical coding conduct, and they demonstrate a commitment to coding integrity.

Steps to Accurate Coding

Regardless of health care setting, the *steps to accurate coding* begin with a review of the entire patient record (manual or electronic) before selecting diagnoses, procedures, and services to which codes are assigned. Depending on the setting, coders perform retrospective coding, concurrent coding, or a combination of both.

Retrospective coding is the review of records to assign codes after the patient is discharged from the health care facility (e.g., hospital inpatient) or released from same-day outpatient care (e.g., hospital outpatient surgery unit). It is most commonly associated with inpatient hospital stays because accurate coding requires verification of diagnoses and procedures by reviewing completed face sheets, discharge summaries, operative reports, pathology reports, and progress notes in the patient records.

Concurrent coding is the review of records and/or use of encounter forms and chargemasters to assign codes during an inpatient stay (e.g., hospital) or an outpatient encounter (e.g., hospital outpatient visit for laboratory testing or x-rays, physician office visit). It is typically performed for outpatient encounters because encounter forms (e.g., physician office) and chargemasters (e.g., hospital emergency department visit, hospital outpatient visit for laboratory testing) are completed in "real time" by health care providers as part of the charge-capture process.

- *Encounter forms* are used to record data about office procedures and services provided to patients.
- *Chargemasters* contain a computer-generated list of procedures, services, and supplies and corresponding revenue codes along with charges for each.

 NOTE:

Information about encounter forms and chargemasters is located in Chapter 20 of this textbook, along with samples of each.

Coding Quality

According to the American Hospital Association, "The importance of understanding and following the basic ICD-10-CM, and ICD-10-PCS coding principles cannot be overemphasized in the training of coders and in quality control activities undertaken to improve the accuracy of data reported for internal and external hospital use. The measures for coding accuracy include (a) adherence to ICD-10-CM and ICD-10-PCS coding principles and instructions, (b) attention to specificity in code selection where indicated by physician documentation in the medical record [patient record], (c) grasp of medical terminology, and (d) absence of clerical-type errors, such as those due to carelessness in reading or in transposing [letters and] numbers. Auditing of coded diagnostic and procedural information for accuracy should not be confused with the review for relevancy in sequencing of the codes at hand. They are separate tasks linked together in the data reporting process."

The statement located in (b) of the aforementioned quote is significant because it means that coders are expected to review the *entire* record when assigning codes to diagnoses and procedures documented on the face sheet and in the discharge summary. Thus, coders should review the face sheet, discharge summary, and other documentation (e.g., progress notes, operative reports, pathology reports, laboratory data) to assign the most specific codes possible.

EHR Results in Greater Implementation of Concurrent Coding

Concurrent coding was introduced for inpatient coding just after the inpatient prospective payment system (using diagnosis-related groups) was implemented on October 1, 1983. Coders from the health information department worked part of the day on nursing units, accessing paper-based manual medical records to begin the process of assigning codes to diagnoses and procedures. On discharge of the patient from the hospital, the coders performed a final review of the patient record to ensure accuracy of reported codes. Because the paper-based manual patient record can be handled by just one individual at a time, coders "competed" with nurses, physicians, and other health care providers for access to the record. As a result, concurrent coding as a process was discontinued in some facilities because it was inefficient.

Today, implementation of the electronic health record (EHR) has resulted in a resurgence of concurrent coding practices because coders (still located in the health information department) access patient records in an electronic format. They no longer "compete" with other health care providers for access to the record and,

as a result, efficiency associated with the concurrent coding concept has been realized. In practice, coders remain at their work stations in the health information department (and *remote coders* use their at-home work stations) to access patient EHRs to begin the discharge coding process. Rising health care costs created an impetus for concurrent coding processes because it is a much faster method for coders to review and verify the accuracy of codes on discharge of inpatients based on concurrent coding work performed (according to an established schedule) up until the date of discharge. For tertiary-care facilities that provide complex health care (e.g., transplant surgery) and quaternary-care facilities that provide highly specialized care (e.g., experimental medicine), both of which are also characterized as providing high-cost care (e.g., transplant surgery), having the ability to submit codes for reimbursement purposes within hours (instead of days) of inpatient discharge significantly and positively impacts their accounts receivables (and their "bottom line"). In addition, community-based hospitals also realize the benefits of concurrent coding.

Remember! Coders must avoid assumption coding, and when a problem with documentation quality is noted (e.g., conflicting diagnostic statements on the discharge summary, face sheet, and elsewhere in the record) the physician query process is initiated (discussed below).

EXAMPLE 1: The provider documented *congestive heart failure* on the face sheet of the patient record. On review of progress notes that document the patient's response to treatment, the coder finds documentation of *acute and chronic diastolic and systolic congestive heart failure* in the discharge progress note. Instead of reporting a code for *congestive heart failure*, report the more specific code for *acute and chronic diastolic and systolic congestive heart failure*.

EXAMPLE 2: The provider documented *malnutrition* on the discharge summary in the patient record. On review of progress notes, the coder finds documentation of *moderate malnutrition*. Instead of reporting the nonspecific code for *malnutrition*, report the more specific code for *moderate malnutrition*.

Avoid Assumption Coding

Coders are prohibited from performing **assumption coding**, which is the assignment of codes based on assuming, from a review of clinical evidence in the patient's record, that the patient has certain diagnoses or received certain procedures/services even though the provider did not specifically document those diagnoses or procedures/services. According to the *Compliance Program Guidance for Third-Party Medical Billing Companies*, published by the Department of Health & Human Services' Office of the Inspector General, assumption coding creates risk for fraud and abuse because the coder assumes certain facts about a patient's condition or procedures/services, although the physician has not specifically documented the level of detail to which the coder assigns codes. (Coders can avoid fraudulent assumption coding by implementing the physician query process discussed in the following section.)

EXAMPLE: An elderly patient is admitted to the hospital for treatment of a fractured femur. Upon examination, the physician documents that the skin around the fractured femur site has split open. X-ray of the left femur reveals a displaced fracture of the shaft. The patient underwent fracture reduction and full-leg casting. The physician documents *open Type I fracture of shaft, left femur* as the final diagnosis.

The coder assigns code S72.302B for the *open Type I fracture of shaft, left femur*, which is correct. The coder assigns code 0QS90ZZ for the *fracture reduction and full leg casting procedure*, which is incorrect because its code description is *reposition left femoral shaft, open approach (no device), femur (shaft)*. Although the patient has an open fracture, the physician did *not* perform an open reduction procedure. (An open reduction involves making a surgical incision to align displaced bones, and it may require external fixation to heal properly.) In this case, the coder incorrectly "assumed" that an open reduction was performed because the patient's open fracture was treated. The code that should be assigned for this procedure is 0QS9XZZ because its code description is *reposition left femoral shaft, external approach*. (A closed reduction involves casting the affected limb to stabilize the fracture for healing, and it might also require the physician to pull back two ends of bone that are touching each other and/or to correct any wide angles.)

Physician Query Process

When coders have questions about documented diagnoses and procedures or services, they use a **physician query process** to contact the responsible physician to request clarification about documentation and the code(s) to be assigned. The electronic health record (EHR) allows for development of an *automated* physician query process, which is used by utilization managers (or case managers), clinical documentation improvement specialists, and coders to obtain clarification about patient record documentation. Integrating the automated physician query process with the EHR allows physicians to more easily receive and reply to queries, which results in better and timely responses from physicians.

 NOTE:

The query should not lead the physician to a desired outcome.

- A leading query would be phrased as, "Is the patient's anemia due to blood loss?" and leads the physician to add due to blood loss to the anemia diagnosis for more specific code assignment and possible increased reimbursement.
- A nonleading query would be phrased as, "Can the cause of the patient's anemia be specified? The history documents symptoms of fatigue, headaches, inflamed tongue, and lightheadedness. The CBC reveals low hemoglobin levels." This query allows the physician to determine whether the anemia can be qualified according to type.

The following guidelines should be followed when activating the physician query process:

- Establish a policy to indicate when a coder should generate a physician query, such as when documentation in the patient's record fails to meet one of the following five criteria (according to AHIMA's practice brief, entitled *Managing an Effective Query Process*):
  - *Legibility* (e.g., illegible handwritten patient record entries)
  - *Completeness* (e.g., abnormal test results but clinical significance of results is not documented)

- ○ *Clarity* (e.g., signs and symptoms are present in the patient record, but a definitive diagnosis is not documented)
- ○ *Consistency* (e.g., discrepancy among two or more treating providers regarding a diagnosis, such as a patient who presents with shortness of breath and the consulting physician documents pneumonia as the cause while the attending physician documents congestive heart failure as the cause)
- ○ *Precision* (e.g., clinical documentation indicates a more specific diagnosis than is documented, such as a sputum culture that indicates bacterial pneumonia and the diagnosis does not indicate the cause of the pneumonia)

- Query the physician when the following are noted by the coder and when provider documentation in the patient record is not present (according to AHIMA's practice brief, entitled *Managing an Effective Query Process*):
  - ○ Clinical indicators of a diagnosis (e.g., lab, x-ray) but the diagnosis is not documented
  - ○ Clinical evidence for a higher degree of specificity or severity (e.g., progress notes) but specificity or severity is not documented in the diagnosis
  - ○ Cause-and-effect relationship between two conditions or an organism but the relationship is not documented in the diagnosis (e.g., due to, with)
  - ○ An underlying cause when a patient is admitted with symptoms (e.g., shortness of breath is documented instead of diagnosed pneumonia)
  - ○ Treatment is documented without a corresponding diagnosis for medical necessity (e.g., antibiotics for a secondary diagnosis of UTI, which is not documented as a diagnosis)
  - ○ Lack of present on admission (POA) indicator status (e.g., history did not indicate diagnoses that were present on admission, such as chronic asthma) (The POA indicator status is discussed in textbook Chapter 20.)

 NOTE:

> Utilization managers (or case managers) are responsible for coordinating inpatient care to ensure the appropriate utilization of resources, delivery of health care services, and timely discharge or transfer. They usually have a bachelor's degree (e.g., nursing), professional licensure (e.g., RN), and clinical practice experience.
>
> Utilization managers work closely with physicians on a daily basis, and they are a logical choice to facilitate the physician query process. In this role, they serve as the liaison for coders (and physicians) by helping coders write appropriate queries and clarifying queries for physicians so that responses are timely and complete.

- Determine whether the query will be generated concurrently (during inpatient hospitalization) or retrospectively (after patient discharge).
- Designate an individual who will serve as the physician's contact during the physician query process (e.g., coding supervisor, utilization manager). Remember that the coder's role is to assign codes based on documentation and that asking for clarification is appropriate, but making an assumption about codes to be assigned is considered fraud. That means that coders should ask physicians open-ended questions to avoid leading the physicians by indicating a preference for a particular response. Coders do not make clinical assumptions—that is the sole responsibility of the physician.

Use a physician query form (Figure 1-1A, Figure 1-1B), not scrap paper, to document the coder's query and the physician's response. If the completed query form is filed in the patient's record, determine whether it is considered an official part of the record and subject to disclosure by those requesting copies of records or whether it is an administrative form that is not subject to disclosure. The query form could also be stored in an administrative file in the coding supervisor's office and the information resulting from the query documented kept in the patient record by the physician (e.g., an addendum to the discharge summary). The length of time that the completed query form is retained is determined by each health care organization.

> **EXAMPLE:** A patient is admitted with severe dyspnea (shortness of breath), chest pain, and fever. Upon physical examination, the physician documents rhonchi (gurgling sound in the lungs), wheezing, and rales (clicking, bubbling, or rattling sounds in the lungs). Laboratory data during the hospitalization include a culture and sensitivity report of sputum that documents the presence of gram-negative bacteria. A review of the physician orders reveals documentation of appropriate medications to treat *pneumonia due to gram-negative bacteria*. The medication administration record (MAR) documents administration of the medications, and the physician progress notes document the patient's positive response to medications (and resolution of the pneumonia). The physician documents *viral pneumonia* as the final diagnosis.

Depending on the health care facility's coding policy and procedure, the coder has two options.

1. If the coding policy and procedure allow coders to use the entire patient record as the basis of assigning codes to final diagnoses and procedures, because documentation in the record supports a final diagnosis of *pneumonia due to gram-negative bacteria* (instead of viral pneumonia), the coder would assign the code for that condition.

2. If the coding policy and procedure require coders to generate a *physician query* when the final diagnosis (on the face sheet or in the discharge summary) differs from documentation found in the patient

---

PHYSICIAN QUERY FORM

Patient Name: John Public   Date: April 14, YYYY
Admission Date: 03/30/YYYY   Coder: Lynn Smith
Patient Number: 123456   Email Address: lsmith@clinic.org
                                                   Office Number: (101) 555-1234

Dear Dr. _____ Hughes _____ ,

The diagnosis or procedure of _____ pneumonia _____ requires more specific information in order to assign the most accurate and complete code. The following information is documented in the discharge summary.
The patient had signs and symptoms of upper respiratory infection upon admission.
_____
_____
_____
_____

I have the following question(s) about this record:
RSV testing was positive for respiratory syncytial virus. Based on your clinical
judgment, can you provide a diagnosis that represents the RSV positive finding?
If so, please document the condition and causative organism (if known) in the patient
record.
_____
_____

Please respond to this question in the space below, and also document an amendment in the patient record (if appropriate):
Patient has RSV. This is now documented in an addendum to the discharge summary in
the patient record.
_____
_____
_____
_____

FIGURE 1-1A Sample open-ended physician query form

PHYSICIAN QUERY: CHEST PAIN DIAGNOSIS CLARIFICATION

Hospital:	ANYWHERE CLINIC	Patient Number:	123456
Physician:	Dr. Hughes	Admission Date:	03/31/YYYY
Patient Name:	John Public	Discharge Date:	04/04/YYYY
Doctor:	Hughes	Date of Query:	April 5, YYYY

The patient record reflects the following clinical finding(s) (to be completed by coder):

Clinical Indicators: / **Location of Documentation in current record:**

- Chest pain (e.g., description, location, level of exertion) — History and Physical Examination
- Signs/Symptoms (e.g., diaphoresis, palpitations, etc.) — Admission Progress Note
- Shortness of breath (e.g., respiratory rate, activity) — History and Physical Examination
- Abnormal test results (e.g., EKG, cardiac cath, chest x-ray) — EKG report and Chest x-ray report (negative)
- Abnormal lab findings (e.g., troponin, CK and CK-MBs) — Laboratory report (cardiac enzymes negative)
- Abnormal EGD (e.g., esophagitis, esophageal varices) — Not applicable
- Treatment prescribed (e.g., nitroglycerine) — Not applicable

TO THE PHYSICIAN: The following may be a factor in determining and reporting the severity of illness of your patient (to be completed by physician, if applicable).

There is clinical documentation of **chest pain** in the patient record. Clarification of documentation is initiated to the provider when there is conflicting, incomplete, or ambiguous information in the patient record. Please use your clinical judgment in responding to this query. (**Note:** This physician query does not imply that any particular answer is desired or expected.)

Please respond to **ALL 4 sections below.** Per CMS guidelines or facility policy, please document your response in the patient record (e.g., progress note, dictated report).

Section 1: Specificity
- ☐ Cardiac
- ☐ Chest wall
- ☐ Musculoskeletal
- ☒ Psychogenic
- ☐ Atypical
- ☐ Traumatic
- ☐ Other:
- ☐ Unknown

Section 2: Etiology
- ☐ Unstable angina
- ☐ Acute MI
- ☐ Costochondritis
- ☐ Exacerbation of COPD
- ☐ Pneumonia
- ☒ Anxiety
- ☐ GERD
- ☐ Other:
- ☐ Unknown

Section 3: Acuity
- ☐ Acute
- ☐ Acute on chronic
- ☐ Chronic
- ☒ Other: *related to Anxiety*
- ☐ Unknown

Section 4: Present on Admission (POA)
- ☒ Yes
- ☐ No
- ☐ Clinically undetermined
- ☐ Unknown

Coder Name:	Sally Smith, CCS	Extension: 1234	Date: April 5, YYYY
Physician Signature:	*Mark Hughes, M.D.*		Date: *April 6, YYYY*

Permission to reprint granted by Medical Audit Resource Services, Inc.

FIGURE 1-1B Sample multiple choice physician query form

---

record, the coder would submit the following query to the physician, which allows the physician an opportunity to correct the documented final diagnosis if warranted. In this case, the physician changed *viral pneumonia* to *pneumonia due to gram-negative bacteria* (using the proper procedure for amending the patient record).

The assignment of a code to pneumonia due to *gram-negative bacteria* results in reimbursement of about $3,500, and the assignment of a code to *viral pneumonia* results in reimbursement of about $2,500. Not querying the physician would have resulted in a loss of $1,000 to the facility.

This case also includes documentation of signs and symptoms, which are due to the pneumonia. Thus, the coder would *not* assign codes to symptoms of dyspnea, chest pain, fever or signs of rhonchi, wheezing, and rales.

Clinical Documentation Improvement Program

The purpose of a *clinical documentation improvement (CDI) program* is to help health care facilities comply with government programs (e.g., RAC audits, ARRA/HITECH) and other initiatives (Joint Commission accreditation) with the goal of improving health care quality. As part of a CDI program, the CDI specialist initiates concurrent and retrospective reviews of inpatient and outpatient records to identify conflicting, incomplete, or nonspecific provider documentation. Concurrent reviews are performed on patient care units (to access paper-based patient records) or remotely (to access EHRs). The CDI program helps ensure that patient diagnoses and procedures are supported by ICD-10-CM and ICD-10-PCS codes, and CDI specialists use a physician query form to communicate with physicians (and other health care providers) with the intended result of improving documentation, coding, reimbursement, and severity of illness (SOI) and risk of mortality (ROM) classifications. CDI programs are usually associated with acute health care facilities; however, they are also implemented in alternate health care settings (e.g., acute rehabilitation facility, skilled nursing facility). A *clinical documentation improvement (CDI) specialist* is responsible for performing inpatient record reviews for the purpose of:

- implementing documentation clarification and specificity processes (as part of the physician query process);
- using and interpreting clinical documentation improvement statistics;
- conducting research and providing education to improve clinical documentation; and
- ensuring compliance with initiatives that serve to improve the quality of health care, which include:
  - complying with fraud and abuse regulations;
  - enforcing privacy and security of patient information; and
  - monitoring a *health information exchange (HIE)*.

Coding Compliance Program

A *coding compliance program* ensures that the assignment of codes to diagnoses, procedures, and services follows established coding guidelines, such as those published by the Centers for Medicare & Medicaid Services (CMS). Health care organizations write *policies* (guiding principles that indicate "what to do") and *procedures* (processes that indicate "how to do it") to assist in implementing the coding compliance stages of detection, correction, prevention, verification, and comparison.

- *Detection* is the process of identifying potential coding compliance problems. For example, a coder notices that some patient records contain insufficient or incomplete documentation, which adversely impacts coding specificity. The coder brings these records to the attention of the coding compliance officer (e.g., coding supervisor), who implements the next stage of the coding compliance program.
- *Correction* is based on the review of patient records that contain potential coding compliance problems, during which specific compliance issues are identified and problem-solving methods are used to implement necessary improvements (corrections). For example, the coding compliance officer conducts a careful review of the patient records that contain insufficient or incomplete documentation. She determines that all of them are the responsibility of a physician new to the practice, and she prepares educational material specific to documentation issues noted during her review of the patient records.

- *Prevention* involves educating coders and providers so as to prevent coding compliance problems from recurring. For example, the coding compliance officer schedules a meeting with the physician responsible for insufficient or incomplete documentation, and educates the physician about the specific areas of insufficient or incomplete documentation that adversely impact medical coding. This meeting is conducted in a nonconfrontational manner, with education and correction as its goals.

- *Verification* provides an "audit trail" that the detection, correction, and prevention functions of the coding compliance program are being actively performed. For example, the coding compliance officer maintains a file that contains the following:
  - Original codes assigned based on insufficient and incomplete documentation
  - Educational materials prepared specific to the documentation issues
  - Minutes of the educational meeting with the responsible physician
  - Final codes assigned based on sufficient and complete documentation
  - Remittance advice from third-party payer, which contains adjudication (decision about reimbursement, including possible claims denial)

- *Comparison* requires the analysis of internal coding patterns over specified periods of time (e.g., quarterly) as well as the analysis of external coding patterns by using external benchmarks (trends). For example, the coding compliance officer reviews reports of quarterly medical audits to determine whether the new physician's documentation has improved. Such reports contain the results of claims submission, which indicate the number of claims denials based on nonspecific codes submitted as a result of insufficient and incomplete documentation. In addition, the coding compliance officer obtains benchmark data (reports) from third-party payers and compares the coding practices in her facility with those of similar providers; if reimbursement to similar providers is significantly higher (or lower) than that paid to her provider, she initiates the *detection* process in an attempt to identify related coding compliance problems.

An effective coding compliance program monitors coding processes for completeness, reliability, validity, and timeliness.

- *Completeness* ensures that codes are assigned to all *reportable* diagnoses, procedures, and services documented in the patient record. For example, coders review the entire patient record to assign the most specific codes possible.

- *Reliability* allows for the same results to be consistently achieved. For example, when the same patient record is coded by different coding professionals, they assign identical diagnosis and procedure/service codes.

- *Validity* confirms that assigned codes accurately reflect the patient's diagnoses, procedures, and services. For example, coders do *not* assign codes to diagnoses that were not medically managed or treated during an encounter.

- *Timeliness* means that patient records are coded in accordance with established policies and procedures to ensure timely reimbursement.

Computer-Assisted Coding

Computer-assisted coding (CAC) uses software to automatically generate medical codes by "reading" transcribed clinical documentation provided by health care practitioners (Figure 1-2). CAC uses "natural language processing" technology to generate codes that are reviewed and validated by coders for reporting on third-party payer claims. Similar to the medical editor's role in ensuring the accuracy of reports produced from speech recognition technology, the coder's role changes from that of data entry to validation or audit. The coder reviews and approves the CAC-assigned codes, improving efficiency and offering expanded

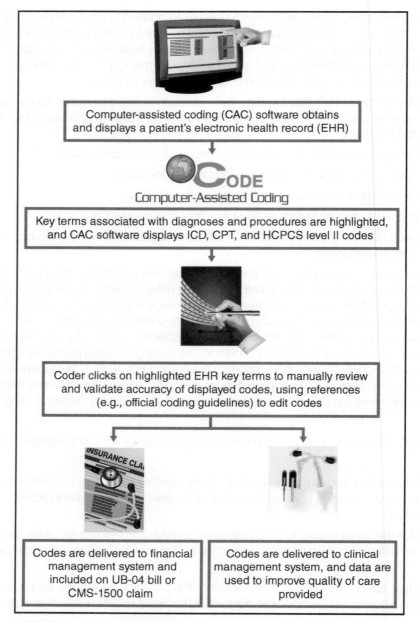

FIGURE 1-2 Computer-assisted coding (CAC)

career opportunities for enthusiastic coders. Thus, coders will use basic data analytic skills to turn data (e.g., CAC-assigned code) into action (coder-reviewed and approved code) using a logical and efficient method.

Coding auditors performed **evidence-based coding**, also referred to as **evidence-verification coding**, which involves clicking on codes that CAC software generates (Figure 1-3) to review electronic health record documentation (evidence) used to generate the code. When it is determined that documentation supports the CAC-generated code, the coding auditor clicks to accept the code. When documentation does not support the CAC-generated code, the coding auditor replaces it with an accurate code. For example, when the CAC-generated ICD-10-CM code does not indicate laterality or does not include a manifestation code, the coding auditor edits codes to ensure accurate reporting.

FIGURE 1-3 Sample screen from Optum360 Enterprise computer-assisted coding (CAC) software

Exercise 1.3 – Coding Systems and Processes

Instructions: Match the code set description with its type. Answers may be assigned more than once.

_____ 1. Race, ethnicity, type of facility, and type of unit

_____ 2. Substances, equipment, supplies, or other items

_____ 3. Actions taken to prevent, diagnose, treat, or manage diseases, injuries, and impairments

_____ 4. Causes of injury, disease, impairment, or other health-related problems

_____ 5. Diseases, injuries, impairments, other health-related problems, and their manifestations

a. Large code set

b. Small code set

Other Classification Systems, Databases, and Nomenclatures

In addition to the ICD-10-CM, ICD-10-PCS, HCPCS level II national, and CPT coding systems, health care providers use the following classifications, clinical vocabularies, databases, and nomenclatures:

- *Alternative Billing Codes* (ABC codes)
- *Clinical Care Classification* (CCC) *System*
- *Current Dental Terminology* (CDT)
- *Diagnostic and Statistical Manual of Mental Disorders* (DSM)
- *Health Insurance Prospective Payment System* (HIPPS) Rate Codes
- *International Classification of Diseases for Oncology, Third Edition* (ICD-O-3)

- *International Classification of Functioning, Disability and Health* (ICF)
- Logical Observation Identifiers Names and Codes (LOINC)
- *National Drug Codes* (NDC)
- RxNorm
- *Systematized Nomenclature of Medicine Clinical Terms* (SNOMED CT)
- Unified Medical Language System (UMLS)

 NOTE:

Clinical vocabularies include clinical phrases or words along with their meanings.

Alternative Billing Codes (ABC Codes)

The *Alternative Billing Codes* (ABC codes) classify services not included in the CPT manual to describe the service, supply, or therapy provided; they may also be assigned to report nursing services and alternative medicine procedures. Codes are five characters in length, consisting of letters, and are supplemented by two-digit code modifiers to identify the practitioner performing the service.

HIPAA authorized the Secretary of DHHS to permit exceptions from HIPAA transaction and code set standards to commercialize and evaluate proposed modifications to those standards. The ABC code set was granted that exception in 2003, and the codes were being commercialized and evaluated through 2005. The intent was for ABC codes to be adopted as part of the electronic code set (as HCPCS level I and level II were in 2000); however, in 2006, ABC codes could no longer be used in electronic claims processing.

EXAMPLE: During an office visit, an acupuncture physician assessed the health status of a new client and developed a treatment plan, a process that took 45 minutes. ABC code ACAAC-1C is assigned.

Clinical Care Classification (CCC) System

The *Clinical Care Classification* (CCC) *System* provides a new standardized framework and a unique coding structure for assessing, documenting, and classifying home health and ambulatory care. Previously called the *Home Health Care Classification* (HHCC) *System*, CCC consists of two interrelated taxonomies:

- CCC of Nursing Diagnoses
- CCC of Nursing Interventions

CCC care components represent functional, health, behavioral, physiological, and psychological patterns of patient care. The care components serve as a standardized framework for mapping and linking the interrelated CCC taxonomies to each other and to other health-related classifications. They are used to track and measure patient/client care holistically over time, across settings, population groups, and geographic locations.

EXAMPLE: 73-year-old female patient discharged from the hospital after treatment for acute myocardial infarction presents today for the scheduled outpatient cardiac rehabilitation sessions. Assign CCC code C08.1 (cardiac rehabilitation).

Current Dental Terminology (CDT)

The *Current Dental Terminology* (CDT) is published by the American Dental Association (ADA) as an annual revision. It classifies dental procedures and services. Dental providers and ambulatory care settings use the CDT to report procedures and services. CDT codes are also included in HCPCS level II, beginning with the first digit of D. The CDT also includes the Code on Dental Procedures and Nomenclature (Code), instructions for use of the Code, questions and answers, ADA dental claim form completion instructions, and tooth numbering systems.

EXAMPLE: Patient underwent incision and drainage of intraoral soft tissue abscess. CDT code D7510 is assigned.

Diagnostic and Statistical Manual of Mental Disorders (DSM)

The *Diagnostic and Statistical Manual of Mental Disorders* (DSM) is published by the American Psychiatric Association as a standard classification of mental disorders used by mental health professionals in the United States. The first edition was published in 1952, and subsequent revisions have been published as:

- DSM-II (1968)
- DSM-III (1980)
- DSM-III-R (1987)
- DSM-IV (1994)
- DSM-IV-TR (2000) (This includes a *text revision* to correct DSM-IV errors, the updating of codes according to ICD-9-CM or ICD-10-CM annual revisions, and so on.)
- DSM-5 (2014)

    DSM-5 is designed for use in a variety of health care settings and consists of three major components:

- Diagnostic classification
- Diagnostic criteria sets
- Descriptive text

    DSM-5 is a multiaxial classification that allows for the collection and classification of information as:

- Axis I: Mental disorders or illnesses, such as substance abuse
- Axis II: Personality disorders or traits, such as mental retardation
- Axis III: General medical illnesses, such as hypertension
- Axis IV: Life events or problems, such as divorce
- Axis V: Global assessment of functioning, or GAF, such as occupational

---

EXAMPLE: A patient is admitted to the hospital with the diagnosis to agoraphobia with panic attacks. The 38-year-old female also has the diagnosis of hypertension and diabetes mellitus. The patient has an avoidant personality disorder as well, as a result of the agoraphobia. After extensive therapy, the clinician has decided that the patient may be discharged. The clinician believed that the patient's condition could have been attributed to her recent divorce and the death of a close relative. He thinks that her anticipated level of functioning will be quite poor, as in the past year she has had trouble in social and occupational functioning. DSM-5 codes are assigned as follows:

Axis I: Agoraphobia with panic attacks, F40.01

Axis II: Avoidant personality disorder, F60.6

Axis III: Hypertension, I10, and diabetes mellitus, E11.9

Axis IV: Recent divorce and death of close relative

Axis V: Poor

Health Insurance Prospective Payment System (HIPPS) Rate Codes

The *Health Insurance Prospective Payment System* (HIPPS) rate codes are alphanumeric codes consisting of five digits. Each HIPPS code contains intelligence, with certain positions of the code indicating the case-mix group itself and other positions providing additional information (e.g., information about the clinical assessment used to arrive at the code). HIPPS was created as part of the prospective payment system for skilled nursing facilities in 1998. Additional HIPPS codes were created for other prospective payment systems, including a system for home health agencies in October 2000, and one for inpatient rehabilitation facilities in January 2002. The HIPPS represents specific sets of patient characteristics (or case-mix groups) on which payment determinations are made under several prospective payment systems. HIPPS codes are not assigned from a coding manual; they are created when information for a data set is entered into software.

EXAMPLE: The home health prospective payment system (HHPPS) requires entry of the Outcome and Assessment Information Set (OASIS) data set into grouper software, which generates the five-digit alphanumeric HIPPS code that is entered on the UB-04 claim. For example, HIPPS code HAEJ1 is entered on the UB-04 claim.

International Classification of Diseases for Oncology, Third Edition (ICD-O-3)

The *International Classification of Diseases for Oncology, Third Edition* (ICD-O-3) was implemented in 2001 as a classification of neoplasms used by cancer registries throughout the world to record incidence of malignancy and survival rates. The data produced are used to provide information for cancer control programs (e.g., National Comprehensive Cancer Control Program), research activity, treatment planning, and health economics. (The first edition of ICD-O was published in 1976, and a revision of topography codes was published in 1990.) ICD-O-3 codes classify a tumor in the following way:

- Primary site (four-character topography code)
- Morphology (six-character code)
  - Four-digit histology (cell type) code
  - One-digit behavior code (such as malignant, benign, and so on)
  - One-digit aggression code (differentiation or grade)

EXAMPLE: Fibrosarcoma of the left knee. ICD-O-3 codes C49.2 (Knee, NOS) and M8810/39 (Fibroscarcoma, NOS) are assigned.

ICD-O Morphology Codes

ICD-O morphology codes indicate the type of cell that has become neoplastic and its biologic activity; in other words, the kind of tumor that developed and how it behaves. There are three parts to a complete morphology code:

- M as the first character of each morphology code
- 4-digit cell type (histology) (e.g., 8010)
- 1-digit behavior (e.g., /o)
- 1-digit grade, differentiation, or phenotype (e.g., /x1)

A common root codes the cell type of a tumor, an additional digit codes the behavior, and yet an additional digit codes the grade, differentiation, or phenotype to provide supplementary information about the tumor.

Cancer and Carcinoma

The words *cancer* and *carcinoma* are often (incorrectly) used interchangeably. For example, squamous cell cancer is often used for squamous cell carcinoma. Both conditions happen to have the same ICD-10-CM code. However, a condition such as "spindle cell cancer" could refer to "spindle cell sarcoma" or "spindle cell carcinoma." Each condition has an entirely different ICD-10-CM code assigned to it.

Behavior

The behavior of a tumor is the way it acts within the body. Pathologists use a variety of observations to characterize the behavior of a tumor. A tumor can grow in place without the potential for spread (/0, benign); it can be malignant but still growing in place (/2, noninvasive or in situ); it can invade surrounding tissues (/3, malignant, primary site); or it can disseminate from its point of origin and begin to grow at another site (/6, metastatic).

Fifth-Digit Behavior Codes for Neoplasms

Code	Behavior of Neoplasm
/0	Benign
/1	Uncertain whether benign or malignant Borderline malignancy Low malignant potential Uncertain malignant potential
/2	Carcinoma in situ Intraepithelial Noninfiltrating Noninvasive
/3	Malignant, primary site
/6	Malignant, metastatic site Malignant, secondary site
/9	Malignant, uncertain whether primary or metastatic site

 NOTE:

Cancer registries collect data on malignant and in situ neoplasms, or /2 and /3 behavior codes. They do not collect data about behavior codes /6, malignant, metastatic site, or /9, malignant, uncertain whether primary or metastatic site. For example, carcinoma that has spread to the lung and for which the site of origin is unknown is assigned ICD-10-CM code C80.1 (unknown primary site) and ICD-O code M-8010/3 (carcinoma). (The /3 signifies the existence of a malignant neoplasm of a primary site.)

Use of Behavior Code in Pathology Laboratories

Pathologists are usually interested in "specimen coding" (whereas a cancer registry identifies just the primary tumor). A pathologist receives the following tissue specimens on the same patient:

- Biopsy of supraclavicular lymph node
- Resection of fundus of stomach
- Resection of upper lobe bronchus

The pathologist has to track each of these specimens (while the cancer registry tracks only the primary cancer). Each pathological specimen is coded with the appropriate topography and morphology; for example, the term "metastatic" in the pathological diagnosis for tissue specimen, "supraclavicular lymph node (biopsy)," results in assignment of behavior character /6.

Tissue Specimen	Pathological Diagnosis	Codes
Supraclavicular lymph node (biopsy)	Metastatic signet ring cell adenocarcinoma, most likely from stomach (metastatic site)	C77.0 M8490/6
Fundus of stomach (resection)	Signet ring cell adenocarcinoma (primary site)	C16.1 M8490/3
Upper lobe bronchus (resection)	Metastatic signet ring cell adenocarcinoma (metastatic site)	C34.10 M8490/6

Code for Histologic Grading and Differentiation

The highest grade code is assigned according to the description documented in the diagnostic statement. The sixth digit of the morphology code is a single-digit code number that designates the grade of malignant neoplasms. Only malignant tumors are graded. The practice of assigning codes for Histologic grading varies greatly among pathologists throughout the world, and many malignant tumors are not routinely graded.

Sixth Digit Code for Histologic Grading and Differentiation

Code	Grade	Differentiation
1	I	Well differentiated Differentiated, NOS
2	II	Moderately differentiated Moderately well differentiated Intermediate differentiation
3	III	Poorly differentiated
4	IV	Undifferentiated anaplastic
9		Grade or differentiation not determined, not stated or not applicable

Differentiation describes how much or how little a tumor resembles the normal tissue from which it arose. There is great variability in pathologists' use of differentiation descriptors. In general, adverbs such as *well, moderately,* and *poorly* indicate degrees of differentiation, which map to grades I, II, and III. Adjectives such as *undifferentiated* and *anaplastic* usually map to grade IV. Grading codes are assigned to all malignant neoplasms listed in ICD-O *if the diagnosis documents the grade and/or differentiation*.

> **EXAMPLE:** The diagnosis *squamous cell carcinoma, grade* II, which is described as *moderately well differentiated squamous cell carcinoma*, is assigned morphology code M-8070/32.

When a diagnosis indicates two different degrees of grading or differentiation, the higher number is assigned as the grading code.

> **EXAMPLE:** *Moderately differentiated squamous cell carcinoma with poorly differentiated areas* is assigned grading code 3, and the morphology code is M-8070/33.

This same sixth-digit column is also used to indicate cell lineage for leukemias and lymphomas, which provides useful ICD-O-3 comparison data (with ICD-O-2). Cell lineage is implicit in the four-digit histology code, and an additional grade of differentiation (sixth digit) code is not required. However, some registries assign the sixth digit to identify cases in which the diagnosis is supported by immunophenotypic data. In such instances, the immunophenotype code takes precedence over other diagnostic terms for grade or differentiation (e.g., well differentiated, grade III).

Sixth Digit for Immunophenotype Designation for Lymphomas and Leukemias

Code	Designation
5	T-cell
6	B-cell
	Pre-B
	B-precursor
7	Null cell
	Non T-non B
8	NK cell
	Natural killer cell
9	Cell type not determined, not stated, or not applicable

International Classification of Functioning, Disability and Health (ICF)

The *International Classification of Functioning, Disability and Health* (ICF) classifies health and health-related domains that describe body functions and structures, activities, and participation. (The ICF was originally published as the *International Classification of Injuries, Disabilities, and Handicaps (ICIDH)* in 1980.) The ICF complements ICD-10, looking beyond mortality and disease.

> **EXAMPLE:** A trauma patient is evaluated two years after the initial injury, and the physician determines that the patient has a severe impairment in mental function as well as a severe impairment of the upper extremity. The patient experiences moderate difficulty in bathing without the use of assistive devices. Products for education are a moderate barrier for this patient. The following ICF codes are assigned:
>
> - b175.3 (severe impairment in mental function)
> - s730.3 (severe impairment of the upper extremity)
> - a5101.2 (moderate difficulty bathing without use of assistive devices)
> - e145.2 (products for education are a moderate barrier)

Logical Observation Identifiers Names and Codes (LOINC)

Logical Observation Identifiers Names and Codes (LOINC) is an electronic database and universal standard that is used to identify medical laboratory observations and for the purpose of clinical care and management. Developed in 1994, it is currently maintained by the Regenstrief Institute, a U.S. non-profit medical research organization. Health care providers use LOINC codes when reportable disease results are sent to state and federal public health laboratories.

The Centers for Disease Control and Prevention (CDC) has developed a LOINC panel specifically for public health case reporting called the Reportable Condition Mapping Tool (RCMT). This panel should be of considerable assistance to health care providers in identifying the correct LOINC code for their reports. Laboratories are also required to archive LOINC codes for test results they receive from other laboratories to which they have referred specimens and, similarly, referral laboratories should provide their clients with LOINC codes when sending results.

> **EXAMPLE:** The complete blood count (CBC) laboratory test of blood (without differential) is assigned LOINC code 24317-0.

National Drug Codes (NDC)

The *National Drug Codes* (NDC) is published by a variety of vendors, and the coding system is in the public domain. It is managed by the Food and Drug Administration (FDA) and was originally established as part of an out-of-hospital drug reimbursement program under Medicare Services as a universal product identifier for human drugs. The current edition is limited to prescription drugs and a few selected over-the-counter (OTC) products. Pharmacies use NDC to report transactions, and some health care professionals also report NDC on claims.

> **EXAMPLE:** Aspirin tablets, 800 milligrams, is assigned NDC code 64125-*106-01. (There are many different NDC codes for aspirin, depending on dosage, manufacturer, and so on.)

RxNorm

RxNorm is a nomenclature that provides normalized names for clinical drugs and links its names to many of the drug vocabularies commonly used in pharmacy management and drug interaction software, including those of First Databank, Micromedex, MediSpan, Gold Standard Drug Database, and Multum. By providing links among these vocabularies, RxNorm can mediate messages among systems that do not use the same software and vocabulary.

RxNorm is a normalized naming system for generic and branded drugs, and it is a tool for supporting semantic interoperation among drug terminologies and pharmacy knowledge base systems. The National Library of Medicine (NLM) produces RxNorm. The NLM receives drug names from many data sources, analyzes and processes the data, and outputs the data into RxNorm files in a standard format.

Purpose of RxNorm

RxNorm is a terminology built on and derived from other terminologies. RxNorm reflects and preserves the meanings, drug names, attributes, and relationships from its sources. Hospitals, pharmacies, and other organizations use computer systems to record and process drug information. Because these systems use many different sets of drug names, it can be difficult for one system to communicate with another. To address this challenge, RxNorm provides normalized names and unique identifiers for medicines and drugs. The goal of RxNorm is to allow computer systems to communicate drug-related information efficiently and unambiguously.

Scope of RxNorm

RxNorm contains the names of prescription and many over-the-counter drugs available in the United States.

RxNorm includes generic and branded:

- Clinical drugs (pharmaceutical products given to or taken by a patient with therapeutic or diagnostic intent)
- Drug packs (packs that contain multiple drugs, or drugs designed to be administered in a specified sequence)
- Radiopharmaceuticals, bulk powders, contrast media, food, dietary supplements, and medical devices, such as bandages and crutches, which are out of scope for RxNorm

 NOTE:

RxNorm also includes the National Drug File—Reference Terminology (NDF-RT), created for the Veterans Health Administration. NDF-RT is a terminology used to code clinical drug properties, including mechanism of action, physiologic effect, and therapeutic category.

EXAMPLE: When Synthroid is entered in the RxNorm database, results display levothyroxine as the ingredient and Levothyroxine Sodium as the precise ingredient. In addition, all possible dosages of the ingredient and brand name are listed under the clinical drug component, branded drug component, clinical drug or pack, and branded drug or pack. Oral product or pill is listed below the dose form group, with expanded information listed below the clinical dose form group and branded dose form group.

Systematized Nomenclature of Medicine Clinical Terms (SNOMED CT)

The *Systematized Nomenclature of Medicine Clinical Terms* (**SNOMED CT**) is a comprehensive and multilingual clinical terminology of body structures, clinical findings, diagnoses, medications, outcomes, procedures, specimens, therapies, and treatments. It combines the content and structure of a previous revision of SNOMED with the following medical nomenclatures:

- United Kingdom's *National Health Service's Clinical Terms Version 3* (formerly called *Read Codes*, developed in the early 1980s by Dr. James Read to record and retrieve primary care data in a computer)
- *Logical Observation Identifier Names and Codes (LOINC®)* database, which provides a universal code system for reporting laboratory and other clinical observations

SNOMED CT supports the development of comprehensive high-quality clinical content in patient records; it provides a standardized way to represent clinical phrases documented by clinicians, facilitating automatic interpretation (e.g., computer-assisted coding).

Unified Medical Language System (UMLS)

The **Unified Medical Language System (UMLS)** is a set of files and software that allows many health and biomedical vocabularies and standards to enable interoperability among computer systems. UMLS can be used to enhance or develop applications, including electronic health records, classification tools, dictionaries, and language translators. The UMLS is used to link health information, medical terms, drug names, and billing codes across different computer systems.

EXAMPLE 1: UMLS is used to link billing codes, drug names, medical terms, and health information across different computer systems, such as among a patient's health care provider, pharmacy, and third-party payer or patient care coordination among several departments within a hospital.

EXAMPLE 2: UMLS uses include search engine retrieval, data mining, public health statistics reporting, and medical terminology research.

The UMLS contains three tools, called Knowledge Sources, which include the following:

- Metathesaurus (terms and codes from many vocabularies, including CPT, ICD-10-CM, LOINC, MeSH®, RxNorm, and SNOMED CT) (MeSH is the National Library of Medicine's controlled vocabulary thesaurus.)
- Semantic network (broad categories, which are semantic types, and their relationships, which are semantic relations)
- SPECIALIST lexicon and lexical tools (natural language processing tools)

Exercise 1.4 – Other Classification Systems and Databases

Instructions: Match the classification or database description with its name.

_____ 1. Classifies dental procedures and services	**a.** ABC codes
_____ 2. Classifies health and health-related domains that describe body functions and structures, activities, and participation	**b.** CCC
	c. CDT
_____ 3. Classifies services not included in the CPT manual to describe the alternative medical service, supply, or therapy provided	**d.** DSM
	e. HIPPS
	f. ICD-O-3
_____ 4. Electronic database and universal standard used to identify medical laboratory observations and for clinical care and management	**g.** ICF
	h. LOINC
_____ 5. Implemented in 2001 to classify neoplasms	**i.** RxNorm
_____ 6. Links health information, medical terms, drug names, and billing codes across different computer systems	**j.** UMLS
_____ 7. Provides new standardized framework and unique coding structure for assessing, documenting, and classifying home health and ambulatory care	

(continues)

Exercise 1.4 – *continued*

_____ 8. Represents specific sets of patient characteristics (or case-mix groups) on which payment determinations are made under several prospective payment systems

_____ 9. Standard classification of mental disorders used by mental health professionals in the United States

_____ 10. Allows computer systems to communicate drug-related information efficiently and unambiguously

Documentation as Basis for Coding

Health care providers are responsible for documenting and authenticating legible, complete, and timely patient records in accordance with federal regulations (e.g., Medicare CoP) and accrediting agency standards (e.g., The Joint Commission). The provider is also responsible for correcting or editing errors in patient record documentation.

A **patient record** (or **medical record**) is the business record for a patient encounter (inpatient or outpatient) that documents health care services provided to a patient. It stores patient demographic data and documentation that supports diagnoses, and justifies treatment. It also contains the results of treatment provided. (**Demographic data** are patient identification information that is collected according to facility policy and includes information such as the patient's name, date of birth, and mother's maiden name.) The primary purpose of the record is to provide for **continuity of care**, which involves documenting patient care services so that others who treat the patient have a source of information on which to base additional care and treatment. The record also serves as a communication tool for physicians and other patient care professionals. It assists in planning individual patient care and documenting a patient's illness and treatment. Secondary purposes of the record do not relate directly to patient care and include:

- Evaluating the quality of patient care
- Providing data for use in clinical research, epidemiology studies, education, public policy making, facilities planning, and health care statistics
- Providing information to third-party payers for reimbursement
- Serving the medicolegal interests of the patient, facility, and providers of care

Documentation includes dictated and transcribed, keyboarded or handwritten, and computer-generated notes and reports recorded in the patient's records by a health care professional. Documentation must be dated and authenticated (with a legible signature or electronic authentication).

In a teaching hospital, documentation must identify what service was furnished, how the teaching physician participated in providing the service, and whether the teaching physician was physically present when care was provided. A **teaching hospital** is engaged in an approved graduate medical education (GME) residency program in medicine, osteopathy, dentistry, or podiatry. A **teaching physician** is a physician (other than another resident physician) who supervises residents during patient care. A **resident physician** is an individual who participates in an approved GME program. A **hospitalist** is a physician who provides care for hospital inpatients. They are often internists (e.g., internal medicine specialists) who handle a patient's entire admission process, including examining the patient, reviewing patient history and medications, writing admission orders, counseling the patient, and performing other tasks that would have required the primary care physician to travel to the hospital to coordinate the inpatient admission. Similar to the concept of emergency physicians practicing in the hospital's emergency department, hospitalists are based in the hospital and provide inpatient care. Thus, their practice is location-based instead of organ-centered (e.g., neurology) or age-centered (e.g., gerontology).

Medical Necessity

Documentation in the patient record serves as the basis for coding. The information in the record must support codes submitted on claims for third-party payer reimbursement processing. The patient's diagnosis must also justify diagnostic and therapeutic procedures or services provided. This is called **medical necessity** and requires providers to document services or supplies that are proper and needed for the diagnosis or treatment of a medical condition; provided for the diagnosis, direct care, and treatment of a medical condition; consistent with standards of good medical practice in the local area; and not mainly for the convenience of the physician or health care facility.

It is important to remember the familiar phrase, "If it wasn't documented, it wasn't done." The patient record serves as a medicolegal document and a business record. If a provider performs a service but does not document it, the patient (or third-party payer) can refuse to pay for that service, resulting in lost revenue for the provider. In addition, because the patient record serves as an excellent defense of the quality of care administered to a patient, missing documentation can result in problems if the record has to be admitted as evidence in a court of law.

EXAMPLE OF MISSING PATIENT RECORD DOCUMENTATION: A representative from XYZ Insurance Company reviewed 100 outpatient claims submitted by the Medical Center to ensure that all services billed were documented in the patient records. Upon reconciliation of claims with patient record documentation, the representative denied payment for 13 services (totaling $14,000) because reports of the services billed were not found in the patient records. The facility must pay back the $14,000 it received from the payer as reimbursement for the claims submitted.

EXAMPLE OF MEDICAL NECESSITY: The patient underwent an x-ray of his right knee, and the provider documented "severe right shoulder pain" in the record. The coder assigned a CPT code to the "right knee x-ray" and an ICD code to the "right shoulder pain." In this example, the third-party payer will deny reimbursement for the submitted claim because the *reason* for the x-ray (shoulder pain) does not match the *type* of x-ray performed. For medical necessity, the provider should have documented a diagnosis such as "right knee pain."

Patient Record Formats

Health care facilities and physicians' offices usually maintain either manual or automated records, and sometimes maintain a hybrid record. A **manual record** is paper-based, while an **automated record** uses computer technology. A **hybrid record** consists of both paper-based and computer-generated (electronic) documents, which means the facility or office creates and stores some patient reports as paper-based records (e.g., handwritten progress notes, physician orders, and graphic charts) and some documents using a computer (e.g., transcribed reports and automated laboratory results). A variety of formats are used to maintain manual records, which include the source-oriented record (SOR), problem-oriented record (POR), and integrated record. Automated record formats include the electronic health record (EHR) (or computer-based patient record, CPR), electronic medical record (EMR), and document imaging. Hybrid records use a combination format, such as the POR for paper-based reports and EMR for computer-stored reports.

 NOTE:

True EHRs are generated by multiple providers using specialized software, and results are stored electronically in a format that is easily retrievable and viewable by users.

Manual Record Formats

Source-oriented record (SOR) (or **sectionalized record**) reports are organized according to documentation (or data) source (e.g., ancillary, medical, and nursing). Each documentation (or data) source is located in a labeled section.

The **problem-oriented record (POR)** systematic method of documentation consists of four components:

- Database
- Problem list
- Initial plan
- Progress notes

The POR **database** contains patient information collected on each patient, including the following:

- Chief complaint
- Present conditions and diagnoses
- Social data
- Past, personal, medical, and social history
- Review of systems
- Physical examination
- Baseline laboratory data

The POR **problem list** serves as a table of contents for the patient record because it is filed at the beginning of the record and contains a numbered list of the patient's problems, which helps to index documentation throughout the record. The POR **initial plan** contains the strategy for managing patient care and any actions taken to investigate the patient's condition and to treat and educate the patient. The initial plan consists of three categories:

- **Diagnostic/management plans**: Plans to learn more about the patient's condition and the management of the conditions.
- **Therapeutic plans**: Specific medications, goals, procedures, therapies, and treatments used to treat the patient.
- **Patient education plans**: Plans to educate the patient about conditions for which the patient is being treated.

The POR **progress notes** are documented for each problem assigned to the patient, using the SOAP structure:

- **Subjective (S)**: Patient's statement about how he or she feels, including symptomatic information (e.g., "I have a headache.").
- **Objective (O)**: Observations about the patient, such as physical findings, or lab or x-ray results (e.g., chest x-ray negative).
- **Assessment (A)**: Judgment, opinion, or evaluation made by the health care provider (e.g., acute headache).
- **Plan (P)**: Diagnostic, therapeutic, and education plans to resolve the problems (e.g., patient to take Tylenol as needed for pain).

A **discharge note** is documented in the progress notes section of the POR to summarize the patient's care, treatment, response to care, and condition on discharge—documentation of all problems is included. A **transfer note** is documented when a patient is being transferred to another facility. It summarizes the reason for admission, current diagnoses and medical information, and reason for transfer.

Integrated record reports are arranged in strict chronological date order (or in reverse date order), which allows for observation of how the patient is progressing (e.g., responds to treatment) based on test results. Many facilities integrate only physician and ancillary services (e.g., physical therapy) progress notes, which require entries to be identified by appropriate authentication (e.g., complete signature of the professional documenting the note as Mary Smith, RRT, registered respiratory therapist).

Automated Record Formats

The **electronic health record (EHR)** is a collection of patient information documented by a number of providers at different facilities regarding one patient. It is a multidisciplinary (many specialties) and multienterprise (many facilities) approach to record keeping. The EHR provides access to complete and accurate health problems, status, and treatment data; it contains alerts (e.g., of drug interaction) and reminders (e.g., prescription renewal notice) for health care providers. According to the *Journal of Contemporary Dental Practice*, February 15, 2002, some professionals prefer to "use *electronic* instead of the earlier term *computer-based* because *electronic* better describes the medium in which the patient record is managed."

The **electronic medical record (EMR)** is created on a computer, using a keyboard, a mouse, an optical pen device, a voice-recognition system, a scanner, or a touch screen. Records are created using vendor software, which also assists in provider decision making (e.g., alerts, reminders, clinical decision support systems, and links to medical knowledge). Numerous vendors offer EMR software, mostly to physician office practices that require practice management solutions (e.g., appointment scheduling, claims processing, clinical notes, patient registration).

Document imaging often supplements the EHR or EMR by converting paper records (e.g., consent to treatment signed by patients) to an electronic format using laser technology to create the image; a **scanner** is used to capture paper record images onto the storage media. The paper record must be prepared for scanning (e.g., removal of staples) so documents can pass through the scanner properly using a document feeder that is attached to the scanner; each report is pulled through the scanner so the image is saved. Each scanned page is **indexed**, which means it is identified according to a unique identification number (e.g., patient record number). A unique feature is that documents for the same patient do *not* have to be scanned at the same time. Because each scanned page is indexed, the complete patient record can be retrieved even when a patient's reports are scanned at a later time.

Documentation Cloning Is an EMR/EHR Concern

Electronic Health Records Provider Fact Sheet. (Permission to reuse in accordance with http://www .cms.gov content reuse and linking policy.)

Medicare administrative contractors noted the frequency of electronic medical records (EMRs) and electronic health records (EHRs) that contain identical documentation across services. This was likely the result of *documentation cloning*, which involves using the EMR/EHR to bring information from previous patient encounters forward to the current encounter without updating that information. Documentation must reflect patient conditions and treatment for each encounter. Bringing forward previous documentation and simply changing the date in the EHR or EMR is unacceptable. The U.S. Department of Health and Human Services, Office of Inspector General (HHS-OIG) indicated its staff continue paying close attention to EMR/EHR documentation cloning.

Exercise 1.5 – Documentation as Basis for Coding

Instructions: If the statement in the first column indicates a primary purpose of the patient record, enter *a*. If the statement indicates a secondary purpose of the patient record, enter *b*.

_____ 1. Continuity of patient care

_____ 2. Evaluating quality of patient care

_____ 3. Providing data for use in clinical research

_____ 4. Serving medicolegal interests of patient, facility, and providers

_____ 5. Submitting information to payers for reimbursement

a. Primary purpose

b. Secondary purpose

Health Data Collection

Health data collection is performed by health care facilities and providers for the purpose of administrative planning, submitting statistics to state and federal government agencies (and other organizations), and reporting health claims data to third-party payers.

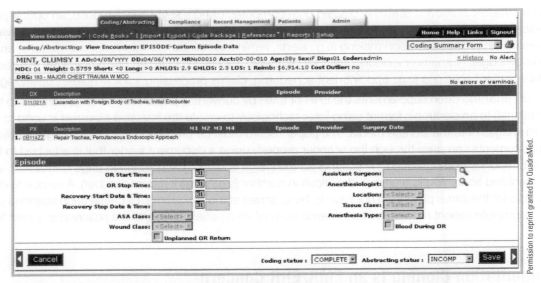

FIGURE 1-4 Sample data entry screen with ICD-10-CM and ICD-10-PCS codes and descriptions

Reporting Hospital Data

Hospitals and other health care facilities use **automated case abstracting software** to collect and report inpatient and outpatient data for statistical analysis and reimbursement purposes. Data are entered in an abstracting software program (Figure 1-4), and the facility's billing department imports it to the **UB-04** (or **CMS-1450**) claim (Figure 1-5) for submission to third-party payers. The facility's information technology department generates reports (Figure 1-6), which are used for statistical analysis. The UB-04 (or CMS-1450) is a standard claim (uniform bill) submitted by health care institutions to payers for inpatient and outpatient services. (The UB-04 is based on the UB-92, which was developed in 1992 and discontinued in 2007. There was also a UB-82, which was developed in 1982 and discontinued when the UB-92 was implemented.)

> **EXAMPLE:** Procedure data reports, profit and loss statements, and patient satisfaction surveys are used by health care planning and forecasting committees to determine the types of procedures performed at their facilities and the costs associated with providing such services. As a result of report analysis, procedures that contribute to a facility's profits and losses can be determined; in addition, some services may be expanded while others are eliminated.

Reporting Physician Office Data

Computerized physicians' offices use medical management software to enter claims data and either electronically submit CMS-1500 claims data to third-party payers or print paper-based CMS-1500 claims that are mailed or faxed to clearinghouses or payers for processing. The **CMS-1500** is a standard claim submitted by physicians' offices to third-party payers. **Medical management software** (e.g., MediSoft, The Medical Manager) is a combination of practice management and medical billing software that automates the daily workflow and procedures of a physician's office or clinic. The software automates the following functions:

- Appointment scheduling (e.g., initial and follow-up appointments) (Figure 1-7)
- Claims processing (e.g., CMS-1500 claims processing) (Figure 1-8)
- Patient invoicing (e.g., automated billing) (Figure 1-9)
- Patient management (e.g., patient registration) (Figure 1-10)
- Report generation (e.g., accounts receivable aging report) (Figure 1-11)

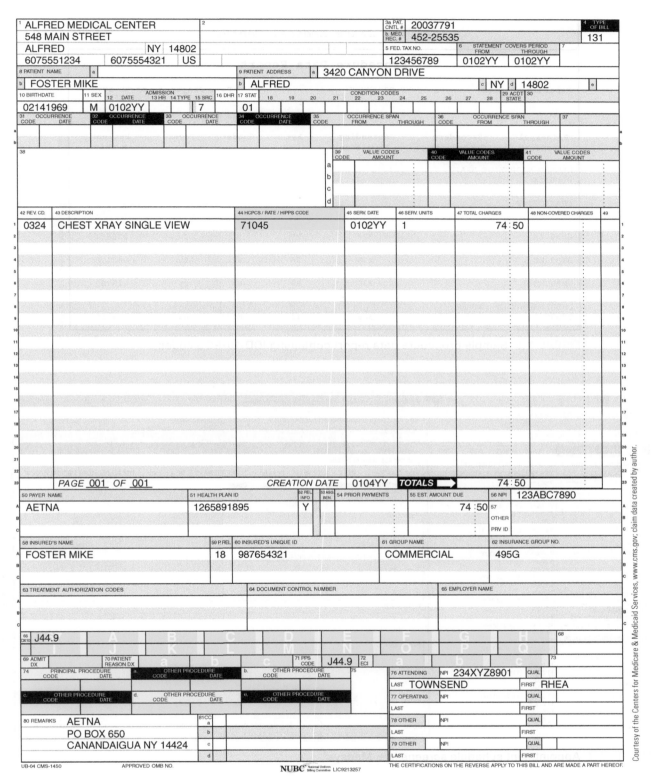

FIGURE 1-5 UB-04 claim with sample patient data in highlighted form locators that also contain ICD-10-CM and CPT codes

Alfred State Medical Center

Procedure Data Report

Reporting Period   0301YYYY-0301YYYY   Date Prepared   03-02-YYYY

Page   1 of 5

Principal Procedure	Secondary Procedures	Attending Physician	Age	Gender	Payer	Patient Number
CLOSED BIOPSY OF BRAIN 00B03ZX		248	42	F	01	562359
CRANIOTOMY 0N800ZZ		235	56	F	03	231587
0N800ZZ		326	27	M	02	239854
0N800ZZ		236	08	F	05	562198
0N800ZZ		236	88	M	05	615789
DEBRIDEMENT OF SKULL 0NB00ZZ		326	43	M	03	653218

FIGURE 1-6 Sample procedure data report containing ICD-10-PCS codes

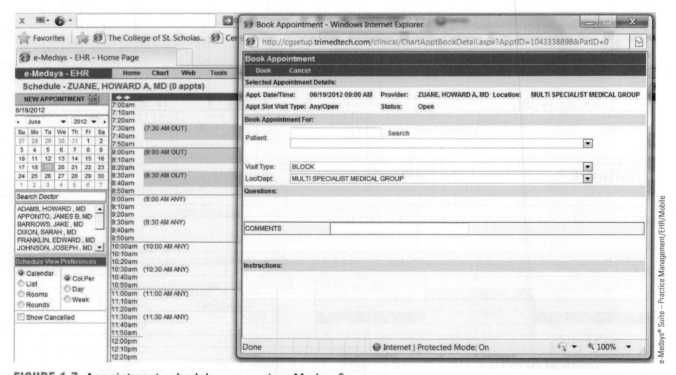

FIGURE 1-7 Appointment schedule screens in e-Medsys®

Medical assistants and insurance specialists use medical management software to collect physician office data for reimbursement purposes by locating patient information, inputting ICD-10-CM, CPT, and HCPCS level II codes for diagnoses and procedures/services, and generating and processing CMS-1500 claims. Medical management software generates claims for a variety of medical specialties, and claims can be printed and mailed

FIGURE 1-8 Claims processing screen

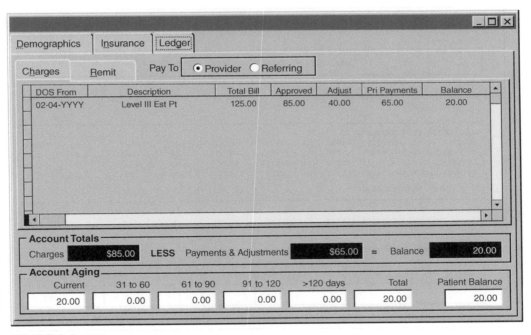

FIGURE 1-9 Billing screen

to clearinghouses, TPAs, or third-party payers for processing. The software also allows for submission of HIPAA-compliant electronic claims to clearinghouses, TPAs, or third-party payers.

When records are reviewed to select ICD-10-CM, CPT, and HCPCS level II codes for reporting to third-party payers, documentation in the physician office patient record serves as the basis for coding. Coders are responsible for reviewing patient records to select the appropriate diagnoses and procedures/services to which codes are assigned. Information in the record must support the codes submitted on claims for third-party payer

FIGURE 1-10 Patient registration screen in e-Medsys®

FIGURE 1-11 Accounts receivable aging report

reimbursement processing. The patient's diagnosis must justify diagnostic or therapeutic procedures or services provided (medical necessity), and the provider must document services or supplies that:

- are proper and needed for the diagnosis or treatment of a medical condition;
- are provided for the diagnosis, direct care, and treatment of a medical condition;
- meet the standards of good medical practice in the local area; and
- are not mainly for the convenience of the physician or health care facility.

Claims can be denied if the medical necessity of procedures or services is not established. Each procedure or service reported on the CMS-1500 claim must be linked to a condition that justifies the necessity for performing that procedure or providing that service. If the procedures or services delivered are determined to be unreasonable and unnecessary, the claim is denied. On the UB-04 claim, procedures/services are not linked; however, payers often request copies of patient records to review documentation to verify diagnoses, procedures, and services reported on the claim.

Exercise 1.6 – Health Data Collection

Instructions: Complete each statement.

1. Appointment scheduling and claims processing are processes associated with medical _____ software.
2. Hospital coders and abstractors use automated case _____ software to collect and report inpatient and outpatient data for statistical analysis and reimbursement purposes.
3. Physicians' offices submit data to third-party payers on the _____ claim.
4. Hospitals submit data to third-party payers on the _____ claim.
5. Claims are denied if _____ necessity of procedures or services is not established.

Summary

A coder is expected to master the use of coding systems, coding principles and rules, government regulations, and third-party payer requirements to ensure that all diagnoses, services, and procedures documented in patient records are accurately coded for reimbursement, research, and statistical purposes. To prepare for entry into the profession, students are encouraged to join a professional association. They usually pay a reduced membership fee and receive most of the same benefits as active members. The benefits of joining a professional association include eligibility for scholarships and grants, opportunity to network with members, free publications, reduced certification exam fees, and website access for members only.

Coding systems and medical nomenclatures are used by health care facilities, health care providers, and third-party payers to collect, store, and process data for a variety of purposes. A coding system organizes a medical nomenclature according to similar conditions, diseases, procedures, and services; it contains codes for each. A medical nomenclature includes clinical terminologies and clinical laboratories that are used by health care providers to document patient care; *clinical terminologies* include designations, expressions, symbols, and terms used in the field of medicine, and *clinical vocabularies* include clinical phrases or words along with their meanings. Codes include numeric and alphanumeric characters that are reported to health plans for health care reimbursement and to external agencies for data collection and internally for education and research. Coding is the assignment of codes to diagnoses, services, and procedures based on patient record documentation.

Health care providers are responsible for documenting and authenticating legible, complete, and timely patient records in accordance with federal regulations and accrediting agency standards. The provider is also responsible for correcting or editing errors in patient record documentation. Health data collection is performed by health care facilities to do administrative planning, to submit statistics to state and federal government agencies, and to report health claims data to third-party payers for reimbursement purposes.

Internet Links

Alternate Billing Codes (ABC codes) Go to: *www.abccodes.com,* click on the Why ABC Codes link.

AHA Central Office Go to: *www.ahacentraloffice.org* to review resources available at the AHA Central Office website. The American Hospital Association's (AHA) Central Office serves as the official U.S. clearinghouse for proper use of ICD-10-CM, ICD-10-PCS, and HCPCS level II codes for health care providers.

AAPC: *www.aapc.com*

American Association of Medical Assistants (AAMA): *www.aama-ntl.org*

American Health Information Management Association (AHIMA): *www.ahima.org*

American Medical Billing Association (AMBA): *www.americanmedicalbillingassociation.com*

American Medical Technologists (AMT): *www.americanmedtech.org*

Clinical Care Classification (CCC): *www.sabacare.com*

Current Dental Terminology (CDT): Go to *www.ada.org,* click on the Publications link, and then click on the CDT: Code on Dental Procedures and Nomenclature link.

Diagnostic and Statistical Manual of Mental Disorders (DSM): *www.dsm5.org*

Health Insurance Prospective Payment System (HIPPS) Rate Codes: Go to *www.cms.gov,* click on the Medicare link, locate the Medicare Fee-for-Service Payment heading, click on the Prospective Payment Systems - General Information link, and click on the HIPPS Codes link.

International Classification of Diseases for Oncology (ICD-O-3): Go to *www.who.int,* click on the Health topics link, click on the letter C link, click on the Classifications link, scroll down to the Derived Classifications heading, and click on the International Classification of Diseases for Oncology, 3rd Edition (ICD-O-3) link.

International Classification of Functioning, Disability and Health (ICF): Go to *www.who.int,* click on the Health topics link, click on the letter I link, and click on the International Classification of Functioning, Disability and Health (ICF) link.

Medical Association of Billers (MAB): *https://mabillers.com*

National Drug Codes (NDC): Go to *www.fda.gov,* and use the Search feature to enter National Drug Codes to navigate to the National Drug Code Directory.

National Cancer Institute's Surveillance, Epidemiology, and End Results (SEER) Training Modules: Go to *training.seer.cancer.gov,* click on the Cancer Registration & Surveillance Modules link, and click on the Coding Primary Site & Tumor Morphology link.

PlatoCode: Go to *www.platocode.com* to learn more about computer assisted coding (CAC).

RxNorm: Go to *www.nlm.nih.gov,* and enter RxNorm in the Search box.

UMLS: Go to *www.nlm.nih.gov,* and enter UMLS in the Search box.

Review

Multiple Choice

Instructions: Circle the most appropriate response.

1. The Health Insurance Portability and Accountability Act of 1996 (HIPAA) requires _____ types of code sets to be adopted for the purpose of encoding data elements.

    a. two   **b.** three   **c.** four   **d.** five

2. Which is considered to be a small code set according to HIPAA?
   - **a.** Actions taken to prevent, diagnose, treat, and manage diseases and injuries
   - **b.** Causes of injury, disease, impairment, or other health-related problems
   - **c.** Diseases, injuries, impairments, and other health-related problems
   - **d.** Race, ethnicity, type of facility, and type of unit

3. Which is a code set adopted by HIPAA for use by clearinghouses, health plans, and providers?
   - **a.** ABC codes
   - **b.** CMIT
   - **c.** NDC
   - **d.** SNOMED

4. The purpose of adopting standard code sets was to:
   - **a.** establish a medical nomenclature to standardize HIPAA data submissions.
   - **b.** improve data quality and simplify claims submission for providers.
   - **c.** increase costs associated with processing health insurance claims.
   - **d.** regulate health care clearinghouses and third-party administrators.

5. According to HIPAA, health plans that do not accept standard code sets are required to modify their systems to accept all valid codes or to contract with a(n):
   - **a.** electronic data interchange.
   - **b.** health care clearinghouse.
   - **c.** insurance company.
   - **d.** third-party administrator.

6. Which type of clinical terminologies and clinical vocabularies are used by health care providers to document patient care?
   - **a.** Classification system
   - **b.** Demographic data
   - **c.** Medical nomenclature
   - **d.** *Nosologia Methodica*

7. The requirement that the patient's diagnoses justify diagnostic and/or therapeutic procedures or services provided is called:
   - **a.** continuity of care.
   - **b.** facilities planning.
   - **c.** medical necessity.
   - **d.** policy making.

8. Which is the business record for a patient encounter (inpatient or outpatient) that documents health care services provided to a patient?
   - **a.** Demographic data
   - **b.** Financial record
   - **c.** Health care statistics
   - **d.** Medical record

9. The primary purpose of the record is _____, which involves documenting patient care services so that others who treat the patient have a source of information on which to base additional care and treatment.
   - **a.** continuity of care
   - **b.** medical necessity
   - **c.** medicolegal
   - **d.** quality of care

10. Which is a secondary purpose of the medical record that does not relate directly to patient care?
    - **a.** Clinical research
    - **b.** Continuity of care
    - **c.** Discharge note
    - **d.** Hybrid record

11. Which type of medical record format stores documentation in labeled sections?
    - **a.** Integrated record
    - **b.** Problem-oriented record
    - **c.** Source-oriented record
    - **d.** SOAP notes

12. A progress note contains diagnoses of muscle strain and weakness. This statement would be located in the _____ portion of the POR progress note.
    - **a.** Assessment
    - **b.** Objective
    - **c.** Plan
    - **d.** Subjective

13. A progress note contains documentation that the patient is to be followed up with in the physician's office two weeks after discharge from the hospital. This statement would be located in the _____ portion of the POR progress note.
    - **a.** Assessment
    - **b.** Objective
    - **c.** Plan
    - **d.** Subjective

14. A progress note contains documentation that the EKG showed elevated T-wave changes. This statement would be located in the _____ portion of the POR progress note.

    a. Assessment   **b.** Objective   **c.** Plan   **d.** Subjective

15. Which is documented in the progress note section of the POR to summarize the patient's care, treatment, response to care, and condition on discharge?

    a. Demographic data   **c.** Medical necessity
    b. Discharge note   **d.** Transfer note

16. Which is used to capture paper record images onto storage media?

    a. EHR   **c.** Documentation cloning
    b. EMR   **d.** Scanner

17. To provide the maximum benefit to students, internships are typically _____ work experiences that are arranged by academic program faculty.

    a. elective   **c.** optional
    b. nonpaid   **d.** voluntary

18. To whom does the student report at the professional practice experience (or internship) site?

    a. Supervisor   **c.** Physician
    b. Patient   **d.** Program faculty

19. Which is a benefit of joining a professional association?

    a. Free certification examination fees
    b. Opportunities to network with other members
    c. Reduced benefits as compared with nonmembers
    d. Website-only access to professional journals

20. Which processes health care claims and performs related business functions for a health plan?

    a. Health care clearinghouse
    b. Health care provider
    c. Third-party administrator
    d. Third-party payer

21. Which classifies dental procedures and services?

    a. CDT   **c.** HCPCS
    b. CPT   **d.** ICD-10-PCS

22. Which is a standard classification of mental disorders used by mental health professionals in the United States?

    a. ABC   **c.** DSM
    b. CCC   **d.** ICF

23. Which is an electronic database and universal standard used for clinical care and management?

    a. LOINC   **c.** READ
    b. SNOMED   **d.** UMLS

24. Hospitals and other health care facilities use automated case abstracting software to:

    a. collect and report data for statistical analysis and reimbursement purposes.
    b. generate claims data for electronic submission to health care providers.
    c. justify diagnostic or therapeutic procedures or services provided to patients.
    d. submit standard claims to providers for inpatient and outpatient services.

25. Which is the standard claim submitted by physicians' offices to third-party payers?

    a. CMS-1450   **c.** UB-04
    b. CMS-1500   **d.** UB-92

PART II

ICD-10-CM and ICD-10-PCS Coding Systems

Part II of *3-2-1 Code It!* contains the following individual chapters that cover ICD-10-CM and ICD-10-PCS coding.

2: Introduction to ICD-10-CM and ICD-10-PCS Coding, 44

3: ICD-10-CM and ICD-10-PCS Coding Conventions, 84

4: Chapter-Specific Coding Guidelines: ICD-10-CM Chapters 1–10, 113

5: Chapter-Specific Coding Guidelines: ICD-10-CM Chapters 11–21, 156

6: ICD-10-CM and ICD-10-PCS Hospital Inpatient Coding, 209

7: ICD-10-CM Outpatient and Physician Office Coding, 265

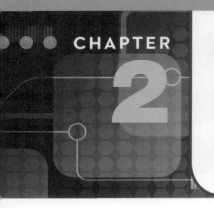

CHAPTER 2

Introduction to ICD-10-CM and ICD-10-PCS Coding

Chapter Outline

Overview of ICD-10-CM and ICD-10-PCS

ICD-10-CM Index to Diseases and Injuries

ICD-10-CM Tabular List of Diseases and Injuries

ICD-10-CM Official Guidelines for Coding and
  Reporting

ICD-10-PCS Index and Tables

ICD-9-CM Legacy Coding System

Chapter Objectives

At the conclusion of this chapter, the student should be able to:

1. Define key terms related to the introduction of ICD-10-CM and ICD-10-PCS coding.
2. Explain the purpose of assigning ICD-10-CM and ICD-10-PCS codes.
3. Locate main terms for diagnostic statements using the ICD-10-CM Index to Diseases and Injuries.
4. Assign diagnosis codes using the ICD-10-CM Index to Diseases and Injuries and the ICD-10-CM Tabular List of Diseases and Injuries.
5. Explain general ICD-10-CM official guidelines for coding and reporting.
6. Assign procedure codes using the ICD-10-PCS Index and Tables.
7. Use general equivalence mappings (GEMs) as part of the ICD-9-CM legacy coding system.

Key Terms

category

combination code

Cooperating Parties
  for the ICD-10-CM/
  PCS

encoder

encounter

essential modifier

etiology

general equivalence
  mapping (GEM)

ICD-10 Coordination
  and Maintenance
  Committee

Index to Diseases and
  Injuries

*International
  Classification of
  Diseases (ICD)*

laterality

legacy classification
  system

legacy coding system

main term

Medicare Prescription
  Drug, Improvement,
  and Modernization
  Act (MMA)

morbidity

mortality

multiple codes

nonessential modifier

| Official ICD-10-CM Guidelines for Coding and Reporting | Official ICD-10-PCS Guidelines for Coding and Reporting placeholder | residual effect sequela subcategory | subterm Tabular List of Diseases and Injuries |

Introduction

There are two related classifications of diseases with similar titles. The ***International Classification of Diseases (ICD)*** is published by the World Health Organization (WHO) and is used to classify **mortality** (death) data from death certificates. WHO published the tenth revision of ICD in 1994 with a new name, *International Statistical Classification of Diseases and Related Health Problems*, and reorganized its 3-digit categories. (Although the name of the publication was changed, the familiar abbreviation ICD was kept.)

The *International Classification of Diseases, Tenth Revision, Clinical Modification* (ICD-10-CM) was developed in the United States and is used to code and classify **morbidity** (disease) data from inpatient and outpatient records, including physician office records. ICD-10-CM is a closed classification system that is used in the United States to classify diagnoses, which means that ICD-10-CM provides just one place to classify each condition.

All health care settings use ICD-10-CM to report diagnoses. The *International Classification of Diseases, Tenth Revision, Procedure Classification System* (ICD-10-PCS) is used to code and classify procedure data from hospital inpatient records only. (ICD-10-CM and ICD-10-PCS are abbreviated as ICD-10-CM/PCS.)

ICD-10-CM and ICD-10-PCS Official Guidelines for Coding and Reporting are used as a companion to ICD-10-CM and ICD-10-PCS, respectively, to ensure accurate coding. This chapter includes an overview about official guidelines for coding and reporting along with details about general ICD-10-CM diagnosis coding guidelines. (ICD-10-CM coding conventions are covered in Chapter 3. ICD-10-CM chapter-specific diagnosis coding guidelines are covered in Chapters 4 and 5. ICD-10-PCS coding guidelines are covered in more detail in Chapter 6.)

 NOTE:

Provider offices and health care facilities (e.g., hospitals) use ICD-10-CM to code diagnoses. Hospitals use ICD-10-PCS to code inpatient procedures. (Provider offices and outpatient health care settings use CPT and HCPCS level II to code procedures and services.) ICD-10-CM and ICD-10-PCS are abbreviated as ICD-10-CM/PCS.

Overview of ICD-10-CM and ICD-10-PCS

ICD-10-CM is a clinical modification of WHO's *International Classification of Diseases, Tenth Revision* (ICD-10). The term *clinical* is used to emphasize the modification's intent. This means that the coding system serves as a useful tool in the classification of morbidity data for indexing of patient records, reviewing quality of care, and compiling basic health statistics. Used to describe the clinical picture of the patient, ICD-10-CM and ICD-10-PCS codes are more precise than those needed for statistical groupings and trends analysis.

ICD-10-CM is divided into two main parts:

- Index to Diseases and Injuries, which is an alphabetical list of terms and corresponding codes, and includes a Neoplasm Table, Table of Drugs and Chemicals, and an Index to External Causes
- Tabular List of Diseases and Injuries, which is a sequential, alphanumeric list of codes divided into chapters based on body system or condition

 NOTE:

Official ICD-10-CM Guidelines for Coding and Reporting, which serve as a companion document to ICD-10-CM, are discussed later in this chapter.

ICD-10-PCS is divided into two main parts:

- Index, which is an alphabetic list of procedures according to general type of procedure (e.g., resection), or a more commonly used term (e.g., appendectomy), and includes the first three or four values of the code (or directs the user to see another term)
- Tables, which are organized according to sections that contain rows that specify valid combinations of code values

NOTE:

Official ICD-10-PCS Guidelines for Coding and Reporting, which serve as a companion document to ICD-10-PCS, are discussed later in this chapter.

ICD-10-CM and ICD-10-PCS (ICD-10-CM/PCS)

The *International Classification of Diseases, Tenth Revision, Clinical Modification* (ICD-10-CM) and the *International Classification of Diseases, Tenth Revision, Procedure Coding System* (ICD-10-PCS) are abbreviated as ICD-10-CM/PCS. ICD-10-CM/PCS also enhances accurate payment for services rendered and facilitates evaluation of medical processes and outcomes. The term *clinical* emphasizes the modification's intent, which is to:

- Describe the clinical picture of the patient, which means the codes must be more precise than those needed only for statistical groupings and trend analysis.
- Serve as a useful tool in the area of classification of morbidity data for indexing of medical records, medical care review, and ambulatory and other medical care programs, as well as for basic health statistics.

NOTE:

The Centers for Medicare & Medicaid Services (CMS) shortens the name of the classification systems to *International Classification of Diseases, 10th Edition, Clinical Modification/Procedure Coding System*, abbreviating it as ICD-10-CM/PCS.

ICD-10-CM is the diagnosis classification system developed by the Centers for Disease Control and Prevention (CDC) for use in *all* U.S. health care treatment settings. ICD-10-CM codes require up to 7 characters, are entirely alphanumeric, and have new coding conventions (e.g., Excludes1 and Excludes2 notes).

ICD-10-CM and ICD-10-PCS incorporate specificity and clinical information, resulting in:

- Decreased need to include supporting documentation with claims
- Enhanced ability to conduct public health surveillance
- Improved ability to measure health care services
- Increased sensitivity when refining grouping and reimbursement methodologies

ICD-10-CM and ICD-10-PCS also provide codes to allow comparison of mortality and morbidity data, and provide data for:

- Conducting research
- Designing payment systems
- Identifying fraud and abuse
- Making clinical decisions
- Measuring care furnished to patients
- Processing claims
- Tracking public health

NOTE:

In ICD-10-PCS, *multiaxial* means the codes contain independent characters, with each axis retaining its meaning across broad ranges of codes (to the extent possible). There is no decimal used in ICD-10-PCS codes. The letters I and O are *never* used in ICD-10-PCS because they are too easily confused with the numbers 1 and 0.

ICD-10-PCS was developed by the CMS for use in the United States for inpatient hospital settings *only*. ICD-10-PCS uses a multiaxial 7-character alphanumeric code structure (e.g., 047K04Z) that provides a unique code for all substantially different procedures. It also allows new procedures to be easily incorporated as new codes. ICD-10-PCS contains more than 87,000 seven-character alphanumeric procedure codes.

ICD-10-CM (1) includes health-related conditions, (2) provides greater specificity at the sixth character level, and (3) adds a seventh character extension (for some codes). Assigning the sixth and seventh characters when available for ICD-10-CM codes is mandatory because they report information documented in the patient record.

EXAMPLE 1: The diagnosis is stage 3 pressure ulcer of the right lower back. In ICD-10-CM, combination code L89.133 is reported to classify the condition along with its depth, location, and laterality (e.g., right side).

ICD-10-CM Tabular List of Diseases and Injuries
L89.133 Pressure ulcer of right lower back, stage 3
Healing pressure ulcer of right lower back, stage 3
Pressure ulcer with full thickness skin loss involving damage or necrosis of subcutaneous tissue, right lower back

EXAMPLE 2: The diagnosis is mechanical breakdown of right femoral arterial graft. In ICD-10-CM, combination code T82.312A is reported, and the right side is classified.

ICD-10-CM Tabular List of Diseases and Injuries
The appropriate 7th character is to be added to each code from category T82.
A   initial encounter
D   subsequent encounter
S   sequela
T82.3   Mechanical complication of other vascular grafts
T82.31   Breakdown (mechanical) of other vascular grafts
T82.310   Breakdown (mechanical) of aortic (bifurcation) graft (replacement)
T82.311   Breakdown (mechanical) of carotid arterial graft (bypass)
T82.312   Breakdown (mechanical) of femoral arterial graft (bypass)
T82.318   Breakdown (mechanical) of other vascular grafts
T82.319   Breakdown (mechanical) of unspecified vascular grafts

Coding Manuals, Encoders, and Computer-Assisted Coding

Many publishers produce their own versions of ICD-10-CM and ICD-10-PCS coding manuals. Companies also publish **encoders**, which automate the coding process by using the search feature to locate and verify codes.

EXAMPLE: ICD-10-CM codes need to be assigned for a physician office visit because the provider selected only the appropriate CPT evaluation and management service code on the encounter form. The reason for the visit was "flu," and the patient's respiratory symptoms had been documented.

Using Optum360's *EncoderPro.com Expert* software and selecting ICD-10-CM as the Code Set Search, "flu" was entered in the search box. A list of ICD-10-CM codes was generated, and "J11.1 Influenza due to unidentified influenza virus with other respiratory manifestations" was selected to review its tabular list entry. Upon review of that tabular entry, which included the J11.1 code, description, and notes (e.g., Use additional code), J11.1 is selected as the code to be reported on the claim. (Codes associated with the "Use additional code" notes were not documented in the patient record and, thus, not reported.)

Computer-assisted coding (CAC) software analyzes the electronic health record (EHR) or electronic medical record (EMR) to generate codes for documented terms and phrases. Coders use data analytic skills to review CAC-generated codes and determine which are to be reported. Data analytic skills allow coders to review codes generated by CAC software, compare codes to documentation in the electronic health record, and select appropriate codes to report for reimbursement purposes.

Format and Structure of ICD-10-CM

ICD-10-CM is divided into two main parts:

- Index to Diseases and Injuries, which is an alphabetical list of terms and their corresponding codes (and includes a Neoplasm Table, Table of Drugs and Chemicals, and an Index to External Causes)
- Tabular List of Diseases and Injuries, which is a sequential, alphanumeric list of codes organized according to chapters based on body system or condition

 NOTE:

ICD-10-PCS Tables are organized into sections (e.g., medical and surgical, obstetrics, imaging), each of which contains a code table. Refer to the ICD-10-PCS Index and Tables heading later in this chapter for more information about the organization and structure of the ICD-10-PCS coding system.

Updating ICD-10-CM and ICD-10-PCS

The National Center for Health Statistics (NCHS) and the Centers for Medicare & Medicaid Services (CMS) are the U.S. Department of Health & Human Services (DHHS) agencies that comprise the **ICD-10 Coordination and Maintenance Committee,** which is responsible for overseeing all changes and modifications to

EXAMPLE OF COMPUTER-ASSISTED CODING: A physician office EMR note is pasted into the Find-A-Code, LLC, *Code-A-Note* CAC product, and the Scan Notes link is clicked to generate a list of possible ICD-10-CM and CPT codes. The list of ICD-10-CM codes requires the coder to compare documentation to codes and then select appropriate codes to be reported. (Likewise, the list of CPT codes requires coder review and selection. In this case, the provider had already selected the appropriate CPT evaluation and management service code from the encounter form.)

ICD-10-CM and ICD-10-PCS. The NCHS works with the WHO to coordinate official disease classification activities for ICD-10-CM. Activities include the use, interpretation, and periodic revision of the classification system. CMS is responsible for annually updating the ICD-10-PCS procedure classification. The Committee also updated the ICD-9-CM and ICD-10-CM/PCS general equivalency mappings (GEMs) through 2018 for ICD-10-CM and ICD-10-PCS.

The **Medicare Prescription Drug, Improvement, and Modernization Act (MMA)** requires all code sets (e.g., ICD-10-CM, ICD-10-PCS) to be valid at the time services are provided. This means that April 1 and October 1 coding updates for ICD-10-CM/PCS must be implemented immediately so accurate codes are reported on claims. (HIPAA legislation also requires the reporting of codes on health insurance claims.)

It is crucial that updated coding manuals be purchased and billing systems be updated with coding changes so that billing delays (e.g., due to waiting for new coding manuals to arrive) and claims rejections are avoided. If outdated codes are submitted on claims, providers and health care facilities will incur administrative costs associated with resubmitting corrected claims and delayed reimbursement for services provided.

- Coders should consider using updateable coding manuals, which publishers offer as a subscription service. These coding manuals are usually stored in a three-ring binder so that coders can remove outdated pages and add newly printed pages provided by the publisher.

- Another option is to purchase encoder software, which publishers also offer as a subscription service. Coders routinely download the most up-to-date encoder software, which contains edits for new, revised, and discontinued codes. An *encoder* automates the coding process using computerized or web-based software; instead of manually looking up conditions (or procedures) in the coding manual index, the coder uses the software's search feature to locate and verify diagnosis and procedure codes.

- Automating the medical coding process is the goal of *computer-assisted coding (CAC)*, which uses a natural language processing engine to "read" patient records and generate ICD-10-CM, ICD-10-PCS, HCPCS level II, and CPT codes. Because of this process, coders become coding auditors (or coding editors), responsible for ensuring the accuracy of codes reported to payers. (CAC can be compared to speech recognition technology that has transitioned the role of medical transcriptionists in certain fields, such as radiology, to that of medical editors.)

History of the International Classification of Diseases (ICD)

The WHO's original intent for ICD was that it would serve as a statistical tool for the international collection and exchange of mortality (death) data. A subsequent revision was expanded to accommodate data collection for morbidity (disease) statistics. The seventh revision (ICD-7), published by WHO in 1955, was clinically modified for use in the United States after a joint study was conducted to evaluate the efficiency of indexing hospital diseases (cataloging diseases and procedures by code). The study participants included the American Hospital Association (AHA) and the American Association of Medical Record Librarians (AAMRL) (now called the American Health Information Management Association, or AHIMA). Results of that study led to the 1959 publication of the International Classification of Diseases, Adapted for Indexing Hospital Records (ICDA), by the federal Public Health Service. The ICDA uniformly modified ICD-7, and it gave the United States a way to classify patient operations and treatments.

An eighth edition of ICD (ICD-8), published by WHO in 1965, lacked the depth of clinical data required for America's emerging health care delivery system. In 1968, two widely accepted modifications were published in the United States: the Eighth Revision of the International Classification of Diseases, Adapted for Use in the United States (ICDA-8), and the Hospital Adaptation of ICDA (H-ICDA).

Hospitals used either of these two systems until 1979, when ICD-9-CM was implemented. The ninth revision of the ICD (ICD-9), published by WHO in 1975, once again prompted the development of a clinical modification. This time the incentive resulted from a process initiated in 1977 by the National Center for Health Statistics (NCHS) for hospital indexing and the retrieval of case data for clinical studies. After more than 30 years since its adoption in the United States, ICD has proven to be indispensable to anyone interested in payment schedules for the delivery of health care services to patients.

The WHO published ICD-10 in 1994 with a new name (*International Statistical Classification of Diseases and Related Health Problems*) and reorganized its 3-digit categories. Although the title was amended to clarify content and purpose and to reflect development of codes and descriptions beyond diseases and injuries, the familiar abbreviation "ICD" was kept.

ICD-10 contains clinical detail, expands information about previously classified diseases, and classifies diseases discovered since the last revision. ICD-10 also incorporates organizational changes and new features, but its format and conventions remain largely unchanged. ICD-10 chapter titles, organization, and includes notes are similar to ICD-9. The greatest difference is that the new ICD-10 codes are alphanumeric, new excludes1 and excludes2 notes were added, and there is more detail in ICD-10-CM than in ICD-9-CM.

A number of other countries have already adopted ICD-10, including the United Kingdom (1995), France (1997), Australia (1998), Germany (2000), and Canada (2001). ICD-10-CM and ICD-10-PCS provide significant improvements through greater detailed information and the ability to expand in order to capture additional advancements in clinical medicine. The change from ICD-9-CM to the NCHS-developed ICD-10-CM and the CMS-developed ICD-10-PCS (Procedure Coding System) took effect October 1, 2015.

Mandatory Reporting of ICD-10-CM Codes

The Medicare Catastrophic Coverage Act of 1988 mandated the reporting of diagnosis codes on Medicare claims; in subsequent years, private third-party payers adopted similar requirements for claims submission.

Reporting ICD-10-CM codes on submitted claims (Figure 2-1) ensures the medical necessity of procedures and services provided to patients during an encounter. An **encounter** is a face-to-face contact between a patient and a health care provider (e.g., physician, nurse practitioner) who assesses and treats the patient's condition. Medicare defines medical necessity as "the determination that a service or procedure rendered is reasonable and necessary for the diagnosis or treatment of an illness or injury."

21. DIAGNOSIS OR NATURE OF ILLNESS OR INJURY Relate A-L to service line below (24E) ICD Ind. **0**					22. RESUBMISSION CODE ORIGINAL REF. NO.	
A. **S63501A**	B. **E119**	C.	D.		23. PRIOR AUTHORIZATION NUMBER	
E.	F.	G.	H.			
I.	J.	K.	L.			

24. A. DATE(S) OF SERVICE From / To			B. PLACE OF SERVICE	C. EMG	D. PROCEDURES, SERVICES, OR SUPPLIES (Explain Unusual Circumstances) CPT/HCPCS | MODIFIER	E. DIAGNOSIS POINTER	F. $ CHARGES	G. DAYS OR UNITS	H. EPSDT Family Plan	I. ID. QUAL.	J. RENDERING PROVIDER ID. #
1	05 01 YYYY		11		99214	A B	125 00	1		NPI	
2	05 01 YYYY		11		82947	B	95 00	1		NPI	
3	05 01 YYYY		11		S8451	A	105 00	1		NPI	
4										NPI	
5										NPI	
6										NPI	

Courtesy of the Centers for Medicare & Medicaid Services, www.cms.gov, claim data created by author.

FIGURE 2-1 CMS-1500 claim Blocks 21 (ICD-10-CM codes) and 24E (Diagnosis Pointer for CPT codes in 24D), which illustrate medical necessity of procedures and services

NOTE:

The Administrative Simplification subtitle of the Health Insurance Portability and Accountability Act of 1996 (HIPAA) mandated the adoption of code set standards in the Transactions and Code Sets final rule published in the *Federal Register*. The final rule modifies the standard medical data code sets for coding diagnoses and inpatient hospital procedures by concurrently adopting the *International Classification of Diseases, 10th Revision, Clinical Modification* (ICD-10-CM) for diagnosis coding (including the *Official ICD-10-CM Guidelines for Coding and Reporting*, as maintained and distributed by the U.S. Department of Health and Human Services) and the *International Classification of Diseases, 10th Revision, Procedure Coding System* (ICD-10-PCS) for inpatient hospital procedure coding (including the *Official ICD-10-PCS Guidelines for Coding and Reporting*, as maintained and distributed by the HHS).

Medical Necessity

Today's concept of medical necessity determines the extent to which individuals with health conditions receive health care services. (The concept was introduced in the 1970s when health insurance contracts intended to exclude care, such as voluntary hospitalizations prescribed primarily for the convenience of the provider or patient.) *Medical necessity* is the measure of whether a health care procedure or service is appropriate for the diagnosis and treatment of a condition. This decision-making process is based on the payer's contractual language and the treating provider's documentation. Generally, the following criteria are used to determine medical necessity:

- *Purpose:* The procedure or service is performed to treat a medical condition.
- *Scope:* The most appropriate level of service is provided, taking into consideration potential benefit and harm to the patient.
- *Evidence:* The treatment is known to be effective in improving health outcomes.
- *Value:* The treatment is cost-effective for this condition when compared to alternative treatments, including no treatment.

 NOTE:

Cost-effective does not necessarily mean least expensive.

EXAMPLE: A 70-year-old male patient with type 1 diabetes mellitus is treated at the physician's office for severe wrist pain resulting from a fall. When the physician asks the patient whether he has been regularly taking his insulin and checking his blood glucose levels, the patient says that most of the time he takes his insulin and sometimes he forgets to check his blood glucose levels. The physician orders a blood glucose test to be done in the office, which reveals elevated blood glucose levels. The physician provides counseling and education to the patient about the importance of taking his daily insulin and checking his blood glucose levels. The physician also orders an x-ray of the wrist, which proves to be negative for a fracture. The physician provides the patient with a wrist brace and instructs the patient to follow up in the office within four weeks.

The insurance specialist reports ICD-10-CM codes for type 1 diabetes mellitus and sprained wrist along with CPT and/or HCPCS level II codes for an office visit, blood glucose lab test, and the wrist brace. If the only diagnosis reported on the claim (Figure 2-1) was a sprained wrist, the blood glucose lab test would be rejected for payment by the insurance company as an unnecessary medical procedure.

Exercise 2.1 – Overview of ICD-10-CM and ICD-10-PCS

Instructions: Complete each statement.

1. ICD-10-CM and ICD-10-PCS were adopted in the year _____ to replace ICD-9-CM.

2. The ICD-10 Coordination and _____ Committee is responsible for overseeing all changes to ICD-10-CM and ICD-10-PCS.

3. The U.S. Department of Health & Human Services agency responsible for overseeing all changes and modifications to ICD-10-CM is _____.

4. The Medicare Prescription Drug, Improvement, and _____ Act (MMA) requires all code sets to be valid at the time services are provided, which means that midyear (April 1) and end-of-year (October 1) coding updates must be implemented immediately so accurate codes are reported on claims.

5. Updateable coding manuals, which publishers offer as an annual _____ service, are popular because coders can remove outdated pages and insert updated pages into the binders.

6. The coding process is automated when computerized or web-based _____ software is used instead of coding books to locate codes manually; the coder uses the software's search feature to locate and verify codes.

7. The reporting of _____ codes on Medicare claims was originally mandated by the Medicare Catastrophic Coverage Act of 1988 while reporting of ICD-10-CM/PCS codes was mandated by HIPAA and the MMA.

8. Reporting ICD-10-CM codes on submitted claims ensures the medical_____ of procedures and services provided to patients during an encounter, which is defined as "the determination that a service or procedure rendered is reasonable and necessary for the diagnosis or treatment of an illness or injury."

9. A patient is seen in the office for the following conditions: chest pain, chronic hypertension, and controlled diabetes mellitus. The provider orders a blood glucose level, chest x-ray, and EKG. For medical necessity, the chest x-ray would be linked to the _____.

10. A patient is seen in the hospital emergency department for treatment of multiple lacerations; the patient also complains of dizziness and a severe headache that is unrelieved by pain medications. The emergency department physician orders a brain scan and performs extensive suturing. For medical necessity, the suturing would be linked to the _____.

ICD-10-CM Index to Diseases and Injuries

The ICD-10-CM **Index to Diseases and Injuries** (Figure 2-2) is an alphabetical list of main terms and their corresponding codes. Main terms are printed in boldfaced type, and subterms and qualifiers are indented below main terms. The ICD-10-CM index is subdivided into two parts (Table 2-1):

- Index to Diseases and Injuries, which includes a Table of Neoplasms and a Table of Drugs and Chemicals

- Index to External Causes of Injuries

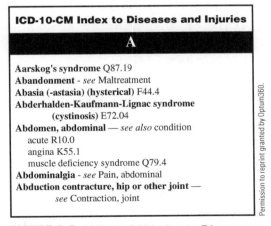

FIGURE 2-2 ICD-10-CM Index to Diseases and Injuries (partial)

Main terms in the Index to Diseases and Injuries are listed in alphabetical order, which means hyphens within main terms are ignored, but a single space within a main term is not ignored. When numerical characters and words appear below a main term, they are listed in alphabetical order. A code listed next

TABLE 2-1 ICD-10-CM Index to Diseases and Injuries

Index to Diseases and Injuries (contains two tables)
Table of Neoplasms
Table of Drugs and Chemicals
Index to External Causes of Injuries

Courtesy of the Centers for Medicare & Medicaid Services, www.cms.gov.

to a main term in the index is referred to as a *default code*. The *default code* represents the code for the condition most commonly associated with the main term, or it may represent an unspecified code for the condition. (The Tabular List of Diseases and Injuries must always be referenced so that the most accurate and complete code is assigned.) If a condition is documented in a medical record (for example, appendicitis) without any additional information, such as acute or chronic, the default code should be assigned (after reviewing the Tabular List of Diseases and Injuries).

The Table of Neoplasms is organized alphabetically according to anatomical site. For each site, there are six possible code numbers according to whether the neoplasm in question is malignant, benign, in situ, of uncertain behavior, or of unspecified nature. The Table of Drugs and Chemicals is an alphabetic index of medicinal, chemical, and biological substances that result in poisonings (and associated external causes) and external causes of adverse effects. The Index to External Causes of Injuries is a separate index (from the Index to Diseases and Injuries) that contains main terms for external causes of morbidities (diseases) (e.g., burns) and injuries (e.g., motorcycle accident) in alphabetic order. (The Table of Neoplasms, Table of Drugs and Chemicals, and Index to External Causes of Injuries are described in more detail in Chapter 3 of this textbook.)

EXAMPLE 1: ICD-10-CM Index to Disease and Injuries main terms are listed in alphabetical order, such as:

```
Catatonic
Cat-scratch
```

The hyphen in "Cat-scratch" is ignored, resulting in sequencing of that main term after "Catatonic".

```
Bee sting (with allergic or anaphylactic shock) —see Toxicity, venom,
   arthropod, bee
Beer-drinkers' heart (disease) I42.6
Begbie's disease (exophthalmic goiter) —see Hyperthyroidism, with, goiter
```

The space between "bee" and "sting" is considered, resulting in that main term being sequenced above "Beer-drinkers' heart (disease)".

EXAMPLE 2: ICD-10-CM Index to Diseases and Injuries numbered cranial nerves are listed in alphabetical order below the main term "Disorder", subterm "nerve", and second qualifier "cranial".

```
Disorder (of) —see also Disease
  nerve G58.9
    cranial G52.9
      eighth —see subcategory H93.3
```

(continues)

```
eleventh G52.8
fifth G50.9
first G52.0
fourth NEC —see Strabismus, paralytic, fourth nerve
multiple G52.7
ninth G52.1
second NEC —see Disorder, nerve, optic
seventh NEC G51.8
sixth NEC —see Strabismus, paralytic, sixth nerve
specified NEC G52.8
tenth G52.2
third NEC —see Strabismus, paralytic, third nerve
twelfth G52.3
```

Main Terms, Subterms, and Qualifiers

ICD-10-CM and ICD-10-PCS index **main terms** (e.g., conditions) are printed in boldfaced type and are followed by the code. Main terms may or may not be followed by a listing of parenthetical terms, which serve as nonessential modifiers of the main term. **Nonessential modifiers** are qualifying words contained in parentheses after the main term that do not have to be included in the documented diagnostic or procedural statement for the code listed after the parentheses to be assigned.

Subterms (or **essential modifiers**) qualify the main term by listing alternative sites, etiology, or clinical status. A subterm is indented two spaces under the main term. Second qualifiers are indented two spaces under a subterm, and third qualifiers are indented two spaces under a second qualifier (Figure 2-3). Care must be taken when moving from the bottom of one column to the top of the next column or when turning to the next page of the index. The main term will be repeated and followed by —continued. When moving from one column to another, watch carefully to determine whether the subterm has changed or new second or third qualifiers appear.

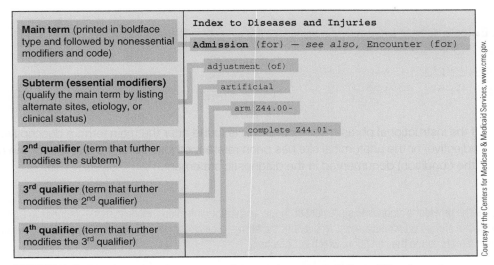

FIGURE 2-3 Display of main terms, subterms (nonessential modifiers), and qualifiers in the ICD-10-CM Index to Diseases and Injuries

EXAMPLE: CONTINUATION OF TERMS IN ICD-10-CM INDEX TO DISEASES AND INJURIES: ICD-10-CM Index to Diseases and Injuries entries are organized according to main terms, subterms, second qualifiers, and third qualifiers. Refer to the index entry for "stricture, anus (sphincter) K62.4" and note the indented subterm and qualifiers. Notice that when the main term continues at the top of a column (or on the next page of the Index to Diseases and Injuries), the word —*continued* appears after the main term. The subterms and qualifiers are indented below the main term.

Start of Main Term in Disease Index		Continuation of Main Term (Next Page)	
Main term:	`Stricture` (*see also*	**Main Term:**	`Stricture` — *continued*
Continuation line:	`Stenosis)`	**Subterm:**	`urethra (organic)` `(spasmodic)` —*see also* `Stricture, urethra,` `male N35.919`
Subterm:	`anus (sphincter) K62.4`	**Second qualifier:**	`postprocedural`
Second qualifier:	`congenital Q42.3`	**Third qualifier:**	`male N99.114`
Third qualifier:	`with fistula Q42.2`	**Fourth qualifier:**	`meatal N35.111`

Basic Steps for Using the ICD-10-CM Index to Diseases and Injuries

It is important to remember that you should never code directly from the Index to Diseases and Injuries. After locating a code in the index, go to that code in the Tabular List of Diseases and Injuries to find important instructions (e.g., includes notes) and to verify the code selected. Instructions may require the assignment of additional codes or indicate conditions that are classified elsewhere.

Step 1   Review patient record documentation to locate the main term in the ICD-10-CM Index to Diseases and Injuries.

Begin the coding process in the Index to Diseases and Injuries by locating the condition's boldfaced main term and then reviewing subterms and qualifiers listed below the main term to locate the proper disease or injury. Refer the patient record to locate documentation that supports the selection of subterms and qualifiers.

EXAMPLE: The underlined terms in the following conditions are main terms:
Verbal agnosia
Intussusception, ileocolic
Status (post) angioplasty

Step 2   If the instructional phrase —*see condition* is found after the main term, a descriptive term (an adjective) or the anatomical site has been referenced instead of the disorder or the disease (the condition) documented in the diagnostic statement.

EXAMPLE: The provider's diagnostic statement is "upper respiratory infection." In the ICD-10-CM Index to Diseases and Injuries, look up the phrase *upper respiratory*. Notice that the term —*see condition* appears next to the phrase *upper respiratory*. This instruction directs you to the condition, which is "infection."

Step 3   When the condition in the diagnostic statement is not easily found in the index, use the main terms below to locate the code.

Abnormal	Findings	Neoplasm
Anomaly	Foreign body	Obstruction
Complication	Infection	Pregnancy
Delivery	Injury	Sequelae
Disease	Late effect(s)	Syndrome
Disorder	Lesion	Wound

Step 4   Select and verify the code in the ICD-10-CM Tabular List of Diseases and Injuries.

 NOTE:

- When the ICD-10-CM index entry includes a hyphen, such as Abruptio placentae O45.9-, review of the tabular list is required to assign the fifth character.
- To locate a code that describes an external cause of illness or injury, refer to the separate Index to External Causes, such as "car sickness" as the cause of "vomiting."

Exercise 2.2 – ICD-10-CM Index to Diseases and Injuries

Instructions: Complete each statement.

1. The alphabetical listing of main terms or conditions printed in boldfaced type that may be expressed as nouns, adjectives, or eponyms is called the ICD-10-CM _____ to Diseases and Injuries.

2. Adverse effects and poisonings associated with medicinal, chemical, and biological substances are located in the ICD-10-CM Table of _____ and Chemicals.

3. Main terms in the ICD-10-CM Index to Diseases and Injuries are listed in _____ order, which means hyphens within main terms are ignored, but a single space within a main term is not ignored.

4. When numerical characters and words appear under a main term or subterm, they are listed in _____ order.

5. Main terms are printed in _____ type and are followed by the code.

6. Qualifying words that are contained in parentheses after the main term, which do not have to be included in the diagnostic statement for the code listed after the parentheses to be assigned, are called _____ modifiers.

7. Subterms are considered _____ modifiers, and they qualify the main term by listing alternative sites, etiology, or clinical status.

8. The provider documents "congenital asplenia." The main term in the ICD-10-CM index is _____.

9. The provider documents "history of malignancy." The main term in the ICD-10-CM index is _____.

10. When the instructional phrase —see condition is found after the main term in the index, a descriptive term (an adjective) or the anatomic site has been referenced instead of the disorder or the _____ (the condition) documented in the diagnostic statement.

ICD-10-CM Tabular List of Diseases and Injuries

The ICD-10-CM **Tabular List of Diseases and Injuries** (Table 2-2) contains 21 chapters. Chapters in ICD-10-CM classify diseases and injuries according to specific body systems as well as **etiology** (cause of disease).

 NOTE:

> ICD-10, created by the WHO, has 22 chapters. ICD-10-CM excludes the ICD-10 chapter, *Codes for Special Purposes, U00–U99.*

ICD-10-CM disease and injury codes consist of 3 characters, and most are followed by a decimal point and between 1 and 4 additional characters. (ICD-10-PCS procedure codes contain 7 characters, and there is no decimal point.) The ICD-10-CM Tabular List of Diseases and Injuries is a sequential list of alphanumeric codes contained within chapters that are organized according to body system or condition. The ICD-10-CM Tabular List of Diseases and Injuries (Figure 2-4) uses an indented format for ease of reference and contains category codes, subcategory codes, and codes. Organization of the tabular list includes:

- Major topic headings, which are printed in bold uppercase letters and followed by groups of ICD-10-CM 3-character disease categories within a chapter (e.g., Intestinal Infectious Diseases, A00–A09). *The first character of an ICD-10-CM code is always a letter.*

TABLE 2-2 ICD-10-CM Tabular List of Diseases and Injuries

Chapter Number	Range of Codes	Chapter Title
Chapter 1	A00–B99	Certain Infectious and Parasitic Diseases
Chapter 2	C00–D49	Neoplasms
Chapter 3	D50–D89	Diseases of the Blood and Blood-forming Organs and Certain Disorders Involving the Immune Mechanism
Chapter 4	E00–E89	Endocrine, Nutritional, and Metabolic Diseases
Chapter 5	F01–F99	Mental, Behavioral, and Neurodevelopmental Disorders
Chapter 6	G00–G99	Diseases of the Nervous System
Chapter 7	H00–H59	Diseases of the Eye and Adnexa
Chapter 8	H60–H95	Diseases of the Ear and Mastoid Process
Chapter 9	I00–I99	Diseases of the Circulatory System
Chapter 10	J00–J99	Diseases of the Respiratory System
Chapter 11	K00–K95	Diseases of the Digestive System
Chapter 12	L00–L99	Diseases of the Skin and Subcutaneous Tissue
Chapter 13	M00–M99	Diseases of the Musculoskeletal System and Connective Tissue
Chapter 14	N00–N99	Diseases of the Genitourinary System
Chapter 15	O00–O9A	Pregnancy, Childbirth, and the Puerperium
Chapter 16	P00–P96	Certain Conditions Originating in the Perinatal Period
Chapter 17	Q00–Q99	Congenital Malformations, Deformations, and Chromosomal Abnormalities
Chapter 18	R00–R99	Symptoms, Signs, and Abnormal Clinical and Laboratory Findings, Not Elsewhere Classified
Chapter 19	S00–T88	Injury, Poisoning, and Certain Other Consequences of External Causes
Chapter 20	V00–Y99	External Causes of Morbidity
Chapter 21	Z00–Z99	Factors Influencing Health Status and Contact with Health Services

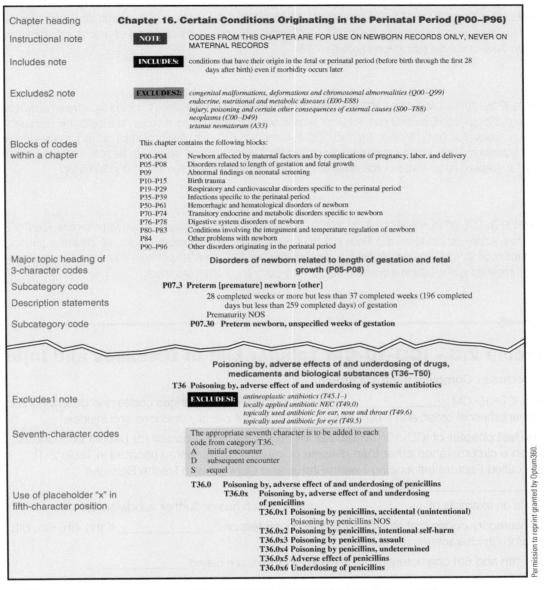

FIGURE 2-4 Sample page from ICD-10-CM Tabular List of Diseases and Injuries

- Categories, subcategories, and codes, which contain a combination of letters and numbers.
  - A **category** contains 3 characters.
  - A 3-character category code that has no further subdivision is a valid code. For example, code I10 (hypertension) has no further subdivisions and is a valid code.
  - A **subcategory** contains 4, 5, or 6 characters. Subcategory codes that require additional characters are invalid if the 5th, 6th, and/or 7th character(s) are absent.
  - Codes may contain 3, 4, 5, 6, or 7 characters.
    - The final level of subdivision is a code.
    - All codes in the ICD-10-CM tabular list are boldfaced.
  - Codes that have an applicable 7th character are referred to as codes (not subcategories).
  - Codes that have applicable 7th characters are invalid if the "x" placeholder(s) and/or the 7th character are missing. (A **placeholder** involves use of the letter "x" in certain ICD-10-CM codes to allow for future expansion.)

EXAMPLE 1: ICD-10-CM CATEGORY AND SUBCATEGORY CODES: Go to Figure 2-4, refer to the *Disorders of newborn related to length of gestation and fetal growth (P05–P08)* range of codes, and locate the 4-character subcategory code (P07.3) and the 5-character subcategory code (P07.30).

EXAMPLE 2: ICD-10-CM 6-CHARACTER CODES: Go to Figure 2-4, refer to the *Poisoning by, adverse effects of and underdosing of drugs, medicaments and biological substances (T36–T50)* range of codes, and locate the 6-character subcategory codes (T36.0x1, T36.0x2, T36.0x3, T36.0x4, and T36.0x5), which also contain "x" as a placeholder to allow for future expansion. Then, locate the seventh characters (A, D, and S), one of which is to be added to each code from category T36 (depending on status of encounter or whether the condition is a sequela) (e.g., T36.0x1A).

EXAMPLE 3: USE OF PLACEHOLDER "X" IN ICD-10-CM CODES: Go to Figure 2-4, and refer to code *T36.0x1 Poisoning by penicillins, accidental (unintentional).* Code T36.0x1A requires "x" as a placeholder in the 5th-character position. Thus, reporting the code as T36.01A (without the "x" placeholder in the 5th-character position) is an invalid code, which is incorrect if reported and results in a denied claim for third-party payer reimbursement.

Exercise 2.3 – ICD-10-CM Tabular List of Diseases and Injuries

Instructions: Complete each statement.

1. The ICD-10-CM _____ of Diseases and Injuries arranges codes and descriptions in alphanumerical order, and it contains 21 chapters that classify diseases and injuries.

2. The last chapter of ICD-10-CM tabular list codes that are reported for patient encounters when a circumstance other than disease or injury is documented (located in Table 2-1) are called Factors Influencing Health Status and Contact with Health Services or _____ codes.

3. I10 is an example of a _____ code, which has no further subdivisions.

4. Subcategory codes that require additional characters are _____ if the 4th, 5th, 6th, and/or 7th character(s) are absent.

5. The 5th and 6th characters of "x" in code O40.1xx0 are called _____.

ICD-10-CM Official Guidelines for Coding and Reporting

The Centers for Medicare & Medicaid Services (CMS) and the National Center for Health Statistics (NCHS) are the agencies in the U.S. Department of Health & Human Services (DHHS) that develop official guidelines for coding and reporting using ICD-10-CM. The *Official ICD-10-CM Guidelines for Coding and Reporting* (and the *Official ICD-10-PCS Guidelines for Coding and Reporting*) are approved by the four organizations that make up the **Cooperating Parties for the ICD-10-CM /PCS**. They include the American Hospital Association (AHA), American Health Information Management Association (AHIMA), CMS, and NCHS. The guidelines are a set of rules developed to accompany and complement the official conventions and instructions provided within ICD-10-CM. They clarify the coding and sequencing instructions in ICD-10-CM and provide additional coding guidance. The health care provider is responsible for complete and accurate patient record documentation, and the coder is responsible for assigning complete and accurate codes that are supported by documentation.

Coders review the entire patient record to determine the reason for an encounter and the conditions treated. This means that if the provider documents a disease (or procedure) on the face sheet or in the discharge summary, the coder reviews other reports (e.g., progress notes, laboratory data, operative report, pathology report) to assign appropriate codes, including level of specificity. Quite often the provider will document additional information about a disease (or procedure) elsewhere in the patient record that contributes to the assignment of a specific code (e.g., laterality, acute or chronic nature).

 NOTE:

Official ICD-10-PCS Guidelines for Coding and Reporting are detailed in Chapter 6.

The ICD-10-CM *Official Guidelines for Coding and Reporting* are organized into four sections and one appendix.

- Section I includes the structure and conventions of the classification and general guidelines that apply to the entire classification and chapter-specific guidelines that correspond to the chapters as they are arranged in the classification.
- Section II includes guidelines for selection of the principal diagnosis for nonoutpatient settings. (Nonoutpatient settings include acute care hospitals, long-term care facilities, home health care agencies, nursing homes, and so on.) (The selection of principal diagnosis is discussed in Chapter 6.)
- Section III includes guidelines for reporting additional diagnoses (e.g., coexisting conditions, complications) in nonoutpatient settings. (The coding of additional diagnoses is discussed in Chapter 6.)
- Section IV includes guidelines for outpatient diagnosis coding and reporting. (Outpatient diagnosis coding is discussed in Chapter 7.)
- Appendix I includes present on admission (POA) reporting guidelines. (POA reporting is discussed in Chapter 20.)

A joint effort between the health care provider and the coder is essential to achieving complete and accurate documentation, code assignment, and reporting of diagnoses and procedures. The coding guidelines were developed to assist both the health care provider and the coder in identifying diagnoses and procedures that are to be reported. The importance of consistent, complete documentation in the patient record is crucial because without such documentation, accurate coding cannot be achieved. In addition, the entire record must be reviewed to determine the specific reason for the encounter and the conditions treated. (The term *encounter* is used in the coding guidelines for all health care settings, including inpatient hospital admissions. The term *provider* is used in the coding guidelines to mean physician or any qualified health care practitioner who is legally accountable for establishing the patient's diagnosis.)

 HIPAA Alert!

The HIPAA regulations for electronic transactions require providers and third-party payers, including Medicare administrative contractors (MACs), to adhere to the *Official Guidelines for Coding and Reporting*. Thus, a violation of the coding guidelines is technically a HIPAA violation. Because some third-party payers and MACs do not appear to be aware of (or understand) this HIPAA provision, to obtain appropriate reimbursement for submitted ICD-10-CM (and ICD-10-PCS) codes, you may need to point out specific provisions in the regulation that reference the coding guidelines. For example, the Z51 (Encounter for other aftercare and medical care) codes in ICD-10-CM can be reported as a first-listed code for outpatient care. If third-party payers and MACs deny claims that report Z51 codes contact the regional CMS office or HIPAA enforcement office (located at CMS) for resolution.

Exercise 2.4 – ICD-10-CM Official Guidelines for Coding and Reporting

Instructions: Complete each statement.

1. The *Official Guidelines for Coding and Reporting* are approved by the _____ for ICD-10-CM to accompany and complement the official conventions and instructions provided within ICD-10-CM.

2. Coding guidelines use the term _____ for all health care settings, including inpatient hospital admissions.

3. Coding guidelines use the term _____ to mean physician or any qualified health care practitioner who is legally accountable for establishing the patient's diagnosis.

4. The _____ regulations for electronic transactions require providers and third-party payers, including Medicare administrative contractors (MACs), to adhere to the *Official Guidelines for Coding and Reporting*.

5. Section I of the *Official Guidelines for Coding and Reporting* includes the _____ and conventions of the classification and general guidelines that apply to the entire classification and chapter-specific guidelines that correspond to the chapters as they are arranged in the classification.

6. Section II of the *Official Guidelines for Coding and Reporting* includes guidelines for selection of the _____ diagnosis for nonoutpatient settings.

7. Section III of the *Official Guidelines for Coding and Reporting* includes guidelines for reporting _____ diagnoses in nonoutpatient settings.

8. Inpatient care requires the reporting of additional diagnoses, which are called comorbidities and _____.

9. Section IV of the *Official Guidelines for Coding and Reporting* covers _____ coding and reporting.

10. Appendix I of the *ICD-10-CM Official Guidelines for Coding and Reporting* covers present on _____ reporting guidelines.

General ICD-10-CM Diagnosis Coding Guidelines

The *International Classification of Diseases (ICD)* was originally created to track diseases for statistical reporting purposes. Its origin is based on the Bertillon *International Statistical Classification of Causes of Death*. In 1948, the World Health Organization (WHO) assumed responsibility for revisions and the official name of the classification system was changed to the *International Classification of Diseases*. The NCHS created the clinical modification (CM) of ICD-9, and ICD-9-CM was implemented in 1979. *ICD-10-CM and ICD-10-PCS replaced ICD-9-CM on October 1, 2015* (Figure 2-5). ICD-10-CM contains additional clinical information as compared with ICD-10. ICD-10-PCS was developed to report inpatient procedure codes; its content is included in Chapter 6.

The general coding guidelines are followed when assigning ICD-10-CM diagnosis codes for inpatient, outpatient, and physician office settings.

Locating a Code in ICD-10-CM—Use of Both Index and Tabular List

Use both the index and the tabular list when locating and assigning codes because relying on just the index or tabular list results in coding errors and less specificity when selecting codes.

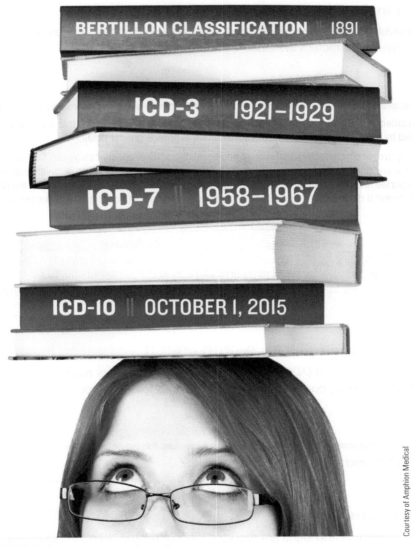

FIGURE 2-5 History of ICD coding

Locate Each Term in the Alphabetic Index

Locate each term in the ICD-10-CM disease index first, and verify the code selected in the tabular list. Make sure you read and are guided by coding conventions (e.g., excludes1, excludes2) that appear in either the index or the tabular list.

> 📝 **NOTE:**
>
> Use *both* the ICD-10-CM index and tabular list because the index does not always provide the complete code. Selection of the complete code, including laterality (e.g., bilateral, right side, left side) and any applicable seventh character is done using the tabular list. A dash (-) at the end of a code in the index indicates that additional character(s) are required. Even if a dash is *not* included at the index entry, refer to the tabular list to verify whether additional character(s) are required.

EXAMPLE: The ICD-10-CM Index to Diseases and Injuries entry for *diabetes mellitus* lists code E11.9, as verified in the tabular list.

Level of Detail in Coding

Pay attention to the level of detail when assigning codes because diagnosis codes are to be reported using the highest number of digits or characters available.

 NOTE:

ICD-10-CM codes contain three, four, five, six, or seven characters. Codes with three characters are called categories, and they may be further subdivided by assigning up to four additional characters to provide greater detail.

Codes with four, five, or six characters that require additional character(s) are subcategories. Codes that do *not* require additional character(s) are simply called *codes*. (It might be helpful to think of such *codes* as *complete codes* or *valid codes*.) A three-character code is reported only if it is not further subdivided. Where fourth through seventh characters are provided, they *must* be assigned. A code is invalid if the complete number of characters required for that code have not been assigned.

EXAMPLE: ICD-10-CM category M1a (chronic gout) requires the assignment of a fourth, fifth, sixth, and seventh character to complete the code. It is incorrect to report a category M1a code without the fourth through seventh characters. Thus, you would assign code M1a.0110 to a patient diagnosed with idiopathic chronic gout of the right shoulder, without tophus.

Codes from A00.0 through T88.9, Z00–Z99.8

Appropriate codes from ICD-10-CM (A00.0 through T88.9, Z00–Z99.8) are reported to identify diagnoses, symptoms, conditions, problems, complaints, or other reason(s) for the encounter.

 NOTE:

Codes V00 through Y99 are reported for external causes of morbidity.

Signs and Symptoms

Codes that describe symptoms and signs are reported when a related definitive diagnosis has not been established (or confirmed) by the provider.

 NOTE:

ICD-10-CM Chapter 18 (Symptoms, Signs, and Abnormal Clinical and Laboratory Findings, Not Elsewhere Classified) contains many, but not all, codes for signs and symptoms. Some codes are found in other ICD-10-CM chapters (e.g., acute neoplasm-related pain, G89.3).

EXAMPLE: The patient is seen at a physician's office for an initial visit, complaining of pain and limited range of motion of her right little finger knuckle. The physician examines the joint and notices a solid mass. He orders an x-ray to rule out ganglion. Upon the follow-up visit, the x-ray results reveal no arthritis or stalklike growth. The diagnosis is ganglion cyst, little finger knuckle joint, right. The patient is scheduled for outpatient surgery to remove the ganglion.

For the initial visit, assign ICD-10-CM codes for pain (M79.644), stiffness (M25.641), and mass of the little finger knuckle joint (R22.31). For the follow-up visit, assign ICD-10-CM code M67.441 to the ganglion cyst, little finger knuckle joint, right. Code M67.441 is reported as a definitive diagnosis, which means signs and symptoms codes for pain, limited range of motion, or mass of the little finger knuckle joint are *not* reported on the claim for the follow-up visit.

Conditions That Are an Integral Part of a Disease Process

Signs and symptoms that are associated with a disease process should *not* be assigned as additional codes (unless otherwise instructed by ICD-10-CM) because they are included in the disease process.

> **EXAMPLE:** The patient is seen at the hospital's emergency department (ED) with a complaint of shortness of breath. A chest x-ray reveals pneumonia, and the ED physician prescribes an antibiotic. Assign ICD-10-CM code J18.9 to the pneumonia, and do not assign a code for the shortness of breath because it is a symptom of pneumonia.

Conditions That Are *Not* an Integral Part of a Disease Process

Conditions that are not considered an integral part of a disease process, such as additional signs and symptoms that may not be associated routinely with a disease process, should be coded when present (e.g., severe headache for which treatment or medical management is provided is coded when the patient is diagnosed with pneumonia).

> **EXAMPLE:** The patient is seen at the physician's office for follow-up care of her controlled hypertension. During the visit, she tells the physician that she has been experiencing some insomnia. The physician discussed possible reasons for the insomnia with the patient, who admitted to being under extreme stress recently. The patient was reluctant to take over-the-counter or prescription medications for the insomnia, and the physician suggested alternative solutions. The physician also instructed the patient to return in two weeks for follow-up of the insomnia. Assign ICD-10-CM code I10 to the hypertension. In addition, assign ICD-10-CM code G47.00 to the insomnia because it is not a symptom of hypertension and it was medically managed during the visit.

Multiple Coding for a Single Condition

The etiology/manifestation coding convention requires that two codes be reported to completely describe a single condition that affects multiple body systems.

> **EXAMPLE:** The diagnosis amyloid neuritis requires ICD-10-CM codes E85.1 and G63 be reported in that order. (Remember: italicized codes in the tabular list are never sequenced first.)

In addition, other single conditions require more than one code to be reported, such as those associated with "use additional code" notes found in the tabular list. These codes are not part of an etiology/manifestation pair where a secondary code is useful to describe a condition fully. The sequencing rule for "use additional code" is the same as the etiology/manifestation pair in that a secondary code should be reported, if known. A "use additional code" note will usually be found at the infectious disease code, indicating the need to report the organism code as a secondary code.

 NOTE:

> Multiple codes also may need to be reported for ICD-10-CM *sequelae*, complications, and obstetrical cases to describe more fully the patient's conditions. (Refer to specific guidelines below for further instruction.)

> **EXAMPLE:** For a diagnosis of urinary tract infection due to *Escherichia coli*, report ICD-10-CM codes N39.0 and B96.20, in that order.

"Code first" notes are also located below certain ICD-10-CM codes in the tabular lists that are not specifically manifestation codes but may be due to an underlying cause. When a "code first" note is present *and* an underlying condition is documented in the patient record, the underlying condition is reported first, if known.

EXAMPLE: The physician documents rheumatic pneumonia in the patient's record. Upon review of the index and tabular list, assign ICD-10-CM codes I00 and J17 for the condition, in that order.

 NOTE:

For bacterial infections not included in ICD-10-CM Chapter 2, a secondary code from category B96 (Other bacterial agents as the cause of diseases classified elsewhere) may be required to identify the bacterial organism causing the infection.

"Code, if applicable, any causal condition first" notes in the ICD-10-CM tabular list indicates that this code may be assigned as a first-listed or principal diagnosis when the causal condition is unknown or not applicable. If a causal condition is known, the code for that condition should be reported as the first-listed or principal diagnosis.

EXAMPLE: The patient is diagnosed with urinary incontinence and congenital ureterocele. Assign ICD-10-CM codes Q62.31 and R32 (although generating a physician query could result in a more specific urinary incontinence code), in that order.

Acute and Chronic Conditions

If the same condition is described as both acute (or subacute) and chronic and separate subentries exist in the ICD-10-CM index at the same indentation level, code both and sequence the acute (or subacute) code first.

EXAMPLE: The diagnoses acute gastritis and chronic gastritis are assigned ICD-10-CM codes K29.00 and K29.50, in that order.

Combination Code

Assign combination codes when available and multiple codes as needed. A **combination code** is a single code that is used to classify two diagnoses (or procedures), a diagnosis with an associated secondary process (manifestation), or a diagnosis with an associated complication. Combination codes are located by referring to subterm entries in the ICD-10-CM index and by following "includes" and "excludes" notes in the ICD-10-CM tabular list. Assign two or more **multiple codes** to completely classify the elements of a complex diagnosis statement, which contain words or phrases such as *due to, incidental to, secondary to*, and *with*. Make sure you carefully review tabular list entries, which provide guidance regarding the assignment of multiple codes.

Make sure you assign only the combination code when that code fully identifies the diagnostic conditions involved or when the index so directs. Do not report multiple codes when ICD-10-CM provides a combination code that clearly identifies all of the elements documented in the diagnosis. When a combination code lacks necessary specificity in describing the manifestation or a complication, an additional code should be reported as a secondary code.

EXAMPLE 1: COMBINATION CODE: Assign ICD-10-CM combination code K80.00 to the diagnosis acute cholecystitis and cholelithiasis because the code description includes both conditions. (The fifth-character 0 is assigned to this code because there is no mention of obstruction in the diagnostic statement.)

EXAMPLE 2: MULTIPLE CODES: The diagnosis trigonitis due to *Escherichia coli* is assigned ICD-10-CM codes N30.30 and B96.20, in that order.

Sequelae (Late Effects)

A **sequela** is the **residual effect** (condition produced) after the acute phase of an illness or injury has terminated. *There is no time limit on when a sequela code can be used.* The residual may be apparent early (e.g., hemiparesis in cerebral infarction), or it may occur months or years later (e.g., scarring due to a previous burn).

Coding of a sequela generally requires two codes sequenced in the following order:

- Residual condition or nature of the sequela is sequenced first.
- Sequela code is sequenced second.

An exception to the above guidelines are those instances where the code for the sequela is followed by a manifestation code identified in the ICD-10-CM tabular list, or the sequela code has been expanded (at the fourth-, fifth-, or sixth-character levels) to include the manifestation(s). *The code for the acute phase of an illness or injury that led to the sequela is never used with a code for the late effect.*

In the ICD-10-CM Index to Diseases and Injuries, the main term is *Sequela (of)* and it includes a "*—see also* condition" instruction because in the tabular list seventh-character "S" is added to condition codes for which sequelae (residual conditions) are treated. (Historically, ICD-9-CM referred to a sequela as a *late effect* of an illness or injury.)

 NOTE:

- The code for the acute phase of an illness or injury that led to the sequela is never reported with a code for the sequela (because treatment for the acute phase has ended).
- Do not confuse sequelae with complications that are associated with current acute illness or injuries and usually develop from problems that occur during the course of medical or surgical care (e.g., postoperative wound infection).
- Multiple codes are assigned to classify a sequela when no combination code exists, such as "headaches due to intracranial injury without loss of consciousness that occurred several years ago" for which ICD-10-CM codes G44.309 and S06.9x0S are both assigned. (In ICD-10-CM, the sequelae of injuries are classified by assigning an S as the seventh character of the injury code.)
- A combination code is assigned to classify a sequela when it exists, such as "nondominant left-sided paralysis due to previous CVA" for which ICD-10-CM I69.864 only is assigned.

EXAMPLE: The patient was in an accident last year and sustained fractures of the left femur and right tibia, which healed without incident. The patient presents with stiffness of the left hip and numbness of the left leg. Assign codes to the stiffness of the left hip (M25.652); numbness of the left leg (R20.0); and sequela of fracture, femur (S72.92xS).

Impending or Threatened Condition

Code any condition described at the time of encounter/visit as "impending" or "threatened" as follows:

- If the condition did occur, code as confirmed diagnosis.
- If the condition did not occur, reference the disease index to determine if the condition has a subentry term for *impending* or *threatened* and also reference main term entries for *impending* and *threatened*.
- If subterms for *impending* or *threatened* are listed, assign the listed code.
- If subterms for *impending* or *threatened* are not listed, code the existing underlying condition(s), and *not* the condition described as *impending* or *threatened* (except for inpatient cases when impending/threatened conditions are coded).

EXAMPLE: The patient is treated for impending myocardial infarction (MI) and is assigned ICD-10-CM code I20.0 because the MI diagnosis has not been confirmed.

Reporting Same Diagnosis Code More Than Once

Each unique ICD-10-CM diagnosis code is reported only once for an encounter. This applies to bilateral conditions *when there are no distinct ICD-10-CM codes identifying laterality* or two different conditions that are classified to the same ICD-10-CM diagnosis code.

> **EXAMPLE:** On March 14, the patient was diagnosed with bilateral lung abscesses. Even though both lungs contain abscesses, assign ICD-10-CM code J85.2 only once.

Laterality

ICD-10-CM codes that indicate **laterality** specifically classify conditions that occur on the left, right, or bilaterally. If a bilateral ICD-10-CM code is not provided *and the condition is bilateral*, assign separate codes for both the left and right side. If the side is not identified in the patient record, assign a code for unspecified side.

When a patient has a bilateral condition and each side is treated during separate encounters, assign the bilateral code (because the condition still exists on both sides) for the first encounter. After one side has been successfully treated, assign the unilateral code for the second encounter (because the condition now exists on just one side). However, if treatment on the first side did not resolve the condition, assign the bilateral code for the second and subsequent encounters until that side is successfully treated.

> **EXAMPLE:** *Bilateral contusion of fallopian tubes, initial encounter* is assigned ICD-10-CM code S37.522A.

When a patient has a bilateral condition *and each side is treated during separate encounters*, assign the "bilateral" code for the encounter during which the first side is treated (because the condition still exists on both sides). For the second encounter during which the other side is treated (and after the other side has been successfully treated and because the condition no longer exists on that side), assign the appropriate unilateral code for the side where the condition still exists. The bilateral code is not assigned for the subsequent encounter because the patient no longer has the condition at the previously treated site. However, if treatment for the first side did not completely resolve the condition, reporting the bilateral code would still be appropriate.

> **EXAMPLE:** The patient was diagnosed with bilateral cataracts. On May 5, the patient successfully underwent cataract surgery of the left eye. The ICD-10-CM code for *cataracts, bilateral eyes*, is reported for the May 5 encounter. On July 5, the patient successfully underwent cataract surgery of the right eye. The ICD-10-CM code for *cataract, left eye*, is reported for the July 5 encounter.

Documentation by Clinicians Other Than the Patient's Provider

Code assignment is based on the documentation by patient's provider (e.g., physician or other qualified health care practitioner legally accountable for establishing the patient's diagnosis). There are a few exceptions, such as codes for the body mass index (BMI), depth of nonpressure chronic ulcers, pressure ulcer stage, coma scale, and NIH stroke scale (NIHSS) codes may be based on documentation from clinicians who are not the patient's provider (e.g., physician, other qualified health care practitioner legally accountable for establishing the patient's diagnosis) *because such information is typically documented by other clinicians involved in the care of the patient* (e.g., dietitians document BMI, nurses document pressure ulcer stages, emergency medical technician documents coma scale). However, associated diagnosis (e.g., overweight, obesity, acute stroke, pressure ulcer) must be documented by the patient's provider. If conflicting documentation is evident in the patient record, either from the same clinician or different clinicians, query the patient's attending provider for clarification.

For social determinants of health, such as information found in categories Z55-Z65, Persons with potential health hazards related to socioeconomic and psychosocial circumstances, code assignment may be based on medical record documentation from clinicians involved in the care of the patient who are not the patient's provider since this information represents social information, rather than medical diagnoses.

The BMI, coma scale, National Institutes of Health stroke scale (NIHSS) codes, and categories Z55-Z65 are reported only as secondary diagnoses.

> **EXAMPLE:** Patient's BMI of 39.4 was documented by the dietician, and patient has an established diagnosis of morbid obesity. Report ICD-10-CM codes E66.01 and Z68.39, in that order.

Syndromes

Follow the alphabetic index guidance when coding syndromes. In the absence of index guidance, assign codes for the documented manifestations of the syndrome. Additional codes for manifestations that are *not an integral part of the disease process* may also be assigned when the condition does not have a unique code.

> **EXAMPLE 1:** Patient is diagnosed with Alagille's syndrome, which is defined as a congenital liver malformation. ICD-10-CM index main term *syndrome* and subterm *Alagille's* lists code Q44.7 (described as *other congenital malformations of liver* in the ICD-10-CM tabular list, where Alagille's syndrome is also listed as an inclusion term).

> **EXAMPLE 2:** Patient is diagnosed with Barlow's syndrome, which is defined as mitral valve prolapse. ICD-10-CM index main term *syndrome* does **not** contain a subterm for *Barlow's*. Therefore, go to ICD-10-CM index main term *prolapse* and subterm *mitral valve* where code I34.1 is listed and described as nonrheumatic mitral (valve) prolapse in the ICD-10-CM tabular list. (Be sure to locate the definition of any syndrome, such as Barlow's syndrome, when it is not specifically listed in the ICD-10-CM index.)

Documentation of Complications of Care

Complications of care codes are based upon documentation of a relationship between a condition and the procedure unless otherwise instructed by ICD-10-CM. Not all conditions that occur during or following medical care or surgery are classified as complications. There must be a cause-and-effect relationship between the condition and procedure or service provided along with documentation that the condition is a complication. If a complication is not clearly documented, query the provider for clarification.

> **EXAMPLE 1:** The patient is seen today for dehiscence of a surgical amputation stump, which means that the surgical incision separated. In the ICD-10-CM index, go to main term *dehiscence (of)* and subterm *amputation stump*, which lists code T87.81 (described as *Dehiscence of amputation stump* in the ICD-10-CM tabular list). Another way to locate the code in the ICD-10-CM is to go to main term *complication(s) (from) (of)*, subterm *amputation stump*, and second qualifier *dehiscence*, which lists code T87.81.

> **EXAMPLE 2:** The patient underwent left hip replacement surgery last month and is seen today for an initial encounter to evaluate instability of the left hip joint prosthesis. It is determined that the joint prosthesis was recalled due to a mechanical defect. Surgical intervention to replace the joint prosthesis is scheduled. For this initial encounter, in the ICD-10-CM index, go to main term *complication*, subterm *joint prosthesis*, second qualifier *mechanical*, and third qualifier *instability* where code T84.02- is listed. Review of the ICD-10-CM tabular list indicates that code T84.023A (Instability of internal left knee prosthesis, initial encounter) is to be reported.

Borderline Diagnosis

If the provider documents a *borderline diagnosis* at the time of discharge, code the diagnosis as confirmed unless ICD-10-CM provides a specific entry. If a borderline condition has a specific index entry in ICD-10-CM, it should be coded as such. Since borderline conditions are not uncertain diagnoses, no distinction is made between the care setting (inpatient versus outpatient). Whenever the documentation is unclear regarding a borderline condition, coders are encouraged to query for clarification.

> **EXAMPLE:** The patient is diagnosed with borderline diabetes mellitus. In the ICD-10-CM index, go to main term *borderline* and subterm *diabetes mellitus*, which lists code R73.03 (described as *Prediabetes* in the ICD-10-CM tabular list).

Use of Sign/Symptom/Unspecified Codes

Assigning codes to signs, symptoms, and unspecified conditions is acceptable, and it is sometimes even necessary. Specific diagnosis codes should be reported when supported by available patient record documentation and clinical knowledge of the patient's health condition. However, there are instances when signs, symptoms, or unspecified codes are the best choices for accurately reflecting the encounter. Each encounter should be coded to the level of certainty known. When a definitive diagnosis is *not* established during an encounter, report codes for signs and/or symptoms instead.

When a specific code cannot be assigned because sufficient clinical information about a particular health condition is unknown or unavailable, report the appropriate unspecified code instead. Unspecified codes are reported when they most accurately reflect what is known about the patient's condition at the end of an encounter. It is inappropriate to assign a more specific code that is *not* supported by the patient record documentation. It is also inappropriate for a provider to order diagnostic testing that is medically *un*necessary to determine a more specific code.

> **EXAMPLE:** The patient is diagnosed with pneumonia, and the specific type was not able to be determined by the end of an encounter. Report code J18.9 (Pneumonia, unspecified organism).

Coding for Health Care Encounters in Hurricane Aftermath

a. Use of External Cause of Morbidity Codes

An external cause of morbidity code should be assigned to identify the cause of the injury(ies) incurred as a result of the hurricane. The use of external cause of morbidity codes is supplemental to the application of ICD-10-CM codes. External cause of morbidity codes are never to be recorded as a principal diagnosis (first-listed in non-inpatient settings). The appropriate injury code should be sequenced before any external cause codes. The external cause of morbidity codes capture how the injury or health condition happened (cause), the intent (unintentional or accidental; or intentional, such as suicide or assault), the place where the event occurred, the activity of the patient at the time of the event, and the person's status (e.g., civilian, military). They should not be assigned for encounters to treat hurricane victims' medical conditions when no injury, adverse effect or poisoning is involved. External cause of morbidity codes should be assigned for each encounter for care and treatment of the injury. External cause of morbidity codes may be assigned in all health care settings. For the purpose of capturing complete and accurate ICD-10-CM data in the aftermath of the hurricane, a health care setting should be considered as any location where medical care is provided by licensed health care professionals.

b. Sequencing of External Causes of Morbidity Codes

Codes for cataclysmic events, such as a hurricane, take priority over all other external cause codes except child and adult abuse and terrorism and should be sequenced before other external cause of injury codes. Assign as many external cause of morbidity codes as necessary to fully explain each cause.

> **EXAMPLE 1:** If an injury occurs as a result of a building collapse during the hurricane, external cause codes for both the hurricane and the building collapse should be assigned, with the external causes code for hurricane being sequenced as the first external cause code.

For injuries incurred as a direct result of the hurricane, assign the appropriate code(s) for the injuries, followed by the code X37.0-, Hurricane (with the appropriate 7th character), and any other applicable external cause of injury codes. Code X37.0- also should be assigned when an injury is incurred as a result of flooding caused by a levee breaking related to the hurricane. Code X38.-, Flood (with the appropriate 7th character), should be assigned when an injury is from flooding resulting directly from the storm. Code X36.0.-, Collapse of dam or man-made structure, should not be assigned when the cause of the collapse is due to the hurricane. Use of code X36.0- is limited to collapses of man-made structures due to earth surface movements, not due to storm surges directly from a hurricane.

c. Other External Causes of Morbidity Code Issues

For injuries that are not a direct result of the hurricane, such as an evacuee that has incurred an injury as a result of a motor vehicle accident, assign the appropriate external cause of morbidity code(s) to describe the cause of the injury, but do not assign code X37.0-, Hurricane. If it is not clear whether the injury was a direct result of the hurricane, assume the injury is due to the hurricane and assign code X37.0-, Hurricane, as well as any other applicable external cause of morbidity codes. In addition to code X37.0-, Hurricane, other possible applicable external cause of morbidity codes include:

W54.0-　　Bitten by dog

X30-　　Exposure to excessive natural heat

X31-　　Exposure to excessive natural cold

X38-　　Flood

d. Use of Z codes

Z codes (other reasons for health care encounters) may be assigned as appropriate to further explain the reasons for presenting for health care services, including transfers between health care facilities. The *ICD-10-CM Official Guidelines for Coding and Reporting* identify which codes may be assigned as principal or first-listed diagnosis only, secondary diagnosis only, or principal/first-listed or secondary (depending on the circumstances). Possible applicable Z codes include:

Z59.0　　Homelessness

Z59.1　　Inadequate housing

Z59.5　　Extreme poverty

Z75.1　　Person awaiting admission to adequate facility elsewhere

Z75.3　　Unavailability and inaccessibility of health care facilities

Z75.4　　Unavailability and inaccessibility of other helping agencies

Z76.2　　Encounter for health supervision and care of other healthy infant and child

Z99.12　　Encounter for respirator [ventilator] dependence during power failure

The external cause of morbidity codes and the Z codes listed above are not an all-inclusive list. Other codes may be applicable to the encounter based upon the documentation. Assign as many codes as necessary to fully explain each health care encounter. Since patient history information may be very limited, use any available documentation to assign the appropriate external cause of morbidity and Z codes.

ICD-10-PCS Index and Tables

The *International Classification of Diseases, 10th Revision, Procedure Coding System (ICD-10-PCS)* was developed by the Centers for Medicare & Medicaid Services (CMS) for use in the United States for inpatient hospital settings *only*. ICD-10-PCS uses a multiaxial 7-character alphanumeric code structure (e.g., 047K04Z) that provides a unique code for all substantially different procedures. It also allows new procedures to be easily incorporated as new codes. ICD-10-PCS contains more than 87,000 seven-character alphanumeric procedure codes.

 NOTE:

- The letters I and O are never used in ICD-10-PCS because they are too easily confused with the numbers 1 and 0. Decimals are also never used in ICD-10-PCS codes.
- ICD-10-PCS uses a "build-a-code" approach to classify procedures, which means one character is assigned to each of seven axes (multiaxial) (e.g., code 02700ZZ is assigned for open dilation of one coronary artery).
- ICD-10-PCS requires detailed knowledge of medical terminology and anatomy and physiology, and its unique vocabulary of operations (sometimes called "root operations" in professional literature) also requires mastery.

Development of ICD-10-PCS

The development of ICD-10-PCS incorporates four major attributes:

- *Completeness*. There are unique codes for all substantially different procedures.
- *Expandability*. As new procedures are developed, the structure of ICD-10-PCS allows them to be easily incorporated as unique codes.
- *Multiaxial*. ICD-10-PCS codes consist of independent characters, with each individual axis retaining its meaning across broad ranges of codes to the extent possible.

> **EXAMPLE:** The Medical and Surgical Section axes include:
> 1. Section (medical and surgical)
> 2. Body system (e.g., heart and great vessels)
> 3. Operation (e.g., dilation)
> 4. Body part (e.g., skin)
> 5. Approach (e.g., open)
> 6. Device (e.g., drainage device)
> 7. Qualifier (e.g., anterior)
>
> However, the Imaging Section axes include:
> 1. Section (imaging)
> 2. Body system (e.g., respiratory system)
> 3. Type (e.g., fluoroscopy)
> 4. Body part (e.g., lungs, right)
> 5. Contrast (e.g., low osmolar)
> 6. Qualifier (e.g., laser)
> 7. Qualifier (e.g., intraoperative)

- *Standardized terminology*. ICD-10-PCS includes definitions of the terminology used, and while the meaning of specific words varies in common usage, each term is assigned a specific meaning.

Development of ICD-10-PCS followed the below-listed general principles:

- *Diagnostic information is not included in procedure code descriptions*. Instead, ICD-10-CM diagnosis codes classify diseases, disorders, injuries, signs, symptoms, external causes, and so on.

- *"Not otherwise specified" (NOS) options are not provided.* A minimal level of specificity is required for each component of the procedure.
- *Use of "not elsewhere classified" (NEC) is limited.* ICD-10-PCS specifies all significant components of a procedure, generally eliminating the need for an NEC code option. Some NEC options are included in ICD-10-PCS where necessary (e.g., "other device" because new devices are frequently developed).
- *Level of specificity is enhanced.* All procedures currently performed can be assigned a specific code in ICD-10-PCS. The frequency (or infrequency) with which a procedure is performed is *not* a consideration. Thus, a unique code is classified for each variation of a procedure performed.

Structure of ICD-10-PCS Codes

ICD-10-PCS has a 7-character alphanumeric code structure, and the code assigned is the result of a build-a-code process instead of verifying codes in a tabular list of codes (after locating the procedure name in an index).

- Each character contains up to 34 possible values (because characters in positions 2–7 can have different meanings in different sections).

EXAMPLE: In the Medical and Surgical Section of ICD-10-PCS, the character in position 1 is the number 0 (for Medical and Surgical Section). The character in position 2 refers to body system (e.g., central nervous system, peripheral nervous system, and so on).

In the Physical Rehabilitation and Diagnostic Audiology Section, the character in position 1 is the letter F (for Physical Rehabilitation and Diagnostic Audiology Section). The character in position 2 refers to "section qualifier" (e.g., rehabilitation or diagnostic audiology).

- Each value represents a specific option for the general character definition.

EXAMPLE: In the Administration Section of ICD-10-PCS, the character in position 2 refers to body system, and it contains just three values:

- ○ Circulatory system, assigned number 0.
- ○ Indwelling device, assigned letter C.
- ○ Physiological systems and anatomical regions, assigned letter E.

- The 10 digits 0–9 and the 24 letters A–H, J–N, and P–Z may be used in each of the 7 characters, depending on the documented procedure. *The letters O and I are not used so as to avoid confusion with the digits 0 and 1.*
- A code is built by selecting a specific value for each of the 7 characters (Table 2-3). Thus, a step-by-step "build-a-code" approach is used when assigning ICD-10-PCS procedure codes. As such, a number or a letter is assigned to *each* of the 7 characters of an ICD-10-PCS code based on documentation of the procedure performed.

ICD-10-PCS procedures are first divided into sections (Table 2-3, column 1), which identify the general type of procedure (e.g., medical and surgical, obstetrics, imaging). *The first character of the 7-character procedure code always specifies the section.* While characters 2–7 have the same meaning within a section, they may have different meanings in different sections (Table 2-3, columns 2–7). Within all sections, the third character specifies either the operation, type (of procedure performed), or modality. Characters 4–7 provide additional information (e.g., body part, approach) that formulate the procedure code.

Then, depending on the ICD-10-PCS section in which a procedure is classified, the values of characters 2–7 may vary (Table 2-3, columns 2–7). However, the values of characters 2–7 *within a particular section* remain the same.

TABLE 2-3 Value Assigned to Each Character in a 7-Character ICD-10-PCS Code

Character 1	Character 2	Character 3	Character 4	Character 5	Character 6	Character 7
Medical and Surgical Section	Body system	Operation	Body part	Approach	Device	Qualifier
Obstetrics Section	Body system	Operation	Body part	Approach	Device	Qualifier
Placement Section	Body system	Operation	Body region	Approach	Device	Qualifier
Administration Section	Body system	Operation	Body system/ region	Approach	Substance	Qualifier
Measurement and Monitoring Section	Body system	Operation	Body system	Approach	Function/ Device	Qualifier
Extracorporeal or Systemic Assistance and Performance Section	Body system	Operation	Body system	Duration	Function	Qualifier
Extracorporeal or Systemic Therapies Section	Body system	Operation	Body system	Duration	Qualifier	Qualifier
Osteopathic Section	Body system	Operation	Body region	Approach	Method	Qualifier
Other Procedures Section	Body system	Operation	Body region	Approach	Method	Qualifier
Chiropractic Section	Body system	Operation	Body region	Approach	Method	Qualifier
Imaging Section	Body system	Type	Body part	Contrast	Qualifier	Qualifier
Nuclear Medicine Section	Body system	Type	Body part	Radionuclide	Qualifier	Qualifier
Radiation Therapy Section	Body system	Modality	Treatment site	Modality qualifier	Isotope	Qualifier
Physical Rehabilitation and Diagnostic Audiology Section	Section qualifier	Type	Body system/ region	Type qualifier	Equipment	Qualifier
Mental Health Section	Body system	Type	Qualifier	Qualifier	Qualifier	Qualifier
Substance Abuse Treatment Section	Body system	Type	Qualifier	Qualifier	Qualifier	Qualifier
New Technology	Body system	Operation	Body part	Approach	Device/ Substance/ Technology	Qualifier

Format of ICD-10-PCS Coding Manual

The ICD-10-PCS coding manual contains two separate parts:

- Index
- Tables

The Centers for Medicare and Medicaid Services (CMS) also publish the following reference addenda:

- Edits made to the current year's definitions, index, and tables
- ICD-10-PCS conversion table (to assist with data retrieval)
- ICD-10-PCS codes file (text file containing the valid ICD-10-PCS codes and their full code titles)
- General equivalence mappings (of ICD-10-CM to ICD-9-CM and vice versa)
- ICD-10-PCS official guidelines for coding and reporting

Build-a-Code Using ICD-10-PCS

The ICD-10-PCS index allows the first 3–5 values, and sometimes all 7 characters, of a 7-character procedure code to be located alphabetically according to general type of procedure (e.g., excision), commonly used medical terms (e.g., appendectomy), or body part (e.g., adductor brevis muscle).

 NOTE:

- Some ICD-10-PCS tables are extensive, and coders must continue on to the next page of the coding manual to build an accurate code. (Coders say "a table bleeds onto the next page" to describe this.)
- In ICD-10-PCS, the term "procedure" refers to the complete specification of the 7 characters that comprise a complete code. The first character of the 7-character procedure code always specifies the section. Then, depending on the ICD-10-PCS section in which a procedure is classified, the values of characters 2–7 may vary. However, the values of characters 2–7 within a particular section remain the same.

The first 3–5 values of a 7-character procedure code as listed in the index entry direct the coder to a specific location in the ICD-10-PCS tables, which must be used to construct a complete and valid 7-character code. When the sixth character of an ICD-10-PCS code indicates a device, a device character is assigned only when a device is inserted (e.g., pacemaker, drain). In many cases, ICD-10-PCS tables include just one option for a device, the letter Z (no device). (Sometimes the coder is directed to a different main term by the instructional note *see*, which is located next to a main term.) It is important to realize that the letters I and O are *never* used in ICD-10-PCS because they are too easily confused with the numbers 1 and 0. Decimals are also *never* used in ICD-10-PCS codes.

Each ICD-10-PCS table identifies the first three values of the 7-character code (e.g., 027). Thus, locating the first 3 values of the 7-character code in the index allows the corresponding table to be located. Tables are organized beginning with numbers (0–9) as the first character, then letters (A–Z, except letters I and O). This means that a table 001 (in the Medical and Surgical Section) precedes table B00 (in the Imaging Section). The table is then used to determine the complete code by assigning the last 4 values, which is based on documentation of the procedure performed. ICD-10-PCS tables contain rows that specify the valid combinations of code values. Within a *body system* (or *section qualifier*, for the Physical Rehabilitation and Diagnostic Section Audiology Section), the three rows of text above each table specify values for characters 1–3 of an ICD-10-PCS code. The fifth row labels characters 4–7 of a possible code. Subsequent rows in the table specify valid combinations of values for characters 4–7 (Figure 2-6).

EXAMPLE: The patient underwent an *open procedure of the spinal canal to insert a subarachnoid-peritoneal shunt using synthetic substitute for the purpose of decreasing cerebrospinal fluid levels via bypass (using the shunt) to the peritoneal cavity*, which is assigned ICD-10-PCS code 001U0J6. Refer to each step and the yellow-highlighted items below to *build-a-code*.

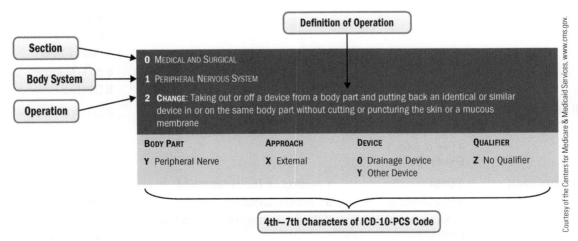

FIGURE 2-6 ICD-10-PCS table 012 with rows that specify valid combination of code values

Step 1   After identifying the name of the procedure performed in the operative report, locate the main term in the ICD-10-PCS Index.

Step 2   After following any instructional notes (e.g., *see*) present after a main term, locate the appropriate main term, subterm, and qualifier to identify the first 3 (or 4–5) values of a 7-character code.

Step 3   Locate the ICD-10-PCS table that corresponds to the first 3 values of a 7-character code, and review the procedure performed to assign a character to each position in the complete 7-character code.

ICD-10-PCS code 001U0J6 is assigned because 001 represents the table, 4th character U represents the spinal canal where the shunt was inserted, 0 represents an open approach (documented in the example), J represents use of a synthetic substitute (documented in the example), and 6 represents the peritoneal cavity. Thus, the shunt was inserted so fluid could move (be bypassed) from the spinal canal to the peritoneal cavity.

Section	0 Medical and Surgical		
Body System	0 Central Nervous System		
Operation	1 Bypass: Altering the route of passage of the contents of a tubular body part		

Body Part	Approach	Device	Qualifier
6 Cerebral Ventricle	0 Open 3 Percutaneous 4 Percutaneous Endoscopic	7 Autologous Tissue Substitute J Synthetic Substitute K Nonautologous Tissue Substitute	0 Nasopharynx 1 Mastoid Sinus 2 Atrium 3 Blood Vessel 4 Pleural Cavity 5 Intestine 6 Peritoneal Cavity 7 Urinary Tract 8 Bone Marrow B Cerebral Cisterns
6 Cerebral Ventricle	0 Open 3 Percutaneous 4 Percutaneous Endoscopic	Z No Device	B Cerebral Cisterns
U Spinal Canal	0 Open 3 Percutaneous 4 Percutaneous Endoscopic	7 Autologous Tissue Substitute J Synthetic Substitute K Nonautologous Tissue Substitute	2 Atrium 4 Pleural Cavity 6 Peritoneal Cavity 7 Urinary Tract 9 Fallopian Tube

Exercise 2.5 – ICD-10-PCS Index and Tables

Instructions: Complete each statement.

1. The *International Classification of Diseases, 10th Revision, Procedure Coding System* is abbreviated as _____.

2. ICD-10-PCS is an entirely new procedure classification system developed by CMS for use in the United States for hospital _____ settings only.

3. ICD-10-PCS uses a multiaxial alphanumeric code structure that contains _____ characters and provides a unique code for all substantially different procedures.

4. The letters I and _____ are never used in ICD-10-PCS codes.

5. Refer to steps 1 through 3 on the previous pages, and use the build-a-code method to assign an ICD-10-PCS code for an *open procedure of the spinal canal to insert a subarachnoid-pleural shunt using autologous tissue substitute for the purpose of decreasing cerebrospinal fluid levels via bypass (using the shunt) to the peritoneal cavity:* _____.

ICD-9-CM Legacy Coding System

As a result of implementing the ICD-10-CM and ICD-10-PCS coding systems, the *International Classification of Diseases, Ninth Revision, Clinical Modification* (ICD-9-CM) became a **legacy coding system** (or **legacy classification system**), which means it is used to archive data but is no longer supported or updated by the ICD-9-CM Coordination and Maintenance Committee. However, because ICD-9-CM was used since 1979 in the United States to classify inpatient and outpatient/physician office diagnoses (Volumes 1 and 2) and inpatient procedures (Volume 3), *general equivalence mappings (GEMs)* (discussed below) will be annually published by the National Center for Health Statistics (NCHS) and Centers for Medicare & Medicaid Services (CMS).

ICD-9-CM was over 30 years old, had outdated and obsolete terminology, used outdated codes that produced inaccurate and limited data, and was inconsistent with current medical practice. It did not accurately describe diagnoses or inpatient procedures of care delivered in the 21st century. ICD-9-CM did not provide the necessary detail about patients' medical conditions or procedures performed on hospitalized inpatients; thus, effective October 1, 2015, provider offices and health care facilities (e.g., hospitals) adopted ICD-10-CM to code diagnoses. (Hospitals use ICD-10-PCS to code inpatient procedures. Provider offices and outpatient health care settings use CPT and HCPCS level II to code procedures and services.)

General Equivalence Mappings (GEMs)

NCHS and CMS annually publish **general equivalence mappings (GEMs)**, which are translation dictionaries or crosswalks of codes that can be used to roughly identify ICD-10-CM codes for their ICD-9-CM equivalent codes (and vice versa). (GEMs published by the NCHS and CMS do not contain code descriptions; however, other publishers include code descriptions to facilitate code translation.) GEMs facilitate the location of corresponding diagnosis codes between two code sets. In some areas of the classification, the correlation between codes is close, and since the two code sets share the conventions of organization and formatting common to both revisions of ICD, translating between them is straightforward.

EXAMPLE 1: There is straightforward correspondence between the two code sets for the conditions, *Salmonella meningitis.*

ICD-9-CM to ICD-10-CM General Equivalence Mapping	
ICD-9-CM Diagnosis Code and Description	**ICD-10-CM Diagnosis Code and Description**
003.21 Salmonella meningitis	A02.21 Salmonella meningitis

EXAMPLE 2: In other areas of the two code sets, such as obstetrics, entire chapters are organized according to a different axis of classification, and translating between them offers a series of possible codes that must be verified in the appropriate tabular list (ICD-9-CM or ICD-10-CM) or table of codes (ICD-10-PCS) to identify the correct code. (Think about translating the English language into Chinese or any other foreign language, and you will see the problems inherent in such translation.)

ICD-9-CM to ICD-10-CM General Equivalence Mapping	
ICD-9-CM Disease Code and Description	**ICD-10-CM Disease Code and Description**
649.51 Spotting complicating pregnancy, delivered, with or without mention of antepartum complication	O26.851 Spotting complicating pregnancy, first trimester
	O26.852 Spotting complicating pregnancy, second trimester
	O26.853 Spotting complicating pregnancy, third trimester

EXAMPLE 3: Procedures located in ICD-9-CM Volume 3 that correspond to ICD-10-PCS codes are contained within its general equivalent mapping.

ICD-9-CM to ICD-10-PCS General Equivalence Mapping	
ICD-9-CM Procedure Code and Description	**ICD-10-PCS Procedure Code and Description**
47.11 Laparoscopic incidental appendectomy	0DTJ4ZZ Resection of Appendix, Percutaneous Endoscopic Approach

Exercise 2.6 – ICD-9-CM Legacy Coding System

Instructions: Use the diagnosis GEM depicted in the table below to complete each statement.

ICD-9-CM to ICD-10-CM General Equivalence Mapping	
ICD-9-CM Diagnosis Code and Description	**ICD-10-CM Diagnosis Code and Description**
078.81 Epidemic vertigo	A88.1 Epidemic vertigo
078.82 Epidemic vomiting syndrome	R11.11 Vomiting without nausea
078.88 Other specified diseases due to *Chlamydiae*	A74.89 Other chlamydial diseases
078.89 Other specified diseases due to viruses	A98.3 Marburg virus disease
	A98.4 Ebola virus disease
	B33.8 Other specified viral diseases

1. ICD-9-CM code 078.82 maps to ICD-10-CM code _____.
2. ICD-9-CM code 078.81 maps to ICD-10-CM code _____.
3. ICD-9-CM code 078.88 maps to ICD-10-CM code _____.
4. ICD-10-CM code A74.89 maps to ICD-9-CM code _____.
5. ICD-10-CM code B33.8 maps to ICD-9-CM code _____.

Summary

The *International Classification of Diseases, 10th Revision, Clinical Modification* (ICD-10-CM) and the *International Classification of Diseases, 10th Revision, Procedure Coding System* (ICD-10-PCS), abbreviated as ICD-10-CM/PCS, replaced ICD-9-CM effective October 2015. ICD-10-CM is a clinical modification of the World Health Organization's *International Classification of Diseases, Ninth Revision* (ICD-9). ICD-10-CM/PCS includes many more codes and applies to more users than ICD-9-CM because it is designed to collect data on every type of health care encounter (e.g., inpatient, outpatient, hospice, home health care, and long-term care). The ICD-10-CM Tabular List of Diseases and Injuries contains 21 chapters. It is a sequential list of codes contained within chapters based on body system or condition, and codes are then organized within major topic headings, categories, subcategories, and codes. ICD-10-CM disease and injury codes consist of three characters, but most are followed by a decimal point and between one and four additional characters. ICD-10-CM Index to Diseases and Injuries entries are organized according to main terms, subterms, second qualifiers, third qualifiers, and fourth qualifiers.

ICD-10-PCS is a procedure classification system developed by the Centers for Medicare & Medicaid Services (CMS) for use in the United States for inpatient hospital settings *only*. It uses a multiaxial 7-character alphanumeric code structure (e.g., 047K04Z) that provides a unique code for all substantially different procedures. It also allows new procedures to be easily incorporated as new codes. ICD-10-PCS contains more than 87,000 seven-character alphanumeric procedure codes.

Medical necessity is the measure of whether a health care procedure or service is appropriate for the diagnosis or treatment of a condition. This decision-making process is based on the payer's contractual language and the treating provider's documentation. Generally, the following criteria are used to determine medical necessity: purpose, scope, evidence, and value.

The DHHS agencies CMS and NCHS prepare guidelines for coding and reporting using ICD-10-CM and ICD-10-PCS that are approved by the four organizations that comprise the cooperating parties for the ICD-10-CM/PCS. The organizations include the AHA, AHIMA, CMS, and NCHS. The guidelines should be used as a companion document when coding from ICD-10-CM and ICD-10-PCS. The guidelines are rules that were developed to accompany and complement the official conventions and instructions provided in ICD-10-CM and ICD-10-PCS. They are based on coding and sequencing instructions in ICD-10-CM and ICD-10-PCS, but provide additional instruction. Adherence to these guidelines when assigning ICD-10-CM and ICD-10-PCS diagnosis and procedure codes is required in accordance with MMA legislation.

A joint effort between the health care provider and the coder is essential to achieving complete and accurate documentation, code assignment, and reporting of diagnoses and procedures. Consistent, complete documentation in the patient record is crucial because without such documentation, accurate codes cannot be assigned. In addition, the entire patient record must be reviewed to determine the specific reason for the encounter and the conditions treated so that appropriate codes are assigned. *Encoder* software automates the coding process, allowing coders to use a search function to locate and verify codes. *Computer-assisted coding (CAC)* software analyzes EHR or EMR documentation to generate codes for terms and phrases, and coders use data analytic skills to review CAC-generated codes and determine which are to be reported.

Upon implementation of ICD-10-CM and ICD-10-PCS, ICD-9-CM became a *legacy coding system (or legacy classification system)*, which means it is used as archive data but is no longer supported or updated. *General equivalence mappings (GEMs)*, which are translation dictionaries or crosswalks of codes that can be used to roughly identify ICD-10-CM codes for their ICD-9-CM equivalent codes (and vice versa), are annually published by NCHS and CMS.

Internet Links

Coding Clinic Advisor: *https://www.codingclinicadvisor.com*

ICD-10-CM and ICD-10-PCS encoder (subscription-based): *www.encoderpro.com* (free trial available)

ICD-10-CM/PCS updates: Go to *www.cdc.gov*, scroll to the Science at CDC heading, click on the Data & Statistics link, scroll to Tools and click on the Classification of Diseases, Functioning, and Disability link, and click on any of the ICD links.

ICD-10-CM/PCS: Go to *www.cms.gov*, click on Medicare, click on ICD-10 under Coding, and click on links in the first column to locate coding manual PDF files, general equivalence mappings (GEMs), and more.

Review

Multiple Choice (ICD-10-CM)

Instructions: Circle the most appropriate response.

1. ICD-10-CM was developed to code and classify _____ data from inpatient and outpatient records, including physician office records.
   - **a.** morbidity
   - **b.** mortality
   - **c.** procedure
   - **d.** service

2. Which entities work together to coordinate official ICD-10-CM disease classification activities?
   - **a.** National Center for Health Statistics (NCHS) and the Centers for Medicare & Medicaid Services (CMS)
   - **b.** National Center for Health Statistics (NCHS) with the World Health Organization (WHO)
   - **c.** U.S. Department of Health & Human Services (DHHS)
   - **d.** World Health Organization (WHO)

3. General equivalence mappings are translation dictionaries or _____ of codes.
   - **a.** appendices
   - **b.** crosswalks
   - **c.** indexes
   - **d.** tabular lists

4. Outcome of delivery, follow-up, history, and vaccination are examples of ICD-10-CM:
   - **a.** external causes of morbidity.
   - **b.** factors influencing health status.
   - **c.** conditions originating in the perinatal period.
   - **d.** symptoms, signs, and abnormal findings.

5. The Table of Neoplasms is located in the:
   - **a.** ICD-10-CM Index to Diseases and Injuries.
   - **b.** ICD-10-CM Tabular List of Disease and Injuries.
   - **c.** ICD-10-PCS Index.
   - **d.** ICD-10-PCS Tables.

6. Review the ICD-10-CM Index to Diseases and Injuries entry for main term *Contusion*, and locate subterm "arm" below it. Which ICD-10-CM code appears next to the subterm?
   - **a.** S40
   - **b.** S40.0
   - **c.** S40.02
   - **d.** S40.02-

7. A patient is diagnosed with tactile agnosia involving her body image and other senses. Referring to the ICD-10-CM Index to Diseases and Injuries, which is the main term for this condition?
   - **a.** agnosia
   - **b.** body image
   - **c.** other sense
   - **d.** tactile

8. A patient is diagnosed with *traumatic hematoma with intact skin surface*. Referring to the ICD-10-CM Index to Diseases and Injuries, which is the main term for this condition?
   - **a.** hematoma
   - **b.** intact
   - **c.** skin surface
   - **d.** traumatic

9. ICD-10-CM _____ codes are reported by all health care settings.
    - a. disease
    - b. medical equipment
    - c. procedure
    - d. service

10. Adhering to official coding guidelines is:
    - a. at the discretion of a health care facility's operating procedures.
    - b. mandated by the cooperating parties.
    - c. not necessary if the facility has a 90 percent or higher coding accuracy rate.
    - d. required by the Health Insurance Portability and Accountability Act.

11. Which organization publishes the ICD-10-CM Official Guidelines for Coding and Reporting?
    - a. American Hospital Association
    - b. American Medical Association
    - c. Centers for Medicare and Medicaid Services
    - d. National Center for Health Statistics

12. Using both the ICD-10-CM index and tabular list when assigning codes results in:
    - a. accurate code assignment.
    - b. coding errors.
    - c. less specificity when selecting codes.
    - d. selection of laterality for all codes.

13. When a related definitive diagnosis has not been established (or confirmed) by the provider, codes are assigned to:
    - a. canceled procedures.
    - b. hierarchical conditions.
    - c. ruled out diagnoses.
    - d. signs and symptoms.

14. When the same condition is described as both acute (or subacute) and chronic, and the ICD-10-CM index contains subentries for each:
    - a. assign a code to the acute (or subacute) condition only.
    - b. generate a physician query to determine sequencing.
    - c. code both and sequence the acute (or subacute) code first.
    - d. report codes for both, and sequence the chronic condition first.

15. When a residual effect is documented after the acute phase of injury or illness has ended, a code for the _____ condition is sequenced first.
    - a. acute
    - b. diagnostic
    - c. qualified
    - d. residual

Multiple Choice (ICD-10-PCS)

1. ICD-10-PCS are reported for:
    - a. emergency department services.
    - b. hospital inpatient procedures.
    - c. outpatient same day surgery.
    - d. physician office encounters.

2. ICD-10-PCS uses a _____ 7-character alphanumeric code structure that provides a unique code for all substantially different procedures.
    - a. anatomic
    - b. complex
    - c. methodological
    - d. multiaxial

3. The ICD-10-PCS index is arranged:
    a. alphabetically.
    b. anatomically.
    c. by service or procedure.
    d. numerically.

4. The development of ICD-10-PCS incorporates an attribute of completeness, which means there are _____ codes for all substantially different procedures.
    a. combination
    b. independent
    c. repetitive
    d. unique

5. The development of ICD-10-PCS incorporates an attribute of standardized terminology, which means definitions of the terminology used are included, and while the meaning of specific words varies in common usage:
    a. as new procedures are developed, they are incorporated into existing codes.
    b. each term is assigned a specific meaning.
    c. codes consist of characters with each individual axis having a different.
    d. there are combination codes for all substantially different procedures.

6. ICD-10-PCS includes the general principle that:
    a. all significant components of a surgical procedure are included in the code reported for substantially different procedures.
    b. diagnostic information is incorporated into code descriptions so that combination diagnosis/procedure codes are assigned.
    c. documentation of a minimal level of specificity is not needed to build a code for each component of a surgical procedure.
    d. level of specificity is enhanced so that all procedures currently performed can be assigned a specific and unique code.

7. Which are excluded from use in ICD-10-PCS?
    a. alphanumeric characters
    b. capital letters I and O
    c. lower case letters I and o
    d. numbers 1 and 0

8. ICD-10-PCS codes:
    a. contain decimals.
    b. do not contain decimals.
    c. have letters in position one only.
    d. include numbers in position seven only.

9. Which is an example of an ICD-10-PCS of a body system?
    a. anterior
    b. lungs
    c. osmolar
    d. respiratory

10. Go to ICD-10-PCS table 001, and identify the code for a percutaneous endoscopic bypass procedure from cerebral ventricle to cerebral cisterns using with nonautologous tissue substitute.
    a. 00163KB
    b. 00164KB
    c. 00163ZB
    d. 00164ZB

Matching

Instructions: Match the format in Column 2 with each line of the ICD-10-CM Tabular List of Diseases and Injuries entry in Column 1.

Tabular List of Diseases and Injuries Entry

_____ 1.   DISEASES OF THE NERVOUS SYSTEM (G00-G99)

_____ 2.   EPISODIC AND PAROXYSMAL DISORDERS (G40-G47)

_____ 3.   G43 Migraine

_____ 4.   G43.C Periodic headache syndromes
                      in child or adult

_____ 5.   G43.C0 Periodic headache syndromes in
                        child or adult, not intractable

Format

a. Category
b. Chapter title
c. Section title
d. Subcategory
e. Code

Coding Practice: ICD-10-CM

Instructions: Underline the main term, and use the ICD-10-CM index and tabular list to assign the appropriate code. Remember! When a code in an ICD-10-CM index entry contains a hyphen (e.g., O45.9-), review the tabular list to assign the fifth character.

_____   **1.** Abdominal hernia

_____   **2.** Abnormal nonfasting glucose tolerance test

_____   **3.** Acute otitis media

_____   **4.** Hyperplasia of endometrium

_____   **5.** Traumatic fracture (closed), right humerus shaft (initial encounter)

_____   **6.** Congenital fibrocystic disease of the lung

_____   **7.** Degenerative arthritis

_____   **8.** Fibrocystic disease of right and left breasts

_____   **9.** Hereditary epistaxis

_____   **10.** Personal history of cancer

Coding Practice: ICD-10-PCS

Instructions: Underline the main term, and use the ICD-10-PCS index and tables to assign the appropriate code. Remember! The ICD-10-PCS index entry contains just the first three characters of a code, which directs coders to the appropriate table to "build a code."

_____   **1.** Open biopsy, left axillary lymph node

_____   **2.** Open cholecystectomy, total

_____   **3.** Cystoscopy

_____   **4.** Exploratory laparotomy, open

_____   **5.** Intravenous right pyelogram (using fluoroscopy)

_____   **6.** Incidental appendectomy (open)

_____   **7.** Open biopsy of left frontal nasal sinus

_____   **8.** Percutaneous biopsy of prostate

_____   **9.** Right frontal craniotomy (open approach)

_____   **10.** Transurethral biopsy of bladder

ICD-10-CM and ICD-10-PCS Coding Conventions

Chapter Outline

Format and Typeface
Eponyms
Abbreviations
Punctuation
Boxed Notes
Tables
Includes Notes
Excludes1 and Excludes2 Notes
Inclusion Terms

Other, Other Specified, and
    Unspecified Codes
Etiology and Manifestation Rules
And
Due To
In
With
Cross-References
Code Assignment and Clinical Criteria

Chapter Objectives

At the conclusion of this chapter, the student should be able to:

1. Define key terms related to ICD-10-CM and ICD-10-PCS coding conventions.
2. Identify ICD-10-CM and ICD-10-PCS coding conventions.
3. Define ICD-10-CM and ICD-10-PCS coding conventions.
4. Interpret ICD-10-CM and ICD-10-PCS coding conventions for accurate code assignment.

Key Terms

coding conventions
  abbreviations
    NEC (not elsewhere
      classifiable)
    NOS (not otherwise
      specified)
  and
  boxed note
  code also
  cross-references
    see
    see also
    see category

    see condition
  use
  default code
  due to
  eponym
  etiology and
    manifestation rules
    code first underlying
      disease
    code, if applicable,
      any causal
      condition first

in diseases classified
  elsewhere
use additional
  code
excludes1 note
excludes2 note
format
in
includes note
inclusion term
manifestation
modifier

other
other specified
punctuation
  brackets
  colon
  parentheses
syndrome
tables
trust the index
typeface
unspecified code
with

Introduction

 NOTE:

When reviewing examples and completing exercises and review questions in this chapter, use your ICD-10-CM and ICD-10-PCS coding manuals to locate disease and procedure index entries and verify codes in the respective tabular list or tables.

The ICD-10-CM and ICD-10-PCS coding conventions (rules) can usually be found at the beginning of any ICD-10-CM or ICD-10-PCS coding manual. Coders are required to reference this material when reviewing case scenarios (and patient records) to assign ICD-10-CM and ICD-10-PCS codes. It is also helpful to coders when health care providers become familiar with coding conventions (and guidelines). When a coder initiates a physician query, an understanding of coding conventions and guidelines helps ensure the assignment of accurate codes for certain conditions and diagnoses.

Coding conventions for ICD-10-CM and ICD-10-PCS are general rules used in the classification, and they are independent of the coding guidelines (covered in Chapters 2 and 4–7 of this textbook). The conventions are incorporated into ICD-10-CM and ICD-10-PCS as instructional notes. General ICD-10-CM coding conventions include the following:

- *Default codes*: In ICD-10-CM, a code listed next to a main term in the ICD-10-CM indexes is referred to as a **default code**. The default code represents that condition that is most commonly associated with the main term, or is the unspecified code for the condition. If a condition is documented in a patient record (e.g., appendicitis) without any additional information, such as acute or chronic, the default code should be assigned.

- *Syndromes*: In ICD-10-CM, coders should follow the alphabetic index guidance when assigning codes to **syndromes**, which is an association of clinically recognizable features such as signs (observed by others), symptoms (reported by the patient), and/or characteristics that often occur together, so that the presence of one or more features alerts the health care provider as to the possible presence of the others. Coders follow ICD-10-CM index guidance when assigning codes to a syndrome, *and in the absence of index guidance, assign codes for the documented manifestations of the syndrome.*

Specific ICD-10-CM and/or ICD-10-PCS coding conventions include the following:

- Format and typeface
- Eponyms
- Abbreviations
- Punctuation
- Boxed notes
- Tables
- Excludes1 and excludes2 notes
- Includes notes
- Inclusion terms
- Other, other specified, and unspecified codes
- Etiology and manifestation rules
- And
- Due to
- In
- With
- Cross-references, including, *see, see also, see* category, *see* condition, and *use*
- Code assignment and clinical criteria

Format and Typeface

Each ICD-10-CM and ICD-10-PCS index uses an indented **format** for ease in reference (Figure 3-1). All ICD-10-CM Index to Diseases and Injuries subterms associated with an index entry's main term are indented two spaces, with any 2nd and 3rd qualifiers associated with the main term further indented by two and four spaces, respectively. In addition, if an index entry requires more than one line, the additional text is printed on the next line and indented five spaces.

ICD-10-CM and ICD-10-PCS also makes use of the boldface and italic **typeface** for ease in reference. Boldface type is used for main term entries in the ICD-10-CM and ICD-10-PCS alphabetical indexes, all codes and descriptions in the ICD-10-CM tabular list, and sections and characters in ICD-10-PCS tables. Italicized type is used for all ICD-10-CM tabular list excludes1 and excludes2 notes and to identify manifestation codes, which are codes that should not be reported as the first-listed or principal diagnoses.

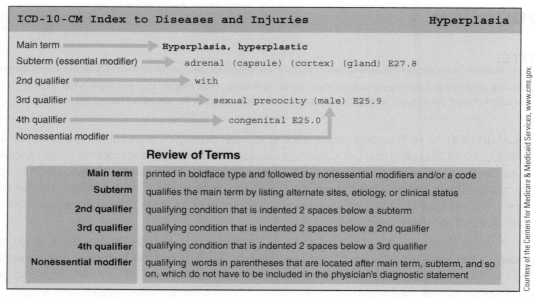

FIGURE 3-1 Display of main terms, subterms, qualifiers, nonessential modifiers in ICD-10-CM Index to Diseases and Injuries

Additional terms are indented below the term to which they are linked in the ICD-10-CM tabular list; if a definition or disease requires more than one line, that text is printed on the next line and indented five spaces.

EXAMPLE 1: ICD-10-CM INDEX TO DISEASES AND INJURIES—INDENTED FORMAT AND BOLDFACE: Locate main term *ulcer* in the ICD-10-CM Index to Diseases and Injuries, and notice that it is boldfaced. Also, notice that subterm *aphthous (oral) (recurrent) K12.0* is indented two spaces below the "U" of main term *ulcer*. Then, notice that second qualifier *genital organ(s)* is further indented two spaces.

EXAMPLE 2: ICD-10-CM TABULAR LIST OF DISEASES AND INJURIES—INDENTED FORMAT AND BOLDFACE: Locate *code K12.0 Recurrent Oral Aphthae* in the ICD-10-CM Tabular List of Diseases and Injuries, and notice that it is in boldface and its synonyms (e.g., Bednar's aphthae) are indented.

EXAMPLE 3: ICD-10-PCS INDEX—INDENTED FORMAT AND BOLDFACE: Locate main term *Laparotomy* in the ICD-10-PCS index, and notice that it is boldfaced and subterm *Drainage* is indented two spaces below the "L" of *Laparotomy*.

 ICD-10 Alert!

The indented format is *not* used in the ICD-10-PCS tables.

EXAMPLE 4: ICD-10-PCS TABLES—BOLDFACE: Locate ICD-10-PCS table 001, and notice that the first three characters and descriptions are boldfaced. Then, notice that additional characters located in columns and rows are also boldfaced.

Exercise 3.1 – Format and Typeface

Exercise 3.1A – ICD-10-CM

Instructions: Assign an ICD-10-CM code to each statement. Make sure you appropriately interpret the use of indented format and typeface in the ICD-10-CM disease index.

Exercise 3.1 – *continued*

_____ 1. Acariasis infestation

_____ 2. Pityriasis rubra pilaris

_____ 3. Admission for adjustment of artificial leg

_____ 4. Adjustment disorder with anxiety

_____ 5. Anorexia nervosa

Exercise 3.1B – ICD-10-PCS

Instructions: Assign an ICD-10-PCS code to each statement. Make sure you appropriately interpret the use of indented format and typeface in the ICD-10-PCS index.

_____ 1. High forceps delivery

_____ 2. Magnetic resonance imaging (MRI), left breast

_____ 3. Termination of pregnancy (by) dilation and curettage

_____ 4. Heart transplantation, allogenic

_____ 5. Ultrasonography, abdomen

Eponyms

 ICD-10 Alert!

There are no eponyms (e.g., Billroth procedure) in ICD-10-PCS.

Eponyms are diseases or syndromes that are named for people. They are listed in alphabetical order as main terms in the ICD-10-CM Index to Diseases and Injuries. They are also listed as subterms below main terms *Disease* and *Syndrome* in the index. A description of the disease, syndrome, or procedure is usually included in parentheses following the eponym.

EXAMPLE: ICD-10-CM INDEX TO DISEASES AND INJURIES—EPONYM: The Index to Diseases and Injuries entry for *Christmas disease* can be located in alphabetical order. It can also be located under main term *Disease*. (Upon review of code D67 and its description in the Tabular List of Diseases and Injuries, Christmas disease is included as an synonym below the code description.)

Exercise 3.2 – Eponyms

Instructions: Assign an ICD-10-CM code to each statement. Make sure that you appropriately interpret the use of eponyms in the ICD-10-CM disease index.

_____ 1. Costen's complex

_____ 2. Madelung's deformity

_____ 3. Coats' disease

_____ 4. Kaschin-Beck disease

_____ 5. Meniere's disease, right ear

Abbreviations

The ICD-10-CM indexes and tabular list contain **abbreviations** to save space. The abbreviation **NEC (not elsewhere classifiable)** means "other" or "other specified" and identifies codes that are to be assigned when information needed to assign a more specific code cannot be located in the code book. When a specific code is not available in the disease index for a condition, the coder is directed to the "other specified" code in the tabular list.

ICD-10 Alert! ━━

> The NEC abbreviation does not appear in the ICD-10-PCS index or tables.

EXAMPLE 1: ICD-10-CM INDEX TO DISEASES AND INJURIES—NEC ABBREVIATION: The Index to Diseases and Injuries entry for *aberrant, artery, basilar* contains the NEC abbreviation in front of code Q28.1, which means a more specific code cannot be assigned in the code book. When verifying code Q28.1 in the Tabular List of Diseases and Injuries, notice that the code description is *Other malformations of precerebral vessels* and that the NEC abbreviation does not appear in the code description. Code Q28.1 is assigned to *aberrant basilar artery* because the index's NEC abbreviation directs the coder to that code.

EXAMPLE 2: ICD-10-CM TABULAR LIST OF DISEASES AND INJURIES—NEC ABBREVIATION: Locate code Q28.8 in the tabular list, and notice that the NEC abbreviation is included next to *Congenital aneurysm, specified site NEC* below the code description.

The ICD-10-CM disease index and tabular list contain the abbreviation **NOS (not otherwise specified),** which is the equivalent of "unspecified." It identifies codes that are to be assigned when information needed to assign a more specific code cannot be obtained from the provider. Because selecting a code from the disease index based on limited documentation results in the coder being directed to an "unspecified" code in the tabular list, the coder should contact the physician to request that additional documentation be provided so that a more specific diagnosis or procedure code can be assigned. A review of the patient record to assign a more specific code is also an important part of the coding process (e.g., laboratory data, radiology reports, operative report, pathology report).

NOTE:

> It is appropriate to ask the physician for clarification about a diagnosis if the patient's record contains documentation (e.g., laboratory data) to support the assignment of a more specific code.

ICD-10 Alert! ━━

> The NOS abbreviation does not appear in the ICD-10-PCS index or tables.

EXAMPLE 1: ICD-10-CM INDEX TO DISEASES AND INJURIES—NOS ABBREVIATION: The index entry for *Bronchomycosis NOS B49 [J99]* directs the coder to B49, which is an *unspecified* code.

EXAMPLE 2: ICD-10-CM TABULAR LIST OF DISEASES AND INJURIES—NOS ABBREVIATION: Locate code A03.9 in the tabular list, and notice the NOS abbreviation appears after *dysentery*.

Exercise 3.3 – Abbreviations

Instructions: Assign an ICD-10-CM code to each statement. Make sure that you appropriately interpret the use of abbreviations in the ICD-10-CM disease index and tabular list.

_____ **1.** Purpura

_____ **2.** Femoral hernia

_____ **3.** ST elevation myocardial infarction, anterior wall

_____ **4.** Hyperinsulinism

_____ **5.** Laceration, right eyeball (initial encounter)

Punctuation

ICD-10-CM includes the following **punctuation**:

- Brackets
- Parentheses
- Colons

Brackets are used to identify manifestation codes in the ICD-10-CM Index to Diseases and Injuries. A **manifestation** is a condition that occurs as the result of another condition, and manifestation codes are always reported as secondary codes. The code and description may or may not appear in italics in the tabular list. When code descriptions are not italicized in the tabular list, make sure you sequence the codes according to the sequence in the index entry.

 NOTE:

When reporting manifestation codes, do not enclose them in brackets.

CORRECT: E85.4

          I43

INCORRECT: E85.4

          [I43]

EXAMPLE: ICD-10-CM INDEX TO DISEASES AND INJURIES—BRACKETS: The index entry for *Amyloid heart (disease) E85.4 [I43]* indicates that two codes should be reported: E85.4 and I43. Because code I43 appears in brackets, it is reported as a secondary code. When verifying code I43 in the tabular list, notice that its description is italicized and includes a *Code first underlying disease,* such as: instruction is provided, prompting you to report code I43 as the second code.

Brackets are used in the ICD-10-CM indexes and tabular list to enclose abbreviations, synonyms, alternative wording, or explanatory phrases.

EXAMPLE 1: ICD-10-CM INDEX TO DISEASES AND INJURIES—SQUARE BRACKETS: The index entry for *Abnormal, electrocardiogram [ECG] [EKG] R94.31* encloses abbreviations in square brackets.

EXAMPLE 2: ICD-10-CM TABULAR LIST OF DISEASES AND INJURIES—SQUARE BRACKETS: Code I45.89 uses square brackets to enclose the abbreviation for *atrioventricular* as [*AV*].

Parentheses are used in both the ICD-10-CM indexes and tabular list and ICD-10-PCS index to enclose nonessential modifiers, which are supplementary words that may be present in or absent from the physician's statement of a disease or procedure without affecting the code to which it is assigned. The nonessential modifiers in the indexes apply to subterms that are located below a main term; *however, when a nonessential modifier and a subterm are mutually exclusive, the subterm takes precedence.*

EXAMPLE 1: ICD-10-CM INDEX TO DISEASES AND INJURIES—PARENTHESES (supplementary terms): Index entry *abasia (-astasia) (hysterical) F44.4* contains two nonessential modifiers in parentheses, which means that the terms may be present or absent from the provider's diagnostic statement.

EXAMPLE 2: ICD-10-CM INDEX TO DISEASES AND INJURIES—PARENTHESES (mutually exclusive modifiers): Index entry *Enteritis* contains nonessential modifier *acute* in parentheses and essential modifier *chronic* as a subterm; nonessential modifier *acute* does *not* have to be included in the provider's diagnosis statement to report code K52.9.

EXAMPLE 3: ICD-10-CM TABULAR LIST OF DISEASES AND INJURIES—PARENTHESES: Code I47.9 contains a nonessential modifier, (*-Hoffman*), in parentheses, which means that the term may be present or absent from the provider's diagnostic statement.

EXAMPLE 4: ICD-10-PCS INDEX—PARENTHESES: Index entry *acromion (process)* contains a nonessential modifier in parentheses, which means the term may be present or absent from the provider's procedural statement.

A **colon** is used after an incomplete term or phrase in the ICD-10-CM disease index and tabular list when one or more of the **modifiers** (additional terms) following the colon is needed to make the condition assignable to a given category.

EXAMPLE 1: ICD-10-CM INDEX TO DISEASES AND INJURIES—COLON: The 2nd qualifier *with retinal:* (located after index main term *Detachment* and subterm *retina (without retinal break) (serous) H33.2-*) requires the type of detachment (e.g., giant break H33.03-) to be documented in the patient record so that a specific code can be selected.

EXAMPLE 2: ICD-10-CM TABULAR LIST OF DISEASES AND INJURIES—COLON: Underneath category *A40 Streptococcal sepsis*, a colon is used in the *Code first:* instruction to indicate conditions (e.g., postprocedural streptococcal sepsis, T81.4-) that are to be reported first when documented in the patient record.

Exercise 3.4 – Punctuation

Instructions: Assign an ICD-10-CM code to each statement. Make sure that you appropriately interpret the use of punctuation in the ICD-10-CM disease index and tabular list.

_____ 1. Acquired acanthosis
_____ 2. Malaria fever
_____ 3. Dimorphous leprosy
_____ 4. Acute pyogenic thyroiditis
_____ 5. Neuritis due to beriberi

Boxed Notes

Certain main terms in the ICD-10-CM disease index, including the Table of Neoplasms, are followed by **boxed notes,** which define terms and provide coding instruction.

EXAMPLE: ICD-10-CM INDEX TO DISEASES AND INJURIES—BOXED NOTE:

- The Index to Diseases and Injuries main term *Epilepsy* contains a boxed note that includes terms that are to be considered equivalent to intractable, such as *pharmacoresistant*.

- The Table of Neoplasms contains a boxed note that clarifies how to use the columns and rows in the table.

Exercise 3.5 – Boxed Notes

Instructions: Assign an ICD-10-CM code to each statement. Make sure that you interpret the content of boxed notes in the ICD-10-CM disease index, which includes the Table of Neoplasms.

_____ 1. Pharmacoresistant epilepsy

_____ 2. Treatment-resistant epilepsy

_____ 3. Refractory epilepsy with status epilepticus

_____ 4. Poorly controlled epilepsy with status epilepticus

_____ 5. Malignant mesonephroma, right ovary (primary malignancy)

_____ 6. Malignant embryoma, right kidney (primary malignancy)

_____ 7. Bowen's disease

Tables

The ICD-10-CM disease index includes **tables**, which organize subterms, 2nd qualifiers, and 3rd qualifiers and their codes in columns and rows to make it easier to select the proper code. ICD-10-PCS also uses tables, but not in its index; instead of a tabular list of codes, ICD-10-PCS tables are used to assign procedure codes (Figure 3-2).

SECTION	0	Medical and Surgical
BODY SYSTEM	J	Subcutaneous Tissue and Fascia
OPERATION	H	*Insertion*: putting in a nonbiological appliance that monitors, assists, performs, or prevents a physiological function but does not physically take the place of a body part

Body Part	Approach	Device	Qualifier
S Subcutaneous Tissue and Fascia, Head and Neck V Subcutaneous Tissue and Fascia, Upper Extremity W Subcutaneous Tissue and Fascia, Lower Extremity	0 Open 3 Percutaneous	1 Radioactive Element 3 Infusion Device Y Other Device	Z No Qualifier
T Subcutaneous Tissue and Fascia, Trunk	0 Open 3 Percutaneous	1 Radioactive Element 3 Infusion Device V Infusion Pump Y Other Device	Z No Qualifier

FIGURE 3-2 Sample ICD-10-PCS table

	Malignant Primary	Malignant Secondary	Ca *in situ*	Benign	Uncertain Behavior	Unspecified Nature
Notes—						
The list below gives the code numbers for neoplasms by anatomical site. For each site there are six possible code numbers according to whether the neoplasm in question is malignant, benign, *in situ*, of uncertain behavior, or of unspecified nature. The description of the neoplasm will often indicate which of the six columns is appropriate; e.g., malignant melanoma of skin, benign fibroadenoma of breast, carcinoma *in situ* of cervix uteri.						
Where such descriptors are not present, the remainder of the Index should be consulted where guidance is given to the appropriate column for each morphologic (histological) variety listed; e.g., Mesonephroma —*see* Neoplasm, malignant; Embryoma —*see also* Neoplasm, uncertain behavior; Disease, Bowen's —*see* Neoplasm, skin, *in situ*. However, the guidance in the Index can be overridden if one of the descriptors mentioned above is present; e.g., malignant adenoma of colon is coded to C18.9 and not to D12.6 as the adjective "malignant" overrides the Index entry "Adenoma —*see also* Neoplasm, benign."						
Codes listed with a dash -, following the code have a required additional character for laterality. The tabular must be reviewed for the complete code.						
Neoplasm, neoplastic	C80.1	C79.9	D09.9	D36.9	D48.9	D49.9
abdomen, abdominal	C76.2	C79.8-	D09.8	D36.7	D48.7	D49.9
cavity	C76.2	C79.8-	D09.8	D36.7	D48.7	D49.89
organ	C76.2	C79.8-	D09.8	D36.7	D48.7	D49.89
viscera	C76.2	C79.8-	D09.8	D36.7	D48.7	D49.89
wall —*see also* Neoplasm, abdomen,						
wall, skin	C44.509	C79.2-	D04.5	D23.5	D48.5	D49.2
connective tissue	C49.4	C79.8-	—	D21.4	D48.1	D49.2
skin	C44.509	—	—	—	—	—
basal cell carcinoma	C44.519	—	—	—	—	—
specified type NEC	C44.599	—	—	—	—	—
squamous cell carcinoma	C44.529	—	—	—	—	—

FIGURE 3-3 ICD-10-CM Table of Neoplasms (partial)

ICD-10-CM organizes the following main terms in tables, which are located at the end of the Index to Diseases and Injuries (before the Index to External Causes of Injuries):

- Table of Neoplasms
- Table of Drugs and Chemicals

The Table of Neoplasms is an alphabetic index of anatomical sites for which there are six possible codes according to whether the neoplasm in question is malignant, benign, *in situ*, of uncertain behavior, or of unspecified nature. The description of the neoplasm will often indicate which of the six columns is appropriate (e.g., malignant melanoma of skin, benign fibroadenoma of breast, carcinoma *in situ* of cervix uteri) (Figure 3-3).

The Table of Drugs and Chemicals in ICD-10-CM is an alphabetic index of medicinal, chemical, and biological substances that result in poisonings and adverse effects as well as underdosings. The first column of the table lists generic names of drugs and chemicals (although some publishers have added brand names) with six columns for *Poisoning: Accidental (Unintentional)* (poisoning that results from an inadvertent overdose, wrong substance administered/taken, or intoxication that includes combining prescription drugs with nonprescription drugs or alcohol); *Poisoning: Intentional Self-harm* (poisoning that results from a deliberate overdose, such as a suicide attempt, of substance[s] administered/taken or intoxication that includes purposely combining prescription drugs with nonprescription drugs or alcohol); *Poisoning: Assault* (poisoning inflicted by another person who intended to kill or injure the patient); *Poisoning: Undetermined* (subcategory used if the patient record does not document whether the poisoning was intentional or accidental); *Adverse Effect* (development of a pathological condition that results from a drug or chemical substance that was properly administered or taken); and *Underdosing* (taking less of a medication than is prescribed by a provider or a manufacturer's instruction) (Figure 3-4).

NOTE:

Tables appear in the ICD-10-CM Index to Diseases and Injuries, and their use is further discussed in Chapters 5–7 of this textbook. ICD-10-PCS also uses tables to facilitate the assignment of procedure codes, but the tables do not appear in the ICD-10-PCS index.

Substance	Poisoning, Accidental (unintentional)	Poisoning, Intentional Self-harm	Poisoning, Assault	Poisoning, Undetermined	Adverse Effect	Underdosing
1-Propanol	T51.3x1	T51.3x2	T51.3x3	T51.3x4	—	—
2-Propanol	T51.2x1	T51.2x2	T51.2x3	T51.2x4	—	—
2, 4-D (dichlorophen-oxyacetic acid)	T60.3x1	T60.3x2	T60.3x3	T60.3x4	—	—
2, 4-toluene diisocyanate	T65.0x1	T65.0x2	T65.0x3	T65.0x4	—	—
2, 4, 5-T (trichloro-phenoxyacetic acid)	T60.1x1	T60.1x2	T60.1x3	T60.1x4	—	—
3, 4-methylenedioxymethamphetamine	T43.641	T43.642	T43.643	T43.644	—	—
14-hydroxydihydro-morphinone	T40.2x1	T40.2x2	T40.2x3	T40.2x4	T40.2x5	T40.2x6
ABOB	T37.5x1	T37.5x2	T37.5x3	T37.5x4	T37.5x5	T37.5x6
Abrine	T62.2x1	T62.2x2	T62.2x3	T62.2x4	—	—
Abrus (seed)	T62.2x1	T62.2x2	T62.2x3	T62.2x4	—	—
Absinthe	T51.0x1	T51.0x2	T51.0x3	T51.0x4	—	—
beverage	T51.0x1	T51.0x2	T51.0x3	T51.0x4	—	—
Acaricide	T60.8x1	T60.8x2	T60.8x3	T60.8x4	—	—
Acebutolol	T44.7x1	T44.7x2	T44.7x3	T44.7x4	T44.7x5	T44.7x6
Acecarbromal	T42.6x1	T42.6x2	T42.6x3	T42.6x4	T42.6x5	T42.6x6
Aceclidine	T44.1x1	T44.1x2	T44.1x3	T44.1x4	T44.1x5	T44.1x6
Acedapsone	T37.0x1	T37.0x2	T37.0x3	T37.0x4	T37.0x5	T37.0x6
Acefylline piperazine	T48.6x1	T48.6x2	T48.6x3	T48.6x4	T48.6x5	T48.6x6

Courtesy of the Centers for Medicare & Medicaid Services, www.cms.gov.

FIGURE 3-4 ICD-10-CM Table of Drugs and Chemicals (partial)

Exercise 3.6 – Tables

Instructions: Assign an ICD-10-CM code to each statement. Use the ICD-10-CM Table of Neoplasms to first locate the anatomic site for questions 1–5, then select the appropriate column to identify the code, and refer to the tabular list to assign the code. Use the Table of Drugs and Chemicals to locate the drug for questions 6 and 7, then refer to the tabular list in the appropriate column to identify the code, and refer to the tabular list to assign the code.

_____ **1.** Ethmoid sinus tumor

_____ **2.** Basal cell carcinoma, skin of external cheek

_____ **3.** Carcinoma of liver

_____ **4.** Prostate cancer

_____ **5.** Poisoning due to inhalation of paint fumes (initial encounter)

_____ **6.** Circulatory collapse due to therapeutic use of magnesium sulfate (oral) (initial encounter)

_____ **7.** Accidental overdose of antidepressants (initial encounter)

Includes Notes

An **includes note** appears in the ICD-10-CM tabular list below certain categories to further define, clarify, or provide examples about the content below a code category.

EXAMPLE: ICD-10-CM TABULAR LIST OF DISEASES AND INJURIES—INCLUDES NOTE: The includes note located below category code *H80 Otosclerosis* in the Tabular List of Diseases and Injuries indicates that *otospongiosis* is classified to that same category. This means that the provider could document *otosclerosis* or *otospongiosis*, and a code from category H80 would be assigned.

Exercise 3.7 – Includes Notes

Instructions: Assign an ICD-10-CM code to each statement. Make sure that you appropriately interpret the use of includes notes in the ICD-10-CM tabular list.

_____ 1. Meningoencephalitis
_____ 2. Nephrosclerosis
_____ 3. Anastomotic ulcer
_____ 4. High blood pressure
_____ 5. Acute pharyngitis

Excludes1 and Excludes2 Notes

NOTE:

ICD-10-PCS does not use excludes notes.

The ICD-10-CM Tabular List of Diseases and Injuries contains two types of excludes notes. Each note has a different definition for use. However, they are similar in that they both indicate that codes excluded from each other are independent of each other.

An **excludes1 note** is a pure excludes. It means "not coded here" and indicates mutually exclusive codes, in other words—two or more conditions that cannot be reported together.

EXAMPLE 1: ICD-10-CM TABULAR LIST OF DISEASES AND INJURIES—EXCLUDES1 NOTE: Locate ICD-10-CM code **Q03 Congenital hydrocephalus** in the tabular list, and find the Excludes1 note for *acquired hydrocephalus (G91.-)*. Hydrocephalus diagnosed in a newborn is assigned a code from Q03.0–Q03.9. For hydrocephalus that develops later in life, a code from G91.0 to G91.9 is assigned. A congenital form of a disease is not reported with an acquired form of the same condition. Thus, the excluded code is never reported with the code located above the Excludes1 note.

Coding Tip

An excludes1 note instructs you to assign one code or the other *except when documentation supports existence of both conditions.*

EXAMPLE 2: ICD-10-CM TABULAR LIST OF DISEASES AND INJURIES—EXCLUDES1 NOTE: Locate ICD-10-CM code **E10 Type 1 diabetes mellitus** in the tabular list, and find the Excludes1 note for *type 2 diabetes mellitus (E11.-)*. Type 1 diabetes mellitus is classified to a code from E10.1x to E10.9. Thus, a code for type 2 diabetes mellitus (E11.0x–E11.9) would never be assigned with a code for type 1 diabetes mellitus.

An exception to the excludes1 definition is the circumstance when two or more documented conditions are unrelated to one another. If it is not clear whether the conditions for which an excludes1 note exists in ICD-10-CM are related or not, query the provider.

EXAMPLE 1: ICD-10-CM TABULAR LIST OF DISEASES AND INJURIES—EXCLUDES1 EXCEPTION: The Excludes1 note for code range R40–R46 in the tabular list states that symptoms and signs constituting part of a pattern of mental disorder (F01–F99) cannot be assigned with the R40–R46 codes. However, if dizziness (R42) is not a component of the mental health condition (e.g., dizziness is unrelated to bipolar disorder), then separate codes may be assigned for both dizziness and bipolar disorder.

EXAMPLE 2: ICD-10-CM TABULAR LIST OF DISEASES AND INJURIES—EXCLUDES1 EXCEPTION: Code range I60–I69 (Cerebrovascular Diseases) has an Excludes1 note for traumatic intracranial hemorrhage (S06.-). Codes in I60–I69 should not be used for a diagnosis of traumatic intracranial hemorrhage. However, if the patient has both a current traumatic intracranial hemorrhage and sequelae from a previous stroke, it would be appropriate to assign both a code from S06.- and I69.-.

An **excludes2 note** means "not included here" and indicates that although the excluded condition is not classified as part of the condition it is excluded from, a patient may be diagnosed with all conditions at the same time. Therefore, when an excludes2 note appears under a code, it may be acceptable to assign both the code and the excluded code(s) together if supported by the medical documentation.

 Coding Tip

An excludes2 note instructs you to assign more than one code when medical documentation supports all conditions.

EXAMPLE: ICD-10-CM TABULAR LIST OF DISEASES AND INJURIES—EXCLUDES2 NOTE: Locate ICD-10-CM code **M19.14 Post-traumatic osteoarthritis, right hand** in the tabular list, and find the Excludes2 note for post-traumatic osteoarthritis of first carpometacarpal joint (M18.2-, M18.3-). The Excludes2 note means that because a patient can be diagnosed with both "post-traumatic osteoarthritis of the hand" and "post-traumatic osteoarthritis of the first carpometacarpal joint," it is acceptable to assign codes to both conditions if supported by medical documentation.

Exercise 3.8 – Excludes1 and Excludes2 Notes

Instructions: Assign an ICD-10-CM code to each statement. Make sure that you appropriately interpret the use of excludes1 and excludes2 notes in the ICD-10-CM tabular list.

_____ 1. Cardiovascular disease of native coronary artery

_____ 2. Arteritis

_____ 3. Absence of menstruation

_____ 4. Herpetiformis dermatosis

_____ 5. Dextrocardia

_____ 6. Meningeal tuberculoma. Tuberculoma of brain and spinal cord.

_____ 7. Malignant neoplasm of dorsal surface of base of tongue

_____ 8. Sucrase-isomaltase deficiency. Congenital lactase deficiency.

_____ 9. Psychotic disorder with hallucinations. Paranoid schizophrenia.

_____ 10. Hemorrhage from the throat. Hemoptysis.

Inclusion Terms

 ICD-10 Alert!

Although inclusion terms are _not_ technically associated with the ICD-10-CM index, the index contains many more terms that do not appear in the tabular list.

ICD-10 Alert! ⎯⎯⎯⎯⎯⎯⎯⎯⎯⎯⎯⎯⎯⎯⎯⎯⎯⎯⎯⎯⎯⎯⎯⎯⎯⎯

ICD-10-PCS does not contain inclusion terms.

Lists of inclusion terms are included below certain codes in the ICD-10-CM tabular list. The **inclusion terms** indicate some of the conditions for which that code may be assigned. They may be synonyms with the code title, or, in the case of "other specified" codes, the terms may also provide a list of various conditions included within a code. The list of inclusion terms in the tabular list is not exhaustive. The index may provide additional terms that may also be assigned to a given code.

The ICD-10-CM disease index is an important supplement to the tabular list because it contains many diagnostic terms that do not appear in the tabular list. The inclusion terms listed below codes in the tabular list are not meant to be exhaustive, and additional terms found only in the disease index may also be assigned to a tabular list code. This concept is called **trust the index**, because when you find a term and a code in the disease index, and the term is not repeated in the tabular list (below a category or subcategory), that code can still be assigned. The tabular list would be too cumbersome to use if all disease index terms were included below categories and subcategories.

EXAMPLE 1: ICD-10-CM TABULAR LIST OF DISEASES AND INJURIES—INCLUSION TERMS: The following inclusion terms are located in the Tabular List of Diseases and Injuries for diagnosis code M54.5, Low back pain:

- Loin pain
- Lumbago NOS

EXAMPLE 2: ICD-10-CM TABULAR LIST OF DISEASES AND INJURIES—INCLUSION TERMS (conditions classified to "other specified" subcategory codes): If the provider documents *polyalgia* as the patient's condition, assign code M79.89 even though the code description indicates it is an *other specified* code.

EXAMPLE 3: ICD-10-CM INDEX TO DISEASES AND INJURIES AND TABULAR LIST OF DISEASES AND INJURIES— *TRUST THE INDEX*: Locate the index entry for *infection, fish tapeworm, larval B70.1*. Then, go to the tabular list to verify code B70.1, where you will notice that *infection due to fish tapeworm, larval* is not listed as an inclusion term. The coder has to *trust the index* and assign code B70.1 for the documented condition.

Exercise 3.9 – Inclusion Terms

Instructions: Assign an ICD-10-CM code to each statement. Make sure that you appropriately interpret the use of inclusion terms in the ICD-10-CM tabular list.

_____   **1.** Acute amebic dysentery

_____   **2.** Disseminated blastomycosis

_____   **3.** Megakaryocytic (thrombocytic) leukemia, acute

_____   **4.** GM2 gangliosidosis, juvenile

_____   **5.** Congenital toxoplasmosis

Other, Other Specified, and Unspecified Codes

 ICD-10 Alert!

> The *other, other specified,* and *unspecified* coding convention does not appear in ICD-10-PCS.

When **other** or **other specified** appears in a code description, the code is assigned when patient record documentation provides detail for which a specific code does not exist in ICD-10-CM. The ICD-10-CM tabular list "other and other specified codes" often contains a fourth and/or fifth character of 8 or 9. ICD-10-CM index entries that contain the abbreviation NEC are classified to "other" codes in the tabular lists. These index entries represent specific disease entities for which no specific code exists in the tabular list, so the term is included within an "other" code.

Unspecified codes are assigned because patient record documentation is insufficient to assign a more specific code. ICD-10-CM tabular list codes designated as "unspecified" often contain a fourth character of 8 or 9 or a fifth character of 9. (Before assigning an unspecified code, ask the provider to document additional information so that a more specific code can be reported.) When an ICD-10-CM tabular list category does not contain an unspecified code, the "other specified" code may represent both "other and unspecified." In ICD-10-CM, "other and unspecified" category and subcategory codes require assignment of extra character(s) to classify the condition.

When the ICD-10-CM index directs the coder to an "other, other specified, or unspecified code" in the tabular list, it is important to review the record carefully (or ask the physician for clarification of documentation) to determine if a more specific code can be assigned. This is referred to as "moving up the ladder of specificity" of codes in the tabular list.

EXAMPLE: ICD-10-CM TABULAR LIST OF DISEASES AND INJURIES—OTHER, OTHER SPECIFIED, AND UNSPECIFIED CODES:

- D64.89 is an *other specified* code.
- D64.9 is an *unspecified* code.
- I70.9- is an *other and unspecified* code.

Exercise 3.10 – Other, Other Specified, and Unspecified Codes

Instructions: Assign an ICD-10-CM code to each statement. Make sure that you appropriately interpret the use of other, other specified, and unspecified codes in the ICD-10-CM tabular list.

_____ 1. Intussusception of appendix
_____ 2. Ectopic pregnancy, week 6
_____ 3. Hepatorenal syndrome (postpartum condition)
_____ 4. Arterial atheroembolism
_____ 5. Glaucoma

Etiology and Manifestation Rules

Etiology and manifestation rules include the following notes in the ICD-10-CM Tabular List of Diseases and Injuries:

- Code first underlying disease
- Code, if applicable, any causal condition first

- Use additional code
- In diseases classified elsewhere

To classify certain conditions completely, codes must be assigned to the underlying *etiology* (cause or origin of disease) and multiple body system manifestations (resulting symptoms or conditions) due to the underlying etiology. For such conditions, the underlying condition is sequenced first, if applicable, followed by the manifestation. Wherever an etiology and manifestation combination of codes exists, the tabular list etiology code contains a **use additional code** note and the manifestation code contains a **code first underlying disease** note. These instructional notes assist coders in the proper sequencing of the codes: etiology code followed by manifestation code. In most cases, the manifestation code will have in its title an **in diseases classified elsewhere** note, which indicates that the manifestation codes are a component of the etiology/manifestation coding convention. A manifestation code that does not contain *in diseases classified elsewhere* in its title will contain a "use additional code" note. (Make sure you sequence the manifestation code after the etiology code.)

 NOTE:

> Manifestation codes that include the instruction *code first underlying condition* are never reported first on health insurance claims. They must be reported in conjunction with an underlying condition (etiology) code, and they must be listed after the underlying condition code.

The instruction to **code, if applicable, any causal condition first** requires the causal condition to be sequenced first if present. A *causal condition* is a disease (e.g., diabetes mellitus) that manifests (or results in) another condition (e.g., diabetic cataracts). If no causal condition is documented, the code that contains the instruction (*code, if applicable, any causal condition first*) may be reported without the causal condition code. (This differs from the instruction to *code first underlying condition*, which does not allow for the code that contains the instruction to be reported without first sequencing the underlying condition.)

Etiology/manifestation conditions are listed together in the ICD-10-CM Index to Diseases and Injuries; the etiology code is listed first, followed by the manifestation codes in brackets. (The manifestation code listed in brackets is always sequenced second.)

EXAMPLE 1: ICD-10-CM INDEX TO DISEASES AND INJURIES AND TABULAR LIST OF DISEASES AND INJURIES—ETIOLOGY/ MANIFESTATION CODES: Diagnostic statement *idiopathic pulmonary hemosiderosis* includes two codes in the ICD-10-CM index: E83.1 [J84.03]. Code J84.03 is enclosed in brackets in the index, which indicates it is the manifestation code and is reported second. The ICD-10-CM tabular list entry for J84.03 is in italics, and it contains a *code first underlying disease* note.

 NOTE:

> A **code also** note alerts the coder that more than one code may be required to fully describe the condition. Code sequencing depends on the circumstances of the encounter.

EXAMPLE 2: ICD-10-CM TABULAR LIST OF DISEASES AND INJURIES—USE ADDITIONAL CODE: The patient is diagnosed with *benign hypertrophy of the prostate with urge and stress incontinence*. Locate subcategory code N40.1 in the ICD-10-CM tabular list, and notice that the *use additional code . . .* note instructs you to report an additional code. Therefore, assign codes N40.1 and N39.46. Next, notice that category code N39.4 in the tabular list includes a *code also any associated overactive bladder (N32.81)* note. Because the diagnostic statement (above) does not include *overactive bladder*, do not assign code N32.81.

EXAMPLE 3: ICD-10-CM TABULAR LIST OF DISEASES AND INJURIES—CODE, IF APPLICABLE, ANY CAUSAL CONDITION FIRST: A patient with an alcohol addiction (F10.20) was seen in the office, complaining of urinary incontinence. The physician determined that the condition was nonorganic in origin and most likely the result of the patient being too inebriated to realize he had urinated while unconscious. Code F98.0 is assigned to urinary incontinence that is of nonorganic origin. Code R32 is assigned to urinary incontinence that is organic in nature (e.g., due to urethritis, N34.2).

Exercise 3.11 – Etiology and Manifestation Rules

Instructions: Assign an ICD-10-CM code to each statement. Make sure that you appropriately interpret etiology and manifestation rules in the ICD-10-CM disease index and tabular list.

_____ 1. Tetanic cataract in hypoparathyroidism

_____ 2. Cardiac sarcoidosis

_____ 3. Uremic pericarditis

_____ 4. Congenital syphilitic peritonitis

_____ 5. Typhoid osteomyelitis

And

When the word **and** appears in category titles and code descriptions in the ICD-10-CM Tabular List of Diseases and Injuries, ICD-10-PCS Index, and ICD-10-PCS Tables, it is interpreted as meaning *and/or*.

EXAMPLE 1: ICD-10-CM TABULAR LIST OF DISEASES—AND: The word *and* in category code J04 (Acute laryngitis and tracheitis) means that codes are reported for conditions of the larynx, trachea, or larynx and trachea.

EXAMPLE 2: ICD-10-PCS INDEX—AND: The word *and* in subterm *use* Bursa and Ligament, Shoulder, Left (located below main term Acromioclavicular ligament) means that the body part character (located in an ICD-10-PCS table) is reported for procedures performed on the bursa, ligament, or bursa and ligament.

EXAMPLE 3: ICD-10-PCS TABLES—AND: The word *and* in the table for section 0 (Medical and Surgical), value N (Head and Facial Bones) means that the body part character is assigned for procedures performed on head bones, facial bones, or head and facial bones.

Exercise 3.12 – And

Exercise 3.12A – ICD-10-CM

Instructions: Assign an ICD-10-CM code to each statement. Make sure that you appropriately interpret the use of the subterm *and* in the ICD-10-CM tabular list.

_____ 1. Venereal disease of the rectum due to chlamydia

_____ 2. Malignant neoplasm of costal cartilage

_____ 3. Acromegaly

_____ 4. Parietoalveolar pneumopathy

_____ 5. Carcinoma *in situ* of scalp

(continues)

Exercise 3.12 – *continued*

Exercise 3.12B – ICD-10-PCS

Instructions: Assign an ICD-10-PCS code to each statement. Make sure you appropriately interpret the use of the subterm *and* in the ICD-10-PCS index and tables.

_____ 1. Ultrasonography of head

_____ 2. Insertion of oropharyngeal (mouth and throat) airway

_____ 3. Open division of muscle, left upper arm

_____ 4. Repair of skin, right hand

_____ 5. Open biopsy, tonsils

Due To

 ICD-10 Alert!

The *due to* instruction does not appear in the ICD-10-PCS Index.

The subterm **due to** is located in the ICD-10-CM Index to Diseases and Injuries in alphabetical order to indicate the presence of a cause-and-effect (or causal) relationship between two conditions. When the disease index includes *due to* as a subterm, the code is assigned only if the physician documented the causal relationship between two conditions, such as meningitis due to adenovirus. It is possible that a patient could have meningitis along with an unrelated adenovirus at the same time. (The *due to* phrase is included in tabular list code descriptions, but it is not a coding instruction.)

 NOTE:

The ICD-10-CM disease index also includes subterm *in* (*due to*) to indicate the presence of a cause-and-effect (or causal) relationship between two conditions.

ICD-10-CM occasionally presumes a causal relationship between two conditions. This means that the physician is not required to document *due to* in the diagnostic statement, such as when the patient has hypertension and chronic renal failure. This condition is coded as hypertensive renal failure, which is interpreted as hypertension due to chronic renal failure.

EXAMPLE 1: ICD-10-CM INDEX TO DISEASES AND INJURIES—DUE TO: When the physician documents *pneumonitis due to inhalation of regurgitated food*, a causal relationship exists and code J69.0 is assigned.

EXAMPLE 2: ICD-10-CM INDEX TO DISEASES AND INJURIES—IN (DUE TO): When the physician documents *anemia in moderate chronic kidney disease*, a causal relationship exists, and codes N18.3 and D63.1 are assigned.

Exercise 3.13 – Due To

Instructions: Assign an ICD-10-CM code to each statement. Make sure that you appropriately interpret the use of subterm *due to* in the ICD-10-CM disease index.

_____ 1. Cirrhosis due to Wilson's disease

_____ 2. Bubo due to *Haemophilus ducreyi*

_____ 3. Carnitine deficiency due to hemodialysis

_____ 4. Hypothyroidism due to irradiation therapy

_____ 5. Airway obstruction due to laryngospasm

In

When the word **in** appears in the ICD-10-CM disease index, it is located in alphabetical order below the main term. To assign a code from the list of qualifiers below the word *in*, the physician must document both conditions in the patient's record. The word "in" is interpreted to mean "associated with" or "due to" when it appears in a code title, the index, or an instructional note in the tabular list. Thus, ICD-10-CM classifies certain conditions as if there were a cause-and-effect relationship present because they occur together much of the time (e.g., pneumonia in Q fever).

EXAMPLE: ICD-10-CM INDEX TO DISEASES AND INJURIES—IN: Locate main term *pneumonia* in the index, and notice that the word *in* appears in alphabetical order above a list of second qualifiers. To assign a code from the list, the physician must document a relationship between both conditions, such as *pneumonia in measles* (or *postpneumonia measles*) to which combination code B05.2 is assigned. (Other conditions that occur together may require the assignment of multiple codes, one for the etiology and another for the manifestation.)

 ICD-10 Alert!

The *in* instruction does not appear in ICD-10-PCS.

Exercise 3.14 – In

Instructions: Assign an ICD-10-CM code to each statement. Make sure that you appropriately interpret the use of subterm *in* when reviewing the ICD-10-CM disease index.

_____ 1. Bicornis uterus in pregnancy, week 12

_____ 2. Adenocarcinoma in adenomatous polyposis coli

_____ 3. Uterine fibroid tumor in pregnancy (antepartum, second trimester, week 14)

_____ 4. Keratoconjunctivitis in exanthema

_____ 5. Nephrosis in epidemic hemorrhagic fever

With

When the word **with** appears in the ICD-10-CM Index to Diseases and Injuries, it is located immediately below either the main term or a subterm, not in alphabetical order. In the ICD-10-PCS Index, the word *with* appears in the main term or indented in alphabetical order below the main term or a subterm. To assign a code from the list of qualifiers below the word *with*, the physician must document the presence of both conditions (or procedures) in the patient's record.

The word "with" is interpreted to mean "associated with" or "due to" when it appears in a code title, the index, or an instructional note in the tabular list. Thus, ICD-10-CM presumes a causal relationship between the two conditions linked by the term "with" in the index or tabular list. Such conditions should be coded as related even in the absence of provider documentation explicitly linking them, *unless the documentation clearly states the conditions are unrelated or when another official coding guideline exists that specifically requires a documented linkage between two conditions* (e.g., sepsis guideline for "acute organ dysfunction that is not clearly associated with the sepsis"). For conditions not specifically linked by these relational terms in the classification or when an official coding guideline requires that a linkage between two conditions be explicitly documented, provider documentation must link the conditions in order to code them as related.

EXAMPLE 1: ICD-10-CM INDEX TO DISEASES AND INJURIES—WITH: Locate main term *measles* in the index, and notice that the word *with* appears above a list of second qualifiers. To assign a code from the list, the physician must document both conditions, such as *measles with keratitis* (B05.81). The physician could also document:

- Measles keratitis
- Measles associated with keratitis
- Measles and keratitis

EXAMPLE 2: ICD-10-PCS INDEX—WITH: Locate main term *phacoemulsification, lens* in the index, and notice the terms *with* (and *without*) appear as subterms. The subterm entries refer coders to ICD-10-PCS tables 08R or 08D, depending on the procedure performed.

 ICD-10 Alert!

Subterm *with* occasionally appears in the ICD-10-PCS Index.

Exercise 3.15 – With

Exercise 3.15A – ICD-10-CM

Instructions: Assign an ICD-10-CM code to each statement. Make sure you appropriately interpret the use of subterm *with* in the ICD-10-CM index.

_____ 1. Appendicitis with perforation
_____ 2. Thyrotoxicosis with uninodular adenomatous goiter
_____ 3. Traumatic hemothorax with pneumothorax (initial encounter)
_____ 4. Adjustment disorder with anxiety
_____ 5. Skull agenesis with anencephalus (or anencephaly)

Exercise 3.15 – *continued*

Exercise 3.15B – ICD-10-PCS

Instructions: Assign an ICD-10-PCS code to each statement. Make sure you appropriately interpret the use of subterm *with* in the ICD-10-PCS index. For ICD-10-PCS answers, enter the code found in the index entry; it may be less than seven characters in length.

_____ 1. Computer-assisted procedure of the lower extremity with computerized tomography

_____ 2. Herniorrhaphy with synthetic substitute

_____ 3. Interrogation, cardiac rhythm related device, with cardiac function testing

_____ 4. Phacoemulsification of right lens, with intraocular lens implant

_____ 5. Vasotomy with ligation

Cross-References

The ICD-10-CM and ICD-10-PCS indexes include **cross-references**, which instruct the coder to refer to another entry in the index (e.g., *see, see also, see* condition) or to the tabular list (e.g., *see* category) to assign the correct code.

- The *see* instruction after a main term directs the coder to refer to another term in the ICD-10-CM and ICD-10-PCS indexes to locate the code. The coder must go to the referenced main term to locate the correct code.

- The *see also* instruction is located after a main term or subterm in the ICD-10-CM indexes and directs the coder to another main term (or subterm) that may provide additional useful index entries. The *see also* instruction does not have to be followed if the original main term (or subterm) provides the correct code.

- The *see category* instruction directs the coder to the ICD-10-CM tabular list, where a code can be selected from the options provided there.

- The *see condition* instruction directs the coder to the main term for a condition, found in the ICD-10-CM disease index.

- The *use* instruction directs the coder to a body part or a device in the ICD-10-PCS index. The coder must go to the appropriate ICD-10-PCS table to assign a character for the body part or device referenced in the index.

EXAMPLE 1: ICD-10-CM INDEX TO DISEASES AND INJURIES—*SEE*: Locate main term *Laceration* and subterm *blood vessel* in the ICD-10-CM index. Notice that a cross-reference directs you to "*See* Injury, blood vessel," which is at a different location in the index where the code can be found.

EXAMPLE 2: ICD-10-CM INDEX TO DISEASES AND INJURIES—*SEE ALSO*: The *see also* instruction is optional if the correct code can be located below the main term (e.g., laceration of lower back, S31.010). If the correct code cannot be located, the *see also* cross-reference directs the coder to a different location in the index where the code can be found.

EXAMPLE 3: ICD-10-CM INDEX TO DISEASES AND INJURIES—*SEE* CATEGORY: Locate main term *pyelitis*, subterm *with*, and second qualifier *calculus* in the ICD-10-CM index. Notice that a cross-reference directs you to *see* category N20. To assign the correct code, review category N20 in the tabular list to select the appropriate fourth character.

EXAMPLE 4: ICD-10-CM INDEX TO DISEASES AND INJURIES—*SEE* CONDITION: Locate main term *Accidental* in the ICD-10-CM index, and notice that a cross-reference directs you to *see* condition, which means the patient record needs to be reviewed to determine the condition (e.g., fracture).

EXAMPLE 5: ICD-10-PCS INDEX—*SEE*: Locate main term *Abdominohysterectomy* in the ICD-10-PCS index, and notice that a cross-reference directs you to *see* Resection, Uterus 0UT9, which is at a different location in the index. (The four characters 0UT9 direct the coder to the 0UT Excision table in ICD-10-PCS.)

EXAMPLE 6: ICD-10-PCS INDEX—*USE*: Locate main term *Abdominal esophagus* in the ICD-10-PCS index. Notice that a cross-reference directs you to *use* Esophagus, Lower, which is a body part that is assigned a character from an ICD-10-PCS table (e.g., Bypass table). Go to main term *Bypass*, and locate subterms *esophagus* and *lower* to identify an ICD-10-PCS table (from which the code is built, and for which a character is selected for body part *lower esophagus*).

Exercise 3.16 – Cross-References

Exercise 3.16A – ICD-10-CM

Instructions: Enter the ICD-10-CM index cross-reference instruction for each ICD-10-CM main term. For example, an ICD-10-CM cross-reference instruction is *see* Laceration.

_____   1. Abnormal, abnormality, abnormalities

_____   2. Toxicosis

_____   3. Strangulation, strangulated

_____   4. Undescended testicle

_____   5. Proteinuria complicating pregnancy

Exercise 3.16B – ICD-10-PCS

Instructions: Enter the ICD-10-PCS index cross-reference instruction for each ICD-10-PCS main term. For example, an ICD-10-PCS cross-reference instruction is *use* Esophagus, Lower.

_____   1. Ablation

_____   2. Achillorrhaphy

_____   3. Canthorrhaphy

_____   4. Accessory obturator nerve

_____   5. Cardiac event recorder

Code Assignment and Clinical Criteria

The assignment of a diagnosis code is based on the physician's diagnostic statement that the condition exists. The physician's statement that the patient has a particular condition is sufficient. Code assignment is *not* based on clinical criteria used by the physician to establish the diagnosis.

EXAMPLE: The patient is admitted to the hospital for "severe confusion" (R41.0). The physician documented "Alzheimer's disease with dementia and behavioral disturbances" (G30.9, F02.81) as the discharge diagnoses. Clinical criteria (e.g., brain imaging study) are not documented in the hospital record. Codes G30.9 and F02.81 are reported instead of code R41.0 because code assignment is based on the physician's diagnostic statement that the condition exists, not clinical criteria. In this case, the physician used *pattern recognition* to establish the discharge diagnoses. This involves the physician using experience to recognize a "pattern" of clinical characteristics; it is based on certain signs and/or symptoms typically associated with a disease process.

EXERCISE 3.17 – Code Assignment and Clinical Criteria

Instructions: Assign an ICD-10-CM code to each statement. Make sure that you appropriately interpret the intent of the *code assignment and clinical criteria* coding convention.

_____ 1. Patient admitted for difficulty breathing and fever. Physician's discharge diagnosis is pneumonia.

_____ 2. Patient admitted with malaise. Physician's discharge diagnosis is depression.

_____ 3. Patient admitted with severe headache. Physician's discharge diagnosis is intractable migraine.

_____ 4. Patient admitted with abdominal pain and fever. Physician's discharge diagnosis is acute appendicitis.

_____ 5. Patient admitted with pain and swelling, left ankle. Physician's discharge diagnosis is sprain, left ankle.

Summary

Coding conventions are general rules used in the ICD-10-CM and ICD-10-PCS classifications, independent of official coding guidelines. An indented format is used for ease in reference in the ICD-10-CM and ICD-10-PCS indexes.

ICD-10-CM contains eponyms and abbreviations. Punctuation in ICD-10-CM includes parentheses, brackets, square brackets, and colons. Certain main terms in the ICD-10-CM disease index, including the Table of Neoplasms, are followed by boxed notes, which contain special instructions. The ICD-10-CM disease index contains a Table of Neoplasms and a Table of Drugs and Chemicals. The ICD-10-PCS index does not contain tables, and instead of a tabular list of codes, ICD-10-PCS contains tables (discussed in Chapter 6 of this textbook). The ICD-10-CM tabular list contains includes notes, excludes1 and excludes2 notes, and inclusion terms.

"Other" and "other specified" codes are assigned when patient record documentation provides detail for which a specific code does not exist in ICD-10-CM. "Unspecified" codes are assigned because patient record documentation is insufficient for the assignment of a more specific code. Etiology and manifestation codes contain the following notes in the ICD-10-CM tabular list: code first underlying disease; code, if applicable, any causal condition first; use additional code; and in diseases classified elsewhere. When the word *and* appears in category titles and code descriptions in the ICD-10-CM indexes and tabular list, it is interpreted as meaning "and/or." The instruction *due to* is located in ICD-10-CM as a subterm (in alphabetical order) to indicate the presence of a cause-and-effect relationship between two conditions. The word *in* as it appears in the ICD-10-CM disease index is located in alphabetical order below the main term. The word *with* appears in the ICD-10-CM and ICD-10-PCS indexes immediately below the main term, and it is not in alphabetical order. A causal relationship is presumed between two conditions linked by terms *in, with*, and *due to* in the index and tabular list; such conditions are coded as related even when physician documentation explicitly linking them is absent (unless the documentation clearly states the conditions are unrelated) or when another official coding guideline exists that specifically requires a documented linkage between two conditions. For conditions not specifically linked by the terms *with* and *due to* in ICD-10-CM or when an official coding guideline requires that a linkage between two conditions be explicitly documented, physician documentation must link the conditions to code them as related. Cross-reference terms in the ICD-10-CM and ICD-10-PCS indexes instruct the coder to refer to another entry in the index or to go directly to the tabular list or table, respectively, to assign or build the correct code.

The code assignment and clinical criteria coding convention bases the assignment of a diagnosis code on the physician's diagnostic statement that the condition exists, not clinical criteria used to establish the diagnosis.

Internet Links

ICD-10-CM/PCS updates: Go to **www.cms.gov**, click on the Medicare link, click on the ICD-10 link under Coding, and scroll down to click on this year's ICD-10-CM or ICD-10-PCS link.

JustCoding News free e-newsletter: Go to **www.justcoding.com**, and click on the eNewsletter Signup link at the top of the page.

Review

Matching – ICD-10-CM

Instructions: Match the format in Column 2 with each line of the ICD-10-CM Index to Diseases and Injuries entries in Column 1.

ICD-10-CM Index to Diseases and Injuries

		Format
_____ 1.	`Abnormal, abnormality, abnormalities` (*see*	a. 2nd qualifier
_____ 2.	*also* `Anomaly)`	b. 3rd qualifier
_____ 3.	`chromosome, chromosomal Q99.9`	c. Continuation line
_____ 4.	`sex Q99.8`	d. Main term
_____ 5.	`female phenotype Q97.9`	e. Subterm

Multiple Choice – ICD-10-CM

Instructions: Circle the most appropriate response.

1. If an index entry is too long to fit on one line, additional text is:
   a. edited so that the content fits onto just one line.
   b. located on the next line, flush with the preceding line.
   c. moved to the second line and indented two spaces.
   d. printed on the next line and indented five spaces.

2. A coder locates a code in the ICD-10-CM disease index, which contains the abbreviation NEC. Upon verification of the code in the tabular list, the coder assigns that code. Which coding convention explains this code assignment?
   a. Information needed to assign a more specific code has not been obtained from the provider.
   b. The coder is directed to an "other specified" code by the index when a specific code is not available in the tabular list.
   c. Use of a more general code is indicated when the coder is unsure about information contained in documentation.
   d. Whenever a specific code is not available in the index for a condition, the coder is directed to the "other specified" code in the tabular list.

3. When the ICD-10-CM tabular list contains the abbreviation NOS, which coding convention explains the code assignment?
   a. If the coder is not sure about the information contained in the documentation, use of a more general code is indicated.
   b. Information to assign a more specific code was not documented by the provider, resulting in assignment of an "unspecified" code.
   c. The coder is directed to an "other specified" code by the index when a specific code is not available in the tabular list.
   d. Whenever a specific code is not available in the index for a condition, the coder is directed to the "other specified" code in the tabular list.

4. The use of a colon in the ICD-10-CM tabular list:
    a. identifies the use of manifestation codes, which are to be sequenced second.
    b. indicates that one or more additional terms are to be included in the diagnostic statement to classify a condition or procedure.
    c. means that the words following the colon may be present in or absent from the provider's diagnostic statement.
    d. suggests the use of synonyms, alternative wording, or explanatory phrases.

5. *Includes* notes appear:
    a. below an ICD-10-CM category in the tabular list.
    b. after main terms in the ICD-10-CM index.
    c. above an ICD-10-CM code in the tabular list.
    d. underneath essential modifiers in the ICD-10-CM index.

6. *Excludes1* and *Excludes2* notes appear in the:
    a. ICD-10-CM and ICD-10-PCS indexes.
    b. ICD-10-CM index and tabular list.
    c. ICD-10-CM tabular list only.
    d. ICD-10-CM index only.

7. *Trust the index* is an ICD-10-CM concept that is used when:
    a. a subterm located in the index is not listed in the tabular list.
    b. additional information was not obtained from the provider.
    c. insufficient documentation prevents the assignment of a more specific code.
    d. the coder is directed to the "other specified" code in the tabular list.

8. Unspecified codes:
    a. are classified as "other" codes in the ICD-10-CM tabular list.
    b. contain the NEC abbreviation in the ICD-10-CM index.
    c. result when a code is not found in the ICD-10-CM index for a specified condition.
    d. often contain a fourth or fifth character of 8 or 9.

9. Etiology codes:
    a. are designated in the ICD-10-CM index by brackets.
    b. classify a condition that occurs as the result of another condition.
    c. contain a *use additional code* instruction in the ICD-10-CM tabular list.
    d. must be sequenced second as the underlying condition code.

10. The *see also* instruction in the ICD-10-CM index follows a subterm and refers the coder to another main term that:
    a. allows for assignment of a secondary code.
    b. contains the code that is to be assigned.
    c. may provide additional useful index entries.
    d. must be followed to assign the correct code.

11. Upon review of the ICD-10-CM Index to Diseases and Injuries entry below, the coder locates main term *Retained* and notes the "*see* Retention" instruction, which means the coder should:

ICD-10-CM Index to Diseases and Injuries
Retained —*see also* Retention
Retention, retained
foreign body —*see also* Foreign body, retained
current trauma —code as Foreign body, by site or type

    a. generate a physician query to ask the physician to document a more specific diagnosis.
    b. go to main term *Retention* in the ICD-10-CM index to begin locating the code.
    c. locate the main term in the ICD-9-CM index, and use the GEM to assign the code.
    d. review the ICD-10-CM Tabular List of Diseases and Injuries to locate the code.

12. A patient was using a nail gun and accidentally nailed the fleshy skin between his left thumb and forefinger to the roof on his home. He was able to pull the flesh free, but the nail remained embedded in the skin of his left hand. Upon review of the ICD-10-CM entry below and main term *Foreign body*, the coder follows the instructional note to "*see* Puncture, by site"; the coder follows the instruction by locating "Puncture, hand S61.439" and reviews index entries to identify the code. Next, the coder should:

ICD-10-CM Index to Diseases and Injuries
Foreign body
in
puncture wound —*see* Puncture, by site, with foreign body
soft tissue (residual) M79.5
Puncture
hand S61.439
with
foreign body S61.449
finger —*see* Puncture, finger
left S61.432
with
foreign body S61.442

    a. assign code M79.5 after verifying it.
    b. locate code S61.449 in the tabular list.
    c. look up code S61.439 in the tabular list.
    d. verify code S61.442 in the tabular list.

13. Upon review of the ICD-10-CM tabular list entry below, which code would be assigned for a patient who was struck in the right eye with a plastic straw three months ago and is being seen today for pain and swelling, right eye, due to a tiny piece of plastic embedded in the soft tissue?

ICD-10-CM Tabular List of Diseases and Injuries

H05.5 **Retained (old) foreign body following penetrating wound of orbit**
Retrobulbar foreign body
Use additional code to identify the type of retained foreign body (Z18.-)
  EXCLUDES1 *current penetrating wound of orbit (S05.4–)*
  EXCLUDES2 *retained foreign body of eyelid (H02.81–)*
    retained intraocular foreign body
      (H44.6–, H44.7–)
  H05.50 **Retained (old) foreign body following penetrating wound of unspecified orbit**
  H05.51 **Retained (old) foreign body following penetrating wound of right orbit**
  H05.52 **Retained (old) foreign body following penetrating wound of left orbit**
  H05.53 **Retained (old) foreign body following penetrating wound of bilateral orbits**

    a. H02.81–
    b. H05.50
    c. H05.51
    d. S05.4–

14. Upon review of the ICD-10-CM index entry below, which code would be selected for a patient diagnosed with *hypotension due to hemodialysis*?

ICD-10-CM Index to Diseases and Injuries

Hypotension (arterial) (constitutional) I95.9
  chronic I95.89
  due to (of) hemodialysis I95.3
  drug-induced I95.2
  iatrogenic I95.89
  idiopathic (permanent) I95.0

    a. I95.2
    b. I95.3
    c. I95.89
    d. I95.9

15. Upon review of the ICD-10-CM index entry below, which action should the coder take to locate the code for *strangulated hernia*?

ICD-10-CM Index to Diseases and Injuries
Strangulation, strangulated —*see also* Asphyxia, traumatic
appendix K38.8
bladder-neck N32.0
bowel or colon K56.2
food or foreign body —*see* Foreign body, by site
hemorrhoids —*see* Hemorrhoids, with complication
hernia —*see also* Hernia, by site, with obstruction
with gangrene —*see* Hernia, by site, with gangrene
intestine (large) (small) K56.2
with hernia —*see* also Hernia, by site, with obstruction
with gangrene —*see* Hernia, by site, with gangrene

    a. Follow the *see also* instruction, and go to Asphyxia, traumatic.
    b. Follow the *see also* instruction, and locate Hernia, by site, with obstruction.
    c. Locate code K56.2 in the ICD-10-CM Tabular List of Diseases and Injuries.
    d. Report code K56.2 in addition to the strangulated hernia code.

Multiple Choice – ICD-10-PCS

Instructions: Circle the most appropriate response.

1. ICD-10-PCS coding conventions are general rules used in the classification that are:
    a. dependent on coding guidelines.
    b. included in ICD-10-PCS as default codes and syndromes.
    c. incorporated into ICD-10-PCS as instructional notes.
    d. must be referenced in a written physician query.

2. In the ICD-10-PCS index, subterms are indented below _____.
    a. code descriptions.   **c.** instructional notes.
    b. codes.   **d.** main terms.

3. ICD-10-PCS makes use of boldface for
    a. code descriptions in the index.
    b. codes in the tabular list of procedures.
    c. instructional notes in tables.
    d. main term entries in the index.

4. The ICD-10-PCS index uses a(n) _____ for ease in reference when locating subterms.
    a. boxed note   **c.** inclusion term
    b. excludes instruction   **d.** indented format

5. Parentheses are used in ICD-10-PCS index to enclose _____, which are supplementary words that may be present in or absent from the physician's statement of a disease or procedure without affecting the code to which it is assigned.
    a. eponyms   **c.** nonessential modifiers
    b. mutually exclusive terms   **d.** NOS abbreviation

6. ICD-10-PCS codes are reported by using the
    a. appropriate table to build a code.   **c.** neoplasm table.
    b. drug and chemicals table.   **d.** tabular list of procedures.

7. When the word *and* appears in category titles and code descriptions in the ICD-10-PCS Index and Tables, it is interpreted as meaning:
   a. and/or.
   b. due to.
   c. in.
   d. with.

8. In the ICD-10-PCS Index, the word *with* is located
   a. as an instructional notation to provide coding direction.
   b. in alphabetical order below the main term or a subterm.
   c. just below the main term or subterm, not in alphabetic order.
   d. within provider documentation as a requirement for coding.

9. The *see* instruction after a main term directs the coder to refer to another term in the ICD-10-PCS index to locate the code, and the coder:
   a. has the option to follow the instructor or not to build the code.
   b. is directed to the tabular list of procedures to locate the code.
   c. must go to that referenced main term to locate the correct code.
   d. selects the original code in the index or goes to the table.

10. Which instruction directs the coder to a body part or a device in the ICD-10-PCS index?
    a. *see*
    b. *see also*
    c. *see category*
    d. *use*

11. A patient underwent *angiectomy of the lower veins*. Which instruction should the coder follow in the ICD-10-PCS Index?

ICD-10-PCS Index
Angiectomy
see Excision, Upper Arteries 03B
see Excision, Lower Arteries 04B
see Excision, Upper Veins 05B
see Excision, Lower Veins 06B
see Excision, Heart and Great Vessels 02B

   a. *see* Excision, Upper Arteries 03B
   b. *see* Excision, Lower Arteries 04B
   c. *see* Excision, Upper Veins 05B
   d. *see* Excision, Lower Veins 06B

12. A patient underwent *continuous cardiac assistance facilitated by use of an impellor pump*. Which code should be verified in the ICD-10-PCS Tables?

ICD-10-PCS Index
Assistance
Cardiac
Continuous
Balloon Pump 5A02210
Impeller Pump 5A0221D
Other Pump 5A02216
Pulsatile Compression 5A02215

   a. 5A02210
   b. 5A0221D
   c. 5A02216
   d. 5A02215

13. A patient underwent *autologous vein graft in the heart using autologous venous tissue.* Which instruction should the coder follow in the ICD-10-PCS Index?

ICD-10-PCS Index
Autologous vein graft
use Autologous Venous Tissue in Heart and Great Vessels
use Autologous Venous Tissue in Upper Arteries
use Autologous Venous Tissue in Lower Arteries
use Autologous Venous Tissue in Upper Veins
use Autologous Venous Tissue in Lower Veins

    a. *use* Autologous Venous Tissue in Heart and Great Vessels
    b. *use* Autologous Venous Tissue in Upper Arteries
    c. *use* Autologous Venous Tissue in Lower Arteries
    d. *use* Autologous Venous Tissue in Upper Veins

14. The patient underwent an angiotripsy procedure of the right brachial artery. Review the following ICD-10-PCS Index entry, and select the appropriate cross-reference.

ICD-10-PCS Index
Angiotripsy
—*See* Occlusion, Upper Arteries 03L
—*See* Occlusion, Lower Arteries 04L

    a. *See* Occlusion, Upper Arteries 03L
    b. *See* Occlusion, Lower Arteries, 04L

15. The patient underwent replacement of a spinal canal drainage device. Review the following ICD-10-PCS Table entry, and using the build-a-code approach, which ICD-10-PCS code would be assigned?

ICD-10-PCS Table

Central Nervous System 001–00X

0	**Medical and Surgical**
0	**Central Nervous System**
2	**Change:** Taking out or off a device from a body part and putting back an identical or similar device in or on the same body part without cutting or puncturing the skin or a mucous membrane

Body Part	Approach	Device	Qualifier
0 Brain	X External	0 Drainage Device	Z No Qualifier
E Cranial Nerve		Y Other Device	
U Spinal Canal			

    a. 0020X0Z
    b. 002EX0Z
    c. 002UX0Z
    d. 002UXYZ

Chapter-Specific Coding Guidelines: ICD-10-CM Chapters 1–10

CHAPTER

4

Chapter Outline

ICD-10-CM Chapter-Specific Diagnosis
Coding Guidelines

ICD-10-CM Chapter 1: Certain Infectious and
Parasitic Diseases (A00–B99)

ICD-10-CM Chapter 2: Neoplasms (C00–D49)

ICD-10-CM Chapter 3: Diseases of the Blood and
Blood-Forming Organs and Certain Disorders
Involving the Immune Mechanism (D50–D89)

ICD-10-CM Chapter 4: Endocrine, Nutritional,
and Metabolic Diseases (E00–E89)

ICD-10-CM Chapter 5: Mental, Behavioral, and
Neurodevelopmental Disorders (F01–F99)

ICD-10-CM Chapter 6: Diseases of the Nervous
System (G00–G99)

ICD-10-CM Chapter 7: Diseases of the Eye and
Adnexa (H00–H59)

ICD-10-CM Chapter 8: Diseases of the Ear and
Mastoid Process (H60–H95)

ICD-10-CM Chapter 9: Diseases of the
Circulatory System (I00–I99)

ICD-10-CM Chapter 10: Diseases of the
Respiratory System (J00–J99)

Chapter Objectives

At the conclusion of this chapter, the student should be able to:

1. Define key terms related to chapter-specific coding guidelines for ICD-10-CM chapters 1 through 10.
2. Assign ICD-10-CM codes to certain infectious and parasitic diseases according to chapter-specific coding guidelines.
3. Assign ICD-10-CM codes to neoplasms according to chapter-specific coding guidelines.
4. Assign ICD-10-CM codes to diseases of the blood and blood-forming organs and certain disorders involving the immune mechanism according to chapter-specific coding guidelines.
5. Assign ICD-10-CM codes to endocrine, nutritional, and metabolic diseases according to chapter-specific coding guidelines.
6. Assign ICD-10-CM codes to mental, behavioral, and neurodevelopmental disorders according to chapter-specific coding guidelines.
7. Assign ICD-10-CM codes to diseases of the nervous system according to chapter-specific coding guidelines.

8. Assign ICD-10-CM codes to diseases of the eye and adnexa according to chapter-specific coding guidelines.

9. Assign ICD-10-CM codes to diseases of the ear and mastoid process according to chapter-specific coding guidelines.

10. Assign ICD-10-CM codes to diseases of the circulatory system according to chapter-specific coding guidelines.

11. Assign ICD-10-CM codes to diseases of the respiratory system according to chapter-specific coding guidelines.

Key Terms

benign	metastatic cancer	secondary malignancy	uncertain behavior
carcinoma (Ca) *in situ*	neoplasm	type 1 diabetes mellitus	unspecified nature
contiguous sites	overlapping sites	type 2 diabetes mellitus	
malignant	primary malignancy		

Introduction

This chapter includes content about the following chapter-specific coding guidelines for ICD-10-CM Chapters 1 through 10. Chapter-specific coding guidelines are used as a companion to the ICD-10-CM coding manual, which contains coding conventions to ensure accurate coding. (ICD-10-CM/PCS structure and conventions were discussed in Chapter 3.)

- Certain Infectious and Parasitic Diseases (A00–B99)
- Neoplasms (C00–D49)
- Diseases of the Blood and Blood-forming Organs and Certain Disorders Involving the Immune Mechanism (D50–D89)
- Endocrine, Nutritional, and Metabolic Diseases (E00–E89)
- Mental, Behavioral, and Neurodevelopmental Disorders (F01–F99)
- Diseases of the Nervous System (G00–G99)
- Diseases of the Eye and Adnexa (H00–H59)
- Diseases of the Ear and Mastoid Process (H60–H95)
- Diseases of the Circulatory System (I00–I99)
- Diseases of the Respiratory System (J00–J99)

The *Official ICD-10-CM Guidelines for Coding and Reporting* (and the *Official ICD-10-PCS Guidelines for Coding and Reporting*) are rules that were developed to accompany and complement the official conventions and instructions located in the classification system. They are based on coding and sequencing instructions in the classification system but provide additional instruction. Adherence to these guidelines when assigning diagnosis and procedure codes is required under HIPAA. ICD-10-CM diagnosis codes were adopted for all health care settings. (ICD-10-PCS procedure codes were adopted for inpatient procedures reported by hospitals.) A joint effort between the health care provider and the coder is essential to achieve complete and accurate documentation.

 NOTE:

- ICD-10-PCS procedure coding guidelines are located in Chapter 6 because they impact inpatient hospital coding only.
- When reviewing examples and completing exercises and review questions in this chapter, use your ICD-10-CM coding manual to locate index entries and to verify codes in the tabular list.

ICD-10-CM codes assigned to patient encounters must be supported by documentation in the patient's record. Third-party payers require submitted claims to demonstrate medical necessity for treatment, which means that a diagnosis code must be reported for each procedure or service code included on the claim. (ICD-10-PCS procedure codes are reported for inpatient hospital procedures, and its codes and coding guidelines are discussed in Chapter 6. HCPCS level II and CPT codes are reported on outpatient claims and are discussed in Chapters 8–19.)

 NOTE:

The following additional content is located on the Student Companion Site at http://login.cengage.com.
- *Alternate Health Care Facilities and Coding Guidelines*
- *HIV-Related Conditions and Opportunistic Infections*
- *Morphology of Neoplasms*

ICD-10-CM Chapter-Specific Diagnosis Coding Guidelines

In addition to coding conventions and general coding guidelines, the *Official ICD-10-CM Guidelines for Coding and Reporting* contain chapter-specific coding guidelines that clarify the assignment of disease codes. Unless otherwise indicated in an individual chapter-specific guideline, the chapter-specific guidelines apply to all health care settings. Some of the guidelines include the following terms, which apply to the reporting of inpatient and outpatient diagnoses (covered in this chapter and Chapters 6 and 7). The terms are briefly defined below to clarify their use in the chapter-specific guidelines.

- *Principal diagnosis*: Reported for inpatient care, it is "that condition established after study to be chiefly responsible for occasioning the admission of the patient to the hospital for care."
- *Secondary diagnoses*: Additional conditions that affect patient care in terms of requiring clinical evaluation, therapeutic treatment, diagnostic procedures, extended length of hospital stay, or increased nursing care and/or monitoring.
- *First-listed diagnosis*: Reported for outpatient care instead of the principal diagnosis, it is the diagnosis, condition, problem, or other reason for an encounter or visit documented in the medical record to be chiefly responsible for the services provided. (The first-listed diagnosis was previously called the *primary diagnosis*.)

ICD-10-CM Chapter-Specific Coding Guidelines

To locate the ICD-10-CM chapter-specific coding guidelines online, go to www.cdc.gov, click on the letter *I* link, and click on the ICD-10-CM link. Scroll down and click on the ICD-10-CM Guidelines link, which will open as an Adobe PDF file.

The *ICD-10-CM Official Guidelines for Coding and Reporting* publication includes a table of contents that organizes the chapter-specific guidelines according to the chapters in the ICD-10-CM classification system (Table 4-1). Although the chapter-specific guidelines have not been created for every ICD-10-CM chapter, the title of each ICD-10-CM chapter is included in the table of contents with the statement "Reserved for future guideline expansion." Refer to the chapter-specific guidelines when assigning ICD-10-CM diagnosis codes.

(continues)

ICD-10-CM Chapter-Specific Coding Guidelines (*continued*)

TABLE 4-1 Portion of Chapter-Specific Coding Guidelines Table of Contents from *ICD-10-CM Official Guidelines for Coding and Reporting*

C. Chapter-Specific Coding Guidelines	17
1. Chapter 1: Certain Infectious and Parasitic Diseases (A00–B99)	17
a. Human Immunodeficiency Virus (HIV) Infections	17
b. Infectious agents as the cause of diseases classified to other chapters	19
c. Infections resistant to antibiotics	19
d. Sepsis, Severe Sepsis, and Septic Shock	20
e. Methicillin resistant *Staphylococcus aureus* (MRSA) conditions	21
2. Chapter 2: Neoplasms (C00–D49)	25
a. Treatment directed at the malignancy	26
b. Treatment of secondary site	26
c. Coding and sequencing of complications	26
d. Primary malignancy previously excised	27

Courtesy of the Centers for Medicare & Medicaid Services, www.cms.gov

ICD-10-CM Chapter 1: Certain Infectious and Parasitic Diseases (A00–B99)

NOTE:

Infections are also classified in other ICD-10-CM chapters, such as Chapter 10, Diseases of the Respiratory System.

This ICD-10-CM chapter classifies the following infectious and parasitic diseases (Table 4-2):

- Intestinal infectious diseases
- Tuberculosis
- Certain zoonotic bacterial diseases
- Other bacterial diseases
- Infections with a predominantly sexual mode of transmission
- Other spirochetal diseases
- Other diseases caused by chlamydiae
- Rickettsioses
- Viral and prion infections of the central nervous system
- Arthropod-borne viral fevers and viral hemorrhagic fevers

- Viral infections characterized by skin and mucous membrane lesions
- Other human herpesviruses
- Viral hepatitis
- Human immunodeficiency virus (HIV) disease
- Other viral diseases
- Mycoses
- Protozoal diseases
- Helminthiases
- Pediculosis, acariasis, and other infestations
- Sequelae of infectious and parasitic diseases
- Bacterial and viral infectious agents
- Other infectious diseases

TABLE 4-2 Organisms

Organism	Definition
Bacteria	• Single-celled organisms that in certain conditions cause illnesses such as strep throat, most ear infections, and bacterial pneumonia • Some bacteria are considered helpful (e.g., intestinal *Escherichia coli*)
Chlamydia	• Infection caused by a parasitic bacteria called *Chlamydia trachomatis* • Affects male and female genitals
Fungi	• Opportunistic pathogens such as Aspergillus, Candida, and Cryptococcus that cause infections in immunocompromised people such as cancer patients, transplant recipients, and people with AIDS • Pathogens such as endemic mycoses, histoplasmosis, coccidioidomycosis, and superficial mycoses that cause infections in healthy people
Helminths	• Parasitic worms that usually lodge in the intestines • Include roundworm, pinworm, *Trichnella spiralis* (causes thrichinosis), tapeworm, and fluke
Mycoplasmas	• Surface parasites of the human respiratory and urogenital tracts • Mainly affect children aged 5 to 9 years • Spread by close personal contact • Have a long incubation period

Protozoans	• Single-celled organisms (e.g., ameba) that cause parasitic diseases in people with AIDS
	   o Toxoplasmosis
	   o Cryptosporidiosis
	• *Pneumocystis jiroveci* pneumonia (PJP) is caused by fungi
	   o Does not respond to antifungal treatment
	   o Formerly known as *Pneumocystis carinii pneumonia* (PCP)

Rickettsias	• Intracellular parasites that grow and reproduce only in living cells of their host • Named for U.S. pathologist Howard T. Ricketts, who died of typhus in 1910 while investigating the spread of the disease • Typhus fever is caused by *Rickettsia prowazekii* when transmitted to humans by lice • Rocky Mountain spotted fever is a rickettsial disease transmitted to humans by ticks
Viruses	• Submicroscopic parasites that cause disease • Contain DNA or RNA, are surrounded by protein, and use host cells to replicate • Include varicella (chickenpox virus), cold viruses, hepatitis viruses, herpesviruses, and human immunodeficiency virus (HIV)

ICD-10-CM Chapter-Specific Coding Guidelines

Chapter 1: Certain Infectious and Parasitic Diseases (A00–B99)

a. Human Immunodeficiency Virus (HIV) infections

1) Code only confirmed cases

Code only confirmed cases of HIV infection/illness. This is an exception to the hospital inpatient guideline Section II, H (Uncertain Diagnosis). In this context, "confirmation" does not require documentation of positive serology or culture for HIV; the provider's diagnostic statement that the patient is HIV positive, or has an HIV-related illness is sufficient.

(continues)

ICD-10-CM Chapter-Specific Coding Guidelines (*continued*)

2) Selection and sequencing of HIV codes

EXAMPLE: A 38-year-old symptomatic HIV-positive female patient was seen in follow-up at the office. The patient was discharged from the hospital last week after inpatient treatment of *Pneumocystis jiroveci* pneumonia (PJP). Lab tests today reveal CBC hemoglobin of 9.0, hematocrit 27, and normal WBC differential and platelets. Hepatitis A, B, and C tests negative. Cytomegalovirus (CMV) test negative. Rapid plasma reagin test negative. Decreased reticulocytes of 0.3 noted. Normal peripheral smear. Parvovirus B19 antibody test negative. Comprehensive metabolic panel was normal. CD4 test revealed somewhat depressed T helper cell level of 460. Viral load is 22,000. Erythropoietin level elevated at 120 milliunits per milliliter. Patient was started on medications of nevirapine plus Combivir.

In this example, the provider's statement of a "symptomatic HIV-positive female patient" is sufficient to assign ICD-10-CM code B20 for HIV infection. Because the PJP is resolved, a code to that HIV-related condition is not assigned.

(a) Patient admitted for HIV-related condition

If a patient is admitted for an HIV-related condition, the principal diagnosis should be B20, Human immunodeficiency virus [HIV] disease, followed by additional diagnosis codes for all reported HIV-related conditions.

EXAMPLE: A 42-year-old HIV-positive male underwent treatment for septic arthritis of the left shoulder. Culture and sensitivity lab test revealed *Klebsiella pneumoniae* as the bacterial agent. Because septic arthritis is considered an opportunistic infection in an HIV-positive patient, sequence the HIV code (B20) first and then the opportunistic infection codes (M00.812 and B96.1).

(b) Patient with HIV disease admitted for unrelated condition

If a patient with HIV disease is admitted for an unrelated condition (such as a traumatic injury), the code for the unrelated condition (e.g., the nature of injury code) should be the principal diagnosis. Other diagnoses would be B20 followed by additional diagnosis codes for all reported HIV-related conditions.

EXAMPLE: A 53-year-old female patient with symptomatic HIV disease undergoes treatment for a closed left wrist fracture. In this example, a fracture is not considered an opportunistic infection or disease in an HIV-positive patient, and it is considered a condition unrelated to HIV status. Therefore, sequence the closed left wrist fracture code (S62.102A) and then the HIV code (B20).

(c) Whether the patient is newly diagnosed

Whether the patient is newly diagnosed or has had previous admissions/encounters for HIV conditions is irrelevant to the sequencing decision.

(d) Asymptomatic human immunodeficiency virus

Z21, Asymptomatic human immunodeficiency virus [HIV] infection, is to be applied when the patient without any documentation of symptoms is listed as being "HIV positive," "known HIV," "HIV test positive," or similar terminology. Do not use this code if the term *AIDS* is used or if the patient is treated for any HIV-related illness or is described as having any condition(s) resulting from their HIV-positive status; use B20 in these cases.

EXAMPLE: A 42-year-old female HIV-positive asymptomatic patient undergoes routine CD4 testing to determine current levels. In this example, even though the patient is HIV-positive, she is also asymptomatic, which means that there are no documented symptoms. Therefore, assign code Z21 for asymptomatic HIV status. *Do not assign code B20, which is assigned to patients diagnosed as HIV positive who are treated for HIV-related illness(es) or to patients described as having AIDS.*

(e) Patients with inconclusive HIV serology

Patients with inconclusive HIV serology, but no definitive diagnosis or manifestations of the illness, may be assigned code R75, Inconclusive laboratory evidence of human immunodeficiency virus [HIV].

EXAMPLE: A 52-year-old asymptomatic male patient was seen in the office after having undergone HIV testing, the results of which proved inconclusive. Patient is scheduled for repeat HIV test. In this example, assign code R75 for an inconclusive laboratory evidence of HIV and code Z11.4 for "screening for HIV status" because the patient is being seen to determine his HIV status. If HIV counseling was provided during the encounter, code Z71.7 would also be assigned. If the patient was determined to be in a high-risk group for HIV, such as *high risk bisexual behavior*, code Z72.53 would also be assigned.

(f) Previously diagnosed HIV-related illness

Patients with any known prior diagnosis of an HIV-related illness should be coded to B20. Once a patient has developed an HIV-related illness, the patient should always be assigned code B20 on every subsequent admission/encounter. Patients previously diagnosed with any HIV illness (B20) should never be assigned to R75 (inconclusive laboratory evidence of human immunodeficiency virus [HIV]) or Z21 (asymptomatic human immunodeficiency virus [HIV] infection status).

EXAMPLE: A 29-year-old female HIV-positive patient was seen in the office to undergo routine CD4 testing. She has a past history of having been treated for HIV wasting syndrome and Hodgkin disease. The patient is currently asymptomatic. In this example, because the patient has known prior diagnoses of HIV-related illnesses, assign code B20 for HIV disease. *Although the patient is currently asymptomatic, according to official coding guidelines, it is incorrect to assign code R75 for inconclusive HIV test or code Z21 for asymptomatic HIV status.*

(g) HIV infection in pregnancy, childbirth, and the puerperium

During pregnancy, childbirth or the puerperium, a patient admitted (or presenting for a health care encounter) because of an HIV-related illness should receive a principal diagnosis code of O98.7-, Human immunodeficiency [HIV] disease complicating pregnancy, childbirth and the puerperium, followed by B20 and the code(s) for the HIV-related illness(es). Codes from Chapter 15 (of ICD-10-CM) always take sequencing priority. Patients with asymptomatic HIV infection status admitted (or presenting for a health care encounter) during pregnancy, childbirth, or the puerperium should be assigned codes O98.7- and Z21.

EXAMPLE: A 33-year-old HIV-positive patient in her second trimester received inpatient treatment for cytomegalovirus (CMV) disease. The patient was discharged to follow up with Dr. Jones regarding the CMV, and she will continue to receive prenatal care from Dr. Miller. When a pregnant patient is admitted for an HIV-related illness, assign code O98.512 for "other maternal viral disease complicating pregnancy, childbirth, or the puerperium." Then, assign code B20 for HIV disease and code B25.9 for the HIV-related condition of CMV.

When this patient is admitted for delivery, even if she has an asymptomatic HIV infection status upon admission, assign code O98.72 for the delivery and code B20 for HIV disease (because she was admitted during her antepartum period for treatment of an HIV-related condition). (The case of an HIV-positive patient who delivers and who has not been treated for an HIV-related condition in the past is assigned codes O98.72 and Z21.) (An outcome of delivery code is also assigned.)

(h) Encounters for testing for HIV

If a patient is being seen to determine his/her HIV status, use code Z11.4, Encounter for screening for human immunodeficiency virus [HIV]. Use additional codes for any associated high risk behavior. If a patient with signs or symptoms is being seen for HIV testing, code the signs and symptoms. An additional counseling

(continues)

ICD-10-CM Chapter-Specific Coding Guidelines (*continued*)

code Z71.7, Human immunodeficiency virus [HIV] counseling, may be used if counseling is provided during the encounter for the test.

When a patient returns to be informed of his/her HIV test results and the test result is negative, use code Z71.7, Human immunodeficiency virus [HIV] counseling. If the results are positive see previous guidelines and assign codes as appropriate.

b. **Infectious agents as the cause of diseases classified to other chapters**

Certain infections are classified in chapters other than Chapter 1 and no organism is identified as part of the infection code. In these instances, it is necessary to use an additional code from ICD-10-CM Chapter 1 to identify the organism. A code from category B95, *Streptococcus*, *Staphylococcus*, and *Enterococcus* as the cause of diseases classified to other chapters, B96, Other bacterial agents as the cause of diseases classified to other chapters, or B97, Viral agents as the cause of diseases classified to other chapters, is to be used as an additional code to identify the organism. An instructional note will be found at the infection code advising that an additional organism code is required.

EXAMPLE: A patient is diagnosed with urinary tract infection due to *Escherichia coli*. Assign codes N39.0 (Urinary tract infection, site unspecified) and B96.20 (Unspecified *Escherichia coli* [*E. coli*] as the cause of diseases classified elsewhere), in that order. (An instruction note below code N39.0 in the ICD-10-CM tabular list directs the coder to use an additional code to identify the infectious agent.)

c. **Infections resistant to antibiotics**

Many bacterial infections are resistant to current antibiotics. It is necessary to identify all infections documented as antibiotic resistant. Assign a code from category Z16, Resistance to antimicrobial drugs.

d. **Sepsis, Severe Sepsis, and Septic Shock**

1) **Coding of Sepsis and Severe Sepsis**

(a) **Sepsis**

For a diagnosis of sepsis, assign the appropriate code for the underlying systemic infection. If the type of infection or causal organism is not further specified, assign code A41.9, Sepsis, unspecified organism. A code from subcategory R65.2, Severe sepsis, should not be assigned unless severe sepsis or an associated acute organ dysfunction is documented.

EXAMPLE 1: Patient is diagnosed with sepsis due to gonococcus, and code A54.86 (Gonococcal sepsis) is reported because the infection is specified. Do not report A41.9 (Sepsis, unspecified organism).

EXAMPLE 2: Patient is diagnosed with gram-negative sepsis with acute respiratory failure. Report codes A41.50 (Gram-negative sepsis, unspecified), R65.20 (Sepsis without septic shock), and J96.00 (Acute respiratory failure, unspecified whether with hypoxia or hypercapnia), in that order.

(i) Negative or inconclusive blood cultures and sepsis

Negative or inconclusive blood cultures do *not* preclude a diagnosis of sepsis in patients with clinical evidence of the condition; however, the provider should be queried.

(ii) Urosepsis

The term *urosepsis* is a nonspecific term. It is not to be considered synonymous with sepsis. It has no default code in the ICD-10-CM Index to Diseases and Injuries. Should a provider use this term, he/she must be queried for clarification.

(iii) Sepsis with organ dysfunction

If a patient has sepsis and associated acute organ dysfunction or multiple organ dysfunction (MOD), follow the instructions for coding severe sepsis.

(iv) Acute organ dysfunction that is not clearly associated with the sepsis

If a patient has sepsis and an acute organ dysfunction, but the patient record documentation indicates that the acute organ dysfunction is related to a medical condition other than the sepsis, do not assign a code from subcategory R65.2, Severe sepsis. An acute organ dysfunction must be associated with the sepsis in order to assign the severe sepsis code. If the documentation is not clear as to whether an acute organ dysfunction is related to the sepsis or another medical condition, query the provider.

(b) Severe sepsis

The coding of severe sepsis requires a minimum of two codes: a code for the underlying systemic infection, followed by a code from subcategory R65.2, Severe sepsis. If the causal organism is not documented, assign code A41.9, Sepsis, unspecified organism, for the infection. Additional code(s) for the associated acute organ dysfunction are also required. Due to the complex nature of severe sepsis, some cases may require querying the provider prior to assignment of the codes.

2) Septic shock

(a) Septic shock generally refers to circulatory failure associated with severe sepsis, and therefore, it represents a type of acute organ dysfunction.

For cases of septic shock, the code for the systemic infection should be sequenced first, followed by code R65.21, Severe sepsis with septic shock or code T81.12, Postprocedural septic shock. Any additional codes for the other acute organ dysfunctions should also be assigned. As noted in the sequencing instructions in the ICD-10-CM tabular list, the code for septic shock *cannot* be assigned as a principal diagnosis.

EXAMPLE: Patient is diagnosed with septic shock due to Enterococcus. Report codes A41.81 (Sepsis due to Enterococcus) and R65.21 (Severe sepsis with septic shock), in that order.

3) Sequencing of severe sepsis

If severe sepsis is present on admission, and meets the definition of principal diagnosis, the underlying systemic infection should be assigned as principal diagnosis followed by the appropriate code from subcategory R65.2 as required by the sequencing rules in the ICD-10-CM tabular list. A code from subcategory R65.2 can never be assigned as a principal diagnosis.

When severe sepsis develops during an encounter (it was not present on admission) the underlying systemic infection and the appropriate code from subcategory R65.2 should be assigned as secondary diagnoses.

Severe sepsis may be present on admission but the diagnosis may not be confirmed until sometime after admission. If the documentation is not clear whether severe sepsis was present on admission, the provider should be queried.

4) Sepsis or severe sepsis with a localized infection

If the reason for admission is sepsis or severe sepsis and a localized infection, such as pneumonia or cellulitis, a code(s) for the underlying systemic infection should be assigned first and the code for the localized infection should be assigned as a secondary diagnosis. If the patient has severe sepsis, a code from subcategory R65.2 should also be assigned as a secondary diagnosis. If the patient is admitted with a localized infection, such as pneumonia, and sepsis/severe sepsis doesn't develop until after admission, the localized infection should be assigned first, followed by the appropriate sepsis/severe sepsis codes.

EXAMPLE: Patient is diagnosed with acute liver failure due to severe sepsis from Pseudomonas. Report codes A41.52 (Sepsis due to pseudomonas), R65.20 (Severe sepsis without septic shock), K72.00 (Acute and subacute hepatic failure without coma), in that order.

(continues)

ICD-10-CM Chapter-Specific Coding Guidelines (*continued*)

5) Sepsis due to a postprocedural infection

(a) Documentation of causal relationship

As with all postprocedural complications, code assignment is based on the provider's documentation of the relationship between the infection and the procedure.

(b) Sepsis due to a postprocedural infection

For infections following a procedure, a code from T81.40 to T81.43, Infection following a procedure, or a code from O86.00 to O86.03, Infection of obstetric surgical wound, that identifies the site of the infection should be coded first, if known. Assign an additional code for sepsis following a procedure (T81.44) or sepsis following an obstetrical procedure (O86.04). Use an additional code to identify the infectious agent. If the patient has severe sepsis, the appropriate code from subcategory R65.2 should also be assigned with the additional code(s) for any acute organ dysfunction.

For infections following infusion, transfusion, therapeutic injection, or immunization, a code from subcategory T80.2, Infections following infusion, transfusion, and therapeutic injection, or code T88.0-, Infection following immunization, should be coded first, followed by the code for the specific infection. If the patient has severe sepsis, the appropriate code from subcategory R65.2 should also be assigned, with the additional codes(s) for any acute organ dysfunction.

If a postprocedural infection has resulted in postprocedural septic shock, assign the codes indicated above for sepsis due to a postprocedural infection, followed by code T81.12-, Postprocedural septic shock. Do not assign code R65.21, Severe sepsis with septic shock. Additional code(s) should be assigned for any acute organ dysfunction.

(c) Postprocedural infection and postprocedural septic shock

In cases where a postprocedural infection has occurred and has resulted in severe sepsis and postprocedural septic shock, the code for the precipitating complication such as code T81.4-, Infection following a procedure, or O86.0-, Infection of obstetrical surgical wound should be coded first followed by code R65.20, Severe sepsis without septic shock. A code for the systemic infection should also be assigned.

If a postprocedural infection has resulted in postprocedural septic shock, the code for the precipitating complication such as code T81.4-, Infection following a procedure, or O86.0-, Infection of obstetrical surgical wound should be coded first followed by code T81.12-, Postprocedural septic shock. A code for the systemic infection should also be assigned.

6) Sepsis and severe sepsis associated with a noninfectious process (condition)

In some cases a noninfectious process (condition), such as trauma, may lead to an infection which can result in sepsis or severe sepsis. If sepsis or severe sepsis is documented as associated with a noninfectious condition, such as a burn or serious injury, and this condition meets the definition for principal diagnosis, the code for the noninfectious condition should be sequenced first, followed by the code for the resulting infection. If severe sepsis is present a code from subcategory R65.2 should also be assigned with any associated organ dysfunction(s) codes. It is not necessary to assign a code from subcategory R65.1, Systemic inflammatory response syndrome (SIRS) of non-infectious origin, for these cases.

If the infection meets the definition of principal diagnosis it should be sequenced before the non-infectious condition. When both the associated non-infectious condition and the infection meet the definition of principal diagnosis either may be assigned as principal diagnosis.

Only one code from category R65, Symptoms and signs specifically associated with systemic inflammation and infection, should be assigned. Therefore, when a non-infectious condition leads to an infection resulting in severe sepsis, assign the appropriate code from subcategory R65.2, Severe sepsis. Do not additionally assign a code from subcategory R65.1, Systemic inflammatory response syndrome (SIRS) of non-infectious origin.

EXAMPLE: Patient experienced an abrasion, left inner thigh, after playing soccer. The area developed into a boil that ruptured, and the patient presented to the emergency department with fever, headache, muscle aches, fatigue, shivering, and a generalized sick feeling. She was admitted as a hospital inpatient, and skin culture grew Methicillin-resistant *Staphylococcus aureus* (MRSA). Inpatient diagnoses included abrasion, left inner thigh, and sepsis due to MRSA. Report code A41.02 for the sepsis and code S70.312A for the abrasion, in that order because sepsis is the reason, after study, for inpatient hospitalization.

For a patient who received initial treatment at her physician's office for the abrasion of left inner thigh, code S70.312A is reported first for that office encounter. If a skin culture was positive for MRSA, code A49.02 for the MRSA infection would be also reported.

7) Sepsis and septic shock complicating abortion, pregnancy, childbirth, and the puerperium

See Section I.C.15. Sepsis and septic shock complicating abortion, pregnancy, childbirth and the puerperium.

8) Newborn sepsis

See Section I.C.16. f. Bacterial sepsis of Newborn.

e. **Methicillin-Resistant *Staphylococcus aureus* (MRSA) conditions**

1) **Selection and sequencing of MRSA codes**

(a) **Combination codes for MRSA infection**

When a patient is diagnosed with an infection that is due to methicillin-resistant *Staphylococcus aureus* (MRSA), and that infection has a combination code that includes the causal organism (e.g., septicemia, pneumonia) assign the appropriate code for the condition (e.g., code A41.02, Sepsis due to Methicillin-resistant *Staphylococcus aureus*, or code J15.212, Pneumonia due to Methicillin-resistant *Staphylococcus aureus*). Do not assign code B96.52, Methicillin-resistant *Staphylococcus aureus*, as an additional code because the code includes the type of infection and the MRSA organism. Do not assign a code from subcategory Z16.11, Resistance to penicillins, as an additional diagnosis.

See Section C.1. for instructions on coding and sequencing of sepsis and severe sepsis.

(b) **Other codes for MRSA infection**

When there is documentation of a current infection (e.g., wound infection, stitch abscess, urinary tract infection) due to MRSA, and that infection does not have a combination code that includes the causal organism, assign the appropriate code to identify the condition along with code B95.62, Methicillin-resistant *Staphylococcus aureus* infection as the cause of diseases classified elsewhere, for the MRSA infection. Do not assign a code from subcategory Z16.11, Resistance to penicillins.

(c) **Methicillin-susceptible *Staphylococcus aureus* (MSSA) and MRSA colonization**

The condition or state of being colonized or carrying MSSA or MRSA is called colonization or carriage, while an individual person is described as being colonized or being a carrier.

Colonization means that MSSA or MSRA is present on or in the body without necessarily causing illness. A positive MRSA colonization test might be documented by the provider as "MRSA screen positive" or "MRSA nasal swab positive."

Assign code Z22.322, Carrier or suspected carrier of Methicillin-resistant *Staphylococcus aureus*, for patients documented as having MRSA colonization. Assign code Z22.321, Carrier or suspected carrier of Methicillin-susceptible *Staphylococcus aureus*, for patients documented as having MSSA colonization. Colonization is not necessarily indicative of a disease process or as the cause of a specific condition the patient may have unless documented as such by the provider.

(continues)

ICD-10-CM Chapter-Specific Coding Guidelines (*continued*)

(d) MRSA colonization and infection

If a patient is documented as having both MRSA colonization and infection during a hospital admission, code Z22.322, Carrier or suspected carrier of Methicillin-resistant *Staphylococcus aureus*, and a code for the MRSA infection may both be assigned.

f. Zika virus infections

1) Code only confirmed cases

Code only a confirmed diagnosis of Zika virus (A92.5, Zika virus disease) as documented by the provider. (This is an exception to the hospital "uncertain diagnosis" inpatient guideline. In that context, "confirmation" does not require documentation of the type of test performed; the provider's diagnostic statement that the condition is confirmed is sufficient.) The Zika virus code should be assigned regardless of the stated mode of transmission. If the provider documents "suspected," "possible," or "probable" Zika, do *not* assign code A92.5. Instead, assign code(s) explaining the reason for encounter (e.g., fever, rash, joint pain) or code Z20.821, Contact with and (suspected) exposure to Zika virus.

EXAMPLE 1: After testing, the patient is diagnosed with the Zika virus. Report code A92.5 (Zika virus disease).

EXAMPLE 2: Patient is diagnosed with congenital Zika virus disease. Report code P35.4 (congenital Zika virus disease).

EXAMPLE 3: Patient states she has symptoms of headache, right shoulder joint pain, and fever. Temperature in the office is not elevated. She explains she just returned from a tropical vacation and is concerned about the Zika virus because she got mosquito bites on both lower legs. Examination revealed the bites to be well healed. Zika test is negative. Patient was instructed to take ibuprofen as directed and to follow up with the office if her symptoms worsen. Report code Z20.821 (Contact with and [suspected] exposure to Zika virus) **or** codes R51 (Headache) and M25.511 (Pain in right shoulder).

Exercise 4.1 – Certain Infectious and Parasitic Diseases

Instructions: Assign the appropriate ICD-10-CM code(s).

_____ 1. AIDS

_____ 2. Botulism

_____ 3. Lyme disease

_____ 4. Postmeasles pneumonia

_____ 5. Rabies

ICD-10-CM Chapter 2: Neoplasms (C00–D49)

This ICD-10-CM chapter classifies malignant, *in situ*, and benign neoplasms according to anatomical site (e.g., breast) and body system (e.g., urinary tract). Neoplasms are also classified according to primary, secondary, and unspecified sites as well as uncertain and unspecified behavior.

 NOTE:

> Functionally active malignant neoplasms behave like their surrounding tissue, such as a thyroid tumor that secretes thyroxine and causes hyperthyroidism.

Neoplasms are new growths or tumors in which cell reproduction is out of control, and they are classified according to appearance and growth pattern (Figure 4-1). For coding purposes, the provider should specify whether the tumor is benign (noncancerous, nonmalignant, or noninvasive) or **malignant** (cancerous, invasive, or capable of spreading to other parts of the body).

Another term associated with neoplasms is *lesion*, which is defined as "any discontinuity of tissue (e.g., skin or organ) that may or may not be malignant." Index entries for *lesion* contain subterms according to anatomical site (e.g., organs or tissue), and the term *lesion* should be referenced if the diagnostic statement does not confirm a malignancy. In addition, conditions that are examples of benign lesions and are listed as separate index entries include adenosis, cys, dysplasia, mass (unless the word neoplasm is included in the diagnostic statement), and polyp.

Do not first reference the neoplasm table to assign codes for benign conditions. Instead, locate the specific term in the disease index, and then locate the subterm for the specific organ or body area. When the specific organ or body area is *not* listed as subterm, follow the instructions provided (e.g., *see, see also,* or *see category*).

EXAMPLE: The provider documents "liver mass" as the final diagnosis because the pathology report of examined tissue is not yet available. A "mass" is not a "neoplasm." In the ICD-10-CM index, locate main term *Mass* and subterm *liver* to assign R16.0 (after verifying it in the tabular list). (When pathology reports are available, assign a more appropriate code.)

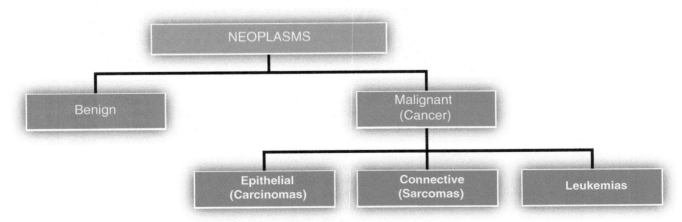

FIGURE 4-1 Classification of neoplasms

The ICD-10-CM Table of Neoplasms (Figure 4-2) is indexed by anatomical site and contains four cellular classifications: malignant, benign, uncertain behavior, and unspecified nature. The malignant classification is subdivided into three divisions: primary, secondary, and carcinoma *in situ*. The six neoplasm classifications are defined as follows:

- **Primary malignancy**: Original tumor site.

 NOTE:

Malignant tumors are considered primary unless otherwise documented as metastatic or secondary.

- **Secondary malignancy** (or **metastatic cancer**): Tumor that has metastasized, or spread, to a secondary site either adjacent to the primary site or to a remote region of the body.
- **Carcinoma (Ca)** *in situ*: Malignant tumor that is localized, circumscribed, encapsulated, and noninvasive, but has not spread to deeper or adjacent tissues or organs.
- **Benign**: Noninvasive, nonspreading, nonmalignant tumor.
- **Uncertain behavior**: Subsequent morphology or behavior that cannot be predicted based on the submitted specimen; the tissue appears to be in transition, and the pathologist cannot establish a definitive diagnosis. (To assign a code from this column, the pathology report must specify "uncertain behavior" of the neoplasm.)
- **Unspecified nature**: A neoplasm is identified, but the results of pathology examination are not available; thus, there is no indication as to histology or nature of the tumor. (Assign a code from the unspecified behavior column when pathology results are pending.)

	Malignant Primary	Malignant Secondary	Ca *in situ*	Benign	Uncertain Behavior	Unspecified Behavior
Neoplasm, neoplastic	C80.1	C79.9	D09.9	D36.9	D48.9	D49.9

Note: The list below gives the code number for neoplasms by anatomical site. For each site there are six possible code numbers according to whether the neoplasm in question is malignant, benign, *in situ*, of uncertain behavior, or of unspecified nature. The description of the neoplasm will often indicate which of the six columns is appropriate; e.g., malignant melanoma of skin, benign fibroadenoma of breast, carcinoma in situ of cervix uteri. Where such descriptors are not present, the remainder of the Index should be consulted where guidance is given to the appropriate column for each morphological (histological) variety listed; e.g., Mesonephroma –*see* Neoplasm, malignant; Embryoma –*see also* Neoplasm, uncertain behavior; Disease, Bowen's –*see* Neoplasm, skin, *in situ*. However, the guidance in the Index can be overridden if one of the descriptors mentioned above is present; e.g., malignant adenoma of colon is coded to C18.9 and not to D12.6 as the adjective "malignant" overrides the Index entry "Adenoma –*see also* Neoplasm, benign." Codes listed with a dash (–), following the code have a required additional character for laterality. The Tabular must be reviewed for the complete code.

	Malignant Primary	Malignant Secondary	Ca *in situ*	Benign	Uncertain Behavior	Unspecified Behavior
abdomen, abdominal	C76.2	C79.8-	D09.8	D36.7	D48.7	D49.89
cavity	C76.2	C79.8-	D09.8	D36.7	D48.7	D49.89
organ	C76.2	C79.8-	D09.8	D36.7	D48.7	D49.89
viscera	C76.2	C79.8-	D09.8	D36.7	D48.7	D49.89
wall–*see also* Neoplasm, abdomen, wall, skin	C44.509	C79.2-	D04.5	D23.5	D48.5	D49.2
connective tissue	C49.4	C79.8-	—	D21.4	D48.1	D49.2
skin	C44.509					
basal cell carcinoma	C44.519	—	—	—	—	—
specified type NEC	C44.599	—	—	—	—	—
squamous cell carcinoma	C44.529	—	—	—	—	—

Courtesy of the Centers for Medicare & Medicaid Services, www.cms.gov

FIGURE 4-2 ICD-10-CM Table of Neoplasms (partial)

To use the Table of Neoplasms, first identify the classification (e.g., malignant), and then locate the site of the neoplasm. Some diagnostic statements specifically document "neoplasm" classification, while others do not provide a clue. If the diagnostic statement classifies the neoplasm, the coder can refer directly to the neoplasm table to assign the proper code (after verifying the code in the tabular list).

When the diagnostic statement does not classify the neoplasm, the coder must refer to the disease index entry for the condition documented (instead of the neoplasm table) (e.g., lipoma). That entry either will contain a code number that can be verified in the tabular list or will refer the coder to the proper neoplasm table entry under which the code can be located.

EXAMPLE 1: For non-Hodgkin lymphoma, go to main term *Lymphoma* in the ICD-10-CM index, subterm *non-Hodgkin*, and verify code C85.9 in the tabular list to assign the fifth character for the anatomical site.

EXAMPLE 2: For adrenal gland adenolymphoma, go to main term *Adenolymphoma* in the ICD-10-CM index, and follow the instruction to *see Neoplasm, benign*, and verify code D35.00 in the tabular list.

ICD-10-CM Index

Lymphoma
   non-Hodgkin *–see also* Lymphoma, by type C85.9-
Adenolymphoma
   specified site *–see* Neoplasm, benign, by site
   unspecified site D11.9

 Coding Tip

Assigning codes from the neoplasm table is a two-step process. First, classify the neoplasm by its behavior (e.g., malignant or benign); then classify the neoplasm by its anatomical site (e.g., acoustic nerve). To classify the neoplasm's behavior, review the provider's diagnostic statement (e.g., carcinoma of the throat) and locate the term *carcinoma* in the disease index. The entry will classify the behavior, directing you to the proper column in the Table of Neoplasms. (If the neoplasm is malignant, you still need to determine primary, secondary, or *in situ* based on documentation in the patient's record.)

Primary and Secondary Malignancies

A malignancy is coded as a primary site if the diagnostic statement documents

- Metastatic *from* a site
- Spread *from* a site
- *Primary neoplasm* of a site
- A malignancy for which there is no specific classification
- A *recurrent* tumor

EXAMPLE: For "carcinoma of cervical lymph nodes, metastatic from the breast," the primary site is female breast and the secondary site is cervical lymph nodes.

Secondary malignancies are metastatic and indicate that a primary cancer has spread (metastasized) to another part of the body. Cancer described as *metastatic from* a site is *primary of* that site. Assign one code to the primary neoplasm and a second code to the secondary neoplasm of the specified site (if secondary site is known) or unspecified site (if secondary site is unknown). (Remember that sequencing of codes depends on which site is being treated.)

EXAMPLE 1: For "metastatic carcinoma from left female breast to lung," assign two codes.

- Primary malignant neoplasm of female breast (C50.912)
- Secondary neoplasm of lung (C78.00)

EXAMPLE 2: For "metastatic carcinoma from left female breast," assign two codes.

- Primary malignant neoplasm of left female breast (C50.912)
- Secondary neoplasm of unspecified site (C79.9)

Cancer described as *metastatic to* a site is considered *secondary of* that site. Assign one code to the secondary site and a second code to the specified primary site (if primary site is known) or unspecified site (if primary site is unknown).

EXAMPLE: For "metastatic carcinoma to right lung," assign two codes.

- Primary malignant neoplasm of unspecified site (C80.1)
- Secondary neoplasm of right lung (C78.01)

When anatomical sites are documented as *metastatic*, assign *secondary* neoplasm code(s) to those sites and assign an *unspecified site* code to the primary malignant neoplasm.

EXAMPLE: For "metastatic renal carcinoma, right kidney, of right lung," assign two codes.

- Primary renal carcinoma, right kidney (C64.1)
- Secondary neoplasm of right lung (C78.01)

Anatomical Site Is Not Documented

If the cancer diagnosis does not contain documentation of the anatomical site but the term *metastatic* is documented, assign codes for "unspecified site" for both the primary and secondary sites.

EXAMPLE: For "metastatic chromophobe adenocarcinoma," assign two codes.

- Secondary neoplasm of unspecified site (C79.9)
- Primary chromophobe adenocarcinoma of unspecified site (C75.1)

Inoperable Primary Site with Metastasis

When the primary neoplasm site is considered inoperable and is not treated, assign a code for the metastatic site first.

> **EXAMPLE:** For "carcinoma of fundus of stomach (inoperable) with metastasis to liver," assign two codes.
>
> - Secondary malignant neoplasm of liver (C78.7)
> - Malignant neoplasm of fundus of stomach (C16.1)

Reexcision of Tumors

A reexcision of a tumor occurs when the pathology report recommends that the surgeon perform a second excision to widen the margins of the original tumor site. The reexcision is performed to ensure that all tumor cells have been removed and that a clear border (margin) of normal tissue surrounds the excised specimen. Use the diagnostic statement found in the report of the original excision to code the reason for the reexcision. The pathology report for the reexcision may not specify a malignancy at that time, but the patient is still under treatment for the original neoplasm.

 Coding Tip

1. Read all notes in the neoplasm table that apply to the condition you are coding.
2. Never assign a code directly from the neoplasm table (or index).
3. Report only those codes that represent the current status of the neoplasm.
4. Assign a neoplasm code if the tumor has been excised and the patient is still undergoing radiation or chemotherapy treatment.
5. Assign an ICD-10-CM Z code if the tumor is no longer present or if the patient is not receiving treatment but is returning for follow-up care (e.g., personal history of a malignancy).
6. The classification documented on a pathology report overrides the morphology classification entry in the index.

Morphology of Neoplasms

The World Health Organization (WHO) has published an adaptation of the International Classification of Diseases for Oncology (ICD-O) that contains a coded nomenclature for the morphology of neoplasms. (Refer to the Student Companion Web Site at *http://login.cengage.com* for the morphology of neoplasms codes document.) The morphology codes consist of five characters, and these codes are reported to state cancer registries and other entities for cancer research purposes. The first four characters identify the histological type of the neoplasm, and the fifth character indicates behavior of the neoplasm (e.g., M8000/0). The one-character behavior codes include:

/0 Benign

/1 Uncertain whether benign or malignant

Borderline malignancy

/2 Carcinoma *in situ*

Intraepithelial

Noninfiltrating

Noninvasive

/3 Malignant, primary site

/6 Malignant, metastatic site

     Secondary site

/9 Malignant, uncertain whether primary or metastatic site

> **EXAMPLE:** Malignant chordoma is assigned morphology code M9370/3. However, benign chordoma is assigned morphology code M9370/0.

When a morphological diagnosis contains two qualifying adjectives that result in more than one morphology code, the higher morphology code is assigned.

> **EXAMPLE:** Transitional cell epidermoid carcinoma is assigned morphology code M8120/3 (Transitional cell carcinoma NOS), while epidermoid carcinoma is assigned morphology code M8070/3 (Epidermoid carcinoma NOS). In this situation, the higher morphology code (M8120/3) is used because it is usually more specific.

ICD-10-CM Chapter-Specific Coding Guidelines

Chapter 2: Neoplasms (C00-D49)

General guidelines

Chapter 2 of the ICD-10-CM contains the codes for most benign and all malignant neoplasms. Certain benign neoplasms, such as prostatic adenomas, may be found in the specific body system chapters. To properly code a neoplasm, it is necessary to determine from the record if the neoplasm is benign, *in situ*, malignant, or of uncertain histologic behavior. If malignant, any secondary (metastatic) sites should also be determined.

Primary malignant neoplasms overlapping site boundaries

A primary malignant neoplasm that overlaps two or more contiguous (next to each other) sites should be classified to the subcategory/code .8 ('overlapping lesion'), unless the combination is specifically indexed elsewhere. For multiple neoplasms of the same site that are not contiguous, such as tumors in different quadrants of the same breast, codes for each site should be assigned.

> **EXAMPLE: Contiguous sites** (or **overlapping sites**) occur when the origin of the tumor (primary site) involves two adjacent sites. For a female patient who is diagnosed with a single primary malignant neoplasm of the right breast that extends from the lower-outer quadrant into the adjacent axillary tail, report code C50.811 (Malignant neoplasm of overlapping sites of right female breast) because the sites are contiguous.
>
> For a male patient who is diagnosed with two malignant neoplasms of left breast, one at the upper-outer quadrant and another at the lower-outer quadrant, report codes C50.422 (Malignant neoplasm of upper-outer quadrant of left male breast) and C50.522 (Malignant neoplasm of lower-outer quadrant of left male breast) because the sites are **not** contiguous.

Malignant neoplasm of ectopic tissue

Malignant neoplasms of ectopic tissue are to be coded to the site of origin mentioned; e.g., ectopic pancreatic malignant neoplasms involving the stomach are coded to malignant neoplasm of pancreas, unspecified (C25.9).

The neoplasm table in the ICD-10-CM Alphabetic Index should be referenced first. However, if the histological term is documented, that term should be referenced first, rather than going immediately to the neoplasm table, in order to determine which column in the neoplasm table is appropriate. For example, if the documentation indicates "adenoma," refer to the term in the ICD-10-CM Alphabetic Index to review the entries under this term and the instructional note to "see also neoplasm, by site, benign." The table provides the proper code based on the type of neoplasm and the site. It is important to select the proper column in the table that corresponds to the type of neoplasm. The ICD-10-CM tabular list should then be referenced to verify that the correct code has been selected from the table and that a more specific site code does not exist.

See Section I.C.21. Factors influencing health status and contact with health services, Status, for information regarding Z15.0, codes for genetic susceptibility to cancer.

a. Treatment directed at the malignancy

If the treatment is directed at the malignancy, designate the malignancy as the principal diagnosis.

The only exception to this guideline is if a patient admission/encounter is solely for the administration of chemotherapy, immunotherapy, or external beam radiation therapy, assign the appropriate Z51.-- code as the first-listed or principal diagnosis, and the diagnosis or problem for which the service is being performed as a secondary diagnosis.

b. Treatment of secondary site

When a patient is admitted because of a primary neoplasm with metastasis and treatment is directed toward the secondary site only, the secondary neoplasm is designated as the principal diagnosis even though the primary malignancy is still present.

EXAMPLE: Patient with primary uterine adnexal cancer (that has not resolved) receives treatment today for metastatic (secondary) cancer of the liver. Report code C78.7 for liver cancer and C57.4 for uterine cancer, in that order.

c. Coding and sequencing of complications

Coding and sequencing of complications associated with the malignancies or with the therapy thereof are subject to the following guidelines:

1) Anemia associated with malignancy

When admission/encounter is for management of an anemia associated with the malignancy, and the treatment is only for anemia, the appropriate code for the malignancy is sequenced as the principal or first-listed diagnosis followed by the appropriate code for the anemia (such as code D63.0, Anemia in neoplastic disease).

EXAMPLE: Patient is diagnosed with anemia due to malignant neoplasm of mandible. Report code C41.1 for mandible cancer and code D63.0 for anemia in neoplastic disease. (The ICD-10-CM tabular list instruction states to "code first neoplasm.")

2) Anemia associated with chemotherapy, immunotherapy, and radiation therapy

When the admission/encounter is for management of an anemia associated with an adverse effect of the administration of chemotherapy or immunotherapy and the only treatment is for the anemia, the anemia code is sequenced first followed by the appropriate codes for the neoplasm and the adverse effect (T45.1X5-, Adverse effect of antineoplastic and immunosuppressive drugs).

EXAMPLE: Patient with Burkitt-type mature B-cell leukemia, in relapse, is admitted today for treatment of anemia due to antineoplastic chemotherapy. Report code D64.81 for anemia, C91.A2 for leukemia, and T45.1x5A for adverse effect, in that order.

When the admission/encounter is for management of an anemia associated with an adverse effect of radiotherapy, the anemia code should be sequenced first, followed by the appropriate neoplasm code and code Y84.2, Radiological procedure and radiotherapy as the cause of abnormal reaction of the patient, or of later complication, without mention of misadventure at the time of the procedure.

(continues)

ICD-10-CM Chapter-Specific Coding Guidelines (*continued*)

EXAMPLE: Patient with Burkitt-type mature B-cell leukemia, in relapse, is admitted today for treatment of anemia related to radiation therapy. Report codes D64.89 for anemia, C91.A2 for leukemia, and Y84.2 for radiotherapy as cause of abnormal reaction, in that order.

3) Management of dehydration due to the malignancy

When the admission/encounter is for management of dehydration due to the malignancy and only the dehydration is being treated (e.g., intravenous rehydration), the dehydration is sequenced first, followed by the code(s) for the malignancy.

4) Treatment of a complication resulting from a surgical procedure

When the admission/encounter is for treatment of a complication resulting from a surgical procedure, designate the complication as the principal or first-listed diagnosis if treatment is directed at resolving the complication.

d. Primary malignancy previously excised

When a primary malignancy has been previously excised or eradicated from its site and there is no further treatment directed to that site and there is no evidence of any existing primary malignancy at that site, a code from category Z85, Personal history of malignant neoplasm, should be used to indicate the former site of the malignancy. Any mention of extension, invasion, or metastasis to another site is coded as a secondary malignant neoplasm to that site. The secondary site may be the principal or first-listed diagnosis, with the Z85 code used as a secondary code.

EXAMPLE: Patient underwent left radical mastectomy last year, and is seen today for metastatic carcinoma to the right lung. Report codes C78.01 (Secondary neoplasm of right lung), Z85.3 (Personal history of malignant neoplasm of right female breast), and Z90.11 (Acquired absence of right breast and nipple), in that order. Code Z90.11 is typically due to status post right mastectomy.

e. Admissions/Encounters involving chemotherapy, immunotherapy, and radiation therapy

1) Episode of care involves surgical removal of neoplasm

When an episode of care involves the surgical removal of a neoplasm, primary or secondary site, followed by adjunct chemotherapy or radiation treatment during the same episode of care, the code for the neoplasm should be assigned as principal or first-listed diagnosis.

2) Patient admission/encounter solely for administration of chemotherapy, immunotherapy, and radiation therapy

If a patient admission/encounter is solely for the administration of chemotherapy, immunotherapy, or radiation therapy, assign code Z51.0, Encounter for antineoplastic radiation therapy, or Z51.11, Encounter for antineoplastic chemotherapy, or Z51.12, Encounter for antineoplastic immunotherapy as the first-listed or principal diagnosis. If a patient receives more than one of these therapies during the same admission, more than one of these codes may be assigned, in any sequence.

The malignancy for which the therapy is being administered should be assigned as a secondary diagnosis.

If a patient admission/encounter is for the insertion or implantation of radioactive elements (e.g., brachytherapy) the appropriate code for the malignancy is sequenced as the principal or first-listed diagnosis. Code Z51.0 should not be assigned.

3) Patient admitted for radiation therapy, chemotherapy or immunotherapy and develops complications

When a patient is admitted for the purpose of external beam radiotherapy, immunotherapy, or chemotherapy and develops complications such as uncontrolled nausea and vomiting or dehydration, the principal or first-listed diagnosis is Z51.0, Encounter for antineoplastic radiation therapy, or Z51.11, Encounter for antineoplastic chemotherapy, or Z51.12, Encounter for antineoplastic immunotherapy, followed by any codes for the complications.

When a patient is admitted for the purpose of insertion or implantation of radioactive elements (e.g., brachytherapy) and develops complications such as uncontrolled nausea and vomiting or dehydration, the principal or first-listed diagnosis is the appropriate code for the malignancy followed by any codes for the complications.

f. Admission/encounter to determine extent of malignancy

When the reason for admission/encounter is to determine the extent of the malignancy, or for a procedure such as paracentesis or thoracentesis, the primary malignancy or appropriate metastatic site is designated as the principal or first-listed diagnosis, even though chemotherapy or radiotherapy is administered.

g. Symptoms, signs, and ill-defined conditions listed in ICD-10-CM Chapter 18 associated with neoplasms

Symptoms, signs, and ill-defined conditions listed in ICD-10-CM Chapter 18 characteristic of, or associated with, an existing primary or secondary site malignancy cannot be used to replace the malignancy as principal or first-listed diagnosis, regardless of the number of admissions or encounters for treatment and care of the neoplasm.

See section I.C.21. Factors influencing health status and contact with health services, Encounter for prophylactic organ removal.

h. Admission/encounter for pain control/management

See Section I.C.6. for information on coding admission/encounter for pain control/management.

i. Malignancy in two or more noncontiguous sites

A patient may have more than one malignant tumor in the same organ. These tumors may represent different primaries or metastatic disease, depending on the site. Should the documentation be unclear, the provider should be queried as to the status of each tumor so that the correct codes can be assigned.

j. Disseminated malignant neoplasm, unspecified

Code C80.0, Disseminated malignant neoplasm, unspecified, is for use only in those cases where the patient has advanced metastatic disease and no known primary or secondary sites are specified. It should not be used in place of assigning codes for the primary site and all known secondary sites.

k. Malignant neoplasm without specification of site

Code C80.1, Malignant (primary) neoplasm, unspecified, equates to Cancer, unspecified. This code should only be used when no determination can be made as to the primary site of a malignancy. This code should rarely be used in the inpatient setting.

l. Sequencing of neoplasm codes

1) Encounter for treatment of primary malignancy

If the reason for the encounter is for treatment of a primary malignancy, assign the malignancy as the principal/first-listed diagnosis. The primary site is to be sequenced first, followed by any metastatic sites.

EXAMPLE: Patient is admitted for treatment of "oat cell carcinoma of the lung with spread to the brain." The primary site is lung, and the secondary site is brain.

2) Encounter for treatment of secondary malignancy

When an encounter is for a primary malignancy with metastasis and treatment is directed toward the metastatic (secondary) site(s) only, the metastatic site(s) is designated as the principal/first-listed diagnosis. The primary malignancy is coded as an additional code.

(continues)

ICD-10-CM Chapter-Specific Coding Guidelines (*continued*)

EXAMPLE: A female patient is admitted for treatment of "metastatic carcinoma from right breast to right lung." The primary site is the right breast and continues to display evidence of cancer. Report codes C78.01 (Secondary neoplasm of right lung) and C50.911 (Malignant neoplasm of unspecified site of right breast), in that order.

3) Malignant neoplasm in a pregnant patient

When a pregnant woman has a malignant neoplasm, a code from subcategory O9A.1-, Malignant neoplasm complicating pregnancy, childbirth, and the puerperium, should be sequenced first, followed by the appropriate code from Chapter 2 to indicate the type of neoplasm.

4) Encounter for complication associated with a neoplasm

When an encounter is for management of a complication associated with a neoplasm, such as dehydration, and the treatment is only for the complication, the complication is coded first, followed by the appropriate code(s) for the neoplasm.

The exception to this guideline is anemia. When the admission/encounter is for management of an anemia associated with the malignancy, and the treatment is only for anemia, the appropriate code for the malignancy is sequenced as the principal or first-listed diagnosis followed by code D63.0, Anemia in neoplastic disease.

5) Complication from surgical procedure for treatment of a neoplasm

When an encounter is for treatment of a complication resulting from a surgical procedure performed for the treatment of the neoplasm, designate the complication as the principal/first-listed diagnosis. See the guideline regarding the coding of a current malignancy versus personal history to determine if the code for the neoplasm should also be assigned.

6) Pathologic fracture due to a neoplasm

When an encounter is for a pathological fracture due to a neoplasm, and the focus of treatment is the fracture, a code from subcategory M84.5, Pathological fracture in neoplastic disease, should be sequenced first, followed by the code for the neoplasm.

If the focus of treatment is the neoplasm with an associated pathological fracture, the neoplasm code should be sequenced first, followed by a code from M84.5 for the pathological fracture.

m. Current malignancy versus personal history of malignancy

When a primary malignancy has been excised but further treatment, such as an additional surgery for the malignancy, radiation therapy or chemotherapy is directed to that site, the primary malignancy code should be used until treatment is completed.

When a primary malignancy has been previously excised or eradicated from its site, there is no further treatment (of the malignancy) directed to that site, and there is no evidence of any existing primary malignancy at that site, a code from category Z85, Personal history of malignant neoplasm, should be used to indicate the former site of the malignancy.

Subcategories Z85.0–Z85.7 should only be assigned for the former site of a primary malignancy, not the site of a secondary malignancy. Codes from subcategory Z85.8-, may be assigned for the former site(s) of either a primary or secondary malignancy included in this subcategory.

See Section I.C.21. Factors influencing health status and contact with health services, History (of)

n. Leukemia, multiple myeloma, and malignant plasma cell neoplasms in remission versus personal history

The categories for leukemia, and category C90, Multiple myeloma and malignant plasma cell neoplasms, have codes indicating whether or not the leukemia has achieved remission. There are also codes Z85.6, Personal history of leukemia, and Z85.79, Personal history of other malignant neoplasms of lymphoid, hematopoietic and related tissues. If the documentation is unclear, as to whether the leukemia has achieved remission, the provider should be queried.

See Section I.C.21. Factors influencing health status and contact with health services, History (of)

o. **Aftercare following surgery for neoplasm**

   See Section I.C.21. Factors influencing health status and contact with health services, Aftercare

p. **Follow-up care for completed treatment of a malignancy**

   See Section I.C.21. Factors influencing health status and contact with health services, Follow-up

q. **Prophylactic organ removal for prevention of malignancy**

   See Section I.C.21. Factors influencing health status and contact with health services, Prophylactic organ removal

r. **Malignant neoplasm associated with transplanted organ**

   A malignant neoplasm of a transplanted organ should be coded as a transplant complication. Assign first the appropriate code from category T86.-, Complications of transplanted organs and tissue, followed by code C80.2, Malignant neoplasm associated with transplanted organ. Use an additional code for the specific malignancy.

Exercise 4.2 – Neoplasms

Instructions: Assign the appropriate ICD-10-CM code(s).

_____   1. Carcinoma *in situ*, cervix uteri (neoplasm)

_____   2. Choriocarcinoma (female patient)

_____   3. Hemangioma

_____   4. Kaposi's sarcoma

_____   5. Lipoma, skin of abdomen

ICD-10-CM Chapter 3: Diseases of the Blood and Blood-Forming Organs and Certain Disorders Involving the Immune Mechanism (D50–D89)

This ICD-10-CM chapter classifies the following:

- Nutritional anemias
- Hemolytic anemias
- Aplastic and other anemias and other bone marrow failure syndromes
- Coagulation defects, purpura, and other hemorrhagic conditions
- Other disorders of blood and blood-forming organs
- Intraoperative and postprocedural complications of the spleen
- Certain disorders involving the immune mechanism

Bone marrow is the principal site for hemopoietic cell proliferation and differentiation. One of the largest organs in the human body, hemopoietic tissue is responsible for producing erythrocytes (red blood cells), neutrophils, eosinophils, basophils, monocytes, platelets, and lymphocytes.

Anemia refers to a lower-than-normal erythrocyte count or level of hemoglobin in the circulating blood. A clinical sign rather than a diagnostic entity, anemia can be classified by three morphological variations of the erythrocyte: size (volume), hemoglobin content, and shape. These variations give clinicians clues to the specific type of anemia. In laboratory blood tests, erythrocyte size is gauged by estimating the volume of red cells in the circulating blood.

- Red cell volume (or mean corpuscular volume) is estimated by dividing the patient's hematocrit (percentage of red blood cells in whole blood) by the red blood cell count (RBC). Normal values are normocytic, abnormally low values are microcytic, and abnormally high values are macrocytic.

- Hemoglobin content refers to the average amount of hemoglobin in each red blood cell. This value, called the mean cell hemoglobin, is calculated by dividing the patient's hemoglobin by the number of red blood cells. Normal values are normochromic, less-than-normal values are hypochromic, and greater-than-normal values are hyperchromic.

- Shape is determined by microscopy. Normally, red blood cells have a smooth, concave shape. Erythrocytes with irregular shapes are called poikilocytes, a general term meaning "abnormally shaped." Terms referring to specific abnormal cell shapes include *acanthocytes, leptocytes, nucleated erythrocytes, macro-ovalocytes, schistocytes, helmet cells, teardrop cells, sickle cells*, and *target cells*.

Once the cell morphology is determined, the anemia can be further classified based on certain physiological and pathological criteria.

EXAMPLE: Constitutional aplastic anemia (D61.09) is classified physiologically as an anemia of hypoproliferation and pathologically as inborn error of heredity.

The term *coagulation defect* refers to deficiencies or disorders of hemostasis. A complicated process involving substances in the injured tissues, formed elements of blood (platelets and monocytes), and the coagulation proteins, coagulation requires the production of thrombin, a substance that stabilizes the platelet plug and forms the fibrin clot. Together they mechanically block the extravasation of blood from ruptured vessels. The coagulation process can be interrupted by a genetic or disease-caused protein deficiency, by an increase in the catabolism of coagulation proteins, or by antibodies directed against the coagulation proteins. Many proteins are involved in coagulation, many of which are identified by the term *factor* followed by a Roman numeral. The appropriate Roman numeral followed by the suffix *a* indicates the activated form of a coagulation factor.

EXAMPLE: When protein factor II (prothrombin) is activated by the enzyme thrombin, it is designated factor IIa.

The term *purpura* refers to a condition characterized by hemorrhage, or extravasation of blood, into the tissues, producing bruises and small red patches on the skin. Purpura may be associated with thrombocytopenia or can occur in a nonthrombocytopenic form. Thrombocytopenia is a decrease of the number of platelets in the circulating blood and may be primary (hereditary or idiopathic) or secondary to a known cause.

Diseases of white blood cells refer to increases, decreases, or genetic or idiopathic anomalies of white blood cells not associated with malignant disease classified to categories C81–C96, *Malignant neoplasms of lymphoid, hematopoietic and related tissue.*

ICD-10-CM Chapter-Specific Coding Guidelines

Chapter 3: Diseases of the Blood and Blood-Forming Organs and Certain Disorders Involving the Immune Mechanism (D50–D89)

Reserved for future guideline expansion.

Exercise 4.3 – Diseases of the Blood and Blood-Forming Organs and Certain Disorders Involving the Immune Mechanism

Instructions: Assign the appropriate ICD-10-CM code(s).

_____ 1. Acquired polycythemia

_____ 2. Acute posthemorrhagic anemia

_____ 3. Agranulocytosis

_____ 4. Chronic simple anemia

_____ 5. Chronic congestive splenomegaly

ICD-10-CM Chapter 4: Endocrine, Nutritional, and Metabolic Diseases (E00–E89)

This ICD-10-CM chapter classifies the following:

- Disorders of thyroid gland
- Diabetes mellitus
- Other disorders of glucose regulation and pancreatic internal secretion
- Disorders of other endocrine glands
- Intraoperative complications of endocrine system
- Malnutrition
- Other nutritional deficiencies
- Overweight, obesity, and other hyperalimentation
- Metabolic disorders
- Postprocedural endocrine and metabolic complications and disorders, not elsewhere classified

The endocrine system includes specialized organs and body tissues that produce, secrete, and store hormones. Hormones regulate the body's development, control the function of various tissues, support reproduction, and regulate metabolism. Hormones from the endocrine system are secreted into the blood, where proteins keep them intact and regulate their release. Other changes in the body also influence hormone secretions.

EXAMPLE: NORMAL HORMONE FUNCTION: Parathyroid hormone causes the body to increase the level of calcium in blood. As calcium levels rise, the secretion of parathyroid hormone decreases.

Nutritional deficiencies in ICD-10-CM Chapter 4 cover deficiencies in vitamins, minerals, and protein-calorie malnutrition. Metabolic diseases in ICD-10-CM Chapter 4 cover a wide range of diseases, including problems with amino acid and carbohydrate transport; lipoid metabolism; plasma protein metabolism; gout; mineral metabolism; and fluid, electrolyte, and acid-base imbalances. Cystic fibrosis, porphyrin, purine and pyrimidine metabolism, and obesity are also classified.

ICD-10-CM Chapter-Specific Coding Guidelines

Chapter 4: Endocrine, Nutritional, and Metabolic Diseases E00–E89

a. Diabetes mellitus

The diabetes mellitus codes are combination codes that include the type of diabetes mellitus, the body system affected, and the complications affecting that body system. As many codes within a particular category as are necessary to describe all of the complications of the disease may be used. They should be sequenced based on the reason for a particular encounter. Assign as many codes from categories E08–E13 as needed to identify all of the associated conditions that the patient has.

1) Type of diabetes

The age of a patient is not the sole determining factor, though most type 1 diabetics develop the condition before reaching puberty. For this reason, type 1 diabetes mellitus is also referred to as juvenile diabetes.

EXAMPLE: For **type 1 diabetes mellitus**, the patient's body is *unable to produce insulin*, and code E10.9 (Type 1 diabetes mellitus without complications) is reported if there are no complications.

2) Type of diabetes mellitus not documented

If the type of diabetes mellitus is not documented in the patient record, the default is E11.-, Type 2 diabetes mellitus.

EXAMPLE: For **type 2 diabetes mellitus**, the patient's body is *unable to properly use insulin produced*, and code E11.9 (Type 2 diabetes mellitus without complications) is reported if there are no complications.

3) Diabetes mellitus and the use of insulin and oral hypoglycemics

If the documentation in a patient record does not indicate the type of diabetes but does indicate that the patient uses insulin, code E11, Type 2 diabetes mellitus, should be assigned. An additional code should be assigned from category Z79 to identify the long-term (current) use of insulin or oral hypoglycemic drugs. If the patient is treated with both oral medications and insulin, only the code for long-term (current) use of insulin should be assigned. Code Z79.4 should not be assigned if insulin is given temporarily to bring a type 2 patient's blood sugar under control during an encounter.

EXAMPLE: Patient has type 2 diabetes mellitus without complications and has used insulin for long-term management. Report code E11.9 for diabetes and Z79.4 for use of insulin.

4) Diabetes mellitus in pregnancy and gestational diabetes

See Section I.C.15. Diabetes mellitus in pregnancy.
See Section I.C.15. Gestational (pregnancy induced) diabetes.

5) Complications due to insulin pump malfunction

(a) Underdose of insulin due to insulin pump failure

An underdose of insulin due to an insulin pump failure should be assigned T85.6-, Mechanical complication of other specified internal and external prosthetic devices, implants and grafts, that specifies the type of pump malfunction, as the principal or first-listed code, followed by code T38.3x6-, Underdosing of insulin and oral hypoglycemic [antidiabetic] drugs. Additional codes for the type of diabetes mellitus and any associated complications due to the underdosing should also be assigned.

EXAMPLE: Type 1 diabetic patient is seen for an elevated blood sugar level due to a malfunctioning insulin pump. Report codes T85.615A for mechanical breakdown of insulin pump, T38.3x6A for underdosing of insulin, and E10.65 for type 1 diabetes with hyperglycemia, in that order.

(b) Overdose of insulin due to insulin pump failure

The principal or first-listed code for an encounter due to an insulin pump malfunction resulting in an overdose of insulin should also be T85.6-, Mechanical complication of other specified internal and external prosthetic devices, implants and grafts, followed by code T38.3x1-, Poisoning by insulin and oral hypoglycemic [antidiabetic] drugs, accidental (unintentional).

EXAMPLE: Type 1 diabetic patient is treated for hypoglycemia due to malfunctioning insulin pump. Report code T85.614A for mechanical breakdown of insulin pump, T38.3x1A for poisoning by insulin (accidental), and E10.649 for diabetes with hypoglycemia (without coma).

6) Secondary diabetes mellitus

Codes under category E08, Diabetes mellitus due to underlying condition, E09, Drug or chemical induced diabetes mellitus, and E13, Other specified diabetes mellitus, identify complications/manifestations associated with secondary diabetes mellitus. Secondary diabetes is always caused by another condition or event (e.g., cystic fibrosis, malignant neoplasm of pancreas, pancreatectomy, adverse effect of drug, or poisoning).

(a) Secondary diabetes mellitus and the use of insulin or oral hypoglycemic drugs

For patients with secondary diabetes mellitus who routinely use insulin or oral hypoglycemic drugs, an additional code from category Z79 should be assigned to identify the long-term (current) use of insulin or oral hypoglycemic drugs. If the patient is treated with both oral medications and insulin, only the code for long-term (current) use of insulin should be assigned. Code Z79.4 should not be assigned if insulin is given temporarily to bring a secondary diabetic patient's blood sugar under control during an encounter.

(b) Assigning and sequencing secondary diabetes codes and its causes

The sequencing of the secondary diabetes codes in relationship to codes for the cause of the diabetes is based on the Tabular List instructions for categories E08, E09 and E13.

(i) Secondary diabetes mellitus due to pancreatectomy

For postpancreatectomy diabetes mellitus (lack of insulin due to the surgical removal of all or part of the pancreas), assign code E89.1, Postsurgical hypoinsulinemia. Assign a code from category E13 and a code from subcategory Z90.41-, Acquired absence of pancreas, as additional codes.

(ii) Secondary diabetes due to drugs

Secondary diabetes may be caused by an adverse effect of correctly administered medications, poisoning, or sequela of poisoning.

See Section I.C.19.e. for coding of adverse effects and poisoning, and section I.C.20. for external code reporting.

Courtesy of the Centers for Medicare & Medicaid Services, www.cms.gov.

Exercise 4.4 – Endocrine, Nutritional, and Metabolic Diseases

Instructions: Assign the appropriate ICD-10-CM code(s).

_____ 1. Diabetes mellitus, type 1, with hyperglycemia

_____ 2. Diabetes mellitus, type 2

_____ 3. Hyperprolactinemia

_____ 4. Morbid obesity due to excess calories

_____ 5. Polycystic ovaries

ICD-10-CM Chapter 5: Mental, Behavioral, and Neurodevelopmental Disorders (F01–F99)

This ICD-10-CM chapter classifies the following:

- Mental disorders due to known physiological conditions
- Mental and behavioral disorders due to psychoactive substance use
- Schizophrenia, schizotypal, delusional, and other non-mood psychotic disorders
- Mood [affective] disorders
- Anxiety, dissociative, stress-related, somatoform, and other nonpsychotic mental disorders
- Behavioral syndromes associated with physiological disturbances and physical factors
- Disorders of adult personality and behavior
- Intellectual disabilities
- Pervasive and specific developmental disorders
- Behavioral and emotional disorders with onset usually occurring in childhood and adolescence
- Unspecified mental disorders

ICD-10-CM Chapter-Specific Coding Guidelines

Chapter 5: Mental, Behavioral, and Neurodevelopmental Disorders (F01–F99)

a. **Pain disorders related to psychological factors**

Assign code F45.41, for pain that is exclusively related to psychological disorders. As indicated by the Excludes1 note under the category G89, a code from category G89 should not be assigned with code F45.41. Code F45.4, Pain disorders related to psychological factors, should be used with a code from category G89, Pain, not elsewhere classified, if there is documentation of a psychological component for a patient with acute or chronic pain.

See Section I.C.6. Pain.

b. **Mental and behavioral disorders due to psychoactive substance use**

1) **In remission**

Selection of codes for "in remission" for categories F10–F19, Mental and behavioral disorders due to psychoactive substance use (categories F10–F19 with -.11, -.21) requires the provider's clinical judgment. The appropriate codes for "in remission" are assigned only on the basis of provider documentation (as defined in the Official Guidelines for Coding and Reporting) unless otherwise instructed by the classification.

Mild substance use disorders in early or sustained remission are classified to the appropriate codes for substance abuse in remission, and moderate or severe substance use disorders in early or sustained remission are classified to the appropriate codes for substance dependence in remission.

2) **Psychoactive substance use, abuse and dependence**

When the provider documentation refers to use, abuse and dependence of the same substance (e.g. alcohol, opioid, cannabis, etc.), only one code should be assigned to identify the pattern of use based on the following hierarchy:

- If both use and abuse are documented, assign only the code for abuse.
- If both abuse and dependence are documented, assign only the code for dependence.
- If use, abuse and dependence are all documented, assign only the code for dependence.
- If both use and dependence are documented, assign only the code for dependence.

EXAMPLE: Patient is diagnosed with cannabis use, abuse, and dependence. Report code F12.20 for cannabis dependence only.

3) Psychoactive substance use, unspecified

As with all other unspecified diagnoses, the codes for unspecified psychoactive substance use disorders (F10.9-, F11.9-, F12.9-, F13.9-, F14.9-, F15.9-, F16.9-, F18.9-, F19.9-) should only be assigned based on provider documentation and when they meet the definition of a reportable diagnosis (*see Section III, Reporting Additional Diagnoses*). These codes are to be used only when the psychoactive substance use is associated with a physical, mental, or behavioral disorder, and such a relationship is documented by the provider.

EXAMPLE: The patient sprained her left ankle during a party where she says she was drinking and became intoxicated. Provider's diagnoses is left ankle sprain and alcohol use with intoxication. Report codes S93.402A for the sprained ankle and F10.929 for the alcohol use with intoxication.

c. Factitious Disorder

Factitious disorder imposed on self or Munchausen's syndrome is a disorder in which a person falsely reports or causes his or her own physical or psychological signs or symptoms. For patients with documented factitious disorder on self or Munchausen's syndrome, assign the appropriate code from subcategory F68.1-, Factitious disorder imposed on self.

Munchausen's syndrome by proxy (MSBP) is a disorder in which a caregiver (perpetrator) falsely reports or causes an illness or injury in another person (victim) under his or her care, such as a child, an elderly adult, or a person who has a disability. The condition is also referred to as "factitious disorder imposed on another" or "factitious disorder by proxy." The perpetrator, not the victim, receives this diagnosis. Assign code F68.A, Factitious disorder imposed on another, to the perpetrator's record. For the victim of a patient suffering from MSBP, assign the appropriate code from categories T74, Adult and child abuse, neglect and other maltreatment, confirmed, or T76, Adult and child abuse, neglect and other maltreatment, suspected.

See Section I.C.19.f. Adult and child abuse, neglect and other maltreatment

Exercise 4.5 – Mental, Behavioral, and Neurodevelopmental Disorders

Instructions: Assign the appropriate ICD-10-CM code(s).

_____ **1.** Alzheimer's disease

_____ **2.** Paranoid schizophrenia

_____ **3.** Alcoholic delirium tremens

_____ **4.** Episodic cocaine abuse

_____ **5.** Major depressive disorder, recurrent episode

ICD-10-CM Chapter 6: Diseases of the Nervous System (G00–G99)

This ICD-10-CM chapter classifies the following:

- Inflammatory diseases of the central nervous system
- Systemic atrophies primarily affecting the central nervous system
- Extrapyramidal and movement disorders
- Other degenerative diseases of the nervous system
- Demyelinating diseases of the central nervous system
- Episodic and paroxysmal disorders
- Nerve, nerve root, and plexus disorders
- Polyneuropathies and other disorders of the peripheral nervous system
- Diseases of myoneural junction and muscle
- Cerebral palsy and other paralytic syndromes
- Other disorders of the nervous system

ICD-10-CM Chapter-Specific Coding Guidelines

Chapter 6: Diseases of the Nervous System (G00–G99)

a. Dominant/nondominant side

Codes from category G81, *Hemiplegia and hemiparesis*, and subcategories, G83.1, *Monoplegia of lower limb*, G83.2, *Monoplegia of upper limb*, and G83.3, *Monoplegia, unspecified*, identify whether the dominant or nondominant side is affected. Should the affected side be documented, but not specified as dominant or nondominant, and the classification system does not indicate a default, code selection is as follows:

- For ambidextrous patients, the default should be dominant.
- If the left side is affected, the default is non-dominant.
- If the right side is affected, the default is dominant.

EXAMPLE: Patient is diagnosed with spastic hemiplegia, right side. Patient is left-handed. Report code G81.13 (Spastic hemiplegia affecting right nondominant side).

b. Pain – Category G89

1) General coding information

Codes in category G89, Pain, not elsewhere classified, may be used in conjunction with codes from other categories and chapters to provide more detail about acute or chronic pain and neoplasm-related pain, unless otherwise indicated below.

If the pain is not specified as acute or chronic, post-thoracotomy, postprocedural, or neoplasm-related, do not assign codes from category G89.

A code from category G89 should not be assigned if the underlying (definitive) diagnosis is known, unless the reason for the encounter is pain control/management and *not* management of the underlying condition.

(a) Category G89 codes as principal or first-listed diagnosis

Category G89 codes are acceptable as principal diagnosis or the first-listed code:

- When pain control or pain management is the reason for the admission/encounter (e.g., a patient with displaced intervertebral disc, nerve impingement, and severe back pain presents for injection of steroid into the spinal canal). The underlying cause of the pain should be reported as an additional diagnosis, if known.

- When a patient is admitted for the insertion of a neurostimulator for pain control, assign the appropriate pain code as the principal or first-listed diagnosis. When an admission or encounter is for a procedure aimed at treating the underlying condition and a neurostimulator is inserted for pain control during the same admission/encounter, a code for the underlying condition should be assigned as the principal diagnosis and the appropriate pain code should be assigned as a secondary diagnosis.

(b) **Use of category G89 codes in conjunction with site-specific pain codes**

(i) **Assigning category G89 codes and site-specific pain codes**

Codes from category G89 may be used in conjunction with codes that identify the site of pain (including codes from Chapter 18) if the category G89 code provides additional information. For example, if the code describes the site of the pain but does not fully describe whether the pain is acute or chronic, both codes should be assigned.

(ii) **Sequencing of category G89 codes with site-specific pain codes**

The sequencing of category G89 codes with site-specific pain codes (including Chapter 18 codes), is dependent on the circumstances of the encounter/admission as follows:

- If the encounter is for pain control or pain management, assign the code from category G89 followed by the code identifying the specific site of pain (e.g., encounter for pain management for acute neck pain from trauma is assigned code G89.11, Acute pain due to trauma, followed by code M54.2, Cervicalgia, to identify the site of pain).

- If the encounter is for any other reason except pain control or pain management, and a related definitive diagnosis has not been established (confirmed) by the provider, assign the code for the specific site of pain first, followed by the appropriate code from category G89.

2) **Pain due to devices, implants, and grafts**

See Section I.C.19. Pain due to medical devices.

3) **Postoperative pain**

The provider's documentation should be used to guide the coding of postoperative pain, as well as *Section III. Reporting Additional Diagnoses* and *Section IV. Diagnostic Coding and Reporting in the Outpatient Setting.* The default for post-thoracotomy and other postoperative pain not specified as acute or chronic is the code for the acute form.

Routine or expected postoperative pain immediately after surgery should not be coded.

(a) **Postoperative pain not associated with specific postoperative complication**

Postoperative pain not associated with a specific postoperative complication is assigned to the appropriate postoperative pain code in category G89.

(b) **Postoperative pain associated with specific postoperative complication**

Postoperative pain associated with a specific postoperative complication (such as painful wire sutures) is assigned to the appropriate code(s) found in Chapter 19, Injury, Poisoning, and Certain Other Consequences of External Causes. If appropriate, use additional code(s) from category G89 to identify acute or chronic pain (G89.18 or G89.28).

4) **Chronic pain**

Chronic pain is classified to subcategory G89.2. There is no time frame defining when pain becomes chronic pain. The provider's documentation should be used to guide the use of these codes.

5) **Neoplasm-related pain**

Code G89.3 is assigned to pain documented as being related, associated with or due to cancer, primary or secondary malignancy, or tumor. This code is assigned regardless of whether the pain is acute or chronic.

This code may be assigned as the principal or first-listed code when the stated reason for the admission/ encounter is documented as pain control/pain management. The underlying neoplasm should be reported as an additional diagnosis.

(continues)

ICD-10-CM Chapter-Specific Coding Guidelines (*continued*)

When the reason for the admission/encounter is management of the neoplasm and the pain associated with the neoplasm is also documented, code G89.3 may be assigned as an additional diagnosis. It is not necessary to assign an additional code for the site of the pain.

See Section I.C.2. for instructions on the sequencing of neoplasms for all other stated reasons for the admission/encounter (except pain control/pain management).

EXAMPLE: Patient with metastatic bone cancer has related chronic pain and is seen today for management of pain medication. Report codes G89.3 for neoplasm-related pain and C79.51 for secondary malignant neoplasm of bone.

6) Chronic pain syndrome

Central pain syndrome (G89.0) and chronic pain syndrome (G89.4) are different than the term "chronic pain," and therefore codes should only be used when the provider has specifically documented this condition.

See Section I.C.5. Pain disorders related to psychological factors.

Exercise 4.6 – Diseases of the Nervous System

Instructions: Assign the appropriate ICD-10-CM code(s).

_____ 1. Central pain syndrome
_____ 2. Bell's palsy
_____ 3. Acute pain due to trauma; cervicalgia
_____ 4. Congenital quadriplegia
_____ 5. Intraspinal abscess

ICD-10-CM Chapter 7: Diseases of the Eye and Adnexa (H00–H59)

This ICD-10-CM chapter classifies the following:

- Disorders of eyelid, lacrimal system, and orbit
- Disorders of conjunctiva
- Disorders of sclera, cornea, iris, and ciliary body
- Disorders of lens
- Disorders of choroid and retina
- Glaucoma
- Disorders of vitreous body and globe
- Disorders of optic nerve and visual pathways
- Disorders of ocular muscles, binocular movement, accommodation, and refraction
- Visual disturbances and blindness
- Other disorders of eye and adnexa
- Intraoperative and postprocedural complications and disorders of eye and adnexa, not elsewhere classified

ICD-10-CM Chapter-Specific Coding Guidelines

Chapter 7: Diseases of the Eye and Adnexa (H00–H59)

a. Glaucoma

1) Assigning glaucoma codes

Assign as many codes from category H40, Glaucoma, as needed to identify the type of glaucoma, the affected eye, and the glaucoma stage.

2) Bilateral glaucoma with same type and stage

When a patient has bilateral glaucoma and both eyes are documented as being the same type and stage, and there is a code for bilateral glaucoma, report only the code for the type of glaucoma, bilateral, with the seventh character for the stage. When a patient has bilateral glaucoma and both eyes are documented as being the same type and stage, and the classification does not provide a code for bilateral glaucoma (e.g., subcategories H40.10 and H40.20) report only one code for the type of glaucoma with the appropriate seventh character for the stage.

3) Bilateral glaucoma stage with different types or stages

When a patient has bilateral glaucoma and each eye is documented as having a different type or stage, and the classification distinguishes laterality, assign the appropriate code for each eye rather than the code for bilateral glaucoma. When a patient has bilateral glaucoma and each eye is documented as having a different type, and the classification does not distinguish laterality (i.e., subcategories H40.10, H40.11, and H40.20), assign one code for each type of glaucoma with the appropriate seventh character for the stage.

When a patient has bilateral glaucoma and each eye is documented as having the same type, but different stage, and the classification does not distinguish laterality (i.e., subcategories H40.10 and H40.20), assign a code for the type of glaucoma for each eye with the seventh character for the specific glaucoma stage documented for each eye.

4) Patient admitted with glaucoma and stage evolves during the admission

If a patient is admitted with glaucoma and the stage progresses during the admission, assign the code for highest stage documented.

EXAMPLE: Patient is admitted for treatment of primary open-angle glaucoma, left eye, with progression from mild to moderate. Report code H40.1122 for the higher stage of moderate glaucoma.

5) Indeterminate stage glaucoma

Assignment of the seventh character "4" for "indeterminate stage" should be based on the clinical documentation. The seventh character "4" is used for glaucomas whose stage cannot be clinically determined. This seventh character should not be confused with the seventh character "0," unspecified, which should be assigned when there is no documentation regarding the stage of the glaucoma.

b. Blindness

If "blindness" or "low vision" of both eyes is documented but the visual impairment category is not documented, assign code H54.3, Unqualified visual loss, both eyes. If "blindness" or "low vision" in one eye is documented but the visual impairment category is not documented, assign a code from H54.6-, Unqualified visual loss, one eye. If "blindness" or "visual loss" is documented without any information about whether one or both eyes are affected, assign code H54.7, Unspecified visual loss.

EXAMPLE: For a patient diagnosed with right eye low vision and left eye normal vision, report code H54.61.

Exercise 4.7 – Diseases of the Eye and Adnexa

Instructions: Assign the appropriate ICD-10-CM code(s).

_____   1. Primary open-angle glaucoma, mild stage, right eye
_____   2. Vitreous hemorrhage, left eye
_____   3. Degenerative myopia, bilateral eyes
_____   4. Alternating exotropia
_____   5. Cystoid macular degeneration, bilateral eyes

ICD-10-CM Chapter 8: Diseases of the Ear and Mastoid Process (H60–H95)

This ICD-10-CM chapter classifies the following:

- Diseases of external ear
- Diseases of middle ear and mastoid
- Diseases of inner ear
- Other disorders of the ear
- Intraoperative and postprocedural complications and disorders of the ear and mastoid process, not elsewhere classified

ICD-10-CM Chapter-Specific Coding Guidelines

Chapter 8: Diseases of the Ear and Mastoid Process (H60–H95)

Reserved for future guideline expansion.

Exercise 4.8 – Diseases of the Ear and Mastoid Process

Instructions: Assign the appropriate ICD-10-CM code(s).

_____   1. Swimmer's ear, right ear
_____   2. Acute serous otitis media, left ear
_____   3. Central perforation of tympanic membrane, left ear
_____   4. Vertigo of central origin
_____   5. Granulation of postmastoidectomy cavity, left ear

ICD-10-CM Chapter 9: Diseases of the Circulatory System (I00–I99)

This ICD-10-CM chapter classifies the following:

- Acute rheumatic fever
- Chronic rheumatic heart diseases
- Hypertensive diseases
- Ischemic heart diseases
- Pulmonary heart disease and diseases of pulmonary circulation
- Other forms of heart disease
- Cerebrovascular diseases
- Diseases of arteries, arterioles, and capillaries
- Diseases of veins, lymphatic vessels, and lymph nodes, not elsewhere classified
- Other and unspecified disorders of the circulatory system

ICD-10-CM Chapter-Specific Coding Guidelines

Chapter 9: Diseases of the Circulatory System (I00–I99)

a. Hypertension

The classification presumes a causal relationship between hypertension and heart involvement and between hypertension and kidney involvement, as the two conditions are linked by the term "with" in the Alphabetic Index. These conditions should be coded as related even in the absence of provider documentation explicitly linking them, unless the documentation clearly states the conditions are unrelated. For hypertension and conditions not specifically linked by relational terms such as "with," "associated with" or "due to" in the classification, provider documentation must link the conditions in order to code them as related.

1) Hypertension with heart disease

Hypertension with heart conditions classified to I50.- or I51.4, I51.7, I51.89, I51.9, are assigned to a code from category I11, Hypertensive heart disease. Use an additional code from category I50, Heart failure, to identify the type of heart failure in those patients with heart failure. The same heart conditions (I50.-, I51.4–I51.7, I51.89, I51.9) with hypertension are coded separately if the provider has specifically documented that they are unrelated to the hypertension. Sequence according to the circumstances of the admission/encounter.

EXAMPLE: Patient is diagnosed with acute right heart failure and has hypertension, which is managed by medication. Report codes I11.0 for hypertensive heart failure and I50.811 for acute right heart failure, in that order.

2) Hypertensive chronic kidney disease

Assign codes from category I12, Hypertensive chronic kidney disease, when both hypertension and a condition classifiable to category N18, Chronic kidney disease (CKD), are present. CKD should not be coded as hypertensive if the provider indicates the CKD is not related to the hypertension.

The appropriate code from category N18 should be used as a secondary code with a code from category I12 to identify the stage of chronic kidney disease.

See Section I.C.14. Chronic kidney disease.

If a patient has hypertensive chronic kidney disease and acute renal failure, an additional code for the acute renal failure is required.

EXAMPLE 1: Patient is hospitalized for hypertensive end-stage renal disease (ESRD). Report codes I12.0 for hypertensive ESRD and N18.6 for ESRD.

(continues)

ICD-10-CM Chapter-Specific Coding Guidelines (*continued*)

EXAMPLE 2: Patient treated for ESRD and also has hypertension due to hyperthyroidism. Report codes N18.6 for ESRD, I10 for hypertension, and E05.90 for hyperthyroidism.

3) Hypertensive heart and chronic kidney disease

Assign codes from combination category I13, Hypertensive heart and chronic kidney disease, when there is hypertension with both heart and kidney involvement. Assume a relationship between the hypertension and the chronic kidney disease, whether or not the condition is so designated. If heart failure is present, assign an additional code from category I50 to identify the type of heart failure.

The appropriate code from category N18, Chronic kidney disease, should be used as a secondary code with a code from category I13 to identify the stage of chronic kidney disease.

See Section I.C.14. Chronic kidney disease.

The codes in category I13, Hypertensive heart and chronic kidney disease, are combination codes that include hypertension, heart disease and chronic kidney disease. The Includes note at I13 specifies that the conditions included at I11 and I12 are included together in I13. If a patient has hypertension, heart disease and chronic kidney disease, then a code from I13 should be used, not individual codes for hypertension, heart disease and chronic kidney disease, or codes from I11 or I12.

For patients with both acute renal failure and chronic kidney disease, an additional code for acute renal failure is required.

4) Hypertensive cerebrovascular disease

For hypertensive cerebrovascular disease, first assign the appropriate code from categories I60-I69, followed by the appropriate hypertension code.

5) Hypertensive retinopathy

Subcategory H35.0, Background retinopathy and retinal vascular changes, should be used with a code from category I10–I15, Hypertensive disease to include the systemic hypertension. The sequencing is based on the reason for the encounter.

6) Hypertension, secondary

Secondary hypertension is due to an underlying condition. Two codes are required: one to identify the underlying etiology and one from category I15 to identify the hypertension. Sequencing of codes is determined by the reason for admission/encounter.

7) Hypertension, transient

Assign code R03.0, Elevated blood pressure reading without diagnosis of hypertension, unless patient has an established diagnosis of hypertension. Assign code O13.-, Gestational [pregnancy-induced] hypertension without significant proteinuria, or O14.-, Pre-eclampsia, for transient hypertension of pregnancy.

8) Hypertension, controlled

This diagnostic statement usually refers to an existing state of hypertension under control by therapy. Assign the appropriate code from categories I10–I15, Hypertensive diseases.

9) Hypertension, uncontrolled

Uncontrolled hypertension may refer to untreated hypertension or hypertension not responding to current therapeutic regimen. In either case, assign the appropriate code from categories I10–I15, Hypertensive diseases.

10) Hypertensive crisis

Assign a code from category I16, Hypertensive crisis, for documented hypertensive urgency, hypertensive emergency or unspecified hypertensive crisis. Code also any identified hypertensive disease (I10–I15). The sequencing is based on the reason for the encounter.

11) Pulmonary Hypertension

Pulmonary hypertension is classified to category I27, Other pulmonary heart diseases. For secondary pulmonary hypertension (I27.1, I27.2-), code also any associated conditions or adverse effects of drugs or toxins. The sequencing is based on the reason for the encounter, except for adverse effects of drugs (See Section I.C.19.e.).

b. Atherosclerotic coronary artery disease and angina

ICD-10-CM has combination codes for atherosclerotic heart disease with angina pectoris. The subcategories for these codes are I25.11, Atherosclerotic heart disease of native coronary artery with angina pectoris and I25.7, Atherosclerosis of coronary artery bypass graft(s) and coronary artery of transplanted heart with angina pectoris.

When using one of these combination codes it is not necessary to use an additional code for angina pectoris. A causal relationship can be assumed in a patient with both atherosclerosis and angina pectoris, unless the documentation indicates the angina is due to something other than the atherosclerosis.

If a patient with coronary artery disease is admitted due to an acute myocardial infarction (AMI), the AMI should be sequenced before the coronary artery disease.

See Section I.C.9. Acute myocardial infarction (AMI)

c. Intraoperative and postprocedural cerebrovascular accident

Medical record documentation should clearly specify the cause-and-effect relationship between the medical intervention and the cerebrovascular accident in order to assign a code for intraoperative or postprocedural cerebrovascular accident.

Proper code assignment depends on whether it was an infarction or hemorrhage and whether it occurred intraoperatively or postoperatively. If it was a cerebral hemorrhage, code assignment depends on the type of procedure performed.

d. Sequelae of cerebrovascular disease

1) Category I69, sequelae of cerebrovascular disease

Category I69 is used to indicate conditions classifiable to categories I60–I67 as the causes of sequela (neurologic deficits), themselves classified elsewhere. These "late effects" include neurologic deficits that persist after initial onset of conditions classifiable to categories I60–I67. The neurologic deficits caused by cerebrovascular disease may be present from the onset or may arise at any time after the onset of the condition classifiable to categories I60–I67.

Codes from category I69, Sequelae of cerebrovascular disease, that specify hemiplegia, hemiparesis and monoplegia identify whether the dominant or nondominant side is affected. Should the affected side be documented, but not specified as dominant or nondominant, and the classification system does not indicate a default, code selection is as follows:

- For ambidextrous patients, the default should be dominant.
- If the left side is affected, the default is non-dominant.
- If the right side is affected, the default is dominant.

2) Codes from category I69 with codes from I60–I67

Codes from category I69 may be assigned on a health care record with codes from I60–I67, if the patient has a current cerebrovascular disease and deficits from an old cerebrovascular disease.

3) Codes from category I69 and Personal history of transient ischemic attack (TIA) and cerebral infarction (Z86.73)

Codes from category I69 should not be assigned if the patient does not have neurologic deficits.

See Section I.C.21.4. History (of) for use of personal history codes.

(continues)

ICD-10-CM Chapter-Specific Coding Guidelines (*continued*)

e. Acute myocardial infarction (AMI)

1) **Type 1 ST elevation myocardial infarction (STEMI) and non-ST elevation myocardial infarction (NSTEMI)**

The ICD-10-CM codes for type 1 acute myocardial infarction (AMI) identify the site, such as anterolateral wall or true posterior wall. Subcategories I21.0-I21.2 and code I21.3 are used for type 1 ST elevation myocardial infarction (STEMI). Code I21.4, Non-ST elevation (NSTEMI) myocardial infarction, is used for type 1 non-ST elevation myocardial infarction (NSTEMI) and nontransmural MIs.

If a type 1 NSTEMI evolves to STEMI, assign the STEMI code. If a type 1 STEMI converts to NSTEMI due to thrombolytic therapy, it is still coded as STEMI.

For encounters occurring while the myocardial infarction is equal to, or less than, four weeks old, including transfers to another acute setting or a postacute setting, and the myocardial infarction meets the definition for "other diagnoses" (*see Section III, Reporting Additional Diagnoses*), codes from category I21 may continue to be reported. For encounters after the 4 week time frame and the patient is still receiving care related to the myocardial infarction, the appropriate aftercare code should be assigned, rather than a code from category I21. For old or healed myocardial infarctions not requiring further care, code I25.2, Old myocardial infarction, may be assigned.

2) **Acute myocardial infarction, unspecified**

Code I21.9, Acute myocardial infarction, unspecified, is the default for the unspecified term acute myocardial infarction or unspecified site. If only type 1 STEMI or transmural MI without the site is documented, assign code I21.3, ST (STEMI) elevation myocardial infarction of unspecified site.

3) **AMI documented as nontransmural or subendocardial but site provided**

If an AMI is documented as nontransmural or subendocardial, but the site is provided, it is still coded as a subendocardial AMI.

See Section I.C.21.3. for information on coding status post administration of tPA in a different facility within the last 24 hrs.

4) **Subsequent acute myocardial infarction**

A code from category I22, Subsequent ST elevation (STEMI) and non-ST elevation (NSTEMI) myocardial infarction, is to be used when a patient who has suffered an AMI has a new AMI within the 4 week time frame of the initial AMI. A code from category I22 must be used in conjunction with a code from category I21. The sequencing of the I22 and I21 codes depends on the circumstances of the encounter.

Do not assign code I22 for subsequent myocardial infarctions other than type 1 or unspecified. For subsequent type 2 AMI assign only code I21.A1. For subsequent type 4 or type 5 AMI, assign only code I21.A9.

If a subsequent myocardial infarction of one type occurs within 4 weeks of a myocardial infarction of a different type, assign the appropriate codes from category I21 to identify each type. Do not assign a code from I22. Codes from category I22 should only be assigned if both the initial and subsequent myocardial infarctions are type 1 or unspecified.

5) **Other types of myocardial infarction**

The ICD-10-CM provides codes for different types of myocardial infarction. Type 1 myocardial infarctions are assigned to codes I21.0–I21.4.

Type 2 myocardial infarction (myocardial infarction due to demand ischemia or secondary to ischemic imbalance) is assigned to code I21.A1, Myocardial infarction type 2 with the underlying cause coded first. Do not assign code I24.8, Other forms of acute ischemic heart disease, for the demand ischemia. Sequencing of type 2 AMI or the underlying cause is dependent on the circumstances of admission. If a type 2 AMI is described as NSTEMI or STEMI, only assign code I21.A1. Codes I21.01–I21.4 should only be assigned for type 1 AMIs.

Acute myocardial infarctions type 3, 4a, 4b, 4c and 5 are assigned to code I21.A9, Other myocardial infarction type.

The "Code also" and "Code first" notes should be followed related to complications, and for coding of postprocedural myocardial infarctions during or following cardiac surgery.

Exercise 4.9– Diseases of the Circulatory System

Instructions: Assign the appropriate ICD-10-CM code(s).

_____   **1.** Acute ST elevation myocardial infarction, inferolateral wall, initial episode of care

_____   **2.** Acute rheumatic endocarditis

_____   **3.** Aphasia, late effect of cerebrovascular disease

_____   **4.** Hypertension

_____   **5.** Mitral and aortic valve insufficiency

ICD-10-CM Chapter 10: Diseases of the Respiratory System (J00–J99)

This ICD-10-CM chapter classifies the following:

- Acute upper respiratory infections
- Influenza and pneumonia
- Other acute lower respiratory infections
- Other diseases of upper respiratory tract
- Chronic lower respiratory diseases
- Lung diseases due to external agents
- Other respiratory diseases principally affecting the interstitium
- Suppurative and necrotic conditions of the lower respiratory tract
- Other diseases of the pleura
- Intraoperative and postprocedural complications and disorders of respiratory system, not elsewhere classified
- Other diseases of the respiratory system

The respiratory system is responsible for pulmonary ventilation and the exchange of oxygen and carbon dioxide between the lungs and ambient air. The organs of the respiratory system also perform nonrespiratory functions such as warming and moisturizing the air passing into the lungs, providing airflow for the larynx and vocal cords for speech, and releasing excess body heat in the process of thermoregulation for homeostasis. The lungs also perform important metabolic and embolic filtering functions.

Coding Guidance Related to E-cigarette, or Vaping, Product Use

CMS released official diagnosis coding guidance for health care encounters and deaths related to *e-cigarette, or vaping, product use associated lung injury (EVALI)*. For EVALI patients, assign the code for the specific condition, such as:

- J68.0 (Bronchitis and pneumonitis due to chemicals, gases, fumes and vapors; includes chemical pneumonitis)
- J69.1 (Pneumonitis due to inhalation of oils and essences; includes lipoid pneumonia)
- J80 (Acute respiratory distress syndrome)
- J82 (Pulmonary eosinophilia, not elsewhere classified)
- J84.114 (Acute interstitial pneumonitis)
- J84.89 (Other specified interstitial pulmonary disease)

For patients with acute lung injury but without further documentation identifying a specific condition (e.g., bronchitis, pneumonitis), assign code J68.9 (Unspecified respiratory condition due to chemicals, gases, fumes, and vapors).

Poisoning and Toxicity

Acute nicotine exposure can be toxic, and children and adults have been poisoned by swallowing, breathing, or absorbing e-cigarette liquid through their skin or eyes. For these patients assign a code from subcategory T65.291- (Toxic effect of other nicotine and tobacco, accidental [unintentional]; includes Toxic effect of other tobacco and nicotine NOS). For a patient with acute tetrahydrocannabinol (THC) toxicity, assign a code from subcategory T40.7X1- (Poisoning by cannabis [derivatives], accidental [unintentional]).

Substance Use, Abuse, and Dependence

For patients with documented substance use, abuse, or dependence, assign additional codes identifying the substance(s) used. When provider documentation refers to use, abuse, and dependence of the same substance (e.g., nicotine, cannabis, etc.), assign just one code to identify the pattern of use based on the following hierarchy:

- If both use and abuse are documented, assign only the code for abuse
- If both abuse and dependence are documented, assign only the code for dependence
- If use, abuse, and dependence are all documented, assign only the code for dependence
- If both use and dependence are documented, assign only the code for dependence.

More than one code is to be assigned when the patient is diagnosed with use, abuse, and dependence of multiple substances.

EXAMPLE 1: For a patient who is diagnosed with both cannabis-related disorders and nicotine-related disorders, report a code from each of categories F12 (Cannabis related disorders) and F17 (Nicotine dependence).

EXAMPLE 2: For a patient who is diagnosed with vaping of nicotine, report a code from subcategory F17.29 (Nicotine dependence, other tobacco product) (because electronic nicotine delivery systems [ENDS] are non-combustible tobacco products).

Signs and symptoms

For patients presenting with signs and symptoms (e.g., fever) and where a definitive diagnosis has not been established, assign appropriate code(s) for each of the presenting signs and symptoms (e.g., R06.00, Dyspnea, unspecified).

ICD-10-CM Chapter-Specific Coding Guidelines

Chapter 10: Diseases of the Respiratory System (J00–J99)

a. Chronic obstructive pulmonary disease [COPD] and asthma

1) Acute exacerbation of chronic obstructive bronchitis and asthma

The codes in categories J44 and J45 distinguish between uncomplicated cases and those in acute exacerbation. An acute exacerbation is a worsening or a decompensation of a chronic condition. An acute exacerbation is not equivalent to an infection superimposed on a chronic condition, though an exacerbation may be triggered by an infection.

EXAMPLE: Patient is diagnosed with COPD with acute exacerbation. Code J44.1 is reported.

b. Acute respiratory failure

1) Acute respiratory failure as principal diagnosis

A code from subcategory J96.0, Acute respiratory failure, or subcategory J96.2, Acute and chronic respiratory failure, may be assigned as a principal diagnosis when it is the condition established after study to be chiefly responsible for occasioning the admission to the hospital, and the selection is supported by the Alphabetic Index and Tabular List. However, chapter-specific coding guidelines (such as obstetrics, poisoning, HIV, newborn) that provide sequencing direction take precedence.

EXAMPLE: Patient is diagnosed with acute and chronic respiratory failure for which code J96.20 is reported.

2) Acute respiratory failure as secondary diagnosis

Respiratory failure may be listed as a secondary diagnosis if it occurs after admission, or if it is present on admission but does not meet the definition of principal diagnosis.

3) Sequencing of acute respiratory failure and another acute condition

When a patient is admitted with respiratory failure and another acute condition (e.g., myocardial infarction, cerebrovascular accident, aspiration pneumonia), the principal diagnosis will not be the same in every situation. This applies whether the other acute condition is a respiratory or nonrespiratory condition. Selection of the principal diagnosis will be dependent on the circumstances of admission. If both the respiratory failure and the other acute condition are equally responsible for occasioning the admission to the hospital and there are no chapter-specific sequencing rules, the guideline regarding two or more diagnoses that equally meet the definition for principal diagnosis (Section II, C.) may be applied in these situations.

If the documentation is not clear as to whether acute respiratory failure and another condition are equally responsible for occasioning the admission, query the provider for clarification.

c. Influenza due to certain identified influenza viruses

Code only confirmed cases of influenza due to certain identified influenza viruses (category J09), and due to other identified influenza virus (category J10). This is an exception to the hospital inpatient guideline Section II, H. (Uncertain Diagnosis).

In this context, "confirmation" does not require documentation of positive laboratory testing specific for avian or other novel influenza A or other identified influenza virus. However, coding should be based on the provider's diagnostic statement that the patient has avian influenza, or other novel influenza A, for category J09, or has another particular identified strain of influenza, such as H1N1 or H3N2, but not identified as novel or variant, for category J10.

If the provider records "suspected" or "possible" or "probable" avian influenza, or novel influenza, or other identified influenza, then the appropriate influenza code from category J11, Influenza due to unidentified influenza virus, should be assigned. A code from category J09, Influenza due to certain identified influenza viruses, should not be assigned nor should a code from category J10, Influenza due to other identified influenza virus.

d. Ventilator associated pneumonia

1) Documentation of ventilator associated pneumonia

As with all procedural or postprocedural complications, code assignment is based on the provider's documentation of the relationship between the condition and the procedure.

Code J95.851, Ventilator associated pneumonia, should be assigned only when the provider has documented ventilator associated pneumonia (VAP). An additional code to identify the organism (e.g., *Pseudomonas aeruginosa*, code B96.5) should also be assigned. Do not assign an additional code from categories J12–J18 to identify the type of pneumonia.

Code J95.851 should not be assigned for cases where the patient has pneumonia and is on a mechanical ventilator and the provider has not specifically stated that the pneumonia is ventilator-associated pneumonia. If the documentation is unclear as to whether the patient has a pneumonia that is a complication attributable to the mechanical ventilator, query the provider.

2) Ventilator associated pneumonia develops after admission

A patient may be admitted with one type of pneumonia (e.g., code J13, Pneumonia due to Streptococcus pneumonia) and subsequently develop VAP. In this instance, the principal diagnosis would be the appropriate code from categories J12–J18 for the pneumonia diagnosed at the time of admission.

Code J95.851, Ventilator associated pneumonia, would be assigned as an additional diagnosis when the provider has also documented the presence of ventilator associated pneumonia.

Exercise 4.10 – Diseases of the Respiratory System

Instructions: Assign the appropriate ICD-10-CM code(s).

_____ 1. Acute frontal sinusitis
_____ 2. Allergic rhinitis due to pollen
_____ 3. Chronic obstructive pulmonary disease
_____ 4. Atelectasis
_____ 5. Croup

Summary

Chapter-specific coding guidelines clarify the assignment of ICD-10-CM disease codes. Unless otherwise indicated in an individual chapter-specific guideline, the ICD-10-CM chapter-specific guidelines apply to all health care settings.

Internet Links

ICD-10-CM/PCS updates: Go to *www.cdc.gov*. Click on Diseases & Conditions, click on the Data & Statistics link, scroll to the Tools heading, click on the Classification of Diseases, Functioning, and Disability link, and click on any of the ICD links.

ICD-10-CM Official Guidelines for Coding and Reporting (including chapter-specific coding guidelines): Go to *www.cdc.gov*. Enter "ICD-10-CM official guidelines" in the Search box, and click Search Now. Scroll down and click on the most current ICD-10-CM Guidelines link.

MedLine Plus Interactive Tutorials (for diseases and procedures): Go to *www.nlm.nih.gov*. Click on the Medline Plus link, click on Videos & Tools, and click to select any video, tool, game, or tutorial activity.

Review

Multiple Choice

Instructions: Select the most appropriate response after locating the ICD-10-CM code(s) for each disease.

1. Gram-negative septicemia due to *E. coli*.
   a. A41.4   b. A41.50   c. A41.51   d. A41.9

2. Metastatic carcinoma from the lung.
   a. C34.90, C79.9   c. D49.9, C34.90
   b. C79.9, D49.1   d. D49.9, C80.1

3. Type 2 diabetes mellitus with iritis.
   a. E08.39   b. E09.39   c. E10.39   d. E11.39

4. Anemia, neutropenia, and thrombocytopenia.
   a. D61.09   c. D64.9, D70.9, D69.6
   b. D61.9   d. P61.4, D70.4, D69.3

5. Alcohol-induced delirium tremens.
   a. F10.121, F10.20   c. F10.96, F10.26
   b. F10.231   d. G25.1, F10.20

6. Hemiparesis due to old spinal cord injury, lumbar region.
    a. G81.90, S34.01xS   **c.** G81.90, S34.109S
    b. G81.90, S30.9xxS   **d.** G81.90, S34.119S

7. Cerebral thrombosis.
    a. I66.09   **b.** I66.19   **c.** I66.29   **d.** I66.9

8. Human immunodeficiency virus disease.
    a. B20   **b.** R75   **c.** Z20.6   **d.** Z21

9. Primary open-angle glaucoma, right eye, mild stage
    a. H40.1111   **b.** H44.511   **c.** P15.3   **d.** Q15.0

10. Acute nasopharyngitis.
    a. J00   **b.** J02.9   **c.** J31.1   **d.** J31.2

11. Acute serous otitis media, left ear, with central perforated eardrum.
    a. H65.06   **c.** H72.02
    b. H65.05, H72.02   **d.** S09.22XA

12. Central pain syndrome.
    a. F45.41   **b.** G89.0   **c.** M79.10   **d.** R52

13. Spastic hemiplegia affecting left dominant side.
    a. G80.9   **b.** G81.02   **c.** G81.12   **d.** G81.92

14. Munchausen's by proxy.
    a. F68.10   **b.** F68.13   **c.** F68.A   **d.** F68.9

15. Postpancreatectomy diabetes mellitus.
    a. E13.9   **c.** E89.1, E13.9, Z90.41
    b. E89.1   **d.** Z90.41

Coding Practice – Diseases

Instructions: Assign the appropriate ICD-10-CM code(s) to each disease.

_____ 1. Classical hemophilia

_____ 2. Malignant neoplasm, right breast (female)

_____ 3. Multiple personality

_____ 4. Pneumonia due to streptococcus, group B

_____ 5. Postsurgical hypothyroidism

_____ 6. Pulmonary arteriosclerosis

_____ 7. Sand flea infestation

_____ 8. Cholera due to Vibrio cholerae 01, biovar eltor

_____ 9. Arachnoid cyst

_____ 10. Hypertensive emergency

_____ 11. Day blindness

_____ 12. Chronic mucoid otitis media, left ear

_____ 13. Hypertensive heart failure

_____ 14. Hypertensive end-stage renal disease

_____ 15. Acute respiratory failure

Chapter-Specific Coding Guidelines: ICD-10-CM Chapters 11–21

Chapter Outline

ICD-10-CM Chapter 11: Diseases of the Digestive System (K00–K95)

ICD-10-CM Chapter 12: Diseases of the Skin and Subcutaneous Tissue (L00–L99)

ICD-10-CM Chapter 13: Diseases of the Musculoskeletal System and Connective Tissue (M00–M99)

ICD-10-CM Chapter 14: Diseases of the Genitourinary System (N00–N99)

ICD-10-CM Chapter 15: Pregnancy, Childbirth, and the Puerperium (O00–O9A)

ICD-10-CM Chapter 16: Certain Conditions Originating in the Perinatal Period (P00–P96)

ICD-10-CM Chapter 17: Congenital Malformations, Deformations, and Chromosomal Abnormalities (Q00–Q99)

ICD-10-CM Chapter 18: Symptoms, Signs, and Abnormal Clinical and Laboratory Findings, Not Elsewhere Classified (R00–R99)

ICD-10-CM Chapter 19: Injury, Poisoning, and Certain Other Consequences of External Causes (S00–T88)

ICD-10-CM Chapter 20: External Causes of Morbidity (V00–Y99)

ICD-10-CM Chapter 21: Factors Influencing Health Status and Contact with Health Services (Z00–Z99)

Chapter Objectives

At the conclusion of this chapter, the student should be able to:

1. Define key terms related to chapter-specific coding guidelines for ICD-10-CM Chapters 11 through 21.
2. Assign codes to diseases of the digestive system according to chapter-specific guidelines.
3. Assign codes to diseases of the skin and subcutaneous tissue according to chapter-specific guidelines.
4. Assign codes to diseases of the musculoskeletal system and connective tissue according to chapter-specific guidelines.
5. Assign codes to diseases of the genitourinary system according to chapter-specific guidelines.
6. Assign codes to pregnancy, childbirth, and the puerperium according to chapter-specific guidelines.
7. Assign codes to certain conditions originating in the perinatal period according to chapter-specific guidelines.

8. Assign codes to congenital malformations, deformations, and chromosomal abnormalities according to chapter-specific guidelines.
9. Assign codes to symptoms, signs, and abnormal clinical and laboratory findings, not elsewhere classified, according to chapter-specific guidelines.
10. Assign codes to injury, poisoning, and certain other consequences of external causes according to chapter-specific guidelines.
11. Assign codes to external causes of morbidity according to chapter-specific guidelines.
12. Assign codes to factors influencing health status and contact with health service according to chapter-specific guidelines.

Key Terms

closed fracture	fracture	nonunion	perinatal period
compound fracture	malunion	open fracture	simple fracture

Introduction

This chapter includes content about chapter-specific coding guidelines for ICD-10-CM Chapters 11 through 21. Chapter-specific coding guidelines are used as a companion to the ICD-10-CM coding manual, which contains coding conventions to ensure accurate coding. (ICD-10-CM/PCS structure and conventions were discussed in Chapter 3.)

- Diseases of the Digestive System (K00–K95)
- Diseases of the Skin and Subcutaneous Tissue (L00–L99)
- Diseases of the Musculoskeletal System and Connective Tissue (M00–M99)
- Diseases of the Genitourinary System (N00–N99)
- Pregnancy, Childbirth, and the Puerperium (O00–O9A)
- Certain Conditions Originating in the Perinatal Period (P00–P96)
- Congenital Malformations, Deformations, and Chromosomal Abnormalities (Q00–Q99)
- Symptoms, Signs, and Abnormal Clinical and Laboratory Findings, Not Elsewhere Classified (R00–R99)
- Injury, Poisoning, and Certain Other Consequences of External Causes (S00–T88)
- External Causes of Morbidity (V00–Y99)
- Factors Influencing Health Status and Contact with Health Service (Z00–Z99)

ICD-10-CM Chapter 11: Diseases of the Digestive System (K00–K95)

This ICD-10-CM chapter classifies the following:

- Diseases of oral cavity and salivary glands
- Diseases of esophagus, stomach, and duodenum
- Diseases of appendix
- Hernia
- Noninfective enteritis and colitis
- Other diseases of intestines
- Diseases of peritoneum and retroperitoneum

- Diseases of liver
- Disorders of gallbladder, biliary tract, and pancreas
- Other diseases of the digestive system

The alimentary tract (or digestive tract) is the long, muscular tube that begins at the mouth and ends at the anus. Major digestive organs include the pharynx, esophagus, stomach, and intestines. Accessory, or secondary, organs include the salivary and parotid glands; jaw; teeth; and supporting structures of the teeth, tongue, liver, gallbladder and biliary tract, pancreas, and peritoneum. Structures that support the digestive process from outside this continuous tube are also included in this system: gallbladder, pancreas, and liver. (These organs provide secretions that are critical to food absorption and use by the body.)

EXAMPLE: The following are examples of diseases that interfere with the digestive function, and they are classified in ICD-10-CM Chapter 11.

- Dental caries (tooth decay), assigned ICD-10-CM code K02.9, has a direct effect on digestion because the disease process interferes with mastication, the mechanical breakdown of food by chewing.

- Portal hypertension, assigned ICD-10-CM code K76.6, is high blood pressure in the liver's portal circulatory system. Although it does not directly affect digestion, portal hypertension is included because it represents a disease of a digestive system organ. Portal hypertension has no apparent effect on the digestive process until the disease has progressed to the point that the liver can no longer perform its function as a digestive organ. (Portal hypertension can be caused by cirrhosis of the liver and other conditions that cause obstruction to the portal vein, such as cancer.)

ICD-10-CM Chapter-Specific Coding Guidelines

Chapter 11: Diseases of the Digestive System (K00–K95)

Reserved for future guideline expansion.

Courtesy of the Centers for Medicare & Medicaid Services, www.cms.gov.

Exercise 5.1 – Diseases of the Digestive System

Instructions: Assign the appropriate ICD-10-CM code(s).

_____ 1. Crohn's disease

_____ 2. Canker sore

_____ 3. Acute gastrojejunal ulcer, with perforation

_____ 4. Gastroesophageal reflux

_____ 5. Inguinal hernia

ICD-10-CM Chapter 12: Diseases of the Skin and Subcutaneous Tissue (L00–L99)

This ICD-10-CM chapter classifies the following:

- Infections of the skin and subcutaneous tissue
- Bullous disorders

- Dermatitis and eczema
- Papulosquamous disorders
- Urticaria and erythema
- Radiation-related disorders of the skin and subcutaneous tissue
- Disorders of skin appendages
- Intraoperative and postprocedural complications of skin and subcutaneous tissue
- Other disorders of the skin and subcutaneous tissue

ICD-10-CM Chapter-Specific Coding Guidelines

Chapter 12: Diseases of the Skin and Subcutaneous Tissue (L00–L99)

a. Pressure ulcer stage codes

1) Pressure ulcer stages

Codes in category L89, Pressure ulcer, are combination codes that identify the site and stage of the pressure ulcer. The ICD-10-CM classifies pressure ulcer stages based on severity, which is designated by stages 1–4, deep tissue pressure injury, unspecified stage, and unstageable.

Assign as many codes from category L89 as needed to identify all the pressure ulcers the patient has, if applicable. *See Section I.B.14 for pressure ulcer stage documentation by clinicians other than patient's provider.*

EXAMPLE: Patient is diagnosed with stage 4 pressure ulcer, right elbow, and stage 2 pressure ulcer, left elbow. Report codes L89.014 for the right elbow pressure ulcer and L89.022 for the left elbow pressure ulcer.

2) Unstageable pressure ulcers

Assignment of the code for unstageable pressure ulcer (L89.--0) should be based on the clinical documentation. These codes are used for pressure ulcers whose stage cannot be clinically determined (e.g., the ulcer is covered by eschar or has been treated with a skin or muscle graft). This code should not be confused with the codes for unspecified stage (L89.--9). When there is no documentation regarding the stage of the pressure ulcer, assign the appropriate code for unspecified stage (L89.--9).

EXAMPLE 1: Patient is diagnosed with pressure ulcer, right elbow, which cannot be staged due to presence of skin graft. Report code L89.010 (Pressure ulcer of right elbow, unstageable).

EXAMPLE 2: Patient is diagnosed with pressure ulcer, right upper back. Report code L89.119 (Pressure ulcer of right upper back, unspecified stage) because the provider did not document the stage. (A physician query should be generated to request staging information.)

3) Documented pressure ulcer stage

Assignment of the pressure ulcer stage code should be guided by clinical documentation of the stage or documentation of the terms found in the Alphabetic Index. For clinical terms describing the stage that are not found in the Alphabetic Index, and there is no documentation of the stage, the provider should be queried.

4) Patients admitted with pressure ulcers documented as healed

No code is assigned if the documentation states that the pressure ulcer is completely healed at the time of admission.

5) Pressure ulcers documented as healing

Pressure ulcers described as healing should be assigned the appropriate pressure ulcer stage code based on the documentation in the medical record. If the documentation does not provide information about the stage of the healing pressure ulcer, assign the appropriate code for unspecified stage.

(continues)

ICD-10-CM Chapter-Specific Coding Guidelines (*continued*)

If the documentation is unclear as to whether the patient has a current (new) pressure ulcer or if the patient is being treated for a healing pressure ulcer, query the provider.

For ulcers that were present on admission but healed at the time of discharge, assign the code for the site and stage of the pressure ulcer at the time of admission.

6) **Patient admitted with pressure ulcer evolving into another stage during the admission**

If a patient is admitted to an inpatient hospital with a pressure ulcer at one stage and it progresses to a higher stage, two separate codes should be assigned: one code for the site and stage of the ulcer on admission and a second code for the same ulcer site and the highest stage reported during the stay.

7) **Pressure-induced deep tissue damage**

For pressure-induced deep tissue damage or deep tissue pressure injury, assign only the appropriate code for pressure-induced deep tissue damage (L89.--6).

b. **Non-pressure chronic ulcers**

1) **Patients admitted with non-pressure ulcers documented as healed**

No code is assigned if the documentation states that the non-pressure ulcer is completely healed at the time of admission.

2) **Non-pressure ulcers documented as healing**

Non-pressure ulcers described as healing should be assigned the appropriate non-pressure ulcer code based on the documentation in the medical record. If the documentation does not provide information about the severity of the healing non-pressure ulcer, assign the appropriate code for unspecified severity.

If the documentation is unclear as to whether the patient has a current (new) non-pressure ulcer or if the patient is being treated for a healing non-pressure ulcer, query the provider.

For ulcers that were present on admission but healed at the time of discharge, assign the code for the site and severity of the non-pressure ulcer at the time of admission.

3) **Patient admitted with non-pressure ulcer that progresses to another severity level during the admission**

If a patient is admitted to an inpatient hospital with a non-pressure ulcer at one severity level and it progresses to a higher severity level, two separate codes should be assigned: one code for the site and severity level of the ulcer on admission and a second code for the same ulcer site and the highest severity level reported during the stay.

See Section I.B.14 for pressure ulcer stage documentation by clinicians other than patient's provider.

Courtesy of the Centers for Medicare & Medicaid Services, www.cms.gov.

Exercise 5.2 – Diseases of the Skin and Subcutaneous Tissue

Instructions: Assign the appropriate ICD-10-CM code(s).

_____ **1.** Alopecia areata

_____ **2.** Carbuncle, left foot

_____ **3.** Decubitus ulcer

_____ **4.** Impetigo

_____ **5.** Keloid

ICD-10-CM Chapter 13: Diseases of the Musculoskeletal System and Connective Tissue (M00–M99)

This ICD-10-CM chapter classifies the following:

- Infectious arthropathies
- Inflammatory polyarthropathies
- Osteoarthritis
- Other joint disorders
- Dentofacial anomalies [including malocclusion] and other disorders of jaw
- Systemic connective tissue disorders
- Deforming dorsopathies
- Spondylopathies
- Other dorsopathies
- Disorders of muscles
- Disorders of synovium and tendon
- Other soft tissue disorders
- Disorders of bone density and structure
- Other osteopathies
- Chondropathies
- Other disorders of the musculoskeletal system and connective tissue
- Intraoperative and postprocedural complications and disorders of musculoskeletal system, not elsewhere classified
- Biomechanical lesions, not elsewhere classified

Localized osteoarthrosis is classified as primary or secondary. Primary osteoarthritis (or polyarticular degenerative arthritis) has an unknown etiology (cause), which means it is idiopathic. It affects apophyseal joints (joints with nodular or bony eminence) of the hips, knees, spine, and small joints of the hands and feet. Secondary osteoarthritis (or monarticular arthritis) is caused by external or internal injuries (acute or chronic trauma) or disease processes and is confined to the joints of one area. Disease processes include endocrine, infectious, metabolic, and neuropathic disease, as well as disease processes that alter the normal structure and function of hyaline cartilage (e.g., chondrocalcinosis, gout, and Paget's disease).

> **EXAMPLE:** A patient is diagnosed with degenerative joint disease, bilateral knees. Assign ICD-10-CM code M17.0 (Bilateral osteoarthritis of knee).

ICD-10-CM Chapter-Specific Coding Guidelines

Chapter 13: Diseases of Musculoskeletal and Connective Tissue (M00–M99)

a. Site and laterality

Most of the codes within Chapter 13 have site and laterality designations. The site represents the bone, joint or the muscle involved. For some conditions where more than one bone, joint or muscle is usually involved, such as osteoarthritis, there is a "multiple sites" code available. For categories where no multiple site code is provided and more than one bone, joint or muscle is involved, multiple codes should be used to indicate the different sites involved.

(continues)

ICD-10-CM Chapter-Specific Coding Guidelines (*continued*)

EXAMPLE: Patient is diagnosed with enteropathic arthropathies of the left knee, ankle, and foot. Report code M07.69 for enteropathic arthropathies of multiple sites.

1) Bone versus joint

For certain conditions, the bone may be affected at the upper or lower end (e.g., avascular necrosis of bone, M87, Osteoporosis, M80, M81). Though the portion of the bone affected may be at the joint, the site designation will be the bone, not the joint.

EXAMPLE: Patient is diagnosed with avascular necrosis of bone (osteonecrosis), right index finger joint. Report code M87.844, Other osteonecrosis, right finger(s).

b. Acute traumatic versus chronic or recurrent musculoskeletal conditions

Many musculoskeletal conditions are a result of previous injury or trauma to a site, or are recurrent conditions. Bone, joint or muscle conditions that are the result of a healed injury are usually found in ICD-10-CM Chapter 13. Recurrent bone, joint or muscle conditions are also usually found in ICD-10-CM Chapter 13. Any current, acute injury should be coded to the appropriate injury code from ICD-10-CM Chapter 19. Chronic or recurrent conditions should generally be coded with a code from ICD-10-CM Chapter 13. If it is difficult to determine from the documentation in the record which code is best to describe a condition, query the provider.

c. Coding of Pathologic Fractures

7th character A is for use as long as the patient is receiving active treatment for the fracture. While the patient may be seen by a new or different provider over the course of treatment for a pathological fracture, assignment of the 7th character is based on whether the patient is undergoing active treatment and not whether the provider is seeing the patient for the first time.

7th character, D is to be used for encounters after the patient has completed active treatment and is receiving routine care for the fracture during the healing or recovery phase. The other 7th characters, listed under each subcategory in the Tabular List, are to be used for subsequent encounters for routine care of fractures during the healing and recovery phase as well as treatment of problems associated with the healing, such as malunions, nonunions, and sequelae.

Care for complications of surgical treatment for fracture repairs during the healing or recovery phase should be coded with the appropriate complication codes.

See Section I.C.19. Coding of traumatic fractures.

d. Osteoporosis

Osteoporosis is a systemic condition, meaning that all bones of the musculoskeletal system are affected. Therefore, site is not a component of the codes under category M81, Osteoporosis without current pathological fracture. The site codes under category M80, Osteoporosis with current pathological fracture, identify the site of the fracture, not the osteoporosis.

1) Osteoporosis without pathological fracture

Category M81, Osteoporosis without current pathological fracture, is for use for patients with osteoporosis who do not currently have a pathologic fracture due to the osteoporosis, even if they have had a fracture in the past. For patients with a history of osteoporosis fractures, status code Z87.310, Personal history of (healed) osteoporosis fracture, should follow the code from M81.

2) Osteoporosis with current pathological fracture

Category M80, Osteoporosis with current pathological fracture, is for patients who have a current pathologic fracture at the time of an encounter. The codes under M80 identify the site of the fracture. A code from category M80, not a traumatic fracture code, should be used for any patient with known osteoporosis who suffers a fracture, even if the patient had a minor fall or trauma, if that fall or trauma would not usually break a normal, healthy bone.

Exercise 5.3 – Diseases of the Musculoskeletal and Connective Tissue

Instructions: Assign the appropriate ICD-10-CM code(s).

_____ 1. Arthralgia, left hand, left lower leg, and left ankle

_____ 2. Claw foot, left (acquired)

_____ 3. Contracture of joint, left hip

_____ 4. Kissing spine

_____ 5. Muscle spasm, back

ICD-10-CM Chapter 14: Diseases of the Genitourinary System (N00–N99)

This ICD-10-CM chapter classifies the following:

- Glomerular diseases
- Renal tubulo-interstitial diseases
- Acute kidney failure and chronic kidney disease
- Urolithiasis
- Other disorders of kidney and ureter
- Other diseases of the urinary system
- Diseases of male genital organs
- Disorders of breast
- Inflammatory diseases of female pelvic organs
- Noninflammatory disorders of female genital tract
- Intraoperative and postprocedural complications and disorders of genitourinary system, not elsewhere classified

ICD-10-CM Chapter-Specific Coding Guidelines

Chapter 14: Diseases of the Genitourinary System (N00–N99)

a. Chronic kidney disease

   1) Stages of chronic kidney disease (CKD)

     The ICD-10-CM classifies CKD based on severity. The severity of CKD is designated by stages 1–5. Stage 2, code N18.2, equates to mild CKD; stage 3, code N18.3, equates to moderate CKD; and stage 4, code N18.4, equates to severe CKD. Code N18.6, End stage renal disease (ESRD), is assigned when the provider has documented end-stage renal disease (ESRD).

     If both a stage of CKD and ESRD are documented, assign code N18.6 only.

EXAMPLE: Patient is diagnosed with stage 2 CKD, for which code N18.2 is reported.

(continues)

ICD-10-CM Chapter-Specific Coding Guidelines (*continued*)

2) Chronic kidney disease and kidney transplant status

Patients who have undergone kidney transplant may still have some form of CKD because the kidney transplant may not fully restore kidney function. Therefore, the presence of CKD alone does not constitute a transplant complication. Assign the appropriate N18 code for the patient's stage of CKD and code Z94.0, Kidney transplant status. If a transplant complication such as failure or rejection is documented, see Section I.C.19.g. for information on coding complications of a kidney transplant. If the documentation is unclear as to whether the patient has a complication of the transplant, query the provider.

EXAMPLE: Patient is diagnosed with stage 1 chronic kidney disease (CKD) of transplanted kidneys. Report codes N18.1 for CKD and Z94.0 for kidney transplant status.

3) Chronic kidney disease (CKD) with other conditions

Patients with CKD may also suffer from other serious conditions, most commonly diabetes mellitus and hypertension. The sequencing of the CKD code in relationship to codes for other contributing conditions is based on the conventions in the Tabular List.

EXAMPLE: Patient is diagnosed with diabetes mellitus due to chronic kidney disease (CKD), stage 1. Report codes E08.22 for diabetes mellitus due to CKD and N18.1 for stage 1 CKD, in that order.

See I.C.9. Hypertensive chronic kidney disease.
See I.C.19. Chronic kidney disease and kidney transplant complications.

Exercise 5.4 – Diseases of the Genitourinary System

Instructions: Assign the appropriate ICD-10-CM code(s).

_____   **1.** Abscess of epididymis
_____   **2.** Chronic cystic mastitis, right breast
_____   **3.** Chronic prostatitis
_____   **4.** Diverticulitis of bladder
_____   **5.** Excessive menstruation with regular cycle

ICD-10-CM Chapter 15: Pregnancy, Childbirth, and the Puerperium (O00–O9A)

This ICD-10-CM chapter classifies the following, which occur during pregnancy, childbirth, and the six weeks immediately following childbirth:

- Pregnancy with abortive outcome
- Supervision of high-risk pregnancy
- Edema, proteinuria, and hypertensive disorders in pregnancy, childbirth, and the puerperium
- Other maternal disorders predominantly related to pregnancy

- Maternal care related to the fetus and amniotic cavity and possible delivery problems
- Complications of labor and delivery
- Encounter for delivery
- Complications predominantly related to the puerperium
- Other obstetric conditions, not elsewhere classified

Obstetrical Discharges

All obstetrical discharges require a code from ICD-10-CM Chapter 15, and these codes are *never* reported on the baby's record.

- When the pregnancy is incidental to the encounter, assign code Z33.1 (Pregnant state, incidental).
- When an obstetrical patient's encounter is related to her pregnancy, report a code from O00–O9A first, followed by codes for secondary conditions.
- When the obstetrical patient delivers, assign an outcome of delivery code from category Z37 as a secondary code.

ICD-10-CM Chapter-Specific Coding Guidelines

Chapter 15: Pregnancy, Childbirth, and the Puerperium (O00–O9A)

a. General rules for obstetric cases

1) **Codes from Chapter 15 and sequencing priority**

Obstetric cases require codes from Chapter 15, codes in the range O00–O9A, Pregnancy, Childbirth, and the Puerperium. Additional codes from other chapters may be used in conjunction with Chapter 15 codes to further specify conditions. Should the provider document that the pregnancy is incidental to the encounter, code Z33.1, Pregnant state, incidental, should be used in place of any Chapter 15 codes. It is the provider's responsibility to state that the condition being treated is not affecting the pregnancy.

EXAMPLE: Patient is at 30 weeks gestation and is treated for urinary tract infection (UTI) due to *Escherichia coli* (*E. coli*). Report codes O23.43 for third trimester UTI, B96.20 for *E. coli*, and Z3A.30 for 30 weeks of gestation of pregnancy.

2) **Chapter 15 codes used only on the maternal record**

Chapter 15 codes are to be used only on the maternal record, never on the record of the newborn.

3) **Final character for trimester**

The majority of codes in Chapter 15 have a final character indicating the trimester of pregnancy. The time frames the trimesters are indicated at the beginning of the chapter. If trimester is not a component of a code it is because the condition always occurs in a specific trimester, or the concept of trimester of pregnancy is not applicable. Certain codes have characters for only certain trimesters because the condition does not occur in all trimesters, but it may occur in more than just one.

Assignment of the final character for trimester should be based on the provider's documentation of the trimester (or number of weeks) for the current admission/encounter. This applies to the assignment of trimester for pre-existing conditions as well as those that develop during or are due to the pregnancy. The provider's documentation of the number of weeks may be used to assign the appropriate code identifying the trimester.

Whenever delivery occurs during the current admission, and there is an "in childbirth" option for the obstetric complication being coded, the "in childbirth" code should be assigned.

(continues)

ICD-10-CM Chapter-Specific Coding Guidelines (*continued*)

EXAMPLE: Patient is treated for malnutrition in pregnancy during her third trimester at 37 weeks. Report codes O25.13 for the pregnancy and Z3A.37 for the weeks of gestation.

4) **Selection of trimester for inpatient admissions that encompass more than one trimester**

In instances when a patient is admitted to a hospital for complications of pregnancy during one trimester and remains in the hospital into a subsequent trimester, the trimester character for the antepartum complication code should be assigned on the basis of the trimester when the complication developed, not the trimester of the discharge. If the condition developed prior to the current admission/encounter or represents a pre-existing condition, the trimester character for the trimester at the time of the admission/encounter should be assigned.

5) **Unspecified trimester**

Each category that includes codes for trimester has a code for "unspecified trimester." The "unspecified trimester" code should rarely be used, such as when the documentation in the record is insufficient to determine the trimester and it is not possible to obtain clarification.

6) **7th character for fetus identification**

Where applicable, a 7th character is to be assigned for certain categories (O31, O32, O33.3–O33.6, O35, O36, O40, O41, O60.1, O60.2, O64, and O69) to identify the fetus for which the complication code applies. Assign 7th character "0":

- For single gestations
- When the documentation in the record is insufficient to determine the fetus affected and it is not possible to obtain clarification.
- When it is not possible to clinically determine which fetus is affected.

b. **Selection of OB principal or first-listed diagnosis**

1) **Routine outpatient prenatal visits**

For routine outpatient prenatal visits when no complications are present, a code from category Z34, Encounter for supervision of normal pregnancy, should be used as the first-listed diagnosis. These codes should not be used in conjunction with Chapter 15 codes.

2) **Supervision of high-risk pregnancy**

Codes from category O09, Supervision of high-risk pregnancy, are intended for use only during the prenatal period. For complications during the labor or delivery episode as a result of a high-risk pregnancy, assign the applicable complication codes from Chapter 15. If there are no complications during the labor or delivery episode, assign code O80, Encounter for full-term uncomplicated delivery.

For prenatal outpatient visits for patients with high-risk pregnancies, a code from category O09, Supervision of high-risk pregnancy, should be used as the first-listed diagnosis.

Secondary Chapter 15 codes may be used in conjunction with these codes if appropriate.

3) **Episodes when no delivery occurs**

In episodes when no delivery occurs, the principal diagnosis should correspond to the principal complication of the pregnancy, which necessitated the encounter. Should more than one complication exist, all of which are treated or monitored, any of the complication codes may be sequenced first.

4) **When a delivery occurs**

When an obstetric patient is admitted and delivers during that admission, the condition that prompted the admission should be sequenced as the principal diagnosis. If multiple conditions prompted the admission, sequence the one most related to the delivery as the principal diagnosis. A code for any complication of the delivery should be assigned as an additional diagnosis. In cases of cesarean delivery, if the patient was admitted with a condition that resulted in the performance of a cesarean procedure, that condition should be selected as the principal diagnosis. If the reason for the admission was unrelated to the condition resulting in the cesarean delivery, the condition related to the reason for the admission should be selected as the principal diagnosis.

5) Outcome of delivery

A code from category Z37, Outcome of delivery, should be included on every maternal record when a delivery has occurred. These codes are not to be used on subsequent records or on the newborn record.

c. Pre-existing conditions versus conditions due to the pregnancy

Certain categories in Chapter 15 distinguish between conditions of the mother that existed prior to pregnancy (pre-existing) and those that are a direct result of pregnancy. When assigning codes from Chapter 15, it is important to assess if a condition was pre-existing prior to pregnancy or developed during or due to the pregnancy in order to assign the correct code.

Categories that do not distinguish between pre-existing and pregnancy-related conditions may be used for either. It is acceptable to use codes specifically for the puerperium with codes complicating pregnancy and childbirth if a condition arises postpartum during the delivery encounter.

d. Pre-existing hypertension in pregnancy

Category O10, Pre-existing hypertension complicating pregnancy, childbirth and the puerperium, includes codes for hypertensive heart and hypertensive chronic kidney disease. When assigning one of the O10 codes that includes hypertensive heart disease or hypertensive chronic kidney disease, it is necessary to add a secondary code from the appropriate hypertension category to specify the type of heart failure or chronic kidney disease.

See Section I.C.9. Hypertension.

e. Fetal conditions affecting the management of the mother

1) Codes from category O35 and O36

Codes from categories O35, Maternal care for known or suspected fetal abnormality and damage, and O36, Maternal care for other fetal problems, are assigned only when the fetal condition is actually responsible for modifying the management of the mother (i.e., by requiring diagnostic studies, additional observation, special care, or termination of pregnancy). The fact that the fetal condition exists does not justify assigning a code from this series to the mother's record.

2) *In utero surgery*

In cases when surgery is performed on the fetus, a diagnosis code from category O35, Maternal care for known or suspected fetal abnormality and damage, should be assigned identifying the fetal condition. Assign the appropriate procedure code for the procedure performed.

No code from Chapter 16, the perinatal codes, should be used on the mother's record to identify fetal conditions. Surgery performed *in utero* on a fetus is still to be coded as an obstetric encounter.

f. HIV infection in pregnancy, childbirth, and the puerperium

During pregnancy, childbirth, or the puerperium, a patient admitted because of an HIV-related illness should receive a principal diagnosis from subcategory O98.7-, Human immunodeficiency [HIV] disease complicating pregnancy, childbirth and the puerperium, followed by the code(s) for the HIV-related illness(es).

Patients with asymptomatic HIV-infection status admitted during pregnancy, childbirth, or the puerperium should receive codes of O98.7- and Z21, Asymptomatic human immunodeficiency virus [HIV] infection status.

g. Diabetes mellitus in pregnancy

See section I.C.4.a.3 for information on the long term use of insulin and oral hypoglycemic.

h. Long term use of insulin and oral hypoglycemics

Code Z79.4, Long-term (current) use of insulin, or code Z79.84, Long term (current) use of oral hypoglycemic drugs, should also be assigned if the diabetes mellitus is being treated with insulin or oral medications. If the patient is treated with both oral medications and insulin, only the code for insulin-controlled should be assigned.

(continues)

ICD-10-CM Chapter-Specific Coding Guidelines (*continued*)

i. Gestational (pregnancy-induced) diabetes

Gestational (pregnancy-induced) diabetes can occur during the second and third trimesters of pregnancy in women who were not diabetic prior to pregnancy. Gestational diabetes can cause complications in the pregnancy similar to those of pre-existing diabetes mellitus. It also puts the woman at greater risk of developing diabetes after the pregnancy. Codes for gestational diabetes are in subcategory O24.4, Gestational diabetes mellitus. No other code from category O24, Diabetes mellitus in pregnancy, childbirth, and the puerperium, should be used with a code from O24.4.

The codes under subcategory O24.4 include diet controlled, insulin controlled, and controlled by oral hypoglycemic drugs. If a patient with gestational diabetes is treated with both diet and insulin, only the code for insulin-controlled is required. If a patient with gestational diabetes is treated with both diet and oral hypoglycemic medications, only the code for "controlled by oral hypoglycemic drugs" is required.

Code Z79.4, Long-term (current) use of insulin, or code Z79.84, Long-term (current) use of oral hypoglycemic drugs, should not be assigned with codes from subcategory O24.4.

An abnormal glucose tolerance in pregnancy is assigned a code from subcategory O99.81, Abnormal glucose complicating pregnancy, childbirth, and the puerperium.

j. Sepsis and septic shock complicating abortion, pregnancy, childbirth and the puerperium

When assigning a Chapter 15 code for sepsis complicating abortion, pregnancy, childbirth, and the puerperium, a code for the specific type of infection should be assigned as an additional diagnosis. If severe sepsis is present, a code from subcategory R65.2, Severe sepsis, and code(s) for associated organ dysfunction(s) should also be assigned as additional diagnoses.

EXAMPLE: For a patient diagnosed as right tubal pregnancy with pelvic sepsis due to Enterococcus, report codes O00.101 (Right tubal pregnancy without intrauterine pregnancy), O08.82 (Sepsis following ectopic and molar pregnancy), and B95.2 (Enterococcus).

k. Puerperal sepsis

Code O85, Puerperal sepsis, should be assigned with a secondary code to identify the causal organism (e.g., for a bacterial infection, assign a code from category B95–B96, Bacterial infections in conditions classified elsewhere). A code from category A40, Streptococcal sepsis, or A41, Other sepsis, should not be used for puerperal sepsis. If applicable, use additional codes to identify severe sepsis (R65.2-) and any associated acute organ dysfunction.

l. Alcohol, tobacco, and drug use during pregnancy, childbirth, and the puerperium

1) Alcohol use during pregnancy, childbirth, and the puerperium

Codes under subcategory O99.31, Alcohol use complicating pregnancy, childbirth, and the puerperium, should be assigned for any pregnancy case when a mother uses alcohol during the pregnancy or postpartum. A secondary code from category F10, Alcohol related disorders, should also be assigned to identify manifestations of the alcohol use.

2) Tobacco use during pregnancy, childbirth, and the puerperium

Codes under subcategory O99.33, Smoking (tobacco) complicating pregnancy, childbirth, and the puerperium, should be assigned for any pregnancy case when a mother uses any type of tobacco product during the pregnancy or postpartum. A secondary code from category F17, Nicotine dependence, should also be assigned to identify the type of nicotine dependence.

3) Drug use during pregnancy, childbirth, and the puerperium

Codes under subcategory O99.32, Drug use complicating pregnancy, childbirth, and the puerperium, should be assigned for any pregnancy case when a mother uses drugs during the pregnancy or postpartum. This can involve illegal drugs, or inappropriate use or abuse of prescription drugs. Secondary code(s) from categories F11–F16 and F18–F19 should also be assigned to identify manifestations of the drug use.

m. Poisoning, toxic effects, adverse effects and underdosing in a pregnant patient

A code from subcategory O9A.2, Injury, poisoning and certain other consequences of external causes complicating pregnancy, childbirth, and the puerperium, should be sequenced first, followed by the appropriate injury, poisoning, toxic effect, adverse effect or underdosing code, and then the additional code(s) that specifies the condition caused by the poisoning, toxic effect, adverse effect or underdosing.

See Section I.C.19. Adverse effects, poisoning, underdosing and toxic effects.

n. Normal delivery, code O80

1) Encounter for full term uncomplicated delivery

Code O80 should be assigned when a woman is admitted for a full-term normal delivery and delivers a single, healthy infant without any complications antepartum, during the delivery, or postpartum during the delivery episode. Code O80 is always a principal diagnosis. It is not to be used if any other code from Chapter 15 is needed to describe a current complication of the antenatal, delivery, or postnatal period. Additional codes from other chapters may be used with code O80 if they are not related to or are in any way complicating the pregnancy.

2) Uncomplicated delivery with resolved antepartum complication

Code O80 may be used if the patient had a complication at some point during the pregnancy, but the complication is not present at the time of the admission for delivery.

3) Outcome of delivery for O80

Z37.0, Single live birth, is the only outcome of delivery code appropriate for use with O80.

EXAMPLE: Patient was admitted to the hospital and delivered a liveborn male infant. Report codes O80 (Encounter for full-term uncomplicated delivery) and Z37.0 (Single live birth).

o. The peripartum and postpartum periods

1) Peripartum and postpartum periods

The postpartum period begins immediately after delivery and continues for six weeks following delivery. The peripartum period is defined as the last month of pregnancy to five months postpartum.

2) Peripartum and postpartum complication

A postpartum complication is any complication occurring within the six-week period.

EXAMPLE: Patient is discharged from the hospital after third-trimester delivery of a single live female. Complications occurred during delivery, including "ablatio placenta" and "delayed postpartum bleed." Report codes O45.93 (Premature separation of placenta, unspecified, third trimester), O72.2 (Delayed and secondary postpartum hemorrhage), and Z37.0 (Single live birth).

3) Pregnancy-related complications after 6-week period

Chapter 15 codes may also be used to describe pregnancy-related complications after peripartum or postpartum period if the provider documents that a condition is pregnancy related.

4) Admission for routine postpartum care following delivery outside hospital

When the mother delivers outside the hospital prior to admission and is admitted for routine postpartum care and no complications are noted, code Z39.0, Encounter for care and examination of mother immediately after delivery, should be assigned as the principal diagnosis.

(continues)

ICD-10-CM Chapter-Specific Coding Guidelines (*continued*)

5) Pregnancy associated cardiomyopathy

Pregnancy associated cardiomyopathy, code O90.3, is unique in that it may be diagnosed in the third trimester of pregnancy but may continue to progress months after delivery. For this reason, it is referred to as peripartum cardiomyopathy. Code O90.3 is only for use when the cardiomyopathy develops as a result of pregnancy in a woman who did not have pre-existing heart disease.

p. Code O94, Sequelae of complication of pregnancy, childbirth, and the puerperium

1) Code O94

Code O94, Sequelae of complication of pregnancy, childbirth, and the puerperium, is for use in those cases when an initial complication of a pregnancy develops a sequelae requiring care or treatment at a future date.

2) After the initial postpartum period

This code may be used at any time after the initial postpartum period.

3) Sequencing of code O94

This code, like all late effect codes, is to be sequenced following the code describing the sequelae of the complication.

q. Termination of pregnancy and spontaneous abortions

1) Abortion with liveborn fetus

When an attempted termination of pregnancy results in a liveborn fetus, assign code Z33.2, Encounter for elective termination of pregnancy and a code from category Z37, Outcome of Delivery.

2) Retained products of conception following an abortion

Subsequent encounters for retained products of conception following a spontaneous abortion or elective termination of pregnancy, without complications, are assigned the appropriate code from category O03.4, Incomplete spontaneous abortion without complication, or code O07.4, Failed attempted termination of pregnancy without complication. This advice is appropriate even when the patient was discharged previously with a discharge diagnosis of complete abortion.

If the patient has a specific complication associated with the spontaneous abortion or elective termination of pregnancy in addition to retained products of conception, assign the appropriate complication code (e.g., O03.-, O04.-, O07.-) instead of code O03.4 or O07.4.

3) Complications leading to abortion

Codes from Chapter 15 may be used as additional codes to identify any documented complications of the pregnancy in conjunction with codes in categories in O07 and O08.

EXAMPLE: For a patient diagnosed with pelvic infection following ectopic pregnancy, report code O08.0 (Genital tract and pelvic infection following ectopic and molar pregnancy).

r. Abuse in a pregnant patient

For suspected or confirmed cases of abuse of a pregnant patient, a code(s) from subcategories O9A.3, Physical abuse complicating pregnancy, childbirth, and the puerperium, O9A.4, Sexual abuse complicating pregnancy, childbirth, and the puerperium, and O9A.5, Psychological abuse complicating pregnancy, childbirth, and the puerperium, should be sequenced first, followed by the appropriate codes (if applicable) to identify any associated current injury due to physical abuse, sexual abuse, and the perpetrator of abuse.

See Section I.C.19.f. Adult and child abuse, neglect and other maltreatment.

Exercise 5.5 – Pregnancy, Childbirth, and the Puerperium

Instructions: Assign the appropriate ICD-10-CM code(s).

_____   1. Amnionitis

_____   2. Engorgement of female breasts (postpartum)

_____   3. Gestational hypertension, third trimester

_____   4. Incoordinate uterine contractions

_____   5. Laceration of cervix (obstetric)

ICD-10-CM Chapter 16: Certain Conditions Originating in the Perinatal Period (P00–P96)

This ICD-10-CM chapter classifies the following:

- Newborn affected by maternal factors and by complications of pregnancy, labor, and delivery
- Disorders of newborn related to length of gestation and fetal growth
- Abnormal findings on neonatal screening

 NOTE:

Codes from ICD-10-CM Chapter 16 are reported for the baby's encounter *only.*

- Birth trauma
- Respiratory and cardiovascular disorders specific to the perinatal period
- Infections specific to the perinatal period
- Hemorrhagic and hematological disorders of newborn
- Transitory endocrine and metabolic disorders specific to newborn
- Digestive system disorders of newborn
- Conditions involving the integument and temperature regulation of newborn
- Other problems with newborn
- Other disorders originating in the perinatal period

This chapter classifies conditions that begin during the perinatal period even if death or morbidity occurs later. The **perinatal period** is the interval of time occurring before, during, and up to 28 days following birth. These codes classify causes of morbidity and mortality in the fetus or newborn. Additional codes can be assigned from other ICD-10-CM chapters to further specify the newborn's condition.

ICD-10-CM Chapter-Specific Coding Guidelines

Chapter 16: Certain Conditions Originating in the Perinatal Period (P00–P96)

For coding and reporting purposes, the perinatal period is defined as "before birth through the 28th day following birth." The following guidelines are provided for reporting purposes.

(continues)

ICD-10-CM Chapter-Specific Coding Guidelines (*continued*)

a. General perinatal rules

1) Use of Chapter 16 codes

They are *never* for use on the maternal record. Codes from Chapter 15, the obstetrics chapter, are never permitted on the newborn record. Chapter 16 codes may be used throughout the life of the patient if the condition is still present.

2) Principal diagnosis for birth record

When coding the birth episode in a newborn record, assign a code from category Z38, Liveborn infants according to place of birth and type of delivery, as the principal diagnosis. A code from category Z38 is assigned only once, to a newborn at the time of birth. If a newborn is transferred to another institution, a code from category Z38 should not be used at the receiving hospital.

A code from category Z38 is used only on the newborn record, not on the mother's record.

EXAMPLE: Single liveborn infant via vaginal delivery was diagnosed with Down syndrome. Report codes Z38.00 (single liveborn via vaginal delivery) and Q90.9 (Down syndrome).

3) Use of codes from other chapters with codes from Chapter 16

Codes from other chapters may be used with codes from Chapter 16 if the codes from the other chapters provide more specific detail. Codes for signs and symptoms may be assigned when a definitive diagnosis has not been established. If the reason for the encounter is a perinatal condition, the code from Chapter 16 should be sequenced first.

EXAMPLE: The patient is a 1-day-old single liveborn infant, delivered vaginally, who is diagnosed with transient tachypnea of newborn and cradle cap. Report codes Z38.00 for the single liveborn infant status, P22.1 for tachypnea, and L21.0 for cradle cap (seborrhea capitis).

4) Use of Chapter 16 codes after the perinatal period

Should a condition originate in the perinatal period, and continue throughout the life of the patient, the perinatal code should continue to be used regardless of the patient's age.

5) Birth process or community-acquired conditions

If a newborn has a condition that may be either due to the birth process or community-acquired and the documentation does not indicate which it is, the default is "due to the birth process" and the code from Chapter 16 should be used. If the condition is "community-acquired," a code from Chapter 16 should not be assigned.

6) Code all clinically significant conditions

All clinically significant conditions noted on routine newborn examination should be coded. A condition is clinically significant if it requires or has:

- Clinical evaluation
- Therapeutic treatment
- Diagnostic procedures
- Extended length of hospital stay
- Increased nursing care and/or monitoring
- Implications for future health care needs

Note: The perinatal guidelines listed above are the same as the general coding guidelines for "additional diagnoses," except for the final point regarding implications for future health care needs. Codes should be assigned for conditions that have been specified by the provider as having implications for future health care needs.

b. Observation and evaluation of newborns for suspected conditions not found

1) Use of Z05 codes

Assign a code from category Z05, Observation and evaluation of newborns and infants for suspected conditions ruled out, to identify those instances when a healthy newborn is evaluated for a suspected condition that is determined after study not to be present. Do not use a code from category Z05 when the patient has identified signs or symptoms of a suspected problem; in such cases code the sign or symptom.

2) Z05 on other than the birth record

A code from category Z05 may also be assigned as a principal or first-listed code for readmissions or encounters when the code from category Z38 code no longer applies. Codes from category Z05 are for use only for healthy newborns and infants for which no condition after study is found to be present.

3) Z05 on a birth record

A code from category Z05 is to be used as a secondary code after the code from category Z38, Liveborn infants according to place of birth and type of delivery.

c. Coding additional perinatal diagnoses

1) Assigning codes for conditions that require treatment

Assign codes for conditions that require treatment or further investigation, prolong the length of stay, or require resource utilization.

2) Codes for conditions specified as having implications for future health care needs

Assign codes for conditions that have been specified by the provider as having implications for future health care needs.

Note: This guideline should not be used for adult patients.

d. Prematurity and fetal growth retardation

Providers utilize different criteria in determining prematurity. A code for prematurity should not be assigned unless it is documented. Assignment of codes in categories P05, Disorders of newborn related to slow fetal growth and fetal malnutrition, and P07, Disorders of newborn related to short gestation and low birth weight, not elsewhere classified, should be based on the recorded birth weight and estimated gestational age.

Codes from category P05 should not be assigned with codes from category P07.

When both birth weight and gestational age are available, two codes from category P07 should be assigned, with the code for birth weight sequenced before the code for gestational age.

e. Low birth weight and immaturity status

Codes from category P07, Disorders of newborn related to short gestation and low birth weight, not elsewhere classified, are for use for a child or adult who was premature or had a low birth weight as a newborn and this is affecting the patient's current health status.

See Section I.C.21. Factors influencing health status and contact with health services, Status.

f. Bacterial sepsis of newborn

Category P36, Bacterial sepsis of newborn, includes congenital sepsis. If a perinate is documented as having sepsis without documentation of congenital or community acquired, the default is congenital and a code from category P36 should be assigned. If the P36 code includes the causal organism, an additional code from category B95, Streptococcus, Staphylococcus, and Enterococcus as the cause of diseases classified elsewhere, or B96, Other bacterial agents as the cause of diseases classified elsewhere, should not be assigned. If the P36 code does not include the causal organism, assign an additional code from category B96. If applicable, use additional codes to identify severe sepsis (R65.2-) and any associated acute organ dysfunction.

g. Stillbirth

Code P95, Stillbirth, is only for use in institutions that maintain separate records for stillbirths. No other code should be used with P95. Code P95 should not be used on the mother's record.

Exercise 5.6 – Certain Conditions Originating in the Perinatal Period

Instructions: Assign the appropriate ICD-10-CM code(s).

_____   1. Cyanotic attacks of newborn

_____   2. Exceptionally large baby

_____   3. Facial palsy, newborn

_____   4. Feeding problems in newborn

_____   5. Fetal blood loss

ICD-10-CM Chapter 17: Congenital Malformations, Deformations, and Chromosomal Abnormalities (Q00–Q99)

This ICD-10-CM chapter classifies the following congenital malformations (and deformations) according to body system (e.g., nervous system), along with cleft lip and cleft palate, and chromosomal abnormalities. Congenital malformations may be the result of genetic factors (chromosomes), teratogens (agents causing physical defects in the embryo), or both. The malformations may be apparent at birth or hidden and identified sometime after birth. Regardless of origin, dysmorphology (clinical structural abnormality) is generally the primary indication of a congenital anomaly; in many cases, a syndrome may be classified according to a single anatomical anomaly rather than a complex of symptoms.

ICD-10-CM does not differentiate between intrinsic abnormalities (defects related to the fetus) or extrinsic abnormalities (defects that are the result of intrauterine problems). ICD-10-CM also does make a distinction in the classification of an anomaly as compared to a deformity. An anomaly is a malformation caused by abnormal fetal development (e.g., transposition of great vessels, or spina bifida). A deformity is an alteration in structure caused by an extrinsic force, such as intrauterine compression. The force may cause a disruption in a normal fetal structure, including congenital amputations from amniotic bands. In some cases, assigning two codes is necessary to describe the condition.

ICD-10-CM Chapter-Specific Coding Guidelines

Chapter 17: Congenital Malformations, Deformations, and Chromosomal Abnormalities (Q00–Q99)

Assign an appropriate code(s) from categories Q00–Q99, Congenital malformations, deformations, and chromosomal abnormalities, when a malformation/deformation or chromosomal abnormality is documented. A malformation/deformation/or chromosomal abnormality may be the principal/first-listed diagnosis on a record or a secondary diagnosis.

When a malformation/deformation or chromosomal abnormality does not have a unique code assignment, assign additional code(s) for any manifestations that may be present.

When the code assignment specifically identifies the malformation/deformation or chromosomal abnormality, manifestations that are an inherent component of the anomaly should not be coded separately. Additional codes should be assigned for manifestations that are not an inherent component.

Codes from Chapter 17 may be used throughout the life of the patient. If a congenital malformation or deformity has been corrected, a personal history code should be used to identify the history of the malformation or deformity. Although present at birth, a malformation/deformation/chromosomal abnormality may not be identified until later in life.

Whenever the condition is diagnosed by the provider, it is appropriate to assign a code from codes Q00–Q99.

For the birth admission, the appropriate code from category Z38, Liveborn infants, according to place of birth and type of delivery, should be sequenced as the principal diagnosis, followed by any congenital anomaly codes, Q00–Q99.

EXAMPLE 1: Patient is diagnosed with Apert's syndrome (or acrocephalosyndactyly), which is a group of congenital syndromes that include peaking at the head due to premature closure of skull sutures and fusion or webbing of digits. Apert's syndrome is a single anatomical anomaly of a multicomplex syndrome, which can include fusion in the hands and facial anomalies. Report Q87.0 for Apert's syndrome.

EXAMPLE 2: Thalidomide phocomelia results from influence of the drug thalidomide on the developing fetus during the perinatal period. It is a congenital birth defect in which the hands and feet are attached to abbreviated arms and legs, respectively. To classify this condition, multiple codes are reported, including:

- Q71.13, Congenital absence of upper arm and forearm with hand present, bilateral
- Q72.13, Congenital absence of thigh and lower leg with foot present, bilateral
- P04.18, Newborn affected by other maternal medication

Codes Q71.13 and Q72.13 classify the limb deformities. Code P04.18 classifies the transmission of the drug across the placenta, which in this case resulted in the limb deformities.

Courtesy of the Centers for Medicare & Medicaid Services, www.cms.gov.

Exercise 5.7 – Congenital Malformations, Deformations, and Chromosomal Abnormalities

Instructions: Assign the appropriate ICD-10-CM code(s).

_____ 1. Anomalies of aortic arch (tortuous)

_____ 2. Congenital heart block

_____ 3. Congenital hydrocephalus

_____ 4. Cystic eyeball, congenital

_____ 5. Fissure of tongue, congenital

ICD-10-CM Chapter 18: Symptoms, Signs, and Abnormal Clinical and Laboratory Findings, Not Elsewhere Classified (R00–R99)

This chapter includes symptoms, signs, and abnormal clinical and laboratory findings, abnormal tumor markers, and ill-defined and unknown causes of mortality. In general, codes from this chapter are used to report symptoms, signs, and ill-defined conditions that point with equal suspicion to two or more diagnoses or represent important problems in medical care that may affect management of the patient. In addition, this chapter classifies abnormal findings that are reported without a corresponding definitive diagnosis. Codes for such findings can be located in the alphabetic index under the following terms:

- Abnormal, abnormality, abnormalities
- Decrease, decreased

- Elevation
- Findings, abnormal, without diagnosis

Codes from this chapter are used to report symptoms and signs that existed on initial encounter but proved to be transient and without a specified cause. Also included are provisional diagnoses for patients who fail to return for further investigation, cases referred elsewhere for further investigation before being diagnosed, and cases in which a more definitive diagnosis was not available for other reasons. Do not assign a code from ICD-10-CM categories R00–R99 when the symptoms, signs, and abnormal findings pertain to a definitive diagnosis.

ICD-10-CM Chapter-Specific Coding Guidelines

Chapter 18: Symptoms, Signs, and Abnormal Clinical and Laboratory Findings, Not Elsewhere Classified (R00–R99)

Chapter 18 includes symptoms, signs, abnormal results of clinical or other investigative procedures, and ill-defined conditions regarding which no diagnosis classifiable elsewhere is recorded. Signs and symptoms that point to a specific diagnosis have been assigned to a category in other chapters of the classification.

a. Use of symptom codes

Codes that describe symptoms and signs are acceptable for reporting purposes when a related definitive diagnosis has not been established (confirmed) by the provider.

EXAMPLE 1: The patient is seen in the office for severe headaches, which occur daily, and fatigue. Report codes R51 (headache) and R53.83 (fatigue).

EXAMPLE 2: The patient complains of abdominal pain, the physical examination reveals abdominal rigidity, and after workup the patient is diagnosed with acute appendicitis. Report code K35.80 (acute appendicitis). Do **not** assign symptom code R10.9 (abdominal pain) or sign code R19.30 (abdominal rigidity).

b. Use of a symptom code with a definitive diagnosis code

Codes for signs and symptoms may be reported in addition to a related definitive diagnosis when the sign or symptom is not routinely associated with that diagnosis, such as the various signs and symptoms associated with complex syndromes. The definitive diagnosis code should be sequenced before the symptom code.

Signs or symptoms that are associated routinely with a disease process should not be assigned as additional codes, unless otherwise instructed by the classification.

EXAMPLE: The patient is diagnosed with adenoviral pneumonia and epistaxis. Report codes J12.0 (adenoviral pneumonia) and R04.0 (epistaxis). (Epistaxis is not routinely associated with pneumonia and is coded separately.)

c. Combination codes that include symptoms

ICD-10-CM contains a number of combination codes that identify both the definitive diagnosis and common symptoms of that diagnosis. When using one of these combination codes, an additional code should not be assigned for the symptom.

d. **Repeated falls**

Code R29.6, Repeated falls, is for use for encounters when a patient has recently fallen and the reason for the fall is being investigated. Code Z91.81, History of falling, is for use when a patient has fallen in the past and is at risk for future falls. When appropriate, both codes R29.6 and Z91.81 may be assigned together.

e. **Coma scale**

The coma scale codes (R40.2-) can be used in conjunction with traumatic brain injury codes, acute cerebrovascular disease or sequelae of cerebrovascular disease codes. These codes are primarily for use by trauma registries, but they may be used in any setting where this information is collected. The coma scale may also be used to assess the status of the central nervous system for other non-trauma conditions, such as monitoring patients in the intensive care unit. The coma scale codes should be sequenced after the diagnosis code(s).

These codes, one from each subcategory, are needed to complete the scale. The 7th character indicates when the scale was recorded.

The 7th character should match for all three codes.

At a minimum, report the initial score documented on presentation at your facility. This may be a score from the emergency medicine technician (EMT) or in the emergency department. If desired, a facility may choose to capture multiple Glasgow coma scale scores.

Assign a code from subcategory R40.24, Glasgow coma scale, total score, when only the total score is documented in the medical record and not the individual score(s).

Do not report codes for individual or total Glasgow coma scale scores for a patient with a medically induced coma or a sedated patient.

See Section I.B.14 for coma scale documentation by clinicians other than patient's provider.

f. **Functional quadriplegia**

GUIDELINE HAS BEEN DELETED EFFECTIVE OCTOBER 1, 2017.

g. **SIRS due to non-infectious process**

The systemic inflammatory response syndrome (SIRS) can develop as a result of certain non-infectious disease processes, such as trauma, malignant neoplasm, or pancreatitis. When SIRS is documented with a non-infectious condition, and no subsequent infection is documented, the code for the underlying condition, such as an injury, should be assigned, followed by code R65.10, Systemic inflammatory response syndrome (SIRS) of non-infectious origin without acute organ dysfunction, or code R65.11, Systemic inflammatory response syndrome (SIRS) of non-infectious origin with acute organ dysfunction. If an associated acute organ dysfunction is documented, the appropriate code(s) for the specific type of organ dysfunction(s) should be assigned in addition to code R65.11. If acute organ dysfunction is documented, but it cannot be determined if the acute organ dysfunction is associated with SIRS or due to another condition (e.g., directly due to the trauma), the provider should be queried.

h. **Death NOS**

Code R99, Ill-defined and unknown cause of mortality, is only for use in the very limited circumstance when a patient who has already died is brought into an emergency department or other health care facility and is pronounced dead upon arrival. It does not represent the discharge disposition of death.

i. **NIHSS Stroke Scale**

The NIH stroke scale (NIHSS) codes (R29.7- -) can be used in conjunction with acute stroke codes (I63) to identify the patient's neurological status and the severity of the stroke. The stroke scale codes should be sequenced after the acute stroke diagnosis code(s).

At a minimum, report the initial score documented. If desired, a facility may choose to capture multiple stroke scale scores.

See Section I.B.14. for NIHSS stroke scale documentation by clinicians other than patient's provider.

Exercise 5.8 – Symptoms, Signs, and Abnormal Clinical and Laboratory Findings, Not Elsewhere Classified

Instructions: Assign the appropriate ICD-10-CM code(s).

_____ 1. Abnormal reflex

_____ 2. Ataxia

_____ 3. Elevated prostate specific antigen

_____ 4. Failure to thrive (child)

_____ 5. Elevated blood pressure reading

ICD-10-CM Chapter 19: Injury, Poisoning, and Certain Other Consequences of External Causes (S00–T88)

This chapter classifies the following:

- Injuries
- Effects of foreign body entering through natural orifice
- Burns and corrosions
- Frostbite
- Poisonings by, adverse effects of, and underdosing of drugs, medicaments, and biological substances
- Toxic effects of substances chiefly nonmedicinal as to source
- Other and unspecified effects of external causes
- Certain early complications of trauma
- Complications of surgical and medical care, not elsewhere classified

 NOTE:

Injury and poisoning codes are not assigned for complications of surgical wounds (e.g., postoperative infection). (For such conditions, refer to main term *Complication* in the ICD-10-CM index.)

Separate codes are assigned for each injury except when a combination code is provided in ICD-10-CM. When multiple codes are assigned, the code for the most serious injury is sequenced first (as determined by the provider and based on treatment provided).

Fractures

A **fracture** is a break in a bone resulting from two possible causes.

- Direct or indirect application of undue force against the bone (injury)
- Pathological changes resulting in spontaneous fractures (disease process)

The provider always determines whether a fracture is open or closed, which is one of the first determinations made. A **closed fracture** (or **simple fracture**) is contained beneath the skin and has intact ligaments and skin, while an **open fracture** (or **compound fracture**) indicates an associated open wound.

NOTE:

ICD-10-CM Chapter 19 classifies **malunion** (or **nonunion**) of fractured bones, which is the failure of the ends of a fractured bone to heal (unite) by adding a seventh character (e.g., S72.001k, S72.001p).

The following terms typically describe closed fractures:

- *Comminuted fracture:* A splintering of the fractured bone
- *Depressed fracture:* Portion of the skull broken and driven inward from a forceful blow
- *Fissured fracture:* Fracture that does not split the bone
- *Greenstick fracture:* Occurs in children; the bone is somewhat bent and partially broken
- *Impacted fracture:* One fractured bone end wedged into another
- *Linear fracture:* Fracture that is in a straight line
- *Slipped epiphysis:* Separation of the growth plate, which is the growing end of the bone, or epiphysis, from the shaft of the bone; occurs in children and young adults who still have active epiphyses
- *Spiral fracture:* Fracture resembles a helix or has a corkscrew shape

 Coding Tip

If there is no documentation whether a fracture is open or closed, the fracture is coded as closed.

An open fracture is classified as a compound fracture because it contains a wound that leads to the fracture or has broken bone ends protruding through the skin. There is a very high risk of infection with open fractures because the tissues are exposed to contaminants (toxins). There may be foreign bodies (or missiles) embedded in the tissues that must be removed during surgery, and puncture wounds may also be present.

Open and closed fractures may both be described as "complicated," which means a bone fragment has injured an internal organ.

EXAMPLE: Fractured ribs that injure internal organs is a complicated fracture.

Burns

Burns (ICD-10-CM categories T20–T32) are classified according to the following:

- Depth
  - First-degree (erythema)
  - Second-degree (blistering)
  - Third-degree (full-thickness involvement)
  - Extent (percentage of body surface involved) (Figure 5-1)
  - Agent (e.g., chemicals, fire, sun) (assigned an external cause code)

Adverse Effects, Poisonings, Underdosings, and Toxic Effects

Certain drugs, medicinal substances, and biological substances (or combinations of them) may cause toxic reactions. Such drug toxicity is classified in ICD-10-CM as

- *Adverse effects* (or adverse reaction): Appearance of a pathological condition caused by ingestion or exposure to a chemical substance properly administered or taken

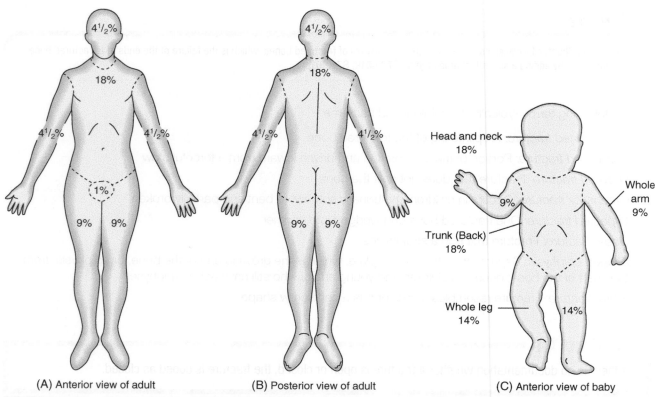

(A) Anterior view of adult   (B) Posterior view of adult   (C) Anterior view of baby

FIGURE 5-1 The rule of nines is used to calculate the percentage of body surface affected by burns (ICD-10-CM category T32). (Percentage assignments are modified to accommodate infants and children who have proportionately larger heads than adults or for patients who have large buttocks, thighs, or abdomen.)

- *Poisonings:* Occur as the result of an overdose, wrong substance administered or taken; or intoxication, which involves combining prescribed drugs with nonprescribed drugs or (ethyl) alcohol
- *Underdosings:* Taking less of a medication than is prescribed by a provider or a manufacturer's instruction
- *Toxic effects:* When a harmful substance is ingested or comes in contact with a person

 Coding Tip

To locate the code for an adverse effect, go to main term *Effect, adverse* in the ICD-10-CM Index to Diseases and Injuries, and locate the appropriate subterm (e.g., drugs and medicinals). Or, go to main term *Reaction*, and locate the appropriate subterm(s) (e.g., *drug NEC*). Then, assign the appropriate code from the Table of Drugs and Chemicals, Therapeutic Use column.

 Coding Tip

To locate the code for a poisoning or toxic effect, go to the Table of Drugs and Chemicals, determine the circumstances for the poisoning (e.g., accidental, intentional self-harm, assault, undetermined), and assign the code from the appropriate Poisoning column. If more than one substance is documented as causing the poisoning, assign codes from the Table of Drugs and Chemicals for *each* substance. Verify each code in the ICD-10-CM Tabular List of Diseases and Injuries.

Substance	Poisoning, Accidental (unintentional)	Poisoning, Intentional Self-harm	Poisoning, Assault	Poisoning, Undetermined	Adverse Effect	Underdosing
1-propanol	T51.3x1	T51.3x2	T51.3x3	T51.3x4	—	—
2-propanol	T51.2x1	T51.2x2	T51.2x3	T51.2x4	—	—
2, 4-D (dichloro-phenoxyacetic acid)	T60.3x1	T60.3x2	T60.3x3	T60.3x4	—	—
2, 4-toluene diisocyanate	T65.0x1	T65.0x2	T65.0x3	T65.0x4	—	—
2, 4, 5-T (trichloro-phenoxyacetic acid)	T60.1x1	T60.1x2	T60.1x3	T60.1x4	—	—
14-hydroxydihydromorphinone	T40.2x1	T40.2x2	T40.2x3	T40.2x4	T40.2x5	T40.2x6
ABOB	T37.5x1	T37.5x2	T37.5x3	T37.5x4	T37.5x5	T37.5x6
Abrine	T62.2x1	T62.2x2	T62.2x3	T62.2x4	—	—
Abrus (seed)	T62.2x1	T62.2x2	T62.2x3	T62.2x4	—	—
Absinthe	T51.0x1	T51.0x2	T51.0x3	T51.0x4	—	—
beverage	T51.0x1	T51.0x2	T51.0x3	T51.0x4	—	—
Acaricide	T60.8x1	T60.8x2	T60.8x3	T60.8x4	—	—
Acebutolol	T44.7x1	T44.7x2	T44.7x3	T44.7x4	T44.7x5	T44.7x6
Acecarbromal	T42.6x1	T42.6x2	T42.6x3	T42.6x4	T42.6x5	T42.6x6
Aceclidine	T44.1x1	T44.1x2	T44.1x3	T44.1x4	T44.1x5	T44.1x6
Acedapsone	T37.0x1	T37.0x2	T37.0x3	T37.0x4	T37.0x5	T37.0x6
Acefylline piperazine	T48.6x1	T48.6x2	T48.6x3	T48.6x4	T48.6x5	T48.6x6

Courtesy of the Centers for Medicare & Medicaid Services, www.cms.gov

FIGURE 5-2 ICD-10-CM Table of Drugs and Chemicals (partial)

Coding Tip

- The term *intoxication* often indicates that ethyl alcohol (e.g., beer, wine) was involved (e.g., alcohol intoxication) or that an accumulation effect of a medication in the patient's bloodstream occurred (e.g., Coumadin intoxication). When this occurs, assign a code from the appropriate Poisoning column of the ICD-10-CM Table of Drugs and Chemicals. In this situation, intoxication means "poisoning."

- When an accumulation effect of a medication occurs, assign the manifestation code first (e.g., dizziness) and a code from the ICD-10-CM Adverse Effect column in the Table of Drugs and Chemicals.

- When less of a medication than is prescribed by a provider or a manufacturer's instruction is taken, first code the medical condition for which the (*underdosing*) drug was prescribed by referring to the appropriate entry in the ICD-10-CM index. Then, code the medication by referring to the Underdosing column in the Table of Drugs and Chemicals (highlighted in yellow in Figure 5-2).

Refer to the Table of Drugs and Chemicals in the ICD-10-CM index (Figure 5-2) when assigning codes for adverse effects, poisonings, and toxic effects.

Coding Tip

The ICD-10-CM Table of Drugs and Chemicals contains a listing of the generic names of the drugs or chemicals. (Some publishers add brand names to the table.)

For adverse effects, first code the nature of the adverse effect (e.g., rash), followed by the chemical substance by referring to the Therapeutic Use column of the Table of Drugs and Chemicals. If more than one substance is documented as causing the adverse effect, assign codes from the Table of Drugs and Chemicals for *each* substance.

EXAMPLE: Gastritis due to prescribed tetracycline. In this statement, gastritis is the adverse effect (or manifestation) of the properly administered drug tetracycline. ICD-10-CM codes are reported as K29.70 (gastritis) and T36.4x5A (adverse effect of tetracycline), in that order.

For poisonings and toxic effects in ICD-10-CM, go to the appropriate Poisoning column of the Table of Drugs and Chemicals to assign the code. If more than one substance is documented as causing the poisoning or toxic effect, assign codes from the Table of Drugs and Chemicals for *each* substance. Next code the result or manifestation of the poisoning or toxic effect (e.g., coma).

EXAMPLE: Accidental (unintentional) overdose of tetracycline resulting in severe vomiting. ICD-10-CM codes are reported as T36.4x1A (unintentional accidental poisoning by tetracycline) and R11.2 (vomiting), in that order.

ICD-10-CM Chapter-Specific Coding Guidelines

Chapter 19: Injury, Poisoning, and Certain Other Consequences of External Causes (S00–T88)

a. Application of 7th Characters in Chapter 19

Most categories in Chapter 19 have a 7th character requirement for each applicable code. Most categories in this chapter have three 7th character values (with the exception of fractures): A, initial encounter, D, subsequent encounter and S, sequela. Categories for traumatic fractures have additional 7th character values. While the patient may be seen by a new or different provider over the course of treatment for an injury, assignment of the 7th character is based on whether the patient is undergoing active treatment and not whether the provider is seeing the patient for the first time.

For complication codes, active treatment refers to treatment for the condition described by the code, even though it may be related to an earlier precipitating problem. For example, code T84.50XA, Infection and inflammatory reaction due to unspecified internal joint prosthesis, initial encounter, is used when active treatment is provided for the infection, even though the condition relates to the prosthetic device, implant, or graft that was placed at a previous encounter.

7th character "A", initial encounter is used for each encounter where the patient is receiving active treatment for the condition. Examples of active treatment are: surgical treatment, emergency department encounter, and continuing treatment by the same or a different physician.

7th character "D" subsequent encounter is used for encounters after the patient has completed active treatment of the condition and is receiving routine care for the condition during the healing or recovery phase. Examples of subsequent care are: cast change or removal, an x-ray to check healing status of fracture, removal of external or internal fixation device, medication adjustment, other aftercare and follow up visits following treatment of the injury or condition.

EXAMPLE: Patient whose right maxillary fracture was initially treated 8 weeks ago returns again today for routine follow-up care; x-ray was performed to check the fracture's healing status, and results indicate the fracture is healing well. Report code S02.40CD (Maxillary fracture, right side, subsequent encounter for fracture with routine healing). (External cause of injury codes would also be reported to classify activity and place of occurrence.)

The aftercare Z codes should not be used for aftercare for conditions such as injuries or poisonings, where 7th characters are provided to identify subsequent care. For example, for aftercare of an injury, assign the acute injury code with the 7th character "D" (subsequent encounter).

7th character "S", sequela, is for use for complications or conditions that arise as a direct result of a condition, such as scar formation after a burn. The scars are sequelae of the burn. When using 7th character "S", it is necessary to use both the injury code that precipitated the sequela and the code for the sequela itself. The "S" is added only to the injury code, not the sequela code. The 7th character "S" identifies the injury responsible for the sequela. The specific type of sequela (e.g. scar) is sequenced first, followed by the injury code.

See Section I.B.10 Sequelae, (Late Effects).

b. Coding of injuries

When coding injuries, assign separate codes for each injury unless a combination code is provided, in which case the combination code is assigned. Codes from category T07, Unspecified multiple injuries should not be assigned in the inpatient setting unless information for a more specific code is not available. Traumatic injury codes (S00-T14.9) are not to be used for normal, healing surgical wounds or to identify complications of surgical wounds.

The code for the most serious injury, as determined by the provider and the focus of treatment, is sequenced first.

1) Superficial injuries

Superficial injuries such as abrasions or contusions are not coded when associated with more severe injuries of the same site.

EXAMPLE: Patient is diagnosed with abrasions and contusions of the upper right arm and closed greenstick fracture of shaft, right humerus. Report code S42.311A (Greenstick fracture of shaft of humerus, right arm, initial encounter for closed fracture) with external cause of injury codes for activity and place of occurrence. Do not assign codes to the abrasions and contusions.

2) Primary injury with damage to nerves/blood vessels

When a primary injury results in minor damage to peripheral nerves or blood vessels, the primary injury is sequenced first with additional code(s) for injuries to nerves and spinal cord (such as category S04), and/or injury to blood vessels (such as category S15). When the primary injury is to the blood vessels or nerves, that injury should be sequenced first.

3) Iatrogenic injuries

Injury codes from Chapter 19 should not be assigned for injuries that occur during, or as a result of, a medical intervention. Assign the appropriate complication code(s).

c. Coding of traumatic fractures

The principles of multiple coding of injuries should be followed in coding fractures. Fractures of specified sites are coded individually by site in accordance with both the provisions within categories S02, S12, S22, S32, S42, S49, S52, S59, S62, S72, S79, S82, S89, S92 and the level of detail furnished by medical record content. A fracture not indicated as open or closed should be coded to closed. A fracture not indicated whether displaced or not displaced should be coded to displaced.

More specific guidelines are as follows:

1) Initial vs. subsequent encounter for fractures

Traumatic fractures are coded using the appropriate 7th character extension for initial encounter (A, B, C) for each encounter where the patient is receiving active treatment for the fracture. Examples of active treatment are: surgical treatment, emergency department encounter, and evaluation and continuing (ongoing) treatment by the same or different physician. The appropriate 7th character for initial encounter should also be assigned for a patient who delayed seeking treatment for the fracture or nonunion.

Fractures are coded using the appropriate 7th character extension for subsequent care for encounters after the patient has completed active treatment of the fracture and is receiving routine care for the fracture during the healing or recovery phase.

Care for complications of surgical treatment for fracture repairs during the healing or recovery phase should be coded with the appropriate complication codes.

(continues)

ICD-10-CM Chapter-Specific Coding Guidelines (*continued*)

Care of complications of fractures, such as malunion and nonunion, should be reported with the appropriate 7th character extensions for subsequent care with nonunion (K, M, N) or subsequent care with malunion (P, Q, R).

Malunion/nonunion: The appropriate 7th character for initial encounter should also be assigned for a patient who delayed seeking treatment for the fracture or nonunion.

The open fracture designations in the assignment of the 7th character for fractures of the forearm, femur and lower leg, including ankle are based on the Gustilo open fracture classification. When the Gustilo classification type is not specified for an open fracture, the 7th character for open fracture type I or II should be assigned (B, E, H, M, Q).

A code from category M80, not a traumatic fracture code, should be used for any patient with known osteoporosis who suffers a fracture, even if the patient had a minor fall or trauma, if that fall or trauma would not usually break a normal, healthy bone.

See Section I.C.13. Osteoporosis.

The aftercare Z codes should not be used for aftercare for traumatic fractures. For aftercare of a traumatic fracture, assign the acute fracture code with the appropriate 7th character.

2) Multiple fractures sequencing

Multiple fractures are sequenced in accordance with the severity of the fracture.

3) Physeal fractures

For physeal fractures, assign only the code identifying the type of physeal fracture. Do not assign a separate code to identify the specific bone that is fractured. (A *physeal fracture* is a growth-plate fracture.)

d. Coding of burns and corrosions

The ICD-10-CM makes a distinction between burns and corrosions. The burn codes are for thermal burns, except sunburns, that come from a heat source, such as a fire or hot appliance. The burn codes are also for burns resulting from electricity and radiation. Corrosions are burns due to chemicals. The guidelines are the same for burns and corrosions.

Current burns (T20–T25) are classified by depth, extent and by agent (X code). Burns are classified by depth as first degree (erythema), second degree (blistering), and third degree (full-thickness involvement). Burns of the eye and internal organs (T26–T28) are classified by site, but not by degree.

1) Sequencing of burn and related condition codes

Sequence first the code that reflects the highest degree of burn when more than one burn is present.

(a) When the reason for the admission or encounter is for treatment of external multiple burns, sequence first the code that reflects the burn of the highest degree.

(b) When a patient has both internal and external burns, the circumstances of admission govern the selection of the principal diagnosis or first-listed diagnosis.

(c) When a patient is admitted for burn injuries and other related conditions such as smoke inhalation and/ or respiratory failure, the circumstances of admission govern the selection of the principal or first-listed diagnosis.

2) Burns of the same anatomic site

Classify burns of the same anatomic site and on the same side but of different degrees to the subcategory identifying the highest degree recorded in the diagnosis (i.e., for second and third degree burns of right thigh, assign only code T24.311-).

3) Nonhealing burns

Nonhealing burns are coded as acute burns.

Necrosis of burned skin should be coded as a nonhealed burn.

4) Infected burn

For any documented infected burn site, use an additional code for the infection.

5) Assign separate codes for each burn site

When coding burns, assign separate codes for each burn site. Category T30, Burn and corrosion, body region, unspecified, is extremely vague and should rarely be used.

Codes for burns of "multiple sites" should only be assigned when the medical record documentation does not specify the individual sites.

6) Burns and corrosions classified according to extent of body surface involved

Assign codes from category T31, Burns classified according to extent of body surface involved, or T32, Corrosions classified according to extent of body surface involved, when the site of the burn is not specified or when there is a need for additional data. It is advisable to use category T31 as additional coding when needed to provide data for evaluating burn mortality, such as that needed by burn units. It is also advisable to use category T31 as an additional code for reporting purposes when there is mention of a third-degree burn involving 20 percent or more of the body surface.

Categories T31 and T32 are based on the classic "rule of nines" in estimating body surface involved: head and neck are assigned nine percent, each arm nine percent, each leg 18 percent, the anterior trunk 18 percent, posterior trunk 18 percent, and genitalia one percent. Providers may change these percentage assignments where necessary to accommodate infants and children who have proportionately larger heads than adults, and patients who have large buttocks, thighs, or abdomen that involve burns.

7) Encounters for treatment of sequela of burns

Encounters for the treatment of the late effects (sequelae) of burns or corrosions (i.e., scars or joint contractures) should be coded with a burn or corrosion code with the 7th character "S" for sequela.

8) Sequelae with a late effect code and current burn

When appropriate, both a code for a current burn or corrosion with 7th character "A" or "D" and a burn or corrosion code with 7th character "S" may be assigned on the same record (when both a current burn and sequelae of an old burn exist). Burns and corrosions do not heal at the same rate and a current healing wound may still exist with sequela of a healed burn or corrosion.

9) Use of an external cause code with burns and corrosions

An external cause code should be used with burns and corrosions to identify the source and intent of the burn, as well as the place where it occurred.

e. Adverse effects, poisoning, underdosing, and toxic effects

Codes in categories T36–T65 are combination codes that include the substance that was taken as well as the intent. No additional external cause code is required for poisonings, toxic effects, adverse effects and underdosing codes.

1) Do not code directly from the Table of Drugs and Chemicals

Do not code directly from the Table of Drugs and Chemicals. Always refer back to the Tabular List.

2) Use as many codes as necessary to describe

Use as many codes as necessary to describe completely all drugs, medicinal or biological substances.

3) If the same code would describe the causative agent

If the same code would describe the causative agent for more than one adverse reaction, poisoning, toxic effect or underdosing, assign the code only once.

4) If two or more drugs, medicinal or biological substances

If two or more drugs, medicinal or biological substances are taken, code each individually unless a combination code is listed in the Table of Drugs and Chemicals.

If multiple unspecified drugs, medicinal or biological substances were taken, assign the appropriate code from subcategory T50.91, Poisoning by, adverse effect of and underdosing of multiple unspecified drugs, medicaments and biological substances.

(continues)

ICD-10-CM Chapter-Specific Coding Guidelines (*continued*)

5) The occurrence of drug toxicity is classified in ICD-10-CM as follows:

(a) Adverse effect

When coding an adverse effect of a drug that has been correctly prescribed and properly administered, assign the appropriate code for the nature of the adverse effect followed by the appropriate code for the adverse effect of the drug (T36–T50). The code for the drug should have a 5th or 6th character "5" (for example T36.0X5-). Examples of the nature of an adverse effect are tachycardia, delirium, gastrointestinal hemorrhaging, vomiting, hypokalemia, hepatitis, renal failure, or respiratory failure.

(b) Poisoning

When coding a poisoning or reaction to the improper use of a medication (e.g., overdose, wrong substance given or taken in error, wrong route of administration), first assign the appropriate code from categories T36–T50. The poisoning codes have an associated intent as their 5th or 6th character (accidental, intentional self-harm, assault and undetermined). If the intent of the poisoning is unknown or unspecified, code the intent as accidental intent. The undetermined intent is only for use if the documentation in the record specifies that the intent cannot be determined. Use additional code(s) for all manifestations of poisonings.

If there is also a diagnosis of abuse or dependence of the substance, the abuse or dependence is assigned as an additional code.

Examples of poisoning include:

(i) Error was made in drug prescription

Errors made in drug prescription or in the administration of the drug by provider, nurse, patient, or other person.

(ii) Overdose of a drug intentionally taken

If an overdose of a drug was intentionally taken or administered and resulted in drug toxicity, it would be coded as a poisoning.

(iii) Nonprescribed drug taken with correctly prescribed and properly administered drug

If a nonprescribed drug or medicinal agent was taken in combination with a correctly prescribed and properly administered drug, any drug toxicity or other reaction resulting from the interaction of the two drugs would be classified as a poisoning.

(iv) Interaction of drug(s) and alcohol

When a reaction results from the interaction of a drug(s) and alcohol, this would be classified as poisoning.

See Section I.C.4. if poisoning is the result of insulin pump malfunctions.

(c) Underdosing

Underdosing refers to taking less of a medication than is prescribed by a provider or a manufacturer's instruction. Discontinuing the use of a prescribed medication on the patient's own initiative (not directed by the patient's provider) is also classified as an underdosing. For underdosing, assign the code from categories T36–T50 (fifth or sixth character "6").

Codes for underdosing should never be assigned as principal or first-listed codes. If a patient has a relapse or exacerbation of the medical condition for which the drug is prescribed because of the reduction in dose, then the medical condition itself should be coded.

Noncompliance (Z91.12-, Z91.13-, and Z91.14-) or complication of care (Y63.6–Y63.9) codes are to be used with an underdosing code to indicate intent, if known.

(d) Toxic effects

When a harmful substance is ingested or comes in contact with a person, this is classified as a toxic effect. The toxic effect codes are in categories T51–T65.

Toxic effect codes have an associated intent: accidental, intentional self-harm, assault and undetermined.

f. Adult and child abuse, neglect and other maltreatment

Sequence first the appropriate code from categories T74.- (Adult and child abuse, neglect and other maltreatment, confirmed) or T76.- (Adult and child abuse, neglect and other maltreatment, suspected) for abuse, neglect and other maltreatment, followed by any accompanying mental health or injury code(s).

If the documentation in the medical record states abuse or neglect it is coded as confirmed (T74.-). It is coded as suspected if it is documented as suspected (T76.-).

For cases of confirmed abuse or neglect an external cause code from the assault section (X92–Y09) should be added to identify the cause of any physical injuries. A perpetrator code (Y07) should be added when the perpetrator of the abuse is known. For suspected cases of abuse or neglect, do not report external cause or perpetrator code.

If a suspected case of abuse, neglect or mistreatment is ruled out during an encounter code Z04.71, Encounter for examination and observation following alleged physical adult abuse, ruled out, or code Z04.72, Encounter for examination and observation following alleged child physical abuse, ruled out, should be used, not a code from T76.

If a suspected case of alleged rape or sexual abuse is ruled out during an encounter, code Z04.41, Encounter for examination and observation following alleged adult rape, or code Z04.42, Encounter for examination and observation following alleged child rape, should be used, not a code from T76.

If a suspected case of forced sexual exploitation or forced labor exploitation is ruled out during an encounter, code Z04.81, Encounter for examination and observation of victim following forced sexual exploitation, or code Z04.82, Encounter for examination and observation of victim following forced labor exploitation, should be used, not a code from T76.

See Section I.C.15. Abuse in a pregnant patient.

g. Complications of care

1) General guidelines for complications of care

(a) Documentation of complications of care

See Section I.B.16. for information on documentation of complications of care.

2) Pain due to medical devices

Pain associated with devices, implants or grafts left in a surgical site (for example painful hip prosthesis) is assigned to the appropriate code(s) found in Chapter 19, Injury, poisoning, and certain other consequences of external causes. Specific codes for pain due to medical devices are found in the T code section of the ICD-10-CM. Use additional code(s) from category G89 to identify acute or chronic pain due to presence of the device, implant or graft (G89.18 or G89.28).

3) Transplant complications

(a) Transplant complications other than kidney

Codes under category T86, Complications of transplanted organs and tissues, are for use for both complications and rejection of transplanted organs. A transplant complication code is only assigned if the complication affects the function of the transplanted organ. Two codes are required to fully describe a transplant complication: the appropriate code from category T86 and a secondary code that identifies the complication.

Pre-existing conditions or conditions that develop after the transplant are not coded as complications unless they affect the function of the transplanted organs.

See Section I.C.21. for transplant organ removal status.

See Section I.C.2. for malignant neoplasm associated with transplanted organ.

(b) Kidney transplant complications

Patients who have undergone kidney transplant may still have some form of chronic kidney disease (CKD) because the kidney transplant may not fully restore kidney function. Code T86.1- should be assigned for documented complications of a kidney transplant, such as transplant failure or rejection or other transplant

ICD-10-CM Chapter-Specific Coding Guidelines (*continued*)

complication. Code T86.1- should not be assigned for post kidney transplant patients who have chronic kidney disease (CKD) unless a transplant complication such as transplant failure or rejection is documented. If the documentation is unclear as to whether the patient has a complication of the transplant, query the provider.

Conditions that affect the function of the transplanted kidney, other than CKD, should be assigned from subcategory T86.1, Complications of transplanted organ, Kidney, and a secondary code that identifies the complication.

For patients with CKD following a kidney transplant, but who do not have a complication such as failure or rejection, *see Section I.C.14. Chronic kidney disease and kidney transplant status.*

4) **Complication codes that include the external cause**

As with certain other T codes, some of the complications of care codes have the external cause included in the code. The code includes the nature of the complication as well as the type of procedure that caused the complication. No external cause code indicating the type of procedure is necessary for these codes.

5) **Complications of care codes within the body system chapters**

Intraoperative and postprocedural complication codes are found within the body system chapters with codes specific to the organs and structures of that body system. These codes should be sequenced first, followed by a code(s) for the specific complication, if applicable.

Complication codes from the body system chapters should be assigned for intraoperative and postprocedural complications (e.g., the appropriate complication code from Chapter 9 would be assigned for a vascular intraoperative or postprocedural complication) unless the complication is specifically indexed to a T code in Chapter 19.

Exercise 5.9 – Injury, Poisoning, and Certain Other Consequences of External Causes

Instructions: Assign the appropriate ICD-10-CM code(s). (Do *not* enter codes for external cause of diseases and injuries.)

_____   1. Closed fracture of mandible, subcondylar, right (initial encounter)

_____   2. Closed dislocation of clavicle (initial encounter)

_____   3. Concussion with brief loss of consciousness (30 minutes) (initial encounter)

_____   4. Foot burn, left, blisters, epidermal loss (second-degree) (initial encounter)

_____   5. Heart laceration without penetration of heart chambers (initial encounter)

_____   6. Hives resulting from penicillin taken as prescribed (initial encounter)

_____   7. Coma due to overdose of barbiturates during an attempted suicide (initial encounter)

_____   8. Adverse reaction to pertussis vaccine (initial encounter)

_____   9. Cardiac arrhythmia due to interaction of prescribed ephedrine and ethyl alcohol intoxication (accident) (initial encounter)

_____   10. Stupor due to overdose of Nytol (accident) (initial encounter)

Chapter 20: External Causes of Morbidity (V00–Y99)

ICD-10-CM Chapter 20 classifies the reporting of *external causes of morbidity* codes, which are reported as secondary codes for use in any health care setting.

This ICD-10-CM chapter classifies the following:

- Accidents
- Transport accidents
- Pedestrian injured in transport accident
- Pedal cycle rider injured in transport accident
- Motorcycle rider injured in transport accident
- Occupant of three-wheeled motor vehicle injured in transport accident
- Car occupant injured in transport accident
- Occupant of pick-up truck or van injured in transport accident
- Occupant of heavy transport vehicle injured in transport accident
- Bus occupant injured in transport accident
- Other land transport accidents
- Water transport accidents
- Air and space transport accidents
- Other and unspecified transport accidents
- Other external causes of accidental injury
- Slipping, tripping, stumbling, and falls
- Exposure to inanimate mechanical forces
- Exposure to animate mechanical forces
- Accidental non-transport drowning and submersion
- Exposure to electric current, radiation, and extreme ambient air temperature and pressure
- Exposure to smoke, fire, and flames
- Contact with heat and hot substances
- Exposure to forces of nature
- Accidental exposure to other specified factors
- Intentional self-harm
- Assault
- Event of undetermined intent
- Legal intervention, operations of war, military operations, and terrorism
- Complications of medical and surgical care
- Misadventures to patients during surgical and medical care
- Medical devices associated with adverse incidents in diagnostic and therapeutic use
- Surgical and other medical procedures as the cause of abnormal reaction of the patient, or of later complication, without mention of misadventure at the time of the procedure
- Supplementary factors related to causes of morbidity classified elsewhere

EXAMPLE: A patient fell off the toilet in the downstairs bathroom of her single-family house during an attempt to coax her cat to come down from the top of a cabinet. It apparently worked because the cat jumped off the cabinet and landed on the patient. However, the patient was so surprised that she screamed and fell off the toilet onto the floor. The patient landed on her left arm due to the fall and experienced extremely sharp pain. She was evaluated in the emergency department where she was diagnosed with a closed nondisplaced comminuted fracture of the shaft of the humerus, left. She received treatment and was discharged home to follow-up with her primary care physician in the office.

For ICD-10-CM, report the injury (fracture) (S42.355A), cause of injury (fall) (W18.11xA), and place of occurrence (bathroom of patient's home) (Y92.012). ICD-10-CM's level of specificity results in different codes for other locations in the patient's home (e.g., bathroom). (Seventh-character A is reported during the entire period when the patient receives active treatment.)

The ICD-10-CM place of injury codes for this case indicate that the patient's health insurance policy should be billed, not a liability or workers' compensation policy. If the place of occurrence had been at a grocery store or other place of business, the business's liability insurance would be billed (instead of the patient's health insurance). If the place of occurrence had been at the patient's employment setting, workers' compensation would be billed.

ICD-10-CM Chapter-Specific Coding Guidelines

Chapter 20: External Causes of Morbidity (V00–Y99)

The external causes of morbidity codes should never be sequenced as the first-listed or principal diagnosis.

External cause codes are intended to provide data for injury research and evaluation of injury prevention strategies. These codes capture how the injury or health condition happened (cause), the intent (unintentional or accidental; or intentional, such as suicide or assault), the place where the event occurred, the activity of the patient at the time of the event, and the person's status (e.g., civilian, military).

There is no national requirement for mandatory ICD-10-CM external cause code reporting. Unless a provider is subject to a state-based external cause code reporting mandate or these codes are required by a particular payer, reporting of ICD-10-CM codes in Chapter 20, External Causes of Morbidity, is not required. In the absence of a mandatory reporting requirement, providers are encouraged to voluntarily report external cause codes, as they provide valuable data for injury research and evaluation of injury prevention strategies.

a. General external cause coding guidelines

1) Used with any code in the range of A00.0–T88.9, Z00–Z99

An external cause code may be used with any code in the range of A00.0–T88.9, Z00–Z99, classification that is a health condition due to an external cause. Though they are most applicable to injuries, they are also valid for use with such things as infections or diseases due to an external source, and other health conditions, such as a heart attack that occurs during strenuous physical activity.

EXAMPLE: Patient stated she got out of bed to walk to the bathroom and tripped on a wooden bed post in her bedroom but did not fall. Diagnosis is sprained great toe, right. Report codes S93.501A (sprain, initial encounter), W18.49xA (tripping, initial encounter), Y93.01 (walking) and Y92.003 (home).

2) External cause code used for length of treatment

Assign the external cause code, with the appropriate 7th character (initial encounter, subsequent encounter, or sequela) for each encounter for which the injury or condition is being treated.

Most categories in Chapter 20 have a 7th character requirement for each applicable code. Most categories in this chapter have three 7th character values: A, initial encounter, D, subsequent encounter, and S, sequela. While the patient may be seen by a new or different provider over the course of treatment for an injury or condition, assignment of the 7th character for external cause should match the 7th character of the code assigned for the associated injury or condition for the encounter.

EXAMPLE: Patient returned to the office for routine follow-up care of sprained great toe, right; she had tripped at home and stubbed her toe. Report codes S93.501D (sprain, subsequent encounter) and W18.49xD (tripping, subsequent encounter).

3) Use the full range of external cause codes

Use the full range of external cause codes to completely describe the cause, the intent, the place of occurrence, and if applicable, the activity of the patient at the time of the event, and the patient's status, for all injuries, and other health conditions due to an external cause.

4) Assign as many external cause codes as necessary

Assign as many external cause codes as necessary to fully explain each cause. If only one external code can be recorded, assign the code most related to the principal diagnosis.

5) The selection of the appropriate external cause code

The selection of the appropriate external cause code is guided by the Alphabetic Index of External Causes and by Inclusion and Exclusion notes in the Tabular List.

6) External cause code can never be a principal diagnosis

An external cause code can never be a principal (first-listed) diagnosis.

7) Combination external cause codes

Certain of the external cause codes are combination codes that identify sequential events that result in an injury, such as a fall which results in striking against an object. The injury may be due to either event or both. The combination external cause code used should correspond to the sequence of events regardless of which caused the most serious injury.

8) No external cause code needed in certain circumstances

No external cause code from Chapter 20 is needed if the external cause and intent are included in a code from another chapter (e.g., T36.0x1-Poisoning by penicillins, accidental (unintentional)).

b. Place of occurrence guideline

Codes from category Y92, Place of occurrence of the external cause, are secondary codes for use after other external cause codes to identify the location of the patient at the time of injury or other condition.

Generally, a place of occurrence code is assigned only once, at the initial encounter for treatment. However, in the rare instance that a new injury occurs during hospitalization, an additional place of occurrence code may be assigned. No 7th characters are used for Y92. Only one code from Y92 should be recorded on a medical record. A place of occurrence code should be used in conjunction with an activity code, Y93.

Do not use place of occurrence code Y92.9 if the place is not stated or is not applicable.

c. Activity code

Assign a code from category Y93, Activity code, to describe the activity of the patient at the time the injury or other health condition occurred.

An activity code is used only once, at the initial encounter for treatment. Only one code from Y93 should be recorded on a medical record.

The activity codes are not applicable to poisonings, adverse effects, misadventures, or sequelae.

Do not assign Y93.9, Unspecified activity, if the activity is not stated.

A code from category Y93 is appropriate for use with external cause and intent codes if identifying the activity provides additional information about the event.

d. Place of occurrence, activity, and status codes used with other external cause code

When applicable, place of occurrence, activity, and external cause status codes are sequenced after the main external cause code(s).

(continues)

ICD-10-CM Chapter-Specific Coding Guidelines (*continued*)

Regardless of the number of external cause codes assigned, there should be only one place of occurrence code, one activity code, and one external cause status code assigned to an encounter.

e. If the reporting format limits the number of external cause codes

If the reporting format limits the number of external cause codes that can be used in reporting clinical data, report the code for the cause/intent most related to the principal diagnosis. If the format permits capture of additional external cause codes, the cause/intent, including medical misadventures, of the additional events should be reported rather than the codes for place, activity, or external status.

f. Multiple external cause coding guidelines

More than one external cause code is required to fully describe the external cause of an illness or injury. The assignment of external cause codes should be sequenced in the following priority:

If two or more events cause separate injuries, an external cause code should be assigned for each cause. The first-listed external cause code will be selected in the following order:

External codes for child and adult abuse take priority over all other external cause codes.

See Section I.C.19., Child and Adult abuse guidelines.

External cause codes for terrorism events take priority over all other external cause codes except child and adult abuse.

External cause codes for cataclysmic events take priority over all other external cause codes except child and adult abuse and terrorism.

External cause codes for transport accidents take priority over all other external cause codes except cataclysmic events, child and adult abuse, and terrorism.

Activity and external cause status codes are assigned following all causal (intent) external cause codes.

The first-listed external cause code should correspond to the cause of the most serious diagnosis due to an assault, accident, or self-harm, following the order of hierarchy listed above.

g. Child and adult abuse guideline

Adult and child abuse, neglect and maltreatment are classified as assault. Any of the assault codes may be used to indicate the external cause of any injury resulting from the confirmed abuse.

For confirmed cases of abuse, neglect and maltreatment, when the perpetrator is known, a code from Y07, Perpetrator of maltreatment and neglect, should accompany any other assault codes.

See Section I.C.19. Adult and child abuse, neglect and other maltreatment.

h. Unknown or undetermined intent guideline

If the intent (accident, self-harm, assault) of the cause of an injury or other condition is unknown or unspecified, code the intent as accidental intent. All transport accident categories assume accidental intent.

1) Use of undetermined intent

External cause codes for events of undetermined intent are only for use if the documentation in the record specifies that the intent cannot be determined.

i. Sequelae (Late Effects) of external cause guidelines

1) Sequelae external cause codes

Sequelae are reported using the external cause code with the 7th character extension "S" for sequela. These codes should be used with any report of a late effect or sequela resulting from a previous injury.

See Section I.B.10 Sequela (Late Effects).

2) Sequela external cause code with a related current injury

A sequela external cause code should never be used with a related current nature of injury code.

3) Use of sequela external cause codes for subsequent visits

Use a late effect external cause code for subsequent visits when a late effect of the initial injury is being treated. Do not use a late effect external cause code for subsequent visits for follow-up care (e.g., to assess healing, to receive rehabilitative therapy) of the injury when no late effect of the injury has been documented.

j. **Terrorism guidelines**

1) **Cause of injury identified by the Federal Government (FBI) as terrorism**

When the cause of an injury is identified by the Federal Government (FBI) as terrorism, the first-listed external cause code should be a code from category Y38, Terrorism. The definition of terrorism employed by the FBI is found at the inclusion note at the beginning of category Y38. Use additional code for place of occurrence (Y92.-). More than one Y38 code may be assigned if the injury is the result of more than one mechanism of terrorism.

2) **Cause of an injury is suspected to be the result of terrorism**

When the cause of an injury is suspected to be the result of terrorism, a code from category Y38 should not be assigned.

Suspected cases should be classified as assault.

3) **Code Y38.9, terrorism, secondary effects**

Assign code Y38.9, Terrorism, secondary effects, for conditions occurring subsequent to the terrorist event. This code should not be assigned for conditions that are due to the initial terrorist act.

It is acceptable to assign code Y38.9 with another code from Y38 if there is an injury due to the initial terrorist event and an injury that is a subsequent result of the terrorist event.

k. **External cause status**

A code from category Y99, External cause status, should be assigned whenever any other external cause code is assigned for an encounter, including an Activity code, except for the events noted below. Assign a code from category Y99, External cause status, to indicate the work status of the person at the time the event occurred. The status code indicates whether the event occurred during military activity, whether a non-military person was at work or whether an individual, including a student or volunteer, was involved in a non-work activity at the time of the causal event.

A code from Y99, External cause status, should be assigned, when applicable, with other external cause codes, such as transport accidents and falls. The external cause status codes are not applicable to poisonings, adverse effects, misadventures or late effects.

Do not assign a code from category Y99 if no other external cause codes (cause, activity) are applicable for the encounter.

An external cause status code is used only once, at the initial encounter for treatment. Only one code from Y99 should be recorded on a medical record.

Do not assign code Y99.9, Unspecified external cause status, if the status is not stated.

Courtesy of the Centers for Medicare & Medicaid Services, www.cms.gov.

Exercise 5.10 – External Causes of Morbidity

Instructions: Assign the appropriate ICD-10-CM external cause V through Y code(s).

_____ 1. Fall from skateboard at public park (initial encounter)

_____ 2. Burning bedclothes resulting from cooking in kitchen of mobile home (initial encounter)

_____ 3. Explosion in watercraft (initial encounter)

_____ 4. Fall from ladder (initial encounter)

_____ 5. Left foot injury taking place on baseball field (accident) (initial encounter)

Chapter 21: Factors Influencing Health Status and Contact with Health Services (Z00–Z99)

This ICD-10-CM chapter classifies circumstances other than a disease, injury or external cause classifiable to categories A00–Y89, which are recorded as "diagnoses" or "problems." Certain Z codes in ICD-10-CM can be reported as a first-listed or additional diagnosis for outpatient care. The chapter classifies the following:

- Persons encountering health services for examinations
- Genetic carrier and genetic susceptibility to disease
- Resistance to antimicrobial drugs
- Estrogen receptor status
- Retained foreign body fragments
- Persons with potential health hazards related to communicable diseases
- Persons encountering health services in circumstances related to reproduction
- Encounters for other specific health care
- Persons with potential health hazards related to socioeconomic and psychosocial circumstances
- Do not resuscitate status
- Blood type
- Body mass index (BMI)
- Persons encountering health services in other circumstances
- Persons with potential health hazards related to family and personal history and certain conditions influencing health status

 NOTE:

Verify history of codes in the tabular list before reporting. Also do not confuse personal history of with family history of codes.

Reporting Z Codes

Such circumstances can arise when the following occurs, for which reporting a Z code is appropriate:

- A person who may or may not be sick encounters the health services for some specific purpose.
  - Limited care or service for a current condition
  - Donation of an organ or tissue
  - Prophylactic vaccination (immunization)
  - Discussion of a problem which is in itself not a disease or injury
- A situation or problem is present that influences the person's health status but is not in itself a current illness or injury.
- A person with a known disease or injury, whether it is current or resolving, encounters the health care system for a specific treatment of that disease or injury (e.g., dialysis for renal disease, chemotherapy for malignancy, or a cast change).
- Some circumstance or problem is present that influences the person's health status but is not in itself a current illness or injury. Such factors may be elicited during population surveys, when the person may or may not be currently sick, or may be recorded as an additional factor to be borne in mind when the person is receiving care for some current illness or injury classifiable to ICD-10-CM categories A00–Y99.

   In this situation, the ICD-10-CM Z code should be assigned as an other (additional) code and is not selected as the principal diagnosis for inpatient cases or the first-listed diagnosis for outpatient cases.

For example, such circumstances include personal history of certain diseases or a person with an artificial heart valve *in situ*.

 Coding Tip

Refer to ICD-10-CM index main terms to begin assigning a Z code. Common main terms include:

Admission	Donor	Outcome of delivery
Aftercare	Encounter for	Pregnancy
Attention to	Examination	Procedure (surgical) not done
Carrier (suspected) of	Exposure	Prophylactic
Checking	Fitting	Removal
Checkup	Follow-up	Resistance, resistant
Closure	History, family	Routine postpartum follow-up
Contact	History (personal) of	Screening
Contraception, contraceptive	Maladjustment	Status
Counseling	Newborn	Test(s)
Dialysis	Observation	Vaccination

ICD-10-CM Chapter-Specific Coding Guidelines

Chapter 21: Factors Influencing Health Status and Contact with Health Services (Z00–Z99)

N o t e : The chapter-specific guidelines provide additional information about the use of Z codes for specified encounters.

a. Use of Z codes in any healthcare setting

Z codes are for use in any healthcare setting. Z codes may be used as either a first-listed (principal diagnosis code in the inpatient setting) or secondary code, depending on the circumstances of the encounter. Certain Z codes may only be used as first-listed or principal diagnosis.

b. Z Codes indicate a reason for an encounter

Z codes are not procedure codes. A corresponding procedure code must accompany a Z code to describe any procedure performed.

c. Categories of Z codes

1) Contact/Exposure

Category Z20 indicates contact with or exposure to communicable diseases. These codes are for patients who do not show any sign or symptom of a disease but have been exposed to it by close personal contact with an infected individual or are in an area where a disease is epidemic.

Category Z77, Other contact with and (suspected) exposures hazardous to health, indicates contact with and suspected exposures hazardous to health.

Contact/exposure codes may be used as a first-listed code to explain an encounter for testing, or, more commonly, as a secondary code to identify a potential risk.

2) Inoculations and vaccinations

Code Z23 is for encounters for inoculations and vaccinations. It indicates that a patient is being seen to receive a prophylactic inoculation against a disease. Procedure codes are required to identify the actual

(continues)

ICD-10-CM Chapter-Specific Coding Guidelines (*continued*)

administration of the injection and the type(s) of immunizations given. Code Z23 may be used as a secondary code if the inoculation is given as a routine part of preventive health care, such as a well-baby visit.

EXAMPLE: Five-year-old male patient seen for annual well-child visit during which provider planned to administer a flu vaccine. The mother refused to allow the vaccine to be administered. Report codes Z00.129 (Routine infant or child health check) and Z28.82 (Vaccination not carried out because of caregiver refusal). (If the vaccine had been administered, code Z23 would be reported.)

3) Status

Status codes indicate that a patient is either a carrier of a disease or has the sequela or residual of a past disease or condition. This includes things such as the presence of prosthetic or mechanical devices resulting from past treatment. A status code is informative because the status may affect the course of treatment and its outcome. A status code is distinct from a history code. The history code indicates that the patient no longer has the condition.

A status code should not be used with a diagnosis code from one of the body system chapters *if the diagnosis code includes the information provided by the status code*. For example, code Z94.1, Heart transplant status, should not be used with code T86.2, Complications of transplanted heart. The complication code indicates that the patient is a heart transplant patient.

For encounters for weaning from a mechanical ventilator, assign a code from subcategory J96.1, Chronic respiratory failure, followed by code Z99.11, Dependence on respirator [ventilator] status.

The status Z codes/categories are:

Z14   Genetic carrier

Genetic carrier status indicates that a person carries a gene, associated with a particular disease, which may be passed to offspring who may develop that disease. The person does not have the disease and is not at risk of developing the disease.

Z15   Genetic susceptibility to disease

Genetic susceptibility indicates that a person has a gene that increases the risk of that person developing the disease.

Codes from category Z15 should not be used as principal or first-listed codes. If the patient has the condition to which he/she is susceptible, and that condition is the reason for the encounter, the code for the current condition should be sequenced first. If the patient is being seen for follow-up after completed treatment for this condition, and the condition no longer exists, a follow-up code should be sequenced first, followed by the appropriate personal history and genetic susceptibility codes. If the purpose of the encounter is genetic counseling associated with procreative management, code Z31.5, Encounter for genetic counseling, should be assigned as the first-listed code, followed by a code from category Z15.

Additional codes should be assigned for any applicable family or personal history.

Z16   Resistance to antimicrobial drugs

This code indicates that a patient has a condition that is resistant to antimicrobial drug treatment. Sequence the infection code first.

Z17   Estrogen receptor status

Z18   Retained foreign body fragments

Z19   Hormone sensitivity malignancy status

Z21   Asymptomatic HIV infection status

   This code indicates that a patient has tested positive for HIV but has manifested no signs or symptoms of the disease.

Z22   Carrier of infectious disease

   Carrier status indicates that a person harbors the specific organisms of a disease without manifest symptoms and is capable of transmitting the infection.

Z28.3   Underimmunization status

Z33.1   Pregnant state, incidental

   This code is a secondary code only for use when the pregnancy is in no way complicating the reason for visit.

   Otherwise, a code from the obstetrics chapter is required.

Z66   Do not resuscitate

   This code may be used when it is documented by the provider that a patient is on do not resuscitate status at any time during the stay.

Z67   Blood type

Z68   Body mass index (BMI)

   BMI codes should only be assigned when there is an associated, reportable diagnosis (such as obesity) meets the definition of a reportable diagnosis (see Section III, Reporting Additional Diagnoses). Do not assign BMI codes during pregnancy. *See Section I.B.14 for BMI documentation by clinicians other than the patient's provider.*

Z74.01 Bed confinement status

Z76.82 Awaiting organ transplant status

Z78   Other specified health status

   Code Z78.1, Physical restraint status, may be used when it is documented by the provider that a patient has been put in restraints during the current encounter.

   Please note that this code should not be reported when it is documented by the provider that a patient is temporarily restrained during a procedure.

Z79   Long-term (current) drug therapy

   Codes from this category indicate a patient's continuous use of a prescribed drug (including such things as aspirin therapy) for the long-term treatment of a condition or for prophylactic use. It is not for use for patients who have addictions to drugs. This subcategory is not for use of medications for detoxification or maintenance programs to prevent withdrawal symptoms in patients with drug dependence (e.g., methadone maintenance for opiate dependence). Assign the appropriate code for the drug dependence instead.

   Assign a code from Z79 if the patient is receiving a medication for an extended period as a prophylactic measure (such as for the prevention of deep vein thrombosis) or as treatment of a chronic condition (such as arthritis) or a disease requiring a lengthy course of treatment (such as cancer). Do not assign a code from category Z79 for medication being administered for a brief period of time to treat an acute illness or injury (such as a course of antibiotics to treat acute bronchitis).

Z88   Allergy status to drugs, medicaments and biological substances

   Except: Z88.9, Allergy status to unspecified drugs, medications and biological substances status

(continues)

ICD-10-CM Chapter-Specific Coding Guidelines (*continued*)

Z89   Acquired absence of limb

Z90   Acquired absence of organs, not elsewhere classified

Z91.0-   Allergy status, other than to drugs and biological substances

Z92.82   Status post administration of tissue plasminogen activator (tPA) (recombinant [rtPA]) in a different facility within the last 24 hours prior to admission to a current facility.

> Assign code Z92.82, Status post administration of tPA (rtPA) in a different facility within the last 24 hours prior to admission to current facility, as a secondary diagnosis when a patient is received by transfer into a facility and documentation indicates they were administered tPA within the last 24 hours prior to admission to the current facility.
>
> This guideline applies even if the patient is still receiving the tPA at the time they are received into the current facility.
>
> The appropriate code for the condition for which the tPA was administered (such as cerebrovascular disease or myocardial infarction) should be assigned first.
>
> Code Z92.82 is only applicable to the receiving facility record and not to the transferring facility record.

Z93   Artificial opening status

Z94   Transplanted organ and tissue status

Z95   Presence of cardiac and vascular implants and grafts

Z96   Presence of other functional implants

Z97   Presence of other devices

Z98   Other postprocedural states

> Assign code Z98.85, Transplanted organ removal status, to indicate that a transplanted organ has been previously removed. This code should not be assigned for the encounter in which the transplanted organ is removed. The complication necessitating removal of the transplant organ should be assigned for that encounter.
>
> *See section I.C.19. for information on the coding of organ transplant complications.*

Z99   Dependence on enabling machines and devices, not elsewhere classified

> **Note:** Categories Z89–Z90 and Z93–Z99 are for use only if there are no complications or malfunctions of the organ or tissue replaced, the amputation site or the equipment on which the patient is dependent.

4) History (of)

There are two types of history Z codes, personal and family. Personal history codes explain a patient's past medical condition that no longer exists and is not receiving any treatment but that has the potential for recurrence and, therefore, may require continued monitoring.

Family history codes are for use when a patient has a family member(s) who has had a particular disease that causes the patient to be at higher risk of also contracting the disease.

Personal history codes may be used in conjunction with follow-up codes, and family history codes may be used in conjunction with screening codes to explain the need for a test or procedure. History codes are also acceptable on any medical record regardless of the reason for visit. A history of an illness, even if no longer present, is important information that may alter the type of treatment ordered.

EXAMPLE 1: Patient with a history of colon cancer, removed two years ago, is seen for follow-up examination to determine whether there is recurrence. Report codes Z08 (Encounter for follow-up examination after completed treatment for malignant neoplasm) and Z85.038 (Personal history of other malignant neoplasm of large intestine).

EXAMPLE 2: Patient has extensive family history of ovarian cancer (e.g., mother, aunts, and sisters) and elects to undergo screening as a preventive measure. Report codes Z12.73 (Encounter for screening for malignant neoplasm of ovary) and Z80.41 (Family history of malignant neoplasm of ovary).

The history Z code categories are:

Z80	Family history of primary malignant neoplasm
Z81	Family history of mental and behavioral disorders
Z82	Family history of certain disabilities and chronic diseases (leading to disablement)
Z83	Family history of other specific disorders
Z84	Family history of other conditions
Z85	Personal history of malignant neoplasm
Z86	Personal history of certain other diseases
Z87	Personal history of other diseases and conditions
Z91.4-	Personal history of psychological trauma, not elsewhere classified
Z91.5	Personal history of self-harm
Z91.81	History of falling
Z91.82	Personal history of military deployment
Z92	Personal history of medical treatment

Except: Z92.0, Personal history of contraception

Except: Z92.82, Status post administration of tPA (rtPA) in a different facility within the last 24 hours prior to admission to a current facility

5) Screening

Screening is the testing for disease or disease precursors in seemingly well individuals so that early detection and treatment can be provided for those who test positive for the disease (e.g., screening mammogram).

The testing of a person to rule out or confirm a suspected diagnosis because the patient has some sign or symptom is a diagnostic examination, not a screening. In these cases, the sign or symptom is used to explain the reason for the test.

A screening code may be a first-listed code if the reason for the visit is specifically the screening exam. It may also be used as an additional code if the screening is done during an office visit for other health problems. A screening code is not necessary if the screening is inherent to a routine examination, such as a Pap smear done during a routine pelvic examination.

Should a condition be discovered during the screening, then the code for the condition may be assigned as an additional diagnosis.

The Z code indicates that a screening exam is planned. A procedure code is required to confirm that the screening was performed.

The screening Z code categories are:

| Z11 | Encounter for screening for infectious and parasitic diseases |
| Z12 | Encounter for screening for malignant neoplasms |

(continues)

ICD-10-CM Chapter-Specific Coding Guidelines (*continued*)

Z13   Encounter for screening for other diseases and disorders

Except: Z13.9, Encounter for screening, unspecified

Z36   Encounter for antenatal screening for mother

6) Observation

There are three observation Z code categories. They are for use in very limited circumstances when a person is being observed for a suspected condition that is ruled out. The observation codes are not for use if an injury or illness or any signs or symptoms related to the suspected condition are present. In such cases, the diagnosis/ symptom code is used with the corresponding external cause code.

The observation codes are to be used as principal diagnosis only. The only exception to this is when the principal diagnosis is required to be a code from category Z38, Liveborn infants according to place of birth and type of delivery. Then a code from category Z05, Encounter for observation and evaluation of newborn for suspected diseases and conditions ruled out, is sequenced after the Z38 code. Additional codes may be used in addition to the observation code but only if they are unrelated to the suspected condition being observed.

Codes from subcategory Z03.7, Encounter for suspected maternal and fetal conditions ruled out, may be used either as a first listed or as an additional code assignment depending on the case. They are for use in very limited circumstances on a maternal record when an encounter is for a suspected maternal or fetal condition that is ruled out during that encounter (for example, a maternal or fetal condition may be suspected due to an abnormal test result). These codes should not be used when the condition is confirmed. In those cases, the confirmed condition should be coded. In addition, these codes are not for use if an illness or any signs or symptoms related to the suspected condition or problem are present. In such cases, the diagnosis/symptom code is used.

Additional codes may be used in addition to the code from subcategory Z03.7, but only if they are unrelated to the suspected condition being evaluated.

Codes from subcategory Z03.7 may not be used for encounters for antenatal screening of mother. *See Section I.C.21.c.5. Screening.*

For encounters for suspected fetal condition that are inconclusive following testing and evaluation, assign the appropriate code from category O35, O36, O40, or O41.

The observation Z code categories are:

Z03   Encounter for medical observation for suspected diseases and conditions ruled out

Z04   Encounter for examination and observation for other reasons

Except: Z04.9, Encounter for examination and observation for unspecified reason

Z05   Encounter for observation and evaluation of newborn for suspected diseases and conditions ruled out

7) Aftercare

Aftercare visit codes cover situations when the initial treatment of a disease or an injury has been performed and the patient requires continued care during the healing or recovery phase, or for the long-term consequences of the disease. The aftercare Z code should not be used if treatment is directed at a current, acute disease or injury. The diagnosis code is to be used in these cases. Exceptions to this rule are codes Z51.0, Encounter for antineoplastic radiation therapy, and codes from subcategory Z51.1, Encounter for antineoplastic chemotherapy and immunotherapy. These codes are to be first-listed, followed by the diagnosis code when a patient's encounter is solely to receive radiation therapy, chemotherapy or immunotherapy for the treatment of a neoplasm. If the reason for the encounter is more than one type of antineoplastic therapy, code Z51.0 and a code from subcategory Z51.1 may be assigned together, in which case one of these codes would be reported as a secondary diagnosis.

The aftercare Z codes should also not be used for aftercare for injuries. For aftercare of an injury, assign the acute injury code with the appropriate 7th character (for subsequent encounter).

The aftercare codes are generally first-listed to explain the specific reason for the encounter. An aftercare code may be used as an additional code when some type of aftercare is provided in addition to the reason for admission and no diagnosis code is applicable. An example of this would be the closure of a colostomy during an encounter for treatment of another condition.

Aftercare codes should be used in conjunction with other aftercare codes or diagnosis codes to provide better detail on the specifics of an aftercare encounter visit, unless otherwise directed by the classification. The sequencing of multiple aftercare codes depends on the circumstances of the encounter.

Certain aftercare Z code categories need a secondary diagnosis code to describe the resolving condition or sequela. For others, the condition is included in the code title.

Additional Z code aftercare category terms include fitting and adjustment, and attention to artificial openings.

Status Z codes may be used with aftercare Z codes to indicate the nature of the aftercare. For example, code Z95.1, Presence of aortocoronary bypass graft, may be used with code Z48.812, Encounter for surgical aftercare following surgery on the circulatory system, to indicate the surgery for which the aftercare is being performed. A status code should not be used when the aftercare code indicates the type of status, such as using Z43.0, Encounter for attention to tracheostomy, with Z93.0, Tracheostomy status.

EXAMPLE: Patient is diagnosed with right breast cancer, undergoes mastectomy, and is admitted today for chemotherapy. Report codes Z51.11 (Encounter for antineoplastic chemotherapy) and C50.911 (Malignant neoplasm of unspecified site of right female breast), in that order.

The aftercare Z category/codes are:

Z42	Encounter for plastic and reconstructive surgery following medical procedure or healed injury
Z43	Encounter for attention to artificial openings
Z44	Encounter for fitting and adjustment of external prosthetic device
Z45	Encounter for adjustment and management of implanted device
Z46	Encounter for fitting and adjustment of other devices
Z47	Orthopedic aftercare
Z48	Encounter for other postprocedural aftercare
Z49	Encounter for care involving renal dialysis
Z51	Encounter for other aftercare and medical care

8) Follow-up

The follow-up codes are used to explain continuing surveillance following completed treatment of a disease, condition, or injury. They imply that the condition has been fully treated and no longer exists. They should not be confused with aftercare codes, or injury codes with a seventh character for subsequent encounter, that explain current treatment for a healing condition or its sequela. Follow-up codes may be used in conjunction with history codes to provide the full picture of the healed condition and its treatment. The follow-up code is sequenced first, followed by the history code.

A follow-up code may be used to explain multiple visits. Should a condition be found to have recurred on the follow-up visit, then the diagnosis code for the condition should be assigned in place of the follow-up code.

(continues)

ICD-10-CM Chapter-Specific Coding Guidelines (*continued*)

The follow-up Z code categories are:

Z08   Encounter for follow-up examination after completed treatment for malignant neoplasm

Z09   Encounter for follow-up examination after completed treatment for conditions other than malignant neoplasm

Z39   Encounter for maternal postpartum care and examination

9) Donor

Codes in category Z52, Donors of organs and tissues, are used for living individuals who are donating blood or other body tissue. These codes are only for individuals donating for others, not for self-donations. They are not used to identify cadaveric donations.

10) Counseling

Counseling Z codes are used when a patient or family member receives assistance in the aftermath of an illness or injury, or when support is required in coping with family or social problems. They are not used in conjunction with a diagnosis code when the counseling component of care is considered integral to standard treatment.

The counseling Z codes/categories are:

Z30.0-   Encounter for general counseling and advice on contraception

Z31.5   Encounter for procreative genetic counseling

Z31.6-   Encounter for general counseling and advice on procreation

Z32.2   Encounter for childbirth instruction

Z32.3   Encounter for childcare instruction

Z69   Encounter for mental health services for victim and perpetrator of abuse

Z70   Counseling related to sexual attitude, behavior and orientation

Z71   Persons encountering health services for other counseling and medical advice, not elsewhere classified

Note: Code Z71.84, Encounter for health counseling related to travel, is to be used for health risk and safety counseling for future travel purposes.

Z76.81   Expectant mother prebirth pediatrician visit

11) Encounters for obstetrical and reproductive services

See Section I.C.15. Pregnancy, Childbirth, and the Puerperium, for further instruction on the use of these codes.

Z codes for pregnancy are for use in those circumstances when none of the problems or complications included in the codes from the Obstetrics chapter exist (a routine prenatal visit or postpartum care). Codes in category Z34, Encounter for supervision of normal pregnancy, are always first-listed and are not to be used with any other code from the OB chapter. Codes in category Z3A, Weeks of gestation, may be assigned to provide additional information about the pregnancy.

The outcome of delivery, category Z37, should be included on all maternal delivery records. It is always a secondary code. Codes in category Z37 should not be used on the newborn record.

Codes in category Z3A, Weeks of gestation, may be assigned to provide additional information about the pregnancy. Category Z3A codes should not be assigned for pregnancies with abortive outcomes (categories O00–O08), elective termination of pregnancy (code Z33.2), nor for postpartum conditions, as category Z3A is not applicable to these conditions. The date of the admission should be used to determine weeks of gestation for inpatient admissions that encompass more than one gestational week.

Z codes for family planning (contraceptive) or procreative management and counseling should be included on an obstetrical record either during the pregnancy or the postpartum stage, if applicable.

Z codes/categories for obstetrical and reproductive services are:

Z30	Encounter for contraceptive management
Z31	Encounter for procreative management
Z32.2	Encounter for childbirth instruction
Z32.3	Encounter for childcare instruction
Z33	Pregnant state
Z34	Encounter for supervision of normal pregnancy
Z36	Encounter for antenatal screening of mother
Z3A	Weeks of gestation
Z37	Outcome of delivery
Z39	Encounter for maternal postpartum care and examination
Z76.81	Expectant mother prebirth pediatrician visit

12) Newborns and infants

See Section I.C.16. Newborn (Perinatal) Guidelines, for further instruction on the use of these codes.

Newborn Z codes/categories are:

Z76.1	Encounter for health supervision and care of foundling
Z00.1-	Encounter for routine child health examination
Z38	Liveborn infants according to place of birth and type of delivery

13) Routine and administrative examinations

The Z codes allow for the description of encounters for routine examinations, such as a general check-up, or examinations for administrative purposes, such as a preemployment physical. The codes are not to be used if the examination is for diagnosis of a suspected condition or for treatment purposes. In such cases, the diagnosis code is used. During a routine exam, should a diagnosis or condition be discovered, it should be coded as an additional code. Preexisting and chronic conditions and history codes may also be included as additional codes as long as the examination is for administrative purposes and not focused on any particular condition.

Some of the codes for routine health examinations distinguish between "with" and "without" abnormal findings. Code assignment depends on the information that is known at the time the encounter is being coded. For example, if no abnormal findings were found during the examination, but the encounter is being coded before test results are back, it is acceptable to assign the code for "without abnormal findings." When assigning a code for "with abnormal findings," additional code(s) should be assigned to identify the specific abnormal finding(s).

Preoperative examination and preprocedural laboratory examination Z codes are for use only in those situations when a patient is being cleared for a procedure or surgery and no treatment is given.

The Z codes/categories for routine and administrative examinations are:

EXAMPLE: Patient undergoes outpatient chest x-ray the day after his routine physical examination. The patient has no signs or symptoms, and the physician ordered the x-ray. Report code Z01.89 (Encounter for other specified special examinations) as the first-listed diagnosis.

(continues)

ICD-10-CM Chapter-Specific Coding Guidelines (*continued*)

Z00　　Encounter for general examination without complaint, suspected or reported diagnosis

Z01　　Encounter for other special examination without complaint, suspected or reported diagnosis

Z02　　Encounter for administrative examination

    Except: Z02.9, Encounter for administrative examinations, unspecified

Z32.0-　Encounter for pregnancy test

14) Miscellaneous Z codes

The miscellaneous Z codes capture a number of other health care encounters that do not fall into one of the other categories. Certain of these codes identify the reason for the encounter, others are for use as additional codes that provide useful information on circumstances that may affect a patient's care and treatment.

Prophylactic organ removal

For encounters specifically for prophylactic removal of an organ (such as prophylactic removal of breasts due to a genetic susceptibility to cancer or a family history of cancer), the principal or first-listed code should be a code from category Z40, Encounter for prophylactic surgery, followed by the appropriate codes to identify the associated risk factor (such as genetic susceptibility or family history).

If the patient has a malignancy of one site and is having prophylactic removal at another site to prevent either a new primary malignancy or metastatic disease, a code for the malignancy should also be assigned in addition to a code from subcategory Z40.0, Encounter for prophylactic surgery for risk factors related to malignant neoplasms. A Z40.0 code should not be assigned if the patient is having organ removal for treatment of a malignancy, such as the removal of the testes for the treatment of prostate cancer.

Miscellaneous Z codes/categories are:

Z28　　Immunization not carried out

    Except: Z28.3, Underimmunization status

Z29　　Encounter for other prophylactic measures

Z40　　Encounter for prophylactic surgery

Z41　　Encounter for procedures for purposes other than remedying health state

    Except: Z41.9, Encounter for procedure for purposes other than remedying health state, unspecified

Z53　　Persons encountering health services for specific procedures and treatment, not carried out

Z55　　Problems related to education and literacy

Z56　　Problems related to employment and unemployment

Z57　　Occupational exposure to risk factors

Z58　　Problems related to physical environment

Z59　　Problems related to housing and economic circumstances

Z60　　Problems related to social environment

Z62　　Problems related to upbringing

Z63　　Other problems related to primary support group, including family circumstances

Z64	Problems related to certain psychosocial circumstances
Z65	Problems related to other psychosocial circumstances
Z72	Problems related to lifestyle

Note: These codes should be assigned only when the documentation specifies that the patient has an associated problem.

Z73	Problems related to life management difficulty
Z74	Problems related to care provider dependency
	Except: Z74.01, Bed confinement status
Z75	Problems related to medical facilities and other health care
Z76.0	Encounter for issue of repeat prescription
Z76.3	Healthy person accompanying sick person
Z76.4	Other boarder to healthcare facility
Z76.5	Malingerer [conscious simulation]
Z89.84-	Oral health risk factors
Z91.1-	Patient's noncompliance with medical treatment and regimen
Z91.83	Wandering in diseases classified elsewhere
Z91.89	Other specified personal risk factors, not elsewhere classified

See Section I.B.14 for Z55-Z65 Persons with potential health hazards related to socioeconomic and psychosocial circumstances, documentation by clinicians other than the patient's provider.

15) Nonspecific Z codes

Certain Z codes are so nonspecific, or potentially redundant with other codes in the classification, that there can be little justification for their use in the inpatient setting. Their use in the outpatient setting should be limited to those instances when there is no further documentation to permit more precise coding. Otherwise, any sign or symptom or any other reason for visit that is captured in another code should be used.

Nonspecific Z codes/categories are:

Z02.9	Encounter for administrative examinations, unspecified
Z04.9	Encounter for examination and observation for unspecified reason
Z13.9	Encounter for screening, unspecified
Z41.9	Encounter for procedure for purposes other than remedying health state, unspecified
Z52.9	Donor of unspecified organ or tissue
Z86.59	Personal history of other mental and behavioral disorders
Z88.9	Allergy status to unspecified drugs, medicaments and biological substances status
Z92.0	Personal history of contraception

16) Z codes that may only be principal/first-listed diagnosis

The following Z codes/categories may only be reported as the principal/first-listed diagnosis, except when there are multiple encounters on the same day and the medical records for the encounters are combined:

Z00	Encounter for general examination without complaint, suspected or reported diagnosis
	Except: Z00.6

(continues)

ICD-10-CM Chapter-Specific Coding Guidelines (*continued*)

Z01	Encounter for other special examination without complaint, suspected or reported diagnosis
Z02	Encounter for administrative examination
Z03	Encounter for medical observation for suspected diseases and conditions ruled out
Z04	Encounter for examination and observation for other reasons
Z31.81	Encounter for male factor infertility in female patient
Z31.82	Encounter for Rh incompatibility status
Z31.83	Encounter for assisted reproductive fertility procedure cycle
Z31.84	Encounter for fertility preservation procedure
Z33.2	Encounter for elective termination of pregnancy
Z34	Encounter for supervision of normal pregnancy
Z38	Liveborn infants according to place of birth and type of delivery
Z39	Encounter for maternal postpartum care and examination
Z40	Encounter for prophylactic surgery
Z42	Encounter for plastic and reconstructive surgery following medical procedure or healed injury
Z51.0	Encounter for antineoplastic radiation therapy
Z51.1-	Encounter for antineoplastic chemotherapy and immunotherapy
Z52	Donors of organs and tissues Except: Z52.9, Donor of unspecified organ or tissue
Z76.1	Encounter for health supervision and care of foundling
Z76.2	Encounter for health supervision and care of other healthy infant and child
Z99.12	Encounter for respirator [ventilator] dependence during power failure

Courtesy of the Centers for Medicare & Medicaid Services, www.cms.gov.

Exercise 5.11 – Factors Influencing Health Status and Contact with Health Services

Instructions: Assign the appropriate ICD-10-CM code(s).

_____   1. Bone marrow donor

_____   2. Chemotherapy encounter

_____   3. Examination for summer camp

_____   4. Exposure to smallpox (laboratory)

_____   5. Family history of stroke

Summary

Chapter-specific coding guidelines clarify the assignment of ICD-10-CM disease codes. Unless otherwise indicated in an individual chapter-specific guideline, the ICD-10-CM chapter-specific guidelines apply to all health care settings.

Internet Links

ICD-10-CM/PCS updates: Go to *www.cdc.gov*. Click on Diseases & Conditions, click on the Data & Statistics link, scroll to the Tools heading, click on the Classification of Diseases, Functioning, and Disability link, and click on any of the ICD links.

ICD-10-CM Official Guidelines for Coding and Reporting (including chapter-specific coding guidelines): Go to *www.cdc.gov*. Click on the CDC A-Z Index link, and click on the letter *I*. Then click on the *ICD-10-CM (International Classification of Disease, Tenth Revision)* link. Scroll down and click on the most current ICD-10-CM Guidelines link.

MedLine Plus Interactive Tutorials (for diseases and procedures): Go to *www.nlm.nih.gov*. Click on the Medline Plus link, click on Videos & Tools, and click to select any video, tool, game, or tutorial activity.

Review

Multiple Choice

Instructions: Circle the most appropriate response after locating the ICD-10-CM code(s) for each disease.

1. Male patient admitted for ligation of vas deferens sterilization procedure.
   - **a.** Z30.2
   - **b.** Z31.09
   - **c.** Z31.42
   - **d.** Z31.89

2. Diverticulitis of the colon with hemorrhage.
   - **a.** K57.20
   - **b.** K57.21
   - **c.** K57.32
   - **d.** K57.33

3. Acute prostatitis due to streptococci.
   - **a.** N41.0, B95.5
   - **b.** N41.1, B95.5
   - **c.** N41.8, B95.5
   - **d.** N41.9, B95.5

4. Spontaneous delivery of full-term pregnancy (single liveborn).
   - **a.** O80, Z37.0
   - **b.** O82, Z37.0
   - **c.** Z34.00, Z37.0
   - **d.** Z34.90, Z38.00

5. Hard corn of right little toe.
   - **a.** L84
   - **b.** M20.5x1
   - **c.** M20.61
   - **d.** M21.271

6. Herniated cervical intervertebral disc. No evidence of myelopathy.
   - **a.** M50.00
   - **b.** M50.10
   - **c.** M50.20
   - **d.** M50.30

7. Congenital partial dislocation of the hip.
   - **a.** Q65.1
   - **b.** Q65.2
   - **c.** Q65.4
   - **d.** Q65.5

8. Liveborn infant, born in taxi cab, and then admitted for evaluation. Discharged in excellent condition after treatment of transitory tachypnea of the newborn.
   - **a.** Z38.00, P22.1
   - **b.** Z38.01, P22.1
   - **c.** Z38.1, P22.1
   - **d.** Z38.2, P22.1

9. Abnormal mammogram.
   - **a.** R92.0
   - **b.** R92.1
   - **c.** R92.2
   - **d.** R92.8

10. First- and second-degree burns of right forearm, initial encounter.
    a. T22.019A
    b. T22.011A
    c. T22.111A, T22.211A
    d. T22.211A

11. Stage 4 chronic kidney disease (CKD) patient undergoes outpatient renal dialysis.
    a. N18.4, Z99.2
    b. N18.6, Z49.31
    c. N18.9, Z91.15
    d. N19, Z99.2

12. Family history of sudden cardiac death (SCD).
    a. Z82.41
    b. Z82.49
    c. Z86.74
    d. Z87.898

13. Personal history of thrombophlebitis.
    a. I80.9
    b. Z09, Z82.49
    c. Z82.49
    d. Z86.72

14. Patient injured while swimming. Select the activity code.
    a. Y92.016
    b. Y92.026
    c. Y93.11
    d. Y93.14

15. Patient fell while at a bank. Select the place of occurrence code.
    a. Y92.214
    b. Y92.510
    c. Y92.513
    d. Y92.61

Coding Practice – Diseases

Instructions: Assign the appropriate ICD-10-CM code(s) to each disease, injury, or reason for treatment.

_____   1. Fitting of cardiac pacemaker

_____   2. Gray syndrome from chloramphenicol administration in newborn as prescribed (initial encounter)

_____   3. Injury by shotgun, undetermined whether accidental or intentional (shooting) (initial encounter)

_____   4. Irritable bowel syndrome

_____   5. Medial dislocation of tibia, proximal end, open (initial encounter)

_____   6. Motor vehicle traffic accident involving a collision with a pedestrian (initial encounter)

_____   7. Nausea with vomiting

_____   8. Personal history of penicillin allergy

_____   9. Polyarticular juvenile rheumatoid arthritis, acute

_____   10. Polycystic kidney, autosomal recessive

_____   11. Spontaneous abortion, complicated by excessive hemorrhage, complete

_____   12. Preterm labor with preterm delivery of liveborn twins, third trimester

_____   13. Uterine prolapse, first degree

_____   14. Staphylococcal scalded skin syndrome

_____   15. Infective myositis, right shoulder, streptococcus

ICD-10-CM and ICD-10-PCS Hospital Inpatient Coding

Chapter Outline

Acute Care Facilities (Hospitals)

Inpatient Diagnosis Coding Guidelines

Inpatient Procedure Coding Guidelines

ICD-10-PCS Procedure Coding

Coding Inpatient Diagnoses and Procedures

Chapter Objectives

At the conclusion of this chapter, the student should be able to:

1. Define key terms related to ICD-10-CM and ICD-10-PCS hospital inpatient coding.
2. Explain the differences among acute care inpatient settings.
3. Interpret inpatient diagnosis coding guidelines when assigning ICD-10-CM codes.
4. Interpret inpatient procedure coding guidelines when assigning ICD-10-PCS codes.
5. Assign ICD-10-PCS codes to procedures.
6. Assign ICD-10-CM and ICD-10-PCS codes for acute care (hospital) inpatient cases.

Key Terms

acute care facility (ACF)

acute care hospital

admitting diagnosis

ancillary service

axis of classification

bed count

bed size

behavioral health care hospital

comorbidity

complication

critical access hospital (CAH)

general hospital

Index

inpatient

long-term acute care hospital (LTACH)

long-term hospital

maximizing reimbursement

multiaxial structure

multihospital system

newborn patient

optimizing reimbursement

other (additional) diagnoses

other significant procedure

principal diagnosis

principal procedure

rehabilitation hospital

secondary procedure

short-term hospital

single hospital

specialty hospital

subacute care patient

swing bed

tables

Uniform Hospital Discharge Data Set (UHDDS)

value

Introduction

This chapter defines inpatient acute care settings and includes an interpretation of the guidelines for sequencing diagnosis (and procedures, as required by some third-party payers) published in the Center for Medicare and Medicaid Services (CMS) *ICD-10-CM Official Guidelines for Coding and Reporting* and *ICD-10-PCS Official Guidelines for Coding and Reporting.*

 NOTE:

The following additional content is located on the Student Companion Site at **http://login.cengage.com**.
- *ICD-10-PCS Operations, Definitions, Explanations, and Examples*
- *Tutorial: How to Code a Hospital Inpatient Record*

Coding guidelines discussed in this chapter are to be used as a companion to the official version of the ICD-10-CM and ICD-10-PCS, which contain coding conventions to ensure accurate coding.

 NOTE:

Students enrolled in medical assistant and medical office administration academic programs may notice that their instructor skips this chapter. Content about hospital outpatients, ambulatory surgery patients, emergency care patients, and observation care patients are discussed in Chapter 7.

Acute Care Facilities (Hospitals)

An **acute care facility (ACF)** is a hospital that provides health care services to patients who have serious, sudden, or acute illnesses or injuries and/or who need certain surgeries. ACFs provide a full range of health care services including ancillary services, emergency and critical care, surgery, and obstetrics (labor and delivery). **Ancillary services** are diagnostic and therapeutic services provided to inpatients and outpatients (e.g., laboratory, physical therapy). Most hospital inpatient stays are short (fewer than 30 days), although some patients may stay for a longer time if medically necessary. Because each inpatient day is expensive, a utilization or case manager closely monitors patient care to determine whether acute health care services are required.

 NOTE:

Inpatient health care settings include:
- Acute care hospitals
- Critical access hospitals (CAHs)
- Behavioral health care facilities
- Hospice inpatient care
- Long-term acute care facilities

 NOTE:

Content about other than acute care inpatient settings (e.g., home health care, hospice) is located on the Student Companion Site at **http://login.cengage.com**.

Hospitals have an organized medical and professional staff, and inpatient beds are available 24 hours per day. The primary function of hospitals is to provide inpatient medical, nursing, and other health-related services to patients for surgical and nonsurgical conditions; hospitals usually provide some outpatient services as well. Hospitals are categorized as (1) **single hospitals** (hospitals are self-contained and not part of larger organizations) and (2) **multihospital systems** (where two or more hospitals are owned, managed, or leased by a single organization; these may include acute, long-term, pediatric, rehabilitation, or psychiatric care facilities).

Another consideration when discussing hospital organization is to identify the *population served by a health care facility*, which means that health care is provided to specific groups of people in that some hospitals specialize in the treatment of children (e.g., pediatric hospitals), while others have special units (e.g., burn unit). The hospital **bed size** (or **bed count**) is the total number of inpatient beds for which the facility is licensed by the state; the hospital must be equipped and staffed to care for these patient admissions. The hospital's average length of stay (LOS) determines classification as a

- **Short-term hospital** (or **acute care hospital**): Average LOS of 4–5 days and a total LOS of fewer than 25 days.
- **Long-term hospital** (or long-term acute care hospital or LTACH): Average LOS is more than 25 days.

> **EXAMPLE:** Patient was admitted 4/5/YYYY and discharged on 4/10/YYYY. To calculate the LOS, count the day of admission but not the day of discharge. This patient's LOS is 5 days.

Hospitals are also categorized by type.

- **Critical access hospitals (CAHs)** are located more than 35 miles from any hospital or another CAH, or they are state-certified as being a necessary provider of health care to area residents. (The requirement is reduced to 15 miles in areas where only secondary roads are available or in mountainous terrains.) CAHs must provide emergency services 24 hours per day and maintain no more than 15 inpatient beds (except swing-bed facilities, which can have up to 25 inpatient beds if no more than 15 are used at any one time for acute care). Inpatients are restricted to 96-hour stays unless a longer period is required due to inclement weather or the development of another emergency condition. (A **swing bed** allows a rural hospital to admit a nonacute care patient.)
- **General hospitals** provide emergency care, perform general surgery, and admit patients for a range of problems from fractures to heart disease based on licensing by the state.
- **Long-term acute care hospitals (LTACH)** provide care designed specifically for patients who need functional restoration or rehabilitation and medical management for an average of 3 to 6 weeks.
- **Specialty hospitals** concentrate on a particular population of patients (e.g., children) or diseases (e.g., cancer).
- **Rehabilitation hospitals** admit patients who are diagnosed with trauma (e.g., car accident) or disease (e.g., stroke) and need to learn how to function.
- **Behavioral health care hospitals** specialize in treating individuals with mental health diagnoses.

Hospital patients who receive care while residing in the facility are categorized as inpatients, newborn patients, and subacute care patients.

- **Inpatients** stay overnight in the facility for 24 or more hours and are provided with room and board and nursing services.
- **Newborn patients** receive infant care upon birth, and, if necessary, they receive neonatal intensive care (either within the hospital or as the result of transfer to another hospital).
- **Subacute care patients** receive specialized long-term acute care such as chemotherapy, injury rehabilitation, ventilator (breathing machine) support, wound care, and other types of health care services provided to seriously ill patients. Subacute care facilities look like *mini-intensive care units*, and they usually do not offer the full range of health care services available in acute care facilities (e.g., emergency departments [EDs], obstetrics, and surgery). Subacute care costs less than acute care, and patients are often transferred directly from an intensive care unit. Medicare will reimburse subacute care facilities if care provided is appropriate and medically necessary.

Medicare Part A Hospital Inpatient Order and Physician Certification

Coverage and reimbursement of Medicare Part A hospital inpatient services requires physician certification of *medical necessity* that such services be provided on an inpatient basis. A critical element of physician certification is the *practitioner order*, which is an inpatient admission order that must be documented by the provider in the patient record. In 2014, CMS issued a final rule (CMS-1599-F) called the *2-Midnight Rule*, which modified and clarified the policy about Medicare Administrative Contractor (MAC) review of inpatient hospital and critical access hospital (CAH) admissions for payment purposes. Under the final rule, surgical procedures, diagnostic tests, and other treatments (in addition to services designated as inpatient-only) are generally appropriate for inpatient hospital admission and payment under Medicare Part A *when the physician expects the beneficiary to require a stay that crosses at least two midnights and admits the beneficiary to the hospital based upon that expectation.* The rule was published as a response to facilities' and beneficiaries' concerns about increasingly long stays as outpatients (e.g., observation care) due to hospital uncertainties about payment.

Physician certification requires physician authentication of the practitioner order, documentation of a reason for inpatient services, estimated or actual length of time the beneficiary requires as an inpatient in the hospital, and plans for posthospital care.

For inpatient CAH services only, the physician must certify that the beneficiary may reasonably be expected to be discharged or transferred to a hospital within 96 hours after admission to the CAH. For inpatient rehabilitation facilities (IRF) services only, the documentation that IRFs are already required to complete to meet the IRF coverage requirements (e.g., preadmission screening physician review and concurrence, the post-admission physician evaluation, and the required admission orders) may be used to satisfy the certification and recertification statement requirements.

Exercise 6.1 – Acute Care Facilities (Hospitals)

Instructions: Complete each statement.

1. The type of hospital that provides health care services to patients who have serious, sudden, or acute illnesses or injuries and/or who need certain surgeries is called a(n) _____ care facility.

2. Diagnostic and therapeutic services provided to inpatients and outpatients (e.g., laboratory, physical therapy) are called _____ services.

3. Hospitals that are self-contained and not part of larger organizations are called _____; while two or more hospitals owned, managed, or leased by a single organization are called multihospital systems.

4. The total number of inpatient beds for which a facility is licensed by the state is called the hospital _____ size or count.

5. A hospital's average length of stay (LOS) determines whether the hospital is classified as a(n) _____ or acute (average LOS of 4–5 days and a total LOS of fewer than 25 days) hospital.

6. A hospital is classified as _____ when the average LOS is more than 25 days.

7. A patient was admitted on May 30 and discharged on June 3 of the same year. The LOS is calculated as _____ days.

8. A swing bed allows a rural hospital to admit a(n) _____ care patient.

9. Patients who are diagnosed with trauma or disease and who need to learn how to function are usually admitted to _____ hospitals.

10. A health care facility that concentrates on a particular population of patients (e.g., children) or disease (e.g., cancer) is called a(n) _____ hospital.

Inpatient Diagnosis Coding Guidelines

The circumstances of inpatient admission govern the sequencing of diagnoses. The **Uniform Hospital Discharge Data Set (UHDDS)** was established by the federal government to define data collected for inpatient hospitalizations (e.g., age, gender, race, diagnoses, procedures, payment sources). UHDDS definitions have always been used by acute care hospitals to report inpatient data elements in a standardized manner. Since the creation of the UHDDS in 1985, the application of the UHDDS definitions has been expanded to include all nonoutpatient settings (e.g., acute care, short-term, long-term, and psychiatric hospitals; home health agencies; rehabilitation facilities; and skilled nursing facilities and nursing homes).

Circumstances associated with an inpatient admission govern the sequencing of the following diagnoses:

- Admitting diagnosis
- Principal diagnosis
- Other (additional) diagnoses (or secondary diagnoses, which include comorbidities and complications)

 Coding Tip

Inpatient and outpatient health care settings require different diagnosis definitions (e.g., principal diagnosis versus first-listed diagnosis) because of the time frame available for patient care and treatment. The first-listed diagnosis, reported as an ICD-10-CM code for outpatient and physician office care, is defined in Chapter 7.

The attending physician does not document final diagnoses until an inpatient is discharged from the hospital; by that time, a definitive diagnosis has usually been established. Because inpatient coding guidelines prohibit the coding of signs and symptoms when a definitive diagnosis has been established, signs and symptoms are seldom documented as the principal diagnosis on inpatient charts. In addition, qualified (uncertain) diagnoses can be coded as principal and other diagnoses for hospital inpatients because physicians use hospital resources to treat the patient for these types of conditions and because hospital reimbursement is based on the utilization and consumption of resources. (In the outpatient setting, the physician usually does not have time to establish a definitive diagnosis during one encounter. Thus, signs and symptoms are often reported as the first-listed diagnosis for third-party payer reimbursement purposes.)

 NOTE:

The attending physician is responsible for documenting the list of final diagnoses in the patient record.

Admitting Diagnosis

The **admitting diagnosis** is the provisional or tentative diagnosis upon which initial patient care is based. It is obtained from the patient's attending physician by the admissions office staff, who enter it in a field on the inpatient face sheet. The admitting diagnosis may be a sign (e.g., fever, cough, rash) or symptom (chest pain, sore throat, numbness) (instead of a definitive diagnosis). One admitting diagnosis ICD-10-CM code is reported on the UB-04.

Principal Diagnosis

The **principal diagnosis** is defined in the UHDDS as "that condition established after study to be chiefly responsible for occasioning the admission of the patient to the hospital for care." The most important part of the definition is the phrase *after study*, which directs the coder to review all patient record documentation associated with an inpatient hospitalization to determine the clinical reason for the admission. The circumstances of admission that impact selection of the principal diagnosis include the chief complaint and the patient's signs and symptoms on admission, which are documented on the history and physical examination. In addition, the entire patient record is reviewed to determine which condition was *established after study*; this means that the coder reviews ancillary test results (e.g., laboratory, x-ray) and other reports (e.g., operative report, pathology report) to select the principal diagnosis. If selection of the principal diagnosis is unclear, the physician should be queried and the outcome of the query corroborated with supporting documentation in the patient record. One principal diagnosis code is reported on the UB-04.

NOTE:

> When determining the principal diagnosis, ICD-10-CM coding conventions take precedence over official coding guidelines.

HIPAA Alert!

HIPAA regulations for electronic transactions require providers and payers (including MACs) to adhere to the *Official Guidelines for Coding and Reporting*. Thus, a violation of the coding guidelines is a HIPAA violation. Unfortunately, some payers do not appear to be aware of or understand this HIPAA provision. Payers should be informed of the provision in the HIPAA regulation that references the use of coding guidelines. If payers deny claims because certain codes are reported as principal diagnosis, contact your regional CMS office or the HIPAA enforcement office (at CMS) to alert them about the HIPAA violation.

EXAMPLE: A 51-year-old male patient presented to the ED, complaining of ringing in his ears, dizziness, blurred vision, confusion, and difficulty walking. Upon evaluation by the ED physician, the patient stated that these symptoms started suddenly just two hours ago. Past history revealed that the patient takes medication for hypercholesterolemia and hypertension. The patient used to smoke two packs of cigarettes daily until 5 years ago, when he quit. Physical examination revealed blood pressure of 175/110. When asked, the patient stated that he had been taking his hypertension medication as prescribed.

Patient underwent carotid ultrasound to evaluate the blood flow of the carotid arteries, and results indicated the need for carotid angiogram to measure blockage of the carotid arteries. The ED physician transferred the case to a cardiologist, who performed a bilateral carotid angiogram that revealed 90% blockage of the right carotid artery and 20% blockage of the left carotid artery. The patient was admitted to the hospital and scheduled for carotid angioplasty with insertion of carotid stent in the morning, which was performed uneventfully. Final diagnoses were documented as carotid artery occlusion, hypertension, and hypercholesterolemia. Procedures performed included carotid ultrasound, carotid angiogram, and carotid angioplasty.

In this example, the principal diagnosis is the carotid artery occlusion (I65.29). Other diagnoses (or secondary diagnoses) include hypertension (I10) and hypercholesterolemia (E78.00). Do not assign codes to the symptoms of ringing in his ears, dizziness, blurred vision, confusion, and difficulty walking because they are associated with the carotid artery occlusion. Signs and symptoms are often documented in the patient's record, but they are not coded if they are considered part of an established diagnosis.

Codes for Symptoms, Signs, and Ill-Defined Conditions

Codes for symptoms, signs, and ill-defined conditions from ICD-10-CM Chapter 18 are *not* to be reported as the principal diagnosis when a related definitive diagnosis has been established.

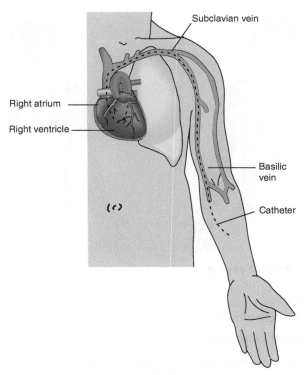

FIGURE 6-1 Cardiac catheterization

EXAMPLE: The patient is admitted as a hospital inpatient after having been treated in the ED for chest pain and a positive electrocardiogram (EKG), which revealed anterolateral MI. The patient underwent cardiac catheterization (Figure 6-1) during hospitalization and subsequent quadruple coronary artery bypass graft surgery. The principal diagnosis for this case is acute anterolateral MI, first episode. The chest pain is not assigned a code because it is a symptom of the MI.

Two or More Interrelated Conditions, Each Potentially Meeting the Definition for Principal Diagnosis

When two or more interrelated *inpatient* conditions (e.g., diseases located in the same ICD-10-CM chapter, manifestations associated with a certain disease) potentially meet the definition of principal diagnosis, either condition may be sequenced first unless the circumstances of the admission, the therapy provided, or the ICD-10-CM index or tabular list indicates otherwise.

EXAMPLE: A patient is admitted as a hospital inpatient with chest pain, fever, and shortness of breath. Chest x-ray reveals exacerbated congestive heart failure (CHF). Physical examination reveals acute bronchitis. The patient's prior history and current EKG findings are consistent with unstable angina (Figure 6-2). All three conditions of CHF, acute bronchitis, and unstable angina were treated with medications, and all three diagnoses equally meet the criteria for the definition of principal diagnosis. The coder can code and sequence any one of the three diagnoses as the principal diagnosis.

As an alternative scenario, this patient underwent coronary arteriography that revealed coronary artery disease and 95% blockage of two prominent arterial branches. Subsequently, the patient was taken to the operating room for percutaneous transluminal coronary angioplasty (PTCA). In this scenario, the coronary arteriography diagnostic workup and PTCA treatment criteria clearly distinguish coronary artery disease, identified as the etiology (cause) of the patient's unstable angina, as the principal diagnosis.

Two or More Diagnoses That Equally Meet the Definition for Principal Diagnosis

In the unusual instance when two or more *inpatient* diagnoses *equally* meet the criteria for principal diagnosis, *as determined by one or more of the following*, any one of the diagnoses may be reported as the principal diagnosis:

FIGURE 6-2 Patterns of angina

- Circumstances of admission
- Diagnostic workup and/or therapy provided
- ICD-10-CM index, tabular list, or other coding guidelines do not provide sequencing direction

Determining which of several diagnoses to report as the principal diagnosis when multiple diagnoses equally meet the criteria for selection as the principal diagnosis is called **optimizing reimbursement**, and it is permitted under the inpatient prospective payment system (IPPS), which uses diagnosis-related groups (DRGs). (DRGs are discussed in Chapter 20.) (Trauma cases often result in several diagnoses, any one of which could be selected and reported as the principal diagnosis.) **Maximizing reimbursement** is *not* permitted because it involves (1) selecting and reporting as principal diagnosis the code that results in the highest level of reimbursement for the facility, whether that diagnosis meets the criteria for selection or not, or (2) assigning a higher-paying code (upcoding) to a diagnosis (or ICD-10-PCS, CPT, or HCPCS level II code to a procedure) even if patient record documentation does not support that code selection. (Under the IPPS, upcoding and maximizing reimbursement is called *DRG creep*.)

EXAMPLE 1: OPTIMIZING REIMBURSEMENT: The patient was admitted to the hospital after an automobile accident, initial evaluation was performed in the ED, and the patient was diagnosed with fractured left femur and fractured right humerus. Inpatient treatment included an open reduction internal fixation of the fractured left femur and open reduction internal fixation of the fractured right humerus. In this case, either the fractured left femur or the fractured right humerus could be reported as the principal diagnosis. The best practice would be to assign codes to each diagnosis and procedure, enter them into the diagnosis-related grouper, determine which would result in optimal reimbursement for the hospital, and report that code as the principal diagnosis.

EXAMPLE 2: MAXIMIZING REIMBURSEMENT AND UPCODING: The patient was admitted as a hospital inpatient for treatment of urosepsis, which is a urinary tract infection (UTI). (A secondary code is assigned to indicate the cause of the infection, such as *Escherichia coli*.) The DRG reimbursement rate is approximately $2,300. Using encoder and DRG grouper software, the coder may notice that the code for sepsis results in the higher DRG rate of approximately $6,400. If the code for sepsis is reported as principal diagnosis, this case would most likely be reviewed to verify accuracy of the reported code. Upon review, the error would be discovered and the hospital could be subject to sanctions (e.g., loss of Medicare participating provider status) and fines.

Two or More Comparative or Contrasting Conditions

In those rare instances when two or more *inpatient* contrasting or comparative diagnoses are documented as *either/or* (or similar terminology), they are coded as if the diagnoses were confirmed. The diagnoses are sequenced according to the circumstances of the admission. If no further determination can be made as to which diagnosis should be principal, either diagnosis may be sequenced first.

> **EXAMPLE:** An elderly patient was treated for complaints of chest pain and shortness of breath, and the physician documented "acute asthma or acute pneumonia" on the patient's record. The patient died before diagnostic workup could be initiated, and the family declined to have the patient undergo an autopsy. Assign an ICD-10-CM code to both conditions, and either diagnosis may be sequenced as the principal diagnosis to optimize reimbursement.

Original Treatment Plan Not Carried Out

Even though treatment may not have been carried out during an inpatient stay due to unforeseen circumstances, the condition which, after study, occasioned the admission to the hospital is sequenced as the principal diagnosis.

> **EXAMPLE:** The patient was scheduled for surgery due to severe ureteritis. After administration of anesthesia, the patient was prepped for an endoscopic biopsy of the right ureter. The endoscope passed easily into the urinary bladder but was unable to advance to the right ureter due to ureteral blockage. The surgeon removed the endoscope, and the patient was taken to the recovery room.
>
> In this example, the surgery was halted because after the cystourethroscope was advanced through the urinary bladder, it could not be advanced into the ureter. The principal diagnosis is ureteritis, and the significant other diagnosis is ureteral blockage.

Complications of Surgery and Other Medical Care

When an inpatient admission is for treatment of a complication resulting from surgery or other medical care, the complication code is sequenced as the principal diagnosis. If the complication is classified to the ICD-10-CM T80–T88 series and the code lacks the necessary specificity in describing the complication, an additional code for the specific complication should be assigned.

> **EXAMPLE:** A 54-year-old male patient was admitted to the hospital for severe stomach pain, nausea, vomiting, and fever of 102 degrees. The abdomen was rigid and distended. Past history revealed that two months ago, the patient had undergone open cholecystectomy for cholecystitis with cholelithiasis. Laboratory tests revealed elevated white blood cell count. Patient was scheduled for exploratory laparotomy, which revealed the presence of abscessed stitches. Cultures taken were positive for *Staphylococcus aureus*.
>
> In this example, the principal diagnosis is abscessed stitches, which is a complication of the open cholecystectomy. The significant other diagnoses include staphylococcal infection and postoperative status. The principal procedure is exploratory laparotomy, and the significant other procedure is reopening of recent laparotomy site.

Uncertain Diagnosis (or Qualified Diagnosis)

If the principal diagnosis documented at the time of discharge is uncertain or qualified with words such as *probable, suspected, likely, questionable, possible, still to be ruled out,* compatible with, consistent with, or other similar terms indicating uncertainty, code the diagnosis as if it existed or was established. The basis for this guideline is the diagnostic workup, arrangements for further workup or observation, and initial therapeutic approach that correspond most closely with the established diagnosis.

 NOTE:

> The *uncertain diagnosis* guideline applies only to diagnoses reported for inpatient admissions to acute short-term, acute long-term, and psychiatric *hospitals*. Other nonoutpatient health care settings (e.g., home health care, rehabilitation hospitals, skilled nursing facilities, nursing homes) and all outpatient health care settings do not assign codes to uncertain diagnoses. They assign codes to signs and symptoms when a provider has not documented a definitive diagnosis.

> **EXAMPLE:** A 24-year-old female was admitted due to fever of 102 degrees for a period of two days, as well as chills. The patient has a past history of having undergone a recent laparoscopic appendectomy, for which she was prescribed postoperative antibiotics. She had completed the prescription when she spiked a fever and started experiencing chills. Review of systems reveals complaints of painful urination for two days. The patient states that she has frequent UTIs. Although the urine culture was negative, it is likely that this patient has a UTI, which has to be treated aggressively given her postoperative status.
>
> Patient received intravenous ciprofloxacin and aminoglycoside for a period of 72 hours, after which she improved and was discharged for follow-up in the office. She was prescribed an oral antibiotic to be continued 10 days after discharge. Final diagnosis is possible UTI. In this example, although the final diagnosis of possible UTI is uncertain (or qualified), it is the principal diagnosis. The other significant diagnosis is postoperative surgical status.

Admission from Observation Unit

Admission Following Medical Observation. When a patient is admitted to an observation unit for a medical condition that either worsens or does not improve *and* is subsequently admitted as an inpatient to the same hospital for this same medical condition, the principal diagnosis would be the medical condition that led to the hospital inpatient admission.

Admission Following Postoperative Observation. When a patient is admitted to an observation unit to monitor a condition (or complication) that develops following outpatient surgery and is subsequently admitted as an inpatient of the same hospital, hospitals should apply the Uniform Hospital Discharge Data Set (UHDDS) definition of principal diagnosis as "that condition established after study to be chiefly responsible for occasioning the admission of the patient to the hospital for care."

Admission from Outpatient Surgery

When a patient undergoes surgery in the hospital's outpatient surgery department and is subsequently admitted for continuing inpatient care at the same hospital, the following guidelines should be followed in selecting the principal diagnosis for the inpatient admission:

- If the reason for the inpatient admission is a complication, assign the complication as the principal diagnosis.
- If no complication, or other condition, is documented as the reason for the inpatient admission, assign the reason for the outpatient surgery as the principal diagnosis.
- If the reason for the inpatient admission is another condition unrelated to the surgery, assign the unrelated condition as the principal diagnosis.

Admissions/Encounters for Rehabilitation

When the purpose for the admission or encounter is rehabilitation, sequence first the code for the condition for which the service is being performed. However, if the condition for which the rehabilitation service is being provided is no longer present, report the appropriate aftercare code as the first-listed or principal diagnosis unless the rehabilitation service is being provided following an injury. For rehabilitation services following active treatment of an injury, assign the injury code with the appropriate seventh character for subsequent encounter as the first-listed or principal diagnosis.

> **EXAMPLE 1:** The patient is admitted for rehabilitation services for right-sided dominant hemiplegia following a cerebrovascular infarction. Report code I69.351 as the first-listed or principal diagnosis.

> **EXAMPLE 2:** The patient is admitted for rehabilitation services due to severe degenerative osteoarthritis of the hip. The patient previously underwent hip replacement surgery. Report aftercare code Z47.1 as the first-listed or principal diagnosis.

> **EXAMPLE 3:** A patient underwent initial rehabilitation following hip replacement for right intertrochanteric femur fracture, and code S72.141A (Displaced intertrochanteric fracture of right femur, initial encounter for closed fracture) was reported. The patient returns at a later date for additional rehabilitation, and code S72.141D (Displaced intertrochanteric fracture of right femur, subsequent encounter for closed fracture with routine healing) is reported as the first-listed or principal diagnosis.

Other (Additional) Diagnoses with Documentation That Supports Reporting

For reporting purposes, the definition for *other (additional) diagnoses* is interpreted as additional conditions that affect patient care by requiring one or more of the following:

- Clinical evaluation
- Therapeutic treatment
- Diagnostic procedures
- Extended length of hospital stay
- Increased nursing care and/or monitoring

The UHDDS defines **other (additional) diagnoses** as "all conditions that coexist at the time of admission, that develop subsequently, or that affect the treatment received and/or the length of stay." Diagnoses related to an earlier episode that have no bearing on the current hospital stay are not coded. Up to 17 secondary diagnoses are reported on a UB-04 claim. The UB-04 claim contains separate fields for entry of three external cause of morbidity ICD-10-CM codes (in addition to the 17 secondary diagnosis codes).

 NOTE:

DRG grouper software allows for the entry of one principal diagnosis ICD-10-CM code and up to 24 other (additional) diagnosis ICD-10-CM codes.

The Centers for Medicare & Medicaid Services (CMS) has developed a standard list of other (additional) diagnoses that are recognized as comorbidities and/or complications (CCs) or major comorbidities and/or complications (MCCs) for Medicare-severity diagnosis-related groups (MS-DRGs) (discussed in Chapter 20). When a CC or MCC is present as a secondary diagnosis, it can affect MS-DRG assignment. A **comorbidity** is a condition that coexists at the time of admission (e.g., diabetes mellitus, hypertension, asthma), and a **complication** is a condition that occurs during the course of the inpatient hospital episode (e.g., fractured hip resulting from fall while gait training, postoperative infection, hospital-acquired staphylococcal infection).

MS-DRGs with CC or MCC require a substantial increase in utilization of hospital resources, and the reimbursement for these DRGs reflects an increase in payment. While just one CC or MCC can change a *MS-DRG without CC or MCC* to an *MS-DRG with CC or MCC*, there are a number of stand-alone MS-DRGs that are not affected by the presence or absence of CCs. For stand-alone MS-DRGs, the MS-DRG (and reimbursement amount) will change (and increase) only if the principal diagnosis is changed or a significant surgical procedure is reported.

EXAMPLE: An 86-year-old female was admitted to the hospital with complaints of severe shortness of breath, dyspnea, and chest pain. Upon evaluation, the attending physician determined that the patient has a history of intrinsic asthma and is currently experiencing acute exacerbation of that condition. The patient also has a past history of hypertension, for which she takes medication. Last year the patient was treated in the hospital's pain clinic on an outpatient basis for cluster headaches, which have not recurred. Patient received respiratory therapy and drug therapy for the asthma. The physician also ordered medications and patient education for the hypertension and blood pressure monitoring three times per nursing shift. The final diagnoses documented upon discharge include acute exacerbation of intrinsic asthma and hypertension.

In this example, the principal diagnosis is acute exacerbation of intrinsic asthma and the comorbidity (coexisting condition or other significant diagnosis) is hypertension. The hypertension increased nursing care and monitoring because medications were administered, patient teaching was performed, and the patient's blood pressure was taken three times per shift.

Coding Tip

When other diagnoses are documented and no supporting documentation can be found in the patient record, make sure you query the physician to determine whether the diagnosis is to be coded and reported. For example, when a patient is admitted for treatment of an acute condition (e.g., trauma, illness) and the physician notes positive findings on the physical examination (e.g., tendonitis) that are not treated during the hospitalization, do not code the positive findings because they do not impact the episode of care.

Previous Conditions Stated as a Diagnosis

If the provider has documented a diagnosis in the list of diagnoses on the discharge summary or the face sheet in the patient record, it should ordinarily be coded. However, some providers document diagnoses for resolved conditions or chronic diagnoses and status-post procedures from previous admissions that have no bearing on the current inpatient stay. Such conditions are not coded and reported for reimbursement purposes. However, family and personal history codes are reported as secondary codes *if* the historical condition or family history impacts current care or influences the patient's treatment.

EXAMPLE: A 92-year-old female patient was admitted as a hospital inpatient for acute MI of the anterolateral wall. The patient's history is negative for cardiovascular or respiratory complaints, and she states that she has not had an MI in the past. The patient does have a past history of localized uterine adenocarcinoma 20 years ago, for which she underwent vaginal hysterectomy. The final diagnosis is acute anterolateral wall MI, initial episode of care.

In this example, the principal diagnosis is acute anterolateral wall MI, initial episode of care. The localized uterine adenocarcinoma is not assigned a neoplasm code from ICD-10-CM Chapter 2. Instead, it is appropriate to assign a code for history of uterine cancer.

Abnormal Findings

Abnormal findings (e.g., ancillary tests such as laboratory, x-ray, pathologic, and other diagnostic results) are not coded and reported unless the provider documents their clinical significance. If the ancillary test findings are outside the normal range and the attending provider has ordered other tests to evaluate the condition or prescribed treatment, it is appropriate to ask the provider whether the abnormal finding should be added.

EXAMPLE: A 49-year-old male patient was admitted as a hospital inpatient for acute pneumonia due to *Staphylococcus aureus*, which was evaluated and successfully treated. During hospitalization, the patient underwent an EKG that was interpreted by the cardiologist as being normal. The EKG report did document abnormal T-wave changes.

In this example, the principal diagnosis is acute pneumonia due to *S. aureus*. The coder should query the physician to determine if a code should be assigned to "abnormal T-wave changes" as documented on the EKG. It is likely that the coder will be told by the physician that such changes are commonly associated with EKGs performed on anxious patients and that this male patient was quite ill, which could cause anxiety.

 NOTE:

In the outpatient setting, the provider interprets diagnostic test results, and codes are assigned for such encounters.

Uncertain Diagnosis (as Other/Additional Diagnosis)

If the diagnosis documented at the time of discharge is qualified as "probable," "suspected," "likely," "questionable," "possible," "still to be ruled out," "compatible with," "consistent with," or other similar terms indicating uncertainty, code the condition as if it existed or was established. The bases for these guidelines are the diagnostic workup, arrangements for further workup or observation, and initial therapeutic approach that correspond most closely with the established diagnosis.

 NOTE:

The "uncertain diagnosis" is applicable only to inpatient admissions to short-term, acute, long-term care, and psychiatric hospitals. ("Uncertain diagnosis" is also called "qualified diagnosis.")

Exercise 6.2 – Inpatient Diagnosis Coding Guidelines

Instructions: Match the case scenario with the sequencing guideline.

_____ 1. Patient undergoes appendectomy and develops postoperative wound infection.

_____ 2. Patient admitted with acute asthma and acute CHF, both of which were treated.

_____ 3. The patient is admitted for rehabilitation services for left-sided dominant hemiplegia following a stroke.

_____ 4. Patient admitted and treated for acute gastroenteritis has extremely low potassium level. (Physician query initiated.)

_____ 5. Patient admitted with acute gastroenteritis versus acute gastric ulcer; patient treated symptomatically.

_____ 6. Elderly patient admitted with recent history of severe abdominal pain for which testing was performed. Final diagnoses are peritonitis and acute ulcerative colitis.

_____ 7. Patient admitted for treatment of acute MI and receives medication and patient education for previously diagnosed insulin-dependent diabetes mellitus.

_____ 8. Patient admitted with right lower quadrant pain and elevated fever. Possible ectopic pregnancy. Possible acute appendicitis.

_____ 9. Patient admitted for treatment of fractured hip; has a past history of cholecystitis with cholecystectomy one year ago.

_____ 10. Patient with a diagnosis of multiparity, admitted for elective sterilization, was found to have elevated temperature, and surgery was canceled.

a. Abnormal findings

b. Complications of surgery and other medical care

c. Original treatment plan not carried out

d. Other (additional) diagnoses reported

e. Previous conditions stated as diagnoses

f. Rehabilitation admission/ encounter

g. Two or more comparative or contrasting conditions coded as if the diagnosis is confirmed

h. Two or more diagnoses equally meeting definition for principal diagnosis

i. Two or more interrelated conditions equally meeting definition of principal diagnosis

j. Uncertain, or qualified, diagnosis

Inpatient Procedure Coding Guidelines

Depending on state reporting requirements, when the circumstances of inpatient admission govern the sequencing of procedure codes, UHDDS definitions are used to report inpatient data elements in a standardized manner. Circumstances associated with an inpatient hospital admission govern the sequencing of

- Principal procedure
- Significant other procedures (or secondary procedures)

> **EXAMPLE:** New York State's (NYS) *Statewide Planning and Research Cooperative System (SPARCS)* is a comprehensive data reporting system that was established in 1979 in cooperation with the health care industry and state government. Initially created to collect information on discharges from hospitals, SPARCS now collects patient-level detail on patient characteristics, diagnoses and treatments, services, and charges for every NYS hospital discharge, ambulatory surgery patient, and emergency department admission. SPARCS created *output data dictionaries*, which include definitions, codes and values, and edit applications for inpatient and outpatient *output data elements*. For electronic claims purposes, SPARCS requires reporting of the principal procedure and significant other procedures. The SPARCS outpatient data dictionary's definition of these terms is based on the federal government's UHDDS definition.

 NOTE:

Inpatient procedures are classified using ICD-10-PCS. Outpatient and physician office settings report CPT and HCPCS level II codes for procedures/services (discussed in Chapters 8–19).

 NOTE:

All operating room procedures performed that are surgical in nature, carry a procedural risk, carry an anesthetic risk, or require specialized training are assigned ICD-10-PCS codes and reported.

Principal Procedure and Significant Other Procedures

When required for reimbursement purposes, the principal procedure is sequenced first, followed by other significant procedure(s) (when more than one procedure is reported on an inpatient claim). The following instructions should be applied in the selection of **principal procedure**, and they provide clarification regarding the importance of the relation to the principal diagnosis when more than one procedure is performed:

1. When the procedure is performed for definitive treatment of both the principal diagnosis and secondary diagnosis, sequence the procedure performed for definitive treatment most related to principal diagnosis as the principal procedure.

2. When the procedure is performed for definitive treatment and diagnostic procedures are performed for both the principal diagnosis and secondary diagnosis, sequence the procedure performed for definitive treatment most related to principal diagnosis as the principal procedure.

3. When a diagnostic procedure was performed for the principal diagnosis, and a procedure is performed for definitive treatment of a secondary diagnosis, sequence the diagnostic procedure as the principal procedure because the procedure most related to the principal diagnosis takes precedence.

4. When no procedures performed were related to the principal diagnosis, but procedures were performed for definitive treatment or diagnostic procedures were performed for the secondary diagnosis, sequence the procedure performed for definitive treatment of the secondary diagnosis as the principal procedure.

Other significant procedures (or **secondary procedures**)

- Are surgical in nature (e.g., incision, excision, amputation)
- Carry a procedural (or operative) risk
- Carry an anesthetic risk
- Require highly trained personnel
- Require special facilities or equipment

One principal procedure is reported on a paper-based UB-04 claim, and up to five significant procedures can be reported on the same paper-based UB-04 claim. Similarly, one principal procedure is reported on an electronic claim, but up to 14 significant procedures can be reported on the same electronic claim.

 NOTE:

DRG grouper software allows for the entry of one ICD-10-PCS principal procedure code and up to 24 other (additional) ICD-10-PCS procedure codes. Upon implementation of MS-DRGs, CMS eliminated the requirement to sequence principal and secondary procedures. However, third-party payers might still require procedure codes to be sequenced properly.

EXAMPLE: A 64-year-old male patient presented to the ED complaining of ringing in his ears, dizziness, blurred vision, confusion, and difficulty walking. Upon evaluation by the ED physician, the patient stated that these symptoms started about 24 hours ago. Past history revealed that the patient takes medication for hypercholesterolemia and hypertension. Physical examination revealed blood pressure of 180/115. When asked, the patient stated that he had been taking his hypertension medication as prescribed. Patient underwent carotid ultrasound to evaluate the blood flow of the carotid arteries, and results indicated the need for carotid angiogram to measure blockage of the carotid arteries.

The ED physician transferred the case to a cardiologist, who admitted the patient to the hospital and performed a bilateral carotid angiogram. Angiogram revealed 92% blockage of the right carotid artery and 24% blockage of the left carotid artery. The patient was admitted to the hospital and scheduled for carotid angioplasty with insertion of carotid stent in the morning, which was performed uneventfully. Final diagnoses were documented as carotid artery occlusion, hypertension, and hypercholesterolemia. Procedures performed included carotid ultrasound, carotid angiogram, and carotid angioplasty.

In this example, the principal procedure is carotid angioplasty, Other significant procedures include insertion of carotid stent and carotid angiogram. (The carotid ultrasound is not categorized as an operating room procedure and is not reported.)

Exercise 6.3 – Inpatient Procedure Coding Guidelines

Instructions: Complete each statement.

1. Depending on state reporting requirements, when the circumstances of inpatient admission govern the sequencing of procedure codes, _____ definitions are used to report inpatient data elements in a standardized manner.

2. Inpatient procedures are classified using _____.

3. Outpatient and physician office settings report _____ and HCPCS level II codes for procedures and services.

4. When CMS implemented _____, they discontinued the practice of sequencing procedure codes for reimbursement purposes.

5. When required for reimbursement purposes, the principal procedure is sequenced _____.

6. The principal procedure is defined as being performed for _____ treatment rather than for diagnostic or exploratory purposes, necessary to treat a complication, or most closely related to the principal diagnosis.

(continues)

Exercise 6.3 – *continued*

7. Other significant procedures (or secondary procedures) are defined as _____, carrying a procedural (or operative) risk, carrying an anesthetic risk, requiring highly trained personnel, and/or requiring special facilities or equipment.

8. A paper-based UB-04 claim allows for the reporting of one principal procedure and _____ significant procedure(s).

9. An electronic inpatient claim allows for reporting of one principal procedure and up to _____ significant procedures.

10. The number of other (secondary) significant procedure codes that can be reported in DRG grouper software is _____.

ICD-10-PCS Procedure Coding

The *International Classification of Diseases, 10th Revision, Procedure Classification System* (ICD-10-PCS) is used by hospitals to code and classify procedure data from inpatient records only. ICD-10-PCS codes use a **multiaxial structure** for its seven-character alphanumeric codes, which means a value from each of seven hierarchies (positions) is assigned to construct a code. As a result, unique codes are constructed for all substantially different procedures, and the multiaxial structure allows new procedures to be easily incorporated as new codes.

The ICD-10-PCS coding manual contains the following:

- Index
- Tables

ICD-10-PCS Index

The ICD-10-PCS **Index** (Figure 6-3) organizes main terms in alphabetical order, providing the first three or four characters (and sometimes all seven characters) of a code as well as direction to a specific location in the tables. The index is used to access the tables, and it mirrors the structure of the tables so it follows a consistent pattern of organization and use of hierarchies. The index is organized as an alphabetical lookup, and the two types of main terms used are

- Based on the value of the third character, which is the *root operation* (e.g., bypass, excision, incision)
- Common procedure terms (e.g., appendectomy, cholecystectomy), which usually provide direction to a root operation main term

Purpose of ICD-10-PCS Index

The purpose of the ICD-10-PCS index is to locate the appropriate table that contains all information necessary to construct a procedure code. The ICD-10-PCS tables must always be consulted to construct the most appropriate valid code. It is not possible to construct a procedure code by using just the alphabetic index.

Main Terms

The ICD-10-PCS index reflects the structure of the tables and is organized as an alphabetical listing. The index is based on the value of the third character, contains common procedure terms, lists anatomical sites, and uses device terms. The main terms in the alphabetic index are root operations, root procedure types, or common procedure names. Examples of main terms in the ICD-10-PCS index include:

- **Resection** (root operation)
- **Fluoroscopy** (root type)
- **Prostatectomy** (common procedure name)
- **Brachial artery** (body part)
- **Bard® Dulex™ mesh** (device)

```
┌─────────────────────────────────────────────────────┐
│                  ICD-10-PCS Index                     │
├─────────────────────────────────────────────────────┤
│                        A                              │
├─────────────────────────────────────────────────────┤
```

Abdominal aortic plexus *use* Nerve, Abdominal Sympathetic
Abdominal esophagus *use* Esophagus, Lower
Abdominohysterectomy *see* Resection, Uterus 0UT9
Abdominoplasty
    see Alteration, Wall, Abdominal 0W0F
    see Repair, Wall, Abdominal 0WQF
    see Supplement, Abdominal Wall 0WUF
Abductor hallucis muscle
    use Foot Muscle, Right
    use Foot Muscle, Left
AbioCor® Total Replacement Heart *use* Synthetic Substitute
Ablation *see* Destruction
Abortion
    Abortifacient 10A07ZX
    Laminaria 10A07ZW
    Products of Conception 10A0
    Vacuum 10A07Z6
Abrasion *see* Extraction
Absolute Pro Vascular (OTW) Self-Expanding Stent System
    use Intraluminal Device
Accessory cephalic vein
    use Cephalic Vein, Right
    use Cephalic Vein, Left
Accessory obturator nerve *use* Lumbar Plexus
Accessory phrenic nerve *use* Phrenic Nerve
Accessory spleen *use* Spleen

Courtesy of the Centers for Medicare & Medicaid Services, www.cms.gov

FIGURE 6-3 ICD-10-PCS Index (partial)

The ICD-10-PCS index provides at least the first three or four values of the code, and some entries may provide complete valid codes. However, the user should always consult the appropriate ICD-10-PCS table to verify that the most appropriate valid code has been selected.

Root Operation and Procedure Type Main Terms

For the *Medical and Surgical* and related sections, the root operation values are used as main terms in the index. The subterms under the root operation main terms are body parts. For the *Ancillary* section of the tables, the main terms in the index are the general type of procedure performed. Examples of root operations (e.g., destruction) and procedure type (e.g., biofeedback) as main terms in the ICD-10-PCS index include:

- **Destruction**

    Acetabulum

        Left 0Q55

        Right 0Q54

    Adenoids 0C5Q

    Ampulla of Vater 0F5C

- **Biofeedback** GZC9ZZZ

ICD-10-PCS Index Coding Conventions

See The ICD-10-PCS index includes common procedure names, such as *appendectomy* or *fundoplication*. These common terms are listed as main terms with a *see* reference directing coders to ICD-10-PCS root operations as possible valid code tables based on the objective of the procedure. Examples of common procedure names as main terms in the ICD-10-PCS index include:

- **Tendonectomy**

  see Excision, Tendons 0LB

  see Resection, Tendons 0LT

Use The ICD-10-PCS index includes anatomical sites and device terms. When these terms appear as main terms in the ICD-10-PCS index, they contain a *use* reference as an additional reference when constructing a procedure code using the ICD-10-PCS tables. The *use* reference does *not* direct coders to another main term in the Index, but it provides guidance regarding the selection of character values *within* an ICD-10-PCS table. Examples of common body part and device main terms in the ICD-10-PCS index include:

- **Epitrochlear lymph node**

  use Lymphatic, Right Upper Extremity

  use Lymphatic, Left Upper Extremity

- **CoAxia NeuroFlo catheter**

  use Intraluminal Device

- **SynCardia Total Artificial Heart**

  use Synthetic Substitute

 NOTE:

- The ICD-10-PCS index contains a hierarchical alphabetical lookup for locating a table that includes supplemental procedure terms (e.g., appendectomy) that correspond to root operation options. (The hierarchy includes boldfaced main terms, indented subterms, and indented qualifiers.)
- It is *not* possible to construct an ICD-10-PCS procedure code from the index. The purpose of the index is to locate the appropriate table that contains all information necessary to construct a procedure code.
- Coders are *not* required to consult the index before proceeding to the tables to construct an ICD-10-PCS code. A valid code can be constructed directly from the tables (by locating the appropriate section, body system, and root operation table). However, the index provides guidance to the appropriate table.

ICD-10-PCS Tables

ICD-10-PCS **tables** (Figure 6-4) are used to construct a complete and valid code (using a build-a-code approach). Tables include terms (and definitions) and rows, which contain **values** that are characters (individual letters and numbers) assigned to each of seven unique hierarchies (positions) needed to construct a valid ICD-10-PCS code. The first three rows of each table list values and descriptions of the first three characters of codes in that table; subsequent rows list values (and descriptions) for the fourth through seventh characters of the ICD-10-PCS code.

EXAMPLE: Refer to Figure 6-4, and notice that the first three characters in the upper portion of the table are 001. This indicates that codes will be constructed for procedures in the Medical and Surgical *section*, Central Nervous System *body system*, and Bypass *root operation* (defined in the table). Use the table in Figure 6-4 to construct an ICD-10-PCS code for the procedural statement (below) by assigning the fourth through seventh character values for each element of the procedure.

(continues)

Section	0	Medical and Surgical
Body System	0	Central Nervous System
Operation	1	Bypass: Altering the route of passage of the contents of a tubular body part

Body Part	Approach	Device	Qualifier
6 Cerebral Ventricle	0 Open 3 Percutaneous 4 Percutaneous Endoscopic	7 Autologous Tissue Substitute J Synthetic Substitute K Nonautologous Tissue Substitute	0 Nasopharynx 1 Mastoid sinus 2 Atrium 3 Blood Vessel 4 Pleural Cavity 5 Intestine 6 Peritoneal Cavity 7 Urinary Tract 8 Bone Marrow B Cerebral Cisterns
6 Cerebral Ventricle	0 Open 3 Percutaneous 4 Percutaneous Endoscopic	Z No Device	B Cerebral Cisterns
U Spinal Canal	0 Open 3 Percutaneous 4 Percutaneous Endoscopic	7 Autologous Tissue Substitute J Synthetic Substitute K Nonautologous Tissue Substitute	2 Atrium 4 Pleural Cavity 6 Peritoneal Cavity 7 Urinary Tract 9 Fallopian Tube

Courtesy of the Centers for Medicare & Medicaid Services, www.cms.gov

FIGURE 6-4 ICD-10-PCS table (sample)

EXAMPLE *(continued)*

After *open incision into the cerebral ventricle, a synthetic shunt was inserted to allow excess cerebrospinal fluid (CSF) to flow* (bypass) *into the peritoneal cavity* (to decrease CSF pressure). ICD-10-PCS code 00160J6 is constructed by assigning a character for each value of the seven-character code:

Section	Body System	Root Operation	Body Part	Approach	Device	Qualifier
Medical and Surgical	Central Nervous System	Bypass	Cerebral Ventricle	Open	Synthetic Substitute	Peritoneal Cavity
0	0	1	6	0	J	6

ICD-10-PCS tables are organized in sections (Figure 6-5) that identify the general type of procedure, and each of the seven characters in a table has a specific meaning (Figure 6-6). Within a section, all character meanings remain constant. (The first character of the ICD-10-PCS procedure code *always* specifies the section.) Within an ICD-10-PCS table, valid values include all combinations of choices for the fourth through seventh characters that are contained in the same row of a table.

- The columns in ICD-10-PCS tables contain values for the fourth through seventh characters.
- The rows in ICD-10-PCS tables delineate valid combinations of values.
- Any combination of values not contained in a single row of the tables is invalid.

 Coding Tip

Construct valid ICD-10-PCS codes using a *build-a-code* approach to assign values to each of the seven unique hierarchies (positions).

ICD-10-PCS SECTIONS	
0	Medical and Surgical
1	Obstetrics
2	Placement
3	Administration
4	Measurement and Monitoring
5	Extracorporeal or Systemic Assistance and Performance
6	Extracorporeal or Systemic Therapies
7	Osteopathic
8	Other Procedures
9	Chiropractic
B	Imaging
C	Nuclear Medicine
D	Radiation Therapy
F	Physical Rehabilitation and Diagnostic Audiology
G	Mental Health
H	Substance Abuse Treatment
X	New Technology

Courtesy of the Centers for Medicare & Medicaid Services, www.cms.gov

FIGURE 6-5 ICD-10-PCS sections

Meaning of Each Character Within a Section						
Section (1st)	2nd	3rd	4th	5th	6th	7th
Medical and Surgical	Body system	Operation	Body part	Approach	Device	Qualifier
Obstetrics	Body system	Operation	Body part	Approach	Device	Qualifier
Placement	Body system	Operation	Body region	Approach	Device	Qualifier
Administration	Body system	Operation	Body system/ region	Approach	Substance	Qualifier
Measurement and Monitoring	Body system	Operation	Body system	Approach	Function/ Device	Qualifier
Extracorporeal or Systemic Assistance and Performance	Physiological system	Operation	Body system	Duration	Function	Qualifier
Extracorporeal or Systemic Therapies	Physiological system	Operation	Body system	Duration	Qualifier	Qualifier
Osteopathic	Body system	Operation	Body region	Approach	Method	Qualifier
Other Procedures	Body system	Operation	Body region	Approach	Method	Qualifier
Chiropractic	Body system	Operation	Body region	Approach	Method	Qualifier
Imaging	Body system	Type	Body part	Contrast	Qualifier	Qualifier
Nuclear Medicine	Body system	Type	Body part	Radionuclide	Qualifier	Qualifier
Radiation Therapy	Body system	Modality	Treatment site	Modality qualifier	Isotope	Qualifier
Physical Rehabilitation and Diagnostic Audiology	Section qualifier	Type	Body system/ region	Type qualifier	Equipment	Qualifier
Mental Health	Body system	Type	Qualifier	Qualifier	Qualifier	Qualifier
Substance Abuse Treatment	Body system	Type	Qualifier	Qualifier	Qualifier	Qualifier
New Technology	Body system	Operation	Body part	Approach	Device/ Substance/ Technology	Qualifier

Courtesy of the Centers for Medicare & Medicaid Services, www.cms.gov

FIGURE 6-6 Meaning of first through seventh characters within each ICD-10-PCS section

EXAMPLE: Refer to Figure 6-7, which contains a portion of a Medical and Surgical section table, and notice that 0JHT3VZ is a valid code, but 0JHW3VZ is *not* a valid code. The "V" in code 0JHW3VZ is not a valid value for sixth character device because it is associated with the subcutaneous tissue and fascia, trunk body part.

Section	0	Medical and Surgical
Body System	J	Subcutaneous Tissue and Fascia
Operation	H	**Insertion:** Putting in a nonbiological appliance that monitors, assists, performs, or prevents a physiological function but does not physically take the place of a body part

Body Part	Approach	Device	Qualifier
S Subcutaneous Tissue and Fascia, Head and Neck	0 Open	1 Radioactive Element	Z No Qualifier
V Subcutaneous Tissue and Fascia, Upper Extremity	3 Percutaneous	3 Infusion Device	
W Subcutaneous Tissue and Fascia, Lower Extremity		Y Other Device	
T Subcutaneous Tissue and Fascia, Trunk	0 Open	1 Radioactive Element	Z No Qualifier
	3 Percutaneous	3 Infusion Device	
		V Infusion Pump	
		Y Other Device	

FIGURE 6-7 Portion of ICD-10-PCS Medical and Surgical section table

All seven characters *must* contain valid values (selected from the appropriate table) to construct a valid ICD-10-PCS procedure code. If documentation is incomplete for coding purposes, query the physician for the necessary information. However, according to ICD-10-PCS coding guidelines, the coder is *not* required to query the physician when the correlation between documentation and defined ICD-10-PCS terms is clear (e.g., surgeon documents "partial resection" and coder determines that "partial resection" is root operation "excision").

- Columns in the ICD-10-PCS tables contain values for characters 4 through 7.
- Rows in the ICD-10-PCS tables delineate valid combinations of values.
- Any combination of values *not* contained in a single row of the ICD-10-PCS tables is invalid (and results in construction of an invalid code if used).

ICD-10-PCS inpatient coding guidelines are organized as follows:

- Structure
- Values
- Index
- Tables
- Medical and surgical section guidelines
- Obstetrics section guidelines

Structure of ICD-10-PCS Codes

ICD-10-PCS codes contain seven characters. Each character is associated with an **axis of classification** (e.g., section, body part, root operation), which specifies information about the procedure performed. Within a defined code range, a character specifies the same type of information for that axis of classification.

All seven characters must be specified to construct a valid code. If documentation is incomplete for coding purposes, query the physician for the necessary information to construct a valid code.

EXAMPLE: The fifth *axis of classification* specifies the approach in the Medical and Surgical section.

ICD-10-PCS Values

One of 34 possible *values* may be assigned to each axis of classification in the seven-character code. The values include numbers 0 through 9 and the alphabet (except for letters I and O because they are easily confused with numbers 1 and 0, respectively). The number of unique values used in an axis of classification differs as needed.

> **EXAMPLE:** Refer to Figure 6-7 where the fifth axis of classification for table 0JH specifies the approach.

ICD-10-PCS Coding Conventions

ICD-10-PCS codes are composed of seven characters. Each character is an axis of classification that specifies information about the procedure performed. Within a defined code range, a character specifies the same type of information in that axis of classification.

> **EXAMPLE:** The fifth axis of classification specifies the approach in sections 0 through 4 and 7 through 9 of ICD-10-PCS.

One of 34 possible values can be assigned to each axis of classification in the seven-character code. The values include numbers 0 through 9 and the alphabet (except I and O because they are easily confused with the numbers 1 and 0). The number of unique values used in an axis of classification differs as needed.

> **EXAMPLE:** Where the fifth axis of classification specifies the approach, seven different approach values are currently used to specify the approach.

The valid values for an axis of classification can be added to as needed (by CMS). If a significantly distinct type of device is used in a new procedure, a new device value can be added to the system.

> **EXAMPLE:** There are currently no *device* values listed in the *Medical and Surgical* section, *Skin and Breast* body system, and *Repair* root operation. In future, perhaps CMS will add *surgical glue* as a device. That means instead of selecting value Z for the device, the coder would select the appropriate value for surgical glue (or some other new device).

As with words in their context, the meaning of any single value is a combination of its axis of classification and any preceding values on which it may be dependent.

> **EXAMPLE:** The meaning of a body part value in the *Medical and Surgical* section is **always** dependent on the body system value. Thus, body part value 0 in the *Central Nervous and Cranial Nerves* body system specifies *Brain*, while body part value 0 in the *Peripheral Nervous* body system specifies *Cervical Plexus*.

As ICD-10-PCS is expanded to become increasingly detailed, over time more values will depend on preceding values for their meaning.

> **EXAMPLE:** In the Lower Joints body system, device value 3 in the root operation Insertion specifies Infusion Device, while device value 3 in the root operation Replacement specifies Ceramic Synthetic Substitute.

The purpose of the alphabetic index is to locate the appropriate table that contains all information necessary to construct a procedure code. The ICD-10-PCS tables should always be consulted to find the most appropriate valid code.

It is not required to consult the index first before proceeding to the tables to complete the code. A valid code may be chosen directly from the tables.

All seven characters must be specified to be a valid code. If the documentation is incomplete for coding purposes, the physician should be queried for the necessary information.

Within an ICD-10-PCS table, valid codes include all combinations of choices in characters 4 through 7 contained in the same row of the table.

> **EXAMPLE:** For Table 0JH, code 0JHT3VZ is valid; however, 0JHW3VZ is not a valid code because character V is not present in the Device column for Body Part character W (Subcutaneous Tissue and Fascia, Lower).

"And," when used in a code description, means "and/or" except when used to describe a combination of multiple body parts for which separate values exist for each body part.

EXAMPLE 1: Lower Arm and Wrist Muscle means lower arm and/or wrist muscle, such as Table 0K5 where body parts 9 (Lower Arm and Wrist Muscle, Right) and B (Lower Arm and Wrist Muscle, Left) are listed in the first column.

EXAMPLE 2: Skin and Subcutaneous Tissue used as a qualifier, where there are separate body part values for "Skin" and "Subcutaneous Tissue," such as Table 0KX where qualifiers 0 (Skin), 1 (Subcutaneous Tissue), and 2 (Skin and Subcutaneous Tissue) are listed in the last column.

Many of the terms used to construct codes are defined within ICD-10-PCS. It is the coder's responsibility to determine what the documentation in the medical record equates to in the PCS definitions. The physician is not expected to use the terms used in PCS code descriptions, nor is the coder required to query the physician when the correlation between the documentation and the defined PCS terms is clear.

EXAMPLE: When the physician documents "partial resection," the coder can independently correlate "partial resection" to root operation Excision without querying the physician for clarification.

Medical and Surgical Section Coding Guidelines

Coding guidelines associated with the *Medical and Surgical* section of ICD-10-PCS include:

- Body system
- Root operation
- Body part
- Approach
- Device

Body System—General Coding Guidelines

Procedure codes in the *Anatomical Regions, General; Anatomical Regions, Upper Extremities;* and *Anatomical Regions, Lower Extremities* body systems are used *only when*

- The procedure is performed on an anatomical region rather than a specific body part.
- Insufficient information is available to support the assignment of a value to a specific body part.

EXAMPLE: Chest tube drainage of the pleural cavity is coded to root operation Drainage, which is located in body system Anatomical Regions, General.

Where general body part values "upper" and "lower" are provided as an option in the Upper Arteries, Lower Arteries, Upper Veins, Lower Veins, Muscles and Tendons body systems, "upper" or "lower" *specify body parts located above or below the diaphragm*, respectively.

EXAMPLE: The jugular veins are located above the diaphragm (in the neck), and they are assigned values from the *Upper Veins* body system in the *Medical and Surgical* section. The saphenous veins are located below the diaphragm (in the legs), and they are assigned values from the *Medical and Surgical* section and *Lower Veins* body system.

Root Operation—General Coding Guidelines

To determine the appropriate root operation, apply the *complete* definition and explanation of the root operation (located in the ICD-10-PCS tables). The root operation is specified in the third character, and in the *Medical and Surgical* section of ICD-10-PCS, there are 31 different root operations. The root operation identifies the objective of the procedure, and each root operation has a precise definition (Table 6-1), which was created specifically for ICD-10-PCS and may differ from those found in medical dictionaries and other resources.

- Components of a procedure that are included in the root operation's definition or explanation as integral to that root operation are *not* coded separately. (However, an exception to this guideline includes *mastectomy followed by breast reconstruction*, for which both the resection *and* reconstruction of the breast are coded separately.)

TABLE 6-1 Medical and Surgical Section Root Operations and Definitions

Root Operation	Definition
Alteration	Modifying the natural anatomical structure of a body part without affecting the function of the body part
Bypass	Altering the route of passage of the contents of a tubular body part
Change	Taking out or off a device from a body part and putting back an identical or similar device in or on the same body part without cutting or puncturing the skin or a mucous membrane
Control	Stopping, or attempting to stop, postprocedural or other acute bleeding
Creation	Putting in or on biological or synthetic material to form a new body part that to the extent possible replicates the anatomic structure or function of an absent body part
Destruction	Physical eradication of all or a portion of a body part by the direct use of energy, force, or a destructive agent
Detachment	Cutting off all or a portion of the upper or lower extremities
Dilation	Expanding an orifice or the lumen of a tubular body part
Division	Cutting into a body part without draining fluids and gases from the body part in order to separate or transect a body part
Drainage	Taking or letting out fluids and gases from a body part
Excision	Cutting out or off, without replacement, a portion of a body part
Extirpation	Taking or cutting out solid matter from a body part
Extraction	Pulling or stripping out or off all or a portion of a body part by the use of force
Fragmentation	Breaking solid matter in a body part into pieces
Fusion	Joining together portions of an articular body part rendering the articular body part immobile
Insertion	Putting in a nonbiological appliance that monitors, assists, performs, or prevents a physiological function but does not physically take the place of a body part
Inspection	Visually or manually exploring a body part
Map	Locating the route of passage of electrical impulses and locating functional areas in a body part
Occlusion	Completely closing an orifice or lumen of a tubular body part
Reattachment	Putting back in or on all or a portion of a separated body part to its normal location or other suitable location
Release	Freeing a body part from an abnormal physical constraint
Removal	Taking out or off a device from a body part by cutting or by use of force
Repair	Restoring, to the extent possible, a body part to its normal anatomical structure and function
Replacement	Putting in or on biological or synthetic material that physically takes the place and/or function of all or a portion of a body part
Reposition	Moving to its normal location or other suitable location all or a portion of a body part
Resection	Cutting out or off, without replacement, all of a body part
Restriction	Partially closing an orifice or lumen of a tubular body part
Revision	Correcting, to the extent possible, a malfunctioning or displaced device
Supplement	Putting in or on biological or synthetic material that physically reinforces and/or augments the function of a portion of a body part
Transfer	Moving, without taking out, all or a portion of a body part to another location to take over the function of all or a portion of a body part
Transplantation	Putting in or on all or a portion of a living body part taken from another individual or animal to physically take the place and/or function of all or a portion of a similar body part

EXAMPLE: During an *open left knee joint replacement procedure using a synthetic substitute*, the original knee joint was resected. Index main term *Replacement*, subterm *Joint*, second qualifier *Knee*, third qualifier *Left* list values 0SRD. Go to ICD-10-PCS Table 0SR to construct code 0SRD0JZ for the joint replacement procedure *only*. (The resection of the original joint is *not* assigned a separate code.)

- Procedural steps necessary to reach the operative site *and* to close the operative site are *not* coded separately.

> **EXAMPLE:** A laparotomy is performed to reach the site where an open liver biopsy (diagnostic) is carried out. Index main term *Biopsy* and its subterm provide a cross reference to *see Excision with qualifier Diagnostic*. Index main term *Excision* and subterm *Liver* list values 0FB0. Go to ICD-10-PCS Table 0FB to construct code 0FB00ZX for the open liver biopsy *only*.
>
> - The index cross reference for main term *Biopsy* included the term *Diagnostic*, which means seventh qualifier value X is assigned instead of Z.
> - The laparotomy is *not* coded separately.

Root Operation—Multiple Procedures

During the same operative episode, codes are constructed for multiple procedures performed *if* the

- Same root operation (e.g., excision, replacement) is performed on different body parts, as defined by distinct values of the body part axis of classification.

> **EXAMPLE:** Two different ICD-10-PCS codes are constructed for diagnostic excision (e.g., biopsy) of the liver and of the pancreas.
> - Index main term *Biopsy* and its subterm provide a cross reference to *see Excision with qualifier Diagnostic*. Index main term *Excision* and subterm *Liver* list values 0FB0. Go to ICD-10-PCS Table 0FB to construct code 0FB00ZX for the liver biopsy.
> - Index main term *Excision* and subterm *Pancreas* list values 0FBG. Return to ICD-10-PCS Table 0FB to construct code 0FBG0ZX for the pancreatic biopsy.
> - The index cross reference for main term *Biopsy* included the term *Diagnostic*, which means seventh qualifier value X is assigned (instead of Z).

- Same root operation is repeated at different body sites that are included in the same body part axis of classification.

> **EXAMPLE:** Two ICD-10-PCS codes are constructed for *biopsies of the right sartorius muscle and right gracilis muscle*, both of which are classified to the *Upper Leg Muscle, Right* body part.
> - Index main term *Biopsy* and its subterm provide a cross reference to *see Excision with qualifier Diagnostic*. Index main term *Excision*, subterm *Muscle*, second qualifier *Upper Leg*, and third qualifier *Right* list values 0KBQ. Go to ICD-10-PCS Table 0KB to construct both codes 0KBQ3ZX (right sartorius muscle) and 0KBQ3ZX (right gracilis muscle).
> - The codes are identical (and both are reported) because the biopsy was performed on two different muscles, which are considered two different body sites within the same *Upper Leg Muscle, Right*, body part axis of classification.
> - The index cross reference for main term *Biopsy* included the term *Diagnostic*, which means seventh qualifier value X is assigned (instead of Z).

 NOTE:

> Root operation names and definitions were created specifically for ICD-10-PCS and may differ from those found in medical dictionaries and other resources.

- Multiple root operations with distinct objectives are performed on the same body part.

EXAMPLE: Two codes are constructed for *Endoscopic destruction of lesion, sigmoid colon*, and *bypass of sigmoid colon, open.*

- Index main term *Destruction*, subterm *Colon*, and second qualifier *Sigmoid* list values 0D5N. Go to ICD-10-PCS Table 0D5 to construct code 0D5N8ZZ.
- Index main term *Bypass*, subterm *Colon*, and second qualifier *Sigmoid* list values 0D1N. Go to ICD-10-PCS Table 0D1 to construct code 0D1N0ZN.

- The intended root operation is attempted using one approach, but it is converted to a different approach.

EXAMPLE: *Laparoscopic cholecystectomy converted to an open cholecystectomy* is assigned two codes: one for the percutaneous endoscopic *Inspection* root operation and a different code for the open *Resection* root operation.

- Index main term *Inspection* and subterm *Gallbladder* list values 0FJ4. Go to ICD-10-PCS Table 0FJ to construct code 0FJ44ZZ.
- Index main term *Resection* and subterm *Gallbladder* list values 0FT4. Go to ICD-10-PCS Tables 0FT to construct code 0FT40ZZ.

Root Operation—Discontinued or Incomplete Procedures

- When the intended procedure is discontinued or otherwise not completed, code the procedure to the root operation performed.

EXAMPLE: A planned *total abdominal hysterectomy was discontinued after resecting just the uterus, leaving the ovaries and fallopian tubes intact* because there was no evidence of dysplasia. Index main term *Hysterectomy* and subterm *total* provide a cross reference to *see Resection, Uterus 0UT9.* Go to ICD-10-PCS Table 0UT to construct code 0UT90ZZ. (If bilateral ovaries and fallopian tubes had also been resected, codes 0UT20ZZ and 0UT70ZZ would also be constructed.)

- When a procedure is discontinued before any other root operation is performed, assign a code to the *Inspection* root operation of the body part or anatomical region inspected.

EXAMPLE: A planned *aortic valve replacement procedure was discontinued after initial thoracotomy, but before any incision was made into the heart muscle*, due to the patient becoming hemodynamically unstable. Index main term *Inspection* and subterm *Mediastinum* list values 0WJC. Go to ICD-10-PCS Table 0WJ to construct code 0WJC0ZZ.

- Do not go to index main term *Thoracotomy* because its cross reference is to *see Drainage, Anatomical Regions, General 0W9*, which was not the procedure performed.
- The coding guideline provides direction to locate index main term *Inspection*, and the subterm is the body part or anatomical region that was inspected.

Root Operation—Biopsy Procedures

Biopsy procedures are coded using the root operations Excision, Extraction, or Drainage and the qualifier Diagnostic.

EXAMPLE 1: Fine needle aspiration biopsy of lung is coded to the root operation Drainage with qualifier Diagnostic.

EXAMPLE 2: Biopsy of bone marrow is coded to the root operation Extraction with qualifier Diagnostic.

EXAMPLE 3: Lymph node sampling for biopsy is coded to the root operation Excision with qualifier Diagnostic.

Root Operation—Biopsy Followed by More Definitive Treatment

If a diagnostic excision, extraction, or drainage procedure (biopsy) is followed by a more definitive procedure (e.g., destruction, excision, resection) *at the same procedure site*, assign separate codes for the biopsy and the more definitive treatment.

> **EXAMPLE:** For *open biopsy of left breast with open left partial mastectomy*, assign a code for the biopsy *and* a separate code for the partial mastectomy.
>
> * Index main term *Biopsy* provides a cross reference to *see Excision with qualifier Diagnostic*. Index main term *Excision*, subterm *Breast*, and second qualifier *Left* list values 0HBU. Go to ICD-10-PCS Table 0HB to construct code 0HBU0ZX. (The index cross reference for main term *Biopsy* included the term *Diagnostic*, which means seventh qualifier value X is assigned instead of Z.)
> * Index main term *Mastectomy* and subterm *partial* provides a cross reference to *see Excision, Skin and Breast 0HB*. Go to ICD-10-PCS Table 0HB to construct code 0HBU0ZZ.

Root Operation—Overlapping Body Layers

When root operations Excision, Extraction, Repair, or Inspection are performed on overlapping layers of the musculoskeletal system, the body part specifying the *deepest layer* is coded.

> **EXAMPLE:** For an *open excisional debridement of the skin, subcutaneous tissue, and muscle, left foot*, assign just one code for the procedure performed on the *Muscle* body part (because muscle is the deepest layer). Index main term *Debridement* and subterm *Excisional* include cross reference *see Excision*. Thus, index main term *Excision*, subterm *Muscle*, second qualifier *Foot*, and third qualifier *Left* list values 0KBW. Go to ICD-10-PCS Table 0KB to construct code 0KBW0ZZ.

Root Operation—Bypass Procedures

Bypass procedures are coded by identifying the body part bypassed *from* and the body part bypassed *to*.
* The fourth character (body part) specifies the body part bypassed *from*.
* The seventh character qualifier specifies the body part bypassed *to*.

> **EXAMPLE:** For an *open bypass from stomach to jejunum*, stomach is the body part (fourth character) and jejunum is the qualifier (seventh character). Index main term *Bypass*, subterm *Stomach* list values 0D16. Go to ICD-10-PCS Table 0D1 to construct code 0D160ZA.

Root Operation—Coronary Bypass Procedures

Coronary artery bypass procedures are coded differently than other bypass procedures that are described in the previous guideline. Rather than identifying the body part bypassed from, the *body part identifies the number of coronary arteries bypassed to*, and the *qualifier specifies the vessel bypassed from*.
* The fourth character (body part) value classifies the number of coronary arteries bypassed *to*.
* The seventh character qualifier classifies the vessel bypassed *from*.

 Coding Tip

> Coronary artery bypass procedures are classified the *opposite* of other bypass procedures (as explained in the above *Root Operation—Bypass Procedures* coding guideline) because the fourth character body part classifies the number of coronary arteries bypassed *to*, and the seventh character qualifier classifies the vessel bypassed *from*.

> **EXAMPLE:** For an *open aortocoronary artery bypass of left anterior descending coronary artery and obtuse marginal coronary artery, using synthetic substitute for each bypass*, the two coronary arteries are the body part (fourth character) and aorta is the qualifier (seventh character). Index main term *Bypass*, subterm *Artery*, second qualifier *Coronary*, third qualifier *Two Arteries* list values 0211. Go to ICD-10-PCS Table 021 to construct code 02110JW.

When multiple coronary arteries are bypassed, a separate procedure code is assigned for each coronary artery *that uses a different device and/or qualifier.*

> **EXAMPLE:** For an *open aortocoronary artery bypass and open right internal mammary coronary artery bypass using synthetic substitute for each bypass*, assign two codes because there are different seventh character qualifier values for the aorta and for the right internal mammary artery. Index main term *Bypass*, subterm *Artery*, second qualifier *Coronary*, and third qualifier *One Artery* list values 0210. Go to ICD-10-PCS Table 021 to construct both codes 02100JW and 02100J8. (Index third qualifier *Two Arteries* is *not* used because the seventh character qualifiers differ for each code.)

Root Operation—Control vs. More Definitive Root Operations

Root operation *Control* is defined as *stopping, or attempting to stop, postprocedural or other acute bleeding.* If an attempt to stop postprocedural or other acute bleeding is unsuccessful, and to stop the bleeding requires performing a more definitive root operation, such as *Bypass, Detachment, Excision, Extraction, Reposition, Replacement,* or *Resection,* then the more definitive root operation is coded instead of *Control.*

> **EXAMPLE:** The ICD-10-PCS code for *open splenectomy to stop bleeding* is constructed using the *Medical and Surgical* section, *Lymphatic and Hemic Systems* body system, and *Resection* root operation. Index main term *Splenectomy* contains a subterm cross reference to *see Resection, Lymphatic and Hemic Systems,* which list values 07T. Go to ICD-10-PCS Table 07T to construct code 07T P0ZZ.
>
> • Although the objective of the procedure was to *stop postprocedural bleeding*, the *Control* root operation is not used because the spleen was resected.
>
> • If surgical cautery or sutures had been performed to stop postprocedural bleeding, the code would have been constructed using the *Control* root operation in the *Anatomical Regions, General* body system and *Medical and Surgical* system.

Root Operation—Excision vs. Resection

ICD-10-PCS contains specific body parts for anatomical subdivisions of a body part (e.g., lobes of the lungs or liver, regions of the intestine). The resection of a specific body part is coded whenever all of that body part is cut out or off (instead of coding an excision of a less specific body part).

> **EXAMPLE:** For a *total open left upper lung lobectomy, Resection* is the root operation and *Upper Lung Lobe, Left* is the body part (instead of the *Excision* root operation and *Lung, Left* body part). Index main term *Resection*, subterm *Lung*, second qualifier *Upper Lobe*, and third qualifier *Left* list values 0BTG. Go to ICD-10-PCS Table 0BT to construct code 0BTG0ZZ.

Root Operation—Excision for Graft

When an autograft is obtained from a different body part in order to complete the objective of the procedure, a separate procedure is coded *except when the seventh character qualifier value in the ICD-10-PCS table fully specifies the site from which the autograft was obtained.*

> **EXAMPLE:** For an *open aortocoronary bypass with open excision of right greater saphenous vein (for use as aortocoronary bypass graft material)*, the *excision of saphenous vein* is assigned a separate code.
>
> • Index main term *Bypass*, subterm *Artery*, second qualifier *Coronary*, third qualifier *One Artery* list values 0210. Go to ICD-10-PCS Table 021 to construct code 021009W.
>
> • Index main term *Excision*, subterm *Vein*, second qualifier *Saphenous*, and third qualifier *Right* list values 06BP. Go to ICD-10-PCS Table 06B to construct code 06BP0ZZ.

EXAMPLE: For a *replacement of breast with autologous deep inferior epigastric artery perforator (DIEP) flap*, the excision of the DIEP flap is *not* coded separately because seventh qualifier Deep Inferior Epigastric Artery Perforator Flap in the Replacement table specifies the site of the autograft harvest.

Root Operation—Fusion Procedures of the Spine

The body part coded for a *spinal vertebral joint(s) rendered immobile by a spinal fusion procedure* is classified according to the level of the spine (e.g., thoracic). There are distinct body part values for a single vertebral joint and for multiple vertebral joints at each spinal level.

EXAMPLE: Go to ICD-10-PCS Table 0RG, and locate values 1, 2, and 4 for body parts *Cervical Vertebral Joint, Cervical Vertebral Joints, 2 or more*, and *Cervicothoracic Vertebral Joint*, respectively.

When multiple vertebral joints are fused, a separate procedure code is assigned for *each vertebral joint that uses a different device and/or qualifier.*

EXAMPLE: *Open fusion of lumbar vertebral joint, posterior approach, anterior column, synthetic substitute* and *open fusion of lumbar vertebral joint, posterior approach, posterior column, synthetic substitute* are each assigned separate codes. Index main term *Fusion* and subterm *Lumbar Vertebral* list values 0SG0. Go to ICD-10-PCS Table 0SG to construct codes 0SG00JJ and 0SG00J1.

Combinations of devices and materials are often used on a vertebral joint to render the joint immobile. When combinations of devices are used on the *same* vertebral joint, the device value assigned to the procedure code is as follows:

- If an interbody fusion device is used to render the joint immobile (alone or containing other material like bone graft), refer to device value *Interbody Fusion Device*.

EXAMPLE: *Open fusion of lumbar vertebral joint, posterior approach, anterior column, using a cage style interbody internal fusion device containing morsellized bone graft* is assigned a device value for *Interbody Internal Fusion Device*. Index main term *Fusion*, and subterm *Lumbar Vertebral* 0SG0. Go to ICD-10-PCS Table 0SG to construct code 0SG00AJ.

- If bone graft is the *only* device used to render the joint immobile, refer to device value *Nonautologous Tissue Substitute* or *Autologous Tissue Substitute*.

EXAMPLE: *Open fusion of the right elbow joint using bone graft material from a bone bank* is assigned a device value for *Nonautologous Tissue Substitute*. Index main term *Fusion*, subterm *Elbow*, and second qualifier *Right* list values 0RGL. Go to ICD-10-PCS Table 0RG to construct code 0RGL0KZ.

- If a mixture of autologous and nonautologous bone graft (with or without biological or synthetic extenders or binders) is used to render the joint immobile, refer to device value *Autologous Tissue Substitute*.

EXAMPLE: *Open fusion of the left temporomandibular joint using both autologous bone graft and bone bank bone graft* is assigned a device value for *Autologous Tissue Substitute*. Index main term *Fusion*, subterm *Temporomandibular*, and second qualifier *Left* list values 0RGD. Go to ICD-10-PCS Table 0RG to construct code 0RGD07Z.

Root Operation—Inspection Procedures

Inspection of a body part(s) that is performed to achieve the objective of a procedure is *not* coded separately.

EXAMPLE: For *fiberoptic bronchoscopy with irrigation of bronchus*, code only the *irrigation of bronchus* procedure. Index main term *Irrigation* and subterm *Respiratory Tract, Irrigating Substance* list values 3E1F. Go to ICD-10-PCS Table 3E1 to construct code 3E1F88Z.

- The bronchus is a part of the respiratory tract.
- Do *not* assign a code for the bronchoscopy.

- When *multiple tubular body parts are inspected*, the most distal body part inspected is assigned a body part value.

  EXAMPLE: For *cystoureteroscopy with inspection of urethra, urinary bladder and ureters*, code only the inspection of the ureter (ureteroscopy) because it is distal to both the urethra and the urinary bladder. Index main term *Ureteroscopy* lists code 0TJ98ZZ. Go to ICD-10-PCS Table 0TJ to construct code 0TJ98ZZ (to verify its accuracy).

- When *multiple nontubular body parts in a region are inspected*, the body part that specifies the entire area inspected is assigned a body part value.

  EXAMPLE: Exploratory laparotomy with percutaneous endoscopic inspection of abdominal contents is assigned the *Peritoneal Cavity* body part value. Index main term *Laparotomy* provides a cross reference for *Exploratory* to *see Inspection, Peritoneal Cavity 0WJG*. Go to ICD-10-PCS Table 0WJ to construct code 0WJG4ZZ.

- When both an inspection procedure and another procedure are performed on the same body part during the same operative episode, if the inspection procedure is performed using a different approach than the other procedure, the inspection procedure is coded separately.

  EXAMPLE: For *percutaneous endoscopic inspection of the duodenum and open biopsy of the duodenum*, two codes are assigned. (The duodenum is part of the lower intestinal tract.)

  - Index main term *Inspection*, subterm *Intestinal Tract*, and second qualifier *Lower* list values 0DJD. Go to ICD-10-PCS Table 0DJ to construct code 0DJD4ZZ.
  - Index main term *Biopsy* contains a cross reference to *see Excision with qualifier Diagnostic*. Index main term *Excision* and subterm *Duodenum* list values 0DB9. Go to ICD-10-PCS Table 0DB to construct code 0DB90ZX. (The index cross reference for main term *Biopsy* included the term *Diagnostic*, which means seventh qualifier value X is assigned instead of Z.)

Root Operation—Occlusion vs. Restriction for Vessel Embolization Procedures

- When the objective of an embolization procedure is to completely close a vessel, a value for root operation *Occlusion* is assigned.

  EXAMPLE: *Percutaneous tumor embolization, left axillary artery*, is assigned a value for root operation *Occlusion* because the objective of the procedure is to cut off the blood supply to the vessel. Index main term *Embolization* includes a cross reference to *see Occlusion*. Index main term *Occlusion*, subterm *Artery*, second qualifier *Axillary*, and third qualifier *Left* list values 03L6. Go to ICD-10-PCS Table 03L to construct code 03L63ZZ.

- When the objective of an embolization procedure is to narrow the lumen of a vessel, a value for root operation *Restriction* is assigned.

  EXAMPLE: *Clipping of right popliteal artery with intraluminal device, open*, is assigned a value for root operation *Restriction* because the objective of the procedure is to narrow the lumen of the vessel at the site of the aneurysm where it is abnormally wide (not to close off the vessel entirely). Index main term *Clipping, aneurysm* includes a cross reference to *see Restriction*. Index main term *Restriction*, subterm *Artery*, second qualifier *Popliteal*, and third qualifier *Right* list values 04VM. Go to ICD-10-PCS Table 04V to construct code 04VM0DZ.

Root Operation—Release Procedures

In root operation *Release*, a value is assigned to the body part being freed, *not* to the tissue being manipulated or cut to free the body part.

> **EXAMPLE:** *Open lysis of ascending colon adhesions* is assigned a value for the *Ascending Colon* body part. Index main term *Lysis* includes a cross reference to *see Release*. Index main term *Release*, subterm *Colon*, and second qualifier *Ascending* list values 0DNK. Go to ICD-10-PCS Table 0DN to construct code 0DNK0ZZ.

Root Operation—Release vs. Division

- When the sole objective of the procedure is to free a body part *without cutting into the body part*, a value is assigned to root operation *Release*.

> **EXAMPLE:** *Freeing of vagus nerve root from surrounding scar tissue via open approach to relieve pain* is coded to root operation *Release*. Index main term *Release*, subterm *Nerve*, and second qualifier *Vagus* list values 00NQ. Go to ICD-10-PCS Table 00N to construct code 00NQ0ZZ.

- When the sole objective of the procedure is to separate or transect a body part, a value is assigned to root operation *Division*.

> **EXAMPLE:** *Severing a vagus nerve root via open approach* to stop hiccups is coded to the root operation *Division*. Index main term *Division*, subterm *Nerve*, and second qualifier *Vagus* list values 008Q. Go to ICD-10-PCS Table 008 to construct code 008Q0ZZ.

Root Operation—Reposition for Fracture Treatment

The reduction of a displaced fracture is coded to root operation *Reposition*, and the application of a cast or splint in conjunction with the reposition procedure is *not* coded separately. Treatment of a nondisplaced fracture is coded to the procedure performed.

> **EXAMPLE 1:** *Open insertion of pin as an internal fixation device in a nondisplaced fracture of left fibula* is coded to root operation *Insertion of device in*. Index main term *Insertion of device in*, subterm *Fibula*, second qualifier *Left* list values 0QHK. Go to ICD-10-PCS Table 0QH to construct code 0QHK04Z.

> **EXAMPLE 2:** *Applying a cast to a nondisplaced right radial fracture* is coded to root operation *Immobilization* in the *Placement* section. Index main term *Casting* includes a cross reference to *see Immobilization*. Index main term *Immobilization*, subterm *Arm*, second qualifier *Lower,* and third qualifier *Right* list values 2W3CX. Go to ICD-10-PCS Table 2W3 to construct code 2W3CX2Z.

Root Operation—Transplantation vs. Administration

- Inserting a mature and functioning living body part taken from another individual or animal is coded to root operation *Transplantation*.

> **EXAMPLE:** For *left kidney transplant, allogeneic,* Index main term *Transplantation*, subterm *Kidney*, and second qualifier *Left* list values 0TY10Z. Go to ICD-10-PCS Table 0TY to verify code 0TY10Z0.

- Inserting autologous or nonautologous cells is coded to the *Administration* section (and root operation *Transfusion*).

> **EXAMPLE:** *Percutaneous autologous bone marrow transplant via central venous line* is coded to the *Administration* section. Index main term *Bone marrow transplant* includes a cross reference to *see Transfusion*. Index main term *Transfusion*, subterm *Vein*, second qualifier *Central*, third qualifier *Blood,* and fourth qualifier *Whole* list values 3024. Go to ICD-10-PCS Table 302 to construct code 30243G0.

Root Operation—Transfer Procedures Using Multiple Tissue Layers

The root operation *Transfer* contains qualifiers that can be used to specify when a transfer flap is composed of more than one tissue layer, such as a musculocutaneous flap (or a myocutaneous flap). For the transfer of multiple tissue layers including skin, subcutaneous tissue, fascia, or muscle, *the procedure is coded to the body part value that describes the deepest tissue layer in the flap, and the qualifier describes the other tissue layer(s) in the transfer flap.*

> **EXAMPLE:** A musculocutaneous flap transfer is coded to the appropriate body part value in body system *Muscles*, and the qualifier describes additional tissue layers from the transfer flap, such as 0KXG0Z5 (open *latissimus dorsi myocutaneous flap transfer to trunk muscle, left*).

Body Part—General Guidelines

- When a procedure is performed on a portion of a body part that does not have a separate body part value, code the body part value corresponding to the whole body part.

> **EXAMPLE:** A procedure performed on the alveolar process of the mandible is assigned a value for body part *Mandible*. Index main term *Alveolar process of mandible* includes a cross reference to *use Mandible, Left* or *use Mandible, Right*.

- If the prefix *peri* is combined with a body part to identify the site of the procedure, the procedure is coded to the body part named. However, a procedure site described as periurethral where documentation indicates vulvar tissue (not urethral tissue) as the procedure site, vulva is selected as the body part (instead of urethra). In addition, a procedure site documented as *involving the periosteum* is coded to the documented bone as the body part.

> **EXAMPLE:** A procedure site identified as *perirenal* is assigned a value for the body part *Kidney*.

- If a procedure is performed on a continuous section of a tubular body part, code the body part value corresponding to the furthest anatomical site from the point of entry.

> **EXAMPLE:** A procedure performed on a continuous section of artery from the femoral artery to the external iliac artery, with the point of entry at the femoral artery, is coded to the *External Iliac* body part.

Body Part—Branches of Body Parts

Where a specific branch of a body part does not have its own body part value in ICD-10-PCS, the body part is typically coded to the closest proximal branch that has a specific body part value. In the cardiovascular body systems, if a general body part is available in the correct root operation table, and coding to a proximal branch would require assigning a code in a different body system, the procedure is coded using the general body part value.

> **EXAMPLE 1:** A procedure performed on the *mandibular branch of the trigeminal nerve* is assigned a value for body part *Trigeminal Nerve*.

> **EXAMPLE 2:** Occlusion of the bronchial artery is coded to body part value Upper Artery in body system Upper Arteries, *not to body part value Thoracic Aorta, Descending in body system Heart and Great Vessels.*

Body Part—Bilateral Body Part Values

Bilateral body part values are available for a limited number of body parts. If the identical procedure is performed on contralateral body parts, and a bilateral body part value exists for that body part, just one code is assigned using the bilateral body part value. If no bilateral body part value exists, each procedure is assigned a separate code using the appropriate body part value.

EXAMPLE 1: An identical procedure performed on both fallopian tubes is assigned a value for body part *Fallopian Tube, Bilateral.*

EXAMPLE 2: An identical procedure performed on both knee joints is assigned two different codes, which means assigning values for body part *Knee Joint, Right* and *Knee Joint, Left* to each code.

Body Part—Coronary Arteries

The coronary arteries are classified as a single body part that is further specified by number of arteries treated. One procedure code specifying multiple arteries is used when the same procedure is performed, including the same device and qualifier values.

EXAMPLE 1: An angioplasty of two distinct coronary arteries with placement of two stents is assigned a code as *Dilation of Coronary Arteries, Two Arteries, with two Intraluminal Devices.*

EXAMPLE 2: An angioplasty of two distinct coronary arteries, one with stent placement and one without, is assigned two separate codes as *Dilation of Coronary Artery, One Artery with Intraluminal Device,* and *Dilation of Coronary Artery, One Artery with No Device.*

Body Part—Tendons, Ligaments, Bursae, and Fascia Near a Joint

Procedures performed on tendons, ligaments, bursae, and fascia supporting a joint are coded to the body part in the respective body system that is the focus of the procedure. Procedures performed on joint structures themselves are coded to the body part in the joint body systems.

EXAMPLE 1: *Repair of anterior cruciate ligament, left knee* is assigned a value from body part *Knee Bursae and Ligament* in the body system *Bursae and Ligaments.*

EXAMPLE 2: A *knee arthroscopy with shaving of articular cartilage* is assigned a value from body part *Knee Joint* in body system *Lower Joints.*

Body Part—Skin, Subcutaneous Tissue, and Fascia Overlying a Joint

When a procedure is performed on skin, subcutaneous tissue, or fascia overlying a joint, assign a value to body parts as indicated below:

- Shoulder is assigned a value for body part *Upper Arm*.
- Elbow is assigned a value for body part *Lower Arm*.
- Wrist is assigned a value for body part *Lower Arm*.
- Hip is assigned a value for body part *Upper Leg*.
- Knee is assigned a value for body part *Lower Leg*.
- Ankle is assigned a value for body part *Foot*.

Body Part—Fingers and Toes

When a body system does not contain a separate body part value for the fingers, procedures performed on the fingers are assigned value(s) for body part *Hand*. If a body system does not contain a separate body part value for the toes, procedures performed on the toes are assigned value(s) for body part *Foot*.

> **EXAMPLE:** *Excision of finger muscle* is assigned a value for body part *Hand Muscle* in body system *Muscles*.

Body Part—Upper and Lower Intestinal Tract

For gastrointestinal body system, general body part values *Upper Intestinal Tract* and *Lower Intestinal Tract* are provided as an option for the root operations *Change, Inspection, Removal,* and *Revision.* The upper intestinal tract includes the portion of the gastrointestinal tract from the esophagus down to and including the duodenum. The lower intestinal tract includes the portion of the gastrointestinal tract from the jejunum down to and including the rectum and anus.

> **EXAMPLE:** Change of a device in the jejunum is coded as 0D2DXUZ, using body part *lower intestinal tract*.

Approach

The technique used to reach the site of the procedure is called the *approach*, and there are seven different approaches.

- *Open*: Cutting through the skin or mucous membrane and any other body layers necessary to expose the site of the procedure
- *Percutaneous*: Entry, by puncture or minor incision, of instrumentation through the skin or mucous membrane and any other body layers necessary to reach the site of the procedure
- *Percutaneous Endoscopic*: Entry, by puncture or minor incision, of instrumentation through the skin or mucous membrane and any other body layers necessary to reach and visualize the site of the procedure
- *Via Natural or Artificial Opening*: Entry of instrumentation through a natural or artificial external opening to reach the site of the procedure
- *Via Natural or Artificial Opening Endoscopic*: Entry of instrumentation through a natural or artificial external opening to reach and visualize the site of the procedure
- *Via Natural or Artificial Opening Endoscopic with Percutaneous Endoscopic Assistance*: Entry of instrumentation through a natural or artificial external opening to reach and visualize the site of the procedure, and entry, by puncture or minor incision, of instrumentation through the skin or mucous membrane and any other body layers necessary to aid in the performance of the procedure
- *External*: Procedures performed directly on the skin or mucous membrane and procedures performed indirectly by the application of external force through the skin or mucous membrane

An approach also includes the following three components:

- *Access location*: For procedures performed on an internal body part, the access location specifies the external site through which the site of the procedure is reached. There are two general types of access locations.
  - Skin or mucous membranes, which can be cut or punctured to reach the procedure site
  - External openings, which are natural (e.g., mouth) or artificial (e.g., colostomy stoma)
- *Method*: For procedures performed on an internal body part, the method specifies how the external access location is entered, including:
  - Open method, which specifies cutting through skin or mucous membrane and any other intervening body layers necessary to expose the site of the procedure

NOTE:

Punctures and minor incisions are not considered open approaches because they do not expose the site of the procedure.

- ○ Instrumentation method, which specifies the entry of instrumentation through an access location (e.g., puncture, minor incision, external opening) to the internal procedure site
- *Type of instrumentation*: For procedures performed on an internal body part, instrumentation refers to specialized equipment used to perform the procedure (e.g., sigmoidoscope)

Approach—Open Approach with Percutaneous Endoscopic Assistance

Procedures performed using the open approach with percutaneous endoscopic assistance are coded to the approach *Open*.

EXAMPLE: *Laparoscopic-assisted sigmoidectomy* is assigned a value for approach *Open*.

Approach—External Approach

- Procedures performed within an orifice on structures that are visible without the aid of any instrumentation are coded to the approach *External*.

EXAMPLE: *Resection of tonsils* is assigned a value for approach *External*.

- Procedures performed indirectly by the application of external force through the intervening body layers are coded to the approach *External*.

EXAMPLE: Closed reduction of fracture is assigned a value for approach *External*.

Approach—Percutaneous Procedure via Device

Procedures performed percutaneously via a device placed for the procedure are coded to the approach *Percutaneous*.

EXAMPLE: *Fragmentation of kidney stone performed via percutaneous nephrostomy* is assigned a value for approach *Percutaneous*.

Device

The sixth character device value is assigned for devices that remain after the procedure is completed. There are four general types of devices.

- Biological or synthetic material that takes the place of all or a portion of a body part (e.g., skin grafts and joint prosthesis)
- Biological or synthetic material that assists or prevents a physiological function (e.g., IUD)
- Therapeutic material that is not absorbed by, eliminated by, or incorporated into a body part (e.g., radioactive implant)
- Mechanical or electronic appliances used to assist, monitor, take the place of, or prevent a physiological function (e.g., cardiac pacemaker, orthopedic pins)

Device—General Guidelines

A device value is assigned *only if a device remains after the procedure is completed*. If no device remains, the *No Device* device value is assigned. In limited root operations, the classification provides qualifier values *Temporary and Intraoperative* to be used for specific procedures that involve clinically significant devices where the purpose of the device is to be utilized for a brief duration during the procedure or current inpatient stay.

When a device (that is intended to remain after the procedure is completed) requires removal before the end of the operative episode during which it was inserted (e.g., inadequate device size, surgical complication), both the insertion and removal of the device are coded.

> **EXAMPLE:** Patient underwent right hip replacement, open. During the operative episode, the surgeon determined that the inserted internal fixation device was too small, and it was removed. A larger device was inserted, and the surgeon determined that it was stable. Report codes 0SH904Z and 0SP904Z.

Materials such as sutures, ligatures, radiological markers, and temporary postoperative wound drains are considered integral to the performance of a procedure; thus, they are *not* coded as devices.

> **EXAMPLE:** Patient underwent surgical excision of a sebaceous cyst, face. After successful removal skin layers were sutured. Report code 0HB1XZZ only. (Do **not** report a separate code for suture of skin layers.)

Procedures performed on a device only, and not on a body part, are classified to root operations *Change, Irrigation, Removal*, or *Revision*, and they are coded to the procedure performed.

> **EXAMPLE:** *Irrigation of percutaneous nephrostomy tube* is classified to root operation *Irrigation, indwelling device* in the *Administration* section. Index main term *Irrigation*, subterm *Genitourinary Tract, Irrigating Substance* list values 3E1K. Go to ICD-10-PCS Table 3E1 to construct code 3E1K38Z.

Device—Drainage Device

A separate procedure to insert a drainage device is assigned a value for root operation *Drainage* and a value for device *Drainage Device*.

> **EXAMPLE:** *Percutaneous insertion of peritoneal cavity drainage device*. Index main term *Drainage*, subterm *Peritoneal Cavity* list values 0W9G. Go to ICD-10-PCS Table 0W9 to construct code 0W9G30Z.
>
> Notice that ICD-10-PCS Index main term *Insertion of device in* and subterm *Peritoneal Cavity* list values 0WHG, which directs you to ICD-10-PCS Table 0WH. However, Table 0WH is **not** used to construct the code because drainage devices are not classified in its column 3 *Device* column.

Obstetrics Section Coding Guidelines

The Obstetrics section includes two additional root operations.

- *Abortion*: Artificially terminating a pregnancy
- *Delivery*: Assisting the passage of the products of conception from the genital canal

A cesarean section is *not* a separate root operation because the underlying objective is *Extraction* (e.g., pulling out all or a portion of a body part).

Obstetrics Section—Products of Conception

Procedures performed on the products of conception are coded to the *Obstetrics* section. Procedures performed on a pregnant female, other than those performed on the products of conception, are coded to the appropriate root operation in the *Medical and Surgical* section.

> **EXAMPLE 1:** *Amniocentesis* is assigned a value from body part *Products of Conception* in the *Obstetrics* section.

> **EXAMPLE 2:** *Repair of obstetric urethral laceration* is assigned a value from body part *Urethra* in the *Medical and Surgical* section.

Obstetrics Section—Procedures Following Delivery or Abortion

Procedures performed following a delivery or abortion for (1) curettage of the endometrium or (2) evacuation of retained products of conception are coded to the *Obstetrics* section, *Pregnancy* body system, *Extraction* root operation, and *Products of Conception, Retained* body part.

   Diagnostic or therapeutic dilation and curettage performed during times *other than* the postpartum or post-abortion period are coded in the *Medical and Surgical* section, *Female Reproductive* body system, *Extraction* root operation, and *Endometrium* body part.

> **EXAMPLE 1:** After delivery of a healthy male term infant, the patient underwent endometrial dilatation and curettage (D&C) to remove retained placenta. D&C code 10D17ZZ is constructed using values from the *Obstetrics* section, *Pregnancy* body system, *Extraction* root operation, and *Products of Conception, Retained* body part.

> **EXAMPLE 2:** A 58-year-old patient underwent diagnostic D&C. Code 0UDB7ZX is constructed using values from the *Medical and Surgical* section, *Female Reproductive* body system, *Extraction* root operation, and *Endometrium* body part.

Placement Section

The Placement section includes seven root operations.

- *Change*: Taking out or off a device from a body part and putting back an identical or similar device in or on the same body part without cutting or puncturing the skin or a mucous membrane
- *Compression*: Putting pressure on a body region
- *Dressing*: Putting material on a body region for protection
- *Immobilization*: Limiting or preventing motion of an external body region
- *Packing*: Putting material in a body region or orifice
- *Removal*: Taking out or off a device from a body part
- *Traction*: Exerting a pulling force on a body region in a distal direction

Administration Section

The Administration section includes three root operations.

- *Introduction*: Putting in or on a therapeutic, diagnostic, nutritional, physiological, or prophylactic substance except blood or blood products
- *Irrigation*: Putting in or on a cleansing substance
- *Transfusion*: Putting in blood or blood products

Measurement and Monitoring Section

The Measurement and Monitoring section includes two root operations.

- *Measurement*: Determining the level of a physiological or physical function at a point in time
- *Monitoring*: Determining the level of a physiological or physical function repetitively over a period of time

Extracorporeal or Systemic Assistance and Performance Section

The Extracorporeal or Systemic Assistance and Performance section includes three root operations.

- *Assistance*: Taking over a portion of a physiological function by extracorporeal means
- *Performance*: Completely taking over a physiological function by extracorporeal means
- *Restoration*: Returning, or attempting to return, a physiological function to its natural state by extracorporeal means; this root operation contains a single procedure code that identifies *extracorporeal cardioversion*

Extracorporeal or Systemic Therapies Section

The Extracorporeal or Systemic Therapies section includes 11 root operations.

- *Atmospheric Control*: Extracorporeal control of atmospheric pressure and composition
- *Decompression*: Extracorporeal elimination of undissolved gas from body fluids; this root operation involves just one type of procedure, *treatment for decompression sickness* (or *the bends*) in a hyperbaric chamber
- *Electromagnetic Therapy*: Extracorporeal treatment by electromagnetic rays
- *Hyperthermia*: Extracorporeal raising of body temperature; *hyperthermia* describes both a temperature imbalance treatment and an adjunct radiation treatment for cancer. For temperature imbalance treatment, assign a code from the Extracorporeal Therapy section; for adjunct radiation treatment, assign a code from the Radiation Therapy section.
- *Hypothermia*: Extracorporeal lowering of body temperature
- *Perfusion*: extracorporeal treatment by diffusion of therapeutic fluid
- *Pheresis*: Extracorporeal separation of blood products; *pheresis has* two main purposes: the treatment of diseases when too much of a blood component is produced (e.g., leukemia) and the removal of a blood product (e.g., platelets) from a donor for transfusion into another patient.
- *Phototherapy*: Extracorporeal treatment by light rays; *phototherapy* involves using a machine that exposes blood to light rays outside the body, recirculates it, and then returns it to the body.
- *Shock Wave Therapy*: Extracorporeal treatment by shock waves
- *Ultrasound Therapy*: Extracorporeal treatment by ultrasound
- *Ultraviolet Light Therapy*: Extracorporeal treatment by ultraviolet light

Osteopathic Section

The Osteopathic section includes just one root operation, *treatment*, which is the manual treatment to eliminate or alleviate somatic dysfunction and related disorders.

Other Procedures Section

The Other Procedures section has just one root operation, *other procedures*, which are methodologies that attempt to remediate or cure a disorder or disease.

Chiropractic Section

The Chiropractic section has just one root operation, *manipulation*, which is a manual procedure that involves a directed thrust to move a joint past the physiological range of motion, without exceeding the anatomical limit.

Imaging Section

The Imaging section includes five root types.

- *Computerized Tomography (CT Scan)*: Computer-reformatted digital display of multiplanar images developed from the capture of multiple exposures of external ionizing radiation
- *Fluoroscopy*: Single plane or bi-plane real-time display of an image developed from the capture of external ionizing radiation on fluorescent screen. The image may also be stored by either digital or analog means.
- *Magnetic Resonance Imaging (MRI)*: Computer reformatted digital display of multiplanar images developed from the capture of radiofrequency signals emitted by nuclei in a body site excited within a magnetic field
- *Plain Radiography*: Planar display of an image developed from the capture of external ionizing radiation on photographic or photoconductive plate
- *Ultrasonography*: Real-time display of images of anatomy or flow information developed from the capture of reflected and attenuated high-frequency sound waves

Nuclear Medicine Section

The Nuclear Medicine section includes seven root types.

- *Nonimaging Uptake*: Introduction of radioactive materials into the body for measurements of organ function, from the detection of radioactive emissions
- *Nonimaging Nuclear Medicine Probe*: Introduction of radioactive materials into the body for the study of distribution and fate of certain substances by the detection of radioactive emissions; alternatively, measurement of absorption of radioactive emissions from an external source
- *Nonimaging Assay*: Introduction of radioactive materials into the body for the study of body fluids and blood elements, by the detection of radioactive emissions
- *Planar Nuclear Medicine Imaging*: Introduction of radioactive materials into the body for single-plane display of images developed from the capture of radioactive emissions
- *Positron Emission Tomography (PET) Imaging*: Introduction of radioactive materials into the body for three-dimensional display of images developed from the simultaneous capture, 180 degrees apart, of radioactive emissions
- *Systemic Nuclear Medicine Therapy*: Introduction of unsealed radioactive materials into the body for treatment
- *Tomographic (Tomo) Nuclear Medicine Imaging*: Introduction of radioactive materials into the body for three-dimensional display of images developed from the capture of radioactive emissions

Radiation Therapy Section

The Radiation Therapy section includes the following modalities: beam radiation, brachytherapy, stereotactic radiosurgery, and other radiation. Coding guidelines impact the use of brachytherapy.

Brachytherapy

Brachytherapy is the treatment of cancer by inserting radioactive implants directly into tissue, and it is coded to the modality Brachytherapy in the Radiation Therapy section. When a radioactive brachytherapy source is left in the body at the end of the procedure, it is coded separately to the root operation Insertion with the device value Radioactive Element.

EXAMPLE: For example, brachytherapy with implantation of a low dose rate brachytherapy source left in the body at the end of the procedure is coded to the applicable treatment site in the Radiation Therapy section using modality Brachytherapy, modality qualifier Low Dose Rate, and the applicable isotope value and qualifier value. The implantation of the brachytherapy source is coded separately to device Radioactive Element in the appropriate Insertion table of the Medical and Surgical section. The Radiation Therapy section code identifies the specific modality and isotope of the brachytherapy, and root operation Insertion code identifies the implantation of the brachytherapy source that remains in the body at the end of the procedure.

An exception to brachytherapy guideline is the implantation of Cesium-131 brachytherapy seeds embedded in a collagen matrix to the treatment site after resection of a brain tumor; the implantation is coded to root operation Insertion with device Radioactive Element, Cesium-131 Collagen Implant. This procedure is coded to root operation Insertion because the device identifies both the implantation of the radioactive element and a specific brachytherapy isotope that is not included in the Radiation Therapy section tables.

A separate procedure to place a temporary applicator for delivering brachytherapy is coded to root operation Insertion and device Other Device. For example, an intrauterine brachytherapy applicator placed during a separate procedure from the brachytherapy procedure is coded to Insertion of Other Device, and the brachytherapy is coded separately using modality Brachytherapy in the Radiation Therapy section.

An intrauterine brachytherapy applicator placed concomitantly with delivery of the brachytherapy dose is coded with a single code using modality Brachytherapy in the Radiation Therapy section.

Physical Rehabilitation and Diagnostic Audiology Section

The Physical Rehabilitation and Diagnostic Audiology section includes the following root types.

- *Activities of Daily Living Assessment*: Measurement of functional level for activities of daily living
- *Activities of Daily Living Treatment*: Exercise or activities to facilitate functional competence for activities of daily living
- *Caregiver Training*: Educating caregiver with the skills and knowledge used to interact with and assist the patient
- *Cochlear Implant Treatment*: Application of techniques to improve the communication abilities of individuals with cochlear implant
- *Device Fitting*: Fitting of a device designed to facilitate or support achievement of a higher level of function
- *Hearing Aid Assessment*: Measurement of the appropriateness and/or effectiveness of a hearing device
- *Hearing Assessment*: Measurement of hearing and related functions
- *Hearing Treatment*: Application of techniques to improve, augment, or compensate for hearing and related functional impairment
- *Motor and/or Nerve Function Assessment*: Measurement of motor, nerve, and related functions
- *Motor Treatment*: Exercise or activities to increase or facilitate motor function
- *Speech Assessment*: Measurement of speech and related functions
- *Speech Treatment*: Application of techniques to improve, augment, or compensate for speech and related functional impairment
- *Treatment*: Use of specific activities or methods to develop, improve, and restore the performance of necessary functions, compensate for dysfunction, and minimize debilitation
- *Vestibular Assessment*: Measurement of the vestibular system and related functions
- *Vestibular Treatment*: Application of techniques to improve, augment, or compensate for vestibular and related functional impairment

Mental Health Section

The Mental Health section includes the following mental health procedures and services:

- *Biofeedback*: Provision of information from the monitoring and regulating of physiological processes in conjunction with cognitive-behavioral techniques to improve patient functioning or well-being

- *Counseling*: Application of psychological methods to treat an individual with normal developmental issues and psychological problems in order to increase function, improve well-being, alleviate distress, maladjustment or resolve crises
- *Crisis Intervention*: Treatment of a traumatized, acutely disturbed or distressed individual for the purpose of short-term stabilization
- *Electroconvulsive Therapy*: Application of controlled electrical voltages to treat a mental health disorder
- *Family Psychotherapy*: Treatment that includes one or more family members of an individual with a mental health disorder by behavioral, cognitive, psychoanalytic, psychodynamic or psychophysiological means to improve functioning or well-being
- *Group Psychotherapy*: Treatment of two or more individuals with a mental health disorder by behavioral, cognitive, psychoanalytic, psychodynamic or psychophysiological means to improve functioning or well-being
- *Hypnosis*: Induction of a state of heightened suggestibility by auditory, visual and tactile techniques to elicit an emotional or behavioral response
- *Individual Psychotherapy*: Treatment of an individual with a mental health disorder by behavioral, cognitive, psychoanalytic, psychodynamic or psychophysiological means to improve functioning or well-being
- *Light Therapy*: Application of specialized light treatments to improve functioning or well-being
- *Medication Management*: Monitoring and adjusting the use of medications for the treatment of a mental health disorder
- *Narcosynthesis*: Administration of intravenous barbiturates in order to release suppressed or repressed thoughts
- *Psychological Tests*: Administration and interpretation of standardized psychological tests and measurement instruments for the assessment of psychological function

Substance Abuse Treatment Section

The Substance Abuse Treatment section includes seven root types.

- *Detoxification Services*: Not a treatment modality but helps the patient stabilize physically and psychologically until the body becomes free of drugs and the effects of alcohol
- *Individual Counseling*: Comprising several techniques, which apply various strategies to address drug addiction
- *Group Counseling*: Provides structured group counseling sessions and healing power through the connection with others
- *Family Counseling*: Provides support and education for family members of addicted individuals. Family member participation is seen as critical to substance abuse treatment.
- *Individual Psychotherapy*: Includes behavior, cognitive/behavioral, cognitive, interactive, interpersonal, psychoanalysis, psychodynamic, psychophysiological, and supportive types
- *Medication Management*: Management of prescription drug dosages through laboratory testing and other evaluation and management services
- *Pharmacotherapy*: Management of mental disorders using pharmacological agents

New Technology

ICD-10-PCS Section X contains stand-alone codes to uniquely identify procedures that are requested as a result of the New Technology Application Process or that capture services not routinely classified in ICD-10-PCS.

After Section X codes have served their purpose, proposals to delete the codes and create new codes in the existing ICD-10-PCS tables will be addressed at ICD-10 Coordination and Maintenance meetings.

The structure of ICD-10-PCS Section X codes includes:

- First character – letter X
- Second character – body system value
- Third character – root operation value
- Fourth character – body part value
- Fifth character – approach value
- Sixth character – device/substance/technology value
- Seventh character – information indicating the year created (e.g., New Technology Group 3 codes were created for use in fiscal year 2018, beginning October 1, 2017)

General Guidelines

Section X (New Technology) codes fully represent the specific procedure described in the code title, and they do not require additional codes from other sections of ICD-10-PCS. When section X contains a code title that fully describes a specific new technology procedure, and it is the only procedure performed, only the section X code is reported for the procedure. There is no need to report an additional code in another section of ICD-10-PCS.

> **EXAMPLE:** Ceftazidime-Avibactam anti-infective was administered via a central vein. ICD-10-PCS code XW04321 (Introduction of Ceftazidime Avibactam Anti-infective into Central Vein, Percutaneous Approach, New Technology Group 1) is reported. A separate code from ICD-10-PCS Table 3E0 in the Administration section is *not* coded.

When multiple procedures are performed, New Technology section X codes are reported by following the ICD-10-PCS multiple procedures guideline.

> **EXAMPLE 1:** When dual filter cerebral embolic filtration is used during transcatheter aortic valve replacement (TAVR), code X2A5312 (Cerebral Embolic Filtration, Dual Filter in Innominate Artery and Left Common Carotid Artery, Percutaneous Approach, New Technology Group 2) is reported for the cerebral embolic filtration. A separate ICD-10-PCS code *is reported* for the TAVR procedure.

> **EXAMPLE 2:** When a magnetically controlled growth rod (MCGR) is placed during a spinal fusion procedure, a code from table XNS, Reposition of the Bones, is reported for the MCGR. A separate ICD-10-PCS code *is reported* for the spinal fusion procedure.

Exercise 6.4 – ICD-10-PCS Procedure Coding

Instructions: Underline the main term in each procedure statement and construct the appropriate ICD-10-PCS procedure code(s).

_____ 1. Bilateral augmentation mammoplasty using synthetic substitute, open approach

_____ 2. Percutaneous biopsy of spleen

_____ 3. Injection of neurolytic agent (nerve block) into peripheral nerve

_____ 4. Laparoscopic oophorectomy, left

_____ 5. Open stripping of varicose veins, left saphenous vein

_____ 6. Open biopsy of prostate

_____ 7. Esophagoscopy

_____ 8. Parathyroidectomy, complete, via open approach

_____ 9. Partial breech extraction with high forceps

_____ 10. Partial left hip joint replacement, synthetic substitute

(continues)

Exercise 6.4 – *continued*

_____ 11. Percutaneous nephrostomy with fragmentation of stone in right kidney pelvis

_____ 12. Drainage of bilateral ethmoid sinuses (percutaneous approach)

_____ 13. Insertion of implantable heart assist system into heart, open approach

_____ 14. Repair of pterygium of conjunctiva, left eye

_____ 15. Left tympanoplasty (via natural opening)

Coding Inpatient Diagnoses and Procedures

ICD-10-CM and ICD-10-PCS (abbreviated as ICD-10-CM/PCS) codes are assigned to inpatient cases to collect statistical data for education and research, determine third-party payer reimbursement, and facilitate health care financial planning. ICD-10-CM/PCS codes assigned to an inpatient case are entered into automated case abstracting software using a data entry screen (Figure 6-8) and diagnosis-related groups (DRGs) are assigned for reimbursement purposes. The ICD-10-CM/PCS codes are then transmitted to the facility's billing department where the inpatient UB-04 claim is generated for submission to third-party payers (to obtain reimbursement).

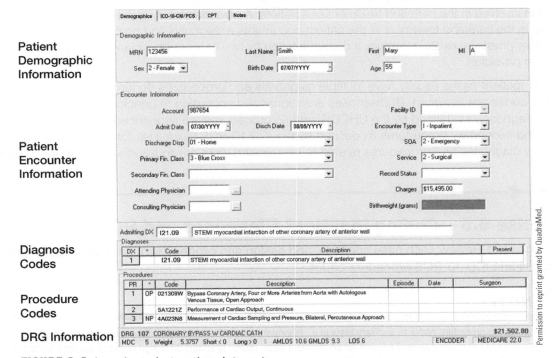

FIGURE 6-8 Inpatient abstracting data entry screen

 NOTE:

As a result of data entry, the facility's information technology (IT) department has the capability of producing customized reports and summary data for education, quality management, research, and statistical purposes. Statistical data allow the facility to conduct financial planning to determine which facility services to expand or deactivate.

 NOTE:

Refer to textbook Chapter 20 for a discussion about the inpatient prospective payment system (IPPS), which includes DRGs, major diagnostic categories (MDCs), outliers, IPPS 3-day payment window (IPPS 72-hour rule), Medicare-severity DRGs (MS-DRGs), IPPS transfer rule, hospital-acquired conditions (HACs), present on admission (POA) indicator, and value-based purchasing (VBP).

When assigning ICD-10-CM/PCS codes, coders carefully review patient records to locate diagnoses and procedures to which codes are assigned.

 NOTE:

> Coders are prohibited from assigning codes to diagnoses and procedures that are not documented by the physician. This is called *assumption coding*, and it is considered fraudulent because the coder has mistakenly assumed certain facts about a patient's diagnosis or procedure even though documentation does not support codes assigned.

Coders should consider the following when assigning ICD-10-CM/PCS to diagnoses and procedures.

- *Incomplete documentation.* When patient record documentation is incomplete for coding purposes, generate a *physician query* to clarify documentation. (Refer to textbook Chapter 1 for more information about the physician query process.)

- *Coding specificity.* When patient record documentation supports the assignment of a specific code, it is appropriate to assign that code. For example, when a physician documents *closed fracture of left femur* in the discharge summary, and review of the x-ray report identifies the fracture site (e.g., shaft of femur). In addition, codes based on other physician (e.g., consultant) documentation may be assigned *as long as there is no conflicting documentation from the attending physician.*

- *Physician documentation.* It is appropriate to base the assignment of codes on documentation by any physician involved in the care and treatment of a patient. A physician query is unnecessary if a physician involved in the care and treatment of the patient documents a diagnosis and no conflicting documentation by another physician exists. However, if documentation by two or more physicians conflicts, query the attending physician.

Hospital inpatient cases usually have multiple diagnoses and procedures documented. Once ICD-10-CM/PCS codes are assigned, (1) diagnoses are sequenced according to principal diagnosis and other (additional) diagnoses as defined by the UHDDS, and (2) procedures are sequenced according to principal procedure and secondary procedures as defined by the *ICD-10-PCS Guidelines for Coding and Reporting.* (Definitions of diagnoses and procedures related to sequencing were previously discussed in this chapter.)

Exercise 6.5 – Coding Inpatient Diagnoses and Procedures

Instructions: Review each case scenario, and assign and properly sequence the ICD-10-CM diagnosis and ICD-10-PCS procedure codes.

 NOTE:

> Do not assign procedure codes to ancillary tests (e.g., laboratory tests, x-rays) because they do not impact DRG assignment or the reimbursement amount for an inpatient case. (Some hospitals do assign codes to ancillary tests even though doing so does not impact the level of reimbursement received; therefore, you should be aware of this practice.)

1. Patient admitted for treatment of AIDS-related conditions and underwent diagnostic fiberoptic bronchoscopy with cell washings for specimen collection. Final diagnoses included AIDS-related *Pneumocystis jiroveci* and oral candidiasis.

   _____

2. Patient admitted with slurred speech and weakness on the right side. Patient is right-handed. CT scan reveals left carotid artery occlusion with cerebral infarction. Patient discharged to inpatient rehabilitation facility for continued treatment of dysphasia and right hemiparesis.

   _____

(continues)

Exercise 6.5 – *continued*

1. Patient was seen during an initial encounter after having sustained a closed fracture of the distal radius, left, due to a fall from the roof of his single-family house while cleaning gutters. X-ray of the left lower arm revealed nondisplaced fracture of distal radius with fracture fragments in good alignment. The physician determined that reduction was unnecessary, and a plaster splint was applied as a stabilizing device.

   _____

2. Patient admitted for treatment of diabetic toe (skin) ulcer, left, with gangrene of the bone. The underlying cause was type 1 diabetic peripheral neuropathy with long-term insulin use. Patient underwent a complete left foot amputation.

   _____

3. Patient admitted following repeated temporal lobe seizures. History revealed that the patient had had 18 seizures within the past 24 hours. He has had seizures since the age of 16, previously well controlled with long-term use of phenobarbital. Blood levels indicate an acceptable therapeutic level. During hospitalization, patient continued to seize at least hourly. Patient was immediately transferred to the neurology unit of tertiary care hospital due to localization-related intractable epilepsy with complex partial seizures.

   _____

Summary

Inpatient health care settings include acute care facilities (hospitals), behavioral health care facilities, hospice inpatient care, and long-term acute care hospitals (LTACHs). CMS publishes official ICD-10-CM and ICD-10-PCS guidelines for coding and reporting, which provide direction about assignment of diagnosis and procedure codes and the sequencing of diagnosis codes for reimbursement purposes. Depending on state reporting requirements, when the circumstances of inpatient admission govern the sequencing of procedure codes, UHDDS definitions are used to report inpatient data elements in a standardized manner, including sequencing of the principal diagnosis and other (additional) diagnoses. Circumstances associated with an inpatient admission also govern the sequencing of principal procedure and significant other procedures (or secondary procedures).

Internet Links

HCPro, Inc.: Go to *www.hcmarketplace.com*, and click on the Sign up for our FREE e-Newsletters link. Enter your contact information, and click on the box located in front of JustCoding News: Inpatient (along with other e-Newsletters that interest you) to subscribe.

NYS DOH SPARCS: Go to *www.health.ny.gov*, click on the Search link, and enter SPARCS in the search box to locate information about the Statewide Planning and Research Cooperative System (SPARCS).

Virtual Pediatric Hospital: *www.virtualpediatrichospital.org*

Review

Multiple Choice (ICD-10-CM)

Instructions: Circle the most appropriate response.

1. Fever of unknown origin. Rule out tuberculosis. (Final diagnosis at time of inpatient hospital discharge.)
   - **a.** A15.0
   - **b.** R50.9
   - **c.** R50.9, A15.0
   - **d.** Z03.89

2. Primary pancreatic cancer.
   a. C25.1   b. C25.9   c. C77.2   d. C79.89

3. Graves disease with thyrotoxic crisis.
   a. E05.01   b. E05.09   c. E05.00, E05.91 d. E05.00

4. Acute posthemorrhagic anemia.
   a. D50.0   b. D61.9   c. D62   d. D64.9, R58

5. Anorexia nervosa.
   a. F50.00   b. F50.9   c. R63.0   d. R63.3

6. Hypertensive heart disease with CHF. Old anterior wall MI, diagnosed on EKG (currently presenting no symptoms).
   a. I50.9, I10   c. I10, I11.9, I50.9
   b. I11.0, I50.9, I25.2   d. I50.9, I10, I25.2

7. Congenital hydrocephalus.
   a. G91.0   b. G91.9   c. Q03.8   d. Q03.9

8. Respiratory distress syndrome of newborn.
   a. J80   b. P22.0   c. P27.8   d. P28.81

9. Stab wound (from knife) of thoracic aorta.
   a. S21.109A, X99.9xxA   c. S25.00xA, X99.1xxA
   b. S31.000A, X99.9xxA   d. S29.001A, X99.8xxA

10. Neonatal cerebral ischemia.
   a. G45.8   b. G45.9   c. I67.82   d. P91.0

Multiple Choice (ICD-10-PCS)

Instructions: Circle the most appropriate response.

1. Partial splenectomy, open.
   a. 07BP3ZZ   b. 07BP4ZX   c. 07BP0ZZ   d. 07TP0ZZ

2. Needle biopsy of cerebral meninges.
   a. 00B13ZX   b. 00B13ZZ   c. 00C13ZZ   d. 00D13ZZ

3. Complete substernal thyroidectomy.
   a. 0GBG0ZX, 0GBH0ZX   b. 0GBH0ZZ   c. 0GPKX0Z   d. 0GTK0ZZ

4. Percutaneous myringotomy with placement of tube in right tympanic membrane.
   a. 099700Z   b. 099730Z   c. 099740Z   d. 099770Z

5. Diagnostic lingula bronchial drainage via endoscopy.
   a. 0BJ08ZZ   b. 0B998ZX   c. 3E1L38Z   d. 3E1F88Z

6. Repair of direct inguinal hernia, right side, via percutaneous endoscopic approach.
   a. 0YQ50ZZ   b. 0YQ53ZZ   c. 0YQ54ZZ   d. 0YQ64ZZ

7. Extracorporeal shock wave lithotripsy of the right kidney pelvis (external approach).
   a. 0TF3XZZ   b. 0TF6XZZ   c. 0TFDXZZ   d. 0WFRXZZ

8. Classical cesarean section by hysterotomy.
   a. 10207YZ   b. 10900ZC   c. 10A00ZZ   d. 10D00Z0

9. Excision of pilonidal abscess.
   a. 0H98X0Z   b. 0H90X0Z   c. 0HB8XZZ   d. 0HC0XZZ

10. Open temporomandibular joint (TMJ) repair, right.
   a. 0RQC0ZZ   b. 0MM00ZZ   c. 0C00X7Z   d. 0KQ00ZZ

Coding Practice—Hospital Inpatient Cases (ICD-10-CM)

Instructions: Review each case scenario, and assign the ICD-10-CM diagnosis codes.

1. A 70-year-old female presented to the hospital with fever, myalgia, arthralgia, tachycardia, and dehydration and was believed to be septic. This patient has a history of hypertension, CHF, and migraines. Routine medications include Lasix 40 milligrams by mouth each morning, if needed, for significant pedal edema and Isordil 20 milligrams by mouth four times a day.

    A variety of studies were obtained to further delineate the source of her problem. Urine cultures were negative. Blood cultures grew *Escherichia coli*. The blood urea nitrogen level was 22, and a random glucose was 149. An anterior-posterior film of the chest taken at the same time showed acute pulmonary edema.

    The patient received intravenous fluids. The patient's routine medications were continued, and she received intravenous antibiotics. On the fourth day of her hospital stay, it was believed that the patient had reached maximal hospital benefit and was therefore switched to oral antibiotics and was discharged. The patient left the hospital in good condition.

    DISCHARGE DIAGNOSES:

    _____ Septicemia due to *Escherichia coli*   _____ Hypertensive heart disease

    _____ Dehydration   _____ with heart failure

2. A 2-year-old male presented with fever, vomiting, and abdominal pain. The patient was severely dehydrated with a blood urea nitrogen level of 54, indicating acute renal failure. Blood cultures obtained grew *Staphylococcus aureus*. The patient was treated with a 10-day course of intravenous vancomycin. The patient also received intravenous fluids and had improved renal function. Upon admission, the patient was noted to have a rash on his buttocks and was treated with topical ointment. The patient improved and was discharged.

    DISCHARGE DIAGNOSES:

    _____ Sepsis due to *Staphylococcus aureus*   _____ Dehydration

    _____ Severe sepsis with septic shock   _____ Diaper rash

    _____ Acute kidney failure

3. A 94-year-old male was admitted to the hospital with a chief complaint of abdominal pain and loss of weight. The patient had a history of coronary artery disease and myocardial infarction. There is no history of coronary bypass surgery. The patient had a nebulizer at home and takes metoprolol. These medications were continued during the patient's stay. Physical examination revealed abdomen to be tender to palpation in the left mid and lower quadrants with some rebound. Bowel sounds were present, and there was no guarding. Blood pressure was normal. Pulse, respirations, and temperature were normal.

    During hospitalization, EKG showed sinus rhythm with myocardial changes of ischemia. Sputum cytology was suggestive of adenocarcinoma, compatible with bronchoalveolar growth. Chest x-ray showed metastatic lesions and chronic obstructive lung disease in both lung fields. Barium enema showed adenocarcinoma of proximal sigmoid colon. Abdominal series showed no evidence of obstruction, but moderate dilation of his transverse colon was evident. Patient was seen in consultation, and it was decided to do as little as possible at this time due to the patient's age and lung conditions. The patient agreed with this approach and requested discharge to home to receive hospice care.

    DISCHARGE DIAGNOSES:

    _____ Carcinoma of sigmoid colon   _____ Chronic obstructive lung disease

    _____ Probable metastatic bronchogenic   _____ Coronary artery disease
    carcinoma, right lung
                                                              _____ Previous myocardial infarction
    _____   and left lung

4. This patient is a 43-year-old female with a long history of joint pain. Lately she had been feeling very tired and weak. She also has had intermittent abdominal pain with nausea and vomiting. Her joint exam showed tenderness of the knees. She denied any problems suggestive of hypothyroidism (myxedema). The patient's hematocrit was 27.6, serum iron was found to be decreased at 27, and thyroid functions were found to be markedly low. Upper GI series showed a 4-millimeter ulcer at the posterior wall of the duodenal bulb. The patient was transfused 2 units of packed red cells. She was started on ferrous sulfate 300 milligrams twice a day. She was also begun on Tagamet for the ulcer. Further questioning revealed that she had indeed been hypothyroid in the past and has been on thyroid medication until stopped by another physician. The patient was restarted on Synthroid 0.2 milligrams per day. She was discharged on the sixth hospital day.

   DISCHARGE DIAGNOSES:

   _____ Hypothyroidism

   _____ Anemia due to myxedema

   _____ Acute duodenal ulcer

   _____

5. This patient is a 14-year-old African American male who was admitted due to sickle cell crisis and acute chest syndrome. His mother has sickle cell anemia, and his father has the sickle cell trait. Because of this, the patient was tested at birth; a blood sample was drawn, and it was sent to the laboratory for hemoglobin electrophoresis to obtain a definitive diagnosis. Unfortunately, the test was positive for sickle cell disease. The patient was given intravenous fluids and was started on Darvocet for pain management. When the Darvocet failed to keep his pain at an acceptable level, he was switched to Vicodin. The patient is to be discharged with follow-up in the pediatrician's office tomorrow.

   DISCHARGE DIAGNOSES:

   _____ Sickle cell crisis with acute chest syndrome

   _____ Family history of sickle cell anemia

   _____

6. A 31-year-old white male presented to the emergency room reportedly having taken 8 to 10 naproxen at home in a suicide attempt. He reported that he had been having trouble with his wife, and he is unemployed. He had apparently become despondent over this and attempted to take his own life with his girlfriend's pills. The patient is admitted to the telemetry unit due to paroxysmal ventricular tachycardia. The patient was started on metaraminol for the tachycardia. Fortunately, the patient seemed to sustain no other ill effects from the naproxen. The mental health service was consulted, and an appointment was made for outpatient services. He was given Prozac to treat his depression. At this time, the patient does not appear to be a threat to himself or to others. He appears remorseful and denies any suicidal ideations. He was discharged in good condition.

   DISCHARGE DIAGNOSES:

   _____ Suicide attempt with naproxen

   _____ Paroxysmal ventricular tachycardia

   _____ Depression

   _____ Unemployment

   _____ Marital relationship problems

   _____ Home (place of occurrence)

   _____

7. A 52-year-old male bus driver is admitted to receive a course of electroconvulsive therapy for his depressive symptomatology. This patient was seen approximately one year ago in consultation; at that time, he was showing early evidence of moderate involutional depressive psychotic reaction. He has had several admissions since that time, and on each occasion, he had been drinking excessively. It appears that he attempts to use alcohol as a tranquilizer. During the first two days of his admission, he continued to show marked depressive symptomatology and he was started on electroconvulsive therapy. After treatment, he showed a mitigation of his depressive symptomatology. He was discharged home on Pertofrane 25 milligrams twice a day and was instructed to call for follow-up care. Condition on discharge was improved.

DISCHARGE DIAGNOSIS:

_____ Moderate involutional depressive psychotic reaction, recurrent

---

8. A 71-year-old male presented to the hospital with the chief complaint of increasing confusion. The patient has been wandering away from home and has displayed aggressive behavior to his family members. The patient is a known type 2 diabetic, which is controlled on Orinase 0.5 milligrams daily. The patient is thin and emaciated. During his period of hospitalization, the patient was uncooperative in all aspects. He refused food and medications. He was confused and seemed slightly paranoid. The family was consulted about the patient's worsening dementia, and the decision was made to transfer the patient to the state psychiatric hospital for care. The patient was transferred on the fifth hospital day.

DISCHARGE DIAGNOSES:

_____ Alzheimer's disease

_____ with senile dementia and aggressive behavior

_____ Diabetes mellitus, type 2

_____ Wandering away from home

---

9. An 84-year-old female was admitted to the hospital because of severe dizziness and weakness. The patient has had previous brain stem transient ischemic attacks and also has completed radiation for what was assumed to be cancer of the endometrium. The patient is currently receiving short-term chemotherapy for the endometrial carcinoma on an outpatient basis, and she was administered her chemotherapy during this inpatient stay. The patient had 3+ hyperreflexia and rotary nystagmus on admission. The urinalysis showed white blood cells and bacteria. Her urine culture grew *Klebsiella pneumoniae*. The patient was started on Velosef. Over the next several days, the dizziness cleared, but the patient continued to be quite weak. Gait training physical therapy was started, and she was eventually able to walk with her walker without assistance. Her reflexia had come back down to 1+, which is her usual state. The patient had no more nystagmus and was switched from heparin to Persantine. The patient was discharged home and was to be seen as an outpatient in one month.

DISCHARGE DIAGNOSES:

_____ Brain stem transient ischemic attack

_____ Endometrial carcinoma

_____ Urinary tract infection

_____ due to *Klebsiella pneumoniae*

10. This patient is a practical nurse who presented to the hospital because her blood pressure was 240/140 at home. Her blood pressure at admission was 220/120. This patient has had multiple strokes, and her first stroke was 5 years ago. This patient has a history of hypertension and paroxysmal atrial fibrillation. She was started on intravenous Aldomet, Dyazide, Catapres, and Lanoxin. Her blood pressure lowered to 190/98. On admission, her radial, brachial, popliteal, and femoral pulses were 2–4. The next day, the femoral pulse was decreased to 1–4, and the posterior tibial pulses were not palpable. The leg on the left side was clammy and cold. There was minimal cyanosis over the heel of the left foot. Possible femoral and popliteal artery embolism had to be ruled out, and it was decided to transfer the patient.

DISCHARGE DIAGNOSES:

_____ Hypertensive crisis

_____ Possible bilateral iliofemoral emboli

_____ Hemiplegia, nondominant left side, following previous cerebrovascular accident

_____ Aphasia, following previous cerebrovascular accident

_____ Paroxysmal atrial fibrillation

_____

11. A 47-year-old male corrections officer presented to the emergency room with an acute onset of chest pain. The pain was described as a crushing pain and was accompanied with radiation of the pain into the jaw and diaphoresis. He does not have a history of previous myocardial infarction (MI). His risk factors include morbid obesity, hypertension, and hypercholesterolemia. The patient takes metoprolol and Lipitor. The cardiologist was consulted, and the patient was found to have an acute ST elevation anterior wall MI. The patient was admitted to the intensive care unit and was observed on telemetry. On the second day of hospitalization, the patient was thought to be stable for transfer. The patient was transferred for coronary angiography and possible angioplasty.

DISCHARGE DIAGNOSES:

_____ Acute ST elevation anterior wall myocardial infarction

_____ Hypertension

_____ Hypercholesterolemia

_____ Morbid obesity

_____

12. A 16-month-old infant was admitted from the emergency room because of nausea and vomiting and some cough. She was felt to have acute bronchitis due to respiratory syncytial virus (RSV) with possible pneumonia. This child was hospitalized previously with meningitis but has had no other serious illnesses until the present time. She has no prior history of diabetes or tuberculosis. Her parents are alive and well. The physical examination revealed generalized sibilant rales. The patient's chest x-ray was normal. Pneumonia was ruled out. Her urinalysis was normal. Her hematocrit was 34. The low hematocrit was thought to be due to the persistent vomiting and lack of iron intake from her diet. The patient was given penicillin and Phenergan injections. She was also given nebulizer treatments every 6 hours on an as-needed basis. The patient was started on clear liquids, and she progressed to a general diet. After the first few days, the vomiting ceased. She was discharged with prescriptions for ferrous gluconate, ampicillin, and Phenergan.

DISCHARGE DIAGNOSES:

_____ Acute bronchitis due to RSV

_____ Nutritional anemia due to inadequate dietary iron intake

_____ Nausea and vomiting

_____

13. The patient is a 77-year-old male admitted to the hospital due to shortness of breath and progressive chest pain. The patient has had evidence of acute bronchitis with discolored sputum for 5 days and, despite antibiotics, was not improving. With this, he developed an increasing need for nitroglycerin. During his hospitalization, the patient was treated with intravenous antibiotics, steroids, theophylline, and hand-held nebulizer with Alupent. The patient improved with the cough clearing nicely. Unfortunately, several days prior to discharge, he developed severe precordial chest pain typical of his angina. This required three nitroglycerin plus morphine to stop the pain. The EKG showed significant ischemic distress, which cleared over the next few hours, and there was no evidence of damage by isoenzyme study. The patient was monitored on telemetry and increased his activity slowly. The patient improved and was discharged to home on Procardia 10 milligrams every other day, nitroglycerin patch 5 milligrams daily, Isordil 10 milligrams every other day, Lasix 40 milligrams daily, Theo-Dur 300 milligrams twice a day, prednisone in a decreasing dose, and Velosef 500 milligrams twice a day and is to be seen in the office in one week.

DISCHARGE DIAGNOSES:

_____ Chronic obstructive pulmonary disease with acute bronchitis

_____ Arteriosclerotic cardiovascular disease, native coronary artery, with progressive angina

_____ Mitral insufficiency

14. This patient was admitted to the hospital due to severe low back pain and a great amount of indigestion. She has had frequent episodes of abdominal pain in the past, but this is more severe and has failed to respond to therapy as an outpatient. She is known to have esophageal hiatus hernia and polyps of the gallbladder in addition to her osteoporosis and stenosis of the lumbar spine, all of which were medically managed during the inpatient stay. The physical examination revealed a 74-year-old white woman who appeared to be acutely and chronically ill. She had epigastric tenderness with no masses palpable. The patient's EKG was normal. An upper gastrointestinal series showed a small sliding hiatal hernia and a duodenal ulcer with considerable evidence for an active ulcer. The gallbladder showed abnormal filling defects, which were consistent with polyps. The x-rays of the spine showed a great deal of osteoporosis and stenosis of the lumbar spine. The patient was given Demerol and Phenergan for the pain and was started on intravenous Prevacid. She was given Dalmane 30 milligrams at bedtime and a calcium supplement one time daily. She was started on a bland diet. The patient has slowly improved as far as the back pain. She is now up and about and is having less indigestion since therapy for the ulcer was begun. The patient is being discharged to be followed as an outpatient. She will continue on a bland diet and will be discharged on Prevacid, Carafate, a calcium substitute, and Darvocet.

DISCHARGE DIAGNOSES:

_____ Acute duodenal ulcer

_____ Sliding esophageal hiatus hernia

_____ Gallbladder polyps

_____ Osteoporosis

_____ Spinal stenosis of the lumbar region

15. This patient is an 84-year-old female who was admitted to the hospital because of extreme weakness and inability to eat. The patient had been a resident of the nursing home when she suddenly developed progression of her symptoms of weakness. She refused to eat. Several days later she was not responding well. Laboratory studies done at that time revealed the hemoglobin to be 8.4 and her white count to be 14,700. There were significant abnormalities of her blood work that included a blood urea nitrogen level of 181, a sodium level of 149, a potassium level of 5.1, and glucose of 232. The patient was admitted to the hospital and hydrated with intravenous fluids. With that, her hemoglobin dropped to a low of 6. The patient was given a total of 4 units of packed red blood cells, and this brought her blood count up to 14.3. With appropriate hydration, there was a continual decline of her blood urea nitrogen level and improvement of her electrolytes. Despite this, she did not seem to be as strong as expected. We were trying to switch her from intravenous to oral medication. The next day, it became apparent that despite the intravenous fluids and blood transfusions, the patient was not responding. Her blood urea nitrogen level was beginning to rise, and she was becoming less responsive. Her breathing began to slow, and she became completely unresponsive. At 1:10 A.M. of the next morning, she was pronounced dead.

DISCHARGE DIAGNOSES:

_____ Acute renal failure   _____ End-stage renal disease

_____ Dehydration   _____ Anemia in chronic kidney disease

Coding Practice—Hospital Inpatient Cases (ICD-10-CM and ICD-10-PCS)

Instructions: Review each case scenario, and assign and properly sequence the ICD-10-CM diagnosis and ICD-10-PCS procedure codes.

1. This is a 62-year-old patient seen in the office because of urinary difficulty. The patient noticed that he had to strain when he had to urinate. He has been having this problem off and on during the past year. Also, sometimes he has to move his bowels when he urinates because of the strain. His urinary stream is very slow. He has no history of dysuria or hematuria. His past history reveals that he has high blood pressure, and he is taking medication for that with occasional Valium. He also has been complaining of some pain in the lower back at the area of the coccyx bone. On his physical examination, the abdomen was soft with no tenderness or mass palpable. He has normal external genitalia with a rectally grade III smooth prostate gland. The patient's urological workup was done as an outpatient, and this showed an essentially normal upper urinary tract and enlarged prostate. He is admitted to the hospital for transurethral resection of the prostate. On the day of admission, under general anesthesia, transurethral resection of the prostate (via artificial opening) to trim away excess prostate tissue only was performed. Postoperatively, the patient did well. When his catheter was removed, he was able to void well without any difficulty. The pathology report revealed benign prostatic hyperplasia. Because of a tender coccyx bone, he did have several x-rays, which were negative. The pain was improved by injecting Aristocort and Novocain into this area. The patient's hypertension medication was continued. The patient was discharged and will be seen in the office in 3 weeks.

DISCHARGE DIAGNOSES:

_____ Benign hyperplasia of the prostate with urinary obstruction

_____   and straining to void   _____ Coccygodynia

_____   and poor urinary stream   _____ Hypertension

PROCEDURE:

_____ Transurethral resection of the prostate

2. The patient is a 23-year-old white female, gravida 2, para 1, who has had no problems with her pregnancy until two days prior to admission. She began with some spotting, which progressed to heavier bleeding with cramping. The cramping became severe on the morning of admission; she began to bleed excessively then, and she presented herself to the emergency room. At that point, it was believed that she had had an incomplete abortion. At the time of admission, she was a well-developed, well-nourished white female in no apparent distress. Her vital signs are stable. She is afebrile. Her pertinent physical findings included a negative abdominal exam and a pelvic exam that revealed blood, clots, and mucus in the external cervical canal and in the vaginal vault. The bimanual exam was deferred until the time of surgery when sterile conditions could be met. She was taken to the operating room after her complete blood count and urinalysis showed nothing unusual. In the operating room, a dilatation and curettage was done without problem. Postoperatively, she has done fine. She has had no unusual vaginal bleeding. She has had no problem with ambulation to the bathroom. Her abdomen is soft and nontender this morning. She feels fine. She is discharged to home in good condition.

DISCHARGE DIAGNOSIS:

_____ Incomplete spontaneous abortion with excessive vaginal bleeding

PROCEDURE:

_____ Dilatation and curettage to remove retained products of conception

---

3. The patient is a 25-year-old white female, gravida 1, whose pregnancy has been benign. She had gone into spontaneous labor late in the evening and came to the obstetric unit at about 0230 hours. She was dilated a fingertip. She came to 50% effacement, and labor picked up every few minutes. By 8 o'clock in the morning, she was only 2 to 3 centimeters dilated. This continued until late in the afternoon. She was station minus 2 and had good contractions for several hours with no further progression of labor. Pelvimetry showed borderline cephalopelvic disproportion. It was finally decided to do a cesarean section. She was taken to the operating room and underwent a low transverse incision with delivery of a live female child. She had an essentially uneventful postoperative course. Her incision has been healing well, and her bowels have been moving. The abdomen is soft and nontender. The patient was anxious to go home and was discharged to home to be seen in the office for her 2-week postpartum check.

DISCHARGE DIAGNOSES:

_____ Borderline cephalopelvic disproportion with obstructed labor

_____ Failure to progress at labor

_____ Single livebirth

PROCEDURE:

_____ Cesarean section, low

4. A 35-year-old white male had a mass on his right wrist for quite some time. It had become tender and quite achy. It was, therefore, recommended that this be excised under axillary block anesthesia. Incidentally, he also had a mass of the skin of the nose and requested removal of the mass. The patient was admitted to undergo these surgeries under local anesthesia following excision of the ganglion cyst. His orthopedic examination at the time of admission revealed him to have a 1 × 2–centimeter fluctuant but fairly firm mass of the radial volar aspect of the right wrist, which was just proximal to the flexor crease. This was nonpulsatile. He also had what appeared to be a sebaceous cyst involving the skin on the tip of the nose. The patient's preoperative chest x-ray, complete blood count, and urinalysis were all within normal limits. An x-ray of the right wrist revealed no bony abnormality, but it did reveal a soft tissue mass on the lateral aspect of the wrist. The patient underwent the operative procedures described above, the first under axillary block and the other two under local anesthetic. The patient tolerated the procedures well and left the operating room in good condition. The pathology report revealed a ganglion cyst of the wrist and a sebaceous cyst of the nose. He was discharged the next day with instructions to return to the office for follow-up.

DISCHARGE DIAGNOSES:

_____ Ganglion cyst, right wrist

_____ Sebaceous cyst, nose

PROCEDURES:

_____ Excision, ganglion cyst, right wrist

_____ Excision, lesion, skin of nose

5. This patient has had a decubitus gangrenous ulcer on the dorsum of his left heel that had not improved and was, in fact, getting worse. He was given intensive medical treatment as an outpatient, but the entire foot became more swollen and red, and he was brought to the hospital for more intensive therapy. Studies revealed a *Staphylococcus aureus* infection from the wound culture. He was treated for cellulitis with intravenous vancomycin and following surgery was placed on gentamicin and intravenous Vibramycin. These medications were effective in controlling his infection and improving the cellulitis. They were not, however, able to improve the ulcer. Whirlpool treatments and dressing changes also failed to improve the ulcer. It was ultimately decided that an above-the-knee amputation was necessary. After 5 days of intravenous antibiotics, the patient was taken to the operative suite, where it was determined that below-the-knee amputation of the left leg was appropriate, and that procedure was performed. He is now being transferred to a rehabilitation facility for continued care. His leg stump sutures will be removed as able, probably in about 2 weeks.

DISCHARGE DIAGNOSES:

_____ Gangrenous decubitus ulcer of the left heel
            stage IV

_____ *Staphylococcus aureus* infection

PROCEDURE:

_____ Below-the-knee amputation, left leg

6. A 62-year-old white female had been hospitalized 5 months previously with a subcapital fracture of the right hip. She underwent open reduction with internal fixation of the fracture. The fracture healed, but she continued to have difficulty with pain over the ends of the Gouffon pins. She was admitted for surgical removal of these pins. Postoperatively, her blood pressure dropped in the recovery room. This was treated with and responded to ephedrine. For the rest of her hospitalization, she had no further problems with her blood pressure. Her incision began to drain serous-type drainage. She was dangled on the side of her bed on her first postoperative day and was transferred out of bed and into the chair on her second postoperative day, and subsequently started on physical therapy for gait training with a walker. Serous drainage persisted from the hip, and a culture of the wound from her right hip incision grew *Escherichia coli*. She was treated with cephalothin for this postoperative infection. She was ultimately discharged to home with care by the visiting nurse, who will do twice-a-week dressing changes.

DISCHARGE DIAGNOSES:

_____ Painful Gouffon pins of the right hip (initial encounter)

_____ Postoperative hypotension

_____ Postoperative wound infection, right hip

_____   due to *Escherichia coli* (initial encounter)

_____ Surgical complication (Gouffon pins)

PROCEDURE:

_____ Open removal of Gouffon pins, right hip

---

7. A 64-year-old male was admitted to the hospital, complaining of right knee pain. X-rays revealed that he had degenerative arthritis of the right knee. His options were discussed with him. He decided to undergo a right total knee replacement with insertion of a molded polyethylene synthetic knee implant. He underwent the procedure without incident. Postoperatively, he has done well. He began with physical therapy, ambulating with a walker. He was afebrile, and his wound was clean, dry, and intact upon discharge. He was stable upon discharge. He will have a home health nurse come to his house to remove his staples in 2 weeks' time. He should continue to work on range of motion and strengthening of his right leg. He should ambulate with the assistance of a walker. The patient should call immediately if he notices any redness, pain, or swelling around his incision.

DISCHARGE DIAGNOSIS:

_____ Degenerative primary osteoarthritis of right knee

PROCEDURE:

_____ Total knee replacement, right knee

---

8. The patient is a male infant who was born during this admission via cesarean section. The day after delivery he appeared jaundiced. His blood was drawn, and he was found to have an elevated bilirubin level. The patient was treated with phototherapy and was discharged the next day with great improvement of his bilirubin level. He is scheduled to see the pediatrician in 2 days for a repeat bilirubin test.

DISCHARGE DIAGNOSES:

_____ Term male, born by cesarean section

_____ Hyperbilirubinemia

PROCEDURE:

_____ Phototherapy of a newborn

---

9. A 22-year-old white male was involved in a motorcycle-truck accident and was admitted with open comminuted type IIIA fractures of the shaft of the left tibia and fibula; a closed Colles' fracture of the distal radius on the right arm; and a laceration of the tongue, which was approximately 1 inch in length. He was the driver of the motorcycle, and he lost control and hit a parked truck in a parking lot. The remainder of his physical and history was essentially noncontributory. He was started on lactated Ringer's and D5% dextrose and given 1 gram of Kefzol. His tetanus immunization was up-to-date. The laboratory studies included an EKG that was read as abnormal with nonspecific myocardial changes in the inferolateral region, not felt to be significant or warranting further follow-up. His chest x-ray was grossly normal on admission. The cervical spine was normal. He was taken to the operating room, where he underwent an open reduction and internal fixation of the fractured tibia and fibula, casting of the right radial fracture, and suturing of the tongue laceration. The patient was treated for a full 10 days with intravenous Keflex. His wounds looked good. His postreduction x-rays revealed good position of the right wrist and left leg fractures. He was discharged to follow-up in the office in 10 days. At that time, he will have an x-ray of the right wrist and left lower leg. He was given a prescription for Talwin 50 milligrams by mouth every four hours as needed for pain.

DISCHARGE DIAGNOSES:

_____ Traumatic open comminuted type IIIA fractures, left tibia shaft

_____   and fibula

_____ Traumatic Colles' closed, distal radius, right (initial encounter)

_____ Laceration, tongue, approximately 1 inch in length (initial encounter)

_____ Motorcycle driver injured in collision (initial encounter)

_____ Parking lot (place of occurrence)

PROCEDURES:

_____ Open reduction, internal fixation, left tibia

_____   and fibula

_____ Suture repair, tongue laceration

_____ Immobilization using cast, right upper extremity

---

10. A 70-year-old white female with pancreatic head carcinoma, confirmed by previous percutaneous fine needle aspiration and determined to be unresectable. The patient was also found to have probable metastasis to the lower lobe of the left lung, and she was admitted now for resection of the lower lobe of the left lung. The patient had a history of hypothyroidism and diet-controlled diabetes. During hospitalization, the patient was continued on Levoxyl, and a "no-concentrated-sweets diet" was ordered. The patient was taken to the operative suite, where a partial left lower lobe lung resection was performed. Pathology from this procedure revealed adenocarcinoma. The patient had an uneventful postoperative course and was discharged with an appointment to see the oncologist to discuss radiation and chemotherapy options.

DISCHARGE DIAGNOSES:

_____ Metastatic left lung cancer

_____   with pancreatic adenocarcinoma as primary site

_____ Hypothyroidism

_____ Diet-controlled type 2 diabetes mellitus

PROCEDURE:

_____ Left lower lung lobe resection (open)

ICD-10-CM Outpatient and Physician Office Coding

Chapter Outline

Outpatient Care

Outpatient Diagnostic Coding and Reporting Guidelines

Chapter Objectives

At the conclusion of this chapter, the student should be able to:

1. Define key terms related to ICD-10-CM outpatient and physician office coding.
2. Explain the differences among outpatient and physician office health care settings.
3. Assign ICD-10-CM diagnosis codes according to outpatient coding and reporting guidelines.

Key Terms

ambulatory care

ambulatory patient

ambulatory surgery
    patient

clinic outpatient

Data Elements for
    Emergency Department
    Systems (DEEDS)

*Diagnostic Coding and
    Reporting Guidelines
    for Outpatient Services*

emergency patient

first-listed diagnosis

inconclusive diagnosis

observation patient

Outcome and Assessment
    Information Set (OASIS)

outpatient

outpatient care

preadmission testing
    (PAT)

primary care

primary care provider

qualified diagnosis

referred outpatient

triage

Uniform Ambulatory
    Care Data Set
    (UACDS)

Introduction

This chapter defines outpatient care settings and interprets the *Diagnostic Coding and Reporting Guidelines for Outpatient Services*, published in the Centers for Medicare and Medicaid Services (CMS) *ICD-10-CM Official Guidelines for Coding and Reporting*.

It is important to remember that coding guidelines are to be used as a companion to the official version of the *International Classification of Diseases, Tenth Revision, Clinical Modification* (ICD-10-CM), which contains coding conventions and instructions to ensure accurate coding.

ICD-10-CM codes are assigned to outpatient and physician office diagnoses for health care financial planning, reimbursement, and statistical purposes. (Outpatient reimbursement systems are discussed in Chapter 20 after students have learned how to assign HCPCS level II and CPT codes to procedures and services.) Patient demographic data and codes are reported to third-party payers on the CMS-1500 claim to generate reimbursement.

 NOTE:

> Outpatient health care settings, such as home health care and hospice, use the UB-04 claim instead of the CMS-1500 claim.

Coders review patient records to locate conditions and diseases to which ICD-10-CM codes are assigned. Coders also assign HCPCS level II and CPT codes to procedures and services (discussed in Chapters 8–19). Similar to the inpatient coding process, outpatient coders may not assign codes to conditions and diseases when the provider does not specifically document the diagnoses or procedures/services. Such *assumption coding* is considered fraud, and the coder should query the physician to determine whether the documented diagnosis should be edited so a more specific code can be assigned. (Refer to Chapter 1 for more information about the physician query process.)

 NOTE:

> The **Uniform Ambulatory Care Data Set (UACDS)** was established by the federal government as a standard data set for ambulatory care facility records. Its goal is to improve data comparison for ambulatory and outpatient care settings.
>
> Home health agencies (HHAs) report data according to the **Outcome and Assessment Information Set (OASIS)**, which is a core set of comprehensive assessments for adult home care patients that is used to
>
> - Measure patient outcomes for Outcome-Based Quality Improvement (OBQI)
> - Conduct patient assessment, patient care planning, and internal HHA performance improvements
> - Generate agency-level case mix reports that contain aggregate statistics about various patient characteristics such as demographic, health, or functional status at start of care
>
> HHAs use Home Assessment and Validation and Entry (HAVEN) data entry software to report OASIS data.
>
> Hospital-based emergency departments report **Data Elements for Emergency Department Systems (DEEDS)** for uniform collection of data to reduce incompatibility in emergency department records.

Outpatient Care

Outpatient care (or **ambulatory care**) includes any health care service provided to a patient who is not admitted as an inpatient to a facility. Such care may be provided in a physician's office, a stand-alone health care facility, a hospital outpatient or emergency department (ED), or the patient's home. Regardless of health care setting, official coding guidelines classify all of these visits as *encounters*. Claims submitted to third-party payers for encounters contain diagnosis and procedure/service codes. When a payer conducts a record review and requests clarification about documented diagnoses and procedures/services, the health care provider is the individual authorized to clarify diagnoses and procedures/services. (Coders edit submitted codes when payers deny claims due to incomplete or inaccurate coding.)

Primary Care Services

Primary care includes both preventive and acute care services, which are often provided as outpatient care and are referred to as the *point of first contact*. Services are usually provided by a general practitioner or another health professional (e.g., nurse practitioner) who has first contact with a patient seeking medical treatment, including general dental, ophthalmic, and pharmaceutical services. These services are usually provided in an office setting where the care is continuous (e.g., quarterly office visits for a chronic condition) and comprehensive (e.g., preventive and medical care). The **primary care provider** manages and coordinates the patient's care, including referring the patient to a medical specialist (Table 7-1) for consultation and a second opinion. Primary care services include the following:

- Annual physical examinations
- Early detection of disease
- Family planning
- Health education

- Immunizations
- Treatment of minor illnesses and injuries
- Vision and hearing screening

Hospital Outpatient Services

Hospital outpatients include ambulatory patients, ambulatory surgery patients, emergency patients, and observation care patients. The maximum length of stay of an outpatient is 23 hours, 59 minutes, and 59 seconds. **Ambulatory patients** (or **outpatients**) are treated and usually released the same day and do not stay overnight in the hospital. **Ambulatory surgery patients** undergo certain procedures that can be performed on an outpatient basis, with the patient treated and released the same day. An ambulatory surgery patient who requires a longer stay must be admitted to the facility as an inpatient. **Emergency patients** are treated for urgent problems (e.g., trauma) and are either released the same day or admitted to the hospital as inpatients. **Observation patients** receive services furnished on a hospital's premises that are ordered by a physician (or another authorized individual), including use of a bed and periodic monitoring by nursing or other staff, and that are reasonable and necessary to evaluate the outpatient's condition or determine the need for possible admission as an inpatient.

Outpatient care allows patients to receive care in one day without the need for inpatient hospitalization. Care is provided in either a freestanding or a hospital-based facility and includes the following (Table 7-2):

- Ambulatory surgical centers (freestanding)
- Hospital-based outpatient department
- Hospital-based ED
- Hospital-based ambulatory surgery program
- Hospital-based partial hospitalization program
- Hospital-owned physician practice
- Hospital-owned satellite clinics
- Industrial health clinic
- Neighborhood health centers
- Physicians' offices
- Public health departments
- Satellite clinics
- Staff model health maintenance organizations (HMOs)
- Urgent care centers

TABLE 7-1 Medical Specialties

Medical Specialty	Description
Allergy & Immunology	Evaluation and treatment of immune system disorders (e.g., asthma, anaphylaxis, eczema, rhinitis, and adverse reactions to drugs/foods/insect stings)
Anesthesiology	Assessment of patient risks for undergoing surgery, management of pain relief, monitoring of patients during and after surgery (postanesthesia recovery), and resuscitative care of patients with cardiac or respiratory emergencies (assessment of need for artificial ventilation)
Colon & Rectal Surgery	Diagnosis and medical/surgical treatment of diseases in the intestinal tract, colon, rectum, anal canal, perianal region, and related organs and tissues (e.g., liver)
Dermatology	Diagnosis and treatment of skin disorders (e.g., contact dermatitis and benign and malignant lesions, or growths) and cosmetic disorders of the skin (e.g., scars)
Family Practice	Management of an individual's or family's total health care, including geriatrics, gynecology, internal medicine, obstetrics, pediatrics, and psychiatry, with an emphasis on preventive and primary care
General Surgery	Management of conditions for which general surgery is warranted (e.g., appendectomy, tonsillectomy, and hernia repair), including diagnosis and preoperative, intraoperative, and postoperative care to surgical patients
Gynecology	Diagnosis and treatment (includes preventive management) of female reproductive and urinary system disorders
Internal Medicine	Management of common and complex illnesses of patients of all ages (e.g., cancer; infections; and diseases of blood, digestive system, heart, joints, kidneys, and respiratory and vascular systems). Primary care internal medicine includes disease prevention, mental health, substance abuse, and wellness. Subspecialties include the following: • Adolescent medicine • Immunology • Cardiovascular medicine • Infectious disease • Critical care medicine • Nephrology • Electrophysiology • Oncology • Endocrinology • Pulmonary medicine • Gastroenterology • Rheumatology • Geriatrics • Sports medicine • Hematology
Medical Genetics	Diagnosis and treatment of patients with genetically linked diseases
Neurology	Diagnosis and treatment of disorders of the nervous system
Obstetrics	Management of pregnancy, from prenatal to puerperium
Ophthalmology	Diagnosis and treatment of eye disorders
Orthopedics	Diagnosis and treatment of musculoskeletal disease and injury
Otorhinolaryngology	Diagnosis and treatment of ear, nose, and throat diseases
Plastic & Reconstructive Surgery	Surgery for the purpose of reconstructing, repairing, or restoring body structures
Psychiatry	Diagnosis and treatment of behavioral health diseases
Radiology	Diagnosis of diseases and injuries, using radiological methods (e.g., electromagnetic radiation, x-ray, radionuclides, and ultrasound). Treatment of diseases (e.g., cancer), using radiant energy (e.g., radiation oncologist)
Thoracic Surgery	Surgical management of disease within the chest (e.g., coronary artery disease and lung cancer)
Urology	Diagnosis and treatment of disorders of the genitourinary system and the adrenal gland

TABLE 7-2 Freestanding, Hospital-Based, and Hospital-Owned Ambulatory Facilities

Type of Facility	Characteristics
Freestanding Centers and Facilities	
Ambulatory surgery center	• Surgery is performed on an outpatient basis. • Patients arrive on the day of procedure, undergo surgery in an operating room, and recover under the care of nursing staff.
Cardiovascular center	• Provides ambulatory cardiovascular services to include diagnosis and treatment, disease prevention, research, education, and cardiac rehabilitation. • Diagnostic and treatment services include cardiac catheterization, Coumadin care, echocardiography, enhanced external counterpulsation (EECP), heart scans, pacemaker care, and percutaneous transluminal coronary angioplasty (PTCA).
Clinical laboratory	• Performs diagnostic testing in microbiology, clinical chemistry, and toxicology, which are ordered by physicians on samples of body fluids, tissues, and wastes. • Information obtained from tests helps physicians diagnose illness, monitor treatment, and check general health. Results from tests are reported to physicians, who interpret them and explain them to patients. • Directed by a pathologist; testing is performed by certified professional technologists and technicians.
Imaging center	• Provides radiographic (e.g., x-rays) and other imaging services (e.g., magnetic resonance imaging) to ambulatory patients. • May also provide training and participate in national research projects.
Industrial health clinic	• Located in a business setting (e.g., factory). • Emphasis is on employee health and safety.
Infusion center	• Dispenses and administers prescribed medications by continuous or intermittent infusion to ambulatory patients. • Infusion is supervised by a licensed health care professional (e.g., registered nurse). • Also called ambulatory infusion centers (AICs).
Neighborhood health center	• Health care is provided to economically disadvantaged and treatment is family-centered because illnesses may result indirectly from crowded living conditions, unsanitary facilities, and other socioeconomic factors. • Family care team consisting of a physician, nurse, and social worker provides continuity of care to families.
Pain management center	• Specializes in treatment of acute and chronic pain syndromes, using proven medications and procedures. • Usually uses a multidisciplinary approach involving participating specialists such as physiatrists, psychiatrists, neurologists, neurosurgeons, internists, and physical and occupational therapists.
Physician's office	• Solo physicians' practices do not have physician partners or employment affiliations with other practice organizations. • Single-specialty group physician practices consist of two or more physicians who provide patients with one specific type of care (e.g., primary care). • Multispecialty group physician practices offer various types of medical specialty care in one organization, and they may be located in more than one location.
Primary care center	• Offers adult and family care medicine in internal medicine, pediatrics, and family practice. • Internal medicine physicians specialize in the care of adults. • Pediatricians provide comprehensive services for infants, children, and adolescents. • Family practitioners provide care for the entire family and focus on general medicine, obstetrics, pediatrics, and geriatrics.
Public health department	• Provides preventive medicine services such as well-baby clinics. • Care includes immunizations and routine checkups.

(continues)

TABLE 7-2 *(continued)*

Type of Facility	Characteristics

Radiology center	• Provides image-guided procedures, as follows:
	  ◦ Computerized tomography (CT scan), in which the source of x-ray beams rotates around the patient, the beams are detected by sensors, and information from sensors is computer-processed and displayed as an image on a video screen.
	  ◦ Magnetic resonance imaging (MRI), which uses a large magnet that surrounds the patient, along with radiowaves and a computer, to produce images.
	  ◦ Mammography, which is a method for detecting early-stage breast abnormalities.
	  ◦ Nuclear medicine, which uses very small amounts of radioactive materials or radiopharmaceuticals to study organ function and structure and to treat disease. (Radiopharmaceuticals are substances that are attracted to specific organs, bones, or tissues.)
	  ◦ Positron emission tomography (PET), which measures radioactive tracers (e.g., radioactive glucose) injected into the body.
	  ◦ Radiography (x-ray), which detects disease or injury in the body when an image (x-ray film) is produced as the result of passing a small amount of radiation through the body to expose sensitive film on the other side.
	  ◦ Ultrasonography, which uses high-frequency sound waves to study parts of the body, including the heart and vessels, to generate an image of the area being studied.
	• Directed by a radiologist and staffed by registered x-ray technicians.

Rehabilitation facility	• Provides occupational, physical, and speech therapy to patients with orthopedic injuries, work-related injuries, sports-related injuries, and various neurologic and neuromuscular conditions. • Occupational therapy provides services to patients who have experienced loss of function resulting from injury or disease. Physical therapy uses physical agents of exercise, massage, and other modalities. Speech/language pathology provides services to evaluate, diagnose, plan, and provide therapy to patients with speech, language, and swallowing difficulties.
Staff model health maintenance organization (HMO)	• Similar to large, multispecialty group practices. • May be partially owned by physician employees, with the physicians typically functioning as employees of either the physician group owning the practice or the insurer. • Most physicians are paid a salary.
Student health center	• Provides health care to full- and part-time students who become ill or injured. • Services usually include allergy injections, contraception and counseling, health education, immunizations, HIV testing, laboratory services, routine medications, primary care and preventive medicine, screening for sexually transmitted diseases (STDs), smoking cessation, and women's health care.
Urgent care center (or emergency care center)	• Immediate care is provided by an on-duty physician (usually salaried). • May be owned by private corporations (e.g., Humana) in states where they are permitted or by nonprofit facilities (e.g., municipal hospital).
Hospital-Based Departments and Programs	
Ambulatory surgery	• Elective surgery is performed on patients who are admitted and discharged the same day (e.g., biopsy); both general and local anesthesia are administered. • Also called short-stay or day surgery. • Patients undergo **preadmission testing (PAT)** to register with Admitting, undergo preoperative nursing assessment, and receive preanesthesia evaluation by an anesthesiologist. As part of PAT, phlebotomists draw blood samples for preoperative testing and electrocardiograms and chest x-rays are performed if ordered. PAT results are documented in the patient's record and are available to the patient care team prior to the patient's surgery.
Emergency department	• Crisis care is provided 24 hours per day by an on-duty physician to patients who have sustained trauma or have urgent problems (e.g., heart attack). • Patients initially undergo **triage**, which is an organized method of identifying and treating patients according to urgency of care required.

TABLE 7-2 *(continued)*

Type of Facility	Characteristics
Outpatient department	• **Clinic outpatients** receive scheduled diagnostic and therapeutic care (e.g., chemotherapy, kidney dialysis). • **Referred outpatients** receive diagnostic (e.g., laboratory tests) or therapeutic care (e.g., physical therapy) because such care is unavailable in the primary care provider's office; follow-up is done at the primary care provider's office.
Partial hospitalization program	• Program for hospital patients who regularly use the hospital facilities for a substantial number of daytime or nighttime hours (e.g., behavioral health, geriatric, and rehabilitative care).
Hospital-Owned Facilities	
Hospital-owned physician practice	• Hospital-owned practices are at least partially owned by the hospital. • Physicians participate in a compensation plan provided by the hospital.
Satellite clinics	• Ambulatory care centers that are established remotely from the hospital. • Primary care is provided by an on-duty physician (usually salaried).

Exercise 7.1 – Outpatient Care

Instructions: Complete each statement.

1. Care provided in a physician's office, a stand-alone health care facility, a hospital outpatient or emergency department, or the patient's home is classified as _____ care.

2. Both preventive and acute care are often provided as outpatient care and are referred to as the point of first contact, which is categorized as _____ care.

3. The physician who manages and coordinates the patient's care, including referring the patient to a medical specialist for consultation and a second opinion, is called the _____.

4. Patients who are treated and released the same day and do not stay overnight in the hospital are called _____ patients.

5. Patients who undergo certain procedures that can be performed on an outpatient basis, with the patient treated and released the same day, are called _____ patients.

6. Patients who are treated for urgent problems (e.g., trauma) and are either released the same day or admitted to the hospital as inpatients are called _____ patients.

7. Patients who receive services furnished on a hospital's premises that are ordered by a physician (or another authorized individual), including use of a bed and periodic monitoring by nursing or other staff, and that are reasonable and necessary to evaluate the outpatients' conditions or determine the need for possible admission as inpatients (and who are in the unit no longer than 23 hours, 59 minutes, and 59 seconds), are called _____ patients.

8. An organized method of identifying and treating patients according to urgency of care required is called _____.

9. Patients who receive scheduled diagnostic and therapeutic care are called _____ outpatients.

10. Patients who receive diagnostic or therapeutic care because such care is unavailable in the primary care provider's office are called _____ outpatients.

Outpatient Diagnostic Coding and Reporting Guidelines

The *Diagnostic Coding and Reporting Guidelines for Outpatient Services* were developed by the federal government and approved for use by hospitals and providers for coding and reporting hospital-based outpatient services and provider-based office visits. Although the guidelines were originally developed for use in submitting government claims, insurance companies have also adopted them (sometimes with variation).

NOTE:

Because variations may contradict official coding guidelines, review health insurance company's coding guidelines when employed.

Selection of First-Listed Condition

In the outpatient setting, the **first-listed diagnosis** is reported (instead of the inpatient setting's *principal diagnosis*); it is the diagnosis, condition, problem, or other reason for encounter/visit documented in the patient record to be chiefly responsible for the services provided. It is determined in accordance with ICD-10-CM *coding conventions* (or rules) as well as general and disease-specific coding guidelines. It reflects the reason for the encounter, which often is a sign or symptom. Because diagnoses are often not established at the time of the patient's initial encounter or visit, two or more visits may be required before a diagnosis is confirmed.

NOTE:

When reviewing the coding guidelines, the terms *encounter* and *visit* are used interchangeably in coding guidelines when describing outpatient and physician office services.

Coding guidelines for inconclusive or qualified diagnoses (e.g., probable, suspected, rule out) were developed for inpatient reporting only; they do not apply to outpatients.

An outpatient is a person treated in one of four settings.

- *Ambulatory surgery center*: Patient is released prior to a 24-hour stay and length of stay must be 23 hours, 59 minutes, and 59 seconds or less
- *Health care provider's office* (e.g., physician)
- *Hospital clinic, ED, outpatient department, same-day surgery unit*: Length of stay must be 23 hours, 59 minutes, and 59 seconds or less
- *Hospital observation status or hospital observation unit*: Patient's length of stay is 23 hours, 59 minutes, and 59 seconds or less unless documentation for additional observation is medically justified

NOTE:

- *Outpatient Surgery*: When a patient presents for outpatient surgery, code the reason for the surgery as the first-listed diagnosis (reason for the encounter) even if the surgery is canceled due to a contraindication (e.g., patient's blood pressure increases unexpectedly upon administration of anesthesia).
- *Observation Stay*: When a patient is admitted for observation for a medical condition, assign a code for the medical condition as the first-listed diagnosis.

  When a patient presents for outpatient surgery and develops complications requiring admission to observation, code the reason for the surgery as the first-listed diagnosis (reason for the encounter) followed by codes for the complications (e.g., respiratory distress) as secondary diagnoses.

EXAMPLE: A patient underwent outpatient laparoscopic cholecystectomy for acute cholecystitis. During recovery from surgery, the patient's temperature spiked at 101 degrees, and she was admitted for observation care and administered intravenous antibiotics. Wound culture grew *Escherichia coli*. The first-listed diagnosis is acute cholecystitis (K81.0), and the secondary diagnosis is postoperative infection of superficial incisional surgical site (T81.41xA) due to *Escherichia coli* (B96.20), which is a complication of surgery.

EXAMPLE 1: The patient was seen in the physician's office with a complaint of chest pain over the past few days. She explained that when she is laying in bed is when she really notices the pain, especially if she snacked later at night. EKG was negative. Cardiac enzyme lab test and chest x-ray were ordered. The physician suspects gastroesophageal reflux disease. The first-listed ICD-10-CM code reported for this case is chest pain (R07.9).

The patient returned to the physician's office for follow-up on his complaint of chest pain and was told cardiac enzyme lab test and chest x-ray were negative. The physician documented gastroesophageal reflux disease (GERD) as the patient's diagnosis. The first-listed ICD-10-CM code reported for this case is GERD (K21.9).

EXAMPLE 2: A patient received ED care for an injury to the right arm, which upon x-ray revealed closed displaced oblique fracture of the shaft of the right humerus (S42.331A). While receiving treatment for the fracture, the physician also medically managed the patient's chronic obstructive asthma (J44.9).

The first-listed diagnosis code is S42.331A and the secondary diagnosis code is J44.9.

Codes from A00.0 Through T88.9, Z00–Z99

The appropriate code or codes from the ICD-10-CM Tabular List of Diseases (A00.0 through T88.9, Z00–Z99) must be used to identify diagnoses, symptoms, conditions, problems, complaints, or other reason(s) for the encounter/visit.

Accurate Reporting of ICD-10-CM Diagnosis Codes

For accurate reporting of ICD-10-CM diagnosis codes, the documentation should describe the patient's condition, using terminology that includes specific diagnoses as well as symptoms, problems, or reasons for the encounter. There are ICD-10-CM codes to describe all of these.

Codes That Describe Signs and Symptoms

Codes that describe symptoms and signs, as opposed to definitive diagnoses, are acceptable for reporting purposes when the physician has not documented an established diagnosis or confirmed diagnosis.

In ICD-10-CM, Chapter 18 (Symptoms, Signs, and Abnormal Clinical and Laboratory Findings Not Elsewhere Classified) (R00–R99) contains many, but not all, codes for symptoms.

Some symptom codes are located in other ICD-10-CM chapters, which can be found by properly using the ICD-10-CM Index to Diseases and Injuries.

EXAMPLE: A 52-year-old female patient presented with feeling flushed off and on, headaches, difficulty falling asleep and remaining asleep, and some confusion. Her last menstruation was eight months ago. The physician's diagnosis was symptomatic menopause (N95.1), which contains a "use additional code" directing the coder to also assign codes for associated symptoms, in this case feeling flushed (R23.23), headaches (R51), sleeplessness (G47.01), and confusion (R41.0).

Encounters for Circumstances Other Than a Disease or Injury

ICD-10-CM provides codes to deal with encounters for circumstances other than a disease or an injury.

Factors Influencing Health Status and Contact with Health Services (Z00–Z99) are provided to deal with occasions when circumstances other than a disease or injury are recorded as diagnosis or problems.

EXAMPLE: A patient was seen in the office because she was very concerned that she might have been exposed to someone who was diagnosed with the Zika virus. The physician determined that the patient presents no signs or symptoms of the Zika virus. ICD-10-CM code Z20.828, Contact with and (suspected) exposure to other viral communicable diseases, is reported as the first-listed diagnosis.

Level of Detail in Coding

ICD-10-CM diagnosis codes contain 3, 4, 5, 6, or 7 characters.

1. *ICD-10-CM codes with 3, 4, 5, 6, or 7 characters*: Disease codes with three characters are included in ICD-10-CM as the heading of a category of codes that may be further subdivided by the use of fourth, fifth, sixth, or seventh characters to provide greater specificity.

2. *Use of full number of characters required for a code*: A three-character code is to be assigned only if it cannot be further subdivided. A code is invalid if it has not been coded to the full number of characters required for that code, including the seventh character extension, if applicable (with appropriate use of placeholder "x").

EXAMPLE: A patient was diagnosed with a crushing injury of the skull (initial encounter). ICD-10-CM category S07 (Crushing injury of head) and subcategory code S07.1 requires "X" placeholders to be entered in front of seventh-character A to report a valid code, S07.1xxA.

S07 Crushing injury of head
    Use additional code for all associated injuries, such as:
    intracranial injuries (S06.-)
    skull fractures (S02.-)
    The appropriate 7th character is to be added to each code from category S07
    A - initial encounter
    D - subsequent encounter
    S - sequela
    S07.0 Crushing injury of face
    S07.1 Crushing injury of skull
    S07.8 Crushing injury of other parts of head
    S07.9 Crushing injury of head, part unspecified

ICD-10-CM Code for the Diagnosis, Condition, Problem, or Other Reason for Encounter/Visit

Report first the ICD-10-CM code for the diagnosis, condition, problem, or other reason for encounter documented in the patient record as chiefly responsible for the services provided. Then report additional codes that describe any coexisting conditions that were treated or medically managed or that influenced the treatment of the patient during the encounter, called comorbidities. In some cases, the first-listed diagnosis may be a sign or symptom when a diagnosis has not been established (confirmed) by the provider.

EXAMPLE: During a physician's office encounter, the patient's severe headaches were evaluated. The patient explained that the onset of the headaches was sudden, and they could be due to stress. She had recently changed jobs. The patient's hypertension was also medically managed during the encounter. The first-listed ICD-10-CM code is R51 (headache), and hypertension (I10) is reported as a secondary code.

Uncertain Diagnoses

Do *not* code diagnoses documented as probable, suspected, questionable, rule out, or working diagnosis, compatible with, consistent with, or other similar terms indicating uncertainty, all of which are considered **inconclusive diagnoses** or **qualified diagnoses**. Instead, code condition(s) to the highest degree of certainty for that encounter/visit, such as symptoms, signs, abnormal test results, or other reasons for the visit.

 NOTE:

This differs from coding practices used by short-term, acute care, long-term, and psychiatric hospitals, where qualified diagnoses are coded and reported.

EXAMPLE:

For Qualified Diagnosis:	Code the Following Documented Sign or Symptom:
Suspected pneumonia	Shortness of breath, wheezing
Questionable Raynaud's	Numbness of hands
Possible wrist fracture	Wrist pain and swelling
Rule out pneumonia	Chest pain and fever

Qualified or uncertain diagnoses are a necessary part of the hospital and office chart until a specific diagnosis can be determined. Although qualified diagnoses are routinely coded for hospital inpatient admissions and reported on the UB-04 claim, CMS *specifically prohibits the reporting of qualified diagnoses on the CMS-1500 claim submitted for outpatient care*. CMS regulations permit the reporting of patients' signs and/or symptoms instead of the qualified diagnoses.

An additional incentive for not coding qualified diagnoses resulted from the Missouri case of *Stafford v. Neurological Medicine Inc.*, 811 F. 2d 470 (8th Cir., 1987). In this case, the diagnosis stated in the physician's office chart was *rule out brain tumor*. The claim submitted by the office listed the diagnosis code for *rule out brain tumor*, although test results were available that proved a brain tumor did not exist. The physician assured the patient that although she had lung cancer, there was no metastasis to the brain. Some time after the insurance company received the provider's claim, it was inadvertently sent to the patient. When the patient received the claim, she was so devastated by the diagnosis that she committed suicide. Her husband sued and was awarded $200,000 on the basis of *negligent paperwork* because the physician's office had reported a *qualified or uncertain diagnosis*.

Chronic Diseases

Chronic diseases treated on an ongoing basis may be coded and reported as many times as the patient receives treatment and care for the condition(s).

EXAMPLE: The patient is seen for a physician office encounter, which is a 6-month follow-up encounter for hypertension and diabetes mellitus. Examination is negative, and the patient states she feels well. Blood pressure is 120/75 and blood glucose is was 95. Because hypertension (I10) and diabetes mellitus (E11.9) are chronic conditions, a code for each condition is reported for this encounter (even though the patient's blood pressure and glucose level are normal).

Code All Documented Conditions That Coexist

Code all documented conditions that coexist at the time of the encounter/visit and that require or affect patient care, treatment, or management. Do not code conditions that were previously treated and no longer exist. However, history codes ICD-10-CM categories Z80–Z87 may be reported as secondary codes if the historical condition or family history has an impact on current care or influences treatment.

EXAMPLE: The patient was seen for an outpatient encounter in follow-up for acute bronchitis due to rhinovirus. Past history of chronic asthma has resolved. Report acute bronchitis (J20.6) as the first-listed diagnosis and personal history of chronic asthma (Z87.09) as the secondary diagnosis.

 NOTE:

Third-party payers review claims for "family history of" codes to determine reimbursement eligibility. Some plans reimburse for conditions that may not normally be eligible for payment when family history of a related condition is documented in the patient's record and reported on the claim.

Patients Receiving Diagnostic Services Only

For patients receiving *diagnostic services only* during an encounter, report first the diagnosis, condition, problem, or other reason for encounter that is documented as being chiefly responsible for the outpatient services provided during the encounter. (This is the *first-listed diagnosis*.) Codes for other diagnoses (e.g., chronic conditions) may be reported as additional diagnoses.

For encounters for routine laboratory/radiology testing in the absence of any signs, symptoms, or associated diagnosis, assign Z01.89- (Encounter for other specified special examinations). If routine testing is performed during the same encounter as a test to evaluate a sign, symptom, or diagnosis, it is appropriate to assign both the Z code and the code describing the reason for the nonroutine test.

For outpatient encounters for diagnostic tests that have been interpreted by a physician and for which the final report is available at the time of coding, code any confirmed or definitive diagnoses documented in the interpretation. *Do not code related signs and symptoms as additional diagnoses.*

EXAMPLE: A patient diagnosed with probable anemia is seen in follow-up to discuss positive Ferritin laboratory test results. The physician's diagnosis is erythroblastic anemia (D56.1).

Patients Receiving Therapeutic Services Only

For patients receiving *therapeutic services only* during an outpatient encounter, sequence first the diagnosis, condition, problem, or other reason for encounter chiefly responsible for the outpatient services provided during the encounter.

Assign codes to other diagnoses (e.g., chronic conditions) that are treated or medically managed or that would affect the patient's receipt of therapeutic services during this encounter.

The only exception to this rule is when the reason for encounter is for chemotherapy, radiation therapy, or rehabilitation. For these services, the appropriate ICD-10-CM Z code for the service is listed first and the diagnosis or problem for which the service is being performed is reported second.

EXAMPLE: The patient was diagnosed with thyroid cancer last month, and today she underwent the first in a series of radiation therapy treatments as an outpatient. Encounter for antineoplastic radiation therapy (Z51.0) is the first-listed diagnosis, and malignant neoplasm of thyroid gland (C73) is the secondary diagnosis.

Patients Receiving Preoperative Evaluations Only

For patients receiving *preoperative evaluations only*, assign and report first the appropriate code from ICD-10-CM subcategory Z01.81- (Encounter for preprocedural examinations) to describe the preoperative consultations.

Assign an additional code for the condition that describes the reason for the surgery. Also assign additional code(s) to any findings discovered during the preoperative evaluation.

EXAMPLE: A patient scheduled for reduction mammoplasty due to massive hypertrophy of the right and left breasts underwent preoperative evaluation during today's outpatient encounter. Findings were negative, and the patient was cleared for surgery. Report codes Z01.818 (Encounter for pre-procedural examination) and N62 (Hypertrophy of breast).

 NOTE:

Preadmission testing (PAT) is routinely completed prior to an inpatient admission or outpatient surgery to facilitate patient treatment and reduce length of stay. As an incentive, some payers provide higher reimbursement for PAT, making it important to assign codes properly.

Ambulatory Surgery (or Outpatient Surgery)

For *ambulatory surgery* (or *outpatient surgery*), assign a code to the diagnosis for which the surgery was performed. If the postoperative diagnosis is different from the preoperative diagnosis when the diagnosis is confirmed, assign a code to the postoperative diagnosis instead (because it is more definitive).

> **EXAMPLE:** A patient diagnosed with uterine polyps and dysfunctional uterine bleeding underwent outpatient laparoscopic hysterectomy surgery. Pathology report results confirmed benign polyps and revealed adenocarcinoma, uterine endometrium. Adenocarcinoma, uterine endometrium, which is a primary malignancy (C54.1) is reported as the first-listed diagnosis, followed by polyp of corpus uteri (N84.0).

Routine Outpatient Prenatal Visits

For routine outpatient prenatal visits when no complications are present, report a code from ICD-10-CM category Z34 (Encounter for supervision of normal pregnancy) as the first-listed diagnosis. *Do not report this code in combination with ICD-10-CM Chapter 15 codes.*

For routine prenatal outpatient visits for patients with high-risk pregnancies, report an ICD-10-CM code from category O09 (supervision of high-risk pregnancy) as the first-listed diagnosis. A code from ICD-10-CM Chapter 15 may also be reported as a secondary diagnosis, if appropriate.

Encounters for General Medical Examinations with Abnormal Findings

The subcategories for encounters for general adult medical examinations (Z00.0) and encounter for routine child health examinations (Z00.12-) provide codes for with and without abnormal findings. Should a general medical examination result in an abnormal finding, the code for general medical examination with abnormal finding should be assigned as the first-listed diagnosis. An *examination with abnormal findings* refers to a condition or diagnosis that is newly identified or a change in severity of a chronic condition (e.g., uncontrolled hypertension, acute exacerbation of COPD) during a routine physical examination. A secondary code for the abnormal finding should also be assigned.

> **EXAMPLE:** During this 72-year-old patient's annual health examination, the physician noted an abnormally high blood pressure of 145/95. The blood pressure was taken again at the conclusion of the examination, and it was still abnormally high (143/97). All other findings during examination were negative. The physician prescribed Hyzaar and scheduled the patient for a follow-up office visit within one month. Encounter for general adult medical examination with abnormal findings (Z00.01) is reported as the first-listed diagnosis, and code hypertension (I10) is reported as the secondary diagnosis.

Encounters for Routine Health Screenings

Screening is the testing for disease or disease precursors in seemingly well individuals so that early detection and treatment can be provided for those who test positive for the disease (e.g., screening mammogram).

The testing of a person to rule out or confirm a suspected diagnosis because the patient has some sign or symptom is a diagnostic examination, not a screening. In these cases, the sign or symptom is used to explain the reason for the test.

A screening code may be a first-listed code if the reason for the visit is specifically the screening exam. It may also be used as an additional code if the screening is done during an office visit for other health problems. A screening code is not necessary if the screening is inherent to a routine examination, such as a Pap smear done during a routine pelvic examination.

Should a condition be discovered during the screening, the code for the condition may be assigned as an additional diagnosis.

The Z code indicates that a screening exam is planned. A procedure code is required to confirm that the screening was performed.

The screening Z codes/categories include the following:

- Z11   Encounter for screening for infectious and parasitic diseases
- Z12   Encounter for screening for malignant neoplasms
- Z13   Encounter for screening for other diseases and disorders

    Except: Z13.9, Encounter for screening, unspecified
- Z36   Encounter for antenatal screening for mother

EXAMPLE: The patient undergoes screening for alcoholism during an outpatient encounter. She explains that she has a family history of chronic alcoholism on both sides of her family. She states that she does not drink to excess, and clarifies that she does enjoy a glass of wine most evenings. Screening for alcoholism (Z13.39) is reported as the first-listed code, and family history of alcohol abuse and dependence (Z81.1) is reported as the secondary diagnosis.

Exercise 7.2 – Diagnostic Coding and Reporting Guidelines for Outpatient Services: Hospital-Based and Physician Office

Instructions: Select the first-listed diagnosis for each case scenario.

1. The patient underwent office treatment for removal of a skin lesion from her face. She also received a renewed prescription for her chronic asthma.
    a. chronic asthma
    b. skin lesion
2. Dr. Smith ordered a chest x-ray to rule out pneumonia; he also documented shortness of breath in the record.
    a. rule out pneumonia
    b. shortness of breath
3. Sally Jones fell out of a tree and sustained a fractured humerus, left, which was treated in the emergency department (ED). While in the ED, the physician noted severe swelling of the arm.
    a. fractured humerus, left
    b. swelling of the arm
4. Cindy Frasier was seen in the office, complaining of severe stomach pain and vomiting. The physician diagnosed gastroenteritis.
    a. gastroenteritis
    b. stomach pain and vomiting
5. Tom Noble was treated in the outpatient department for urinary frequency. The physician documented probable cystitis in the record.
    a. probable cystitis
    b. urinary frequency
6. The patient was treated on an outpatient basis for both acute and chronic bronchitis, for which each was assigned an ICD-10-CM diagnosis code.
    a. acute bronchitis
    b. chronic bronchitis
7. Eric Fischer was treated for back pain in the physician's office. The physician documented that Eric's previously diagnosed influenza had completely resolved.
    a. back pain
    b. influenza

8. Scott Taylor was seen for complaints of dizziness, shakiness, and fainting spells; his blood was drawn and sent to the lab to have a blood glucose level performed. Lab results revealed blood glucose level of 325, Scott was placed on oral insulin, and the physician documented diabetes mellitus in the record.

    a. diabetes mellitus

    b. dizziness

    c. fainting spells

    d. shakiness

9. Tina Day had an encounter for outpatient chemotherapy for treatment of breast cancer.

    a. breast cancer

    b. encounter for outpatient chemotherapy

10. Joe Daly's preoperative diagnosis was cholelithiasis, for which he underwent laparoscopic cholecystectomy. The postoperative diagnosis was acute cholecystitis with cholelithiasis.

    a. acute cholecystitis with cholelithiasis

    b. cholelithiasis

Summary

Outpatient care includes any health care service provided to a patient who is not admitted to a facility. Such care may be provided in a physician's office, a stand-alone health care facility, a hospital outpatient or emergency department, or the patient's home. The CMS *Diagnostic Coding and Reporting Guidelines for Outpatient Services: Hospital-Based and Physician Office* were developed by the federal government and have been approved for use by hospitals and providers for coding and reporting hospital-based outpatient services and provider-based office visits. Although the guidelines were originally developed for use in submitting government claims, insurance companies have also adopted them (sometimes with variation). The CMS Coding Guidelines for Outpatient Diagnostic Tests includes instructions and examples that are to be used when assigning ICD-10-CM codes for diagnostic test results. The instructions and examples provide guidance regarding the appropriate assignment of ICD-10-CM diagnosis codes to simplify coding for diagnostic tests, consistent with the CMS *Diagnostic Coding and Reporting Guidelines for Outpatient Services: Hospital-Based and Physician Office.*

Internet Links

Encoder Pro: *www.EncoderPro.com*

Find-A-Code: *www.findacode.com*

HCPro, Inc.: Go to *www.hcmarketplace.com*, and click on the "Sign up for our FREE e-Newsletters" link. Enter your contact information, and click on the box located in front of *JustCoding News: Outpatient* (along with other e-Newsletters that interest you) subscribe.

Medical Information Bureau (MIB): *www.mib.com*

National Practitioner Data Bank (NPDB) and the Healthcare Integrity and Protection Data Bank (HIPDB): *www.npdb-hipdb.com*

Web-based training courses (free from CMS): Go to *https://learner.mlnlms.com*, and click on the Need an account? link.

Review

Multiple Choice

Instructions: Select the most appropriate response.

1. A patient was seen on an outpatient basis to have lab tests performed. The next day the patient underwent an outpatient procedure. Due to complications, he was admitted to the hospital. One week after discharge from the hospital, he was seen in the physician's office for a follow-up visit. Coding guidelines classify all of these visits as

   a. admissions.   **b.** appointments.   **c.** claims.   **d.** encounters.

2. A patient's record underwent review because the outpatient diagnosis about multiple injuries was unclear. Who is authorized to clarify the diagnosis?

   a. Health care provider   **c.** Insurance company
   b. HIM supervisor   **d.** Outpatient coder

3. A patient is diagnosed with osteoarthritis, and the encounter is assigned code M19.90. When referring to the ICD-10-CM index and following tabular list entries, the code assignment of M19.90 was

   ---

   INDEX TO DISEASES

   Osteoarthritis M19.90

   TABULAR LIST OF DISEASES

   M19   Other and unspecified osteoarthritis
            EXCLUD   *polyarthritis (M15.-)*
            EXCLUD   *arthrosis of spine (M47.-)*
                        hallux rigidus (M20.2)
                        osteoarthritis of spine (M47.-)

   M19.9 Osteoarthritis, unspecified site
        M19.90 Unspecified osteoarthritis, unspecified site
               Arthrosis NOS
               Arthritis NOS
               Osteoarthritis NOS
        M19.91 Primary osteoarthritis, unspecified site
               Primary osteoarthritis NOS
        M19.92 Post-traumatic osteoarthritis, unspecified site
               Post-traumatic osteoarthritis NOS
        M19.93 Secondary osteoarthritis, unspecified site
               Secondary osteoarthritis NOS

   ---

   a. correct because M19.9 is listed in the index as the code for osteoarthritis.
   b. correct because no further information was available in the patient record to assign a more specific code.
   c. invalid because upon verifying M19.90 in the tabular list, the coder should have assigned a sixth digit.
   d. incorrect because the tabular list's excludes1 note directs the coder to assign a code for polyarthritis (M15.-)

4. In ICD-10-CM, code Z85.020 (personal history of malignant carcinoid tumor of stomach) is reported as a _____.

    a. complication   **b.** first-listed   **c.** primary   **d.** secondary

5. When a definitive diagnosis has not been established or confirmed by the provider, which should be reported?

    a. Codes that describe symptoms and signs
    b. None because code assignment must wait until a diagnosis is confirmed
    c. Office visit only
    d. Qualified diagnosis, such as rule out, possible, or suspected

Use these tabular list entries to answer the question that follows.

6. When referring to the ICD-10-CM index and following tabular list entries, duodenitis with bleeding (K29.81) is an example of a _____ code.

> ### INDEX TO DISEASES AND INJURIES
>
> **Duodenitis** (nonspecific) (peptic) K29.80
>   with bleeding K29.81

> ### TABULAR LIST OF DISEASES AND INJURIES
>
> **K29.8 Duodenitis**
>   **K29.80 Duodenitis without bleeding**
>   **K29.81 Duodenitis with bleeding**

    a. combination   **b.** history   **c.** late effect   **d.** multiple

7. When a bacterial organism is documented as the cause of a condition (e.g., UTI), it is

    a. coded as either a first-listed or a secondary code.
    b. coded as a first-listed diagnosis only.
    c. reported as a secondary code, below the code for the condition.
    d. not coded because bacterial organisms are always classified in the disease code.

8. When determining the first-listed diagnosis, the ICD-10-CM coding conventions and _____ guidelines take precedence over the official outpatient guidelines.

    a. drugs and adverse effects
    b. eponyms and procedure/surgical
    c. external cause of injury and poisoning
    d. general and disease-specific

9. For accurate reporting of ICD-10-CM diagnosis codes,

    a. a definitive diagnosis must be documented by the physician who provides care to the patient.
    b. all diagnosis and condition codes must contain seven characters.
    c. A00.0 through T88.9 and Z00–Z99.89 are used to classify the encounter.
    d. definitive diagnoses in addition to all signs and symptoms are classified.

10. Which section of the ICD-10-CM tabular list would be referenced to assign codes that deal with encounters for circumstances other than a disease or an injury?

    a. Index to Diseases and Injuries
    b. Neoplasm Table
    c. Factors Influencing Health Status and Contact with Health Services
    d. Table of Drugs and Chemicals

11. An encounter is reported with codes for symptoms listed first, followed by an unrelated secondary condition code. Thus, the reason for the visit has
    a. been confirmed, and a coexisting condition was treated or medically managed during the same encounter.
    b. been confirmed, and the patient also exhibited unrelated signs and symptoms during the same encounter.
    c. not been confirmed at the time of coding, and a coexisting condition was treated or medically managed during the same encounter.
    d. not been confirmed at the time of coding, and the patient also exhibited unrelated signs and symptoms during the same encounter.

12. A woman is examined for a routine prenatal visit, with no apparent complications. Which would be the reason for this encounter?
    a. Complications of pregnancy and childbirth
    b. Encounter for pregnancy test, result positive
    c. Personal history of complications of pregnancy
    d. Supervision of normal uncomplicated pregnancy

13. Which is assigned when the provider documents a reason for a patient seeking health care that is not a disorder or disease?
    a. Conditions that are ruled out   c. External causes of morbidity
    b. Diagnoses that are qualified   d. Factors influencing health status

14. The "x" character in an ICD-10-CM code is called a(n) _____.
    a. eponym   b. modifier   c. placeholder   d. qualifier

15. Which ICD-10-CM Index to Diseases and Injuries entry (below) identifies the second qualifier?

    Stricture (*see also* Stenosis)
        aqueduct of Sylvius (congenital) Q03.0
            with spina bifida —*see* Spina bifida, by site, with hydrocephalus

    a. Aqueduct of Sylvius   c. Stricture
    b. Stenosis   d. With spina bifida

16. The patient is seen in the office because of chronic asthma. Coding guidelines for chronic conditions state that such codes
    a. are not to be reported if the condition is already being medically managed.
    b. may be reported as additional diagnosis only if medically managed.
    c. may be reported as first-listed if medically managed during the encounter.
    d. should never be reported on an outpatient claim.

17. A patient complains of nausea and abdominal pain and undergoes an endoscopy for suspected hiatal hernia. The test results were negative, so the physician instructed the patient to return next week to be tested for gastroesophageal reflux disease. To code this encounter to the highest degree of accuracy and completeness, which would be reported?
    a. Gastroesophageal reflux disease
    b. Hiatal hernia
    c. Nausea and abdominal pain
    d. Nausea and vomiting and gastroesophageal reflux disease

18. Urinary tract infection due to *E. coli* is coded as _____.
    a. B96.20   c. N39.0
    b. B96.20, N39.0   d. N39.0, B96.20

19. Well-child visit is coded as _____.
    a. Z00.129   c. Z71.89
    b. Z00.2   d. Z00.00

20. The patient is diagnosed with pneumonia. A sputum specimen is sent to a pathologist and growth of strep-tococcus, type B, is confirmed and documented in the patient's record. Use your ICD-10-CM coding manual to determine which code is reported for this diagnosis.

    a. J13   c. J17, A40.1

    b. J15.3   d. J18.9

Coding Practice

Instructions: Review each case scenario, and assign and properly sequence the ICD-10-CM diagnosis codes, including ICD-10-CM external cause codes, as appropriate.

Coding Practice — Ambulatory Surgery Center (ASC)

1. SUBJECTIVE: 20-year-old female patient with past medical history significant for asthma underwent total thyroidectomy due to feelings of fatigue and weight gain for the past six months.

   OBJECTIVE: Thyroid function tests revealed that the patient was hypothyroid with a thyroid-stimulating hormone level of 110.2, free thyroxine index of 0.9, and total T3 of 0.41. The patient also has a palpable mass in the left lobe of the thyroid, and thyroid ultrasound revealed diffuse enlargement of the thyroid gland and microcalcifications. Thyroid lobes were biopsied bilaterally; based on those results, the patient underwent total thyroidectomy.

   DIAGNOSES: Hypothyroidism. Enlargement of thyroid gland. History of asthma.

2. SUBJECTIVE: 42-year-old female with past family history of gastric polyposis underwent upper gastrointestinal endoscopy, which revealed multiple gastric polyps in the fundus and body.

   OBJECTIVE: Biopsies of the gastric polyps were submitted for pathological examination.

   DIAGNOSES: Multiple gastric (stomach) polyps. Family history of gastric polyposis.

3. This 35-year-old states that her menstrual periods have been regular, and she had been taking birth control pills until January of this year. Since that time, she has been using other methods of birth control that are unsatisfactory to her. She and her husband also desire tubal ligation for prevention of further pregnancies.

   PHYSICAL EXAMINATION reveals a morbidly obese white female in no obvious distress; heart and lungs normal to auscultation; abdomen flat; on pressure, the cervix protrudes to the opening of the vaginal os; otherwise, the uterus was average size. Patient was taken to surgery and underwent laparoscopic bilateral tubal ligation. She was discharged in stable condition to be seen by Dr. Baker for follow-up care next week.

   DIAGNOSES: Elective sterilization. Morbid obesity.

4. A 53-year-old male is admitted with a right inguinal hernia. Laboratory results were within normal limits. Right inguinal herniorrhaphy was performed, and the patient did well; there were no complications. He was discharged to be seen in the office in several days for suture removal. No specific diet or medication was prescribed. The patient was advised to avoid any strenuous activities.

   DIAGNOSIS: Right inguinal hernia.

5. This 31-year-old white female is admitted to the ambulatory surgery unit with chief complaint of multiparity. She states that she wants to undergo a sterilization procedure. She underwent laparoscopic tubal fulguration, bilateral. There are no familial diseases such as epilepsy, diabetes, bleeding tendency, tuberculosis, or heart attacks. She smokes a pack of cigarettes a day and takes no alcohol. She is married, but now separated.

She has been in good health and has had no other problems. Her menses are every 28 days and last 4 days. No clots or pains. Her last period was January 1. She has two children living and well, ages 11 and 5.

DIAGNOSES: Encounter for sterilization procedure. Multiparity. History of tobacco use.

Coding Practice — Chiropractic Office

Special Instructions: Also assign external cause codes for any applicable activity performed, external cause status, place of occurrence, and/or type of accident.

1. A 37-year-old civilian contractor was hired by a home owner. While lifting boards from his truck while on the job in the private driveway at a single family residence, he began to experience acute burning pain in his neck from this sudden strenuous movement. His symptoms persisted, and he was seen by his chiropractor who checked the range of motion in his neck and noted restriction in lateral bending and rotation. Neurologic screening revealed decreased sensation at the left thumb and first finger. Reflexes were normal (intact), but there was some muscle weakness in the arm. Patient underwent magnetic resonance imaging (MRI), which was negative, and received chiropractic treatment.

    DIAGNOSIS: Cervical disc syndrome.

---

2. A 15-year-old high school student was playing in a basketball game one evening on the basketball court at his public high school; when he went up for a rebound, he collided with another player. He felt his neck "wrench" backward, and he experienced immediate pain in both sides of his neck. That evening he felt pain and stiffness in his neck, and he had trouble turning his head.

    DIAGNOSIS: Acute cervical sprain. (Initial encounter.)

---

3. A 48-year-old online college professor who sits at a computer, keyboarding all day in her office at the college, has been experiencing neck pain accompanied by soreness and stiffness in her upper back. She became concerned when she began to experience numbness and tingling in her left arm, especially at night. History reveals no weakness in her arms and minor arm pain. All neurologic signs are normal, and the patient has full range of motion in her neck except for some restriction when she bends her head to the left. Tight and very tender muscles in the upper back and along both side of the neck are palpated. There are also joint restrictions in the middle back. Chiropractic treatment was provided.

    DIAGNOSES: Cervical neck strain. Myalgia, upper back.

---

4. A 77-year-old individual experiences neck pain and seeks chiropractic treatment. Upon examination, all neurologic signs are normal. There is restricted joint motion and tight muscles along both sides of the neck and into the upper and midback. Previous x-ray of the neck revealed osteoarthritis. The patient undergoes chiropractic treatment.

    DIAGNOSIS: Osteoarthritis, cervical spine.

---

5. A 25-year-old college student is seen for chiropractic treatment. She complains of neck stiffness, shoulder and back pain, and headaches. Neck x-rays are negative. Chiropractic treatment included adjustment and heat therapy.

    DIAGNOSIS: Neck sprain. (Initial encounter.)

Coding Practice — Hospital Emergency Department

1. SUBJECTIVE: 15-year-old male patient with previous diagnoses of congenital cataracts and retinal detachments had experienced an episode of orbital hemorrhage, which was treated in the past. He arrived in the ED today after developing pain behind his right eye yesterday.

   OBJECTIVE: Physical examination revealed no redness of the eye. The left pupil is deviated medially with a steamy anterior chamber. This is the normal appearance, according to the mother. There was no sight in that eye. Funduscopic examination shows a pigmented retina in the right eye, but no evidence of hemorrhage or optic disc cupping. Schiotz tonometry showed a right orbital pressure of 21 and left orbital pressure of 0. There was no cervical lymphadenopathy. Tympanic membranes were clear. Chest was clear, and heart is regular rate and rhythm. There is full range of motion of the neck. No palpable temporal arteries; no abrasions or swelling. There has been no fever.

   ASSESSMENT: Headache, etiology unknown.

   PLAN: I called his primary care physician, who explained that this has been a problem in the past and that neurologically, the patient has been evaluated for this type of problem but nothing was ever found. He believed that the pressure of 21 was okay and that the patient could be discharged on some sort of analgesic. The patient is scheduled to be seen by him in two weeks.

   DIAGNOSIS: Headache.

---

2. SUBJECTIVE: 25-year-old male was working with a heavy sledgehammer in the garden on his personal property when he noted pain in his right shoulder area. The pain developed suddenly as he was swinging the hammer rather vigorously. The pain has persisted over the past three weeks. At certain times, it was somewhat better, but it became painful once again. The patient has continued working, which involves swinging this sledgehammer.

   OBJECTIVE: Physical examination reveals tenderness over the anterior joint line; there is no swelling or abnormal mass present. The rotator cuff does not seem involved, as the patient can tolerate extreme downward pressure on his elbows without any pain whatsoever. What really causes the patient's pain is bringing the arms apart when they are in the midline in front of his chest. Distal neurovascular status is intact. X-ray of the shoulder was negative.

   DIAGNOSIS: Pain, right shoulder. Probable strain, deltoid muscle, and possibly the deeper muscles of the anterior shoulder area.

   TREATMENT: The patient was given a prescription for Motrin 600 milligrams three times daily and advised to apply heat to the area once or twice each day. He is also to rest the arm as much as possible; however, he says he must work and will not take time off. He was told that this pain may last for a number of weeks before it resolves completely. He is to return to see Dr. Callus if there are any problems.

---

3. SUBJECTIVE: This 48-year-old man is a patient of mine who complains of midsternal chest pain but no radiation. This has occurred intermittently today since 10 P.M. and did not occur reliably with exertion. He has not been exerting himself too much, as he is a pastor at a Baptist church. He complains of feeling quite warm, but has had no diaphoresis or shortness of breath. He previously had his gallbladder removed. He has been taking Inderal 40 milligrams four times each day, and he took Isordil sublingually with mixed results during the day today. He says that Tylenol will help somewhat with the pain in the midsternal area.

   OBJECTIVE: Physical examination reveals a mildly anxious middle-aged male in little distress. The neck is supple; carotids are two plus without bruits. Chest is symmetrical in expansion, and lungs show few abnormal sounds and some rales in the right base. Heart is regular rate and rhythm; S1 and S2 and 2/4; no murmurs, clicks, heaves, gallops, or rubs were appreciated. The abdomen is soft and nontender. There is a right upper quadrant surgical scar; no masses or organomegaly noted. EKG was done and read as normal. Chest x-ray shows slightly increased density at right lower lobe. He was given Mylanta without any change in his pain.

DIAGNOSIS: Bronchitis and early pneumonia on the right.

___

4. SUBJECTIVE: This 22-year-old female twisted her ankle yesterday while playing softball at a local baseball field. She states that she developed pain in the ankle subsequent to this injury and has been on crutches prior to her arrival in the ED this morning. She denies any previous significant injuries to the ankle.

    OBJECTIVE: Physical examination reveals a healthy, cooperative 22-year-old female in no acute distress. There is tenderness about the left ankle. There is no ecchymoses or swelling present. There is tenderness beneath both malleoli and anteriorly across the ankle. X-rays of the ankle show no evidence of fracture.

    PLAN: The patient was instructed to use crutches for seven days and to avoid any weight-bearing and then begin partial weight-bearing. If she is uncomfortable, she is to return to using crutches for several more days before attempting weight-bearing. She is to elevate the leg and use ice compresses, and she was advised to be reevaluated if she is not able to walk comfortably in 7 to 10 days.

    DIAGNOSIS: Sprain, left ankle.

___

5. SUBJECTIVE: This is a 28-year-old female who was handed a knife by her husband, blade first, while cooking at home in their kitchen; she accidentally punctured her left ring finger on the blade.

    OBJECTIVE: Patient has a superficial puncture wound over the lateral aspect of the left fourth finger. The area has been cleansed well, and a bandage was applied.

    ASSESSMENT: Puncture wound, left ring finger. (Initial encounter.)

    PLAN: Patient is to watch for any signs of infection and follow up with her primary care physician.

___

Coding Practice — Hospital Outpatient Department

1. A 39-year-old female patient undergoes a screening electrocardiogram (EKG) as an outpatient. She has a family history of cardiovascular disease. EKG results were negative. The nonspecific T-wave changes illustrated on the EKG were explained to the patient as probably due to anxiety and positional changes.

___

2. A 42-year-old male patient diagnosed with systemic lupus erythematosus received a scheduled transfusion of erythrocytes and platelets in the ambulatory transfusion clinic.

___

3. A 54-year-old male previously diagnosed with arteriosclerotic heart disease (ASHD) underwent scheduled right and left cardiac catheterization as an outpatient. The patient has no past history of previous coronary artery bypass graft (CABG) surgery. Cardiac catheterization results revealed 40% blockage of the right coronary artery, 70% blockage of the left main coronary artery, and 80% blockage of the left anterior descending coronary artery. Surgical intervention options to treat the blockages were discussed with the patient, and the patient will be admitted in two days to undergo triple CABG.

___

4. A 62-year-old patient with known congestive heart failure registered for outpatient services at the heart failure clinic and receives lifestyle modification counseling about his diet and activities. He received instruction from

the dietician about following a low-sodium, low-fat diet, and he was also counseled to avoid tobacco and heavy alcohol use. His current medications were reviewed, and his diuretic dosage was adjusted.

5. A 45-year-old patient registered as an outpatient to undergo scheduled hemodialysis. The patient was born with just one kidney, which failed when she was 30 years old. She previously underwent a kidney transplant, which also failed. Currently, dialysis is her only option as she awaits the availability of another kidney for transplant. The hemodialysis takes three hours and is uneventful.

Coding Practice — Hospital Same Day Surgery

1. This 5-year-old white male is admitted with the chief complaint of recurrent bouts of tonsillitis and tonsils so large that food gets stuck in them and he chokes on it. He has had a sore throat now for four to five weeks, and this is the second time this year that this has happened. He has consulted Dr. Blair, and she advised that the patient undergo tonsillectomy and adenoidectomy (T&A). The patient has no ear problems, and he has not had strep throat that his father knows of.

   PAST MEDICAL HISTORY: He has had no operations, serious illnesses, or injuries.

   FAMILY HISTORY: He has had no familial diseases such as cancer, tuberculosis, epilepsy, diabetes, bleeding tendency, or heart attacks.

   SOCIAL HISTORY: The patient is in kindergarten. He lives with his parents and has no social problems.

   SYSTEMIC REVIEW: The father states that his son has been in good health and has had no other problems.

   PHYSICAL EXAMINATION: Reveals his tonsils to be huge. There is evidence that he had an anterior lymphadenopathy.

   LABORATORY STUDIES: Urinalysis negative. Bleeding time 1 minute 30 seconds. Partial prothrombin time 30 seconds. Hemoglobin 12.3 grams, hematocrit 37 volume percent, white blood count 6500 with 34 polys. Chest x-ray normal. The patient was prepared for surgery and taken to the operating room where, under satisfactory general intratracheal anesthesia, T&A was performed. Following the operation, he had an uncomplicated postoperative recovery. He had no bleeding, he was afebrile, tonsillar fossa are clean, and he has had no anesthetic complications.

   DIAGNOSIS: Greatly hypertrophied tonsils and adenoids.

2. This is an 89-year-old white male who was apparently in good health except for pneumonia in 1938 and had never had any serious medical problems since then. For about a month prior to outpatient surgery, he developed urgency and frequency upon urination and marked nocturia every hour, followed finally by the passing of blood in the urine. He was seen in the emergency room (ER) last week due to passing blood in the urine every day for several days and having a great deal of difficulty voiding. ER treatment involved inserting a Foley catheter, from which 400 cc of grossly bloody urine was evacuated.

   PHYSICAL EXAMINATION: Reveals a degree of blindness due to cataracts. The testes are atrophic. Prostate is a grade II benign, enlarged gland.

   LABORATORY AND X-RAY FINDINGS: BUN 62, blood sugar 155, CO_2 14, creatinine 3.6. Urinalysis reveals many red blood cells per high-power field and WBC 4–6. Urine culture reveals innumerable enterococci. Complete blood count reveals hemoglobin of 11.9 grams, hematocrit of 35. Blood gases reveal pH of 7.38, pCO_2 of 22.9, PO_2 of 91, HCO of 313. WBC of 12,200. EKG was negative. Drip infusion IVP revealed poorly functioning kidneys and one bladder diverticulum with elevation of the bladder floor consistent with a large prostate gland. Chest x-ray showed bilateral basal pulmonary infiltration and calcification of the thoracic aorta. Upper gastrointestinal and gallbladder series and small bowel series revealed small active ulcer crater of the lesser curvature of the pyloric canal. Patient underwent cystoscopy and retropubic prostatectomy.

DIAGNOSES: Benign prostatic hypertrophy. Chronic renal insufficiency secondary to benign prostatic hypertrophy. Urinary tract infection.

---

3. This 48-year-old male patient has had an anal fissure for several months and is complaining of pain and bleeding. This has not responded to conservative measures, and he is scheduled to undergo outpatient fissurectomy and hemorrhoidectomy.

PHYSICAL EXAMINATION: Reveals no other pertinent positive findings except the presence of obesity, anal fissure, and hemorrhoids. X-ray of the chest was unremarkable. Barium enema studies were unremarkable. EKG showed no abnormality. Lab results revealed blood sugar 92, BUN 14, normal electrolytes, and normal enzymes. CBC and differential were normal. Urinalysis was essentially unremarkable. After adequate workup, the patient was taken to surgery; under endotracheal anesthesia, a fissurectomy, hemorrhoidectomy, and sphincterotomy were performed. Post-op, the patient was voiding and comfortable. The patient was prescribed Tylenol with Codeine, Metamucil, sitz baths, and limited activity. The patient will be followed in my office.

DIAGNOSES: Anal fissure. First-degree bleeding hemorrhoids.

---

4. This 51-year-old white female has noticed a steady enlargement on the left side of the neck for the past year. A thyroid scan revealed a cold nodule in the right lobe, and carcinoma is to be ruled out. The patient also complains of some difficulty with pain in the neck and on swallowing.

PHYSICAL EXAMINATION: Reveals a large mass in the left lobe of the thyroid and a questionable mass on the right side. The patient was taken to surgery, where at the time of exploration, both lobes of the thyroid were markedly enlarged and revealed multiple nodules. A total thyroidectomy was performed after identifying the parathyroid glands and protecting them. The patient was discharged and instructed to return for follow-up examination within two weeks. She was placed on Synthroid 0.15 daily and no other medication.

DIAGNOSES: Nodular colloid goiter, left and right lobes of thyroid. Degenerating follicular adenoma, right lobe of thyroid.

---

5. Patient was diagnosed as missed abortion at 20 weeks' gestation. The patient was noted to have grown appreciably in the last month of her prenatal care, and it was noted that she had begun bleeding three days before being seen in the office yesterday. At the time of the office visit, she was passing clots. The cervix was dilated, and she was developing a foul-smelling discharge but no morbidity. She was scheduled for outpatient surgery, during which pregnancy was removed with curettage of the uterus. The patient was discharged in satisfactory condition. Her hemoglobin was 13.8 gm, white blood cell count was normal differential. Pathology revealed products of conception and degenerated decidual and placental tissue.

DIAGNOSIS: Missed abortion.

Coding Practice — Physician Office

1. This 38-year-old man was accidentally poked in his left eye by his nine-month-old little girl yesterday when she came to visit him in his office on a college campus, where he teaches. He says that she was very excited about seeing him, and when she reached up to be lifted into his arms, her finger accidentally poked him in the eye and her fingernail scratched his eyeball. He had to teach a class after he saw her, or he would have

been in my office earlier. He states, "My eye is killing me!" Since that time, he has pain in his left eye and a lot of watering. He has had no changes in vision, no blurriness noted, and he is otherwise well. Physical examination shows the conjunctiva to be inflamed. Funduscopic examination is normal, and extraocular movements are intact. Stain with fluorescein shows positive corneal abrasion. I administered an ophthalmic topical analgesic to relieve his discomfort and Chloromycetin ointment to the eye to prevent infection. He was fitted with an eye patch, and he is to see me tomorrow for a recheck.

DIAGNOSIS: Corneal laceration.

2. This 15-year-old male was struck on the left leg by a stick yesterday, which created a puncture wound in the skin of his leg. The patient presents today with swelling and localized redness around the wound. Physical exam reveals a healthy and cooperative 15-year-old male in no acute distress with a small puncture-type wound approximately 5 millimeters in length on the anterior aspect of the left leg, just proximal to the knee. The wound is noted to have a small amount of induration, approximately 2 centimeters in diameter around the area with localized redness. There is no discomfort to motion of the knee.

DIAGNOSIS: Puncture wound, left knee. (Initial encounter.)

PLAN: The patient was instructed to use warm soaks to that knee several times each day and have it rechecked if it becomes worse. He will return or be seen sooner if the knee does not appear to improve. He was started on Keflex 500 milligrams four times daily.

3. This 34-year-old male, who has had a hydrocele in the past and had been seen and treated by Dr. Wise, returns now for continued pain and swelling in the hydrocele, which is causing poor sleep habits. Apparently, the patient has been given some kind of "fluid pill" for the discomfort.

OBJECTIVE: Patient has a tender, swelling right scrotal region about the size of a grapefruit, which is very tense.

ASSESSMENT: Right-sided hydrocele.

PLAN: The patient is to wear tight, supportive underwear; take Tylenol #3 for pain; and see Dr. Wise for evaluation.

4. This man cut his left thumbnail and thumb with a powered hand saw today, which flapped back the lateral aspect of the thumb. The thumb was cleansed, numbed, and one stitch put through the nail, fixing the flap in place. He is currently on his tetanus immunizations. He will return to the office to have the stitch removed in six to eight days unless he experiences symptoms, in which case he is to call the office to be seen.

DIAGNOSIS: Laceration, thumbnail and thumb, left.

5. This 1-year-old little girl injured her hand while "playing the drum" by banging away at pots and pans on the floor of the kitchen while her mother was nearby preparing last evening's meal. The child slept fitfully last night, and this morning her left hand is somewhat swollen and painful to touch. X-ray was taken and is negative for fracture. I treated her with a sling, ice, and elevation, which will continue at home. She will be rechecked as needed. She left the office in good condition.

Coding Practice — Stand-Alone Radiology Center

1. A 50-year-old male patient underwent ultrasound of neck and ultrasound-guided placement of internal jugular dialysis catheter. Indication for radiographic procedures is chronic renal failure and occluded dialysis access graft. Real-time ultrasound examination was done of the neck and showed patency of both internal jugular veins. Following sterile prep and drape and infiltration with local anesthetic, puncture was done of the lower aspect of the right internal jugular vein using a 21-gauge needle. Using Seldinger technique, the tract was dilated and a 14 French dialysis catheter was introduced and positioned within the right atrium. The catheter was secured with a silk suture and irrigated and the patient sent for dialysis.

_____

2. Gallbladder cholecystogram shows moderate concentration of dye in the gallbladder, no evidence of stone, and moderate hypertrophic change of lumbar spine. Small intestinal pattern is normal below the level of the duodenum. Impression is hypertrophic gallbladder with no diagnostic evidence of stones.

_____

3. Patient underwent upper gastrointestinal study due to severe stomach pain. Study reveals esophagus and stomach to be normal in appearance, and first portion of duodenum is normal. There is moderate deformity of the medial aspect of the second portion of the duodenum with moderate flattening of the mucosal pattern in this area, but without any definite evidence of ulceration. The duodenal loop is not significantly widened, but there does appear to be slight extrinsic pressure and probable stiffening of the medial wall of the second portion of the duodenum.

IMPRESSION: Second portion of duodenum is consistent with residues of recurrent pancreatitis with probable exacerbation of the pancreatitis at this time. The possibility of neoplasm arising in the head of the pancreas is not excluded.

_____

4. Patient underwent excretory urogram for complaints of urinary incontinence. Urogram revealed that both kidneys appear to concentrate Renografin media in a satisfactory manner. Renal collecting system on the left appears grossly normal. Visualized lateral contour of right kidney appears normal. Renal pelvis and ureters are of normal caliber. Urinary bladder is moderately distended, normal in contour, and shows some indentation on its dome, probably due to the adjacent uterus. There is moderate post voiding residual. Impression is normal right and left calices, small post voiding residual with indentation on dome of urinary bladder, possibly due to an enlarged uterus.

_____

5. Patient underwent opaque right knee arthrogram for severe pain and limited mobility. Following shaving and scrubbing of the knee in the usual manner, local anesthetic was infiltrated along the lateral approach to the patellofemoral joint. A needle was directed through the anesthetized tissue and into the joint with subsequent removal of 30 cc of pink-colored joint fluid. Then, 11 cc of Renografin 76 was injected and films taken in various projections. Fissures are demonstrated in the posterior segment of the medial meniscus. Cruciate ligaments and lateral meniscus appear intact. Impression is knee joint effusion and rupture of posterior segment of right medial meniscus. (Initial encounter.)

_____

Coding Practice — Stand-Alone Urgent Care Center

1. SUBJECTIVE: A 45-year-old female was seen complaining of severe pain of the right knee and ankle after having been in a motorcycle accident earlier today in the driveway of her home. She has difficulty bearing weight on her right leg.

OBJECTIVE: Multiple abrasions are noted on both forearms. Two lacerations are noted on the left elbow, approximately 2 centimeters in length. She has a sprain of the right knee, lower leg, and ankle. X-rays of the right knee, lower leg, and ankle were negative. Multiple views revealed no bony abnormality. There was slight soft tissue swelling over the lateral malleolus.

TREATMENT: The lacerations on the left elbow were 1 inch long and 1/2 inch long. They were closed with interrupted 4-0 Prolene sutures after thorough cleansing. The abrasions were cleansed. She was given a tetanus toxoid booster, and a sterile dressing was applied. The patient is to be rechecked by her primary care physician in 48 hours. She left in good condition.

DIAGNOSES: Multiple abrasions, arms and legs. Laceration, left elbow. Sprain, right knee, lower leg, and ankle.

---

2. The patient is a 41-year-old male seen for treatment of a scratch on the dorsum of his right hand that occurred about a week ago. It did not seem to bother him, and he did not think too much of it. He was building a piece of furniture at home and accidentally stepped on the edge of a piece of 2×4 wood and the opposite end raised up and struck his right hand about two days ago, and it stung a little bit and became a little swollen. It was rather tender today and looking a bit red. He was quite concerned because he has had blood poisoning once before due to an infected hair follicle on his hand. I instructed him to come to the urgent care center for evaluation. The patient does have swelling and induration around the area where he had the original scratch. It is red and warm, but there is no streaking that I can see in the lymphatic channels. I think he is developing an infection there, or cellulitis.

IMPRESSION: Cellulitis, right hand. (Initial encounter.)

DISPOSITION: Hot soaks three or four times each day. Amoxil 250 milligrams three times each day for a week. If it should progressively worsen and become more swollen, the patient should call and have it checked again to be sure he isn't developing an abscess; otherwise, we'll give him a few days. If it hasn't cleared within five to seven days, he is to let me know.

---

3. This 44-year-old male presents with a chief complaint of back pain. HPI: 44-year-old gentleman states that he went fishing Wednesday. He did not fall or injure himself, but Thursday he was feeling quite bad with right flank pain radiating into the back of his leg and into the testicle. He stated that he had no change in the color of his urine and that the pain actually started to subside. Friday, he had another recurrence of pain, and it gradually worsened and stayed with him. Today, it was much worse, he was unable to work, and he came to the urgent care center for evaluation and treatment. The patient walks leaning to the right where his pain is. He has a significant amount of difficulty in hyperextension and also forward bending. It does not hurt him too much to bend to the right, but it hurts him quite a bit to bend to the left. He has a lot of tenderness in the sacroiliac region and also in the superior rim of the ilium and the sacrum. X-rays of the area appear normal to my eye. The radiology report is not back at this time.

PLAN: We will treat him with Tylenol with Codeine, two tablets every four hours as needed, and Flexeril 10 milligrams three times a day. He should not work tomorrow or Monday, and perhaps he will be able to return to work on Tuesday. He was instructed to call the urgent care center if he gets any worse. He is instructed to schedule a follow-up visit in one week. He left the urgency care center in satisfactory condition.

DIAGNOSIS: Sacroiliac inflammation.

---

4. This 15-year-old male presents to the urgent care center with the complaint of a cyst on his right cheek. Over the past two days, the patient has developed a reddened, tender mass on the right cheek, just lateral to the nose. Physical exam reveals an erythematous, tender mass approximately 7 millimeters in diameter on the right cheek. It is hard and tender, but does not seem to be fluctuant at this time.

DIAGNOSIS: Infected sebaceous cyst, right cheek.

PLAN: The patient was instructed to use warm soaks frequently, and he was given a prescription for tetracycline 250 milligrams four times daily. He was instructed to see Dr. Smith in two days. He is to return sooner if he has further difficulty.

---

5. This young lady was accidentally hit in her nose and mouth two days ago by another resident while playing baseball outside of the detention center where she resides; she has had intermittent nosebleeds since that time. She was brought to the urgent care center and examined. There was moderate swelling in the nose and quite a bit of edema and swelling in the nasal mucosa, but there is no active bleeding noted at the present time. No treatment was given other than Dimetapp one every 12 hours, and the patient was told to avoid taking aspirin. She is to take Tylenol and apply ice to her nose. The detention center staff person who accompanied the patient to the urgent care center was told to call if the patient experienced further problems.

Health Care Procedure Coding System (HCPCS) Level II Coding System

8: HCPCS Level II Coding System, 294

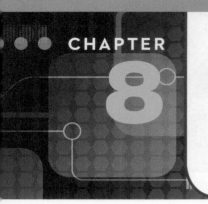

HCPCS Level II Coding System

Chapter Outline

Overview of HCPCS

HCPCS Level II Codes

Assigning HCPCS Level II Codes

Determining Payer Responsibility

Chapter Objectives

At the conclusion of this chapter, the student should be able to:

1. Define key terms related to HCPCS level II coding.
2. Provide an overview about the use of HCPCS codes.
3. List the HCPCS levels and their components.
4. Assign HCPCS level II procedure and services codes for outpatient care.
5. Determine payer responsibility based on HCPCS level II code assignment.

Key Terms

advance beneficiary notice (ABN)

certificate of medical necessity (CMN)

DME MAC medical review policies

durable medical equipment, prosthetics, orthotics, and supplies (DMEPOS)

durable medical equipment, prosthetics, orthotics, and supplies (DMEPOS) dealer

HCPCS level I

HCPCS level II miscellaneous codes

HCPCS level II modifiers

HCPCS level II permanent national codes

HCPCS level II temporary codes

local coverage determinations (LCDs)

Medicare Benefit Policy Manual

Medicare National Coverage Determinations Manual

Medicare Pricing, Data Analysis, and Coding (PDAC) contractor

national coverage determinations (NCDs)

orthotics

prosthetics

transitional pass-through payment

Introduction

The HCPCS level II coding system contains alphanumeric codes that were developed to complement the Current Procedural Terminology (CPT) coding system. It is also called the HCPCS national coding system. HCPCS level II was introduced in 1983 after Medicare found that its payers used more than 100 different coding systems, making it difficult to analyze claims data. HCPCS level II furnishes health care providers and suppliers with a standardized language for reporting professional and nonphysician services, procedures, supplies, and equipment. (Most state Medicaid programs and many commercial payers also use the HCPCS level II coding system.)

NOTE:

When reviewing examples and completing exercises and review questions in this chapter, use your HCPCS Level II coding manual to locate index entries and to verify them in the tabular list.

NOTE:

Instruction about the HCPCS level II coding system is sequenced prior to CPT Chapters 9–19 in this textbook to familiarize students with HCPCS level II modifiers that must be added to CPT codes and HCPCS level II codes that must be reported with CPT codes. Examples, exercises, and review questions in Chapters 9–19 of this textbook require students to report HCPCS level II modifiers and codes, where appropriate. (Code ranges included in parentheses after section titles in the textbook and workbook chapters may differ from your HCPCS level II coding manual.)

Overview of HCPCS

Two levels of codes are associated with HCPCS, commonly referred to as HCPCS level I and II codes. Most of the procedures and services are reported using CPT (HCPCS level I) codes. However, CPT does not describe durable medical equipment, prosthetics, orthotics, supplies (DMEPOS), and certain other services. Therefore, the Centers for Medicare & Medicaid Services (CMS) developed HCPCS level II codes to report DMEPOS and other services.

HCPCS Level I

HCPCS level I includes the CPT codes developed and published by the American Medical Association (AMA). The AMA is responsible for the annual update of this coding system and its two-digit modifiers. (CPT was defined in Chapter 1 of this textbook, and its content is covered in Chapters 9–19.)

HCPCS Level II

HCPCS level II (or HCPCS national coding system) was created in 1983 to describe common medical services and supplies not classified in CPT. HCPCS level II codes are five characters in length, and they begin with the letters *A–V* followed by four numbers. The codes identify services performed by physician and nonphysician providers (e.g., nurse practitioners, speech therapists), services provided by ambulance companies, and supplies and equipment provided by durable medical equipment (DME) companies, which are called durable medical equipment, prosthetics, orthotics, and supplies (DMEPOS) dealers. *Durable medical equipment (DME)* is defined by Medicare as equipment that

- Can withstand repeated use
- Is primarily used to serve a medical purpose
- Is used in the patient's home
- Would not be used in the absence of illness or injury

Durable medical equipment, prosthetics, orthotics, and supplies (DMEPOS) include artificial limbs, braces, medications, surgical dressings, and wheelchairs. **Durable medical equipment, prosthetics, orthotics, and supplies (DMEPOS) dealers** supply patients with DME (e.g., canes, crutches, walkers, commode chairs, and blood-glucose monitors). DMEPOS claims are submitted to DME Medicare administrative contractors (MACs) (previously called durable medical equipment regional carriers, or DMERCs) that were awarded contracts by CMS. Each DME MAC covers a specific geographic region of the country and is responsible for processing DMEPOS claims for its specific region.

NOTE:

> When claims are to be submitted to one of the four DME MACs, DMEPOS dealers that have coding questions should check with the **Medicare Pricing, Data Analysis, and Coding (PDAC) contractor** (formerly called the Statistical Analysis Durable Medical Equipment Regional Carrier, or SADMERC), which assists suppliers and manufacturers in determining HCPCS codes to be used. The PDAC has a toll-free help line for this purpose at (877) 735-1326.

When people refer to HCPCS codes, they are most likely referring to HCPCS level II codes. CMS is responsible for the annual updates to HCPCS level II codes and the two-character alphanumeric modifiers. HCPCS level II codes are further discussed in this chapter.

HCPCS Level III

Effective December 31, 2003, HCPCS level III local codes were no longer required. They had the same structure as level II codes, but were assigned by local Medicare carriers (LMCs) (now called Medicare administrator contractors or MACs), which process Medicare claims. HCPCS level III codes began with the letters *W, X, Y,* or *Z.* (Some third-party payers continue to use the HCPCS level III codes.)

Exercise 8.1 – Overview of HCPCS

Instructions: Complete each statement.

1. HCPCS level II codes are considered _____ codes.
2. HCPCS level II codes describe procedures, services, and _____.
3. CPT codes are included as HCPCS _____ codes.
4. HCPCS level II codes are _____ characters in length.
5. HCPCS level II codes begin with the letters _____.

HCPCS Level II Codes

The HCPCS level II coding system classifies similar medical products and services for the purpose of efficient claims processing. Each code contains a description, and the codes are used primarily for billing purposes. The codes describe the following:

- DME devices, accessories, supplies, and repairs; prosthetics; orthotics; and medical and surgical supplies
- Medications
- Provider services

- Temporary Medicare codes (e.g., Q codes)
- Other items and services (e.g., ambulance services)

 NOTE:

DMEPOS dealers report HCPCS level II codes to identify equipment reported on claims submitted to private or public health insurers.

HCPCS is *not* a reimbursement methodology or payment system; it is important to understand that just because codes exist for certain products or services, coverage (e.g., payment) is not guaranteed. The HCPCS level II coding system

- Ensures uniform reporting of medical products or services on claims
- Has code descriptors that identify similar products or services (instead of specific products or brand/trade names)
- Is not a reimbursement methodology for making coverage or payment determinations (Each payer makes determinations on coverage and payment outside this coding process.)

Responsibility for HCPCS Level II Codes

HCPCS level II codes are developed and maintained by the *CMS HCPCS Workgroup*, which is comprised of representatives of the major components of CMS, Medicaid state agencies, and the Pricing, Data Analysis and Coding (PDAC). HCPCS level II codes are revised annually, and the revised codes are implemented each January. (The revision involves adding and deleting codes and revising code descriptors.)

HCPCS level II codes do not carry the copyright of a private organization; they are in the public domain, which allows many publishers to print annual coding manuals. Each publisher may elect to color-code the print or pages, include supplemental explanatory material, or provide reimbursement information from the *Medicare Benefit Policy Manual* for Part B or the *Medicare National Coverage Determinations Manual*. The ***Medicare Benefit Policy Manual*** provides direction about services and procedures to be reimbursed by the MAC. The ***Medicare National Coverage Determinations Manual*** indicates whether a service is covered or excluded under the Medicare program.

Some publishers include the following HCPCS level II references in their version of the coding manual:

- General instructions or guidelines for each section
- Appendix that summarizes additions, deletions, and terminology revisions in level II codes
- Separate tables of drugs or deleted codes
- Symbols to identify codes excluded from Medicare coverage
- Codes for which payment is left to the discretion of the responsible MAC
- Codes with special coverage instructions
- Current HCPCS level II modifiers

CMS has stated that it is not responsible for any errors that might occur in or from the use of these private printings of HCPCS level II codes.

Types of HCPCS Level II Codes

HCPCS level II codes are organized according to type depending on the purpose of the codes and the entity responsible for establishing and maintaining them. The four types are as follows:

- Permanent national codes
- Miscellaneous codes
- Temporary codes
- HCPCS level II modifiers

NOTE:

HCPCS level II previously included dental codes (D codes), which are copyrighted by the American Dental Association. Effective 2012, purchase of a separate *Current Dental Terminology* (CDT) coding manual is usually required to assign dental codes.

Permanent National Codes

HCPCS level II permanent national codes are maintained by the CMS HCPCS Workgroup, which unanimously makes decisions about additions, revisions, and deletions. Because HCPCS level II is a national coding system, none of the parties, including CMS, can make unilateral decisions regarding permanent national codes, which are intended for use by all private and public health insurers.

Miscellaneous Codes

HCPCS level II miscellaneous codes include *miscellaneous/not otherwise classified* codes that are reported when a DMEPOS dealer submits a claim for a product or service for which there is no existing HCPCS level II code. Miscellaneous codes allow DMEPOS dealers to submit a claim for a product or service as soon as it is approved by the Food and Drug Administration (FDA) even though there is no code that describes the product or service. The use of miscellaneous codes also helps avoid the inefficiency of assigning codes for items or services that are rarely furnished or for which MACs expect to receive few claims.

Claims that contain miscellaneous codes are manually reviewed by the payer, and the following must be provided for use in the review process:

- Complete description of product or service
- Pricing information for product or service
- Documentation to explain why the item or service is needed by the beneficiary

Before reporting a miscellaneous code on a claim, a DMEPOS dealer should check with the payer to determine if a specific code has been identified for use (instead of a miscellaneous code).

Temporary Codes

HCPCS level II temporary codes (Table 8-1) are maintained by the CMS and other members of the CMS HCPCS Workgroup, independent of permanent level II codes. Permanent national codes are updated once a year on January 1, but temporary codes allow payers the flexibility to establish codes on a quarterly basis throughout the year. Such codes are needed before the next January 1 annual update. Approximately 35 percent of the HCPCS level II codes are temporary codes. Certain sections of the HCPCS level II codes were set aside to allow CMS HCPCS Workgroup members to develop temporary codes, and decisions regarding the number and type of temporary codes and the way they are used are made independently by each CMS HCPCS Workgroup member. Temporary codes serve the purpose of meeting short time frame operational needs of a particular payer.

Although the CMS HCPCS Workgroup may decide to replace temporary codes with permanent codes, if permanent codes are not established, the temporary codes remain "temporary" indefinitely.

 NOTE:

- Decisions regarding temporary codes are made by an internal CMS HCPCS Workgroup, and other payers may also use these codes.
- Whenever a permanent code is established by the CMS HCPCS Workgroup to replace a temporary code, the temporary code is deleted and cross-referenced to the new permanent code.

HCPCS Level II Modifiers

HCPCS level II modifiers are attached to any HCPCS level I (CPT) or II (national) code to provide additional information regarding the product or service reported. Modifiers supplement the information provided by an HCPCS code descriptor to identify specific circumstances that may apply to an item or a service. HCPCS level II

TABLE 8-1 Categories of HCPCS Level II Temporary Codes

Category	Descriptions
C codes	• Reported to Medicare administrative contractors (MACs) for hospital outpatient department procedures and services, including device categories, new technology procedures, and drugs, biologicals, and radiopharmaceuticals that do not have other HCPCS code assignments, which are provided exclusively for Outpatient Prospective Payment System (OPPS) purposes.
G codes	• Identify professional and outpatient health care procedures and services that do not have codes identified in CPT. • G codes can be reported to all payers.
H codes	• Reported to state Medicaid agencies that are mandated by state law to establish separate codes for identifying mental health services (e.g., alcohol and drug treatment services).
K codes	• Reported to MACs when existing permanent national codes do not include codes needed to implement a medical review coverage policy.
Q codes	• Identify services that would not ordinarily be assigned a CPT code (e.g., drugs, biologicals, and other types of medical equipment or services). • Q codes can be reported to all payers.
S codes	• Used by private payers when no HCPCS level II codes exist to report drugs, services, and supplies, but codes are needed to implement private payer policies and programs for claims processing. • S codes are reported to BCBS, Medicaid, and private third-party payers.
T codes	• Reported to state Medicaid agencies when no HCPCS level II permanent codes exist, but codes are needed to administer the Medicaid program. • T codes are not reported to Medicare, but they can be reported to private third-party payers.

modifiers contain alpha or alphanumeric characters (Figure 8-1) (unlike CPT modifiers, which contain numeric characters only, as covered in Chapter 9). (Modifiers are located in an appendix of the HCPCS level II coding manual and the CPT coding manual.)

HCPCS Level II Modifiers

AA	Anesthesia services performed personally by anesthesiologist
AD	Medical supervision by a physician: more than 4 concurrent anesthesia procedures
AE	Registered dietician
AF	Specialty physician
AG	Primary physician
AH	Clinical psychologist

Permission to reprint granted by Optum360.

FIGURE 8-1 Sample listing of HCPCS level II modifiers

 NOTE:

Because modifiers are attached to HCPCS level II codes, chapter content about modifiers precedes content about the assignment of HCPCS level II codes.

EXAMPLE: A clinical psychologist provides 45 minutes of group psychotherapy in a partial hospitalization setting. Report G0410-AH.

Coding Tip

- HCPCS level II alpha and alphanumeric modifiers may also be added to CPT codes to further define the procedure or service reported (e.g., 69436-RT, tympanostomy, right ear).
- Refer to the HCPCS level II and CPT coding manuals for a comprehensive list of modifiers.
- Encoder software often contains guidance regarding selection of modifiers. For example, www.EncoderPro.com contains a clickable Ⓜ icon that displays a list of applicable modifiers for a code.

General Guidelines for Modifier Use

Not all HCPCS level I and II codes require modifiers. The CMS has clarified the use of modifiers when codes are reported for outpatient hospital services. (These rules also apply to the use of modifiers when reporting codes for physician services. Modifiers for physician services that differ from those used to report outpatient hospital services are clarified here.)

- Do not add a modifier to a code when its description indicates multiple occurrences, such as:
  - Two or more lesions
  - Multiple extremities
  - Different body parts

EXAMPLE: 11600 Excision malignant lesion, trunks, arms, or legs; excised diameter 0.5 cm or less.

- Modifiers -GN, -GO, and -GP are added to codes reported for an outpatient plan of care.
  - Speech language therapy (-GN)
  - Occupational therapy (-GO)
  - Physical therapy (-GP)
- The following modifiers are added to codes reported for hospital outpatient surgical procedures *from the CPT Surgery section and certain codes from the CPT Medicine section (e.g., cardiac catheterization) only*:
  - Modifier -50 (Bilateral procedure)
  - Modifier -73 (Discontinued outpatient hospital/ambulatory surgery center (ASC) procedure prior to the administration of anesthesia)
  - Modifier -74 (Discontinued outpatient hospital/ambulatory surgery center (ASC) procedure after administration of anesthesia)

Coding Tip

- For physician services, the following modifiers are added to codes reported for Surgery and Medicine procedures:
  - -50 (Bilateral procedure)
  - -52 (Reduced services)
  - -53 (Discontinued procedure)

- Modifiers are added to codes reported for procedures and services when they
  - Add more information regarding the anatomical site of the procedure

EXAMPLE: Cataract surgery on the right or left eye. Add modifier -RT (right side) or -LT (left side) to the CPT code reported for cataract surgery. (Modifiers -LT and -RT are used to identify procedures performed on the left or right side of the body, respectively.)

  - Help to eliminate duplicate billing

EXAMPLE: Add modifier -76 (Repeat Procedure or Service by Same Physician or Other Qualified Health Care Professional) to the reported code when the same procedure is performed more than once by the same physician.

  - Help to eliminate unbundling

EXAMPLE: When codes Q0081 (Infusion therapy, using other than chemotherapeutic drugs, per visit) and 36000 (Introduction of needle or intracatheter, vein) are reported on the same claim, the payer will deny payment for one of the codes because they are duplicate services. Adding modifier -59 (distinct procedural service) to code 36000, *if that procedure was performed for a reason other than as part of the IV infusion*, ensures appropriate processing of the claim and reimbursement for both procedures.

- Report modifiers on the hard copy UB-04 (CMS-1450) in Form Locator 44 (next to Form Locators where HCPCS codes are entered). (There is space for two modifiers on each hard copy UB-04.) For electronic claims, the UB-04 flat file allows entry of modifiers as record type 61, field numbers 6 and 7. (There is space for two modifiers, one in field 6 and one in field 7.)

EXAMPLE: Modifier LT (left side) is reported as LT in form locator 44 of the UB-04.

42 REV. CD.	43 DESCRIPTION	44 HCPCS / RATE / HIPPS CODE	45 SERV. DATE	46 SERV. UNITS	47 TOTAL CHARGES	48 NON-COVERED CHARGES	49
0360	BREAST RECONSTRUCTION DIEP FLAP	S2068 LT	0505YY	1	477500		

Courtesy of the Centers for Medicare and Medicaid Services, www.cms.gov; claim data created by author.

- Report modifier(s) in Block 24D of the CMS-1500 claim, spacing once after the CPT or HCPCS level II code. (Space once between modifiers when multiple modifiers are added to the same code.)
- Do not report the dash that precedes a modifier.

EXAMPLE: Modifier -AH (clinical psychologist) is reported as AH in form locator 24D of the CMS-1500.

24.	A DATE(S) OF SERVICE						B Place of Service	C Type of Service	D PROCEDURES, SERVICES, OR SUPPLIES (Explain Unusual Circumstances) CPT/HCPCS MODIFIER	E DIAGNOSIS POINTER	F $ CHARGES	G DAYS OR UNITS	H EPSDT Family Plan	I EMG	J COB	K RESERVED FOR LOCAL USE
	From MM	DD	YY	To MM	DD	YY										
1									G0410 AH							

Courtesy of the Centers for Medicare & Medicaid Services, www.cms.gov; claim data created by author.

- When multiple modifiers are added to a code, the most specific modifier is listed first. For example, the following HCPCS level II modifiers are added (instead of modifier -LT or -RT):
  - -E1 through -E4 (indicate upper/lower and laterality of eyelids)
  - -FA and -F1 through -F9 (indicate hand digits and laterality, such as -FA for *left hand, thumb*)
  - -LC (left circumflex coronary artery)
  - -LD (left anterior descending coronary artery)
  - -RC (right coronary artery)
  - -TA and -T1 through -T9 (indicate feet digits and laterality, such as -T1 for *left foot, 2nd digit*)

Modifiers Added to Surgical Procedures

Add modifier -50 (Bilateral procedure) to codes for procedures that are performed on both sides of a paired organ or body part during the same operative session (and when the code description does *not* include *bilateral* terminology).

> **EXAMPLE:** Patient underwent correction of hallus valgus (bunion), right and left feet. Since this procedure was performed bilaterally, report 28292-50. (*Do not report 28292-RT and 28292-LT.*)

The following rules clarify the use of modifier -50:

- Do not add modifiers -RT and -LT to a code when modifier -50 is added to that code.
- Add modifier -50 to surgical procedures only (CPT Surgery section codes, 10004–69990).
- Modifier -50 is *not* added to surgical procedure codes when the code description contains the following terminology:
  - Bilateral
  - Unilateral or bilateral
- Modifier -LT or -RT is added to the code that identifies a procedure performed on just one of two paired organs (e.g., ears, eyes, nostrils, kidneys, lungs, or ovaries).

> **EXAMPLE:** Code 69100 is eligible for modifier -50 if the procedure is performed on both ears. However, if a procedure (e.g., biopsy) is performed on the right or left ear, report code 69100-RT or 69100-LT.

 Coding Tip

- Do not add modifier -50 to codes reported for Evaluation and Management, Anesthesia, Radiology, Pathology and Laboratory, or Medicine procedures and services. Do not add modifier -50 to HCPCS level II codes.
- Modifier -LT or -RT is added to the code for a procedure that is performed on just one side.
- Do not add directional modifiers (e.g., -50, -LT, -RT, -) to CPT codes when a description includes paired and nonpaired body parts or organs, such as "12031, Repair, intermediate, wounds of scalp, axillae, trunk and/or extremities (excluding hands and feet); 2.5 cm or less."

- Modifiers for discontinued procedures for outpatient hospital/ambulatory surgery center (ASC) (-73 and -74) are added to diagnostic and surgical procedure codes so hospitals can be reimbursed for expenses incurred during the preparation of a patient for surgery, which includes scheduling a room for performing the procedure.
  - Add modifier -73 when an outpatient hospital/ambulatory surgery center (ASC) diagnostic or surgical procedure is terminated after a patient has been prepared for surgery (including sedation when provided) and taken to the room where the procedure is to be performed, but before the administration of anesthesia (e.g., local, regional block, or general anesthesia).
  - Add modifier -74 when an outpatient hospital/ambulatory surgery center (ASC) procedure is terminated after the administration of anesthesia (e.g., local, regional block, or general anesthesia) or after the procedure was started (incision made, intubation started, or scope inserted).
  - Do *not* add modifier -73 or -74 to a code for the *elective* cancellation of a procedure.

Coding Tip

- Add modifiers -73 and -74 to codes reported from the CPT Surgery section and to certain codes reported from the CPT Medicine section (e.g., cardiac catheterization). Do not add modifiers -73 and -74 to codes reported for CPT Evaluation and Management, Anesthesia, Radiology, or Pathology and Laboratory procedures and services.

- When services are discontinued in the physician's office, report modifier -52 (reduced services) or -53 (discontinued procedure) (instead of modifier -73 or -74).

- Add modifier -76 to the code for a procedure or service that was repeated during a separate operative session on the same day by the same physician. Add modifier -77 to the code for a procedure or service that was repeated during a separate operative session on the same day by another physician. The following rules apply to adding modifier -76 or -77:
  - Adding modifier -76 or -77 is based on whether the physician performing the procedure is the same or different.
  - The repeated procedure must be the same as the originally performed procedure. (On the claim, the code for the original procedure is entered for the original date of the procedure. Then it is entered again, with the appropriate modifier, for the date the procedure was repeated.)

Modifiers Added to Radiology Services

The following modifiers are added to codes for CPT Radiology services:

- -52 (reduced services)
- -59 (distinct procedural service)

 NOTE:

The following HCPCS level II modifiers define specific subsets of the -59 CPT modifier:

- XE (Separate encounter, a service that is distinct because it occurred during a separate encounter)
- XS (Separate structure, a service that is distinct because it was performed on a separate organ/structure)
- XP (Separate practitioner, a service that is distinct because it was performed by a different practitioner)
- XU (Unusual non-overlapping service, the use of a service that is distinct because it does not overlap usual components of the main service)

CMS will continue to recognize the -59 modifier; however, CPT instructions state that modifier -59 should not be used when a more descriptive modifier (e.g., -XE) is available.

- -76 (repeat procedure by same physician or other qualified health care professional)
- -77 (repeat procedure by another physician or other qualified health care professional)
- HCPCS level II modifiers

When a radiology procedure is canceled, report a code to describe the extent of the procedure performed. If no code exists for what was done, report the intended code and add modifier -52.

EXAMPLE: The physician orders a chest x-ray, two views (code 71046). Just the frontal view is performed because the patient started feeling faint and needed to lie down. Report code 71045 (Radiologic examination, chest; single view).

Reporting HCPCS Level II Modifiers

HCPCS level II modifiers are added to HCPCS level I (CPT) and level II (national) codes. When more than one HCPCS level II modifier applies, report the code on more than one line of the UB-04 claim, with the appropriate HCPCS level II modifier.

EXAMPLE: Patient underwent simple drainage of a finger abscess, left-hand thumb and second finger (code 26010). On the UB-04, report the code on two lines as follows:

- 26010 FA
- 26010 F1

 NOTE:

On the CMS-1500, report the code and multiple modifiers on just one line of Block 24D, such as 26010 FA F1.

Do not add modifiers -LT or -RT to

- Allergy and clinical immunology codes
- Ambulance codes
- Codes that do not specify a limb or paired organ
- Drug administration codes (J and Q codes)
- DME (HCPCS level II E codes) that do not specify a limb
- Evaluation and management codes
- Immunization and vaccines/toxoid codes
- Medicine codes that contain *right* or *left* in the code description
- Orthotics/prosthetics codes that do not specify a limb
- Osteopathic and chiropractic manipulation codes
- Pathology and laboratory codes
- Physical medicine and rehabilitation codes
- Supply codes
- Temporary procedure and service codes (G codes) that do not specify a limb

Exercise 8.2 – HCPCS Level II Codes

Instructions: Complete each statement.

1. HCPCS level II codes are developed and maintained by the _____.
2. Services and procedures that are reimbursed by a MAC can be found in the _____.
3. Whether a service is covered or excluded under the Medicare program can be found in the _____.
4. HCPCS level II _____ are attached to any HCPCS level I (CPT) or II (national) code to provide additional information regarding the product or service reported.
5. HCPCS level II and CPT codes and multiple modifiers are reported on the same line of Block 24D on the _____ claim, such as 26010 FA F1.
6. HCPCS level II miscellaneous codes are reported when a(n) _____ submits a claim for a product or service for which there is no existing HCPCS level II code.
7. HCPCS level II temporary codes allow payers the flexibility to establish codes that are needed before the next _____ update.
8. Refer to Figure 8-1, and identify the modifier that is added to a code when a procedure is performed by a registered dietician: _____.

(continues)

Exercise 8.2 – *continued*

9. Modifier _____ is added to codes for procedures that are performed on both sides during the same operative session.

10. HCPCS level II _____ are added to HCPCS level I (CPT) and level II (national) codes.

Assigning HCPCS Level II Codes

Some services must be reported by assigning both a CPT and an HCPCS level II code. The most common scenario uses the CPT code for the administration of an infusion or injection and the HCPCS level II code to identify the medication. Most drugs have qualifying terms such as *dosage limits* that could alter the quantity reported (Figure 8-2).

- If a drug is administered in a 70-mg dose and the HCPCS level II code description states "per 50 mg," the quantity billed is 2.
- If just 15 mg of a drug were administered and the HCPCS level II code description stated "up to 20 mg," the quantity billed is 1.

 NOTE:

CMS developed HCPCS level II codes for Medicare, but commercial payers also adopted them.

Imagine how much money providers lose by reporting only the CPT code for injections. Unless the payer or insurance plan advises the provider that it does not pay separately for the medication injected, always report this combination of codes. It is possible that a particular service would be assigned a CPT code and a level II HCPCS code. Which one should you report? The answer is found in the instructions from the payer. Most commercial payers require the CPT code. Medicare gives HCPCS level II codes the highest priority if the CPT code is general and the HCPCS level II code is more specific.

Most supplies are included in the charge for the office visit or the procedure. CPT provides code 99070 for all supplies and materials exceeding those usually included in the primary service or procedure performed. However, this CPT code may be too general to ensure correct payment. If the office provides additional supplies when performing a service, the HCPCS level II codes may identify the supplies in sufficient detail to secure proper reimbursement.

Although CMS developed this system, some HCPCS level I and II services are not payable by Medicare. Medicare may also place qualifications or conditions on payment for some services. As an example, an electrocardiogram (ECG) is a covered service for a cardiac problem but is not covered when performed as part of a routine examination. Also, the payment for some services may be left to the discretion of the MAC. Two CMS

DRUGS ADMINISTERED OTHER THAN ORAL METHOD
J0475 Injection, baclofen, 10 mg
J0476 Injection, baclofen, 50 mcg for intrathecal trial
J0480 Injection, basiliximab, 20 mg
J0485 Injection, belatacept, 1 mg
J0490 Injection, belimumab, 10 mg
J0500 Injection, dicyclomine HCl, up to 20 mg
J0515 Injection, benztropine mesylate, per 1 mg
J0520 Injection, bethanechol chloride, Mytonachol or Urecholine, up to 5 mg

FIGURE 8-2 Sample listing of HCPCS level II J codes

publications assist MACs in correctly processing claims: the *Medicare National Coverage Determinations Manual* advises the MAC as to whether a service is covered or excluded under Medicare regulations, and the MCM directs the MAC to pay or reject a service, using a specific "remark" or explanation code.

There are more than 4,000 HCPCS level II codes, but you may find that no code exists for the procedure or service you need to report. Unlike CPT, HCPCS level II does not have a consistent method of establishing codes for reporting "unlisted procedure" services. If the MAC does not provide special instructions for reporting these services in HCPCS, report them with the proper "unlisted procedure" code from CPT. Remember to submit documentation explaining the procedure or service when using the "unlisted procedure" codes.

HCPCS Level II Index

Because of the wide variety of services and procedures described in HCPCS level II, the alphabetical index (Figure 8-3) is very helpful in finding the correct code. The various publishers of the reference may include an expanded index that lists "alcohol wipes" and "wipes," as well as "Ancef" and "cefazolin sodium," making the search for codes easier and faster. Some references also include a table of drugs (Figure 8-4) that lists J codes assigned to medications. Some publishers print brand names beneath each generic description, and others provide a special expanded index of the drug codes.

It is important never to code directly from the index and always to verify the code in the appropriate code section of the coding manual. You may want to review the HCPCS level II references from several publishers and select the one that best meets your needs and is easiest for you to use. If you have difficulty locating

Index
Abdomen
dressing holder/binder, A4461, A4463
pad, low profile, L1270
Abduction
control, each, L2624
rotation bar, foot, L3140-L3170
Ablation
ultrasound, C9734

FIGURE 8-3 Sample listing of HCPCS level II index entries

Drug Name	Unit Per	Route	Code
10% LMD	500 mL	IV	**J7100**
4-Factor Prothrombin Complex Concentrate	1 IU	IV	**C9132**
5% Dextrose and .45% Normal Saline	1000 mL	IV	**S5010**
5% Dextrose in Lactated Ringers	1000 mL	IV	**J7121**
5% Dextrose with Potassium Chloride	1000 mL	IV	**S5012**

FIGURE 8-4 Sample listing of HCPCS level II table of drugs

Contents

Introduction ix

    The HCPCS System ix

    HCPCS Levels of Codes ix

    Modifiers ix

    Why You Should Be Using HCPCS xiii

    How to Use HCPCS Level II xiv

    New, Changed, and Deleted Codes xiv

Transportation Services Including Ambulance 1

Medical and Surgical Supplies 3

    Miscellaneous Supplies 3

    Vascular Catheters 5

    Incontinence Appliances and Care Supplies 5

    External Urinary Supplies 6

    Ostomy Supplies 6

    Additional Miscellaneous Supplies 6

    Supplies for Oxygen and Related Respiratory Equipment 7

    Supplies for Other Durable Medical Equipment 8

    Supplies for Radiologic Procedures 8

    Supplies for End Stage Renal Disease 9

    Additional Ostomy Supplies 10

    Additional Incontinence Appliances/Supplies 11

    Supplies for Either Incontinence or Ostomy Appliances 11

    Diabetic Shoes, Fitting, and Modifications 11

    Dressings 12

Respiratory Durable Medical Equipment, Inexpensive and Routinely Purchased 13

Administrative, Miscellaneous and Investigational 16

    Supplies for Radiology Procedures 16

    Miscellaneous Service Component 16

    Enteral and Parenteral Therapy 17

    Enteral Formulae and Enteral Medical Supplies 17

    Parenteral Nutrition Solutions and Supplies 17

    Enteral and Parenteral Pumps 18

C Codes for Use only Under the Hospital OPPS 19

Durable Medical Equipment 20

    Canes 20

    Crutches 20

    Walkers 20

    Attachments 20

    Commodes 21

    Decubitus Care Equipment 21

    Heat/Cold Application 21

Courtesy of the Centers for Medicare & Medicaid Services, www.cms.gov.

FIGURE 8-5 Sample HCPCS level II coding manual table of contents

the service or procedure in the HCPCS level II index, review the table of contents (if available in your coding manual) to locate the code section (Figure 8-5). Or, page through the tabular list to familiarize yourself with the procedures and services classified in the coding manual. Read the code descriptions very carefully before selecting a code.

HCPCS Level II Code Sections

HCPCS level II code sections are identified by an alphabetical first character (e.g., *B* for *enteral and parenteral therapy* and *C* for *outpatient PPS*). Some code sections are logical, such as *R* for *radiology*, whereas others, such as *J* for *drugs*, appear to be arbitrarily assigned.

Transportation Services Including Ambulance (A0000–A0999)

The Transportation Services Including Ambulance section of HCPCS level II includes codes for ancillary transportation-related fees, ground and air ambulance, and nonemergency transportation (e.g., automobile, bus, taxi, and wheelchair van).

> **EXAMPLE:** A Medicaid patient received emergency transport from her home to the hospital emergency department in an ambulance that contained basic life support (BLS). Report code A0429-RH. (The origin was the patient's residence, and the destination was the hospital; therefore, modifier -RH is added to code A0429.)

Medical and Surgical Supplies (A4000–A8999)

The Medical and Surgical Supplies section of HCPCS level II includes codes for DME-related supplies, accessories, maintenance, and repair (to ensure proper functioning of DME); medical supplies and accessories; and surgical supplies and accessories.

> **EXAMPLE:** A 68-year-old patient who is undergoing treatment for unresected liver cancer was supplied with a refill kit for an implantable infusion pump. Report code A4220.

 NOTE:

Some supplies are included during the administration of an evaluation and management (E/M) service, and separate HCPCS level II codes are not assigned (e.g., sterile gauze). E/M services are assigned separate CPT codes, which is discussed in Chapter 10.

Administrative, Miscellaneous, and Investigational (A9000–A9999)

The Administrative, Miscellaneous, and Investigational section of HCPCS level II includes codes for miscellaneous supplies, supplies for radiological procedures, and miscellaneous service components.

> **EXAMPLE:** A 72-year-old patient was provided with artificial saliva, 30 milliliters. Report code A9155.

Enteral and Parenteral Therapy (B4000–B9999)

The Enteral and Parenteral Therapy section of HCPCS level II includes codes for enteral and parenteral infusion pumps, enteral and parenteral supplies, enteral formulae, and parenteral nutritional solutions.

> **EXAMPLE:** The patient was supplied with a fiber additive for enteral formula. Report code B4104.

CMS Hospital Outpatient Payment System (C1000–C9999)

The Hospital Outpatient Payment System section of HCPCS level II includes codes for biologicals, devices, and drugs eligible for transitional pass-through payments for hospitals, as well as items included in the new technology APCs under the OPPS. **Transitional pass-through payments** are temporary additional payments (over and above the OPPS payment) made for certain innovative medical devices, drugs, and biologicals provided to Medicare beneficiaries.

> **EXAMPLE:** Patient underwent insertion of a directional transluminal atherectomy catheter. Report code C1714.

Coding Tip

The OPPS requires hospitals and ambulatory surgery centers to report product-specific HCPCS level II "C codes" to obtain reimbursement for biologicals, devices, drugs, and other items associated with implantable device technologies. Reporting C codes in conjunction with CPT procedure codes greatly improves the quality of claims data Medicare uses to establish future APC payments. Outpatient coding edits (updated on a quarterly basis) identify C codes that should be billed with CPT procedure codes.

Applications are also submitted to CMS for "new" biologicals, devices, and drugs for consideration of "transitional pass-through payment status" and items for consideration of "new-technology APC designation." If certain criteria are met and CMS approves the "new" biologicals, devices, drugs, and items, C codes are assigned and published in program memorandums.

Durable Medical Equipment (E0100–E9999)

The Durable Medical Equipment section of HCPCS level II includes codes for equipment (e.g., artificial kidney machines, oxygen and related respiratory equipment, and pacemakers) and supplies (e.g., bath and toilet aids, commodes, cranes, crutches, hospital beds, and walkers).

> **EXAMPLE:** The patient was supplied with a pair of aluminum underarm crutches. Report code E0114.

Temporary Procedures/Professional Services (G0000–G9999)

The Temporary Procedures/Professional Services section of HCPCS level II includes codes for professional health care procedures and services that either do not have codes identified in the CPT or require the reporting of G codes (instead of CPT codes).

> **EXAMPLE:** A patient became a Medicare beneficiary on March 1 and underwent an initial preventive physical examination (IPPE) and in-office electrocardiogram (ECG) on May 30. Report codes G0402 and G0403. (Make sure you report the appropriate ICD-10-CM Z code as the first-listed diagnosis.)

Behavioral Health and/or Substance Abuse Treatment Services (H0001–H9999)

The Behavioral Health and/or Substance Abuse Treatment Services section of HCPCS level II includes codes used by state Medicaid agencies mandated by state law to establish separate codes for identifying mental health services that include alcohol and drug treatment services.

> **EXAMPLE:** A patient underwent alcohol assessment prior to participating in psychotherapy. Report code H0001.

Drugs Other Than Chemotherapy Drugs (J0100–J8999)

The Drugs Other Than Chemotherapy Drugs section of HCPCS level II includes codes for drugs that ordinarily cannot be self-administered, chemotherapy drugs, immunosuppressive drugs, inhalation solutions, and other miscellaneous drugs and solutions.

> **EXAMPLE:** A female home health patient received an injection of 10 mcg of teriparatide (brand name Forteo) for treatment of osteoporosis. Report code J3110.

Chemotherapy Drugs (J9000–J9999)

The Chemotherapy Drugs section of HCPCS level II includes codes reported for the administration of chemotherapy.

> **EXAMPLE:** The patient was administered 5 milligrams of oral aprepitant. Report code J8501.

Temporary Codes Assigned to DME Regional Carriers (MACs) (K0000–K9999)

The Temporary Codes Assigned to Regional Carriers (MACs) section of HCPCS level II includes codes for durable medical equipment (DME), as established by DME MACs (formerly DMERCs), when permanent national codes do not include codes needed to implement a DME MAC medical review policy.

> **EXAMPLE:** The patient was supplied with a standard wheelchair. Report code K0001.

Orthotics (L0000–L4999)

The Orthotics section of HCPCS level II includes codes for orthopedic shoes, orthotic devices and procedures, and scoliosis equipment. **Orthotics** is the branch of medicine that deals with the design and fitting of orthopedic (relating to bone disorders) devices (e.g., braces). Several orthotic procedures subsections include "addition" codes, which means they are reported in addition to base codes from the same subsection or a previous subsection.

> **EXAMPLE:** Patient underwent a halo procedure during which the cervical halo was incorporated into a jacket vest. Patient also received a magnetic resonance image compatible system during the same encounter. Report codes L0810 and L0859.
>
> Because the description for code L0859 states "Addition to halo procedure, magnetic resonance image compatible system," it must be reported in addition to another HCPCS level II code, such as L0810.

Prosthetics (L5000–L9999)

The Prosthetics section of HCPCS level II includes codes for prosthetic devices, implants, and procedures. **Prosthetics** is the branch of medicine that deals with the design, production, and use of artificial body parts (e.g., artificial limbs). Several prosthetic procedures subsections include "addition" codes, meaning that they are reported in addition to base codes from the same subsection or from a previous subsection.

> **EXAMPLE:** The patient received a below-knee PTB type socket, nonalignable system, pylon, no cover, SACH (solid ankle cushion heel) foot, plaster socket, direct-formed. The patient also received a test socket, below knee, during the same encounter. Report codes L5500 and L5620.
>
> Because the description for code L5620 states "Addition to lower extremity, test socket, below knee," it must be reported in addition to another HCPCS level II code, such as L5500.

Other Medical Services (M0000–M1999)

The Other Medical Services section of HCPCS level II includes codes for cellular therapy, fabric wrapping of an abdominal aneurysm, intragastric hypothermia, intravenous (IV) chelation therapy, and prolotherapy.

- *Cellular therapy* involves injecting processed tissue from animal embryos, fetuses, or organs for the purpose of rejuvenating diseased tissue; its therapeutic effect has not been established.
- *Fabric wrapping of an abdominal aneurysm* is performed to reinforce an aneurysm with a fabric-wrapped stent (a small, flexible mesh tube used to "patch" the blood vessel). This procedure has largely been replaced with other more effective treatment methods.
- *Intragastric hypothermia* is a form of gastric freezing for the treatment of chronic peptic ulcer disease; CMS considers this procedure obsolete.
- *IV chelation therapy* is also called chemical endarterectomy, and it is performed to treat arteriosclerosis; it is considered experimental in the United States.
- *Prolotherapy* is a form of nonsurgical ligament reconstruction as a treatment for chronic pain; its therapeutic effect has not yet been established.

> **EXAMPLE:** The patient received cellular therapy services. Report code M0075.

Laboratory Services (P0000–P9999)

The Laboratory Services section of HCPCS level II includes codes for chemistry, microbiology, and toxicology tests; screening Papanicolaou smears; and miscellaneous blood tests.

> **EXAMPLE:** The patient underwent screening cervical Papanicolaou smear, which was interpreted by the physician. Report code P3001.

Temporary Codes Assigned by CMS (Q0035–Q9999)

The Temporary Codes Assigned by CMS section of HCPCS level II are reported until permanent codes are available. Effective 2001, casting supplies were removed from the practice expenses for all HCPCS codes, including CPT codes for fracture management, casts, and splints. This means that when CPT codes are reported for services that include the provision of a cast or splint, codes Q4001–Q4051 are also reported to provide reimbursement to providers for the supplies used in creating casts.

> **EXAMPLE:** A Medicare patient received brachytherapy services, which included the administration of radioisotopes. Report code Q3001.
>
>   CPT code 79900 was deleted in 2005, and HCPCS level II code Q3001 was created to report the administration of radioisotopes during brachytherapy. Report as the first-listed procedure the appropriate CPT brachytherapy code from 77316–77318 and/or 77750–77799.

Diagnostic Radiology Services (R0000–R9999)

The Diagnostic Radiology Service section of HCPCS level II includes codes that are reported for the transportation of portable x-ray and/or EKG equipment, including testing.

> **EXAMPLE:** The provider transported portable EKG equipment to the nursing facility for the purpose of testing his patients. Report code R0076.
>
>   When more than one patient undergoes EKG testing, report code R0076, but prorate the single allowed transportation cost among all patients. For example, if the single allowed transportation cost is $50 and five patients underwent EKG testing, the prorated cost for each patient is $10.

Temporary National Codes Established by Private Payers (S0000–S9999)

The Temporary National Codes (Non-Medicare) section of HCPCS level II includes codes reported to non-Medicare third-party payers (e.g., Blue Cross/Blue Shield, commercial payers, and Medicaid) for drugs, services, and supplies that are not classified in CPT or another section of HCPCS level II.

> **EXAMPLE:** The patient was administered butorphanol tartrate (trade name Stadol NS), nasal spray, 25 mg. Report code S0012.

Temporary Codes Established by Medicaid (T1000–T9999)

The Temporary Codes Established by Medicaid section of HCPCS level II includes codes that are reported to Medicaid state agencies for behavioral health, home health, hospice, long-term care, nursing, and other services; substance abuse treatment; supplies; and certain training-related procedures that are not classified in CPT or another section of HCPCS level II.

> **EXAMPLE:** The Medicaid patient required sign language services for 30 minutes. Report codes T1013 and T1013 (because the description of code T1013 states "per 15 minutes"). (On the CMS-1500 or UB-04 claim, T1013 is reported once and 2 is entered in the units column.)

Vision Services (V0000–V2999)

The Vision Services section of HCPCS level II includes codes for vision-related supplies (e.g., contact lenses, intraocular lenses, lenses, and spectacles).

> **EXAMPLE:** The patient was supplied with a custom plastic prosthetic eye. Report code V2623.

Hearing Services (V5000–V5999)

The Hearing Services section of HCPCS level II includes codes that describe hearing tests and related supplies and equipment, speech-language pathology screenings, and repair of augmentative communicative systems.

> **EXAMPLE:** The audiologist dispenses a monaural, in-the-ear (ITE) hearing aid for a patient diagnosed with sensorineural hearing loss, combined types. Report codes V5050 and V5241.

Exercise 8.3 – Assigning HCPCS Level II Codes

Instructions: Complete each statement.

1. Some services must be reported by assigning both a CPT and an HCPCS level II code; the most common scenario uses a CPT code for administration of a(n) _____ and the HCPCS level II code to identify the _____.

2. If a drug is administered in a 100-mg dose and the HCPCS level II code description states "per 50 mg," the quantity billed is _____.

3. If just 10 mg of a drug were administered and the HCPCS level II code description stated "up to 15 mg," the quantity billed is _____.

4. The charge for office visit or procedure usually includes _____ used to perform the procedure or service.

5. Although CMS developed this system, some HCPCS level I and II services are not payable by _____.

6. Some HCPCS level II coding manuals include a table of drugs that lists J codes assigned to _____.

7. If you have difficulty locating the service or procedure in the HCPCS level II index, review the _____ to locate the code section and read the code descriptions very carefully before selecting a code.

8. Codes sections in HCPCS level II are identified by a(n) _____.

9. CMS developed the level II codes for Medicare, but _____ also adopted them.

10. If no code exists for a procedure or service, report the proper "unlisted procedure" code from _____ and submit documentation explaining the procedure or service.

Determining Payer Responsibility

The specific HCPCS level II code determines whether the claim is sent to the primary MAC that processes provider claims or the DME MAC that processes DMEPOS dealer claims. Providers and DMEPOS dealers obtain annual lists of valid HCPCS level II codes, which include billing instructions for services.

NOTE:

The emphasis on keeping seniors in their own homes led to a rapid expansion in DME services and dealers, and many of the larger DME companies operated in several states and sent their claims to multiple Medicare administrator contractors (MACs). Unfortunately, a few DME companies formed for the sole purpose of collecting as much money as possible from the Medicare program and then closed down. When CMS began to investigate and pursue fraudulent claims, it became apparent that DME billings were out of control. CMS decided to have all DME claims processed by only four DME MACs to reduce fraudulent claims.

When the doctor treats a Medicare patient for a broken ankle and supplies the patient with crutches, two claims are generated. The claim for the fracture care, or professional service, is sent to the primary MAC; the claim for the crutches is sent to the DME MAC. The physician must register with both, review billing rules, comply with claims instructions, and forward claims correctly to secure payment for both services. If the physician is not registered with the DME MAC to provide medical equipment and supplies, the patient is given a prescription for crutches to take to a local DMEPOS dealer.

Some services, such as cosmetic procedures, are excluded as Medicare benefits by law and will not be covered by either MAC. Splints and casts for traumatic injuries have CPT numbers that are used to report these supplies or services to the primary MAC. Because the review procedure for adding new codes to level II is a much shorter process, new medical and surgical services may first be assigned a level II code and then incorporated into CPT at a later date.

Patient Record Documentation

The patient record includes documentation that justifies the medical necessity of procedures, services, and supplies coded and reported on an insurance claim. This means that the diagnoses reported on the claim must justify diagnostic and therapeutic procedures or services provided. The patient's record should include documentation of the following:

- Patient history, including review of systems
- Physical examination, including impression
- Diagnostic test results, including analysis of findings
- Diagnoses, including duration (e.g., acute or chronic) and comorbidities that impact care
- Patient's prognosis, including potential for rehabilitation

When DMEPOS items are reported on a claim, the DMEPOS dealer must keep the following documents on file:

- Provider order for DMEPOS item, signed and dated
- Signed advance beneficiary notice if medical necessity for an item cannot be established

When the provider reports DMEPOS items on a claim, the provider must keep the following documents on file:

- Diagnosis establishing medical necessity for the item
- Clinical notes that justify the DMEPOS item ordered
- Provider order for DMEPOS item, signed and dated
- Signed advance beneficiary notice if medical necessity for an item cannot be established

NOTE:

An **advance beneficiary notice (ABN)** is a waiver signed by the patient acknowledging that because medical necessity for a procedure, service, or supply cannot be established (e.g., due to nature of patient's condition, injury, or illness), the patient accepts responsibility for reimbursing the provider or DMEPOS dealer for costs associated with the procedure, service, or supply.

U.S. DEPARTMENT OF HEALTH & HUMAN SERVICES
CENTERS FOR MEDICARE & MEDICAID SERVICES

CERTIFICATE OF MEDICAL NECESSITY

FORM APPROVED
OMB NO. 0938-0679

DMERC 01.02A

HOSPITAL BEDS

SECTION A   Certification Type/Date: INITIAL __/__/__   REVISED __/__/__

PATIENT NAME, ADDRESS, TELEPHONE and HIC NUMBER	SUPPLIER NAME, ADDRESS, TELEPHONE and NSC NUMBER
(__ __) ___ ___-___ HICN _____	(__ __) ___ ___-___ NSC # _____

| PLACE OF SERVICE _____
 NAME and ADDRESS of FACILITY if applicable (See reverse | HCPCS CODE
 _____
 _____
 _____ | PT DOB __/__/__; Sex ___ (M/F); HT.___(in.); WT.___(lbs.)

 PHYSICIAN NAME, ADDRESS (Printed or Typed)

 PHYSICIAN'S UPIN: _____
 PHYSICIAN'S TELEPHONE #: (__ __) ___ ___-___ |

SECTION B   Information in this Section May Not Be Completed by the Supplier of the Items/Supplies.

EST. LENGTH OF NEED (# OF MONTHS): _____ 1-99 (99=LIFETIME)   DIAGNOSIS CODES (ICD-9): _____ _____ _____ _____

ANSWERS	ANSWER QUESTIONS 1, AND 3-7 FOR HOSPITAL BEDS (Circle **Y** for Yes, **N** for No, or **D** for Does Not Apply)
	QUESTION 2 RESERVED FOR OTHER OR FUTURE USE.
Y N D	1. Does the patient require positioning of the body in ways not feasible with an ordinary bed due to a medical condition which is expected to last at least one month?
Y N D	3. Does the patient require, for the alleviation of pain, positioning of the body in ways not feasible with an ordinary bed?
Y N D	4. Does the patient require the head of the bed to be elevated more than 30 degrees most of the time due to congestive heart failure, chronic pulmonary disease, or aspiration?
Y N D	5. Does the patient require traction which can only be attached to a hospital bed?
Y N D	6. Does the patient require a bed height different than a fixed height hospital bed to permit transfers to chair, wheelchair, or standing position?
Y N D	7. Does the patient require frequent changes in body position and/or have an immediate need for a change in body position?

NAME OF PERSON ANSWERING SECTION B QUESTIONS, IF OTHER THAN PHYSICIAN (Please Print):
NAME: _____   TITLE: _____   EMPLOYER: _____

SECTION C   Narrative Description Of Equipment And Cost

(1) Narrative description of all items, accessories and options ordered; (2) Supplier's charge; and (3) Medicare Fee Schedule Allowance for each item, accessory, and option. (See Instructions On Back)

SECTION D   Physician Attestation and Signature/Date

I certify that I am the physician identified in Section A of this form. I have received Sections A, B and C of the Certificate of Medical Necessity (including charges for items ordered). Any statement on my letterhead attached hereto, has been reviewed and signed by me. I certify that the medical necessity information in Section B is true, accurate and complete, to the best of my knowledge, and I understand that any falsification, omission, or concealment of material fact in that section may subject me to civil or criminal liability.
PHYSICIAN'S SIGNATURE _____   DATE __/__/__   (SIGNATURE AND DATE STAMPS ARE NOT ACCEPTABLE)

CMS-841 (04/96)

FIGURE 8-6 Sample certificate of medical necessity required of DMEPOS dealer

DMEPOS Claims

For certain items or services reported on a claim submitted to the DME MAC, the DMEPOS dealer must receive a signed certificate of medical necessity (CMN) (Figure 8-6) from the treating physician before submitting a claim to Medicare. A copied, electronic, faxed, or original certificate of medical necessity (CMN) must be maintained by the DMEPOS dealer and must be available to the DME MAC on request. The **certificate of medical necessity (CMN)** is a prescription for DME, services, and supplies.

DME MAC medical review policies include **local coverage determinations (LCDs)** and **national coverage determinations (NCDs)**, both of which define coverage criteria, payment rules, and documentation required as applied to DMEPOS claims processed by DME MACs for frequently ordered DMEPOS equipment, services, and supplies. (National policies are included in the *Medicare Benefit Policy Manual, Medicare Program Integrity Manual,* and *Medicare National Coverage Determinations Manual.*) If DMEPOS equipment, services, or supplies do not have medical review policies established for coverage, the general coverage criteria applies. The DMEPOS equipment, services, or supplies must

- Fall within a benefit category
- Not be excluded by statute or by national CMS policy
- Be reasonable and necessary to diagnose and/or treat an illness or injury or to improve the functioning of a malformed body

The DME MACs are required to follow national CMS policy when it exists; when there is no national CMS policy on a subject, DME MACs have the authority and responsibility to establish local policies. Because many DMEPOS dealers operate nationally, the CMS requires that medical review policies published by the DME MACs to be identical in all four regions.

Exercise 8.4 – Determining Payer Responsibility

Instructions: Complete each statement below.

1. The specific _____ code determines whether the claim is sent to the primary MAC that processes provider claims or the DME MAC that processes DMEPOS dealer claims.
2. Providers and DMEPOS dealers obtain annual lists of valid HCPCS level II codes, which include _____ instructions for services.
3. CMS decided to have all DME claims processed by only four DME MACs to reduce _____ claims.
4. When a physician treats a Medicare patient for a fractured femur and supplies the patient with crutches, two claims are generated. The physician's claim for the fracture care is sent to the _____, and the claim for the crutches is sent to the _____.
5. For certain items or services reported on a claim submitted to the DME MAC, the DMEPOS dealer must receive a signed _____.

Summary

Three levels of codes are associated with HCPCS, commonly referred to as HCPCS level I, II, and III codes. HCPCS level I includes the five-digit Current Procedural Terminology (CPT) codes developed and published by the American Medical Association (AMA). HCPCS level II codes (or HCPCS national codes) were created in 1983 to describe common medical services and supplies not classified in CPT. (Effective December 31, 2003, HCPCS level III local codes were no longer required; however, some third-party payers continue to use them.)

The HCPCS level II coding system classifies similar medical products and services for the purpose of efficient claims processing. Each code contains a description, and the codes are used primarily for billing purposes. The codes describe DME devices, accessories, supplies, and repairs; prosthetics; orthotics; medical and surgical supplies; medications; provider services; temporary Medicare codes (e.g., Q codes); and other items and services (e.g., ambulance services). Some services must be reported by assigning both a CPT and an HCPCS level II code. The most common scenario uses the CPT code for the administration of an injection and the HCPCS code to identify the medication.

The specific HCPCS level II code determines whether the claim is sent to the primary Medicare administrative contractor (MAC) that processes provider claims or the DME MAC that processes DMEPOS dealer claims. Providers and DMEPOS dealers obtain annual lists of valid level II codes, which include billing instructions for services.

Internet Links

CMS Online Manual System: Go to *www.cms.gov* and click on the Regulations & Guidance link, then click on the Manuals link below the Guidance heading.

HCPCS coding system: Go to *www.cms.gov* and click on the Medicare link, then scroll down to the Coding heading, and click on the HCPCS – General Information link.

Noridian Medicare Durable Medical Equipment: Go to *www.noridianmedicare.com* and click on the Durable Medical Equipment, Orthotics and Supplies link below the Jurisdiction A or Jurisdiction D heading.

Review

Multiple Choice

Instructions: Circle the most appropriate response.

1. Which would be assigned to report DMEPOS on insurance claims?
   a. CPT codes
   b. HCPCS level I codes
   c. HCPCS level II codes
   d. HCPCS level III codes

2. Which provides suppliers and manufacturers with assistance in determining HCPCS codes to be reported?
   a. CMS
   b. DME MAC
   c. DMEPOS dealers
   d. PDAC

3. Which temporary codes are reported to all payers?
   a. G codes
   b. G codes and Q codes
   c. H codes and K codes
   d. H codes, S codes, and T codes

4. When both a CPT code and an HCPCS level II code are available for a procedure, service, or supply, the coder should assign the:
   a. code according to payer instructions.
   b. CPT code.
   c. HCPCS level II code.
   d. more specific code.

5. Which are reported to generate transitional pass-through payments under the Outpatient Prospective Payment System?
   a. C codes
   b. G codes
   c. Q codes
   d. S codes

6. HCPCS level II "addition" codes are included in subsections of _____ codes.
   a. alcohol and drug abuse treatment services
   b. cellular therapy and chelation therapy
   c. enteral and parenteral therapy
   d. orthotics and prosthetics procedures

7. HCPCS level II modifiers:
   a. contain alphanumeric characters only.
   b. contain numeric characters only.
   c. may also be added to CPT codes.
   d. may be attached to HCPCS level II codes only.

8. Which processes claims for providers?
   a. DME MAC
   b. DMEPOS dealer
   c. DMERC
   d. primary MAC

9. Which processes claims for DMEPOS dealers?
   a. DME MAC
   b. LMC
   c. primary MAC
   d. SADMERC

10. Which is an example of a certificate of medical necessity?
   a. Advance beneficiary notice signed by the patient
   b. Local medical review policy
   c. National coverage determination
   d. Prescription for DMEPOS from treating physician

11. A patient was supplied with an air pressure mattress. Report code _____.
   a. E0181   **b.** E0184   **c.** E0185   **d.** E0186

12. Magnetic resonance imaging without contrast followed by with contrast, left breast. Report code _____.
   a. C8903-LT   **b.** C8904-LT   **c.** C8905-LT   **d.** C8908-LT

13. A patient received an injection of hydrocortisone acetate, 15 mg, for contact dermatitis. Report code(s) _____.
   a. J1700   **c.** J1720
   b. J1700, J1700   **d.** J1720, J1720

14. A patient received a gradient compression stocking, full length/chap style 30–40 mmHg. Report code _____.
   a. A6531   **b.** A6534   **c.** A6537   **d.** A6539

15. A patient required catheterization for the collection of a specimen. Report code _____.
   a. A4300   **b.** A4305   **c.** P9612   **d.** P9615

16. A patient received 2 mg leuprolide acetate for treatment of prostate cancer. Report code(s) _____.
   a. J1950   **b.** J9217   **c.** J9218, J9218   **d.** J9219

17. A patient in a drug and alcohol rehabilitation hospital received an injection of methadone by the treating physician. Report code _____.
   a. H0020   **b.** H0029   **c.** H0033   **d.** J1230

18. An eight-year-old boy is fitted with a long-arm plaster cast. Service is performed in part by a resident under the direction of a teaching physician. Report code _____.
   a. Q4007   **b.** Q4007-GC   **c.** Q4008-GC   **d.** Q4010

19. The patient's family received 30 minutes of family training and counseling, which was provided for the purpose of child development. Report code(s) _____.
   a. T1025   **c.** T1027
   b. T1026   **d.** T1027, T1027

20. A patient received a hand-held low-vision aid. Report code _____.
   a. V2020   **b.** V2510   **c.** V2600   **d.** V2610

Coding Practice I

Instructions: Underline the main term, and assign HCPCS level II code(s) to each statement.

Transport Services Including Ambulance (A0000–A0999)

_____ **1.** Ambulance transport of patient from physician's office to hospital emergency department, including advanced life support, level 2.

_____ **2.** Ambulance transport of newborn from rural hospital to a children's specialty hospital.

_____ **3.** Patient received basic life support (BLS) during emergency transport from his home to the hospital via ambulance.

_____ 4. Patient received life-sustaining oxygen in an ambulance during transport to the hospital from a skilled nursing facility.

_____ 5. Patient transported in wheelchair van from residential assisted living facility to physician's office.

Medical and Surgical Supplies (A4000–A9999)

_____ 1. Patient was administered an injection using a sterile 3-cc syringe with needle.

_____ 2. RN swabbed the patient's upper torso with one pint of pHisoHex solution in preparation for an office procedure.

_____ 3. Physician inserted a cervical cap for contraceptive use.

_____ 4. Patient purchased a brand-new replacement adapter for her breast pump from a local DMEPOS dealer.

_____ 5. Patient was supplied with a sterile eye pad.

Administrative, Miscellaneous, and Investigation [Supplies] (A9000–A9999)

_____ 1. Patient underwent diagnostic radiology procedure, which required injection of one 30-mCi dose of ammonia N-13 as the radiopharmaceutical diagnostic imaging agent.

_____ 2. Patient rented prescribed exercise equipment from a local DMEPOS dealer.

_____ 3. Patient was administered a 2-millicurie I-131 sodium iodide capsule as the radiopharmaceutical diagnostic agent prior to a diagnostic radiology procedure.

_____ 4. Patient was injected with contrast material prior to echocardiography.

_____ 5. Patient was administered one dose of an oral multivitamin.

Enteral and Parenteral Therapy (B4000–B9999)

_____ 1. Patient was provided with parenteral nutrition administration kits for two days of care.

_____ 2. Patient received 1 unit of nutritionally incomplete/modular nutrients enteral formula via enteral feeding tube.

_____ 3. A new enteral infusion pump with alarm was attached to the patient's enteral feeding tube system.

_____ 4. Patient was provided with a new gravity-fed enteral feeding supply kit, one day.

_____ 5. A Levine-type stomach tube was used during the procedure.

CMS Hospital Outpatient Payment System (C1000–C9999)

_____ 1. One brachytherapy source of high-dose-rate iridium-192 was inserted into the patient by the radiation oncologist.

_____ 2. A cardiac event recorder was implanted in the patient as a medically necessary service/supply.

_____ 3. Implantable breast prosthesis was provided during surgery.

_____ 4. Patient underwent left breast MRI without contrast, followed by left breast MRI with contrast.

_____ 5. A short-term hemodialysis catheter was inserted in the patient's right forearm (patient is left-handed).

Durable Medical Equipment (E0100–E9999)

_____ 1. "Patient helper" trapeze bars and a grab bar were attached to the patient's bed.

_____ 2. An adult oxygen tent was supplied to the patient.

_____ 3. A bilirubin light with photometer was used to treat the patient.

_____ 4. Provider reported a dispensing fee for use of a DME nebulizer with compressor (covered drug).

_____ 5. Patient purchased a new folding walker, which has adjustable and fixed-height features.

Temporary Procedures/Professional Services (G0000–G9999)

_____ 1. A complete CBC, automated, was performed.

_____ 2. Trimming of five dystrophic nails.

_____ 3. Patient received 20 minutes of individual smoking cessation counseling as part of a demonstration project.

_____ 4. Patient underwent colorectal cancer screening via flexible sigmoidoscopy.

_____ 5. Patient underwent full positron emission tomography (PET) imaging for initial diagnosis of breast cancer.

Behavioral Health and/or Substance Abuse Treatment Services (H0001–H9999)

_____ 1. Patient received 30 minutes of behavioral health counseling and therapy as provided through his employee assistance program.

_____ 2. Patient received 18 hours of partial hospitalization care for mental health crisis.

_____ 3. One day of psychiatric health care facility services was provided to the patient.

_____ 4. Three days of respite care services were provided to the patient in the hospice unit of the hospital.

_____ 5. Patient received 30 minutes of activity therapy delivered as part of outpatient physical therapy plan of care.

Drugs Other Than Chemotherapy Drugs (J0100–J8999) and Chemotherapy Drugs (J9000–J9999)

_____ 1. Injection, caffeine citrate, 5 mg.

_____ 2. Injection, gamma globulin, intramuscular, 1 cc.

_____ 3. Injection, paricalcitol, 1 mcg.

_____ 4. Injection, torsemide, 10 mg/mL.

_____ 5. Injection, doxorubicin HCl, 10 mg.

Temporary Codes Assigned to DME Regional Carriers (K0000–K9999)

_____ 1. Repair service of 10-year-old DMEPOS device required supply of complete front caster assembly for wheelchair with two semipneumatic tires.

_____ 2. Patient was supplied with one IV hanger.

_____ 3. Patient was supplied with two leg straps for use with her wheelchair.

_____ 4. Patient rented a prescribed lightweight portable motorized wheelchair.

_____ 5. A replacement alkaline battery, 1.5 volt, was provided for the patient-owned external infusion pump.

Orthotics (L0000–L4999)

_____ 1. Patient was provided with a cervical wire frame, semirigid, for occipital/mandibular support.

_____ 2. Patient purchased a prescribed custom-fabricated thoracic rib belt.

_____ 3. Patient underwent halo procedure (cervical halo incorporated into Milwaukee orthosis).

_____ 4. Patient purchased a prescribed 2-inch neoprene heel and sole elevation lift.

_____ 5. In conjunction with a previously furnished orthotics prosthetic device, patient was supplied with a posterior solid ankle, plastic, custom-fabricated, ankle foot orthosis (AFO).

Prosthetics (L5000–L9999)

_____ 1. Patient was fitted with a knee disarticulation prosthesis that contained a molded socket, external knee joint, shin, and solid ankle cushion heel (SACH) foot.

_____ 2. Patient (adult) was fitted with an Otto Bock electric hand, myoelectrically controlled.

_____ 3. Patient was fitted with a partial foot prosthesis that contained a shoe insert with longitudinal arch, toe filler.

_____ 4. Patient was provided with a glove (for terminal device), right-hand prosthesis.

_____ 5. During breast reconstruction surgery, a silicone breast prosthesis was inserted.

Other Medical Services (M0000–M0301)

_____ 1. Intragastric hypothermia using gastric freezing.

_____ 2. Cellular therapy.

_____ 3. Chemical endarterectomy via intravenous (IV) chelation therapy.

_____ 4. Fabric wrapping of abdominal aneurysm.

_____ 5. Prolotherapy.

Pathology and Laboratory Services (P0000–P9999)

_____ 1. Catheterization for collection of specimen was performed for one patient.

_____ 2. Screening Pap smear, cervical, by technician under physician supervision.

_____ 3. Infusion of 250 mL of 5% albumin (human).

_____ 4. Two units of platelets were infused.

_____ 5. Two units of whole blood were used during transfusion.

Temporary Codes Assigned by CMS (Q0000–Q9999)

_____ 1. Patient received chemotherapy administration, push technique.

_____ 2. Patient underwent a collagen skin test.

_____ 3. Patient injected with 1 mL of 50 mg of teniposide.

_____ 4. As part of fracture treatment, 10-year-old patient received short-arm plaster splint.

_____ 5. Potassium hydroxide (KOH) preparation included as part of patient's treatment.

Diagnostic Radiology Services (R0000–R9999)

_____ 1. Transportation of portable chest x-ray and radiology technician to nursing home; 20 patients underwent x-ray.

_____ 2. Transportation of portable EKG equipment to nursing facility; five patients underwent EKG.

_____ 3. Transportation of portable x-ray equipment and radiology technician to patient's home; husband and wife underwent x-ray.

Temporary National Codes Established by Private Payers (S0000–S9999)

_____ 1. Allogenic cord blood-derived stem cell transplantation.

_____ 2. Echosclerotherapy.

_____ 3. Gastrointestinal fat absorption study.

_____ 4. Global fee for extracorporeal shock wave lithotripsy (ESWL) treatment of kidney stone.

_____ 5. Harvesting of multivisceral organs from cadaver donor with preparation and maintenance of allografts.

Temporary National Codes Established by Medicaid (T1000–T9999)

_____ 1. Patient underwent 15 minutes of family training and counseling for child development.

_____ 2. Human breast milk processing, storage, and distribution.

_____ 3. Intramuscular medication administration by home health licensed practical nurse (LPN).

_____ 4. Patient received 30 minutes of private-duty nursing from a registered nurse (RN).

_____ 5. Waiver of utility services to support medical equipment and assistive technology/devices.

Vision Services (V0000–V2999)

_____ 1. Bifocal lenses, bilateral, 5.25 sphere, 2.12 cylinder, two lenses.

_____ 2. Deluxe frame.

_____ 3. Photochromatic tinting of two lenses.

_____ 4. Processing, preserving, and transporting corneal tissue.

_____ 5. Reduction of ocular prosthesis.

Hearing Services (V5000–V5999)

_____ 1. Patient underwent assessment for hearing aid.

_____ 2. Provision of binaural, behind-the-ear hearing aid.

_____ 3. Provision of digitally programmable monaural hearing aid, analog, in the canal (ITC).

_____   **4.** Dispensing fee, binaural contralateral routing of signals (BICROS).

_____   **5.** Patient purchased prescribed telephone amplifier assistive listening device.

Coding Practice II

Instructions: Review each SOAP note to identify medications administered, procedures performed, and services provided. Assign appropriate HCPCS level II code(s) and modifier(s) to each medication, procedure, and service. (Do *not* assign CPT codes to procedures or services.)

1. SUBJECTIVE: The patient is an 89-year-old white female resident of the county nursing facility. I was asked to see her today because the nursing staff had noticed the patient was having difficulty breathing and was coughing up purulent material. A chest x-ray was ordered, and the mobile x-ray service arrived and took the x-ray while I was seeing my other patients.

OBJECTIVE: The patient appears ill. Temperature is 100.7.

CHEST: Scattered rhonchi throughout all lung fields, with severely diminished breath sounds in the left lower lung. Expiratory and inspiratory wheezes present.

HEART: Within normal limits.

ABDOMEN: No tenderness on palpation.

EXTREMITIES: Mild dependent edema is noted; otherwise within normal limits.

ASSESSMENT: The chest x-ray revealed a density consistent with left lower lobe pneumonia.

PLAN: The patient was administered an injection of Zithromax 500 milligrams. The cough does not seem to be bothersome to the patient right now, so the nursing staff will wait and watch. The nursing staff is to monitor her for any signs of increased fever, lethargy, or medication reaction. They are to encourage fluids and keep the patient up in a chair as much as possible when she is not sleeping. The staff is to contact me immediately if the patient's symptoms worsen.

_____

2. SUBJECTIVE: This 45-year-old construction worker was seen in the office today on an emergency basis because he stepped on a sharp edge of steel and lacerated his right foot. He states that he cannot recall his last tetanus shot.

OBJECTIVE: Examination of the right foot reveals a laceration of approximately 3.5 cm at the lateral edge of the foot that extends medially across the heel.

PROCEDURE: The right heel was cleansed with pHisoHex and prepped with Betadine. The wound edges were infiltrated with 1% Xylocaine. After adequate anesthesia was obtained, the laceration was repaired with 3-0 nylon sutures. The wound was dressed with gauze and secured with paper tape.

ASSESSMENT: Laceration of right heel, repaired in the office.

PLAN: The patient was given a tetanus shot today. He was given instructions on wound care and signs of infection and was also given reference sheets on the same. He is to be non-weight-bearing for the next three days and was given a pair of wooden crutches. He will return to the office in three days for reevaluation. The patient was also reminded to call immediately if pain increases or if he shows any signs of fever.

_____

PART IV

Current Procedural Terminology (CPT) Coding System

9: Introduction to CPT Coding, 324

10: CPT Evaluation and Management, 360

11: CPT Anesthesia, 418

12: CPT Surgery I, 457

13: CPT Surgery II, 501

14: CPT Surgery III, 548

15: CPT Surgery IV, 593

16: CPT Surgery V, 639

17: CPT Radiology, 693

18: CPT Pathology and Laboratory, 737

19: CPT Medicine, 765

Introduction to CPT Coding

Chapter Outline

History of CPT

Overview of CPT

Organization of CPT

CPT Index

CPT Appendices

CPT Symbols

CPT Sections, Subsections, Categories,
   and Subcategories

CPT Modifiers

National Correct Coding Initiative (NCCI)

Chapter Objectives

At the conclusion of this chapter, the student should be able to:

1. Define key terms related to the introduction of CPT coding.
2. Identify key dates and events in the history of CPT.
3. Provide an overview about CPT.
4. Explain the organization of CPT.
5. Apply CPT index rules and conventions to identify main terms, subterms, qualifiers, cross-references, and code ranges.
6. Describe the types of codes included in each of the CPT appendices.
7. Interpret CPT symbols.
8. Summarize the contents of CPT sections, subsections, categories, and subcategories.
9. Add CPT modifiers to codes.
10. Describe how the national correct coding initiative impacts CPT code assignment.

Key Terms

add-on code	Appendix F of CPT	Appendix O of CPT	Category I code
Appendix A of CPT	Appendix J of CPT	Appendix P of CPT	Category II code
Appendix B of CPT	Appendix K of CPT	blue reference symbol (⟳)	Category III code
Appendix C of CPT	Appendix L of CPT	bullet symbol (•)	column 1/column 2 edit
Appendix D of CPT	Appendix M of CPT	Category I PLA symbol	descriptive qualifiers
Appendix E of CPT	Appendix N of CPT	(↑↓)	

duplicate PLA symbol (⚹)

flash symbol (𝒩)

forbidden (or prohibitory) symbol (⊘)

functional modifier

green reference symbol (⊜)

guidelines

horizontal triangle symbols (▶◀)

inferred words

informational modifiers

mutually exclusive edit

National Correct Coding Initiative (NCCI)

notes

Notice of Exclusions from Medicare Benefits (NEMB)

number symbol (#)

plus symbol (+)

pricing modifier

range of codes

red reference symbol (⊜)

semicolon (;)

single code

special report

star symbol (★)

triangle symbol (▲)

unlisted procedure

unlisted service

Introduction

This chapter introduces the Current Procedural Terminology (CPT) coding system (or HCPCS level I), a proprietary coding system published annually by the American Medical Association (AMA). (Exceptions to the January 1 annual release of CPT codes include (1) Category II codes and the Medicine section vaccine product codes that are also released on July 1, and (2) Category II codes that are released three times each year.) Current Procedural Terminology (CPT) is a listing of descriptive terms and identifying codes for reporting medical services and procedures. It provides a uniform language that describes medical, surgical, and diagnostic services to facilitate communication among providers, patients, and third-party payers.

 NOTE:

When reviewing examples and completing exercises and review questions in this chapter (and in Chapters 11–19), use your CPT coding manual to locate index entries and to verify codes in the tabular.

History of CPT

The AMA first published CPT in 1966, and subsequent editions expanded its descriptive terms and codes for diagnostic and therapeutic procedures. Five-digit codes were introduced in 1970, replacing the four-digit classification. In 1983, CPT was adopted as part of the Healthcare Common Procedure Coding System (HCPCS) (as HCPCS level I) and its use was mandated for reporting Medicare Part B physician services. In 1986, HCPCS was required for reporting to Medicaid agencies, and the Omnibus Budget Reconciliation Act (OBRA) of 1986 mandated that CPT codes be reported for outpatient hospital surgical procedures.

The Health Insurance Portability and Accountability Act of 1996 (HIPAA) named CPT and HCPCS level II as the procedure code sets for physician services, physical and occupational therapy services, radiological procedures, clinical laboratory tests, other medical diagnostic procedures, hearing and vision services, and transportation services including ambulance. (Also included are ICD-10-CM as the code set for all diagnoses and ICD-10-PCS for inpatient procedures.)

CMS enforced regulations resulting from the Medicare Prescription Drug, Improvement, and Modernization Act (MMA) in October 2004, which required that new, revised, and deleted CPT codes be implemented each January 1. It is important to purchase updated coding manuals to avoid billing delays and claims rejections. If outdated codes are submitted on claims, providers and health care facilities will incur administrative costs associated with resubmitting corrected claims and delayed reimbursement for services provided.

 NOTE:

The AMA's CPT Editorial Board publishes an "early release" of new and revised codes (e.g., vaccination codes) each July and January (for implementation six months later). Early release codes are further discussed later in this chapter.

Exercise 9.1 – History of CPT

Instructions: Match the year with the event.

_____ 1. Introduction of five-digit CPT codes.

_____ 2. Elimination of 90-day grace period for new/revised/ deleted CPT codes.

_____ 3. AMA first published CPT.

_____ 4. Required reporting CPT codes for outpatient surgical procedures.

_____ 5. Mandated reporting CPT codes for Medicare services.

a. 1966
b. 1970
c. 1983
d. 1986
e. 2004

Overview of CPT

CPT codes are used to report services and procedures performed on patients by the following types of providers:

- Home health care and hospice agencies
- Outpatient hospital departments (e.g., ambulatory surgery, emergency department, and outpatient laboratory or radiographic procedures)
- Physicians who are employees of a health care facility (e.g., Veterans Administration Medical Centers physicians)
- Physicians who see patients in their offices or clinics and in other health care settings (e.g., home health care, hospice, long-term care, professional services provided to hospital inpatients, and so on)

CPT codes and descriptions are based on consistency with contemporary medical practice and is performed by clinical providers throughout the country. The assignment of CPT codes simplifies reporting and assists in the accurate identification of procedures and services for third-party payer consideration. As such, procedures and services reported on a claim must be linked to the ICD-10-CM code that justifies the need for the service or procedure. This demonstrates medical necessity for the service or procedure provided so the payer can judge whether the claim should be paid.

When reporting CPT codes, some services are considered integral to the standard of practice, which means that certain medical and surgical services are not assigned CPT codes. Such services include the following:

- Administering local, topical, or regional anesthetic (by physician performing procedure)
- Administering sedatives (by physician performing procedure)
- Applying, managing, and removing postoperative dressings and analgesic devices
- Cleansing, shaving, and prepping of skin
- Documenting preoperative, intraoperative, and postoperative procedures provided
- Draping and positioning of patient
- Inserting and removing drains, suction devices, dressings, and pumps into same site
- Inserting intravenous access for medication
- Irrigating a wound
- Providing surgical approach, closure, cultures, and supplies (unless CMS policy states otherwise)

CPT Categories

CPT is compatible with electronic data interchange (EDI), the electronic health record (EHR), and reference/research databases. CPT is used to track new technology and performance measures.

In 2000, the AMA completed the CPT-5 Project, resulting in the establishment of three categories of CPT codes.

- **Category I codes** (e.g., 99201): Procedures/services identified by a five-digit CPT code and descriptor nomenclature; these are codes traditionally associated with CPT and organized into six sections.
- **Category II codes** (e.g., 0001F): Optional "performance measurements" tracking codes that are assigned an alphanumeric identifier with a letter in the last field (e.g., 1000F); these codes will be located after the Medicine section.

> **EXAMPLE:** A physician counsels a patient who smokes during an evaluation and management (E/M) service. Report CPT Category II code 4000F (tobacco use cessation intervention, counseling). If the physician also prescribes a smoking cessation medication, report code 4001F (tobacco use cessation intervention, pharmacologic therapy). (CPT Category II codes are reported in addition to the CPT E/M service and other procedure code.)

NOTE:

According to the AMA, CPT Category II codes minimize administrative burdens because they facilitate data collection about quality of care. Services and test results are assigned codes that support performance measures and that contribute to good patient care. CPT Category II codes also relate to compliance with state or federal law.

- **Category III codes** (e.g., 0058T): Contain "emerging technology" temporary codes assigned for data collection purposes that are assigned an alphanumeric identifier with a letter in the last field (e.g., 0042T); these codes are located after the Category II codes, and they will be archived after five years if they are not accepted for placement within Category I sections of CPT.

> **EXAMPLE:** Prior to 2005, Category III code 0012T was reported for a surgical arthroscopy of the knee with osteochondral autograft(s). In 2005, code 0012T was deleted and a Category I code 29866 was created with a code description of "arthroscopy, knee, surgical; osteochondral autograft(s) (eg mosaicplasty) (including harvesting of the autograft[s])."

NOTE:

According to the AMA, Category III codes allow for data collection of "emerging technology" services and procedures, which are conducted as part of ongoing or planned research. Effective 2006, modifiers are reported with Category III codes.

The CPT Editorial Panel also approves the "early release" of new CPT codes. All changes provided as an "early release" take effect on the implementation date, which is six months after the "early release" of the codes. This means that codes included in an "early release" in January are implemented for use in July (and codes included in an "early release" in July are implemented the following January). To assist users in reporting the most recently approved codes, the AMA's CPT website will feature updates of the CPT Editorial Panel's actions and early release of the codes in July and January during a given CPT cycle. These dates for early release correspond with the quarterly CPT Editorial Panel's meetings for each CPT cycle (May, August, November, and February).

Exercise 9.2 – Overview of CPT

Instructions: Complete each statement.

1. CPT codes and descriptions are based on consistency with contemporary medical practice as performed by clinical _____ throughout the United States.

2. The assignment of CPT codes simplifies reporting and assists in the accurate identification of procedures and services for third-party _____ consideration.

3. CPT codes for procedures and services that are reported on a claim must be linked to the ICD-10-CM code that justifies the need for the service or procedure, which demonstrates medical _____ for the service or procedure provided.

4. Category _____ codes contain optional "performance measurements" tracking codes that are assigned an alphanumeric identifier with a letter in the last field.

5. Category _____ codes contain "emerging technology" temporary codes, which are assigned for data collection purposes and contain an alphanumeric identifier with a letter in the last field.

Organization of CPT

To assign CPT codes, it is necessary to become familiar with CPT's organizational characteristics.

- CPT sections
- CPT code number format
- Boldfaced type
- Italicized type
- Cross-reference term
- Single codes and code ranges
- Inferred words
- Guidelines
- Unlisted procedures and services
- Notes
- Descriptive qualifiers

CPT Category I Codes

CPT organizes Category I procedures and services into six sections.

- Evaluation and Management (E/M) (99201–99499)
- Anesthesia (00100–01999, 99100–99140)
- Surgery (10004–69990)
- Radiology (including Nuclear Medicine and Diagnostic Ultrasound) (70010–79999)
- Pathology and Laboratory (80047–89398, 0001U–0138U)
- Medicine (90281–99199, 99500–99607)

 NOTE:

The E/M section is located at the beginning of CPT because these codes are reported by all specialties.

 NOTE:

Medicine section codes 99100–99140 classify qualifying circumstances for anesthesia and are reported with Anesthesia section codes.

CPT Category II Codes

CPT Category II codes are supplemental tracking codes used for performance measurement. Category II codes are assigned for certain services or tests results, which support nationally established performance measures that have proven to contribute to quality patient care. CPT Category II codes are alphanumeric and consist of four digits followed by the alpha character F. The reporting of Category II codes is optional and not a substitute for the assignment of CPT Category I codes. When reported on the CMS-1500 claim, the submitted charge is zero ($0.00). CPT Category II codes are arranged according to the following categories:

- Modifiers (1P–8P), reported with CPT Category II codes only
- Composite Codes (0001F–0015F)
- Patient Management (0500F–0584F)
- Patient History (1000F–1505F)
- Physical Examination (2000F–2060F)
- Diagnostic/Screening Processes or Results (3006F–3776F)
- Therapeutic, Preventive, or Other Interventions (4000F–4563F)
- Follow-up or Other Outcomes (5005F–5250F)
- Patient Safety (6005F–6150F)
- Structural Measures (7010F–7025F)
- Nonmeasure Code Listing (9001F–9007F)

The purpose of reporting Category II codes is to facilitate the collection of information about the quality of patient care (e.g., appropriate services provided to patients based on diagnosis). The use of Category II is expected to decrease the time required for patient record abstracting and review, thus minimizing the administrative burden on health care providers for tracking patient care quality.

EXAMPLE: Dr. Ryan is a dermatologist who is participating in a nationwide quality management study about malignant melanoma. CPT Category II code 0015F is reported for each patient who receives melanoma follow-up services, which include obtaining a history about new or changing moles (code 1050F), performing a complete physical skin examination (code 2029F), and providing patient counseling to perform a monthly skin self-examination (code 5005F). Thus, codes 0015F, 1050F, 2029F, and 5005F are reported on the CMS-1500 claim, and the charge for each is zero ($0.00). In addition, reason for encounter ICD-10-CM code(s) and CPT Category I service/procedure code(s) are reported on the same CMS-1500 claim with appropriate charges entered for each CPT Category I code.

 NOTE:

Some payers deny claims that contain CPT category II codes. Providers can save the codes as part of a spreadsheet or data base for internal data capture purposes.

CPT Category III Codes

CPT Category III codes are temporary codes for emerging technology, procedures, and services. The codes facilitate data collection on and assessment of new services and procedures during the FDA approval process or to confirm that a procedure/service is generally provided. According to the CPT coding manual, the "procedure or service is currently or recently performed on humans; and at least one additional criteria (listed in the CPT coding manual) has been met." CPT Category III codes are alphanumeric and consist of four digits followed by the alpha character T, and they range from 0042T–0504T. In 2002, CMS began designating certain CPT Category III codes as covered by Medicare, which means charges are entered when reporting the codes on a CMS-1500 claim.

In the past, researchers were hindered by the length and requirements of the CPT approval process. Thus, CPT Category III (temporary) codes facilitate the reporting of emerging technology, procedures, and services.

They are generally retired if the emerging technology, procedure, or service is not assigned a CPT Category I code within five years. When a Category III code is available, it must be reported instead of an unlisted CPT Category I code (because reporting an unlisted code does not offer the opportunity for collection of specific data). Category III codes were initially released in July 2001 and are included as a separate section in CPT (following the Category II codes). (HCPCS level II codes also describe emerging technology, procedures, and services; when a HCPCS level II code exists, it must be reported for Medicare claims.)

> **EXAMPLE:** The patient's physician administered breath test for heart transplant rejection. Report Category III code 0085T and its charge on the CMS-1500 claim.

CPT Code Number Format

A five-digit code number and a narrative description identify each procedure and service listed in Category I of CPT. Most procedures and services contain stand-alone descriptions. To save space, some descriptions are not printed in their entirety next to a code number. Instead, the entry is indented and the coder must refer back to the common portion of the code description that is located before the semicolon.

> **EXAMPLE 1:** STAND-ALONE CODE DESCRIPTION:
>
> 27870   Arthrodesis, ankle, open

> **EXAMPLE 2:** INDENTED CODE DESCRIPTION:
>
> 27780   Closed treatment of proximal fibula or shaft fracture; without
>   manipulation
> 27781   with manipulation
>
> The code description for 27781 is *closed treatment of proximal fibula or shaft fracture with manipulation*.

Exercise 9.3 – Organization of CPT

Instructions: Complete each statement.

1. CPT organizes Category I procedures and services into _____ sections.
2. The Evaluation and Management section of CPT is located at the beginning of CPT because these codes are reported by all _____.
3. Medicine section codes 99100–99140, which classify *Qualifying Circumstances for Anesthesia*, are explained in the _____ section guidelines.
4. Refer to CPT code 55605. Its code description is _____.
5. Refer to CPT code 47562 and review all code descriptions through code 47570. The description for code 47562 is "Laparoscopy, surgical; cholecystectomy." The code description for 47562 includes a semicolon, which means the description for code 47563 is _____
   _____
   _____.

CPT Index

The CPT index (Figure 9-1) is organized by alphabetical main terms printed in boldface. The main terms represent procedures or services, organs, anatomical sites, conditions, eponyms, or abbreviations. The main term may be followed by indented terms that modify the main term; these are called *subterms*.

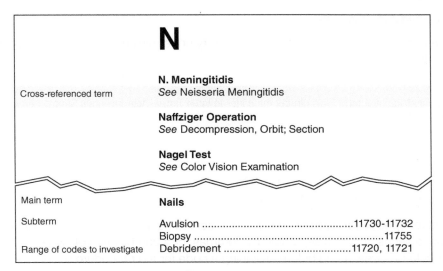

FIGURE 9-1 Selection from CPT index

The CPT index organizes procedures and services according to

- Procedure or service (e.g., arthroscopy)
- Organ or other anatomical site (e.g., ankle)
- Condition (e.g., wound)
- Synonyms (e.g., finger joint or intercarpal joint)
- Eponyms (e.g., Billroth I or II)
- Abbreviations (e.g., EKG)

To locate a CPT code, review patient record documentation to locate the service and/or procedure performed and locate the main term in the index (located in the back of the coding manual).

> **EXAMPLE:** For the procedure "surgical temporomandibular joint (TMJ) arthroscopy," refer to the CPT index and locate main term *Temporomandibular Joint (TMJ)*, subterm *Arthroscopy*, and qualifier *Surgical* 29804. Next, verify code 29804 in the tabular portion of the coding manual before reporting it on a claim for submission to a third-party payer. (A diagnosis code must be reported on the claim to justify medical necessity of the procedure.)

Coding Tip

The descriptions of all codes listed in the index for a specific procedure must be carefully investigated before selecting a final code. CPT coding must never be performed solely from the index.

Boldfaced Type

Main terms in the CPT index are printed in boldfaced type. CPT category and subcategory titles and code numbers are also printed in boldfaced type.

Italicized Type

Italicized type is used for the cross-reference term *See* in the CPT index.

Cross-Reference Term

See is a cross-reference that directs coders to an index entry under which codes are listed. No codes are listed under the original entry.

> **EXAMPLE:** The instructional term *See* directs the coder to index entry "Arteriovenous Shunt" because no codes are listed for the abbreviation *AV Shunt*.
>
> **AV Shunt**
> *See* Arteriovenous Shunt

Single Codes and Code Ranges

Index code numbers for specific procedures may be represented as a **single code** number, a **range of codes** separated by a dash, a series of codes separated by commas, or a combination of single codes and ranges of codes. All codes should be investigated before assigning a code for the procedure or service.

> **EXAMPLE:** The main term *Acid fast stain* contains just one code. Subterm *esophagus*, which is located below main term *Acid perfusion test*, contains two codes separated by commas. Main term *Acid Reflux Test* contains a range of codes.
>
> **Acid-Fast Stain**
> Analysis 88312
> **Acid Perfusion Study**
> Esophagus 91013, 91030
> **Adenoids**
> Excision 42830-42836

Inferred Words

To save space in the CPT index when referencing subterms, **inferred words** are used.

> **EXAMPLE:** The word *(of)* in parentheses is inferred and does not actually appear in the CPT index.
>
> **Abdomen**
> Exploration (of) 49000,49010

Exercise 9.4 – CPT Index

Instructions: Indicate whether each statement is true (T) or false (F).

_____   1. The cross-reference that directs coders to refer to a different index entry because no codes are found under the original entry is called *See*.

_____   2. Main terms appear in *italics* in the CPT index.

_____   3. Inferred words appear in the CPT index to assist coders in assigning appropriate codes.

_____   4. The main term may be followed by indented terms, known as subterms, which modify the main term.

_____   5. Cross-reference terms are printed in bold in the CPT index.

CPT Appendices

CPT contains appendices, located after CPT Category III codes. Insurance specialists should carefully review these appendices to become familiar with coding changes that affect the practice annually.

- **Appendix A** (Modifiers) contains a list of CPT modifiers and detailed descriptions. Place a marker at the beginning of Appendix A because you will refer to it often.
- **Appendix B** (Summary of Additions, Deletions, and Revisions) contains annual CPT coding changes that include added, deleted, and revised CPT codes. Carefully review Appendix B of the current CPT manual because it will serve as the basis for updating interoffice documents and billing tools.
- **Appendix C** (Clinical Examples) contains clinical examples for codes found in the E/M section.
- **Appendix D** (Summary of CPT Add-on Codes) contains a list of add-on codes that are identified throughout CPT with a ✚ symbol. An **add-on code** is reported when another procedure is performed in addition to the primary procedure during the same operative session and must never be reported as a stand-alone code. (Do not report modifier -50 with add-on codes. For bilateral procedures, the add-on code is reported twice. Modifier -51 is also not reported with add-on codes because payers have already discounted the payment.) Modifier -51 (multiple procedures) is *not* added to add-on codes.
- **Appendix E** (Summary of CPT Codes Exempt from Modifier 51) contains a list of codes that are exempt from modifier -51 reporting rules and that are identified throughout CPT with a forbidden (⊘) symbol.
- **Appendix F** (Summary of CPT Codes Exempt from Modifier 63) contains a list of codes that are exempt from modifier -63.
- *Appendix G* (Summary of CPT Codes That Include Moderate (Conscious) Sedation) was removed from the CPT coding manual.
- *Appendix H* (Alphabetic Clinical Topics Listing) was removed from the CPT coding manual and relocated to the AMA website with access available only to AMA members (who must be physicians, medical graduates, and medical students).
- *Appendix I* (Genetic Testing Code Modifiers) was removed from the CPT coding manual.
- **Appendix J** (Electrodiagnostic Medicine Listing of Sensory, Motor, and Mixed Nerves) contains an electrodiagnostic medicine listing of sensory, motor, and mixed nerves that are reported for motor and nerve studies codes. There is also a table that indicates the "type of study and maximum number of studies" generally performed for needle electromyogram (EMG), nerve conduction studies, and other EMG studies. The AMA's *CPT Changes 2006: An Insider's View* calls this table a ". . . tool to detect outliers."
- **Appendix K** (Product Pending FDA Approval) contains a list of products that are pending FDA approval but that have been assigned CPT codes. In the CPT manual, these codes are preceded by the flash symbol (⚡).
- **Appendix L** (Vascular Families) contains a list of vascular families that is intended to assist in the selection of first-, second-, third-, and beyond third-order branch arteries.
- **Appendix M** (Renumbered CPT Codes–Citations Crosswalk) contains a summary of crosswalked deleted and renumbered codes from 2007 to 2009. (The AMA discontinued the practice of deleting and renumbering codes in 2010.)
- **Appendix N** (Summary of Resequenced CPT Codes) contains a list of CPT codes that do not appear in numeric order. CPT codes are resequenced (instead of deleted and renumbered) so that existing codes can be relocated to a more appropriate location. In the CPT manual, out-of-sequence codes are preceded by the number symbol (#).

- **Appendix O** (Multianalyte Assays With Algorithmic Analyses, MAAA) includes administrative codes for procedures that by their nature are typically unique to a single clinical laboratory or manufacturer.
- **Appendix P** (CPT codes That May Be Used For Synchronous Telemedicine Services) includes codes for electronic communication using interactive telecommunications equipment (e.g., audio, video). In the CPT manual, these codes are preceded by the star (★) symbol. Modifier -95 is reported with Appendix P codes.

Exercise 9.5 – CPT Appendices

Instructions: Match the appendix with its description.

_____ 1. Contains a list of CPT modifiers and detailed descriptions

_____ 2. Contains CPT codes that may be used for synchronous telemedicine services

_____ 3. Contains added, deleted, and revised CPT codes

_____ 4. Contains codes that are exempt from modifier -51 reporting rules and that are identified in CPT with a ⊘ symbol

_____ 5. Contains a crosswalk of resequenced codes that are identified with a **#** symbol

a. Appendix A
b. Appendix B
c. Appendix E
d. Appendix N
e. Appendix P

CPT Symbols

Symbols (Figure 9-2 contains a partial selection) are located throughout the CPT coding manual.

- A **bullet symbol** located to the left of a code number identifies new procedures and services added to CPT.

▲ A **triangle symbol** located to the left of a code number identifies a code description that has been revised.

►◄ **Horizontal triangle symbols** surround revised guidelines and notes. These symbols are *not* used for revised code descriptions.

 NOTE:

Review your CPT coding manual to locate codes preceded by the bullet, triangle, and horizontal triangle symbols.

; To save space in CPT, some code descriptions are not printed in their entirety next to a code number. Instead, the entry is indented, and the coder must refer back to the common portion of the code description that is located before the **semicolon**. The common portion begins with a capital letter, and the abbreviated (or subordinate) descriptions are indented and begin with lowercase letters.

Symbol:	CPT Entry:	
Use of semicolon	**11000**	Debridement of extensive eczematous or infected skin; up to 10% of body surface
Use of plus symbol	**✚ 11001**	each additional 10% of the body surface, or part thereof (List separately in addition to code to primary procedure)
Use of -51 modifier exemption symbol	⊘ **20974**	Electrical stimulation to aid bone healing, noninvasive (nonoperative)

FIGURE 9-2 Selection from CPT illustrating symbols

EXAMPLE:

```
20910    Cartilage graft; costochondral
20912         nasal septum
```

 Coding Tip

CPT is printed using proportional spacing, and careful review of code descriptions to locate the semicolon may be necessary.

- For a patient who undergoes costochondral cartilage graft procedure, report code 20910.
- For a patient who undergoes a nasal septum cartilage graft procedure, report code 20912.

  For a patient who undergoes costochondral and nasal septum cartilage graft procedures during the same operative session, report codes 20910 and 20912-51. (Modifier -51 indicates that a multiple procedure was performed. The payer will discount reimbursement for the procedure assigned code 20912.)

+ The **plus symbol** identifies add-on codes (Appendix D of CPT) for procedures that are commonly, but not always, performed at the same time and by the same surgeon as the primary procedure. Parenthetical notes, located below add-on codes, often identify the primary procedure to which add-on codes apply.

EXAMPLE: For a patient who undergoes posterior osteotomy of the spine, two cervical vertebral segments, report codes 22210 and 22216.

```
22210    Osteotomy of spine, posterior or posterolateral approach,
         1 vertebral segment; cervical
22212       thoracic
22214       lumbar
+ 22216     each additional vertebral segment (List separately in addition to
            primary procedure)
         (Use 22216 in conjunction with codes 22210, 22212, 22214)
```

 Coding Tip

- Do not report codes identified with + (add-on codes) as stand-alone codes; they must be reported with a primary code.
- Do not add modifier -51 to codes identified with the + symbol because payers discount reimbursement for such add-on codes; adding modifier -51 to codes that have the + symbol incorrectly reduces reimbursement even more.
- Do not report modifier -50 with add-on codes; instead, report the add-on code twice.

⊘ This **forbidden** (or **prohibitory**) **symbol** identifies codes (Appendix E of CPT) that are exempt from modifier -51. These codes are reported in addition to other codes, but they are not classified as add-on codes.

EXAMPLE: The patient underwent emergency endotracheal intubation.

```
⊘ 20974    Electrical stimulation to aid bone healing, noninvasive
           (nonoperative)
```

When code 20974 is reported with other procedures performed during the same encounter, do not add modifier -51.

★ The **star symbol** indicates that a code may be reported for synchronous telemedicine services. (CPT Appendix P contains a list of CPT codes that may be used for synchronous telemedicine services.)

> **EXAMPLE:** Patient underwent psychiatric diagnostic evaluation using synchronous telemedicine services. Report code 90791-95.
>
> ★ 90791   Psychiatric diagnostic evaluation

✐ The **flash symbol** indicates codes that classify products pending FDA approval but that have been assigned a CPT code.

> **EXAMPLE:** Patient was administered an influenza virus vaccine, pandemic formulation
>
> ✐ 90587   Dengue vaccine, quadrivalent, live, 3 dose schedule, for subcutaneous use

\# The **number symbol** indicates out-of-numerical sequence codes.

> **EXAMPLE:** Patient underwent excision of 4-cm subcutaneous soft tissue tumor of the neck.
>
> 21555   Excision, tumor, soft tissue of neck or anterior thorax, subcutaneous; less than 3 cm
>
> \# 21552   3 cm or greater

NOTE:

Prior to 2010, when a new code was added and there was no available code in a "code range," a new range of codes was added to accommodate the new code(s). This meant that all codes in a range were deleted (and added as new codes) for certain procedures even though the procedure text and meaning or applicability of the procedure had not changed. Payers typically interpreted a new range of codes as "new codes" to CPT, resulting in payment denials.

The new policy of creating out-of-numerical sequence codes facilitates historical data analysis, reduces the number of codes that providers must revise (e.g., superbill, encounter form), and eliminates the need for payers to modify related reimbursement policies resulting in reduced claims denials.

Resequenced codes appear "out of sequence" in the print version of CPT, but that means the codes will be located with concepts to which they are related. CPT code description content determines placement of out-of-sequence codes.

⊃ The **green reference symbol** located below a code description in some CPT coding manuals indicates that the coder should refer to the *CPT Assistant* monthly newsletter.

⊃ The **blue reference symbol** located below a code description in some CPT coding manuals indicates that the coder should refer to the *CPT Changes: An Insider's View* annual publication that contains all coding changes for the current year.

⊃ The **red reference symbol** located below a code description in some CPT coding manuals indicates that the coder should refer to the *Clinical Examples in Radiology* quarterly newsletter.

> **EXAMPLE:**
>
> 73551   Radiologic examination, femur; 1 view
> ⊃ *Clinical Examples in Radiology* Fall 15:9, Summer 16:8
> ⊃ *CPT Changes: An Insider's View* 2016
> ⊃ *CPT Assistant* Aug 16:7, Nov 16:10

⋈ The **duplicate PLA symbol** identifies duplicate proprietary laboratory analyses (PLA) tests. PLA codes are included in Appendix O, and they contain the proprietary name of the procedure. Descriptor language of some PLA codes are identical, and codes are differentiated only by listed proprietary names in Appendix O. Such codes are denoted by the symbol.

↑↓ The **Category I PLA symbol** is used to identify CPT category I codes.

 NOTE:

CPT 2020 does not contain codes preceded by the arrow symbol.

 NOTE:

Although PLA codes are included in the Pathology and Laboratory section of CPT, they do not fulfill Category I criteria unless the arrow symbol precedes the code.

Exercise 9.6 – CPT Symbols

Instructions: Match the symbol with its description

_____ 1. Identifies a code that may be used for synchronous telemedicine services

_____ 2. Identifies add-on codes

_____ 3. Identifies codes that are exempt from modifier -51

_____ 4. Identifies codes that classify products pending FDA approval

_____ 5. Identifies new procedures and services added to CPT

_____ 6. Identifies revised code descriptions

_____ 7. Refers coders to *Clinical Examples in Radiology* newsletter

_____ 8. Indicates an out-of-numeric sequence code

_____ 9. Refers coders to *CPT Assistant* newsletter and/or *CPT Changes: An Insider's View* annual publication of coding changes for current year

_____ 10. Surround revised guidelines and notes

a. ★
b. ▲
c. •
d. +
e. ⊘
f. ⟋
g. ▶◀
h. #
i. ⊃
j. ⊃

CPT Sections, Subsections, Categories, and Subcategories

CPT Category I codes are organized according to six sections that are subdivided into subsections, categories, and subcategories (Figure 9-3). Guidelines are located at the beginning of each CPT section, and the following are located in CPT subsections, headings or categories, subheadings or subcategories, and codes:

- Notes
- Descriptive qualifiers

Section	**Surgery**
Subsection	**Integumentary System**
Category	**Skin, Subcutaneous and Accessory Structures**
Subcategory	**Incision and Drainage**
Note	(For excision, see 11400, et seq)
Descriptive qualifier (underlined phrase)	10060 Incision and drainage of abscess (eg, carbuncle, suppurative hidradenitis, cutaneous or subcutaneous abscess, cyst, furuncle, or paronychia); <u>simple or single</u>

FIGURE 9-3 Selection from CPT illustrating sections, subsections, categories, subcategories, notes, and descriptive qualifiers

NOTE:

CPT is inconsistent in its use of subsection, category, and subcategory terminology. For example, the CPT E/M section guideline *Classification of Evaluation and Management (E/M) Services* refers to categories and subcategories (instead of the more logical subsections and categories). (Many years ago, the E/M section was a subsection of the Medicine section. When the codes were relocated to the beginning of the CPT coding manual for easy reference, the E/M section was created. The category and subcategory terminology associated with the E/M codes was retained.)

To complicate matters, CPT refers to "headings and subheadings" in some section guidelines and "categories and subcategories" in other section guidelines. In addition, the Surgery guidelines include "Subsection Information," which refers to "subheadings or subsections." It would be more logical if the latter phrase had been written as "subheadings or subcategories."

HIPAA Alert!

HIPAA designated CPT as a national code set for reporting outpatient (including physician's office) procedures and services. It further designated *CPT Assistant* as an official source of coding guidelines. CPT guidelines and notes and *CPT Assistant* coding guidelines take precedence over payer-specific rules for reporting codes. However, payers are selective about the guidelines and notes they implement for reimbursement purposes. Thus, payer-specific reimbursement rules often contradict CPT guidelines and notes and *CPT Assistant* coding guidelines. This means coders must review and follow payer-specific reimbursement rules for reporting codes to obtain appropriate reimbursement.

EXAMPLE: Cautery was used to correct everted lacrimal puncta (small openings in the inner canthus of eyelids that channel tears), right and left eye. (There are two puncta in each eye, an upper and a lower punctum.) Code 68705 is assigned. According to *CPT Assistant*, the puncta code is reported four times. However, Medicare reimbursement rules require the code to be reported twice with modifier -50 (Bilateral Procedure) added to each code.

PROCEDURES, SERVICES, OR SUPPLIES	
CPT/HCPCS	MODIFIER
68705	
68705	
68705	
68705	

PROCEDURES, SERVICES, OR SUPPLIES	
CPT/HCPCS	MODIFIER
68705	50
68705	50

Courtesy of the Centers for Medicare & Medicaid Services, www.cms.gov; claim data created by author.

This is just one of many cases where official CPT coding guidelines differ from payer reimbursement rules. To obtain appropriate reimbursement, make sure you determine payer reimbursement rules for submitting codes.

CPT Guidelines

Guidelines located at the beginning of each CPT section should be carefully reviewed before assigning a code. **Guidelines** define terms and explain the assignment of codes for procedures and services located in a particular section (Figure 9-4). This means that guidelines in one section do not apply to another section in CPT.

Unlisted Procedures and Services

An **unlisted procedure** or **unlisted service** code is assigned when the provider performs a procedure or service for which there is no CPT code. When an unlisted procedure or service code is reported, a **special report** (e.g., copy of the procedure report) must accompany the claim to describe the nature, extent, and need for the procedure or service.

 NOTE:

- Do not add a modifier to CPT unlisted procedure/service codes because they do not include specific descriptions that would justify modifying their meaning.
- Medicare and third-party payers often require providers to report HCPCS level II national codes instead of unlisted procedure or service CPT codes.

Notes

Instructional **notes** appear throughout CPT sections to clarify the assignment of codes. They are typeset in two patterns (Figure 9-5).

- A *blocked unindented note* is located below the title of a subsection, heading (or category), or subheading (or subcategory). It contains instructions that apply to all codes in the subsection, heading/category, or subheading/subcategory.

- An *indented parenthetical* note is located below the
  - Title of a subsection, heading (or category), and subheading (or subcategory)
  - Code description (and the note applies to that code only unless the note indicates otherwise)

- A *parenthetical note* is located in the code description to provide an example. Such notes contain the abbreviation "eg," and terminology in the example is *not* required to appear in the procedural statement documented by the provider.

 Coding Tip

Within a code series, parenthetical notes provide information about deleted codes.

Surgery Guidelines

Guidelines to direct general reporting of services are presented in the **Introduction**. Some of the commonalities are repeated here for the convenience of those referring to this section on **Surgery**. Other definitions and items unique to Surgery are also listed.

Services

Services rendered in the office, home, or hospital, consultations, and other medical services are listed in the **Evaluation and Management Services** section (99201–99499), beginning on page 11. "Special Services, Procedures and Reports" (99000–99082) are listed in the **Medicine** section.

Follow-Up Care for Therapeutic Surgical Procedures

Follow-up care for therapeutic surgical procedures includes only that care which is usually a part of the surgical service. Complications, exacerbations, recurrence, or the presence of other diseases or injuries requiring additional services should be separately reported.

Supplied Materials

Supplies and materials (eg, sterile trays/drugs), over and above those usually included with the procedure(s) rendered are reported separately. List drugs, trays, supplies, and materials provided. Identify as 99070 or specific supply code.

FIGURE 9-4 Portion of CPT Surgery Guidelines

Cardiovascular System	
Blocked unindented note	Selective vascular catheterizations should be coded to include introduction and all lesser order selective catheterizations used in the approach (eg, the description for a selective right middle cerebral artery catheterization includes the introduction and placement catheterization of the right common and internal carotid arteries).
	Additional second and/or third order arterial catheterizations within the same family of arteries supplied by a single first order artery should be expressed by 36218 or 36248. Additional first order or higher catheterizations in vascular families supplied by a first order vessel different from a previously selected and coded family should be separately coded using the conventions described above.
Indented parenthetical note located below subsection title	(For monitoring, operation of pump and other nonsurgical services, see 99190–99192, 99291, 99292, 99354–99360)
	(For other medical or laboratory related services, see appropriate section)
	(For radiological supervision and interpretation, see 75600–75970)
	(For anatomic guidance of arterial and venous anatomy, see Appendix L)

Heart and Pericardium

Pericardium

33020   Pericardiotomy for removal of clot or foreign body

Parenthetical note located below code description   (primary procedure)

FIGURE 9-5 Selection from CPT illustrating different types of instructional notes

Descriptive Qualifiers

Descriptive qualifiers are terms that clarify the assignment of a CPT code. They can occur in the middle of a main clause or after the semicolon and may or may not be enclosed in parentheses. Make sure you read all code descriptions very carefully to properly assign CPT codes that require descriptive qualifiers.

EXAMPLE: The underlining in code descriptions for 17000 and 17003 identify descriptive qualifiers for each.

```
17000    Destruction (eg, laser surgery, electrosurgery, cryosurgery,
         chemosurgery, surgical curettement), premalignant lesions (eg,
         actinic keratoses); first lesion

+ 17003    second through 14 lesions, each (List separately in addition to
         code for first lesion)
```

 Coding Tip

Coders working in a provider's office should highlight descriptive qualifiers in CPT that pertain to the office's specialty. This will help ensure that qualifiers are not overlooked when codes are assigned.

Exercise 9.7 – CPT Sections, Subsections, Categories, and Subcategories

Instructions: Indicate whether the statement is true (T) or false (F).

_____   1. The major sections of CPT are nuclear medicine, surgery, medicine, pathology, and radiology.

Exercise 9.7 – *continued*

_____ 2. When a parenthetical statement within a code description begins with "eg", one of the terms that follows must be included in the provider's description of the surgery for the code number to apply.

_____ 3. When an unlisted procedure or service code is reported, a special report (e.g., copy of the procedure report) must accompany the claim.

_____ 4. A blocked unindented note is located below a subsection, category, or subcategory, and contains instructions that apply to all codes in the subsection, category, or subcategory.

_____ 5. All descriptive qualifiers for a particular code are found in an indented code description.

CPT Modifiers

CPT modifiers clarify services and procedures performed by providers. Although the CPT code and description remain unchanged, modifiers indicate that the description of the service or procedure performed has been altered.

- CPT modifiers are reported as two digits added to the five-digit CPT code (e.g., 99213-25).
- HCPCS level II modifiers are reported as two characters added to the five-digit CPT code (e.g., 11760-TA). (HCPCS level II modifiers were explained in Chapter 8.)

EXAMPLE: A patient undergoes repair of nasal septal perforations (30630), which was unsuccessful. Three months later, the patient undergoes repeat repair of nasal septal perforations by a different surgeon (30630-77). The same CPT code is assigned, and a modifier is added to indicate the repeat procedure.

When reporting codes with more than one modifier, enter the **functional modifier** (or **pricing modifier**), which assists in reimbursement decision making (e.g., assistant surgeon). Next, enter **informational modifiers**, which clarify aspects of the procedure or service provided for the payer (e.g., procedure performed on right or left side only). (Medicare carriers originally created the terms *functional modifier, pricing modifier*, and *informational modifier*, which means some payers do not use the terms.)

EXAMPLE: A patient fractured his left femur. An assistant surgeon participated in the open treatment and internal fixation of the femoral fracture, proximal end, neck. Report code 27236-80-LT.
Modifier -80, Assistant Surgeon, is a functional modifier that impacts the reimbursement rate paid by the third-party payer. Modifier -LT is an informational modifier, which indicates that the surgery was performed on the patient's left side. It does not impact the reimbursement amount paid to the physician.

When multiple modifiers are added to a CPT (or HCPCS level II) code and an informational modifier is listed first, third-party payers manually review the claim. Manual review slows claims processing and results in reimbursement delays to physicians.

Not all CPT modifiers apply to each section of CPT. Table 9-1 summarizes CPT modifiers in numeric order and identifies applicable CPT sections that are recommended for each. (Coders should contact third-party payers to obtain a list of modifiers and applicable CPT sections because each payer has different reporting requirements.)

The AMA and CMS develop new modifiers on a continuous basis, and next available numbers are assigned. This means that there is no relationship among groups of modifier numbers. Reviewing modifiers in strict numeric order does not allow for comparison of those that are related to one another in terms of content; therefore, Table 9-2 organizes modifiers according to reporting similarity.

EXAMPLE: Mrs. T has a history of gallbladder disease. After several hours of acute pain, she was referred to Dr. S for an evaluation of her condition. Dr. S performed a complete history and physical examination and decided to admit the patient to the hospital for an immediate workup for cholecystitis. When the results of laboratory tests and sonogram were received, the patient was scheduled for an emergency laparoscopic cholecystectomy.

 NOTE:

In an attempt to simplify the explanation of modifiers, wording in the example does not correspond word for word with descriptions found in CPT.

The surgeon was Dr. S, and the assistant surgeon was Dr. A. The surgery was successful, and the patient was discharged the next day and told to return to the office in seven days. Four days later, Mrs. T returned to Dr. S's office complaining of chest pains. Dr. S performed another examination and ordered the necessary tests. After reviewing the test results and confirming with the patient's primary care physician, it was determined that the patient was suffering from mild angina.

Dr. S reports the following services (Figure 9-6):

- Initial hospital visit, comprehensive, with medical decision making of high complexity (99223-57) (Modifier -57 indicates that the decision to perform surgery was made during the hospital evaluation.)

- Laparoscopic cholecystectomy (47562)

- Office visit, established patient, expanded problem focused, with medical decision making of low complexity (99213-24) (Modifier -24 indicates that the patient received an E/M service by the same physician during a postoperative period. Reexamination revealed the problem to be unrelated to the normal postoperative care provided to a cholecystectomy patient. The diagnosis linked to this visit is angina.)

Dr. A reports (Figure 9-7) the following service:

- Laparoscopic cholecystectomy 47562-80 (Modifier -80 indicates that Dr. A is the assistant surgeon.)

PROCEDURES, SERVICES, OR SUPPLIES	
(Explain Unusual Circumstances)	
CPT/HCPCS	MODIFIER
99223	57
47562	
99213	24

Courtesy of the Centers for Medicare & Medicaid Services, www.cms.gov; claim data created by author.

FIGURE 9-6 Completed Block 24D of CMS-1500 claim

PROCEDURES, SERVICES, OR SUPPLIES	
(Explain Unusual Circumstances)	
CPT/HCPCS	MODIFIER
47562	80

Courtesy of the Centers for Medicare & Medicaid Services, www.cms.gov; claim data created by author.

FIGURE 9-7 Completed Block 24D of CMS-1500 claim

TABLE 9-1 CPT Modifiers in a Quick View Format

Modifier	Title of Modifier
-22	Increased Procedural Services
-23	Unusual Anesthesia
-24	Unrelated Evaluation and Management Service by the Same Physician or Other Qualified Health Care Professional During a Postoperative Period
-25	Significant, Separately Identifiable Evaluation and Management Service by the Same Physician or Other Qualified Health Care Professional on the Same Day of the Procedure or Other Service
-26	Professional Component
-27	Multiple Outpatient Hospital E/M Encounters on the Same Date
-32	Mandated Services
-33	Preventive Services
-47	Anesthesia by Surgeon
-50	Bilateral Procedure
-51	Multiple Procedures
-52	Reduced Services
-53	Discontinued Procedure
-54	Surgical Care Only
-55	Postoperative Management Only
-56	Preoperative Management Only
-57	Decision for Surgery
-58	Staged or Related Procedure or Service by the Same Physician or Other Qualified Health Care Professional During the Postoperative Period
-59	Distinct Procedural Service
-62	Two Surgeons
-63	Procedure Performed on Infants Less Than 4 kg
-66	Surgical Team
-73	Discontinued Outpatient Hospital/Ambulatory Surgery Center (ASC) Procedure Prior to the Administration of Anesthesia
-74	Discontinued Outpatient Hospital/Ambulatory Surgery Center (ASC) Procedure After Administration of Anesthesia
-76	Repeat Procedure or Service by Same Physician or Other Qualified Health Care Professional
-77	Repeat Procedure by Another Physician or Other Qualified Health Care Professional
-78	Unplanned Return to the Operating/Procedure Room by the Same Physician or Other Qualified Health Care Professional Following Initial Procedure for a Related Procedure During the Postoperative Period
-79	Unrelated Procedure or Service by the Same Physician or Other Qualified Health Care Professional During the Postoperative Period
-80	Assistant Surgeon
-81	Minimum Assistant Surgeon
-82	Assistant Surgeon (when qualified resident surgeon not available)
-90	Reference (Outside) Laboratory
-91	Repeat Clinical Diagnostic Laboratory Test
-92	Alternative Laboratory Platform Testing
-95	Synchronous Telemedicine Service Rendered Via a Real-Time Interactive Audio and Video Telecommunication System
-96	Habilitative Services
-97	Rehabilitative Services
-99	Multiple Modifiers

TABLE 9-2 Organization of CPT Modifiers According to Reporting Similarity

Modifier	Description	Interpretation	Coding Tips and Examples
Special Evaluation and Management (E/M) Cases			
-24	Unrelated Evaluation and Management Service by the Same Physician or Other Qualified Health Care Professional During a Postoperative Period	Assign to indicate that an E/M service was performed during the standard postoperative period for a condition unrelated to the surgery. The *service* to which the modifier is attached *must be* linked to a diagnosis that is *unrelated* to the surgical diagnosis previously submitted. Make sure you submit a copy of documentation with the claim to explain the circumstances.	EXAMPLE: One week after surgical treatment to release a frozen shoulder, patient received level 3 evaluation and management services for treatment of the flu. Report code 99213-24.
-25	Significant, Separately Identifiable Evaluation and Management Service by the Same Physician or Other Qualified Health Care Professional on the Same Day of the Procedure or Other Service	Assign when a documented E/M service was performed on the same day as another procedure because the patient's condition required the assignment of a significant, separately identifiable, additional E/M service that was provided "above and beyond the other service provided or beyond the usual preoperative and postoperative care associated with the procedure performed." The documented history, examination, and medical decision making must "stand on its own" to justify reporting modifier -25 with the E/M code. The E/M service provided must be "above and beyond" what is normally performed during a procedure.	EXAMPLE: During a routine annual examination, it was discovered that the 65-year-old established patient had an enlarged liver expanding the scope of level 4 evaluation and management services. Report codes 99397 and 99214-25. (Make sure you submit supporting documentation to the payer.)
-57	Decision for Surgery	Assign when the reported E/M service resulted in the *initial* decision to perform surgery on the day before *or* the day of surgery, to exempt it from the global surgery package.	EXAMPLE: The patient received level 4 evaluation and management services for chest pain in the emergency department, and a decision was made to insert a coronary artery stent. Report code 99284-57.
Greater, Reduced, or Discontinued Services			
-22	Increased Procedural Services	Assign when a procedure *requires greater than usual service(s).* Documentation that would support using this modifier includes difficult, complicated, extensive, unusual, or rare procedure(s).	EXAMPLE: The patient experienced blood loss of 600 cc, which required intraoperative transfusions. Report the CPT surgery code with modifier -22.
-52	Reduced Services	Report when a service has been partially reduced or eliminated at the provider's discretion and does not completely match the CPT code description. (Attach a copy of documentation to the claim.)	EXAMPLE: A surgeon removed a coccygeal pressure ulcer and performed a coccygectomy. However, the surgeon did not use a primary suture or perform a skin flap closure because the wound had to be cleansed for a continued period of time postoperatively. Report code 15920-52. (When the surgeon eventually performs the wound closure procedure, an appropriate code would be reported.)
-53	Discontinued Procedure	Report when a provider has elected to terminate a procedure because of extenuating circumstances that threaten the well-being of the patient. NOTE: This modifier applies only to provider office settings and is not reported for elective cancellation (e.g., by the patient) prior to anesthesia induction and/or surgical preparation in the operating suite.	EXAMPLE: The surgeon inserted the colonoscope and removed it right away because the patient had not been properly prepared for the procedure. Report code 45378-53. (The patient received instruction about properly preparing for the colonoscopy procedure, and the procedure was rescheduled.)
-73	Discontinued Outpatient Hospital/Ambulatory Surgery Center (ASC) Procedure Prior to the Administration of Anesthesia	Report to describe discontinued procedures *prior to the administration of any anesthesia* because of extenuating circumstances threatening the well-being of the patient. (Also report an ICD-10-CM code to document the reason the procedure was halted.) NOTE: This modifier applies only to hospital and ASC outpatient settings and is *not* reported for elective cancellation (e.g., by the patient) prior to anesthesia induction or surgical preparation in the operating suite.	EXAMPLE: Hospital outpatient developed a heart arrhythmia prior to anesthesia administration, and the laparoscopic cholecystectomy procedure was canceled. Report code 47562-73.

(continues)

TABLE 9-2 *(continued)*

Modifier	Description	Interpretation	Coding Tips and Examples
-74	Discontinued Outpatient Hospital/Ambulatory Surgery Center (ASC) Procedure After the Administration of Anesthesia	Report to describe discontinued procedures *after the administration of anesthesia* due to extenuating circumstances. (Also report an ICD-10-CM code to document the reason the procedure was halted.) NOTE: This modifier applies only to hospital and ASC outpatient settings.	**EXAMPLE:** ASC outpatient was prepped and draped, and general anesthesia was administered. The anesthesiologist noted a sudden increase in blood pressure, and the laparoscopic cholecystectomy procedure was terminated. Report code 47562-74.

Global Surgery

- Global surgery modifiers apply to the four areas related to the CPT *surgical package* (Figure 9-8), which includes local infiltration; metacarpal/digital block or topical anesthesia when used; the procedure; and normal, uncomplicated follow-up care.

- Global surgery modifiers do *not* apply to obstetrical coding, where the CPT description of specific codes clearly describes separate antepartum, postpartum, and delivery services for both vaginal and cesarean deliveries.

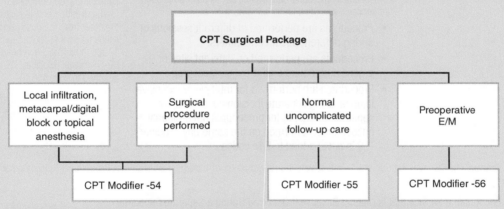

FIGURE 9-8 Modifiers that apply to components of the CPT surgical package

-54	Surgical Care Only	Report when a provider performed only the surgical portion of surgical package and personally administered required local anesthesia. Different provider(s) will have performed preoperative evaluation and/or provided postoperative care.	**EXAMPLE:** While on vacation, John Jones sustained a tibial shaft fracture and underwent closed treatment by Dr. Charles. Upon return to his hometown, John received follow-up care from Dr. Smith, a local orthopedist. Dr. Charles reports code 27750-54.
-55	Postoperative Management Only	Report when a provider other than the surgeon is responsible for postoperative management only of a surgery performed by another provider. Documentation in the patient's chart should detail the date of transfer of care to calculate the percentage of the fee to be billed for postoperative care. (The modifier is added to the surgical procedure code. Modifier -55 does *not* apply when a second provider occasionally covers for the surgeon and where no transfer of care occurs.)	**EXAMPLE:** While on vacation, John Jones sustained a tibial shaft fracture and underwent closed treatment by Dr. Charles. Upon return to his hometown, John received follow-up care from Dr. Smith, a local orthopedist. Dr. Smith reports code 27750-55.

(continues)

TABLE 9-2 (*continued*)

Global Surgery

Modifier	Description	Interpretation	Coding Tips and Examples
-56	Preoperative Management Only	Report when a provider *other than* the operating surgeon performs preoperative care and evaluation of the patient for surgery (e.g., preoperative clearance).	**EXAMPLE:** Dr. Berger preoperatively cleared his patient during a level 4 E/M service for scheduled surgery by Dr. Charles. Dr. Berger reports code 99214-56.

Special Surgical and Procedural Events

Modifier	Description	Interpretation	Coding Tips and Examples
-58	Staged or Related Procedure or Service by the Same Physician or Other Qualified Health Care Professional During the Postoperative Period	Report to indicate that additional related surgery was required during the postoperative period of a previously completed surgery and was performed by the same provider. Documentation should include one of the following: • Original plan for surgery included additional stages to be performed within postoperative period of first stage of procedure. • Underlying disease required a second related, but unplanned, procedure to be performed. • Additional related therapy is required after the performance of a procedure.	**CODING TIP:** Do not report modifier -58 if the CPT code description describes multiple sessions of an event. **EXAMPLE:** A surgical wound is not healing properly because of the patient's underlying diabetes. Patient was told prior to the original surgery that if this happened, additional surgery would be required for subcutaneous tissue debridement of the wound. Report code 11042-58 for debridement surgery.
-59	Distinct Procedural Service	Report when same provider performs one or more *distinctly independent procedures* on the same day as other procedures or services, according to the following criteria: • Procedures are performed at different sessions or during different patient encounters. • Procedures are performed on different sites or organs and require a different surgical prep. • Procedures are performed for multiple or extensive injuries, using separate incisions/excisions; for separate lesions; or for procedures not ordinarily encountered/performed on the same day. Modifier -59 is *never* added to E/M codes.	**EXAMPLE:** Patient has two basal cell carcinomas removed, one from the forehead with a simple closure (11640) and the other from the nose requiring adjacent tissue transfer (14060). Report codes 14060, 11640-51 (forehead), and 11640-59-51 (nose). (Modifier -XS could also be attached to code 11640.)

NOTE: CMS has defined HCPCS level II modifiers to selectively identify subsets of modifier -59 (Distinct Procedural Services) for Medicare claims, as follows:

- -XE Separate Encounter, a Service that is Distinct Because it Occurred During a Separate Encounter
- -XS Separate Structure, a Service that is Distinct Because it was Performed on a Separate Organ/Structure
- -XP Separate Practitioner, a Service that is Distinct Because it was Performed by a Different Practitioner
- -XU Unusual Non-Overlapping Service, the Use of a Service that is Distinct Because it Does Not Overlap Usual Components of the Main Service

EXAMPLE: A patient receives an antibiotic infusion as an outpatient and is discharged. She returns later that same day and receives another separate antibiotic infusion. Modifier -XE is reported with each CPT medication administration (infusion) code and each HCPCS level II drug (e.g., clindamycin).

Modifier	Description	Interpretation	Coding Tips and Examples
-63	Procedure Performed on Infants Less Than 4 kg	Report when infant weighs less than 4 kilograms (kg) because procedures performed may require increased complexity and provider work. (Refer to CPT Appendix A for the list of codes to which modifier -63 applies.)	**EXAMPLE:** Baby Girl Markel's weight was 3.5 kg at the time she underwent diagnostic thoracoscopy. Report 32601-63.
-78	Unplanned Return to the Operating/Procedure Room by the Same Physician or Other Qualified Health Care Professional Following Initial Procedure for a Related Procedure During the Postoperative Period	Report for unplanned circumstances that require return to operating room for complications of initial operation. (Also report an ICD code to document the surgical complication that necessitated a return to operating room.) NOTE: This modifier applies only to hospital outpatient settings.	**EXAMPLE:** Surgical sutures did not hold, and a 12-cm layer closure of axillary wound was performed. Report code 12034-78.

(continues)

TABLE 9-2 (*continued*)

Special Surgical and Procedural Events			
Modifier	**Description**	**Interpretation**	**Coding Tips and Examples**
-79	Unrelated Procedure or Service by the Same Physician or Other Qualified Health Care Professional During the Postoperative Period	Report when a new procedure or service is performed by a provider during the normal postoperative period of a previously performed but unrelated surgery. NOTE: This modifier applies only to hospital outpatient settings.	**EXAMPLE:** Six weeks following cataract surgery performed on the left eye, the patient underwent diathermic repair of retinal detachment, right eye. Report code 67101-79.

Bilateral and Multiple Procedures			
-27	Multiple Outpatient Hospital E/M Encounters on the Same Date	Report for patients who receive multiple E/M services performed by *different providers* on the same day. NOTE: This modifier applies only to hospital outpatient settings.	**EXAMPLE:** A patient was seen in the hospital's emergency department and received level 4 evaluation and management services due to a fractured ankle. The patient was seen later the same day in the urgent care center and provided with level 3 evaluation and management services due to a migraine that did not respond to prescribed medication taken at home. Report codes 99284-27 and 99213-27.
-50	Bilateral Procedure	Report this directional modifier when a procedure was performed bilaterally *during the same session and when the code description does not specify that the procedure is bilateral.* Modifier -50 is *not* reported with add-on codes, designed with a plus symbol in CPT. For bilateral procedures, report the add-on code twice.	**EXAMPLE:** Patient underwent bilateral arthrodesis of the knees. Report code 27580-50 (or report HCPCS level II national modifiers as codes 27580-LT and 27580-RT).

NOTE: Directional modifiers (e.g., -50, -LT, -RT) are reported with CPT and HCPCS level II codes when the code description includes anatomic structures that are found bilaterally (e.g., kidneys, breasts, eyes). When code descriptions include anatomic structures that are found bilaterally *along with those not found bilaterally, do not report directional modifiers with the CPT or HCPCS level II code.*

EXAMPLE 1: Laparoscopic retroperitoneal lymph node biopsy. Report code 38570. Retroperitoneal lymph nodes are located in the abdomen, which is not a paired anatomic structure; thus, a directional modifier is not reported.

EXAMPLE 2: Percutaneous arterial line inserted into left radial artery. Report code 36620. Although the anatomic structure described in the physician's procedure statement is bilateral, the code description of 36620 is "arterial catheterization or cannulation for sampling, monitoring or transfusion (separate procedure); percutaneous." Because this code is reported for *any* artery, including those that are not bilateral anatomic structures (e.g., brachiocephalic artery), a directional modifier is *not* reported.

-51	Multiple Procedures	Report when multiple procedures *other than E/M services* are performed during a single patient encounter by the same provider. The procedures performed are characterized as • Multiple related surgical procedures performed at the same session • Surgical procedures that are performed in combination, whether through the same or another incision, or that involve the same or different anatomy • Combination medical and surgical procedures performed at the same session	**EXAMPLE:** Patient underwent right tibial shaft fracture repair and arthrodesis of left knee. Report codes 27750 and 27580-51.

Repeat Services			
-76	Repeat Procedure or Service by Same Physician or Other Qualified Health Care Professional	Report when a procedure was repeated because of special circumstances involving the original service and the same physician performed the repeat procedure.	**EXAMPLE:** A repeat EKG is performed due to changes in the patient's condition or the need to assess the effect of therapeutic procedures. Report code 93041-76.
-77	Repeat Procedure by Another Physician or Other Qualified Health Care Professional	Report when a physician *other than the original physician* performs a repeat procedure because of special circumstances involving the original study or procedure.	**EXAMPLE:** Patient underwent past sterilization procedure (e.g., tubal ligation) but became pregnant. After C-section delivery, she underwent a second sterilization procedure. Report code 58611-77 for the second sterilization procedure.

(continues)

TABLE 9-2 (*continued*)

Multiple Surgeons

Modifier	Description	Interpretation	Coding Tips and Examples
-62	Two Surgeons	Report when two primary surgeons are required during an operative session, each performing distinct parts of a reportable procedure. Ideally, the surgeons represent different specialties.	**EXAMPLE:** A spinal surgeon and a general surgeon work together as primary surgeons to perform an anterior spinal fusion of L5-S1. The spinal surgeon also inserts an intervertebral synthetic cage and performs iliac bone grafting. Each surgeon reports code 22558-62. The spinal surgeon also reports codes 22853 and 20937.
-66	Surgical Team	Report when surgery performed is highly complex and requires the services of a skilled team of three or more surgeons. The procedure reported on the claim for each participating surgeon must include this modifier. The operative reports must document the complexity of the surgery and refer to the actions of each team member.	**EXAMPLE:** Reattachment of severed forearm. Each surgeon reports code 20802-66.
-80	Assistant Surgeon	Report when one physician assists another during an operative session. The assistant surgeon reports the same CPT code as the operating physician.	**EXAMPLE:** Dr. Landry assisted Dr. Bartron during single coronary artery bypass surgery. Dr. Landry reports code 33510-80. (Dr. Bartron reports code 33510 without the modifier.)
-81	Minimum Assistant Surgeon	Report when primary operating physician has planned to perform a surgical procedure alone, but circumstances arise that require the services of an assistant surgeon for a short time. The second surgeon reports the same CPT code as the operating physician.	**EXAMPLE:** Dr. Kelly begins an invasive cholecystectomy procedure and discovers that the gallbladder is the size of a hot dog bun, which necessitates calling Dr. Pietro to assist for a short time. Dr. Pietro reports code 47600-81. (A gallbladder is supposed to be the size of your little finger.)
-82	Assistant Surgeon (when qualified resident surgeon not available)	Report when a qualified resident surgeon is unavailable to assist with a procedure. In teaching hospitals, the physician acting as the assistant surgeon is usually a qualified resident surgeon. If circumstances arise (e.g., rotational changes) and a qualified resident surgeon is not available, another surgeon may assist with a procedure. The nonresident-assistant surgeon reports the same CPT code as the operating physician.	**EXAMPLE:** Resident surgeon Dr. Smith was to assist surgeon Dr. Manlin with a routine laparoscopic appendectomy. Dr. Smith was temporarily reassigned to the emergency department, and Dr. Manlin's partner assisted with the procedure. Code 44970-82 is reported.

Preventive Services

Modifier	Description	Interpretation	Coding Tips and Examples
-33	Preventive Service	Alerts third-party payers that the procedure or service was preventive under applicable laws and that patient cost sharing (e.g., coinsurance, copayment, deductible) does not apply when furnished by in-network providers.	**EXAMPLE:** The patient's primary care provider provided 20 minutes of smoking and tobacco use cessation counseling. Report code 99407-33.

Professional and Technical Components

Modifier	Description	Interpretation	Coding Tips and Examples
-26	Professional Component	Report when the provider either interprets test results or operates equipment for a procedure. *Do not report this modifier when a specific separately identifiable code describes the professional component of a procedure (e.g., 93010).*	**EXAMPLE:** Independent radiologist Dr. Minion interprets a 3-view chest x-ray that was performed by another provider. Dr. Minion reports code 71047-26.

Mandated Services

Modifier	Description	Interpretation	Coding Tips and Examples
-32	Mandated Services	Report when services (e.g., second or third opinion for a surgical procedure) provided were mandated by a third party (e.g., attorney or payer).	**EXAMPLE:** A patient's primary care provider recommends respiratory therapy. The payer requires the patient to undergo a level 3 evaluation and management service by a respiratory specialist. Code 99243-32 is reported.

(continues)

TABLE 9-2 *(continued)*

Unusual Anesthesia			
Modifier	**Description**	**Interpretation**	**Coding Tips and Examples**
-23	Unusual Anesthesia	Report when circumstances (e.g., extent of service or patient's physical condition) require anesthesia for procedures that usually require either no anesthesia or local anesthesia.	**EXAMPLE:** The 30-year-old patient has an intellectual disability and requires the administration of general anesthesia for ventral hernia repair (instead of regional anesthesia). Code 00832-23 is reported.
-47	Anesthesia by Surgeon	Report when the surgeon provides regional or general anesthesia in addition to performing the surgical procedure. Modifier -47 is added to the CPT surgery code. It is not reported with Anesthesia codes 00100–01999.	**EXAMPLE:** The surgeon administers the regional anesthesia and performs the spigelian hernia repair. Code 49590-47 is reported.
Laboratory Services			
-90	Reference (Outside) Laboratory	Report when a laboratory test is performed by an outside or reference laboratory.	**EXAMPLE:** The provider orders a CBC. Arrangements are made with an outside lab to perform the CBC and bill the physician. The physician reports code 85025-90. (Code 36415 is also reported for routine venipuncture.)
-91	Repeat Clinical Diagnostic Laboratory Test	Report when a clinical diagnostic laboratory test is repeated on the same day to obtain subsequent (multiple) test results. *This modifier is not reported when lab tests are repeated to confirm initial results* (e.g., due to equipment problems).	**EXAMPLE:** The patient underwent serial (repeated) lab tests for cardiac enzyme testing every six hours. Report codes 82657, 82657-91, and 82657-91.
-92	Alternative Laboratory Platform Testing	Report when laboratory testing is performed using a kit or transportable instrument that wholly or in part consists of a single-use, disposable analytical chamber. Such testing does not require permanent dedicated space because the testing materials can be carried or transported to the patient care area.	**EXAMPLE:** The laboratory technician brought the HIV-1 testing materials to the emergency department and performed an HIV-1 test on Mary Jones. Report code 86701-92.
Multiple Modifiers			
-99	Multiple Modifiers	Report to alert third-party payers that more than four modifiers are added to a procedure or service code. The CMS-1500 claim allows up to four modifiers to be listed after a CPT or HCPCS level II code (Figure 9-9).	**EXAMPLE:** An assistant surgeon (-80) reports an unusual service (-22), bilateral (-50), surgeon-provided general anesthesia services (-47) for lumbar hernia repair procedure (49540). • On the CMS-1500 claim, report as 49540 22 47 50 99 and 49540 80.

Courtesy of the Centers for Medicare & Medicaid Services, www.cms.gov; claim data created by author.

FIGURE 9-9 Block 24D of CMS-1500 claim, with multiple modifiers entered

• The UB-04 claim allows up to three modifiers to be listed after a CPT or HCPCS level II code in Form Locator 44 (Figure 9-10).

• On the UB-04, report as 49540 22 47 99, 49540 and 49540 50 80.

Courtesy of the Centers for Medicare & Medicaid Services, www.cms.gov; claim data created by author.

FIGURE 9-10 Form Locators 44 of UB-04 claim, with multiple modifiers reported

(continues)

TABLE 9-2 *(continued)*

Telemedicine			
Modifier	**Description**	**Interpretation**	**Coding Tips and Examples**
-95	Synchronous Telemedicine Service Rendered Via a Real-Time Interactive Audio and Video Telecommunication System	Synchronous telemedicine service is real-time interaction between a provider and a patient who is located at a distant site from the provider.	**EXAMPLE:** Patient underwent psychiatric diagnostic evaluation with medical services. Report code 90792-95.

Habilitative and Rehabilitative Services			
-96	Habilitative Services	Report for *habilitative services*, which (1) help patients learn skills and functioning for daily living that they have not yet developed and (2) help patients keep, learn, or improve skills and functioning for daily living.	**EXAMPLE:** Thirty-month old child received speech therapy due to a limited expressive vocabulary (speech delay). Report code 92507-96.
-97	Rehabilitative Services	Report for *rehabilitative services*, which help patients keep, relearn, or improve skills and functioning for daily living that have been lost or impaired because of illness, injury, or disability.	**EXAMPLE:** Patient received 15 minutes of direct one-on-one patient contact for therapeutic activities to improve functional performance as the result of a stroke. Report code 97530-97.

Exercise 9.8 – CPT Modifiers

Instructions: Assign appropriate modifier(s) to each statement. Do *not* assign CPT codes.

_____   1. Assistant surgeon reporting patient's cesarean section, delivery only

_____   2. Cholecystectomy reported during postoperative period for treatment of leg fracture

_____   3. Treatment for chronic conditions at same time preventive medicine is provided

_____   4. Inpatient visit performed by surgeon, with decision to perform surgery tomorrow

_____   5. Office consultation as preoperative clearance for surgery

_____   6. Postoperative management of vaginal hysterectomy

_____   7. Repeat gallbladder x-ray series, same physician

_____   8. Arthroscopy of right elbow and closed fracture reduction of left wrist

_____   9. Needle core biopsy of right and left breasts

_____   10. Consultation required by payer

National Correct Coding Initiative (NCCI)

To promote national correct coding methodologies and control the improper assignment of codes that results in inappropriate reimbursement of Medicare Part B claims, the Centers for Medicare & Medicaid Services (CMS) implemented the **National Correct Coding Initiative (NCCI)**. NCCI edits (Table 9-3) are used to process Medicare Part B claims for hospital outpatient and physician services, and NCCI coding policies are based on the following:

- Analysis of standard medical and surgical practice
- Coding conventions included in CPT
- Coding guidelines developed by national medical specialty societies (e.g., CPT advisory committee, which contains representatives of major medical societies)
- Local and national coverage determinations
- Review of current coding practices

The NCCI was initially developed for use by Medicare administrative contractors (MACs) that process Medicare Part B claims for physician office services. NCCI edits were added to the Outpatient Code Editor (OCE) in August 2000, and they are used by MACs to process Medicare Part B claims for outpatient hospital procedures and services. (Some OCE edits that apply to outpatient hospital services claims differ from comparable edits in the NCCI used to process physician office services claims.)

NOTE:

Locate Medlearn articles that contain OCE updates by going to www.cms.gov and clicking on the Outreach & Education link, then clicking on the Medicare link, followed by the MLN Matters Articles link.

NOTE:

In 2010, 23 Medicare administrative contractors (MACs) replaced the 23 fiscal intermediaries (FIs) that processed hospital inpatient and outpatient claims for Medicare Part A and Part B services and 17 Medicare carriers that processed physician claims for Medicare Part B services. MACs process both hospital inpatient/outpatient and physician Medicare Part A and Part B claims, and are abbreviated as A/B MACs. In addition, MACs also process durable medical equipment claims and home health/hospice claims, abbreviated as DME MACs and HH&H MACs, respectively. (Although FIs and carriers continue to be referenced on government and private websites and newsletters, MACs replaced both entities in 2010.)

TABLE 9-3 Partial Listing of National Correct Coding Initiative (NCCI) Edits

NCCI Edit	Description	Disposition of Claim
1	Invalid diagnosis code	Return to Provider
2	Diagnosis and age conflict	Return to Provider
3	Diagnosis and sex conflict	Return to Provider
4	Medicare secondary payer alert	Suspend
19	Mutually exclusive procedure that is not allowed by CCI even if appropriate modifier is present	Line Item Rejection
20	Component of a comprehensive procedure that is not allowed by CCI even if appropriate modifier is present	Line Item Rejection
39	Mutually exclusive procedure that would be allowed by CCI if appropriate modifier were present	Line Item Rejection
40	Component of a comprehensive procedure that would be allowed by CCI if appropriate modifier were present	Line Item Rejection

Carefully review parenthetical notes below CPT code descriptions to locate procedures that are separately reported (in addition to the major procedure performed). When reporting codes for outpatient hospital services and physician office services, use OCE software or NCCI software, respectively, to identify bundled codes for procedures and services considered necessary to accomplish the major procedure. Bundled procedure codes are *not* separately coded and reported with the major procedure code. Reporting bundled procedure codes in addition to the major procedure code is *unbundling*, which is characterized as abuse or fraud depending upon intent. The OCE edits are packaged with commercial software, such as Optum360's Encoder Pro Expert. The NCCI edits are available at www.cms.gov. Click on the Medicare link, scroll down to the Coding heading, and click on the National Correct Coding Initiative Edits. (The OCE and NCCI edits are available for purchase from the National Technical Information Service [NTIS] at www.ntis.gov.) (Additional content about the NCCI is located in Chapter 20 of this textbook.)

CMS Posts Correct Coding Initiative (CCI) Edits on Internet

The Centers for Medicare & Medicaid Services (CMS) has made it easier for physicians and other providers to bill properly and be paid promptly for their services to people with Medicare coverage. CMS has posted CCI edits that are used to identify questionable claims and adjust payments to reflect what would have been paid if the claim had been filed correctly. The edits, known as the National Correct Coding Initiative (NCCI), identify pairs of services that normally should not be billed by the same physician for the same patient on the same day. The NCCI also promotes uniformity among the contractors that process Medicare claims in interpreting Medicare payment policies.

The posting of NCCI edits is the most recent in a series of steps CMS has taken to use the Internet creatively to reduce the regulatory burden on physicians and make it easier for them to work with Medicare to improve services to beneficiaries. CMS has also added a Physician Fee Schedule Look-Up Tool to its website (www.cms.gov) that makes it possible for physicians to determine in advance what they will be paid for a particular service or range of services. The Medicare Physician Fee Schedule Look-Up Tool provides unadjusted payment rates as well as payment rates by geographic location.

While the NCCI is a cornerstone of efforts to ensure that Medicare and beneficiaries do not pay twice for the same service or for duplicative services, CMS believes physicians should have easy access to the edits used to identify incorrect claims. The NCCI includes two types of edits:

- **Column 1/column 2 edits**: Code pairs that should not be billed together because one service inherently includes the other; previously called comprehensive/component edits
- **Mutually exclusive edits**: Code pairs that, for clinical reasons, are unlikely to be performed on the same patient on the same day (e.g., two different types of testing that yield equivalent results)

CPT codes representing services denied based on NCCI edits may not be billed to Medicare beneficiaries. Since these denials are based on incorrect coding rather than medical necessity, the provider cannot submit an *Advance Beneficiary Notice (ABN)* to seek payment from a Medicare beneficiary. An ABN is a form completed and signed by a Medicare beneficiary each time a provider believes a normally covered service will not be covered *and* the provider wants to bill the beneficiary directly for the service. In addition, because the denials are based on incorrect coding (rather than a legislated Medicare benefit exclusion), the provider *cannot* seek payment from the beneficiary even if a Notice of Exclusions from Medicare Benefits (NEMB) was obtained.

A **Notice of Exclusions from Medicare Benefits (NEMB)** is a form completed and signed by a Medicare beneficiary before items, procedures, and services excluded from Medicare benefits are provided; it alerts Medicare beneficiaries in advance that Medicare does not cover certain items and services because they do not meet the definition of a Medicare benefit or because they are specifically excluded by law. NEMB is completed when an ABN is not appropriate.

The NCCI edits, which are updated quarterly, were previously available to physicians and other providers on a paid subscription basis; but they are now available to anyone with a computer. The NCCI edits are posted as a spreadsheet

(continues)

that allows users to sort by procedural code and effective date. A *Find* feature allows users to look for a specific code. The NCCI edit files are also indexed by procedural code ranges to allow for easy navigation.

The website also includes links to documents that explain the edits, including the following:

- Medicare Claims Processing Manual
- NCCI Edits Program Transmittals
- NCCI FAQs (frequently asked questions)
- NCCI Policy Manual for Part B MACs

(Courtesy of the Centers for Medicare & Medicaid Services, www.cms.gov)

EXAMPLE: Code 67911 describes the "Correction of lid retraction." A parenthetical note below the code description advises that if autogenous graft materials are obtained during the same operative session, tissue graft code 15769, 20920, or 20922 is reported in addition to code 67911.

According to the Medicare Code Editor (MCE), *other procedures necessary to accomplish* the "correction of lid retraction" are included in code 67911, such as full-thickness graft placement (15260). Those procedures are not separately coded and reported when performed during the same operative session as the "correction of lid retraction."

Unbundling CPT Codes

Providers are responsible for reporting the CPT (and HCPCS level II) code that most comprehensively describes the services provided. NCCI edits determine the appropriateness of CPT code combinations for claims submitted to MACs. NCCI edits are designed to detect *unbundling*, which involves reporting multiple codes for a service when a single comprehensive code should be assigned. The practice of unbundling occurs when coders unintentionally report multiple codes when coding guidelines are misinterpreted *or* when multiple codes are intentionally reported to maximize reimbursement.

- Unbundling occurs when one service is divided into its component parts and a code for each component part is reported as if they were separate services.

EXAMPLE: A 64-year-old female patient undergoes total abdominal hysterectomy with bilateral salpingectomy and oophorectomy. Review CPT Surgery code descriptions for 58150, 58700, and 58720. Reporting codes 58700 and 58720 in addition to 58150 is considered unbundling. If all three codes were submitted on a claim, reimbursement for codes 58700 and 58720 would be disallowed (and the provider might be subject to allegations of fraud and abuse, depending upon intent).

- Unbundling occurs when a code for the separate surgical approach (e.g., laparotomy) is reported in addition to a code for the surgical procedure. Procedures performed to gain access to an area or organ system are not separately reported.

EXAMPLE: A 54-year-old female patient underwent excision of ileoanal reservoir with ileostomy, which required lysis of adhesions to gain access to the site of surgery. Review CPT Surgery code descriptions for 45136 and 44005. Report CPT code 45136 only because code 44005 is considered a component part of the total procedure (45136). Reporting both codes would be considered unbundling.

Exercise 9.9 – National Correct Coding Initiative

Instructions: Complete each statement.

1. To promote national correct coding methodologies and control the improper assignment of codes that result in inappropriate reimbursement of Medicare Part _____ claims, CMS implemented the NCCI.

2. The NCCI was initially developed for use by Medicare administrative contractors (MACs) that process Medicare Part B claims for physician office services; in August 2000, NCCI edits were added to the Outpatient Code _____ for use by MACs to process Medicare Part B claims for outpatient hospital services.

3. The NCCI code pairs that should not be billed together because one service inherently includes the other are called column 1/column 2 edits, while the NCCI code pairs that, for clinical reasons, are unlikely to be performed on the same patient on the same day are called _____ edits.

4. When a submitted claim for reimbursement is denied because of incorrect coding rather than medical necessity, the provider cannot submit an Advance Beneficiary Notice (ABN) or a Notice of Exclusions from Medicare _____ to seek payment from a Medicare beneficiary.

5. A 34-year-old male underwent upper gastrointestinal endoscopy, which included visualization of the esophagus, stomach, and duodenum. During endoscopy, brushings collected esophageal specimens and esophageal biopsy was performed. Upon review of CPT Surgery code descriptions for 43235 and 43239, the coder assigned 43239 only (because 43235 is considered a component of the total procedure, 43239). Reporting both codes would be considered _____.

Summary

CPT codes are reported for services and procedures provided by home health care and hospice agencies, outpatient hospital departments, physicians who are employees of a health care facility, and physicians who see patients in their offices or clinics and in patients' homes. To promote national correct coding methodologies and to control the improper assignment of codes that result in inappropriate reimbursement of Medicare Part B claims, the Centers for Medicare & Medicaid Services (CMS) implemented the National Correct Coding Initiative (NCCI).

CPT organizes Category I procedures and services into six sections: Evaluation and Management (E/M), Anesthesia, Surgery, Radiology (including Nuclear Medicine and Diagnostic Ultrasound), Pathology and Laboratory, and Medicine. The CPT index is organized by alphabetical main terms printed in boldface, and appendices are located after Category III codes.

CPT sections are subdivided into subsections, categories, and subcategories. Guidelines, notes, and descriptive qualifiers are also found in CPT sections, subsections, categories, and subcategories. Two-character modifiers are added to CPT codes to clarify services and procedures performed by providers. Symbols are located throughout the CPT coding book.

Internet Links

JustCoding.com: Go to *www.justcoding.com*, and sign up for the free e-newsletter by clicking on the "eNewsletter Signup" link.

Medicare PFS look-up: Go to *www.cms.gov*, and click on the Medicare link. Scroll down to the Medicare Fee-for-Service Payment heading, and click on the Physician Fee Schedule Look-Up Tool link.

MedlinePlus: *www.medlineplus.gov*

National Correct Coding Initiative (NCCI) Edits: Go to *www.cms.gov*, and click on the Medicare link. Scroll down to the Coding heading, and click on the National Correct Coding Initiative Edits link.

Review

Multiple Choice

Instructions: Circle the most appropriate response.

1. Which mandated that CPT codes be reported for outpatient hospital surgical procedures?
    a. Health Insurance, Portability, and Accountability Act of 1996 (HIPAA)
    b. Healthcare Common Procedure Coding System (HCPCS)
    c. Medicare Prescription Drug, Improvement, and Modernization Act (MMA)
    d. Omnibus Budget Reconciliation Act (OBRA) of 1986

2. New, revised, and deleted CPT codes that are provided as an "early release" in July by the CPT Editorial Panel are intended to take effect:
    a. after the FDA approves the product.
    b. immediately upon "early release."
    c. 6 months later.
    d. within a 90-day grace period.

3. The E/M section is located at the beginning of CPT because these codes are:
    a. reported by all specialties.
    b. sequenced first on all claims.
    c. the most frequently reported.
    d. used to establish medical necessity.

4. *Arthroscopy, ankle,* and *wound* are examples of _____ in the CPT index.
    a. cross-references
    b. main terms
    c. qualifiers
    d. subterms

5. Which is the best example of a CPT index cross-reference term?
    a. Also   b. And   c. See   d. See also

6. When a range *or* series of single codes is listed in the CPT index for a procedure or service:
    a. a cross-reference will direct the coder to another index entry.
    b. each code must be verified in the CPT manual before a code is assigned.
    c. the range of codes is separated by a comma.
    d. the series of single codes is separated by a dash.

7. Codes identified throughout CPT with a forbidden (⊘) symbol are summarized in Appendix _____.
    a. C   **b.** D   **c.** E   **d.** F

8. Horizontal triangles (▶◀):
    a. identify a code description that has been revised.
    b. mark revisions that are included in Appendix B.
    c. surround new procedures and services that have been added to CPT.
    d. surround new or revised text.

9. Codes identified with a plus symbol (+):
    a. are exempt from modifier -51.
    b. are reported as stand-alone codes.
    c. contain parenthetical notes.
    d. identify add-on codes.

10. A code identified by a star symbol (★) indicates that:
    a. anesthesia is considered medically necessary and payable.
    b. a code may be used for synchronous telemedicine services.
    c. general anesthesia was administered by an anesthesiologist.
    d. no other anesthesia procedures or services may be reported.

11. Which are located at the beginning of each CPT section, define terms, and explain the assignment of codes for procedures and services located in a particular section?
    a. Descriptive qualifiers   **c.** Notes
    b. Guidelines   **d.** Unlisted procedures or services

12. Which are typeset as a blocked unindented or a blocked indented parenthetical pattern?
    a. Descriptive qualifiers   **c.** Notes
    b. Guidelines   **d.** Unlisted procedures or services

13. Which requires the submission of a special report that describes the nature, extent, and need for the procedure or service?
    a. Descriptive qualifier   **c.** Note
    b. Guideline   **d.** Unlisted procedure or service

14. Which code is assigned for "unattended sleep study, interpretation only"?
    a. 95805   **b.** 95805-90   **c.** 95806   **d.** 95806-26

15. A patient was seeking loss-of-wages benefits due to injuries sustained in a motor vehicle accident. The insurance company requested a second opinion regarding injuries and sent the patient for an Independent Medical Exam (IME), where a level 3 outpatient consultation service was provided. The IME physician reviewed medical records from the emergency department, the primary care physician, and pain management center. The IME report was sent to the insurance company. Which code is assigned?
    a. 99243-26   **b.** 99243-32   **c.** 99243-77   **d.** 99243-90

16. A patient presented to the physician's office for removal of ten skin tags on his torso. During the procedure, the patient became anxious and the procedure was discontinued. No skin tags were removed. Which code is reported?
    a. 11200-52   **b.** 11200-53   **c.** 11200-73   **d.** 11200-74

17. The patient underwent osteotomy of cervical spine, anterior approach, single segment, by two surgeons. Which code is reported?
    a. 22220-62   **b.** 22220-66   **c.** 22220-80   **d.** 22220-81

18. The patient underwent a T7 index (total thyroxine) lab test, which was sent to an outside laboratory but was billed by the physician's office. Which code is reported?
    a. 84436-90   b. 84436-91   c. 84439-90   d. 84437-91

19. If payment of a service or procedure is denied based on National Correct Coding Initiative (NCCI) edits, the provider:
    a. can seek payment from a Medicare beneficiary if an Advance Beneficiary Notice (ABN) or a Notice of Exclusions from Medicare Benefits (NEMB) is obtained.
    b. can seek payment from the beneficiary if a Notice of Exclusions from Medicare Benefits (NEMB) is obtained.
    c. can submit an Advance Beneficiary Notice (ABN) to seek payment from a Medicare beneficiary.
    d. cannot seek payment from a Medicare beneficiary even if an Advance Beneficiary Notice (ABN) or a Notice of Exclusions from Medicare Benefits (NEMB) is obtained.

20. National Correct Coding Initiative (NCCI) edits were developed to promote national correct coding methodologies and control the improper assignment of codes that results in inappropriate reimbursement of Medicare Part _____ claims.
    a. A   b. B   c. C   d. D

CPT Index

Instructions: Refer to the CPT index to respond to each case.

1. Patient underwent debridement of infected subcutaneous tissue, lower left leg. Use the CPT index to identify the following:
    a. Main term _____
    b. Subterm _____
    c. 2nd qualifier _____
    d. 3rd qualifier _____
    e. Code range _____

2. Patient underwent arthrodesis of the elbow. Use the CPT index to identify the following:
    a. Main term _____
    b. Subterm _____
    c. Code range _____

3. Patient underwent Kocher pylorectomy. Use the CPT index to locate the cross-reference for the procedure. Then identify the main term, subterm, and code range.
    a. Main term _____
    b. Cross-reference _____
    c. Main term _____
    d. Subterm _____
    e. Code range _____

4. Patient underwent abdominal hysterectomy with resection of both ovaries due to malignancy. Use the CPT index to locate the following:
    a. Main term _____
    b. Subterm _____
    c. 2nd qualifier _____
    d. Code range _____

5. Patient underwent PET scan, brain. Use the CPT index to locate the cross-reference for the procedure. Then identify the main term, subterm, and code range.

   a. Main term _____

   b. Cross-reference _____

   c. Main term _____

   d. Subterm _____

   e. Code range _____

CPT Symbols

Instructions: Interpret the use of CPT symbols to respond to each case.

1. A 60-year-old patient presents to the physician's office for a vaccination, and the coder notices the flash (✗) precedes the code to be assigned. The flash (✗) symbol that precedes the code means it is pending FDA _____.

2. A 37-year-old female presents to a local hospital for the birth of her second child. After a difficult labor, the patient undergoes a cesarean section. The patient also undergoes a subtotal hysterectomy due to endometriosis. Codes 59510 and 59525 are reported. The plus (+) symbol that precedes code 59525 means it is a(n) _____ code and modifier -51 is not added to the code.

3. A patient undergoes a genetics counseling for a period of 30 minutes. Code 96040 is reported. The star (★) symbol precedes code 96040, which means that _____ services were provided.

4. A patient presents to the emergency department (ED) following an accident in his garage. The patient was working under his car when the jack failed, and the car fell on the patient's chest. The patient requires 65 minutes of critical care time during which he is evaluated and undergoes emergency endotracheal intubation. The patient is admitted as an inpatient and scheduled for an exploratory laparotomy with possible splenectomy. Codes 99291 and 31500 are reported for the ED visit. The forbidden (⊘) symbol precedes code 31500, which means that modifier _____ is not added to the code.

5. Patient underwent initial closed treatment of a temporomandibular dislocation. Code 21480 is reported. The semicolon (;) symbol in the code description is used to save space; thus, the description of code 21480 is closed treatment of temporomandibular dislocation; initial or _____.

CPT Modifiers

Instructions: Assign CPT modifiers to each case.

1. A patient undergoes simple repair of multiple skin lacerations, left foot and toes. The patient also undergoes intermediate repair of left heel laceration. The patient is discharged home after suturing, bandaging, and placing in a soft cast. Codes assigned include 12041 and 12002. Modifier _____ is added to code 12002.

2. An 80-year-old male patient undergoes bilateral mastotomy with deep exploration. Code 19020 is assigned. Modifier _____ is added to code 19020.

3. A patient undergoes magnetic resonance imaging (MRI), lower left leg. Dr. Miller interprets the MRI and documents a report. Modifier _____ is added to the CPT code reported for the MRI.

4. Patient underwent incision and drainage (I&D) of a Bartholin's gland abscess done on April 5. The global period is 30 days. The abscess recurred; on April 28, the patient underwent repeat I&D by the same surgeon. Code 56420 was reported for the procedure performed on April 5. Modifier _____ is added to code 56420 for the procedure performed on April 28.

5. A male patient underwent biopsy of the prostate gland on October 11, performed by Dr. Smith. The global period is zero days. The pathology results were of uncertain behavior; per the pathologist's recommendations, the patient underwent repeat biopsy on November 15, by Dr. Jones, to obtain a larger sample. Code 55700 was reported for the procedure performed on October 11. Modifier _____ is added to code 55700 for the procedure performed on November 15.

CPT Evaluation and Management

Chapter Outline

Overview of Evaluation and Management Section

Evaluation and Management Section Guidelines

Evaluation and Management Levels of Service

Evaluation and Management Categories and Subcategories

Chapter Objectives

At the conclusion of this chapter, the student should be able to:

1. Define key terms related to the CPT Evaluation and Management section.
2. Explain the organization of the CPT Evaluation and Management section.
3. Interpret CPT Evaluation and Management section guidelines.
4. Select CPT Evaluation and Management levels of service for documented patient care.
5. Assign CPT Evaluation and Management service codes and modifiers.

Key Terms

advance care planning

care plan oversight services

case management

chief complaint (CC)

clinical examples

comprehensive examination

comprehensive history

concurrent care

consultation

contributory components

coordination of care

counseling

critical care

critical illness or injury

delivery/birthing room attendance and resuscitation services

detailed examination

detailed history

Documentation Guidelines for Evaluation and Management Services

emergency department service

established patient

expanded problem focused examination

expanded problem focused history

extent of examination

extent of history

face-to-face time

family history

history

history of present illness (HPI)

home services

hospital discharge service

hospital inpatient service

infant

inpatient neonatal and pediatric critical care and intensive service

intensivist

interfacility transport

intraservice time

key components

low birth weight

medical decision making (MDM)	partial hospitalization	problem focused examination	special evaluation and management services
nature of the presenting problem	past medical history	problem focused history	standby service
neonate	pediatric critical care patient transport	professional services	system review
newborn care services	physical examination	prolonged services	transfer of care
new patient	place of service (POS)	referral	type of service (TOS)
observation service	preoperative clearance	review of systems (ROS)	unit/floor time
office or other outpatient services	preventive medicine services	social history	very low birth weight

Introduction

The Evaluation and Management (E/M) section (codes 99201–99499) is located at the beginning of the CPT coding manual because these codes describe services most frequently provided by physicians and other qualified health care professionals. This makes it easier to locate these frequently reported codes. Accurate assignment of E/M codes is essential to the success of a provider's practice because most of the revenue generated by the office is based on provision of these services. Before assigning E/M codes, make sure you review the guidelines (located at the beginning of the E/M section) and apply any notes (located below category and subcategory titles).

 Coding Tip

Notes located beneath categories and/or subcategories in the CPT coding manual apply to all codes in the categories or subcategories. Parenthetical notes that are located below a specific code apply to that code only unless the note indicates otherwise.

Most E/M services are cognitive services. This means that the provider must acquire information from the patient, use reasoning skills to process the information, interact with the patient to provide feedback, and respond by creating an appropriate plan of care. E/M services do *not* include significant procedural services (e.g., diagnostic tests or surgical procedures), which are coded separately. However, some services that arise directly from the E/M service provided are included (e.g., cleansing traumatic lesions, closing lacerations with adhesive strips, applying dressings, and providing counseling and educational services).

Overview of Evaluation and Management Section

CPT 1992 introduced the E/M level of service codes, replacing the office visit codes that were included in the Medicine section of past editions of CPT. The E/M section is organized according to *place of service (POS)* (e.g., office, hospital, home, nursing facility, emergency department, critical care), *type of service (TOS)* (e.g., office or other outpatient service, hospital observation service, preventive medicine service), *content of service* (e.g., detailed history and examination), and miscellaneous services (e.g., prolonged provider service, care plan oversight service). The E/M *level of service* reflects the amount of work involved in providing health care to a patient, and selecting the appropriate level of service requires determining the extent of history and examination performed as well as the complexity of medical decision making.

Documentation in the patient record must support the E/M level of service reported. The Centers for Medicare & Medicaid Services (CMS) often refers to E/M codes by level numbers, and the level often corresponds to the last digit of the CPT code (e.g., 99204 is a level 4 E/M service).

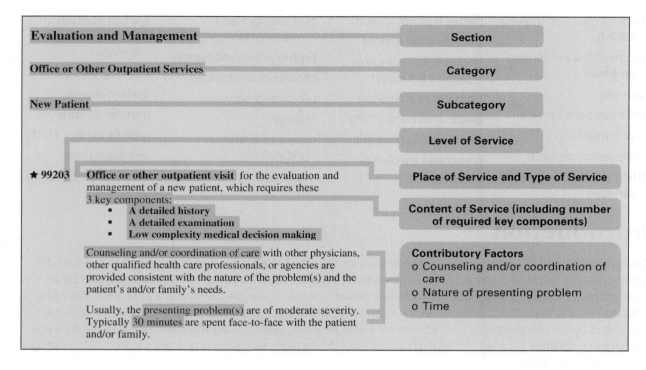

Accurate assignment of E/M codes depends on: (1) identifying the place of service (POS) and/or type of service (TOS) provided to the patient, (2) determining whether the patient is new or established to the practice, (3) reviewing the patient's record for documentation of level of service components, and (4) applying CMS's Documentation Guidelines for Evaluation and Management Services.

 NOTE:

Refer to the Office or Outpatient Services category of E/M, and notice that it contains two subcategories (New Patient and Established Patient). Each subcategory contains five codes. Each code represents an E/M level of service ranked from lowest to highest. CMS would consider E/M code 99201 a level 1 service.

Place of Service (POS)

Place of service (POS) refers to the physical location where health care is provided to patients (e.g., office or other outpatient settings, hospitals, nursing facilities [NFs], home health care, or emergency departments [EDs]).

> **EXAMPLE 1:** The provider treated the patient in her office.
> *Place of Service*: Office
> *E/M Category*: Office or Other Outpatient Services

> **EXAMPLE 2:** The patient received care in the hospital's ED.
> *Place of Service*: Hospital ED
> *E/M Category*: Emergency Department Services

Type of Service (TOS)

Type of service (TOS) refers to the kind of health care services provided to patients (e.g., critical care, inpatient care, nursing facility care, observation care, and preventive care).

EXAMPLE 1: The patient underwent an annual physical examination in the provider's office.

> *Type of Service*: Preventive care
>
> *E/M Category*: Preventive Medicine Services

EXAMPLE 2: The hospital inpatient was transferred to the regular medical-surgical unit where he was recovering from surgery. He suddenly stopped breathing and required respirator management by his provider.

> *Type of Service*: Critical care
>
> *E/M Category*: Critical Care Services

Sometimes *both the TOS and POS* must be identified before the proper code can be assigned.

EXAMPLE 1: Dr. Smith completed Josie Black's history and physical examination on the first day of her inpatient admission.

> *Place of Service*: Hospital
>
> *Type of Service*: Initial inpatient care
>
> *E/M Category*: Hospital Inpatient Services
>
> *E/M Subcategory*: Initial Hospital Care

EXAMPLE 2: Dr. Charles saw Josie Black (age 38) in her office to perform an annual physical examination.

> *Place of Service*: Office
>
> *Type of Service*: Preventive medicine
>
> *E/M Category*: Preventive Medicine Services

⚠ Coding Tip

The CPT Medicine section includes codes describing specialty services (e.g., ophthalmology, psychiatry) that require E/M. When codes for specialty services are reported, a separate E/M service from the CPT E/M section is *not* reported on the same date *unless a significant, separately identifiable E/M service was provided (and modifier -25 is attached).*

Exercise 10.1 – Overview of Evaluation and Management Section

Instructions: Use your CPT coding manual to complete each statement.

1. When a 49-year-old female patient is seen in the provider's office for an annual physical examination, the coder should refer to the E/M category entitled _____ Medicine Services.

2. For a 24-year-old male patient who received immediate care in the hospital emergency room, the coder should refer to the E/M category entitled _____ Department Services.

3. Codes for E/M levels of service reflect the amount of work involved in providing health care to a patient, and correct coding primarily involves determining the extent of history and _____ performed and the complexity of medical decision making.

(continues)

Exercise 10.1 – *continued*

4. CMS often refers to E/M codes by level numbers, and the level often corresponds to the last digit of the CPT code. Therefore, code 99215 is a level _____ service.

5. The physical location where health care is provided to patients is called the _____ of service.

6. The kind of health care services provided to patients is called the _____ of service.

7–10. Mary Smith was seen in her primary care provider's office two months ago when she underwent a routine physical examination. She returns today with complaints of severe abdominal pain and discomfort. Diagnostic testing revealed Crohn's disease, and a treatment plan was discussed. Identify each of the following for services provided to Mary Smith today.

7. Type of Service: _____ visit

8. Place of Service: physician's _____

9. E/M Category: _____ or Other Outpatient Services

10. E/M Subcategory: _____ patient

Evaluation and Management Section Guidelines

The E/M section guidelines are located at the beginning of the section and include the following contents:

- Classification of Evaluation and Management (E/M) services
- Definitions of commonly used terms
- Unlisted service
- Special report
- Clinical examples
- Instructions for selecting a level of E/M service

Classification of E/M Services

The E/M section of CPT is organized into categories, including office and other outpatient visits, hospital observation and inpatient services, and emergency department services. Many categories contain subcategories (e.g., new and established patients and team conferences and telephone calls). Each category of E/M contains five-digit numeric codes ranging from 99201 to 99499; most code descriptions include the place and/or type of service, content of service (e.g., detailed history and detailed examination), nature of presenting problem, and time typically required to provide the service. E/M codes classify provider services according to the extent of work (e.g., counseling, history, or physical) and the intensity of the medical encounter (e.g., complexity of medical decision making). This means that a provider who performs and documents extensive work in the diagnosis and treatment of a patient (e.g., comprehensive history and examination, and medical decision making of high complexity) can assign a higher-level E/M code than a provider who performs and documents less extensive work.

Assigning E/M codes can be difficult and confusing; although guidelines and notes include definitions and instructions for selecting codes, they were perceived as insufficient to guarantee consistent coding by providers and reliable medical review by payers. In response, CMS developed *Documentation Guidelines for Evaluation and Management Services*, which explain how E/M codes are assigned according to elements associated with comprehensive multisystem and single-system examinations. The first set of documentation guidelines created by CMS in 1995 was criticized by providers as containing unclear criteria for single-system examinations. CMS then created an alternative set of documentation guidelines in 1997, which was also criticized as being confusing and requiring extensive counting of services and other elements. CMS, therefore, instructed Medicare administrative contractors to use both sets of guidelines when reviewing records, and providers were instructed to use whichever set of guidelines was most advantageous to their practice reimbursement. (The American Medical Association [AMA] continues to work with CMS to develop an acceptable approach for classifying E/M services.)

NOTE:

CMS has streamlined evaluation and management payment and reduced clinician burden effective October 1, 2020, which means that separate, complex documentation will no longer be required for office and other outpatient services. A single rate will be paid for E/M office and other outpatient levels 2 through 4 services for new and established patients, and a separate payment rate will be maintained for level 5 services to account for the care and needs of complex patients. Practitioners will document level 2 through 5 encounters using medical decision making or time *instead of applying current 1995 or 1997 E/M documentation guidelines.* (Practitioners can also continue to use the E/M documentation guidelines if they prefer.)

Minimum supporting documentation requirements are for an E/M office and other outpatient level 2 history, examination, and/ or medical decision making. When time is used to justify the encounter's level, practitioners will document medical necessity of the encounter *and that the required amount of time was spent face-to-face with the patient.*

Add-on codes will be implemented to describe additional resources inherent in encounters for primary care and non-procedural specialized medical care, and they will not be restricted by physician specialty. Add-on codes are reportable only with E/M office and other outpatient level 2 through 4 services, and their use generally will not impose new per-encounter documentation requirements. A new "extended visit" add-on code will also be implemented for use with E/M office and other outpatient level 2 through 4 services *only* to account for the additional resources required when practitioners need to spend extended time with the patient.

Definitions of Commonly Used Terms

The E/M guidelines organize definitions of commonly used terms in alphabetical order (except for new and established patient terms). The following terms are discussed below:

- New and established patient
- Concurrent care

The following terms are discussed under the "Levels of Evaluation and Management Services" heading in this chapter:

- Key components
  - History
    - Chief complaint
    - History of present illness
    - Family history
    - Past history
    - Social history
    - Systems review (review of systems)
  - Examination
  - Medical decision making
- Contributory components
  - Counseling
  - Coordination of care
  - Nature of presenting problem
  - Time

New and Established Patient

A **new patient** is one who has *not* received any professional services from the provider or from another provider of the exact same specialty and subspecialty who belongs to the same group practice, within the past three years. (A provider includes physicians and other qualified health care professionals who report E/M service codes.)

An **established patient** is one who *has* received professional services from the provider or from another provider of the same exact specialty and subspecialty who belongs to the same group practice, within the past three years.

Coding Tip

- **Professional services** are face-to-face services provided by physicians and other qualified health care professionals (e.g., nurse practitioner, physician assistant), and the services are reported by assigning an E/M code.

- Definitions of new and established patients include professional services rendered by other physicians and other qualified health care professionals of the exact same specialty and subspecialty in the same group practice.

- CPT Evaluation and Management section guidelines contain a decision tree that can be used to determine new versus established patients.

EXAMPLE 1: Sally Dunlop had a prescription renewed by Dr. Smith's office on January 1, 2015, but she did not see the physician. She has been Dr. Smith's patient since her initial office visit on March 15, 2012. On December 1, 2015, Dr. Smith treated Sally during an office visit.

New Patient: March 15, 2012

New Patient: December 1, 2015

Although the patient had the prescription renewed on January 1, 2015, because there was no face-to-face service provided Sally Dunlop is considered a new patient for the December 1, 2015, visit.

EXAMPLE 2: Dr. Charles and Dr. Black share a practice. Dr. Charles is a general surgeon who treated Mary Smith in the office on July 1, 2015. Mary was first seen by the practice on February 15, 2012, when Dr. Black, also a general surgeon, provided preventive care services to her. Mary returned to the practice on November 1, 2015, for her annual physical examination conducted by Dr. Black.

New Patient: February 15, 2012, and July 1, 2015.

Established Patient: November 1, 2015

EXAMPLE 3: Dr. Corey left Alfred Medical Group to join Buffalo Physician Group as a family practitioner. At Buffalo Physician Group, when Dr. Corey provides professional services to patients, are those patients considered new or established?

Answer: Patients who have not received professional services from Dr. Corey and other qualified health care professionals or other physicians of the exact same specialty and subspecialty at Buffalo Physician Group are considered new.

Patients who have been treated by such a provider at Buffalo Physician Group within the past three years are considered established. If any of Dr. Corey's patients from the Alfred Medical Group choose to seek care from him at the Buffalo Physician Group (and services were provided to them during the past three years), they will be considered established patients.

Concurrent Care and Transfer of Care

Concurrent care is the provision of similar services, such as hospital inpatient visits, to the same patient by more than one provider on the same day. CMS permits the provision of concurrent care by two or more providers on the same day even if the providers are of the same specialty. To avoid reimbursement denials by third-party payers and Medicare administrative contracts, the attending physician is to add modifier -AI (Principal Physician of Record) to the E/M code reported. When possible, each provider should also report different ICD-10-CM diagnosis codes from those reported by other providers who provide E/M services to the patient on the same day.

EXAMPLE: Laurie Birch was admitted to the hospital on October 5 for an acute myocardial infarction. On October 7, her attending physician (a cardiologist) wrote a physician's order requesting a psychiatrist to consult with the patient regarding her anxiety and depression. The cardiologist's insurance specialist should report the ICD-10-CM code for "acute myocardial infarction" to justify inpatient E/M services provided to the patient (and add modifier -AI, Principal Physician of Record, to the CPT code reported). The psychiatrist's insurance specialist should report the ICD-10-CM codes for "anxiety and depression" to justify inpatient consultation E/M services provided to the patient. If each provider reported the ICD-10-CM code for "acute myocardial infarction," the provider who submitted the claim first would be reimbursed (and the other provider's claim would be denied).

Transfer of care occurs when a provider who is managing some or all of a patient's problems relinquishes that responsibility to another provider who explicitly agrees to accept this responsibility and who, from the initial encounter, is *not* providing consultative services. The provider transferring care no longer manages these problems but may continue to manage other conditions.

EXAMPLE: Sally Southern was admitted to the hospital on March 1 by her surgeon for total thyroidectomy that was performed on March 2. During admission, the patient's severe anxiety and depression was initially co-managed with a psychiatrist. Late evening on March 2, the attending physician transferred management of the patient's anxiety and depression to the psychiatrist. At discharge on March 5, the attending physician reported CPT surgery codes for the total thyroidectomy surgery and CPT E/M codes for management of the thyroid condition. The psychiatrist reported CPT E/M codes for management of the patient's anxiety and depression.

Unlisted Service

An unlisted service code is assigned when the provider furnishes an E/M service for which there is no CPT code. When an unlisted procedure or service code is reported, a special report (e.g., copy of documented encounter note record) must accompany the claim to describe the nature of, extent of, and need for the procedure or service.

 Coding Tip

Payers often require providers to report HCPCS level II codes (if available) instead of unlisted procedure or service CPT codes.

Special Report

When an unlisted service code is reported, a special report must be submitted with the insurance claim to demonstrate medical appropriateness. The provider should document the following elements in the special report:

- Complexity of patient's symptoms
- Description of nature of, extent of, and need for service
- Diagnostic and therapeutic procedures performed
- Follow-up care
- Patient's final diagnosis and concurrent problems
- Pertinent physical findings
- Time, effort, and equipment required to provide the service

Clinical Examples

Appendix C of the CPT coding manual contains **clinical examples** of E/M service codes. Along with a careful review of the E/M code descriptions, they assist providers in selecting the appropriate code for documented E/M services. The AMA cautions providers that the clinical examples "do not encompass the entire scope of medical practice." They can be used in addition to documented key components (history, examination, and/or medical decision making) that are required to determine a particular level of service.

Exercise 10.2 – Evaluation and Management Section Guidelines

Instructions: Complete each statement.

1. Tim Turner was seen by Dr. Chambers on February 5 of this year for follow-up of his type 2 diabetes mellitus. Tim has been Dr. Chambers' patient since 1984, when he was seen for an initial visit. Tim returned to the office each year since 1984 for an annual physical examination until last year, when he was diagnosed with type 2 diabetes mellitus. Since then, Tim has returned for a recheck office visit with Dr. Chambers every three months. Tim is considered a(n) _____ (new or established) patient for Dr. Chambers' practice.

2. Kristin Broome was seen by Dr. Marlot on March 8 six years ago for treatment of influenza. She returned on January 5 one year later for her annual physical examination, which included a prescription for birth control pills. Kristin called the office on April 10 of that same year to request that the local pharmacy be called so she could receive a refill of her birth control pills. Dr. Marlot called in the prescription that afternoon. Kristin next returned to the office on April 15 of this year for an annual physical examination. Kristin is considered a(n) _____ (new or established) patient for Dr. Marlot's practice.

3. Dr. Peterson, Dr. Slatterly, and Dr. Vaughan are members of the Medex Pediatric Group Practice. Eric Webb is a 15-year-old boy who was initially seen by Dr. Vaughan on August 5 of last year for a sports physical. Eric returned to the office on September 10 of this year and was seen by Dr. Peterson for treatment of an ear infection. Eric is considered a(n) _____ (new or established) patient for Dr. Peterson's practice.

4–5. Sandy Tyler was admitted to the hospital on July 4 for treatment of a fractured pelvis, which he sustained while parasailing earlier in the day. On July 5, his attending physician (an orthopedic surgeon) wrote a physician's order requesting a neurologist to consult with the patient regarding numbness of his left foot.

    4. The orthopedic surgeon reports the diagnosis of _____ pelvis to justify inpatient E/M services.

    5. The neurologist reports the diagnosis of _____, left foot, to justify inpatient E/M consultation services.

Evaluation and Management Levels of Service

E/M categories and subcategories contain codes that are classified according to levels of service for reporting to third-party payers. Although the last number of some E/M codes represents the level of service (e.g., code 99213 is a level 3 E/M service), the levels within categories and subcategories are not interchangeable. Levels of E/M service include conferences with or about patients, evaluations, examinations, preventive adult and pediatric health supervision, treatments, and other medical services (e.g., determining the need for and location of appropriate care, such as hospice care for a terminally ill patient).

Typically, just one E/M code is reported each day by a provider who provides outpatient services. When a separately identifiable E/M service is provided *in addition to a surgical procedure*, the E/M code is reported with modifier -25.

EXAMPLE 1: A physician sutured a patient's 2.5-cm scalp wound in the ED and performed a comprehensive neurological history and exam of the patient. The patient had sustained head trauma as the result of a car accident, and EMT personnel documented that he had been unconscious at the scene. Medical decision making was of high complexity. Report code 12001 for the simple repair of the scalp wound, and report code 99285-25 for the E/M service provided.

EXAMPLE 2: A physician sutured a 5-cm laceration of a patient's left hand and confirmed that the patient was up-to-date regarding tetanus toxoids immunization status. Report code 12002 for the simple repair of the skin laceration, hand. Do *not* report an E/M code because the patient was not evaluated other than for confirmation of her tetanus immunization status.

Impact of OPPS on Reporting Hospital Clinical and Emergency Department CPT Evaluation and Management Codes

With implementation of the outpatient prospective payment system (OPPS) in 2000, CMS recognized that the majority of CPT code descriptors are applicable to both physician and facility resources associated with specific services. However, CMS also acknowledged that they believe CPT Evaluation and Management (E/M) codes were defined to reflect the activities of physicians and *do not necessarily fully describe the range and mix of services provided by hospitals during visits of clinic or emergency department patients or critical care encounters.* CMS advised *hospitals to develop internal billing and coding guidelines* that determine the levels of clinic and emergency department visits to be reported. Guidelines created by hospitals follow the intent of CPT code descriptors and are designed to reasonably relate the intensity and volume of hospital resources and services to the different levels of effort represented by the codes. (Hospital outpatient encounters, except for emergency department encounters, are assigned HCPCS level II code G0463, Hospital outpatient clinic visit for assessment and management of a patient.)

 NOTE:

> CMS modified the definition of an established patient for hospital clinics or emergency departments as *one who has been registered as an inpatient or outpatient of the hospital within the past three years.*

CMS originally planned to develop a national set of facility-specific codes and guidelines; however, CMS soon recognized the challenge in developing such guidelines. Thus, CMS will simplify the reporting of E/M codes, effective with CPT 2021.

The levels of E/M services code descriptions include seven components, six of which determine the E/M level of service code to be assigned.

- History
- Examination
- Medical decision making
- Counseling
- Coordination of care
- Nature of presenting problem
- Time

The **key components** of history, examination, and medical decision making are required when selecting an E/M level of service code. **Contributory components** include counseling, coordination of care, nature of presenting problem, and time; they are used to select the appropriate E/M service code when patient record documentation indicates that they were the focus of the visit.

Key Components

E/M code selection is based on three key components.

- Extent of history
- Extent of examination
- Complexity of medical decision making

All three key components must be considered when assigning codes for new patients. For established patients, two of the three key components must be considered. This means that documentation in the patient's chart must support the key components used to determine the E/M code selected.

The E/M code reported to a payer must be supported by documentation in the patient's record (e.g., SOAP or clinic note, diagnostic test results, or operative findings). Although providers are responsible for selecting the E/M code at the time patient care is rendered, insurance specialists audit records to make sure that the appropriate level of E/M code was reported to the third-party payer.

Extent of History

A **history** is an interview of the patient that includes the following elements: history of present illness (HPI) (including the patient's chief complaint, CC), a **review of systems (ROS)**, and a past/family/social history (PFSH) (Table 10-1). The **extent of history** (Figure 10-1A) is categorized according to four types.

- **Problem focused history**: Chief complaint, brief history of present illness or problem
- **Expanded problem focused history**: Chief complaint, brief history of present illness, problem pertinent system review
- **Detailed history**: Chief complaint, extended history of present illness, problem pertinent system review extended to include a limited number of additional systems, pertinent past/family/social history directly related to patient's problem
- **Comprehensive history**: Chief complaint, extended history of present illness, review of systems directly related to the problem(s) identified in the history of the present illness in addition to a review of all additional body systems, complete past/family/social history

TABLE 10-1 History Elements, Definitions, and Examples

History Element	Definition	Example
Chief complaint (CC)	Patient's description of medical condition stated in the patient's own words.	EXAMPLE: Patient states, "My knee gives out, and it really hurts when I walk."
History of present illness (HPI)	Chronological description of patient's present condition from time of onset to present. HPI should include location, quality, severity, duration of the condition, timing, modifying factors, context, and associated signs and symptoms.	EXAMPLE: Patient states that for the past several months, his left knee has caused discomfort, especially when walking. Previous evaluation resulted in a diagnosis of probable torn cartilage. Today the knee is very bruised, and the patient complains of severe pain that started one week ago and is constant. The knee is painful when the patient is either resting or walking. Nothing helps reduce the pain. The patient has taken prescription Motrin and has tried using a heating pad as well as an ice pack. He states that nothing helps. Patient denies current injury.

Item	Documentation
location	left knee
quality	bruised, painful
severity	extremely severe
duration	one week
timing	constant
context	resting or walking
modifying factors	nothing makes it better

TABLE 10-1 *(continued)*

History Element	Definition	Example
Past medical history	Summary of past illnesses, operations, injuries, treatments, and known allergies.	**EXAMPLE:** Reveals a healthy individual who has been hospitalized in the past x3 for childbirth; the patient has no known allergies, has no history of diseases, and is not currently on any medications.
Family history	A review of the medical events in the patient's family, including diseases that may be hereditary or that may present a risk to the patient.	**EXAMPLE:** Patient states that father died at age 51 of heart disease and that mother is living and well.
Social history	An age-appropriate review of past and current activities such as daily routine, dietary habits, exercise routine, marital status, occupation, sleeping patterns, smoking, use of alcohol and other drugs, and sexual activities.	**EXAMPLE:** Patient has history of marijuana use as a teenager and currently drinks alcohol socially; previous history of smoking cigarettes (quit three years ago).
System review [ROS]	Inventory by systems to document subjective symptoms stated by the patient. Provides an opportunity to gather information that the patient may have forgotten to mention or that may have seemed unimportant. The ROS includes: • constitutional • cardiovascular • skin • gastrointestinal • head • genitourinary • eyes • musculoskeletal • ears • neurological • nose • endocrine • mouth • psychological • throat • hematologic/lymphatic • breasts • allergic/immunologic • respiratory	**EXAMPLE:** Respiratory: The patient denies shortness of breath. **NOTE:** Providers should not document *negative* or *normal* in response to ROS items. Instead, they should document a statement relative to the item. **NOTE:** The *constitutional* as performed during a system review includes nonspecific symptoms that indicate a person is unwell, such as general aches. During a physical examination, the *constitutional* includes the patient's vital signs (e.g., blood pressure, pulse, and respirations).

Extent of Examination

A **physical examination** (Table 10-2) is an assessment of the patient's organ (e.g., lungs) and body systems (e.g., cardiovascular). The **extent of examination** (Figure 10-1B) is categorized according to four types.

- **Problem focused examination:** A limited examination of the affected body area or organ system
- **Expanded problem focused examination:** A limited examination of the affected body area or organ system and other symptomatic or related organ system(s)
- **Detailed examination:** An extended examination of the affected body area(s) and other symptomatic or related organ system(s)
- **Comprehensive examination:** A general multisystem examination or a complete examination of a single organ system

SELECTING EXTENT OF HISTORY: To select extent of history, review the following elements documented in the patient record. If an element is not documented, it cannot be considered when selecting the level of E/M service code.
- History of Present Illness (HPI)
- Review of Systems (ROS)
- Past, Family, and Social History (PFSH)

HISTORY OF PRESENT ILLNESS (HPI): Review the patient's record, and for each documented HPI element listed below, enter an **x** in the box located in front of the element on this form.

- ☐ **Duration:** of pain/discomfort or illness; length of time condition has persisted (e.g., pain began 3 days ago)
- ☐ **Location:** of pain/discomfort (e.g., is pain diffuse/localized, unilateral/bilateral, does it radiate or refer?)
- ☐ **Quality:** a description of the quality of the symptom (e.g., is pain described as sharp, dull, throbbing, stabbing, constant, intermittent, acute or chronic, stable, improving or worsening)
- ☐ **Severity:** use of self-assessment scale to measure subjective levels (e.g., "on a scale of 1–10, how severe is the pain?"), or comparison of pain quantitatively with previously experienced pain
- ☐ **Timing:** establishing onset of pain and chronology of pain development (e.g., migraine in the a.m.)
- ☐ **Context:** where was the patient and what was he doing when pain began (e.g., was patient at rest or involved in an activity; was pain aggravated or relieved, or does it recur, with a specific activity; did situational stress or some other factor precede or accompany the pain)
- ☐ **Modifying factors:** what has patient attempted to do to relieve pain (e.g., heat vs. cold; does it relieve or exacerbate pain; what makes the pain worse; have over-the-counter drugs been attempted - with what results)
- ☐ **Associated signs/symptoms:** clinician's impressions formulated during the interview may lead to questioning about additional sensations or feelings (e.g., diaphoresis associated with indigestion or chest pain, blurred vision accompanying a headache, etc.)
- _____ **Total Score:** Enter the number of **x**'s entered above. Place an **x** in front of the HPI type below.
  - ☐ BRIEF HPI (1–3 elements)
  - ☐ EXTENDED HPI (4 or more elements)

REVIEW OF SYSTEMS (ROS): Review the clinic or SOAP note in the patient's record, and for each documented ROS element listed below, enter an **x** in the box located in front of the element on this form.

- ☐ Constitutional symptoms
- ☐ Allergic or immunologic
- ☐ Cardiovascular
- ☐ Ears, nose, throat, mouth
- ☐ Endocrine
- ☐ Eyes
- ☐ Gastrointestinal
- ☐ Genitourinary
- ☐ Hematologic/Lymphatic
- ☐ Integumentary (including breasts)
- ☐ Musculoskeletal
- ☐ Neurological
- ☐ Psychiatric
- ☐ Respiratory

- _____ **Total Score:** Enter the number of **x**'s entered above. Place an **x** in front of the ROS type below.
  - ☐ NONE
  - ☐ PROBLEM PERTINENT ROS (1 body system documented)
  - ☐ EXTENDED ROS (2–9 body systems documented)
  - ☐ COMPLETE ROS (all body systems documented)

PAST, FAMILY, AND/OR SOCIAL HISTORY (PFSH): Review the clinic or SOAP note in the patient's record, and for each documented PFSH element (below), enter an **x** in the box located in front of the element on this form.
- ☐ Past history (current medications, drug allergies, immunizations, and prior illnesses/ injuries, hospitalizations, surgeries)
- ☐ Family history (health status/cause of death of relatives, specific disease related to CC, HPI, ROS, hereditary diseases for which patient is at risk)
- ☐ Social history (alcohol use, current employment, illicit drug use, level of education, nutritional status, occupational history, sexual history, tobacco use)

- _____ **Total Score:** Enter the number of **x**'s entered above. Place an **x** in front of the PFSH type below.
  - ☐ NONE
  - ☐ PERTINENT PFSH (1 history area documented)
  - ☐ COMPLETE PFSH (2 or 3 history areas documented)

Circle the type of HPI, ROS, and PFSH. Select the Extent of History. (Note: 3 of 3 elements must be met or exceeded.)

HPI	Brief	Brief	Extended	Extended
ROS	None	Problem Pertinent	Extended	Complete
PFSH	None	None	Pertinent	Complete
EXTENT OF HISTORY	PROBLEM FOCUSED	EXPANDED PROBLEM FOCUSED	DETAILED	COMPREHENSIVE

FIGURE 10-1A Extent of history

Courtesy of the Centers for Medicare & Medicaid Services, www.cms.gov

TABLE 10-2 Physical Examination Elements and Examples

Element	Example
General Survey	Reveals well-developed, somewhat obese, elderly, white male in severe distress with severe substernal discomfort and pain in upper arms. Conscious. Alert. Appears to be stated age. No deformity. Patient cannot sit or stand still because he is in such agony. Gait affected only by pain; otherwise it is normal. Carriage normal. Age 67. Sex male. Height 5'11". Weight 188 lbs. Temperature 98.0°F orally. Pulse 56 and regular. Blood pressure 150/104.
Skin	Reveals pale, cool, moist surface with no cyanosis or jaundice. No eruption. No tumors.
Head	Hair, scalp, skull within normal limits. Facies anxious.
Eyes	Pupils round, regular, equal. Pupils react normally to light and accommodation. Extraocular muscles intact. Corneae, sclerae, conjunctivae clear. Fields intact. Ophthalmoscopic examination reveals fundi discs to be well outlined.
Ears	Examination reveals grossly intact hearing. No lateralization. External canals and ears, and left membrana tympanica clear. No tumor.
Nose and Sinuses	Inspection reveals grossly intact sense of smell. No deformity. No tenderness. Septum benign. Only residual mucus in both nostrils. No tumor. Sinuses within normal limits.
Mouth	Mouth edentulous. Lips, gums, buccal mucosa, and tongue within normal limits.
Throat	Examination reveals posterior oropharynx and tonsils to be very red and inflamed. Palate and uvula benign. Larynx not visualized.
Neck	Reveals cervical structures to be supple with no masses, scars, or abnormal glands or pulsations.
Chest	Chest inspection reveals it to have normal expansion. Thorax observation reveals it to be somewhat obese but with normal shape and symmetry without swellings or tumors or significant lymphadenopathy. Respiratory motions normal. Palpable tactile fremitus physiologically normal.
Breasts	Felt to be symmetrical and without masses or tenderness. Nipples normal. No axillary lymphadenopathy.
Lungs	Investigation reveals lungs clear on inspection, palpation, percussion, and auscultation.
Heart	Examination reveals heart to be indicated as normal since the area of cardiac dullness is normal in size, shape, and location. Heart rate slow. Rhythm regular. No accentuation of A2 and P2.
Abdomen	Appearance is slightly obese with no striae. Has a well-healed herniorrhaphy scar on the right inguinal area. No tenderness, guarding, rigidity, or rebound phenomena. No abnormal abdominal masses palpable. No organomegaly. No distention. No herniae. Bowel sounds are normal.
Genitalia	Reveals male type and circumcised penis. Scrotum, testes, and epididymes appear to be normal in size, shape, and color without skin lesions or tumors.
Rectal	Inspection proves sphincter tone good. Lumen clear. Hemorrhoids, internal and external, found on examination.
Extremities	Examination reveals no loss of motor function of the extremities or back. Patient can sit, stand, squat, and walk, although it causes excruciating pain, and this is in the substernal chest area. Patient advised to avoid doing these things. No evidence of injury. No paralysis. Patient squirms and moves constantly in his agony. He cannot sit long nor can he stand in one position. Extremities exam reveals them to be intact. Shoulder girdle inspection reveals no tenderness, muscle spasms, or abnormality or motion. No crepitation. Examination of the back reveals a slight infected and tender pilonidal cyst over the sacrum. No deformity or limitation of motion of the back noted. No other tenderness. Arms, hands, legs, and feet investigation reveals no deformity, fracture, dislocations, injury, tremors, atrophic muscles, swelling, tenderness, muscle spasms, or abnormality of motion.
Lymphatics	System check reveals lymph glands to be normal throughout.
Blood Vessels	Investigation reveals veins to be normal. Arteries are arteriosclerotic and all peripheral pulses are palpable and undiminished.
Neurological	Examination reveals the patient generally conscious, cooperative, mentally alert, and reasonably intelligent, although he seems to be somewhat confused. Cranial nerves intact. Superficial and deep tendon reflexes intact and equal bilaterally. No pathological reflexes. No abnormality of the sensory perception or of the associated movements, or of the autonomic or endocrine systems felt to be due to neurological disorder. IMPRESSION: Acute myocardial infarction. Essential hypertension. Arteriosclerosis. Pilonidal cyst with mild infection. Internal and external hemorrhoids. NOTE: Impression is documented at the end of a history and physical examination report. It is not an element of the physical examination.

SELECTING EXTENT OF EXAMINATION: To select the level of examination, first determine whether a *single organ examination* (e.g., specialist exam, such as ophthalmologist) or a *general multisystem examination* (e.g., family practitioner) was completed.

SINGLE ORGAN SYSTEM EXAMINATION: Refer to single organ system examination requirements in CMS's *1997 Documentation Guidelines for Evaluation and Management Services.* Place an **x** in front of the appropriate exam type below.

☐ PROBLEM FOCUSED EXAMINATION (1–5 elements identified by a bullet)
☐ EXPANDED PROBLEM FOCUSED EXAMINATION (at least 6 elements identified by a bullet)
☐ DETAILED EXAMINATION (at least 12 elements identified by a bullet)
☐ COMPREHENSIVE EXAMINATION (all elements identified by a bullet; document every element in each box with a shaded border and at least 1 element in each box with an unshaded border)

NOTE: for eye and psychiatric examinations, at least 9 elements in each box with a shaded border and at least 1 element in each box with a shaded or unshaded border is documented

GENERAL MULTISYSTEM EXAM: Refer to the general multisystem examination requirements in CMS's *1997 Documentation Guidelines for Evaluation and Management Services.* Place an **x** in front of the organ system or body area for up to the total number of allowed elements (e.g., up to 2 marks can be made for the Neck exam).

☐ Constitutional (2)   ☐ Gastrointestinal (5)   ☐ Psychiatric (4)
☐ Cardiovascular (7)   ☐ Genitourinary (M–3; F–6)   ☐ Respiratory (4)
☐ Chest (Breasts) (2)   ☐ Musculoskeletal (6)   ☐ Skin (2)
☐ Eyes (3)   ☐ Neck (2)
☐ Ears, nose, mouth, throat (6) ☐ Neurological (3)

_____ **Total Score:** Enter the number of **x**'s entered above. Place an **x** in front of the Examination type below.

☐ PROBLEM FOCUSED EXAMINATION (1–5 elements identified by a bullet on CMS's *E/M Documentation Guidelines*)
☐ EXPANDED PROBLEM FOCUSED EXAMINATION (at least 6 elements identified by a bullet on CMS's *E/M Documentation Guidelines*)
☐ DETAILED EXAMINATION (at least 2 elements identified by a bullet from each of 6 organ systems or body areas or at least 12 elements identified by a bullet in 2 or more systems or areas, on CMS's *E/M Documentation Guidelines*)
☐ COMPREHENSIVE EXAMINATION (documentation of all elements identified by a bullet in at least 9 organ systems or body areas, and documentation of at least 2 elements identified by a bullet from each of 9 organ systems or body areas, on CMS's *E/M Documentation Guidelines*)

FIGURE 10-1B Extent of examination

Complexity of Medical Decision Making

Medical decision making (MDM) refers to the complexity of establishing a diagnosis and selecting a management option as measured by the

- Number of diagnoses or management options
- Amount and complexity of data to be reviewed
- Risk of complications and/or morbidity or mortality

Complexity of medical decision-making criteria (Figure 10-1C) reflects the provider's level of uncertainty, volume of data to review, and risk to the patient. Documentation in the patient's record includes:

- Laboratory, imaging, and other test results that are significant to the management of the patient care
- List of known diagnoses as well as those that are suspected
- Opinions of other providers who have been consulted
- Planned course of action for the patient's treatment (plan of treatment)
- Review of patient records obtained from other facilities

The provider is responsible for determining the complexity of medical decision making, and that decision must be supported by documentation in the patient's chart. CPT includes a table in the E/M guidelines that can assist

Criteria to Determine Minimal, Low, Moderate, and High Levels of Medical Decision Making

	Minimal	Low	Moderate	High
Number of Diagnoses	• One self-limited or minor problem (e.g., cold, insect bite)	• Two or more self-limited minor problems • One stable chronic illness (e.g., controlled hypertension) • Acute, uncomplicated illness or injury (e.g., allergic rhinitis, simple sprain)	• One or more chronic illnesses with mild exacerbation, progression, or side effects of treatment • Two or more stable chronic illnesses • Undiagnosed new problem with uncertain prognosis (e.g., breast lump) • Acute illness with systemic symptoms (e.g., pyelonephritis) • Acute complicated injury (e.g., head injury with unconsciousness)	• One or more chronic illnesses with severe exacerbation, progression, or side effects of treatment • Acute or chronic illnesses or injuries that pose a threat to life or bodily function (e.g., acute myocardial infarction) • An abrupt change in neurological status (e.g., seizure)
Amount/ Complexity of Data to Be Reviewed	• Lab tests requiring venipuncture • Chest x-ray • ECG/EEG • Urinalysis • Ultrasound • KOH prep	• Physiologic tests not under stress (e.g., pulmonary function tests) • Noncardiovascular imaging studies with contrast (e.g., barium enema) • Superficial needle biopsies • Clinical lab tests requiring arterial puncture • Skin biopsies	• Physiologic tests under stress (e.g., cardiac stress test) • Diagnostic endoscopies with no identified risk factors • Deep needle or incisional biopsies • Cardiovascular imaging studies with contrast and no identified risk factors • Obtain fluid from body cavity (e.g., thoracentesis)	• Cardiovascular imaging studies with contrast with identified risk factors • Cardiac electrophysiologic tests • Diagnostic endoscopies with identified risk factors • Discography
Management Options	• Rest • Gargles • Elastic bandages • Superficial dressings	• Over-the-counter drugs • Minor surgery with no identified risk factors • Physical therapy • Occupational therapy • IV fluids without additives	• Minor surgery with identified risk factors • Elective major surgery (open, percutaneous, or endoscopic) with no identified risk factors • Prescription drug management • Therapeutic nuclear medicine • IV fluids with additives • Closed treatment of fracture or dislocation without manipulation	• Elective major surgery (open, percutaneous, or endoscopic) with identified risk factors • Emergency major surgery (open, percutaneous, or endoscopic) • Parenteral controlled substances • Drug therapy requiring intensive monitoring for toxicity • Decision not to resuscitate or to de-escalate care because of poor prognosis

FIGURE 10-1C Complexity of medical decision making

Courtesy of the Centers for Medicare & Medicaid Services, www.cms.gov

TABLE 10-3 Complexity of Medical Decision Making

Two of Three Elements Must Be Met or Exceeded			
Number of Diagnoses or Management Options	**Amount/Complexity of Data to Be Reviewed**	**Risk of Complications and/ or Morbidity/Mortality**	**Medical Decision Making**
Minimal	Minimal or none	Minimal	Straightforward
Limited	Limited	Low	Low complexity
Multiple	Moderate	Moderate	Moderate complexity
Extensive	Extensive	High	High complexity

in determining complexity of medical decision making (Table 10-3). Once the key components for extent of history and examination are determined, the type of medical decision making can be selected, as follows:

- Straightforward
- Low complexity
- Moderate complexity
- High complexity

EXAMPLE OF MEDICAL DECISION-MAKING DOCUMENTATION

Review the progress note to identify:

- diagnoses documented.
- whether data were reviewed.
- management options available to treat the patient.
- any risk of complications, morbidity, or mortality.

PROGRESS NOTE

SUBJECTIVE: The patient states that she has had an upset stomach for the past five days, and that it just won't go away. The patient denies recent changes in dietary habits or activities. She states that she was recently notified by her son that he is getting a divorce, and she admits that she is very upset about this news.

OBJECTIVE: GI: Normal bowel sounds. No rigidity. Some pain upon deep organ palpation. No organomegaly. Upon review of the record, it was noted that the patient has not complained about this problem in the past.

ASSESSMENT: Dyspepsia due to anxiety.

PLAN: (1) Gaviscon Extra Strength Relief Formula Liquid, 2 to 4 teaspoonfuls 4 times a day after meals and at bedtime. Follow with half a glass of water or other liquid. (2) Referral to James Kaplan, PhD, Clinical Psychologist. (3) Follow-up appointment in one month.

Notice that documentation included a review of data, a diagnosis, and management options. The risk of complications, morbidity, or mortality were not documented.

Assigning the E/M Code

Once the extent of history, extent of examination, and complexity of medical decision making are determined, select the appropriate E/M code (Figure 10-1D).

Select the E/M code based on extent of history and examination and complexity of medical decision making:					
History	Problem focused	Expanded problem focused	Expanded problem focused	Detailed	Comprehensive
Examination	Problem focused	Expanded problem focused	Expanded problem focused	Detailed	Comprehensive
Medical Decision Making	Straightforward	Low complexity	Moderate complexity	Moderate complexity	High complexity
Go to the appropriate E/M category/subcategory, and select the code based upon the information above					

FIGURE 10-1D E/M code selection based on extent of history, extent of examination, and complexity of medical decision making

EXAMPLE: Use Figures 10-1A, 10-1B, 10-1C, and 10-1D and Table 10-3 to determine extent of history and examination and complexity of medical decision making for a patient who is seen by his general practitioner.

SUBJECTIVE: The patient is a 35-year-old established male patient seen today with a CC of severe snoring. He says that this has gone on for years and that he's finally ready to do something about it because he awakens during the night from it and his wife is also losing sleep from his snoring. He says that he wakes up in the morning feeling very tired and notices that he gets very tired during the day. ROS reveals allergies. He denies smoking or alcohol use. He is on no medications.

OBJECTIVE: Blood pressure is 126/86. Pulse is 82. Weight is 185. EYES: Pupils equal, round, and reactive to light and accommodation; extraocular muscles intact. EARS & NOSE: Tympanic membranes normal; oropharynx benign. NECK: Supple without jugular venous distention, bruits, or thyromegaly. RESPIRATORY: Breath sounds are clear to percussion and auscultation. EXTREMITIES: Without edema; pulses intact.

ASSESSMENT: Possible sleep apnea.

PLAN: Patient to undergo sleep study in two weeks. Results to be evaluated by Dr. Jones, ENT specialist, to determine whether patient is candidate for laser-assisted uvuloplasty (LAUP) surgery.

To assign the E/M code, the following is determined:

- **NEW OR ESTABLISHED PATIENT:** This is an established patient.

- **EXTENT OF HISTORY:** HPI elements include quality, severity, timing, and context; extended HPI (four elements) is documented. ROS elements include allergic; problem pertinent ROS (one body system) is documented. PFSH elements include documentation of social history; pertinent PFSH (one history area) is documented for a score of 1. Because three of three HPI/ROS/PFSH types must be selected to determine the higher-level extent of history, expanded problem focused history is assigned.

- **EXTENT OF EXAMINATION:** Constitutional (1), Eyes (1), ENT (2), Neck (1), Respiratory (1), Cardiovascular (1); expanded problem focused examination (six elements) is documented.

- **COMPLEXITY OF MEDICAL DECISION MAKING:** Undiagnosed new problem with uncertain prognosis is documented (possible sleep apnea). Although "physiologic test not under stress" (sleep study) is documented as being ordered, results are not reviewed by this provider. In addition, this provider will not follow through on management options because the patient is referred to an ENT specialist. Therefore, complexity of medical decision making is straightforward because two of three elements are required and just one element is documented.

- **E/M CODE ASSIGNED:** 99213 (Two of three key components are required.)

 NOTE:

The E/M CodeBuilder located in Appendix I will help you to select the correct E/M code.

Contributory Components

The contributory components of counseling, coordination of care, nature of presenting problem, and time play an important role in selecting the E/M code when documentation in the patient record indicates that they were the focus of the visit. Counseling and/or coordination of care components drive CPT code selection only when they dominate the encounter (e.g., office visit), requiring that more than 50 percent of the provider's time be spent on such components. In such circumstances, the provider must be sure to carefully document these elements so as to support the higher-level code selected. (Some E/M code descriptions include notes about time and nature of the presenting problem to assist in determining the appropriate code number to report.)

Counseling

CPT defines **counseling** as it relates to E/M coding as a discussion with a patient and/or family concerning one or more of the following areas:

- Diagnostic results, impressions, and recommended diagnostic studies
- Prognosis
- Risks and benefits of management (treatment) options
- Instructions for management (treatment) and follow-up
- Importance of compliance with chosen management (treatment) options
- Risk factor reduction
- Patient and family education

 Coding Tip

Do not confuse E/M counseling with psychotherapy. Psychotherapy codes are located in the CPT Medicine section and are reported for behavioral health modification or the treatment of mental disease.

Providers typically select the level of E/M code based on extent of history and examination and complexity of medical decision making. However, some patients require counseling services (e.g., nutrition instruction, smoking cessation, and weight management) during an E/M visit. If provided, such counseling should be properly documented and the appropriate level of E/M code selected.

EXAMPLE: Sherry Salins is a 52-year-old established female patient who was diagnosed with type 2 diabetes mellitus five years ago. She has never been able to control her diabetes with diet and exercise alone and was prescribed oral insulin upon onset. During today's expanded problem focused history and examination E/M office visit, Sherry informed me that she is determined to reduce the amount of oral insulin she takes daily, and she requested nutrition instruction and weight counseling. I subsequently spent 45 minutes (of the 70-minute office visit) discussing the fundamentals of nutrition and weight as related to diabetes mellitus. Sherry is scheduled to return in one month for recheck, and she was provided with a referral to a nutritionist as well as a weight counselor.

The patient received 45 minutes of counseling services *in addition to the expanded problem focused E/M service (code 99213), which was 25 minutes in length.* The 45 minutes of additional time represents more than 50 percent of the time associated with the total 70-minute office visit. Thus, code 99215 is reported because its description states *40 minutes face-to-face time with patient.*

Coordination of Care

When the provider makes arrangements with other providers or agencies for services to be provided to a patient, this is called **coordination of care**.

EXAMPLE: Dr. Smith writes a discharge order for inpatient Carol Clark to be discharged home and to receive home health care. Dr. Smith spends 30 minutes contacting the home health agency to make the appropriate arrangements for the patient and instructing the hospital to send copies of the patient's record to the home health care agency.

NOTE:

Time spent with the patient (and/or persons responsible for the patient) is the key factor to selecting a level of E/M services *when counseling and/or coordination of care consists of more than 50% of face-to-face time*. The extent of counseling and/or coordination of care must be documented in the patient record.

Nature of the Presenting Problem

CPT defines **nature of the presenting problem** as "a disease, condition, illness, injury, symptom, sign, finding, complaint, or other reason for the encounter, with or without a diagnosis being established at the time of the encounter." The *nature of the presenting problem* is considered when determining the number of diagnoses or management options for medical decision-making complexity (Table 10-3). Five types of presenting problems are recognized.

- *Minimal*: A problem may not require the presence of the provider, but service is provided under the provider's supervision (e.g., patient who comes to the office once a week to have blood pressure taken and recorded).

- *Self-limited or minor*: A problem that runs a definite and prescribed course, is transient in nature, and is not likely to permanently alter health status or that has a good prognosis with management/compliance (e.g., patient diagnosed with adult-onset diabetes mellitus controlled by diet and exercise).

- *Low severity*: A problem where the risk of morbidity without treatment is low, there is little to no risk of mortality without treatment, and full recovery without functional impairment is expected (e.g., patient diagnosed with eczema that does not respond to over-the-counter medications).

- *Moderate severity*: A problem where the risk of morbidity without treatment is moderate, there is moderate risk of mortality without treatment, uncertain prognosis, and increased probability of prolonged functional impairment (e.g., 35-year-old male patient diagnosed with chest pain on exertion).

- *High severity*: A problem where the risk of morbidity without treatment is high to extreme, there is a moderate to high risk of mortality without treatment, and high probability of severe, prolonged functional impairment (e.g., infant hospitalized with a diagnosis of respiratory syncytial virus).

Time (Face-to-Face versus Unit/Floor)

Intraservice time is a variable that includes *face-to-face time and unit/floor time*. **Face-to-face time** is the amount of time the office or outpatient care provider spends with the patient and/or family. **Unit/floor time** is the amount of time the provider spends at the patient's bedside rendering services and managing the patient's care on the unit or floor (e.g., reviewing test results). Unit/floor time applies to inpatient hospital care, hospital observation care, initial and subsequent inpatient hospital E/M services, and nursing facility services.

As mentioned above, although the key components of history, examination, and medical decision making usually determine the E/M code, visits consisting predominantly of counseling and/or coordination of care are the exception. When counseling and/or coordination of care dominates (more than 50 percent) the provider patient and/or family encounter, it can be considered a key factor in selecting a particular E/M code. The extent of counseling must be documented in the patient's chart to support the E/M code selected.

EXAMPLE: Anne Sider is seen by Dr. Cyrix in the office for her three-month check-up. (She has chronic hypertension controlled by diet and exercise.) During the visit, Dr. Cyrix notes that the patient seems distracted and stressed, and he asks her about these symptoms. Anne starts to cry and spends 10 minutes telling Dr. Cyrix that her "life is falling apart" and that she wakes up in the middle of the night with a pounding heart, feeling as though she's going to die. Dr. Cyrix spends the next 45 minutes (of the 70-minute visit) counseling Anne about these symptoms. He determines that Anne is suffering from panic attacks, so he prescribes a medication and contacts ABC Counseling Associates to arrange an appointment for mental health counseling.

In this example, a routine three-month check-up (for which code 99212 or 99213 would be selected) evolves into a higher-level service (for which code 99215 can be reported). The provider must carefully document all aspects of this visit, which

(continues)

EXAMPLE (continued)

includes the recheck for hypertension, provision of counseling, coordination of care provided, and length of time spent face-to-face with the patient. (The coder should report an ICD-10-CM disease code from category Z70, in addition to the hypertension disease code, when counseling and/or coordination of care dominates the patient encounter *and is documented by the provider.*)

To properly bill an E/M level of service for an encounter based on time, the provider must provide counseling and/or coordination of care *in the presence of the patient* and document the following:

- Total length of time for the encounter
- Length of time spent coordinating care and/or counseling patient
- Issues discussed
- Relevant history, exam, and medical decision making (if performed)

EXAMPLE: Lucy Moreno is a 45-year-old established female patient who was seen in the office on April 22 for problem focused history and examination as follow-up for her diagnosis of lower back pain. Patient states that she is having great difficulty managing her pain, and she says that she realizes part of the problem is that she needs to lose 50 pounds. I discussed a variety of weight loss management options with the patient, including an appropriate exercise program, and she is scheduled to return in one month for recheck. Today's visit was 30 minutes in length, more than half of which was spent discussing weight loss management. Report code 99214.

Exercise 10.3 – Levels of Evaluation and Management Services

Instructions: Complete each of the following.

1. Refer to the Evaluation and Management section of CPT and identify a code for each level of service listed.
   a. Office or other outpatient visit, new patient, level 4 _____
   b. Office or other outpatient visit, established patient, level 1 _____
   c. Hospital inpatient services, initial hospital care, level 2 _____
   d. Home visit, new patient, level 5 _____
   e. Emergency department services, level 3 _____

2. An 89-year-old diabetic female presented to the hospital emergency room for evaluation of a very painful lower left arm. An x-ray revealed a left ulnar fracture. After taking a detailed history and performing a detailed exam, the physician reduced the fracture and applied a short-arm cast. Medical decision making was of moderate complexity. A CPT Surgery code was reported on the claim.
   a. Should an E/M code also be reported for this case? (Yes or No) _____
   b. If so, which code? _____

3. A 14-year-old male presented to his primary care provider's office for treatment of 3-cm laceration, which the physician sutured. The physician also administered a tetanus toxoid after confirming that the patient's tetanus immunization status was not up-to-date. Codes for treatment of the laceration and administration of the tetanus toxoid were assigned from the CPT Surgery and Medicine sections, respectively.
   a. Should an E/M code also be reported for this case? (Yes or No) _____
   b. If so, which code? _____

4. The three key components that determine an E/M code include extent of history, extent of examination, and complexity of medical decision _____.

5. When assigning an E/M code for a new patient, the number of key components that must be considered is _____ out of three.

Exercise 10.3 – *continued*

6. When an E/M code is assigned for an established patient, the number of key components that must be considered is _____ out of three.

7. Name the contributory components that are considered when determining an E/M code; they are not considered key components: counseling, coordination of care, nature of presenting problem, and _____.

8. Dr. Kuhl performed a level 3 E/M service to treat an 18-year-old established female patient in the office for a urinary tract infection. Urine culture revealed *Escherichia coli* bacteria. The patient was prescribed antibiotics and instructed to return for recheck in 10 days.

   a. The CPT E/M category and subcategory is Office or Other Outpatient Services, _____ Patient.

   b. The appropriate CPT code is _____.

9. Review the case below and answer the questions to assign the E/M office or other outpatient code. (You will have to identify the elements documented in the case to determine the level of history, level of examination, and complexity of medical decision making.)

   SUBJECTIVE: A 54-year-old female patient is seen in the office for routine three-month follow-up for evaluation and management of type 2 diabetes mellitus and hypertension. The patient has no new complaints today; she denies chest pain, headache, numbness of the extremities, shortness of breath, or visual changes. The patient states that she has remained on the diet recommended during the last E/M visit and that she is regularly exercising. Home monitoring of blood pressure and glucose levels are within normal limits.

   OBJECTIVE: Blood pressure 130/78. Weight 145. Pulse 78, regular. HEAD, EYES, EARS, NOSE, THROAT: Pupils equal, round, and reactive to light and accommodation. External auditory canals and tympanic membranes negative. Oropharynx benign. NECK: Supple. No bruits, jugular venous distention, or thyromegaly. CHEST: Breath sounds clear to auscultation and percussion. No rubs, rales, rhonchi, or wheezing. HEART: No click, gallop, irregularity, murmur, or rub. EXTREMITIES: Distal pulses intact. No cyanosis, clubbing, or edema. NEUROLOGICAL: Deep tendon reflexes within normal limits and symmetrical. No decreased lower extremity sensation noted. LAB RESULTS: Fasting blood sugar 132. Urinalysis within normal limits.

   ASSESSMENT: Type 2 diabetes mellitus, controlled. Benign hypertension.

   PLAN: Glucotrol 5 milligrams daily, every morning. Procardia XL 30 milligrams daily. Relafen 1,000 milligrams daily. Continue home glucose monitoring. SMA-7 and glycosylated hemoglobin today. Return for routine follow-up in three months.

   a. Is this patient new or established? _____
   b. What is the extent of history? _____
   c. What is the extent of examination? _____
   d. What is the complexity of medical decision making? _____
   e. Which E/M code is assigned? _____

10. A home care physician provided E/M home care services to a new 54-year-old male patient who complained of dyspnea due to cirrhosis of the liver and ascites. The home care physician spent 60 minutes reviewing the patient's record, taking a comprehensive history, and performing a comprehensive examination. Medical decision making was of moderate complexity. The home care physician then spent an additional 20 minutes documenting the home visit report and coordinating care with the patient's primary care physician. Assign the appropriate CPT code.

Evaluation and Management Categories and Subcategories

The E/M section (99201–99499) contains notes unique to each category and subcategory. *Remember to review notes before assigning an E/M code.* (As discussed in Chapter 9, CPT refers to E/M subsections and categories as categories and subcategories, respectively.)

 NOTE:

> The star (★) symbol in front of CPT codes in the office or other outpatient services category indicates that these codes may be reported for telemedicine services, and modifier -95 is added to each code when services are provided via telemedicine.

Office or Other Outpatient Services

The *Office or Other Outpatient Services* category of E/M includes the following subcategories:

- New Patient
- Established Patient

Office or other outpatient services are provided in a physician or other provider's office, a hospital outpatient department, or another ambulatory care facility (e.g., stand-alone ambulatory care center). Before assigning an E/M level of service code from this category, make sure you apply the definition of *new* and *established patient* and consider the following:

- When a patient receives two E/M services from the same provider on the same day and the patient's problem is the same for each encounter, report just one E/M service. (Providers in the same group practice who are in the same exact specialty and same subspecialty submit claims as though they are a single provider.) This means that when E/M office or other outpatient services are provided to the same patient multiple times on the same day for the same problem by the same provider, the highest-level E/M service is reported. *(An exception to this rule is reporting of critical service codes with an E/M service code.)*

- When multiple E/M office or other outpatient services are provided to the same patient on the same day by the same provider and the patient's problems are different for each E/M service, report multiple E/M codes. To justify medical necessity, make sure you link the appropriate diagnosis or condition code to its respective E/M code. Add modifier -25 to the second and subsequent E/M codes.

- When the patient receives office or other outpatient E/M services *on the same day that the patient is admitted to the hospital as an inpatient by the same provider*, report an E/M code for the initial hospital care only. Do not report an office or other outpatient E/M service code.

- When the provider performs a comprehensive exam in the office and the patient is later admitted to the hospital *on another day as a planned admission*, report a lower-level-of-service initial hospital care E/M code for the hospital admission (because the provider already performed and reported the predominant portion of the E/M during the office encounter). (When the patient is admitted on another day but the admission is unplanned, report the appropriate E/M code for the office visit and an appropriate-level-of-service E/M code for the initial hospital care.)

 Coding Tip

> The provider does not have to redocument the history, review of symptoms, and past/family/social history documented during a previous encounter if the provider documents that the previous information was reviewed and then updates the information. The period of time since the previous encounter should generally be no more than one or two years. In addition, the provider should indicate in the current note where the previous documentation can be found (e.g., Refer to office records dated April 14, YYYY.).

EXAMPLE 1: Dr. Smith provides a level 3 E/M service to a new patient in the office for treatment of anxiety. The patient is prescribed medication and referred to a psychologist for therapy. The same patient returns four hours later because she is having difficulty dealing with her anxiety, and Dr. Smith provides a level 2 E/M service and 30 minutes of counseling. The insurance specialist should report code 99203 on the insurance claim. (An E/M code for the return visit four hours later is not reported because the patient's problem was the same as for the first visit.)

EXAMPLE 2: An 89-year-old established patient receives level 3 E/M services from Dr. James to evaluate her blood pressure medication. The same patient returns five hours later and receives level 4 E/M services from Dr. James to evaluate hip pain due to falling at home. The insurance specialist should report 99213 and 99214-25 because this patient received E/M services for two different problems. (The payer may request copies of the patient record to verify the claim.)

EXAMPLE 3: An established patient receives level 4 E/M services in the office from Dr. Peterson and is later admitted to the hospital, where Dr. Peterson provides level 3 initial hospital care E/M services. The insurance specialist should report code 99223 on the insurance claim. (An office or other outpatient services E/M code is not reported.)

Teaching Physicians and Resident Physicians

A *teaching physician* is a physician (other than another resident) who involves and supervises resident physicians in the care of his or her patients. A *resident physician* (or *resident*) is an individual who participates in an approved graduate medical education (GME) program.

Teaching physicians are no longer required to rewrite in its entirety the key elements of a resident physician's E/M documentation. However, a teaching physician cannot bill for a resident physician's history or physical exam *unless present for a significant portion of the exam*. The teaching physician can select an E/M level of service based on time spent later reviewing the resident's documented history and exam (as part of the medical decision-making process), adding it to the history and examination performed by the provider. (These conditions also apply when *any* provider reviews a history and examination performed, for example, six months previously.)

Teaching physicians are also required to substantiate any services reported on a claim by documenting a summary note of services provided personally or directly observed. The summary note can confirm or revise the HPI, physical examination, and medical decision-making activities. (For services such as a single surgical procedure and/or diagnostic test, the teaching physician can indicate his or her physical presence during the key portion of the procedure or test.)

EXAMPLE 1: When all required elements are obtained personally by a teaching physician without a resident present, the teaching physician documents the E/M service as if in a nonteaching setting. The teaching physician's documentation should also include a statement such as, "I performed a history and physical examination of the patient and discussed his management with the resident. I reviewed the resident's note and agree with the documented findings and plan of care."

EXAMPLE 2: When all required elements are obtained by the resident in the presence of or jointly with the teaching physician and documented by the resident, the teaching physician documents that he or she was present during performance of critical or key portion(s) of the service and that he or she was directly involved in the management of the patient's care. The teaching physician's note should also reference the resident's note. The combination of entries must be adequate to substantiate the level of service billed and the medical necessity of the service. The teaching physician's documentation should also include a statement such as, "I was present with resident during the history and exam. I discussed the case with the resident and agree with the findings and plan as documented in the resident's note."

EXAMPLE 3: When selected required elements of the service (e.g., history and physical examination) are obtained by the resident *in the absence of the teaching physician*, the resident documents the services provided. The teaching physician must independently perform the critical or key portion(s) of the service with or without the resident present and discuss the case with the resident. In this situation, the teaching physician must document that he or she personally saw the patient, personally performed critical or key portions of the service, and participated in the management of the patient. The teaching physician's note should also reference the resident's note. For payment consideration by the third-party payer, the combined entries of the teaching physician and resident must be adequate to substantiate the level of service billed and the medical necessity of the service. The teaching physician's documentation should also include a statement such as, "I saw and evaluated the patient. Discussed with resident and agree with resident's findings and plan as documented in the resident's note."

Code 99211

Code 99211 is commonly thought of as a "nurse visit" because it is typically reported when ancillary personnel provide E/M services. However, the code can be reported when the E/M service is rendered by any other provider (e.g., nurse practitioner, physician assistant, or physician). CMS "incident to" guidelines apply when the 99211 E/M level of service is provided by ancillary personnel in the office. The guidelines state that the physician and other qualified health care professional must be physically present in the suite of offices when the service is provided. Documentation of a 99211 level of service includes a CC and a description of the service provided. Because the presenting problem is considered of minimal severity, documentation of a history and examination is not required.

EXAMPLE 1: The office nurse takes and documents the patient's vital signs (blood pressure, height, weight, and body temperature). Report CPT code 99211.

EXAMPLE 2: The patient comes to the physician's office, and the office nurse administers the monthly injection of testosterone enanthate (1 mg). The patient had received E/M level 3 services from the physician last week. Report HCPCS level II national code J3121 only. Do not report CPT code 99211 because the only service provided was the injection and the patient did not require or receive other E/M services (e.g., taking vital signs).

Hospital Observation Services

The *Hospital Observation Services* category includes the following subcategories:

- Observation Care Discharge Services
- Initial Observation Care
- Subsequent Observation Care

 NOTE:

Observation care is a service that is provided to a patient (e.g., initial observation care). It is *not* a patient status (e.g., inpatient, outpatient). For example, both outpatients and emergency department patients receive observation services.

Observation services are provided in a hospital outpatient setting, and the patient is considered an outpatient. Observation status is "an outpatient in a bed" because services include use of a bed (including overnight use of a bed) and hourly monitoring by a hospital's nursing or other staff that is reasonable and necessary to evaluate an outpatient's condition or determine the need for possible admission to the hospital as an inpatient. An observation patient may improve and be released *or* be admitted as an inpatient, which requires documentation of a proper admission order that serves as a rationale for an inpatient stay; the word "Admit" as an admission order for inpatient hospitalization is insufficient. Observation services are reimbursed only when ordered by a physician (or another individual authorized by state licensure law and hospital staff bylaws to admit patients to the hospital or to order outpatient tests). Medicare says that "the decision whether to discharge a patient from the hospital following resolution of the reason for the observation care or to admit the patient as an inpatient can be made in less than 48 hours, usually less than 24 hours," after which the provider must order an inpatient admission.

 Coding Tip

No differentiation is made as to patient status (new versus established) when assigning hospital observation services codes.

EXAMPLE: A patient underwent open reduction internal fixation (ORIF) in the hospital's outpatient surgery department. The surgeon ordered observation care due to unusual postoperative pain, and the patient is discharged home the next day. CPT codes reported for this encounter include the ORIF procedure, initial observation care, and observation care discharge services. (ICD-10-CM codes reported include the reason for surgery and the reason for observation care, which was postoperative pain.)

 Coding Tip

When observation care is initiated during an encounter for another service (e.g., outpatient surgery), Evaluation and Management services provided by the provider initiating observation care are considered part of the initial observation care *when performed on the same date.* This rule applies to the supervising provider (who places the patient under observation); other providers who render services to patients under observation will report such services separately. For example, a thoracic surgeon who provides consultative services to a patient under observation reports codes for those services to the payer.

> **EXAMPLE:** A patient is treated in the emergency department (ED) and is then placed under observation in the hospital. Reply only the observation service code because the ED service is included in that observation service.

 Coding Tip

A patient who is referred by a provider for hospital observation services, bypassing the outpatient or emergency department, is considered a "direct admission to observation." This can occur when the patient receives E/M services in the provider's office and the provider determines that the patient's status requires observation services. Instead of reporting an office or other outpatient service E/M code, the provider reports an observation service code.

The following services are *not* reported as observation services, and claims submitted for such services will be denied as being not reasonable or necessary: ⚠

- Services *not* reasonable or necessary for the diagnosis or treatment of the patient but provided for the convenience of the patient, patient's family, or provider (e.g., patient is waiting for transfer to nursing facility [NF] or physician is busy when patient is physically ready for discharge).
- Services covered by Medicare Part A (e.g., medically appropriate inpatient admission).
- Services that are bundled with another Medicare Part B service (e.g., postoperative monitoring during standard recovery period of four to six hours). (Such services are billed as recovery room services.)

- Services provided to patients who undergo diagnostic testing in a hospital outpatient department (e.g., routine preparation services furnished prior to the testing and recovery afterward).
- Therapeutic services associated with other treatments (e.g., chemotherapy).
- Standing orders for observation following outpatient surgery. (Such services are provided as part of outpatient surgery services.)

Observation Care Discharge Services

Observation care discharge services include documentation of the following:

- Final examination of the patient
- Discussion of the hospital stay
- Instructions for continuing care

Services also include preparation of discharge records. The *observation care discharge* code is reported when patient discharge is on a date other than for initial observation care.

 Coding Tip

For patients who are admitted and discharged from observation care on the same date, report codes from the Observation or Inpatient Care Services (including Admission and Discharge Services) subcategory of the Hospital Inpatient Services category.

Initial Observation Care

Initial observation care codes are reported for patients who are admitted for observation services on one date and discharged from observation status on a different date. Reference times are included in descriptions of initial observation care codes, which means the service can be based on time (instead of key components of history, examination, and medical decision making) *when counseling and/or coordination of care dominates (more than 50 percent of) the physician/patient encounter*. This means that the insurance specialist assigns a code from range 99218–99220 along with code 99217.

Subsequent Observation Care

Subsequent observation care codes 99224–99226 are reported when a patient receives observation services for a second calendar day and is *not* admitted as a hospital inpatient or discharged from observation services.

> **EXAMPLE:** A patient was treated in the hospital's ED for acute asthmatic bronchitis at 9:30 PM on May 14. The ED physician determined that the patient needed to be observed for a period of six to eight hours after provision of emergency treatment. The patient received a detailed level of observation services and was discharged from observation services at 5 AM on May 15. Report codes 99218 and 99217.

CMS's Quick Guide to Coding Observation Care Services		
For Patients Admission/Discharged on the:	**Whose Length of Observation Time Is:**	**Report Codes:**
Same date	<8 hours	99218–99220
Same date	>8 hours	99234–99236
Different dates	Any length of time	99218–99220 and 99224–99226 and 99217

Hospital Inpatient Services

Hospital inpatient services codes are reported by acute care hospitals, inpatient psychiatric facilities, comprehensive inpatient rehabilitation facilities, and partial hospitalization settings. The Hospital Inpatient Services category of E/M includes the following subcategories:

- Initial Hospital Care
- Subsequent Hospital Care
- Observation or Inpatient Care Services (Including Admissions and Discharge Services)
- Hospital Discharge Services

NOTE:

When more than one provider (e.g., attending physician and a consultant) delivers inpatient services on the same date of service, the attending physician adds modifier -AI (Principal Physician of Record) to the reported E/M code.

Hospital inpatient services are provided to hospital inpatients, including partial hospitalization services; they are indicated when the patient's condition requires services and/or procedures that cannot be performed in any other POS without putting the patient at risk. **Partial hospitalization** is a short-term, intensive treatment program where individuals who are experiencing an acute episode of an illness (e.g., geriatric, psychiatric, or rehabilitative) can receive medically supervised treatment during a significant number of daytime or nighttime hours. This type of program is an alternative to 24-hour inpatient hospitalization and allows the patients to maintain their everyday life without the disruption associated with an inpatient hospital stay.

Coding Tip

No differentiation is made as to patient status (new versus established) when assigning hospital inpatient services codes.

Reporting Codes for Hospitalist Services

The Society of Hospital Medicine defines hospitalists as physicians whose primary focus is the general medical care of hospitalized patients; their activities include patient care, teaching research, and leadership related to hospital medicine. Hospitalists may be employed directly by the hospital, serve as independent contractors, or be part of a group practice of hospitalists.

EXAMPLE: An orthopedic surgeon admits a 40-year-old patient from the emergency department on May 1 and schedules surgery on May 2 to repair a hip fracture. She requests that Dr. Jones, an internal medicine hospitalist, evaluate the patient on May 1 for chronic bronchitis and to provide preoperative clearance.

The orthopedic surgeon reports a code for the initial hospital care (99221–99223), and the hospitalist reports a code for the inpatient consultation (99251–99255) or a code for the hospital inpatient service (99221–99223, 99231–99233), depending on which code the payer accepts. [If the hospitalist had provided E/M services to a Medicare patient, he would report a code from the Initial Hospital Care (99221–99239) subcategory instead of the Inpatient Consultations or Hospital Inpatient Services subcategory.]

Initial Hospital Care

Initial hospital care services cover the first inpatient encounter the provider has with the patient for each admission. An initial hospital care code is reported once per hospitalization by the provider. In addition, providers may not bill for both an admission visit and a discharge visit on the same day; for a patient who is admitted and discharged on the same date, report a code from the Observation or Inpatient Care Services (including Admission and Discharge Services) subcategory (99234–99236). When a patient placed under observation is admitted as an inpatient by the same provider on the same day he or she is placed under observation, report an initial hospital care code (99221–99223) only for that day.

A hospital inpatient is someone who is admitted and discharged and has a length of stay (LOS) of one or more days.

- Initial hospital care codes cover all E/M services provided to a patient by the same provider for a *planned admission*, regardless of where other E/M services were performed (e.g., preoperative history and examination performed in the office just days prior to an elective surgical admission). Report an initial hospital care E/M code only. (An exception is when a surgeon is the primary care provider during an inpatient admission, for which a CPT Surgery code is reported *only*, and inpatient E/M codes are not reported by the surgeon.)

- When a patient receives office or other outpatient E/M services *on the same day as an inpatient admission to the hospital by the same provider*, report an E/M code for the initial hospital care only. *Do not report an office or other outpatient E/M service code.*

- When the provider performs a comprehensive exam in the office and the patient is later admitted to the hospital on another day as a *planned* admission, report a lower-level-of-service initial hospital care E/M code for the hospital admission (because the provider already performed and reported the predominant portion of the E/M during the office encounter).

- When the provider provides E/M services in the office and the patient is later admitted to the hospital on another day as an *unplanned* admission, report the appropriate E/M code for the office visit and an appropriate level-of-service E/M code for the initial hospital care.

Providers involved in care of the patient but not designated as the attending physician report services from a different category of E/M depending on where services were rendered (e.g., ED services).

> **EXAMPLE:** On the day of inpatient admission, Dr. Thompson provided initial hospital care E/M level 3 services to a 42-year-old male patient who was admitted for antibiotic therapy to treat pneumonia due to *Klebsiella pneumoniae* bacteria. Report code 99223.
>
> If Dr. Thompson had provided level 4 or 5 E/M services to the patient in the office, which resulted in admission the next day, the reported code would be 99214 or 99215 for the office or other outpatient services encounter and code 99221 for the initial hospital care service.

Subsequent Hospital Care

Subsequent hospital care includes the review of the patient's record for changes in the patient's condition, the results of diagnostic studies, and/or the reassessment of the patient's condition since the last assessment performed by the provider.

- Code 99231 is reported for a stable, recovering, or improving patient.
- Code 99232 is reported for a patient who did not readily respond to inpatient therapy or who developed a minor complication during the inpatient stay.
- Code 99233 is reported for a patient who is considered unstable because he or she developed a significant complication or a new problem. (Such patients are transferred to NFs or discharged home to receive home health care services.)

EXAMPLE: Dr. Thompson provided subsequent hospital care level 2 services to the 42-year-old male patient who was admitted for antibiotic therapy to treat pneumonia due to *Klebsiella pneumoniae* bacteria. Report code 99232.

Observation or Inpatient Care Services (Including Admission and Discharge Services)

When *observation or inpatient care services* are provided to patients who are admitted and discharged on the same date, report a code from 99234 to 99236.

- When a patient is admitted as a hospital inpatient after receiving observation services on the same date, report only an initial hospital care code. (That code should reflect the services provided by the provider during the patient's observation status.)

- When a patient receives observation services on the same date as the result of services provided at another site of service (e.g., physician's office, hospital ED, or NF), report only an observation or an inpatient care services code. (That code should reflect the services provided by the provider at the other site.)

EXAMPLE 1: A patient receives treatment in the hospital ED for an acute asthma attack. The ED physician orders a blood gas analysis laboratory test and an injection of medication to help the patient breathe more easily. The ED physician then orders the patient to be placed in the hospital outpatient observation unit to monitor the patient's breathing and to ensure that the treatment resolves the patient's problem. Five hours later, the ED physician examines the patient, who has normal vital signs and has resumed normal breathing. The patient is discharged to follow up with his primary care provider (PCP). The patient's record reveals documentation of a comprehensive history, comprehensive examination, and medical decision making that is of moderate complexity. Report code 99235 only. (*Do not report ED services code 99283 for this encounter.*)

EXAMPLE 2: A 38-year-old female patient undergoes a scheduled hospital ambulatory surgical procedure and is taken to the recovery room, where she has difficulty awakening from anesthesia and an elevated blood pressure. Both conditions persist during the usual recovery period, and the surgeon orders the ED physician to evaluate the patient. The patient is placed in the hospital's outpatient observation unit, and the ED physician orders the nursing staff to monitor the patient's condition and note any continued abnormalities that could indicate a drug reaction or other postsurgical complications. After four hours in the observation unit, the patient is no longer lethargic, has a normal blood pressure, and shows no signs of postsurgical complications. The ED physician discharges the patient from the observation unit to home. The patient record documents a comprehensive history, comprehensive examination, and medical decision making of high complexity. Report code 99236. (The coverage of outpatient observation services began when the patient was placed in the observation unit. Services provided to the patient in the hospital's outpatient surgical suite and recovery room are not considered observation status services.)

EXAMPLE 3: A patient is scheduled to undergo outpatient cataract extraction surgery. The patient expresses a preference for spending the night following the procedure at the hospital despite the fact that the procedure does not require an overnight stay. The hospital registered and treated the patient on an outpatient basis to perform the surgery and then permitted the patient to remain at the hospital overnight. Do not report a code for the overnight stay because it is not covered as medically necessary observation status services. (When a patient is accommodated in this manner, make sure that you notify the patient in advance that the overnight stay is not medically necessary and that the patient will be charged for the additional services. If the patient experiences complications postsurgically that necessitate an inpatient admission, the patient is admitted and a Medicare Part A claim is submitted.)

Hospital Discharge Services

Hospital discharge services include the final examination of the patient, discussion of the hospital stay with the patient and/or caregiver, instructions for continuing care provided to the patient and/or caregiver, and preparation of discharge records, prescriptions, and referral forms. Hospital discharge day management codes are reported for services provided by the provider as part of the final hospital discharge of a patient.

Coding Tip

Do not report a hospital E/M visit and a hospital discharge day management code for the same date of service.

EXAMPLE 1: Dr. Taylor provided 30 minutes of hospital discharge day management services to a 44-year-old female patient who was admitted for management of newly diagnosed type 2 diabetes mellitus. The patient responded well to inpatient insulin treatment and, upon examination, is discharged in improved condition. The patient was provided with discharge instructions for diabetes care, including the administration of insulin injections at home. Follow-up appointment in 10 days was scheduled. Report code 99238.

EXAMPLE 2: Dr. Collins provided 70 minutes of hospital discharge day management services to a 94-year-old female patient who was admitted for surgical treatment of a fractured pelvis. During inpatient hospitalization, the patient developed pneumonia, which was successfully treated. Arrangements were made to transfer the patient to an NF for follow-up care. Orders for pain management were provided to the NF. The patient was informed that Dr. Collins would visit her tomorrow to perform a comprehensive nursing facility assessment. Report code 99239.

Consultations

The *Consultations* category of E/M includes the following subcategories:

- Office or Other Outpatient Consultations
- Inpatient Consultations

 NOTE:

Medicare and some other payers no longer allow providers to report codes from the Consultations category of CPT. Providers (e.g., specialists) who deliver consultation services to such patients in a(n)

- Office or hospital outpatient setting are to report codes from the Office or Other Outpatient Services category
- Inpatient setting are to report codes from the Hospital Inpatient Services category
- Nursing facility setting are to report codes from the Nursing Facility Services category

The attending physician reports modifier -AI (Principal Physician of Record) with the initial hospital care code or initial nursing facility care code to distinguish the admitting or attending physician's service from those who provide consultation services.

The OIG reported that most consultation services reported to Medicare in 2001 were inappropriate, and subsequent education efforts to improve reporting failed to produce desired results. Other third-party payers will likely adopt the elimination of CPT's consultation codes. It is unknown whether the AMA will eliminate the "Consultations" category from a future revision of CPT.

EXAMPLE: On May 1, Mary Smith was seen in the hospital's emergency department (ED) and received level 4 Evaluation and Management services from Dr. Axel (ED physician). This Medicare patient complained of severe shortness of breath, chest pain radiating down the left arm, back pain, and extreme anxiety. The patient was admitted to the hospital on May 1, and Dr. Rodney (attending physician) provided level 2 initial hospital care. The patient was experiencing severe anxiety during admission, and Dr. Coleman was asked to provide psychiatric consultation; he provided level 1 inpatient consultation services. Dr. Axel reported code 99284, Dr. Rodney reported code 99222-AI, and Dr. Coleman reported code 99221.

A **consultation** is an examination of a patient by a health care provider, usually a specialist, for the purpose of advising the referring or attending physician in the evaluation and/or management of a specific problem with a known diagnosis. Consultants may initiate diagnostic and/or therapeutic services as necessary during the consultative encounter. The following criteria are used to define a consultation:

- The consultation is requested by another provider or source such as a third-party payer. (If the consultation is mandated by a payer or other source, attach modifier -32 to the consultation code.)

- The consultant renders an opinion or advice.
- The consultant initiates diagnostic or therapeutic services.
- The requesting provider has documented in the patient's record the request and the need for the consultation.
- The consultant's opinion, advice, and any services rendered are documented in the patient's record and communicated to the requesting provider or source, generally in the form of a written report.

Coding Tip

- Do not confuse a consultation with a referral. A **referral** is a recommendation to transfer a patient's care from one provider to another. A referring provider does not schedule the appointment or document a request for referral. A referral is not a consultation. To ensure proper coding of the encounter, call the referring provider to inquire whether a consultation was intended instead of a referral.
- No differentiation is made as to patient status (new versus established) when assigning consultation codes.
- When a confirmatory consultation is required by a third-party payer or another party, add modifier -32 to the appropriate code from the Consultations category (non-Medicare patient), Office or Other Outpatient Services category (Medicare office or hospital outpatient), Inpatient Hospital Care subcategory (Medicare inpatient), or Initial Nursing Facility Care subcategory (Medicare nursing facility patient).

Office or Other Outpatient Consultations

The *Office or Other Outpatient Consultation* category includes services provided in the following health care settings:

- Physician's office
- Outpatient or other ambulatory care facility
- Hospital observation services
- Home services
- Domiciliary, rest home, or custodial care
- Emergency department

Coding Tip

- When a consultant provides follow-up office or other outpatient consultation services, report codes from Office or Other Outpatient Services, Established Patient (99211–99215).
- When office or other outpatient consultation services are provided to Medicare patients, report codes from the Office or Other Outpatient Services category.
- Guidelines about consultation requests and documentation also apply to consulting providers who report codes from the Office or Other Outpatient Services category.

For a code from the Office or Other Outpatient Consultations category to be reported, the consultation request must be initiated by the attending physician or another health care provider and the attending physician must document all consultation requests in the patient's record. The consultant must document a written report that includes the name of the person requesting the consultation, the reason for the consultation, and the way the findings were communicated to the referring health care provider. Any specifically identifiable diagnostic or therapeutic service performed on the same day as the examination may be billed separately. These separate services must be linked to the appropriate diagnosis to ensure that medical necessity criteria are met. (Some Medicare administrative contractors and third-party payers may disallow payment when surgical procedures and E/M services are performed during the encounter.)

EXAMPLE: On March 15, a 42-year-old female patient was seen by Dr. Verde, her general practitioner, due to symptoms of chest pain and heart palpitations. Dr. Verde determined that the patient needed to be evaluated by a specialist and arranged for the patient to be seen in consultation by Dr. Falco, a cardiologist. Dr. Falco provided a level 4 office or other outpatient consultation service to the patient on March 20 and ordered diagnostic testing to establish a definitive diagnosis. (The payer allows CPT consultation codes to be reported.) Code 99244 is reported for the visit to Dr. Falco's office. (If, upon review of diagnostic testing results, Dr. Falco establishes a definitive diagnosis that requires the provision of further E/M services to the patient, report codes from the Office or Other Outpatient Services category of E/M.)

 Coding Tip

- When a consultant provides consultation services in the hospital's emergency department (ED) (at the request of the ED physician), report a code from the Office or Other Outpatient Consultations category of the Consultations subsection.

- When a consultant assumes responsibility for a portion or all management of the case, subsequent care provided by the consultant is reported with the appropriate office or other outpatient services or subsequent hospital care code.

- A **preoperative clearance** occurs when a surgeon requests that a specialist or another provider (e.g., general practitioner) examine a patient and indicate whether the patient can withstand the expected risks of a specific surgery. This is considered a consultation even if the physician performing the preoperative clearance is the patient's primary care provider. (A written request must be documented in the patient's record.)

 NOTE:

A history and physical examination is often performed by the patient's surgeon (in the office or at the hospital).

Inpatient Consultations

Inpatient consultation codes are reported when consultation services are provided to non-Medicare inpatients, nursing facility residents, or partial hospitalization patients. Just one inpatient consultation code is reported by a consulting provider per non-Medicare admission. When consulting providers participate in the patient's inpatient care, report codes from the Subsequent Hospital Care or Subsequent Nursing Facility subcategory of E/M, depending on health care setting. When follow-up care is provided in the consultant's office, report a code from the Office or Other Outpatient Services category of E/M.

 Coding Tip

- When an inpatient consultation is provided to Medicare patients, consultants report a code from the Initial Hospital Care category or the Initial Nursing Facility Care category.

- Guidelines about consultation requests and documentation also apply to consulting physicians who report codes from the Initial Hospital Care or Initial Nursing Facility Care category.

EXAMPLE: A 52-year-old female patient was admitted to the hospital by her primary care provider (PCP) to control her type 2 diabetes mellitus and to evaluate possible gangrene of her left foot. The provider ordered inpatient consultation services from an orthopedic surgeon, who provided level 4 E/M initial inpatient consultation services during evaluation of the patient. The orthopedic surgeon told the patient and her PCP that immediate surgical debridement was necessary. (Surgical debridement was performed.) (The payer allows CPT consultation codes to be reported.) Report code 99254-57 for the consultation services, along with a code from the CPT Surgery section for surgical debridement. (Modifier -57 is attached to code 99254 because the E/M services resulted in a decision to perform surgery. When the orthopedic surgeon provides inpatient and office E/M services to the patient postoperatively, do not report E/M codes. Such follow-up care is part of the global period of surgery; the orthopedic surgeon is paid a fee for having performed the surgery and providing routine follow-up care.)

 Coding Tip

- When consultation services are provided to a nursing facility resident, just one inpatient consultation code (for health plans that allow CPT consultation codes to be reported) or one Medicare patient Initial Nursing Facility Care code may be reported per nursing facility admission, regardless of the length of time the resident remains in the facility (e.g., years). For additional consultation services, report subsequent nursing care visit codes (even when months or years have passed since the initial consultation service).

- For follow-up inpatient consultation services, report codes from the Subsequent Hospital Care subcategory of E/M.

Emergency Department Services

Emergency department services are provided in a hospital, which is open 24 hours for the purpose of providing unscheduled episodic services to patients who require immediate medical attention. A *medical emergency* is the sudden and unexpected onset of a medical condition or the acute exacerbation of a chronic condition that is threatening to life, limb, or sight and that requires immediate medical treatment or that manifests painful symptomatology requiring immediate palliative effort to relieve suffering. A *maternity emergency* is a sudden unexpected medical complication that puts the mother or fetus at risk. A *psychiatric inpatient admission* is an emergency when, based on a psychiatric evaluation performed by a provider (or another qualified mental health care professional with hospital admission authority), the patient is at immediate risk of serious harm to self or others as a result of a mental disorder, and requires immediate continuous skilled observation at the acute level of care.

While ED physicians employed by the facility usually provide ED services, any physician who provides services to a patient registered in the ED may report the ED services codes. This means that the physician does not have to be assigned to the hospital's ED. When services provided in the ED are determined not to be an actual emergency, ED services codes (99281–99288) are still reportable if ED services were provided. Typically, the hospital reports a lower-level ED services code for nonemergency conditions.

EXAMPLE: A 54-year-old female patient presented to the hospital ED with the symptoms of abdominal discomfort, severe shortness of breath, and numbness in both hands. The ED physician provided level 5 E/M services, which included diagnostic workup. Report code 99285.

If a physician provides emergency services to a patient in the office, it is not appropriate to assign codes from the Emergency Department Services category of E/M. If the patient's primary care provider (PCP) asks the patient to meet him in the hospital's ED as an alternative to the physician's office and the patient is not registered as a patient in the ED, the physician should report a code from the Office or Other Outpatient Services category of E/M. ED services codes are reported only if the patient receives services in the hospital's ED.

When the same physician provides ED services on the same day as a comprehensive nursing facility assessment, do not report an ED services code. Any E/M services provided at a site other than the NF are included in reimbursement for initial nursing facility care when performed on the same date as the nursing facility admission. (When a different physician provides ED services in addition to services provided by a physician at the NF, each physician reports an appropriate E/M code.)

When a patient's PCP directs the patient to go to the hospital's ED to receive care and that physician is subsequently asked by the ED physician to evaluate the patient and advise the ED physician as to whether the patient should be admitted to the hospital or be sent home, assign codes as follows:

- If the patient is admitted to the hospital by the patient's PCP, the PCP should report a code for the appropriate level of the initial hospital care (99221–99223) only. All E/M services provided by the PCP in conjunction with an inpatient admission are considered part of initial hospital care when performed on the same date as the admission. The ED physician who treated the patient in the ED should report the appropriate ED services code.

- If the ED physician, based on the advice of the patient's PCP who came to the ED to evaluate the patient, sends the patient home, the ED physician should report the appropriate ED services code. The patient's PCP should also report an ED services code that describes the services provided in the ED. If the PCP does not come to the hospital to evaluate the patient but provides advice to the ED physician via telephone, the PCP should not report any E/M code.

When an ED physician requests that another provider evaluate an emergency patient, the other provider should report a consultation services code if criteria for providing a consultation have been met (or an appropriate Office or Other Outpatient code if the health plan does not allow CPT consultation codes to be reported). If those criteria are not met and the patient is discharged from the ED or admitted to the hospital by another provider, the provider contacted by the ED physician should report an ED services code. If the consulted provider admits the patient to the hospital and the criteria for a consultation have not been met, the provider should report an initial hospital care code.

Other Emergency Services

Other emergency services code 99288 is reported when the provider is in two-way communication contact with ambulance or rescue crew personnel located outside the hospital. The provider directs performance of the following procedures:

- Administration of intramuscular, intratracheal, or subcutaneous drugs
- Administration of intravenous fluids
- Cardiac and/or pulmonary resuscitation
- Electrical conversion of arrhythmia
- Endotracheal or esophageal obturator airway intubation
- Telemetry of cardiac rhythm

Coding Tip

- No differentiation is made as to patient status (new versus established) when assigning ED services codes.

- Usually Medicare administrative contractors and third-party payers do not provide a separate payment for services reported as code 99288 because they are considered included in the payment for services (e.g., emergency department services reported with CPT codes or ambulance services reported with HCPCS level II codes).

Critical Care Services

Critical care is the direct delivery of medical care by a provider to a patient who is critically ill or injured and who requires the full, exclusive attention of the provider. A **critical illness or injury** is one that acutely impairs one or more vital organ systems, jeopardizing the patient's survival. Critical care involves high-complexity medical decision making to assess and manage life-threatening conditions (e.g., central nervous system failure, circulatory failure, shock, renal failure, hepatic failure, metabolic failure, respiratory failure, postoperative complications, overwhelming infection, and other vital system functions), to treat single or multiple vital organ system failure, or to prevent further deterioration of vital functions. Critical care is usually, but not always, provided in a critical care area (e.g., coronary care unit, intensive care unit [ICU], pediatric intensive care unit [PICU], respiratory care unit, or emergency care facility). Payers will reimburse critical care services provided in any location as long as the care provided meets the definition of critical care and supporting documentation is in the patient's record.

Critical care services are reported when a provider directly delivers medical care for a critically ill or critically injured patient. Critical care services can be provided on multiple days even if no changes are made to the treatment rendered to the patient, as long as the patient's condition requires the direct delivery of critical care services by the provider. Time spent away from the patient's bedside that is documented in the patient's record qualifies as critical care services (e.g., time spent with family members or surrogate decision makers to obtain the patient's history or to discuss treatment options). The documented progress note must include any family discussion to a specific treatment issue and *explain why the discussion was necessary on that day*.

 NOTE:

Critical care services require personal management by the provider. They are life- and organ-supporting interventions that require personal assessment and manipulation by the provider. Withdrawal of or failure to initiate these interventions on an urgent basis would likely result in sudden and clinically significant or life-threatening deterioration in the patient's condition. The service is of such intensity that the provider must devote his or her full attention to the patient and, therefore, cannot render services to any other patient during that same period of time.

Critical care time may be continuous or interrupted; the time spent engaged in critical care services is directly related to the patient's care, whether that time was spent at the immediate bedside or elsewhere on the floor or unit. The following services performed elsewhere by the provider represent critical care:

- Spending time at the nursing station reviewing test results
- Discussing the patient's care with other medical staff
- Documenting critical care services in the patient's record
- Obtaining the patient's medical history and discussing treatment options with family members if the discussion is absolutely necessary for the treatment decision under consideration that day

Critical care services include the following procedures, which are not coded or reported separately:

- Blood gases
- Chest x-rays
- Gastric intubation
- Information data stored in computers (e.g., EKGs, blood pressures, and hematological data)
- Interpretation of cardiac output measurements
- Pulse oximetry
- Temporary transcutaneous pacing
- Vascular access procedures
- Ventilatory management

TABLE 10-4 Critical Care Services: Total Duration of Critical Care and Codes

Total Duration of Critical Care	Codes
Less than 30 minutes	Assign appropriate E/M code(s)
30–74 minutes	99291
75–104 minutes	99291, 99292
105–134 minutes	99291, 99292, 99292
135–164 minutes	99291, 99292, 99292, 99292
165–194 minutes	99291, 99292, 99292, 99292, 99292
194 minutes or longer	99291 and 99292 as appropriate based on total duration of time

Coding Tip

- Just because a patient is located in a critical care unit does not mean that he or she is receiving critical care; if the patient is stable, report the appropriate subsequent hospital care service code.

- Report services, such as Swan-Ganz catheterization (93503) and intubation (31500), when provided in addition to critical care services codes.

When a patient receives critical care services while located in a critical care unit, on a medical or surgical unit, or in the hospital ED, the critical care services codes are reported *in addition to initial hospital care, subsequent hospital care, and/or initial inpatient consultations service codes.* (Add modifier -25 to the E/M level of service code to report it as a separately identified service provided to the patient.) Comprehensive documentation of critical care services provided is crucial, including the length of time the provider spent providing services. Critical care services codes are selected according to the total duration of time the provider spent delivering services to the patient, even if the time spent was not continuous (Table 10-4). To calculate duration of time, the provider must devote his or her full attention to the patient and cannot provide services to any other patient during that same period of time.

Coding Tip

- Critical care code 99292 is reported for up to 30 minutes each beyond the first 74 minutes. Throughout CPT, interpret length of time, burn percentage, number of lesions, and so on, as "up to" the number in the code description.

- If critical care services are provided on the same date as a surgical procedure that has a global period and the services are related to the reason for surgery, critical care services are bundled (included) in the reimbursement for the surgical procedure. In this situation, do not report codes for critical care services.

- If critical care services provided are unrelated to the reason for surgery, report codes for services provided (in addition to the surgery code). Attach modifier -24 or -25 to the critical care services code(s). (The surgeon must document that the critical care was unrelated to the surgical procedure performed or was beyond the typical work of pre- or postoperative care associated with the procedure.)

- If the surgeon is also an intensivist, the surgeon should not report codes for critical care services provided to his or her patient during the pre- or postoperative period. Such critical care services are included in the global surgical fee.

Coding Tip *(continued)*

- If a surgeon requires the assistance of another intensivist, the intensivist should report codes for critical care services provided. An **intensivist** is a provider who has received extensive training and experience in critical care and who specializes in the care of critically ill patients, usually in an intensive care unit (ICU). Usually an intensivist has completed a fellowship in critical care following completion of a residency in internal medicine, pulmonary medicine, anesthesia, or surgery. Most intensivists are board-certified or board-eligible in critical care medicine.

- Critical care services (99291–99292) are reported for services provided to patients whose age is over 24 months.

- To report critical care services for patients 24 months and younger, refer to codes 99466–99467 and 99485–99486 for critical care pediatric patient transport or codes 99468–99480 for inpatient neonatal, infant, and pediatric critical care services.

EXAMPLE 1: Mary Jones is seen in the hospital ED for trauma as the result of an automobile accident. Level 4 emergency department E/M services are provided, and the ED physician also provides 60 continuous minutes of critical care services. Report the appropriate ED level of service code along with codes 99284-25 and 99291.

EXAMPLE 2: Dr. Smith delivers critical care services to his patient on June 15 from 8–9 AM, 10:30–10:45 AM, and 3:00–3:45 PM. To assign a critical care services code to this case, total the minutes of critical care services directly delivered by the provider. Codes 99291, 99292, and 99292 are reported.

Nursing Facility Services

Nursing facility services are provided at a nursing facility (NF), skilled nursing facility (SNF), intermediate care facility/mentally retarded (ICF/MR), long-term care facility (LTCF), or psychiatric residential treatment facility. NFs provide convalescent, rehabilitative, or long-term care for patients, and a comprehensive assessment must be completed on each patient that meets the resident's medical, nursing, mental, and psychological needs. The patient's functional capacity, identification of potential problems, and nursing plan to enhance (or at least maintain) the patient's physical and psychosocial functions are assessed and documented. The assessments are written when the patient is admitted or readmitted to the facility or when a reassessment is necessary because of a substantial change in the patient's status.

Coding Tip

No differentiation is made as to patient status (new versus established) when assigning nursing facility services codes.

NOTE:

Medicare and some other payers do not allow providers to report codes from the Consultations category. Thus, inpatient consultation services for Medicare and other affected nursing facility residents are reported with codes from the Initial Nursing Facility Care subcategories. (Coders should determine whether health plans allow CPT codes from the Consultations category to be reported.)

When more than one provider (e.g., attending physician and a consultant) delivers inpatient services on the same date of service, the attending physician adds modifier -AI (Principal Physician of Record) to the reported E/M code.

Coding Tip

- Report a code for hospital discharge services (99238–99239), observation care discharge (99217), or observation or inpatient hospital care (same day admission/discharge) (99234–99236) and initial nursing facility care (99304–99306) *if a patient is discharged and admitted to an NF, an SNF, an ICF, or an LTCF on the same date.*

- Do not report codes for ED or office or other outpatient services with initial nursing facility care when provided on the same day for the same patient by the same provider. E/M services provided at sites other than the NF are bundled into initial nursing facility care when performed on the same date as the nursing facility admission by the same provider.

- Do not report codes for initial or subsequent nursing facility care and initial hospital care on the same date for the same patient by the same provider. Payment for initial hospital care services includes all work performed by the provider in all sites of service on that date.

- Report a code for subsequent nursing facility care when the evaluation of the patient's assessment plan is not required and/or when the patient has not had a major or permanent change of health status.

- For discharge from a nursing facility, report code 99315 or 99316. If the patient has expired, report code 99315 or 99316 if the primary service provided by the provider is pronouncement of death, completion of the death summary, and discussion with the deceased patient's family. The provider must personally visit the patient and document pronouncement of death before midnight on the date the patient expired.

EXAMPLE: The nursing facility assessment code (99318) is reported when the nursing facility patient's attending physician conducts an annual assessment. The attending physician is responsible for reviewing and affirming the patient's plan of care.

Third-party payers usually reimburse E/M services provided in a nursing facility when the purpose of the visit is to fulfill the minimum federal requirement of at least one provider visit every 30 days for the first three months and at least once every 60 days thereafter and/or the service is reasonable and necessary for the diagnosis or treatment of illness or injury or to improve the functioning of a malformed body member and all of the following conditions are fulfilled:

- The service requires the skill of a physician.

- The service is sufficiently well documented to satisfy the criteria of the CMS 1995 or 1997 *Evaluation and Management Documentation Guidelines* for the level of service and code reported.

- The service is performed by the attending physician, a consulting physician requested by the attending physician, or a named physician requested by the patient or the patient's interested family member or legal guardian.

For an E/M service in an NF to be considered reasonable and necessary, it must be furnished in accordance with accepted standards of medical practice for the diagnosis or treatment of the patient's condition or with the goal of improving the function of a malformed body member, be ordered and furnished by qualified personnel, and meet, but not exceed, the patient's medical need.

EXAMPLE: On October 14, a 97-year-old female patient was transferred from the hospital to the NF in stable condition. The patient's attending physician provided hospital discharge day management services and provided a level 2 initial nursing facility care service. On November 14, the attending physician provided level 1 subsequent nursing facility care. The patient expired on November 30, and the attending physician was not in attendance. Report codes 99305 (10/14) and 99307 (11/14). (A discharge service code is not reported.)

Domiciliary, Rest Home (e.g., Boarding Home), or Custodial Care Services

Domiciliary, rest home (e.g., boarding home), or custodial care services are provided to residents of a facility that provides room, board, and other personal assistance services, usually on a long-term basis. These codes include E/M management services provided to residents of an assisted living facility, group home, or custodial care and intermediate care facilities.

Coding Tip

Differentiate between new and established patients when assigning codes.

Assisted living facilities offer nonmedical senior housing that assists residents with tasks such as cooking and laundry and provides reminders to take medications. *Assisted living* is a general term for living arrangements in which some services are available to residents who still live independently within the assisted living complex. In most cases, assisted living residents pay a regular monthly rent and then pay additional fees for the services (e.g., home health) they require. *Group homes* (*boarding homes* or *rest homes*) are group living arrangements designed to meet the needs of people who cannot live independently but who do not require nursing facility services. These homes offer a wider range of services than assisted living facilities, and most provide help with activities of daily living (e.g., eating, walking, bathing, and toileting). In some cases, private long-term care insurance and medical assistance programs help pay for group home services. *Custodial care* and *intermediate care facilities* offer non-skilled care services, which include helping residents with activities of daily living (ADL) (e.g., bathing, eating, dressing, toileting, and transferring from bed to wheelchair).

EXAMPLE: A 92-year-old established female patient who resides in an assisted living facility received E/M level 1 services from her primary care physician on December 4. Report code 99334 for the December 4 E/M service.

Domiciliary, Rest Home (e.g., Assisted Living Facility), or Home Care Plan Oversight Services

Codes 99339–99340 are reported for care plan oversight services provided for patients who reside at home or in a domiciliary, facility, or rest home. These codes are not reported for home health or hospice patients or for nursing facility residents.

Home Services

Home services are provided to individuals and individuals and families in their place of residence to promote, maintain, or restore health and/or to minimize the effects of disability and illness, including terminal illness. Home services for Medicare patients are provided by nurses, doctors, social workers, therapists, and home health aides. Services are ordered by a provider (instead of treatment in a hospital or SNF) and may result in a shorter acute care hospital or SNF LOS. Home health care programs must be organized, administered, and supervised by a hospital or qualified licensed personnel under the medical direction of a provider. Home services allow patients to recuperate while remaining at home. Since most home health care is temporary and part-time, in addition to providing direct care, the home health staff teaches patients (and their families or others) how to continue needed care (e.g., medication administration, wound care, and therapy).

Coding Tip

Differentiate between new and established patients when reporting codes for home services.

The home health care provider is responsible for documenting a plan of care and reviewing data. If the written plan of care was not initially prepared by the provider (e.g., prepared by the home health agency), the patient record must include documentation of the provider's contribution to the development of the plan and/or a review of the specific items entered into the plan. It is not sufficient for a home health agency to maintain documentation in its records for the physician. The provider must maintain his or her own records, including periodic summary reports provided by the home health agency. Documentation of all face-to-face E/M home services visits and any telephone communications with the patient or caretakers must be documented in the patient's record. This documentation must indicate an ongoing knowledge of any changes in the patient's condition, drugs, or other needs and the way they are being addressed.

> **EXAMPLE:** A primary care physician provides level 2 home services to a 72-year-old established patient to evaluate the status of the patient's wound healing. The patient has been receiving daily skilled wound care. The physician determines that an additional 10 days of daily skilled wound care is needed, and he documents that order for the home health agency. Report code 99348.

Home Health Agency Face-to-Face Encounters for Medicare Beneficiaries

For Medicare purposes, certifying providers are responsible for documenting all face-to-face encounters with patients in the patient record, and the encounter must occur no more than 90 days prior to the home health start of care date or within 30 days after the start of care. Such face-to-face encounters can be performed using telehealth services at an approved originating site, which is the location of an eligible Medicare beneficiary at the time such services occur. Originating sites must be located in Rural Health Professional Shortage Areas or in counties outside of metropolitan statistical areas, and they can include provider offices, hospitals, critical access hospitals (CAHs), rural health clinics (RHCs), federally qualified health centers (FQHCs), hospital-based or CAH-based renal dialysis centers, skilled nursing facilities (SNFs), and community mental health centers (CMHCs). Nonphysician providers (e.g., certified nurse-midwives, nurse practitioners, physician assistants) can also provide face-to-face E/M home services, but they must inform the certifying physician of any clinical findings exhibited by the patient during the encounter. Then, the provider must document the encounter and countersign the certification. Documentation requirements include:

- Date of face-to-face encounter between the provider and the patient
- Brief narrative describing how the patient's observed clinical condition supports the patient's homebound status and need for skilled services
- Documentation of the encounter (e.g., handwritten, keyboarded, or EHR format) by the certifying provider on the signed/dated certification form or as a signed/dated addendum to the certification

Certifying providers are permitted to verbally communicate the brief narrative describing how the patient's observed clinical condition supports the patient's homebound status and need for skilled services to the home health agency (HHA). The HHA provider documents the encounter on the certification form, and the certifying provider must sign the form.

Prolonged Services

Provider services involving patient contact that are considered beyond the usual service in either an inpatient or outpatient setting may be reported as **prolonged services**. Codes for prolonged services are reported *in addition to* other provider services (e.g., office or other outpatient services and hospital inpatient services). Prolonged services are reported only when the time involved *exceeds* the typical time associated with an E/M service by at least 30 minutes. Prolonged services of less than 30 minutes total duration on a given date are not separately reported because the work involved is included in the total work for the E/M service code. In addition, prolonged services of less than 15 minutes beyond the first hour and less than 15 minutes beyond the final 30 minutes are not reported separately.

Coding Tip

The patient's record must include documentation that supports the E/M level of service code reported, as well as the duration and content of prolonged services that the physician furnished.

- Time the office staff spends with the patient or time the patient remains unaccompanied in the office is not reported using prolonged services codes.

- Time spent waiting for inpatient test results, changes in the patient's condition, end of therapy, or use of facilities is not reported using prolonged services codes.

Prolonged Service with Direct Patient Contact

Prolonged service with direct patient content add-on codes (Table 10-5) are reported when a physician or other qualified health care professional provides prolonged service(s) involving direct patient contact that is provided beyond the usual service in either the inpatient or outpatient setting. *Direct patient contact* includes face-to-face and additional non-face-to-face services on the patient's floor or unit in the hospital or nursing facility during the same encounter. *This service is reported in addition to the primary procedure and any other services provided during the same encounter.*

> **EXAMPLE 1:** A physician provided level 3 office or other outpatient services to an acutely ill established patient who was treated for an asthma attack with intermittent bronchial dilation and subcutaneous epinephrine. The physician provided intermittent direct services over a period of 65 minutes. Report codes 99213 and 99354.

> **EXAMPLE 2:** A physician provided level 3 initial hospital care services to an acutely ill 4-year-old patient who was admitted with respiratory distress, requiring direct contact by the physician. Total duration of time was 115 minutes. Report codes 99223, 99356, and 99357.

Prolonged Service Without Direct Patient Contact

Prolonged service without direct patient contact codes are reported for the total duration of time during which the physician or other qualified health care professional provided services *without direct patient contact* (e.g., extensive record review) on an outpatient or inpatient basis occurring before and/or after direct patient care.

> **EXAMPLE:** A physician provided level 4 office or other outpatient services to an established elderly male patient who was seen for senile dementia, hypertension, diabetes mellitus, and arrhythmia. It becomes clear during the encounter that the patient needs to be placed in an SNF immediately. The patient's wife becomes upset when the physician discusses this recommendation with her, and the physician spends 45 minutes talking with her about what she and the patient can expect regarding SNF care. The physician also calls the local SNF to arrange for patient admission and to coordinate the patient's plan of care; 15 minutes are spent during this phone call. The total duration of time providing non-face-to-face contact was 65 minutes. Report codes 99214 and 99358.

TABLE 10-5 Prolonged Services Without Direct Patient Contact: Total Duration of Services and Codes

Total Duration of Prolonged Services Without Direct Face-to-Face Contact	Code(s)
Less than 30 minutes	Not reported separately
30–74 minutes (30 minutes–1 hr. 14 minutes)	99358 × 1
75–104 minutes (1 hr. 15 minutes–1 hr. 44 minutes)	99358 × 1 AND 99359 × 1
105 minutes or more (1 hr. 45 minutes or more)	99358 × 1 AND 99359 × 2

Prolonged Clinical Staff Services with Physician or Other Qualified Health Care Professional Supervision

Prolonged Clinical Staff Services with Physician or Other Qualified Health Care Professional Supervision codes are reported for an office or outpatient setting when clinical staff (e.g., dietician) have prolonged face-to-face time with patients. The physician or qualified health care professional (e.g., nurse practitioner) must provide direct supervision of clinical staff.

Code 99415 is reported (in addition to the E/M service code) for up to the first 45 to 60 minutes of prolonged clinical staff service on a given date, even if the time spent by the clinical staff is not continuous on that date. (Code 99416 is *not* reported for 44 minutes or less of clinical staff time.)

Code 99416 is reported for each additional 15 to 30 minutes of prolonged clinical staff service beyond the first hour, and it is an add-on code, which means it must be reported with code 99415. (Code 99416 is *not* reported for 14 minutes or less of clinical staff time.)

> **EXAMPLE:** An established patient received E/M services for obesity, and code 99213 was reported for the nurse practitioner's provision of services. The patient is participating in a weight loss program, and the dietician provided 80 minutes of face-to-face time counseling services, under the nurse practitioner's supervision, during the same encounter. Code 99415 was reported for the first 60 minutes of the dietician's time, and code 99416 was also reported for the next 20 minutes of the dietician's time. Thus, the CMS-1500 claim reported codes 99213, 99415, and 99416 for this one encounter.

 NOTE:

Codes 99415 and 99416 are *not* reported by physician or other qualified health care professionals, such as nurse practitioners and physician assistants. Instead, codes 99354–99359 are reported by physicians and other qualified health care professionals.

Standby Services

Standby services involve a physician or other qualified health care professional spending a prolonged period of time *without patient contact* waiting for an event to occur that will require the physician's services. Such services must be requested by another provider (e.g., attending physician) and are reported only if the standby time is 30 minutes or longer. However, if a physician who provides standby services performs surgery, the standby services are included in the surgical procedure's global period. Standby services include the following:

- Operative standby: Surgeon is requested to stand by in the event surgery is required, such as for a trauma case.
- Pathology standby: Pathologist is requested to stand by to evaluate a frozen section while the patient is in the operating room.
- Diagnostics standby: Cardiologist is requested to stand by to monitor diagnostics, such as telemetry.
- Obstetrics standby: Surgeon is requested to stand by in the event that a cesarean section is required.
- Pediatrics standby: Pediatrician is requested to stand by in the event that services are needed after the delivery of a high-risk newborn.

Code 99360 is reported in addition to codes 99460 (history and examination of normal newborn) and 99465 (newborn resuscitation), *but not* 99464 (attendance at delivery and initial stabilization of newborn).

> **EXAMPLE:** An obstetric surgeon was called in for consultation by the patient's attending physician (a family practitioner) and provided 30 minutes of standby services due to fetal distress, as noted on the fetal monitor. During standby, the fetal distress resolved, the patient went into active labor, and the patient's attending physician (not the obstetric surgeon) delivered the baby vaginally. The insurance specialist should report 99360 for the obstetric surgeon (because no cesarean section was required).

Case Management Services

According to CPT, "**case management** is a process in which a physician or another qualified health care professional is responsible for direct care of a patient, and for coordinating and managing access to, initiating, and/or supervising other health care services needed by the patient." Case management services include medical team conferences. (Anticoagulant management codes were relocated to the CPT Medicine section.)

EXAMPLE: The physician participated in a 30-minute interdisciplinary medical team conference of mental health professionals to discuss a 49-year-old patient's plan of care. Report code 99367.

Care Plan Oversight Services

Care plan oversight services codes are reported by one individual who supervises the home health, hospice, or nursing facility care plan of a patient or resident during a given period of time (e.g., 30 days). One individual may report care plan oversight services for a given period of time, which reflects the sole or predominant supervisory role with a particular patient or resident. Codes are not reported for the supervision of residents in nursing facilities or patients receiving home health care *unless recurrent supervision of therapy is required*.

EXAMPLE: The physician reviewed and revised the hospice agency care plan for a 64-year-old female patient with terminal breast cancer. Care plan oversight services required 25 minutes of the physician's time. Report code 99377.

Preventive Medicine Services

Preventive medicine services include routine examinations or risk management counseling for children and adults who exhibit no overt signs or symptoms of a disorder while presenting to the medical office for a preventive medical physical. Such services are also called *wellness visits*. Discussion of risk factors such as diet and exercise counseling, family problems, substance abuse counseling, and injury prevention are an integral part of preventive medicine. Care must be taken to select the proper code according to the age of the patient and the patient's status (new versus established).

 Coding Tip

- Determine the patient's status (new versus established) when assigning preventive medicine services codes.
- Preventive medicine services are not reported when a patient who is receiving treatment for a specific disorder returns to the office for a "recheck of a known problem."

When a significant abnormality or preexisting condition is treated during the same encounter as a preventive medicine service (e.g., annual physical exam), it is appropriate to report an office or other outpatient services code (99201–99215) in addition to the preventive medicine services code. To report both codes, the preventive medicine services portion of the visit must be complete and comprehensive and the workup for the significant problem must meet the required key components for assignment of codes 99201–99215. Attach modifier -25 to the code reported from 99201 to 99215, and link the appropriate diagnosis code to justify medical necessity.

EXAMPLE 1: A 24-year-old new patient receives preventive medicine services from a family practitioner. Report code 99385.

EXAMPLE 2: A 45-year-old established patient receives preventive medicine services as part of an annual physical exam; during examination, the physician notices a breast lump. The physician provides level 3 E/M office or other outpatient services to evaluate the breast lump, which include additional examination and discussion of diagnostic testing plans with the patient. Report codes 99396 and 99213-25.

Counseling Risk Factor Reduction and Behavior Change Intervention

Counseling risk factor reduction and behavior change intervention services are reported by physicians or other qualified health care professionals who provide face-to-face services to promote patients' health and prevent illness or injury. They are distinct from other E/M services (e.g., level 3 new patient E/M service), which can be reported separately by adding modifier -25.

- Risk factor reduction services are reported for patients who do not have a specific illness, but for whom such counseling might otherwise be used as part of treatment. Patient issues include family problems, substance use, sexual practices, and so on.
- Behavior change interventions are provided to patients who exhibit a behavior that is often considered an illness (e.g., obesity, substance abuse or misuse, tobacco use or addiction).

EXAMPLE 1: A patient who has been identified as being the adult child of an alcoholic receives preventive medicine individual counseling lasting 60 minutes. Report code 99404.

EXAMPLE 2: A patient who has a two-pack per day history of smoking cigarettes receives individual behavior change intervention counseling as part of his level 3 E/M service for treatment of type 2 diabetes mellitus. Report codes 99213 and 99406-25.

Non-Face-to-Face Services

Non-face-to-face services include telephone services, online digital evaluation and management services, and interprofessional telephone/Internet/electronic health record consultations, digitally stored data services/remote physiologic monitoring, and remote physiologic monitoring treatment management services. Telephone services are provided by a provider to an established patient using the telephone. Online medical evaluations are provided by a provider to an established patient using Internet resources to respond to a patient's online inquiry. Interprofessional telephone/Internet/electronic health record consultations occur when a patient's treating physician requests the opinion and/or treatment advice of a physician with specific specialty expertise (e.g., consultant) to assist in the diagnosis and/or management of the patient's problem without the need for the patient's face-to-face contact with the consultant.

EXAMPLE 1: A physician called an established patient to discuss the results of laboratory testing and to revise the instructions for taking a prescribed medication. The call was 12 minutes in duration. The patient had previously been seen in the office 10 days ago, and is scheduled to return to the office for follow-up in 2 months. Report code 99442.

EXAMPLE 2: A patient emailed her physician to ask whether her prescribed Effexor could be increased from 75 to 150 mg per day, per the recommendation of her marriage counselor. The counselor suggested that 75 mg per day was not a therapeutic dosage for the patient, and her physician agreed and instructed the patient to take two 75-mg capsules daily. The patient had previously been seen by the physician in the office 30 days ago, and she is scheduled to receive office E/M services in 60 days as part of her routine care. The physician spent 5 minutes providing online digital E/M services. Report code 99421.

EXAMPLE 3: A patient received an Internet assessment and management service that was provided by an ENT specialist during 60 minutes of medical consultative discussion and review with the patient's treating physician, including a verbal and written report. Report code 99449. (Do not add modifier -95 to code 99449 because the star symbol does not precede the code in the coding manual. The code includes "Internet assessment and management service" in its description.)

EXAMPLE 4: A physician provided remote physiologic monitoring of a patient's parameters, including blood pressure and respiratory flow rate. Initial set-up and patient education on the use of equipment was provided. Report code 99453. (Modifier -95 does not apply.)

EXAMPLE 5: The patient received remote physiologic monitoring treatment management services for a period of 20 minutes from her physician on May 1, facilitated by interactive communication between patient and physician during the entire month. Report code 99457.

Special Evaluation and Management Services

According to CPT, **special evaluation and management services** are provided for establishment of baseline information prior to life or disability insurance certificates being issued and for examination of a patient with a work-related or medical disability problem. During special evaluation and management services, the examining provider does *not* assume active management of the patient's health problems.

> **EXAMPLE 1:** A life insurance company's representative examines a 27-year-old male patient in his home to determine whether a base life insurance policy will be issued. Report code 99450.

> **EXAMPLE 2:** A 42-year-old male who had sustained an on-the-job injury about 10 years ago is evaluated by a court-appointed workers' compensation physician to determine whether the patient's current condition is considered work related. Report code 99456.

Newborn Care Services

Newborn care services are provided to newborns in a variety of health care settings (e.g., hospital, birthing center, and home birth).

> **EXAMPLE 1:** A 34-year-old female patient was admitted to the hospital on May 19 for vaginal delivery, which resulted in a healthy 10-pound newborn boy. The pediatrician provided newborn care services on May 19 to complete a history and examination of the infant, and on the morning of May 20, the patient and her infant boy were discharged home. Report codes 99460 and 99462 for the newborn case.

> **EXAMPLE 2:** A 34-year-old female patient delivered a healthy 8-pound newborn girl at home, and the physician in attendance performed a physical examination of the neonate and provided instruction to the parents about initial care. The patient and her daughter are scheduled to follow up in the office in three days. Report code 99461 for the newborn case.

Delivery/Birthing Room Attendance and Resuscitation Services

Delivery/birthing room attendance and resuscitation services include attendance at delivery, initial stabilization of the newborn, and delivery/birthing room resuscitation. When delivery room attendance services (99464) or delivery room resuscitation services (99465) are required, they are reported in addition to newborn care services codes.

> **EXAMPLE:** Per the request of the patient's delivering physician, a pediatrician was in attendance at the delivery to provide initial stabilization of the newborn. The pediatrician reports code 99464.

Inpatient Neonatal Intensive Care Services and Pediatric and Neonatal Critical Care Services

Inpatient neonatal and pediatric critical care and intensive services are delivered to critically ill neonates and infants by a provider. A **neonate** is a newborn, up to 28 days old. An **infant** is a very young child, up to one year old. The definitions for critical care services codes provided to neonates are the same as those provided to adults. (Refer to the previous section of this chapter for discussion of critical care services definitions and coding guidelines.) Inpatient neonatal and pediatric critical care and intensive services begin on the date of admission,

 Coding Tip

- When a neonate or an infant is no longer considered critically ill (e.g., attains a body weight that exceeds 5,000 grams), report subsequent hospital care codes (99231–99233) for inpatient services provided.
- For infants with less than 5,000 grams body weight, who are no longer considered critically ill, report subsequent intensive care services codes (99478–99480).

and codes are reported once per day per patient. These codes are reported for each 24-hour period, not according to total duration of critical care; the appropriate code is reported once per day per patient.

Pediatric Critical Care Patient Transport

Pediatric critical care patient transport includes the physical attendance and direct face-to-face care delivered by a provider during the interfacility transport of a critically ill or critically injured patient, aged 24 months or younger. **Interfacility transport** is the transfer of a patient from one health care facility to another (e.g., community hospital to children's hospital), and it usually involves use of an ambulance or a helicopter.

> **EXAMPLE:** A 4-month-old infant requires pediatric critical care patient transport services due to respiratory failure. The infant's pediatrician provided critical care services during a 95-minute interfacility transfer from a rural community hospital, where the patient was initially treated to stabilize him, to a specialty children's hospital in a city located 70 miles away. Report codes 99466 and 99467.

Inpatient Neonatal and Pediatric Critical Care

Inpatient neonatal critical care services are provided to patients 28 days of age or less. *Inpatient pediatric critical care services* are provided to patients 29 days of age through less than six years of age.

Initial and Continuing Intensive Care Services

Continuing intensive care services codes are reported for services provided subsequent to the day of admission to **very low birth weight** (less than 1,500 grams) or **low birth weight** (1,500–2,500 grams) infants who are no longer considered critically ill.

> **EXAMPLE:** A 25-day-old infant weighing 1,400 grams received subsequent intensive care services from her pediatrician on days two and three of her inpatient admission. Report 99478, 99478.

Cognitive Assessment and Care Plan Services

Cognitive assessment and care plan services are provided when the comprehensive evaluation of a patient who exhibits signs and symptoms of cognitive impairment is required to confirm or establish a diagnosis, including etiology and severity of the condition.

> **EXAMPLE:** Patient underwent cognitive assessment and care planning at her apartment in an assisted living facility. All of the required elements of assessment and care planning were performed and documented. Report code 99483.

Care Management Services

Care management services are provided by providers, other qualified health care professionals, and clinical staff. Services include patient-centered management and support services that are provided to patients who reside at home or in a domiciliary, rest home, or assisted living facility (e.g., coordinating patient care with a home health agency). Chronic care management services and complex chronic care management services are provided to patients.

Chronic care management services are provided when the patient's medical and/or psychological needs require establishment, implementation, revision, or monitoring of the care plan. Such patients receive services for two or more chronic conditions or episodic health conditions, which are expected to be managed for a period of at least 12 months or until the death of the patient and that place the patient at significant risk of acute exacerbation or decompensation, death, or functional decline. Code 99490 is reported when at least 20 minutes of clinical staff time during the calendar month is spent providing chronic care management activities.

Complex chronic care management services are provided to patients who require the establishment or substantial revision of a comprehensive care plan and for which medical decision making of moderate or high complexity was provided. Codes 99487–99489 are reported when a minimum of 60 minutes of clinical staff care management services were provided under the direction of a physician or other qualified health care professional.

EXAMPLE: Established patient received level 3 physician office services for treatment of acute bronchitis. During the same encounter, the provider medically managed the patient's brittle type 1 diabetes mellitus and chronic asthma. Patient's comprehensive care plan was revised to provide education to explain that over-the-counter (OTC) medications cannot be combined with prescribed medications for her acute bronchitis because of the risk to stability of her chronic conditions. The patient had numerous questions about not using OTC medications and how they might impact her chronic conditions; the physician provided education and counseling for 30 minutes to ensure that all of the patient's questions were answered and that the patient understood her treatment plan. Report codes 99213 and 99490.

Psychiatric Collaborative Care Management Services

Psychiatric collaborative care management services are provided when a patient has a diagnosed psychiatric disorder that requires behavioral health care assessment; establishment, implementation, revision, and monitoring of a care plan; and provision of brief interventions (Table 10-6).

TABLE 10-6 Psychiatric Collaborative Care Management Services: Total Duration of Care and Codes

Type of Service	Total Duration of Collaborative Care Management over Calendar Month	Code(s)
Initial – 70 minutes	Less than 36 minutes	Not reported separately
	36–85 minutes (36 minutes–1 hr. 25 minutes)	99492
Initial plus each additional increment up to 30 minutes	86–115 minutes (1 hr. 26 minutes–1 hr. 55 minutes)	99492 × 1 AND 99494 × 1
Subsequent – 60 minutes	Less than 31 minutes	Not reported separately
	31–75 minutes (31 minutes–1 hr. 15 minutes)	99493
Subsequent plus each additional increment up to 30 minutes	76–105 minutes (1 hr. 16 minutes–1 hr. 45 minutes)	99493 × 1 AND 99494 × 1

EXAMPLE: Patient received 1 hour and 45 minutes of initial psychiatric collaborative care management, which included completion and documentation of all required elements was provided for the patient. (One hour and 45 minutes = 105 minutes.) Report codes 99492, 99494.

Transitional Care Management Services

Transitional care management services are provided to patients in their community setting (e.g., home, assisted living facility). Services are provided for medical and/or psychosocial problems that require moderate or high complexity medical decision making during transitions in care from an inpatient hospital setting, partial hospital, observation status in a hospital, or skilled nursing facility.

EXAMPLE: A patient was discharged from a nursing facility to her home. The provider coordinated home health care services, educated the primary caregiver about follow-up care, and communicated with the patient via telephone on the day after discharge. Medical decision making was of moderate complexity. Report code 99495 (in addition to an appropriate code for nursing facility E/M services).

Advance Care Planning

Advance care planning includes face-to-face services between a physician or other qualified health care professional and a patient, family member, or surrogate for counseling and discussing advance directives, with or without completing relevant legal forms (e.g., health care proxy).

EXAMPLE: The patient and her daughter met with the patient's primary care physician for 30 minutes of advance care planning, which included an explanation and discussion of the patient's health care proxy. Report code 99497.

General Behavioral Health Integration Care Management

General behavioral health integration care management services are provided by clinical staff for patients with behavioral health and substance abuse conditions, and codes are reported by the supervising physician or other qualified health care professional. Services provided require care management services (face-to-face or non-face-to-face) of 20 or more minutes in a calendar month, a treatment plan, and specified elements of the CPT code description, which include:

- initial assessment or follow-up monitoring, including the use of applicable validated rating scales
- behavioral health care planning in relation to behavioral/psychiatric health problems, including revision for patients who are not progressing or whose status changes
- facilitating and coordinating treatment such as psychotherapy, pharmacotherapy, counseling and/or psychiatric consultation
- continuity of care with a designated member of the care team

Other Evaluation and Management Services

Code 99499 is assigned when the E/M service provided is not described in any other listed E/M codes.

Exercise 10.4 – Evaluation and Management Categories and Subcategories

Instructions: Indicate whether each statement is true (T) or false (F).

_____ 1. When a physician provides more than one Evaluation and Management (E/M) service for the same patient on the same day and the patient's problem is the same for each encounter, report an E/M service code for each encounter.

_____ 2. When a physician provides two E/M office or other outpatient services to the same patient on the same day and the patient's problems are different for each E/M service, report multiple E/M codes and attach modifier -51 to the second code.

_____ 3. When the patient receives office or other outpatient E/M services *and is admitted to the hospital as an inpatient by the same physician*, report an E/M code for the initial hospital care only.

_____ 4. When the provider performs a comprehensive exam in the office and the patient is later admitted to the hospital *on another day*, void the previously submitted claim on which the office E/M code was reported and report a higher level of service initial hospital care E/M code for the hospital admission.

_____ 5. The provider does not have to redocument the history, review of symptoms, and past/family/social history documented during a previous encounter *if the provider documents that the previous information was reviewed and then updates the information*.

_____ 6. Teaching physicians are required to rewrite in entirety the key elements of a resident physician's E/M documentation.

_____ 7. Code 99211 is commonly thought of as a "nurse visit" because it can be reported only when a nurse provides office E/M services for an established patient.

_____ 8. Observation services are provided in a hospital outpatient setting, and the patient is considered an outpatient.

Exercise 10.4 – *continued*

_____ 9. A patient who is referred by a physician for hospital observation services, bypassing the outpatient or emergency department, is considered a "direct admission to observation."

_____ 10. Initial observation care codes are reported for patients who are admitted and discharged from observation services on the same date.

_____ 11. Subsequent hospital care includes the review of the patient's record for changes in the patient's condition, the results of diagnostic studies, and/or the reassessment of the patient's condition since the last assessment performed by the physician.

_____ 12. When a patient is admitted as a hospital inpatient after receiving observation services on the same date, report only an initial hospital care code.

_____ 13. A hospital discharge day management code is reported with a subsequent hospital care services code on the same date.

_____ 14. For a code from the Office or Other Outpatient Consultations category to be reported, the consultation request must be initiated by the attending physician or another health care provider and the attending physician must document all consultation requests in the patient's record.

_____ 15. Initial inpatient consultation codes are reported when consultation services are provided to acute care hospital inpatients only.

_____ 16. Reporting emergency department (ED) services codes is not restricted to ED physicians employed by the hospital.

_____ 17. When a physician provides emergency services to a patient in the office, a code from the Emergency Department Services category of E/M should be reported.

_____ 18. Critical care services require personal management by the physician.

_____ 19. A neonate is a newborn, up to one year old.

_____ 20. Do not report a subsequent nursing facility service code and an initial hospital care service code on the same date for the same patient.

_____ 21. Medical services are usually provided to residents of an assisted living facility by the facility's staff.

_____ 22. Documentation of all face-to-face E/M home services visits and any telephone communications with the patient or caretakers must be documented in the patient's record.

_____ 23. Codes for prolonged services are reported instead of other physician services, such as hospital inpatient services.

_____ 24. When a physician who provides standby services performs surgery, the standby services are included in the surgical procedure's global period.

_____ 25. Case management services include team conferences.

_____ 26. Care plan oversight services codes are classified separately from other E/M codes when the physician is involved in direct patient examinations.

_____ 27. Preventive medicine services are reported when a patient who is receiving treatment for a specific disorder returns to the office for a "recheck of a known problem."

_____ 28. Newborn care code 99460 is reported for birthing center care only.

_____ 29. During special evaluation and management services, the examining provider assumes active management of the patient's health problems.

_____ 30. Code 99499 is assigned when the E/M service provided is not described in any other listed E/M codes.

Summary

The E/M section is organized according to place of service (e.g., office, hospital, home, nursing facility, emergency department, or critical care), type of service (e.g., new or initial encounter, follow-up or subsequent encounter), and miscellaneous services (e.g., prolonged physician service or care plan oversight service). The Evaluation and Management (E/M) section guidelines are located at the beginning of the section and include the following contents: classification of E/M services, definitions of commonly used terms, unlisted service, special report, clinical examples, and instructions for selecting a level of E/M service.

E/M categories and subcategories contain codes that are classified according to level of services for reporting to third-party payers. Although the last number of some E/M codes represents the level of service (e.g., code 99213 is a level 3 E/M service), the levels within categories and subcategories are not interchangeable. Levels of E/M services include conferences with or about patients, evaluations, examinations, preventive adult and pediatric health supervision, treatments, and other medical services (e.g., determining the need for and/or location of appropriate care, such as hospice care for a terminally ill patient). The E/M section (99201–99499) contains notes unique to each category and subcategory. *Remember to review notes before assigning an E/M code.*

 NOTE:

Medicare and some other payers no longer allow providers to report codes from the Consultations category. Thus, providers (e.g., specialists) who deliver consultation services to office patients, hospital outpatients, hospital inpatients, or nursing facility residents are to report codes from the Office or Other Outpatient Services category, Initial Hospital Care subcategory, or Initial Nursing Facility Care subcategory of CPT. (Coders should determine whether health plans allow CPT consultation codes to be reported.) When more than one provider (e.g., attending physician and a consultant) delivers services to a Medicare inpatient or nursing facility resident on the same date of service, the attending physician adds modifier -AI (Principal Physician of Record) to the reported E/M code.

Internet Links

American Academy of Family Physicians (AAFP): *www.aafp.org*

American Academy of Pediatrics (AAP): *www.aap.org*

Documentation Guidelines for E/M Services: Go to *http://login.cengage.com*, and use the login instructions located in the Preface to locate an online version of the documentation guidelines for E/M services on the Student Companion Site.

E/M CodeBuilder: Go to *http://login.cengage.com*, and use the login instructions located in the Preface to locate an online version of the E/M CodeBuilder on the Student Companion Site.

Medicare Learning Network (MLN): Go to *www.cms.gov*, click on the Outreach & Education link, click on the "Get training" link below the Learn heading, and then click on the Medicare Learning Network® (MLN) link.

Review

Multiple Choice

Instructions: Circle the most appropriate response.

1. The E/M level of service reflects the:
    a. amount of work involved in providing health care to a patient.
    b. kind of health care services provided to a patient.
    c. physical location where health care is provided to a patient.
    d. type of condition for which the patient is being treated.

2. Concurrent care is the provision of similar services to:
    a. different patients by the same provider on the same day.
    b. the same patient by more than one provider on the same day.
    c. the same patient by the same provider on different days.
    d. the same patient by the same provider on the same day.

3. Dr. Benjamin practiced at Hopewell Medical Center until 2002, when he began to practice with Dr. Evans at the Lakewood Clinic. Which would be considered a new patient at Lakewood Clinic?
    a. Debra injured her back two years ago and has been under continuous treatment at another facility. She had her records transferred to Lakewood Clinic and is going to be seen by Dr. Evans for continuing treatment of her chronic condition.
    b. Henrique, who had last seen Dr. Benjamin at Hopewell Medical Center in April 2001, is treated by Dr. Benjamin at the Lakewood Clinic in March 2004.
    c. Martha had a physical performed on June 1, 2003, by Dr. Benjamin and is seen by Dr. Evans on September 30, 2005, for a sinus condition.
    d. Sheryl was treated last month by Dr. Evans. This week she needs to be seen again, but Lakewood Clinic is closed for the holiday. She is seen by an on-call physician who is covering for Dr. Evans.

4. *Problem focused*, *expanded problem focused*, *detailed*, and *comprehensive* are terms used to describe which components of an E/M level of service code?
    a. Extent of exam
    b. Extent of history
    c. Extent of history and extent of exam
    d. Review of systems

5. Which contributory component would be considered when determining the number of diagnoses or management options for medical decision-making complexity?
    a. Coordination of care
    b. Counseling
    c. Nature of the presenting problem
    d. Time

6. There are seven components to a level of E/M service code description. Which are considered key components when selecting the E/M code?
    a. Counseling, coordination of care, and nature of presenting problem
    b. History, exam, and medical decision making
    c. History, exam, and time
    d. Medical decision making, time, and nature of presenting problem

7. Time is a contributing factor in E/M code selection for which scenario?
    a. A patient had an encounter solely for the purpose of discussing treatment options for a recently diagnosed condition.
    b. After Dr. Harris diagnosed Ellen with an ear infection, he explained the prognosis and wrote a prescription for an antibiotic.
    c. Dr. Bender showed frightened little Jimmy the x-ray of his broken arm and explained why a cast would help him get better.
    d. Dr. Knolles spent 10 minutes reviewing information on drugs to find one that the patient could tolerate.

8. Documentation of the review of systems is used to establish:
    a. complexity of medical decision making.
    b. extent of examination performed.
    c. extent of history obtained.
    d. presence of contributing factors.

9. A physician discussed the results of diagnostic testing with his patient. This portion of the encounter is considered:
    a. coordination of care.
    b. counseling.
    c. examination.
    d. history of present illness.

10. Which is reported using a non-face-to-face service code?

   a. A patient came into the emergency department with severe pain in the lower back. She told the physician that she had recently had an MRI at that facility but hadn't received the results yet. The physician looked up the test results and verified that a displaced disc was causing the pain.

   b. A patient involved in a motor vehicle accident came to the emergency department with complaints of a sore neck and blurry vision. The patient was diagnosed with whiplash. The attending physician requested an ophthalmology consultation during the encounter, but no physicians were available so he scheduled the consultation for the following day. He instructed the patient to follow up with her primary care physician if symptoms persisted.

   c. A physician called the patient at home to discuss the results of her lab tests. After reviewing the reports, he believed that further testing was necessary and advised her to make an appointment as soon as possible.

   d. During an encounter, a physician recommended physical therapy to a patient with rheumatoid arthritis. She expressed concern over which facility she should contact and how she would get there. Before she left, the physician provided her with names and numbers of facilities she could contact for treatment, as well as agencies that would assist in her transportation needs.

11. A patient is admitted with head injury. On the initial visit, the physician observes that the patient is unconscious and is bleeding from the right ear. The physician spends 70 minutes treating the patient and coordinating care, during which time a comprehensive history and exam are obtained. Which E/M code is reported?

   a. 99221   b. 99222   c. 99223   d. 99285

12. A six-year-old child is seen by her family physician for her annual check-up and immunizations. Her last encounter was one year ago. Which E/M code is reported?

   a. 99211   b. 99251   c. 99383   d. 99393

13. A patient with severe chest pain is admitted for observation. A comprehensive history and examination are performed. Medical decision making is moderate. The patient is released the same day. Which E/M code is reported?

   a. 99202   b. 99219   c. 99222   d. 99235

14. A 38-year-old patient with neck stiffness and pain radiating down the right arm presents to the neurosurgeon for an office consultation, and the health plan allows CPT consultation codes to be reported. A detailed history and exam are obtained during the 40-minute encounter. Which E/M code is reported?

   a. 99204   b. 99221   c. 99243   d. 99244

15. A patient was seen in the emergency department after she burned her hand with scalding water. An expanded problem focused history and exam were performed. Medical decision making was of low complexity. Which E/M code is reported?

   a. 99213   b. 99232   c. 99282   d. 99283

16. A physician performs a scheduled follow-up visit to a 65-year-old patient in a nursing facility who is recovering from pneumonia. The patient has responded well to the treatment, and no complications are noted. Which E/M code is reported?

   a. 99307   b. 99308   c. 99324   d. 99341

17. A new patient presents to the physician's office with complaints of severe earache, jaw pain, and facial swelling. The physician obtains a detailed history of the chief complaint, an extended review of systems, and a problem pertinent past/family/social history and performs a detailed exam. Medical decision making is of low complexity. Which E/M code is reported?

   a. 99203   b. 99204   c. 99205   d. 99214

18. An established patient has a four-month office check-up for medical management of high triglyceride levels. A brief history of present illness and a problem pertinent review of systems are obtained. The physician counsels the patient on diet and exercise and advises the patient to return again in four months. Which E/M code is reported?

    a. 99202   **b.** 99213   **c.** 99214   **d.** 99232

19. A subsequent hospital visit is required for a 58-year-old patient admitted with an esophageal neoplasm who has begun to spit up blood. Metastasis is suspected. Which E/M code is reported?

    a. 99233   **b.** 99236   **c.** 99255   **d.** 99285

20. An inpatient follow-up consultation is performed for a 70-year-old Medicare patient who is experiencing foot drop after leg surgery. The foot has regained normal positioning. Which E/M code is reported?

    a. 99221   **b.** 99231   **c.** 99241   **d.** 99251

Coding Practice

Instructions: Review each case and assign CPT code(s) and appropriate modifier(s).

Outpatient and Other Visits

1. A 4-year-old female established patient received Evaluation and Management services in her physician's office, which included a problem focused history, an expanded problem focused exam, and medical decision making (MDM) of a low level. The patient is diagnosed with influenza.

   _____

2. A 16-year-old outpatient who is a new patient to the office complains of severe facial acne. The history and physical examination are expanded problem focused. The physician must consider related organ systems in addition to the integumentary system in order to treat the condition. With minimal number of diagnoses to consider and the minimal amount of data to review, the physician's decision making is straightforward with regard to the treatment of this patient.

   _____

Hospital Inpatient and Observation Services

3. A patient was in an automobile accident and is complaining of a minor headache and no other apparent injuries. History gathered from bystanders states that the patient was not wearing a seat belt and hit his head on the windshield. A 15-minute loss of consciousness was noted. The patient was then admitted for 24-hour observation to rule out head injury. A comprehensive history and exam are performed by the physician. The MDM is of moderate complexity.

   _____

4. A 55-year-old female came in with the complaint of severe abdominal pain. The patient was admitted on 05/07 to observation due to the severity and location of her pain. The admitting physician performed a comprehensive history and a detailed examination and documented medical decision making of a moderate complexity given the amount of possible diagnoses, including appendicitis, gastric ulcer, cholelithiasis, and pyelonephritis. Various diagnostic tests were ordered and done, including barium enema, upper gastrointestinal endoscopy, and KUB (kidneys, ureters, bladder) x-ray. No disease or disorder was found, and the patient was discharged from observation on 05/08. The patient reported a decrease in her pain after 30 hours of IV analgesics and antispasmodics. The physician documented that the patient should follow up with her primary care physician in two days or return to the hospital if the pain worsens. The physician also documented a final detailed examination of the patient and dictated a discharge summary report.

   _____

5. A 50-year-old female patient was admitted to the hospital on 10/10 with a diagnosis of pneumonia due to *Staphylococcus aureus*, at which time she received level 2 E/M services from her attending physician. On 10/11 and 10/12, the patient received level 2 E/M services. On 10/13, the patient was discharged from the hospital in improved condition to follow up with the physician at home; the physician spent 30 minutes performing discharge day management functions.

_____

6. An established patient is seen in the hospital on day two of his hospital stay. The patient had been admitted through the emergency department with status asthmaticus and had been undergoing extensive respiratory therapy over the past 24 to 30 hours. The physician performs a detailed interval history and a detailed physical exam. The possibility of pneumonia complicating the asthma must be considered. The patient's respiratory condition is still unstable. The MDM complexity was high.

_____

Consultations

7. A 52-year-old patient was sent to a surgeon for an office consultation concerning hemorrhoids, and the health plan allows CPT consultation codes to be reported. An expanded problem focused history and examination were performed. The consultant recommended treating with medication after a straightforward MDM.

_____

8. A 13-year-old male was admitted yesterday for a tympanotomy. Postsurgically, the child developed fever and seizures of unknown origin. A pediatric consultation was requested, and the health plan allows CPT consultation codes to be reported. This was done on the second hospital admission day and 24 hours after surgery. The history of present illness (HPI) was extended with a complete review of systems (ROS). A complete past/family/social history (PFSH) was elicited from the mother as part of a comprehensive history. A comprehensive examination was conducted on all body areas and organ systems. The MDM complexity was high.

_____

Emergency Department Visits

9. A patient in the emergency department (ED) has a temperature of 103°F and is in acute respiratory distress. Symptoms include shortness of breath, chest pain, and gasping. The physician is unable to obtain a history or perform a comprehensive physical examination because the patient's condition is critical. The MDM complexity is high.

_____

10. With two-way communication, the physician directs the emergency medical technicians (EMTs) in an ambulance en route to the emergency department with a patient in apparent cardiac arrest.

_____

11. A patient presents with the complaint of hematemesis. The patient also has a rapid pulse rate and low blood pressure. In the ED, critical care is provided by the ED attending to raise the patient's blood pressure and decrease blood loss. This is done for 70 minutes before the patient is transferred to the surgical suite for an endoscopic procedure to evaluate his esophagus. The ED physician also documents a detailed examination and MDM of high complexity. Due to the patient's medical condition, he is unable to provide any history; no family is present to provide information.

_____

Critical Care Services

12. A physician is called to the intensive care unit to provide care for a patient who received second- and third-degree burns over 50 percent of his body due to a chemical fire. The patient is in respiratory distress and is suffering from severe dehydration. The physician provides support for two hours. Later that day, the physician returns and provides an additional hour of critical care support to the patient.

Nursing Facility Services

13. A 72-year-old patient suffered a cerebral vascular accident (CVA). Today the patient is admitted to a skilled nursing facility (SNF) for rehab and medical care. The patient was just discharged from an acute care facility. The SNF medical director documents a comprehensive history, including the patient's chief complaint of paralysis and weakness, an extended HPI, and a complete ROS. A detailed exam of the patient's cardiovascular, respiratory, musculoskeletal, neurological, and genitourinary systems is documented. The physician orders a multidisciplinary rehabilitation care plan for the patient and the continued treatment of the patient's other medical conditions, including hypertension and diabetes. The MDM complexity is high.

14. Subsequent follow-up care is provided for a comatose patient transferred to a long-term care center from the hospital two days ago. The resident shows no signs of consciousness on examination but appears to have developed a minor upper respiratory tract infection with a fever and rales heard on auscultation. The physician performs an expanded problem focused history and a problem focused interval examination with respiratory status and status of related organ systems such as cardiovascular. The physician is concerned that the respiratory infection could progress to pneumonia and orders the appropriate treatment. The MDM complexity is moderate.

Domiciliary Care, Rest Home, Assisted Living Visits

15. A new patient diagnosed with mild intellectual disabilities and self-abuse is sent to a custodial care facility for admission. The patient's family is no longer able to care for the patient at home. The care facility physician documents a problem focused history with a problem focused exam. The medical decision-making documented was straightforward.

16. A 21-year-old patient with a recent history of drug abuse is admitted to a rehab center for treatment. In the patient's second week of treatment, she complains of back pain and is seen by the same physician who evaluated her medically upon admission. At this time, the physician documents a problem focused interval history, an expanded problem focused examination, and MDM of moderate complexity.

Home Visits

17. A 64-year-old female patient has diabetes and has been having problems adjusting her insulin doses. She has had an onset of dizziness and sensitivity to light. Her primary care physician, who has treated her for this condition during the past four years, makes a home visit today. At this visit, the physician gathers a brief HPI and a problem pertinent ROS during the problem focused history. The physical exam focuses on the body systems currently affected by the diabetes. The patient's condition is moderately severe and the MDM complexity is of a moderate level.

18. A 15-year-old new patient has cystic fibrosis and is having problems with her Pulmozyme dosage. This medication is used to thin the mucus that clogs her lungs. The patient is having moderate throat pain and slight tightness in her chest. The physician makes a home visit to gather HPI and ROS and pertinent past personal medical information for a detailed history. The detailed exam focuses on the body systems currently affected by the cystic fibrosis and related organ systems: ears, nose, throat, mouth, respiratory, gastrointestinal, and cardiovascular. The MDM complexity is of a moderate level.

Prolonged Services

19. An established patient with a history of asthma presents in an office visit with acute bronchospasm and moderate respiratory distress. The physician conducts a problem focused history followed by a detailed examination, which shows a respiratory rate of 30. Office treatment is initiated: intermittent bronchial dilation and subcutaneous epinephrine. This service requires the physician to have intermittent direct contact with the patient over a two-hour period. The MDM complexity is moderate.

20. A patient was in the delivery room ready to give birth. When the physician had the patient start pushing, possible complications for the infant were noted and the hospital pediatric neonatal specialist was notified of a possible need for her evaluation of this newborn. The pediatric specialist was notified at 9:20 AM. At 10 AM, she was informed via phone call from the OB/GYN that the infant had normal Apgar scores of 9 and 9.

Case Management Services

21. A 72-year-old patient with a history of breast cancer has a suspicious mass in her uterus. A biopsy was done. The determination was that the patient had a carcinoma *in situ* of the uterus. The physician who conducted the surgery called a face-to-face meeting with his fellow surgeons and discussed the case and the patient's outcome for 30 minutes.

22. A 14-year-old boy twisted his ankle while playing soccer. He received level 3 E/M services from his physician the next morning for which code 99213 was reported on the CMS-1500 claim generated immediately after the visit. The physician ordered an x-ray of the ankle, and the child left the office after the x-ray but did not see the physician. Later that afternoon the patient and his mother came into the office and met with the physician, an orthopedic surgeon, and a rehabilitation therapist. Medical discussion was 45 minutes in duration.

Care Plan Oversight: Patient Under Care of Home Health Agency, Hospice, or Nursing Facility

23. A 75-year-old patient was just diagnosed with type 1 diabetes. This means that the patient will have to give himself insulin shots. The physician supervised the coordination of home health care, which required 30 minutes of his time.

24. A 50-year-old female has brain cancer, and the physician supervised the coordination of hospice services, which required 45 minutes of his time.

Preventive Medicine Services

25. A 13-year-old new patient presents for a well-check examination. The patient does not report any medical complaints.

_____

26. A 75-year-old established patient presents for his annual physical examination. The patient's chronic conditions are well controlled with diet and exercise.

_____

Non-Face-to-Face Physician Services

27. A physician called an established patient to inform her that the results of a chest x-ray were negative. The call was 5 minutes in duration. The patient had previously been seen in the office 10 days ago.

_____

28. A patient emailed his physician to ask whether taking 500 mg of cinnamon tablets daily would be acceptable, given the prescribed medications he takes. The physician replied (5 minutes), approving his taking 500 mg of cinnamon tablets daily. The patient had previously been seen by the physician in the office 15 days ago, and he is scheduled to receive office E/M services in 60 days as part of his routine care.

_____

Life/Disability Insurance Eligibility Visits

29. A 58-year-old man was seen by his private physician for an examination as part of his claim for long-term medical disability. The patient has chronic obstructive lung disease with severe emphysema and has been unable to work during the past year. The physician documents a comprehensive medical history and a detailed examination. The physician reviews the patient's current medical treatment plan and recommends that it continue. All of the necessary documentation required by the insurance company is completed, including the physician's opinion that the patient would be unable to work in the future, as his pulmonary function is markedly impaired in spite of continual respiratory and pharmacologic therapy.

_____

Newborn Care Services

30. A full-term healthy newborn girl received initial and subsequent hospital care services on July 7 and July 8, respectively.

_____

CPT Anesthesia

Chapter Outline

Anesthesia Terminology

Overview of Anesthesia Section

Anesthesia Section Guidelines

Anesthesia Subsections

Chapter Objectives

At the conclusion of this chapter, the student should be able to:

1. Define key terms related to the CPT Anesthesia section.
2. Define terminology associated with types of anesthesia.
3. Provide an overview about the Anesthesia section, focusing on organization, services included and excluded, and monitored anesthesia care.
4. Interpret Anesthesia section guidelines.
5. Assign CPT Anesthesia section codes and modifiers.

Key Terms

airway management

A-line

analgesia

analgesic

anesthesia

anesthesia conversion factor

anesthesia time unit

anesthesiologist

anesthetic

arteriography

base unit value

Bier block

cannula

capnography

caudal anesthesia

central nervous system (CNS)

central venous access device (CVAD)

central venous pressure catheter

central venous pressure (CVP) line

certified registered nurse anesthetist (CRNA)

cleft lip

concurrent medically directed anesthesia procedure

contrast medium

dura mater

electroconvulsive therapy (ECT)

emergency condition

endotracheal tube (ET)

epidural anesthesia

external catheter

extracorporeal shock wave lithotripsy (ESWL)

extradural procedure

field block

fluid management

general anesthesia

heparin

hypovolemia

implanted port

infiltration anesthesia

internal catheter

interventional therapeutic radiological procedure

intra-arterial cannula

intra-arterial catheter

intra-arterial line

intracranial	monitored anesthesia care (MAC)	plexus anesthesia	radiopaque
intravenous regional anesthesia	nerve plexus	postanesthesia evaluation	regional anesthesia
lesion	nontunneled catheter	postoperative pain management	saddle block anesthesia
lithotripter	one lung ventilation (OLV)	preanesthesia evaluation	sedation
local anesthesia	organ harvest	pulmonary wedge pressure	shock therapy
lumbar puncture (LP)	panniculectomy	pulse oximetry	spinal anesthesia
lumen	panniculus adiposus	pump oxygenator	spinal tap
mass spectrometry	pannus	qualifying circumstance	surface anesthesia
modifying unit	peripheral nerve block		Swan-Ganz catheter
	physical status modifier		tunneled catheter
			urethrocystoscopy

Introduction

The Anesthesia section is located after the Evaluation and Management section in the CPT coding manual, and the codes range from 00100 to 01999. Anesthesia codes are reported for services related to the administration of anesthesia (including general and regional), the supplementation of local anesthesia, and other supportive anesthesia services. Anesthesia subsections are organized according to anatomical site, except the last four subsections, which are listed as types of procedure. Any qualified health care provider who administers analgesic or anesthetic agents is permitted to report codes from the Anesthesia section of CPT. Providers include anesthesiologists, certified registered nurse anesthetists (CRNAs), surgeons, and other physicians. However, when the same physician (e.g., surgeon) performs the procedure and administers anesthesia, add modifier -47 to the CPT Surgery section code (and do not report a separate code from the Anesthesia section).

Anesthesia Terminology

An **anesthesiologist** is a physician who, after medical school, completes a one-year internship and three-year residency in anesthesia. *Qualified nonphysician anesthetists* includes anesthesiologist's assistants and CRNAs. A **certified registered nurse anesthetist (CRNA)** is a licensed registered nurse (RN) who has earned a bachelor's degree in science or nursing, has at least one year of acute care nursing experience (e.g., intensive care, coronary care, or emergency/trauma), has completed a 24- to 36-month nurse anesthesia program leading to a master's degree, and has passed the national certification exam. (Doctorate programs are also available.)

Patients who undergo surgical or other invasive procedures (e.g., radiological procedure) require anesthesia services so the procedure can be performed. **Anesthesia** is the process of inducing a loss of sensitivity to pain in all or part of the body, resulting from the administration of an **anesthetic** (drug or agent that causes a loss of feeling, awareness, and/or consciousness). An **analgesic** is a drug that reduces pain, such as aspirin, acetaminophen, and ibuprofen; for surgery, other substances (e.g., morphine) are used to cause **analgesia** (loss of pain sensation without loss of consciousness).

Types of Anesthesia

The following types of anesthesia are used in surgical practice:

- General anesthesia
- Local anesthesia
- Regional anesthesia

General anesthesia is used for extensive surgeries and involves the administration of anesthetic agents that are inhaled (e.g., sevoflurane combined with nitrous oxide) or administered intravenously (e.g., propofol). They act as hypnotics, muscle relaxants, and painkillers and serve to block any memory of the surgery. General anesthesia renders a patient unconscious, which means the brain doesn't perceive pain signals. To determine the general anesthetic agents to administer, the patient's age and health must be considered, along with the type of surgery to be performed.

Local anesthesia is appropriate for minor surgeries (e.g., dental work, skin biopsy, and suture of a laceration) and involves applying a topical agent (e.g., lidocaine) on the body's surface or injecting a local anesthetic agent (e.g., procaine) for the purpose of numbing a small part of the body. As a result, pain signals are blocked and the patient remains alert. Local anesthesia administration techniques include:

- **Surface anesthesia**: Topical application of local anesthetic cream, solution, or spray to skin or mucous membranes

- **Infiltration anesthesia**: Topical injection of local anesthetic into tissue

- **Field block**: Subcutaneous injection of local anesthetic in area bordering the field to be anesthetized

- **Peripheral nerve blocks**: Injection of local anesthetic in the vicinity of a peripheral nerve to anesthetize that nerve's area of innervation

- **Plexus anesthesia**: Injection of local anesthetic in the vicinity of a **nerve plexus**, which is a network of intersecting nerves (Figure 11-1)

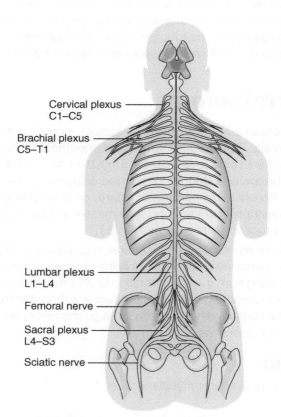

Cervical plexus
C1–C5

Brachial plexus
C5–T1

Lumbar plexus
L1–L4

Femoral nerve

Sacral plexus
L4–S3

Sciatic nerve

FIGURE 11-1 Spinal cord and nerves. (Most spinal nerves are named for the corresponding vertebrae.)

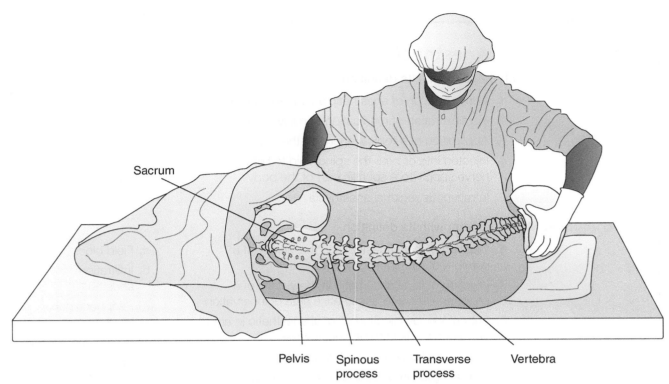

Sacrum

Pelvis   Spinous   Transverse   Vertebra
          process   process

FIGURE 11-2 Correct position for performing a spinal block or inserting an epidural catheter in the lumbar region

Regional anesthesia is appropriate when there is a need to block pain from a large part of the body (e.g., lower extremity and pelvic surgeries). Regional anesthetic agents are injected into or near the spinal fluid and around a nerve or network of nerves to block the nerve supply to a specific part of the body (Figure 11-2). The patient cannot feel pain in that area when a procedure is performed, and the patient remains awake (or sedated). Intravenous (IV) sedation may be administered prior to regional anesthesia to relax the patient and make him or her drowsy, but the patient remains conscious. Regional anesthesia includes the following:

- **Caudal anesthesia**, or **saddle block anesthesia**: Local anesthetic is injected into the caudal canal, which is the sacral portion of the spinal canal; anesthetized area is the umbilicus, below the navel.
- **Epidural anesthesia**: Local anesthetic is injected into the epidural space where it acts primarily on spinal nerve roots; anesthetized area includes the abdomen, chest, and large regions of the body.
- **Spinal anesthesia**: Local anesthetic is injected into cerebrospinal fluid (CSF) at the lumbar spine, where it acts on spinal nerve roots and part of the spinal cord; anesthetized area extends from the legs to the abdomen or chest.
- **Intravenous regional anesthesia**, or **Bier block**: An IV cannula is inserted into the extremity on which the procedure is to be performed and a tourniquet is applied to interrupt blood circulation; then a large volume of local anesthetic is injected into a peripheral vein, anesthetizing the extremity.

Sedation is the administration of medication into a vein to relieve pain and anxiety; it makes the patient feel calm. Such medications may result in the patient not remembering surgical events (even though the patient remains awake). Sedation medications are often administered in addition to other forms of anesthesia.

Exercise 11.1 – Anesthesia Terminology

Instructions: Match the term with its definition.

_____   1. Administration of anesthetic agents that are inhaled

_____   2. Administration of medication to relieve pain/anxiety

_____   3. Application of a topical agent on the body's surface

_____   4. Injected into or near the spinal fluid to block the nerve supply to a specific part of the body

_____   5. Intravenous regional anesthesia

a. Bier block

b. General anesthesia

c. Local anesthesia

d. Regional anesthesia

e. Sedation

Instructions: Match the term with its definition.

_____   6. Injection of local anesthetic in the vicinity of a network of intersecting nerves

_____   7. Injection of local anesthetic in the vicinity of a peripheral nerve to anesthetize area of innervation

_____   8. Subcutaneous injection of local anesthetic in area bordering the field to be anesthetized

_____   9. Topical application of local anesthetic cream to skin

_____   10. Topical injection of local anesthetic into tissue

a. Field block

b. Infiltration anesthesia

c. Peripheral nerve block

d. Plexus anesthesia

e. Surface anesthesia

Overview of Anesthesia Section

The Anesthesia section includes 15 anatomical sites, followed by four additional subsections for radiological procedures, burn excisions or debridement, obstetrics, and other procedures. Codes are organized according to type of procedure (open, closed, endoscopic, and so on), and each anesthesia code relates to corresponding surgical procedures. Because a one-to-one correlation for anesthesia to surgery codes does not exist, one anesthesia code is often reported for many different surgical procedures that share similar anesthesia requirements. The Anesthesia section guidelines also include four codes (99100–99140) that are located in the Medicine section, which are used to report qualifying circumstances for anesthesia.

 Coding Tip

Notes located beneath headings and/or subheadings apply to all codes in the headings or subheadings. Parenthetical notes that are located below a specific code apply to that code only unless the note indicates otherwise.

Anesthesia services include the preparation and monitoring of the patient, and the services included (bundled) in the anesthesia code reported include the following:

- Draping, positioning, prepping, and transporting the patient
- Inserting nasogastric or orogastric tubes

- Inserting peripheral IV lines for fluid and medication administration

- Interpreting laboratory results (e.g., arterial blood gases, hematology, and blood chemistries)

- Interpreting monitored functions (e.g., blood pressure, brain stem evoked response [BSER], capnography, central nervous system [CNS] pressure, Doppler flow, electroencephalogram, heart rate, oximetry, respirations, and temperature)

- Placing airway tubes (e.g., endotracheal tube [ET] and orotracheal tube), including laryngoscopy (direct or endoscopic) for airway management

- Positioning external devices for capnography, cardiac monitoring, CNS evoked responses, Doppler flow, pulse oximetry, and temperature

- Stimulating nerves to determine level of paralysis or localization of nerve(s)

When the above services are provided to surgical patients, they are included as part of the anesthesia service. They are not coded and reported or reimbursed in addition to the anesthesia code. The previously listed services are typically provided on the same date as the surgery performed.

> **EXAMPLE:** A patient with sepsis underwent a sternal debridement surgical procedure for which the CRNA provided general anesthesia services. The procedure ended at 2 PM, and by noon the next day, anesthesia services were concluded. Later that night at 10 PM, the CRNA inserted an ET to establish an airway for the patient. Report codes 00550-P3-QZ and 31500-59.
>
> - Go to the CPT index and locate main term *Anesthesia* and subterm *Sternum* to locate code 00550. Refer to the Anesthesia section guidelines to assign physical status modifier -P3. (Sepsis is considered a severe systemic disease.)
>
> - Go to the CPT index and locate main term *Endotracheal Tube* and subterm *Intubation* to locate code 31500. Modifier -59 is added to code 31500 to alert the payer that insertion of the ET was a distinct procedural service.

Monitored Anesthesia Care (MAC)

Monitored anesthesia care (MAC) is the administration of varying amounts of local, regional, and certain mind-altering drugs by an anesthesiologist or a qualified nonphysician anesthetist (e.g., CRNA) during a patient's diagnostic or therapeutic procedure. CMS defines MAC as "the intraoperative monitoring of the surgical patient's vital physiological signs, in anticipation of the patient's need for general anesthesia or development of adverse physiological patient reaction to the surgery."

During MAC, the anesthesiologist or qualified nonphysician anesthetist administers anesthetic medication through an IV line, monitors the patient's comfort level, and increases or decreases medication as needed (hence the name *monitored anesthesia care*). MAC includes a preoperative visit, intraoperative care, and postoperative anesthesia management. The anesthesiologist or qualified nonphysician anesthetist provides the following services:

- Monitors vital signs and maintains patient's airway and continual evaluation of vital functions

- Diagnoses and treats clinical problems that occur during the procedure

- Administers analgesics, anesthetic agents, hypnotics, sedatives, or other medications as necessary to ensure patient safety and comfort

- Provides other medical services as needed for the safe completion of the procedure

Coding Tip

Because monitored anesthesia care is a physician service provided to an individual patient and is based on medical necessity, reimbursement may be the same amount as for full general anesthesia services if all required services are properly documented. Report the appropriate anesthesia code and add an appropriate physical status modifier along with modifier -QS (monitored anesthesia care). In addition, report a qualifying circumstances code (from the Medicine section) when indicated. When appropriate, add one or more of the HCPCS level II anesthesia modifiers (discussed in the next section of this chapter) to the anesthesia code. Make sure you report the appropriate ICD-10-CM code(s) that support(s) medical necessity for MAC and identify the reason for the surgical procedure.

NOTE:

Monitored anesthesia care is not the same as moderate (conscious) sedation, which is reported with codes from the CPT Medicine section. Refer to Chapters 12 and 19 of this textbook for information about moderate (conscious) sedation.

Exercise 11.2 – Overview of Anesthesia Section

Instructions: Enter a response for each item.

1. Anesthesia services include the preparation and _____ of the patient, along with other services.

2. When services are provided to surgical patients that are not included as part of the anesthesia service code, they are reported separately. Modifier _____ is added to each code to indicate that the service provided was independent of the anesthesia service.

3. When an electromyogram (EMG) is performed to determine nerve dysfunction and report results are documented in the patient's record, the service is included in the reported anesthesia code. True or False?

4. With _____ anesthesia care (MAC), an anesthesiologist participates in care provided to a patient during a diagnostic or therapeutic procedure.

5. When reporting an anesthesia services code for which *monitored anesthesia care* was provided, add modifier _____ to the code along with appropriate CPT and HCPCS level II anesthesia modifiers.

Anesthesia Section Guidelines

Anesthesia services are reported by assigning a five-digit procedure code and adding appropriate modifiers. A physician (e.g., anesthesiologist) is responsible for supervising anesthesia services (which include general and regional), supplementation of local anesthesia, and other supportive services so the patient receives appropriate and optimal anesthesia care. The administration of local infiltration, metacarpal/metatarsal/ digital block, or topical anesthesia by the operating surgeon or obstetrician is included (bundled) in the surgery code; separate codes are not reported. Such anesthesia is not coded or reported separately because it is included in the surgery code (e.g., surgical procedure fee in physician's office, facility charge at an ambulatory surgical center or hospital outpatient department, and accommodation revenue code for a hospital inpatient).

An anesthesiologist's responsibilities include the following services, which are included (bundled) in the anesthesia code:

- Providing **airway management**: Ensuring an open airway to the patient's lungs
- Administering analgesics and general anesthetic drugs and agents
- Providing **fluid management**: Administering IV fluids to avoid dehydration, maintain an effective circulating volume, and prevent inadequate tissue perfusion
- Performing and documenting preanesthesia and postanesthesia evaluations (Figure 11-3) and an anesthesia record (Figure 11-4)
- Monitoring the patient's cardiorespiratory status during surgery to include:
  - Blood pressure and temperature
  - **Capnography** (monitoring carbon dioxide levels)
  - Continuous electrocardiogram
  - Continuous **pulse oximetry** (arterial oxyhemoglobin saturation)
  - Low oxygen and circuit disconnect alarms
  - **Mass spectrometry** (monitors proper levels of the anesthetic)

The anesthesiologist or qualified nonphysician anesthetist is responsible for conducting a **preanesthesia evaluation** of the patient prior to surgery, which includes assessing information from the patient's record, interviewing the patient (e.g., history), conducting a physical examination, evaluating preoperative test results, and ensuring that informed anesthetic consent has been obtained. The preanesthesia evaluation is included (bundled) in the anesthesia services code. If the surgery for which a preanesthesia evaluation was performed is canceled, the anesthesiologist should report an evaluation and management service code (e.g., office or other outpatient consultation or inpatient consultation).

A **postanesthesia evaluation** is also included (bundled) in the anesthesia services code and includes an evaluation of the patient during recovery from anesthesia, as well as evaluation, treatment, and follow-up of possible anesthesia-related complications. When an anesthesiologist or a qualified nonphysician anesthetist provides significant, separately identifiable services (e.g., critical care services, postoperative pain management services, or unrelated ventilator management), the appropriate code(s) are reported for each service.

When a physician (e.g., anesthesiologist) *other than the physician performing the procedure* (e.g., surgeon) provides anesthesia services, report the code(s) from the CPT Anesthesia section. (This means that a surgeon is performing the surgical procedure and the anesthesiologist or qualified nonphysician anesthetist is providing anesthesia services. The surgeon reports the code(s) from the Surgery section, and the anesthesiologist or qualified nonphysician anesthetist reports the code(s) from the Anesthesia section.)

PRE- AND POST-ANESTHESIA EVALUATION RECORD

Addressograph

PRE-ANESTHESIA EVALUATION

HISTORY TAKEN FROM: ☐ Patient ☐ Parent/Guardian ☐ Significant Other ☐ Chart ☐ Poor Historian ☐ Language Barrier

PROPOSED PROCEDURE:

| AGE | GENDER ☐ Male ☐ Female | HEIGHT | WEIGHT | BLOOD PRESSURE | PULSE | RESPIRATIONS | TEMPERATURE | O2 SAT% |

PREVIOUS ANESTHESIA: ☐ None
PREVIOUS SURGERY: ☐ None
CURRENT MEDICATIONS: ☐ None
FAMILY HX – ANES. PROBLEMS: ☐ None
ALLERGIES ☐ None

AIRWAY (Enter ✗ in appropriate boxes)
☐ MP1 ☐ MP2 ☐ MP3 ☐ MP4 ☐ Unrestricted neck ROM ☐ T-M distance = _____
☐ Obesity ☐ ↓ neck ROM ☐ History of difficult airway ☐ Short muscular neck
☐ Teeth poor repair ☐ Teeth chipped/loose ☐ Edentulous ☐ Facial hair

BODY SYSTEM	COMMENTS
RESPIRATORY	☐ WNL Tobacco Use: ☐ Yes ☐ No ☐ Quit _____ Packs/Day for _____ Years
CARDIOVASCULAR	☐ WNL Pre-procedure Cardiac Assessment:
GASTROINTESTINAL	☐ WNL Ethanol Use: ☐ Yes ☐ No ☐ Quit Frequency _____ ☐ History of Ethanol abuse
MUSCULOSKELETAL	☐ WNL
GENITOURINARY	☐ WNL
OTHER	☐ WNL
PREGNANCY	☐ WNL ☐ AROM ☐ SROM ☐ Pitocin Drip ☐ Induction ☐ MgDrip Weeks Gestation: _____ G: _____ P: _____ EDC: _____

DIAGNOSTIC STUDIES
ECG
CHEST X-RAY
PULMONARY STUDIES
LABORATORY STUDIES
PT/PTT/INR:
T&S / T&C:
HCG:
LMP:
UA:
OTHER DIAGNOSTIC TESTS
PLANNED ANESTHESIA/MONITORS
PRE-ANESTHESIA MEDICATION
SIGNATURE OF ANESTHESIOLOGIST OR C.R.N.A.

POST-ANESTHESIA EVALUATION

| Location | Time | B/P | O2Sat | Pulse | Respirations | Temperature |

☐ Awake ☐ Mask O2 ☐ Somnolent ☐ Unarousable ☐ Oral/nasal airway
☐ Stable ☐ NC O2 ☐ Unstable ☐ T-Piece ☐ Intubated ☐ Ventilator
☐ Regional – dermatome level: ☐ Continuous epidural analgesia
☐ Direct admit to hospital room ☐ No anesthesia related complications noted
☐ See notes for anesthesia related concerns ☐ Satisfactory postanesthesia/analgesia recovery

CONTROLLED MEDICATIONS

| Medication | Used | Destroyed | Returned |

SIGNATURE OF ANESTHESIOLOGIST OR C.R.N.A.

ALFRED STATE MEDICAL CENTER ■ 100 MAIN ST, ALFRED NY 14802 ■ (607) 555-1234

FIGURE 11-3 Sample pre- and postanesthesia evaluation record

EXAMPLE: An anesthesiologist provides general anesthesia services for a patient who undergoes carpal tunnel surgery. Report code 01810 (with appropriate modifiers, discussed later in this chapter). (In the CPT index, locate main term *Anesthesia* and subterm *Wrist* to locate code 01810.)

When the surgeon (or another physician) provides general or regional anesthesia *in addition to performing the procedure for which anesthesia is administered*, report the code(s) from the CPT Surgery section and attach modifier -47 to each code. *Do not attach modifier -47 to an anesthesia code.* (This means that the surgeon is performing the surgical procedure and providing general or regional anesthesia services to the same patient during the same operative session. No anesthesiologist or qualified nonphysician anesthetist is in the operating room providing anesthesia services.)

FIGURE 11-4 Sample anesthesia record

EXAMPLE: The surgeon provides regional anesthesia services for a 38-year-old female patient who undergoes a needle biopsy of the thyroid. Report code 60100-47.

- In the CPT index, locate main term *Thyroid Gland* and subterm *Needle Biopsy* to locate code 60100.
- Add modifier -47 to code 60100 to indicate that the physician who performed the surgical procedure also provided anesthesia services.
- Do *not* report code 00322 from the Anesthesia section of CPT.

Reporting Codes for Monitoring or Providing Other Services

When an anesthesiologist or a qualified nonphysician anesthetist (or the surgeon if he or she is providing anesthesia services) performs unusual forms of monitoring or other services, report codes for each procedure or service separately. Add modifier -59 to each code reported in addition to the anesthesia code. Modifier -59 is added to codes that describe distinct procedural services performed during the same encounter, operative session, or patient's stay as the provision of anesthesia services (e.g., endotracheal intubation by anesthesiologist or qualified nonphysician anesthetist after completion of anesthesia services).

EXAMPLE: An anesthesiologist inserts a percutaneous arterial line (catheter) to monitor the patient while providing the anesthesia services during an intracranial surgical procedure. At the conclusion of surgery, the anesthesiologist inserts a Swan-Ganz (flow-directed) cardiac catheter. The anesthesiologist reports codes 00210, 36620-59, and 93503-59.

 NOTE:

Physical status and other modifiers added to anesthesia codes (e.g., -P3, -AA) are discussed later in this chapter.

- In the CPT index, locate main term *Anesthesia* and subterm *Intracranial* to locate code 00210.
- In the CPT index, locate main term *Catheterization*, subterm *Arterial*, and 2nd qualifier *Percutaneous* to locate code 36620.
- In the CPT index, locate main term *Insertion*, subterm *Catheter*, 2nd qualifier *Cardiac*, and 3rd qualifier *Flow Directed* to locate code 93503.
- Modifier -59 indicates that the anesthesiologist provided distinct procedures in addition to anesthesia services on the same date.

Emergency Endotracheal Tube Intubation

An **endotracheal tube (ET)** is an artificial airway used for short-term airway management or mechanical ventilation due to potential or actual respiratory system insufficiency. The indications for endotracheal intubation include administration of medications during cardiopulmonary arrest, airway maintenance, oxygenation and ventilation, and secretion control.

Central Venous Access Devices (CVADs)

A **central venous access device (CVAD)** is a thin plastic tube (or catheter) that is inserted (or placed) into a vein and connected to a monitor. After insertion, a chest x-ray is done to verify that the catheter's tip is in the proper location above the heart. It measures a patient's central venous pressure (CVP) as an indicator of circulating blood volume, the heart's effectiveness as a pump, and the patient's vascular tone and response to treatment. CVADs are inserted due to the absence of a suitable peripheral access for fluid administration (e.g., rapid infusion of a high volume of fluid in a patient with **hypovolemia,** which is abnormally decreased blood volume). CVADs are also used for the administration of medications (e.g., potassium chloride and dopamine) that may be harmful to smaller **lumen** (opening) peripheral veins and/or for the insertion of a pacing wire.

A **central venous pressure (CVP) line** (or **central venous pressure catheter**) is inserted through a vein in the neck (e.g., external or internal jugular vein) or a vein in the upper chest under the collar bone (e.g., subclavian vein) and then into a large central vein in the chest (e.g., superior vena cava). A CVP line can also be inserted through a vein in the leg (e.g., femoral) and then into a large central vein below the chest (e.g., inferior vena cava).

 NOTE:

A CVP line (or CVP catheter) is also called a central venous catheter (CVC) or central venous line (CVL).

CVP lines are inserted as internal or external catheters depending on the patient's condition as well as the frequency and duration of infusions. An **external catheter** or **nontunneled catheter** is not implanted under the patient's skin, and it does not require a needle to be inserted into the skin to deliver medications. It is used when the patient requires frequent infusions that last several hours, and it requires a sterile dressing that must be changed once or twice daily. In addition, external catheters may require periodic injections of **heparin** (anticoagulant that prevents blood clots from developing in the catheter). The Cook (cystotomy catheter) is an example of an external catheter. Some nontunneled catheters require just a saline flush, and others require both a saline and a heparin flush. Blood can be drawn from a nontunneled catheter.

An **internal catheter** (or **tunneled catheter**) is implanted completely under the skin. (The catheter's tip is inserted in the superior vena cava, and the other end is "tunneled" about 6 inches away under the chest's skin and sealed with a Dacron cuff to prevent infection.) An internal catheter requires no special care when it is not being used since it is located completely under the skin. The AshSplit Cath (hemodialysis catheter), Groshong, and Hickman are examples of internal catheters. Some tunneled catheters require just a saline flush, and others require both a saline and heparin flush. Blood can be drawn from a tunneled catheter.

An **implanted port** is a small reservoir that has a rubber plug attached to the catheter that enters the patient's vein below the collar bone and is threaded into the superior vena cava. The port is implanted underneath the skin (local anesthesia and IV sedation). To access the catheter, the site must be located and cleaned and a special needle is inserted through the skin and into the rubber plug. Blood can be drawn from an implanted port.

Intra-Arterial Lines

An **intra-arterial line** (also called **intra-arterial cannula**, or **intra-arterial catheter**, or **A-line**) is a thin plastic tube, cannula, or catheter that is inserted into an artery and connected to a monitor. Its purpose is to measure immediate changes in intra-arterial blood pressure and concentrations of oxygen and carbon dioxide; it also is used to collect frequent blood samples for lab tests. An A-line is inserted when cardiopulmonary status is unstable or when serial (repeat) blood sampling is necessary.

Swan-Ganz Catheterization

A **Swan-Ganz catheter** is a thin, flexible, flow-directed multilumen plastic tube (or catheter) that is advanced from a peripheral vein into the right atrium and then positioned in a branch of the pulmonary artery. The catheter's balloon tip travels through the pulmonary artery, and pulmonary wedge pressure is measured in front of the temporarily inflated and wedged balloon. **Pulmonary wedge pressure** is the indirect measurement of left atrial pressure that is useful in the diagnosis of left ventricular failure and mitral valve disease. The Swan-Ganz catheter serves to obtain diagnostic information about the heart and to provide continuous monitoring of heart function in critically ill patients. The result is that the physician can evaluate circulatory volume due to acute valvular regurgitation, burns, congenital heart disease, heart failure, kidney disease, or shock. It is also used to monitor complications of myocardial infarction and the effects of certain heart medications.

Postoperative Pain Management

Postoperative pain management includes the administration of epidural or subarachnoid medications on the date(s) of service after the date of surgery. It is provided by the surgeon as part of the surgical procedure's global package, which means reimbursement is included in the CPT surgery code reported. When postoperative pain management is performed by the anesthesiologist, the surgeon must document the reason such care was transferred to the anesthesiologist. The anesthesiologist reports code 01996 just once each day that services are provided. Add modifier -59 to code 01996 on the day of *surgery* to indicate that a distinct procedural service was provided (in addition to administration of anesthesia during surgery that day).

Drug Administration Codes

Anesthesiologists and qualified nonphysician anesthetists do not report drug administration CPT Medicine section or HCPCS level II codes for anesthetic agents or other drugs administered from the time of the patient's arrival in the operating room through discharge from postanesthesia care.

Anesthesia Modifiers

All anesthesia services require the following types of modifiers to be reviewed for assignment with reported anesthesia codes:

- HCPCS level II modifiers
- Physical status modifiers
- CPT modifiers

HCPCS Level II Anesthesia Modifiers

When applicable, the following HCPCS level II modifiers are added (as the first modifier) to reported anesthesia codes:

- -AA: Anesthesia services performed personally by anesthesiologist
- -AD: Medically supervised by a physician for more than four concurrent procedures
- -G8: Monitored anesthesia care for a deep, complex, complicated, or markedly invasive surgical procedure

 NOTE:

Do not report modifier -G8 modifier with modifier -QS.

- -G9: Monitored anesthesia care for patient who has history of severe cardiopulmonary condition
- -QK: Medical direction of 2, 3, or 4 concurrent procedures involving qualified individuals
- -QS: Monitored anesthesia care services (can be billed by a qualified nonphysician anesthetist or a physician)

 NOTE:

Monitored anesthesia care involves intraoperative monitoring of vital physiologic signs in anticipation of the need for administration of general anesthesia or to monitor the development of adverse physiologic patient reaction to the surgical procedures.

- -QX: Qualified nonphysician anesthetist service with medical direction by physician

 NOTE:

Assign modifier -QX when the qualified nonphysician anesthetist (e.g., CRNA) alone provides anesthesia service to the patient and the anesthesiologist is not in the operating room with the qualified nonphysician anesthetist but provides medical direction, such as from another operating room.

- -QY: Medical direction of one qualified nonphysician anesthetist by an anesthesiologist

 NOTE:

Assign modifier -QY when the qualified nonphysician anesthetist (e.g., CRNA) and the anesthesiologist both provide anesthesia services to the same patient in the same operating room, and the anesthesiologist provides medical direction for the qualified nonphysician anesthetist.

- -QZ: CRNA service without medical direction by physician

> **EXAMPLE:** A CRNA provided general anesthesia services to an otherwise healthy patient who underwent a vaginal hysterectomy due to uterine fibroids. The CRNA received medical direction from an anesthesiologist. Report code 00944-QX-P1. (Modifier -P1 is a physical status modifier added to the anesthesia code, indicating a "normal healthy patient." Physical status modifiers are discussed in the next section of this chapter.)

Physical Status Modifiers

A **physical status modifier** is added to each reported anesthesia code to indicate the patient's condition at the time anesthesia was administered. The modifier also serves to identify the complexity of services provided. (The physical status modifier is determined by the anesthesiologist or qualified nonphysician anesthetist [e.g., CRNA] and is documented as such in the patient record.) Physical status modifiers are represented by the letter *P* followed by a single digit from 1 to 6 as follows:

- -P1: Normal healthy patient (e.g., no biochemical, organic, physiologic, or psychiatric disturbance)
- -P2: Patient with mild systemic disease (e.g., anemia, chronic asthma, chronic bronchitis, diabetes mellitus, essential hypertension, heart disease that only slightly limits physical activity, or obesity)
- -P3: Patient with severe systemic disease (e.g., angina pectoris, chronic pulmonary disease that limits activity, history of prior myocardial infarction, heart disease that limits activity, poorly controlled essential hypertension, morbid obesity, or diabetes mellitus, type 1)
- -P4: Patient with severe systemic disease that is a constant threat to life (e.g., advanced pulmonary/renal/hepatic dysfunction; congestive heart failure; persistent angina pectoris; or unstable/rest angina)
- -P5: Moribund patient who is not expected to survive without the operation (e.g., abdominal aortic aneurysm)
- -P6: Patient declared brain dead whose organs are being removed for donor purposes

> **EXAMPLE:** An anesthesiologist provided general anesthesia services to a 65-year-old male with mild systemic disease who underwent total knee replacement. Report code 01402-P2.

CPT Modifiers

The following CPT modifiers should be reviewed to determine whether they need to be added to the reported anesthesia codes:

- -23: Unusual anesthesia

 Coding Tip

- When a patient's circumstances warrant the administration of general or regional anesthesia (instead of the usual local anesthesia), add modifier -23 to the anesthesia code. The following may require general or regional anesthesia services (when local anesthesia services are usually provided):
  - Extremely apprehensive patients
  - Individuals with an intellectual disability
  - Patients who have a physical condition (e.g., spasticity or tremors)

> **EXAMPLE:** An anesthesiologist provided general anesthesia services to a 49-year-old male patient with chronic obstructive pulmonary disease who underwent extracorporeal shock wave lithotripsy with water bath. The patient was extremely anxious about the procedure, which normally does not require general anesthesia. Report code 00872-AA-P3-23.

- -59: Distinct procedural service

Coding Tip

- An anesthesiologist or a qualified nonphysician anesthetist reports the anesthesia code with the highest base unit value first. Modifier -59 is added to each separately reported anesthesia code.

- -74: Discontinued outpatient hospital/ambulatory surgery center (ASC) procedure after administration of anesthesia
- -99: Multiple modifiers

Time Reporting

Anesthesia services are reported based on time, which begins when the anesthesiologist or qualified nonphysician anesthetist starts preparing the patient to receive anesthesia and ends when the anesthesiologist or qualified nonphysician anesthetist is no longer in personal attendance. Anesthesia time units are reported for the amount of time the anesthesiologist or qualified nonphysician anesthetist is in personal attendance, providing anesthesia services and reimbursement for anesthesia services varies according to increments of time. (Nonmonitored time is *not* considered when calculating time units.)

NOTE:

Teaching anesthesiologists must be present with the resident physician during all critical or key portions of the anesthesia service, and they must be immediately available to furnish anesthesia services during the entire procedure. Teaching qualified nonphysician anesthetists who are involved with two concurrent cases must be present with the student nurse anesthetist during pre- and postanesthesia care for each case. They are prohibited from being involved in any other activities (e.g., preanesthesia evaluation of the patient for a third case) when two concurrent cases are ongoing.

EXAMPLE: A patient undergoes a cataract extraction and requires 90 minutes of MAC by the anesthesiologist, which includes the administration of a sedative along with a retrobulbar injection for regional block anesthesia. Subsequently, an interval of 30 minutes transpires, during which time the patient does not require monitoring by the anesthesiologist. After this period, monitoring commences for 30 additional minutes until the patient is released to the recovery room. The anesthesiologist reports 120 minutes of time on the claim.

Payment for anesthesia services is based on the sum of an anesthesia code-specific base unit value plus anesthesia time units and modifying units multiplied by the locality-specific anesthesia conversion factor. The formula for calculating the anesthesia fee is as follows: [code-specific base unit value + anesthesia time unit(s) + modifying unit(s)] × locality-specific anesthesia conversion factor (e.g., [5 + 3 + 0] × $17.04 = anesthesia fee).

- The code-specific **base unit value** for anesthesia codes (00100–01999) represents the degree of difficulty associated with providing anesthesia for a surgical procedure (Table 11-1).
- **Anesthesia time units** are based on the total anesthesia time, and they are reported as one unit for each 15 minutes (or fraction thereof) of anesthesia time. (Anesthesia time begins when the anesthesiologist or qualified nonphysician anesthetist begins to prepare the patient for anesthesia care and ends when the anesthesiologist is no longer in personal attendance.)

NOTE:

Anesthesia time reported includes monitoring during administration of regional block anesthesia and during the procedure. Interval and recovery room times are not included when calculating time, although the anesthesiologist or qualified nonphysician anesthetist is required to document the patient's condition on the recovery room record (Figure 11-5).

TABLE 11-1 Sample Portion of Anesthesia Base Unit Values

CPT Code	Description Base Unit Value
00100	5
00102	6
00103	5
00104	4
00120	5

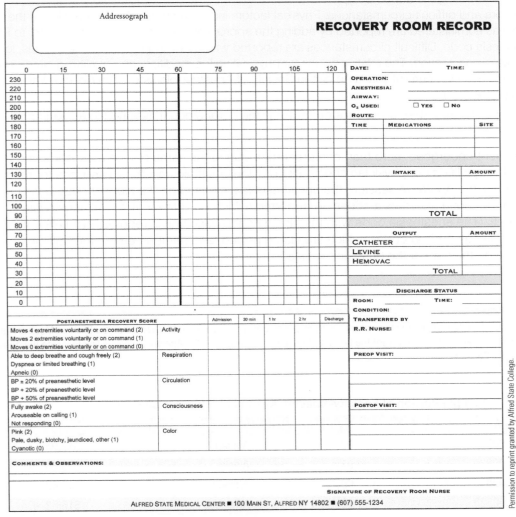

FIGURE 11-5 Sample recovery room record

TABLE 11-2 Sample Portion of Modifying Units and Relative Values

CPT Physical Status Modifier	Relative Value
-P1	0
-P2	0
-P3	1
-P4	2
-P5	3
-P6	0
CPT Qualifying Circumstances Code	Relative Value
99100	1
99116	5
99135	5
99140	2

- **Modifying units** recognize added complexities associated with the administration of anesthesia, including physical factors and difficult circumstances. Physical factors indicating the patient's condition at the time anesthesia was administered are reported by adding the appropriate physical status modifier (P1 to P6) to the anesthesia code. Difficult circumstances are reported with qualifying circumstances codes, located in the CPT Medicine section. The relative values for physical status modifiers and qualifying circumstances codes are located in the current year's American Society of Anesthesiologists (ASA) *Relative Value Guide* publication (Table 11-2).

- The locality-specific **anesthesia conversion factor** is the dollar amount assigned to a geographic location (Table 11-3).

When the patient undergoes more than one procedure during the same operative episode and the anesthesiologist or qualified nonphysician anesthetist provides multiple anesthesia services for the same patient during the same operative session, the anesthesia fee is based on the *highest* code base unit value when multiple stand-alone anesthesia codes are reported (which is added to the total anesthesia time for all services provided). (The anesthesia code with the highest code base unit is reported. The exception is when an anesthesia code has add-on codes, which are also reported, and reimbursement for multiple anesthesia services is based on the sum of the base unit values.)

NOTE:

Base unit values and modifying unit relative values are available as downloadable files at www.cms.gov. Click on Medicare, scroll to the Provider Type heading (located toward the bottom of the page), and click on the Anesthesiologists link to locate the Anesthesia Base Units by CPT Code file.

TABLE 11-3 Sample Portion of Locality-Specific Anesthesia Conversion Factors

Payer Number	Locality Number	Locality Name	Conversion Factor
00500	00	Alabama	$17.04
00830	01	Alaska	$29.66
00832	00	Arizona	$17.83
00520	13	Arkansas	$16.52

Courtesy of the Centers for Medicare & *Medicaid* Services, www.cms.gov

EXAMPLE 1: A 22-year-old female patient who has chronic asthma underwent a planned vaginal delivery on May 14, during which neuraxial labor anesthesia was administered by an anesthesiologist. Report code 01967-P2. (Anesthesia code 01967 has a base unit value of 5, and physical status modifier -P2 has a relative value of 0.) A review of the patient record indicates 45 minutes of anesthesia time, which is calculated as 3 anesthesia time units (45 ÷ 15 = 3). If a conversion factor of $17.45 is assigned to New York State, payment for anesthesia services is calculated as $139.60. The formula for calculating anesthesia services reimbursement is as follows:

```
STEP 1: (5 + 3 + 0) × $17.45
STEP 2: 8 × $17.45
AMOUNT: $139.60
```

EXAMPLE 2: A 22-year-old female patient who has chronic asthma was prepared for a planned vaginal delivery on May 14, during which neuraxial labor anesthesia was administered by an anesthesiologist. Complications required that an emergency cesarean delivery be performed instead of the planned vaginal delivery. Report codes 01968-P2 and 99140 *in addition to* code 01967-P2. (Reimbursement for multiple anesthesia services is based on the sum of each base unit value because code 01968 is an add-on code.) Anesthesia code 01967 has a base unit value of 5, and code 01968 has a base unit value of 2. The total length of anesthesia time for both procedures was 75 minutes, which is calculated as 5 anesthesia time units (75 ÷ 15 = 5). The patient is assigned physical status modifier -P2, which has a relative value of 0, and code 99140 has a relative value of 2. If the conversion factor is $17.45, payment for anesthesia services is calculated as $244.30. The formula for calculating anesthesia services reimbursement is as follows:

```
STEP 1: (5 + 2 + 5 + 2) × $17.45
STEP 2: 14 × $17.45
AMOUNT: $244.30
```

EXAMPLE 3: A 39-year-old male patient who has otherwise been healthy sustained multiple trauma and was administered general anesthesia by an anesthesiologist during cranial surgery and upper abdominal surgery. Both surgical procedures were performed during the same operative session. (Reimbursement for multiple anesthesia services is based on the highest ASA base unit value when anesthesia for two separate procedures is provided.) Assign codes 00210-P5 and 99140. (Do not report code 00790 for the administration of anesthesia for the upper abdominal surgery because it was provided during the same operative episode as anesthesia administered for the cranial surgery.) If anesthesia code 00210 has a base unit value of 11 and code 00790 has a base unit value of 7, use value 11 when determining anesthesia reimbursement (because code 00790 is not reported). The total length of anesthesia time for both procedures was 120 minutes, which is calculated as 8 anesthesia time units (120 ÷ 15 = 8). Physical status modifier -P5 is assigned a relative value of 3, and code 99140 is assigned a relative value of 2. If the conversion factor is $17.45, payment for anesthesia services is calculated as $418.80. The formula for calculating anesthesia services reimbursement is as follows:

```
STEP 1: (11 + 8 + [3 + 2]) × $17.45
STEP 2: (19 + 5) × $17.45
STEP 3: 24 × $17.45
AMOUNT: $418.80
```

Medicare defines **concurrent medically directed anesthesia procedures** as "the maximum number of procedures an anesthesiologist or qualified nonphysician anesthetist medically directs within the context of a single procedure and when the procedures overlap each other." The ASA base unit value is reduced for subsequent anesthesia services when the definition of *concurrent medically directed anesthesia procedures* applies to the submission of multiple anesthesia codes. (Base unit value reduction of services is determined by the third-party payer.)

Anesthesia Services

Assign the appropriate CPT evaluation and management (E/M) code when anesthesia services are provided in an office, home, or hospital; this includes consultation services and other medical services. *Special Services and Reporting* (99000–99091) are included in the CPT Medicine section.

EXAMPLE: Procedures A through C are concurrent medically directed anesthesia procedures provided by an anesthesiologist on May 20. The start and end times for each procedure represent the periods during which anesthesia time is counted.

Procedure	Start Time	End Time	Number of Concurrent Procedures	Base Unit Value Reduction
A	8:00 AM	8:20 AM	2	10%
B	8:10 AM	8:45 AM	2	10%
C	8:30 AM	9:15 AM	2	10%

- During procedure A, the anesthesiologist medically directed two concurrent procedures A and B (from 8:10 AM to 8:20 AM).
- During procedure B, the anesthesiologist medically directed two concurrent procedures A and B from 8:10 AM to 8:20 AM and then procedures B and C from 8:30 AM to 8:45 AM.
- Thus, during each procedure A and B, the anesthesiologist medically directed, at most, two concurrent procedures.

Supplied Materials

When an anesthesiologist or a qualified nonphysician anesthetist provides materials and supplies (e.g., sterile trays and drugs) over and above those usually included with the office visit or other services rendered, report the materials and supplies separately with CPT code 99070 (or appropriate HCPCS Level II code).

Separate or Multiple Procedures

When multiple surgical procedures are performed during the provision of anesthesia services, report the anesthesia code that represents the most complex procedure performed. However, if the additional anesthesia code for multiple surgical procedures performed is an add-on code, report all codes. The time reported for the provision of anesthesia services is the combined total for all procedures performed.

Unlisted Service or Procedure

When the service or procedure performed is not listed in the CPT coding manual, report an unlisted service or procedure code on the claim and attach a special report.

Special Report

When a service is provided that is new, variable, rare, or unusual, a *special report* may be submitted with the claim. The special report should include information that defines or describes the nature, event, and need for the procedure as well as the time, effort, and equipment necessary to provide the service. Special reports accompany claims that contain unlisted service or procedure codes.

Qualifying Circumstances

When anesthesia services are provided during situations or circumstances that make anesthesia administration more difficult, report a **qualifying circumstances** code from the CPT Medicine section (in addition to the anesthesia code). Difficult circumstances depend on factors such as extraordinary condition of patient, notable operative conditions, or unusual risk factors. These codes are reported in addition to the anesthesia codes. Qualifying circumstances codes include the following:

- 99100: Anesthesia for patient of extreme age, under 1 year and over 70
- 99116: Anesthesia complicated by utilization of total body hypothermia
- 99135: Anesthesia complicated by utilization of controlled hypotension
- 99140: Anesthesia complicated by emergency conditions (specify)

NOTE:

For hernia repair procedures performed on infants younger than one year of age at the time of surgery, assign code 00834 or 00836, depending on the infant's age.

NOTE:

An **emergency condition** results when a delay in treatment of the patient would lead to a significant increase in threat to life or body part.

EXAMPLE: A 92-year-old female patient received general anesthesia services from a CRNA and was monitored by an anesthesiologist during total left hip arthroplasty. Report codes 01214-P2-QX and 99100.

Exercise 11.3 – Anesthesia Section Guidelines

Instructions: Match the term with its definition.

_____ 1. Administering intravenous fluids to avoid dehydration

_____ 2. Arterial oxyhemoglobin saturation

_____ 3. Ensuring an open airway to the patient's lungs

_____ 4. Monitoring proper levels of the anesthetic

_____ 5. Monitoring carbon dioxide levels

a. Airway management
b. Capnography
c. Fluid management
d. Mass spectrometry
e. Pulse oximetry

Instructions: Match the type of evaluation with its description. Answers may be assigned more than once.

_____ 6. Conducting a physical examination

_____ 7. Evaluating the patient during anesthesia recovery

_____ 8. Interviewing the patient

_____ 9. Obtaining informed anesthetic consent

_____ 10. Treatment of anesthesia-related complications

a. Preanesthesia evaluation
b. Postanesthesia evaluation

Instructions: Indicate whether each statement is true (T) or false (F).

_____ 11. When an anesthesiologist or a qualified nonphysician anesthetist performs unusual forms of monitoring or other services, the codes are reported separately and modifier -59 is added to each code reported in addition to the anesthesia code.

_____ 12. When local infiltration, metacarpal/metatarsal/digital block, or topical anesthesia is administered by the operating surgeon or obstetrician, it is included in the surgery code.

_____ 13. When a physician (e.g., anesthesiologist) other than the physician performing the procedure provides anesthesia services, report the code(s) from the CPT Anesthesia section.

(continues)

Exercise 11.3 – *continued*

_____ 14. When the surgeon (or other physician) provides general or regional anesthesia in addition to performing the procedure for which anesthesia is administered, report the anesthesia code for the procedure performed and attach modifier -47 to that code.

_____ 15. Anesthesia services are reported based on time, which begins when the anesthesiologist or qualified nonphysician anesthetist is in personal attendance providing anesthesia services, which includes preparing the patient to receive anesthesia and ends when the patient is discharged from the recovery room.

_____ 16. Anesthesia time units are reported for the amount of time the anesthesiologist or qualified nonphysician anesthetist spends administering anesthesia, and reimbursement for anesthesia services varies according to increments of time.

_____ 17. When calculating anesthesia time units, do not include nonmonitored time.

_____ 18. A patient undergoes a surgical procedure that requires 30 minutes of monitored anesthesia care by the anesthesiologist. Then 15 minutes transpires when the patient does not require monitoring by the anesthesiologist. After this interval, the anesthesiologist commences monitoring for 15 additional minutes until the patient is released to the recovery room. The number of anesthesia time units is 3.

_____ 19. Payment for anesthesia services is based on the following formula: [code-specific base unit value + anesthesia time unit(s) + modifying unit(s)] × locality-specific anesthesia conversion factor = anesthesia fee.

_____ 20 A 38-year-old female patient who has diabetes mellitus underwent a planned vaginal delivery on November 14, during which neuraxial labor anesthesia was administered by an anesthesiologist. Code 01967-P2 is reported (base unit value of 5 and relative value of 0). A review of the patient record indicates 60 minutes of anesthesia time. The conversion factor is $17.45. The payment for anesthesia services is calculated as $139.60.

Instructions: Match the physical status modifier with its example.

_____ 21 A patient who is on medication for petit mal seizures undergoes inguinal herniorrhaphy.

_____ 22 A patient with late-stage adenocarcinoma of the left breast undergoes left mastectomy.

_____ 23 A healthy patient undergoes colonoscopy.

_____ 24 A patient with end-stage renal disease undergoes laparoscopic cholecystectomy.

_____ 25 A patient with cardiomyopathy undergoes heart transplant.

a. P1 (normal healthy patient)

b. P2 (patient with mild systemic disease)

c. P3 (patient with severe systemic disease)

d. P4 (patient with severe systemic disease that is a constant threat to life)

e. P5 (moribund patient who is not expected to survive without the operation)

f. P6 (patient declared brain dead whose organs are being removed for donor purposes)

Anesthesia Subsections

The Anesthesia section is organized according to general anatomical areas or services that relate to a number of surgical procedures. For Medicare purposes, just one anesthesia code is usually reported unless the second and subsequent anesthesia codes are add-on codes. When unusual procedures and services are provided by the anesthesiologist, report separate anesthesia codes. The code that describes the anesthesia service for the procedure that has the *highest* base unit value is reported first.

The Anesthesia section includes add-on codes for anesthesia services provided to patients undergoing burn excisions or debridement and obstetrics procedures. The add-on code is reported in addition to the code for the primary anesthesia service.

 Coding Tip

- When an anesthesiologist or a qualified nonphysician anesthetist provides distinct procedural services (e.g., insertion of the Swan-Ganz catheter) in addition to anesthesia services, codes for those services are reported separately and modifier -59 is added to each code.

- Surgical endoscopy/arthroscopy always includes diagnostic endoscopy/arthroscopy. This means that if an anesthesiologist or a qualified nonphysician anesthetist provides anesthesia services for a diagnostic and a surgical endoscopy/arthroscopy that are performed during the same operative session, report just one anesthesia services code with appropriate modifiers. This coding tip applies to the following subsections: knee and popliteal area, lower leg (below knee, includes ankle and foot), shoulder and axilla, and upper arm and elbow.

Head

Anesthesia services for the Head subsection include procedures on the following anatomical sites: accessory sinuses, ears, eyelids, eyes, facial bones, lips, nose, salivary glands, and skull. Codes for anesthesia services provided for electroconvulsive therapy (ECT) and intraoral and intracranial procedures are also included. Refer to Table 11-4 for coding rules associated with Head subsection anesthesia codes.

TABLE 11-4 Sample Coding Rules Associated with Head Subsection Anesthesia Codes

Code	Coding Rule
00102	Code 00102 is reported when anesthesia services are provided for plastic repair of a cleft lip, and code 00172 is reported when a cleft lip repair is performed. To report non-cleft lip repairs, assign code 00300. A **cleft lip** is a congenital deformity of the upper lip that failed to close during development; types include unilateral, bilateral, and median (harelip) and may be accompanied by defects of the maxilla and hard palate. NOTE: Bilateral cleft lip describes the type of defect, not the surgery performed.
00104	When a procedure code for electroconvulsive therapy is reported on a claim that is submitted to a Medicare administrative contractor, it is denied as a noncovered service. This means that code 00104, anesthesia for electroconvulsive therapy, will also be denied by Medicare. **Electroconvulsive therapy (ECT)** (or **shock therapy**) involves briefly applying an electric current to the brain to produce a seizure; its purpose is to relieve depression, schizophrenia, and severe affective disorders.
00170	To justify medical necessity for code 00170, make sure you report an appropriate ICD diagnosis code. Medicare does not cover anesthesia services for the care, filling, removal, replacement, or treatment of teeth or structures directly supporting the teeth.
00190	Code 00190 is reported when anesthesia services are provided during extradural procedures on bone(s) of the skull. An **extradural procedure** is performed on the outer side of the **dura mater**, which is the membrane that forms the outer covering of the **central nervous system (CNS)** (brain and spinal cord).
00218	Code 00218 is reported for anesthesia services provided during any **intracranial** (introduced into or within the skull) procedure performed while the patient is in a seated position.

> **EXAMPLE:** A healthy patient underwent soft tissue biopsy of the accessory sinuses, for which a CRNA provided anesthesia services. The CRNA was supervised by an anesthesiologist. Report code 00164-QX-P1.

Neck

Anesthesia services for the Neck subsection include procedures on the following anatomical sites: integumentary system; muscles and nerves of the head, neck, and posterior trunk; esophagus, thyroid, larynx, trachea, and lymphatic system of the neck; and major vessels of the neck. Refer to Table 11-5 for coding rules associated with Neck subsection anesthesia codes.

> **EXAMPLE:** An anesthesiologist provided anesthesia services to a terminally ill 1-year-old patient who underwent laryngoscopy. Report code 00320-AA-P4.

Thorax (Chest Wall and Shoulder Girdle)

Anesthesia services for the Thorax (Chest Wall and Shoulder Girdle) subsection include procedures on the following anatomical sites: integumentary system on the extremities, anterior trunk, and perineum; breast; clavicle; scapula; and ribs. Anesthesia services for an electrical conversion of arrhythmias procedure are also included. Refer to Table 11-6 for coding rules associated with Thorax (Chest Wall and Shoulder Girdle) subsection anesthesia codes.

TABLE 11-5 Sample Coding Rules Associated with Neck Subsection Anesthesia Codes

Code(s)	Coding Rule
00300	When a patient who undergoes removal of a lesion (abnormal tissue resulting from autoimmune or metabolic disorders, infection, neoplasm, or trauma) that requires an anesthesiologist or a qualified nonphysician anesthetist to provide anesthesia services, report code 00300. When such services are provided, make sure you report an appropriate ICD diagnosis code to justify medical necessity (e.g., patient with intellectual disability who exhibits severe anxiety about undergoing the procedure). (And make sure you are prepared to send the payer a copy of the patient record.) The surgeon who removes a lesion usually provides anesthesia services, which involve administration of local anesthesia. If general or regional anesthesia is administered by the surgeon, add modifier -47 to the surgery code. NOTE: Modifier -47 is never added to an anesthesia code.
00326	When procedures on the larynx and trachea are performed on a patient who is younger than 1 year of age, report 00326. *Do not report code 99100 on the same claim as code 00326.*
00350–00352	Codes 00350–00352 are not reported when anesthesia services are provided during arteriography. Instead, report code 01916.

TABLE 11-6 Sample Coding Rules Associated with Thorax (Chest Wall and Shoulder Girdle) Subsection Anesthesia Codes

Code	Coding Rule
00400	Surgical procedures of the skin are often performed under local anesthesia. When monitored anesthesia care (MAC) is provided by an anesthesiologist or a qualified nonphysician anesthetist due to the patient's age, mental status, or size of the skin lesion, report the appropriate anesthesia code, physical status modifier, and HCPCS level II modifier -QS. Also report a qualifying circumstances code if indicated.
00402	Reconstructive breast procedures are reported with code 00402.
00404	Radical or modified radical breast procedures that do not include internal mammary node dissection are reported with code 00404.
00406	When an internal mammary node dissection is performed *in addition to a radical or modified radical breast procedure*, report code 00406. (If internal mammary node dissection is *not* performed, report code 00404.)

> **EXAMPLE:** A 79-year-old female patient underwent bilateral radical mastectomy with internal mammary node dissection (12 lymph nodes). She was recently diagnosed with metastatic adenocarcinoma of the breast to the lung. The anesthesiologist provided general anesthesia services. Report codes 00406-AA-P5 and 99100.

The surgeon who removes a skin lesion usually provides local anesthesia or MAC. If general or regional anesthesia services are provided by the surgeon, add modifier -47 to the surgery code. (*Do not add modifier -47 to an anesthesia code.*) If general anesthesia, regional anesthesia, or MAC is provided by an anesthesiologist or a qualified nonphysician anesthetist, report the appropriate code, physical status modifier, and qualifying circumstances codes. (Add modifier -QS to the anesthesia code if MAC is provided.) Make sure you report an appropriate ICD diagnosis code to justify medical necessity (e.g., patient with intellectual disability who exhibits severe anxiety about undergoing the procedure).

> **EXAMPLE:** An anesthesiologist provided MAC for a 5-year-old patient who underwent a biopsy of the perineum. Report 00400-AA-QX-P1.
> - If the surgeon had provided MAC, you would have reported code 56605. (*Do not report modifier -QS or modifier -47.*)
> - If the surgeon had provided general or regional anesthesia services, you would have reported code 56605-47.

Intrathoracic

Anesthesia services for the Intrathoracic subsection include procedures on the following anatomical sites: bronchus, coronary arteries, diaphragm, esophagus, great vessels of chest, heart, lungs, mediastinum, pericardial sac, pleura, sternum, and thorax. Refer to Table 11-7 for coding rules associated with Intrathoracic subsection anesthesia codes.

> **EXAMPLE:** A 39-year-old female patient with severe systemic disease underwent sternal debridement for which the anesthesiologist provided general anesthesia services. Report code 00550-AA-P3.

Spine and Spinal Cord

Anesthesia services for the Spine and Spinal Cord subsection include procedures on the following anatomical sites: cervical, thoracic, and lumbar spine and spinal cord. Refer to Table 11-8 for coding rules associated with Spine and Spinal Cord subsection anesthesia codes.

> **EXAMPLE:** General anesthesia services were provided by an anesthesiologist during an otherwise healthy patient's thoracic spine surgery. Report code 00620-AA-P1.

 NOTE:

> When a physician performs spinal manipulation under anesthesia, report code 22505. Other manipulation under anesthesia codes (e.g., 23700, manipulation under anesthesia, shoulder joint, including application of fixation apparatus) actually refers to "reduction" of a fracture, which is typically reimbursed by payers. When spinal manipulation is performed without anesthesia, report code 97140, which is located in the Physical Medicine and Rehabilitation subsection of the CPT Medicine section.

Upper Abdomen

Anesthesia services for the Upper Abdomen subsection include procedures on the following anatomical sites: upper abdominal wall, liver, major abdominal blood vessels, pancreas, and stomach. This subsection also includes anesthesia codes for upper gastrointestinal (GI) endoscopic procedures and hernia repairs and laparoscopy. Refer to Table 11-9 for coding rules associated with Upper Abdomen subsection anesthesia codes.

TABLE 11-7 Sample Coding Rules Associated with Intrathoracic Subsection Anesthesia Codes

Code(s)	Coding Rule
00500	The "procedures on esophagus" described in code 00500 require (intrathoracic) chest incision. For "procedures on esophagus" that do *not* require (intrathoracic) chest incision, report 00320.
00528, 00529	Anesthesia services for endoscopic procedures (e.g., esophagoscopy, bronchoscopy, mediastinoscopy, and thoracoscopy) are usually provided by the surgeon who performs the procedure. If an anesthesiologist or a qualified nonphysician anesthetist provides general or regional anesthesia services, report 00528 or 00529 and the appropriate physical status and HCPCS level II modifiers. (When MAC is provided by the anesthesiologist or qualified nonphysician anesthetist, also add HCPCS level II modifier -QS.)
00530–00534	General anesthesia or monitored anesthesia care may be reimbursed by Medicare if it is determined to be reasonable and necessary. Adequate documentation of medical necessity is reviewed on a case-by-case basis. When pacemaker surgery involves the use of the transthoracic method of implantation (code 00560), which requires open surgery, it is accepted practice that general anesthesia services will be provided. Medicare will reimburse such services, and it is unnecessary to submit special medical documentation to Medicare for consideration. According to Ingenix's *Coding and Payment Guide for Anesthesia Services*, Medicare will reimburse general anesthesia or MAC when the patient's record documents • Diagnoses of other hyperalimentation, intermediate coronary syndrome, pulmonary valve disorders, and/or congestive heart failure • The fact that the patient is uncontrollable under local anesthesia (e.g., small child), is disoriented, or has mental confusion
00528–00529 00540–00541	**One lung ventilation (OLV)** is the isolation of the right or left lung so that one lung is ventilated and the other is allowed to collapse. OLV is performed to (1) improve surgical access so the surgeon can perform lung surgery, (2) prevent the other lung from being contaminated by blood or pus from the diseased lung during surgery (because an anesthetized patient loses the ability to cough and, thus, the ability to prevent infected material or blood from entering the normal lung), or (3) provide intensive care ventilation to prevent the normal lung from being subjected to the high pressure required to ventilate an abnormal lung (e.g., after a single lung transplant). When OLV is provided, assign code 00529 or 00541. When OLV is not provided (because bilateral lung ventilation is provided), assign code 00528 or 00540.
00561	Do not report qualifying circumstances codes 99100 with code 00561, which includes in its description "under one year of age." Also do not report qualifying circumstances code 99116 or 99135 with code 00561 because "total body hypothermia" and "controlled hypotension" are included in general anesthesia services for procedures on the heart, pericardial sac, and great vessels of the chest.
00560–00567	A **pump oxygenator** is a device that substitutes for the heart (pump) and lungs (oxygenator) during open heart surgery. A pump oxygenator is not typically used for coronary artery bypass grafting (CABG) or laser myocardial revascularization surgery, and the patient's beating heart provides circulatory support.

TABLE 11-8 Sample Coding Rules Associated with Spine and Spinal Cord Subsection Anesthesia Codes

Code	Coding Rule
00600	When anesthesia services for diagnostic and therapeutic percutaneous image-guided spine and spinal cord procedures are provided, report codes 01935–01936 instead of 00600.
00604	When anesthesia services are provided for a patient who undergoes cervical spine and cord surgery in a sitting position, report code 00604.
00635	A **lumbar puncture (LP)**, or **spinal tap**, involves inserting a **cannula** (hollow needle) at the L3–L4 or L4–L5 (lumbar vertebrae) to remove cerebrospinal fluid (CSF) for diagnostic or therapeutic purposes (e.g., measure CSF pressure or analyze CSF fluid).
00640	Report code 00640 when anesthesia is provided for closed procedures on the cervical, lumbar, or thoracic spine. Third-party payers do not usually reimburse 00640 when reported for spinal manipulation under anesthesia (SMUA) to treat low back pain or other neuromusculoskeletal disorders by improving range of motion and reducing spinal pain.

TABLE 11-9 Sample Coding Rules Associated with Upper Abdomen Subsection Anesthesia Codes

Code	Coding Rule
00731–00732	Anesthesia services (e.g., sedation) for endoscopic procedures (e.g., upper GI endoscopy) are usually provided by the surgeon who performs the procedure. If an anesthesiologist or a qualified nonphysician anesthetist provides general or regional anesthesia services, report 00731 or 00732 and the appropriate physical status and HCPCS level II modifiers. (When MAC is provided by the anesthesiologist or qualified nonphysician anesthetist, also add HCPCS level II modifier -QS.)
00796	Code 00796 is reported for anesthesia services provided to the recipient of a liver transplant. Assign code 01990 for anesthesia services provided to a brain-dead patient who undergoes liver organ harvest (removal of an organ for transplantation).

EXAMPLE: An anesthesiologist provides general anesthesia services for a patient who undergoes a liver transplant. Report 00796-AA-P5.

Lower Abdomen

Anesthesia services for the Lower Abdomen subsection include procedures on the following anatomical sites: lower abdominal wall, **panniculus adiposus**, or **pannus** (layer of subcutaneous adipose tissue, or fat, below the dermis that contains fat deposits, blood vessels, and nerves). The following anatomical sites are accessed via transabdominal incision: uterus; fallopian tubes; urinary tract, including kidneys and urinary bladder; prostate gland; adrenal glands; lower abdominal vessels; and inferior vena cava. This subsection also includes anesthesia codes for lower intestinal endoscopic procedures and hernia repairs and lower abdomen intraperitoneal procedures including laparoscopy. Refer to Table 11-10 for coding rules associated with Lower Abdomen subsection anesthesia codes.

EXAMPLE: An anesthesiologist provided regional anesthesia services to a diabetic patient who underwent total cystectomy. Report code 00864-AA-P2.

TABLE 11-10 Sample Coding Rules Associated with Lower Abdomen Subsection Anesthesia Codes

Code(s)	Coding Rule
00802	**Panniculectomy** is the surgical removal of excess abdominal panniculus (or pannus), which is a redundant layer of fat tissue (or apron) located at the lowest portion of the abdominal wall. (Patients who have lost significant weight after undergoing a previous gastric restrictive procedure for morbid obesity often develop excess pannus.)
00811–00813	Anesthesia services (e.g., sedation) for endoscopic procedures (e.g., lower intestinal endoscopy and laparoscopy) are often provided by the surgeon who performs the procedure. If an anesthesiologist or a qualified nonphysician anesthetist provides general or regional anesthesia services, report 00811–00813 and the appropriate physical status and HCPCS level II modifiers. (When MAC is provided by the anesthesiologist or qualified nonphysician anesthetist, also add HCPCS level II modifier -QS.)
00834–00836	When a hernia repair is performed on an infant less than 1 year of age, report code 00834 or 00836 (depending on age). *Do not report qualifying circumstances code 99100 with code 00834 or 00836.* For patients 1 year of age or older who undergo hernia repair surgery, report code 00830 or 00832 (depending on type of hernia).
00868	Code 00868 is reported for anesthesia services provided to the recipient of a kidney transplant. Assign code 00862 for anesthesia services provided to a living kidney donor. Assign code 01990 for anesthesia service provided to a brain-dead patient who undergoes a kidney organ harvest.
00872	**Extracorporeal shock wave lithotripsy (ESWL)** uses ultrasound shock waves to crush calculi (stones) located in the bladder, renal pelvis, or ureter. A **lithotripter** is the device that administers a high-voltage electrical discharge through a spark gap under water, which produces a compressive force and breaks apart the stones so they can pass in urine. Typically, the surgeon provides monitored anesthesia care (MAC) to the patient. However, if an anesthesiologist or a qualified nonphysician anesthetist provides general or regional anesthesia services, report 00872 and the appropriate physical status and HCPCS level II modifiers. If MAC is provided by the anesthesiologist, add HCPCS level II modifier -QS.

TABLE 11-11 Sample Coding Rules Associated with Perineum Subsection Anesthesia Codes

Code(s)	Coding Rule
00902	For anesthesia services provided during lower intestinal endoscopic procedures, report code 00810.
00910–00918	When anesthesia services are provided for **urethrocystoscopy** (visualization of urethra and urinary bladder) and the surgeon completes other procedures through the urethrocystocope (e.g., biopsy of urinary bladder), report the appropriate code from range 00910–00918.
00920–00938	When anesthesia services are provided for procedures performed on male genitalia and an open urethral procedure (incision into urethra) is done to access anatomical sites, report the appropriate code from range 00920–00938.

Perineum

Anesthesia services for the Perineum subsection include procedures on the following anatomical sites: anus, rectum, perineum, vulva, vas deferens, seminal vesicles, testes, penis, vagina, labia, cervix, endometrium, uterus, prostate, urethra, urinary bladder, and ureters. Refer to Table 11-11 for coding rules associated with Perineum subsection anesthesia codes.

> **EXAMPLE:** An anesthesiologist provided general anesthesia services to a hypertensive patient who underwent vulvectomy. Report code 00906-AA-P2.

For anesthesia services provided during perineal muscle and nerve procedures, report code 00300. For anesthesia services provided during perineal skin procedures, report code 00400.

> **EXAMPLE 1:** An anesthesiologist provided general anesthesia services to 4-year-old female healthy patient who underwent perineal skin biopsy. Report code 00400-AA-P1.

> **EXAMPLE 2:** An anesthesiologist provided regional anesthesia services to an anxious diabetic patient who underwent left gluteus maximus muscle biopsy. Report code 00300-AA-P2.

Pelvis (Except Hip)

Anesthesia services for the Pelvis (Except Hip) subsection include procedures on the following anatomical sites: anterior or posterior iliac crest, bony pelvis, interpelviabdominal (hindquarter), pelvis, symphysis pubis, sacroiliac joint, acetabulum, and extrapelvic and intrapelvic obturator nerves. (There are no coding rules for the Pelvis [Except Hip] subsection.)

> **EXAMPLE:** An anesthesiologist provided general anesthesia services to a chronic asthmatic patient who underwent an open procedure involving the sacroiliac joint. Report code 01170-AA-P2.

Upper Leg (Except Knee)

Anesthesia services for the Upper Leg (Except Knee) subsection include procedures on the following anatomical sites: hip joint; upper two-thirds of femur; and arteries, veins, nerves, muscles, tendons, fascia, and bursae of upper leg. (There are no coding rules for the Upper Leg [Except Knee] subsection.)

> **EXAMPLE:** An anesthesiologist provided general anesthesia services to an intellectually disabled patient with mild systemic disease who underwent nerve biopsy of the upper leg. Report code 01250-AA-P2.

Knee and Popliteal Area

Anesthesia services for the Knee and Popliteal Area subsection include procedures on the following anatomical sites: arteries, veins, nerves, muscles, tendons, fascia, and bursae of knee and/or popliteal area; lower one-third of femur; knee joint; upper ends of the tibia and fibula; and patella. (There are no coding rules for the Knee and Popliteal Area subsection.)

EXAMPLE: An anesthesiologist provided general anesthesia services to a normal healthy patient who underwent diagnostic arthroscopy, left knee. Report code 01382-AA-P1.

Lower Leg (Below Knee, Includes Ankle and Foot)

Anesthesia services for the Lower Leg (Below Knee, Includes Ankle and Foot) subsection include procedures on the following anatomical sites: lower leg; ankle; foot; and arteries, veins, bones, nerves, muscles, tendons, and fascia of leg, ankle, and foot. (There are no coding rules for the Lower Leg [Below Knee, Includes Ankle and Foot] subsection.)

EXAMPLE: An anesthesiologist provided general anesthesia services to a normal healthy patient who underwent arthroscopic procedure, right ankle. Report code 01464-AA-P1.

Shoulder and Axilla

Anesthesia services for the Shoulder and Axilla subsection include procedures on the following anatomical sites: arteries, veins, nerves, muscles, tendons, fascia, and bursae of shoulder and axillae; humeral head and neck; sternoclavicular joint; acromioclavicular joint; and shoulder joint. (There are no coding rules for the Shoulder and Axilla subsection.)

EXAMPLE: An anesthesiologist provided general anesthesia services to a normal healthy patient who underwent muscle biopsy, left shoulder. Report code 01610-AA-P1.

Upper Arm and Elbow

Anesthesia services for the Upper Arm and Elbow subsection include procedures on the following anatomical sites: arteries, veins, nerves, muscle, tendons, fascia, and bursae of upper arm and elbow; humerus; and elbow. (There are no coding rules for the Upper Arm and Elbow subsection.)

EXAMPLE: An anesthesiologist provided general anesthesia services to a patient with mild systemic disease who underwent excision of tumor of the right humerus. Report code 01758-AA-P2.

Forearm, Wrist, and Hand

Anesthesia services for the Forearm, Wrist, and Hand subsection include procedures on the following anatomical sites: arteries, veins, nerves, muscles, tendons, fascia, and bursae of forearm, wrist, and hand; radius; ulna; wrist; hand bones; distal radius; distal ulna; and hand joints. (There are no coding rules for the Forearm, Wrist, and Hand subsection.)

EXAMPLE: An anesthesiologist provided general anesthesia services to a normal healthy but very anxious patient who underwent diagnostic and surgical arthroscopy with bone biopsy, right wrist. Report code 01830-AA-P1-AA. (Modifier -23 indicates general anesthesia services were provided for a procedure that usually is performed under local anesthesia.)

Radiological Procedures

Anesthesia services for radiological procedures include the following: myelography, discography, and vertebroplasty; diagnostic arteriography/venography; cardiac catheterization, including coronary angiography and ventriculography; noninvasive imaging or radiation therapy; and therapeutic interventional radiology involving the arterial/venous/lymphatic systems. (Refer to Table 11-12 for Radiological Procedures subsection coding rules.)

EXAMPLE: An anesthesiologist provided MAC to a patient with severe systemic disease who underwent cardiac catheterization, including coronary angiography and ventriculography. Report code 01920-AA-QS-P3.

NOTE:

Refer to Chapter 17, CPT Radiology, of this textbook for coding rules about radiological procedures and services.

Coding Tip

- Medicare anesthesia billing guidelines require that just one code be reported for anesthesia services provided in conjunction with radiological procedures.

- Radiological supervision and interpretation codes applicable to radiological procedures being performed are reported by the appropriate provider (e.g., radiologist, cardiologist, neurosurgeon, or radiation oncologist). Such codes are not included (bundled) in anesthesia services codes for radiological procedures, and the appropriate provider must report the radiology procedure or service code.

TABLE 11-12 Sample Coding Rules Associated with Radiological Procedures Subsection Anesthesia Codes

Code(s)	Coding Rule
01916	An **arteriography** is the visualization of an artery via x-ray after injection of a **radiopaque** (cannot be penetrated by electromagnetic radiation) substance. A **contrast medium** is a radiopaque substance (e.g., Renografin dye used for intravenous pyelogram) that obstructs the passage of x-rays so structures containing it appear white on radiographic film. This allows the radiologist to visualize abnormalities and define body structure contours.
01920	CPT code 01920 (Anesthesia for cardiac catheterization including coronary angiography and ventriculography [not to include Swan-Ganz catheter]) is reported for monitored anesthesia care (MAC) in patients who are critically ill or critically unstable. If the physician performing the radiological service inserts a catheter (other than a Swan-Ganz catheter) as part of the anesthesia services provided and a catheter is left in place and used for monitoring purposes, do not report a code for placement of the monitoring catheter (e.g., CPT code 36500).
01922	When anesthesia is required for a CT scan or MRI due to medical necessity (e.g., patient with intellectual disability), report code 01922 (Anesthesia for noninvasive imaging or radiation therapy) with appropriate modifiers.
01924–01933	**Interventional therapeutic radiological procedures** are the therapeutic application of radiation that includes the following aspects: - Analysis and interpretation of radiation equipment performance measurements - Calibration of equipment associated with production and use of radiation - Analysis and interpretation of measurements associated with patient dosages - Radiation safety aspects associated with production and use of radiation
01935–01936	Percutaneous image guided procedures on the spine and spinal cord involve inserting a peripheral intravenous catheter, administering an anxiolytic (antianxiety) medication, and accompanying the patient to the radiology suite. Once in the radiology suite, sedation and analgesic agents (e.g., diagnostic procedures) or general anesthesia (e.g., therapeutic procedures) are administered.

TABLE 11-13 Sample Coding Rule Associated with Burn Excisions or Debridement Subsection Anesthesia Codes

Code(s)	Coding Rule
01952–01953	Code 01953 is reported with code 01952 when the percent of total body surface area or part thereof treated is greater than 9 percent. Do not add modifier -51 (Multiple Procedures) to code 01953 because the word "each" is included in its code description. Be sure to interpret percent of total body surface in code 01952 as up to 4 percent and in code 01953 as up to 9 percent.

Burn Excisions or Debridement

Anesthesia services for burn excisions or debridement procedures include the following: second- and third-degree burn excision or debridement with or without skin grafting according to total body surface area. (Refer to Chapter 12, CPT Surgery I, of this textbook for discussion of total body surface area calculations.) (Refer to Table 11-13 for Burn Excisions or Debridement subsection coding rules.)

EXAMPLE: An anesthesiologist provided general anesthesia services to a 2-year-old type 1 diabetic patient who underwent second-degree burn debridement of the chest, 5 percent of total body surface area. Report code 01952-AA-P2.

Obstetric

Anesthesia services for obstetric procedures include the following: external cephalic version procedure, vaginal delivery, cesarean delivery, urgent hysterectomy following delivery, cesarean hysterectomy without labor analgesia/anesthesia care, abortion procedures, neuraxial labor analgesia/anesthesia for planned vaginal delivery, neuraxial labor analgesia/anesthesia for cesarean delivery following planned vaginal delivery, and cesarean hysterectomy following neuraxial labor analgesia/anesthesia. (Refer to Chapter 16, CPT Surgery V, of this textbook for detailed discussion of obstetric procedures and services.) (Refer to Table 11-14 for Obstetric subsection coding rules.)

EXAMPLE: An anesthesiologist provided general anesthesia services to a normal healthy patient who suffered a miscarriage and underwent surgery to remove the remaining products of conception. Report code 01965-AA-P1.

Other Procedures

Anesthesia services for other procedures include the following: physiologic support for harvesting organ(s) from brain-dead patients, anesthesia for diagnostic/therapeutic nerve blocks and injections, daily hospital management of epidural or subarachnoid continuous drug administration, and unlisted anesthesia procedure(s). (Refer to Table 11-15 for Other Procedures subsection coding rules.)

TABLE 11-14 Sample Coding Rule Associated with Obstetric Subsection Anesthesia Codes

Code(s)	Coding Rule
01967–01969	If documentation supports procedures or services provided, code 01968 is reported with 01967, or code 01969 is reported with 01967 and 01968.

TABLE 11-15 Sample Coding Rules Associated with Other Procedures Subsection Anesthesia Codes

Code	Coding Rule
01996	Report code 01996 when the anesthesiologist or qualified nonphysician anesthetist provides daily hospital management of continuous epidural or subarachnoid drug administration. This management is provided because the anesthesiologist or qualified nonphysician anesthetist inserted an epidural or subarachnoid catheter during a surgical procedure as part of anesthesia services provided.
01999	When reporting code 01999, make sure you submit a copy of the operative report and other pertinent documents to the third-party payer for review.

NOTE:

- To report regional intravenous administration of local anesthetic agents or other medication in the upper or lower extremity, assign an Anesthesia code from the appropriate Anesthesia subsection.
- To report a Bier block for pain management, assign code 64999. A *Bier block* is an intravenous regional block, which involves using a tourniquet to restrict the effects of anesthesia to a region of the body (e.g., leg).
- To report intra-arterial or intravenous injections, including that for pain management, assign a code from 96373 to 96379.

EXAMPLE: An anesthesiologist managed the continuous drug administration of an epidural for a 50-year-old patient who has chronic obstructive pulmonary disease. Report code 01996-AA-P2.

Exercise 11.4 – Anesthesia Subsections

Instructions: Complete each statement below.

1. For Medicare purposes, just one anesthesia code is usually reported unless the second and subsequent anesthesia codes are _____ codes.

2. When an anesthesiologist or a qualified nonphysician anesthetist provides distinct procedural services such as the insertion of a Swan-Ganz catheter in addition to anesthesia services, codes are reported separately and modifier _____ is added to the procedure (e.g., Swan-Ganz catheter) code.

3. When procedures on the larynx and trachea are performed on a patient who is younger than 1 year of age, report qualifying circumstances code 99100 in addition to 00326. True or False?

4. When an internal mammary node dissection is performed *in addition to a radical or modified radical breast procedure*, report anesthesia code _____.

5. Anesthesia services for endoscopic procedures are usually provided by the surgeon who performs the procedure. When monitored anesthesia care (MAC) is provided by the anesthesiologist or qualified nonphysician anesthetist, add HCPCS level II modifier _____ for MAC.

6. When anesthesia services for therapeutic percutaneous image-guided procedure on the spine and spinal cord are provided, report a code from range _____.

7. When anesthesia services are provided to the recipient of a liver transplant, report code _____.

8. When anesthesia services are provided to a brain-dead patient who undergoes a kidney organ harvest, report code _____.

9. When anesthesia is required for a CT scan or MRI due to medical necessity (e.g., patient with intellectual disability), report code _____.

10. When the percentage of total body surface area or part thereof treated for second- and third-degree burns is greater than 9 percent, report code _____ in addition to 01952.

Summary

The Anesthesia section is located after the Evaluation and Management section in the CPT coding manual, and codes (00100 to 01999) with appropriate modifiers are reported for services related to the administration of anesthesia (including general and regional), supplementation of local anesthesia, and other supportive anesthesia services. The Anesthesia section is organized according to general anatomical areas or services that relate to a number of surgical procedures. For Medicare purposes, just one anesthesia code is reported unless the second and subsequent anesthesia codes are add-on codes. When separate anesthesia codes are reported, the code that describes the anesthesia service for the procedure that has the *highest* base unit value is reported first.

A physician (e.g., anesthesiologist) is responsible for supervising anesthesia services (which include general and regional), supplementation of local anesthesia, and other supportive services so the patient receives appropriate optimal anesthesia care. The administration of local infiltration, metacarpal/metatarsal/ digital block, or topical anesthesia by the operating surgeon or obstetrician is included (bundled) in the surgery code; separate codes are not reported. Anesthesia services include the preparation and monitoring of the patient, as well as the following services: draping, positioning, prepping, and transporting the patient; inserting nasogastric or orogastric tubes; inserting peripheral IV lines for fluid and medication administration; interpreting laboratory results; interpreting monitored functions; placing airway tubes, including laryngoscopy for airway management; positioning external devices for capnography, cardiac monitoring, CNS evoked responses, Doppler flow, pulse oximetry, and temperature; and stimulating nerves to determine level of paralysis or localization of nerve(s).

Internet Links

American Society of Anesthesiologists (ASA): Go to *www.asahq.org*, scroll over the Quality & Practice Management heading, and click on the Practice Management link to access coding and billing information.

Medicare Information for Anesthesiologists: Go to *www.cms.gov*, click on the Medicare link, scroll to the Provider Type heading, and click on the Anesthesiologists link.

Review

Multiple Choice

Instructions: Circle the most appropriate response.

1. Local anesthesia administration techniques include:
    a. caudal anesthesia, saddle block anesthesia, and epidural anesthesia.
    b. general anesthesia, local anesthesia, and regional anesthesia.
    c. spinal anesthesia, intravenous regional anesthesia, and Bier block.
    d. surface anesthesia, infiltration anesthesia, field block, peripheral nerve block, and plexus anesthesia.

2. The CPT Anesthesia section includes:
    a. subsections for anatomical sites followed by subsections for procedures.
    b. subsections for procedures followed by subsections for anatomical sites.
    c. subsections for anatomical sites only.
    d. subsections for procedures only.

3. Prior to surgery, a professional assesses information from the patient's record, performs a physical examination, evaluates preoperative test results, and ensures that informed anesthetic consent has been obtained. This service is called:

    a. monitored anesthesia care.
    b. postanesthesia evaluation.
    c. postoperative pain management.
    d. preanesthesia evaluation.

4. The professional who assesses information from the patient's record, performs a physical examination, evaluates preoperative test results, and ensures that informed anesthetic consent has been obtained is called a(n):

    a. anesthesiologist or qualified nonphysician anesthetist.
    b. primary care physician.
    c. registration technician.
    d. surgeon.

5. The information assessed from the patient's record, physical examination performed on the patient, evaluation of preoperative test results, and verification that informed anesthetic consent has been obtained is:

    a. documented in the operative report.
    b. included in the anesthesia code.
    c. part of postanesthesia services.
    d. reported as a separate service.

6. If the surgery for which preanesthesia services are performed is canceled, the anesthesiologist should:

    a. not report any codes.
    b. report an evaluation and management service code instead of an anesthesia code.
    c. report the anesthesia code for the procedure that was canceled.
    d. report the anesthesia code for the procedure that was canceled and add modifier -53 for discontinued procedure.

7. When an anesthesiologist provides anesthesia services for a 5-month-old healthy patient who undergoes a procedure on the larynx and trachea, report code(s):

    a. 00326-AA-P1.
    b. 00326-AA-P1 and 99100.
    c. 99100.
    d. 99100 and 00326-AA-P1.

8. Code 00218 is reported for anesthesia services provided during an _____ procedure, which is performed on the skull while the patient is in a seated position.

    a. endocranial
    b. innercranial
    c. intercranial
    d. intracranial

9. Which is considered a diagnostic radiological procedure?

    a. Analysis and interpretation of measurements associated with patient dosages
    b. Analysis and interpretation of radiation equipment performance measurements
    c. Calibration of equipment associated with production and use of radiation
    d. Visualization of abnormalities and definition of body structure contours

10. Code 00802 is reported for anesthesia services administered during a procedure in which a redundant layer of fat tissue located at the lowest portion of the abdominal wall is surgically removed. This procedure is called a:

    a. panniculectomy.
    b. panniculotomy.
    c. panniculus.
    d. pannus.

11. An anesthesiologist provided anesthesia services on an otherwise healthy patient who underwent left corneal transplant. Which CPT code is assigned?

    a. 00144-AA-P1
    b. 00580-AA-P1
    c. 65410-AA-P1
    d. 65710-AA-P1

12. An anesthesiologist provided anesthesia services on a 30-year-old male patient who underwent thyroidectomy for rare thyroid cancer. Which CPT code is assigned?

    a. 00320-AA-P3
    b. 00322-AA-P3
    c. 01442-AA-P3
    d. 60210-AA-P3

13. An anesthesiologist provided monitored anesthesia care to a patient with history of severe cardiopulmonary condition who underwent a procedure to access central venous circulation. Which CPT code is assigned?

    a. 00530-AA-G9-P3   **c.** 00560-AA-G9-P3

    b. 00532-AA-G9-P3   **d.** 01916-AA-G9-P3

14. An anesthesiologist provided anesthesia services on a patient with mild systemic disease who underwent upper abdomen vascular surgery. Which CPT code is assigned?

    a. 00700-AA-P2   **b.** 00770-AA-P2   **c.** 00880-AA-P2   **d.** 00882-AA-P2

15. An anesthesiologist provided anesthesia services on an otherwise healthy patient who underwent open revision of total hip arthroplasty (both components). Which CPT code is assigned?

    a. 01140-AA-P1   **b.** 01200-AA-P1   **c.** 01210-AA-P1   **d.** 27134-AA-P1

16. An anesthesiologist provided anesthesia services on a patient with mild systemic disease who underwent popliteal thromboendarterectomy. Which CPT code is assigned?

    a. 01440-AA-P2   **b.** 01442-AA-P2   **c.** 01400-AA-P2   **d.** 35303-AA-P2

17. An anesthesiologist provided anesthesia services on an otherwise healthy patient who underwent repair of the Achilles tendon. Which CPT code is assigned?

    a. 01462-AA-P1   **b.** 01472-AA-P1   **c.** 27650-AA-P1   **d.** 28200-AA-P1

18. An anesthesiologist provided anesthesia services on a patient with severe systemic disease who underwent an interthoracoscapular amputation. Which CPT code is assigned?

    a. 01630-AA-P3   **b.** 01636-AA-P3   **c.** 01710-AA-P3   **d.** 23900-AA-P3

19. An anesthesiologist provided anesthesia services to a five-year-old otherwise healthy patient who underwent bilateral orchiopexy. Which CPT code is assigned?

    a. 00926-AA-P1   **b.** 00928-AA-P1   **c.** 00930-AA-P1   **d.** 54650-AA-P1

20. An anesthesiologist provided anesthesia services on an otherwise healthy patient who underwent phleborrhaphy, right wrist. Which CPT code is assigned?

    a. 01782-AA-P1   **b.** 01852-AA-P1   **c.** 15850-AA-P1   **d.** 37650-AA-P1

Coding Practice I—Modifiers

Instructions: Review each case and assign CPT anesthesia code(s) and appropriate modifier(s). (Enter the physical status modifier first, such as 00000-P1-AA.) Some cases require assignment of CPT surgery codes and appropriate modifier(s), per chapter content about anesthesia coding guidelines.

1. While providing regional anesthesia services for a healthy patient who underwent an emergency cesarean section, the anesthesiologist inserted a lumbar catheter to provide continuous epidural analgesia pain management (morphine bolus).

    _____

2. A CRNA (with medical direction by the surgeon) provided general anesthesia services for a controlled diabetic patient who underwent total wrist replacement. At the conclusion of the surgical procedure, the CRNA inserted an epidural catheter to provide continuous postoperative analgesia for pain management. The CRNA monitored the patient's pain management on the day after surgery.

    _____

3. A healthy patient underwent total knee replacement surgery; regional anesthesia services were provided by an anesthesiologist.

    _____

4. An anesthesiologist provided regional pain block for an arthroscopic anterior cruciate ligament repair of the left knee of a healthy 40-year-old male patient. The anesthesiologist also performed a femoral nerve block for postoperative pain management.

_____

5. A patient with chronic asthma underwent a thoracotomy. The CRNA (without medical direction by a physician) provided general anesthesia services and, at the conclusion of the procedure, inserted an epidural catheter for continuous infusion of morphine for postoperative pain control.

_____

Coding Practice II—Anesthesia

Instructions: Review each case and assign the appropriate anesthesia code(s) and physical status modifier(s). Make sure you assign qualifying circumstance code(s) where appropriate. _All anesthesia services were provided by the anesthesiologist, which means that modifier -AA is added to each anesthesia code._ Some cases require assignment of CPT surgery codes and appropriate modifier(s), per chapter content about anesthesia coding guidelines.

Head

1. A 77-year-old healthy male patient with controlled diabetes mellitus underwent intraocular lens transplant surgery for which general anesthesia was administered.

_____

2. A 5-year-old healthy boy was admitted to the pediatrics floor of an acute care hospital and underwent tympanostomy for which general anesthesia was administered.

_____

Neck

3. A 9-month-old female patient underwent tracheostomy under general anesthesia after having sustained injuries in a motor vehicle accident. The child lost consciousness for 60 minutes after the accident and required cardiopulmonary resuscitation.

_____

4. A 47-year-old male patient with a history of hypertension underwent a partial thyroid lobectomy due to a thyroid tumor. General anesthesia was administered.

_____

Thorax

5. A 33-year-old healthy male construction worker fell from a ladder onto a wooden platform. He was brought into the emergency room and diagnosed with a concussion; there was no loss of consciousness. The patient went to the operating room for the complicated removal of wood from the skin of his shoulder. He received general anesthesia.

_____

6. A 14-year-old male is admitted to the pediatrics ward with chest pain, shortness of breath, and possible lordosis. After examination, the diagnosis of pectus excavatum was made. The boy had the condition corrected with an open procedure under general anesthesia.

_____

Intrathoracic

7. A 78-year-old female smoker was admitted for shortness of breath, hypertension, and bloody sputum. She was diagnosed with pneumonia and underwent pneumocentesis performed under general anesthesia.

_____

8. A 45-year-old male with a history of coronary disease and mild hypertension underwent insertion of a permanent pacemaker with epicardial electrodes by thoracotomy. General anesthesia was administered.

_____

Spine and Spinal Cord

9. A 57-year-old female with a history of osteoporosis underwent posterior arthrodesis in the craniocervical (occipital C2) region. General anesthesia was administered.

_____

10. A 25-year-old male heroin addict complaining of severe headaches was admitted to the psychiatric floor of an acute care hospital. After detoxification, the patient still had headaches; increased spinal fluid pressure was noted. He underwent diagnostic lumbar spinal puncture performed under regional anesthesia.

_____

Upper Abdomen

11. An obese 56-year-old male with benign hypertension complained of recurring heartburn. After examination, he was admitted for surgery and underwent a transabdominal repair of a diaphragmatic hernia. General anesthesia was administered.

_____

12. An otherwise healthy 5-year-old female underwent percutaneous liver biopsy under general anesthesia.

_____

Lower Abdomen

13. A 54-year-old female who lost 100 pounds two years ago underwent panniculectomy under general anesthesia. The patient has no significant medical history or chronic conditions.

_____

14. A healthy 36-year-old female underwent tubal ligation under general anesthesia for voluntary sterilization.

_____

Perineum

15. A 45-year-old female presented with moderate vaginal bleeding. After being admitted and tested, she underwent hysteroscopy with endometrium biopsy under general anesthesia.

_____

16. A healthy 38-year-old male requested voluntary sterilization and underwent vasectomy. Regional anesthesia was administered.

_____

Pelvis (Except Hip)

17. A volunteer offered bone marrow to a needy recipient. He underwent bone marrow aspiration of the posterior iliac crest with general anesthesia to provide a sample to test for a match. The donor has no chronic or current medical conditions.

_____

18. An otherwise healthy 14-year-old-male fell while skateboarding and landed on his back. After radiological exam, he was diagnosed with fractured sacroiliac joint. Open treatment of the anterior ring fracture was performed under general anesthesia.

_____

Upper Leg (Except Knee)

19. A 46-year-old female fell while in-line skating and fractured her femur at the proximal end. She underwent open treatment of the femoral fracture with internal fixation under general anesthesia. The patient has type 2 diabetes mellitus, controlled.

_____

20. A 76-year-old female with Parkinson's disease fell while getting out of bed. She was unable to walk and was found two days later by her son. She was dehydrated and disoriented. She was seen and evaluated in the emergency department. She was admitted with the diagnosis of a hip fracture. The patient's hip was repaired with total hip arthroplasty under general anesthesia on the day of admission.

_____

Knee and Popliteal Area

21. A 17-year-old male high school football player's knee was injured during a game. Examination revealed fractured patella. He underwent open treatment of the fractured patella under general anesthesia.

_____

Lower Leg (Below Knee, Includes Ankle and Foot)

22. A 15-year-old female high school gymnast's knee was injured during a meet. Radiological examination revealed torn meniscus. She underwent a surgical arthroscopic procedure of her knee to repair the meniscus, with general anesthesia.

_____

23. A 14-year-old Down syndrome male was stepped on by a horse. Upon radiological exam, it was noted that the boy had a trimalleolar fracture. He underwent closed treatment of the fracture without manipulation under general anesthesia.

_____

24. A 23-year-old female smoker was seen in the emergency room with pain, swelling, and disfigurement in her right lower leg. Radiological exam revealed a fractured tibia. She underwent closed reduction and casting under general anesthesia.

_____

Shoulder and Axilla

25. An otherwise healthy 27-year-old male fell while riding his motorcycle. He complained of right shoulder pain and swelling. Upon radiological exam, it was noted that he had a fractured humerus. He underwent closed treatment of the humeral head under general anesthesia.

_____

26. A healthy 37-year-old female iron worker had an I beam fall on her shoulder. The joint was crushed. She went to the emergency room and was brought to the operating room for interthoracoscapular amputation under general anesthesia.

_____

Upper Arm and Elbow

27. A healthy 21-year-old female college tennis player complained about pain in her left elbow. The joint was swollen and tender. After orthopedic and radiological exam, reconstruction of the lateral collateral ligament was performed under general anesthesia.

_____

28. A 50-year-old bodybuilder heard a pop and felt severe pain in his right upper arm while lifting heavy weights. Radiological exam revealed a ruptured bicep tendon. He underwent reinsertion of the ruptured tendon under general anesthesia.

_____

Forearm, Wrist, and Hand

29. An otherwise healthy 68-year-old male noticed a lump on his left forearm. Examination determined that he was in need of incision and drainage of a bursa. The procedure was performed under general anesthesia.

_____

30. A 47-year-old healthy male factory worker caught his lower left arm in a commercial washing machine. The patient sustained a fracture and dislocated distal radius. The patient underwent open reduction of the fracture and dislocation under general anesthesia.

_____

Radiological Procedures

31. A 57-year-old obese female with hypertension showed coronary problems during a stress test. A cardiac catheterization under general anesthesia was performed.

_____

32. A 63-year-old male was diagnosed with a glioblastoma multiforme. He underwent radiation therapy under regional anesthesia.

_____

Burn Excisions or Debridement

33. A firefighter sustained second-degree burns over 35 percent of his body while on duty. He received general anesthesia during the burn debridement.

_____

34. A 59-year-old female chemical factory worker sustained second-degree burns due to a caustic chemical spill to her left arm. Nine percent of her body was burned. She received general anesthesia during burn excision.

_____

Obstetric

35. A healthy 24-year-old female had a normal vaginal delivery under regional anesthesia.

_____

36. A controlled non-insulin-dependent diabetic 29-year-old female underwent cesarean delivery with general anesthesia.

_____

Other Procedures

37. A 37-year-old male has recurring back pain. He underwent spinal disc surgery and continued to need daily epidural continuous drug anesthesia while in the hospital.

_____

38. An anesthesiologist provided physiologic support for harvesting organs (for organ donation) from a brain-dead patient.

_____

39. A healthy 30-year-old patient underwent insertion of an epidural catheter on the first day of admission. On the second day of admission, the anesthesiologist was responsible for hospital management of continuous epidural drug administration. (Report the Anesthesia code for the second day of admission only.)

_____

40. General anesthesia was administered to a 6-month-old male child with mild systemic disease who underwent anesthesia for a brand new procedure not yet classified in CPT. The patient was observed in recovery by the nursing staff and evaluated by the anesthesiologist before being transferred to the pediatric unit of the hospital. The nursing staff placed an IV line for saline and postoperative pain medication.

_____

CPT Surgery I

Chapter Outline

Overview of Surgery Section

Surgery Guidelines

General Subsection

Integumentary System Subsection

Chapter Objectives

At the conclusion of this chapter, the student should be able to:

1. Define key terms related to the General and Integumentary System subsections of CPT Surgery.
2. Provide an overview about the CPT Surgery section, including its organization, format, and content.
3. Interpret CPT Surgery guidelines.
4. Assign codes from the General subsection of CPT Surgery.
5. Assign codes from the Integumentary System subsection of CPT Surgery.

Key Terms

ablation

acellular dermal
   replacement

actinic keratosis (AK)

adjacent tissue transfer/
   rearrangement

advancement flap

allograft

autograft

bedsore

biopsy

blepharoplasty

chemical peel

chemosurgery

cryosurgery

decubitus ulcer

defect

dermabrasion

destruction

diagnostic procedure

donor site

double pedicle flap

electrosurgery

endoscopy

excision

excisional biopsy

extensive cellulitis

fine-needle aspiration
   (FNA)

flap

free flap

free skin graft

full-thickness skin graft

glabellar frown lines

global period

global surgical package

graft

incision

incisional biopsy

incision and drainage
   (I&D)

introduction

island flap

island pedicle flap

LASER (light
   amplification by
   stimulated emission
   of radiation)

Limberg flap

lumpectomy

microdermabrasion

moderate (conscious) sedation

modified radical mastectomy

Mohs microsurgery

mycocutaneous flap

needle core biopsy

open biopsy

paring and curettement

partial mastectomy

pedicle skin graft

pilonidal cyst

pressure ulcer

primary defect

radical mastectomy

random pattern flap

recipient site

reconstruction

removal

repair

revision

rhomboid flap

rhytidectomy

rotation flap

rule of nines

secondary defect

separate procedure

shaving

simple closure

simple repair

skin substitute graft

split-thickness skin graft

stereotactic localization

stroma

surgical curettement

surgical package

suture

therapeutic surgical procedure

tissue approximation

tissue-cultured autograft

tissue rearrangement

total mastectomy

undermining

V-Y plasty

W-plasty

xenograft

Z-plasty

Introduction

The Surgery section of CPT contains codes and code descriptions for surgical procedures performed by physicians. Because procedures can be performed using a variety of methods and different combinations, the Surgery section contains multiple codes that describe similar procedures. The intention is to allow for coding specificity and to accurately reflect the actual procedure performed. The patient's diagnosis and physical status (e.g., normal, healthy patient versus patient with severe systemic disease) guides the physician, who determines whether just one procedure or multiple procedures will be performed during an encounter (e.g., office visit) or operative session (e.g., ambulatory surgery). The documented operative report and other patient record documentation guide the selection of appropriate codes for reporting to third-party payers. The General subsection classifies fine-needle aspiration (FNA) biopsy procedures. The Integumentary subsection classifies procedures performed on the skin, subcutaneous, and accessory structures, nails, and breasts.

 Coding Tip

- Notes located beneath headings and/or subheadings apply to all codes under the heading or subheading. Parenthetical notes located below a specific code apply to that code only, unless the note indicates otherwise.

Overview of Surgery Section

The CPT Surgery section and its subsections are organized anatomically according to major body area and/or organ system. Categories and subcategories are organized within subsections according to type of procedure. Selecting the appropriate surgery code requires a careful review of the patient record to determine the procedures and services provided. Before referring to the CPT index to begin the process of locating a surgery code, review the documented operative report (Figure 12-1) to determine the following:

- Body system (e.g., digestive)
- Anatomical site (e.g., stomach)

EXAMPLE 1: When reporting the CPT code for "excision of cervical stump," if an abdominal approach was documented in the operative report, assign code 57540. If a vaginal approach was documented, assign code 57550.

```
57540   Excision of cervical stump, abdominal approach;
57545   with pelvic floor repair
```

PREOPERATIVE DIAGNOSIS: Possible uterine polyp.

POSTOPERATIVE DIAGNOSIS: Endometrial polyp.

PROCEDURE: Hysteroscopy with biopsy.

The cervix was dilated and hysteroscope was inserted into the uterus and the lining of the uterus and openings of the fallopian tubes were well visualized. One large polyp was noted on the endometrial wall, and a biopsy was taken. The uterus is of normal size and configuration. Biopsy was submitted for pathology examination. Postoperatively the patient is doing well, and she was taken to the recovery room.

Name of procedure
Surgical approach
Anatomical site

FIGURE 12-1 Sample operative report with name of procedure, surgical approach, and anatomical site highlighted to illustrate how to locate information needed to assign CPT code

EXAMPLE 2: When reporting the CPT code for "removal of a 0.5-cm malignant lesion of the arm," if a surgical excision was documented in the operative report, assign code 11600. If a destruction procedure (e.g., laser ablation) was documented, assign code 17260.

11600   Excision, malignant lesion including margins, trunk, arms, or legs; excised diameter 0.5 cm or less

17260   Destruction, malignant lesion (eg, laser surgery, electrosurgery, cryosurgery, chemosurgery, surgical curettement), trunk, arms or legs; lesion diameter 0.5 cm or less

- Surgical approach (e.g., laparotomy)
- Type of procedure performed (e.g., partial gastrectomy)
- Fact that multiple procedures were performed during the same operative session (e.g., gastroscopy followed by exploratory laparotomy and removal of a portion of the stomach)

CPT code descriptions include the procedure performed, but they do not include the numerous activities integral to the procedure. It would be impractical to list every event common to all procedures of a similar nature in the code's narrative description. Many common activities reflect the principles of medical and surgical care, and while considered acceptable medical/surgical practice, they are not coded separately. In addition, although many activities are common to all procedures, some are integral only to certain groups of procedures.

The services integral to the standard practice of medical/surgical services, for which no separate code is assigned, include:

- Cleansing, shaving, and prepping the patient's skin
- Draping and positioning the patient
- Inserting intravenous access for medication
- Administering sedatives (by physician performing procedure)
- Administering local, topical, and/or regional anesthetic (by physician performing procedure)
- Establishing the surgical approach (identifying anatomical landmarks, making the incision, evaluating the surgical field, and performing simple debridement of traumatized tissue)
- Performing lysis of simple adhesions
- Isolating neurovascular, muscular (including stimulation for identification), bony, or other structures that limits access to surgical field

- Taking surgical cultures
- Irrigating wounds
- Inserting and removing drains, suction devices, dressings, and pumps into same site
- Closing the surgical incision
- Applying, managing, and removing postoperative dressings, including analgesic devices (e.g., peri-incisional TENS unit, institution of patient-controlled analgesia)
- Documenting preoperative, intraoperative, and postoperative reports, which includes providing photographs, drawings, dictation, and transcription necessary to document services provided
- Identifying surgical supplies (unless third-party payer policy states that they are separately coded and reimbursable)

EXAMPLE 1: The physician removed cerumen (earwax) impaction prior to performing a myringotomy. The cerumen impaction prevented access to the tympanic membrane, and its removal was necessary for the successful completion of the myringotomy. Report code 69420 (Myringotomy including aspiration and/or eustachian tube inflation) only. *Do not report a separate code for removal of cerumen impaction.*

EXAMPLE 2: The physician performed a bronchoscopy to assess the patient's lung anatomy prior to performing a lobectomy (single lobe). Report code 32480, which has a CPT code description of "removal of lung, other than total pneumonectomy; single lobe (lobectomy)." *Do not report a code for the bronchoscopy*, which was performed as a scout endoscopy to assess the surgical field and to establish anatomical landmarks, extent of disease, and so on. When an endoscopic procedure is done as part of an open procedure, such as a lobectomy, it is not separately coded and reported.

If an endoscopy is performed initially to diagnose the patient on the same day as the open procedure, the endoscopy is separately coded and reported. Modifier -58 is added to the endoscopy code to indicate that the procedures are staged or planned services. Also, if endoscopic procedures are performed on distinct, separate areas during the same operative session, separately code and report each procedure (e.g., thoracoscopy and mediastinoscopy). However, if a cursory (brief) evaluation of the upper airway is done as part of a bronchoscopy, do not separately code and report procedures (e.g., laryngoscopy or sinus endoscopy).

Organization of Surgery Section

The guidelines located at the beginning of the Surgery section apply to all codes in the section. The basic organization of the Surgery section is by major body system, with headings and subheadings based on anatomical site and/or type of procedure (Table 12-1). The Surgery section contains the following subsections, which represent major body areas, organ systems, or other designations:

- General (10004–10021)
- Integumentary System (10030–19499)
- Musculoskeletal System (20100–29999)
- Respiratory System (30000–32999)
- Cardiovascular System (33016–37799)
- Hemic and Lymphatic Systems (38100–38999)
- Mediastinum and Diaphragm (39000–39599)
- Digestive System (40490–49999)
- Urinary System (50010–53899)
- Male Genital System (54000–55899)
- Reproductive System Procedures (55920)
- Intersex Surgery (55970–55980)

TABLE 12-1 Subheadings Typically Organized Below CPT Surgery Subsections

Subheading	Description
Incision	Cut made into body tissue during surgery using a knife, electrosurgical unit, or laser
Incision and Drainage (I&D)	Cutting open a lesion (e.g., abscess) and draining its contents
Excision	Removing a portion or all of an organ or another tissue (e.g., skin), using a scalpel or another surgical instrument
Introduction	Injecting, inserting, or puncturing body tissue or scoping an organ
Removal	Eliminating tissue (e.g., amputating a body part) or taking something out (e.g., removing implants, such as buried wire, pins, or screws)
Endoscopy	Visualizing a body cavity using an instrument that can be inserted into the body through a small incision or a natural opening (e.g., nose) NOTE: An endoscope is also used as a surgical approach for performing other procedures (e.g., laparoscopic cholecystectomy, sigmoidoscopy with removal of polyps)
Repair	Improving improperly functioning body parts; types of repair include: • **Grafts:** Moving healthy tissue from one site to another to replace diseased or defective tissue • **Suture:** Closing a wound using catgut, glue, silk thread, wire, or other materials (Figure 12-2)
Revision	Modifying a previous procedure (e.g., gastric restrictive procedure) or a device (e.g., shunt)
Reconstruction	Rebuilding a body part, such as the breast
Destruction	**Ablation** (or removal) of benign, premalignant, or malignant tissue; types of destruction include: • **Chemosurgery:** Using chemicals to destroy diseased tissue, such as for skin cancer • **Cryosurgery:** Applying extreme cold, such as liquid nitrogen, to destroy abnormal tissue cells, such as warts or small skin lesions • **Electrosurgery:** Using an electrical device, such as electrocautery, to destroy abnormal tissue • **LASER (light amplification by stimulated emission of radiation):** Using a device that is filled with a gas, liquid, or solid substance that is stimulated to emit light to a specific wavelength to burn, cut, or dissolve tissue • **Surgical curettement:** Scraping abnormal tissue
Other Procedures	Unrelated procedures, which include arthrodesis, Mohs micrographic surgery, manipulation (of fractures/dislocations), splinting, or casting

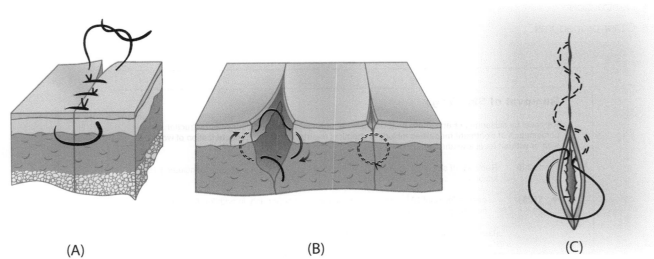

(A)   (B)   (C)

FIGURE 12-2 (A) Simple interrupted sutures (B) Buried sutures (C) Running subcuticular sutures

- Female Genital System (56405–58999)
- Maternity Care and Delivery (59000–59899)
- Endocrine System (60000–60699)
- Nervous System (61000–64999)
- Eye and Ocular Adnexa (65091–68899)
- Auditory System (69000–69979)
- Operating Microscope (69990)

Many of the Surgery subsections contain unique instructions called *notes,* which are located just below the title of the subsection (Figure 12-3), heading, or subheading. Parenthetical notes are located below codes, and they apply to just that code.

> **EXAMPLE:** The note located above code 11200 in the CPT coding manual provides instruction about methods (e.g., scissoring) for removal, which applies to all codes under the heading "Removal of Skin Tags."
>
> The parenthetical note located below code 11201 in the coding manual indicates that code 11201 is reported with 11200, which means that it is never reported as a stand-alone code. This note applies to code 11201 only.

In the Surgery section, procedures are categorized as diagnostic procedures or therapeutic surgical procedures. **Diagnostic procedures** (e.g., arthroscopy, biopsy, and endoscopy) are performed to evaluate the patient's complaints or symptoms and to establish the diagnosis. **Therapeutic surgical procedures** (e.g., removal, repair) are performed to treat specific conditions or injuries; they include the procedure itself and normal, uncomplicated follow-up care.

Surgery section procedures are typically organized according to the following subheadings (below the heading of a subsection). (Some subheadings are not located below each heading, while some headings include additional subheadings, such as fracture and/or dislocation in the Musculoskeletal System subsection.)

- Incision *or* incision and drainage (I&D)
- Excision
- Introduction or removal
- Endoscopy
- Repair, revision, and/or reconstruction
- Destruction
- Other procedures

Removal of Skin Tags

Removal by scissoring or any sharp method, ligature, strangulation, electrosurgical destruction or combination of treatment modalities including chemical destruction or electrocauterization of wound, with or without local anesthesia.

11200	Removal of skin tags, multiple fibrocutaneous tags, any area; up to and including 15 lesions
+ 11201	each additional 10 lesions, or part thereof (List separately in addition to code for primary procedure)
	(Use 11201 in conjunction with 11200)

FIGURE 12-3 Sample note in CPT

Exercise 12.1 – Overview of Surgery Section

Instructions: Complete each statement.

1. The organization of the CPT Surgery section is according to _____.
2. Endoscopy, arthroscopy, and biopsy are considered _____ procedures.
3. Gastric resection and knee replacement surgeries are considered _____ procedures.
4. The patient underwent cystourethroscopy with biopsy of urinary bladder wall. Identify the following:
   a. Body system: _____
   b. Anatomical site: _____
   c. Surgical approach: _____
   d. Type of procedure performed: _____
   e. Name of the procedure: _____
   f. Code number assigned: _____
5. The physician performed lysis of adhesions, exploratory laparotomy, and partial colon resection with end-to-end anastomosis. Identify the following:
   a. Body system: _____
   b. Anatomical site: _____
   c. Surgical approach: _____
   d. Type of procedure performed: _____
   e. Name of the procedure: _____
   f. Code number assigned: _____

Surgery Guidelines

Guidelines located at the beginning of the CPT Surgery section clarify the assignment of codes and explain terms. Surgery guidelines include the following:

- Services
- CPT surgical package definition
- Follow-up care for diagnostic procedures
- Follow-up care for therapeutic surgical procedures
- Supplied materials
- Reporting more than one procedure/service
- Separate procedure
- Unlisted service or procedure
- Special report
- Imaging guidance
- Surgical destruction

Services

Codes for services that are provided in the office, patient's home, hospital, and other health care facilities are located in the Evaluation and Management (E/M) section of the CPT. This section also includes codes for consultations and other medical services. Codes for special services and reports are located in the CPT Medicine section.

CPT Surgical Package Definition

Many services performed are integral to the standard of medical/surgical services, such as the cleansing, shaving, and prepping of skin and the insertion of intravenous access for medication. The CPT **surgical package** usually includes the following services, in addition to the surgical procedure:

- Local infiltration, metacarpal/metatarsal/digital block, or topical anesthesia
- One related E/M service following the decision for surgery, which includes the history and physical, on the date of procedure or immediately prior to performance of the procedure
- Immediate postoperative care, which includes dictating the operative report and talking with the family and other physicians or qualified health care professionals
- Documentation of postoperative physician orders
- Evaluation of the patient in the postanesthesia recovery area
- Typical postoperative follow-up care (e.g., removal of sutures)

 NOTE:

- When reporting a CPT surgery code, surgical package services are included in that code. They are not separately coded and reported.
- Medicare administrative contractors use software that contains prepayment edits to detect the separate billing of services included in the global package.
- When E/M codes are reported for services provided during a global period and a modifier is not added to the code to indicate special circumstances, the claims are denied.

In 1992, the Centers for Medicare & Medicaid Services (CMS) established a national definition for a **global surgical package** (that differs from the definition of the CPT *surgical package*) to ensure that payments are made consistently for the same services across all Medicare administrative contractor jurisdictions. The *global surgical package* definition prevents Medicare payments for services that are more or less comprehensive than intended. The CMS global surgical package includes the surgical procedure and a standard package of preoperative, intraoperative, and postoperative services. In addition, CMS categorizes surgeries as major or minor, and it establishes a postoperative **global period** (0, 10, or 90 days) (Figure 12-4) for each surgical procedure, which includes the following policies:

- The global period for major surgery is 0, 10, or 90 days.
- The global period begins the day following surgery.
- The global period includes a one-day preoperative period.

CPT Code	Brief Description	Global Period
59050	Fetal monitoring with report	XXX
59160	Dilatation and curettage after delivery	010
59200	Insertion of cervical dilator	000
59400	Obstetrical care	MMM
59525	Removal of uterus after cesarean section	ZZZ
59812	Treatment of miscarriage	090
59899	Maternity care procedure	YYY

FIGURE 12-4 Sample of CMS global periods

EXAMPLE: To determine the global period for major surgeries, count the day before the day of surgery, the day of surgery, and the 90 days immediately following the day of surgery. For a date of surgery on January 1, the

- Preoperative day is December 31
- Last day of the 90-day postoperative period is April 1

To arrive at April 1, count January 2–31 as 30 days, February 1–28 as 28 days, March 1–31 as 31 days, and April 1 as 1 day, for a total of 90 days *after the day of surgery.*

- The global period for minor surgery (e.g., endoscopies) is zero or 10 days, and physician visits on the day of a minor surgical procedure or endoscopy are included in reimbursement for the procedure.
- The zero-day global period includes the day of surgery only.

EXAMPLE: To determine the zero-day global period for a minor surgical procedure, count the day of surgery only. For a date of surgery on March 5, the last day of the postoperative period is also March 5.

- The 10-day global period includes the day of surgery and the 10 days that immediately follow the day of surgery.

EXAMPLE: To determine the 10-day global period for a minor surgical procedure, count the day of surgery and the appropriate number of days immediately following the date of surgery. For a date of surgery on March 5, the last day of the postoperative period is March 15.

CMS publishes a list of the global periods (Figure 12-4) for each CPT code in the *Federal Register.* That list also includes the following alphabetical codes in the global period column:

- MMM: Global period policy does not apply; describes services furnished in uncomplicated maternity cases, including antepartum care, delivery, and postpartum care.
- XXX: Global period policy does not apply.
- YYY: Global period is established by each Medicare administrative contract (e.g., unlisted surgery codes).
- ZZZ: CPT code is related to another service provided, which is always included in the global period of the other service.

 NOTE:

When a patient receives treatment for an unrelated condition during the global period, add modifier -24 to the CPT code for an E/M service or add modifier -79 to the CPT code for a surgical procedure/service.

Instructions for the CMS's global surgical package describe the components of a global surgical package and payment rules for minor surgeries, endoscopies, and global surgical packages that are split between physicians. In addition to the global surgical package policy, other payment policies and claims processing requirements were established for other surgical issues, including bilateral and multiple surgeries. The CMS global surgical package includes the following:

- Preoperative services (visits after the decision is made to operate)
- The day before the day of surgery for major procedures
- The day of surgery for minor procedures
- Intraoperative services (includes the operation and all usual and necessary parts of a surgical procedure, such as wound irrigation, insertion and removal of drains, surgical closure, and application and/or removal of postoperative dressings)
- Treatment of complications following surgery (additional services provided by the surgeon during the postoperative period because of the development of complications that do not require additional trips to the operating room)

- Postoperative visits (follow-up visits during the postoperative period that are related to recovery from surgery)
- Postsurgical pain management (provided by the surgeon)
- Miscellaneous services (e.g., dressing changes; local incisional care; removal of operative packing; removal of sutures and staples, tubes, drains, and casts; insertion or removal of urinary catheters and/or nasogastric tubes)

The CMS global surgical package does *not* include the following:

- Initial consultation or evaluation services by the surgeon to determine need for major surgery

 NOTE:

For *minor surgery*, the initial consultation or evaluation services by the surgeon *is included* in the global surgical package.

- Visits unrelated to the diagnosis for which a surgical procedure is performed
- Services provided by other physicians, except when the physicians agree on transfer of care
- Diagnostic tests and procedures, including diagnostic radiological procedures
- Clearly distinct surgical procedures during the postoperative period that are *not* for treatment of complications or procedures done in "stages" (e.g., two or more parts of a procedure planned at the time of the first procedure to occur at a time after the initial surgery, such as a mastectomy, and insertion of a prosthesis during the postoperative global period)
- Treatment for postoperative complications that require a return trip to the operating room
- A required, more extensive procedure when a less extensive procedure fails; in this case, the second procedure is payable separately

It is important to understand that the procedure being performed determines the global follow-up care; the condition being treated does not. The global surgical packages deal with the procedure(s) performed during the global period by the operating surgeon; only the operating surgeon is associated with that particular global period of follow-up care.

EXAMPLE: A patient underwent ventral hernia repair performed by a general surgeon and one week later fractured her ankle. An orthopedic surgeon inserted a pin to repair the fractured ankle. A global follow-up period for the specific surgery performed is associated with the CPT code assigned by each physician. Thus, each physician receives appropriate reimbursement for services provided.

When the patient is seen by the general surgeon for follow-up care related to the ventral hernia repair and such care is provided within the global period, an E/M code for services provided is *not* reported. Payment for such follow-up care is bundled in the CPT code reported for the ventral hernia repair surgery. Likewise, when the patient is seen by the orthopedic surgeon for follow-up care related to the ankle surgery, E/M services are bundled in the CPT code reported for that surgery.

If the patient develops complications subsequent to surgery and receives E/M services within the global period, the respective surgeon should report a CPT code for services provided to receive reimbursement from the third-party payer.

E/M services provided as follow-up to a surgical procedure are included in the reimbursement amount for the surgery, and codes for follow-up E/M services are not reported separately. However, when the patient receives E/M services for an unrelated condition, make sure you report an E/M code to receive reimbursement for services provided.

EXAMPLE: An excision of a malignant lesion on the left arm is performed in the office on May 10. The postoperative global period for code 11606 is 10 days. The patient returns to the office on May 15 and is treated for conjunctivitis. The physician should report an appropriate E/M code and add modifier -24 (Unrelated Evaluation and Management Service by the Same Physician During a Postoperative Period) (e.g., 99213-24).

When an E/M service provided is for the purpose of deciding to perform a major surgical procedure, the E/M service is considered a significant, separately identifiable service. Report an appropriate E/M code and add modifier -57 (decision for surgery) (e.g., 99214-57).

> **EXAMPLE:** A surgeon provided level 5 consultation services to a patient in the office to determine whether surgery was necessary due to complaints of severe abdominal pain. After evaluation, the ambulance is called and the patient is transported to the hospital, where the surgeon performs an emergency gastrotomy with suture repair of a bleeding ulcer. Report code 43501 (Gastrotomy; with suture repair of bleeding ulcer) and 99245-57 (Office consultation for new or established patient, level 5).

Local Infiltration, Metacarpal/Metatarsal/Digital Block, or Topical Anesthesia

Local infiltration, metacarpal/metatarsal/digital block, or topical anesthesia, when provided by the physician performing the procedure, is considered part of the procedure. When the surgeon provides general anesthesia, regional anesthesia, or monitored anesthesia care, add modifier -47 to the surgery code.

NOTE:

When a physician other than the surgeon (e.g., anesthesiologist) provides general anesthesia, regional anesthesia, or monitored anesthesia care, the other physician reports an anesthesia code for services provided. (Refer to Chapter 11 of this textbook for anesthesia coding rules.)

> **EXAMPLE:** A surgeon injected a local anesthetic in preparation for performing an inguinal hernia repair on a 42-year-old patient. The local anesthetic procedure performed by the surgeon is included in the surgical procedure and is not separately coded and reported.

Moderate (conscious) sedation is moderate sedation or analgesia that results in a drug-induced depression of consciousness.

> **EXAMPLE:** A surgeon placed radiotherapy afterloading brachytherapy catheters into the breast for interstitial radioelement following a partial mastectomy, including imaging guidance. The 67-year-old patient required the administration of 30 minutes of moderate (conscious) sedation during the procedure. An independent trained observer monitored the patient's sedation. Report codes 19298, 99156, and 99157.

The management of postoperative pain by the surgeon, including epidural drug administration, is included in the global package with the operative procedure.

Follow-Up Care for Diagnostic Procedures

Diagnostic procedures are performed to evaluate a patient's condition, to determine the nature of a condition, and to distinguish between one disease and another. According to CPT, follow-up care for diagnostic procedures includes only that care related to recovery from the diagnostic procedure itself. Codes for services provided should be reported when a physician treats

- The patient's condition for which the diagnostic procedure was performed
- Other conditions that are not related to the reason for performing the diagnostic procedure

When a patient receives services from the physician who performed the diagnostic procedure and those services are in follow-up to the procedure performed (e.g., suture removal or dressing change), do not report a code for services provided.

Follow-Up Care for Therapeutic Surgical Procedures

Therapeutic surgical procedures are performed for the definitive treatment of a disease or condition rather than for diagnostic or investigative purposes. Follow-up care for therapeutic surgical procedures includes only the care that is typically considered part of the surgical service. The physician generally sees the patient several times as part of normal, uncomplicated follow-up care (e.g., remove sutures, evaluate the results of the surgery, or check for complications). These postoperative visits are included as part of surgery's global period because normal follow-up care services are a necessary component of the surgical process.

Codes for services provided should be reported when a physician treats the following during the postoperative global period:

- Complications (e.g., postoperative wound infection)
- Exacerbations (e.g., macular degeneration that was treated, but worsens, requiring another treatment)
- Recurrence (e.g., return of cancer)
- Presence of other diseases (e.g., appendicitis during global period for gastric resection)
- Injuries (e.g., fracture resulting from car accident)

Supplied Materials

Supplies commonly included in surgical packages (e.g., dressings, tubing, and Steri-Strips) are not coded separately. *Only those supplies and materials provided by the physician over and above the supplies usually included with the procedure rendered are reported separately.* Assign code 99070 to report these supplies or assign specific HCPCS level II national codes for such supplies or drugs.

The CPT Surgery section guidelines do not identify procedures codes for which it is appropriate to report supply items (e.g., surgical trays) separately. Reimbursement of supplies and materials required to perform the procedure is a specific reimbursement issue, which varies from one third-party payer to another. CMS created specific instructions regarding the separate reporting of "supply" items. With the full implementation of the practice expense component of the Medicare Fee Schedule, all supplies, such as surgical trays, are included (e.g., bundled) in the payment for the procedure; Medicare does *not* reimburse the physician for this code. Some non-Medicare payers may still use it; others may alternatively allow CPT code 99070, Supplies and materials (except spectacles), provided by the physician over and above those usually included with the office visit or other services rendered (list drugs, trays, supplies, or materials provided) instead.

> **EXAMPLE:** A patient underwent a repair of recurrent strangulated abdominal incisional hernia with implantation of mesh. Report code 49566 (Repair recurrent incisional or ventral hernia; incarcerated or strangulated), 49568 (Implantation of mesh or other prosthesis for incisional or venetral hernia repair), and HCPCS level II code C1781 (supply of mesh). (Do not add modifier -51 to code 49568 or C1781 because they are exempt from that modifier.)

Reporting More Than One Procedure/Service

When a physician performs more than one procedure or service on the same date, during the same operative session, or during a postoperative period and the surgical package concept applies, report one or more CPT modifiers to receive reimbursement consideration from third-party payers.

 NOTE:

> Refer to Table 9-2 in this text for a comprehensive list of modifiers, descriptions, and examples (including modifiers used for reporting more than one procedure/service).

Add-on Codes

CPT includes a ✚ (plus) symbol next to add-on codes that describe a service that can be reported only in addition to a primary procedure. Add-on codes can also be identified by specific language in the code descriptor, such as *each additional* or *(List separately in addition to primary procedure)*. Add-on codes are never reported as stand-alone codes because they are considered an integral part of another procedure. They are never reported alone because the procedures they describe would not be performed unless another primary procedure was performed.

Add-on codes allow physicians to separately report procedures and services performed in addition to the primary procedure. The key to identifying add-on codes is determining whether the code always has to be reported with another code. If that is the case, the code is considered an add-on code. Also, add-on codes are exempt from the bilaterial procedure and the multiple procedure concept, respectively, which means -50 and -51 are not added. (Add-on codes are reported twice for bilateral procedures.)

> **EXAMPLE:** A patient underwent open treatment of three lumbar vertebral fractures. Report codes 22325, 22328, and 22328.
>
> The description for code 22325 includes "one fractured vertebra," and the description for code 22328 states "each additional fractured vertebrae . . . (List separately in addition to code for primary procedure)." This patient underwent treatment for three vertebral fractures, which requires the reporting of three codes. (Do not add modifier -51 to the 22328 codes because they are exempt from that modifier.)

Separate Procedure

CPT code descriptions that contain the term **separate procedure** in parentheses are commonly performed as an integral component of a comprehensive service or procedure. When the comprehensive procedure or service is performed, do not report as an additional procedure the code that contains the term *(separate procedure)* in its code description.

> **EXAMPLE:** The patient underwent sesamoidectomy and excision of a bone cyst of the middle phalanx of the right hand. Report code 26210.
>
> Do not mistakenly report code 26185 in addition to code 26210. Code 26185 contains the term *(separate procedure)* in its code description. The procedure described in code 26185 is a component part of the more comprehensive "excision of bone cyst" procedure.

When a procedure or service that contains *(separate procedure)* in its code description *is performed independently of or is considered unrelated to or distinct from other procedures performed during the same operative session, report the separate procedure code in addition to codes for other procedures (or services).*

Reporting separate procedure codes may be necessary to classify the following:

- Procedure performed during a different session or patient encounter, procedure or surgery, site, or organ system
- Procedure performed through a separate incision or excision
- Separate lesion excised during the same operative session as removal of another lesion
- Treatment of a separate injury (or area of injury for extensive injuries)

Add modifier -59 to the separate procedure code to indicate that the procedure is not considered a component of another procedure, but is a distinct, independent procedure.

> **EXAMPLE:** A patient underwent a complete salpingo-oophorectomy, bilateral, during the same operative session as a total abdominal hysterectomy. Report code 58150, Total abdominal hysterectomy (corpus and cervix), with or without removal of tube(s), with or without removal of ovary(s). Do not report code 58720, Salpingo-oophorectomy, complete or partial, unilateral or bilateral (separate procedure), because it is considered an integral component of the procedures described for code 58150.

Unlisted Service or Procedure

CPT unlisted service or procedure codes are assigned when no specific code accurately describes the procedure performed. When reporting an unlisted procedure code on an insurance claim, make sure you include a written report (e.g., copy of operative report) that describes the procedure(s) performed. (During the first year that laparoscopic appendectomies and cholecystectomies were performed, no procedure codes were included in CPT. Unlisted procedure codes were reported.)

EXAMPLE: A physician performs a pressure ulcer excision using a technique that is not described by any existing pressure ulcer codes. Report code 15999, and include a copy of the operative report with the claim.

Special Report

When an unlisted procedure code is reported to a third-party payer, attach a special report that describes the procedure performed. Special reports may also be required for procedures and services that are rarely provided, unusual, or new (to establish medical necessity). As a minimum, to document a special report, include the following:

- Adequate description of the nature, extent, and need for the procedure
- Time, effort, and equipment necessary to provide the procedure or service

The following additional items may also be documented in a special report:

- Complexity of symptoms
- Concurrent problems
- Diagnostic and therapeutic procedures

- Final diagnosis
- Follow-up care
- Pertinent physical findings (e.g., location, number, and size of lesions)

EXAMPLE: An ear, nose, and throat specialist performed an experimental procedure on the pharynx of a 14-year-old prodigy opera singer to treat persistent pharyngitis that has not resolved with traditional medical treatment. Conventional procedures to treat the unusual condition are not an option for this patient because they pose too great a risk of damage to the patient's vocal cords. The procedure was approved by the patient's parents, the health care facility at which it was performed, and the third-party payer that will reimburse its costs. Because the procedure is experimental, no CPT code is available. Report 42999, and attach a copy of the transcribed operative report to the claim. The operative report is the "special report" required by the payer to process the claim for reimbursement.

Imaging Guidance

When imaging guidance or imaging supervision and interpretation is performed with a surgical procedure and included in the Surgery code description, the Radiology guidelines apply. Imaging guidance is not reported when nonimaging-guided tracking and localizing systems (e.g., electromagnetic signals) are used. Imaging guidance is reported when an imaging modality (e.g., radiography) is documented as used.

EXAMPLE: Percutaneous breast biopsy, left, with placement of breast clip and imaging of biopsy specimen, including stereotactic guidance. Report code 19081. (Stereotactic guidance is included in code 19081, and a separate Radiology code is *not* reported.)

Surgical Destruction

Surgical destruction is considered part of a surgical procedure, and different methods of destruction are not reported separately unless the technique substantially differs from the standard management of a problem or condition. (CPT codes are available for exceptions due to special circumstances.) Surgical destruction includes the ablation (or removal) of tissues by any method, including chemical treatment, cryosurgery, electrosurgery, or laser.

EXAMPLE: A physician performed argon laser treatments on a patient with a congenital port wine stain. Report code 17106.

Exercise 12.2 – Surgery Guidelines

Instructions: Indicate whether each statement is true (T) or false (F).

_____   1. When services performed are integral to the standard of medical/surgical services, they are coded and reported separately.

_____   2. The CPT surgical package includes typical postoperative follow-up care in addition to the surgical procedure.

_____   3. CMS categorizes surgeries as major or minor, and it establishes a postoperative global period of 0, 10, or 90 days.

_____   4. The CMS global surgical package includes preoperative visits before the decision is made to operate.

_____   5. Visits unrelated to postoperative follow-up for a surgical procedure are included in CMS's global surgical package.

_____   6. It is inappropriate for a physician to report a code for conscious sedation with the surgical service-described CPT code 19298.

_____   7. A diagnostic esophagogastroduodenoscopy was performed to rule out gastric ulcer disease. The findings confirmed the diagnosis, and the physician prescribed medication. The patient was seen in the physician's office one week later for a follow-up visit to determine whether the patient's symptoms had been alleviated by medication. The patient was still experiencing acute pain, and the physician increased the medication dosage. The patient was scheduled for a two-week follow-up visit. The evaluation and management code for the follow-up visit during which the physician increased the dosage of the patient's medication is reported separately.

_____   8. Health care services that are provided above and beyond the original surgical procedure are included in follow-up care for therapeutic procedures.

_____   9. A physician applied sterile dressings after repairing a laceration. The sterile dressings are not separately coded and reported.

_____   10. The patient underwent esophageal dilation for esophageal stricture (43450); next, during the same operative session, the patient also underwent esophagoscopy (43200) to investigate the cause of the esophageal stricture. Upon review of both codes, the physician should report 43450 and 43200-59.

Instructions: Complete each statement.

11. The global period for a minor surgical procedure performed on March 15 is zero days. The last day of the postoperative period is _____.

12. The global period for a minor surgical procedure performed on October 4 is 10 days. The last day of the postoperative period is _____.

13. A surgeon performed an incision and drainage of an abscess in the office. The patient developed an infection of the surgical site that required a return visit within 3 days to the surgeon's office. Which CPT modifier is reported with the E/M visit? _____

14. A surgeon provided level 4 E/M services to a patient in the office, which resulted in the decision for surgery. The physician reports the E/M code adds modifier _____.

15. A physician performed surgery on a patient to destroy 25 lesions. Review the description for code 17004. How many times should code 17004 be reported? _____

General Subsection

The General subsection contains one heading, *Fine Needle Aspiration (FNA) Biopsy*. **Fine-needle aspiration (FNA)** involves the removal of fluid from a cyst or cells from a solid mass. Then the cells are examined cytologically. FNA is a percutaneous procedure that is performed with or without imaging guidance. If the cyst or mass is *not* palpable on physical exam, the procedure is typically performed under imaging guidance using fluoroscopy, ultrasound, or computed tomography (CT).

> **EXAMPLE 1:** A physician aspirates a cyst, without imaging guidance, using FNA technique. Report code 10021.

> **EXAMPLE 2:** A patient presents with a thyroid nodule. Using CT guidance with radiological supervision and interpretation, an FNA is performed on the thyroid nodule; the material is sent for cytologic review. In addition to code 10009, report code 77012 (Computed tomography guidance for needle placement [e.g., biopsy, aspiration, injection, localization device], radiological supervision and interpretation). (Directional modifiers, such as -LT and -RT, are not added to codes in CPT's General subsection.)

Exercise 12.3 – General Subsection

Instructions: Assign the CPT code(s) and appropriate modifier(s) to each statement.

1. A patient presents with a palpable left breast mass for which fine-needle aspiration biopsy is performed.

   _____

2. A patient has a nonpalpable right breast mass that was identified on a previous screening mammogram. Ultrasound exam at that time revealed that the mass is not a simple cyst. Fine-needle aspiration biopsy of the right breast mass is performed under ultrasonic guidance during today's encounter.

   _____

Integumentary System Subsection

The Integumentary System subsection includes dermatological procedures, plastic surgery, and components of multiple surgical procedures (e.g., closure, flaps, grafts, and tissue transfer). Integumentary procedures (Table 12-2) are often performed as staged procedures (e.g., flaps and grafts) due to the complexity of services rendered. Integumentary procedures include incision, biopsy, removal, paring/curettement, shaving, destruction, excision, repair, adjacent tissue rearrangement, grafts, flaps, and specialized services (e.g., burn management, Mohs micrographic surgery). (Refer to the definitions of surgical terms earlier in this chapter. Additional terms are defined in Table 12-2.)

The CPT Surgery Integumentary subsection contains the following headings:

- Skin, Subcutaneous and Accessory Structures
- Nails
- Pilonidal Cyst
- Introduction
- Repair (Closure)
- Destruction
- Breast

Coding Tip

- Do not add HCPCS level II modifiers -LT and -RT to codes in the Skin, Subcutaneous and Accessory Structures; Nails; Pilonidal Cyst; Introduction; Repair (Closure); or Destruction headings—the skin is not a paired organ.
- Add modifiers -50, -LT, or -RT to codes in the Breast heading.
- Add HCPCS level II modifiers -FA through -F9 or -TA through -T9 to codes for procedures performed on the fingernails or toenails.

TABLE 12-2 Integumentary Procedures and Definitions

Integumentary Procedure	Definition
Adjacent tissue transfer/ rearrangement	Closure of defects by relocating a flap of adjacent normal, healthy tissue from a donor site to a nearby (adjacent) defect, such as a traumatic skin wound or the site of excised lesion; a portion of the flap remains intact to provide a blood supply to the grafted site
Biopsy	Removal and examination of tissue to establish a diagnosis, confirm a diagnosis, or determine the extent of a disease; types of skin biopsies include incisional, punch, and tangential (e.g., shaving)
Flap	Relocation of a mass of tissue (usually skin) that has been partially removed from one part of the body so that it retains its own blood supply
Graft	Any tissue or organ used for implantation or transplant
Mohs microsurgery	Technique of excising skin tumors by removing tumor tissue layer by layer, examining the removed portion microscopically for malignant cells, and repeating the procedure until the entire tumor is removed
Paring and curettement	Removal of growths or other material from the wall of a cavity or another surface, as with a curette; paring of lesions (e.g., corns and calluses) seldom, if ever, require local anesthesia
Shaving	Horizontal slicing to remove epidermal and dermal lesions (e.g., without a full-thickness dermal excision); removal includes scissoring or any sharp method

Skin, Subcutaneous and Accessory Structures

The Skin, Subcutaneous and Accessory Structures heading includes the following subheadings: Introduction and Removal, Incision and Drainage (I&D), Debridement, Paring or Cutting, Biopsy, Removal of Skin Tags, Shaving of Epidermal or Dermal Lesions, Excision—Benign Lesions, and Excision—Malignant Lesions.

Introduction and Removal

The *Introduction and Removal* heading includes a code for percutaneous image-guided fluid collection drainage via catheter of soft tissue abscesses, hematomas, seromas, lymphoceles, and cysts.

Incision and Drainage (I&D)

The I&D subheading contains procedures that establish a drainage pathway for fluid that forms at sites of infection. CPT I&D procedures include cutaneous and subcutaneous drainage of cysts, fluid collections, infections, hematomas, pustules, and seromas. When a procedure to excise a lesion results in drainage of an area, either as a part of the procedure or as a way to gain access to the lesion, do not report a code for I&D if the excision or another procedure is performed during the same operative session. It is also inappropriate to report a separate code for an I&D of a hematoma if it is performed during the same operative session as excision, repair, destruction, removal, and so on.

EXAMPLE: A patient undergoes a scheduled procedure to treat a **pilonidal cyst** (entrapped epithelial tissue and hair located in the sacral area at the top of the crease between the buttocks, which can become infected). Treatment options include simple I&D (10080–10081), excision (11770–11772), or a combination of both *if extensive cellulitis is present.*

During simple I&D of a pilonidal cyst, if the provider encounters **extensive cellulitis** (acute inflammation of skin's connective tissue that is caused by infection with bacteria) and the excision of the pilonidal cyst cannot be performed, the provider will prescribe an antibiotic. CPT codes also describe procedures necessary to address complications. Such codes are *not* reported with codes for the original surgery that resulted in the complication. If the original surgery code is reported with the procedure to treat the complication, National Correct Coding Initiative (NCCI) edits will deny reimbursement for the procedure performed to treat the complication.

EXAMPLE: A patient who underwent a thoracotomy developed a surgical wound infection, which required I&D. Report code 10180-78 for I&D of the (skin) wound infection.

Exercise 12.4 – Incision and Drainage

Instructions: Assign the CPT code(s) and any appropriate modifier(s) to each statement.

1. Complex incision and drainage, postoperative wound infection.

   _____

2. Incision and drainage of hematoma, skin.

   _____

3. Incision and removal of foreign body, subcutaneous tissue.

   _____

4. Marsupialization acne surgery.

   _____

5. Simple incision and drainage of five infected cysts.

   _____

Lesion Removal

Lesion removal is coded in CPT by referencing the following subheadings:

- Excision—Debridement
- Paring or Cutting
- Biopsy
- Removal of Skin Tags
- Shaving of Epidermal or Dermal Lesions
- Excision—Benign Lesions
- Excision—Malignant Lesions

A skin lesion (Figure 12-5) is a pathologic change in tissue (e.g., benign or malignant). To accurately code the removal of lesions, review the patient record to locate the following information:

- Method of removing the lesion (e.g., paring, shaving, or debridement)
- Malignant or benign status of lesion if excision method is performed
- Site or body part where lesion is located
- Size of the lesion in centimeters (Figure 12-6)
- Type of wound closure/repair (e.g., simple, intermediate, or complex)

Bulla: (Large blister)
Same as a vesicle only greater than 10 mm
Example:
Contact dermatitis, large second-degree burns, bulbous impetigo, pemphigus

Macule:
Localized changes in skin color of less than 1 cm in diameter
Example:
Freckle

Nodule:
Solid and elevated; however, they extend deeper than papules into the dermis or subcutaneous tissues, greater than 10 mm
Example:
Lipoma, erythema, cyst, wart

Papule:
Solid, elevated lesion less than 1 cm in diameter
Example:
Elevated nevi

Pustule:
Vesicles or bullae that become filled with pus, usually described as less than 0.5 cm in diameter
Example:
Acne, impetigo, furuncles, carbuncles

Ulcer:
A depressed lesion of the epidermis and upper papillary layer of the dermis
Example:
Stage 2 pressure ulcer

Tumor:
The same as a nodule only greater than 2 cm

Example:
Benign epidermal tumor, basal cell carcinoma

Vesicle: (Small blister)
Accumulation of fluid between the upper layers of the skin; elevated mass containing serous fluid; less than 10 mm
Example:
Herpes simplex, herpes zoster, chickenpox

Urticaria, Hives:
Localized edema in the epidermis causing irregular elevation that may be red or pale, may be itchy
Example:
Insect bite, wheal

FIGURE 12-5 Skin lesions

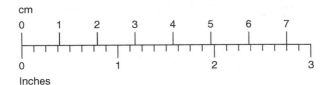

FIGURE 12-6 Lesions are measured in centimeters.
(Note: 2.5 centimeters equals 1 inch.)

NOTE:

- To calculate the size of a lesion, refer to "excised diameter" notes located in CPT Surgery (above the Excision—Benign Lesions heading in the Integumentary System subsection). The "excised diameter" includes the size of the lesion plus its margins.

- Documentation of the "excised diameter" should include dimensions for the greatest size (diameter) of the lesion as well as for the margin around the lesion. *When multiple lesions are removed, do not add together the greatest size (or diameter) of each separate lesion even when excised in one ellipse.*

- The margin is the amount of surrounding tissue that must be removed to adequately excise the lesion, and it is calculated as the shortest distance from the lesion to the edge of the skin ellipse.
  ○ An ellipse is a shape resembling an oval.
  ○ The narrowest amount of tissue removed from each end of the ellipse is measured and used to calculate the "excised diameter" of the lesion.
  ○ When multiple lesions are excised using one ellipse, the narrowest margin between lesions is measured and used *in addition to measurements of each end of the ellipse* to calculate the "excised diameter" of the lesion.

> **EXAMPLE 1:** A 2-cm × 1-cm benign lesion of the cheek was excised in an elliptical fashion with 2-mm margins in all directions. Simple closure was performed. The "excised diameter" is calculated as 2.4 cm because
> - The greatest size (or diameter) of the lesion is 2 cm.
> - The narrowest margin of each end of the ellipse is 2 mm (or 0.2 cm), calculated as 0.2 cm × 2 = 0.4 cm.
> - 2 cm + 0.4 cm = 2.4-cm "excised diameter."
>
> Report CPT code 11443. (Do not report a separate code for the simple closure procedure.)

> **EXAMPLE 2:** One elliptical excision was made to remove two nevi from each of the patient's arms. Lesion A was 3 cm in diameter, and lesion B was 2 cm in diameter. Skin margins were 4 mm at each end of the ellipse, and 2 mm between the two lesions. Simple closure was performed. The "excised diameter" of lesion A is 3.5 cm and lesion B is 2.5 cm because
> - The greatest size (or diameter) of each lesion is 3 cm and 2 cm, respectively. Do not add together the greatest size (or diameter) of separate lesions even when excised in one ellipse.
> - The narrowest margin of each end of the ellipse is 4 mm (or 0.4 cm). Thus, associate 0.4 cm with each lesion.
> - The narrowest margin between the lesions is 2 mm (or 0.2 cm). Thus, associate 0.1 cm (half of 0.2 cm) with each lesion.
> - 3 cm + 0.4 cm + 0.1 cm = 3.5-cm "excised diameter" of lesion A.
> - 2 cm + 0.4 cm + 0.1 cm = 2.5-cm "excised diameter" of lesion B.
>
> Report CPT code 11404 for lesion A and 11403-51 for lesion B. (Do not report a separate code for the simple closure procedure. Do not add modifiers -LT or -RT because the codes' descriptions include anatomic structures that are not paired, such as trunk.)

From a coding perspective, benign lesions include neoplasms, fibrous cysts, or other inflammatory cystic lesions. Malignant lesions are typically described as melanoma, basal cell carcinoma, or squamous cell carcinoma. When surgery is performed on a lesion, select the appropriate code according to the lesion's "excised diameter," which includes the lesion plus its margins. (Do not refer to the pathology report for the diameter because placing a lesion in formalin, the formaldehyde solution used to preserve organic specimens, can result in shrinkage.)

> **EXAMPLE:** A malignant lesion of the nose measuring 1.0 cm in diameter is excised, and the operative report states that skin margins are 1.1 cm. The "excised diameter" of the lesion is 2.1 cm (1.0 + 1.1 = 2.1). Therefore, report code 11643 (Excision, malignant lesion including margins, face, ears, eyelids, nose, lips; excised diameter 2.1 to 3.0 cm).

NOTE:

If an operative report describes the diameter of a lesion as having multiple sides, select the largest size as the diameter (e.g., a lesion described as 2 cm × 3 cm × 5 cm is 5 cm in diameter).

Just one type of removal is reported for each lesion, whether it is destruction (e.g., laser or freezing), debridement, paring, curettement, shaving, or excision. CPT notes describe the nature of each of these forms of removal.

When multiple methods are used to remove one lesion, report a code for just one destruction method. *When multiple distinct lesions are removed using different methods*, report a code for each lesion removal and attach modifier -59 to each code. Modifier -59 indicates different site, different method, or different type of lesion (e.g., benign versus malignant). Make sure the provider has documented the distinct locations of each lesion in the patient's record.

The biopsy of a lesion involves the partial removal of a lesion, and it is frequently performed at the same time as the removal of the entire lesion to obtain a pathologic specimen. The lesion biopsy is performed first, the tissue is submitted to pathology for evaluation and pathologic diagnosis, and then the lesion is completely removed. When a lesion biopsy is performed as part of a lesion removal, it is considered part of the total procedure and is not assigned a separate code. Types of skin biopsies include incisional, punch, and tangential (e.g., shaving) methods. Report only the CPT code for removal of the lesion.

Lesion removal by any method may require simple, intermediate, or complex closure; it is also possible that a tissue transfer procedure will have to be performed. When the lesion removal requires bandaging, strip closure, or simple closure, the closure is included in the lesion excision and is not coded and reported separately. A **simple repair**, or **simple closure** (also called one-layer closure, nonlayered closure, and single-layer closure), involves the use of staples, sutures, and/or tissue adhesives to repair superficial wounds involving epidermis, dermis, and/or subcutaneous tissues.

Simple repair procedures are considered integral to lesion removal. Intermediate and complex repair (closure), when medically necessary, is coded separately. (For Mohs micrographic surgery, all necessary repairs are coded and reported separately.)

Coding Tip

- When a benign or malignant lesion is excised and complex closure is performed during the same operative session, two codes are reported.
  - Excision of benign or malignant lesion
  - Complex closure
- However, when a scar is excised followed by complex closure, report the complex repair code only.
- When multiple lesions are excised during the same operative session, report a code for the excision of each lesion.
- When a malignant lesion is excised and the patient returns for further excision to ensure that the malignancy has been completely resected, report a code for excision of a malignant lesion (adding modifier -58 if surgery was performed within the global surgery period) (even if the pathology report documents no residual malignancy).

Refer to the following table when assigning codes for excision of benign or malignant lesions that require wound repair (closure). When using the table to assign codes, it is important to note that

- When multiple lesions are excised during the same operative session, the number of excision codes must be increased accordingly.
- When intermediate or complex repair (closure) is performed to repair defects resulting from excision of multiple lesions, codes are grouped according to the same anatomical sites.

Type of Procedure	# of Codes	Types of Codes
Simple repair	1	Excision
Intermediate repair	2	Excision Intermediate repair
Complex repair	2	Excision Complex repair

Exercise 12.5 – Lesion Removal

Instructions: Assign the CPT code(s) and any appropriate modifier(s) to each statement.

1. A physician excises a 1-cm benign lesion, left forearm; the defect is closed with a simple repair.
   _____

2. Punch biopsy of a benign skin lesion on the back and another one on the arm.
   _____

3. Excision of a 2.1-cm malignant lesion of the nose and two malignant lesions, including margins, of the chest, each 1.5-cm in diameter, including margins.
   _____

4. Four warts were removed by paring.
   _____

5. A physician excised a 2-cm benign lesion from the face.
   _____

Nails

The Nails heading classifies procedures that are performed to treat a variety of nail conditions, such as infections, trauma, nail dystrophy, and neoplasms. Most nail surgery is performed using local or digital block anesthetic. These procedures are typically performed on toenails but can be done on fingernails as well.

Nondystrophic nails are normal nails with no abnormal development or changes due to aging, injury, or disease. Nail debridement is generally done to treat hypertrophic dystrophic nails and mycotic (fungal) infections. It is performed mechanically by using instruments such as a nail splitter, a nail elevator, and an electrical burr (sander). For lacerations to the nail bed, where the wound extends under the proximal nail fold, a portion or all of the nail plate must be removed in order to visualize the laceration.

 Coding Tip

Report HCPCS level II modifiers (-FA through -F9 and -TA through -T9) with codes for procedures performed on a patient's fingernails and toenails.

Exercise 12.6 – Nails

Instructions: Assign the CPT code(s) and any appropriate modifier(s) to each statement.

1. A diabetic patient was seen by a podiatrist for trimming of nondystrophic nails, which are unaffected by abnormal development or changes in structure or appearance. Following cleansing and drying of all toenails of both feet, clippers are used to cut each nail straight across so that it is in line with the edge of the end of the toe.

   _____

2. Reconstruction of nail bed, second toe on left foot, with graft.

   _____

3. Avulsion of nail plate, simple, 5 nails, right foot.

   _____

4. The physician evacuated blood from a hematoma located beneath a patient's fingernail, second digit, left hand. The physician used an electrocautery needle to pierce the nail plate so the hematoma can drain. Pressure was applied to the nail bed to force the blood from beneath the nail plate. A loose dressing was applied so the area can continue to drain.

   _____

5. Wedge excision of skin of nail fold for ingrown toenail, third digit, right foot.

   _____

Pilonidal Cyst

The Pilonidal Cyst heading contains codes for procedures to report excision. A pilonidal cyst contains a tuft of hair that developed as the result of repeated friction, which caused hairs to penetrate the skin; it occurs primarily in the sacrococcygeal area. (For incision of a pilonidal cyst, report the appropriate code from the Incision and Drainage heading.)

Exercise 12.7 – Pilonidal Cyst

Instructions: Assign the CPT code(s) and any appropriate modifier(s) to each statement.

1. Excision of complicated pilonidal cyst.

   _____

2. Pilonidal sinus excision, simple.

   _____

3. Excision of extensive pilonidal cyst.

   _____

4. The physician shaved hair adjacent to a pilonidal cyst and made an incision to allow drainage of cystic fluid.

   _____

5. The patient presented with an infected pilonidal cyst (complicated). The cyst was incised and drained.

   _____

Introduction

Codes located in the Introduction heading include the following procedures: injection of lesion(s); tattooing; subcutaneous injection of filling material (e.g., collagen); insertion, removal, and replacement of tissue expanders; insertion and removal of implantable contraceptive capsules; subcutaneous hormone pellet implantation; and insertion, removal, and removal with insertion of nonbiodegradable drug delivery implants.

CPT codes for intralesional injection(s) into one or more lesions are reported for the treatment of lesions such as keloids, psoriasis, and acne (cystic or nodular). Drugs are injected directly into the lesion, and it is appropriate to report HCPCS level II national code(s) for medication(s) administered. CPT codes reported are determined by the number of lesions treated (not by the number of injections).

 Coding Tip

- Intralesional injection codes are *not* reported for local anesthetic injection in anticipation of chemotherapy or any other definitive service performed on a lesion or group of lesions (e.g., lesion destruction or removal).

- Do not report lesion injection codes with intralesional chemotherapy codes (from the Medicine section) unless separate lesions are injected with different agents. (Attach modifier -59 to the intralesional chemotherapy code(s) *when performed during the same encounter as lesion injection(s).)*

- The administration (injection) of local anesthesia is included in the surgical procedure performed, and it is not coded separately.

EXAMPLE: A physician performed intralesional injection of eight lesions. Report code 11901. (Code 11901 is a stand-alone code; it does not contain the plus symbol next to the code, which would indicate an add-on code. Do not report 11900 with 11901. Report either 11900 or 11901 based on the number of lesions injected.)

Exercise 12.8 – Introduction

Instructions: Assign the CPT code(s) and any appropriate modifier(s) to each statement.

1. Patient presented for subcutaneous implantation of estradiol and testosterone compressed crystalline pellets.

   _____

2. A patient presented with acne (cystic), and the physician injected drugs directly into six lesions.

   _____

3. Subcutaneous injection of 15.0 cc of collagen was performed.

   _____

4. Five implantable contraceptive capsules were removed.

   _____

5. Intralesional injection, 12 lesions.

   _____

TABLE 12-3 Medical Terms for Adjacent Tissue Transfer/Rearrangement, Flap, and Graft Procedures

Defect	Wound that is the result of surgical intervention or trauma
Donor site	Anatomical site from which healthy skin is removed
Primary defect	Wound resulting from initial surgical intervention (e.g., excision of lesion) or trauma (e.g., deep abrasions)
Recipient site	Anatomical site to which healthy skin is attached
Secondary defect	Wound resulting from removal of tissue to create flap(s) or graft(s)
Stroma	Supporting tissue (matrix) of an organ
Tissue approximation	Method of replacing sutures with material or substance (e.g., surgical glue), which facilitates enhanced cosmetic results and faster healing of defects
Undermining	Process of using a surgical instrument to separate skin and mucosa from its underlying stroma so that the tissue can be stretched and moved to overlay a defect

Repair (Closure)

The Repair (Closure) heading includes the following subheadings, which require knowledge of additional medical terms associated with repair (closure) procedures (Table 12-3):

- Repair—Simple
- Repair—Intermediate
- Repair—Complex
- Adjacent Tissue Transfer or Rearrangement
- Skin Replacement Surgery
- Flaps (Skin and/or Deep Tissues)
- Other Flaps and Grafts
- Other Procedures
- Pressure Ulcers (Decubitus Ulcers)
- Burns, Local Treatment

Simple, Intermediate, Complex Repairs

Coding wound repairs is sometimes confusing because codes for repairs can be stand-alone procedures, separately reportable services when performed with certain other procedures (e.g., excisions requiring complex repair), or they can be an integral part of a more complex procedure and not separately reportable (e.g., surgical wound closure).

To add to the confusion, repairs are also divided into three categories.

- Simple: Superficial, only simple, one layer, primary suturing is required
- Intermediate: One of the deeper layers of subcutaneous tissue and fascia are involved
- Complex: Requiring more than layered closure; e.g., revision, debridement, creation of a defect, or preparation of the site

 NOTE:

- Single-layer closure is coded as an intermediate repair if the wound is heavily contaminated and requires extensive cleaning.
- When a physician documents layered closure, do not assume an intermediate repair code is to be reported. Locate documentation of
  - Closure of subcutaneous tissue or more than one layer of tissue beneath the dermis. Such closure of tissue layers under the skin uses dissolvable sutures before suturing the dermis and epidermis.
  - or
  - Extensive cleaning or removal of foreign matter from a heavily contaminated wound that is closed with a single layer.

Assign codes to report wound closures utilizing sutures, staples, or tissue adhesives (e.g., 2-cyanoacrylate tissue glue) either alone or in combination with one 1 or with adhesive strips.

To report wound repairs, review the patient record to locate the length of the repaired wound(s) in centimeters. Then group the wounds by type of repair (e.g., simple, intermediate, or complex) and anatomical site. Finally, add the lengths of multiple wounds in the same category and report the repair code for the total. Make sure you separately code and report wound repairs that are located in more than one anatomical site; report the most complicated service as the first-listed procedure.

> **EXAMPLE 1:** A complex repair of two scalp lacerations measuring a total of 4 cm is located in the same anatomical site and is the same type of repair. Report code 13121.

> **EXAMPLE 2:** A complex repair of a 6-cm forehead laceration, 3-cm cheek laceration, and 3-cm chin laceration and an intermediate repair of 3.5-cm lacerations to both hands represent two different sites and types of repair. Report codes 13132, 13133, and 12042-59. (Report codes 13132 and 13133 for complex repair of the total 12-cm laceration [forehead, cheek, and chin]. Report code 12042-59 for the intermediate repair of the 3.5-cm lacerations of both hands.)
>
> **NOTE:**
>
> > Modifier -51 is not reported with code 13133 because the plus symbol indicates that the code has *modifier -51 exempt* status. However, modifier -59 is reported with code 12042 because notes below the Repair (Closure) heading state, *When more than one classification of wounds is repaired, list the more complicated as the primary procedure and the less complicated as the secondary procedure, using modifier -59.*

 Coding Tip

Wound closures utilizing adhesive strips (e.g., steri-strips) as the only repair material are reported with an appropriate E/M code.

> **EXAMPLE:** The physician used steri-strips for wound closure, left hand of an established patient. Report code 99213.

 Coding Tip

HCPCS level II national code G0168, Wound closure utilizing tissue adhesive(s) only (e.g., Dermabond surgical glue), is considered a supply code. Therefore, code G0168 is reported in addition to the appropriate wound repair CPT code.

> **EXAMPLE:** Patient sustained a 2.5-centimeter superficial laceration, right leg, which was repaired using Dermabond tissue adhesive. Report codes 12001 and G0168.

Coding Wound Repair (Closure) Procedures

When reporting wound repair (closure) codes, make sure that you do the following:

- Calculate the size of the wound in centimeters, whether angular, curved, or star-shaped.
- Add together the lengths of all wounds for the multiple repair of wounds in the same anatomical site, and report just one code.
- Report the code for the most complicated repair first, followed by less complicated repair codes (with modifier -59).
- Report skin debridement codes when
  - Gross contamination requires prolonged cleansing.
  - Large amounts of devitalized or contaminated tissue are removed.
  - Debridement is performed without immediate primary wound closure.

- Report codes for extensive debridement of subcutaneous tissue, muscle fascia, muscle, and/or bone (including removal of foreign material) at the site of open fracture(s) and/or dislocation(s) *when debridement includes removal of foreign material and is performed to the level of skin and/or subcutaneous tissue* (but may extend to muscle or bone). Documentation must specify precisely the depth of debridement.

- For debridement of skin only (or for active wound care management), without removal of foreign material, report codes from the CPT Medicine section.

- Report codes for the repair of nerves, blood vessels, and tendons (from the specific body system involved, such as nervous, cardiovascular, or musculoskeletal). (However, codes for simple exploration of nerves, blood vessels, and tendons exposed in an open wound are not reported separately.)

- When the physician locates a foreign body and removes it, report a code for its removal only.

EXAMPLE 1: A diabetic male is diagnosed with a 2.0-cm × 2.0-cm posterior left heel ulceration that involves skin, subcutaneous tissues, and the soleus muscle. Debridement at all levels was performed. Report code 11043 for the 4.0-cm treatment area (2.0 cm × 2.0 cm = 4.0 sq cm).

EXAMPLE 2: A motorcyclist lost control on a 2-lane country road that was covered with loose stone. She suffered an open fracture of her right tibia and extensive abrasions directly over the fracture site, which required debridement down to muscle. The debridement procedure is reported with code 11011. (The open fracture repair code is also reported.)

In addition, it is important to remember that

- The simple ligation of vessels in an open wound is included in the wound repair code.

- The simple exploration of nerves, blood vessels, or tendons exposed in an open wound is included in the wound repair code.

- The reported wound repair codes are based on length of the wound (in centimeters), wound site, and complexity of repair.

- Wound repairs usually require local anesthesia, and the physician usually performs a neurovascular exam prior to administering the anesthetic. The administration of the local anesthesia is included in the wound repair code.

When the closure of a lesion excision cannot be accomplished by simple, intermediate, or complex closure, the following methods are used:

- Adjacent tissue transfer or rearrangement (Table 12-4)
- Skin replacement surgery

Adjacent Tissue Transfer or Rearrangement

Adjacent tissue transfer or rearrangement codes include skin excision and are assigned according to anatomical site. To determine the correct code, calculate the combined area (as square centimeters) of the defect to be repaired *and the defect created by the tissue transfer*. Do not report a separate code for excision of a lesion or another defect when an adjacent tissue transfer or a rearrangement procedure is performed.

When a procedure is performed to repair a secondary defect (e.g., site of donor advancement flap), report an additional procedure code for the repair (e.g., full-thickness skin graft).

EXAMPLE 1: Patient previously underwent excision of lesion, chest. Today, the patient undergoes adjacent tissue transfer repair of resulting 1 sq cm skin defect via advancement flap, created from 2 sq cm of adjacent chest tissue. Dressings were applied to both wounds. Report code 14000 (because 1 sq cm + 2 sq cm = 3 sq cm, and the chest is part of the body's trunk).

TABLE 12-4 Adjacent Tissue Transfer or Tissue Rearrangement Methods and Definitions

Adjacent Tissue Transfer Method	Definition
Advancement flap	Movement of tissue in a straight line from donor to defect site using a sliding process; once movement is achieved, the flap is sutured in place; advancement flaps are not rotated or moved sideways.
Double pedicle flap	Maintains blood supply from both ends of the flap incision made to create a curvilinear flap contiguous with the defect; flap is pivoted and sutured in place over the defect.
Free flap	Island flap that is detached from donor site and reattached at recipient site via microvascular anastomosis.
Island flap	Flap consisting of skin and subcutaneous tissue with a pedicle comprised only of nutrient vessels; also called island pedicle flap.
Mycocutaneous flap	Autologous graft consisting of both skin and muscle tissue from the donor site.
Random pattern flap	Mycocutaneous flap with a random pattern of arteries.
Rhomboid flap	Random pattern flap that can be raised on any or all corners of a parallelogram configuration, typically 120 and 60 degrees; also called Limberg flap.
Rotation flap	Incision made to create a curvilinear flap contiguous with the defect; flap is dissected, freed, pivoted, and sutured in place over the defect.
Tissue rearrangement	Defined by anatomical site and size of defect; includes excision of the defect or lesion; terms used to describe transfer or rearrangement include *Z-plasty, W-plasty, V-Y plasty, rotation flap, advancement flap,* and *double pedicle flap.*
V-Y-plasty	After creation of a V-shaped incision, the edges of the incision are drawn together and sutured, converting the incision to a Y shape.
W-plasty	Both edges of the wound or defect are trimmed into the shape of a W or multiple Ws.
Z-plasty	Involves making an incision along with two additional incisions, one above and another below, creating a Z formation.

EXAMPLE 2: Patient previously underwent excision of nasal scar, which resulted in a skin defect. Today, the patient undergoes adjacent tissue transfer repair of the 2 sq cm nasal skin defect using an advancement flap (using 4 sq cm of skin from the left cheek). A full-thickness skin graft (using 6 sq cm of skin from right inner thigh) was required to close the 4 sq cm flap left cheek donor site defect. The right inner thigh was repaired using direct closure. Report codes 14060 (because 2 sq cm + 4 sq cm = 6 sq cm) and 15240-51 (which includes direct closure to repair the right inner thigh).

Skin Replacement Surgery Flaps (Skin and/or Deep Tissues), and Other Flaps and Grafts

CPT graft codes are organized as follows:

- Autograft/tissue cultured autograft
- Acellular dermal replacement
- Allograft/tissue cultured allogeneic skin substitute
- Allograft, skin
- Xenograft, skin

Skin replacement surgery includes surgical preparation and topical placement of an autograft or a skin substitute graft. *Surgical preparation* codes describe initial services performed to prepare a clean and viable wound surface for placement of an autograft, flap, skin substitute graft, or for negative pressure wound therapy. An **autograft** is the transplantation of tissue from the same individual (e.g., harvesting skin from the patient's thigh to graft a defect of the upper arm). **Tissue-cultured autografts** are supplied by laboratories. (Modifier -58 is often added to tissue-cultured autograft codes because labs can grow a limited amount of tissue and such grafts are often performed as staged procedures.) **Skin substitute grafts** include nonautologous human skin grafts (e.g., acellular dermal), non-human skin substitute grafts (e.g., xenograft), and biological products that form a sheet scaffolding for skin growth.

Acellular dermal replacement is a bioengineered artificial skin (e.g., Alloderm). An **allograft** is the transplantation of tissue from someone of the same species (e.g., harvesting skin from another person's thigh to graft a defect on the patient's upper arm). A **xenograft** is the transplantation of tissue from a different species (e.g., harvesting skin from a baboon or a pig to graft a defect on the patient's upper arm).

Types of skin grafts include the following:

- Free skin graft
  - Full-thickness skin graft
  - Split-thickness skin graft
- Pedicle skin graft

Free skin grafts are completely separated from the donor site before being transferred to the recipient site. They are classified as **full-thickness skin grafts** (graft of epidermis and dermis) or **split-thickness skin grafts** (graft of entire epidermis and a portion of the dermis). Full-thickness skin grafts are often harvested from the inguinal folds, supraclavicular region, abdomen, thigh, and postauricular skin (because of the availability of excess skin, which eases primary closure of the donor site). Split-thickness grafts are typically used to repair edematous, infected, or large wounds (e.g., result of burns).

 Coding Tip

- Before reporting codes 15040–15278 for free skin grafts, determine whether the graft is full-thickness or split-thickness, what the size of the recipient area is, and where the location of the recipient area is.
- Surgical preparation codes 15002–15005 are reported for skin replacement surgery that describe initial services for preparing a clean and viable wound surface for the placement of an autograft, flap or skin substitute graft, or for negative pressure wound therapy.
- Although codes 15002–15278 include simple debridement of the recipient area, they do not include repair of the donor site with skin grafts or local flaps. Report additional code(s) when the donor site is repaired in this manner.

Pedicle skin grafts are not immediately completely separated from their donor site. A portion of the graft is transferred to the recipient area, and a remaining portion (the base) is attached to the donor site so that there is a vasculature and nerve supply for the recipient area. Once blood flow to the recipient site is sufficient, the base is grafted to the recipient site.

 Coding Tip

Codes 15600–15630 are reported when the "delay technique" is used to improve the blood supply to the base of a flap. This is accomplished by temporarily obstructing the blood supply to the flap to allow a relatively long flap to be transferred onto a narrow pedicle.

When assigning codes for skin grafts, identify the following:

- Type of graft
  - Permanent or temporary
  - Natural or manufactured graft material
  - Use of skin components (e.g., epidermal, dermal, split-thickness, or full-thickness grafts) (Refer to Figure 12-7 to view full-thickness and split-thickness skin grafts.)
- Recipient site (anatomical location)
- Surface area of the recipient site calculated as square centimeters

Epidermis

Dermis

Hypodermis

Split thickness

Full thickness

Subcutaneous tissue

FIGURE 12-7 Depth of full-thickness and split-thickness skin cross sections

Just one type of skin graft is usually applied to an anatomical location. Thus, primary free skin graft codes are mutually exclusive of one another. When multiple anatomical locations require different grafts, add modifier -59 to the reported code(s) to indicate that different sites underwent grafting.

When a benign or malignant lesion is excised and surgical preparation and free skin grafting are performed, two codes are reported.

- Excision lesion code
- Skin graft code

However, when a benign or malignant lesion is excised with flap closure, just the flap closure code is reported.

Generally, debridement of nonintact skin in anticipation of a skin graft is necessary prior to application of the skin graft and is included in the skin graft. When skin is intact, however, and the graft is being performed after excisional preparation of intact skin, surgical preparation/creation of recipient site codes 15002–15005 are separately reported. CPT codes 15002–15005 do not describe debridement of nonintact, necrotic, or infected skin, nor is their use indicated with other lesion removal codes.

> **EXAMPLE:** A patient with full-thickness burns of the left arm underwent surgical preparation of the burned tissue. After excision and hemostasis, 100 sq cm full thickness free graft with direct closure was performed. Report codes 15002, 15220, 15221, 15221, 15221, and 15221.

Refer to Table 12-5 when assigning codes for tissue rearrangement, free skin grafts, flaps (skin and/or deep tissues), and/or other flaps and grafts. When multiple tissue rearrangement and free skin graft procedures are required during the same operative session, make sure you report each separately. (The total square centimeters for repair of different defects are not added together.)

Other Procedures

"Other procedures" codes classify the following integumentary system procedures:

- Dermabrasion
- Abrasion
- Chemical peel
- Cervicoplasty
- Blepharoplasty
- Rhytidectomy

- Excision, excessive skin and subcutaneous tissue (including lipectomy)
- Graft for facial nerve paralysis
- Removal of sutures under anesthesia
- Dressing change under anesthesia
- Intravenous injection of agent
- Suction-assisted lipectomy

TABLE 12-5 Types of Codes for Tissue Rearrangement, Free Skin Grafts, and Flaps

Type of Procedure	# of Codes	Types of Codes
Adjacent tissue transfer or rearrangement	1	• Adjacent tissue transfer or rearrangement (14000–14350)
Free skin graft	2 or more	• Free skin graft (15050–15278) • Surgical preparation or creation of recipient site *(15002–15005) for burn and wound preparation and management procedures only* • Repair of donor site if local flap or skin graft is required (14000–14350)
Flap (skin and/or deep tissue)	1 or more	• Flap (skin and/or deep tissue) (15570–15738) • Repair of donor site if local flap or skin graft is required (14000–14350)
Other flap and graft	1 or more	• Flap or graft (15740–15777) • Repair of donor site if local flap or skin graft is required (14000–14350)

Dermabrasion (Figure 12-8) is performed for conditions such as acne scarring and wrinkles (facial) and rhytids and general keratosis (facial and other than face). The physician uses a rotary device to sand down raised lesions or thickened tissue, regenerating smoother skin.

EXAMPLE: Patient underwent total face dermabrasion by use of a rotary instrument that penetrates into the dermis layer of skin. Report code 15780.

 Coding Tip

- The code description for code 15783 includes "tattoo removal" as an example. However, dermabrasion to remove a tattoo usually involves the dermis. According to the AMA's *CPT Assistant,* because code 15783 is reported for superficial abrasion, it should not be reported for tattoo removal. Report a code from 15780–15782 for tattoo removal.

- Microdermabrasion is not classified in CPT, which means that unlisted code 17999 is assigned. **Microdermabrasion** is a skin-freshening technique used to repair facial skin that is damaged by the sun and the effects of aging. A sandblaster device is used to spray tiny crystals across the face, mixing gentle abrasion with suction to remove the outer layer of skin.

FIGURE 12-8 Dermabrasion

A **chemical peel** involves the use of chemical agents (e.g., glycolic acid or phenol) to remove wrinkles and abnormal pigmentation. Be sure to determine if treatment is localized to surface layers of the facial skin or the deeper dermal layer.

NOTE:

Actinic keratosis (AK) is a common sun-induced skin lesion of the epidermis that has the potential to become skin cancer. The most commonly performed treatments for AK includes cryosurgery with liquid nitrogen, topical drug therapy, and curettage. However, AK treatments also include dermabrasion, excision, chemical peels, laser therapy, and photodynamic therapy (PDT).

A **blepharoplasty** is any surgical repair of an eyelid. From a coding perspective, blepharoplasty describes the removal of the orbicularis muscle, orbital fat, and excess eyelid skin around the orbit. Make sure you review the operative report to identify the procedure performed and assign appropriate codes. A blepharoptosis repair is performed on the levator muscle of the eyelid. The code selected is based on the surgical approach used to perform the blepharoptosis repair.

EXAMPLE: Patient underwent blepharoplasty of the left lower eyelid, which required the physician to dissect lower eyelid skin to the subcutaneous and muscle fascial layers and excise excess skin. Report code 15820-E2. (HCPCS level II modifier -E2 is reported to indicate that the procedure was performed on the "lower left, eyelid.")

NOTE:

Medicare reimburses services that are reasonable and necessary to diagnose and treat or to improve the functioning of a malformed body member. When blepharoplasty procedures are performed for cosmetic purposes, they are not covered by Medicare. When the function of the eye is impaired by overlying skin or fatty tissue, the repair is deemed medically necessary and is covered by Medicare.

A **rhytidectomy** involves excising a section of skin to eliminate wrinkles and can be done to reduce **glabellar frown lines,** which are vertical furrows in the forehead area between the eyebrows.

Graft procedures for facial nerve paralysis involve the removal of connective tissue (e.g., fascia) from the body. The graft is transplanted to the face to reanimate previously paralyzed areas.

The removal of sutures by the surgeon is included in the global period associated with that procedure. (The removal of sutures by a physician other than the surgeon who initially placed the sutures is usually reported with an E/M code.)

Abdominal panniculectomy (abdominoplasty) is performed to remove fatty tissue and excess skin from the lower to middle portions of the abdomen. This procedure is typically performed on individuals who have lost considerable weight, resulting in loose-hanging folds of skin in the abdominal area. A lipectomy is the removal of localized subcutaneous fat deposits by suction curettage or blunt cannulization to cosmetically correct obesity and other contour defects.

EXAMPLE: Patient underwent lipectomy of the submental fat pad. Report code 15838.

When a physician performs a suction-assisted lipectomy, a liposuction cannula is inserted through the fat deposits, removing excess deposits.

EXAMPLE: Patient underwent suction-assisted lipectomy of the neck. Report code 15876.

Pressure Ulcers (Decubitus Ulcers)

A **pressure ulcer**, or **decubitus ulcer**, or **bedsore**, is an ulceration of the skin and underlying tissue that occurs over a bony prominence (e.g., sacral decubitus). A decubitus ulcer appears in patients confined to bed or immobilized when blood supply is decreased in pressure areas by pressure on the skin, resulting in inflammation and swelling and ultimately necrosis, ulceration, and infection.

The primary excisional procedure of a staged process does not include the flap/graft procedures, which are reported separately. CPT includes notes that provide instruction to report appropriate repair and skin graft codes.

EXAMPLE: Patient underwent excision of ischial pressure ulcer with ostectomy. Report code 15946.

When a muscle or myocutaneous flap is planned for a subsequent session prospectively (e.g., at the time of the original procedure), report the appropriate flap code and add modifier -58 (Staged Procedure).

Burns, Local Treatment

The introduction to the Burns, Local Treatment heading states that the application of materials (e.g., Biobrane) is included. To assign appropriate codes for the treatment of burns, review the medical record to identify the following:

- Percentage of body surface
- Severity (depth) of the burn
  - Partial-thickness burns (e.g., first-degree or second-degree)
  - Full-thickness burns (e.g., third-degree)

To determine the extent of body surface involved, use the **rule of nines**, which divides total body surface area (BSA) into nine segments by percentage (Figure 12-9). When estimating the percentage of the body affected by burns, review the medical record to locate the patient's age. (The surface area for children is estimated differently than that for adults.)

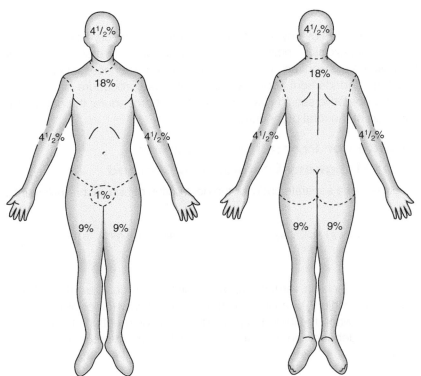

FIGURE 12-9 The rule of nines

EXAMPLE: The physician surgically debrided blisters and devitalized tissue that involved less than 5 percent of the total BSA. Report code 16020.

Exercise 12.9 – Repair (Closure)

Instructions: Assign the CPT code(s) and any appropriate modifier(s) to each statement.

1. Simple repair of 3.0-cm scalp laceration.
   _____

2. A physician performed a 4-cm wound closure on an established patient using adhesive strips during a level 2 E/M established patient office encounter.
   _____

3. Debridement of partial-thickness burn of the right hand involving 1 percent of total body surface.
   _____

4. Full-thickness skin graft, free, including direct closure of donor site, trunk (20 sq cm). Surgical preparation of recipient site, trunk (20 sq cm), was also performed during the same operative session.
   _____

5. Dermabrasion, total face.
   _____

Destruction

Destruction is the ablation of tissue by any method (e.g., electrosurgery, cryosurgery, or laser or chemical treatments). During destruction, excision, incision, removal, repair, or closure procedures, the debridement of nonviable tissue that surrounds a lesion, an injury, or an incision may be necessary to perform the intended procedure. Do not report the debridement codes when the intended procedure (e.g., destruction of lesion) is performed during the same operative session as the debridement procedure; the debridement procedure is considered a necessary part of the total procedure.

Destruction of Benign or Premalignant Lesions and Destruction of Malignant Lesions, Any Method

Each lesion treated is reported as a separate code for the destruction of benign, premalignant, and malignant lesions.

EXAMPLE: The physician uses a small applicator to apply liquid nitrogen directly to the patient's skin to remove a hypertrophic AK lesion. Report code 17000.

During destruction, excision, incision, removal, repair, or closure procedures, the debridement of nonviable tissue that surrounds a lesion, an injury, or an incision may be necessary to perform the intended procedure. Do *not* report a debridement code when the intended procedure (e.g., destruction of lesion) is performed during the same operative session as the debridement procedure. The debridement procedure is considered a necessary part of the total procedure.

EXAMPLE: A physician performed laser surgery to destroy a 0.5-cm malignant facial skin lesion. He also destroyed a premalignant lesion on the skin of the left shoulder. Report codes 17280 and 17000-51.

Mohs Micrographic Surgery

Mohs micrographic surgery is an advanced treatment procedure used to treat basal cell carcinoma and squamous cell carcinoma skin cancers. Dermatologists trained in this technique serve as surgeon, pathologist, and reconstructive surgeon. They use a microscope to trace and ensure the removal of skin cancer to its roots. Mohs micrographic surgery codes are reported instead of excision codes and surgical pathology codes. Reporting Mohs micrographic surgery and surgical pathology codes on the same claim is inappropriate. A Mohs surgeon who obtains a diagnostic biopsy to make the decision to perform surgery reports the diagnostic biopsy code separately. When Mohs surgery is performed in addition to a skin biopsy on the same day, add modifier -59 to the biopsy code, such as 17311 and 11106-59.

> **EXAMPLE:** A patient undergoes Mohs micrographic surgery for basal cell carcinoma of the head (behind the left ear). In the first stage, a layer of tissue is removed and the specimen is subdivided into two smaller specimens for pathologic review. In the subsequent stage, the second layer is excised and subdivided into three smaller specimens for pathologic processing. Report codes 17311 and 17312.

Other Procedures

Other Procedures codes classify cryotherapy, chemical exfoliation for acne, electrolysis epilation, and unlisted procedures. When reporting an unlisted procedure code, include documentation about the procedure performed with the submitted claim.

> **EXAMPLE:** Patient underwent experimental destruction procedure on the skin, which is not currently classified in CPT. Report code 17999.

Exercise 12.10 – Destruction

Instructions: Assign the CPT code(s) and any appropriate modifier(s) to each statement.

1. Destruction of three premalignant facial lesions.

   _____

2. Destruction of 17 skin tags.

   _____

3. Patient underwent removal of five flat warts, using photothermolysis laser (destruction).

   _____

4. Laser surgery destruction of two actinic keratosis lesions, chest.

   _____

5. Electrosurgical destruction of 10 skin tags.

   _____

6. Chemosurgery, 3.8 centimeter malignant lesion, scalp.

   _____

7. Surgical curettement of 1.5 centimeter malignant lesion, trunk.

   _____

8. Cryosurgery, 10.0 centimeter malignant lesion, neck.

   _____

9. Electrosurgery, 0.5 centimeter malignant lesion, nose.

   _____

10. Laser surgery, 2.3 centimeter malignant lesion, left shoulder.

    _____

Breast

Diagnostic testing used to detect breast cancer may include a mammogram, ultrasonography, magnetic resonance imaging (MRI), FNA, core biopsy, or surgical biopsy. Treatment plans can include a local therapy approach such as breast-conserving surgery or mastectomy, radiation therapy (e.g., internal or implant radiation or external radiation), and breast reconstruction (e.g., implant or tissue transfer).

Because of the unique nature of procedures developed to address breast disease, codes in CPT are established for services (e.g., incision, excision, introduction, repair, and reconstruction). FNA biopsies, core biopsies, open incisional or excisional biopsies, and related procedures performed to procure tissue from a lesion for which an established diagnosis exists are not to be reported separately at the time of a lesion excision unless performed on a different lesion or on the contralateral breast. However, if a diagnosis is not established *and the decision to perform the excision or mastectomy is dependent on the results of the biopsy*, the biopsy is separately reported. Modifier -58 is used to indicate that the biopsy and the excision or mastectomy are staged or planned procedures.

Breast Biopsies

Breast biopsies are performed according to the following methods:

- Fine-needle aspiration (FNA) (Figure 12-10A)
- Needle core biopsy
  - Hand-operated needle
  - Stereotactic localization
- Open biopsy
  - Excisional biopsy
  - Incisional biopsy (Figure 12-10B)

Fine-Needle Aspiration (FNA)

FNA of the breast is reported, depending on whether imaging guidance was used during the procedure. FNA uses a thin needle (e.g., 20- or 22-gauge needle), which is inserted through the mass several times. Suction is applied as the needle is withdrawn to obtain strands of single cells for cytologic diagnosis.

 Coding Tip

Do not report code 19100 (needle core breast biopsy) for fine-needle aspiration (FNA) of breast tissue. FNA procedures are reported with codes 10004–10012, 10021, which include single and multiple lesions.

(A) (B)

FIGURE 12-10 (A) Fine-needle aspiration. (B) Incisional biopsy

Needle Core Biopsy

A **needle core biopsy** is obtained using a hand-operated needle (e.g., Trucut or Vim-Silverman) or stereotactic localization. Once the tissue is obtained, it is fixed for routine pathologic section. **Stereotactic localization** is indicated for nonpalpable lesions because it uses specialized three-dimensional imaging to target the lesion. The breast is placed in a fixed position, and a biopsy gun (e.g., 14- or 18-gauge needle) is used to obtain needle core biopsies from the lesion.

Coding Tip

- A biopsy code is assigned for each biopsied site (e.g., three needle core biopsy sites are reported as codes 19100, 19100, and 19100).

- Differentiating a puncture aspiration of a breast cyst, a needle core biopsy of the breast, and fine-needle aspiration of breast tissue can be determined by reviewing the operative report (or documented procedure statement).
  - Codes 10004–10012 and 10021 are assigned for fine-needle aspirations of the breast, depending on whether imaging guidance was used during the procedure.
  - Codes 19000–19001 are assigned for puncture aspirations of breast cysts.
  - Code 19100 is assigned for needle core breast biopsies.
  - Code 19101 describes a breast biopsy obtained through an incision. (However, when an entire lesion is subsequently removed during the same operative session as an excisional biopsy, code 19120 is reported instead of 19101.)

Open Biopsy

An **open biopsy** can be incisional or excisional, depending on the amount of lesion removed. An **excisional biopsy** removes the lump or suspicious area in its entirety. An **incisional biopsy** removes a portion of the lesion by slicing into it or incising it; it is usually performed on large tumors (and the patient undergoes mastectomy later).

Excisional breast surgery includes certain biopsy procedures, the removal of cysts or other benign or malignant tumors or lesions, and the surgical treatment of breast and chest wall malignancies. Biopsy procedures may be percutaneous or open. Open excision of breast lesions without attention to surgical margins, with or without the preoperative placement of radiological markers, is reported with codes 19120, 19125, or 19126.

NOTE:

An excisional biopsy (19120) is not a **lumpectomy**, which is a partial mastectomy (19301–19302).

Coding Tip

- Review the entire operative report and pathology report to determine whether the biopsy was excisional or incisional.

- For an excisional biopsy, report code 19120. (However, if the lesion was identified with preoperative placement of a radiological marker, report codes 19081–19086 and 19125, 19125, or 19126.)

- For an open incisional biopsy, report code 19101. (However, if the operative report indicates that the biopsy was "incisional" and the pathology report indicates that the entire lesion was removed, report code 19120 for an excisional biopsy.)

EXAMPLE 1: The right patient was registered for outpatient surgery on August 1. The patient received an explanation from the surgeon that she would undergo excisional left breast biopsy in the morning and that if pathology results were positive for cancer, the patient would undergo left breast lumpectomy during the late afternoon. The excisional left breast biopsy was performed at 9 AM, and tissue was positive for adenocarcinoma. The patient returned to the operating room at 2 PM and underwent left breast lumpectomy. Report codes 19120-LT (Excisional breast biopsy) and 19301-58-LT (Breast lumpectomy, staged or related procedure performed by the same physician during the postoperative period). (Modifier -58 is added to just one CPT code. The pathologist reports an appropriate code from the Pathology and Laboratory section of CPT.)

> ## ⚠ Coding Tip
>
> Do not report code 19120 for a breast lumpectomy. Code 19120 (excisional biopsy) is reported when the physician makes an incision in the skin of the breast overlying the site of the mass and dissects skin and tissue (from the site of the aberrant tissue, areola, cyst, fibroadenoma, lesion of the duct, nipple, or tumor). This procedure involves excising the lesion and a rim of surrounding normal tissue. When the excision of more than one lesion is performed in different areas of the breast (through separate incision sites), report code 19120 for each excision site.
>
> A breast lumpectomy is a type of partial mastectomy, and it is reported with code 19301. When more than one lumpectomy is performed in different areas of the breast (through separate incision sites), report code 19301 for each excision site. (Modifier -51 is added to the second and subsequent reporting of code 19301 when multiple lumpectomies are performed during the same operative episode.)

EXAMPLE 2: A right breast mass biopsy was sent to the pathologist during the operative procedure for immediate diagnosis. The pathologist examined the specimen and diagnosed a malignancy. Immediate full-thickness (through the dermis) removal of the lesion, including margins, was performed. The procedure included simple (nonlayered) closure of the mass. Report code 19120-RT. (The pathologist reports an appropriate code from the Pathology and Laboratory section of CPT.)

Mastectomy

Mastectomy (Figure 12-11) procedures are classified in CPT as follows:

- Partial mastectomy (including lumpectomy)
- Radical mastectomy
- Simple or total mastectomy
- Modified radical mastectomy

Lumpectomy   Simple or total mastectomy   Modified radical mastectomy   Radical mastectomy

FIGURE 12-11 Types of mastectomy

Partial mastectomy procedures describe open excisions of breast tissue with specific attention to adequate surgical margins. A **partial mastectomy** involves making an incision through skin and fascia over the breast tumor and clamping lymphatic and blood vessels; the physician then excises the tumor mass along with a section of breast tissue. A partial mastectomy is also called a lumpectomy, quadrantectomy, segmental mastectomy, and tylectomy.

> **EXAMPLE:** A sentinel node biopsy is performed as part of an axillary lymphadenectomy during a partial right mastectomy procedure. Report code 19302-RT, which includes removal of the sentinel node and other axillary lymph nodes.

Total mastectomy procedures include complete mastectomy, modified radical mastectomy, simple mastectomy, and subcutaneous mastectomy. A **total mastectomy** is the surgical removal of the entire breast, including the pectoral fascia and a sampling of axillary lymph nodes. Radical mastectomy procedures include the removal of pectoral muscles, axillary lymph nodes, and/or internal mammary lymph nodes. A **radical mastectomy** is a total mastectomy that includes removal of the breast and nipple, pectoralis muscles (major and/or minor), axillary lymph nodes, and internal mammary lymph nodes. A **modified radical mastectomy** is a total mastectomy that includes removal of the breast and nipple, axillary lymph nodes, and pectoralis minor muscle.

Breast Repair and Reconstruction

CPT breast reconstruction codes include the following elements:

- Elevation and transfer of the flap
- Closure of the donor site
- Breast contouring
- Insertion of breast implant or prosthesis, when performed

Breast reconstruction with transverse rectus abdominis myocutaneous flap (TRAM), single pedicle includes closure of donor site. In addition, TRAM flap codes include the following:

- Creation of the breast pocket
- Elevation of the abdominal flap
- Muscle dissection
- Flap transfer
- Fascial closure (donor site) with or without mesh
- Abdominal closure including umbilicoplasty
- Breast contouring

Because excision of lesions is often done during the same operative session as a mastectomy, breast excisions are not separately reported in addition to the mastectomy code *unless performed to establish the malignant diagnosis before proceeding to the mastectomy.* Thus, CPT breast excision codes are not reported in addition to CPT mastectomy codes when performed on the same side. If the breast excision is performed to obtain tissue to determine pathologic diagnosis of malignancy prior to proceeding to a mastectomy, the excision is separately coded and reported with the mastectomy code and modifier -58 is added to the codes.

Use of other integumentary codes for incision and closure are included in the codes that describe various breast excision or mastectomy codes. Because of the frequent need to biopsy lymph nodes or remove muscle tissue in conjunction with mastectomies, these procedures are included in CPT coding for mastectomy. It is inappropriate to separately report ipsilateral lymph node dissection with mastectomy codes. When a breast lesion is identified and treated and medical necessity indicates that biopsy of contralateral nodes should be done, report the biopsy or lymph node dissection codes (and add an appropriate anatomical modifier, such as -LT or -RT for left or right). Breast reconstruction codes also include the insertion of a prosthetic implant, and they are not reported with CPT codes that describe the insertion of breast prosthesis only.

CPT coding for breast procedures generally refers to unilateral procedures; when performed bilaterally, add modifier -50 to the code. (The Repair and/or Reconstruction subheading includes a parenthetical note as a reminder to report modifier -50 when appropriate.) When breast reconstruction is performed unilaterally, add the applicable HCPCS level II modifier -LT (left) or -RT (right) to the procedure code.

Other Procedures

The Other Procedures code classifies an unlisted procedure performed on breast. When reporting an unlisted procedure code, include documentation about the procedure performed with the submitted claim.

> **EXAMPLE:** Patient underwent experimental procedure on the breast, which is not currently classified in CPT. Report code 19499 (and attach a special report to the submitted claim).

Exercise 12.11 – Breast

Instructions: Assign the CPT code(s) and any appropriate modifier(s) to each statement.

1. Excision of two lesions, right breast, identified by the placement of radiological markers for each.
   _____

2. A transverse rectus abdominis myocutaneous flap procedure for right breast reconstruction is performed using a single rectus abdominis muscle to transfer the necessary tissue to form a breast mound.
   _____

3. Lumpectomy, left breast.
   _____

4. Physician performed a partial mastectomy of the right breast with right axillary lymphadenectomy and biopsy of the right sentinel node.
   _____

5. Patient underwent percutaneous left breast biopsy with placement of a breast localization clip under stereotactic guidance.
   _____

Summary

The CPT Surgery section and its subsections are organized anatomically according to major body area or organ system. Guidelines located at the beginning of the CPT Surgery section clarify the assignment of codes and explain terms. The General subsection contains just two codes. The Integumentary System subsection includes dermatological procedures, plastic surgery, and components of multiple surgical procedures (e.g., closure, flaps, grafts, and tissue transfer). Integumentary procedures are often performed as staged procedures (e.g., flaps and grafts) due to the complexity of services rendered.

Internet Links

American Academy of Dermatology (AAD): *www.aad.org*

Medscape: Go to *www.medscape.com*, and click Register to register for free access to Medscape's clinical information and resources.

National Correct Coding Initiative (NCCI) Edits: Go to *www.cms.gov*, and click on the Medicare link, scroll to the Coding heading, and click on the National Correct Coding Initiative Edits link.

ORlive™ BroadcastMed: Go to *www.orlive.com* to view live webcasts in selected health specialties.

SurgeryTheater: Go to *www.surgerytheater.com*, and enter the name of a surgical procedure in the Search field to locate videos of surgical procedures.

Review

Multiple Choice

Instructions: Select the most appropriate response.

1. Which is a therapeutic surgical procedure?
   - **a.** Arthroscopy
   - **b.** Biopsy
   - **c.** Endoscopy
   - **d.** Repair

2. A patient undergoing a surgical procedure was draped and positioned. The surgical area was cleansed and shaved, an IV was started, and a sedative was administered. The surgical approach was identified, and an incision was made. The wound was irrigated, and cultures were taken. The incision was closed, and dressings were applied. The procedure was then dictated and transcribed. A CPT code was assigned to the surgical procedure. Which service is assigned a separate code, in addition to the reported CPT Surgery code?
   - **a.** Administration of a sedative
   - **b.** None of the services are reported separately.
   - **c.** Taking cultures and wound irrigation
   - **d.** Transcription of the dictated report

3. Which modifier indicates a staged procedure or service?
   - **a.** -58
   - **b.** -59
   - **c.** -66
   - **d.** -76

4. When a patient receives treatment for an unrelated condition during the global period, which modifier is added to the CPT code?
   - **a.** -51
   - **b.** -57
   - **c.** -59
   - **d.** -79

5. The CMS global surgical package includes:
   - **a.** diagnostic tests and procedures, including diagnostic radiological procedures.
   - **b.** initial consultation or evaluation of the problem by the surgeon to determine the need for surgery.
   - **c.** the day before the day of surgery for major procedures.
   - **d.** treatment for postoperative complications that require a return trip to the operating room.

6. When an evaluation and management (E/M) service provided is for the purpose of deciding to perform a major surgical procedure, which is reported?
   - **a.** E/M code
   - **b.** E/M code with modifier -57
   - **c.** E/M code with modifier -59
   - **d.** No E/M code is reported because the service is bundled in the surgery code.

7. The code reported for fine-needle aspiration is determined based on whether:
   a. fluid is aspirated from a cyst or cells are aspirated from a solid mass.
   b. imaging guidance is used during the procedure.
   c. the cyst or mass is visible.
   d. the procedure is performed percutaneously.

8. If the operative report describes a lesion as 3.5 cm × 4 cm × 5 cm, which is reported as the diameter?
   a. 3.5 cm   b. 4 cm   c. 5 cm   d. 17.5 cm

9. When Mohs micrographic surgery is performed, Mohs micrographic surgery codes are reported instead of:
   a. a diagnostic biopsy code.
   b. excision codes and a diagnostic biopsy code.
   c. excision codes and surgical pathology codes.
   d. surgical pathology codes.

10. Wound repair is coded with an appropriate evaluation and management code when the sole repair material used is:
    a. adhesive strips.   c. sutures.
    b. staples.   d. tissue adhesives.

11. Evacuation of subungual hematoma. Which CPT code is assigned?
    a. 10140   b. 10160   c. 11740   d. 11750

12. Collagen injection, face, 5.1 cc. Which CPT code is assigned?
    a. 11950   b. 11951   c. 11952   d. 11954

13. Puncture aspiration of abscess on lower left eyelid. Which CPT code is assigned?
    a. 10120-E2   b. 10140-E2   c. 10160-E2   d. 10180-E2

14. Open excision of fibroadenomas, right breast. Which CPT code is assigned?
    a. 19100-RT   b. 19120-RT   c. 19301-RT   d. 21601-RT

15. Suction-assisted abdominal lipectomy. Which CPT code is assigned?
    a. 15876   b. 15877   c. 15878   d. 15879

16. Adjacent tissue transfer of 12 sq cm defect of forehead. Which CPT code is assigned?
    a. 14020   b. 14021   c. 14040   d. 14041

17. Mohs micrographic surgery of upper left arm (first stage) with excision of five specimens. Diagnostic incisional skin biopsy performed the same day. Which CPT code(s) are assigned?
    a. 11106, 17313-51   c. 17313
    b. 17313, 11106-59   d. 17313, 11406

18. Modified radical mastectomy, including axillary lymph nodes, excluding pectoral muscles. Which CPT code is assigned?
    a. 19301   b. 19305   c. 19306   d. 19307

19. Epidermal facial chemical peel. Which CPT code is assigned?
    a. 15788   b. 15789   c. 15792   d. 15793

20. Cryosurgery of two plantar warts. Which CPT code(s) are assigned?
    a. 17000, 17000
    b. 17000, 17003
    c. 17000, 17003-51
    d. 17110

Coding Practice

Instructions: Assign the CPT code(s) and appropriate modifier(s) to each case.

General Surgery

1. Patient underwent fine-needle aspiration to remove fluid sample from a cyst, anterior neck. Physician palpated the cyst, cleansed the site with Betadine solution, and inserted a 25-gauge needle into the cyst. Approximately 2 cc of fluid were removed. The needle was withdrawn, and a small bandage was placed over the insertion area.

_____

2. Patient underwent fine-needle aspiration to remove a cluster of cells from a solid mass, subcutaneous layer of the left upper quadrant, abdomen. Computed tomography imaging guidance for needle placement was performed. Physician palpated the mass, cleansed the area with Betadine solution, and inserted a 22-gauge needle into the solid mass. Approximately 1 cc of tissue was removed. The needle was withdrawn, and a small bandage was placed over the insertion area.

_____

Integumentary System

3. A large mass, soft and movable, located on the patient's back between the lower scapular area and midline on the left, was palpated. An elliptical incision was made, a section of the tissue was removed, and the 4.0-cm cyst was resected completely. Bleeding vessels were clamped and coagulated. Penrose drain was left in the wound, and skin edges were closed along with subcutaneous tissue, using interrupted silk sutures.

_____

4. Patient was prepped and draped; after adequate general endotracheal anesthesia, the body was somewhat flexed at the waist to provide adequate exposure after taping in preparation to separate the buttocks at the sacral crease. A probe was inserted into the inferior sinus, and only 3 to 4 cm of fluid were obtained. The area was prepped for excision, and an oval-shaped piece of skin was excised in total, including the 5.0-cm subcutaneous pilonidal cyst sinus end. Bleeding was controlled with electrocautery, the area was copiously irrigated with Betadine saline solution and suctioned and sponged off, and vertical mattress sutures of Prolene were placed in layers to obliterate the dead space.

_____

5. Local anesthesia was injected using 1 percent lidocaine with epinephrine 1.5 cc. Incision was made along the postauricular sulcus through the drainage point with retraction applied. A 3.0-cm sebaceous cyst was evident, and it was drained. A small bandage was placed over the incision and drainage site.

_____

6. Split-thickness skin graft of about 7 sq cm was removed from the left thigh, and sterile dressings were applied. A 6-cm malignant lesion was removed from the left calf by a wide excision, including at least 1 cm of normal skin all around, taking it all the way down to include fascia and overlying muscle. Bleeding points were carefully ligated, wound was treated with Hibiclens, and skin graft was applied and sutured in place with 4-0 Mersilene sutures.

_____

7. Patient was using a chain saw, which slipped, and the patient sustained a 5.0-cm laceration to the dorsum of the proximal portion of the left index finger, extending through the extensor tendon and capsule. Debridement of tissue was done to facilitate a better repair of this deep laceration. Tendon and capsule were sutured with five 6-0 silk sutures. Bleeders were ligated with plain catgut. Skin was debrided extensively and approximated with seven sutures of 4-0 Dermal.

_____

8. Patient sustained second-degree burn of the right thigh that was less than 5 percent of the total body surface. The skin was completely necrotic. The right thigh was prepared with pHisoHex, and the wound was debrided using a dermatome. Partial thickness, superficial layer of dead skin tissue was removed. Wound was treated with pHisoHex and cleaned, and a sterile outside dressing was applied.

_____

9. Digital nerve block was applied to numb the top of the right great toe and the left great toe. Blunt dissection of the nail plate from the nail bed, right great toe, was performed. Bleeding was cauterized. Right great toe was bandaged. Next, the left great toenail plate was removed from the nail bed, bleeding was cauterized, and left great toe was bandaged.

_____

10. Patient sustained a 3.0-cm scalp laceration and a 2.0-cm neck laceration after being cut with a knife during a bar fight. Local anesthetic was injected around the scalp and neck laceration sites. Wounds were thoroughly cleansed, explored, and irrigated with a saline solution. One-layer suture repair of scalp and neck wounds was performed.

_____

11. An island pedicle flap was formed on the left thigh, and the defect was covered by elevating a flap of skin and subcutaneous tissue. The flap was then rotated into the defect, with transfer being accomplished through a tunnel underneath the skin. The flap was sutured into its new position, and the donor site was closed.

_____

12. Bell's palsy patient underwent harvesting of a graft for residual facial nerve paralysis. Connective tissue fascia was removed from the fascia lata, right leg. Fascia graft was transplanted to the face and sutured into place underneath skin to reanimate paralyzed area of the face.

_____

13. Using surgical curettement, 3.0-cm malignant lesion of the neck was removed.

_____

14. Procedure: Lumpectomy, left breast. Incision was made through skin and fascia over a left breast mass, and lymphatic and blood vessels were clamped. Tumor mass was excised in its entirety along with normal breast tissue. Drainage tube was placed through a separate stab incision. Layered closure was performed, and a sterile dressing was applied.

_____

15. Right breast cyst was palpated, and needle was inserted into skin of the breast overlying the cyst. Needle was inserted into the cyst, and fluid was evacuated into the syringe. Needle was withdrawn, and pressure was applied to the puncture wound.

_____

CHAPTER

13

CPT Surgery II

Chapter Outline

Musculoskeletal System Subsection

Respiratory System Subsection

Chapter Objectives

At the conclusion of this chapter, the student should be able to:

1. Define key terms related to the Musculoskeletal System and Respiratory System subsections of CPT Surgery.
2. Assign codes from the Musculoskeletal System subsection of CPT Surgery.
3. Assign codes from the Respiratory System subsection of CPT Surgery.

Key Terms

allogenous

arthrocentesis

arthrodesis

arthroscopy

artificial ankylosis

arytenoidectomy

arytenoidopexy

augmentation

autogenous

backbench work

bronchoscopy

brushing

bunion

cadaver donor
    pneumonectomy

cell washing

closed fracture
    treatment

concha

direct laryngoscopy

dislocation

extensor tendons

external fixation device

femur

flexor tendons

harvesting

immobilize

indirect laryngoscopy

internal fixation device

knee

laryngoscopy

larynx

LeFort I

LeFort II

LeFort III

ligament

luxation

manipulation

nasal vestibule

non-segmental
    instrumentation

obturator

open fracture treatment

osteogenesis

osteotomy

percutaneous needle
    biopsy

percutaneous skeletal
    fixation

percutaneous
    vertebroplasty

pleura

pleural effusion

pneumocentesis

pneumonectomy

pyramidal fracture

recipient lung
    allotransplantation

reduction

replantation

rhytides

segmental instrumentation	subglottic stenosis	tibia	turbinates
skeletal traction	subluxation	tibial plateau	vertebral augmentation
stabilize	thoracentesis	trachea	
	thoracoscopy	tracheobronchoscopy	

Introduction

The Musculoskeletal System subsection classifies procedures performed on bones, cartilage, joints, ligaments, muscles, and tendons (including casting and strapping). The Respiratory System subsection classifies procedures performed on the nose, accessory sinuses, larynx, trachea and bronchi, lungs, and pleura. CPT guidelines that apply to the subsections are located at the beginning of the Surgery section. Unique coding instructions for Musculoskeletal System or Respiratory System subsections are located in notes below headings or codes.

 NOTE:

The content in Chapters 12 through 15 of this textbook are organized exactly as it appears in the CPT Surgery section. This organization facilitates learning by allowing students to move from one CPT Surgery subsection to the next, in order.

The Other Procedures code below each subheading classifies an unlisted procedure performed on the anatomical site. When reporting an unlisted procedure code, include documentation about the procedure performed with the submitted claim. (Other Procedures subheadings are not included throughout Chapter 14 of this textbook except when codes that describe additional procedures are included.)

 Coding Tip

Notes located beneath headings and/or subheadings apply to all codes under the heading or subheading. Parenthetical notes located below a specific code apply to that code only, unless the note indicates otherwise.

Musculoskeletal System Subsection

The CPT Musculoskeletal System subsection is arranged from head to toe according to body area and includes the following headings:

- General
- Head
- Neck (Soft Tissues) and Thorax
- Back and Flank
- Spine (Vertebral Column)
- Abdomen
- Shoulder
- Humerus (Upper Arm) and Elbow
- Forearm and Wrist

- Hand and Fingers
- Pelvis and Hip Joint
- Femur (Thigh Region) and Knee Joint
- Leg (Tibia and Fibula) and Ankle Joint
- Foot and Toes
- Application of Casts and Strapping
- Endoscopy/Arthroscopy

Each heading includes one or more of the following subheadings:

- Incision
- Excision
- Introduction or Removal
- Repair, Revision, and/or Reconstruction
- Fracture and/or Dislocation (Table 13-1)
- Manipulation
- Arthrodesis
- Amputation
- Other Procedures

 Coding Tip

The Other Procedures code below each subheading often classifies an unlisted procedure performed on the anatomical site. When reporting an unlisted procedure code, attach documentation (e.g., special report) that describes the procedure to the submitted claim.

EXAMPLE: Patient underwent experimental procedure on the spine, which is not currently classified in CPT. Report code 22899.

Musculoskeletal System Notes

Musculoskeletal System subsection notes include definitions of fractures (e.g., closed and open) and clarify that the type of fracture does not necessarily correspond to the type of treatment (e.g., closed, open, or percutaneous) provided. In addition, types of injury codes include open or closed fractures and joint injuries. Musculoskeletal system notes also clarify the excision of subcutaneous soft connective tissue tumors, excision of fascial or subfascial soft tissue tumors, and radical resection of bone tumors.

 Coding Tip

Open and closed fractures may not receive the same type of treatment. Closed fractures can receive open treatment, and open fractures can receive closed treatment. Either type of fracture can receive percutaneous skeletal fixation treatment.

TABLE 13-1 Types of Fractures, Joint Injuries, and Fracture Treatment

Term	Definition
Types of Fractures	
Closed fracture (or simple fracture) (Figure 13-1)	• Broken bone(s) do not protrude through skin • No open wounds • Described clinically as "closed"
Dislocation or **luxation** (Figure 13-1)	• Total displacement of bone from its joint • **Subluxation** is the partial displacement of a bone from its joint
Open fracture (or compound fracture) (Figure 13-1)	• Broken bone(s) that can be seen through an open wound or that protrudes through skin • Clinically requires an injury with sufficient force to penetrate skin, subcutaneous tissue, muscle fascia/muscle, and/or bone or joint
Closed and Open Fracture Treatment	

Closed fracture treatment	• Fracture site is not surgically opened or exposed
	• Three methods of treatment
	   ○ With **manipulation**, or **reduction** (Figure 13-2), which means that the bones are realigned
	   ○ Without manipulation, which means that the bones are not realigned and a cast or strapping device is placed around the limb to **stabilize**, or **immobilize**, it, which secures the bone(s) in fixed position
	   ○ With or without **skeletal traction** (Figure 13-3), which exerts a pulling force on the affected limb to realign bone or joint

Open fracture treatment	• Fracture site is surgically opened or exposed • With or without *manipulation* (reduction) • With or without *skeletal traction*
Percutaneous Skeletal Fixation Fracture Treatment	
External fixation device (Figure 13-4)	• Hardware is inserted through bone and skin and held rigid with cross braces outside of the body • Always removed after the fracture has healed • Removal procedure is included in the global service, which means it is *not* separately coded and reported
Internal fixation device (Figure 13-5)	• Pins, screws, and/or plates are inserted through or within the fracture area to stabilize and immobilize the injury • Often called open reduction with internal fixation, or ORIF

Coding Tip

Fracture management codes are found throughout the Musculoskeletal System subsection. The codes include the following:

- Pinning
- Open or closed treatment of the fracture
- Application and removal of the initial cast or splint
- Normal, uncomplicated follow-up care

Do not report separate codes for each of the above services when provided during the same encounter, because they are included in the fracture treatment code. Codes for treatment of fractures and joint injuries (dislocations) are classified according to type of manipulation (reduction) and stabilization (fixation or immobilization).

FIGURE 13-1 Fractures and dislocations

FIGURE 13-2 Closed manipulation (reduction) of fractured left humerus

FIGURE 13-3 Traction

(A)

(B)

FIGURE 13-4 External fixation (A) Fracture of femur epiphysis (B) External fixation device stabilizes the bone and is removed after the bone has healed

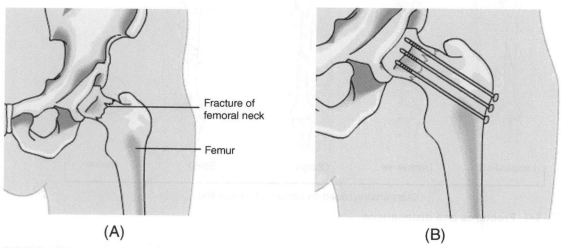

Fracture of femoral neck

Femur

(A)

(B)

FIGURE 13-5 Internal fixation (A) Fracture of femoral neck (B) Internal fixation device (e.g., pins) is placed to stabilize the bone and is not removed after the bone has healed

Exercise 13.1 – Musculoskeletal System Notes

Instructions: Complete each statement.

1. The Musculoskeletal subsection is arranged from head to toe according to _____.
2. Types of injury codes include _____.
3. Open and closed fractures may not receive the same type of _____.
4. Fracture management codes include pinning, open or closed treatment of the fracture, application and removal of the initial cast or splint, and _____.
5. Codes for treatment of fractures and joint injuries are classified according to type of _____ and stabilization.

General

The General heading contains the following subheadings, several of which are unique to the heading:

- Incision
- Wound Exploration—Trauma (e.g., Penetrating Gunshot, Stab Wound)
- Excision
- Introduction or Removal
- Replantation
- Grafts (or Implants)
- Other Procedures

Wound Exploration—Trauma

Wound exploration—trauma codes are reported for the treatment of wound(s) resulting from penetrating trauma (e.g., gunshot or stab wound), and they include the following:

- Surgical exploration and enlargement of the wound
- Extension of dissection (to determine penetration)
- Debridement
- Removal of foreign body(s)
- Ligation or coagulation of minor subcutaneous and/or muscular blood vessel(s) of the subcutaneous tissue, muscle fascia, and/or muscle, not requiring thoracotomy or laparotomy

When major structures or major blood vessels require repair via thoracotomy or laparotomy, do not report the -otomy code. Report the repair code. When a simple, intermediate, or complex repair of wound(s) is performed *only* (without enlargement of wound area, extension of dissection to determine penetration, debridement, removal of foreign body, ligation/coagulation of minor blood subcutaneous/muscular blood vessels), report the appropriate repair code(s) from the Integumentary System section.

EXAMPLE: A patient was treated for a 2.5-cm stab wound located above the base of the neck. The physician extended the wound to explore and assess damage; it was determined that the injury extended to the muscle. Muscle fascia and subcutaneous tissue were closed in layers, and the skin was closed. Report code 20100.

Excision

Report excision codes for epiphyseal bar procedures (performed on bone) and biopsies performed on muscle or bone.

> **EXAMPLE:** Patient underwent open bone biopsy of the right femoral shaft. Report code 20245-RT.

Introduction or Removal

Introduction and removal procedure codes are reported for injection procedures, removal of a foreign body, insertion and application of surgical hardware, arthrocentesis, and aspirations. Surgical injections are performed by inserting a needle directly into a joint or tendon sheath, trigger point, or ganglion cyst (Figure 13-6) to aspirate fluid or inject medications. Codes for injections are based on anatomical site. **Arthrocentesis** is a procedure done to puncture a joint for fluid removal or medication injection.

> **EXAMPLE 1:** A patient underwent aspiration of ganglion cyst, left wrist. Report code 20612-LT.

> **EXAMPLE 2:** Using ultrasound guidance for needle placement, the physician injected patient's left knee joint with 10 mg of Kenalog for therapeutic relief of knee pain. Report codes 20611-LT and HCPCS level II code J3301.

> **EXAMPLE 3:** A patient underwent closed treatment of a femoral shaft fracture with manipulation and application of an uniplane external fixation system. Report codes 27502 and 20692-51. Code 27502 does not specify the use of an external fixation device in its code description; therefore, also report code 20692 with modifier -51.

 NOTE:

Code 20692 is reported in addition to the code for treatment of the fracture or joint injury (unless application of an external fixation system is included in the fracture or joint injury code description).

When a traumatic injury with an open wound requires surgical debridement but the type of fracture requires manipulation and casting (instead of an external or internal fixation device), report the appropriate code for closed fracture treatment *in addition to the appropriate debridement code*.

> **EXAMPLE:** A patient underwent closed treatment of tibial fracture with manipulation, application of a cast, and open wound debridement of 15 sq cm of skin using a scalpel around the fracture site. Report codes 27752 and 97597. There is mention of manipulation; therefore, report code 27752. Report code 97597 for the debridement procedure.

FIGURE 13-6 Ganglion cyst

Replantation

Replantation is the surgical reattachment of a finger, a hand, a toe, a foot, a leg, or an arm that has been completely severed from a person's body. (A severed body part is also called an amputation.) Replantation codes include arthrodesis, cleansing, debridement, internal fixation, and repair of tendons (as well as the surgical reattachment procedure).

EXAMPLE 1: A patient who severed his left arm at the humeral diaphysis in a machine accident underwent replantation of the arm. Wound debridement and shortening were performed on the stump and the amputated part of the arm, along with primary repair of muscles and microsurgical repair of arteries, veins, and nerves and internal fixation. A splint was also applied. Report code 20802-LT.

EXAMPLE 2: A patient who suffered a partially severed right leg in an automobile accident underwent repair of the cruciate and collateral ligaments of the right knee; suture of tendon, right knee; repair of one arterial blood vessel, right knee; and 7.5-cm complex closure of wound. Report codes 27409-RT, 35226-51-RT, 27380-51-RT, and 13121-51-RT. (Modifier -51 is reported to indicate that multiple procedures were performed *in addition* to the first-listed procedure.)

Grafts (or Implants)

Grafts (or implants) codes are reported when **autogenous** (originating in the patient's body) tissue is obtained through separate skin or fascial incisions, *except when the graft procedure code includes **harvesting*** (removing tissue for transplantation) *the graft (or implant) for which a combination code is reported*. Codes with the ✚ (add-on code) symbol mean that modifier -51 is not added. (**Allogenous** grafts involve tissue organ transplanted from one person to another; for example, bone tissue can be obtained from a bone bank. Xenografts are obtained from another species, such as pigs.)

Graft material is harvested (obtained) from bone, cartilage, fascia, or tendon. Harvested bone tissue is transplanted to another site to promote **osteogenesis** (bone growth) or to provide structural stability (e.g., spinal fusion). Harvested cartilage tissue is often used for reconstruction purposes (e.g., facial reconstruction to relieve temporomandibular joint [TMJ] pain). Fascia lata tissue is harvested from gastrocnemius fascia (from the calf) or tensor fascia lata (from the thigh) for soft tissue augmentation (e.g., repair skin defects, such as multiple depressed acne scars or **rhytides**, or wrinkles). (**Augmentation** is the process of enlarging or increasing.) Tendon tissue is harvested for the purpose of repairing another tendon (e.g., reconstruct anterior cruciate ligament).

EXAMPLE: Costochondral cartilage graft was harvested from the left rib of a 4-year-old child for laryngotracheal reconstruction to treat **subglottic stenosis** (narrowing of the airway below the vocal cords, adjacent to the cricoid cartilage). Report codes 31551 and 20910-51.

For bone grafts obtained for spine surgery, just one bone graft code is reported for each operative session (in addition to codes for the definitive procedure, such as spinal fusion) even if graft material is obtained from more than one spinal level (e.g., C1 and C2).

EXAMPLE: A patient diagnosed with spinal stenosis undergoes laminectomy with cervical spine fusion, which requires harvesting a large structural bone graft from the iliac crest (through a separate incision). Report codes 22800, 20902-51, and 20931 in addition to the spinal fusion procedure code. (Do not add modifier -51 to code 20931 because it is an add-on code.)

Other Procedures

Other Procedures codes classify monitoring of interstitial fluid pressure in detection of muscle compartment syndrome, bone graft with microvascular anastomosis, free osteocutaneous flap with microvascular anastomosis, electrical simulation to aid bone healing, low-intensity ultrasound stimulation to aid bone healing, bone tumor ablation, computer-assisted surgical navigation, and an unlisted procedure. When reporting an unlisted procedure code, include documentation about the procedure performed with the submitted claim.

> **EXAMPLE 1:** Patient underwent monitoring of interstitial fluid in detection of muscle compartment syndrome. Report code 20950.

> **EXAMPLE 2:** The patient undergoes bone graft of the left fibula, with microvascular anastomosis. This means that the bone tissue is harvested along with its blood supply (but without overlying skin). (The grafted tissue will be used to reconstruct the patient's right tibial bone, which has a filling defect as the result of trauma; surgery will involve microsurgical anastomosis of blood vessels.) Report code 20955-LT for the "bone graft of left fibula, with microvascular anastomosis."

Exercise 13.2 – General

Instructions: Assign the CPT code(s) and appropriate modifier(s) to each statement.

1. The physician performed an exploration, penetrating wound, neck.

   _____

2. Patient underwent exploration of a penetrating wound of the chest, which involved surgical exploration and enlargement of the wound, debridement, removal of a foreign body, and ligation of subcutaneous tissue.

   _____

3. Open bone biopsy, superficial, left femur.

   _____

4. Patient underwent aspiration of ganglion cyst, right wrist.

   _____

5. Patient received a cortisone injection to a single trigger point, which consisted of the trapezius, deltoid, and latissimus dorsi muscles.

   _____

6. A patient diagnosed with joint contracture of the right ankle underwent application of a multiplane external fixation device.

   _____

7. A patient severed his right index finger while using a chain saw. He underwent successful replantation of the index finger, which included metacarpophalangeal (MCP) joint to insertion of flexor sublimis tendon.

   _____

8. Fascia lata graft was harvested using a stripper.

   _____

Exercise 13.2 – *continued*

9. Patient underwent structural allograft as part of an arthrodesis, posterior technique, craniocervical (occiput-C2).

_____

10. Electrical stimulation procedure was performed to aid bone healing, invasive type.

_____

Head

Head codes classify procedures performed on the skull, facial bones, and temporomandibular joint (TMJ).

Incision

The Incision subheading contains just one code for Arthrotomy, temporomandibular joint. When performed on both sides of the joint, add modifier -50 to the code.

> **EXAMPLE:** A patient underwent TMJ arthrotomy, left, to release scar tissue. Report code 21010-LT.

Excision

Report excision codes for surgery performed on bone and soft tissue of the face and/or scalp.

> **EXAMPLE:** Patient underwent TMJ condylectomy, left. Report code 21050-LT.

Manipulation

The Manipulation subheading contains a code for reporting TMJ manipulation, which requires anesthesia services.

> **EXAMPLE:** Patient underwent therapeutic TMJ manipulation for which general anesthesia was administered. Report code 21073. (Do not report modifier -50, -LT, or -RT with code 21073 because the jaw is not a paired organ or body part.)

Head Prosthesis

Head prosthesis codes describe professional services that involve designing and preparing a prosthesis for a patient. Prostheses are created for rehabilitation patients who have facial, oral, or other anatomical deficiencies that require an artificial ear, eye, or nose or an intraoral **obturator**, which is used to close a gap (e.g., cleft).

> **EXAMPLE:** A patient was fitted for a mandibular resection prosthesis, which was custom prepared by the physician. Report code 21081.

 Coding Tip

When an outside laboratory prepares the prosthetic device, the physician who fits a device reports an appropriate evaluation and management code.

Introduction or Removal

Introduction or removal codes are reported for other introduction or removal procedures, such as application of halo-type appliance for maxillofacial fixation (including removal), interdental fixation device (e.g., arch bar) for conditions other than fracture or dislocation (including removal), or injection procedure for TMJ arthrography.

> **EXAMPLE:** A physician applied a halo-type appliance for maxillofacial fixation, and he removed it 30 days later. Report code 21100. (Do not report a separate code for removal of the halo-type appliance because that procedure is included in the global period for code 21100.)

Repair, Revision, and/or Reconstruction

Reconstruction of the face procedures include LeFort type procedures. **LeFort I** brings the lower midface forward (from the level of the upper teeth) to just above the nostrils. **LeFort II**, or **pyramidal fracture**, is a surgical fracture of the midfacial skeleton at an apex near the superior aspect of the nasal bones. **LeFort III** brings the entire midface forward, from the upper teeth to just above the cheekbones.

> **EXAMPLE:** A patient underwent a LeFort I reconstruction procedure of the midface, which required reconstruction of two pieces without bone graft. Report code 21142.

 NOTE:

- Colpocleisis, also known as a LeFort procedure, involves the surgical repair of a uterine prolapse or a vaginal vault prolapse.
- LeFort I, II, and III fractures are complex bilateral fractures of facial bones that contain large, unstable fragments.
- A Wagstaff-LeFort fracture is an avulsion of the fibula.

Other repair, revision, and/or reconstruction codes are reported for genioplasty, augmentation, and reduction procedures performed on the face, mandible, or forehead. Procedures include reconstruction, osteotomy, arthroplasty, repositioning, augmentation, revision, canthopexy, and reduction.

> **EXAMPLE:** Patient underwent TMJ arthroplasty with allograft. Report code 21242.

Fracture and/or Dislocation

Fracture and/or dislocation codes are reported for treatment of fractures and/or dislocations of the skull, facial bones, and TMJ.

> **EXAMPLE:** A physician performs an open reduction and internal fixation of a left mandibular fracture. Report code 21470-LT.

Exercise 13.3 – Head

Instructions: Assign CPT code(s) and appropriate modifier(s) to each statement.

1. Arthrotomy of temporomandibular joint, right and left sides.

2. Excision of two facial bones (due to bone abscesses).

3. Impression and custom preparation of speech aid prosthesis.

4. Sliding osteotomy genioplasty, single piece.

5. Reconstruction midface, Lefort II with anterior intrusion.

6. Osteotomy of mandible, segmental.

7. Malar augmentation with prosthetic material.

8. Closed treatment of orbit fracture, with manipulation.

9. Closed treatment of maxillary alveolar ridge fracture.

10. Open treatment of mandibular condylar fracture.

Neck (Soft Tissues) and Thorax

The Neck (Soft Tissues) and Thorax heading includes codes for procedures performed on the soft tissues of the neck and thorax (e.g., incision and drainage, excisional biopsies, repairs, revisions, and reconstruction).

Incision

Incision codes are reported for the incision and drainage of abscesses or hematomas, with code 21510 specifically reported for the deep incision with opening of bone cortex of the thorax.

EXAMPLE: Patient underwent incision and drainage of deep abscess, soft tissues of thorax, with partial rib ostectomy. Report code 21502.

Excision

Excision codes are reported for excision of soft tissue of the neck or thorax (e.g., biopsy or excision of tumor), radical resection of a tumor, partial and total excision of ribs, costotransversectomy, ostectomy of sternum, sternal debridement, and radical resection of sternum.

EXAMPLE: Patient underwent costotransversectomy for decompression of paravertebral mass. Report code 21610.

Repair, Revision, and/or Reconstruction

Repair, revision, and/or reconstruction are performed on the soft tissues of the neck (e.g., muscle) and thoracic soft tissues and bones. When procedures are performed to repair superficial wounds, refer to the Integumentary System subsection to assign an appropriate code.

EXAMPLE: Patient underwent open reconstructive repair of pectus excavatum. Report code 21740.

Fracture and/or Dislocation

Fracture and/or dislocation codes are reported for procedures performed to treat rib and sternum fractures or dislocations.

EXAMPLE: Patient underwent open treatment of sternum fracture with skeletal fixation. Report code 21825.

Back and Flank

The Back and Flank heading contains just one subheading.

Excision

Back and Flank excision codes are reported for biopsy, tumor excision, and radical resection of tumor procedures performed on the back and flank. When a drain is inserted and/or the incision is repaired with multiple layers of sutures, staples, or Steri-Strips, do not separately report codes for those procedures; they are bundled in Back and Flank heading codes.

EXAMPLE: Patient underwent soft tissue biopsy of the back, deep. Report code 21925.

Exercise 13.4 – Neck (Soft Tissues) and Thorax and Back and Flank

Instructions: Assign the CPT code(s) and appropriate modifier(s) to each statement.

1. Deep incision with opening of bone cortex, thorax.

   _____

2. Hyoid myotomy and suspension.

   _____

3. Closed treatment of sternum fracture.

   _____

4. Partial excision of rib.

   _____

5. Sternal debridement.

   _____

6. Needle biopsy, soft tissue, thorax.

   _____

7. Excision of tumor, subcutaneous soft tissue of back, 2.5 cm.

   _____

Exercise 13.4 – *continued*

8. The physician removed a 4-cm malignant soft tissue tumor, including adjacent tissue, from the patient's flank. Radical resection was performed to remove the tumor and adjacent tissue. The 5-cm surgical wound was repaired with complex closure.

_____

9. Patient underwent biopsy of superficial soft tissues of the back.

_____

10. Biopsy, soft tissue of flank, deep.

_____

Spine (Vertebral Column)

Spine (Vertebral Column) codes classify procedures performed on the cervical, thoracic, and lumbar spine. Vertebral procedures are sometimes followed by arthrodesis, and they may also include bone grafts and instrumentation. When reporting codes for spinal procedures, make sure you differentiate spinal segments (e.g., T1) and interspaces (e.g., T1–T2 interspace).

- T1–T2 represents two spinal segments of the thoracic vertebrae, at levels 1 and 2.
- L1–L4 represents four spinal segments of the lumbar vertebrae, at levels 1, 2, 3, and 4.
- T1–T2 represents one interspace of the thoracic vertebrae, between levels T1 and T2.
- C1–C2 and C2–C3 represent two interspaces of the cervical vertebrae, between levels C1 and C2 as well as between C2 and C3.

 Coding Tip

- Procedures performed on the bones, connective tissue, and muscles of the spinal column are classified in the Musculoskeletal subsection of CPT.
- Procedures performed on the spinal cord and spinal nerves are classified in the Nervous System subsection of CPT.

The notes located just below the Spine (Vertebral Column) heading should be reviewed before assigning codes.

- Bone graft procedure codes are reported separately, in addition to arthrodesis procedure codes. For bone grafts in other Musculoskeletal categories, review code descriptions and notes.
- Instrumentation procedure codes are reported in addition to primary procedure codes.
- Vertebral procedures may be followed by arthrodesis and may also include bone grafts and instrumentation.
- When an arthrodesis procedure is performed in addition to another procedure, report the arthrodesis procedure code in addition to codes for other procedures performed. (Add modifier -51 to the arthrodesis procedure code[s].)
- When two surgeons collaborate to perform a spinal procedure during the same operative session on the same patient and each performs a distinct part of the procedure, add modifier -62 to the procedure code reported by each surgeon. (Additional procedure codes reported by each surgeon are also reported with modifier -62 if the surgeons continue to work as primary surgeons.)

EXAMPLE 1: Patient underwent arthrodesis of T1–T3 using local autograft from the ribs. Dual rods were inserted with multiple hooks and sublaminar wires. Report codes 22610, 22614, 22614, 22842, and 20936.

Three thoracic segments were fused; therefore, report codes 22610, 22614, and 22614. (Code 22614 is an add-on code; therefore, do not add modifier -51.) Report code 22842 for insertion of dual rods with multiple hooks and sublaminar wires; it is also exempt from the addition of modifier -51. Code 20936 describes the local autograft from the ribs, and it is exempt from modifier -51.

EXAMPLE 2: Surgeon A performed a posterior exposure procedure on Mary Jones by making an incision overlying the lumbar vertebrae, separating the fascia and supraspinous ligaments in line with the incision. He then lifted ligaments and muscles out of the way. Next, Surgeon B performed a posterior discectomy and fusion at L2, and he performed a partial excision of the vertebral body at L3.

- Surgeon A reports code 22612-62.
- Surgeon B reports codes 22612-62 and 22114-51.

Although Surgeon A performed just the posterior exposure part of the procedure, because it is significant to the entire procedure, Surgeon A reports code 22612 with modifier -62. Then, Surgeon B reports code 22612 with modifier -62 because she completed the surgery; she also reports code 22114 with modifier -51.

Incision

Incision codes are reported for the open incision and drainage of deep abscesses (subfascial) of the following sites:

- Cervical
- Thoracic
- Cervicothoracic
- Lumbar
- Sacral
- Lumbosacral

EXAMPLE: A patient underwent open incision and drainage of a deep subfascial abscess, sacral region. Report code 22015.

Excision

The Excision subheading contains a note stating that when two surgeons work together to perform a spinal procedure during the same operative session on the same patient, when each performs a distinct part of the procedure, modifier -62 is added to the procedure code reported by each surgeon. (Additional procedure codes are also reported with modifier -62 if the surgeons continue to work as primary surgeons.)

EXAMPLE: A patient underwent surgical repair of L1–L2 and L3–L4. Dr. Berry performed a posterior exposure of the spine with mobilization of great vessels. Dr. Thomas performed posterior discectomy and spinal fusion at L2–L3 and L4, using anterior interbody technique.

Dr. Berry reports codes 22612-62 and 22614-62. Dr. Thomas reports codes 22612-62 and 22614-62. (Code 22614 is exempt from modifier -51.)

Osteotomy

An **osteotomy** is an incision into bone. Spinal osteotomy involves making incisions in vertebral bone to remove pieces or wedges of bone to correct a deformity such as kyphosis, lordosis, or scoliosis (Figure 13-7). Because the osteotomy codes include corpectomy, discectomy, and laminectomy, separate codes are not reported for these procedures when they are documented in the operative report. Osteotomy codes differentiate anterior and posterior approach.

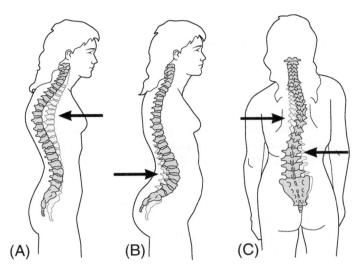

FIGURE 13-7 Spinal deformities (A) Kyphosis (B) Lordosis (C) Scoliosis

Osteotomy procedures include:

- Arthrodesis.
- Instrumentation (report the appropriate code(s) in addition to the primary procedure code).
- Bone graft procedure (report an appropriate code in addition to the primary procedure code).
- Collaboration between two surgeons who perform distinct parts of an anterior spine osteotomy procedure during the same operative session on the same patient (each surgeon adds modifier -62 to reported codes). (Additional procedure codes reported by each surgeon are also reported with modifier -62 if the surgeons continue to work as primary surgeons.)

Spinal osteotomy procedure codes are reported when a portion of the vertebral segment is removed in preparation for re-alignment of the spine as part of spinal deformity correction.

The three sections of the spinal column are defined as *anterior* (anterior two-thirds of vertebral body), *middle* (posterior third of vertebral body and pedicle), and *posterior* (articular facets, lamina, and spinous process).

The Osteotomy subheading also includes a note indicating that when two surgeons work together to perform an anterior spine osteotomy procedure during the same operative session on the same patient *and each performs a distinct part of the procedure*, modifier -62 is added to the appropriate procedure codes (reported by each surgeon).

EXAMPLE 1: Patient underwent spinal osteotomy of spine, posterolateral approach, C1. Report code 22210.

EXAMPLE 2: Patient underwent anterior osteotomy of the spine with discectomy, T1. Report code 22222. (Do not report a separate code for the discectomy procedure.)

EXAMPLE 3: Patient underwent anterior spinal osteotomy, L1–L2. Dr. James performed anterior exposure of the spine with mobilization of great vessels. Dr. Smith performed anterior spinal osteotomy of L1–L2 with discectomy. Then Dr. James performed closure procedures. Dr. James reports codes 22224-62 and 22226-62. Dr. Smith also reports codes 22224-62 and 22226-62. (Code 22226 is an add-on code and exempt from modifier -51.)

Fracture and/or Dislocation

Treatment of fractures and/or dislocations performed during the same operative session include:

- Bone graft procedure.
- Arthrodesis.
- Instrumentation procedure.
- Collaboration between two surgeons who perform distinct parts of an open fracture and/or dislocation procedure (each surgeon adds modifier -62 to reported codes). (Additional procedure codes reported by each surgeon are also reported with modifier -62 if the surgeons continue to work as primary surgeons.)

The Fracture and/or Dislocation subheading also includes a note indicating that when two surgeons work together to treat distinct parts of *open fracture and/or dislocation* procedures during the same operative session and each performs a distinct part of the procedure, modifier -62 is added to the procedure codes. Both surgeons must work together as primary surgeons.

> **EXAMPLE:** Patient underwent open treatment and reduction of T3–T4 vertebral fracture with grafting. Dr. Lawson performed posterior exposure of the spine with mobilization of great vessels. Dr. Timber performed open treatment and reduction of T3–T4 vertebral fracture with spinal allograft. Then Dr. Lawson performed closure procedures. Dr. Lawson reports codes 22327-62 and 22328-62. Dr. Timber also reports codes 22327-62, 22328-62, and 20931. Codes 22328 and 20931 are exempt from modifier -51.

Manipulation

"Manipulation of spine" under anesthesia is performed to treat back pain and other disorders. The idea is that the patient is more relaxed while under anesthesia, and better spinal manipulation results. The code is reported once for manipulation of any region of the spine, including multiple regions during the same operative session. (For "manipulation of the spine *without* anesthesia," report code 97140 from the Medicine section.)

> **EXAMPLE:** Patient underwent lumbar spinal manipulation under anesthesia. Report code 22505.

Percutaneous Vertebroplasty and Vertebral Augmentation

Percutaneous vertebroplasty is the process of injecting a material (e.g., cement) into the vertebral body to reinforce that structure using image guidance. **Vertebral augmentation** is the process of creating a cavity followed by injecting material (e.g., cement) under image guidance. Both procedures are typically performed to relieve pain due to (1) vertebral compression fractures (e.g., pathologic fractures due to osteoporosis) and (2) benign and malignant infiltrating vertebral lesions (e.g., aneurysmal bone cysts, giant cell tumor, hemangioma, metastatic cancer, or myeloma). Codes for percutaneous vertebroplasty and vertebral augmentation include bone biopsy when performed, moderate sedation, and imaging guidance necessary to perform the procedure.

Percutaneous vertebroplasty is usually performed with the patient under conscious sedation; a bone cement (that hardens in about 10 minutes) is injected under pressure directly into a fractured vertebra. The cement causes fragments of fractured vertebra to congeal, providing stability. Bone cement is also injected to fill minor spaces in cancellous bone.

> **EXAMPLE:** Patient underwent percutaneous vertebroplasty under imaging guidance, L1 and L2, to stabilize pathologic fractures due to osteoporosis. Report codes 22510 and 22512. (Code 22512 is exempt from modifier -51 because it is an add-on code.)

Percutaneous Augmentation and Annuloplasty

Percutaneous augmentation and annuloplasty is a minimally invasive technique that is performed under fluoroscopic guidance to treat small tears in the annulus without an associated disc protrusion.

> **EXAMPLE:** Patient underwent percutaneous intradiscal electrothermal annuloplasty, L5, under fluoroscopic guidance. Report code 22526.

Arthrodesis

Arthrodesis, or **artificial ankylosis**, is the surgical fixation (e.g., fusion) of a joint. Arthrodesis may be performed independently of other procedures; when arthrodesis is performed with another procedure, report the arthrodesis code in addition to the definitive procedure and add modifier -51 to the arthrodesis code if applicable. (Some arthrodesis codes are exempt from modifier -51.)

Arthrodesis performed for reasons other than to correct a spinal deformity is classified according to anatomical approach, such as anterior or anterolateral approach, posterior or posterolateral approach, or anterior or posterior interbody technique. Arthrodesis for spinal deformities (e.g., scoliosis and kyphosis) is also reported according to anatomical approach, such as posterior.

- Spinal instrumentation procedures are reported in addition to the arthrodesis code(s). (Modifier -51 is added to some instrumentation codes.)
- Bone graft procedures are reported in addition to the arthrodesis code(s), and modifier -51 is exempt.

> **EXAMPLE:** A physician performed posterior arthrodesis of L5–S1 using autogenous iliac bone graft harvested through a separate incision. Report codes 22612 and 20937. (Code 20937 is exempt from modifier -51.)

Exploration

Just one code is reported for exploration of spinal fusion.

- When spinal instrumentation is performed during the same operative session as the exploration of spinal fusion, report an appropriate spinal instrumentation code.
- When instrumentation reinsertion or removal is reported with other procedures (e.g., arthrodesis, decompression, exploration of fusion), add modifier -51 to the spinal instrumentation code(s).
- When exploration of spinal fusion is performed in addition to other definitive procedures (e.g., arthrodesis), add modifier -51 to the "exploration of spinal fusion" code.

Spinal Instrumentation

Spinal instrumentation includes **segmental instrumentation**, which is a fixation at each end of the construct (structure) and includes at least one additional interposed bony attachment. **Non-segmental instrumentation** is a fixation at each end of the construct (structure) that may span several vertebral segments without attachment to the intervening segments. A *vertebral segment* represents a single complete vertebral bone with its associated articular processes and laminae (e.g., C1). A *vertebral interspace* is the non-bony compartment between two adjacent vertebral bodies and it contains the intervertebral disc, which includes the nucleus pulposus, annulus fibrosus, and two cartilaginous endplates.

> **EXAMPLE:** Patient underwent posterior technique arthrodesis of C1–C2. Autogenous iliac bone graft was used, and it was harvested through a separate incision. Anterior instrumentation of the two vertebral segments was also performed. Report codes 22595, 22845, and 20937. (Do not add modifier -51 to code 20937.)

Exercise 13.5 – Spine (Vertebral Column)

Instructions: Assign the CPT code(s) and appropriate modifier(s) to each statement.

1. Patient underwent arthrodesis at L4–L5 interspace. Posterior interbody technique laminectomy was performed. Discectomy was also performed to prepare the vertebral interspace for fusion.

   _____

2. Physician performed "spinal manipulation under anesthesia," cervical, thoracic, and lumbar spine.

   _____

3. Patient underwent osteotomy and discectomy of a single cervical spine vertebral segment. Anterior approach was used.

   _____

4. Physician performed arthrodesis using posterior technique of atlas-axis (C1–C2) with internal spinal fixation by wiring the spinous processes.

   _____

5. Patient underwent posterior arthrodesis of L2–L3 for spinal deformity, with casting. Morselized autogenous iliac bone graft was harvested through a separate skin incision.

   _____

Abdomen

The Abdomen subheading contains just two headings.

- Excision
- Other Procedures

The excision procedure code is reported for excision of abdominal wall tumor. The "other procedures" code is reported for unlisted procedures.

EXAMPLE: Patient underwent excision of subfascial abdominal wall tumor. Report code 22900.

Shoulder

The Shoulder heading contains codes for procedures performed on the clavicle, scapula, humerus head and neck, sternoclavicular joint, acromioclavicular joint, and shoulder joint.

EXAMPLE: Physician performed removal of a "total shoulder" implant with replacement of a new implant. Report codes 23335 for removal of the implant and 23472-51 for arthroplasty and insertion of a new total shoulder implant.

 NOTE:

To report magnetic resonance imaging (MRI) of the shoulder with intra-articular contrast, report code 23350 (Injection procedure for shoulder arthrography or enhanced CT/MRI shoulder arthrography) in addition to the MRI code (from the Radiology section).

Humerus (Upper Arm) and Elbow

The Humerus (Upper Arm) and Elbow heading includes codes for procedures performed on the humerus, elbow, and head and neck of the radius and olecranon process.

> **EXAMPLE:** Patient underwent closed treatment with manipulation, medial humeral epicondylar fracture. Report code 24565.

Forearm and Wrist

The Forearm and Wrist heading includes codes for procedures performed on the radius, ulna, carpal bones, and joints.

> **EXAMPLE:** A patient was diagnosed with subluxation of extensor carpi ulnaris (ECU) tendon at the wrist. The physician reconstructed the ECU tendon sheath with a retinacular graft harvest from the fourth dorsal compartment. Report code 25275, which includes the procedure for obtaining the graft.

 Coding Tip

- Open carpal tunnel decompression surgery (for carpal tunnel syndrome) is classified in the Nervous System subsection of surgery.
- Surgical endoscopy to release the transverse carpal ligament to treat carpal tunnel syndrome surgery is assigned code 29848, which is located under the Endoscopy/Arthroscopy heading of the Musculoskeletal System subsection.

Hand and Fingers

The Hand and Fingers heading includes codes for procedures performed on the hands and fingers, which include repairs to tendons, nerves, and blood vessels to provide treatment for injuries or to correct deformities. Tendons include two types.

- **Flexor tendons:** Bend the fingers
- **Extensor tendons:** Straighten the fingers

The following procedures are bundled in the tendon repair codes:

- Application of immobilization
- Extension of the excision
- Repair and closure of tendon sheath

Codes for harvesting and inserting tendon grafts from another site, repairing nerves or arteries, and treating fractures are reported in addition to the tendon repair.

> **EXAMPLE:** A patient underwent percutaneous palmar fasciotomy, right hand for Dupuytren's contracture. Report code 26040-RT.

Exercise 13.6 – Abdomen, Shoulder, Humerus (Upper Arm) and Elbow, Forearm and Wrist, and Hand and Fingers

Instructions: Assign the CPT code(s) and appropriate modifier(s) to each statement.

1. The physician performed an excision of a 4-cm subfascial abdominal wall tumor and the surrounding tissue. Incision was repaired in multiple layers with sutures.

2. The physician removed subdeltoid calcareous deposits, left shoulder joint, by incising the raised area over the calcium deposits and removing the calcareous deposits.

3. The physician performed a forequarter interthoracoscapular amputation, right shoulder.

4. The physician performed removal of a deep foreign body, left shoulder.

5. Excision of 2-cm malignant tumor from subcutaneous tissue around right elbow.

6. Percutaneous medial tenotomy for treatment of tennis elbow, right.

7. Patient who sustained left elbow trauma developed an elbow contracture that required manipulation under anesthesia.

8. Percutaneous skeletal fixation of left Colles fracture.

9. Injection procedure performed to prep patient for right wrist arthrography.

10. Left palmar fasciectomy with Z-plasty.

Pelvis and Hip Joint

The Pelvis and Hip Joint heading includes codes for procedures performed on the head and neck of the femur (hip joint). (Codes for procedures performed on the femur and its tibial plateau are located under the Femur [Thigh Region] and Knee Joint heading.)

EXAMPLE: Patient underwent partial hemiarthroplasty of the left hip with insertion of femoral stem prosthesis. Report code 27125-LT. (Insertion of the femoral stem prosthesis is included in code 27125.)

Femur (Thigh Region) and Knee Joint

The Femur (Thigh Region) and Knee Joint heading includes codes for procedures performed on the femur and its tibial plateau and the knee joint. (Codes for procedures performed on the head and neck of the femur are located under the Pelvis and Hip Joint heading.)

NOTE:

Arthroscopic knee surgery is a commonly performed procedure, and codes are located under the Endoscopy/Arthroscopy heading of the Musculoskeletal System subsection.

The **femur** (Figure 13-8) is the long bone of the thigh, and it articulates with the hip bone, tibia, and patella. The **tibial plateau** is the lower portion of the femur that articulates with the **tibia** (larger of the two lower leg bones). The **knee** is a "hinge" joint comprised of bones, cartilage, ligaments, and tendons. **Ligaments** (e.g., medial collateral ligament) are connective tissue that connects bone to bone (e.g., patella to femur), and they control stability of the knee. Trauma to knee joints can result in ligament tears, which require surgical repair (Figure 13-9).

EXAMPLE: Patient was diagnosed with an anterior medial left thigh mass, which was 2 × 2 × 1.5 cm in size. With the patient under local anesthesia, biopsy of the mass above the superficial fascia was performed. Report code 27323-LT (because the mass was removed from "above the superficial fascia").

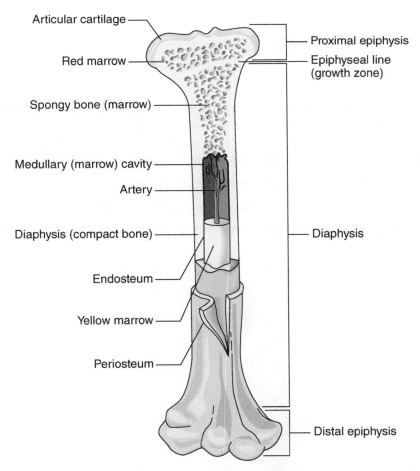

FIGURE 13-8 Structure of femur (long bone), including proximal (near) and distal (far) references to the bone's shaft

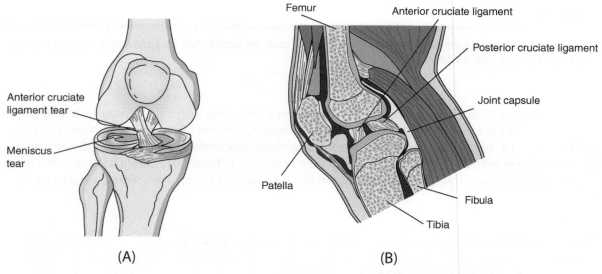

FIGURE 13-9 (A) Meniscus and anterior cruciate ligament tears (B) Knee joint

Leg (Tibia and Fibula) and Ankle Joint

The Leg (Tibia and Fibula) and Ankle Joint heading includes codes for procedures performed on the tibia, fibula, and ankle joint.

> **EXAMPLE:** Patient underwent flexor tenolysis of the right ankle, single tendon. Report code 27680-RT.

Foot and Toes

The Foot and Toes heading includes codes for procedures performed on the feet and toes. Hallux valgus repair codes (28292–28299) are reported to correct **bunions** (Figure 13-10), which are caused by bone inflammation and swelling and result in medial deviation and axial rotation of the first metatarsophalangeal (MTP) joint. Bunion deformities develop differently, and repair requires different levels of complexity and different techniques, as follows:

- Keller procedure: Simple resection of the base of the proximal phalanx with removal of the medial eminence

- McBride procedure: Distal soft tissue release that corrects soft tissue deformity at the MTP joint

- Mitchell procedure: Complex, double cut osteotomy through the neck of the first metatarsal

FIGURE 13-10 Bunion

EXAMPLE: Patient underwent bilateral hallux valgus correction with sesamoidectomy and resection of proximal phalanx base. Report code 28292-50.

Exercise 13.7 – Pelvis and Hip Joint, Femur (Thigh Region) and Knee Joint, Leg (Tibia and Fibula) and Ankle Joint, and Foot and Toes

Instructions: Assign the CPT code(s) and appropriate modifier(s) to each statement.

1. Proximal hamstring release.

2. Partial hip replacement with bipolar arthroplasty to treat right hip fracture.

3. Removal of a foreign body deep in the left thigh.

4. Complete 1 × 1 × 0.5-cm excision of subcutaneous tumor, posterior left thigh.

5. Excision of 2-cm bone cyst with autograft of harvested femur graft, left, which was performed during the same operative session.

6. Decompression fasciotomy of the lateral and posterior compartments, right knee.

7. Percutaneous repair of ruptured Achilles tendon, right.

8. Incision and drainage of infected bursa, left ankle.

9. Distal Chevron osteotomy, right.

10. Partial ostectomy to surgically correct bunionette involving the right fifth metatarsal head.

Application of Casts and Strapping

The Application of Casts and Strapping heading includes codes that are reported when the cast (or splint) application or strapping is a(n)

- Replacement procedure performed during or after the period of follow-up care
- Initial service performed *without restorative treatment or procedure* to stabilize or protect a fracture, a dislocation, or another injury and/or to provide comfort to a patient

EXAMPLE 1: A 5-year-old patient was seen in the office to have his left short-arm cast replaced. He was playing a game he invented called "bop it," which involved knocking his cast on top of one of his bedposts. The cast cracked and had to be replaced. The patient was instructed to stop playing "bop it." Report code 29075-LT.

EXAMPLE 2: A 7-year-old patient injured his left arm while roller-skating. A two-view left forearm x-ray performed at Sylvania Community Hospital's emergency department revealed fractures of the radial and ulnar shafts. A level III emergency department evaluation and management service was provided. The patient's arm was placed in a splint to stabilize the fracture, and the mother was informed that treatment would have to be performed the next day because no orthopedic physician was available in the facility or on call. Report codes 99283, 29125-LT, and 73090-LT. (Do not add modifier -57 to the E/M code [because surgery was not performed] or modifier -51 to the surgery and radiology codes.)

Upon being informed that treatment would not be performed that day, the mother called the facility from which the family normally receives treatment and asked to speak with the orthopedic surgeon on call. That physician called her back within 15 minutes; when the mother explained the circumstances, she was told to bring the x-rays and her child to St. Francis Hospital to meet the surgeon there so he could assess her son and perform treatment. Upon outpatient evaluation and management (level III) of this new patient by the orthopedic surgeon, the mother was informed that same-day treatment was preferred because waiting until the next day would result in swelling, inflammation, and pain, making it more difficult to treat the fractures. Later that day the patient underwent closed manipulation of radial and ulnar shaft fractures under general anesthesia, and a short-arm cast was applied. The patient remained in the hospital until 10 PM, at which time he was released to return home with his parents. Report codes 25565 and 99203-57.

When one physician applies a cast, splint, or strapping device as initial treatment of a fracture or dislocation and a different physician later performs a restorative treatment or procedure, report "treatment of fracture and/or dislocation" code(s) from the appropriate heading in the Musculoskeletal System subsection.

When a physician performs an initial restorative treatment or procedure and an initial cast, splint, or strap is also applied, the physician is responsible for providing all subsequent fracture, dislocation, and/or injury care. Do not report a code for the application of a cast, splint, or strapping device with the initial restorative treatment or procedure; the first cast, splint, or strapping device application is included in the "treatment of fracture and/or dislocation" code.

 Coding Tip

Do not report modifier -58 (staged or related procedure or service by the same physician during the postoperative period) when a temporary cast, splint, or strapping device is applied and the patient later undergoes a restorative treatment or procedure. In addition, do not report evaluation and management service codes unless significant identifiable further services are provided at the time of the cast application or strapping. (Report only the "treatment of fracture and/or dislocation" code.)

Endoscopy/Arthroscopy

The Endoscopy/Arthroscopy heading includes codes for procedures performed using an endoscope or arthroscope. Endoscopy is the visual examination of the interior of a body cavity or an organ. **Arthroscopy** (Figure 13-11) is the visual examination of the inside of a joint.

Endoscopic and arthroscopic procedures are diagnostic or surgical, and CPT notes indicate that surgical endoscopy/arthroscopy always includes diagnostic endoscopy/arthroscopy. An endoscopy/arthroscopy is considered diagnostic when it is performed to visualize an abnormality or to determine the extent of disease. When anything in addition to visualization is performed, the endoscopy/arthroscopy procedure is considered surgical.

EXAMPLE: Patient underwent surgical arthroscopy, left knee, with medical and lateral meniscectomy, which included debridement and shaving of articular cartilage (chondroplasty). Report code 29880-LT.

(A) Arthroscope in use

(B) Internal view of the knee during arthroscopy

**FIGURE 13-11 Arthroscopic surgery (A) The physician views progress on a monitor
(B) Internal view as diseased tissue is removed during surgery**

 Coding Tip

- A surgical endoscopy/arthroscopy always includes a diagnostic endoscopy/arthroscopy. This means that a code for diagnostic endoscopy/arthroscopy is not reported with a code for surgical endoscopy/arthroscopy. A diagnostic endoscopy/arthroscopy code is reported when it is the only endoscopic/arthroscopic procedure performed. (Codes for other procedure codes, other than surgical endoscopy/arthroscopy, can be reported with diagnostic endoscopy/arthroscopy codes.)

- Diagnostic knee arthroscopy is probably the most common type of procedure performed. It is done to examine and diagnose knee joint abnormalities. Diagnostic knee arthroscopy involves inserting an arthroscope through small incisions and using a camera to transmit images onto a monitor so the knee joint's interior can be visualized. During arthroscopic knee surgery, the knee is subdivided into three compartments: medial, lateral, and patellofemoral.

- Surgical knee arthroscopy is often performed to treat diseased or damaged structures of the knee joint (e.g., torn meniscus, meniscal lesions, damaged patella or ligaments, and inflamed or damaged synovium).

Exercise 13.8 – Application of Casts and Strapping and Endoscopy/Arthroscopy

Instructions: Assign the CPT code(s) and appropriate modifier(s) to each statement. (Do not assign CPT E/M codes.)

1. Diagnostic arthroscopy, left elbow, with synovial biopsy.

_____

(continues)

Exercise 13.8 – *continued*

2. Patient's left long-arm cast was removed after getting wet, the site was evaluated, and another long-arm fiberglass cast was reapplied. The same physician who applied the first cast removed the wet cast and applied the new cast.

   _____

3. Physician treated flexion contracture of right small finger proximal interphalangeal joint by applying a cast to stabilize the joint.

   _____

4. Patient with diabetic neuropathic ulcers had rigid total contact leg cast applied, left.

   _____

5. Patient sustained nondisplaced fracture of distal left ulna, and emergency department physician applied a molded splint for immobilization and protection of the fracture. Patient was referred to orthopedic specialist.

   _____

6. Patient underwent arthroscopic repair of large osteochondritis dissecans lesion and talar dome fracture with internal fixation, right.

   _____

7. Surgical arthroscopy of the metacarpophalangeal joint on the right with debridement.

   _____

8. Patient underwent arthroscopic Mumford procedure of distal 1 cm of left clavicle.

   _____

9. Arthroscopic superior labrum anterior/posterior (SLAP) lesion tear repair, right shoulder.

   _____

10. Left knee diagnostic and surgical arthroscopy with partial medial meniscectomy.

    _____

Respiratory System Subsection

The CPT Respiratory System (Figure 13-12) subsection is arranged according to body area from nose to lungs. It includes the following headings:

- Nose
- Accessory Sinuses
- Larynx
- Trachea and Bronchi
- Lungs and Pleura

Respiratory system headings include one or more of the following subheadings:

- Incision
- Excision
- Introduction (and Removal)
- Removal of Foreign Body
- Repair
- Destruction
- Endoscopy
- Other Procedures

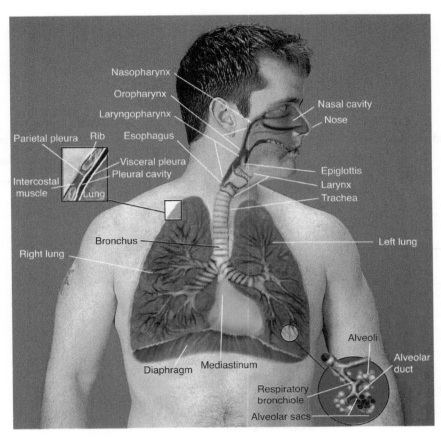

FIGURE 13-12 **Respiratory system**

The Respiratory System subsection's Lungs and Pleura heading also contains the following subheadings:

- Lung Transplantation
- Surgical Collapse Therapy; Thoracoplasty

Respiratory section guidelines define procedures and provide instruction for the selection of appropriate codes, as follows:

- Approach used for lung procedures
- Amount and type of tissue removed
- Difference between diagnostic and therapeutic procedures
- Ways various removal procedures may be performed

Nose

The Nose heading contains codes for procedures that are performed on the nose, nasal septum, intranasal tissue, nasal turbinates, and skin of the nose. (Refer to Figure 13-13 for structure of the upper respiratory system, including nasal anatomy.) Codes for procedures range from simple control of a nosebleed to complex surgery (e.g., rhinoplasty).

 Coding Tip

When the control of bleeding is performed during a procedure on the nose, it is considered an integral part of that procedure and is not separately coded and reported. Thus, codes that classify "control of nasal hemorrhage" are not reported with other procedure codes from the Nose heading.

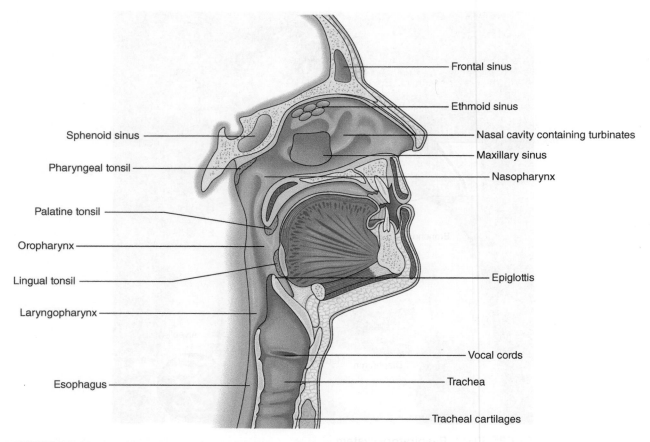

FIGURE 13-13 Structure of the upper respiratory system

Incision

Incision codes are reported for drainage of abscess of hematoma, nasal (internal approach) or nasal septum. A *hematoma* is a localized collection of blood outside of the blood vessels, usually in liquid form within tissue.

> **EXAMPLE:** Patient underwent drainage of a nasal hematoma via internal approach. Report code 30000.

Excision

Turbinates, or **conchae**, are bony plates covered by spongy mucosa with curved margins. There are three turbinates on each side of the **nasal vestibule** (nose's entrance): inferior, middle, and superior. When surgery is performed on turbinates, it is important to identify the type of turbinate procedure and technique used. Turbinates can be removed by resection or excision with or without endoscopy, cauterization, debridement, laser, cryotherapy, radiofrequency reduction, or ablation. Turbinate excision and submucous resection codes (30130, 30140) are typically reported for inferior turbinate surgery. These codes can also be reported separately with other surgical procedures performed on the nose (e.g., sphenoid, maxillary, or frontal sinus procedures; septoplasty). Codes 30130 and 30140 describe unilateral procedures, which means that if the surgery is performed on both sides, modifier -50 (bilateral procedure) is added to the reported code.

> **EXAMPLE:** Patient underwent anterior intranasal ethmoidectomy for chronic sinusitis. A partial inferior turbinate excision was performed to gain access to the ethmoid bone. Report code 31200. (Code 30130 is not reported for the partial inferior turbinate excision because it was performed only to gain access to the ethmoid bone.)

Coding Tip

When a turbinate procedure is performed to gain access to the ethmoid bone, do not report code 30130 or 30140 in addition to the turbinate procedure code(s). However, if a separate diagnosis justifies medical necessity for excision of turbinate (30130) or submucous resection of turbinate (30140), report the appropriate code and add modifier -51. (NOTE: Even if medical necessity justifies reporting codes 30130–30140, some third-party payers will not reimburse the turbinate excision or submucous resection because the code descriptions do not specify middle or superior turbinates.)

> **EXAMPLE:** Patient underwent a total intranasal ethmoidectomy for chronic sinusitis and a complete excision of the inferior turbinate for sleep apnea. Report codes 31201 and 30130-51.

Introduction

Introduction codes are reported for therapeutic injection into nasal turbinate(s), displacement therapy, and insertion of a nasal septum prosthesis.

> **EXAMPLE:** Patient underwent Proetz type displacement therapy. Report code 30210.

Removal of Foreign Body

Removal of foreign body codes are reported for removal of a foreign body from the intranasal area (office type procedure) and that requiring general anesthesia or by lateral rhinotomy.

> **EXAMPLE:** Patient underwent removal of intranasal foreign body via lateral rhinotomy. Report code 30320.

Repair

Nasal repair include rhinoplasty, repair of nasovestibular stenosis, septoplasty, repair of choanal atresia, lysis of intranasal synechia, fistula repair, septal or intranasal dermatoplasty, and repair of nasal septal perforations.

> **EXAMPLE:** Patient underwent bilateral nasal septoplasty with cartilage scoring. Report code 30520-50.

Destruction

Destruction codes are reported for ablation of soft tissue of inferior turbinates superficially or intramurally.

> **EXAMPLE:** Patient underwent submucosal soft tissue ablation of inferior turbinates, bilateral via electrocautery. Report code 30802.

Other Procedures

Other Procedures codes are reported for the control of nasal hemorrhage, therapeutic fracture of nasal inferior turbinate(s), and unlisted procedures of the nose.

> **EXAMPLE:** Patient underwent therapeutic fracture of the nasal inferior turbinates. Report code 30930.

Exercise 13.9 – Nose

Instructions: Assign the CPT code(s) and appropriate modifier(s) to each statement.

1. Physician made therapeutic injections into the right and left turbinates.

2. Excision of polyp from inside of nose, left side, via scalpel. Single-layer closure was also performed.

3. Removal of nasal mucosa from inside left side of nose for biopsy. Some normal tissue adjacent to diseased mucosa is also removed during biopsy.

4. Excision of intranasal lesion via lateral rhinotomy, left.

5. Rhinoplasty for nasal deformity secondary to congenital cleft lip and palate, including columellar lengthening of the tip and septum, with osteotomies.

Accessory Sinuses

The Accessory Sinuses heading contains codes for procedures performed on the maxillary, frontal, ethmoid, and sphenoid sinuses. The Accessory Sinuses heading contains unique coding guidelines for endoscopy procedures. (Refer to Figure 13-13 for location of accessory sinuses.)

Incision

Incision codes classify lavage, sinusotomy, and pterygomaxillary fossa surgery. A *lavage* is the washing out of a body cavity, such as the accessory sinuses, with water or a medicated solution. A *sinusotomy* is a surgical incision of the sinus (e.g., treatment of chronic sinus disease). The *pterygomaxillary fossa* is an opening in the skull, through which arteries and nerves pass.

> **EXAMPLE:** Patient underwent right maxillary sinus lavage by cannulation. Report code 31000-RT.

Excision

Excision codes classify ethmoidectomy and maxillectomy procedures. An *ethmoidectomy* involves removing partitions between the ethmoid sinuses to create larger sinus cavities (e.g., treatment of sinus infections and sinus obstructions). A *maxillectomy* involves removing the upper jaw bone (maxilla) (e.g., treatment of cancer in bones and tissues of roof or hard palate of mouth).

> **EXAMPLE:** Patient underwent total intranasal ethmoidectomy, left. Report code 31201-LT.

Endoscopy

Endoscopy codes classify unilateral procedures unless the code description indicates otherwise. This means that HCPCS level II modifier -LT or -RT is added to the endoscopy code unless the procedure is performed bilaterally and modifier -50 is added to the code.

NOTE:

Modifier -50 is not added to code 31231, Nasal endoscopy, diagnostic; unilateral or bilateral (separate procedure), because "bilateral" is included in its description. However, modifier -LT or -RT can be added to code 31231 if the procedure is performed unilaterally.

Diagnostic endoscopy codes include inspection of the interior of the nasal cavity and its meatus, turbinates, and sphenoethmoid recess. When diagnostic endoscopy is performed, the following procedures are bundled in the reported code: administration of local anesthesia, electrocautery, access to different cavities, and some shaving/debridement. (Extensive shaving/debridement is reported with a separate code and modifier -51.) Report just one code when diagnostic endoscopy is performed on all of these areas on one or both sides.

Surgical sinus endoscopy is performed through the nose, using a fiberoptic endoscopy; it includes sinusotomy (when performed) and diagnostic endoscopy. When a physician performs surgical endoscopy of accessory sinuses, evaluation of nasal access regions (diagnostic endoscopy) is also performed as part of the medically necessary service. Do not report a code for diagnostic endoscopy in addition to the surgical endoscopic procedure. This means that when surgical and diagnostic endoscopies are performed during the same operative session, just one code is reported to classify both procedures.

EXAMPLE: Patient undergoes surgical nasal endoscopy with anterior ethmoidectomy, left; the physician uses the endoscope diagnostically to evaluate other regions of the nasal cavity. Report code 31254-LT. (Do not report code 31231 for the diagnostic nasal endoscopy.)

 NOTE:

Recognize the difference between endoscopic and open surgical approaches. An endoscopic nasal surgical approach utilizes a fiberoptic endoscope instrument, which is inserted through the nostril(s). An open nasal surgical approach is performed by making an incision into skin or tissues inside the nasal cavity.

Anatomically, the middle turbinate is part of the ethmoid bone. Therefore, if the middle turbinate is removed during endoscopic polypectomy or endoscopic ethmoidectomy, a code for removal of the middle turbinate is *not* reported.

EXAMPLE: Patient underwent bilateral nasal surgical endoscopy with total ethmoidectomy and bilateral nasal septoplasty. Report codes 31255-50 and 30520-50-51.

When biopsy of a lesion from the accessory sinuses is obtained as part of an excision, destruction, or other type of removal during the same operative session, do not report a biopsy code in addition to the excision/destruction/removal code. Also, biopsy codes are not separately reported for multiple similar or identical lesions even if the lesions are taken from a different area of the respiratory system.

EXAMPLE: A patient presents with multiple nasal polyps. Patient undergoes bilateral surgical nasal endoscopy with polypectomy and total ethmoidectomy. Report code 31255-50. (Do not report separate procedure code 31237 for the surgical endoscopy with polypectomy because that procedure is bundled with code 31255.) Even though polypectomy may have been performed prior to total ethmoidectomy, the polypectomy procedure is included in the more invasive ethmoidectomy procedure.

Coding Tip

When a sinusotomy is performed in conjunction with a sinus endoscopy, just one code is reported for both services. If the endoscopy was performed to evaluate the sinus cavity prior to sinusotomy, report just the sinusotomy procedure code. CPT instructions state that a surgical sinus endoscopy always includes sinusotomy and diagnostic endoscopy.

Exercise 13.10 – Accessory Sinuses

Instructions: Assign the CPT code(s) and appropriate modifier(s) to each statement.

1. Anterior ethmoidectomy via intranasal approach.

   _____

2. Endoscopic treatment of a nosebleed.

   _____

3. Endoscopic anterior and posterior (total) ethmoidectomy, left, with left maxillary antrostomy.

   _____

4. Nasal endoscopy with biopsy.

   _____

5. Endoscopic frontal nasal exploration with removal of tissue from left frontal sinus and diagnostic endoscopy of left turbinates.

   _____

Larynx

The Larynx (Figure 13-14) heading contains codes for procedures performed on the epiglottis and larynx and inside the trachea.

FIGURE 13-14 View of larynx and vocal cords from above. (A) Vocal cords are open during breathing. (B) Vocal cords vibrate together during speech.

Excision

Excision codes classify laryngotomy, laryngectomy, pharyngolaryngectomy, arytenoidectomy or arytenoidopexy, and epiglottidectomy procedures. A *laryngotomy* involves making a surgical incision into the larynx to provide air passage when breathing is obstructed. A *laryngectomy* involves removal of the larynx (voicebox). A *pharyngolaryngectomy* is the removal of the hypopharynx (laryngeal part of throat) and larynx. An *epiglottidectomy* is the removal of all or part of the epiglottis (e.g., treatment of sleep apnea).

> **EXAMPLE:** Patient underwent total intranasal ethmoidectomy, left. Report code 31201-LT.

According to *CPT Assistant* (October 2001), when a total laryngectomy with bilateral radical neck dissection (31365) is performed, do not add modifier -50 to the code because the larynx is a single midline organ. (A laryngectomy cannot be performed bilaterally.) Instead, report code 31365 for the total laryngectomy and radical neck dissection on one side. Also, report code 38720-59 for the radical neck dissection on the other side. (The description of code 38720 is "Cervical lymphadenectomy [complete].") (Modifier -59 is added to indicate a distinct procedural service.)

An **arytenoidectomy** is the excision of arytenoid cartilage, which is located in the bilateral vocal fold. An **arytenoidopexy** is the surgical fixation of arytenoidal cartilage and/or surrounding muscles. Both procedures are done to treat vocal cord paralysis or to improve patient breathing.

> **EXAMPLE:** Patient underwent endoscopic arytenoidectomy. Report code 31560. (Do *not* report code 31400.)

Introduction

Introduction procedures are performed for emergency endotracheal intubation and to change a tracheotomy tube prior to healing (before an abnormal fistula tract is created by the body).

> **EXAMPLE:** Patient underwent an emergency endotracheal intubation during provision of critical care services. Report code 31500. (Appropriate code[s] from the E/M critical care services subsection would also be reported.)

Endoscopy

Endoscopy codes include the following types of laryngoscopy, and the documented operative report will indicate the instrumentation used:

- Direct
- Indirect
- Use of operating microscope (for magnification)
- Use of fiberoptic scope (that transmits light)

Laryngoscopy is the visualization of the back of the throat, including the **larynx** (voice box) and vocal cords. **Direct laryngoscopy** is the insertion of a flexible or rigid fiberoptic scope or a rigid laryngoscope to visualize throat structures. **Indirect laryngoscopy** is the insertion of a small hand mirror in the patient's mouth at the back of the throat while the physician wears headgear that contains a mirror and light source; the mirror worn by the physician reflects light into the patient's mouth, allowing the physician to visualize the patient's throat.

> **EXAMPLE:** Patient underwent indirect diagnostic laryngoscopy. Report code 31505.

Repair

Repair codes classify laryngoplasty and laryngeal reinnervation procedures. A *laryngoplasty* involves reconstruction of the larynx (voicebox). A *laryngeal reinnervation* supplies a new, functioning nerve supply to a paralyzed larynx; the purpose is to restore phonation (vocalization).

EXAMPLE: Patient underwent cricoid split laryngoplasty. Report code 31587.

Exercise 13.11 – Larynx

Instructions: Assign the CPT code(s) and appropriate modifier(s) to each statement. (Do not assign CPT E/M codes.)

1. Emergency department physician places endotracheal tube for a patient in respiratory distress.

   _____

2. Total laryngectomy with radical neck dissection.

   _____

3. Patient with cricoid split (break in the circular cartilage of the larynx) undergoes laryngoplasty.

   _____

4. Complicated tracheotomy tube change (prior to establishment of fistula tract).

   _____

5. Total laryngectomy with bilateral radical neck dissection.

   _____

Trachea and Bronchi

The Trachea and Bronchi (Figure 13-15) heading contains codes for procedures performed through the trachea and on tracheal cartilage (carinii) and the bronchi.

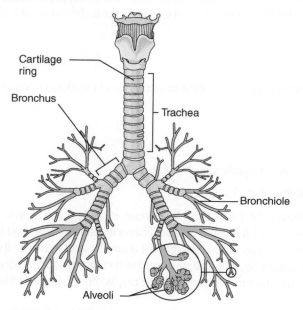

FIGURE 13-15 Trachea, bronchi, bronchial trees, and alveoli (air sacs)

Incision

Incision codes classify tracheostomy, construction of tracheoesophageal fistula and subsequent insertion of an alaryngeal speech prosthesis, tracheal puncture, and tracheostoma revision procedures. A *tracheostomy* involves creating an opening through the neck into the trachea (windpipe); a tracheostomy tube is usually placed into the opening to provide an airway and/or to remove secretions from the lungs. A tracheoesophageal fistula is constructed with insertion of a one-way valve, which is an alaryngeal speech prosthesis, called a *voice button* or a *Blom-Singer prosthesis*, to allow the patient to phonate (vocalize). A *tracheal puncture* involves piercing the trachea with a hollow point needle to aspirate secretions or inject therapeutic agent(s). A *tracheostoma revision* involves incising the stoma area and resecting redundant scar tissue or a poorly healing wound.

EXAMPLE: Patient underwent emergency transtracheal tracheostomy. Report code 31603.

Endoscopy

A **bronchoscopy** (Figure 13-16) is the visual examination of the interior of the bronchus. A tracheoscopy is the visual examination of the interior of the **trachea** (windpipe). A **tracheobronchoscopy** is the visual examination of the interior of the trachea and bronchus. Endoscopy of the trachea and bronchus is performed with either a flexible fiberoptic scope or a rigid scope, with or without cell washings or brushing. A **brushing** involves combing the mucous lining of the trachea or bronchus with a bronchial brush to collect cells. **Cell washing** involves flushing fluid into an area and removing the fluid, using aspiration technique to collect cells.

Endoscopy procedures also involve use of a bronchoscope, with or without fluoroscopic guidance, to visualize all major lobar and segmental bronchi. These procedures may also include obtaining diagnostic specimens as part of the examination. Fiberoptic bronchoscopy services routinely include inspection of the nasal cavity, pharynx, and larynx. When nasal endoscopy or laryngoscopy is performed, in addition to bronchoscopy, report a code for the bronchoscopy procedure only.

Diagnostic endoscopy of the trachea and bronchi performed during the same operative session as a surgical endoscopy is included in the surgical endoscopy. Do not report a code for diagnostic endoscopy when it is performed with surgical endoscopy.

Diagnostic endoscopy is often performed during an open surgical procedure to evaluate (or scout or investigate) the surgical field. Do not report a code for diagnostic endoscopy when it is performed with an open surgical procedure.

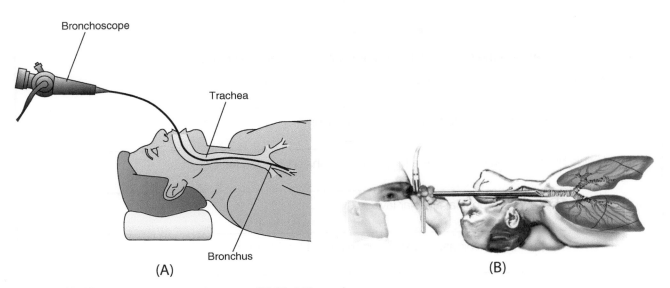

Bronchoscope

Trachea

Bronchus

(A)

(B)

FIGURE 13-16 (A) Flexible bronchoscopy (B) Rigid bronchoscopy

When a surgical endoscopic procedure fails and is converted to an open procedure, do not report a code for the surgical endoscopic procedure. Report only a code for the open procedure.

EXAMPLE: A patient presents with aspiration of a foreign body. A diagnostic bronchoscopy is performed to locate the foreign body, and a surgical bronchoscopy is performed to remove the foreign body. Report code 31635. (Do not report a code for the diagnostic bronchoscopy.)

Bronchial Thermoplasty

Bronchial thermoplasty codes classify procedures that reduce the amount of smooth muscle in the airway walls in asthmatic patients. *Bronchial thermoplasty* involves introducing a catheter with an electrode array into an area of the lung that is to be treated, and radiofrequency energy is used to heat and reduce the amount of smooth muscle.

EXAMPLE: Patient underwent flexible bronchoscopy with bronchial thermoplasty, one lobe, right lung. Report code 31660-RT.

Introduction

Introduction codes classify catheterization, catheter aspiration with bronchial brush biopsy, and transtracheal introduction of needle wire dilator/stent or indwelling tube for oxygen therapy procedures.

EXAMPLE: Patient underwent nasotracheal catheter aspiration to remove sputum from the lungs. Report code 31720. (Do not report modifier -50 because the trachea is not a paired organ.)

Excision, Repair

Excision, Repair codes classify tracheoplasty, carinal reconstruction, bronchoplasty, excision, suture, and revision procedures.

EXAMPLE: Patient underwent carinal reconstruction. Report code 31766.

Exercise 13.12 – Trachea and Bronchi

Instructions: Assign the CPT code(s) and appropriate modifier(s) to each statement.

1. Emergency transtracheal tracheostomy of 18-month-old child.

2. Bronchial brush biopsy via transglottic catheterization.

3. Flexible bronchoscopy to remove a piece of food inhaled into the left bronchus.

4. Bronchoscopy with bronchial alveolar lavage.

5. Bronchoscopy with brushings, biopsy, and removal of foreign body.

Lungs and Pleura

The Lungs and Pleura (Figure 13-17) heading contains codes for procedures performed on the lungs and **pleura** (membrane that envelops the lungs and lines the walls of the pleural cavity).

Incision

Incision codes classify thoracostomy, pneumonostomy, pleural scarification, and decortication procedures. A *thoracostomy* is the construction of an artificial opening through the chest wall, usually for drainage of fluid or release of an abnormal accumulation of air. A *pneumonostomy* is the surgical formation of an artificial opening into a lung (e.g., drainage of abscess). *Pleural scarification* is the injection of a chemical solution into the chest cavity (through a chest tube) to create adhesions between the surface of the lung and inside surface of the chest cavity for the treatment of repeat pneumothorax. *Decortication* is the removal of a constricting membrane or layer of tissue from the surface of the lung to permit the lung to fully expand.

EXAMPLE: Patient underwent pleural scarification for repeat pneumothorax. Report code 32215.

Excision/Resection

Excision/Resection codes classify pleurectomy, decortication and parietal pleurectomy, and biopsy procedures. *Pleurectomy* is the removal of pleura. *Decortication* is the removal of a constrictive fibrinous covering (to allow

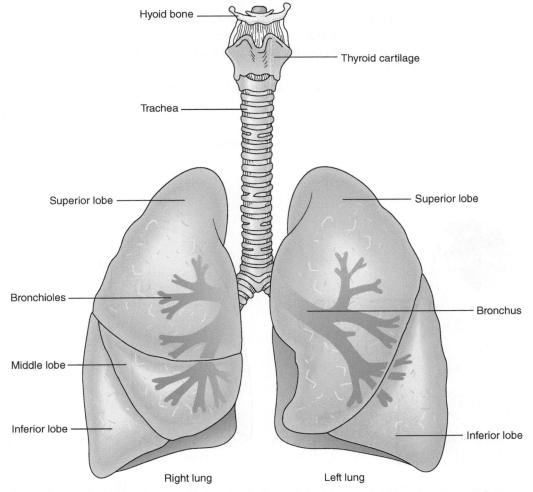

FIGURE 13-17 **External view of lungs. Note three lobes in the right lung and two lobes in the left lung.**

the lungs to expand). A *percutaneous pleural biopsy* involves inserting a long needle through skin into the chest wall to obtain pleural tissue (without direct visualization of the pleura). For **percutaneous needle biopsy**, a long needle is inserted through the skin and into other tissue (e.g., chest wall, lung, or mediastinum) to obtain tissue for diagnostic evaluation. This heading contains a code for "biopsy, pleura; percutaneous needle." However, when fine-needle aspiration is documented, report an appropriate code from the General subsection.

> **EXAMPLE:** Patient underwent parietal pleurectomy. Report code 32310.

Removal

Removal codes classify lung removal, resection and repair of bronchus, resection of apical lung tumor, thoracotomy, and extrapleural enucleation of empyema (empyemectomy) procedures. **Pneumonectomy** is the removal of the entire lung or one or more lobes of the lung. *Thoracotomy* is the surgical incision of the chest wall. *Empyemectomy* is the removal of an *empyema* (abscess in chest cavity between lung and chest wall) in its entirety, including pleural membranes surrounding the abscess.

> **EXAMPLE:** Patient underwent extrapleural pneumonectomy. Report code 32445.

Introduction and Removal

Introduction and Removal codes classify insertion of indwelling tunneled pleural catheter, tube thoracostomy, placement of interstitial device(s) for radiation therapy guidance, thoracentesis, and pleural drainage procedures. **Thoracentesis** (Figure 13-18A) is the surgical puncture of the chest wall with a needle to obtain fluid from the pleural cavity. It is performed to make a diagnostic evaluation or to drain excess fluid from a patient with severe **pleural effusion** (Figure 13-18B) (fluid in the pleural cavity prevents the lung from fully expanding, making it difficult for the patient to breathe).

Pneumocentesis is the puncture of the pleural space with a transthoracic needle to drain *fluid* or to obtain material for diagnostic study.

> **EXAMPLE:** Patient underwent thoracentesis via needle for aspiration of fluid from pleural space (pleural effusion). Report code 32554.

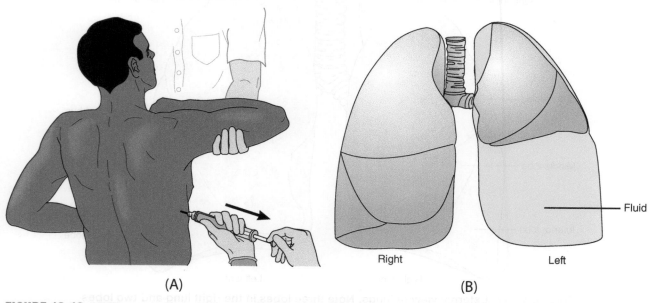

(A)   (B)

FIGURE 13-18 **(A) Thoracentesis (B) Lung with pleural effusion**

Destruction

Destruction codes classify instillation of pleurodesis or fibrinolytic agent procedures. *Pleurodesis agents* (e.g., talc) are instilled to treat recurrent or persistent pneumothorax. *Fibrinolytic agents* (e.g., saline mixture with streptokinase or urokinase) disintegrate or dissolve fibrinous adhesions.

> **EXAMPLE:** Patient underwent instillation of an agent for pleurodesis via chest tube. Report code 32560.

Thoracoscopy (Video-Assisted Thoracic Surgery [VATS])

A **thoracoscopy** is the visual examination of the pleural cavity, and it provides an alternative to open lung or thoracotomy procedures to treat pleural disorders surgically. Surgical thoracoscopy always includes diagnostic thoracoscopy, which means just the surgical thoracoscopy code is reported when both procedures are performed. However, when an open lung procedure, a thoracotomy, or another open chest procedure immediately follows diagnostic thoracoscopy during the same operative episode, report codes for both procedures (and sequence the open procedure first). When a surgical thoracoscopy is converted to an open procedure, report code(s) for the open lung procedure(s) only; do not report a code for the surgical thoracoscopy procedure.

> **EXAMPLE:** Patient presents with lower lateral chest wall pain and shortness of breath. Thoracoscopy with diagnostic biopsy of lobulated lung mass is performed. Biopsy reveals mesothelioma. Report code 32608.

Stereotactic Radiation Therapy

The Stereotactic Radiation Therapy code classifies thoracic target(s) delineation for the purpose of administering stereotactic body radiation therapy. The code is reported just once for an entire course of treatment. *Stereotactic radiation surgery (SRS)* involves identifying and delineating the target(s) for surgery. *Stereotactic body radiation therapy (SBRT)* uses high potent biological radiation to target a malignant tumor (and codes are reported from the Radiology section of CPT). SRS and SBRT procedures usually require the skill of both a surgeon and a radiation oncologist. SRS/SBRT uses a single or up to five fractionated doses of high potent biological radiation, and the high doses of radiation allow a tumor to be precisely localized using four-dimensional imaging. Occasionally, separately reportable *fiducial* (fixed) markers are placed during SRS to ensure proper placement of radiation delivery.

> **EXAMPLE:** Patient underwent thoracic target delineation for stereotactic body radiation therapy. Report code 32701.

Lung Transplantation

Lung transplants include the following distinct components, and a code is assigned to each by the physician who performs the component procedure:

- **Cadaver donor pneumonectomy**, which involves harvesting the allograft (graft such as lung tissue that is transplanted between genetically nonidentical individuals of the same species) and preserving the allograft with cold preservation solution and cold maintenance

- **Recipient lung allotransplantation**, which includes transplantation of a single or double lung allograft and care of the recipient

- **Backbench work** for lung transplantation, which involves preparing the cadaver donor lung allograft prior to lung transplantation and dissecting allograft from surrounding soft tissues to prepare the pulmonary venous/atrial cuff, pulmonary artery, and bronchus

> **EXAMPLE:** Patient with severe respiratory system complications due to cystic fibrosis underwent lung transplant procedure to remove diseased lungs and replace them with healthy lungs from a recently deceased donor. Transplant physician performed donor pneumonectomy including cold preservation from cadaver donor, backbench standard preparation of cadaver donor lung allografts, and double lung transplant with cardiopulmonary bypass. Report code 32854 for the donor and codes 32850 and 32856-51 for the transplant recipient.

Surgical Collapse Therapy; Thoracoplasty

Surgical collapse therapy and thoracoplasty codes classify procedures performed to therapeutically collapse a patient's lung(s).

- *Extrapleural resection of ribs* is the removal of rib(s).
- *Thoracoplasty* is the resection of ribs to allow the chest wall to retract, reducing the size of the pleural space.
- *Pneumonolysis* is the division of tissues that attach the lung to the wall of the chest cavity.
- *Therapeutic pneumothorax* is the injection of air into the pleural space.

EXAMPLE: A patient underwent extraperiosteal pneumonolysis. Report code 32940.

Other Procedures

Other Procedures codes classify total lung lavage, ablation therapy, and unlisted procedures. When a total lung lavage is performed bilaterally, add modifier -50 to code 32997 (because the code description specifies "unilateral"). When bronchoscopic bronchial alveolar lavage is performed, report code 31624 under the Trachea and Bronchi heading.

EXAMPLE: Patient underwent total lung lavage, left. Report code 32997-LT.

Exercise 13.13 – Lungs and Pleura

Instructions: Assign the CPT code(s) and appropriate modifier(s) to each statement.

1. Emergency department physician performed a tube thoracostomy for hemothorax, inserting a tube for drainage.

   _____

2. Total lung lavage, right.

   _____

3. Percutaneous needle biopsy of lung (right side) and fine-needle aspiration of lung (right side).

   _____

4. Diagnostic thoracoscopy with lung biopsy (left side) and surgical thoracoscopy with segmental lobectomy (left side) (both procedures performed during same operative session).

   _____

5. Patient with severe respiratory system complications due to chronic obstructive pulmonary disease underwent unilateral lung transplant (right side) procedure to remove one diseased lung, on the right, and replace it with a healthy lung from a recently deceased donor. Donor lung also required repair of intrathoracic blood vessel. Transplant physician performed donor pneumonectomy including cold preservation from cadaver donor, backbench standard preparation of cadaver donor lung allografts, and single lung transplant without cardiopulmonary bypass.

   _____

Summary

CPT codes in the Musculoskeletal System subsection are reported for procedures on bones, cartilage, joints, ligaments, muscles, and tendons. The subsection is arranged from head to toe according to body area. The Musculoskeletal System subsection also classifies fracture management, casting and strapping, and endoscopy/arthroscopy. The CPT Respiratory System subsection is arranged from nose to lungs according to body area.

Internet Links

American Lung Association: *www.lungusa.org*

Amilcare Gentili, M.D. (Professor of Clinical Radiology): Go to *www.gentili.net* to locate resources about musculoskeletal radiology.

National Institute of Arthritis and Musculoskeletal and Skin Diseases (NIAMS): *www.niams.nih.gov*

Northwest ENT Surgery Center: Go to *nwentsurgerycenter.com*, and click on the ENT Surgical Procedures link to locate videos about surgical procedures performed on the ears, nose, and throat.

YourLungHealth.org: *www.yourlunghealth.org*

Review

Multiple Choice

Instructions: Select the most appropriate response.

1. Which is a type of open fracture treatment?
   - **a.** Closed reduction
   - **b.** Internal fixation
   - **c.** Stabilization
   - **d.** Traction

2. Which is performed to puncture a joint for fluid removal or medication injection?
   - **a.** Arthrocentesis
   - **b.** Arthrodesis
   - **c.** Arthroscopy
   - **d.** Artificial ankylosis

3. Which are included with osteotomy codes (22210–22226), which means that separate codes are not reported when these procedures are performed during the same operative session as the osteotomy?
   - **a.** Arthrocentesis, arthroscopy, artificial ankylosis
   - **b.** Corpectomy, discectomy, laminectomy
   - **c.** Grafting, reduction, stabilization
   - **d.** Skeletal fixation, stabilization, traction

4. Open carpal tunnel decompression surgery (for carpal tunnel syndrome) is classified in which CPT Surgery subsection and/or under which heading?
   - **a.** Integumentary System
   - **b.** Musculoskeletal System
   - **c.** Nervous System
   - **d.** Operating Microscope section

5. The application of casts and strapping are reported when the cast (or splint) or strapping is an initial service performed _____ to stabilize or protect a fracture, a dislocation, or another injury and/or to provide comfort to a patient.
   - **a.** during restorative treatment/procedure
   - **b.** instead of placing a cast (or splint) or strap
   - **c.** when a reduction or manipulation is completed
   - **d.** without restorative treatment/procedure

6. Calcaneus ostectomy for removal of spurs, left foot. Which CPT code is assigned?
    a. 28111-LT   b. 28116-LT   c. 28118-LT   d. 28119-LT

7. Unlisted maxillofacial prosthetic procedure. Which CPT code is assigned?
    a. 21089   b. 21299   c. 22899   d. 23929

8. C3–C4 anterior discectomy performed by two primary surgeons. Which CPT code(s) are reported by Surgeon A?
    a. 22554, 22585-51   c. 22554-62
    b. 22554-62, 22585-51   d. 22554-62, 22585-62

9. Reconstruction of complete shoulder (rotator) cuff avulsion, chronic, right side. Which CPT code(s) are assigned?
    a. 23130-RT, 23420-RT   c. 23410-RT
    b. 23130-RT, 23420-51-RT   d. 23420-RT

10. Incision and drainage of deep abscess, right forearm. Which CPT code is assigned?
    a. 10060   b. 24310-RT   c. 25028-RT   d. 25031-RT

11. When a physician performs surgical nasal/sinus endoscopy with partial ethmoidectomy (anterior) and septo-
    plasty or submucous resection, report the:
    a. septoplasty code (30520).
    b. endoscopy code (31254).
    c. endoscopy code (31254) and the septoplasty code (30520).
    d. endoscopy code (31254) or the septoplasty code (30520).

12. Which is considered part of the ethmoid bone and, if removed during endoscopic polypectomy or
    endoscopic ethmoidectomy, is not coded and reported separately?
    a. Frontal sinus   c. Middle turbinate
    b. Maxillary sinus   d. Nasal vestibule

13. Which is the surgical fixation of arytenoidal cartilage and/or surrounding muscles?
    a. Arytenoidectomy   c. Arytenoidostomy
    b. Arytenoidopexy   d. Arytenoidotomy

14. Which procedure is performed to comb the mucous lining of the trachea or bronchus and uses a
    bronchial brush to collect cells?
    a. Brushing   c. Tracheotomy
    b. Cell washing   d. Bronchoscopy

15. Which component(s) of a lung transplant are reported as distinct code(s) by the physician who performs the
    component procedure(s)?
    a. Cadaver donor pneumonectomy   c. Recipient lung allotransplantation
    b. Backbench work for lung   d. Each of the above
        transplantation

16. Initial cautery to control posterior nasal hemorrhage. Which CPT code is assigned?
    a. 30901   b. 30903   c. 30905   d. 30906

17. Surgical nasal endoscopy with repair of cerebrospinal fluid leak, sphenoid region, right side. Which CPT
    code is assigned?
    a. 31287-RT   b. 31290-RT   c. 31291-RT   d. 31292-RT

18. A 3-year-old child undergoes direct laryngoscopy for aspiration of fluid. Which CPT code is assigned?
    a. 31515   b. 31520   c. 31520-63   d. 31525

19. Catheterization with bronchial brush biopsy. Which CPT code is assigned?
    a. 31623   b. 31717   c. 31720   d. 31725

20. Surgical thoracoscopy with excision of a pericardial cyst. Which CPT code is assigned?
    a. 32604   b. 32658   c. 32659   d. 32661

Coding Practice

Instructions: Assign the CPT code(s) and appropriate modifier(s) to each case.

Musculoskeletal System

1. Patient sustained a stab wound to the neck during a domestic dispute and underwent wound exploration. The stab wound was extended, and examination of surrounding bones, connective tissue, muscles, and nerves revealed normal findings. No foreign bodies were found. The area was debrided and irrigated. Coagulation of minor subcutaneous and muscular blood vessels was achieved with electrocautery. The wound was cleaned and closed with 3-0 Vicryl.

_____

2. Patient underwent reconstruction of the entire forehead and supraorbital rims, requiring grafts, to correct a congenital skeletal deformity. After administration of general anesthesia, scalp and upper eyelid incisions were made to access the surgical site. The forehead bones were reshaped and repositioned, and bone allografts were inserted to augment the forehead and supraorbital rims. Incisions were closed after wires were inserted as fixation devices to maintain the proper shape of the facial bones.

_____

3. A 13-year-old male sustained a fractured right femur during a soccer game and underwent open treatment with insertion of two screws and two pins. After administration of general anesthesia, an incision was made over the fracture site and a metal rod was inserted through the bone's shaft to stabilize it. The rod was secured with screws, and the leg was placed in a cast.

_____

4. Patient underwent incision and drainage of bursa, right knee. Needle was inserted into bursa and fluid was drained from the sac, which was located deep within the knee's soft tissue.

_____

5. Patient underwent knee replacement surgery four months ago. Today "manipulation of the left knee under general anesthesia" was performed to flex the knee joint and increase its range of motion.

_____

6. Two-year-old patient underwent reapplication of a long-leg cast to the left femur, which extended from the thigh to the toes. The patient sustained femur fracture four weeks ago when initial reduction was performed and application of long-leg cast was applied. Today that cast was removed and replaced with a long-leg cast due to the patient's age, to ensure optimal bone healing.

_____

7. Patient underwent open reduction of left tibia fracture four weeks ago. Today the orthopedic surgeon cut a hole in the patient's short-leg cast to check for incisional infection due to patient complaints of pain. No infection was noted.

_____

8. Patient underwent diagnostic arthroscopy of the left elbow due to unexplained pain. Surgeon inserted arthroscope into the left elbow joint to determine presence of disease or injury.

_____

9. Patient underwent removal of a metal sliver from the index finger, right hand. The surgeon made an incision between the first and second bones of the right index finger. Joint exploration revealed the presence of a metal sliver, which was removed.

_____

10. Patient underwent closed treatment of fractured tip of the right radius at distal end, which included application of a short-arm cast.

Respiratory System

1. Patient underwent bilateral diagnostic nasal endoscopy. The physician inserted an endoscope into the left nostril to evaluate nasal structures. The right nostril was also examined.

2. Patient underwent indirect endoscopy of the larynx with biopsy. The physician used a small, round mirror to examine the vocal cords, tongue, and top of the throat for signs of disease or injury. Biopsy of larynx was performed for evaluation and diagnosis.

3. Patient presents with a six-month history of hoarseness. The physician performs a laryngoscopy. The patient is prepped in the usual fashion. A fiberoptic laryngoscope is passed; the vocal cords are examined under direct visualization. Slight swelling is noted. A biopsy sample is taken to be sent to pathology.

4. Patient with a history of recurrent spontaneous left pneumothorax was prepped for a thoracoscopy and underwent parietal pleurectomy. An incision was made at the eighth intercostal space, and a thorascope was inserted to view patient's lungs. No evidence of disease was found in the lobes. Trocars were then placed, and the pleura was stripped away from the chest wall. A nice surface was accomplished. A chest tube was placed for drainage. The remaining incision was closed with mattress sutures of 4-0 nylon.

5. A 45-year-old female nonsmoker has had a cough for the last six months. With the patient placed under intravenous sedation, a bronchoscope was passed in the patient's oral cavity. Primary structures of upper area visualized and found to be normal. The transbronchial area was examined. A biopsy sample was taken of the lobe. The patient had minimal blood loss. The bronchoscope was then removed, and the patient returned to the outpatient area in satisfactory condition.

6. A patient with bilateral vocal cord paralysis presents for removal of arytenoid cartilage. This is being done to improve the patient's breathing. With the patient placed under general anesthesia, the laryngoscope with operating microscope is inserted into the oral cavity. The pharynx and larynx are examined under the microscope. After adequate visualization is established, the arytenoid cartilage is exposed by excision of the mucosa overlying it.

7. A 50-year-old patient has difficulty breathing through the left nostril. The patient has a deformity of the septum and presents for a submucous resection of the septum (SMR). After making an incision, the lining of the septum is detached. The patient's deviated portion of his septum is removed, and the cartilage portion above is scored. Nasal packing is placed.

8. Patient suffers from anosmia. The patient consents to a diagnostic biopsy of intranasal cavity. This procedure is done under local anesthesia delivered to nasal tissue. A small amount of tissue is removed under direct visualization. Minimal bleeding is noted.

9. A 2-year-old patient presents to the office with a marble in his nose, per the mother. Using nasal forceps, the marble is removed.

_____

10. A 5-year-old patient had a cleft lip repair done at 3 months of age. Now the patient has a nasal deformity that requires repair. The physician makes intranasal incisions and pulls back skin from the nasal bone tip. The bone is shaved and lengthened at the tip. The area is irrigated, and nasal packing is placed. The patient has little blood loss.

_____

CPT Surgery III

Chapter Outline

Cardiovascular System Subsection

Hemic and Lymphatic Systems Subsection

Chapter Objectives

At the conclusion of this chapter, the student should be able to:

1. Define key terms related to the Cardiovascular System and the Hemic and Lymphatic Systems subsections of CPT Surgery.
2. Assign codes from the Cardiovascular System subsection of CPT Surgery.
3. Assign codes from the Hemic and Lymphatic Systems subsection of CPT Surgery.

Key Terms

adenoids

adjuvant techniques

aneurysm

angiogenesis

angioscopy

aortic anomaly

aortic sinus

arteriovenous fistula

blood

bone marrow

bone marrow aspiration

bone marrow biopsy

cadaver donor cardiectomy with or without pneumonectomy

cancer staging

cardiac ablation

cardiac tumor

cardiac valve

cardiopulmonary bypass

chyle

commissurotomy

composite graft

coronary artery bypass graft (CABG)

coronary endarterectomy

cross-over vein graft

cutdown

dual chamber

electrophysiology

embolectomy

embolus

en bloc

endocardium

extracorporeal life support (ECLS)

extracorporeal membrane oxygenation (ECMO)

first-order vessels

heart murmur

hemic system

implantable defibrillator

lymph

lymph nodes

lymphatic system

Maze procedure

modified Maze procedure

myocardium

nonselective vascular catheterization

pacemaker

patency

pericardial sac

pericardiectomy

pericardiocentesis

pericardiotomy

pericardium

peripherally

recipient heart with or without lung allotransplantation

reconstruction of the vena cava

saphenopopliteal vein anastomosis

second-order vessels

selective vascular catheterization

septal defects	stentless valve	transmyocardial revascularization (TMR)	valvular regurgitation
septum	sympathectomy		valvular stenosis
shunting procedure	tetralogy of Fallot	transposition of great vessels	valvuloplasty
single chamber	therapeutic apheresis		valvulotomy
sinus of Valsalva	third-order vessels	truncus arteriosus	vascular family
spleen	thrombectomy	tube pericardiostomy	venous anomaly
splenoportography	thromboendarterectomy	tunneled	venous valve transposition
stab phlebectomy	thymus	valvular atresia	ventricular assist device (VAD)
stem cells	tonsils	valvular heart disease	
stented valve		valvular prolapse	visceral arteries

Introduction

The Cardiovascular System subsection classifies procedures performed on the heart and pericardium, valves (e.g., mitral and semilunar), and peripheral vascular vessels (e.g., arteries, veins, and capillaries). The Hemic and Lymphatic Systems subsection classifies procedures performed on the spleen, lymph nodes, and lymphatic channels. CPT guidelines that apply to the subsections are located at the beginning of the Surgery section. Unique coding instructions for the cardiovascular system and hemic and lymphatic system are located in notes below headings or codes.

 Coding Tip

Notes located beneath headings and/or subheadings apply to all codes in the heading or subheading. Parenthetical notes that are located below a specific code apply to that code only unless the note indicates otherwise.

 NOTE:

The Other Procedures code below each subheading classifies an unlisted procedure performed on the anatomical site. When reporting an unlisted procedure code, include documentation about the procedure performed with the submitted claim. (Other Procedures subheadings are not included throughout this chapter except when codes that describe additional procedures are included.)

Cardiovascular System Subsection

Cardiovascular System subsection codes are arranged anatomically and then according to procedure performed. The Cardiovascular System subsection includes the following headings:

- Heart and Pericardium
- Arteries and Veins

Cardiovascular System Notes

Notes located at the beginning of the Cardiovascular System subsection provide instruction about assigning codes for *selective vascular catheterization*. When performed as part of cardiovascular (and radiology) procedures, codes for *selective vascular catheterization* are reported separately.

In addition, parenthetical notes are located just above the Cardiovascular System subsection heading. They serve as reminders to review other codes and sections of CPT to locate additional codes associated with certain cardiovascular system procedures. (Notes are also located throughout the Cardiovascular System subsection as a reminder to report additional surgery codes with some procedures.)

 Coding Tip

During cardiovascular procedures, cardiopulmonary bypass is often required to divert blood from the heart to the aorta, using a pump oxygenator. Because some procedures can be performed without cardiopulmonary bypass, make sure you review the operative report to determine whether to assign the cardiopulmonary bypass code for the procedure performed.

EXAMPLE: Patient underwent repair of cardiac wound with cardiopulmonary bypass. Report code 33305.

Selective Vascular Catheterization

When reporting codes for selective vascular catheterization, knowledge of the flow of blood (Figure 14-1) throughout the body's circulatory system is crucial. (In fact, it's a good idea to reference an anatomy and physiology textbook such as Cengage's *Body Structures & Functions* when assigning codes to procedures

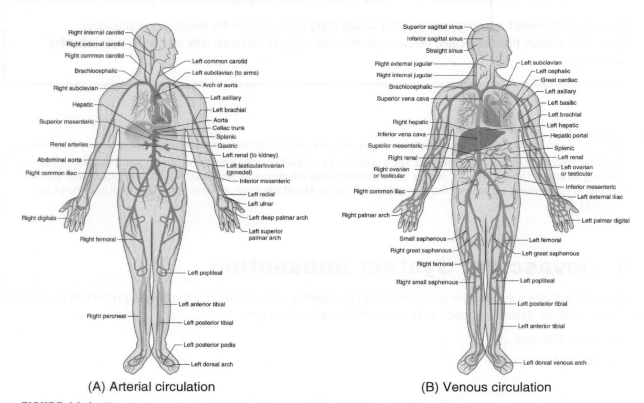

(A) Arterial circulation

(B) Venous circulation

FIGURE 14-1 Circulatory system (A) Arterial circulation (B) Venous circulation

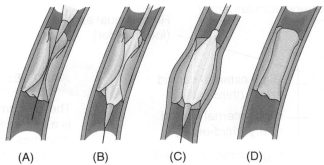

FIGURE 14-2 (A) Insertion of guidewire into and beyond plaque formation in artery (B) Insertion of catheter with attached balloon through plaque formation in artery (C) Expansion of balloon to compress plaque against arterial walls and open the arterial lumen (D) Compressed plaque, creating wider lumen in artery

classified in the Cardiovascular System subsection.) Selective vascular catheterization procedures are classified as "vascular injection procedures" and require separate coding of the following:

- Diagnostic procedure (e.g., carotid angiogram) and/or therapeutic procedure (e.g., balloon dilation via catheter)
- Vascular access (e.g., selective vascular catheterization)

Separate codes are not reported for the administration of local anesthesia, introduction of the needle or catheter, or *injection* of contrast material. (The supply of contrast media *is* assigned an HCPCS level II code.) In addition, CPT codes are assigned to the point of catheter placement (not guidewire insertion); catheters (or sheaths) are inserted into blood vessels to serve as conduits for the administration of fluids (or gases), access by surgical instruments (e.g., stent), and other tasks (e.g., balloon angioplasty). A guidewire might be inserted beyond placement of the catheter, and no images are taken or procedures are performed at the insertion point of the guidewire; thus, code to the point of catheter placement (not guidewire insertion) (Figure 14-2).

Selective vascular catheterization is the insertion and manipulation or guidance of a catheter (that is attached to a guidewire) into the branches of the arterial system (other than the aorta or the vessel punctured) for the purpose of performing diagnostic or therapeutic procedures. Selective vascular catheterization is usually performed under fluoroscopic (moving x-ray) guidance. The code reported for selective vascular catheterization includes introduction of the catheter into the punctured vessel and guidance through all lesser- (or first-) order vessels (to get to the intended vessel that undergoes the diagnostic or therapeutic procedure). Thus, codes are *not* reported for **nonselective vascular catheterization**, which involves introducing the catheter directly into a vessel without further advancement past the punctured vessel or introduction of a catheter into any portion of the aorta or vena cava from any approach (e.g., axillary, brachial, femoral, jugular).

 Coding Tip

When fluoroscopic guidance is provided during selective vascular catheterization, make sure you assign the appropriate supervision and interpretation code from the Radiology Vascular Procedures subsection (codes 75600–75989).

Once the catheter reaches its intended vessel, assign an appropriate code for that selective vascular catheterization. When additional vessels are catheterized for the purpose of performing diagnostic and/or therapeutic procedures, assign codes for selective vascular catheterization of those second- and third- (and beyond) order vessels. First-, second-, and third- (and beyond) order vessel catheterization is discussed next.

FIGURE 14-3 Artery vascular families (A) First-, second-, third-, and fourth-order vessels in the right brachiocephalic artery vascular family (B) First-, second-, and third-order vessels in the left common carotid artery vascular family

A **vascular family** (Figure 14-3) (CPT Appendix L) is a group of vessels that is accessed by the same first-order vessel, and it is supplied by the same primary branch from the aorta. A vascular family can be compared to a tree with branches. The trunk is the aorta, which contains large and small branches. (Think of the aorta as a zero-order vessel because it is a common starting point for catheterization. The femoral artery, as a starting point for catheterization, is an example of another zero-order vessel.) From the starting point, vessels branch outward (similar to a network of streets from a highway) into the following:

- First-order vessels
- Second-order vessels
- Third-order vessels

First-order vessels extend as primary arterial branches from the aorta (e.g., left common carotid artery in the neck and inferior mesenteric artery or common iliac artery in the abdomen). When an *initial* second- or third-order arterial catheterization is performed within a vascular family, report just one code. **Second-order vessels** branch from first-order vessels, and **third-order vessels** branch from second-order vessels. (Refer to Figure 14-3 for an illustration of first-, second-, and third-order vessels of a vascular family.)

Review the operative report to determine which artery (or arteries) underwent diagnostic or therapeutic procedures after having a catheter inserted. Although multiple arteries might be involved in a catheter being threaded from the insertion point to the intended artery, only one code is reported if just one artery undergoes diagnostic or therapeutic procedures.

EXAMPLE: SELECTIVE VASCULAR CATHETERIZATION INTO FIRST-ORDER VESSELS: After being assaulted, a patient presented to the emergency department, complaining of severe upper left flank pain. Patient underwent left renal angiogram. This required insertion of a catheter into the right femoral artery. The catheter was advanced to the right external iliac and common iliac arteries and aorta and into the left renal artery. Contrast media was injected for visualization of the left renal artery upon x-ray. Report code 36251. The right femoral, right external iliac, and right common iliac arteries underwent nonselective catheterization because they were used to access the left renal artery; no diagnostic or therapeutic procedure was performed on them. (Thus, do not assign catheter placement codes for accessing the right femoral, right external iliac, or right common iliac arteries.)

Selective vascular catheterization was achieved by making a small incision in the skin and performing an arterial puncture into the left femoral artery (groin region). A needle containing a stylet (inner wire) was inserted through the skin into the left femoral artery. The stylet was removed and replaced with a guidewire. Under fluoroscopy, the guidewire was advanced through the external iliac artery and common iliac artery and then into the aorta. From the abdominal aorta, the guidewire was advanced into the left renal artery. The needle was removed, and a catheter was inserted over the length of the guidewire until it reached the renal artery. The guidewire was removed, and the catheter was left in place. Under fluoroscopic guidance, contrast media was injected manually with a syringe or with an automatic injector connected to the catheter. (An automatic injector propels a large volume of dye quickly to the angiogram site.) X-rays were taken, and the catheter was slowly and carefully removed. Pressure was applied to the insertion site (to facilitate clotting and to allow the arterial puncture to reseal), and a pressure bandage was applied.

When procedures are performed on multiple arteries along the path of catheterization from first- through to second-, third-, and/or fourth-order vessels, assign an appropriate code for each.

EXAMPLE: A catheter was introduced into the brachiocephalic artery (first-order) and then inserted into the right common carotid artery (second-order) and the right internal carotid artery (third-order) to the cerebral artery (fourth-order), where contrast media was injected to perform a cerebral angiography. In addition to the cerebral angiography code, report just one selective vascular catheterization code for the cerebral artery. The brachiocephalic, right common carotid, and right internal carotid arteries were used to access the (fourth-order) cerebral artery. No diagnostic or therapeutic procedures were performed on them. Therefore, do not assign selective vascular catheterization codes for catheterization of the brachiocephalic, right common carotid, or right internal carotid arteries.

Add-on code 36218 or 36248 (in addition to the primary code 36215–36217 or 36245–36247) is reported when *additional*

- Selective arterial catheterization of second-order, third-order, and beyond (thoracic or brachiocephalic branch) vessels is achieved using a single first-order artery.

- Second-, third-order, and beyond (abdominal, pelvic, or lower extremity artery branch) vessels are accessed during selective arterial catheterization.

EXAMPLE: A catheter was introduced into the left common carotid artery (first-order) and inserted into the left internal carotid artery (second-order). Contrast media was injected and carotid arteriogram performed. The catheter was further advanced into the left cerebral artery (third-order), additional contrast media was injected, and cerebral angiogram was performed. In addition to radiology codes for the carotid arteriogram and cerebral angiogram, report a selective vascular catheterization code for the (second-order) left internal carotid artery and add-on code 36218 for the selective vascular catheterization of the (third-order) cerebral artery. The left common carotid artery was used to access the other two arteries; therefore, a selective vascular catheterization code is *not* assigned.

Coding Tip

When multiple selective arterial catheterization procedures of separate and distinct vascular families are performed during the same operative session, report the appropriate number of units in Form Locator 46 of the UB-04.

> **EXAMPLE:** Selective arterial catheterization of the thoracic artery and the brachiocephalic artery: Report code 36215 and the number of units on the UB-04 claim (Figure 14-4).

42 REV. CO.	43 DESCRIPTION	44 HCPCS/RATES	45 SERV. DATE	46 SERV. UNITS	47 TOTAL CHARGES	48 NON-COVERED CHARGES	49
		36215		02			

Courtesy of the Centers for Medicare & Medicaid Services, www.cms.gov; claim data created by author.

FIGURE 14-4 Reporting selective arterial catheterization code by completing form locators 44 and 46 on the UB-04 claim

Heart and Pericardium

Heart and Pericardium codes classify procedures performed on the heart and pericardium.

Pericardium

The **pericardium**, or **pericardial sac**, is the membrane that surrounds the heart. **Pericardiocentesis** is the insertion of a needle to withdraw fluid from the pericardium. Radiological guidance is often performed with pericardiocentesis, so make sure you report a Radiology code if instructed to do so.

A **tube pericardiostomy** is the insertion of a tube for drainage or specimen collection. A **pericardiotomy** requires thoracotomy as incision for pericardial drainage, fluid collection, or foreign body removal.

Pericardiectomy is the removal of part of the pericardium (to treat chronic pericarditis). Also code the cardiopulmonary bypass if documented in the operative report.

> **EXAMPLE:** Patient underwent pericardiotomy for removal of blood clot. Report code 33020.

Cardiac Tumor

A **cardiac tumor** is a growth that develops in the heart's **endocardium** (inner lining), **myocardium** (muscle layer), or pericardium. The majority of cardiac tumors are benign, although a percentage are malignant. Methods for diagnosing cardiac tumors include complete history and physical examination and diagnostic procedures such as echocardiogram, electrocardiogram, computed tomography (CT scan), magnetic resonance imaging (MRI), chest x-ray, and coronary arteriogram or angiogram.

Benign cardiac tumors include myxoma, rhabdomyoma, and other rare tumors (e.g., fibroma, hemangioma, lipoma, lymphangioma, neurofibroma, and papillary fibroelastoma). Malignant cardiac tumors include cardiac sarcoma, fibrosarcoma, liposarcoma, and rhabdomyosarcoma. Surgical removal of a cardiac tumor is indicated if it causes an arrhythmia or obstructs blood flow through the heart. When a cardiac tumor cannot be removed, a heart transplant may be required.

> **EXAMPLE:** Patient underwent resection of intracardiac liposarcoma, resection with cardiopulmonary bypass. Report code 33120. (Go to CPT Index main term Heart, subterm Cardiopulmonary Bypass, and second qualifier with Tumor Excision/Resection to review code 33120.)

Transmyocardial Revascularization (TMR)

Transmyocardial revascularization (TMR) uses a high-powered laser to create small channels in the heart muscle to increase blood supply to the myocardium. The procedure also promotes **angiogenesis** (growth of new capillaries) as a blood supply to the heart muscle. TMR is performed to treat severe angina (in patients who are not candidates for coronary artery bypass graft [CABG] or angioplasty surgery), and the procedure may be performed with or without cardiopulmonary bypass. (TMR is usually performed with cardiopulmonary bypass.)

EXAMPLE: Patient underwent TMR, by thoracotomy. Report code 33140.

Pacemaker or Implantable Defibrillator

A **pacemaker** (Figure 14-5) regulates the patient's heartbeat to prevent arrhythmias (e.g., atrial fibrillation and bradycardia) and includes a pulse generator (battery and electronic device) and electrodes (leads). An **implantable defibrillator** (Figure 14-6) is similar to a pacemaker in that it includes a pulse generator and electrodes, but it uses a combination of antitachycardia pacing and low-energy cardioversion or defibrillating shocks to regulate the patient's heartbeat and prevent arrhythmias (e.g., ventricular fibrillation and ventricular tachycardia).

Pulse generators for pacemakers and implantable defibrillators are implanted internally under the skin (permanent), or they are attached externally (temporary). The implantable defibrillator pulse generator is often inserted in a "pocket" below the skin in the infraclavicular region or abdomen. Electrodes are inserted through a vein or placed on the surface of the heart. The two types of pacemakers and implantable defibrillators are:

- **Single chamber**: Contains a single electrode that is positioned in the heart's right atrium *or* right ventricle
- **Dual chamber**: Contains two electrodes; one is placed in the right atrium, and the other is placed in the right ventricle

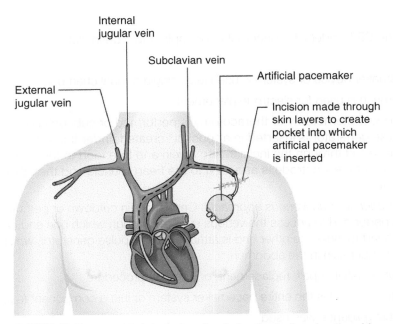

FIGURE 14-5 An artificial pacemaker is implanted under the skin

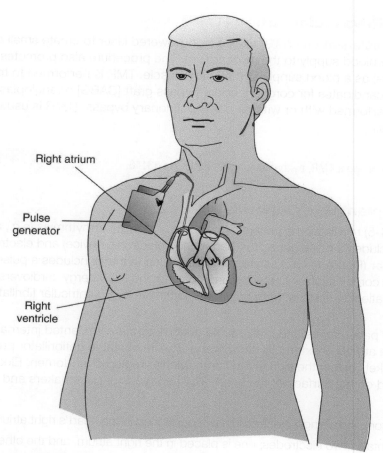

Right atrium

Pulse
generator

Right
ventricle

FIGURE 14-6 Implantable defibrillator

Before assigning the CPT code(s) for pacemaker or implantable defibrillator insertions, determine the following:

- What type of pacemaker device or system is used (e.g., single or dual chamber)
- What surgical approach is used for electrode placement
  - *Epicardial approach*: Sternotomy or thoracotomy is performed or subcostal or xiphoid incision is made and pulse generator is inserted in a "pocket" created under the skin in the upper chest; electrodes are inserted through the incision into a vein and threaded to the heart under fluoroscopic guidance; one end of the electrode is attached to the heart muscle and the other end is attached to the pulse generator.
  - *Endocardial approach (or transvenous approach)*: Cephalic vein cutdown or percutaneous subclavian vein puncture is performed to access the venous system, through which one end of the electrode is attached to the heart muscle; the other end is attached to the pulse generator, which is placed in a "pocket" created under skin in the abdomen.
- Whether insertion is an initial, repair, replacement, or upgrade procedure
- Whether the procedure involves the entire pacemaker system or just a component (e.g., electrode)
- Whether fluoroscopic guidance was used

Coding Tip

- The CPT *Pacemaker or Implantable Defibrillator* subheading contains a table of transvenous procedures with codes that are reported for pacemakers and implantable cardioverter-defibrillator systems, which helps clarify code assignment.

- When implantable defibrillator electrodes are removed, a transvenous extraction may be attempted; however, if unsuccessful, a thoracotomy may be required to remove the electrodes.

- When a pacemaker or implantable defibrillator "battery" is changed, it is actually the pulse generator that is changed. Replacement of a pulse generator is reported with two codes: a code for removal of the pulse generator and a code for insertion of a new pulse generator.

- When pacemaker or implantable defibrillator electrodes are replaced, report appropriate code(s) from 33206–33208, 33210–33214, or 33221. Do not report a separate pacemaker removal code in addition to a replacement code, which would be considered overcoding.

EXAMPLE 1: Patient underwent subcutaneous insertion of permanent dual-chamber pacemaker pulse generator with transvenous placement of existing dual leads in the right atrium and right ventricle. Procedure included fluoroscopic guidance. Report code 33213.

EXAMPLE 2: Patient underwent replacement of a single-chamber pacemaker pulse generator. The existing pocket was reopened, and the pulse generator was disconnected from its single lead and removed. The new pulse generator was inserted into the existing pocket and connected to the single existing lead. The incision was closed with sutures. Report code 33227.

EXAMPLE 3: Single-chamber pacemaker system was replaced with dual-chamber system, including insertion of new pulse generator and new leads. Report code 33214. (Do not report a code for removal of the existing pacemaker system, because it is included in code 33214.)

EXAMPLE 4: Thirty days after initial insertion of transvenous pacemaker, pacemaker electrode was repositioned. Incision is made into the existing pocket; pulse generator and electrode are removed and tested to ensure that they are not defective. Because the electrode is not defective, the generator is replaced in the pocket. The electrode is reattached to the generator, placed in a new position (repositioned) in the right atrium, and retested. The incision is closed with sutures. Report code 33215.

EXAMPLE 5: Single transvenous electrode was repaired for a single-chamber pacemaker. Incision is made into the existing pocket, and the electrode is disconnected from the pulse generator. After repair, the electrode is reattached to the generator and the incision is closed with sutures. Report code 33218.

NOTE:

When evaluation of a pacemaker system is performed, report a code from the Medicine section. The code is reported for an encounter after the insertion procedure to determine whether the pacemaker or implantable defibrillator is functioning properly and/or has to be reprogrammed.

Electrophysiologic Operative Procedures

Electrophysiology is the study of heart arrhythmias; electrophysiologic (EP) procedures analyze heart rhythm abnormalities and include operative ablation or operative incisions and reconstruction of the atria to correct abnormal pathways. The electrophysiology procedure is invasive, similar to a cardiac catheterization, in that electrode catheters are introduced into the right side of the heart from the femoral, brachial, or jugular vein. The catheters positioned in the heart are used to measure and record cardiac rhythm.

- Operative **cardiac ablation (modified Maze procedure)** stops atrial or ventricular fibrillation by using radiofrequency waves (modified electrical energy) to create small scars on the heart's surface. Impulses are redirected and follow a normal electrical pathway through the heart.
- The **Maze procedure** stops atrial fibrillation or atrial flutter by using incisions in heart tissue to stop abnormal heart rhythm.

 NOTE:

When the physician performs an "operative" cardiac ablation (also called a Maze procedure), a code is assigned from the CPT Surgery section of CPT. Cardiac ablation is sometimes called "cardiac catheter ablation"; however, that procedure is assigned a code from the CPT Medicine section.

Both types of EP procedures require thoracotomy to access the heart, and cardiopulmonary bypass may or may not be used.

EXAMPLE: Patient underwent operative ablation of ventricular arrhythmogenic focus with cardiopulmonary bypass. Thoracotomy was used to access the heart. Report code 33261.

Patient-Activated Event Recorder

A patient-activated cardiac event recorder (also called an *insertable loop recorder* or a *cardiovascular monitoring system*) is implanted under the skin (of the patient's chest region, under local anesthesia) and is programmed with a looping memory that records electrocardiogram (ECG) tracings. When the patient experiences symptoms (e.g., irregular heart beats, fainting), the patient activates a hand-held telemetry to initiate ECG recording and storage. The physician retrieves the data, which can be displayed, printed, and/or stored. Cardiac event recorders document the heart's rhythms during transient (infrequent or recurrent) cardiac symptoms (e.g., recurrent syncope). The procedure for inserting and removing an event recorder is similar to that for implanting or removing a pacemaker pulse generator.

 Coding Tip

- Initial implantation of patient-activated event recorders includes programming. When subsequent electronic analysis and/or reprogramming are required, report codes from the Medicine section.
- Holter monitor and external event recording are reported with codes from the Medicine section.

EXAMPLE: Patient underwent insertion, subcutaneous cardiac rhythm monitor, including programming. Report code 33285.

Subcutaneous Cardiac Rhythm Monitor

A subcutaneous cardiac rhythm monitor is a cardiac event recorder or implantable/insertable loop recorder (ILR), which is placed subcutaneously into a small pre-pectoral pocket. It continuously records the patient's electrocardiographic rhythm, and the device is automatically triggered when rapid, irregular, or slow heart rates are detected.

EXAMPLE: Patient underwent insertion of subcutaneous cardiac rhythm monitor, which included programming. Report code 33285.

Implantable Hemodynamic Monitors

An implantable hemodynamic monitor is an intravascular device that is implanted via transcatheter approach. It is used for long-term remote (wireless) pulmonary artery pressure monitoring. (A code from the Medicine section is reported for the weekly remote monitoring of pulmonary artery pressures.)

EXAMPLE: Patient underwent transcatheter implantation of wireless pulmonary artery pressure sensor for long-term hemodynamic monitoring, which included deployment and calibration of the sensor. The physician reviewed recordings of remote monitoring of the wireless pulmonary artery pressure sensor on a weekly basis during the month of July, and he prepared a report that included interpretation and trend analysis. Report codes 33289 and 93264.

Heart (Including Valves) and Great Vessels

Repairs to injuries of the heart and/or great vessels (e.g., stab wounds and gunshot wounds) may or may not require cardiopulmonary bypass during the procedure.

 Coding Tip

To report removal of a thrombus in addition to codes for other cardiac procedures performed during the same operative session, a separate incision into the heart is required (to remove the atrial or ventricular thrombus). Add modifier -59 to the appropriate code when it is reported for "removal of a thrombus with coronary bypass" in addition to codes for other cardiac procedures.

EXAMPLE: Patient underwent repair of cardiac stab wound, with cardiopulmonary bypass. Separate incision was made to remove atrial thrombus. Report codes 33305 and 33315-59.

Cardiac Valves

Cardiac valves are flaps of tissue that keep blood flowing in one direction to allow for the efficient one-way flow of blood through the heart's chambers. **Valvular heart disease** is the abnormality or dysfunction of one or more of the heart's four valves (aortic, mitral, pulmonary, and tricuspid).

- **Valvular atresia:** Valve fails to develop properly and is completely closed at birth
- **Valvular prolapse:** Two valvular flaps do not close properly
- **Valvular regurgitation:** Backflow of blood due to valvular prolapse
- **Valvular stenosis:** Narrowing of one or more cardiac valves

When coding procedures performed on cardiac valves, first determine the valve involved.

- Aortic
- Mitral
- Tricuspid
- Pulmonary

Then determine the type of procedure performed.

- **Valvuloplasty:** Open-heart surgery during which the surgeon removes the damaged valve and replaces it with a prosthetic, homograft or allograft, stented, or stentless valve (Figure 14-7)

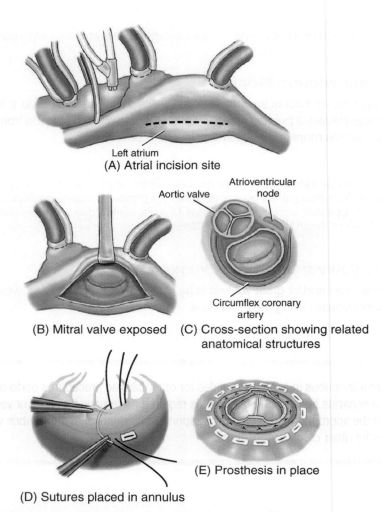

Left atrium
(A) Atrial incision site

Aortic valve

Atrioventricular node

Circumflex coronary artery

(B) Mitral valve exposed   (C) Cross-section showing related anatomical structures

(E) Prosthesis in place

(D) Sutures placed in annulus

FIGURE 14-7 Mitral valve replacement: (A) Atrial incision site; (B) Mitral valve exposed; (C) Cross-section showing related anatomical structures; (D) Sutures placed in annulus; (E) Prosthesis in place

 Coding Tip

When nonsurgical, catheter-based, percutaneous balloon valvuloplasty is performed, report a code from 92986–92990.

- **Valvulotomy**: Open-heart surgery in which an incision is made into a valve to repair valvular damage; includes **commissurotomy**, in which narrowed valve leaflets are widened by carefully opening the fused leaflets with a scalpel

 Coding Tip

When multiple valve procedures are performed during the same operative session, add modifier -51 to the second (and subsequent) valve procedure code(s).

NOTE:

A **stented valve** includes framework on which the replacement valve is mounted to provide support for the valve's leaflets. A **stentless valve** is often an actual heart valve obtained from either a human donor (homograft) or a pig, and it does not contain framework. Stentless valves are preferred because they are less obstructive and have improved long-term performance.

EXAMPLE 1: Patient underwent aortic valvuloplasty with cardiopulmonary bypass. Report code 33390.

EXAMPLE 2: Patient underwent open replacement of the aortic valve with a stentless tissue valve, including cardiopulmonary bypass. Report code 33410.

 NOTE:

A **stentless valve** is often an actual heart valve obtained from either a human donor (homograft) or a pig, and it does not contain framework. (A **stented valve** includes framework on which the replacement valve is mounted to provide support for the valve's leaflets.) Stentless valves are preferred because they are less obstructive and have improved long-term performance.

EXAMPLE 3: Patient underwent right ventricular resection for infundibular stenosis, with commissurotomy. Report code 33476.

Other Valvular Procedures

The Other Valvular Procedures code classifies the repair of non-structural prosthetic valve dysfunction with cardiopulmonary bypass as a separate procedure.

EXAMPLE: Patient underwent repair of non-structural prosthetic valve dysfunction with cardiopulmonary bypass. Report code 33496.

Coronary Artery Anomalies

An **arteriovenous fistula** is an abnormal passageway between an artery and a vein that allows blood to flow directly into a vein. It can occur as a congenital defect or as the result of trauma. (A fistula can also be surgically created to provide a site for vascular access.) An arteriovenous fistula can occur anywhere in the body, but it most often occurs in the legs or arms. The fistula might eventually develop into an **aneurysm** (bulge in an artery that can weaken the arterial wall and eventually burst, resulting in hemorrhage). For example, a coronary arteriovenous fistula (or coronary artery fistula) is a congenital fistula that is often located between the right coronary artery and the right heart.

EXAMPLE: Patient underwent a Takeuchi procedure, which involved constructing an intrapulmonary artery tunnel. Report code 33505.

Endoscopy

When an endoscopic approach is used to harvest veins for coronary artery bypass procedures, report code 33508 as an add-on code.

EXAMPLE: Patient underwent coronary artery bypass graft (CABG) procedure, single coronary venous graft, with endoscopic harvesting of saphenous vein. Report codes 33510 and 33508.

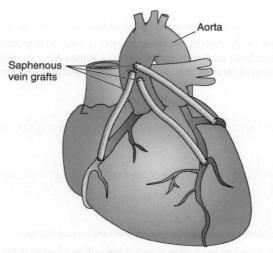

Aorta

Saphenous
vein grafts

FIGURE 14-8 Coronary artery bypass
graft (CABG) using
saphenous vein grafts

Coronary Artery Bypass Graft (CABG) Procedures

The Cardiovascular System subsection contains three headings to classify coronary artery bypass graft (CABG) procedures, which are organized according to type of graft.

- Venous grafting only for coronary artery bypass
- Combined arterial-venous grafting for coronary bypass (add-on codes)
- Arterial grafting for coronary artery bypass

  Coronary artery bypass graft (CABG) (pronounced "cabbage") (Figure 14-8) is a procedure performed to improve the flow of blood to the heart. A blood vessel (called a graft) is removed from the arm, leg, or chest and anastomosed to bypass (detour) the blood flow around a narrowed or blocked coronary artery. (The surgery relieves angina symptoms, improves the patient's ability to exercise, and reduces the patient's risk of a heart attack.) Correctly reporting CABG requires careful review of the operative report to determine the number and type of grafts performed.

Venous Grafting Only for Coronary Artery Bypass

CABG procedures that use venous grafts only are *not* reported when CABG procedures use a combination of arterial and venous grafts during the same procedure.

Combined Arterial-Venous Grafting for Coronary Bypass

The add-on codes reported for combined arterial-venous grafts are always reported in addition to codes from the Arterial Grafting for Coronary Artery Bypass subheading.

Arterial Grafting for Coronary Artery Bypass

Coronary artery bypass procedures that use either arterial grafts only *or* a combination of arterial-venous grafts include the use of the internal mammary artery, gastroepiploic artery, epigastric artery, radial artery, and arterial conduits procured from other sites.

EXAMPLE: Patient underwent CABG procedure for arteriosclerotic heart disease. A single arterial graft was performed. The sternum was opened, the heart was stopped and cooled, and the patient was connected to cardiopulmonary bypass. A long piece of the saphenous vein was harvested, and one end was attached to the ascending aorta. The other end of the graft was attached to the circumflex coronary artery, just below the blocked area. Report codes 33533-LC and 33517.

Coding Tip

HCPCS level II modifiers identify placement of the bypass grafts and are added to the CABG code.

- -LC (left circumflex coronary artery)
- -LD (left anterior descending coronary artery)
- -RC (right coronary artery)

Coronary Endarterectomy

Coronary endarterectomy is performed to remove the inner layer of coronary arteries that contain cholesterol plaques. When a patient's coronary arteries contain extensive cholesterol plaque, a CABG procedure cannot be performed until the plaque is removed via coronary endarterectomy.

> **EXAMPLE:** Patient underwent coronary endarterectomy of the left anterior descending and left circumflex coronary arteries. During the same operative session, the patient also underwent double CABG. The graft sections were obtained from the internal mammary arteries. Report codes 33534-LC-LD, 33572, and 33572.

Single Ventricle and Other Complex Cardiac Anomalies

Procedures performed to correct single ventricle and other complex cardiac anomalies include, for example, the Norwood procedure to repair a single ventricle that has an aortic outflow obstruction and aortic arch hypoplasia. During the procedure, the pulmonary artery is connected to the right ventricle, using a shunt, and the underdeveloped aorta is enlarged and reconstructed.

> **EXAMPLE:** Patient diagnosed with tricuspid atresia undergoes repair that involves closure of the atrial septal defect and anastomosis of the vena cava to the pulmonary artery. Report code 33615.

Congenital Heart Defects

Congenital heart defects include the following:

- Septal defects
- Sinus of Valsalva defects
- Venous anomalies
- Shunting procedures

- Transposition of great vessels
- Truncus arteriosus
- Aortic anomalies

Septal Defects

The **septum** is tissue that separates the heart's left and right sides. **Septal defects** occur when the tissue doesn't completely close between the heart's chambers (atria or ventricles). This allows oxygen-rich blood from one side of the heart (e.g., left atrium) to mix with oxygen-poor blood on the other side (e.g., right atrium). The extra blood flows through the hole, causing a swishing sound, which is called a **heart murmur** (an extra heart sound).

> **EXAMPLE:** Patient underwent repair of atrial septal defect, secundum, with cardiopulmonary bypass, without patch. The right atrium was opened, and the size and location of the atrial septal defect was assessed. Due to the small size of the atrial septal tissue, it was closed with a suture. Report code 33641.

The **tetralogy of Fallot** is a congenital heart condition that includes ventral septal defect, stenosis of the infundibulum, hypertrophy of the right ventricle, and an abnormally positioned aorta.

> **EXAMPLE:** Patient underwent complete repair of tetralogy of Fallot without pulmonary atresia using transannular patch. Report code 33694.

Sinus of Valsalva Defects

The **sinus of Valsalva** (or **aortic sinus**) is an anatomical dilation of the ascending aorta that occurs just above the aortic valve (e.g., left anterior aortic sinus that gives rise to the left coronary artery). Defects include aneurysms and fistulas for which repair and closure procedures are performed.

> **EXAMPLE:** Patient underwent surgical repair of a sinus of Valsalva aneurysm, with cardiopulmonary bypass. Report code 33720.

Venous Anomalies

Venous anomalies are associated with systemic veins and pulmonary veins and include conditions such as

- *Cor triatriatum* (congenital anomaly in which left atrium or right atrium is divided into two parts by a fold of tissue, membrane, or fibromuscular band; referred to as a heart with three atria)
- *Pulmonary vein stenosis* (abnormal thickening and narrowing of walls of pulmonary veins)
- *Scimitar syndrome* (congenital condition in which aberrant vessel connects pulmonary vein in right lung to inferior vena cava)
- *Supravalvular mitral ring* (rare congenital defect characterized by an abnormal ridge of connective tissue on the atrial side of the mitral valve)
- *Total anomalous pulmonary venous return (TAPVR)* (rare congenital defect in which all four pulmonary veins do not connect normally to left atrium but instead drain to the right atrium by way of an abnormal connection)

> **EXAMPLE:** Patient underwent surgical repair of supravalvular mitral ring via resection of left atrial membrane. Report code 33732.

Shunting Procedures

Shunting procedures are performed to move blood from one area to another, and they are performed for conditions such as

- *Atrial septal defect (ASD)* (opening in atrial septum fails to close after birth)
- *Coarctation of the aorta* (part of the aorta has a very narrow section, similar in appearance to an hourglass timer, reducing blood flow)
- *Patent ductus arteriosus (PDA)* (opening between aorta and pulmonary artery fails to close after birth)
- *Tricuspid atresia* (tricuspid valve is deformed, narrow, or missing)
- *Ventricular septal defect (VSD)* (opening in ventricular septum fails to close after birth)

> **EXAMPLE:** Patient underwent a shunt procedure of the descending aorta to the pulmonary artery to correct patent ductus arteriosus. Report code 33762.

Transposition of Great Vessels

The **transposition of great vessels** is the congenital reversal of the aorta and pulmonary artery. The pulmonary arteries are supplied by the left ventricle, and the aorta is supplied by the right ventricle—the opposite of the normal arrangement.

EXAMPLE: Patient underwent repair of transposition of the great arteries with aortic and pulmonary artery reconstruction. Report code 33778.

Truncus Arteriosus

Truncus arteriosus is a congenital malformation in which just one artery arises from the heart to form the aorta and pulmonary artery.

EXAMPLE: Patient underwent total repair of truncus arteriosus. Report code 33786.

Aortic Anomalies

Aortic Anomalies codes classify repair procedures. **Aortic anomalies** result from unusual patterns of aortic development and include conditions such as

- *Tracheal decompression* (or *tracheomalacia*) (softness of cartridge that supports tracheal walls, which can be due to *vascular ring formation* and results in tracheal collapse and decreased airflow)
- *Aberrant vessels* (or *vascular ring formation*) (abnormal growth of vessels, which encircle trachea and esophagus and result in upper airway obstruction)
- *Aortopulmonary septal defect (APSD)* (deficiency in septum between aorta and pulmonary artery, resulting in abnormal communication between them)
- *Patent ductus arteriosus* (opening between aorta and pulmonary artery fails to close after birth)
- *Coarctation of aorta* (part of the aorta has a very narrow section, similar in appearance to an hourglass timer, reducing blood flow)
- *Hypoplastic aortic arch* (or *interrupted aortic arch*) (absence of a portion of the aortic arch, creating a gap between the ascending and descending aorta)

EXAMPLE: Patient underwent surgical division of aberrant vessels with aortopexy to correct tracheomalacia. Report codes 33802 and 33800-51.

Thoracic Aortic Aneurysm

An aneurysm (Figure 14-9) is a bulge in an artery than can weaken the arterial wall and eventually burst, resulting in hemorrhage.

(A)   (B)

FIGURE 14-9 Aortic aneurysm repair (A) Aortic aneurysm (B) Graft repair of aneurysm

EXAMPLE: Patient underwent transverse aortic arch graft to repair thoracic aortic aneurysm. Cardiopulmonary bypass was provided with profound hypothermia, total circulatory arrest, and isolated cerebral perfusion with reimplantation of arch vessel. Report code 33871.

Endovascular Repair of Descending Thoracic Aorta

Endovascular repair of descending thoracic aorta procedures involve the placement of grafts to repair defects of the thoracic aorta (e.g., aneurysm, intramural hematoma, penetrating ulcer, traumatic disruption). When fluoroscopic guidance is used during endovascular repair procedures, report a code from the Radiology section (when the Surgery code does not include such guidance).

 NOTE:

Interventional procedures performed with endovascular repair of the descending thoracic aorta are reported separately (e.g., innominate, carotid, subclavian, visceral, or iliac artery transluminal angioplasty or stenting; arterial embolization; and intravascular ultrasound).

EXAMPLE: Patient underwent placement of proximal extension prosthesis for endovascular repair of descending thoracic aorta dissecting aneurysm, initial extension only. Fluoroscopic guidance confirmed appropriate placement. Report codes 33883 and 75958.

Pulmonary Artery

Pulmonary Artery codes classify procedures performed on the pulmonary artery.

EXAMPLE: Patient underwent repair of pulmonary atresia with ventricular septal defect, by construction or replacement of conduit from right or left ventricle to pulmonary artery. Report code 33920.

Heart/Lung Transplantation

Guidelines for heart/lung transplantation include three components.

- **Cadaver donor cardiectomy with or without pneumonectomy,** which involves harvesting the allograft (graft such as lung tissue that is transplanted between genetically nonidentical individuals of the same species) and preserving the allograft with cold preservation solution and cold maintenance

- Backbench work, which involves preparing the cadaver donor heart and/or lung allograft prior to lung transplantation and dissecting allograft from surrounding soft tissues to prepare the aorta, superior vena cava, inferior vena cava, pulmonary artery, left atrium, and/or trachea for implantation

- **Recipient heart with or without lung allotransplantation,** which includes transplantation of the allograft and care of the recipient

EXAMPLE: Patient with severe cardiomyopathy underwent heart transplant procedure to remove diseased heart and replace with healthy heart from a recently deceased donor. Transplant physician performed donor cardiectomy including cold preservation from cadaver donor, backbench standard preparation of cadaver donor heart allograft, and heart transplant with cardiopulmonary bypass. Report code 33940 for the donor procedure, and report codes 33944 and 33945-51 for procedures performed on the recipient; and modifier -51 is added to code 33945 only. (Cold preservation is a component of the donor organ harvesting procedure, not the backbench preparation.)

When donor cardiectomy and backbench preparation are performed at a facility other than the transplant facility (and the removed organ is transported to the transplant facility), codes 33940 (donor procedure) and 33944 (recipient procedure) are reported by the first facility. Code 33945 (recipient procedure) is reported by the transplant facility.

Extracorporeal Membrane Oxygenation or Extracorporeal Life Support Services

Extracorporeal membrane oxygenation (ECMO) or **extracorporeal life support (ECLS)** provides cardiac and/or respiratory support to the heart and/or lungs, which allow them to rest and recover when patients are sick or injured. The CPT coding manual contains a table of codes for ECMO/ECLS procedures, which helps provide direction to proper codes.

> **EXAMPLE:** Veno-venous extracorporeal life support was initiated by the patient's physician. Report code 33946.

Cardiac Assist

Cardiac assist procedures include the insertion, implantation, and removal of various devices. A **ventricular assist device (VAD)** provides temporary support for the heart by substituting for left or right heart function (e.g., after myocardial infarction).

> **EXAMPLE:** Patient underwent insertion of intra-aortic balloon assist device into the common femoral artery. Device was to the distal aortic arch. Report code 33967.

Exercise 14.1 – Heart and Pericardium

Instructions: Assign the CPT code(s) and appropriate modifier(s) to each statement.

1. Patient undergoes aortic valve replacement with stentless tissue valve, by division. Cardiopulmonary bypass is provided.

2. An 18-year-old patient underwent repair of ductus arteriosus. Posterolateral thoracotomy was performed to access the heart.

3. Patient underwent coronary artery bypass, during which a single arterial and single vein graft was performed.

4. A 7-year-old child underwent repair of pulmonary atresia with ventricular septal defect, and a prosthetic conduit was used.

5. Patient underwent insertion of permanent pacemaker with transvenous electrode(s), ventricular. An additional electrode was inserted in the left ventricle to provide a biventricular (dual chamber) pacing system and attached to the inserted pacemaker.

6. Patient underwent subtotal pericardiectomy with cardiopulmonary bypass.

7. Subcutaneous cardiac rhythm monitor was inserted, including programming, in a 54-year-old male patient.

8. Patient underwent sinus of Valsalva fistula repair, with cardiopulmonary bypass.

9. Operative ablation of ventricular arrhythmogenic focus was performed on a 62-year-old female patient, with cardiopulmonary bypass.

Exercise 14.1 – *continued*

10. Patient underwent transection of pulmonary artery with cardiopulmonary bypass.

_____

11. The physician drained fluid from the pericardial space under ultrasonic guidance.

_____

12. The physician repositions a previously placed transvenous right ventricular electrode.

_____

13. The physician performed an operative ablation of a supraventricular arrhythmia without cardiopulmonary bypass.

_____

14. The physician performed a surgical vascular endoscopy with video-assisted harvesting of a vein for coronary artery bypass surgery (vein only, single coronary venous graft).

_____

15. Patient underwent banding of pulmonary artery.

_____

16. The physician initiated cardiopulmonary bypass, the right atrium was opened, and a stiff ring was inserted for valvuloplasty of the tricuspid valve.

_____

17. Using cardiopulmonary bypass, the physician repaired an artificial prosthetic valve that was malfunctioning due to leakage.

_____

18. The patient was brought to the operating room, and a triple coronary bypass was performed using only venous conduits.

_____

19. The physician performed a coronary endarterectomy (open), left anterior descending artery, during the same operative session as a coronary artery bypass graft procedure (using an arterial graft).

_____

20. The physician performed a Damus-Kaye-Stansel procedure.

_____

21. Using cardiopulmonary bypass, the right atrium was opened and a patch of Dacron was sutured to the edge of the atrial septal defect (secundum) to close it.

_____

22. The physician repaired a hypoplastic aortic arch using prosthetic material, without cardiopulmonary bypass.

_____

23. The surgeon repaired transposition of the great arteries via Jatene-type aortic pulmonary artery reconstruction, including closure of ventricular septal defect.

_____

24. The physician repaired an atrial septal defect and ventricular septal defect with patch closure.

_____

25. Using cardiopulmonary bypass, the physician repaired a thoracoabdominal aortic aneurysm using a prosthetic graft.

_____

Arteries and Veins

The Arteries and Veins subsection also requires an excellent understanding of the anatomy of vascular structures because it is organized according to artery or vein (and approach). Notes at the beginning of the Arteries and Veins subsection indicate the following:

- Codes for procedures performed on arteries and veins include the establishment of both inflow and outflow by whatever procedures are necessary. This means that separate codes for establishing inflow and outflow are not reported.
- The portion of the operative arteriogram that is performed by the surgeon is included in codes for procedures performed on arteries and veins. (When the radiologist participates by supervising and interpreting an arteriogram, a separate code is reported.)
- When a **sympathectomy** (excision of a segment of the sympathetic nerve) procedure is performed, it is included in the codes for aortic procedures. For example, a lumbar sympathectomy might be performed to improve collateral blood supply to the foot when reconstructive surgery is not possible.

Embolectomy/Thrombectomy

An **embolectomy** is the surgical removal of an **embolus** (blood clot that circulates throughout the bloodstream), and a **thrombectomy** (fixed blood clot) is the surgical removal of a thrombus. Before reporting a code, make sure you identify the type of blood vessel (artery or vein) and the approach used to remove the embolus or thrombus (e.g., catheter and/or incision).

EXAMPLE 1: Patient underwent carotid embolectomy with catheter, by neck incision. Report code 34001.

EXAMPLE 2: Patient underwent direct subclavian vein thrombectomy, by neck incision. Report code 34471.

Venous Reconstruction

Venous reconstruction procedures are performed to repair venous valves, the vena cava, and venous transposition. Leg veins contain valves, which contain two leaflets to allow blood to flow in one direction toward the heart. When venous valves become damaged and fail to function properly, the backflow of blood occurs, resulting in varicose veins, pain, leg swelling, hyperpigmentation (skin discoloration), and skin ulcers (breakdown of the skin). Valvuloplasty is performed to repair incompetent valves by opening the vein; exposing the leaflets after dissecting the vein from surrounding tissues; and placing very fine sutures to attach the valve edges to the vein wall, which tightens the valve flaps when the vein is closed.

Reconstruction of the vena cava is performed to correct a congenital defect or to repair the vena cava when the patient sustains trauma or the vena cava is damaged due to long-term drug therapy (e.g., chemotherapy). For example, the obstructed or damaged portion of the vena cava is resected and repaired with an autologous (graft from patient's own body) pericardial patch.

Venous valve transposition is performed to treat chronic deep venous insufficiency. An incision is made to expose the venous valve, and the section of the vein that contains the malfunctioning valve is excised. Then a harvested vein that contains functional valves is anastomosed end-to-end to the remaining vein.

A **cross-over vein graft** procedure involves making an incision to expose the vein's incompetent valve, dividing that section of the vein, and connecting it to a nearby vein that has functioning valves.

A **saphenopopliteal vein anastomosis** involves making an incision to expose the saphenous vein and connecting it to the popliteal vein using end-to-end anastomosis.

EXAMPLE: Patient developed chronic benign superior vena cava syndrome due to long-term use of central venous catheters (CVCs) for administration of chemotherapy. Reconstruction of vena cava was performed by resecting the obstructed segment and placing an autologous pericardial patch. Report code 34502.

Coding Tip

The list of procedures included with and excluded from endovascular repair of an abdominal aortic aneurysm varies slightly from those associated with endovascular repair of an iliac aneurysm. For example, open femoral or iliac artery exposure is included with endovascular repair of an abdominal aortic aneurysm, but it is reported separately when performed with endovascular repair of an iliac aneurysm.

Repair of Aneurysms

The Arteries and Veins heading contains the following subheadings about repair of aneurysms and related procedures:

- Endovascular Repair of Abdominal Aortic Aneurysm
- Fenestrated Endovascular Repair of the Visceral and Infrarenal Aorta
- Endovascular Repair of Iliac Aneurysm
- Direct Repair of Aneurysm or Excision (Partial or Total) and Graft Insertion for Aneurysm, Pseudoaneurysm, Ruptured Aneurysm, and Associated Occlusive Disease

An aneurysm is an abnormal "bulging" of a portion of a vessel, usually due to a weakness or thinning of the vessel wall at that location (Figure 14-10). It can be caused by congenital or acquired weakness of the vessel wall. Minimally invasive procedures are performed to implant endovascular devices (e.g., endovascular graft) for treatment of aortic and iliac aneurysms. Direct (open) repair includes partial or total excision of the arterial segment that contains the aneurysm and insertion of a graft, using end-to-end anastomosis (Figure 14-11).

Because a number of different methods are used to repair abdominal aortic aneurysms, the coder must review the operative report to identify

- Whether an endovascular or direct (open) repair of the abdominal aortic aneurysm was performed
- What the artery and type of exposure were (e.g., open femoral artery exposure for delivery of endovascular prosthesis, by groin incision, unilateral)
- What type of device was used for repair (e.g., modular bifurcated prosthesis)
- What other separately reported procedures or services were provided (e.g., fluoroscopy)

FIGURE 14-10 Three types of aneurysms

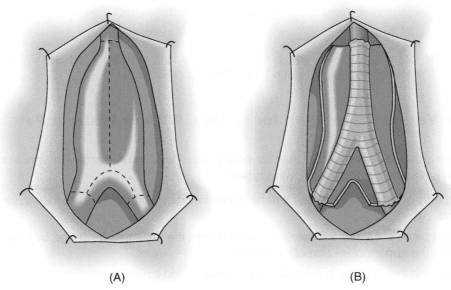

FIGURE 14-11 (A) Surgical resection of aneurysm (B) Grafting of aneurysm

Coding Tip

- Codes for endovascular repair of aneurysms include balloon angioplasty with target treatment zone either before or after graft deployment, distal extensions, manipulation, and positioning.

- When assigning codes for aneurysm repair, review the patient record to determine if the type of repair is direct (open) or endovascular. Direct (open) repairs include procedures performed on the thoracic aorta and all other arteries. Endovascular repairs include procedures performed on the thoracic aorta, abdominal aorta, and the iliac artery.

EXAMPLE 1: Patient underwent open iliac artery exposure for delivery of endovascular prosthesis during endovascular therapy, via abdominal incision (unilateral), with placement of extension prosthesis to treat an infrarenal abdominal aortic aneurysm. Report codes 34820 and 34709-51.

EXAMPLE 2: Patient underwent direct repair with partial excision of aneurysm and graft insertion to treat a left carotid aneurysm. Report code 35001-LT.

Repair Arteriovenous Fistula

An *arteriovenous fistula* is an abnormal connection or passageway between an artery and a vein, which means blood flows directly from an artery into a vein, bypassing the capillaries. A person may be born with an arteriovenous fistula (congenital fistula), or a fistula may develop after birth (acquired fistula due to trauma or other pathology).

EXAMPLE 1: Patient underwent repair of a congenital arteriovenous fistula, neck. Report code 35180.

EXAMPLE 2: Patient sustained a knife wound to the abdomen, and a traumatic arteriovenous fistula developed. Surgical repair of the abdominal arteriovenous fistula was performed. Report code 35189.

Repair Blood Vessel Other Than for Fistula, With or Without Patch Angioplasty

Generally, the *repair of blood vessels (other than for fistula)* is due to an injured artery or vein, such as a lacerated or torn blood vessel. Repairs include the following types:

- Direct (e.g., a partly divided vessel or one that has been lacerated longitudinally can be sutured, with the cut ends anastomosed)
- Vein graft (e.g., a piece of saphenous vein is harvested from the patient and sutured over lacerated blood vessel to bypass the abnormal section of the vessel)
- Graft other than vein (e.g., synthetic graft material is sutured end-to-end to the vessel, replacing the excised portion)

EXAMPLE 1: Patient underwent direct repair of superficial basilic vein, left hand. Report code 35207-LT.

EXAMPLE 2: Patient underwent repair of peroneal artery with synthetic graft, right lower leg. Report code 35286-RT.

Thromboendarterectomy

A **thromboendarterectomy** is the surgical excision of a thrombus and atherosclerotic inner lining from an obstructed artery. It is typically performed to treat calcified plaque or clot formations that don't respond to balloon angioplasty procedures. Coders must carefully review documentation to distinguish between a thrombectomy (e.g., procedure to remove a thrombus or blood clot) and a thromboendarterectomy (e.g., procedure to remove a thrombus and the lining of the artery, including possible placement of a patch graft).

EXAMPLE 1: Patient underwent abdominal aortic thromboendarterectomy with patch graft. Report code 35331.

EXAMPLE 2: Patient underwent carotic thromboendarterectomy with patch graft reoperation 90 days after initial carotid thromboendarterectomy (without patch graft). Report codes 35301 and 35390.

Angioscopy

Angioscopy is the microscopic visualization of substances (e.g., contrast media and radiopaque agents) as they pass through capillaries. The intravenous injection of the substance is performed as part of the procedure.

EXAMPLE: Patient underwent endovascular repair of infrarenal abdominal aortic aneurysm using aorto-aortic tube prosthesis. Prior to performing the therapeutic portion of the procedure, angioscopy was performed to visualize the interior of the aortic arch. Subsequently, under abdominal aortographic guidance, initial third-order vascular catheterization of left infrarenal artery was performed and atherectomy catheter device was advanced to the aorta. In addition to codes for the endovascular repair (34701, 36247-LT, 75625), report code 35400. (Do not add modifier -51 to code 35400.)

Bypass Graft

The Bypass Graft heading includes codes that describe procedures performed on veins and *in situ* veins. Codes also classify the use of "other than vein" material (e.g., synthetic graft) as bypass grafts for arteries. Each code describes the bypass graft anastomosis location (e.g., carotid-vertebral, carotid-subclavian).

EXAMPLE 1: Patient underwent bypass graft, with vein, of the left femoral-popliteal artery. Report code 35556-LT.

EXAMPLE 2: Patient underwent *in situ* vein bypass of the right femoral-popliteal artery. Report code 35583-RT.

EXAMPLE 3: Patient underwent synthetic bypass graft, common carotid-ipsilateral internal carotid arteries. Report code 35601-RT.

Composite Grafts

Add-on codes for composite grafts describe harvesting and anastomosis of multiple vein segments as arterial bypass graft conduits. A **composite graft** is comprised of vein and synthetic graft material *or* segments of veins from two or more locations, such as saphenous vein and femoral vein.

EXAMPLE 1: Patient underwent bypass graft procedure of right femoral-popliteal artery with Gore-Tex synthetic graft and a portion of the right saphenous vein. Report 35556-RT and 35681. (Do not add modifier -51 to code 35681.)

EXAMPLE 2: Patient underwent bypass graft procedure of right femoral-femoral artery. Vein grafts were obtained from the left brachial and left basilic veins. Report codes 35558-RT and 35682-LT. (Do not add modifier -51 to code 35682.)

 NOTE:

The most common material used for "other than vein" includes synthetic materials such as Gore-Tex.

Adjuvant Techniques

Add-on for **adjuvant techniques** are additional procedures or techniques that may be required during a *lower extremity* bypass graft procedure. They are performed to improve the **patency** (open and unblocked status of a blood vessel or another tube in the body) of *lower extremity* synthetic or autogenous arterial bypass grafts.

EXAMPLE 1: Patient underwent right popliteal-tibial bypass grafting with Gore-Tex synthetic graft material. Adjuvant distal vein cuff (DVC) of the popliteal-tibial bypass graft was performed during the same operative session. Report codes 35671-RT and 35685-RT. (Do not report modifier -51 with code 35685.)

EXAMPLE 2: Patient underwent left femoral-popliteal bypass grafting with polytetrafluoroethylene synthetic material. Adjuvant distal arteriovenous fistula (DAVF) of the femoral-popliteal graft was performed during the same operative session. Report codes 35656-LT and 35686-LT. (Do not report modifier -51 with code 35686.)

Arterial Transposition

Arterial transposition and/or reimplantation procedures are performed to improve arterial blood flow. An add-on code is reported for reimplantation procedures involving **visceral arteries**, which supply blood to the intestines, liver, and spleen.

EXAMPLE 1: Patient underwent transposition surgery to anastomose the right vertebral artery to the right subclavian artery. Report code 35693.

EXAMPLE 2: Patient underwent bypass graft surgery of splenorenal artery, during which synthetic graft material was used. Replantation of splenic artery to infrarenal aortic prosthesis was performed during the same operative session to ensure adequate blood supply to the spleen. Report codes 35636 and 35697. (Do not add modifier -51 to code 35697.)

Excision, Exploration, Repair, Revision

Excision, exploration, repair, and revision procedures include reoperations, explorations not followed by surgical repair or for postoperative hemorrhage, repair of grant-enteric fistulas, and thrombectomies of arterial or venous grafts, including revision procedures.

EXAMPLE: Patient underwent exploration for suspected postoperative hemorrhage, chest. Five days ago patient underwent CABG surgery. Report 35820-78.

Vascular Injection Procedures

Vascular injection procedure codes describe common procedures performed to gain venous access for phlebotomy, prophylactic intravenous access, infusion therapy, chemotherapy, and drug administration. They are reported for

- Diagnostic catheterization (e.g., injecting contrast media into vasculature for radiologic imaging)
- Therapeutic (interventional) catheterization (e.g., balloon dilation or stent placement to open narrowed valves and vessels)

NOTE:

When you look up "Vascular Injection" in the CPT index, a code for "Unlisted Services and Procedures" is the only entry. There is also no index entry for "Injection, Vascular" in the CPT index. (Some codes are listed for the "Catheter" entry in the CPT index.) Thus, coders must become familiar with codes and descriptions in the Vascular Injection Procedures heading (and subheadings) of CPT.

CPT also classifies cardiovascular procedures in multiple locations. For example, vascular ultrasound procedures for noncoronary vessels are classified in the Cardiovascular Surgery section, but vascular ultrasound procedures for coronary vessels and cardiac catheterizations are located in the Medicine section.

Vascular injection procedures include the following services, *which are not coded and reported separately:*

- Injection of contrast media, with or without automatic power injection

NOTE:

Although the injection procedure is not reported separately, an HCPCS level II code for provision of contrast media is reported separately.

- Introduction of needles or catheters

NOTE:

Although the introduction of a needle or catheter is not reported separately, a CPT code for selective vascular catheterization is reported separately.

- Necessary local anesthesia
- Necessary pre- and postinjection care specifically related to the injection procedure

The following supplies are reported with HCPCS level II codes if provided during a vascular injection procedure:

- Catheters
- Drugs
- Contrast media

Notes below the Vascular Injection Procedures subheading provide instruction about coding selective vascular catheterization. (Be sure to review previous content about selective vascular catheterization.)

Codes for vascular injection procedures include the following routes:

- Intravenous
- Intra-arterial–intra-aortic (including placement of shunts for dialysis)
- Venous
- Central venous access procedures

Coding Tip

- When two separate access procedures (e.g., punctures of two different vessels) are performed, report a separate code for each.
- When a nonselective vascular catheterization is converted to a selective vascular catheterization, report a code for the selective vascular catheterization only.

Vascular injection procedures include the introduction of the catheter or needle into a blood vessel and insertion into lesser- (first-) order vessels. Then when the catheter is inserted as follows for the purpose of performing diagnostic and/or therapeutic procedures, the code(s) for selective vascular catheterization is reported:

- Second-, third- (and beyond) order vessels (e.g., popliteal angiogram)
- Aorta and first-, second-, third- (and beyond) vessels (e.g., carotid angiogram)

Coding Tip

Codes for cardiac catheterization are reported from the Medicine section of CPT.

Coding Tip

When a catheter is removed from a vessel, do not report a separate code for that procedure. However, when implantable venous access devices and/or subcutaneous reservoirs are removed, report an appropriate code (e.g., code 36589).

EXAMPLE: Patient underwent left arm venogram. Catheter was introduced into the superior vena cava and inserted into the brachiocephalic vein and left subclavian vein. Catheter was manipulated into the left axillary vein, and contrast media was injected. Catheter was further advanced into the left brachial basilic vein, and contrast media was injected. Good visualization of the left axillary and brachial veins was obtained. No deformities were noted. Report code 75820-LT for the left arm venogram. Report code 36011-LT for selective vascular catheterization of the left axillary vein. Report 36012-51-LT for selective vascular catheterization of the left brachial and basilic veins.

CPT code 36200 is reported just once for "introduction of catheter, aorta" regardless of the number of times the catheter is repositioned in the aorta. When multiple vessels are accessed during catheterization, in different vascular families, report the code for the highest level of selectivity in each vascular family.

Venous procedures are coded according to the type of procedure, patient's age, and the puncture site (e.g., 2-year-old patient underwent scalp vein venipuncture, 36405). Make sure you carefully review the patient record and code descriptions to determine whether the procedure was a direct puncture or a cutdown and whether a physician's skill was required.

Therapeutic apheresis is the removal of blood components, cells, or plasma solute and the retransfusion of the remaining components into the patient. Procedure codes are based on blood components.

- White blood cells
- Red blood cells
- Platelets
- Plasmapheresis
- Extracorporeal immunoadsorption and plasma reinfusion
- Extracorporeal selective adsorption or selective filtration and plasma reinfusion

Central Venous Access Procedures

Central venous access procedures include insertion, repair, partial replacement, complete replacement, and/or removal of the catheter or device. The CPT coding manual contains the central venous access procedures table, which provides direction for assignment of proper codes. A venous access device is inserted

- Centrally (e.g., femoral, jugular, or subclavian vein or inferior vena cava)
- Peripherally (e.g., basilic or cephalic vein)

A central venous catheter (CVC) or a central venous access device (CVAD) is used to deliver intravenous fluids and medications and to obtain blood samples. These infusions may be administered for short or prolonged periods, using a single-lumen (allows for infusion of one solution) or multiple-lumen catheter (allows for infusion of several solutions simultaneously).

To be considered a central venous access catheter or device, the tip of the CVC or CVAD must terminate in the subclavian, brachiocephalic, or iliac veins; the superior or inferior vena cava; or the right atrium. (Otherwise, the catheter is considered a midline catheter, MLC.) The device is accessed for use (e.g., administration of medications or hyperalimentation) through a(n)

- Exposed catheter (external to the skin)
- Subcutaneous port
- Subcutaneous pump

CVAD codes are reported according to the patient's age and whether the device is nontunneled (not implanted) or tunneled (implanted).

Peripherally inserted CVADs include peripherally inserted central (venous) catheters (PICCs) and MLCs. The type of catheter inserted depends on the technique used, solutions infused, and duration of the intravenous therapy. Any catheter placed with the tip between the antecubital area and the head of the clavicle is called an MLC. Such placement is typically done for infusion therapy, which is expected to last from 1 to 8 weeks (when the catheter tip doesn't need to terminate in the superior vena cava). The PICC can also be shortened if it is needed for midline placement. It is usually inserted below the antecubital fossa and does not require use of a guidewire.

When reporting codes for central venous access procedures (Table 14-1), make sure you determine the following:

- Patient's age
- Whether the catheter was **tunneled** (implanted) or nontunneled

TABLE 14-1 Coding Central Venous Access Catheters and Devices

Code	Age	Nontunneled	Tunneled (Implanted)	Types of Venous Access Catheters and Devices	Venous Insertion Sites
36555 36556	< 5 ≥ 5	X X		Centrally inserted central venous catheter (CVC), such as • Cook • Leonard • Quinton • Shiley • Triple lumen	• Femoral vein • Inferior vena cava • Jugular vein • Subclavian vein
36557 36558	< 5 ≥ 5		X X	Centrally inserted CVC, without subcutaneous port or pump, such as • Ash Split • Broviac • Double lumen • Groshorg • Hickman • PermCath	• Femoral vein • Inferior vena cava • Jugular vein • Subclavian vein
36560 36561	< 5 ≥ 5		X X	Centrally inserted central venous access device (CVAD), with subcutaneous port, such as • Bard port • Infuse-a-Port • MediPort • Port-a-Cath • Q-Port	• Femoral vein • Inferior vena cava • Jugular vein • Subclavian vein
36563			X	Centrally inserted CVAD, with subcutaneous pump, such as • Chemotherapy pump • Infusion pump • Intravenous pump	• Femoral vein • Inferior vena cava • Jugular vein • Subclavian vein
36565			X	Centrally inserted CVAD requiring two catheters via two separate venous access sites, without subcutaneous port or pump, such as Tesio type catheter	• Femoral vein • Inferior vena cava • Jugular vein • Subclavian vein
36566			X	Centrally inserted CVAD requiring two catheters via two separate venous access sites, with subcutaneous port(s), such as Tesio type catheter, with port	• Femoral vein • Inferior vena cava • Jugular vein • Subclavian vein
36568 36569	< 5 ≥ 5			Peripherally inserted central venous catheter (PICC), without subcutaneous port or pump, such as • Abbott • Angiocath • Jelco • Triple lumen	Superficial veins in the arms, legs, feet, or head, such as • Basilic vein • Cephalic vein • Saphenous vein
36570 36571	< 5 ≥ 5			Peripherally inserted CVAD, with subcutaneous port, such as • Bard port • Infuse-a-Port • Medi-Port • Port-a-Cath • Q-Port	Superficial veins in the arms, legs, feet, or head, such as • Basilic vein • Cephalic vein • Saphenous vein

- Whether the procedure was done via
  - **Cutdown:** Catheter is inserted directly into a vein through an incision
  - **Peripherally:** Catheter is inserted into peripheral vein using a needle or trocar

NOTE:

Tunneled (implantable) venous access ports are typically used for long-term intravenous therapy, and they contain two parts: · catheter and port.

Coding Tip

When blood is collected from a partially or completely implantable venous access device, report code 36591.

Repair of Central Venous Access Device (CVAD) procedures are performed to repair, replace, and/or remove CVADs and central venous catheters (CVCs). These codes do not require selection based on the patient's age or central/peripheral insertion site. However, they do distinguish between nontunneled (with exposed access) and tunneled catheters (require subcutaneous port/pump pocket and connection). They also require knowledge of whether a subcutaneous port or pump was inserted. (Refer to Table 14-1 for a list of centrally inserted and peripherally inserted CVC and CVAD devices.)

> **EXAMPLE:** Patient underwent mechanical removal of a blood clot from a central venous device using venous access. Report code 36595.

Arterial

Arterial blood gases (e.g., arterial blood oxygen, carbon dioxide, and bicarbonate levels) are commonly performed to diagnose the patient's effectiveness of respiration. To report an arterial puncture for the purpose of obtaining a sample for arterial blood gas analysis, report code 36600. During an arterial puncture, a needle is inserted into the artery to obtain a sample of blood; a catheter is *not* inserted into the artery.

NOTE:

A heparin flush is performed to maintain patency of the catheter/port and to reduce the risk of blood clotting in the catheter. When a heparin flush is performed as a part of an injection or infusion procedure, it is not separately coded.

> **EXAMPLE 1:** Patient underwent insertion of a catheter into the artery percutaneously for blood sampling; the catheter was removed after sampling was completed. Report code 36620.

> **EXAMPLE 2:** Patient underwent a cutdown procedure to access an artery after which a catheter was inserted, the artery was sutured, and the incision was closed in layers. Report code 36625.

Intraosseous

Code 36680 is reported when the physician inserts a special needle to puncture the bone marrow cavity (e.g., tibia or femur) to infuse fluids into bone marrow blood vessels.

Hemodialysis Access, Intervascular Cannulation for Extracorporeal Circulation, or Shunt Insertion

Hemodialysis Access procedures include:

- Arteriovenous anastomosis, direct
- Insertion of cannulas for prolonged extracorporeal circulation of membrane oxygenation (ECMO)
- Arteriovenous fistula

Arteriovenous hemodialysis access is created by using autogenous venous tissue or inserting a prosthetic graft.

EXAMPLE 1: Patient underwent forearm vein transposition between the elbow and the wrist. Report code 36820.

EXAMPLE 2: Patient underwent open arteriovenous anastomosis of the right cephalic vein. (The cephalic vein is located in the upper arm.) Report code 36818-RT.

EXAMPLE 3: Patient underwent open arteriovenous anastomosis via left basilic vein transposition. (The basilic vein is in the upper arm.) Report code 36819-LT.

Dialysis Circuit

Dialysis circuit procedures and services are performed as part of Hemodialysis treatment, which involves circulating arteriovenous (AV) blood outside of the body through the *dialysis circuit*, which is created using an arterial-venous anastomosis (called an AV fistula) or by placing a prosthetic graft between an artery and vein (called an AV graft). The dialysis circuit is designed for easy and repetitive access, and it contains two segments, the peripheral dialysis segment and the central dialysis segment.

EXAMPLE: Patient underwent percutaneous mechanical thrombectomy with infusion for thrombolysis. Report code 36904.

Portal Decompression Procedures

Portal decompression procedure codes are reported for the insertion and revision of transvenous intrahepatic portosystemic shunt (TIPS) procedures. A TIPS is inserted to reduce portal pressure associated with portal hypertension. Portal blood flow is diverted into the hepatic vein, which reduces pressure between the portal and systemic circulations.

Coding Tip

Codes 37182 and 37183 include radiological supervision and interpretation (e.g., portography and all associated imaging guidance and documentation). Therefore, do not report Radiology codes 75885 and 75887 with codes 37182 and 37183.

EXAMPLE: Patient underwent insertion of TIPS. Report code 37182.

Transcatheter Procedures

The Transcatheter Procedures subheading contains notes that provide instruction to report codes separately for catheter placement and radiological supervision and interpretation. When transcatheter therapy services are provided, the introduction of the needle and catheter are included in the code for the primary service.

EXAMPLE 1: Patient underwent open transluminal stent placement of the right femoral artery for revascularization with atherectomy and angioplasty of the same vessel. The catheter was introduced into the right femoral artery (second-order artery), and contrast medium was injected. Femoral magnetic resonance angiogram was performed and revealed blockage of the femoral artery. Repeat femoral magnetic resonance angiogram (Figure 14-12), after stent placement, revealed good arterial circulation in the femoral artery. Report codes 37227-RT, 36246-RT, and 73725-RT.

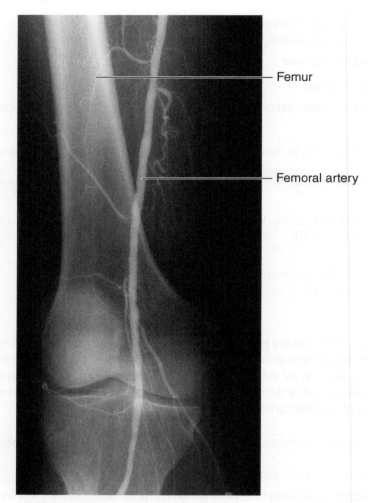

FIGURE 14-12 Femoral angiogram. The use of contrast medium makes arteries visible.

EXAMPLE 2: Patient underwent cerebral thrombolysis as therapy for acute ischemic stroke. Report code 37195.

Endovascular Revascularization (Open or Percutaneous, Transcatheter)

Endovascular revascularization procedures are performed for lower extremity occlusive disease, and include open, percutaneous, and transcatheter methods. The CPT codes are inclusive of all services provided for the vessel treated, and codes from one vascular family are reported for the purpose of revascularization.

- *Iliac Vascular Territory*, which is subdivided into the common iliac, internal iliac, and external iliac arteries
- *Femoral/Popliteal Vascular Territory*, which includes the femoral and popliteal arteries in one extremity
- *Tibial/Peroneal Vascular Territory*, which includes the anterior tibial, posterior tibial, and peroneal arteries

EXAMPLE: Patient underwent percutaneous transluminal angioplasty (PTCA) (Figure 14-13) for endovascular revascularization of the right common iliac, right internal iliac, and right external iliac arteries. Report codes 37220, 37222, 37222. (Code 37220 is the primary endovascular revascularization code, and code 37222 is reported twice for endovascular revascularization of the two additional arteries. Code 37222 is an add-on code and, thus, exempt from modifier -51.)

Vascular Embolization and Occlusion

Vascular Embolization and Occlusion codes classify vascular embolization and occlusion procedures, including arteries, veins, and lymphatics. (This subheading excludes codes for such procedures performed on the central nervous system and the head and neck.)

Catheter threaded into subclavian artery

(1)   (2)   (3)   (4)

Balloon in position in right coronary artery

FIGURE 14-13 Percutaneous transluminal coronary (balloon) angioplasty (PTCA)

EXAMPLE: Patient underwent venous vascular embolization, including radiological supervision and interpretation, intraprocedural roadmapping, and imaging guidance necessary to control venous hemorrhage. Report code 37244.

Intravascular Ultrasound Services

Intravascular ultrasound services (IVUS) of noncoronary vessels are performed during diagnostic evaluation and/or therapeutic intervention. These codes are reported in addition to a code for the primary procedure.

EXAMPLE: Patient undergoes percutaneous transluminal mechanical thrombectomy of dialysis circuit, with diagnostic angiography of dialysis circuit, and intravascular ultrasound service. Report codes 36904 and 37252.

Endoscopy

Endoscopy codes describe vascular endoscopy procedures, and surgical vascular endoscopy always includes diagnostic endoscopy.

EXAMPLE: Patient underwent surgical vascular endoscopy with ligation of subfascial perforator veins. Report code 37500.

Ligation

Ligation of arteries and veins is performed to control bleeding of a ruptured or dissected (torn) artery/vein. Ligation CPT codes describe

- ligation, division, and stripping of the saphenous veins. For a **stab phlebectomy**, multiple tiny incisions are made over varicose vein sites. At each stab site, the varicosity is extracted and then the varicose segment is removed. (The stab phlebectomy procedure is not typically performed on saphenous veins.)
- subfascial ligation of incompetent perforator veins (e.g., connecting superficial veins located below the skin's surface to deep veins in the leg muscle).
- ligation and division of the short saphenous vein at the saphenopopliteal junction. An incision is made in the skin overlying the short saphenous vein at its junction with the saphenopopliteal vein at the knee. Vessels are dissected and ties are placed around the short saphenous vein, which is divided between the ties.
- ligation, division, and/or excision of varicose vein "clusters." These are large varicose veins that cannot be effectively treated using the stab phlebectomy technique because they require a larger incision. An open surgical dissection of the vein cluster is made using long incisions rather than short stab incisions.

EXAMPLE: Patient underwent ligation, division, and stripping of the short saphenous vein, right leg. Report code 37718-RT.

Other Procedures

Other Procedures codes classify penile revascularization, penile venous occlusive procedures, and unlisted procedures involving vascular surgery.

> **EXAMPLE:** Patient underwent penile venous occlusive procedure. Report code 37790.

Exercise 14.2 – Arteries and Veins

Instructions: Assign the CPT code(s) and appropriate modifier(s) to each statement.

1. On the initial treatment day, the physician performed transcatheter therapy, which included arterial infusion for thrombolysis of the inferior vena cava. Radiological supervision and interpretation were included.

   _____

2. A physician performs a right upper extremity arteriogram. Catheter is inserted into the right brachial artery.

   _____

3. Physician uses a transfemoral approach to advance a catheter to the ascending aorta, where nonradioactive contrast media is injected and the descending thoracic aortography and abdominal aortography are performed.

   _____

4. Physician punctures the subclavian vein of a 4-year-old, passes a guidewire centrally, and inserts a central venous catheter (nontunneled).

   _____

5. Patient underwent left renal venogram, which required introduction of a catheter into the inferior vena cava, insertion into the left renal vein, and manipulation into the left suprarenal vein. Contrast media was injected into both veins, and the structures were well visualized. No obstruction or other deformity was noted.

   _____

Hemic and Lymphatic Systems Subsection

The Hemic and Lymphatic Systems subsection headings include the following:

- Spleen
- General
- Transplantation and Post-Transplantation Cellular Infusions
- Lymph Nodes and Lymphatic Channels

The Hemic and Lymphatic Systems subsection contains codes that describe procedures on the spleen, bone marrow transplantation services, the lymph nodes and lymph channels, the mediastinum, and the diaphragm. The **hemic system** is a blood-producing system. **Blood** is tissue that consists of plasma, red blood cells, white blood cells, and platelets (or thrombocytes). The **lymphatic system** (Figure 14-14) consists of the spleen, thymus, tonsils, adenoids, vessels that carry lymph, and lymph nodes. The **spleen** (Figure 14-15) produces mature lymphocytes, destroys worn out red blood cells, and serves as a reservoir for blood. The **thymus** produces T lymphocytes, which are important to the body's immune function. The **tonsils** are located at the back of the throat, and they contain lymphoid tissue that helps fight infections. The **adenoids** are located at the rear of the nose, and they contain

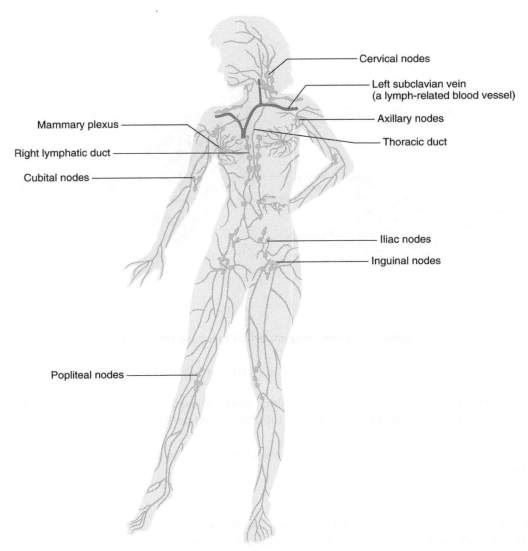

FIGURE 14-14 Lymphatic circulation and major lymph node locations

lymphoid tissue that helps fight infections. **Lymph** is a clear fluid that contains **chyle** (digestive fluid that contains proteins and fats), some red blood cells, and lymphocytes, which help fight infection and disease. **Lymph nodes** are clusters of bean-shaped nodules that act as the body's filtration system, removing cell waste and excess fluid and helping to fight infection. Lymph nodes are located in the

- Back of the head, just above the hairline (occipital region)
- Neck (cervical region)
- Armpits (axillary region)
- Elbow (cubital region)

- Chest (supraclavicular region)
- Abdomen (retroperitoneal region)
- Groin (inguinal region)
- Knee (popliteal region)

Spleen

Spleen codes are reported for the excision or repair of the spleen. (In code 38102, *en bloc* means "as a whole.") These codes include laparoscopic procedures performed on the spleen. A note below the Laparoscopy subheading provides instruction that "surgical laparoscopy always includes diagnostic laparoscopy." This means that when the physician performs diagnostic and surgical laparoscopies during the same operative session, just the code for surgical laparoscopy is reported.

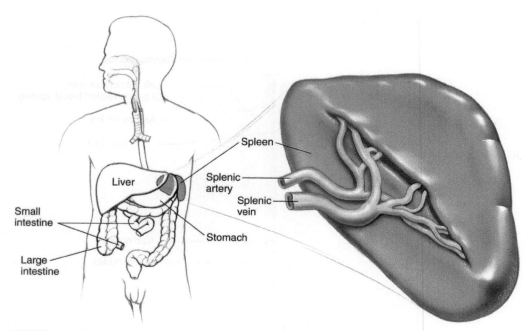

FIGURE 14-15 The spleen performs many important functions related to the immune system.

EXAMPLE: Patient underwent open repair of ruptured spleen with partial splenectomy. Report code 38115.

When a needle is inserted percutaneously and contrast media is injected into the spleen for direct **splenoportography,** the radiographic visualization of the splenic and portal veins results.

EXAMPLE: Patient underwent splenoportography, with percutaneous injection of contrast medium into the spleen. Report codes 75810 and 38200.

General

The General heading includes the Bone Marrow or Stem Cell Services/Procedures subheading. **Bone marrow** is spongy material that fills large bones' cavities and consists of two types.

- *Red marrow:* Produces red blood cells, white blood cells, and platelets
- *Yellow marrow:* Replaces red marrow with fatty tissue that does not produce blood cells

Bone marrow contains two types of **stem cells**.

- *Hemopoietic:* Produce red blood cells, white blood cells, and platelets
- *Stromal:* Produce fat, cartilage, and bone and have the ability to differentiate into many kinds of tissue, such as nervous tissue

Codes are reported for the harvesting, aspiration, biopsy, and transplantation of bone marrow and/or stem cells. Codes are also reported for the steps involved in the preservation, preparation, and purification of bone marrow and stem cells prior to transplantation or reinfusion. Stem cells are harvested from a suitable donor (allogeneic) or the patient's bone marrow (autologous).

A **bone marrow aspiration** uses a needle to remove a sample of the liquid bone marrow for examination under a microscope. A **bone marrow biopsy** involves boring a small hole into a long bone (e.g., hip) and using a large, hollow needle to remove bone marrow for examination under a microscope. When bone marrow aspiration and bone marrow biopsy procedures are performed at the same site through the same skin incision (during the same operative session), report just bone marrow biopsy code. When the bone marrow aspiration and bone marrow biopsy procedures are performed at separate sites (e.g., different bones or separate skins incisions in the same bone), report multiple codes.

EXAMPLE: Progenitor cells (stem cells) were harvested from an umbilical cord after delivery, and they were cryopreserved and kept for transplantation to the neonate later in life or to other recipients. This process required transplantation preparation of hematopoietic progenitor cells and included cryopreservation and storage. Report code 38207.

Transplantation and Post-Transplantation Cellular Infusions

Hematopoietic cell transplantation (HCT) is the autologous or allogeneic infusion of hematopoietic progenitor cells (HPC) obtained from bone marrow, peripheral blood apheresis, or umbilical cord blood. The infusion of HPCs help restore bone marrow function, while allogeneic lymphocyte infusions are often used to treat chronic myelogenic leukemia.

EXAMPLE: Hematopoietic cells previously obtained from the patient's bone marrow were implanted because the recipient's immune system had been suppressed using radiation. The autologous harvested cells are injected into the recipient by intravenous drip therapy in a sterile environment. Report code 38241.

Lymph Nodes and Lymphatic Channels

Capillaries surround cells but are not actually connected to cells, which results in the leakage of watery blood plasma (containing oxygen, proteins, glucose, and white blood cells) or lymph (Figure 14-16). This lymph (fluid) is recirculated away from the body's cells in the lymphatic circulatory system, which contains lymphatic channels, called capillaries and lymphatic vessels. The lymph eventually reaches one of about one hundred lymph nodes located throughout the body, which filter the fluid. (Lymph nodes contain white blood cells that filter debris and foreign cells from lymph.) When a patient becomes infected (e.g., bacteria or virus), the number of white blood cells in lymph nodes increases to billions. The lymph nodes work to fight the infection and release the filtered lymph (fluid) back into the bloodstream. Sometimes lymph nodes become infected or abscessed and require surgical treatment.

EXAMPLE: A patient is diagnosed with cervical lymphadenitis and undergoes incision and drainage. The surgeon makes a skin incision overlying the abscessed cervical lymph node, a needle with a syringe attached is inserted into the lymph node, and the abscess is drained. The wound is closed with Steri-Strips. Report code 38300.

Limited excision of lymph nodes is often performed for **cancer staging**, which is the determination that cancer has or has not spread anatomically from its point of origin. After cancer staging, the complete removal of the lymph nodes, and surgical wound closure is often performed in layers.

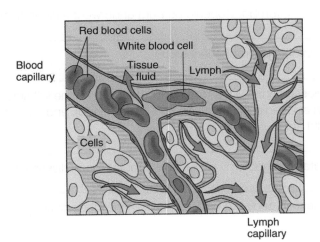

FIGURE 14-16 Lymph circulation showing interaction with blood vessels and cells

Exercise 14.3 – Hemic and Lymphatic

Instructions: Assign the CPT code(s) and appropriate modifier(s) to each statement.

1. Patient underwent bilateral total pelvic lymphadenectomy via laparoscope with multiple periaortic lymph node samplings.

2. Physician conducted a donor search to locate a suitable match for a transplant patient and arranged acquisition of cells.

3. Physician infused a patient with allogeneic lymphocytes.

4. Previously frozen stem cells were thawed, without washing.

5. Bone marrow biopsy, sternum, using trocar.

6. Progenitor cells (allogeneic) were harvested from umbilical and placental blood, cryopreserved, and maintained for transplantation.

7. Physician made a subcostal incision, dissected tissue surrounding the spleen, doubly ligated the vessels, and removed the spleen.

8. Physician sutured lacerations in a ruptured spleen and then resected and removed a damaged segment of the spleen.

9. Physician inserted a catheter into the spleen and injected 20 cubic centimeters of radiopaque dye for splenoportography.

10. Physician performed a total splenectomy.

11. A patient with idiopathic thrombocytopenic purpura underwent a laparoscopic splenectomy.

12. Patient underwent suprahyoid lymphadenectomy.

13. Patient underwent glossectomy with a composite resection on the left side of the neck with mandibular resection and radical neck dissection (Commando), and a modified radical neck dissection on the right side.

14. Patient underwent total laryngectomy with bilateral radical neck dissection.

15. Patient underwent injection of dye to visualize the sentinel node during lymphangiography nuclear imaging test.

Summary

The Cardiovascular System subsection classifies procedures performed on the heart and pericardium, valves (e.g., mitral and semilunar), and peripheral vascular vessels (e.g., arteries, veins, and capillaries). Cardiovascular System subsection codes are arranged anatomically and then according to procedure performed.

The Hemic and Lymphatic Systems subsection classifies procedures performed on the spleen, lymph nodes, and lymphatic channels.

Internet Links

CTSNet Global I Cardiothoracic Community: *www.ctsnet.org*

Medcomp vascular access devices: *www.medcompnet.com*

Vascular & Endovascular Surgery Society: Go to *www.vesurgery.org*, hover over Resources, and click on the FAQs link.

The Gross Physiology of the Cardiovascular System: *www.cardiac-output.info*

The Leukemia & Lymphatic Society: *www.lls.org*

Review

Multiple Choice

Instructions: Select the most appropriate response.

1. When coding cardiovascular system procedures, from which section(s) of CPT are additional procedure codes often reported?
    - **a.** E/M
    - **b.** Anesthesia
    - **c.** Pathology/Laboratory
    - **d.** Radiology, Medicine

2. When reporting codes 33880 and 33881 for endovascular repair of the descending thoracic aorta, review of the code descriptions indicates that which is included?
    - **a.** Descending thoracic aorta extension(s), if required to level of celiac artery origin
    - **b.** Radiological supervision and interpretation
    - **c.** Transcervical retropharyngeal carotid-carotid bypass
    - **d.** Transposition of subclavian to carotid

3. Codes 33500–33507, Coronary Artery Anomalies, include _____ when performed during the same operative session.
    - **a.** arterial embolization
    - **b.** coronary artery bypass grafting
    - **c.** endarterectomy or angioplasty
    - **d.** intravascular ultrasound

4. Review code 33286 (Removal, subcutaneous cardiac rhythm monitor). The parenthetical note below code 33286 provides instruction to assign codes 93285, 93291, or 93298 for:
    - **a.** Holter monitor and external event recording.
    - **b.** initial implantation, including programming.
    - **c.** removal and reinsertion of a pacing cardioverter.
    - **d.** subsequent electronic analysis and/or reprogramming.

5. When the "battery" of a pacemaker or implantable defibrillator is changed, it is actually the _____ that is changed.
    - **a.** catheter
    - **b.** electrode
    - **c.** pacemaker
    - **d.** pulse generator

6. An angioscopy (35400) is performed in addition to a transluminal balloon angioplasty of the renal artery during the same operative session. Codes are reported for:
   a. transluminal balloon angioplasty of renal artery only.
   b. transluminal balloon angioplasty of renal artery and angioscopy.
   c. transluminal balloon angioplasty of renal artery, angioscopy, and injection of contrast medium.
   d. transluminal balloon angioplasty of renal artery, angioscopy, injection of contrast medium, and angiography.

7. A coder reviews the patient record to determine the patient's age, whether the inserted catheter was tunneled or nontunneled, and whether the procedure was performed peripherally or via cutdown. Which procedure is being coded?
   a. Arteriovenous anastomosis
   b. Central venous access
   c. Portal decompression
   d. Therapeutic apheresis

8. Which is the removal of a fixed blood clot?
   a. Atherectomy
   b. Embolectomy
   c. Sympathectomy
   d. Thrombectomy

9. The two types of aneurysm repair are:
   a. arteriovenous and open.
   b. endocardial and endovascular.
   c. endovascular and direct.
   d. transluminal and direct.

10. *En bloc* means:
   a. closed and blocked status of incision.
   b. implanted.
   c. insertion directly into a vein through a blood vessel.
   d. surgical removal as a whole.

11. Injection procedure of radioactive tracer for identification of sentinel node. Which CPT code is assigned?
   a. 36005   b. 38790   c. 38792   d. 38790, 38900

12. Pericardiectomy with cardiopulmonary bypass. Which CPT code(s) are assigned?
   a. 33030, 33935
   b. 33030, 33935-51
   c. 33030, 33935-59
   d. 33031

13. Suture repair of aorta without shunt or cardiopulmonary bypass. Which CPT code is assigned?
   a. 33300   b. 33320   c. 33322   d. 33330

14. A 15-year-old patient is admitted for repair of patent ductus arteriosus by division. Which CPT code is assigned?
   a. 33820   b. 33822   c. 33824   d. 33840

15. Patient with cardiopulmonary insufficiency receives 72 hours of daily management of veno-venous extracorporeal life support (ECLS) provided by his physician. Which CPT code(s) are assigned?
   a. 33946
   b. 33946, 33948, 33948
   c. 33948, 33948, 33948
   d. 33949, 33949, 33949

16. Open biopsy of deep cervical nodes. Which CPT code is assigned?
   a. 38500   b. 38510   c. 38520   d. 38525

17. Patient underwent percutaneous thrombectomy of the arteriovenous fistula. Which CPT code is assigned?
   a. 36825   b. 36831   c. 36832   d. 36904

18. Percutaneous venous transluminal balloon angioplasty performed as a distinct procedural service. Which CPT code is assigned?
   a. 37236-59   b. 37236-79   c. 37248   d. 37248-59

19. Percutaneous transcatheter retrieval of intravascular foreign body. Which CPT code is assigned?
     a. 37184   b. 37187   c. 37195   d. 37197

20. Direct repair of a ruptured aneurysm of the abdominal aorta. Which CPT code is assigned?
     a. 33877   b. 34701   c. 35082   d. 35092

Coding Practice

Instructions: Assign the CPT code(s) and appropriate modifier(s) to each case.

Cardiovascular System

1. A patient presents to the ambulatory surgery center for stripping of the long saphenous veins in the right leg and the long and short saphenous veins in the left leg. The long saphenous veins were stripped from the saphenofemoral junction to the knee.

_____

2. A patient has a 3-year history of mitral regurgitation. The patient presents for mitral valve replacement. The procedure begins with placing the patient on heart-lung bypass machine. After gaining access to the thoracic cavity, the left atrium is identified. The damaged mitral valve is identified and removed. This is replaced with a biprosthetic valve and sewn in. Total time on bypass machine was 2.5 hours.

_____

3. A patient presents for pacemaker insertion due to diagnosis of bradycardia. After intravenous sedation was obtained, the entire left chest and neck were prepped. A standard incision was made in the left deltopectoral groove. A small venotomy was made, and the ventricular and then the atrial leads were placed into position. These were tested and found to be functioning properly. The leads were anchored at exit sites from the vein attached to the pacemaker. The pacemaker was tested, was functioning, and was placed in the subcutaneous pocket. All connections are checked. The patient will have another check before discharge from the hospital tomorrow.

_____

4. A 20-year-old male patient presents for surgical treatment of his patent ductus arteriosus (PDA). Under general anesthesia, a thoracotomy is done for access to the PDA. After the pericardium is opened to get to the mediastinum, the ductus is identified and closed via ligation.

_____

5. A 2-year-old patient presents to the ED after having fallen in a lake, with a near drowning. The patient is in shock. Regular venous access methods have failed, and the emergency department attending physician decides to do a venous cutdown. After a transverse incision over the vein of the patient's ankle is made, a small stab incision is done distal to the first incision. Two sutures are placed around the vein. A cannula is passed though the incision of the vein. The skin is closed in layers with sutures.

_____

6. A 45-year-old patient diagnosed with chronic renal failure underwent surgery to facilitate dialysis access. The surgeon created an arteriovenous fistula by other than direct arteriovenous anastomosis with placement of nonautogenous graft access. The patient was prepped and draped in the usual fashion. Dissection was carried down the brachial artery and basilic vein. Prolene sutures were used to expose the vein. A thermoplastic graft was tunneled subcutaneously. The vein graft was sewn end to side. The graft was flushed with saline and then clamped below the anastomosis. The proximal graft at the 4-mm end was beveled and sewn to the small caliber brachial artery. Anastomosis was secured, and the native artery was flushed up through the graft first. All wounds were closed with Vicryl and nylon sutures.

_____

7. A 57-year-old patient was found to have carotid stenosis after duplex scan and angiogram. The patient presents today for a left carotid thromboendarterectomy with patch angioplasty. The neck area of the patient was prepped. An oblique incision along the sternomastoid muscle was made. Dissection was done through the platysma to the carotid sheath. The hypoglossal and vagus nerves were identified during dissection and preserved with care. The sheath dissection was performed along the anterior border of the left internal jugular vein. The common, external, and internal carotid arteries were dissected. The patient was given heparin, and clamping of the internal carotid did not reveal any changes on EEG monitor. The common and external carotids were clamped. A longitudinal arteriotomy was made. Standard thromboendarterectomy was performed, transecting the proximal end and working distally. The arteriotomy was closed with a patch cut to an ellipse and parachuted into the distal apex. The external and common carotids were opened. There was a good signal in the arteries. No changes were noted on the EEG. The wound was irrigated and closed.

_____

8. The patient had an implantable pacing cardioverter-defibrillator (ICD) placed 6 months ago. The patient now has a malfunction of this device. After adequate anesthesia, an incision was made and the electrodes were removed from the generator. There was a screw problem with the generator that was producing a noise. The leads were tested and found to be working satisfactorily. The original implantable defibrillator pulse generator was removed and then replaced with an implantable defibrillator pulse generator. Both generators were a dual lead system. The ICD was placed back in the pocket, and the wound was closed after irrigation with 3-0 and 4-0 Vicryl.

_____

9. A 35-year-old female patient has been found to have a pericardial cyst via echocardiogram. After adequate anesthesia, a lateral thoracotomy is performed to gain access to the pericardium. The patient's heart is stopped via cardioplegia infused through a heart-lung bypass machine. The pericardial cyst is seen lying next to the diaphragm. It is removed in total. Drainage tubes are placed. The cardioplegia is reversed. The cyst will be sent to pathology for analysis. The wound is closed in layers with Prolene and Vicryl.

_____

10. A patient presents with a history of atherosclerosis. The patient is having surgery to bypass his blocked heart arteries. After anesthesia is administered and the patient is placed on a heart bypass machine, the surgeon makes a thoracic incision. The blockage of the heart is identified. The physician harvests the saphenous vein from the patient's leg to use in the bypass. An opening is made in the aorta. The grafted vein is sutured to the opening in the aorta at one end and below the blockage at the other end.

_____

Hemic and Lymphatic Systems

1. A patient with a history of pancytopenia presents for a bone marrow biopsy. The physician numbs the skin and inserts a needle into the iliac bone. The core of the needle is discharged, and the sample is placed. The needle is withdrawn. The sample is sent for analysis.

   _____

2. A 14-year-old patient was in a motor vehicle crash and suffered blunt abdominal trauma. Due to internal bleeding and a ruptured spleen, the patient requires a splenectomy. After making the initial abdominal incision, the physician identifies the spleen. Splenic blood vessels are tied off. The spleen is removed in total. The remainder of the abdominal cavity is examined for any injuries or bleeding. No injury or additional bleeding is found. The wound is closed in layers.

   _____

3. A 3-year-old patient with a cystic hygroma of the neck presents for dissection. An incision is made in the neck. The tissue surrounding the hygroma is removed via excision. The hygroma is deep in the neurovascular section of the neck. Extensive and deep dissection is required for complete removal. The cyst is accessed and removed. The skin is closed in multiple layers.

   _____

4. A patient underwent pelvic lymphadenectomy, which included removal of all external iliac, hypogastric, and obturator nodes. The patient has a history of ureteral cancer and now has pelvic pain and swelling. The patient is placed in the supine position. An incision is made over the iliac crest. Blood vessels are identified, and bleeders are cauterized. Enlarged pelvic lymph nodes are identified and removed in total. These are sent to pathology. The wound is closed with sutures.

   _____

5. A patient presents for a cervical node removal. The patient's left neck area is prepped and draped in the usual fashion. An incision is made to access the cervical node. A scalene fat pad is identified and removed to access the deeper node. Both the cervical node and the pad are sent to pathology for analysis. The wound is closed in layers.

   _____

6. A patient suffered a fall from 20 feet. The patient has internal bleeding and has consented for a laparoscopic procedure to identify internal structures that may be causing hemorrhage. The patient is placed in the normal lateral decubitus position. A trocar is placed above the umbilical region through an incision. Gas is introduced into the abdominal cavity. Laparoscopic examination identifies damage to the patient's spleen. An additional two incisions are made to insert trocars for the procedure. The spleen is dissected with hemostasis achieved. The spleen is removed via pouch method through the trocar. The three incision sites are closed with sutures.

   _____

7. The patient presents for lymphangiography of the right pelvic lymph nodes. The radiologist accesses the patient's vein and puts dye in to highlight subcutaneous tissues. A lymph vessel is identified. A small incision is made to allow for the introduction of a needle and catheter. More dye is injected into this vessel. The needle and catheter are secured with a suture. The first set of films is done. The second set of films is done on the next day. After the second set of films, the radiologist removes the catheter and sutures the incision site closed.

   _____

8. A patient with a history of chyle in the pleural cavity presents for suturing of his thoracic duct. Via an abdominal incision, the duct is identified and tied off. The incision is closed in layers with sutures.

_____

9. A patient with leukemia requires a bone marrow donor. The physician contacts the national bone marrow donor registry and provides medical information on the patient. The physician receives two potential matches.

_____

10. A patient has an enlarged lymph node of the axillary region. The physician makes an incision over the lymph node area after adequate local anesthesia. The node is identified and found to be inflamed; drainage of the node yields a pustulant material. The area is thoroughly irrigated, and the incision wound is closed with 4-0 Prolene sutures.

_____

CPT Surgery IV

Chapter Outline

Mediastinum and Diaphragm Subsection

Digestive System Subsection

Urinary System Subsection

Chapter Objectives

At the conclusion of this chapter, the student should be able to:

1. Define key terms related to the Mediastinum and Diaphragm, Urinary System, and Digestive System subsections of CPT Surgery.
2. Assign codes from the Mediastinum and Diaphragm subsection of CPT Surgery.
3. Assign codes from the Digestive System subsection of CPT Surgery.
4. Assign codes from the Urinary System subsection of CPT Surgery.

Key Terms

anoscopy

biliary system

bipolar cautery

cheiloplasty

cholecystectomy

closed laparoscopy

cold biopsy forceps

colectomy

colonoscopy

colostomy

complex fistulectomy

continent ileostomy

cystometrogram

cystoscopy

cystourethroscopy

diagnostic endoscopy

diaphragm

digestive system

diverticula

diverticulosis

electrocautery snare

endorectal pull-through

endoscopic retrograde cholangiopancreatography (ERCP)

enterectomy

enterolysis

esophageal varices

esophagogastroduodenoscopy (EGD)

esophagogastroscopy

esophagoscopy

gastrectomy

hepatotomy

hernia

hot biopsy forceps

hypopharynx

ileoanal anastomosis

ileostomy

J-pouch

kidney

Kock pouch

laparoscopy

laser technique

laser-assisted uvulopalatoplasty

lithotripsy

Meckel's diverticulum

mediastinum

mucocutaneous margin

nasopharynx

nephrectomy

Nissen fundoplasty

open laparoscopy

oropharynx

ostomy	rhinoplasty	submuscular fistulectomy	ureterolithotomy
palatopharyngoplasty	second-stage fistulectomy/ fistulotomy	surgical endoscopy	urethra
percutaneous lithotomy		transurethral resection of the prostate (TURP)	urethroplasty
peristalsis	seton	transurethral ureteroscopic lithotripsy	urinary bladder
peritoneoscopy	sigmoidoscopy		urinary system
proctectomy	stoma		uroflowmetry
proctosigmoidoscopy	subcutaneous fistulectomy	upper GI endoscopy	volvulus
pull-through		ureter	Whipple procedure

Introduction

The Mediastinum and Diaphragm subsection classifies procedures performed on the mediastinum and diaphragm. The Digestive System subsection classifies procedures performed on gastrointestinal (GI) tract organs as well as the teeth, palate and uvula, adenoids and tonsils, Meckel's diverticulum and mesentery, appendix, biliary tract, pancreas, abdomen, peritoneum, and omentum. The Urinary System subsection classifies procedures performed on the kidneys, ureters, bladder, and urethra.

CPT guidelines that apply to the subsections are located at the beginning of the Surgery section. Unique coding instructions for the Mediastinum and Diaphragm, Digestive System, and Urinary System subsections are located in notes below headings or codes.

Coding Tip

Notes located beneath headings and/or subheadings apply to all codes in the heading or subheading. Parenthetical notes that are located below a specific code apply to that code only, unless the note indicates otherwise.

NOTE:

The Other Procedures code below each subheading classifies an unlisted procedure performed on the anatomical site. When reporting an unlisted procedure code, include documentation (e.g., special report) about the procedure performed with the submitted claim. (Other Procedures subheadings are not included throughout this chapter of this textbook except when codes that describe additional procedures are included.)

Mediastinum and Diaphragm Subsection

Mediastinum and Diaphragm subsection headings include the following:

- Mediastinum
- Diaphragm

The **mediastinum** is the space in the thoracic cavity between the lungs that contains the aorta, the esophagus, the heart, and other structures.

The **diaphragm** is the thin muscle below the heart and lungs that separates the chest from the abdomen. It functions in respiration by contracting during inspiration, which means that the size of the chest cavity expands when a person is breathing in.

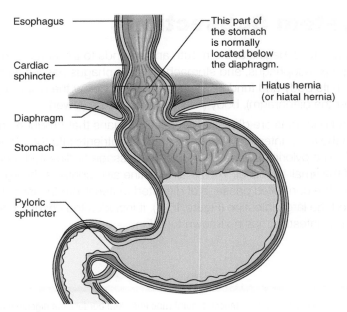

Esophagus

This part of the stomach is normally located below the diaphragm.

Cardiac sphincter

Hiatus hernia (or hiatal hernia)

Diaphragm

Stomach

Pyloric sphincter

FIGURE 15-1 In a hiatus hernia (or hiatal hernia), part of the stomach protrudes through the esophageal opening in the diaphragm.

The repair of two types of hernias is coded from the Mediastinum and Diaphragm heading.

- Hiatus hernia (Figure 15-1)
- Diaphragmatic hernia

EXAMPLE 1: Patient underwent resection of mediastinal cyst. Report code 39200.

EXAMPLE 2: Patient underwent resection of the diaphragm, with simple repair. Report code 39560.

Exercise 15.1 – Mediastinum and Diaphragm

Instructions: Assign the CPT code(s) and appropriate modifier(s) to each statement.

1. The physician performed a complex repair during resection of the diaphragm and closed the residual defect with synthetic graft material.

   _____

2. Mediastinotomy to remove foreign body using transthoracic approach, including median sternotomy.

   _____

3. Patient underwent repair, laceration of diaphragm.

   _____

4. Physician inserted a medastinoscope through an incision in the sternal notch and performed a mediastinal lymph node biopsy.

   _____

5. Physician repaired an acute traumatic diaphragmatic hernia.

   _____

Digestive System Subsection

The **digestive system** (Figure 15-2) begins at the mouth and extends to the anus. The upper digestive tract consists of the mouth, pharynx, esophagus, and stomach. The esophagus passes through the diaphragm and enters the stomach between its body and fundus. The stomach lies below the diaphragm and is composed of the fundus (upper portion under the diaphragm), body (middle), and antrum (lower).

The liver, gallbladder, and pancreas are digestive accessory organs that produce enzymes and substances that assist with digestion in the small intestine. The absorption of nutrients into the bloodstream occurs in the small intestine (Figure 15-3). The pyloric sphincter controls the passage of digested food from the stomach into the duodenum (first part of the small intestine). The small intestine also contains the jejunum and the ileum, where the ileocecal valve allows for the controlled passage of digested material into the large intestine. The last section of the digestive tract is called the large intestine (Figure 15-4). It includes the cecum, colon, rectum, and anus. The appendix, located off the large intestine, has no known function.

 NOTE:

When a lesion of the **mucocutaneous margin** (mucous membrane and skin) borders the digestive tract, it may appear that treatment (e.g., biopsy, destruction, or excision) requires the reporting of codes from multiple subsections of CPT to classify procedures performed. In fact, codes from just *one* of the following CPT subsections are reported:

- Integumentary system
- Digestive system

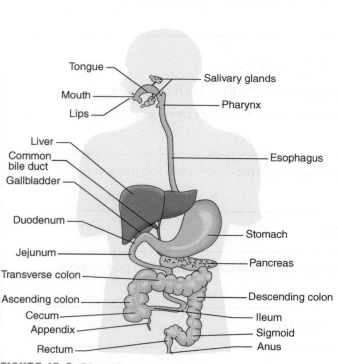

FIGURE 15-2 Digestive system organs

FIGURE 15-3 Small intestine

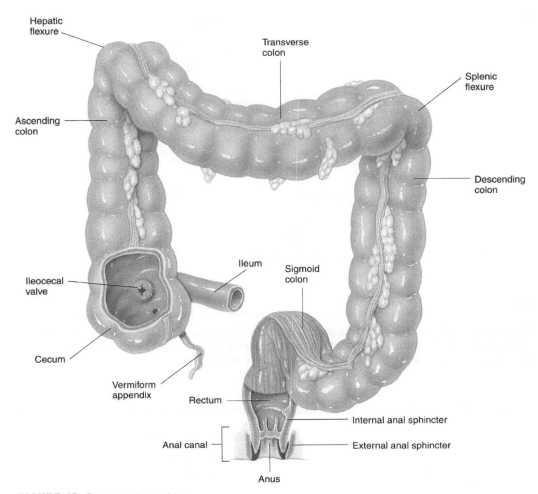

Hepatic flexure
Transverse colon
Splenic flexure
Ascending colon
Descending colon
Ileum
Sigmoid colon
Ileocecal valve
Cecum
Vermiform appendix
Rectum
Internal anal sphincter
Anal canal
External anal sphincter
Anus

FIGURE 15-4 Large intestine

The Digestive System subsection includes procedures to diagnose and treat disorders of the digestive system (e.g., GI endoscopy, laparoscopy, and gastric analysis). Similar to other Surgery subsections, procedures are classified first by anatomical area and then by type.

EXAMPLE: Patient underwent upper GI endoscopy of the esophagus, stomach, and duodenum, with specimen collection via brushing technique. Report code 43235.

Digestive System subsection codes are reported for open, endoscopic, and laparoscopic procedures. The operative report must be carefully reviewed to correctly identify the surgical approach.

EXAMPLE: The following codes are reported for gastrostomy procedures (Figure 15-5). A gastrostomy is the surgical creation of an artificial opening into the stomach. Code descriptions differ based on the surgical approach (underlined in each code description below) used to perform the gastrostomy.

43246   Esophagogastroduodenoscopy, flexible, transoral; with directed placement of percutaneous gastrostomy tube

43653   Laparoscopy, surgical; gastrostomy, without construction of gastric tube (eg, Stamm procedure) (separate procedure)

43830   Gastrostomy, open; without construction of gastric tube (eg, Stamm procedure) (separate procedure)

49440   Insertion of gastrostomy tube, percutaneous, under fluoroscopic guidance including contrast injection(s), image documentation and report

FIGURE 15-5 Gastrostomy

NOTE:

The CPT Medicine section also contains codes for digestive system procedures. They are located under the Gastroenterology heading (91010–91299), which classifies diagnostic tests such as electrogastrography. Such tests are generally included in endoscopic procedures, which means that they are not separately coded and reported.

The following headings contain codes that classify procedures performed on the oral cavity (Figure 15-6):

- Lips
- Vestibule of Mouth
- Tongue and Floor of Mouth
- Dentoalveolar Structures
- Palate and Uvula
- Salivary Glands and Ducts
- Pharynx, Adenoids, and Tonsils

Lips

CPT codes for procedures performed on the lips (e.g., biopsy of lip) include the following subheadings:

- Excision
- Repair (cheiloplasty)
- Other procedures

When a procedure is performed on the *skin* of the lip, report an appropriate code from the Integumentary System subsection. Do *not* report codes from both subsections for the same lip procedure.

EXAMPLE 1: Patient underwent a lip biopsy. Report code 40490.

EXAMPLE 2: Patient underwent incisional biopsy of the skin of the lip. The surgeon removed a skin lesion from the lateral side of the bottom lip. Report code 11106 (from the Integumentary System subsection).

Cheiloplasty is the plastic surgery of the lips. To properly assign codes, review the operative report to determine the vertical height associated with the repair (e.g., up to one-half vertical height or over one-half vertical height).

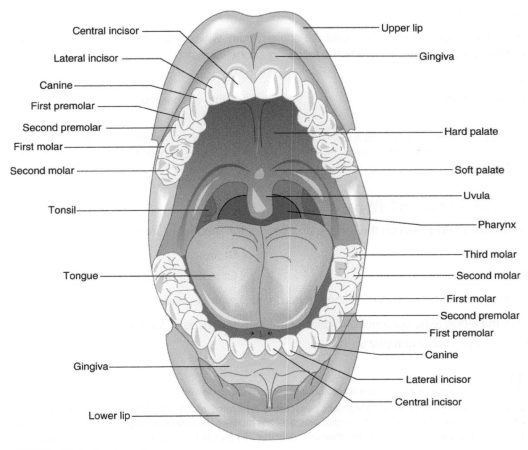

FIGURE 15-6 Oral cavity

The *full-thickness* repair of a lip laceration is reported with a code from the Repair (Cheiloplasty) heading. Do *not* report a code from the Integumentary System subsection instead of *or* in addition to full-thickness repairs of lip lacerations. (Simple and intermediate repairs of *skin* on the lip are reported with codes from the Integumentary System subsection.)

For procedures performed to repair cleft lip and nasal deformities, review the operative report to identify whether the procedure is

- Primary or secondary
- One-stage or two-stage

A primary procedure repairs the cleft lip/nasal deformity without recreating the defect. A secondary procedure re-creates the defect and includes reclosure to repair the cleft lip/nasal deformity. For a **rhinoplasty** (repair of skin defect of the nose using harvested tissue or plastic surgery to change the nose's shape or size), report a code from the Respiratory subsection.

EXAMPLE 1: Patient underwent full-thickness repair of the vermilion border of the upper lip. Patient sustained a laceration while replacing spark plugs in his classic 1967 Pontiac Bonneville. Report code 40650.

EXAMPLE 2: Patient underwent up to half vertical height full-thickness repair of the lower lip due to laceration acquired during a bar fight. The wound extended through the full thickness of the lip, including the vermilion border. Wound size was up to one-half the vertical height of the lip. Report code 40652.

Vestibule of Mouth

Codes for procedures performed on the vestibule of the mouth, which includes mucosal and submucosal tissue (inner lining) of the lips and cheeks, include the following subheadings:

- Incision
- Excision, destruction
- Repair
- Other procedures

EXAMPLE: The patient has a habit of sucking on toothpicks; during a recent automobile accident, a toothpick became embedded in submucosal tissue in his mouth. Patient underwent simple removal of embedded foreign body (toothpick). Report code 40804.

Tongue and Floor of Mouth

Codes for procedures performed on the tongue and floor of the mouth include the following subheadings:

- Incision
- Excision
- Repair
- Other procedures

When reporting codes for excision of a tongue lesion, review the operative report to identify the

- Location of the lesion (e.g., posterior one-third or anterior two-thirds of the tongue)
- Type of excision (partial or complete/total)

 NOTE:

When a partial glossectomy with bilateral radical neck dissection is performed, report code 41135 for the glossectomy and radical neck dissection on one side. (There is just one tongue, which means modifier -50 cannot be added to code 41135.) Report code 38720-59 for the radical neck dissection on the other side. (Modifier -59 is added to indicate a distinct procedural service.)

EXAMPLE: Patient underwent partial glossectomy with unilateral radical neck dissection. Report code 41135.

Dentoalveolar Structures

Codes for procedures performed on dentoalveolar structures (e.g., teeth or gums) include the following subheadings:

- Incision
- Excision, destruction
- Other procedures

(Commonly performed dental procedures are classified in the *Current Dental Terminology* [CDT].)

EXAMPLE: Patient underwent drainage of gum abscess. Report code 41800.

Palate and Uvula

CPT codes for procedures performed on the hard and soft palates and the uvula include the following subheadings:

- Incision
- Excision, destruction
- Repair
- Other procedures

FIGURE 15-7 A child with a cleft palate before and after treatment

A **palatopharyngoplasty** is performed to treat oropharyngeal obstructions; it involves surgically resecting excess tissue from the uvula, soft palate, and pharynx to open the airway (e.g., cure extreme cases of snoring with or without sleep apnea).

 NOTE:

Do *not* report code 42145 (Palatopharyngoplasty) for a **laser-assisted uvulopalatoplasty** procedure, which uses a laser technique to remove tissue from the uvula, soft palate, and pharynx. CPT does not list a specific code for laser-assisted uvulopalatoplasty. Therefore, report HCPCS level II code S2080. Because more than one treatment session may be required to achieve optimal results, subsequent visits to repeat the laser-assisted uvulopalatoplasty are included in the global period for the code reported. Therefore, a code for each repeat session is *not* reported separately.

For codes that describe cleft palate repairs (Figure 15-7), the size and location of the cleft determine the type of repair performed (and reported code).

EXAMPLE: The patient underwent primary plastic repair of cleft lip/nasal deformity, complete, unilateral. During the same operative session, the patient also underwent palatoplasty for cleft palate, with closure of alveolar ridge, soft tissue only. Report codes 40700 and 42205-51.

Salivary Gland and Ducts

Codes for procedures performed to treat conditions involving the salivary gland and salivary ducts (e.g., abscess, cyst, and tumor) include the following subheadings:

- Incision
- Excision
- Repair
- Other procedures

The selection of a code for the excision of a parotid tumor or the parotid gland is based on the following:

- What amount of tissue was excised
- Where the location was (e.g., lateral lobe)
- Whether the procedure included nerve dissection
- Whether the procedure included radical neck dissection

EXAMPLE: For the excision of a parotid tumor with bilateral radical neck dissection, report code 42426 for the excision and radical neck dissection on one side. (There is just one parotid gland, which means that modifier -50 *cannot* be added to code 42426.) Also, report code 38720-59 for the radical neck dissection on the other side. (Modifier -59 is added to indicate that a distinct procedural service was provided.)

Pharynx, Adenoids, and Tonsils

Codes reported for procedures performed on the pharynx, adenoids, and tonsils include the following subheadings:

- Incision
- Excision, destruction
- Repair
- Other procedures

The pharynx contains three segments.

- **Nasopharynx:** Located above the soft palate
- **Oropharynx:** Area between the soft palate and the upper portion of the epiglottis, including the tonsils
- **Hypopharynx:** Extends from the upper edge of the epiglottis to the larynx/esophagus juncture

A variety of techniques and approaches are used when treating conditions of the pharynx (e.g., oral, cervical, thoracic, and horizontal or lateral neck incisions).

EXAMPLE: Patient underwent removal of a lesion of the pharynx via oral approach using curettage. Report code 42808.

Tonsillectomy and Adenoidectomy

Tonsillectomy and adenoidectomy are the most frequently performed procedures coded from this heading. Codes reported for the removal of diseased tonsils or adenoid include the following techniques:

- Cryogenic
- Electrocautery
- Laser

The selection of a tonsillectomy or adenoidectomy code is based on the following:

- Type of procedure performed (e.g., primary or secondary)
- Age of the patient

A primary procedure code is reported the first time the tonsils or adenoids are removed. A secondary procedure code is reported when there is tissue regrowth requiring subsequent removal. The age of the patient is a factor because age increases the complexity (level of difficulty) of the procedure and lengthens the recovery time.

Separate codes are included to report hemorrhage control following tonsillectomy and adenoidectomy procedures. Make sure you report these procedure codes with modifier -78 to indicate the return to the operating room for a related procedure performed during the postoperative (global) period.

Codes reported for the radical resection of tonsils include the removal of the tonsils, tonsillar pillars, retromolar trigone, and any infected portions of the maxilla and mandible. Radical resection may also include a hemi- or total glossectomy and/or a full neck dissection.

 Coding Tip

Tonsillectomy and adenoidectomy are routinely performed bilaterally, and modifier -50 is not added to the codes.

A limited pharyngectomy is performed to remove a small portion of the pharyngeal wall (e.g., pyriform sinus).

EXAMPLE: A 6-year-old patient underwent tonsillectomy and adenoidectomy. Report code 42820.

Exercise 15.2 – Oral Cavity

Instructions: Assign the CPT code(s) and appropriate modifier(s) to each statement.

1. Patient underwent alveoloplasty to remove sharp areas or undercuts of alveolar bone, one quadrant.

2. Surgeon used a scalpel to slice off a cancerous portion of the vermilion border of the patient's lip; mucosal advancement was performed after excision.

3. Surgeon made an incision through submucosal tissue and removed a lesion in the vestibule of the mouth. Wound repair was not required.

4. Patient underwent simple incision of the lingual frenum to free the tongue.

5. Patient underwent incision in the parotid gland to remove a calcified stone.

6. Surgeon repaired a tear at the pharyngeal esophageal junction.

7. Physician drained an abscess near the tonsil.

8. Surgeon removed an 8-year-old patient's tonsils and adenoids.

9. Physician controlled secondary oropharyngeal hemorrhaging, status post-tonsillectomy, by using cellulose sponges that expanded when placed in the tonsillar cavity.

10. Physician performed a tonsillectomy on a 12-year-old male patient.

Esophagus

Codes reported for procedures performed on the esophagus include the following subheadings:

- Incision
- Excision
- Endoscopy
- Laparoscopy
- Repair
- Manipulation
- Other procedures

When assigning codes to procedures performed on the esophagus, review documentation carefully to identify the approach (e.g., incision or endoscopy).

EXAMPLE 1: Patient underwent esophagotomy via cervical approach, with removal of foreign body. Report code 43020.

EXAMPLE 2: Patient underwent cricopharyngeal myotomy via esophagotomy, thoracic approach, with removal of foreign body. Report code 43045.

Endoscopy

Endoscopic procedures performed to visualize digestive system organs generally use a flexible fiberoptic tube. (Rigid instruments are also used to perform endoscopy.) GI endoscopy is performed to diagnose and treat disorders of the GI tract. Codes are assigned according to the type of instrument used and the anatomical area visualized. The codes are classified in CPT as the following series:

- **Esophagoscopy** is the direct visualization of the esophagus from the cricopharyngeus muscle (upper esophageal sphincter) to and including the gastroesophageal junction (and may include examination of the proximal region of the stomach via retroflexion when performed), using an endoscope.
- **Upper GI endoscopy (esophagogastroscopy)** is the direct visualization of the esophagus and the stomach.
- **Esophagogastroduodenoscopy (EGD)** (Figure 15-8) uses a fiberoptic endoscope to visualize the esophagus, stomach, and proximal duodenum.
- **Endoscopic retrograde cholangiopancreatography (ERCP)** involves passing an endoscope through the esophagus, stomach, and duodenum to the ducts of the biliary tree and pancreas. A small plastic tube is passed through the endoscope, through which dye is injected (to allow for visualization of the ducts on x-rays). A radiologist then takes x-rays to diagnose liver, gallbladder, bile duct, and pancreas problems.

Endoscopic procedures are considered diagnostic or surgical, and surgical endoscopy always includes diagnostic endoscopy. This means that when both procedures are performed during the same operative session, report the code for surgical endoscopy only.

- **Diagnostic endoscopy** is performed to visualize an abnormality or determine the extent of disease.
- **Surgical endoscopy** is performed when anything in addition to visualization is performed (e.g., removal of foreign body).

EXAMPLE: Patient underwent diagnostic flexible sigmoidoscopy and biopsy of a lesion during the same operative session. The code for the diagnostic endoscopy (45330) is *not* reported. Only the code for the surgical procedure (45331) is reported.

FIGURE 15-8 Esophagogastroduodenoscopy (EGD)

Endoscopic biopsy codes are reported just once regardless of the number of biopsies performed. Likewise, endoscopic polyp or lesion removal codes are reported just once regardless of the number of polyps or lesions treated.

EXAMPLE 1: Patient underwent flexible esophagoscopy with multiple biopsies. Report code 43202.

EXAMPLE 2: Patient underwent flexible esophagoscopy with removal of five polyps by hot biopsy forceps. Report code 43216 (just once even though five polyps were removed).

EXAMPLE 3: Patient underwent flexible esophagoscopy with removal of three lesions by snare technique. Report code 43217 (just once even though three lesions were removed).

The endoscopic treatment of **esophageal varices** (uneven, enlarged, tortuous veins) (Figure 15-9) includes the following:

- Ligation (similar to the technique used to band hemorrhoids)
- Endoscopic injection of a sclerosing agent (e.g., concentrated saltwater) after passing sclerotherapy needle through scope

EXAMPLE 1: Patient underwent flexible esophagoscopy with band ligation of esophageal varices. Report code 43205.

EXAMPLE 2: Patient underwent direct ligation of esophageal varices. Physician accessed the esophagus through a thoracic incision and ligated the varices with sutures. Report code 43400.

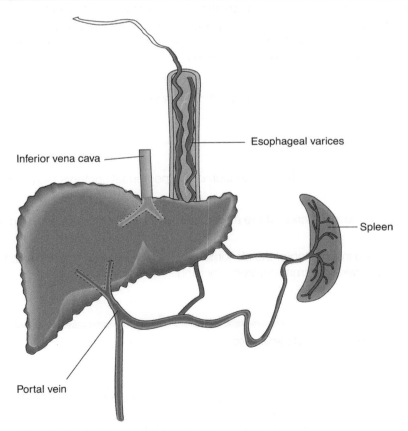

FIGURE 15-9 Esophageal varices

EXAMPLE 3: Patient underwent ligation at the gastroesophageal junction for preexisting esophageal perforation. The physician ligated the junction of the stomach and esophagus, and a gastrostomy was created for feeding. Report code 43405. Do not report code 43653 because its (separate procedure) note means the gastrostomy is included in code 43405.

Procedures performed to treat gastroesophageal reflux disease (GERD) typically use moderate (conscious) sedation and radiofrequency energy delivered via endoscopy. The physician performs an EGD with ultrasound examination, and radiofrequency energy is subsequently applied through the endoscope to the muscle of the lower esophageal sphincter and/or the gastric cardia to treat GERD.

EXAMPLE: Patient underwent upper GI endoscopy of the esophagus, stomach, and duodenum with delivery of thermal energy to the lower esophageal sphincter muscle for treatment of GERD. Report code 43257.

Endoscopic retrograde cholangiopancreatography (ERCP) combines upper gastrointestinal (GI) endoscopy and x-rays to detect and treat bile and pancreatic duct problems, such as blockages due to tumors, gallstones that become stuck in ducts, inflammation and infection due to trauma or illness, sclerosis (scarring) of ducts, and pseudocysts (accumulation of fluid and tissue debris). For example, if gallstones are present in the gallbladder (or bile duct), the doctor can remove them through the endoscope. Biopsies may also be taken for evaluation by the pathologist.

EXAMPLE: Patient underwent diagnostic ERCP with single biopsy. Report code 43261.

When a sphincterotomy of the bile duct or pancreatic duct is performed, it includes a diagnostic ERCP. A guidewire is advanced into the biliary tree, and an electrocautery current is applied to make the incision. However, when the patient undergoes gallstone and pancreatic duct stone removal and a sphincterotomy is performed during the same operative session, two codes are reported.

EXAMPLE: A patient undergoes ERCP basket removal of gallstones following a sphincterotomy. Report codes 43262 and 43264-51.

Laparoscopy

A **laparoscopy**, or **peritoneoscopy**, is the examination of the peritoneal contents using a laparoscope that is inserted through the abdominal wall.

- **Closed laparoscopy** is the insufflation of the abdominal cavity and is performed using a percutaneously placed needle.
- **Open laparoscopy** is the insufflation of the abdomen and is performed using a trocar, which is placed under direct vision after making a small celiotomy incision.

 NOTE:

Surgical laparoscopy always includes diagnostic laparoscopy.

EXAMPLE: Patient underwent surgical laparoscopy with Nissen esophagogastric fundoplasty. Report code 43280. (**Nissen fundoplasty** involves mobilizing the lower end of the esophagus by suturing the fundus of the stomach around the circumference of the lower esophagus at the esophagogastric junction.)

Manipulation

When endoscopic esophageal procedures are performed, the advancement of the endoscope through the esophagus expands any stricture. The dilation is considered an integral part of the esophagoscopy procedure. This means that a code for dilation of the esophagus without the use of an endoscope is *not* reported with a code for endoscopy of the esophagus (even if the operative report documents esophageal dilation during endoscopy).

 NOTE:

Esophageal dilation (without endoscopy) is usually performed under fluoroscopic guidance. Report the appropriate fluoroscopic guidance (x-ray) code in addition to the dilation code, when performed.

EXAMPLE: The physician uses fluoroscopy to insert a guidewire and to dilate the esophagus by passing dilators over the guidewire. Report 43453. (Code 74360 is also reported for fluoroscopy, which is radiological guidance of "intraluminal dilation of strictures and/or obstructions, such as the esophagus.")

Other Procedures

The free transfer of a short segment of jejunum is usually performed after portions of the pharynx or esophagus have been resected (e.g., cervical esophageal and hypopharyngeal carcinoma).

EXAMPLE: Patient underwent free jejunum transfer with microvascular anastomosis. Report code 43496.

Stomach

Codes reported for procedures performed on the stomach include the following subheadings:

- Incision
- Excision
- Laparoscopy
- Introduction
- Bariatric surgery
- Other procedures

Stomach procedures include the following:

- **Gastrectomy** (removal of all or a portion of the stomach), which is typically performed to treat ulcers (Figure 15-10) or malignancy.
- Roux-en-Y gastric bypass and small bowel reconstruction procedures that use a Y-shaped anastomosis, which includes the intestines.
- Surgical laparoscopic procedures performed on the stomach. Codes reported for procedures involving the field of bariatric surgery use laparoscopic techniques to perform gastric restrictive procedures for morbid obesity.
- Naso- or orogastric tube placement that requires a physician's skill and fluoroscopic guidance (reported when the nursing staff is unable to successfully insert the tube). Do not report a code when the nursing staff inserts the tube.
- Gastric restrictive procedures involving placement of an adjustable gastric band.

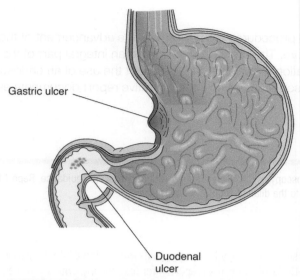

Gastric ulcer

Duodenal
ulcer

FIGURE 15-10 **Gastric and duodenal ulcers**

- Gastric restrictive procedure, which includes two reconstructive anastomoses (biliopancreatic diversion with duodenal switch).
- Gastric bypass procedure, which includes Roux-en-Y gastroenterostomy.

EXAMPLE: Patient underwent surgical laparoscopic gastric restrictive procedure, which included gastric bypass and Roux-en-Y gastroenterostomy (roux limb 150 cm or less). Report code 43644.

Exercise 15.3 – Esophagus and Stomach

Instructions: Assign the CPT code(s) and appropriate modifier(s) to each statement.

1. Physician inserted a flexible esophagoscope into the esophagus and destroyed a lesion, using snare technique.

_____

2. Surgeon made an incision in the left posterior chest wall into the esophagus to remove a foreign body from the esophagus.

_____

3. Physician inserted a balloon endoscopically for tamponade of bleeding esophageal varices.

_____

4. Dr. Smith performed a partial cervical esophagectomy, and then Dr. Jones performed a jejunum transfer with microvascular anastomosis.

_____

5. The physician passed an endoscope through the patient's mouth and visualized the entire esophagus, stomach, duodenum, and jejunum. One lesion was removed using biopsy forceps. Another lesion was removed using a snare.

_____

6. Patient underwent incision of the pyloric muscle.

_____

Exercise 15.3 – *continued*

7. The physician performed an open revision of a previously performed gastric restrictive procedure and reversed the previously partitioned stomach to restore normal gastrointestinal continuity.

   _____

8. Using fluoroscopic guidance, the physician repositioned a gastric feeding tube through the duodenum.

   _____

9. The physician performed a laparoscopic surgical gastric restrictive procedure with gastric bypass and Roux-en-Y gastroenterostomy.

   _____

10. The physician percutaneously placed a gastrostomy tube into the stomach under fluoroscopic guidance including contrast injection(s), image documentation, and report.

   _____

Intestines (Except Rectum)

Codes for procedures performed on the intestines (except rectum) include the following subheadings:

- Incision
- Excision
- Laparoscopy
- Enterostomy—external fistulization of intestines
- Endoscopy, small intestine
- Endoscopy, stomal
- Introduction
- Repair
- Other procedures

   Because codes located in the Intestines (Except Rectum) subsection describe similar-sounding procedures (e.g., enterolysis, enterectomy, and enteroenterostomy), coders must carefully review operative report documentation to ensure correct code assignment.

Incision

Enterolysis (freeing of intestinal adhesions) is classified as a separate procedure code, and it is considered an integral component of hernia repair codes. Therefore, do not report the enterolysis code when other surgical procedures include the lysis of intestinal adhesions. However, if documentation indicates that enterolysis was extensive and added significantly to the procedure, add modifier -22 (Increased Procedural Services) to code 44005. There are, however, some instances when it is appropriate to report the enterolysis code with other intestine procedure codes.

   Codes that describe the surgical treatment of a **volvulus** (twisting or displacement of the intestines, causing obstruction) are located in the Incision subheading.

EXAMPLE: Patient underwent reduction of volvulus (Figure 15-11) via laparotomy. Report code 44050.

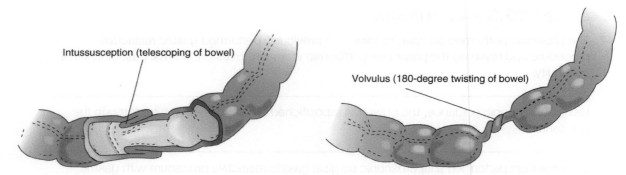

Intussusception (telescoping of bowel)

Volvulus (180-degree twisting of bowel)

FIGURE 15-11 Bowel obstructions can be caused by an intussusception or a volvulus.

Excision

Enterectomy (resection of small bowel segments) procedure codes describe resection of a segment of the intestine, and they require the coder to determine the

- Amount of tissue removed
- Type of repair performed

An *enteroenterostomy* is the creation of an artificial external opening or fistula in the intestines.

> **EXAMPLE:** Patient underwent enterectomy, which involved resection of two segments of the small intestine with anastomosis. Report codes 44120 and 44121.

Colectomy is the removal of part or all of the large intestine (e.g., colon); however, a partial colectomy is more common. Four types of partial colectomies include removal of

- All/part of the right colon (e.g., right colectomy)
- All/part of the left colon (e.g., left colectomy)
- All/part of the rectosigmoid colon (e.g., anterior resection)
- The lower rectosigmoid colon, rectum, and anus (e.g., abdominal perineal resection)

> **EXAMPLE:** Patient underwent total colectomy with proctectomy and ileostomy. Report code 44155.

Laparoscopy

Surgical laparoscopy includes diagnostic laparoscopy, which means if both procedures are documented a code for the surgical laparoscopy only is reported. If a diagnostic laparoscopy (peritoneoscopy) only is performed, report code 49320, which contains the (separate procedure) note.

> **EXAMPLE:** Patient underwent laparoscopic jejunostomy for feeding. Report code 44186.

Enterostomy—External Fistulization of Intestines

An **ostomy** refers to surgically creating an opening in the body for the discharge of body wastes. (A **stoma** is a surgically created opening between the ureter, small intestine, or large intestine through to the abdominal wall.) Ostomy procedures are classified according to the portion of the digestive tract that is brought to the surface. (They may be permanent or temporary.) Types of ostomies are the following:

- **Colostomy:** A portion of the colon or rectum is removed, and the remaining colon is brought to the abdominal wall (Figure 15-12).
- **Ileostomy:** The colon and rectum are removed, and the small intestine is brought to the abdominal wall.

Ascending colostomy

Transverse colostomy

Descending colostomy

Sigmoid colostomy

FIGURE 15-12 Colostomy locations (Blue section may be surgically removed if colostomy is permanent)

A **continent ileostomy**, or **Kock pouch**, is a surgical variation of an ileostomy. A reservoir pouch is created inside the abdomen using a portion of the terminal ileum, a valve is constructed in the pouch, and a stoma is brought through the abdominal wall. A catheter is inserted into the pouch several times each day to empty feces from the reservoir.

EXAMPLE: Patient underwent continent ileostomy. Report code 44316.

Endoscopy, Small Intestine and Endoscopy, Stomal

Jejunal feedings are performed via small intestinal endoscopy. This type of endoscopy is an enteroscopy that is performed beyond the second portion of duodenum. During this procedure, a thin tube is passed through the gastrostomy tube into the stomach and advanced; a direct puncture is *not* made into the jejunum.

EXAMPLE: Patient underwent small intestinal endoscopy with enteroscopy beyond the second portion of the duodenum and single biopsy. Report code 44361.

Introduction

The introduction of a long gastrointestinal (GI) tube with an inflatable balloon at the end (e.g., Miller-Abbott) is performed to clear GI strictures.

> **EXAMPLE:** Patient underwent introduction of a Miller-Abbott GI tube to clear GI strictures. Report code 44500.

Repair

Repair codes are reported for procedures performed to repair the small intestine.

> **EXAMPLE:** Patient underwent the suturing of a single perforation of the small intestine. Report code 44602.

Other Procedures

Other procedures codes are reported for procedures performed to exclude the small intestine from the pelvis by implanting mesh or other prosthesis or by using native tissue. When the small intestine is elevated to prevent damage from radiation therapy, mesh, other prosthesis, or native tissue is used. An instructional note below the code provides instruction to report codes from the Radiology Oncology heading for therapeutic radiation treatment.

> **EXAMPLE:** Patient underwent exclusion of the small intestine from the pelvis with placement of mesh. Report code 44700.

Meckel's Diverticulum and the Mesentery

Diverticula (Figure 15-13) are small pouches (herniations) in the colon that bulge outward through weak spots. **Diverticulosis** is the presence of diverticula in the mucosa and submucosa, through or between fibers of the colon's major muscle layer. Diverticulosis is almost always located in the descending or sigmoid colon.

Meckel's diverticulum is a common congenital abnormality of the GI tract that results in a pouch in the wall of the small bowel that contains remnants of fetal GI tissue. The diverticulum may contain gastric, stomach, ectopic, or pancreatic tissue. Treatment includes excision of Meckel's diverticulum.

> **EXAMPLE:** Patient underwent excision of Meckel's diverticulum. Report code 44800.

Perforation 18%
Hemorrhage 25%

FIGURE 15-13 Diverticula in the sigmoid colon

Appendix

Appendectomies are performed laparoscopically or through an open abdominal incision. An instructional note below states that when an appendectomy is performed during intra-abdominal surgery, it is considered incidental; it is not coded and reported separately. When an appendectomy is performed for an indicated purpose during the same operative session as another major procedure, report the appropriate add-on code.

EXAMPLE 1: Patient underwent laparoscopic appendectomy for acute appendicitis. Report code 44970.

EXAMPLE 2: Patient underwent excision of Meckel's diverticulum. During surgery, the physician noted that the appendix was inflamed and enlarged; an appendectomy was also performed. Report codes 44800 and 44955. (According to Optum360's *Encoder Pro Expert,* modifier -51 is not reported with add-on code 44955. Also, modifier -59 is not added to code 44955 because a separate incision was *not* made to perform the appendectomy.)

Colon and Rectum

Codes reported for procedures performed on the colon and rectum include the following subheadings:

- Incision
- Excision
- Destruction
- Endoscopy
- Laparoscopy
- Repair
- Manipulation
- Other procedures

Endoscopic procedure codes specify the type of instrument used, the purpose of the endoscopy, and the site involved. The CPT coding manual contains a colonoscopy decision tree, which provides direction for assignment of correct codes. When reporting codes for colonoscopies (e.g., colostomy or rectum), the coder must also determine the approach. GI endoscopic procedures involve the small bowel, colon, and rectum and include the following:

- **Proctosigmoidoscopy**: Visual examination of the rectum and sigmoid colon
- **Sigmoidoscopy**: Visual examination of the entire rectum and sigmoid colon and may include a portion of the descending colon (Figure 15-14)
- **Colonoscopy**: Visual examination of the entire colon, from the rectum to the cecum, and may include the terminal ileum (Figure 15-15)

FIGURE 15-14 Sigmoidoscopy

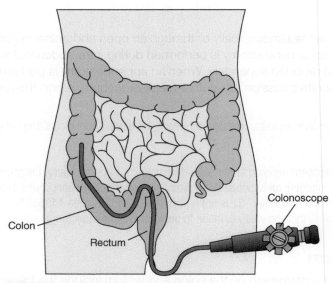

FIGURE 15-15 Colonoscopy (posterior view)

Coding Tip

- When assigning codes for colonoscopy procedures, use the *Colonoscopy Decision Tree* located in the Digestive System subsection of CPT Surgery.

Proctosigmoidoscopy and sigmoidoscopy procedures are typically performed without anesthesia. Colonoscopies usually require sedation to avoid severe patient discomfort.

EXAMPLE: Patient underwent sigmoidoscopy and colonoscopy during the same operative session. Report code 45378 for the colonoscopy only. (Do not report a code for the sigmoidoscopy because the endoscope was passed through the sigmoid colon to perform the colonoscopy. Visual examination of the sigmoid colon was performed on the way to visual examination of the rest of the colon.)

When multiple services are provided during an endoscopic procedure, report a code for each. Multiple services are reimbursed according to multiple endoscopic payment rules (e.g., discounted reimbursement for second and subsequent procedures). An exception to this rule is follow-up treatment of bleeding due to the endoscopic procedure.

Different techniques are used to remove lesions or polyps (Figure 15-16) through an endoscope. A **hot biopsy forceps** uses tweezer-like forceps connected to a monopolar electrocautery unit and a grounding pad. **Bipolar cautery** uses an electric current that flows from one tip of the forceps to the other and does not require a grounding pad. An **electrocautery snare** uses a wire loop to encircle, not grasp, the polyp. **Cold biopsy forceps** does not use electrocoagulation; the polyp is simply pulled from the colon wall. **Laser technique**

FIGURE 15-16 Colon polyp

is most suitable for treatment of rectal lesions and uses a waveguide to deliver the laser beam through the endoscope to the lesion (e.g., YAG laser).

> **EXAMPLE:** Patient underwent removal of a polyp by snare technique during a colonoscopy. During the same operative session, another area of the colon was also biopsied. Report a code for the colonoscopy with polypectomy (45385) and a different code for colonoscopy with biopsy (45380-59). (Modifier -59 is added to code 45380 because the colon biopsy was performed as a distinct and separate procedure, using different instruments, in addition to the removal of the polyp during the colonoscopy.)

A **proctectomy** is the surgical removal of the rectum. (Do not confuse this procedure with a *prostatectomy*, which is the excision of the prostate gland.) An **ileoanal anastomosis** (or **J-pouch**, **pull-through**, or **endorectal pull-through**) is a common alternative to conventional ileostomy, and it is not considered an ostomy because there is no stoma. The colon and most of the rectum are surgically removed, and an internal pouch is created from the terminal portion of the ileum. An opening at the bottom of the pouch is attached (anastomosed) to the anus so that existing anal sphincter muscles can be used for continence.

> **EXAMPLE:** Patient underwent proctopexy via abdominal approach. Report code 45540.

Anus

Codes reported for procedures performed on the anus include the following subheadings:

- Incision
- Excision
- Introduction
- Endoscopy

- Repair
- Destruction
- Other procedures

Anoscopy is a diagnostic procedure during which anal mucosa and the lower rectum are visualized using an anoscope. Anoscopy is typically performed to detect hemorrhoids (Figure 15-17), polyps, anal fissures, and anal bleeding.

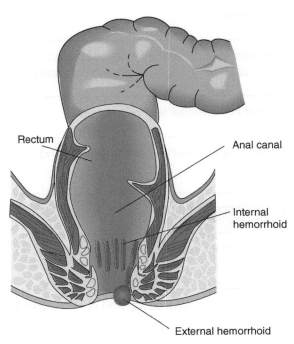

FIGURE 15-17 Hemorrhoids: internal and external

For hemorrhoidectomy procedures, identify what approach was used, where the hemorrhoid(s) were located (e.g., internal or external), and whether a fissurectomy was also performed. The most commonly performed procedure is a hemorrhoidectomy by simple ligature (e.g., rubber band). (Report the appropriate code once regardless of the number of hemorrhoids removed.) Simple hemorrhoidectomy procedures do not include plastic repair; complex and extensive hemorrhoidectomy procedures do require plastic repair. When multiple methods are used to remove multiple hemorrhoids, report a code for each method.

EXAMPLE: Patient underwent hemorrhoidopexy for prolapsing internal hemorrhoids via stapling. Report code 46947.

When reporting codes for the surgical treatment of anal fistulas, apply the following definitions:

- **Subcutaneous fistulectomy**: Removal of an anal fistula, without division of the sphincter muscle
- **Submuscular fistulectomy**: Removal of an anal fistula, including division of the sphincter muscle
- **Complex fistulectomy**: Excision of multiple fistulas
- **Second-stage fistulectomy/fistulotomy**: Use of a **seton**, such as a large silk suture or rubber bands, to cut through the fistula; the seton is left in place until later removal

EXAMPLE: Patient underwent subcutaneous fistulectomy. Report code 46270.

Exercise 15.4 – Intestines (Except Rectum), Meckel's Diverticulum, Mesentery, Appendix, Rectum, and Anus

Instructions: Assign the CPT code(s) and appropriate modifier(s) to each statement.

1. After performing an emergency cesarean section, the physician noticed that the appendix was distended, resulting in medical necessity for an appendectomy performed during the same operative session.

   _____

2. The physician freed intestinal adhesions.

   _____

3. The physician resected two segments of small intestine and performed an anastomosis between the remaining intestinal ends. An open approach was used for this surgery.

   _____

4. The physician repaired a defect in the mesentery with sutures.

   _____

5. The physician performed a laparoscopic partial colectomy with end colostomy and closure of the distal segment.

   _____

6. The physician drained a pelvic abscess through the rectum.

   _____

7. The physician removed a portion of the rectum through combined abdominal and transsacral approaches.

   _____

8. The physician performed rigid proctosigmoidoscopy and obtained brushings.

   _____

Exercise 15.4 – *continued*

9. The physician performed a flexible sigmoidoscopy and removed a polyp. The physician inserted the sigmoidoscope through the anus and advanced the scope into the sigmoid colon. The lumen of the sigmoid colon and rectum were well visualized, and the polyp was identified and removed with hot biopsy forceps. The sigmoidoscope was withdrawn upon completion of the procedure.

_____

10. The physician inserted a colonoscope through the anus and advanced the scope past the splenic flexure. Two polyps were identified and removed by hot biopsy forceps.

_____

Liver

Codes reported for procedures performed to treat liver injuries and diseases, including liver transplantation, include the following subheadings:

- Incision
- Excision
- Liver transplantation
- Repair
- Laparoscopy
- Other procedures

Liver injuries include gunshot wounds, stab wounds, and blunt trauma; treatment includes various methods of hemorrhage control. The management of liver hemorrhage may require a simple suture of the liver wound, or it may require complex suturing of the liver wound or injury, with or without hepatic artery ligation.

Other codes are reported to classify the exploration of a hepatic wound, extensive debridement, coagulation, and/or packing of the liver.

A **hepatotomy** (open drainage of abscess or cyst) is performed in one or two stages, but when it is performed as a two-stage procedure, the code is not reported a second time.

EXAMPLE 1: Patient underwent wedge biopsy of the liver. Report code 47100.

EXAMPLE 2: Patient underwent surgical laparoscopy with ablation of one liver tumor, using cryosurgery under ultrasound guidance. Report codes 47371 and 76940.

EXAMPLE 3: Patient underwent reexploration of a hepatic wound to remove packing material. Report code 47362.

Biliary Tract

Codes reported for procedures performed on the organs and duct system that create, transport, store, and release bile into the duodenum (as part of the digestive process) include the following subheadings:

- Incision
- Introduction
- Endoscopy
- Laparoscopy
- Excision
- Repair
- Other procedures

The **biliary system** includes the following digestive accessory organs and structures (Figure 15-18):

- Gallbladder
- Bile ducts inside the liver
- Bile ducts outside the liver
- Hepatic ducts
- Common bile duct
- Cystic duct

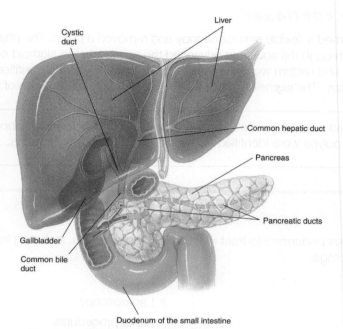

FIGURE 15-18 Digestive accessory organs (liver, gallbladder, and pancreas)

A **cholecystectomy** (surgical removal of the gallbladder) (Figure 15-19) can be performed laparoscopically or as an open procedure. During a cholecystectomy, common duct exploration and dilation procedures are often performed through the same incision. An operative cholangiography may also be performed during the same operative session.

Coding Tip

When a cholecystectomy is attempted laparoscopically and converted to an open procedure, report a code for the open cholecystectomy procedure only.

EXAMPLE: Patient underwent percutaneous extraction of a stone with a basket. Report code 47544.

Pancreas

Codes reported for procedures performed on the pancreas, including pancreas transplantation, include the following subheadings:

- Incision
- Excision
- Introduction
- Repair
- Pancreas transplantation
- Other procedures

The **Whipple procedure** is the excision of the pancreas, duodenum, bile duct, and stomach with reconstruction; code assignment is based on the extent of the excision. The code reported for an internal anastomosis of the pancreatic duct is based on the approach.

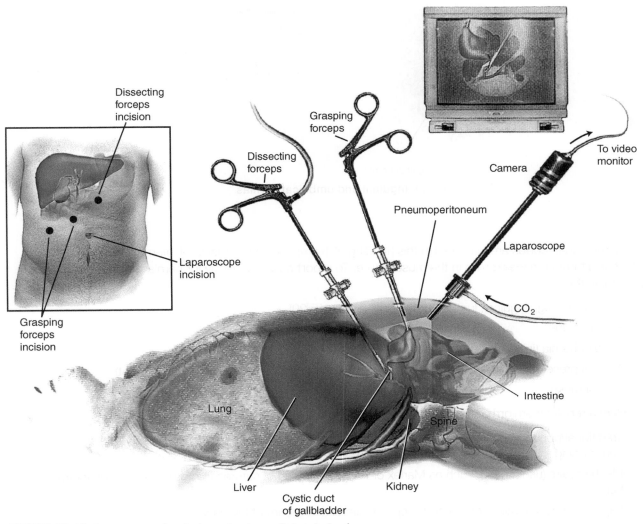

FIGURE 15-19 Laparoscopic cholecystectomy (lateral view)

EXAMPLE: Patient underwent placement of a peripancreatic drain for pancreatitis. Report code 48000.

Abdomen, Peritoneum, and Omentum

Codes reported for procedures performed on the abdomen, peritoneum, and omentum include the following subheadings:

- Incision
- Excision, destruction
- Laparoscopy
- Introduction, revision, removal
- Repair
- Suture
- Other procedures

When reporting codes for procedures in this heading, make sure you review the operative report to determine whether the procedure was performed via laparotomy or laparoscopy.

Umbilical hernia

Inguinal hernia

FIGURE 15-20 Inguinal and umbilical hernias

Hernia repair codes are classified in this heading. A **hernia** is the protrusion of internal organs (e.g., intestines) through a weakening in the musculature. To report codes correctly for hernia repair procedures, determine the

- Hernia site (e.g., inguinal, lumbar, or femoral) (Figure 15-20)
- Patient's age
- Type of hernia (initial or recurrent)
- Clinical presentation of the hernia (e.g., reducible, incarcerated, strangulated, or recurrent)
- Use of mesh

Hernia repairs (herniorrhaphies) include

- Traditional/conventional (physician pushes bulging tissue back into the abdominal cavity and sutures surrounding muscle in place)
- Mesh repairs (uses mesh, such as Marlex or Prolene, instead of sutures to repair incisional or ventral hernias)
- Laparoscopic (typically performed to repair bilateral and recurrent hernias)

 Coding Tip

- Neonatal diaphragmatic hiatal hernia repairs are not classified in the Digestive System subsection. To report codes for these repairs, refer to the Mediastinum and Diaphragm subsection.
- Implantation of mesh or other prosthesis is reported for incisional or ventral hernia repairs. When mesh or other prosthesis is used to repair other types of hernias, do not separately report a code. The mesh code is also reported with Integumentary System codes for closure after debridement of necrotizing soft tissue infection.
- When strangulated organs are repaired in addition to a strangulated hernia, report a code for each procedure performed.
- When a hernia repair is performed during another open abdominal procedure, a code for the hernia repair is reported only if it was performed through a different incisional site. (Add modifier -59, Distinct Procedural Service, to the hernia repair code.) An incidental hernia repair during the course of an abdominal procedure is not coded and reported.

Exercise 15.5 – Liver, Biliary Tract, Pancreas, Abdomen, Peritoneum, and Omentum

Instructions: Assign the CPT code(s) and appropriate modifier(s) to each statement.

1. Hepatotomy for open drainage of abscess or cyst, 1 stage.

   _____

2. Surgeon removed segments II, III, and IV (the whole left lobe) of the liver from a living donor.

   _____

3. The physician performed radiofrequency ablation of a liver tumor via an open laparotomy.

   _____

4. The physician performed laparoscopic cholecystectomy with common bile duct exploration.

   _____

5. The physician performed a cholecystostomy with removal of calculus.

   _____

6. Subsequent to a previous peritoneocentesis (performed at a different operative session), the physician withdrew fluid and performed infusion and drainage of fluid from the abdominal cavity (peritoneal lavage).

   _____

7. The physician reopened a recent laparotomy incision, before the incision had fully healed, to drain a postoperative infection.

   _____

8. The physician performed laparoscopic repair of an initial inguinal hernia, using mesh.

   _____

9. The physician performed a reducible ventral hernia (initial) repair and inserted mesh implantation.

   _____

10. The physician repaired an initial, reducible, inguinal hernia with hydrocelectomy in a 5-month-old infant.

   _____

Urinary System Subsection

The **urinary system** consists of the kidneys, ureters, urinary bladder, and urethra (Figure 15-21). Blood flows through the renal arteries to the kidneys, where waste materials are filtered and urine is formed. Urine is transported from the kidneys to the bladder by the ureters, and the urine ultimately passes out of the body through the urethra.

 NOTE:

The *ureter* is the tube that conveys urine from each kidney to the urinary bladder; there are two ureters. The *urethra* is the tube that conveys urine from the urinary bladder to the outside of the body.

FIGURE 15-21 Urinary system (A) Male (B) Female

A urinary tract infection is a common disorder of the urinary system and may involve different areas of the urinary tract (e.g., urethritis, prostatitis, cystitis, and pyelonephritis). Other urinary system disorders affect the pressure within the urinary system, affect stagnation of flow (stasis), and cause the formation of stones (calculi).

Urinary system function can also be affected by disorders such as obstruction (e.g., benign prostatic hypertrophy or strictures), which typically form in three places within the ureter.

- Ureteropelvic junction (between ureter and renal pelvis)
- Ureterovesical junction (between ureter and bladder)
- Ureter/iliac arteries

Various methods are used to treat urinary disorders, including open procedures and endoscopy or laparoscopy. Diagnostic urodynamic procedures (study of urine storage and voiding functions) include tests such as the following:

- Cystometrogram
- Uroflowmetry
- Urethral pressure profile (UPP)
- Neuromuscular studies
- Voiding pressure (VP) studies

Urinary System subsection procedures are classified according to anatomical site and surgical approach (e.g., open, incision, percutaneous, endoscopic, or laparoscopic). The subsection also separates endoscopy procedures from open procedures.

Many procedures include the phrase *exclusive of radiologic service*, which means that an additional code from the Radiology section is assigned to report the radiologic service performed.

EXAMPLE: Patient underwent renal endoscopy through established nephrostomy, with biopsy. Report code 50555.

The Urinary System subsection includes the following headings:

- Kidney
- Ureter
- Bladder
- Urethra

Kidney

Codes for procedures performed on the kidney include the following subheadings:

- Incision
- Excision
- Renal transplantation
- Introduction
- Repair
- Laparoscopy
- Endoscopy
- Other procedures

The **kidneys** filter and clean the blood, producing urine that carries waste. In renal (kidney) failure, filtration of blood is slowed or stopped (due to obstruction, bacterial infection, or injury). This causes waste products and other toxic substances to build up in the blood. These problems can lead to renal failure, resulting in the need for treatment such as surgery or dialysis.

In the Kidney heading, the removal of urinary calculi (stones) (Figure 15-22) is coded according to the anatomical site (e.g., renal pelvis, bladder, or urethra) and approach (e.g., open incision, percutaneous, or endoscopic).

EXAMPLE: Patient underwent nephrolithotomy to remove urinary stones. Report code 50060.

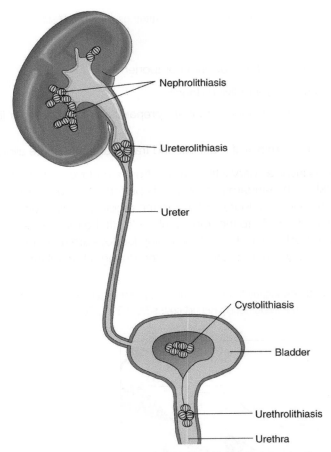

FIGURE 15-22 Common locations of urinary calculi (stone) formation: nephrolithiasis (kidney stone), ureterolithiasis (ureter stone), cystolithiasis (urinary bladder stone), and urethrolithiasis (urethral stone)

Nephrectomy (surgical removal of a kidney) requires review of the operative report to identify the

- Type of procedure (e.g., partial or total)
- Surgical approach (e.g., laparoscopic or open)
- Other structures removed

EXAMPLE: Patient underwent laparoscopic partial nephrectomy. Report code 50543.

When a surgeon performs a retrograde pyelography (or retrograde ureteropyelography), one or both of the ureters are catheterized and contrast is injected slowly through the catheter.

EXAMPLE: Patient underwent injection procedure for ureterogram. Report code 50431-LT.

Extracorporeal shock wave lithotripsy (ESWL) is a nonoperative procedure that uses ultrasonic shock waves to break up stones in the renal pelvis or ureter (Figure 15-23). The patient then passes the stones in urine, with minimal discomfort. **Percutaneous lithotomy** and **lithotripsy** is a two-stage procedure that requires a percutaneous nephrostomy and dilation of the nephrostomy tract. Instruments (e.g., a basket or lithotripter) are inserted via nephrostomy, and the stones are removed.

EXAMPLE: Patient underwent extracorporeal shock wave lithotripsy on the left side to pulverize kidney stones. Report code 50590-LT.

Renal transplantation codes include three distinct components.

- Harvest of the kidney from a cadaver or living donor
- Physician backbench work, which includes standard preparation of a cadaver or living donor allograft prior to transplantation
- Allotransplantation (e.g., organ removal, if required, and transplantation of the allograft)

The procurement of kidneys involves harvesting organs from a cadaver or living donor. Once the kidney is received by the hospital, backbench standard preparation is performed to prepare the kidneys for transplantation. The actual transplantation of the kidney (Figure 15-24) into the recipient is also reported. (When a bilateral kidney transplant is performed, add modifier -50 to the transplant code.) (If the recipient's nonfunctioning kidney is resected, code 50340 is also reported. If both nonfunctioning kidneys are resected, modifier -50 is added to code 50340. Nonfunctioning kidneys are not always resected during a transplant procedure.)

EXAMPLE: Patient underwent left kidney transplant, including backbench standard preparation of living donor renal allograft. Kidney was obtained from a living donor. Report codes 50365-LT, 50325-51-LT (recipient), and 50320-LT (donor).

Shock wave generator

FIGURE 15-23 Extracorporeal shock wave lithotripsy (ESWL)

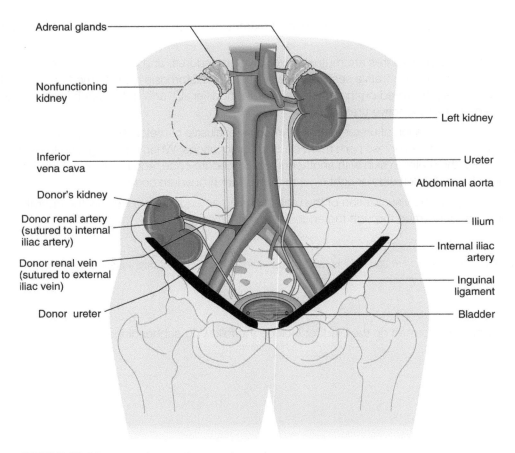

FIGURE 15-24 Renal (kidney) transplantation

Ureter

Codes for procedures performed on the ureter include the following subheadings:

- Incision/Biopsy
- Excision
- Introduction
- Repair
- Laparoscopy
- Endoscopy

The **ureters** convey urine from the kidneys to the urinary bladder. The walls of the ureters contain muscle that propels urine using wavelike motions called **peristalsis**. Procedures performed on the ureters are based on two approaches.

- Open endoscopic
- Laparoscopic

To facilitate the passage of urine through the ureter(s), a physician may insert a ureteral stent. Stents used to relieve or prevent ureteral obstruction can be placed during the course of another diagnostic or therapeutic intervention. Stents may be temporary, and the physician may remove a temporary stent and insert another type of stent (e.g., indwelling).

A **ureterolithotomy** is the surgical removal of stones from the ureter. The procedure should identify the ureteral location from which the stone was removed.

- Upper one-third of ureter
- Middle one-third of ureter
- Lower one-third of ureter

(When stones are removed using the stone basket extraction technique, report code 51065 from the Bladder heading.)

Ureteral anastomosis procedures are mutually exclusive procedures, and codes for these procedures are not usually reported for the same operative session. However, if an anastomosis is performed on one ureter and a different anastomosis is performed on the other ureter, add modifier -LT and -RT to each code (to describe the service performed on the respective ureter).

Ureterostomy, transplantation of ureter to skin, is mutually exclusive of ureterostomy, ureterocolon conduit, and urinary undiversion procedures unless performed on different locations. When reporting a ureterostomy code for the transplantation of the ureter to skin with another ureter procedure code, add modifier -59 (distinct procedural service); and add -LT or -RT (left side or right side) to both ureter procedure codes.

Ureteral endoscopy is the visualization of the ureter(s) using an endoscope. Review the operative report to locate the procedure performed through the endoscope (e.g., biopsy).

> **EXAMPLE:** Patient underwent ureterolysis, with repositioning of ureter for retroperitoneal fibrosis. Report code 50715.

Bladder

Codes for procedures performed on the bladder include the following subheadings:

- Incision
- Removal
- Excision
- Introduction
- Urodynamics
- Repair
- Laparoscopy
- Endoscopy—cystoscopy, urethroscopy, cystourethroscopy
- Transurethral surgery
- Vesical neck and prostate

The **urinary bladder** is a hollow organ that serves as a reservoir for urine until it passes from the body (via urination). Urine enters the urinary bladder from the ureters and exits through the urethra.

Coding Tip

Urethral catheterization codes (51701–51702) are reported only when performed independently.

- When urethral catheterization is performed preceding surgery, a code is not separately reported. Urethral catheterization is considered integral to preoperative services provided and represents the standard of medical practice.
- When urethral catheterization or urethral dilation is necessary to accomplish a more extensive procedure, a code for the urethral catheterization or urethral dilation is not separately reported.

Open excisional procedures of the bladder include the following:

- Excision of urachal cysts and sinuses
- Cystostomy (Figure 15-25)
- Cystectomy
- Pelvic exenteration

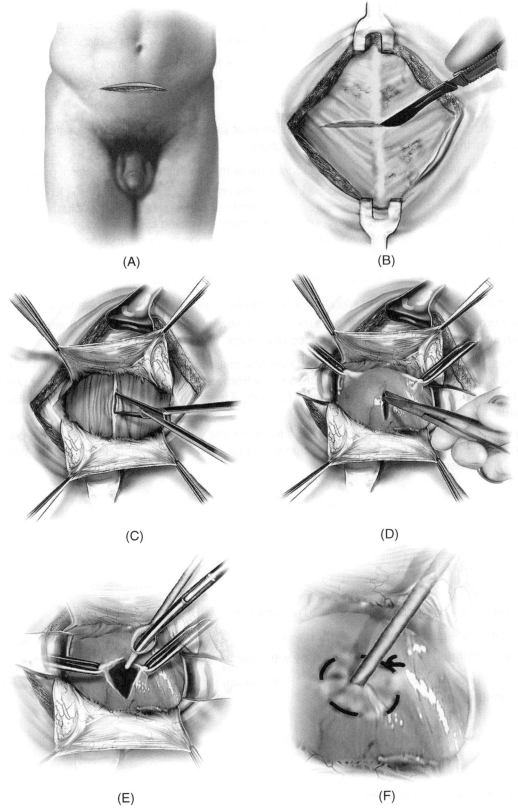

(A)

(B)

(C)

(D)

(E)

(F)

FIGURE 15-25 Open cystostomy (A) Incision site (B) Fascia incised (C) Muscle split
(D) Bladder incised (E) Cystostomy tube inserted (F) Cystostomy tube secured
with purse-string suture

Diagnostic urodynamic procedures are performed to study urine storage and voiding functions, and the codes may be reported separately or in combination when more than one procedure is performed. (Report as many codes as necessary to completely describe procedures performed.) Urodynamics includes the following tests:

- Cystometrogram (CMG)
- Uroflowmetry (UFR)
- Urethral pressure profile studies

- Neuromuscular studies
- Voiding pressure studies

A **cystometrogram** records urinary bladder pressure at various volumes, which is useful in diagnosing bladder outlet obstruction and other voiding dysfunctions.

- A simple cystometrogram measures the bladder's capacity, sensation, and intravesical pressure.
- A complex cystometrogram is a procedure in which the physician uses a rectal probe to differentiate abdominal pressure from bladder pressure. Components of complex cystometry include the placement of the transurethral catheter and anal probe, measurement of voiding cystometry and intra-abdominal pressure, and other provocative maneuvers (e.g., patient position changes and trials of anticholinergics or muscle depressants).

Uroflowmetry measures the amount of urine that flows from the urinary bladder per second.

- Simple uroflowmetry measures voiding time and peak flow using nonautomated equipment.
- Complex uroflowmetry measures/records mean, peak flow, and time to reach peak flow during continuous urination, and it is performed using automated equipment.

UPP studies (urethral closure pressure profile) describe tests for measuring urethral pressure. A UPP records pressures along the urethra using a special catheter. Electromyography studies measure anal or urethral sphincter muscle activity during voiding and urine flow rate. This study is usually performed on patients with voiding dysfunctions.

Voiding pressure studies involve placing a transducer into the urinary bladder to measure the patient's urine flow rate and pressure during emptying of the urinary bladder. Intra-abdominal VP (e.g., rectal, gastric, and intraperitoneal) can also be measured.

EXAMPLE 1: Patient underwent simple uroflowmetry. Report code 51736.

EXAMPLE 2: Patient underwent complex uroflowmetry, which required the use of calibrated electronic equipment. Report code 51741.

Urinary endoscopy procedures are classified according to

- Anatomical area (e.g., urethra, prostate, or ureter)
- Procedure performed (e.g., cystourethroscopy with insertion of indwelling ureteral stent)

Cystoscopy, or **cystourethroscopy** (Figure 15-26), allows for the direct visual examination of the urinary bladder and urethra.

EXAMPLE: A cystourethroscope was passed through the urethra and urinary bladder to examine the urethra, bladder, and ureteral openings. No other procedure was performed. Report code 52000.

Transurethral surgery is performed on the

- Urethra and bladder
- Ureter and pelvis

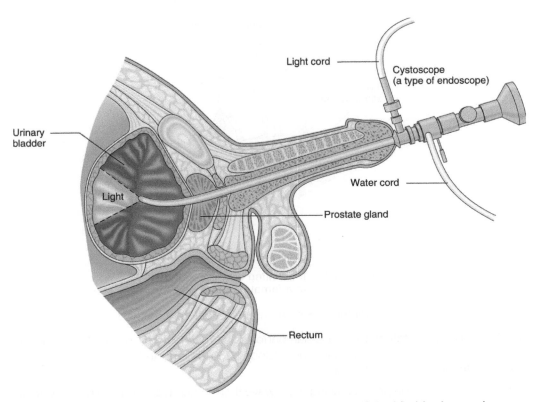

FIGURE 15-26 Use of a cystoscope to examine the interior of the bladder in a male

In addition, a separate subheading for vesical neck and prostate procedures is located under the Bladder heading. It is important to review the operative report to identify the anatomical site for the surgery performed. Diagnostic procedures (e.g., bladder biopsy) and therapeutic procedures (e.g., steroid injection into a urethral stricture) are accomplished using a transurethral approach. Transurethral surgeries include diagnostic cystoscopy, which is not reported separately.

When a physician performs a urethral dilation to determine the size of the cystoscope to be inserted, do not code and report the dilation procedure separately. However, when the physician performs a cystourethroscopy with transurethral dilation for a urethral stricture, assign an appropriate code.

Cystourethroscopy with removal of foreign body, calculus, or ureteral stent from urethra or bladder is classified as simple or complicated.

Before a transurethral therapeutic or diagnostic intervention procedure is performed, a direct visual examination is performed using a cystourethroscope. The cystoscope is passed through the male urethra to visualize the urethra, prostate, and bladder.

Notes in the Ureter and Pelvis subheading clarify the reporting of temporary stents and self-retaining indwelling stents. Indwelling ureteral catheters (Figure 15-27) are inserted into the renal pelvis via the ureter to allow drainage (e.g., when a tumor is impinging on the ureters). Gibbons and double-J stents are the most common ureteral stents.

When a surgeon performs a **transurethral ureteroscopic lithotripsy** (instead of an ESWL), a cystoscope is inserted through the urethra into the bladder and a ureteroscope is passed into the ureters. Instruments passed through the ureteroscope into the ureters are used to manipulate and disintegrate stones (utilizing transcystoscopic electrohydraulic shock waves, ultrasound, or laser).

Transurethral resection of the prostate (TURP) is an initial resection of the prostate gland via transurethral approach using an electrosurgical device. Specific codes classify laser treatment of the prostate gland. TURP codes include vasectomy, meatotomy, cystourethroscopy, urethral calibration, dilation, and/or internal urethrotomy. Codes for these procedures, when performed during the same operative session as a TURP, are not reported separately.

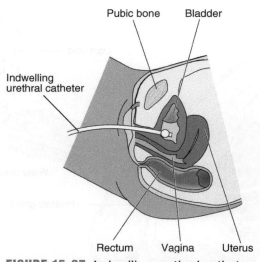

FIGURE 15-27 Indwelling urethral catheter in a female patient

The physician may perform a prostatectomy using a number of different methods.

- Transurethral two-stage prostatectomy: Physician performs a prostatectomy in two stages, and the operative report specifies the first or second stage. (Code 52601 is reported for the first stage, and code 52601-58 is reported for the second stage.)
- Transurethral destruction of the prostate using microwave thermotherapy: Physician uses microwave thermotherapy stylet (inserted in urethra), and the diseased prostate is treated with electromagnetic radiation. (Code 53850)
- Transurethral destruction of the prostate using radiofrequency: Physician uses radiofrequency thermotherapy stylet (inserted in urethra) and prostate is treated with thermal energy vapor. (Code 53852)

Urethra

Codes for procedures performed on the urethra include the following subheadings:

- Incision
- Excision
- Repair
- Manipulation
- Other procedures

The **urethra** is a muscular tube that discharges urine from the urinary bladder. In males, the urethra also serves as a passageway for semen. Codes assigned for urethral procedures will vary depending on the gender of the patient.

EXAMPLE 1: Female patient underwent total urethrectomy, including cystostomy. Report code 53210.

EXAMPLE 2: Male patient underwent total urethrectomy, including cystostomy. Report code 53215.

To report codes properly for urethral excision procedures, locate the diagnosis in the patient's record.

EXAMPLE 1: Patient underwent excision of bulbourethral gland. Report code 53250.

EXAMPLE 2: Patient underwent excision of urethral polyp, distal urethra. Report code 53260.

EXAMPLE 3: Patient underwent excision of urethral caruncle. Report code 53265.

For **urethroplasty** (repair of the urethra), identify

- Whether the procedure was staged
- Which stage of the procedure was performed (e.g., stage one or stage two)

EXAMPLE 1: Patient underwent urethroplasty, first stage, to repair stricture. Report code 53400.

EXAMPLE 2: Patient underwent urethroplasty, second stage, to form a urethra. Procedure included urinary diversion. Report code 53405.

EXAMPLE 3: Patient underwent one-stage urethroplasty to reconstruct a male anterior urethra. Report code 53410.

For dilation of urethral stricture, identify

- What surgical approach was used
- What the patient's gender was
- Whether the dilation was initial or subsequent

EXAMPLE 1: Patient underwent initial dilation of urethral stricture by passage of sound or urethral dilator, male. Report code 53600.

EXAMPLE 2: Patient underwent subsequent dilation of urethral stricture by passage of sound or urethral dilator, male. Report code 53601.

EXAMPLE 3: Patient underwent initial dilation of urethral stricture by passage of filiform and follower, male. Report code 53620.

EXAMPLE 4: Patient underwent initial dilation of female urethra including suppository and instillation. Report code 53660.

 Coding Tip

Urethral repair codes are performed to treat urethral wounds or injuries (urethrorrhaphy). When urethroplasty is performed, do not report a code for urethrorrhaphy because suture to repair wound or injury is included in the urethroplasty service.

Exercise 15.6 – Urinary

Instructions: Assign the CPT code(s) and appropriate modifier(s) to each statement.

1. Physician made an open incision and inserted multiple drain tubes to drain an infection (abscess) from the kidney.

2. The physician pulverized a kidney stone (renal calculus) by directing shock waves through a water cushion that was placed against the left side of the patient's body at the location of the kidney stone.

(continues)

Exercise 15.6 – *continued*

3. The physician removed a kidney stone (calculus) by making an incision in the right kidney.

_____

4. The interventional radiologist inserted a percutaneous nephrostomy catheter into the right renal pelvis for drainage. Fluoroscopic guidance was provided.

_____

5. The physician performed laparoscopic ablation of a solid mass from the posterior hilum of the left kidney.

_____

6. The physician made an incision in the left ureter through the abdominal wall for examination of the ureter and insertion of a catheter for drainage.

_____

7. The physician examined the patient's right and left renal and ureteral structures with an endoscope, which passed through an established opening between the skin and the ureter (ureterostomy). He also inserted a catheter into the ureter.

_____

8. The physician revised a surgical opening between the skin and the right ureter.

_____

9. The physician injected a contrast agent through an opening between the skin and the left ureter (ureterostomy) for ureterography (study of the renal collecting system).

_____

10. The physician made an incision in the left ureter (ureterotomy) to insert a catheter (stent) into the ureter.

_____

11. The physician performed a transurethral resection of a postoperative bladder neck contracture using a resectoscope.

_____

12. The physician inserted a special instrument through the cystourethroscope to fragment a calculus in the ureter using electrohydraulics.

_____

13. The physician inserted a cystourethroscope through the urethra to drain an abscess on the prostate.

_____

14. The physician inserted a suprapubic catheter to aspirate urine.

_____

15. The physician performed a cystourethroscopy with fulguration of the bladder neck and then removed a calculus from the ureter.

_____

16. The physician performed a sling procedure using synthetic material to treat a male patient's urinary incontinence.

_____

17. The physician made an initial attempt to treat a male patient's urethral stricture using a dilator.

_____

18. The physician, in the first of two stages to reconstruct the urethra, identified the area of stricture by urethrography and marked it with ink.

_____

19. The physician performed a transurethral destruction of the prostate using microwave therapy.

_____

20. The physician excised a specimen of tissue from the urethra for biopsy.

_____

Summary

The Mediastinum and Diaphragm subsection classifies procedures performed on the mediastinum and diaphragm (also the titles of subsection headings). The Digestive System subsection includes procedures to diagnose and treat disorders of the digestive system (e.g., gastrointestinal endoscopy, laparoscopy, and gastric analysis). Similar to other Surgery subsections, procedures are classified first by anatomical area and then by type. Digestive System subsection codes are also reported for open, endoscopic, and laparoscopic procedures. The operative report must be carefully reviewed to correctly identify the surgical approach. Urinary System subsection procedures are classified according to anatomical site and surgical approach (e.g., open, incision, percutaneous, endoscopic, or laparoscopic). The subsection also separates endoscopy procedures from open procedures. Many procedures include the phrase "exclusive of radiologic service," which means that an additional code from the Radiology section is assigned to report the radiological service performed.

Internet Links

American College of Gastroenterology (ACG): Go to *www.gi.org*, and click on the Patients link to access information about diseases and treatments.

Society of American Gastrointestinal and Endoscopic Surgeons (SAGES): *www.sages.org*

Urology Care Foundation: *www.urologyhealth.org*

WebSurg's Virtual Surgical University: *www.websurg.com*

Review

Multiple Choice

Instructions: Circle the most appropriate response.

1. Which types of hernias are assigned codes from the Mediastinum and Diaphragm subsection of Surgery?
   a. Abdominal and epigastric
   b. Hiatus and diaphragmatic
   c. Incisional and inguinal
   d. Umbilicus and femoral

2. Procedures performed on the gallbladder, bile ducts, hepatic ducts, and cystic ducts are assigned codes from which heading of the Digestive System subsection of Surgery?
   a. Abdomen, Peritoneum, and Omentum
   b. Biliary Tract
   c. Liver
   d. Ureter

3. Hernia repair codes are classified in which heading of the Digestive System subsection of Surgery?
   a. Abdomen, Peritoneum, and Omentum
   b. Anus
   c. Appendix
   d. Rectum

4. Which procedure(s) has/have age as a factor in determining the correct code?
   a. Colonoscopy
   b. Esophagotomy and esophagoscopy
   c. Palatopharyngoplasty
   d. Tonsillectomy and adenoidectomy

5. When assigning codes for a ureterolithotomy procedure (50610–50630), which correctly describes the location in the ureter from which the stone was removed?
   a. Right or left side of ureter
   b. Upper-left, lower-left, upper-right, or lower-right quadrant of ureter
   c. Upper, middle, or lower one-third of ureter
   d. Upper or lower half of ureter

6. Diagnostic procedures (e.g., uroflowmetry) that are performed to study urine storage and voiding functions are assigned a code from which subheading of the Bladder heading in the Urinary System subsection of Surgery?

    a. Bladder   **c.** Laparoscopy

    b. Endoscopy   **d.** Urodynamics

7. Codes for urethral catheterization are reported when performed _____ another urinary bladder procedure.

    a. in combination with   **c.** preceding surgery for

    b. independently of   **d.** as a more extensive procedure than

8. Which gastrointestinal (GI) endoscopy procedure involves injecting dye through a tube in the endoscope to allow for visualization of the ducts on x-rays?

    a. Endoscopic retrograde cholangiopancreatography (ERCP)

    b. Esophagogastroduodenoscopy (EGD)

    c. Esophagoscopy

    d. Upper GI endoscopy (esophagogastroscopy)

9. When an incomplete therapeutic colonoscopy is performed beyond the splenic flexure, but not to the cecum, and the patient underwent full preparation for a colonoscopy, which modifier is added to the colonoscopy code?

    a. -52   **b.** -53   **c.** -58   **d.** -59

10. When a hernia repair is performed through a different incisional site during another open abdominal procedure, which modifier is added to the hernia repair code?

    a. -51   **b.** -58   **c.** -59   **d.** -79

11. Excision of mediastinal tumor. Which CPT code is assigned?

    a. 39200   **b.** 39220   **c.** 39401   **d.** 39402

12. Destruction of dentoalveolar lesion. Which CPT code is assigned?

    a. 41825   **b.** 41826   **c.** 41827   **d.** 41850

13. Simple revision of colostomy. Which CPT code is assigned?

    a. 44320   **b.** 44322   **c.** 44340   **d.** 44345

14. Incision and drainage of ischiorectal abscess. Which CPT code is assigned?

    a. 45020   **b.** 46040   **c.** 46045   **d.** 46060

15. Proximal subtotal pancreatectomy with total duodenectomy, partial gastrectomy, choledochoenterostomy, and gastrojejunostomy with pancreatojejunostomy. Which CPT code is assigned?

    a. 48150   **b.** 48152   **c.** 48153   **d.** 48154

16. Peritoneoscopy with partial laparoscopic colectomy and anastomosis. Which CPT code(s) are assigned?

    a. 44140   **c.** 49320, 44140

    b. 44204   **d.** 49320, 44204

17. Open drainage of retroperitoneal abscess. Which CPT code is assigned?

    a. 49020   **b.** 49060   **c.** 49405   **d.** 49406

18. Intraoral incision and drainage of hematoma of tongue, submandibular space. Which CPT code is assigned?

    a. 41008   **b.** 41009   **c.** 41015   **d.** 41017

19. Cystourethroscopy with resection of 1.1-cm bladder tumor. Which CPT code is assigned?

    a. 52224   **b.** 52234   **c.** 52235   **d.** 52240

20. Female patient underwent reconstructive urethroplasty. Which CPT code is assigned?

    a. 53410   **b.** 53420   **c.** 53430   **d.** 53431

Coding Practice

Instructions: Assign the CPT code(s) and appropriate modifier(s) to each case.

Mediastinum and Diaphragm

1. A patient is found to have a cystlike lesion per magnetic resonance imaging (MRI) of the mediastinum. This is to be removed. An incision is made by the physician from the shoulder blade to the spinal column of the thoracic area. Muscles are retracted, and the rib cage is exposed. After gaining access to the thoracic cavity, the physician identified the cyst and removed it. The specimen is sent to pathology. The wound is closed in layers.

   _____

2. A 45-year-old male has an acute diaphragmatic hernia. After adequate general anesthesia, an abdominal incision is made in the epigastric region. A moderate amount of abdominal tissue is protruding through the hernia into the diaphragm. These contents are moved back into proper placement. The opening of the diaphragm is closed with sutures.

   _____

3. Via transabdominal approach, the physician performs imbrication by overlapping diaphragm tissue to ensure that the diaphragm is in the correct position and the eventration is corrected.

   _____

4. A lacerated diaphragm tear measuring 2.5 cm is repaired with sutures.

   _____

5. A patient is being seen to confirm the diagnosis of sarcoidosis. An endoscopic examination of her mediastinum is done under general anesthesia. After making an incision in the area of the sternum, the scope is inserted. The trachea, bronchi, and lymph nodes are examined. A lymph node biopsy is taken. The scope is withdrawn, and the incision is closed with sutures.

   _____

Digestive System

1. A patient had the signs and symptoms consistent with a perforated viscus. After discussion, the patient consented to suture repair of the gastric ulcer. The patient was placed in a supine position. After adequate anesthesia, attention was turned to the anterior abdominal wall. A midline incision was made. Gross contamination was visualized. This was suctioned out. The gastric ulcer was visualized, and copious irrigation with 3 liters of warm saline was performed. All gross evidence of contamination was gone. Checking was done, hemostasis was throughout, and the skin incision was closed.

   _____

2. A patient presented with a lesion of the lip; due to the patient's history of smoking, it was determined to remove the lesion and send it to analysis to rule out carcinoma. After adequate anesthesia, a wedge incision was done of the lower lip to remove the lesion. The defect was closed with a small flap and sutures.

   _____

3. A patient with the diagnosis of carcinoma of the stomach presented for a hemigastrectomy. With the patient in the supine position and after adequate level of general anesthesia, the abdomen was prepped and draped in usual sterile fashion. An upper midline incision was made to access the abdominal cavity. The abdominal ligament was retracted to the right side of the incision. The stoma was mobilized. The duodenum was divided away from the stomach. The tumor was identified. The stomach tumor was transected with cautery, and a specimen was sent for evaluation by pathology. The distal margin of the remaining stomach was cleaned. Staples were used to close the curvature area of the stomach. The abdomen was closed with running Prolene for the fascia. The skin was closed with staples.

_____

4. An 18-year-old patient has a history of chronic tonsillitis. Under general anesthesia, the physician separated the tonsils from the tonsil bed by blunt and sharp dissection followed by the snare. No gross bleeding was found. The adenoids were extracted by the adenotome followed by the sharp curette. Again, no gross bleeding was found. The patient had minimal blood loss.

_____

5. A 72-year-old male patient presented to the emergency department with a 14-hour history of acute right inguinal pain and obstructive symptoms. Examination found a tender nonreducible mass in the right groin. He consented to surgical intervention via exploration and correction of possible hernia. After adequate anesthesia, the patient had an oblique preperitoneal incision through the fascia. The peritoneal cavity was entered. A strangulated loop was found along with the femoral hernia. The lower edge of the inguinal ligament was grasped with clamps, and interrupted Prolenes were used to close the femoral defect using Coopers ligament repair. The defect was closed up to the edge of the external iliac vein. Once the repair was completed, the wound was irrigated with saline. The bowel was inspected and appeared to be totally revascularized, with no evidence of necrosis and no need for resection. The femoral hernia sac was reduced and resected using electrocautery. The abdominal wall was closed with interrupted polypropylene sutures for the anterior wall fascia. A Jackson-Pratt drain was brought out through a separate stab wound. The subcutaneous tissue was closed with interrupted 3-0 Vicryl, and the skin was closed with staples.

_____

6. A patient with chronic cholelithiasis presented for a cholecystectomy. An infraumbilical incision was made, and a trocar was inserted into the abdominal cavity. After insufflation of the cavity, the laparoscope was inserted through the trocar. Two additional incisions were made to place trocars—one on the right side and one on the left. The gallbladder was identified. It was noted to be slightly enlarged and grayish in color. Multiple stones were palpable inside the gallbladder. Tissue surrounding the gallbladder was dissected. The cystic duct and artery were clipped and then cut. The gallbladder was dissected from the liver bed and removed through the umbilical trocar site. Careful irrigation of the cavity was done. The patient had minimal blood loss.

_____

7. A 19-year-old patient presented to the hospital with a history of bloody stools of three weeks' duration. The patient was prepped for a sigmoidoscopy. The sigmoidoscope was passed without difficulty to about 40 cm. The entire mucosal lining was erythematous. There was no friability of the overlying mucosa and no bleeding noted anywhere. No pseudopolyps were noted. Biopsies were taken at about 30 cm; these were thought to be representative of the mucosa in general. The scope was retracted; no other abnormalities were seen.

_____

8. A patient with a history of breast cancer presented for a biopsy of her liver to confirm metastatic disease. The abdomen was exposed by an incision through the skin, fascia, and muscle. A wedge-shaped section of the liver was resected. This specimen was sent to pathology.

_____

9. A patient was found to have a sublingual abscess of the mouth. After consent and normal prep, an incision up through the supramylohyoid muscle was made. The superficial abscess was identified, an extraoral incision made, and clear liquid fluid was drained from the abscess.

_____

10. A 45-year-old patient has been diagnosed with a parotid gland mass via examination and radiograph films. The patient presented for excision of this mass. After adequate anesthesia, the initial incision was made near the midpoint of the mandible. Skin flaps were retracted to expose the parotid gland. The facial nerve was visualized. A mass was identified on the lateral lobe of the gland, and it was carefully dissected free from the space with attention not to damage the facial nerve. The mass was sent in total to pathology for analysis.

_____

Urinary System

1. A patient with the complaint of hematuria presented for an endoscopic examination under conscious sedation. A cystourethroscope was passed through the structures of the urinary system. A lesion was identified on the trigone; this was fulgurated. The cystourethroscope was removed.

_____

2. A patient was diagnosed with a urethral calculus as confirmed by x-ray. Endoscopic treatment was warranted to remove this stone. A cystourethroscope was passed through the urethra, and the stone was extracted through the endoscope. The remaining structures of the system were examined and found to be normal. The cystourethroscope was removed.

_____

3. The patient consented to cystoscopy with possible bladder tumor removal. After the endoscope was inserted through the urethra, the bladder was entered. A lesion approximately 3.0 cm in size was identified in the bladder. This was removed via excision and taken out through the scope. Minimal bleeders were cauterized. The remainder of the bladder was normal in appearance. The cystoscope was removed.

_____

4. Imaging was used to assist in the percutaneous insertion of a guidewire, and a catheter was inserted to drain and collect fluid from the right kidney for analysis. The catheter was removed, and a bandage was applied.

_____

5. The patient was placed on a table. Water-filled bellows using coupling gel to make contact with the skin of the patient's right back were positioned at the area of the kidney stone. Shock waves were administered and directed in short bursts toward the bellows for a total of 35 minutes. The process was overseen by the attending physician, who monitored the fragmentation of the stone. The patient was discharged with instructions to drain urine and collect stone fragments.

_____

6. An endoscope was passed through the urethra. The urethra was normal in appearance, as was the bladder upon examination. The cystourethroscope was then directed to the right ureter. Slight narrowing was seen in the distal third of this ureter. A double-J stent was placed in the right ureter. The left ureter was then examined and found to be normal. The stent will be removed at a later date.

_____

7. With the patient under general anesthesia, a midline incision was made over the abdominal cavity wall. After the bladder was accessed, a ureterocele was identified. This was removed via an incision made in the bladder. All bleeders were cauterized. Minimal blood loss was noted. The bladder was closed with absorbable sutures. A urethral Foley catheter was placed. The fascia and muscle were closed with staples. The skin was closed with sutures.

_____

8. The patient consented to a renal biopsy. The skin of the back was punctured with the biopsy needle after administration of anesthesia. The needle was advanced to the right kidney. The core of the needle was used to collect the tissue specimen. The needle core was removed to preserve the specimen for pathology. Another core was inserted in the needle, and the same method was used to collect two more specimens. The skin puncture wound was closed with two sutures.

_____

9. The patient received an incision of his back. After access was gained to the left kidney, it was incised. The kidney was examined; a stone was identified and removed. The remainder of the kidney was found to be normal in appearance. The kidney was closed with sutures. A drainage tube was inserted. The tube was allowed to drain outside the body via access through another small incision. The main incision was closed in layers.

_____

10. A patient presented for the first stage of urethroplasty. After an abdominal incision was made, the urethra was identified. The strictures were seen. An incision was made over the first stricture area. The area was opened wide and sutured to the edge of the mucosa. The second stricture area was handled in the same method. The patient will return in eight weeks for stage two of this repair.

_____

CPT Surgery V

Chapter Outline

Male Genital System Subsection

Reproductive System Procedures Subsection

Intersex Surgery Subsection

Female Genital System Subsection

Maternity Care and Delivery Subsection

Endocrine System Subsection

Nervous System Subsection

Eye and Ocular Adnexa Subsection

Auditory System Subsection

Operating Microscope Subsection

Chapter Objectives

At the conclusion of this chapter, the student should be able to:

1. Define key terms related to the Male Genital System, Reproductive System Procedures, Intersex Surgery, Female Genital System, Maternity Care and Delivery, Endocrine System, Nervous System, Eye and Ocular Adnexa, Auditory System, and Operating Microscope subsections of CPT Surgery.
2. Assign codes from the Male Genital System subsection of CPT Surgery.
3. Assign codes from the Reproductive System Procedures subsection of CPT Surgery.
4. Assign codes from the Intersex Surgery subsection of CPT Surgery.
5. Assign codes from the Female Genital System subsection of CPT Surgery.
6. Assign codes from the Maternity Care and Delivery subsection of CPT Surgery.
7. Assign codes from the Endocrine System subsection of CPT Surgery.
8. Assign codes from the Nervous System subsection of CPT Surgery.
9. Assign codes from the Eye and Ocular Adnexa subsection of CPT Surgery.
10. Assign codes from the Auditory System subsection of CPT Surgery.
11. Assign codes from the Operating Microscope subsection of CPT Surgery.

Key Terms

antepartum care

anterior approach

anterolateral approach

auditory system

Bell's palsy

burr hole

carotid body

carpal tunnel

carpal tunnel syndrome	eye and ocular adnexa	lens	pupil
choroid	eyeball	loop electrodissection conization	retina
ciliary body	eye socket		salpingo-oophorectomy
ciliary muscle	female genital system	male genital system	sclera
cochlear implant	globe	middle ear	septic abortion
conization	hysteroscopy	missed abortion	somatic nerves
conjunctiva	incomplete abortion	myringotomy	stereotaxis
cornea	induced abortion	nervous system	strabismus
corpectomy	inner ear	neuroplasty	sympathetic nerves
costovertebral	intersex surgery	neurorrhaphy	tear apparatus
costovertebral approach	intracapsular cataract extraction (ICCE)	neurostimulator	tenosynovitis
delivery services		ocular adnexa	trachoma
discectomy	iris	ocular implant	transpedicular approach
endocrine system	lacrimal apparatus	omentectomy	
enucleation of the eye	lacrimal puncta	oocyte	tympanoplasty
evisceration of ocular contents	laminectomy	oophorectomy	tympanostomy
	laminotomy	operating microscope	uvea
exenteration of the orbit	lateral extracavitary approach (LECA)	orbit	vaginal birth after cesarean (VBAC)
external ear		orbital implant	
extracapsular cataract extraction (ECCE)	LEEP electrodissection conization	osteophytectomy	varicocele
		postpartum care	vas deferens

Introduction

The Male Genital System subsection classifies procedures performed on the male genitalia and accessory organs. The Reproductive System Procedures subsection classifies the placement of needles into pelvic organs and/or genitalia for subsequent interstitial radioelement application. The Intersex Surgery subsection contains just two codes to classify male-to-female as well as female-to-male sex change procedures. The Female Genital System subsection classifies procedures performed on female genitalia and accessory organs. The Maternity Care and Delivery subsection classifies procedures performed and services provided for obstetrics, including antepartum, delivery, and postpartum care.

 Coding Tip

Notes located beneath headings and/or subheadings apply to all codes in the heading or subheading. Parenthetical notes that are located below a specific code apply to that code only unless the note indicates otherwise.

The Endocrine System subsection includes codes for procedures performed on endocrine glands. The Nervous System subsection includes codes for procedures performed on the central and peripheral nervous systems. The Eye and Ocular Adnexa subsection classifies procedures performed on the eyeball, anterior segment, posterior segment, ocular adnexa, and conjunctiva. The Auditory System subsection includes codes for procedures performed on the external ear, middle ear, internal ear, and temporal bone (middle fossa approach). The Operating Microscope subsection contains a code that is reported in addition to the primary procedure code when an operating microscope is used during a surgical procedure to perform microsurgery techniques.

CPT guidelines that apply to the subsections are located at the beginning of the Surgery section. Unique coding instructions for the Male Genital System, Intersex Surgery, Female Genital System, Maternity Care and Delivery, Endocrine System, Nervous System, Eye and Ocular Adnexa, Auditory System, and Operating Microscope subsections are located in notes below headings or codes.

 NOTE:

> The Other Procedures code below each subheading classifies an unlisted procedure performed on the anatomical site. When reporting an unlisted procedure code, include documentation about the procedure (e.g., special report) performed with the submitted claim. (Other Procedures subheadings are not included throughout this chapter of the textbook except when codes that describe additional procedures are included.)

Male Genital System Subsection

The **male genital system** (Figure 16-1) includes the prostate, seminal vesicles, penis, testicles (testes) (Figure 16-2), epididymis, tunica vaginalis, vas deferens, scrotum, and spermatic cord. Codes are reported for procedures performed on the male genital system. Code assignment is determined according to

- Approach (e.g., incision, destruction, excision, or introduction)
- Reason for surgery

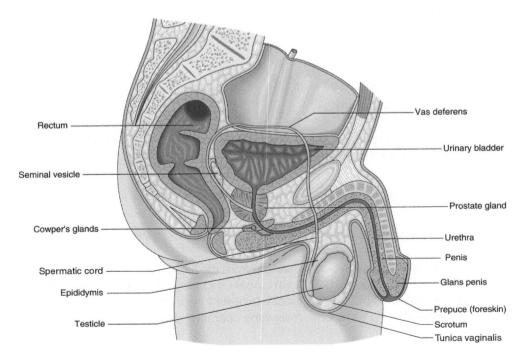

FIGURE 16-1 Male genital system

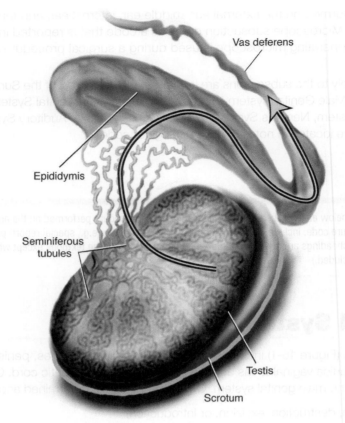

FIGURE 16-2 Male testicle

When an orchiectomy (removal of testis) procedure is performed, identify the following:

- Type of procedure (simple or radical)
- Surgical approach
- Additional procedures performed

EXAMPLE 1: Patient underwent radical orchiectomy (removal of testis) due to testicular tumor, inguinal approach. Report code 54530.

EXAMPLE 2: Patient underwent simple orchiectomy, inguinal approach, which was performed prophylactically to prevent the release of hormones that may promote tumor metastasis. Report code 54520.

EXAMPLE 3: Patient underwent orchiopexy via abdominal approach for intra-abdominal testis. Report code 54650.

EXAMPLE 4 : Patient underwent laparoscopic orchiopexy for intra-abdominal testis. Report code 54692.

The **vas deferens** is the tube that carries spermatozoa from the testis, and it is the structure upon which a vasectomy procedure is performed (Figure 16-3). A **varicocele** (Figure 16-4) is an abnormal dilation of the veins of the spermatic cord in the scrotum. Treatment typically involves ligation of spermatic veins or excision of the varicocele. For excision or ligation of a varicocele, review the operative report to locate the approach.

- Laparoscopic
- Abdominal

FIGURE 16-3 Vasectomy procedure

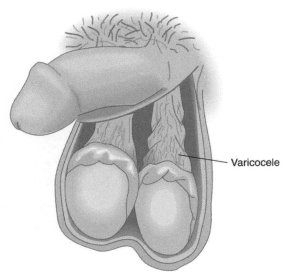

FIGURE 16-4 Varicocele affecting the left testicle

EXAMPLE 1: Patient underwent vasectomy procedure. Report code 55250. (Do not add modifier -50 to the code because its description includes the phrase *unilateral or bilateral.* Code 55250 also includes postoperative semen examination to determine whether the semen contains sperm.)

EXAMPLE 2: The patient underwent ligation of spermatic veins for varicocele. Report code 55530.

Benign conditions of the prostate gland include infection, inflammation, and benign prostatic hyperplasia (BPH) (also called benign prostatic hypertrophy, BPH). Men with benign prostate disease experience difficulty urinating (voiding). The degree of prostate involvement determines the therapeutic approach. For severe BPH, surgical procedures performed to restore urine flow include the following:

- Transurethral resection of the prostate (TURP) (Figure 16-5)
- Subtotal open prostatectomy (subtotal perineal prostatectomy)
- Subtotal prepubic prostatectomy
- Subtotal retropubic prostatectomy

EXAMPLE: Patient underwent transurethral electrosurgical resection of the prostate, including control of postoperative bleeding. During the same operative session, complete vasectomy was performed as well as meatotomy, cystourethroscopy, urethral calibration and dilation, and internal urethrotomy. Report code 52601.

 NOTE:

The code for transurethral electrosurgical resection of the prostate is classified in the Urinary System subsection. The procedure requires the use of an electrocautery knife to resect the prostate. (Report code 52601.)

Prostate cancer treatment may involve surgery, chemical destruction, electrocautery, or radiation. Surgical procedures that are performed to treat localized prostate cancer include radical prostatectomy, laparoscopic radical prostatectomy, and cryoablation.

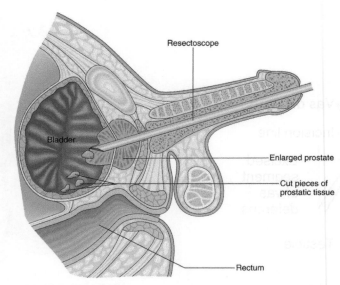

FIGURE 16-5 A transurethral resection of the prostate (TURP) is performed to treat benign prostatic hypertrophy.

A prostate biopsy includes the following types

- Needle
- Punch
- Incisional

The "transperineal placement of needles or catheters into prostate for interstitial radioelement application, with or without cystoscopy" describes a procedure performed for interstitial radioelement application. Code 55875 is reported for the transperineal placement of needles or catheters only. A parenthetical note provides instruction directing the coder to radioelement application codes, which are reported separately from the Radiology section.

Exercise 16.1 – Male Genital System Subsection

Instructions: Assign the CPT code(s) and appropriate modifier(s) to each statement.

1. The physician resected diseased scrotal tissue.

   _____

2. The physician removed a lesion from the left spermatic cord by dissection and excision.

   _____

3. The physician made an incision into the scrotum to search for the right testis, which failed to descend into the scrotum.

   _____

4. The physician performed a radical prostatectomy to remove the entire gland along with the seminal vesicles and the vas deferens. The incision was made between the base of the scrotum and the anus. Local lymph nodes were also removed for analysis.

   _____

5. The physician destroyed extensive condyloma of the penis using local application of a chemical.

   _____

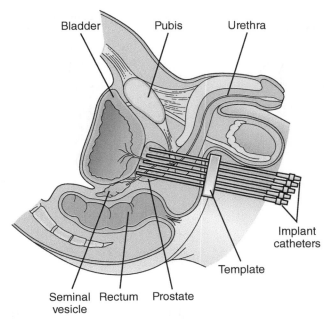

FIGURE 16-6 Insertion of implant catheters through perineum into prostate and seminal vesicles

Reproductive System Procedures Subsection

The reproductive system procedures subsection contains a code to report the placement of needles or catheters into pelvic organs and/or genitalia (Figure 16-6) for subsequent interstitial radioelement application. The code is *not* reported when needles or catheters are inserted into the prostate gland.

> **EXAMPLE:** Patient underwent insertion of catheters into the uterus to facilitate radiation therapy. Report code 55920.

 NOTE:

> Radioactive isotopes (e.g., iodine-125) contained within tiny seeds remain inside the pelvic organs or genitalia to deliver radiation during an extended period of time (e.g., months). This method targets the prescribed body area, minimizing radiation exposure to normal tissue.

Intersex Surgery Subsection

Intersex surgery (Figure 16-7) is performed as a series of staged procedures to transform the normal adult genitalia of one sex to that of the other sex (genital reconstructive surgery or sex reassignment surgery).

- For male-to-female intersex surgery, portions of the male genitalia are removed and female external genitals are formed.
- For female-to-male intersex surgery, a penis and scrotum are formed using pedicle flap grafts and free skin grafts and a prosthesis is inserted.

> **EXAMPLE:** Patient underwent female to male intersex surgery. Report code 55980.

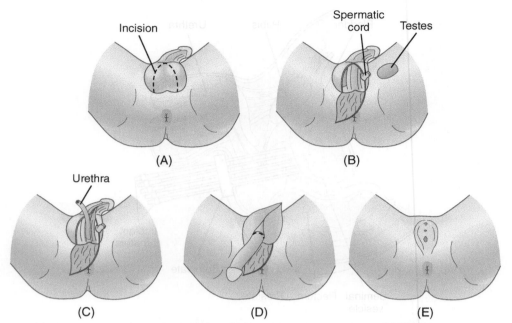

FIGURE 16-7 Sex reassignment surgery: (A) To change male genitalia to female genitalia, an incision is made into the scrotum. (B) The flap of scrotal skin is retracted, and the testes are removed. (C) Skin is then excised from the penis but remains attached, and a shorter urethra is created. (D) All but a stump of the penis is then removed. (E) Excess skin is used to create labia (external genitalia) and the vagina.

Exercise 16.2 – Reproductive System Procedures and Intersex Surgery Subsection

Instructions: Assign the CPT code(s) and appropriate modifier(s) to each statement.

1. A needle was inserted into the patient's bladder to insert a radiopharmaceutical (HCPCS level II code A9699) for the purpose of radiation therapy.

2. Surgery was performed to dissect the penis and remove portions of it to fashion a clitoris-like structure. The urethral opening was moved, and a vagina was created by dissecting and opening the perineum. Labia were created using scrotal skin and adjacent tissue.

3. In the fourth of a series of staged procedures, the physician formed a penis and scrotum using pedicle flap grafts and free skin grafts. Prostheses were placed in the penis and testicles, and the vagina was closed.

Female Genital System Subsection

Female Genital System subsection codes are reported for procedures performed on the **female genital system** (Figure 16-8), including the following: vulva, perineum, introitus, vagina, cervix uteri, corpus uteri, oviduct/ovary (fallopian tube), ovary, and *in vitro* fertilization (IVF).

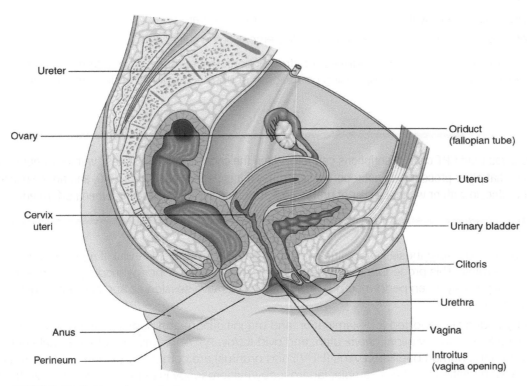

FIGURE 16-8 Female genital system

When reporting codes for procedures performed on the female genital system, review the operative report to identify the following:

- Anatomy on which the procedure was performed (e.g., vulva)
- Surgical approach

 NOTE:

Codes classified in the Female Genital System subsection are reported for procedures performed on women who are *not* pregnant. To report codes for women who are pregnant, refer to the Maternity Care and Delivery subsection.

 Coding Tip

- All laparoscopic procedures and nonobstetrical dilation and curettage procedure codes are classified in the Female Genital System subsection.
- Some female genital procedures are classified in other subsection headings of the CPT coding manual, such as the open destruction of endometriomas, which is located in the Digestive System subsection, Abdomen/Peritoneum/Omentum heading, Excision/Destruction subheading.

For vulvectomy procedure codes, refer to the following definitions when reviewing the operative report (to select the type of procedure performed):

- *Simple procedure*: Removal of skin and superficial subcutaneous tissues
- *Radical procedure*: Removal of skin and deep subcutaneous tissue

- *Partial procedure*: Removal of less than 80 percent of the vulvar area
- *Complete procedure*: Removal of greater than 80 percent of the vulvar area

When an open sling operation is performed for stress incontinence, report a code from the Female Genital System subsection. When a laparoscopic sling operation is performed, report a code from the Urinary System subsection.

Coding Tip

Make sure you read CPT code descriptions carefully. When the code description states "with or without" another procedure, that other procedure is not reported separately if it is performed (e.g., 57240, anterior colporrhaphy, repair of cystocele with or without repair of urethrocele, including cystourethroscopy, when performed).

A pelvic exam under anesthesia is a routine evaluation of the surgical field, and it is reported with a code *only if performed separately*. This procedure is included in all major and most minor gynecological procedures, and it is *not* reported separately when performed during the same operative session as another female genital system surgical procedure.

Endoscopy codes are reported for examination and magnification, and codes distinguish among anatomical sites (e.g., vulva, vagina, cervix uteri, and oviduct/ovary). Abnormalities of the female genital system (e.g., cancer, tumors, human papilloma virus [HPV], and pruritus) are commonly diagnosed and treated with examination and magnification. For example, laparoscopy/hysteroscopy is performed to visualize the corpus uteri (Figure 16-9).

When dilation of the vagina or cervix is performed during the same operative session as another vaginal approach procedure, do not report the dilation procedure separately. When a pelvic examination under anesthesia is performed during the same operative session as a dilation and curettage (Figure 16-10), report the code for the dilation and curettage only.

In the Cervix Uteri heading, **conization** of the cervix (removal of a cone-shaped piece of tissue) is reported for fulguration, dilation and curettage, and repair procedures. Conization procedures can also be performed through use of a cold knife or laser or through loop electrode excision. Make sure you review the operative report carefully to assign the appropriate code.

FIGURE 16-9 Laparoscopy/hysteroscopy

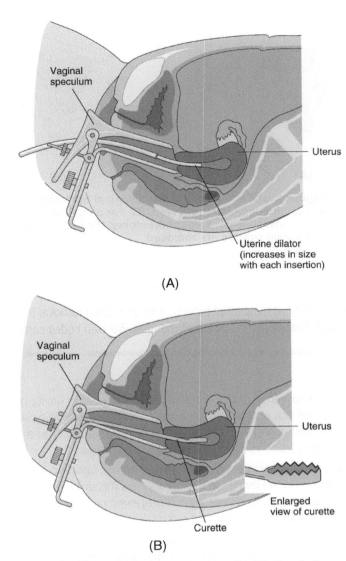

FIGURE 16-10 Dilation and curettage: (A) Dilation is the expansion of the cervical opening. (B) Curettage is the removal of material from the endometrial lining of the uterus.

Coding Tip

Physicians use the terms *loop conization* and *LEEP (loop electrosurgical excision procedure) conization* interchangeably in operative reports. **Loop electrodissection conization** is a deep dissection of the cervix using a loop wire (instead of the traditional surgical scalpel). **LEEP electrodissection conization** is a more superficial dissection of the cervix using a loop wire.

For abdominal hysterectomy procedures, make sure you review the operative report to identify whether the fallopian tubes and/or ovaries were removed during the same operative session as the hysterectomy. Then read the code descriptions carefully to select the appropriate code.

When reporting a code for vaginal hysterectomy (Figure 16-11), determine whether the surgical approach is open or laparoscopic.

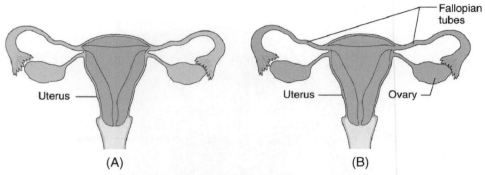

FIGURE 16-11 Vaginal hysterectomies: (A) For a vaginal hysterectomy, just the uterus and cervix are removed. (B) For a vaginal hysterectomy with bilateral salpingo-oophorectomy, the cervix, uterus, fallopian tubes, and ovaries are removed.

 Coding Tip

The code description "with or without removal of tube(s), with or without removal of ovary(s)" indicates that these procedures are bilateral. Therefore, do not report modifier -50 with codes containing such descriptions.

Hysteroscopy is the direct visualization of the cervical canal and uterine cavity using a hysteroscope. It is performed to examine the endometrium and to carry out surgical procedures (e.g., removal of cervical polyp). When a dilation and curettage is performed during the same operative session as a hysteroscopic biopsy or polypectomy, do not report a separate code for the dilation and curettage.

The Oviduct/Ovary heading includes procedures performed on the fallopian tubes. It also includes codes for endoscopic procedures performed on the ovaries. (The Ovary heading does not contain endoscopic codes.) Make sure you review the operative report to differentiate therapeutic procedures performed using surgical laparoscopy or hysteroscopy from those performed for diagnostic laparoscopy.

Review the operative report to determine the surgical approach before coding a tubal ligation procedure (e.g., ligation, transaction, or other occlusion of the fallopian tubes) (Figure 16-12).

FIGURE 16-12 Tubal ligation

- Abdominal or vaginal approach
- Vaginal or suprapubic approach
- Laparoscopic

> **EXAMPLE:** Patient underwent a total abdominal hysterectomy during which routine lysis of adhesions was performed to access the abdomen. Report code 58150. (Do *not* report code 58660.)

Procedures performed on the ovaries are based on surgical approach.

- Open (e.g., oophorectomy performed via open surgery)
- Laparoscopic (e.g., laparoscopic oophorectomy)

An **oophorectomy** (removal of the ovaries) is often performed due to ovarian cancer. An ovarian malignancy is also resected by performing a bilateral **salpingo-oophorectomy** (removal of both fallopian tubes and ovaries) and an **omentectomy** (removal of the omentum).

In vitro fertilization (IVF) procedures are performed during a one- to seven-day period from the time the **oocyte** (immature female reproductive cell, or egg) was aspirated from the ovary until the embryo is transferred to the uterus or is cryopreserved. IVF procedures include both male and female gametes in addition to the subsequent embryos that develop. The physician who performs the oocyte retrieval reports a code for follicle puncture for oocyte retrieval, any method, to describe these services.

 Coding Tip

Any associated laboratory procedures performed during *in vitro* fertilization are reported separately with codes from the Pathology and Laboratory section of CPT.

Exercise 16.3 – Female Genital System Subsection

Instructions: Assign the CPT code(s) and appropriate modifier(s) to each statement.

1. The physician performed a tubal ligation (vaginal approach), postpartum, bilateral, during same hospitalization (as delivery). (Do not code the delivery.)

_____

2. The physician performed colpocentesis to aspirate fluid from the peritoneum through the vaginal wall.

_____

3. The physician aspirated a mature egg from its follicle for *in vitro* fertilization.

_____

4. The physician inserted an intrauterine device (IUD).

_____

5. The physician performed laparoscopic electrical cautery destruction of an ovarian lesion with the assistance of a fiberoptic laparoscope.

_____

Maternity Care and Delivery Subsection

In clinical terms, pregnancy is subdivided into trimesters.

- First trimester (fetal organ development)
- Second trimester (well-baby visits at the physician's office)
- Third trimester (baby maturity and delivery at 38–40 weeks)

In coding terms, the three stages of pregnancy care include services provided as part of total obstetrical care.

- Antepartum care
- Delivery of the baby
- Postpartum care

Total obstetrical care does not include diagnostic procedures (e.g., ultrasound, amniocentesis, or special screening tests), physician office visits for unrelated conditions incidental to pregnancy, and additional visits due to high-risk conditions or medical complications of pregnancy (e.g., cardiac conditions, diabetes mellitus, hyperemesis, hypertension, neurological conditions, premature rupture of membranes, preterm labor, toxemia, or hyperemesis). Codes for these services are separately reported from the Evaluation and Management and Medicine sections of CPT. For treatment of surgical complications associated with pregnancy (e.g., appendectomy, cholecystectomy, hernia repair, or removal of ovarian cyst or Bartholin cyst), codes from the Surgery section are reported separately.

Most procedures in the Maternity Care and Delivery heading include just what is described in the code description. Additional procedures performed on the same day as a maternity care and delivery service are reported separately, except for the following services, which are included in the code for maternity care and delivery:

- Fetal monitoring during labor
- Episiotomy
- Delivery of the placenta

Services that are reported separately when performed during maternity care and delivery include the following:

- Amniocentesis (Figure 16-13)
- Chorionic villus sampling
- Cordocentesis
- Fetal contraction stress test
- Fetal nonstress test
- Insertion of cervical dilator (e.g., laminaria and prostaglandin)
- External cephalic version with or without tocolysis
- Limited or complete obstetric ultrasound
- Fetal biophysical profile
- Fetal echocardiography
- Administration of Rh immune globulin

Antepartum Services

Antepartum care begins with conception and ends with delivery, and it includes the following:

- Initial prenatal history and examination
- Subsequent prenatal history and examinations
- Documentation of weight, blood pressures, and fetal heart tones
- Routine chemical urinalysis (e.g., glucose)
- Monthly visits up to 28 weeks' gestation
- Biweekly visits to 36 weeks' gestation
- Weekly visits until delivery

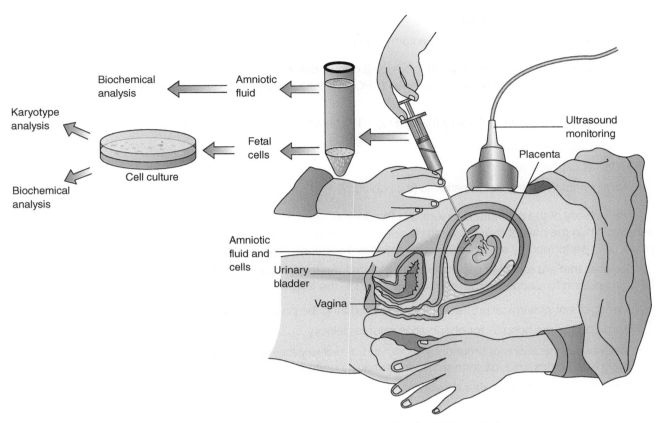

FIGURE 16-13 Amniocentesis and preparation of specimen for amniotic fluid analysis

The previously listed services are included with total obstetrical care, and they are not reported separately. Services that are reported separately with a code from the Evaluation and Management or Surgery section of CPT (in addition to a code for delivery services) include the management of the following:

- Medical problems *unrelated* to pregnancy
- Complications related to pregnancy

EXAMPLE: Patient develops gestational diabetes, which complicates her pregnancy. She requires additional office visits to monitor her blood sugar and weight. Report an appropriate evaluation and management service code for each office visit during which the patient's gestational diabetes is managed.

When a physician provides *antepartum care only* (e.g., patient's care is transferred to another physician or patient relocates out of the area), report an appropriate evaluation and management code for the first through third antepartum care visit. For the fourth and subsequent visits, report code 59425 (Antepartum care only; 4–6 visits) or 59426 (Antepartum care only; 7 or more visits).

Delivery Services

Delivery services (e.g., vaginal delivery, cesarean delivery, and delivery after previous cesarean delivery) begin with the admission of the patient to the hospital and end with delivery of the placenta (Figure 16-14). Services include the following:

- Admission of the patient to the hospital
- Admission history and physical examination

- Management of uncomplicated labor
- Vaginal delivery (with or without episiotomy and/or with or without forceps) or cesarean delivery

The induction of labor (e.g., Pitocin [oxytocin]) during delivery is included in the code for delivery services. The artificial rupture of membranes (AROM) prior to delivery is also included in the delivery services code.

Services provided during delivery that are reported separately include the following:

- Fetal scalp blood sampling
- External cephalic version
- Administration of regional anesthesia (e.g., epidural)

The delivery of the placenta is included in the delivery service, and it is *not* reported in addition to the delivery service. When the patient delivers vaginally prior to admission to the hospital and subsequent delivery of the placenta is performed by a physician in the hospital, a separate code is reported.

Services that are reported separately with a code from the Evaluation and Management or Surgery section of CPT (in addition to a code for delivery services) include the following:

- Management of surgical problems that develop during the postpartum period
- Admission to the hospital for observation prior to delivery
- Medical complications of pregnancy, labor, and/or delivery that require additional resources (e.g., diabetes, hypertension, toxemia, preterm labor, or premature rupture of membranes)
- Tubal ligation performed after delivery

FIGURE 16-14 **Stages of labor (A) Position of the fetus before labor (B) First stage of labor (C) Second stage of labor, fetal delivery (D) Third stage of labor, delivery of the placenta**

Coding Tip

- Multiple births create the potential for complications during pregnancy, and they present coding challenges. (Report the ICD-10-CM diagnosis code for multiple gestation.)

- When performing diagnostic tests on multiple fetuses (e.g., amniocentesis or biophysical profile), more work is usually required because the procedure must be performed and documented for each fetus. To indicate additional work, report the appropriate code with modifier -22 or report the code for each fetus. (Make sure you report an ICD-10-CM diagnosis code that indicates multiple gestation.)

- Codes for multiple births are reported as follows:

  ○ Vaginal delivery of each baby: report code 59400 for Baby A, code 59409-51 for Baby B, code 59409-51 for Baby C, and so on.

  ○ Vaginal delivery followed by cesarean delivery: report code 59510 for Baby B, code 59409-51 for Baby A (and subsequent vaginal delivery codes if additional babies were delivered vaginally, with modifier -51 added to each code). (Code 59510 for cesarean delivery is reported first because that procedure consumes the most resources. If multiple babies are delivered via cesarean, report code 59510 just once.)

  ○ Cesarean delivery of each baby: report code 59510 once (because just one cesarean section is performed). When a cesarean delivery is significantly more difficult, add modifier -22 to the code. (Submit a copy of the operative report with the claim.)

Postpartum Care

Postpartum care begins after vaginal or cesarean section delivery and includes the recovery room visit; any uncomplicated inpatient hospital and outpatient postpartum visits; follow-up care for episiotomy; and repair of cervical, vaginal, or perineal lacerations, including follow-up care. During delivery, if a vaginal laceration occurs and the repair is minimal, it is included in the delivery services. The repair of the vaginal laceration is not coded separately.

Coding Tip

- When a physician provides all or part of the antepartum and/or postpartum care but does not perform the delivery due to termination of pregnancy by abortion or referral to another physician for delivery, report codes from the antepartum and postpartum subheadings.

- When a physician performs only the delivery, report a "delivery only" code.

EXAMPLE: The on-call obstetrician performs an emergency cesarean section on a colleague's patient. The on-call obstetrician reports code 59514. The patient's obstetrician reports codes for antepartum and postpartum care.

Delivery After Previous Cesarean Delivery

Codes for delivery after previous cesarean section are reported whether an attempted vaginal birth (after previous cesarean delivery) is successful or a repeat cesarean is performed. A code is reported for **vaginal birth after cesarean (VBAC)**, which is a planned vaginal birth after previous cesarean section. When the planned VBAC fails, a different code from the heading is reported.

Abortion

Abortion treatment codes are based on the method used and type of abortion.

- **Incomplete abortion:** Miscarriage in which part, but not all, of the uterine contents are expelled
- **Missed abortion:** Miscarriage in which a dead fetus and other products of conception remain in the uterus for four or more weeks
- **Septic abortion:** Abortion-related pelvic and uterine infection

EXAMPLE: Patient underwent treatment for a septic abortion, which was completed surgically. Report code 59830.

- **Induced abortion:** Deliberate termination of pregnancy

Exercise 16.4 – Maternity Care and Delivery Subsection

Instructions: Assign the CPT code(s) and appropriate modifier(s) to each statement.

1. The physician treated an ectopic pregnancy by removing the fallopian tube and ovary through an incision in the lower abdomen.

   _____

2. Using ultrasonic guidance, the physician inserted an amniocentesis needle through the abdominal wall into the interior of the pregnant uterus and directly into the amniotic sac to collect amniotic fluid for diagnostic analysis.

   _____

3. Using ultrasonic guidance, the physician inserted an amniocentesis needle through the abdominal wall into the cavity of the pregnant uterus and into the umbilical vessels to obtain fetal blood.

   _____

4. The physician used an external monitor to record fetal heart rate changes during a fetal nonstress test.

   _____

5. A physician provided all antepartum (7 visits) and postpartum care but did not perform the delivery.

   _____

Endocrine System Subsection

The **endocrine system** (Figure 16-15) includes the following glands:

- Adrenal (2)
- Gonads (ovaries in females, testes in males) (2)
- Pancreas (islets of Langerhans) (1)
- Parathyroid (divided into four lobes) (1)
- Pituitary (divided into two lobes) (1)
- Thymus (1)
- Thyroid (divided into two lobes) (1)

The Endocrine System subsection includes procedures performed on the endocrine glands and the carotid body.

FIGURE 16-15 Endocrine glands

 Coding Tip

Codes for procedures performed on the pituitary and pineal glands are located in the Nervous System subsection.

Thyroid Gland

Thyroid Gland procedures classify increasingly complex procedures involving excision of the thyroid gland.

A "total or subtotal resection" is the removal of both the left and right lobes of the thyroid gland. A "limited neck dissection" is the removal of a limited number of lymph nodes. A "radical neck dissection" is the total removal of lymph nodes from one side (or both sides) of the neck.

 NOTE:

You may recall that when a radical neck dissection is performed during the same operative session as the resection of a unilateral organ (e.g., larynx), modifier -50 is not added to the procedure codes. The thyroid gland is a unilateral organ that contains two lobes. Thus, modifiers -50, -LT, and -RT are *never* added to thyroid gland procedure codes.

EXAMPLE: A physician suspects lymphoma in a patient who has signs of diffuse neck swelling. A large-core needle biopsy of the right lobe of the thyroid gland is performed. The tissue is sent for histopathology. Report code 60100.

Parathyroid, Thymus, Adrenal Glands, Pancreas, and Carotid Body

Codes 60500–60699 are reported for procedures performed on the parathyroid, thymus, adrenal glands, and carotid body. The **carotid body** is tissue that contains many capillaries, and it is located at the point where the carotid artery branches in the neck. It contains cells that sense oxygen and carbon dioxide blood levels so that information is sent to the brain's medulla to regulate heart rate.

Surgery performed on the adrenal glands can be performed as open or laparoscopic procedures. Make sure you review the operative report to identify the surgical approach to report the appropriate code.

The exploration of parathyroid glands is often performed using a cervical approach. In cases where further exploration is needed, the physician uses a transthoracic approach.

EXAMPLE 1: Patient underwent laparoscopic exploration with partial removal of the left adrenal gland, performed from a transabdominal approach. Report code 60650-LT.

EXAMPLE 2: Patient underwent surgical laparoscopy with complete right adrenalectomy, performed from a lumbar approach. Report code 60650-RT.

Exercise 16.5 – Endocrine System Subsection

Instructions: Assign the CPT code(s) and appropriate modifier(s) to each statement.

1. The physician determines the location of a thyroid cyst, using palpation, and aspirates it.

   _____

2. The physician performed a total thyroid lobectomy on the right and a contralateral subtotal lobectomy on the left, including isthmusectomy.

   _____

3. The physician removed remaining thyroid tissue on one side, following an earlier partial thyroidectomy.

   _____

4. Patient underwent large-core needle biopsy of the thyroid gland.

   _____

5. Patient underwent incision and drainage of an infected thyroglossal cyst of the neck, which was the result of incomplete closure of the embryonic thyroglossal duct between the thyroid gland and the back of the tongue.

   _____

6. The physician performed a laparoscopic exploration of the adrenal gland through the abdomen.

   _____

7. The physician explored the parathyroid glands. During the same operative session, a parathyroid autotransplantation was also performed.

   _____

8. Patient underwent partial adrenalectomy with biopsy, dorsal approach.

   _____

9. The physician surgically removed the parathyroid glands.

   _____

10. The physician removed a carotid body tumor, which was located just above the bifurcation of the carotid artery.

    _____

Nervous System Subsection

The **nervous system** (Figure 16-16) includes the following:

- Central nervous system (brain and spinal cord)
- Peripheral nervous system (12 pairs of cranial nerves extending from the brain and 31 pairs of spinal nerves extending from the spinal cord).

FIGURE 16-16 Nervous system (A) Divisions of the nervous system (B) Structure of the central nervous system and peripheral nervous system

Codes for Nervous System subsection procedures are arranged anatomically.

- Skull, meninges, and brain
- Spine and spinal cord
- Extracranial nerves, peripheral nerves, and autonomic nervous system

Nervous system procedures are performed using a variety of approaches (e.g., craniectomy, craniotomy, and laminectomy) and for specific purposes (e.g., decompression and drainage of hematomas).

EXAMPLE: Patient underwent a procedure to create subdural burr holes to drain a hematoma. Report code 61154. (The subdural burr hole is the approach, and drainage of the hematoma is the purpose.)

Skull, Meninges, and Brain

The Skull, Meninges, and Brain (Figure 16-17) heading includes the following subheadings (and for "Surgery of Skull Base," further subdivisions):

- Injection, Drainage, or Aspiration
- Twist Drill, Burr Hole(s), or Trephine
- Craniectomy or Craniotomy
- Surgery of Skull Base

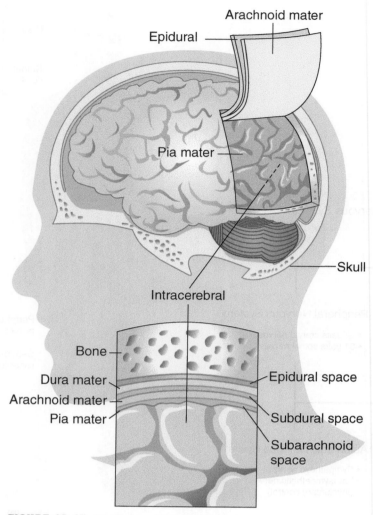

FIGURE 16-17 Skull, meninges, and brain

- ○ Approach Procedures
- ○ Definitive Procedures
- ○ Repair and/or Reconstruction of Surgical Defects of Skull Base
- • Endovascular Therapy
- • Surgery for Aneurysm, Arteriovenous Malformation, or Vascular Disease

- • Stereotaxis
- • Stereotactic Radiosurgery (Cranial)
- • Neurostimulators (Intracranial)
- • Repair
- • Neuroendoscopy
- • Cerebrospinal Fluid (CSF) Shunt

A **burr hole** is a small opening in the skull made with a surgical drill. This procedure is often necessary when intracranial surgery (e.g., craniotomy or craniectomy) is planned. The burr hole provides access to intracranial contents, it alleviates pressure in preparation of further surgery, and it allows the placement of an intracranial pressure monitoring device. (These services are integral to the performance of subsequent services, and they are not to be separately coded or reported.)

When burr holes, punctures, and/or taps are created for the purpose of performing drainage procedures (e.g., hematoma, abscess, or cyst) and additional procedures are performed, the burr hole and drainage procedure is not separately coded and reported (unless it is performed as a staged procedure). In addition, many intracranial procedures include bone grafting; such grafts are not separately coded and reported.

Injection procedures for imaging of CSF flow are reported with code 61026 in addition to codes from the Radiology section (to report the imaging procedure).

EXAMPLE 1: Patient underwent ventricular puncture through previous burr hole with injection of medication. Report code 61026. (The ventricular puncture through a previous burr hole describes the approach to access a specific area of the brain.)

EXAMPLE 2: A patient with an open head injury and a contrecoup subdural hematoma underwent a craniectomy for the open head injury and creation of a burr hole on the opposite side of the skull to drain the subdural hematoma. Report codes 61304 and 61154. (The creation of the contralateral burr hole and drainage of the subdural hematoma is considered a separate service not integral to the craniectomy. Thus, it is assigned a separate code.)

Surgery of Skull Base

Surgery of skull base codes contain important notes that define anatomical areas included (e.g., skull base includes the base of the anterior, middle, and posterior cranial fossae). Notes further indicate that skull base surgery often requires the skills of several different surgical specialties that work together. Skull base surgery requires review of the operative report to identify the following variables:

- What the size of the lesion or tumor is
- What the anatomy of the individual patient is
- Whether this is an initial procedure to treat the condition or a reoperation

Surgery of skull base codes are arranged anatomically (anterior, middle, and posterior cranial fossae), and they are further subdivided according to the following:

- Approach procedures (provide adequate exposure to the intracranial field so the definitive procedure, such as excision of lesion, can be performed)
- Definitive procedures (e.g., resection, excision, transection, ligation, and obliteration), which include primary closure of dura, mucous membranes, and skin
- Repair and/or reconstruction of skull defects of skull base procedures (reported separately when cranioplasty, extensive dural grafting, extensive skin grafts, or local or regional myocutaneous pedicle flaps are required)

When skull base surgery is performed, a code for each procedure is reported by the surgeon who performed that aspect of the procedure: approach procedure, definitive procedure, and repair and/or reconstructive procedure. Generally, one surgeon performs the approach procedure, which exposes the area (e.g., lesion) to be treated. Another surgeon then performs the treatment (e.g., excision of lesion). A third surgeon repairs the defect created by the treatment (e.g., free tissue graft of dural defect created by excision of lesion). When one surgeon performs both the approach procedure and the definitive procedure, that surgeon reports both codes on the same claim; modifier -51 is added to the secondary procedure.

 NOTE:

Skull base surgery procedures are not typically considered "staged" because definitive closure of the surgical field (e.g., dura, subcutaneous tissues, or skin) must be performed to avoid serious infections (e.g., osteomyelitis or meningitis).

EXAMPLE: The operative report documents a right maxillectomy with orbital exenteration, bilateral ethmoidectomies, and a sphenoidectomy. The patient underwent resection of a neoplastic lesion at the base of the anterior cranial fossa, extradural.

The approach procedure code is 61581 because a "craniofacial approach to anterior cranial fossa" includes ethmoidectomy, sphenoidectomy, maxillectomy, and orbital exenteration procedures. (Approach procedures for middle cranial fossa and posterior cranial fossa do include such procedures.) The definitive procedure code is 61600. (Do not report a code for repair and/or reconstruction of surgical defects of skull base because such procedures were not documented.)

Codes distinguish between procedures performed extradurally (outside the dura) or intradurally (within the dura). The dura mater is the outermost, fibrous, and toughest of the three meninges (Figure 16-18) that surround the brain and spinal cord.

Skin Fat Periosteum
(covering over bone)
Bone
Dura mater
Arachnoid mater
Pia mater

Subdural space

Subarachnoid space

Brain

FIGURE 16-18 Meninges (dura mater, arachnoid mater, and pia mater) and other anatomical structures that protect the brain

Some procedure codes in the Surgery of Skull Base heading are add-on procedures. They are not reported alone; they must be reported with another procedure code.

> **EXAMPLE:** A surgeon performed a resection of an infectious lesion of the parasellar area and a transection of the carotid artery in a petrous canal, without repair. (No repair and/or reconstruction of surgical defects of the skull base was required.) Report codes 61607 and 61611. (The approach procedure was performed by a different surgeon; therefore, do not report a code for an approach procedure.) (Code 61611 is exempt from modifier -51.)

Neurostimulators (Intracranial)

Codes describing craniotomy procedures are usually bundled with craniectomy codes. Thus, when a craniotomy is performed during the same operative session as a craniectomy, report only the craniectomy code. Do not report the craniotomy code in addition to the craniectomy code.

> **EXAMPLE:** When a patient undergoes "craniectomy or craniotomy for implantation of neurostimulator electrodes" during the same operative session as the creation of "twist drill or burr hole(s) for implantation of neurostimulator electrodes," only code 61860 is reported. Code 61850 is not reported in addition to code 61860.

Cerebrospinal Fluid (CSF) Shunt

A CSF shunt (Figure 16-19) is used to eliminate excess CSF in cases of hydrocephalus.

> **EXAMPLE:** A child underwent creation of a ventriculo peritoneal shunt. Report code 62223.

Spine and Spinal Cord

The Spine and Spinal Cord heading describes percutaneous procedures performed on the spine, as well as spinal injections and extracranial and peripheral nerve injections. To report procedure codes properly, review the operative report to identify the following:

- What the anatomical site is (e.g., epidural or facet joint nerves)
- Whether the procedure is diagnostic or therapeutic

FIGURE 16-19 A cerebrospinal shunt allows drainage of cerebrospinal fluid (CSF) from the brain into the peritoneal cavity.

- What type of substance is injected (e.g., contrast media or neurolytic substance)
- Whether the injections are continuous

EXAMPLE: Patient underwent percutaneous lysis of epidural adhesions procedure under fluoroscopic guidance on June 14. Hypertonic saline solution was administered during the procedure. Report code 62264. (Do not report a separate code for fluoroscopic guidance.)

Coding Tip

- Report code 01996 from the Anesthesia section for daily hospital management of continuous epidural or subarachnoid drug administration performed with services assigned for the injection of diagnostic or therapeutic substances.

- For a spinal puncture procedure, the administration of local anesthesia is included. Reporting a separate code for the administration of local anesthesia (e.g., nerve block or facet block) is inappropriate.

- When an anesthetic block procedure is performed and cerebrospinal fluid is withdrawn during the same operative session (to make room for the anesthetic), do not report a code for diagnostic lumbar puncture. Report a code for the nerve (or other) block only because the removal of CSF is not done for diagnostic purposes.

- The following subcategories define "partial" for a vertebral corpectomy as the "removal of a substantial portion of the body of the vertebra. In the cervical spine, the amount of bone removed is defined as at least one-half of the vertebral body. In the thoracic and lumbar spine, the amount of bone removed is defined as at least one-third of the vertebral body."

  o Anterior or Anterolateral Approach for Extradural Exploration/Decompression

  o Lateral Extracavitary Approach for Extradural Exploration/Decompression

  o Excision, Anterior or Anterolateral Approach, Intraspinal Lesion

Catheter Implantation

The *implantation* of an epidural or intrathecal catheter placement involves penetration of the dura.

> **EXAMPLE:** Patient underwent implantation of tunneled epidural catheter for long-term medication administration via external pump. Report code 62350.

Reservoir/Pump Implantation

Programmable and nonprogrammable infusion pumps provide long-term access to the vascular or nervous system for the administration of medications. When electronic analysis and reprogramming of a programmable implanted pump is performed at the same time as refilling and maintenance, report a separate code.

> **EXAMPLE:** Patient underwent implantation of a subcutaneous reservoir for intrathecal drug infusion. Report code 62360.

Endoscopic Decompression of Neural Elements and/or Excision of Herniated Intervertebral Discs

Endoscopic decompression of neural elements and/or excision of herniated intervertebral discs includes surgical approaches of percutaneous, endoscopic, and open. Visualization includes direct and indirect.

> **EXAMPLE:** Patient underwent endoscopic decompression of lumbar spinal cord, which included laminotomy and excision of herniated intervertebral disk. Report code 62380.

Posterior Extradural Laminotomy or Laminectomy for Exploration/Decompression of Neural Elements or Excision of Herniated Intervertebral Discs

A **laminotomy** involves the removal of part of the lamina from one side of the vertebra. A **laminectomy** is the excision of the entire posterior arch or lamina of a vertebra. When reporting codes for a laminectomy or laminotomy (hemilaminectomy) procedure, determine the following:

- Anatomical site
- Surgical approach
- Type of procedure performed

 Coding Tip

- A laminotomy is also known as a hemilaminectomy. Therefore, review of the operative report to differentiate between laminectomy and laminotomy (or hemilaminectomy) is required.
- When a laminotomy is performed during the same operative session as a laminectomy, the laminotomy code is not reported separately.

When codes are reported for laminotomy procedures, just one vertebral interspace in a specific area of the spine is accessed. When additional interspace(s) are accessed for laminotomy during the same operative session, report appropriate add-on code(s) in addition to the primary procedure code.

> **EXAMPLE:** Patient underwent hemilaminectomy with decompression of nerve roots and partial facetectomy and excision of herniated intervertebral disc, C1-C2. Report code 63040. (C1-C2 is one interspace; thus, code 63040 is reported once.)

Transpedicular or Costovertebral Approach for Posterolateral Extradural Exploration/Decompression

Extradural exploration/decompression procedures are performed using a transpedicular or costovertebral approach.

- A **transpedicular approach** is performed through and inside the pedicle (segment between transverse process and vertebral body) of a thoracic vertebra to access a thoracic disc. This approach does not require retraction of the spinal cord, but it may involve removal of the lamina and facet joint.

- A **costovertebral approach** is performed where the ribs articulate (connect) with thoracic vertebrae. (**Costovertebral** refers to that area of the thoracic spine where the rib meets the vertebra.) The physician makes an incision laterally to the spine, cutting through epidermis, dermis, subcutaneous tissue, fascia, muscle tissue, and a section of rib.

> **EXAMPLE:** Patient underwent decompression of spinal cord at T1 via costovertebral approach. Report code 63064.

Anterior or Anterolateral Approach for Extradural Exploration/Decompression

A **discectomy** is the removal of an intervertebral disc. Make sure you review the operative report to identify the *number of interspaces removed* (e.g., C1-C2 describes one interspace, and C1-C2 and C2-C3 describe two interspaces) (Figure 16-20).

A **corpectomy** is the removal of a portion of the vertebra and adjacent intervertebral discs. Its purpose is for the decompression of the spinal cord and spinal nerves. A bone graft is placed to reconstruct the spine and provide stability. Make sure you review the operative report to identify the *number of segments removed* (e.g., C1 describes one segment, and C1-C2 describes two segments) (Figure 16-20).

 Coding Tip

- **Osteophytectomy** is the removal of bone spurs to relieve compression of the spinal cord or nerve roots.

- The placement of graft material (obtained from the ilium or the removed rib) into the disc space is reported with a code, when performed. Grafting is performed to allow for proper spacing between vertebrae and to promote spinal fusion.

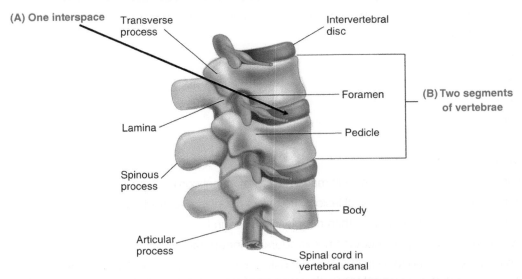

FIGURE 16-20 Interspaces and vertebrae (A) One interspace (B) Two segments of vertebrae

Exploration/decompression procedures are performed using an anterior or anterolateral approach.

- An **anterior approach** involves making an incision overlying the intervertebral disc by cutting through epidermis, dermis, subcutaneous tissue, fascia, and muscle tissue.

- An **anterolateral approach** involves making an incision along (and removing) the rib that corresponds to the vertebra that is located above the compressed intervertebral disc.

> **EXAMPLE:** Patient underwent anterior discectomy with decompression of spinal cord, including osteophytectomy, C2-C3. Report code 63075.

Lateral Extracavitary Approach (LECA) for Extradural Exploration/Decompression

For the **lateral extracavitary approach (LECA)**, a midline incision is made in the area of the affected vertebral segment (e.g., fractured vertebra or vertebral tumor), and the incision is inferiorly curved out to the lateral plane. Paraspinous muscles are mobilized medially (denervating and devascularizing these structures). The muscles are lifted from the spinous process, and they are divided and lifted from the ribs, exposing the vertebral segment.

> **EXAMPLE:** Patient underwent complete vertebral corpectomy with decompression of spinal cord, T1. Report code 63101.

Incision

A laminectomy with cordotomy procedure may be performed as a one-stage or two-stage procedure.

> **EXAMPLE:** Patient underwent one-stage cervical laminectomy procedure with cordotomy and section of one spinothalamic tract. Report code 63194.
>
> On June 10, the patient underwent the first procedure for a two-stage cervical laminectomy procedure with cordotomy and section of both spinothalamic tracts. On June 17, the patient underwent the second of the two-stage procedure. Report code 63198. (Code 63198 is reported just once for this two-stage procedure.)

Excision by Laminectomy of Lesion Other Than Herniated Disc

When reporting codes for excision by laminectomy of lesion other than herniated disc, review the operative report to identify the following:

- Anatomical site
  - Cervical
  - Thoracic
  - Lumbar
  - Sacral
- Type of procedure performed
  - Excision or occlusion of arteriovenous malformation of spinal cord
  - Excision or evacuation of intraspinal lesion other than neoplasm, extradural
  - Excision of intraspinal lesion other than neoplasm, intradural
  - Biopsy/excision of intraspinal neoplasm, extradural or intradural

An add-on code is reported for osteoplastic reconstruction of dorsal spinal elements following a primary intraspinal procedure, such as laminectomy with drainage of intramedullary cyst/syrinx to subarachnoid space. (Do not add modifier -51 to the add-on code.)

EXAMPLE: Patient underwent laminectomy for excision of intraspinal neoplasm, extradural, thoracic. Report code 63276.

Excision, Anterior or Anterolateral Approach, Intraspinal Lesion

An excision code is reported for "vertebral corpectomy (vertebral body resection), partial or complete, for excision of intraspinal lesion, single segment; each additional segment." An add-on code is reported for each additional segment in addition to the code for the single segment. (Do *not* add modifier -51 to the add-on code.)

EXAMPLE: Patient underwent partial vertebral corpectomy for excision of an intraspinal lesion, extradural, C1 and C2. Report codes 63300 and 63308.

Stereotaxis

Stereotaxis uses a stereotactic guidance system to allow the physician to determine three-dimensional coordinates to

- Create a lesion on the spinal cord (to alleviate chronic pain in a particular part of the body).
- Stimulate the spinal cord percutaneously (to create a lesion that will block pain).
- Facilitate the biopsy, aspiration, or excision of a spinal cord lesion.

EXAMPLE: Patient underwent stereotactic percutaneous electrical stimulation of the spinal cord to create a lesion to block severe pain. Report code 63600.

Stereotactic Radiosurgery (Spinal)

Spinal stereotactic radiosurgery uses externally generated ionizing radiation to inactivate or eradicate spinal targets without the need to make an incision.

EXAMPLE: Patient underwent particle beam stereotactic radiosurgery, 1 spinal lesion. Report code 63620.

Neurostimulators (Spinal)

A spinal neurostimulator system includes an electrode and a pulse generator that are implanted along the spine to alleviate pain or control spasms. Neurostimulator codes describe codes for procedures used to implant, revise, and place neurostimulators along the spine. Codes for the implantation or placement and removal or revision of the neurostimulators are reported separately.

EXAMPLE: Patient underwent percutaneous implantation of neurostimulator electrode array, epidural. Report code 63650.

Coding Tip

Initial and subsequent electronic analysis and programming of neurostimulator pulse generators are reported with Medicine section codes.

Repair

When reporting repair codes, do not add modifier -63 (Procedure Performed on Infants Less Than 4 kg). (Modifier -63 is added to indicate significantly increased complexity and physician work associated with procedures performed on infants who weigh less than 4 kg.) It is not appropriate to add modifier -63 to these repair codes because the additional complexity and work is already included in the procedure codes.

EXAMPLE: Patient underwent repair of meningocele,10 cm in diameter. Report code 63702.

Shunt, Spinal CSF

The Shunt, Spinal CSF heading classifies procedures performed on the lumbar spine (not the brain).

EXAMPLE: Patient underwent creation of percutaneous shunt, lumbar, subarachnoid-peritoneal. Report code 63741.

 Coding Tip

For CSF shunt procedures performed on the brain, report codes located under the Skull, Meninges, and Brain heading.

Extracranial Nerves, Peripheral Nerves, and Autonomic Nervous System

The Extracranial Nerves, Peripheral Nerves, and Autonomic Nervous System heading describes procedures performed on these types of nerves. To report procedure codes properly, review the operative report to identify the following:

- Anatomical site (e.g., somatic nerve or sympathetic nerve)
- Type of procedure performed (e.g., injection or neurostimulator implantation)

Introduction/Injection of Anesthetic Agent (Nerve Block), Diagnostic or Therapeutic

The introduction or injection of an anesthetic agent (e.g., nerve block) are performed on somatic and sympathetic nerves for diagnostic and therapeutic reasons (e.g., pain management).

- **Somatic nerves** control voluntary movements (performed by skeletal muscles) and conscious sensation (e.g., hearing, sight, and touch), and they include voluntary motor and sensory nerves.
- **Sympathetic nerves** are part of the involuntary autonomic nervous system and originate in the thoracic and lumbar regions of the spinal cord; they inhibit (or oppose) the physiological effects of the parasympathetic nervous system (e.g., contract blood vessels, increase heart rate, and reduce digestive secretions).

To properly report codes (e.g., nerve blocks), review the operative report to identify the following:

- Type of substance injected (e.g., anesthetic or neurolytic)
- Nerves involved (e.g., somatic or sympathetic)
- Type of block (e.g., single, multiple, or regional)
- Duration of the infusion

EXAMPLE: Patient underwent injection of anesthetic agent, facial nerve. Report code 64402.

 Coding Tip

When injections into an area *surrounding the spinal cord* are performed, report pain management codes (instead of injection into nerve codes).

Neurostimulators (Peripheral Nerve)

A peripheral nerve neurostimulator system includes an electrode and a pulse generator that are implanted along peripheral nerves to alleviate pain or control spasms. Codes for the implantation or placement and removal or revision of the neurostimulators are reported separately.

EXAMPLE: Patient underwent percutaneous implantation of neurostimulator electrode array, cranial nerve. Report code 64553.

 Coding Tip

Initial and subsequent electronic analysis and programming of neurostimulator pulse generators are reported with Medicine section codes.

Destruction by Neurolytic Agent (e.g., Chemical, Thermal, Electrical, or Radiofrequency), Chemodenervation

Procedures that include destruction by neurolytic agent (e.g., chemical, thermal, electrical, or radiofrequency), somatic or sympathetic nerves also include the injection of other therapeutic agents, such as corticosteroids.

EXAMPLE: Patient underwent destruction by neurolytic agent, intercostal nerve. Report code 64620.

Neuroplasty (Exploration, Neurolysis, or Nerve Decompression)

Neuroplasty is the freeing or decompression of an intact nerve from scar tissue. Neuroplasty also includes decompression, exploration, external neurolysis, and/or nerve transposition, which are not coded and reported separately.

 Coding Tip

When internal neurolysis (included in neuroplasty) requires the use of an operating microscope, report add-on code 64727 in addition to the neuroplasty code.

Carpal Tunnel Release

The **carpal tunnel** receives its name from the eight bones in the wrist (carpals) that form a tunnel-like structure. The tunnel is filled with flexor tendons that control finger movement and provide a pathway for the median nerve to reach sensory cells in the hand.

Repetitive flexing and extension of the wrist (e.g., repetitive motion injuries due to a job such as keyboarding or assembly line work) may cause a thickening of the protective sheaths that surround each of the tendons. When the tendon sheaths become swollen (**tenosynovitis**), increased pressure is applied to the median nerve, producing carpal tunnel syndrome.

Carpal tunnel syndrome (Figure 16-21) is a painful progressive condition caused by compression of the median nerve at the wrist. Symptoms usually begin with numbness, pain, and weakness in the hand and wrist. Then pain radiates up the arm. As symptoms worsen, a tingling sensation may result along with decreased grip strength.

 Coding Tip

When the release of the transverse carpal ligament is performed endoscopically, report Musculoskeletal System subsection code 29848.

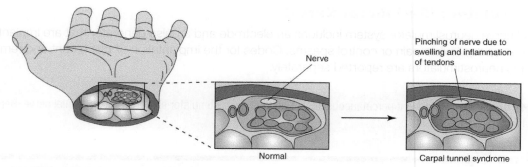

FIGURE 16-21 Carpal tunnel syndrome

Surgical treatment of carpal tunnel syndrome includes surgery to release compression of the median nerve. (Anti-inflammatory drugs and hand/wrist splinting are also used to reduce tendon swelling.)

> **EXAMPLE:** Patient underwent an open procedure that included neuroplasty and transposition of the median nerve at the carpal tunnel. Report code 64721.

Transection or Avulsion

Transection or avulsion procedures involve surgically removing a nerve (e.g., eliminate pain).

> **EXAMPLE:** Patient underwent lingual nerve transection due to continuous pain and burning sensation of the tongue. Report code 64740.

Excision

Excision procedures are performed on somatic and sympathetic nerves.

> **EXAMPLE:** Patient underwent excision of neuroma, digital nerves, left thumb, and left second digit. Report codes 64776-FA and 64778-F1.

Neurorrhaphy and Neurorrhaphy with Nerve Graft, Vein Graft, or Conduit

Neurorrhaphy (repair of nerves) procedures include the suture and anastomosis of proximal nerves (e.g., facial-spinal and facial-hypoglossal). For neurorrhaphy with nerve graft procedures, the operative report should be reviewed to identify the following:

- Anatomical site (e.g., head and neck, hand or foot, or arm or leg)
- Length of the nerve graft (e.g., up to 4 cm in length or more than 4 cm in length)

> **EXAMPLE:** Patient underwent suture of brachial plexus nerve. Report code 64861.

Exercise 16.6 – Nervous System Subsection

Instructions: Assign the CPT code(s) and appropriate modifier(s) to each statement.

1. Burr holes were drilled into the infratentorial area, and an exploratory craniotomy was performed during the same operative session.

_____

Exercise 16.6 – *continued*

2. Burr holes were created, and a ventricular reservoir was implanted.

   _____

3. The physician inserted a subcutaneous pump for connection to a ventricular (brain) catheter.

   _____

4. The physician reprogrammed a shunt on a patient with an implanted programmable cerebrospinal fluid valve and shunt system to decrease the shunt pressure.

   _____

5. The physician aspirated shunt tubing with a needle to determine functioning.

   _____

6. Gill laminectomy with decompression of lumbar nerve roots.

   _____

7. Diagnostic lumbar puncture.

   _____

8. Removal of lamina and insertion of lumboperitoneal (LP) shunt for drainage of excess cerebrospinal fluid.

   _____

9. Replacement of a nonprogrammable epidural drug infusion pump.

   _____

10. Decompression of spinal cord with removal of herniated disc via costovertebral approach, T1.

    _____

11. Nerve block, axillary nerve.

    _____

12. Bilateral lumbar paravertebral facet joint injections, two levels.

    _____

13. Single intercostal nerve block injection.

    _____

14. Excision of sciatic nerve neuroma.

    _____

15. Percutaneous implantation of neurostimulator electrode array, cranial nerve.

    _____

Eye and Ocular Adnexa Subsection

The **Eye and Ocular Adnexa** subsection describes procedures performed on the eyeball, anterior and posterior segment, ocular adnexa, and conjunctivae (Figure 16-22). When reporting codes, review the operative report to identify the following:

- Anatomical site (e.g., eyeball)
- Type of procedure (e.g., retinal repair)

Eye and Ocular Adnexa subsection codes also include surgery to remove eyelid lesions and the repair or reconstruction of orbits, eyeballs, and eyelids.

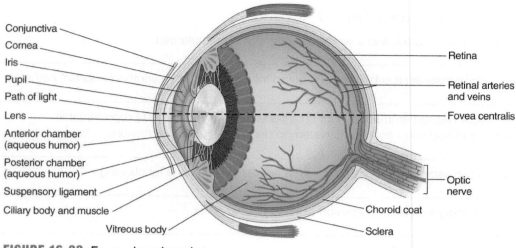

FIGURE 16-22 Eye and ocular adnexa

Coding Tip

Ophthalmologic procedures are also located in the

- Integumentary System subsection (CPT Surgery) (e.g., shaving of epidermal lesions from the eyelid
- Musculoskeletal System subsection (CPT Surgery) (e.g., orbital wall decompression with nasal/sinus endoscopy
- Medicine section (e.g., diagnostic/therapeutic ophthalmologic services

NOTE:

The following HCPCS level II modifiers are added to Eyelid heading codes when appropriate:

- E1 (upper left eyelid)
- E2 (lower left eyelid)
- E3 (upper right eyelid)
- E4 (lower right eyelid)

Eyeball

The **eyeball**, or **globe**, contains the choroid, retina, and sclera. The **sclera** is the white of the eye that comprises the eye's outer layer; it contains fibrous tissue that maintains the eye's shape and protects the eye's inner layers. The **cornea** is the transparent layer on the eye's surface; it covers the iris and pupil and provides focusing power. The **uvea** is the eye's vascular layer, which includes the choroid, ciliary body (ciliary muscle), and iris. The **choroid** is the opaque layer behind the retina that contains blood vessels. The **iris** is colored tissue that surrounds the pupil. The **pupil** is the black opening in the center of the iris that permits light to enter the eye. The **lens** is a clear, flexible, curved structure that focuses images on the retina. The **ciliary body**, or **ciliary muscle**, adjusts the shape of the lens and focuses light rays onto the retina. The **retina** contains nerve tissue.

An **evisceration of ocular contents** includes removal of the contents of the eyeball (choroid, ciliary muscles, iris, lens, retina, and vitreous); the sclera remains intact. (An implant may or may not be placed into the scleral shell.)

An **enucleation of the eye** includes severing the eyeball from extraorbital muscles and the optic nerve and removing it. (An implant may or may not be placed and attached to extraocular muscles.)

An **exenteration of the orbit** includes the removal of orbital contents and may also include removal of bone, muscle, and/or the myocutaneous flap. When a skin graft is placed, report a code from the Integumentary subsection (in addition to the exenteration of the orbit code). When the eyelid is repaired, report a code from the Reconstruction Area of the Eyelids subheading (in addition to the exenteration of the orbit code).

Codes 65125–65175 are reported for procedures performed to modify an ocular implant (e.g., alter the shape of a prosthesis to create a better fit). An **orbital implant** is inserted outside the muscular cone into the eye socket, and an intraocular lens (IOL) is placed. An **ocular implant** is inserted inside the muscular cone.

> **EXAMPLE:** Patient underwent secondary insertion of ocular implant (after having undergone previous evisceration) into the scleral shell. Report code 65130.

CPT differentiates between the removal of a foreign body located in the eye and removal of implanted material (e.g., ocular implant). When coding the removal of a foreign body from the external eyeball, review the operative report to identify the following:

- Where the location is (e.g., intraocular)
- Whether a foreign body is embedded
- Whether a slit lamp was used

Most foreign bodies of the eye are located in the cornea and conjunctiva. Fluorescein staining with slit lamp inspection is used to visualize a corneal foreign body or abrasion.

For laceration repairs of ocular structures, an extensive conjunctival laceration may also include a graft or flap. The repair of a laceration includes use of a conjunctival flap and restoration of anterior chamber by air or saline injection. Do *not* separately code and report these procedures.

> **EXAMPLE:** Patient underwent the removal of foreign body, external eye, superficial conjunctiva. Report code 65205.

Anterior Segment

Anterior Segment heading codes are reported for procedures performed on the anterior segment of the eye, which includes the cornea, anterior chamber, anterior sclera, iris, ciliary body (ciliary muscle), and lens.

- Corneal transplant (e.g., keratoplasty) is a common procedure that includes use of fresh or preserved grafts and preparation of donor material.
- Radial keratotomy (Figure 16-23) corrects myopia; the surgeon makes numerous radial incisions (like the pattern of spokes of a wheel) extending from the pupil to the periphery of the cornea. (The procedure was accidentally discovered by Dr. Svyatoslav Fyodorov, who removed pieces of glass from a patient's eye and noted that the patient's eyesight improved after removal of the glass. The lacerations to the cornea resulted in the improved eyesight.)

(A)

(B)

(C)

FIGURE 16-23 Radial keratotomy (A) Cross-section of eye prior to surgery (B) Small incisions are made in the cornea from the middle outward. (C) Radial keratotomy causes the cornea to become flatter, improving vision.

- Cataract removal codes include the following procedures, which are not separately coded and reported:

    - Anterior and posterior capsulotomy
    - Iridectomy
    - Iridotomy
    - Lateral canthotomy
    - Subconjunctival or subtenon injections

    - Use of viscoelastic agents, enzymatic zonulysis, and other pharmacologic agents
    - Implantation of an IOL prosthesis *when performed during the same operative session*

The following two surgical methods are typically used to remove the lens and cataracts:

- **Intracapsular cataract extraction (ICCE)**: Removal of lens and surrounding capsule
- **Extracapsular cataract extraction (ECCE)**: Removal of lens and anterior portion of capsule

The extracapsular cataract removal with insertion of an IOL (Figure 16-24) is a common procedure. An iridectomy, trabeculectomy, and anterior vitrectomy may also be performed during the same operative session as the cataract removal. Codes for these procedures are *not* reported separately.

 Coding Tip

When an iridectomy is performed to accomplish the cataract extraction, it is considered an integral part of the procedure and is not reported separately.

EXAMPLE: A patient presents with a cataract and evidence of glaucoma, left eye. Trabeculectomy is performed on August 15 as treatment for the glaucoma. Extracapsular cataract extraction with insertion of IOL prosthesis is performed on August 30 as treatment for the cataract. Report codes 66170-LT (August 15) and 66984-LT (August 30). (Code 99070 or C1780 is also reported.)

Posterior Segment

Posterior segment procedures are performed on the vitreous, retina or choroid, and sclera. Vitreous heading codes include the removal and aspiration of vitreous and other fluids. Retina or Choroid heading codes include subheadings for repair, prophylaxis, and destruction. Some retinal detachment repair procedures also include procedures performed on the vitreous.

EXAMPLE: Code 67108 is reported for the repair of a retinal detachment. The code includes the following procedures: vitrectomy, air or gas tamponade, focal endolaser photocoagulation, cryotherapy, drainage of subretinal fluid, scleral buckling, and/or removal of lens by same technique. This means that separate codes are not reported for the included procedures.

FIGURE 16-24 Cataract extraction with placement of intraocular lens

Ocular Adnexa

The **ocular adnexa** includes the orbit, eye muscles, eyelids, eyelashes, conjunctiva, and lacrimal apparatus. The **orbit**, or **eye socket**, is the bony cavity in the skull that contains and protects the eyeball (and its associated blood vessels, muscles, and nerves). The eye muscles work together to enable binocular vision. The eyelids protect the eyeball and keep its surface moist. The eyebrows and eyelashes prevent debris from getting into the eyes. The **conjunctiva** is a mucous membrane that lines the underside of each eyelid and forms a protective covering over the exposed surface of the eyeball. The **lacrimal apparatus**, or **tear apparatus**, contains structures that produce, store, and remove tears.

These codes are reported for procedures performed on the eyelid that involve more than skin. Many of these codes also include surgery to correct **strabismus**, which is improperly aligned eyes, such as cross-eyes (one eye points inward) and walleye (one eye points outward). Such codes are reported for exploration, excision, and decompression procedures performed on the orbit, in addition to injections and orbital implants.

Strabismus surgery is performed on extraocular muscles to realign the eyes. Each strabismus surgery code reflects a procedure performed on one eye (unilateral), which means that modifier -50 is added to the appropriate code when the procedure is performed on both eyes. Two methods are used to correct the alignment of eye muscles.

- Recession: Lengthening the muscle
- Resection: Shortening the muscle

For a recession procedure, the muscle is detached from the attachment site on the surface of the eyeball and reattached along the surface of the eye. For a resection procedure, a small portion of the muscle is removed and the eye muscle is reattached to the original insertion site.

Coding Tip

Codes for the treatment of orbital bone fractures (e.g., frontal, sphenoid, zygomatic, maxilla, ethmoid, and lacrimal) are located in the Musculoskeletal System section.

When it is medically necessary to inject sclerosing agents during the same operative session as surgery to correct glaucoma, that service is included in the glaucoma surgery.

EXAMPLE: Patient underwent removal of an embedded foreign body, left lower eyelid. Report code 67938-E2.

Conjunctiva

Conjunctiva codes are reported for procedures performed on the conjunctiva, including the following:

- Incision and drainage
- Excision and/or destruction
- Injection
- Conjunctivoplasty
- Other procedures
- Lacrimal system

EXAMPLE: Patient underwent incision and drainage of a conjunctival cyst of the right upper eyelid. Report code 68020-E3.

A **trachoma** is a chronic inflammation of the conjunctiva in which granulations form. The physician uses biomicroscopic guidance to remove the conjunctival follicles with a cotton tipped swab or a curette without making an incision. Physicians often use biomicroscopic guidance (e.g., an optical instrument that looks like a microscope with two eyepieces) to treat trachoma. A slit lamp (e.g., a specialized magnifying microscope used to examine the structures of the eye) is also used with the biomicroscope.

NOTE:

Per the CPT note below the "Eye and Ocular Adnexa" subsection, do not report code 69990 (microsurgical techniques requiring use of operating microscope) in addition to codes 65091–68850. Use of the operating microscope is not reported separately because it is considered an essential part of eye and ocular adnexa procedures.

When a subconjunctival injection with a local anesthetic is performed as part of a more extensive anesthetic procedure (e.g., peribulbar or retrobulbar block), do not separately code and report the injection procedure. The injection procedure is considered a routine part of the anesthetic procedure and does not represent a separate service.

Conjunctivoplasty codes describe plastic surgery procedures performed on the conjunctiva. The following procedures are included in conjunctivoplasty codes, which means that they are *not* coded and reported separately: incision and drainage, excision and/or destruction, and injection of conjunctiva.

The lacrimal system keeps the cornea and conjunctiva moist through tear production. Codes reported for procedures performed on the lacrimal system include incision, excision, repair, and probing and/or related procedures.

A common procedure is the repair of the **lacrimal puncta**, which are small openings in the inner canthus of the eyelids that channel tears. There are two puncta in each eye, an upper and lower punctum. Thus, when both puncta in one eye are treated, report the appropriate code twice. According to *CPT Assistant* (June 1996), when all puncta in both eyes are treated (four puncta), codes 68705 and 68760–68761 are reported four times.

EXAMPLE: Patient underwent closure of the lacrimal puncta via laser surgery, both eyes. Report codes 68760, 68760, 68760, and 68760.

Exercise 16.7 – Eye and Ocular Adnexa Subsection

Instructions: Assign the CPT code(s) and appropriate modifier(s) to each statement.

1. Removal of foreign body from cornea of right eye, using a slit lamp.
   _____

2. Repair of corneal laceration with removal of foreign body, left eye.
   _____

3. Modification of ocular implant with replacement of pegs.
   _____

4. Nonmagnetic extraction of an intraocular foreign body from posterior segment of right eye.
   _____

5. A patient complained of sudden onset of tearing and pain in the right eye. After eversion of the upper lid, a small wood fragment was removed.
   _____

6. Cryotherapy destruction of corneal lesion, left eye.
   _____

7. Endoscopic goniotomy, right eye.
   _____

8. Insertion of intraocular lens four weeks after right cataract removal.
   _____

9. Removal of corneal lesion using scleral scissors, left eye.
   _____

(continues)

Exercise 16.7 – *continued*

10. Extracapsular cataract removal with insertion of intraocular lens prosthesis, left eye.

_____

11. Aspiration of vitreous fluid, pars plana approach, right eye.

_____

12. Laser photocoagulation of choroidal lesion, right eye, using fluorescein angiogram as a guide.

_____

13. Diathermy for treatment of a patient with progressive diabetic retinopathy, both eyes.

_____

14. Scleral reinforcement with graft, left eye.

_____

15. Prophylactic treatment of retinal detachment, left eye, using cryotherapy, four sessions.

_____

16. Fine-needle aspiration of orbit, right eye.

_____

17. Strabismus surgery that included a recession procedure of two horizontal muscles, both eyes.

_____

18. Removal of chalazions from right upper eyelid and left upper eyelid.

_____

19. Strabismus surgery was performed for the first time on one horizontal muscle of the right eye and on the superior oblique muscle of the left eye.

_____

20. Strabismus surgery performed on two horizontal muscles during which a transposition procedure was also performed to detach and relocate two rectus muscles next to a paralyzed muscle, right eye.

_____

21. Injection of cortical steroid into subconjunctival space, left eye.

_____

22. Closure of a total of four lacrimal puncta using collagen plugs, both eyes.

_____

23. Bilateral nasolacrimal duct probing with irrigation.

_____

24. Cauterization to correct everted upper and lower lacrimal puncta, left eye.

_____

25. Incision and drainage, conjunctival cyst, right eye.

_____

Auditory System Subsection

The **Auditory System** (Figure 16-25) subsection is organized anatomically according to the following:

- External ear
- Middle ear
- Inner ear
- Temporal bone, middle fossa approach

Subsection notes direct the coder to otorhinolaryngologic service codes in the Medicine section for diagnostic services performed on the auditory system.

FIGURE 16-25 The auditory system

FIGURE 16-26 Removal of impacted cerumen

 Coding Tip

Most procedures classified in the Auditory System subsection are unilateral. Report modifier -LT (Left side), -RT (Right side), or -50 (Bilateral Procedure) as appropriate.

External Ear

The **external ear** includes the auricle (or pinna) and the external auditory meatus (or ear canal). The incision, excision, removal of foreign body, repair, and other procedures are performed on the external ear.

A frequently performed procedure is the "removal of impacted cerumen (separate procedure), one or both ears" (Figure 16-26), which is reported just once when the procedure is performed bilaterally.

EXAMPLE: Patient underwent biopsy, external ear, left. Report code 69100-LT.

(A)   (B)   (C)

FIGURE 16-27 Tympanoplasty (A) Tympanic membrane incision (B) Tube placement (C) Tympanoplasty completed

Middle Ear

The **middle ear** includes the tympanic membrane, auditory ossicles, muscles, and conduction pathways. A commonly performed procedure is "tympanostomy (requiring insertion of ventilation tube), local or topical anesthesia." This procedure is typically performed on children who have chronic ear infections.

A **myringotomy**, or **tympanostomy**, is the surgical incision of the tympanic membrane, and it is usually performed to release pressure or fluid. A **tympanoplasty** is the repair or reconstruction of the eardrum (Figure 16-27).

> **EXAMPLE:** Patient underwent complete mastoidectomy, left ear. Report code 69502-LT.

Inner Ear

The **inner ear** includes the cochlea, saccule, acoustic nerve (e.g., auditory portion), semicircular canals, utricle, and superior and inferior vestibular nerves (e.g., vestibular portion). A labyrinthotomy procedure is performed using a transcanal approach, and all required infusions performed on initial and subsequent days of treatment are included in the reported code.

A **cochlear implant** is an implanted electronic device for treatment of sensory deafness. A vestibular nerve section using a transcranial approach includes the removal of the semicircular canals as well as bone over the internal auditory canal.

> **EXAMPLE:** Patient underwent cochlear device implantation with mastoidectomy, right and left ears. Report code 69930-50.

Temporal Bone, Middle Fossa Approach

Temporal bone, middle fossa approach codes are reported for nerve decompression or repair procedures. A common procedure performed to repair facial nerve damage is total nerve decompression, which is used to treat symptoms of **Bell's palsy** (unilateral paralysis of facial muscles resulting from dysfunction of the 7th cranial nerve, probably due to a viral infection).

> **EXAMPLE:** Patient underwent decompression of the internal auditory canal, left ear. Report code 69960-LT.

Exercise 16.8 – Auditory System Subsection

Instructions: Assign the CPT code(s) and appropriate modifier(s) to each statement.

1. Simple incision and drainage, abscess, left external ear.

   _____

2. Removal of a button from the left ear canal of a 2-year-old child.

   _____

Exercise 16.8 – *continued*

3. Plastic surgeon reduced the size of a protruding right ear.

_____

4. Routine cleaning (simple debridement) of mastoidectomy cavity, right ear.

_____

5. A family physician pierced a 1-year-old girl's ears.

_____

6. With the patient under general anesthesia, the physician removed ventilating tubes from both ears.

_____

7. With the patient under general anesthesia, tympanostomy with insertion of ventilating tubes was performed.

_____

8. Transcanal tympanolysis, right.

_____

9. Replacement of a bone conduction hearing device and removal of old device, left ear.

_____

10. Mobilization of stapes on the left.

_____

11. Decompression of intratemporal nerve, lateral to geniculate ganglion.

_____

12. Physician implanted a cochlear device bilaterally.

_____

13. A physician repaired a tympanic membrane with patch, right ear.

_____

14. Mastoidectomy and tympanoplasty with ossicular chain reconstruction, left ear.

_____

15. Neurectomy of tympanic nerve, left side.

_____

16. Removal of temporal bone tumor, left side.

_____

17. A physician treated a patient who was diagnosed with a tumor of the facial nerve by performing total facial nerve repair and grafting the nerve.

_____

18. Decompression internal auditory canal, right side.

_____

19. A physician performed an endolymphatic sac operation.

_____

20. Transcranial vestibular nerve section.

_____

Operating Microscope Subsection

When an **operating microscope** is used during a surgical procedure to perform microsurgery techniques, report add-on code 69990 in addition to the primary procedure code.

Coding Tip

Do *not* report code 69990 for

- Visualization with a magnifying loupe or corrected vision.
- Procedures for which use of an operating microscope is an inclusive component. (Refer to Operating Microscope heading notes for a list of excluded codes.)

EXAMPLE: Patient underwent vestibular nerve section, transcranial approach, with use of an operating microscope. Report codes 69950 and 69990.

Exercise 16.9 – Operating Microscope Subsection

Instructions: Assign the CPT code(s) and appropriate modifier(s) to each statement.

1. An otolaryngologist used a magnifying loupe to perform a tympanic membrane repair.

2. Diagnostic direct laryngoscopy with use of an operating microscope.

3. The physician uses an operating microscope while performing a partial mastectomy, right breast.

4. Microsurgical epididymovasostomy, bilateral.

5. The physician used an operating microscope to perform a hypophysectomy.

Summary

For procedures performed on the male genital system, code assignment is determined according to approach (e.g., incision, destruction, excision, or introduction) and reason for surgery. Reproductive System Procedures classify the placement of needles into pelvic organs and/or genitalia for subsequent interstitial radioelement application. Intersex surgery is performed as a series of staged procedures to transform the normal adult genitalia of one sex to that of the other sex (genital reconstructive surgery or sex reassignment surgery).

Codes classified in the Female Genital System heading are reported for procedures performed on women who are *not* pregnant. (Codes for women who are pregnant are reported from the Maternity Care and Delivery heading.) When reporting codes for procedures performed on the female genital system, review the operative report to identify the anatomy on which the procedure was performed (e.g., vulva, perineum, introitus, or vagina) and the surgical approach.

The three stages of pregnancy care include services provided as part of total obstetrical care: antepartum care, delivery of the baby, and postpartum care. Total obstetrical care does *not* include diagnostic procedures, physician office visits for unrelated conditions incidental to pregnancy, and additional visits due to high-risk conditions or medical complications of pregnancy. Codes for these services are separately reported from the Evaluation and Management and Medicine sections of CPT. The treatment of surgical complications associated with pregnancy are separately reported with codes from the Surgery section.

The Endocrine System subsection includes procedures performed on the endocrine glands and the carotid body. Codes for Nervous System subsection procedures are arranged anatomically (skull, meninges, and brain; spine and spinal cord; and extracranial nerves, peripheral nerves, and autonomic nervous system). Nervous system procedures are performed using a variety of approaches for specific purposes.

The Eye and Ocular Adnexa subsection describes procedures performed on the eyeball, anterior and posterior segment, ocular adnexa, and conjunctivae. When reporting codes, review the operative report to identify the anatomical site and type of procedure. The Auditory System subsection is organized anatomically according to the external ear; middle ear; inner ear; and temporal bone, middle fossa approach. When an operating microscope is used during a surgical procedure to perform microsurgery techniques, report add-on code 69990 in addition to the primary procedure code when appropriate.

Internet Links

American Academy of Family Physicians: Go to *www.aafp.org*, click on the Practice Management link, and then click on the Medical Billing and Coding link below the Payment for Physicians heading.

American Academy of Otolaryngology—Head and Neck Surgery: *www.entnet.org*

American Association of Neurological Surgeons: *www.aans.org*

American Congress of Obstetricians and Gynecologists: Go to *www.acog.org*, click on the Practice Management link, and then click on the Coding link.

Center for Male Reproductive Medicine (CMRM) and Vasectomy Reversal: *www.malereproduction.com*

Center for Male Reproductive Medicine and Microsurgery: *www.maleinfertility.org*

The Eye Digest: *www.scribd.com/eyeMD*

FamilyDoctor.org: Go to *www.familydoctor.org*, click on the Family Health link, and click on the Pregnancy and Childbirth link to locate articles.

Lacrimedics, Inc.: Go to *www.lacrimedics.com*, and click on the Patients link.

Office on Women's Health: *www.womenshealth.gov*

Society for Endocrinology: *www.endocrinology.org*

Review

Multiple Choice

Instructions: Circle the most appropriate response.

1. The tube that carries spermatozoa from the testis is the:
   a. prostate gland.
   b. urethra.
   c. varicocele.
   d. vas deferens.

2. Which procedure involves the direct visualization of the cervical canal and the uterine cavity and is performed to examine the endometrium?
   a. Colposcopy
   b. Hysteroscopy
   c. LEEP electrodissection conization
   d. Loop electrodissection conization

3. According to the notes below the Maternity Care and Delivery subsection of Surgery, which service is included in codes reported for maternity care and delivery?
    a. Cordocentesis
    b. Episiotomy
    c. Fetal nonstress test
    d. Insertion of cervical dilator

4. How many glands are included in the endocrine system?
    a. 7
    b. 9
    c. 13
    d. 15

5. When more than one interspace is accessed for laminotomy during the same operative session, report the:
    a. appropriate add-on code(s) in addition to the primary procedure code.
    b. primary code once for each interspace accessed.
    c. primary code only.
    d. primary code with modifier -51.

6. Which surgical approach used in extradural exploration/decompression involves making an incision overlying the intervertebral disc and cutting through epidermis, dermis, subcutaneous, fascia, and muscle tissue?
    a. Anterior approach
    b. Anterolateral approach
    c. Costovertebral approach
    d. Transpedicular approach

7. Which nerves are part of the involuntary autonomic nervous system, originate in the thoracic and lumbar regions of the spinal cord, and inhibit the physiological effects of the parasympathetic nervous system?
    a. Cranial
    b. Median
    c. Somatic
    d. Sympathetic

8. Which is the freeing or decompression of an intact nerve from scar tissue?
    a. Neuroma
    b. Neuroplasty
    c. Neurorrhaphy
    d. Neurostimulator

9. When all puncta in both eyes are treated during the same encounter, the appropriate code is reported:
    a. once.
    b. twice.
    c. three times.
    d. four times.

10. Which includes the tympanic membrane, auditory ossicles, muscles, and conduction pathways?
    a. Cochlea
    b. Inner ear
    c. Middle ear
    d. Outer ear

11. Plastic repair of the penis due to epispadias distal to external sphincter. Patient was diagnosed with incontinence. Which CPT code is assigned?
    a. 54360
    b. 54380
    c. 54385
    d. 54390

12. Patient placed under anesthesia and an impacted foreign body removed from vagina. Which CPT code is assigned?
    a. 57110
    b. 57111
    c. 57135
    d. 57415

13. Surgical treatment of ovarian ectopic pregnancy. Vaginal salpingectomy. Which CPT code is assigned?
    a. 59120
    b. 59130
    c. 59140
    d. 59150

14. Excision of thyroglossal duct cyst. Which CPT code is assigned?
    a. 60200
    b. 60280
    c. 60281
    d. 60600

15. Intersex surgery, female to male. Which CPT code(s) are assigned?
    a. 55970
    b. 55980
    c. 54125, 55970
    d. 54125, 55980

16. Replacement of cerebrospinal fluid shunt using operating microscope. Which CPT code(s) are assigned?
    a. 62220, 69990
    b. 62223
    c. 62225
    d. 62230, 69990

17. Insertion of catheters into uterus to facilitate radiation therapy. Which CPT code is assigned?
    a. 49320
    b. 51045
    c. 52005
    d. 55920

18. Laceration repair of conjunctiva by mobilization and rearrangement, with hospitalization. Which CPT code is assigned?

    a. 65270   **b.** 65272   **c.** 65273   **d.** 65285

19. Patient diagnosed as having dislocated lens in left eye. Physician performed intracapsular removal of lens. Which CPT code is assigned?

    a. 66920-LT   **b.** 66930-LT   **c.** 66940-LT   **d.** 66982-LT

20. Transcanal labyrinthectomy. Which CPT code is assigned?

    a. 69801   **b.** 69905   **c.** 69910   **d.** 69915

Coding Practice

Instructions: Assign the CPT code(s) and appropriate modifier(s) to each case.

Male Genital System

1. A biopsy needle was passed up the urethra. Using manual guidance, the surgeon identified the prostate gland and performed a punch biopsy. The needle was withdrawn.

    _____

2. The patient had been diagnosed with hydroceles, which are scheduled to be removed via excision. First, an incision was made of the patient's scrotum. The hydrocele on the right was identified and dissected free. The left side of the patient's body was treated in the same manner for the hydrocele there.

    _____

3. The patient has a papilloma of the penis. This is removed via laser surgery.

    _____

4. After being informed of all of the risks, the parents of a newborn male patient consented to a circumcision. Regional dorsal penile block (anesthesia) was administered by the physician performing the circumcision. The foreskin of the penis was clamped, and excess skin was trimmed. The clamp was left in place, and anti-biotic ointment was applied.

    _____

5. After adequate general anesthesia, the patient's scrotum was incised. The spermatic cord was identified, dissected, and cross-clamped. The right testis was carefully pushed up from the scrotum and excised. All vessels were clamped, and all bleeders were cauterized. The left testis was removed using a similar method. The spermatic cord was cross-clamped and cut.

    _____

6. Patient underwent bilateral vasectomy including postoperative semen examination. The skin over the spermatic cord was injected with a local anesthetic. The scrotum was exposed via an incision, and the tubular structures of this organ were identified. The vas deferens was identified and cut with a small section of the tube removed. The same method was performed on the opposite side.

    _____

7. A prostatectomy was being performed for prostate cancer. An incision was made at the scrotum. A urethrotomy was used to enlarge the penile urethra. The prostate was dissected via the use of an instrument. The prostate as well as supporting anatomical structures were removed. All bleeding was controlled with cauterization. Attention was then directed to pelvic lymph nodes, which were removed on both sides in total for analysis and staging.

    _____

8. Patient underwent reduction of torsion of the left testis. An incision was made in the patient's scrotum. The twisted left testis was identified. The testis was carefully detangled. Excellent blood flow was seen. Four sutures were used to anchor the testis to the wall of the scrotum to prevent further twisting.

9. A patient has a spermatocele. After incising the scrotum, the physician identified the testis and the spermatocele. The spermatocele was dissected from the epididymis.

10. A patient with moderate chordee presents for surgical repair of the penis to straighten the chordee for hypospadias, with mobilization of the urethra.

Reproductive System Procedures and Female Genital System

1. The patient has a diagnosis of recurrent cervical carcinoma with metastatic disease to the ovaries and bladder. After discussing with the patient and informing her of the risks, the patient consented to an abdominal hysterectomy. An incision was made at the pubic area. The fascia and muscle were retracted. The cervix and uterus were identified and excised. The bladder was found to have numerous lesions; it was also removed. The ureters were transplanted to the skin to allow for urine flow. An ileal urinary conduit, in which the ureters are implanted into a segment of small bowel, was done. Patient also underwent placement of needles or catheters into pelvic organs in preparation for subsequent interstitial radioelement application, which will be scheduled postoperatively.

2. An endoscope was inserted into the vulva and passed into the uterus. After gaining access to the cavity, a biopsy of the endometrium was done. The scope was withdrawn.

3. An incision was made in the umbilical region for the insertion of laparoscope; a second incision was made on the right side of the abdomen to pass additional trocars. A Falope ring was inserted and advanced through the trocar to the area of the fallopian tubes. This ring was clamped around the fallopian tubes to provide occlusion.

4. A colposcope was inserted into the patient. This allowed for visualization of the female genital organs. The vagina was found to be normal. The cervix has an area of fibrous tissue, which was biopsied. The endocervical area had an area of inflammation, which was taken away via curettage.

5. After inserting a speculum into the vagina, the physician was able to visualize a vaginal cyst directly. Forceps were used to clamp the cyst. The cyst was excised and sent to pathology for analysis. The speculum was removed.

6. After inserting a speculum into the vagina, the physician identified a Bartholin gland; the cyst was directly visualized. An incision was made, and the cyst was dissected free of the surrounding tissue and mucosa. The wound was closed in layers with absorbable sutures.

7. After insertion of a speculum into the vagina, laser cautery was performed to remove the outer cells of the cervix.

8. The physician performed a salpingostomy and identified a damaged right fallopian tube.

_____

9. After insertion of a speculum into the vagina, a catheter was passed that contained several small embryos. With the use of the catheter, the embryos were inserted into the uterus.

_____

10. After an abdominal incision was made, the left ovary was identified. The ovarian cysts were located and removed in total. The incision was closed with sutures.

_____

Intersex Surgery

1. Second-stage operation was done with the goal of constructing a penis and scrotum. This was done using multiple grafts from the patient's skin and clitoris. A penile prosthesis was implanted into the constructed organ.

_____

2. The new construction of a vagina was the goal in this staged procedure. Using tissue from the patient's penis, a clitoris structure was fashioned. The perineum of the patient was opened to form a vagina. The sides of the vagina were lined with skin grafts to add stability.

_____

Maternity Care and Delivery

1. A neonatologist attached a fetal monitoring electrode to the scalp of the fetus in utero. This was done for seven hours during the labor process. The physician read, interpreted, and made notations on the tracing coming from the electrode data.

_____

2. A patient at 39 weeks' gestation presented in labor. The patient has requested a VBAC (vaginal birth after cesarean). After 20 hours in labor, fetal distress was noted. The patient required a cesarean delivery. All antepartum and postpartum care was provided by the delivering physician.

_____

3. A woman with five fetuses presents for fetal reduction due to her severe preeclampsia. Using the potassium chloride method, two fetal sacs are injected. At the conclusion of the procedure, the woman has three fetal sacs intact.

_____

4. At 11 weeks' gestation, the patient had an incomplete abortion. Due to profuse vaginal bleeding, evacuating the uterus was necessary. Dilation and curettage (D and C) was done with suction of any remaining products of conception.

_____

5. A woman presents after having delivered her baby vaginally en route to the hospital in a private motor vehicle. The newborn was taken directly to the neonatal intensive care unit (NICU) for evaluation. The placenta had not been delivered on route to the hospital. Using abdominal massage, the placenta was delivered.

_____

6. An ectopic pregnancy was confirmed by ultrasound. Via a vaginal approach, the pelvic cavity was visualized and examined. All products of conception were removed using curettage. The pelvic cavity was lavaged with saline solution. The patient's right fallopian tube was affected. This tube was excised.

_____

7. After normal prenatal care, this patient presented in labor at 38 weeks. An episiotomy was done to facilitate delivery. A normal healthy newborn was born via vaginal delivery. The episiotomy was repaired. The patient was discharged with her baby and received postpartum follow-up care in the office.

8. The patient presents for an antepartum visit. This is her fourth scheduled appointment. Her estimated gestational age is 26 weeks. The patient reports heavy vaginal bleeding overnight. After insertion of the speculum, the uterus was examined. Slight bleeding was noted. The patient has had a complete miscarriage. No products of conception are seen. There is no need for surgical intervention.

9. Routine prenatal care was rendered to this patient, who presented at 41 weeks in labor. The patient was examined, and the fetus was found to be in a breech position. The fetus was turned via external abdominal approach into a cephalic position. After the turning of the fetus, an episiotomy was performed. A normal healthy 10-pound infant was born via vaginal delivery. The episiotomy was repaired. Postpartum care was delivered.

Endocrine System

1. The patient's neck was palpated, and a mass was identified on the left. Local anesthesia was administered, and the position of the mass was confirmed again by palpation. A percutaneous core needle was inserted through the skin and underlying tissue into the thyroid mass. The needle was withdrawn with the sample inside the core. The sample will be sent for analysis.

2. After adequate general anesthesia, a cervical incision was made. Skin, fascia, and muscle were retracted to expose the thyroid gland. A severely enlarged left lobe of the thyroid was found. The left lobe was removed in total and sent to pathology for analysis. Parathyroid glands were carefully inspected and found to be normal. These were not removed but were left intact. All bleeders were cauterized. The skin and muscle were closed in layers.

3. After adequate general anesthesia, a midline abdominal incision was made. The retroperitoneal area was identified and found to be normal. The adrenal glands were directly visualized. The left adrenal gland was removed in total. A biopsy sample was taken from the right adrenal gland.

4. After adequate general anesthesia, an incision was made along the thyroglossal duct cyst. A portion of the hyoid bone was removed, and recurrent thyroglossal duct cyst was excised. Wound was packed for secondary closure.

5. After adequate general anesthesia, a cervical incision was made to expose the thyroid and parathyroid glands. The parathyroid glands were directly visualized. The right gland was removed.

6. After several small incisions were made in the patient's back, the laparoscope was introduced. The adrenal gland on the right was identified and examined. It was normal in appearance. The left adrenal gland was found to be enlarged at the tip. This section was removed and passed through the trocar. The scope was removed and the skin incision closed with sutures.

7. After a cervical incision was made, the muscles of the neck were separated to expose the thyroid and parathyroid glands. The right lobe was normal in appearance and size. The left upper thyroid gland had a goiter measuring approximately 3.0 cm. This lobe with the goiter was removed.

_____

8. Based on thyroid biopsy, this patient presented for a total thyroidectomy due to thyroid carcinoma. The neck area was cleaned and draped in the usual fashion. Under general anesthesia, the patient had a cervical incision. A radical neck dissection was performed. After the muscles of the neck were separated, the gland was exposed. Direct visualization showed the gland to be cystic and nodular in nature. The right lobe of the gland was removed first, followed by the left lobe. The parathyroid glands were inspected and appeared to be normal. The thyroid gland in total was removed and sent to pathology for analysis. All bleeders were cauterized. The incision was closed in layers with staples and sutures.

_____

9. Under general anesthesia, a cervical incision at the previous incision site was done. The neck muscles were divided and retracted. The thyroid area was exposed. The absent left lobe of the thyroid was noted. The right lobe of the thyroid was examined. It was found to be very nodular in appearance. This lobe was removed. The parathyroid glands were examined and appeared normal. The specimen of the right lobe was sent to pathology. The muscles were retracted back and closed with staples. The incision was closed in layers.

_____

10. After the patient's adrenal area was accessed through a midline abdominal incision, the retroperitoneal space was explored. A mass was identified adjacent to the left adrenal gland. This was removed. The left adrenal gland, which also appeared abnormal, was removed in total. The incision was closed.

_____

Nervous System

1. After the patient was placed in a prone position, an incision was made over the upper spinal area. The placement of the epidural drug infusion device was in the subcutaneous tissue. The incision was closed with sutures.

_____

2. The greater occipital nerve was identified, and a nerve block (anesthetic agent) injection was performed.

_____

3. The patient presented with a laceration of the digital nerve of the left hand. This was repaired with sutures.

_____

4. A neurostimulator electrode device is placed through the skin to the cranial nerve.

_____

5. The patient presents with a meningocele approximately 4.0 cm in diameter. This was repaired after placing the patient in a prone position and making an incision. Access was gained to the dura of the thoracic spinal region. The bulging tissue was carefully placed into normal position. The incision was closed.

_____

6. The patient was placed on his side. After local anesthesia, the biopsy needle was inserted at the lumbar region. The sheath of the needle was pulled back; cloudy fluid was seen. This fluid was collected in the hollow portion of the needle.

_____

7. This patient presented for drainage of a brain abscess. After a burr hole was drilled, the cranium was accessed to reveal the site of the abscess. The abscess was drained.

_____

8. The patient presented with an arteriovenous (AV) malformation. A craniotomy was performed to gain access to the brain and the site of the malformation. This was done without difficulty. Blood vessels leading to the malformation were identified and ligated. The malformation measured approximately 2.0 cm in size. It was carefully resected supratentorially. The bone portion from the craniotomy was replaced and secured.

_____

9. The patient presented with a nerve compression of the left leg. An incision was made overlying the compressed sciatic nerve midpoint. Scar tissue was identified and dissected free. No adhesions were seen.

_____

10. The patient presented for a replacement of his lumbosubarachnoid shunt, which was performed by first incising at the original incision site. A moderate number of adhesions were seen, which were removed. The old shunt was also removed. A new shunt was placed in the same position.

_____

Eye and Ocular Adnexa

1. The patient presented with a foreign body sensation of the left eye. Under slit lamp examination, a small metallic foreign body was identified. This object was slightly embedded in the lower corneal area. It was removed via a small incision, using the slit lamp for guidance.

_____

2. The patient presented for correction of cross-eyes. The left eye was immobilized with a speculum. Incisions were made in the conjunctiva. The lateral muscle was identified and incised. The lateral muscle was sutured distally to the sclera. The medial rectus muscle was surgically incised and sutured in the same manner.

_____

3. After injection of a local anesthetic agent, the left upper eyelid was examined closely. A large chalazion was seen. The chalazion was resected in total. A moderate area of infection was noted, and this was drained. The infectious area was flushed with saline solution.

_____

4. After the injection of a local anesthetic agent, an incision was made on the patient's right side at the site of the medial canthal tendon. After careful dissection, the lacrimal sac was identified and removed.

_____

5. The patient presented with a corneal lamellar on the right side. This was excised using scleral scissors. Antibiotic ointment was applied.

_____

6. Using a laser, short bursts were administered to the patient's left eye. This iridotomy was performed to allow for the movement of fluid in the anterior chamber and to treat the patient's glaucoma.

_____

7. Using a xenon arc, spots were made on the patient's retina. This provided a good seal of the retinal tear of the right eye.

_____

8. With the patient under local anesthesia, the right lower eyelid is palpated and a foreign body is found in the upper-right quadrant near the posterior surface. The lid was everted and an incision made under the site. The foreign body was removed.

   _____

9. The patient presented with a tumor of the lacrimal gland. An incision was made in the lid crease of the left upper eyelid. This had to be extended down into the lacrimal fossa. An osteotomy was necessary to gain access to the entire mass. The mass was removed in total. The incisional wound was closed.

   _____

10. After making an incision in the patient's left eye at the junction of the cornea and sclera, the eye was entered. The nucleus of the eye lens was removed. The operating microscope was brought into the operating field. The soft portion of the lens was removed. This removed the entire cataract, but the capsule of the eye was left intact. An intraocular lens (IOL) was inserted. The incision was closed, and antibiotic injection was done.

   _____

Auditory System

1. Impacted cerumen was removed from the left ear, using lavage and suction. After removal, the ear canal was inspected. No evidence of infection was seen. The same method was done on the right ear.

   _____

2. The patient presented with a protruding left ear. The posterior auricle was incised. This allowed for the skin fold to be raised away from the ear cartilage. A new skin fold was created using several sutures. This new fold allowed for the ear to be in a more normal position.

   _____

3. The patient reported a buzzing sound from her left ear. Direct examination identified an insect-like foreign object in the canal. Using a cerumen spoon, the object was removed.

   _____

4. Using the punch biopsy method, a specimen was taken from the right external auditory canal.

   _____

5. With the patient under general anesthesia, an incision was made at the left auricular region and tympano-plasty with mastoidectomy was performed. The outer bone of the mastoid was removed, and the mastoid antrum was entered. The tympanic membrane was identified and perforated. The eardrum was brought forward. The middle ear was examined. A cholesteatoma was found and removed. The ossicular chain was identified and examined and found to be normal.

   _____

6. Through the ear canal of the patient's left ear, the aural polyp was identified under direct examination. With an ear snare, the polyp was removed. Antibiotic drops were placed in the canal. Minimal bleeding was noted.

   _____

7. After the patient's right auditory canal was examined, an abscess was noted. This required drainage. An incision was made over the location of this external abscess. The abscess was drained, with a puslike material seen. Antibiotic ointment and dressing were applied.

   _____

8. The patient underwent bilateral myringotomy including aspiration and eustachian tube inflation.

   _____

9. The patient presented with an aural glomus tumor on the left. After an incision of the skin was made posteriorly to the aural, the skin was retracted. The mastoid bone was exposed, and the tegmen (roof of mastoid sinuses) was identified. The tumor was also identified. The tumor was removed in total with forceps and sent to pathology for analysis. The incision was closed.

   _____

10. The patient presented seven months postmastoidectomy for debridement of the left cavity. This was done under direct visualization using suction. Skin and debris were removed from the left side of the mastoid. No infection was observed. The skin and debris removed appeared normal in appearance.

    _____

Operating Microscope

1. The patient underwent transcanal labyrinthotomy with cryosurgery and multiple perfusion of vestibuloactive drugs. After anesthesia, an incision was made posterior to the ear canal on the right and the external ear was exposed. The operating microscope was brought into the field to facilitate the placement of a temporary stapes plate. The cryolaser was used to debride tissue present in the area.

   _____

2. A patient presented with a fistula of the left salivary gland. This area was incised to expose the fistula, and the operating microscope was used to get a better view of the fistula for the purpose of closure.

   _____

3. A neonatal patient presented with a diaphragmatic hernia. Under adequate anesthesia, an abdominal incision was made. The operating microscope was used to identify all vessels and small arteries. This was in part due to the size of the infant. The hernia sac was exposed and dissected free, sutures were placed to close the diaphragmatic hernia defect, and the external incision was closed in layers.

   _____

4. The patient had a malfunctioning valve of the left femoral vein. After an incision was made over the vein site, the operating microscope was used to isolate the exact site of the valve in the femoral vein. The valve was exposed and repaired with sutures.

   _____

5. The patient had an injury to his left pinky finger. The volar plate required repair. The digit was incised at the interphalangeal joint space. The operating microscope was used to identify the area of instability. The plate was sutured to the distal bone. The wound was closed with sutures.

   _____

6. An incision was made over the skin at the site of the injured blood vessel, left hand, third finger. The operating microscope was brought into the field to help identify the vessel and used to assist in the dissection. Direct repair of the vessel with sutures was performed. The surgical incision was closed with sutures.

   _____

7. The infratemporal facial nerve required repair. First, an incision was made to expose the nerve. The operating microscope was then used to facilitate the repair. The surgical incision wound was closed with sutures.

   _____

8. The patient presented with a lesion of the pharynx. The patient's oral cavity was assessed using the operating microscope, and the lesion was identified. After identification, the laser was brought into the field to perform the excision. Minimal bleeding was noted.

_____

9. The patient presented with several small lesions of the epiglottis. Epiglottidectomy was performed using the operating microscope.

_____

10. After an extensor tendon in the patient's left index finger was excised using the operating microscope, a synthetic rod was implanted for delayed tendon graft. The surgical incision was closed with sutures.

_____

11. The patient presented with retained ventilating ear tubes bilaterally. After general anesthesia was administered, the operating microscope was brought into the operating field. The right tympanic membrane was examined under the microscope. The tube was found and removed. The ear canal was irrigated. The left ear was handled in the same method.

_____

12. The patient presented with a cyst of the urachus. This was removed after making an abdominal incision. The urachal portion of the bladder (cord from apex of bladder to the umbilicus) was exposed. The operating microscope was used to identify several small cysts. These were removed under microscopic guidance.

_____

13. Arthrodesis of the metacarpophalangeal joint was performed on the right hand, second digit. After an incision was made over the joint space, the external bony structures of the carpometacarpal joint space were identified. With both the operating microscope and a small screw, the joint was repaired. The surgical incision was closed with sutures.

_____

14. A decompression fasciotomy of the right forearm was performed using the operating microscope to explore the brachial artery.

_____

CPT Radiology

Chapter Outline

Radiology Terminology

Overview of Radiology Section

Radiology Section Guidelines

Radiology Subsections

Chapter Objectives

At the conclusion of this chapter, the student should be able to:

1. Define key terms related to the CPT Radiology Section.
2. Define radiology terminology related to planes of view, positioning and radiographic projection, and radiology procedures.
3. Summarize the organization, format, and content of the CPT Radiology section.
4. Interpret CPT Radiology Section guidelines.
5. Assign codes from the CPT Radiology section.

Key Terms

A-mode

amplitude modulation

angiography

anteroposterior
projection

aortography

arthrography

axial plane

biometric A-scan

biomicroscopy

block

blocking

bone density study

brightness mode

B-scan

cardiac blood pool
imaging

compensator

component coding

computed axial
tomography (CT) (CAT)

computed tomography
angiography (CTA)

contrast agent

contrast material

contrast medium
injection device

corneal pachymetry

coronal plane

cystography

cytoreduction surgery

debulking

diagnostic mammography

Doppler ultrasonography

dosimetry

dual energy x-ray
absorptiometry (DEXA)
(DXA)

echo

epidurography

equivalent dose

external radiation

fluoroscopy

fraction (in radiation
treatment
management)

frontal plane

global service

gray (gy)

gray-scale ultrasound

horizontal plane

hyperthermia

internal radiation

interventional radiologic procedure

intrathecal

lateral projection

magnetic resonance angiography (MRA)

magnetic resonance imaging (MRI)

mammography

megaelectron volt

megavolt

MeV

midsagittal plane

M-mode

motion mode

nuclear imaging

nuclear medicine

oblique projection

parenterally

photons

plane of view

port

positron emission tomography (PET)

posteroanterior (PA) projection

professional component

quantitative A-scan

radiation absorbed dose (rad)

radiation oncology

radiographic projection

radiologic guidance

radiologist

radiology

radionuclide

radiopharmaceutical therapy

real-time scan

roentgen

roentgen-equivalent-man (rem)

sagittal plane

screening mammography

side view

single photon emission computerized tomography (SPECT)

slit lamp exam

supervision and interpretation

systemic radiation therapy

technical component

therapeutic port film

transverse plane

treatment volume determination

ultrasonography

ultrasound

uptake

venography

view

wedge

x-ray

x-ray beam

Introduction

The Radiology section of CPT includes subsections for diagnostic radiology (diagnostic imaging); diagnostic ultrasound; radiologic guidance; breast, mammography; bone/joint studies; radiation oncology; and nuclear medicine. These subsections are further subdivided into anatomical categories. The Diagnostic Radiology (Diagnostic Imaging) subsection includes noninvasive and invasive diagnostic and therapeutic (interventional) procedures, as well as computed (or computerized) tomography and magnetic resonance imaging.

NOTE:

Procedures frequently performed by radiologists that are located in other CPT sections include

- Noninvasive vascular diagnostic studies (93880–93998)
- Invasive (or interventional) radiology services (Surgery section), such as
  - Injection procedures
  - Transcatheter procedures

   The Other Procedures code below each subheading classifies an unlisted procedure performed on the anatomical site. When reporting an unlisted procedure code, include documentation about the procedure performed (e.g., special report) with the submitted claim. (Other Procedures subheadings are not included throughout this chapter of the textbook except when codes that describe additional procedures are included.)

Radiology Terminology

Radiology is a branch of medicine that uses imaging techniques to diagnose and treat disease. A **radiologist** is a physician who has undergone specialized training to interpret diagnostic x-rays, perform specialized x-ray procedures, and administer radiation for the treatment of disease (e.g., cancer). Terms unique to the radiographic procedures include the following:

- Planes of view
- Positioning and radiographic projection

EXAMPLE: Axial is a standard plane of reference for most radiology codes. For example, axial images depict the long axis of the body, from the head to foot.

Planes of View

Terminology that describes **planes of view** (Figure 17-1) used when performing radiology procedures includes the following:

- **Coronal plane** (or **frontal plane**): Divides the body into anterior or ventral and posterior or dorsal portions at a right angle to the sagittal plane, separating the body into front and back; also called ventral or dorsal plane
- **Midsagittal plane**: Vertically divides the body through the midline into two equal left and right halves
- **Sagittal plane**: Vertically divides the body into unequal left and right portions
- **Transverse plane** (or **horizontal plane** or **axial plane**): Horizontally divides the body into superior and inferior portions

FIGURE 17-1 Planes that separate body structures

FIGURE 17-2 Radiographic projections

Positioning and Radiographic Projection

Patients are positioned for radiographic procedures so that a certain part of the body is placed closest to the x-ray film. The patient's position in relation to the camera is the **view** (e.g., code 71045 specifies a single view of the chest). **Radiographic projection** (Figure 17-2) describes the path that the x-ray beam travels through the body, from entrance to exit. An **x-ray beam** is made up of invisible electromagnetic energy waves called **photons**, which are emitted from a radiation machine and are used to produce images (x-rays) and treat disease (e.g., cancer). Radiographic projections include the following:

- **Anteroposterior projection**: Patient is positioned with his or her back parallel to the film; the x-ray beam travels from front to back, or anterior to posterior

- **Lateral projection**, or **side view**: Patient is positioned at a right angle to the film; the x-ray beam travels through the side of the body

- **Oblique projection**: Patient is positioned with the body slanted sideways toward the film, halfway between a parallel and right-angle position; the x-ray beam travels through this angle of the body

- **Posteroanterior (PA) projection**: Patient is positioned facing the film and parallel to it; the x-ray beam travels from back to front, or posterior to anterior

Radiology Procedures

Radiology procedures include

- **Angiography**: X-ray of a blood vessel after injection of contrast material (Figure 17-3)
- **Aortography**: X-ray of the aorta after injection of contrast material
- **Arthrography**: X-ray of a joint after injection of contrast material
- **Computed axial tomography (CT) (CAT)**: X-ray of horizontal and vertical cross-sectional views or "slices" of the body that are computer-processed to create three-dimensional, or 3D, images
- **Computed tomography angiography (CTA)**: X-rays of different angles create cross-sectional images of organs, bones, and tissues to visualize blood flow in arterial and venous vessels throughout the body
- **Cystography**: X-ray of the urinary bladder after injection of contrast material

FIGURE 17-3 Angiography

- **Fluoroscopy**: Continuous x-ray beam generates a movie-like image that is viewed on a monitor; used for invasive procedures such as intravenous/intra-arterial catheterization and extracorporeal shock wave lithotripsy
- **Magnetic resonance imaging (MRI)**: Noninvasive x-ray procedure uses an external magnetic field to produce a two-dimensional view of an internal organ or structure such as the brain or spinal cord
- **Nuclear imaging**: Noninvasive x-ray procedure creates an image by measuring radiation emission, or radiation "uptake," of body areas after the administration of a **radionuclide**, which is a radioactive material, such as an isotope of iodine
- **Positron emission tomography (PET)**: X-ray images of the body are produced after the administration of radioisotopes, which track metabolism or blood flow, not anatomy
- **Single photon emission computerized tomography (SPECT)**: 3D x-ray images of internal organs are produced after administration of a radioactive material, which visualize anatomy *and* function
- **Ultrasound**, or **ultrasonography**: High-frequency sound waves bounce off internal organs and create echoes; the echo pattern is displayed on the ultrasound machine monitor; an **echo** is the effect of a sound that reflects off a distant surface and returns to its source, just like the sound produced when you yell into a well and your voice "bounces back"
- **Venography**: X-ray of a vein is taken after injection of contrast material
- **X-ray**: Radiographic visualization or imaging of internal body structures uses low-dose high-energy radiation (High-dose high-energy radiation is used to treat diseases such as cancer.)

When a radiology procedure is performed, a device called a **block** (e.g., lead apron) made of lead or another heavy metal is placed between the radiation beam and that portion of the patient's body that requires protection from radiation.

The international unit of exposure dose for x-rays or gamma rays is called a **roentgen**, abbreviated as R or r. (Roentgen is named after Professor Wilhelm Konrad Roentgen, who discovered x-rays in 1895.) A unit of **radiation absorbed dose (rad)** is the amount of radiant energy absorbed in a tissue. Newer radiation terminology includes the term **gray**, abbreviated as **gy**, named for British physician L. Harold Gray (1905–1965) (an authority on the use of radiation for cancer treatment). (One gray equals 100 rads.) A **roentgen-equivalent-man (rem)** is the unit of measurement that includes different biological responses to different kinds of radiation. The radiation quantity measured by rem is called an **equivalent dose**. (A millirem is one-thousandth of a rem, the unit for measuring equivalent dose.)

Exercise 17.1 – Radiology Terminology

Instructions: Match each plane of view with its description.

_____ 1. Divides body horizontally into superior and inferior portions

_____ 2. Divides body into anterior and posterior portions

_____ 3. Divides body vertically into unequal left and right portions

_____ 4. Divides body vertically through midline into equal left and right halves

a. Coronal plane

b. Midsagittal plane

c. Sagittal plane

d. Transverse plane

Instructions: Match each radiographic projection with its description.

_____ 5. Patient positioned at right angle to film; x-ray beam travels through side of body.

_____ 6. Patient positioned facing film and parallel to it; x-ray beam travels back to front.

_____ 7. Patient positioned with back parallel to film; x-ray beam travels from front to back.

_____ 8. Patient positioned with body slanted sideways toward the film, halfway between parallel and right-angle position; x-ray beam travels through this angle of the body.

a. Anteroposterior

b. Lateral

c. Oblique

d. Posteroanterior

Instructions: Match each radiology procedure with its description.

_____ 9. X-ray of a vein after injection of contrast material.

_____ 10. X-ray of the urinary bladder after injection of contrast material.

_____ 11. Continuous x-ray beam generates a movie-like image that is viewed on a monitor.

_____ 12. Use of an external magnetic field to produce a two-dimensional x-ray of an internal organ.

_____ 13. High-frequency sound waves bounce off internal organs, creating echoes.

_____ 14. X-ray of the aorta after injection of contrast material.

_____ 15. X-ray of a joint after injection of contrast material.

a. Aortography

b. Arthrography

c. Cystography

d. Fluoroscopy

e. MRI

f. Ultrasound

g. Venography

Overview of Radiology Section

The Radiology section includes subsections for diagnostic radiology (diagnostic imaging); diagnostic ultrasound; radiologic guidance; breast, mammography; bone/joint studies; radiation oncology; and nuclear medicine. Procedure descriptions include the

- Type of service (e.g., modality)
- Anatomical site
- Use of contrast material

Professional Versus Technical Components

For radiology coding, the physician responsible for the professional and technical components of an examination must be determined. (Professional and technical components are reimbursement issues, which means that there are no CPT guidelines or notes explaining the three options.) Radiology procedures include the following three components:

- **Technical component:** Use of equipment and supplies and the employment of radiologic technologists to perform diagnostic imaging examinations and administer radiation therapy treatments
- **Professional component:** Services provided by the physician, which include supervising the performance of a diagnostic imaging procedure, interpreting imaging films, and documenting the imaging report
- **Global service:** Combined technical and professional components, as reported with a CPT Radiology code

Most radiology procedures require both professional and technical components, and the following modifiers are added to radiology codes as appropriate:

- -26 (Professional Component)
- -TC (Technical Component)

 NOTE:

Some radiology codes include only a professional component, and modifier -26 is *not* added to these codes (e.g., therapeutic radiology treatment planning codes and weekly radiation therapy management codes).

Modifier -26 is added to the radiology code when a radiologist interprets the radiographic image and documents a report (but does not perform the radiologic procedure). This indicates that only the professional component was provided.

Modifier -TC is added to the radiology code when the provider performs the radiologic procedure. (A radiologist employed by another facility interprets the radiographic image and documents the report. That radiologist adds modifier -26 to the radiology code.)

When a provider owns the equipment and performs both the technical and the professional components, a global CPT code is reported. A modifier is *not* added to the radiology code. (Hospitals own radiology equipment, and they employ radiologic technicians who perform x-rays and employ or contract with radiologists who interpret radiographic images and document reports.)

 NOTE:

Depending on the contract negotiated between radiologists and the health care facility

- Radiologists are considered employees of the health care facility (e.g., hospital) or contractors.
- The facility submits claims to obtain reimbursement for all services provided to patients (including professional services), or the radiologists use a medical billing service to submit claims for professional services.

EXAMPLE 1: Patient undergoes a complete chest x-ray, minimum of four views (71048), which is performed on an outpatient basis at the hospital. (The patient's primary care provider completed a requisition for the chest x-ray after having evaluated the patient in the office for shortness of breath.) The radiologic technician takes the x-ray, and the radiologist interprets the image and documents an x-ray report. A copy of the x-ray report is mailed to the patient's primary care provider. The hospital reports the x-ray code as a global service.

EXAMPLE 2: Patient undergoes a complete wrist x-ray, minimum of three views (73110), which is performed at a freestanding radiology clinic. (The patient's primary care provider had completed a requisition for the wrist x-ray after evaluating the patient in the office for severe wrist pain earlier that day.) The clinic's radiologic technician takes the x-ray, and the clinic's radiologist interprets the image and documents an x-ray report. A copy of the x-ray report is mailed to the patient's primary care provider. The clinic reports the x-ray code as a global service.

EXAMPLE 3: The patient is seen by her primary care provider, who evaluates a lump on her right pinky finger. The office has x-ray equipment and takes a two-view x-ray of the hand (73120). The x-ray is interpreted by a hand specialist who is located in another office. The primary care provider reports the x-ray code with HCPCS level II modifier -TC (technical component). The hand specialist reports the x-ray code with CPT modifier -26 (professional component) added to it.

Use of Modifiers with Radiology Codes

Modifiers commonly added to Radiology codes include

- -52 (Reduced Services), to indicate that a service is partially reduced at the physician's discretion.

EXAMPLE: Patient underwent ultrasound exam of swollen tonsils. Code 76536 is reported for "Ultrasound, soft tissues of head and neck (eg, thyroid, parathyroid, parotid) real time with image documentation." Because just tonsillar tissue was evaluated, code 76536-52 is reported.

- -76 (Repeat Procedure by Same Physician or Other Qualified Health Care Professional) describes a repeat procedure by the same physician on the same date of service. ("Same physician" refers to either the same physician or a physician in the same specialty or group.)

EXAMPLE: A patient presents to the emergency department (ED) with blunt abdominal trauma. Complete acute abdomen series with supine, erect, and decubitus views and single-view chest x-ray was performed. The patient became unstable several hours later in the ED, and the x-ray was repeated. Code 74022-76 is reported for the repeat x-ray.

 Coding Tip

- Modifier -50 (Bilateral Procedure) is not added when code descriptions specify "bilateral." Radiology code descriptions must be carefully reviewed to determine whether modifier -50 should be added (when code descriptions do not specify "bilateral" and the procedure performed was bilateral).
- HCPCS level II anatomical modifiers -LT (Left) and -RT (Right) are added to radiology codes when appropriate. These modifiers are reported to identify a specific side of the body.

Complete Procedure

The term *complete* as included in radiology code descriptions refers to the number of views required for the study of a designated body part. Code descriptions include language that indicates what constitutes a *complete study* for a specific type of radiologic procedure.

EXAMPLE 1: Code 70120 is reported when a mastoid x-ray of fewer than three views is performed. Code 70130 is reported when a complete mastoid x-ray is performed.

 Coding Tip

Do not confuse use of the term *complete* in the code description with its use in a parenthetical note below a code.

EXAMPLE 2: Code 70332 describes a radiologic diagnostic procedure that contains both radiologic and surgical components. Report code 70332 for the radiologic procedure. Report code 21116 for the injection procedure if it is performed during the same session.

Both components comprise a complete procedure when performed by the same physician (e.g., radiologist), and two codes are reported by that physician. However, when two physicians are involved in performing the procedure, each physician submits the code for the respective portion of the procedure performed.

Evaluation and Management (E/M) Services

When the radiologist provides E/M services as part of the radiographic procedure (e.g., invasive or interventional radiology), a CPT E/M code is *not* reported. The services provided by the radiologist include a minimal history and examination to determine the following:

- Reason for the examination
- Presence of allergies
- Acquisition of informed consent
- Discussion of follow-up
- Review of the patient record

The complexity of medical decision making is usually limited to the following:

- Whether the invasive or interventional procedure should be performed
- Whether any comorbidities (coexisting conditions) may impact the procedure
- What discussion and education took place with the patient

However, when a significant, separately identifiable E/M service is provided by the radiologist *distinct from the radiographic procedure*, an appropriate E/M code is reported (e.g., initial radiation oncology consultation to determine whether to proceed with treatment).

EXAMPLE: The patient's primary care provider requests that a radiologist provide consultation services to render an opinion about the patient's candidacy for a uterine embolization procedure. The radiologist performs a comprehensive history and examination and reviews the patient's record. A pelvic MRI is performed to assist in medical decision making. The radiologist reports a code from the Office or Other Outpatient Consultations category of the CPT E/M section.

Exercise 17.2 – Overview of Radiology Section

Instructions: Complete each statement.

1. Procedure descriptions for codes in the Radiology section include _____, _____, and _____.
2. Services provided by the radiologic technologist include performing diagnostic imaging examinations and administering radiation therapy treatments. This is called the _____ component.
3. Services provided by the physician include supervising the performance of a diagnostic imaging procedure, interpreting imaging films, and documenting the imaging report. This is called the _____ component.
4. The combined technical and professional components, as reported with a CPT radiology code, is called the _____.
5. When a significant, separately identifiable E/M service is provided by the radiologist distinct from the radiographic procedure, the appropriate _____ code is reported.

Radiology Section Guidelines

Guidelines located at the beginning of the Radiology section provide instruction about the following:

- Subject listings
- Separate procedures
- Unlisted service or procedure
- Special report

- Supervision and interpretation, imaging guidance
- Administration of contrast material(s)
- Written report(s)

Instructional notes appear throughout the Radiology section to provide coding clarification and direction.

Subject Listings

When radiologic services are performed by or under the responsible supervision of a physician (e.g., radiologist) or other qualified health care professional, radiology codes are reported.

Separate Procedures

Some procedures listed in the Radiology section of CPT are considered an integral component of a total service or procedure and are identified by the descriptor *separate procedure*. These codes are *not* reported in addition to the code for the primary or total x-ray procedure unless the *separate procedure* is unrelated to or distinct from other procedures/services provided at that time.

> **EXAMPLE:** Patient undergoes laparoscopic cholecystectomy with intraoperative cholangiogram and fluoroscopy. Report codes 47563 (surgeon) and 74300.

Unlisted Procedures

As in other CPT sections, unlisted procedure codes are reported for a service or procedure that is not adequately described or listed in CPT (e.g., 76499, Unlisted diagnostic radiographic procedure).

Special Report

The radiology guidelines repeat the special report instructions found in previous sections. As in other CPT sections, when a service is new, unusual, or rarely provided, it requires a special report to validate the medical necessity and appropriateness of the service (e.g., complexity of symptoms). A special report should include all pertinent information (e.g., the time, effort, and equipment needed; diagnostic and therapeutic procedures performed; and description of the nature, extent, and need for the procedure).

Supervision and Interpretation, Imaging Guidance

Imaging procedures may require a surgical procedure to access the imaged area (e.g., injection of contrast material), or a surgical procedure may require image guidance (e.g., lung biopsy with fluoroscopic guidance). In CPT, many radiological services include image guidance in their code descriptions, which means separate *radiological supervision and interpretation* codes for image guidance are *not* reported.

 NOTE:

The radiological supervision and interpretation concept does *not* apply to Radiation Oncology subsection procedures.

Interventional radiologic procedures (e.g., catheterization, injection of contrast media) are used to diagnose and treat conditions using percutaneous or minimally invasive techniques under imaging guidance. Due to the complexity of interventional radiology services, **component coding** allows for reporting a radiology procedure code *and* a surgical procedure code to completely describe the service provided. Component coding provides a mechanism for reporting interventional services whether the services are performed by a single physician or by different physicians (e.g., one physician performs the procedure and the other performs the imaging supervision and interpretation).

- When two different physicians (e.g., surgeon and radiologist) perform the surgical and radiological components, each physician reports the code(s) for his or her component of the procedure performed. The radiological portion of the procedure is designated as "radiological **supervision and interpretation**."

- When one physician performs the procedure and provides radiological supervision and interpretation, that physician reports codes for both components (from the Surgery section *and* the Radiology section).

EXAMPLE 1: In a hospital outpatient setting, a radiologist performed an injection procedure and supervised and interpreted an antegrade pyelography through a previously placed nephrostomy. The hospital reports code 50431. (Radiologists are salaried hospital employees, and they do not submit insurance claims for reimbursement. The hospital billing department submits the claim.)

EXAMPLE 2: Patient undergoes needle biopsy of the liver under fluoroscopic guidance. Report codes 47000 and 77002.

Administration of Contrast Material(s)

A **contrast agent**, or **contrast material** (or contrast medium), is a radiopaque substance (solid or liquid) that is administered to provide better radiographic visualization of organs studied. The contrast agent is administered orally, rectally, intravenously, percutaneously, or through inhalation or urinary catheterization. A **contrast medium injection device** (Figure 17-4) is used to deliver a predetermined amount of contrast, typically for vascular imaging procedures.

FIGURE 17-4 Contrast medium injection device

NOTE:

Radiologic procedures are performed with contrast, without contrast, or with and without contrast. Separate codes are available in the Radiology section to describe all of these combinations.

Contrast agents are radiopaque (impenetrable by x-rays or other forms of radiation), and they block x-ray beams and provide excellent contrast for body structures. Common contrast agents include

- Barium sulfate (gastrointestinal studies)
- Organic iodine (vascular and renal studies)
- Iodized oils (myelography)

Contrast materials make body structures appear white on x-rays.

 Coding Tip

Radiology codes that contain the description "with contrast" include intravascular, intra-articular, or intrathecal administration of contrast material. When contrast material is administered orally or rectally, the administration of the contrast material is not reported separately. It is included in the radiologic procedure performed.

 NOTE:

The supply of contrast material is not included in radiology procedure codes. HCPCS level II codes are reported for the supply of contrast material (e.g., A4641, A4642, A9500, A9600).

Written Report

The written report, documented and authenticated by the interpreting individual (e.g., radiologist), is considered an integral part of a radiologic procedure or interpretation. Therefore, before reporting the radiology procedure code on an insurance claim, the documented report must be available in the patient's record.

 NOTE:

Code of Federal Regulations, 42 CFR (Conditions of Participation for Hospitals) states, "The radiologist or other practitioner who performs radiology services must sign reports of his or her interpretations. Authentication may include signatures, written initials or computer entry." (Electronic signatures require verification methods to ensure accuracy of the entry, such as encryption.)

Radiology guidelines state that the interpreting individual must sign a written report as an integral part of a radiologic procedure. However, the guidelines do *not* specify content or format.

When a teaching physician reviews a radiographic image interpreted by a resident, the teaching physician is responsible for documenting a note indicating that the image was reviewed with the resident, and the teaching physician agreed with the resident's interpretation. (If the teaching physician disagreed with the resident's interpretation, the teaching physician is responsible for documenting a corrected report.) Before a claim is submitted to Medicare for payment, the radiologic report must be authenticated by the teaching physician (and a statement of agreement with the resident's interpretation must be documented by the teaching physician).

Exercise 17.3 – Radiology Section Guidelines

Instructions: Complete each statement.

1. Radiological procedures that are completed as an integral component of a total service or procedure are called _____ procedures.

2. A radiological procedure that is provided to patients but that is not included in the current edition of the CPT coding manual is called a(n) _____ procedure.

3. A #5 French pigtail catheter was placed via femoral puncture in the abdominal aorta. Abdominal aortography, by serialography, with radiological supervision and interpretation was performed. Identify and assign CPT codes to the surgical and radiological components.

   a. Surgical component: _____

   b. Radiological component: _____

4. Radiology codes that contain the description "with contrast" include the _____, _____, and _____ administration of contrast material.

5. When contrast material is administered orally or rectally, its administration is included in the procedure and is separately reported. TRUE or FALSE.

Radiology Subsections

The Radiology section of CPT includes seven subsections.

- Diagnostic radiology (diagnostic imaging) (70010–76499)
- Diagnostic ultrasound (76506–76999)
- Radiologic guidance (77001–77022)
- Breast, mammography (77053–77067)
- Bone/joint studies (77071–77086)
- Radiation oncology (77261–77799)
- Nuclear medicine (78012–79999)

Radiology is the medical specialty that uses x-rays (e.g., radiant energy) to diagnose and treat injuries and disease. Radiology imaging also includes MRI, magnetic resonance angiography (MRA), CT scan, ultrasound, and nuclear scans. Radiology procedure codes are found under the procedural term (e.g., transluminal atherectomy) or the anatomical site (e.g., chest).

Diagnostic Radiology (Diagnostic Imaging)

The Diagnostic Radiology (Diagnostic Imaging) subsection includes the following headings:

- Head and Neck
- Chest (Figure 17-5)
- Spine and Pelvis
- Upper Extremities
- Lower Extremities
- Abdomen
- Gastrointestinal Tract
- Urinary Tract
- Gynecological and Obstetrical
- Heart
- Vascular Procedures
- Other Procedures

FIGURE 17-5 Lateral chest x-ray. Bones of the spine are white, and soft tissues are shades of gray.

FIGURE 17-6 Abdominal CT scan in which the liver is predominant in the upper left and the stomach is visible in the upper right

The Diagnostic Radiology (Diagnostic Imaging) subsection includes diagnostic and therapeutic procedures, computed tomography (CT) (Figure 17-6), magnetic resonance imaging (MRI), and magnetic resonance angiography (MRA). These diagnostic procedures can be as simple as a routine chest x-ray or as complex as a carotid angiography, which requires selective vascular catheterization.

To code diagnostic radiology procedures accurately, identify the following:

- Anatomical site
- Type of procedure
- Number of views
- Laterality of the procedure (e.g., unilateral or bilateral)
- Use of contrast media

CPT allows for various combinations of codes to address the number and type of radiographic views. For a given radiographic series, the procedure code that most accurately describes what was performed is appropriate.

A variety of combinations of views necessary to obtain medically useful information are classified in the Diagnostic Radiology subsection. A complete review of available codes for radiographic procedures ensures accurate coding so that the most comprehensive code is reported (to describe services performed). Do not report multiple codes to describe a service when a combination code is available.

 NOTE:

A careful review of the radiology code description is required so that the most comprehensive code is reported. Codes 71045–71048 are reported for chest x-ray procedures. The radiologic report will indicate the number of views, such as code 71045 for "Radiological examination, chest; single view."

When radiographic procedures are repeated during the same encounter due to substandard quality, just one code is reported. However, if after reviewing initial films the radiologist elects to obtain additional views to render further interpretation, determine the third-party payer's policy regarding multiple procedures. Generally, the CPT code that describes the total service provided is reported even if the patient was released from the radiology suite and had to return for additional services.

Descriptions of many radiology codes refer to a "minimum" number of views. When more than the minimum number specified in the code description is performed and a more specific code is not available, report one code for the highest level of service. (When additional x-rays are necessary due to a change in the patient's condition, report separate radiology codes as appropriate.)

> **EXAMPLE 1:** A three-view x-ray of the shoulder was obtained. Report code 73030. (Do *not* report codes 73020 and 73030 even though that combination of codes equals three views.)

> **EXAMPLE 2:** The patient presented to the ED with the complaint of severe shortness of breath. A single-view chest x-ray was obtained. A repeat chest x-ray, four views, was obtained several hours later after it was noted that the patient was experiencing labored breathing unrelieved by medication. Report codes 71045 and 71048-59. (Modifier -59 indicates that the second x-ray was a separate procedure.)

Radiographic procedures are performed without contrast, with contrast, or with and without contrast. (Invasive diagnostic imaging that involves the use of contrast material is discussed later.) Separate codes are available to describe all of these combinations of contrast usage.

Preliminary scout radiographs obtained prior to contrast administration or delayed imaging radiographs are often performed. When a CPT code is available to classify scout radiographs, it is reported. If there is no CPT code, the scout radiograph procedures are included in the reported code for the primary procedure.

Fluoroscopy

According to *CPT Assistant*, when radiologic supervision and interpretation are performed during surgical procedures, fluoroscopy (Figure 17-7) is included in the radiologic procedure. This means that codes for physician or other qualified health care professional time during fluoroscopy (76000) are *not* reported in addition to the radiologic procedure code.

© Courtesy of GE Healthcare

FIGURE 17-7 Fluoroscopy unit: Fluoroscopy is a dynamic radiographic examination that allows for visualization of flow of barium through the gastrointestinal tract, injection of a contrast agent into the heart, and so on.

EXAMPLE: Patient underwent a laparoscopic cholecystectomy and an intraoperative cholangiogram with fluoroscopy. Report codes 47563 (surgical component) and 74300. Do *not* report code 76000 (fluoroscopy) because it is included in code 74300.

Interventional Radiologic Procedures

Interventional radiologic procedures involve the administration of contrast material orally (by mouth, such as for an upper GI), rectally (by rectum, such as a barium enema), or **parenterally** (other than by mouth or rectum, such as implantation, infusion, or injection).

 Coding Tip

The administration of oral or rectal contrast material is included as part of the radiologic procedure code. (Do *not* report a separate code for the administration of oral or rectal contrast material.) However, it is acceptable to report an HCPCS level II code for the supply of the contrast material.

When spinal radiologic procedures are performed using CT, MRI, or magnetic resonance angiography (MRA) and the code description includes the phrase *with contrast*, do not report a code for intravenous (IV) injection. The IV injection procedure is included in the radiologic procedure code. However, when an intrathecal injection is performed, report a separate code. (**Intrathecal** refers to the fluid-filled space between layers of tissue that cover the brain and spinal cord.)

EXAMPLE 1: Patient underwent CT of the cervical spine, with IV injection of contrast material. Report code 72126.

EXAMPLE 2: Patient underwent CT of the thoracic spine, with intrathecal injection of contrast material. Report codes 72129 and 62284.

For intra-articular injection of contrast material, report the appropriate joint injection code. When an IV line is placed for administration of contrast material, it is not coded or reported. Placement of the IV line is included in the radiologic procedure code.

EXAMPLE: Patient underwent left femoral venography, which required placement of an IV line and injection of contrast material. Report codes 75820 and 36005. (Do *not* report code 36000 for placement of the IV line.)

 NOTE:

For urogenital radiography, the insertion of a urethral catheter is included in the radiographic procedure code and not separately reported. However, a code from the CPT Surgery section for the injection procedure to administer dye or radionuclide material is reported.

EXAMPLE: Patient underwent cystography (three views), which involved insertion of a catheter through the patient's urethra into the bladder and injection of contrast material. X-rays were taken from various angles at various stages of filling to visualize the bladder. Report codes 74430 and 51600. (Do *not* report a code for catheter insertion.) (The supply of dye is reported with a code from HCPCS level II.)

Computed Tomography (CT) and Computed Tomographic Angiography (CTA)

CT (or CAT) is an x-ray of horizontal and vertical cross-sectional views or "slices" of the body (Figure 17-8), which are computer-processed to create 3D images.

Sagittal   Transverse   Coronal (frontal)

FIGURE 17-8 Computed tomography (CT) sections

CTA (Figure 17-9) is a less invasive technique that uses x-ray beams to image blood vessels. (Until the introduction of CTA, vascular evaluation was performed primarily using invasive angiography procedures, which required catheterization.)

> **EXAMPLE 1:** Patient underwent CT of the abdomen, with contrast material. Report code 74160.

> **EXAMPLE 2:** Patient underwent CTA of the abdomen, first without contrast material and then followed by the injection of contrast material, and image post processing. Report code 74175.

Do not report a code for the injection of contrast material for a "with contrast" CTA procedure. However, the supply of the contrast material is reported separately with an appropriate HCPCS level II code. (The administration of oral or rectal contrast materials does not qualify as "with contrast." Such contrast materials are not typically used in CTA because they obscure the vasculature.)

> **EXAMPLE:** The patient underwent a CTA of the abdominal aorta with contrast material, including bilateral iliofemoral lower extremity runoff. Post processing of the image was performed. Report code 75635.

(A)

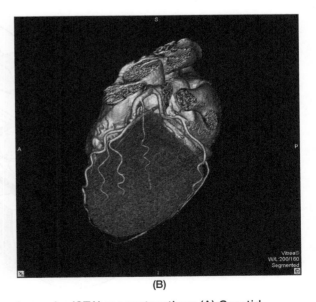

(B)

FIGURE 17-9 Three-dimensional computed tomography angiography (CTA) reconstructions (A) Carotid arteries (B) Coronary arteries

Epidurography

Epidurography is performed to assess the structure of the spine's epidural space prior to percutaneous epidural adhesiolysis (to identify nerve construction or inflammation and the degree of fluid flow in the epidural space). The code for "epidurography, radiological supervision and interpretation" is reported for a formally interpreted contrast study that involves multiplanar imaging, generating hard copy images. When epidurography is performed at *multiple* spinal levels, the code is reported for each spinal region examined (e.g., once for the thoracic region and once for the lumbar region).

> **EXAMPLE:** Using direct fluoroscopy, a catheter is percutaneously placed in the epidural space. Following fluoroscopic confirmation of the needle location, contrast material is injected. Permanent recording of the epidural space is performed. Report code 72275. (Do *not* report code 77003 for fluoroscopic guidance, because fluoroscopy is included as a component of epidurography.)

Magnetic Resonance Imaging (MRI)

Magnetic resonance imaging (MRI) (Figure 17-10) produces high-quality anatomical images. Code descriptions include studies performed without contrast materials, with contrast materials, and without contrast material followed by injection of contrast materials.

> **EXAMPLE:** A diagnostic MRI of the brain (Figure 17-11) was performed without contrast material. Report code 70551.

Magnetic Resonance Angiography (MRA)

Magnetic resonance angiography (MRA) is a noninvasive diagnostic study that is used to evaluate disorders of arterial and venous structures. MRA is performed to visualize the arteries and vessels without invasive procedures, and it is performed on MRI machines that contain hardware and software enhancements. Post processing procedures to create the images are included in MRA codes.

> **EXAMPLE:** Patient underwent MRA of the abdomen with contrast material. Report code 74185.

FIGURE 17-10 Magnetic resonance imaging (MRI) unit, which includes stationary magnet, radio frequency coil, and gradient coils

© Courtesy of GE Healthcare

FIGURE 17-11 Magnetic resonance imaging (MRI) of the brain

Vascular Procedures

Some vascular radiographic procedures performed on the aorta and arteries are designated as selective or nonselective. The radiographic procedure codes are reported in addition to appropriate catheterization codes from the Surgery section. (Chapter 14 of this textbook contains content about coding of arterial catheterization procedures.)

- *Selective vascular catheterization* is the insertion and manipulation or guidance of a catheter into the branches of the arterial system (other than the aorta or the vessel punctured) for the purpose of performing diagnostic (e.g., angiography) or therapeutic (e.g., endarterectomy) procedures. Selective vascular catheterization includes introduction of the catheter and all lesser-order selective catheterizations used in the approach.

EXAMPLE: The insertion of the catheter from the aorta into the right common and internal carotid arteries is a selective vascular catheterization procedure. (The catheter was inserted into the aorta from the brachial artery, which is a nonselective vascular catheterization procedure.)

- *Nonselective vascular catheterization* is the introduction of a catheter into a vessel and guidance of the catheter into lesser- (or first-) order vessels. (A nonselective catheterization code from the Surgery section is *not* reported with a selective radiological supervision and interpretation code.)

EXAMPLE: The introduction of a catheter into the femoral artery and threading of the catheter into the aorta is a nonselective vascular catheterization procedure. (If the catheter is further threaded from the aorta into another vessel, such as the brachiocephalic artery, a selective vascular catheterization procedure is performed.)

For diagnostic angiography or venography (radiological supervision and interpretation) (Figure 17-12), the following interventional procedures are included in the procedure code:

- Contrast injections, angiography, roadmapping, and/or fluoroscopic guidance for the intervention
- Vessel measurement
- Post angioplasty/stent angiography

FIGURE 17-12 Vascular imaging equipment

Codes for the above procedures are not coded separately when performed during the same session as an angiography or a venography.

For diagnostic angiography or venography performed during the same session as an interventional procedure, the angiography or venography is separately coded and reported if

- No prior catheter-based angiographic study is available during a full diagnostic study *and the decision to intervene is based on the diagnostic study*
- A prior angiographic study is available, but documentation indicates the following:
  - The patient's clinical condition has changed since the prior study.
  - There was inadequate visualization of anatomy and/or pathology.
  - There was a clinical change during the procedure that requires new evaluation.

EXAMPLE: Patient underwent selective catheter placement into the left common carotid artery with angiography of ipsilateral (same side) intracranial carotid circulation, extracranial carotid, and cervicocerebral arch. Procedure included associated radiological supervision and interpretation for angiography. Report code 36222-LT. (Do *not* report a separate angiography code.)

Vascular Procedures—Transcatheter Procedures

Therapeutic transcatheter radiological supervision and interpretation code(s) include the following services:

- Contrast injections, angiography/venography, roadmapping, and fluoroscopic guidance for the intervention
- Vessel measurement
- Completion angiography/venography

Codes for the above procedures are *not* coded separately when performed during the same session as a therapeutic transcatheter procedure.

EXAMPLE: Patient underwent angiography through existing catheter for follow-up study for transcatheter therapy, via infusion. Report code 75898.

Other Procedures

Other procedure codes are reported for professional time associated with fluoroscopy, radiological examinations not classified previously in CPT, cineradiography and vineradiography, consultation on x-ray examination, 3D rendering, computed tomography follow-up study, magnetic resonance spectroscopy and elastography, and unlisted fluoroscopic procedures.

EXAMPLE: A 5-year-old child swallowed a coin and underwent single-view nose-to-rectum radiologic examination to detect the foreign object. Report code 76010.

Exercise 17.4 – Diagnostic Radiology (Diagnostic Imaging)

Instructions: Assign the CPT code(s) and appropriate modifier(s) to each statement.

1. Computed tomography guidance for needle placement, radiological supervision, and interpretation.

   _____

2. Orthodontic cephalogram.

   _____

3. Radiologist provided supervision and interpretation of a retrograde angiography, left brachial artery.

   _____

4. Radiological examination, sacrum and coccyx, two views.

   _____

5. Magnetic resonance spectroscopy (MRS).

   _____

Diagnostic Ultrasound

Diagnostic ultrasound uses high-frequency sound waves (e.g., mechanical oscillations) to produce an image. Radiologic ultrasound codes are organized according to anatomical site. Radiologic ultrasound procedures are often performed as follow-up studies for inconclusive diagnostic radiology procedures. They are also performed intraoperatively (e.g., during endoscopic procedures). Ultrasound is also used as guidance for the following:

- Biopsies
- Cyst localization
- Invasive procedures (e.g., ablation of renal cysts, coded as 50541)
- Paracentesis
- Pericardiocentesis
- Placement of radiation therapy fields
- Thoracentesis

Ultrasound display modes include

- **A-mode**, or **amplitude modulation**: One-dimensional display that reflects the length of time a sound reaches a structure and is reflected back
- **B-scan**, or **brightness mode**, or **gray-scale ultrasound**: Two-dimensional display that reflects sound waves bouncing off tissues or organs; the diagnostic ultrasound produces a two-dimensional cross-sectional view of tissues that cannot be seen directly (e.g., used to locate a lesion and determine its shape)
- **M-mode**, or **motion mode**: One-dimensional display that reflects the _movement_ of structures
- **Real-time scan**: Two-dimensional display of structures and movement that indicates the movement, shape, and size of the tissue or organ

Ophthalmic ultrasound includes the following:

- **Biometric A-scan**: Diagnostic ultrasound that produces a one-dimensional view of normal and abnormal eye tissue and precise measurements of the eye's length (e.g., dimensions of an orbital lesion and exact depth of a foreign body)
- **Biomicroscopy**: Optical instrument that looks like a microscope, with two eyepieces

 NOTE:

Biomicroscopy is performed with a **slit lamp exam**, which is a high-intensity light source that can be focused to shine as a slit to look at anterior structures, including the eyelid, sclera, conjunctiva, iris, natural crystalline lens, and cornea.

- *B-scan* (see definition noted previously)
  - **Quantitative A-scan**: Diagnostic ultrasound that produces quantitative data about the posterior eye segment and evaluates tissue consistency, mobility, and vascularity (e.g., size of an orbital lesion)
  - **Corneal pachymetry**: Noninvasive ultrasound procedure that determines thickness of the cornea (e.g., prior to performing LASIK surgery)

Complete and Limited Ultrasound Procedures

To report a code for a "complete" ultrasound, the documented report must contain a description of all elements or the reason that an element could not be visualized (e.g., organ is surgically absent). A complete study includes visualization and diagnostic evaluation of all major structures within the anatomical location.

If fewer/less than the required elements for a complete exam are documented (e.g., limited number of organs or limited portion of region evaluated), report the "limited" code for that anatomical region. A limited study could include a follow-up examination, or it might address just a single quadrant or single diagnostic problem. (A "limited" exam of an anatomical region is not reported during the same session as a "complete" exam of the same region.)

 Coding Tip

The abdomen and retroperitoneum heading include ultrasound codes that are described as one of the following:

- Complete (e.g., entire abdomen)
- Limited (e.g., single organ or single quadrant)

A limited ultrasound of a single organ or a single quadrant is also performed as follow-up to a complete ultrasound procedure. For example, a complete abdominal ultrasound revealed an abnormality of a single organ. Patient was placed on a therapeutic regimen (e.g., medications). A limited abdominal ultrasound of that organ was performed as follow-up to determine whether abnormality still existed.

 NOTE:

ED physicians perform limited ultrasound procedures to evaluate a specific problem, and diagnostic ultrasound results are used to determine subsequent treatment.

EXAMPLE 1: Patient underwent complete ultrasound of the abdominal region, B-scan and real time with image documentation. Report code 76700. (A complete ultrasound of the abdomen describes all major abdominal structures, and organ-specific findings are reported, such as the liver and spleen.)

EXAMPLE 2: Patient underwent limited ultrasound of the abdomen, B-scan and real time with image documentation. Report code 76705. (A limited ultrasound of the abdomen describes a problem-specific study, such as the presence or absence of intraperitoneal fluid.)

 Coding Tip

When there is no corresponding limited ultrasound procedure code for a complete procedure and a limited ultrasound was performed, add modifier -52 (Reduced Services) to the complete code.

> **EXAMPLE:** Patient underwent a nonobstetrical transvaginal ultrasound to confirm an ectopic pregnancy. Report code 76830-52. (A complete transvaginal ultrasound procedure involves evaluation of the uterus, endometrium, adnexa, and ovaries. Because the transvaginal ultrasound was performed to confirm an ectopic pregnancy only, the procedure is limited and modifier -52 [Reduced Services] is added to the complete study code [76830].)

Doppler Ultrasound

Doppler ultrasound is effective in the evaluation of major arteries and veins, of the heart, and in obstetrics for fetal monitoring. **Doppler ultrasonography** evaluates movement by measuring changes in the frequency of echoes reflected from moving structures. It uses diagnostic ultrasound to detect moving structures (e.g., blood cells) and measures their direction and speed. Doppler ultrasound allows for real-time viewing of blood flow, which cannot be obtained by other methods.

 Coding Tip

Austrian mathematician and physicist (Johann) Christian Doppler is known for a principle called the Doppler effect (frequency of a sound wave appears to change as the source moves toward or away from you).

> **EXAMPLE:** Patient underwent ultrasound of transplanted kidney, real time with image documentation, with duplex Doppler studies. Report code 76776.

 Coding Tip

Review Non-Invasive Vascular Diagnostic Studies subsection codes located in the Medicine section to report venous Doppler studies and duplex scans.

Obstetrical Ultrasound Procedures

An ultrasound of the pregnant uterus includes fetal and maternal evaluation for single and multiple gestations, with limited and follow-up exams.

> **EXAMPLE:** Patient underwent fetal biophysical profile with nonstress testing. Report code 76818. The fetal biophysical profile can include assessment of amniotic fluid, fetal breathing, tone, and movement.

Fetal echocardiography is performed ultrasonically according to specific criteria.

> **EXAMPLE:** Patient underwent fetal echocardiography, cardiovascular system, real time with image documentation (2D), with M-mode recording. Report code 76825.

For female patients known to be pregnant (e.g., established diagnosis of pregnancy), it is appropriate to report an obstetrical ultrasound code. However, when a female patient does not have an established diagnosis of pregnancy and undergoes an ultrasound evaluation (e.g., dysmenorrhea or pelvic pain), report a nonobstetrical ultrasound code.

> **EXAMPLE:** A patient with an established diagnosis of pregnancy presents with symptoms that necessitate an ultrasound evaluation of the pelvis. Report a code from obstetrical ultrasound codes 76801–76817 even if the outcome of the procedure is that the patient is not pregnant (e.g., ultrasound confirms that miscarriage occurred).

Ultrasonic Guidance Procedures

Ultrasonic guidance procedures include the use of ultrasound when certain procedures (e.g., ultrasonic guidance for endomyocardial biopsy) are performed.

Report *either* a diagnostic ultrasound *or* a guidance ultrasound code (but not both) for the same patient during the same encounter.

> **EXAMPLE:** Patient underwent ultrasound guidance for endomyocardial biopsy performed during the same encounter. Report codes 93505 and 76932.

Other Procedures

The code for "ultrasound study, follow-up" is *not* reported in addition to other echocardiograph procedures or ultrasound guidance procedures because it classifies a follow-up procedure performed on the same day. Other procedures in this heading include ultrasound bone density measurement and interpretation, targeted ultrasound to detect lesions, elastographic ultrasound, intraoperative ultrasonic guidance, and unlisted ultrasound procedures.

> **EXAMPLE:** Patient underwent elastrographic ultrasound to detect three target lesions. Report codes 76982, 76983, and 76983.

Radiologic Guidance

Radiologic guidance is performed during a procedure to visualize access to an anatomical site. The Radiologic Guidance subsection contains four headings: fluoroscopic guidance, computed tomography guidance, magnetic resonance imaging (MRI) guidance, and other radiologic guidance (Table 17-1).

TABLE 17-1 Type of Radiologic Guidance and the Purpose of Each

Type	Purpose

Fluoroscopic Guidance	• Guidance for placement, replacement, or removal of:
	   o Catheter
	   o Central venous access device (CVAD)
	   o Needle

Computed Tomography Guidance	• Guidance for stereotactic localization • Guidance for needle placement • Guidance and monitoring of parenchymal tissue ablation • Guidance for placement of radiation therapy fields
Magnetic Resonance Imaging (MRI) Guidance	• Guidance for needle placement • Guidance and monitoring of parenchymal tissue ablation
Other Radiologic Guidance	• Stereotactic localization for breast biopsy or needle placement • Mammographic guidance for needle placement, breast

EXAMPLE: A 75-year-old patient underwent fluoroscopic guidance for visualization of the subclavian vein during placement of a nontunneled central venous catheter. Report codes 36556 and 77001. (Do not report modifier -51 with add-on code 77001.)

Breast, Mammography

Mammography (Figure 17-13) is a radiological examination of the soft tissue and internal structures of the breast.

- **Screening mammography** (Figure 17-14A) is performed when a patient presents without signs and symptoms of breast disease (e.g., routine annual screening for early detection of unsuspected breast cancer) and is reported with code 77067.
- **Diagnostic mammography** (Figure 17-14B) includes an assessment of suspected disease (e.g., suspicious mass is palpated on physical examination) and is reported with codes 77065–77066 when an abnormality is found or suspected.

 NOTE:

Mammography code descriptions do not specify male or female, which means that the codes can be reported for either female or male patients.

EXAMPLE: Patient underwent bilateral screening mammography with computer-aided detection, which was reviewed and interpreted by the radiologist. Report code 77067.

FIGURE 17-13 In mammography, the breast is flattened and then radiographed from above

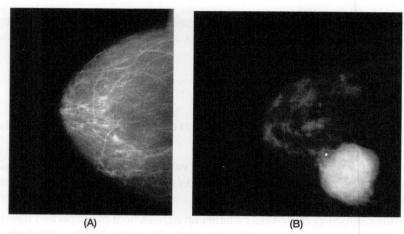

(A)   (B)

FIGURE 17-14 Mammogram images (A) Normal mammogram
(B) Large breast mass is visible, lower right

Bone/Joint Studies

Bone and joint studies are radiological procedures performed to detect bone density, bone age, bone length, vertebral fracture assessment, and bone marrow blood supply. A **bone density study** evaluates diseases of the bone and are used to assess the response of bone disease to treatment. The studies assess bone mass (e.g., density) of the wrist, radius, hip, pelvis, spine, or heel.

Dual energy x-ray absorptiometry (DEXA or **DXA)** is a bone density study that uses two x-ray beams with different levels of energy pulsing alternately (e.g., two-dimensional projection) to create the image. Results are scores that are reported as standard deviations of the bone density of a person at the age of peak bone mass (e.g., 30 years of age). (Both men and women undergo DEXA imaging.) To code DEXA studies properly, determine the type of skeletal bone mass being measured:

- Axial skeleton (e.g., hips, pelvis, or spine)
- Appendicular skeleton (e.g., peripheral bones such as wrist or heel, vertebra)

EXAMPLE 1: Patient underwent DXA bone density study of the hips and pelvis. Report code 77080.

EXAMPLE 2: Nine-day-old infant underwent osseous survey. Report code 77076.

Exercise 17.5 – Diagnostic Ultrasound, Radiologic Guidance, Breast Mammography, and Bone/Joint Studies

Instructions: Assign the CPT code(s) and appropriate modifier(s) to each statement.

1. Radiologist performed a complete abdominal ultrasound, real time, with image documentation.

2. The patient known to have an intrauterine pregnancy based on previous physician evaluation underwent transabdominal real-time ultrasound of pregnant uterus with image documentation, first trimester.

Exercise 17.5 – *continued*

3. Patient underwent fetal biophysical profile, with nonstress testing, due to suspicion that fetus was in distress.

   _____

4. Abdominal ultrasound with real time and image documentation, stomach.

   _____

5. Ophthalmic diagnostic ultrasound for bilateral corneal pachymetry.

   _____

6. Fluoroscopic guidance for needle placement during liver biopsy.

   _____

7. CT guidance for stereotactic localization for treatment during removal of an intracranial lesion.

   _____

8. Magnetic resonance imaging guidance and monitoring for parenchymal tissue ablation of osteoid osteoma (bone tumor), left tibia.

   _____

9. Stereotactic localization guidance for planned breast biopsy, left, one lesion.

   _____

10. Patient underwent limited osseous survey radiologic examination for possible metastases.

    _____

Radiation Oncology

Radiation oncology is the specialty of medicine that utilizes high-energy ionizing radiation in the treatment of malignant neoplasms and certain nonmalignant conditions. Distinct therapeutic modalities (methods) are directed at malignant and benign lesions. Modalities include brachytherapy, hyperthermia, stereotactic radiation, and teletherapy.

Radiation oncology codes include professional services and technical procedures that are organized according to the following types of treatment provided:

- Consultation (clinical management)
- Clinical treatment planning (external and internal sources)
- Medical radiation physics, dosimetry, treatment devices, and special services
- Stereotactic radiation treatment delivery
- Other procedures
- Radiation treatment delivery
- Neutron beam treatment delivery
- Radiation treatment management
- Proton beam treatment delivery
- Hyperthermia
- Clinical intracavitary hyperthermia
- Clinical brachytherapy

Consultation (Clinical Management)

Codes from the CPT E/M, Surgery, and/or Medicine sections are reported by the radiation oncologist who does the following:

- Provides preliminary consultation services
- Evaluates a patient prior to the decision to treat
- Delivers full medical care (in addition to treatment management)

Consultation (clinical management) services provided by the radiation oncologist include evaluation of the patient, determination of the need for radiation therapy, identification of site(s) of treatment, assessment of therapy goal(s), and the coordination and sequencing of combined modality therapy with other oncology specialists. The radiation oncologist subsequently orders and coordinates the technical planning and execution of the treatment with ancillary staff, including radiation therapists, dosimetrists, and physicists. (The treatment is supervised by the radiation oncologist.)

Consultation services provided by radiation oncologists are the same as those provided by other physicians (e.g., a referral is required for initial consultation). The initial consultation is reported with an appropriate CPT Evaluation and Management (E/M) code for outpatient consultation services or inpatient consultation services. (The code is reported just once per course of radiation therapy.) (Refer to Chapter 10 of this textbook for clarification about assignment of consultation codes.)

Once the radiation oncologist has determined the appropriate radiation therapy, the best course of treatment is established. During radiation treatment, patients are monitored closely for adverse reactions that require immediate care. Thus, ongoing patient evaluation is provided as necessary. These services are reported with radiation oncology treatment management codes, *not* E/M service codes.

When a patient completes the course of radiation therapy, the patient continues to see the radiation oncologist during regular follow-up visits. The radiation oncologist monitors the patient's progress and reaction to treatment. This follow-up care is reported with codes from the CPT E/M section (the same as any other established patient follow-up care).

Clinical Treatment Planning (External and Internal Sources)

Clinical treatment planning is performed for each radiation therapy patient, and it includes interpretation of special testing, tumor localization, **treatment volume determination** (region within the body to which radiation therapy is directed), treatment time/dosage determination, choice of treatment modality, determination of number and size of treatment **ports** (sites on the skin where radiation beams enter the body), selection of appropriate treatment devices, and other procedures.

Radiation is administered by a machine outside the body (**external radiation**), is placed inside the body (**internal radiation**) (Figure 17-15), or uses unsealed radioactive materials that travel throughout the body (**systemic radiation therapy**). The internal radiation source is usually sealed in a small container called an *implant* (e.g., thin wire, catheter, ribbon, capsule, or seed) and inserted directly into the body. The type of radiation administered depends on what type of cancer it is, where it is located, how far into the body the radiation has to go, what the patient's general health and medical history are, whether the patient will have other types of cancer treatment, and other factors. Most patients receive external radiation, and some receive both external and internal or systemic radiation therapy.

Clinical treatment planning and tumor mapping are critical to identifying the location, extent, and volume of tumor(s) to be treated and all critical and sensitive structures surrounding them. The radiation oncologist plans the appropriate course of therapy that will allow for maximum benefit while protecting surrounding tissues and structures. Clinical treatment planning may involve ordering and interpreting special tests such as CT scans, lymphangiography, MRI scans, and radionuclide scans and/or surgical exploration with biopsy. Markers may also be placed for the purpose of treatment planning and tumor localization.

 Coding Tip

Debulking (surgical removal of part of a malignant tumor; also called **cytoreduction surgery**) may be performed to enhance the effectiveness of radiation oncology treatment.

FIGURE 17-15 Radium implant devices (A) Colpostat and tandem (B) Placement of colpostat and tandem within vagina and uterus

Therapeutic radiology treatment planning codes are classified according to type of planning, as follows:

- Simple
  - Single treatment area of interest
  - Single port or simple parallel opposed ports
  - Minimal (simple or no) **blocking** (device, such as lead, that shields or protects critical or sensitive organs)
  - No interpretation of special tests for localization of tumor volume

- Intermediate
  - Two separate treatment areas
  - Three or more converging ports

- ○ Multiple blocks to protect critical or sensitive organs
- ○ Special time/dose constraints
- ○ Interpretation of special tests for localization of tumor volume
- Complex
  - ○ Three or more separate treatment areas
  - ○ Highly complex blocking to protect critical or sensitive organs
  - ○ Custom shielding blocks
  - ○ Tangential ports
  - ○ Special **wedges** (treatment beam-modifying devices that act to change the beam intensity profile)
  - ○ Special **compensators** (irregularly shaped beam-modifying devices used to reconfigure beam intensity so it matches irregular tissue contour)
  - ○ Rotational or special beam considerations
  - ○ Combination of therapeutic modalities
  - ○ Interpretation of complex testing procedures (e.g., CT and MRI localization)
  - ○ Possible special laboratory testing

Simulation clinical treatment planning uses a simulator to determine various treatment ports to be used during radiation therapy. The simulator can orient a radiation beam toward a patient according to parameters that imitate the treatment proposed for actual therapy (but it does not deliver radiation therapy). Simulation may be carried out on a dedicated conventional simulator or by use of a CT scanner, radiation therapy treatment unit (e.g., linear accelerator), or other diagnostic imaging equipment (e.g., fluoroscopy, CT, or MRI). Simulation is complex because custom shielding blocks are designed, and the simulation must be coordinated with information from treatment planning CT scans and isodose plan data. Therapeutic radiology simulation-aided field setting codes are classified according to type of setting.

- Simple
  - ○ Simulation of single treatment area
  - ○ Single port or parallel opposed ports
  - ○ Minimal (simple or no) blocking of critical or sensitive organs
- Intermediate
  - ○ Simulation of three or more converging ports
  - ○ Two separate treatment areas
  - ○ Multiple blocking of critical or sensitive organs
- Complex
  - ○ Simulation of tangential (peripheral) portals (or ports)
  - ○ Three or more treatment areas
  - ○ Rotation or arc therapy
  - ○ Three-dimensional (3D)
  - ○ Computer-generated 3D reconstruction of tumor volume and surrounding critical or sensitive normal tissue structures (using CT scans or MRI data in preparation for noncoplanar or coplanar therapy)
  - ○ Simulation uses documented 3D beam's eye view volume-dose displays of multiple or moving beams
  - ○ Documentation with 3D volume reconstruction and dose distribution is required

EXAMPLE: Radiation oncologist provided simple therapeutic radiology treatment planning services, which consisted of a single area of malignancy with a single port or opposing ports parallel to each other and basic or no blocking. Report code 77261.

Medical Radiation Physics, Dosimetry, Treatment Devices, and Special Services

"Medical radiation physics, **dosimetry** (measurement and calculation of radiation treatment doses), treatment devices, and special services" codes are reported by the health care facility (e.g., hospital). There is no professional component for most of these services. (Reimbursement for the radiation oncologist's professional component is included in reimbursement for clinical treatment planning and radiation treatment management codes.)

A basic radiation dosimetry calculation is a photon calculation that includes central axis depth dose, time dose factor (TDF), nominal standard dose (NSD), gap calculation, off-axis and tissue inhomogeneity factors, as well as calculation of nonionizing radiation surface and depth dose. Dosimetry may be repeated during the course of treatment as required. That CPT code is reported as many times as necessary during a course of radiation therapy. However, codes for teletherapy isodose planning services are reimbursed just once per course of treatment.

Intensity modulated radiation therapy (IMRT) uses high-precision radiotherapy to precisely target cancerous tumors with higher radiation doses by using strategically positioned beams to minimize collateral damage to healthy cells. IMRT varies the intensity of radiation exposure depending on whether tumor is present in the beam pathway. The radiation therapy consists of multiple pencil thin beams (or beamlets) calculated to hit tumors with high-dose radiation beams and sensitive normal tissues with modulated lower-intensity beams, leaving them mostly unaffected. Planning for IMRT involves the use of computer programs that calculate the beam angle configurations and dosage intensities. The CPT code reported for an IMRT plan includes dose-volume histograms for target and critical structure partial tolerance specifications. A CPT code is reported for IMRT delivery, and includes guidance and tracking, when performed.

Brachytherapy isodose calculation is also reimbursed just once per course of treatment. The number of units billed for brachytherapy isodose calculation (simple, intermediate, or complex) should equal the number of brachytherapy treatments provided within the billing period. When billing is done for multiple treatment devices, there must be documentation in the clinical record to support the medical necessity of each device or set of devices.

The use of a treatment device is based on the clinical judgment of the radiation oncologist and is influenced by the patient's anatomy and disease state. The selection and use of any treatment device requires medical necessity, radiation oncologist involvement, and a written and signed order for each device. The radiation oncologist must be directly involved in the design, selection, and placement of any device and must document their involvement with each device.

Treatment devices include the following:

- Beam-shaping devices are called blocks, and they are placed in an external radiation beam to modify its shape to either contour the beam around target structures or to shield normal tissues.
- Immobilization devices (e.g., thermoplastic face and body masks, bite-block head holders, Styrofoam body casts, and breast boards) are used to restrict patient movement during treatment.
- Beam-modifying devices include wedges, compensators, and boluses.
- Shielding devices include bite blocks, eye shields, and testicular shields.

Codes for treatment devices are reported at the onset of the treatment. They may be reported again later during the course of treatment if additional or new devices are required.

Codes for medical physics and medical radiation physics consultations are reported for patients undergoing radiation therapy. Although the radiation oncologist orders these procedures, he or she generally has little involvement in the actual procedure. The medical radiation physics measurements are used to evaluate a treatment plan. After these procedures are completed, treatment management and delivery is established. Continuing medical physics consultation is reported "per week of therapy," which means that it may be reported after multiple radiation treatments *if those treatments occurred during one week of treatment. If, however, the multiple radiation treatments occurred over a period of multiple different weeks, the continuing medical physics consultation code would be reported once for each week of treatment.*

> **EXAMPLE:** Radiation oncologist designed and constructed a simple block treatment device. Report code 77332.

Stereotactic Radiation Treatment Delivery

Stereotactic radiation treatment delivery includes the following types:

- *Stereotactic radiosurgery (SRS)*: Radiation therapy that focuses high-powered x-rays onto a small area, such as a brain, liver, lung, or other lesion; it is a single-session treatment that has such a dramatic effect on its target that the result is considered "surgical"; however, it is not actually considered a surgical procedure; also referred to as *gamma knife* or *cyberknife*.

- *Stereotactic body radiation therapy (SBRT)*: Radiation therapy that uses special equipment to position a patient and precisely deliver smaller doses of radiation over several days to bone, liver, and lung tumors in the body; SBRT is not administered to brain tumors; exposure to normal tissue is minimized; also called extracranial *radiotherapy*.

> **EXAMPLE:** Patient underwent radiation treatment delivery, which used stereotactic radiosurgery to deliver one large radiation dose to his brain tumor. Report code 77371.

Radiation Treatment Delivery

Radiation treatment delivery codes are reported for the administration of radiation therapy *per treatment*. A nonphysician may deliver radiation treatment; however, the radiation oncologist is responsible for checking and documenting the accuracy of the treatment. The radiation oncologist must also treat any adverse reactions to treatment and monitor the effects of radiation therapy on the tumor and surrounding tissues. (Radiation treatment delivery includes ongoing patient evaluation, and codes for such evaluation are not reported separately.)

- Radiation treatment delivery is measured in units of **MeV** (**megaelectron volts** or **megavolts**), which is 1 million electron volts.

- **Therapeutic port films** are x-rays taken during delivery of radiation treatment that utilize the treatment beam of the machine. Portal films demonstrate the exact shape, size, and area covered by the treatment beam during an actual treatment.

> **EXAMPLE:** Complex radiation therapy delivery was directed to three distinct treatment areas, and 11 MeV was administered. Report code 77412.

Neutron Beam Treatment Delivery

Neutron beam radiation therapy is an external radiation treatment that uses higher linear energy transfer to treat certain tumors (e.g., salivary gland tumors) due to increased susceptibility, as compared with conventional radiation therapy. An interventional radiologist provides this treatment at a facility equipped with a superconducting accelerator (cyclotron). Pretreatment planning usually involves CT to locate and determine the tumor volume prior to radiation therapy.

> **EXAMPLE:** Patient underwent high-energy neutron radiation treatment delivery 1 isocenter with coplanar geometry and blocking. Report code 77423.

Radiation Treatment Management

Radiation treatment management is reported in units of five fractions or treatment sessions even though the service need not be performed on consecutive days. For radiation treatment management purposes, a **fraction** is a single session of radiation treatment delivered to a specific area of interest. The number of calendar days between treatment fractions is not relevant as long as the treatment is directed to the same area and is part of a single course of therapy. Thus, a claim is submitted with the treatment code for every five treatments. *Multiple fractions* that represent two or more treatment sessions furnished on the same day are counted separately *if there has been a distinct break in therapy sessions*.

> **EXAMPLE:** Radiation treatment management of 20 daily treatments during a 4-week period. Report codes 77427, 77427, 77427, and 77427.

 NOTE:

- When a patient who has completed a course of radiation therapy returns with a recurrent tumor and treatment is provided to the same area, report codes for a separate course of radiation therapy.
- HCPCS level II codes for radioactive materials, when supplied by the radiation oncologist, are reported in addition to codes for radiation therapy.

Reimbursement for weekly radiation therapy management includes payment for normal follow-up care during therapy and for three months following its completion.

> **EXAMPLE:** Radiation oncologist provided radiation therapy management for a course of treatment that consisted of two single sessions (fractions). Report code 77431.

Proton Beam Treatment Delivery

Compared to photon beams, proton beams deliver higher radiation doses to tumors, and proton beams do not exceed the radiation tolerance of normal tissue. Proton beam treatment delivery is a modality that consists of delivering smaller doses to intervening normal tissues and organs. Codes are reported according to the following types of treatment:

- *Simple*: Single treatment area utilizing a single nontangential/oblique port, custom block with or without compensation
- *Intermediate*: One or more treatment areas utilizing two or more ports or one or more tangential/oblique ports, with custom blocks and compensators
- *Complex*: One or more treatment areas using two or more ports per treatment area with matching or patching fields and/or multiple isocenters, with custom blocks and compensators

> **EXAMPLE:** Patient underwent intermediate proton treatment delivery to two treatment areas using two ports per treatment area and custom blocks. Report code 77523.

Hyperthermia and Clinical Intracavitary Hyperthermia

Hyperthermia involves the use of an external heat-generating source (e.g., ultrasound or microwave) to produce localized heating. Hyperthermia is usually performed immediately before or after a session of external beam radiation therapy. Typically, three to six applications of hyperthermia per course of radiation therapy are required. When hyperthermia is generated by intracavitary probe(s), report code 77620.

> **EXAMPLE:** Patient underwent hyperthermia treatment, which was generated by interstitial probe that used 10 interstitial applicators. Report code 77615.

Clinical Brachytherapy

Brachytherapy (Figure 17-16) involves the use of radioactive isotopes for internal radiation, and codes are reported according to the following applications:

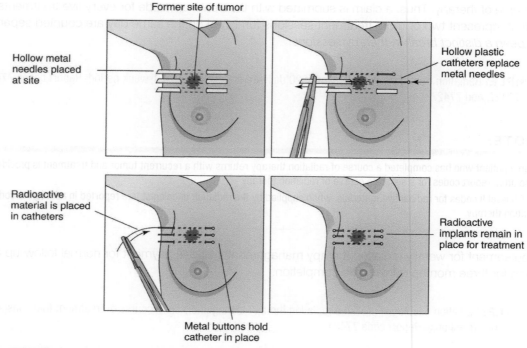

Former site of tumor

Hollow metal needles placed at site

Hollow plastic catheters replace metal needles

Radioactive material is placed in catheters

Radioactive implants remain in place for treatment

Metal buttons hold catheter in place

FIGURE 17-16 Brachytherapy for treatment of breast cancer

- *Simple*: Application has 1 to 4 sources/ribbons
- *Intermediate*: Application has 5 to 10 sources/ribbons
- *Complex*: Application has greater than 10 sources/ribbons

A *source* is an intracavitary placement or permanent interstitial placement. A *ribbon* is a temporary interstitial placement. Intracavitary brachytherapy is performed by placing applicators containing radioactive materials directly into or around a tumor area. A common use of intracavitary brachytherapy is the treatment of carcinoma of the endometrium (uterus) or cervix.

Intracavitary and interstitial applications are seldom used as the sole modality of radiation treatment. Interstitial brachytherapy is performed with needles, ribbons, or wires containing radioactive materials that are inserted directly into and around a cancerous area. The devices remain in place over a period of many days while delivering their relatively low-intensity radiation directly into the tumor. These applications are often used in conjunction with external beam radiation therapy to bring the total dose up to the desired level.

EXAMPLE: Radiation oncologist supervised the handling and loading of a radiation source. Report code 77790.

Exercise 17.6 – Radiation Oncology

Instructions: Assign the CPT code to each statement.

1. A special teletherapy port plan for the total body.

   _____

2. The patient underwent a hyperthermia treatment that was generated by an intracavitary probe.

   _____

Exercise 17.6 – *continued*

3. A therapeutic radiology simulation-aided field setting of a single treatment area with a single port was performed.

_____

4. Patient underwent superficial voltage radiation treatment delivery.

_____

5. The surface application of a radiation source was performed.

_____

Nuclear Medicine

Nuclear medicine involves the use of radioactive elements (e.g., radionuclides and radioisotopes) for diagnostic imaging (e.g., scan) and **radiopharmaceutical therapy** (destroys diseased tissue, such as a malignant neoplasm). The isotope emits gamma rays as it deteriorates, which enables the radiologist to visualize internal abnormalities (e.g., tumors). The images created by the contrast media (radioactive element) are detected by a gamma camera.

Nuclear medicine codes do not include the provision of radium, which means that the nuclear medicine report must be reviewed to identify the diagnostic or therapeutic radiopharmaceutical provided. Then an appropriate HCPCS level II code is reported for the radiopharmaceutical administered. (The injection of the radionuclide is included as part of the procedure, and a separate injection code is *not* reported.)

Common diagnostic nuclear medicine procedures include bone scans, cardiac scans (e.g., thallium scan and MUGA), renal scans, thyroid scans, and hepatobiliary scans (e.g., HIDA scans). Therapeutic nuclear medicine procedures are used to treat diseases such as chronic leukemia, hyperthyroidism, and thyroid cancer.

The Nuclear Medicine subsection contains two headings.

- Diagnostic
- Therapeutic

The Diagnostic heading contains the following subheadings:

- Endocrine System
- Hematopoietic, Reticuloendothelial, and Lymphatic System
- Gastrointestinal System
- Musculoskeletal System
- Cardiovascular System
- Respiratory System
- Nervous System
- Genitourinary System
- Other Procedures

The Therapeutic heading contains no subheadings.

Endocrine System

Nuclear medicine is commonly used to evaluate thyroid function (e.g., thyroid update). **Uptake** is the absorption by a tissue of a substance, material, or mineral and its permanent or temporary retention.

A thyroid uptake test measures thyroid function to determine how much iodine the thyroid absorbs (expressed as a percentage of the administered radioiodine present in the thyroid gland at a specific time after administration). Thyroid imaging (scan) is performed to assess anatomical size and physiologic function. A radioactive tracer (e.g., iodide-123 capsule or technetium-99m injection) is administered, which allows blood flow and vascularity of the thyroid to be monitored by imaging at different intervals.

EXAMPLE: Patient underwent thyroid imaging with vascular flow and radioactive tracer. Report code 78013 (and a HCPCS level II code for the radioactive material administered).

Hematopoietic, Reticuloendothelial, and Lymphatic System

Bone marrow imaging evaluates bone marrow functioning and irregular marrow tissue expansion (e.g., malignancy or infection). A radiopharmaceutical radiotracer (e.g., radiolabeled sulfur colloid) is injected, and images are obtained after a two- to three-hour delay using a special camera (e.g., scintillation or gamma camera). The camera takes images by detecting gamma radiation from the radionuclide in bone marrow as it "scintillates" (e.g., emits energy in a flash of light) when coming in contact with the camera's detector.

For whole blood volume determination, the radiopharmaceutical volume-dilution technique evaluates plasma and red cell volume by using radiolabeled protein tracers (e.g., iodinated serum albumin) and autologous radiolabeled red blood cells. The procedure involves collecting blood and recording blood counts to calculate volumes using formulas that compare the dilution factor from a standard sample of each radiotracer.

A lymphatics and lymph nodes imaging code is reported for lymphoscintigraphy. The injection of a radioactive tracer is included in the lymphoscintigraphy procedure. Modifier -26 (Professional Component) is added to the lymphoscintigraphy code only if the professional component was performed by the physician.

EXAMPLE: Patient underwent a platelet survival study. Report code 78191.

Gastrointestinal System

Tomographic single-photon emission computed tomography (SPECT) is used for evaluation of the anatomy and functionality of the liver. A radiolabeled sulfur colloid is injected, and imaging of the distribution of gamma radiation emitted from the radiopharmaceutical is performed. SPECT imaging is performed by rotating a single- or multiple-head camera around the patient to provide 3D computer-reconstructed views of cross-sectional slices of the liver. For imaging done with a vascular flow test, red blood cells are labeled to enable imaging of the blood flow through the liver.

EXAMPLE: Patient underwent acute gastrointestinal blood loss imaging. Report code 78278.

Musculoskeletal System

Single and dual photon absorptiometry are noninvasive techniques used to measure the absorption of the photon beam (e.g., mono- or dichromatic) by bone material. The device is placed directly on the patient and uses a small amount of radionuclide to measure the bone mass absorption. This provides a measurement of the bone mineral density of cortical bone and can be used to assess an individual's response to treatment at different intervals.

EXAMPLE: Patient underwent a bone density study with single photon absorptiometry, vertebral column and rib cage. Report code 78350.

Cardiovascular System

Myocardial perfusion and cardiac blood pool imaging may be performed at rest or during stress. When performed during exercise and/or pharmacologic stress, report an appropriate stress test code from the Medicine section. **Cardiac blood pool imaging** uses a gamma camera for sampling, which is performed repetitively over several hundred heartbeats during the transition of the radionuclide (e.g., technetium-99m) through the central circulation.

Nuclear imaging for noncardiac vascular flow studies is performed to evaluate arterial or venous peripheral vascular diseases or injuries. In radionuclide angiography, red blood cells are tagged with radioactivity and injected intravenously. A scintillation camera takes a series of dynamic images every two to three seconds immediately after injection, followed by static images.

For myocardial perfusion study, PET myocardial imaging is typically performed on patients with coronary artery disease and left ventricular dysfunction. PET scanning is also used in diagnostic and therapeutic procedures for malignant tumors. PET is a noninvasive nuclear medicine technique that produces 3D images of the distribution of radioactivity (e.g., emission of positrons) similar to a CT scan. However, PET uses radiopharmaceuticals instead of dye and x-rays. When the radiopharmaceutical agent is injected into the blood, a positron scanner detects, measures, and displays metabolism of tissues (e.g., heart and brain) and many types of tumors. PET scans are also used to diagnose dementia. (Report appropriate HCPCS level II codes for radiopharmaceutical diagnostic imaging agents or "tracers," in addition to CPT codes for PET scan procedures.)

EXAMPLE: Patient underwent single-study myocardial imaging, PET, and metabolic evaluation. Report code 78459.

Respiratory System

A pulmonary perfusion imaging procedure is used to diagnose pulmonary emboli (Figure 17-17) and pulmonary trauma. The procedure consists of imaging a patient twice.

- Once after inhalation of a radioactive aerosol to determine pulmonary ventilation
- Once again after injection of a radioactive particulate to determine lung perfusion

The Respiratory System heading contains a combination code that allows accurate reporting of both components of the procedure.

EXAMPLE: Patient underwent particulate pulmonary perfusion imaging. Report code 78580.

Nervous System

Radiology Nervous System codes are reported for brain imaging, cerebral vascular flow, cerebrospinal fluid flow/leakage, and radiopharmaceutical dacryocystography radiographic procedures.

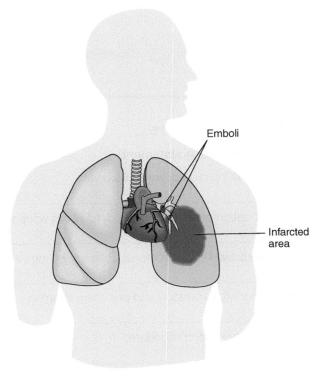

FIGURE 17-17 Pulmonary emboli

EXAMPLE: Patient underwent radiopharmaceutical dacryocystography. Report code 78660.

Genitourinary System

Radiology Genitourinary System codes are reported for kidney imaging, kidney function study, urinary bladder residual study, ureteral reflux study, and testicular imaging radiographic procedures.

EXAMPLE: Patient underwent multiple kidney imaging studies with vascular flow and function, with and without pharmacological angiotensin intervention as a converting enzyme inhibitor. Report code 78709.

Other Procedures

Radiology Other Procedures codes include tomographic SPECT imaging, which allows for evaluation of complex anatomy. A radionuclide is introduced, and the distribution of gamma radiation emitted is detected with a camera that rotates around the patient. A 3D computer reconstructs views of cross-sectional slices of the body. When scanning for an inflammatory process, gallium is the radiopharmaceutical used.

EXAMPLE: Patient underwent single-area, single-day of imaging, tomographic SPECT for radiopharmaceutical localization of a stomach tumor. Report code 78803 (and a HCPCS level II code for the radiopharmaceutical agent).

Therapeutic (Nuclear Medicine)

When radiopharmaceutical therapy is administered orally or intravenously, the reported code includes the mode of administration (e.g., injection or infusion). When intra-arterial, intracavitary, or intra-articular administration is the method used for radiopharmaceutical therapy, an appropriate injection and/or procedure code is reported in addition to the therapy code. When imaging guidance and radiological supervision and interpretation are provided for intra-arterial, intracavitary, or intra-articular administration, appropriate code(s) are reported in addition to the therapy and administration codes.

EXAMPLE: Patient underwent radiopharmaceutical therapy for chronic leukemia, by oral administration. Report code 79005.

Exercise 17.7 – Nuclear Medicine

Instructions: Assign the CPT code to each statement.

1. Therapeutic radiopharmaceutical is injected directly into a vein.

   _____

2. The physician determines the location of the sentinel node(s) using scintigraphy imaging.

   _____

3. The physician administered a radiolabeled monoclonal antibody by intravenous infusion.

   _____

4. Patient underwent aerosol pulmonary ventilation and perfusion imaging.

   _____

5. Patient underwent cardiac shunt detection procedure.

   _____

Summary

Radiology is a branch of medicine that uses imaging techniques to diagnose and treat disease. A radiologist is a physician who has undergone specialized training to interpret diagnostic x-rays, perform specialized x-ray procedures, and administer radiation for the treatment of disease (e.g., cancer). The Radiology section includes subsections for diagnostic radiology (diagnostic imaging); diagnostic ultrasound; radiologic guidance; breast, mammography; bone/joint studies; radiation oncology; and nuclear medicine. Procedure descriptions include the type of service, anatomical site, and use of contrast material. Radiology guidelines are located at the beginning of the section, and they should be carefully reviewed prior to the assigning of codes.

Internet Links

Hospital for Special Surgery: Go to *www.hss.edu*, click on Conditions, and click on a letter that corresponds with the first letter of condition or treatment to be researched.

LearningRadiology: *www.learningradiology.com*

RadiologyInfo.org: *www.radiologyinfo.org*

Review

Multiple Choice

Instructions: Circle the most appropriate response.

1. Which are the types of radiographic projection?
   a. Anteroposterior, lateral, oblique, and posteroanterior
   b. Anteroposterior, posteroanterior, midsagittal, and sagittal
   c. Coronal, midsagittal, sagittal, and transverse
   d. Coronal, transverse, lateral, and oblique

2. Which are the three components of a radiologic procedure?
   a. Coronal, transverse, and lateral
   b. Posteroanterior, midsagittal, and sagittal
   c. Simple, intermediate, and complex
   d. Technical, professional, and global

3. Which is a common contrast agent administered to provide better radiographic visualization of organs studied?
   a. Barium sulfate
   b. Betadine
   c. Iodized sodium
   d. Sulfuric acid

4. Which is the rectal administration of contrast material?
   a. Barium enema
   b. Implantation
   c. Infusion
   d. Injection

5. A patient underwent a procedure in which a special catheter tipped with a hollow tube and rotating blades was used to cut away plaque from the arterial wall. The debris was suctioned out of the body through the tube. Which procedure was performed?
   a. Dual energy x-ray absorptiometry
   b. Epidurography
   c. Transluminal atherectomy
   d. Venography

6. Biometric A-scan, quantitative A-scan, B-scan, and corneal pachymetry are considered:
   a. types of ophthalmic ultrasound.
   b. types of x-rays.
   c. radiographic projections.
   d. ultrasound display modes.

7. Brachytherapy, hyperthermia, stereotactic radiation, and teletherapy are considered:
    a. dosimetry techniques.
    b. external heat-generating sources.
    c. therapeutic modalities for radiation oncology.
    d. treatment devices.

8. The use of equipment and supplies and the employment of radiologic technologists to perform diagnostic imaging examinations and administer radiation therapy treatments is called the _____.
    a. complete procedure   c. professional element
    b. global service   d. technical component

9. In CPT, many radiological services include image guidance in their code descriptions, which means _____ radiological supervision and interpretation codes for image guidance are not reported.
    a. contrast material   c. therapeutic
    b. separate   d. unlisted

10. A patient underwent a nuclear medicine procedure in which radionuclides were administered to destroy a malignant neoplasm. For nuclear medicine purposes, radionuclides are an example of _____ elements and destruction of the malignant neoplasm is considered the _____ procedure.
    a. radioactive, diagnostic
    b. radioactive, radiopharmaceutical
    c. radiopharmaceutical, gamma ray
    d. therapeutic, gamma ray

11. Complete radiological exam of paranasal sinuses. Which CPT code is assigned?
    a. 70140   b. 70160   c. 70210   d. 70220

12. Chest x-ray, four views. Which CPT code is assigned?
    a. 71045   b. 71046   c. 71047   d. 71048

13. Computed tomography of the cervical spine without contrast on a patient, repeated the same day. Which CPT code(s) are assigned?
    a. 70450, 70450-76   b. 72125, 72125-76   c. 72126-76   d. 72127-76

14. Hip x-ray, two views, performed on the right side of the patient. Which CPT code is assigned?
    a. 73501-RT   b. 73502-RT   c. 73521-RT   d. 73525-RT

15. Selective adrenal angiography, left side, with radiological supervision and interpretation. Which CPT code is assigned?
    a. 75726   b. 75731   c. 75733   d. 75736

16. Screening mammography, bilateral breasts. Which CPT code is assigned?
    a. 77065-50   b. 77066   c. 77067   d. 77067-50

17. Red cell survival study. Which CPT code is assigned?
    a. 78110   b. 78120   c. 78130   d. 78140

18. Radiopharmaceutical localization of tumor, tomographic (SPECT), performed twice by the same physician during the same encounter. Which CPT code(s) are assigned?
    a. 78803   c. 78803-77
    b. 78803-51   d. 78803, 78803-76

19. Radiopharmaceutical therapy by intracavitary administration. Which CPT code is assigned?
    a. 79200   b. 79403   c. 79440   d. 79445

20. Therapeutic radiology treatment planning, simple. Which CPT code is assigned?
    a. 77261   b. 77262   c. 77263   d. 77280

Coding Practice

Instructions: Assign the CPT code(s) and appropriate modifier(s) to each case.

Diagnostic Radiology

1. X-RAY OF ABDOMEN: Radiological examination 1-view of abdomen reveals no abnormal soft tissue masses, gas shadows, or calcifications. Liver and spleen not enlarged. Visualized bones appear normal.

   _____

2. X-RAY OF COLON (SINGLE-CONTRAST STUDY): Fluoroscopic and radiographic examination of the colon reveals normal retrograde flow of barium through all segments of the large bowel and into the terminal ileum. No diverticula or other filling defects are demonstrated. Terminal ileum is not unusual. The postevacuation response is normal, and no alteration of the mucosal pattern is demonstrated.

   IMPRESSION: Normal colon and terminal ileum.

   _____

3. GALLBLADDER: Following administration of oral contrast medium, there is satisfactory concentration within the gallbladder. The outline is normal, and no calculi are detected.

   IMPRESSION: Normal gallbladder series.

   _____

4. UPPER GASTROINTESTINAL SERIES: Radiographic examination of upper gastrointestinal tract that includes scout abdominal radiographs, double-contrast study, reveals no abnormalities of the swallowing mechanism or of the entire esophagus. The stomach is readily entered, peristalsis traverses this organ in normal fashion, and a very small sliding type of hiatus hernia of the stomach is seen on one of the radiographs. No reflux of gastric contents into the esophagus or radiographic signs of esophagitis can be seen. The mucosal pattern of the stomach is not unusual. There is a suggestion of a small ulcer crater of the lesser curvature aspect of the pyloric canal of the stomach. No additional site of gastric ulceration or other abnormality is seen. The duodenal bulb fills out well, and this structure is noted to be slightly distorted in configuration; however, no ulcer crater of the duodenal bulb is appreciated. Prolapse of gastric mucosa into the base of the bulb is seen. The remainder of the duodenal loop and the upper jejunum mucosal pattern are within normal limits.

   _____

5. SMALL BOWEL SERIES: Serial films obtained show normal progression of barium through the small intestine. The jejunum and ileum show a normal caliber and position. There is no evidence of filling defect or obstruction. The mucosal pattern is normal.

   IMPRESSION: Normal small bowel series.

   _____

6. CHEST: Two-view radiological examination of the chest show increased markings with some honeycomb formations, probably representing bronchiectasis associated with infiltrate. However, as compared with earlier study, there are no significant changes. Linear atelectasis is seen in the lower lung field. Otherwise, the lung fields remain clear. The heart is enlarged in its transverse diameter, and its CT ratio measures 16.0 cm/30.5 cm. Calcification is seen in the thoracic aorta.

   CONCLUSION: Increased markings in both bases with honeycomb formations, most likely representing bronchiectasis probably superimposed with infiltrate. Close follow-up is recommended.

   _____

7. RIGHT RIB CAGE: AP and oblique views of the right portion of the rib cage show no evidence of fracture or other abnormality of the visualized ribs.

    _____

8. SKULL: Skull in three views shows calvarium to be intact. There is no evidence of any abnormal calcification or increased intracranial pressure. Sella turcica is normal in size and shape. There are a few teeth in the mandible, and there is poor visualization of the lamina dura.

    _____

9. LEFT HAND: Left hand in two views shows some osteoporosis of the visualized bones. There is no evidence of fracture or dislocation. Calcification is seen in the arteries around the wrist.

    _____

10. CHEST: Radiologic examination of chest, one view, at 72 inches shows the heart to be transverse in position. Significant enlargement is not apparent on this study. At both bases, there is noted air-bronchogram effect associated with pulmonary infiltration. The thoracic aorta shows atheromatous calcification, and the right acromioclavicular joint shows degenerative arthrosis, as does the thoracic spine, which also shows a scoliosis with convexity toward the right.

    _____

11. DRIP TECHNIQUE INFUSION UROGRAPHY: Right renal length is approximately 11.3 cm, and the left is approximately 10.8 cm. Right kidney is higher than the left. Following Renografin, there was minimal delay in excretion from the kidneys and rather poor concentration bilaterally throughout the study, particularly on the right. As far as can be seen, the renal collecting structures are grossly normal. Drip infusion urography shows poorly functioning kidneys. For this reason, one cannot fully assess the kidneys or ureters. As far as can be seen, significant pathology is not apparent.

    _____

12. SKULL: Cranial vault is intact. Sella turcica was normal in size and shape. There are no intracranial calcifications.

    _____

13. CERVICAL SPINE: Two views were done; there is no fracture or dislocation identified. Alignment is normal. There is no disc space narrowing. Neural foramina are patent bilaterally. There are no cervical ribs and no soft tissue calcifications in either side of the neck.

    _____

14. LEFT ELBOW IN FRONTAL, LATERAL, OBLIQUE, AND AXIAL PROJECTIONS: The elbow is believed to be negative for fracture or dislocation, but because of some irregularity of ossification in the distal metaphysic, conservative management and reexamination is recommended before use is allowed.

    _____

15. BOTH KNEES IN FRONTAL, OBLIQUE, AND LATERAL PROJECTIONS: There is no fracture or dislocation and no joint effusion.
    IMPRESSION: Negative examination of both knees.

    _____

16. LEFT WRIST RADIOGRAPHED IN FRONTAL AND LATERAL PROJECTIONS: There has been an anatomical reduction of the distal radial epiphysis.

    _____

17. ABDOMINAL SERIES: A three-view radiologic examination of the abdomen shows gross distention of multiple loops of small bowel in the midabdomen with large air fluid levels. I see very little air in the colon past the hepatic flexure. The fact that this patient is only two days after abdominal surgery more or less points to a paralytic ileus, but I cannot absolutely rule out the possibility of a mechanical obstruction without a small bowel study.

CONCLUSION: Multiple dilated loops of small bowel in the midabdomen. The possibility of a mechanical obstruction cannot be ruled out without a small bowel study. A repeat abdominal series would be advisable before any further studies are done.

18. NUCLEAR VENTRICULOGRAM: Following injection of 22 mCi of Tc-99m, ventriculogram was done and ejection fraction was calculated. The study was compared with prior ventricular ejection, which was 42% with a peak ejection velocity of 2.2 EDV/second. This compares with the last reported values of 31%, 33%, and 24%.

19. MASTOIDS: The left mastoid shows a surgical defect, apparently due to simple mastoidectomy. There are many small, residual cloudy areas in the periphery of the mastoidectomy defect and in the attic region and anterior to the knee of the sinus and low in the squama extending toward the root of the zygoma. No sequestrum is noted. The tegmen antri appears defective. The left sinus is in good position. The left internal auditory canal is of normal caliber. There are a few small cells along the sinus groove near the tip; these also appear cloudy. The left malleus and incus are partly outlined. The right mastoid is highly pneumatic with cells extending into the zygoma. The right malleus and incus are partly outlined. The right sinus is in good position. The right internal auditory canal is of normal caliber.

20. CT SCAN: After administration of intravenous contrast dye, soft tissue structures of the neck are identified via computed tomography (CT) scan. The thyroid and parathyroid glands are seen. The right parathyroid gland shows a cyst-like structure.

21. CT SCAN: The lumbar spine has a right curvature of 3 mm. The vertebra at L4 has a moderate amount of bone spur.

CONCLUSION: Scoliosis.

22. X-RAY OF SHOULDER: AP and lateral views of the right shoulder reveal no soft tissue masses or bony abnormalities.

CONCLUSION: Normal right shoulder.

23. X-RAY OF LEFT ANKLE: Lateral, AP, and oblique views reveal fracture of the malleolus bone on the lateral side. Soft tissue swelling is noted at the fracture site. No dislocation is seen.

CONCLUSION: Fracture of left ankle.

24. MRI OF HEART: A complete view of the heart and cardiac structures via magnetic resonance imaging (MRI) revealed no abnormalities. Heart valves were normal in appearance. Cardiac function was normal.

CONCLUSION: Normal imaging of the heart.

Diagnostic Ultrasound

25. ABDOMINAL ULTRASOUND: The pregnant uterus is examined via a transabdominal view. Estimated gestation is 16 weeks. A single fetus is observed. No abnormalities of the fetus or placenta are seen. Real-time imaging is provided during this ultrasound.

---

26. DIAGNOSTIC ULTRASOUND: The scrotum is normal in size. All tissue within appears normal. The testes are normal in appearance. The epididymis appears normal in structure.

Radiation Oncology

27. RADIATION TREATMENT: 4 MeV were delivered to thyroid area.

Nuclear Medicine

28. PET SCAN: The chest region positron emission tomography (PET) scan reveals no soft tissue masses or bony abnormalities. Ribs, mediastinum, and heart are normal.

---

29. NUCLEAR LIVER-SPLEEN SCAN: The liver is of normal size with homogeneous uptake. The spleen is enlarged and is almost the same size as the liver. There is also increased activity in the spleen. I do not see any focal areas of diminished activity, and there is no significant bone marrow uptake.

CONCLUSION: Splenomegaly.

---

30. NUCLEAR MEDICINE: WHOLE BODY BONE AND JOINT SCAN: Uptake was noted in the nasal area of the sphenoid sinuses. The remainder of the scan is normal. No masses, bony abnormalities, or metastatic disease is seen.

CPT Pathology and Laboratory

Chapter Outline

Overview of Pathology and Laboratory Section

Pathology and Laboratory Section Guidelines

Pathology and Laboratory Subsections

Chapter Objectives

At the conclusion of this chapter, the student should be able to:

1. Define key terms related to the CPT Pathology and Laboratory Section.
2. Summarize the organization, format, and content of the CPT Pathology and Laboratory section.
3. Interpret CPT Pathology and Laboratory Section guidelines.
4. Assign codes from the subsections of CPT Pathology and Laboratory.

Key Terms

accession

adjuvant

aliquot

analyte

antibody

antigen

arterial puncture

assay

Bethesda System

block

Chemstrip automated
   urine analyzer

chromosomal breakage
   syndrome

Clinical Laboratory
   Improvement Act of
   1988 (CLIA)

cytogenetics

cytopathology

definitive identification

dipstick

evocative

fluorescence *in situ*
   hybridization (FISH)

Gram stain

gross examination

hematology

immunoglobulin

immunology

microbiology

microtechnique

necropsy

phlebotomy

presumptive
   identification

qualitative assay

quantitative assay

reagent strip automated
   urine analyzer

section

specimen

venipuncture

Introduction

The Pathology and Laboratory section of CPT includes subsections for organ or disease-oriented panels, drug assays, therapeutic drug assays, evocative/suppression testing, consultations (clinical pathology), urinalysis, molecular pathology, genomic sequencing procedures and other molecular multianalyte assays, multianalyte assays with algorithmic analyses, chemistry, hematology and coagulation, immunology, transfusion medicine, microbiology, anatomical pathology, cytopathology, cytogenetic studies, surgical pathology, *in vivo* (e.g., transcutaneous) laboratory procedures, other procedures, reproductive medicine procedures, and proprietary laboratory analyses.

Overview of Pathology and Laboratory Section

CPT pathology and laboratory codes describe services performed on specimens (e.g., body fluids, tissue, or cytological specimens) to evaluate, prevent, diagnose, or treat a disease. A **specimen** (e.g., blood, urine, tissue from an organ) is tissue submitted for laboratory or pathological evaluation. Types of examinations include the following:

- Biophysical
- Chemical
- Cytological
- Hematological

- Immunohematological
- Microbiological
- Pathological
- Serological

> **EXAMPLE:** A wound culture is obtained from the smear of an infected area. The infective organism is identified as the result of growing the organism on a culture plate and microscopically reviewing the specimen or serologically testing the organism (e.g., antistreptolysin O titer).

Most clinical laboratory service codes include a technical component; however, some include both a technical and a professional component. In addition, because many pathology and laboratory procedures can be performed using different methods, patient record documentation must be reviewed along with code descriptions and instructional notes.

New *proprietary laboratory analyses (PLA)* codes were added to CPT effective January 2016 and are available to any clinical laboratory or manufacturer that wants to specifically identify their commercially available tests that are used on human specimens. PLA test codes are published quarterly at the www.amaproductupdates.org website, with new codes effective in the quarter following their publication. The CPT coding manual now includes PLA codes, and new codes will continue to be published quarterly at the AMA's website.

NOTE:

Hospitals include pathology and laboratory codes on a chargemaster, which is used to report services (and supplies) for inpatients, outpatients, and emergency department patients. Coders do not assign codes to pathology and laboratory procedures that are performed on an inpatient basis because such services do not impact diagnosis-related group (DRG) assignment and facility reimbursement.

NOTE:

Depending on the contract negotiated between pathologists and the health care facility

- Pathologists are considered employees of the health care facility (e.g., a hospital) or they are considered contractors.
- The facility submits claims to obtain reimbursement for all services provided to patients (including professional services) *or* the pathologists use a medical billing service to submit claims for professional services.

Specimens

Laboratory codes describe the *performance* of lab tests. These codes do not include *collection of the specimen* (e.g., venipuncture, fingerstick, or lumbar puncture) used to perform the test.

For laboratory-testing purposes, a specimen includes tissue (e.g., blood and urine) that is submitted for individual and separate examinations and/or pathological diagnosis. Specimen collection is reported separately, in addition to the laboratory test performed. Collection methods vary from those requiring no patient preparation to invasive-type procedures, and the reason for the test typically determines the appropriate collection method. Special collection methods (e.g., urethral catheterization or suprapubic aspiration) are indicated when a specimen cannot be obtained by more common techniques.

> **EXAMPLE:** With an indwelling urinary catheter in place, a specimen is obtained by inserting the needle into the catheter. The urine is aspirated and placed in a sterile urine container for laboratory testing.

Venipuncture, or **phlebotomy**, is the puncture of a vein using a needle for the purpose of drawing blood, and it is the most common method of collecting blood specimens. **Arterial puncture** is the puncture of an artery using a needle for the purpose of drawing blood. For safety purposes, after venipuncture, the used needle is placed in an approved *sharps container* made of hard, damage-resistant plastic (Figure 18-1).

Coding Tip

A venipuncture code is reported just once per encounter for each type of specimen, regardless of the number of specimens drawn.

Professional and Technical Components

Certain laboratory procedures contain both a professional (e.g., physician) component and a technical component. The technical component of a laboratory procedure or service includes, but is not limited to, the cost of equipment, supplies, and technician salaries. (CPT guidelines do not address reporting the technical component of a pathology and laboratory procedure or service.)

FIGURE 18-1 Sharps containers

Coding Tip

When a pathology and laboratory procedure or service code description includes both the technical and the professional component, and one of the components was not performed, report the appropriate code with modifier

- -26, to indicate that only the professional component was performed
- -TC, to indicate that only the technical component was performed

Pathologists often oversee the clinical laboratory and assume overall responsibility for test results. When reporting codes for professional and technical components of clinical laboratory services, standard practice is for the pathologist to report the professional component of clinical laboratory services. Clinical pathology professional services include the following:

- Directing and evaluating quality assurance and control procedures (e.g., ensuring that tests and procedures are properly performed, recorded, and reported; validating test methodologies)
- Supervising laboratory technicians
- Recommending follow-up diagnostic tests, when appropriate

The hospital reports the technical component, which represents the hospital's costs (e.g., laboratory equipment, supplies, and nonphysician personnel). The hospital's technical component does *not* include the pathologist's professional services.

NOTE:

Most laboratory services reported with CPT codes are paid by Medicare according to the laboratory fee schedule, which is discussed in Chapter 20 of this textbook.

Coding Tip

Modifier -90, Reference (Outside) Laboratory, is reported to indicate that an outside laboratory performed the service. This modifier is often added to pathology and laboratory codes to indicate that the physician did not perform the actual test, but instead sent the specimen to an outside laboratory.

Pathology and laboratory services can be provided by a physician or by technologists under the supervision of a physician. Although most codes describe clinical laboratory tests, physician laboratory and pathology services are also included. Physician laboratory and pathology services include the following:

- Surgical pathology services
- Cytopathology, hematology, and blood-banking services that require a physician
- Clinical consultation services
- Clinical laboratory interpretation services

Typically, pathology and laboratory specimens are prepared by laboratory personnel with a pathologist assuming responsibility for the integrity of the results. Certain tests are personally reviewed by the pathologist. Very few CPT pathology and laboratory codes require patient contact; however, occasionally a pathologist provides evaluation and management services. Such services are reported with appropriate CPT evaluation and management codes.

Clinical Laboratory Improvement Act of 1988 (CLIA)

To perform certain pathology and laboratory tests (and to submit claims to Medicare and Medicaid), physician office labs must obtain certification under the **Clinical Laboratory Improvement Act of 1988 (CLIA)**. A waiver is available for small office labs that perform only basic testing (e.g., urine dipsticks and fingerstick glucose testing), and a special CLIA waiver number is assigned to these labs. The list of approved tests is updated periodically, which means that physician office labs must determine if they still qualify for a waiver.

 Coding Tip

When reporting CLIA waived services to Medicare or Medicaid, add HCPCS level II modifier -QW to pathology and laboratory codes.

National Coverage Determinations (NCDs)

The Centers for Medicare & Medicaid Services (CMS) developed National Coverage Determinations (NCDs), which define coverage for services and procedures. Medicare administrative contractors (MACs) apply national coverage determinations nationwide, and local coverage decisions (LCDs) supplement the NCDs. Pathology and laboratory NCDs were developed to

- Simplify administrative requirements for clinical diagnostic services.
- Promote national uniformity in processing Medicare claims.

Pathology and Laboratory Section Tables

The following tables are located prior to Pathology and Laboratory section guidelines in the *CPT coding manual*

- Table of Drugs and the Appropriate Qualitative Screening, Confirmatory, and Quantitative Codes
- Molecular Pathology Table

Exercise 18.1 – Overview of Pathology and Laboratory Section

Instructions: Complete each statement.

1. Although most clinical laboratory service codes include a technical component, some include both a technical and a(n) _____ component.

2. Review of patient record documentation is necessary before assigning pathology and laboratory codes because many procedures can be performed using different _____.

3. Hospital coders usually do not assign pathology and laboratory codes because they are included on a(n) _____, which is used by providers to select services provided to patients.

4. CPT laboratory codes describe the performance of lab tests, and they do not include collection of the _____, which is performed using different methods (e.g., venipuncture, fingerstick, or lumbar puncture) and is reported separately.

5. The puncture of a vein using a needle for the purpose of drawing blood as a common method of collecting blood specimens is called venipuncture, or _____.

6. A routine venipuncture (usually performed by a nurse) is assigned code _____, and it is reported in addition to the laboratory procedure code.

Exercise 18.1 – *continued*

7. For a cutdown venipuncture procedure, code _____ is assigned.

8. When a pathology and laboratory procedure code description includes technical and professional components, and both components were not performed, modifier _____ is added to the code to indicate that only the professional component was performed.

9. When an outside laboratory performs pathology and laboratory services, add modifier _____ to the reported code.

10. To perform certain pathology and laboratory tests (and to submit claims to Medicare and Medicaid), physician office labs must obtain certification under the _____.

Pathology and Laboratory Section Guidelines

Guidelines located at the beginning of the Pathology and Laboratory section provide instruction about the following:

- Services in pathology and laboratory
- Separate or multiple procedures
- Unlisted services or procedures
- Special reports

Services in Pathology and Laboratory

Pathology and laboratory services are provided by a physician (e.g., a pathologist) or by technologists under responsible supervision of a physician. The unit of pathology service is a *specimen*, which is tissue that is submitted for individual and separate examination and pathological diagnosis. When multiple specimens are received for pathological examination, each specimen is considered a single unit of service and each is reported with a separate code.

EXAMPLE 1: Two separately identified skin lesions are submitted for individual examination and diagnosis. Report codes 88305 and 88305-59 (Skin, Other Than Cyst/Tag/Debridement/Plastic Repair). (Modifier -59 is added to indicate that the second lesion was evaluated as a "distinct procedural service.")

EXAMPLE 2: The uterus (with or without tubes and ovaries) is considered one specimen and is reported with code 88305 (when the uterus is removed for prolapse and shows no other abnormalities), 88309 (for neoplasia), or 88307 (for other conditions).

EXAMPLE 3: A cell block prepared from cytology fluids, bone marrow aspirates, or fine-needle aspirates is coded as 88305 (Cell block, any source).

(A **block** is a portion of tissue obtained from a specimen that is placed in a support medium, such as paraffin. A **section** is a thin slice of tissue prepared from a block that is examined.)

Separate or Multiple Procedures

It is appropriate to separately code and report multiple pathology and laboratory procedures that are provided on the same date of service. However, it is *not* appropriate to report tests that are repeated simply to confirm initial results (because of an equipment malfunction or technician error) or when a series of tests is performed (e.g., glucose tolerance tests). These services are considered part of the originally ordered test, and codes for repeated tests are not separately coded and reported.

EXAMPLE: The physician ordered an automated hemogram with automated platelet count. The laboratory also conducted a manual platelet count as a confirmatory test for quality control purposes. Report code 85027. (Do not report code 85032, manual platelet count, because it was conducted by the laboratory for quality control purposes.)

Unlisted Service or Procedure

A service or procedure that is provided for which there is no CPT code is reported with an "unlisted service or procedure" code.

EXAMPLE: An unlisted immunology procedure is reported with code 86849 (and a special report is attached to the submitted insurance claim).

Special Report

When an unlisted procedure or service code is reported on a claim, a "special report" is attached to the submitted claim to clarify the service or procedure performed. A service or procedure that is rarely performed, unusual, variable, or new may require a special report to be submitted so the third-party payer can determine the medical appropriateness of the service or procedure. The special report should include a description of the nature, extent, and need for the procedure. In addition, the following items may be included:

- Complexity of symptoms
- Final diagnosis
- Pertinent physical findings
- Diagnostic and therapeutic procedures
- Concurrent problems
- Follow-up care

Modifier -51 and Modifier -91

- Modifier -51 (Multiple Procedures) is *not* added to pathology and laboratory codes.
- Modifier -91 (Repeat Clinical Diagnostic Laboratory Test) is added to pathology and laboratory codes when procedures or services are repeated on the same date of service to obtain multiple results.

EXAMPLE: A patient undergoes a comprehensive metabolic panel laboratory test (80053). Because of abnormal blood urea nitrogen (BUN) test results, the patient undergoes a repeat BUN test as an individual test (84520). Report codes 80053 and 84520-91.

Exercise 18.2 – Pathology and Laboratory Section Guidelines

Instructions: Complete each statement.

1. The unit of pathology service is a(n) _____, which is tissue submitted for individual and separate examination and pathological diagnosis.

2. During the same operative session, the surgeon submitted "incidental appendix" tissue and a section of fallopian tube (as the result of a sterilization procedure) for pathological evaluation. Refer to the notes located below the Surgical Pathology subsection (codes 88300–88399) to determine whether one or two codes are reported. Code 88302 is reported _____ (once/twice).

Exercise 18.2 – *continued*

3. It is appropriate to separately code and report multiple pathology and laboratory procedures that are provided on the same _____.

4. A service or procedure that is provided for which there is no CPT code is reported with a(n) _____ code, and a(n) _____ is attached to the submitted claim.

5. When procedures or services are repeated on the same date of service to obtain multiple results, add modifier -91 to the reported pathology and laboratory code(s). It is *not* appropriate to add modifier _____ to pathology and laboratory codes.

Pathology and Laboratory Subsections

The Pathology and Laboratory section is organized according to type of procedure performed or service provided. Pathology and laboratory procedures are listed alphabetically within each subsection, which include the following:

- Organ or disease-oriented panels
- Drug assay
- Therapeutic drug assays
- Evocative/suppression testing
- Consultations (clinical pathology)
- Urinalysis
- Molecular pathology
- Genomic sequencing procedures and other molecular multianalyte assays
- Multianalyte assays with algorithmic analyses
- Chemistry
- Hematology and coagulation

- Immunology
- Transfusion medicine
- Microbiology
- Anatomical pathology
- Cytopathology
- Cytogenetic studies
- Surgical pathology
- *In vivo* laboratory procedures
- Other procedures
- Reproductive medicine procedures

Organ or Disease-Oriented Panels

Organ or disease-oriented panels subsection codes are reported for a defined group of tests that are administered for a certain purpose. The panels were developed for coding purposes only and are not considered clinical parameters. The tests listed below each panel identify the components of that panel.

To report an organ or disease-oriented panel code, all tests listed below the panel must be performed. No substitutions can be made.

EXAMPLE: Patient underwent a general health panel (80050). A general health panel must include all of the following procedures:

- Comprehensive metabolic panel (80053)
- Blood count, complete (CBC); automated and automated differential WBC count (85025 or 85027 and 85004) *or* CBC, automated and automated differential WBC count (85025 or 85027 and 85004) *or* Blood count, complete (CBC), automated (85027) and appropriate manual differential WBC count (85007 or 85009)
- Thyroid-stimulating hormone (TSH) (84443)

These individual procedure codes are *not* reported in addition to general health panel code 80050.

When only one or several of the tests associated with a panel are performed, do not report the panel code. Instead, report codes for each individual test performed. When additional tests are performed in addition to those listed below the panel, separately code and report the additional tests (in addition to the panel code).

EXAMPLE 1: Patient underwent a glucose test and a sodium test. Report codes 82947 and 84295. (Do *not* report basic metabolic panel code 80048.)

EXAMPLE 2: Patient underwent a basic metabolic panel test and an albumin test. Report codes 80048 and 82040.

Drug Assay and Therapeutic Drug Assays

CPT codes reported for drug procedures are located in three subsections of pathology and laboratory, and code selection is dependent on the purpose and type of patient results obtained.

- Therapeutic drug assays
- Drug assay
- Chemistry

An **assay** (e.g., lab test) is the measurement of the amount of a constituent in a specimen. Therapeutic drug assay procedures are performed to monitor the patient's clinical response to a known, prescribed medication. The two major categories include the following:

(1) *Presumptive drug class procedures* identify possible use or non-use of a drug or drug class. They may be followed by a definitive test in order to specifically identify drugs or metabolites.

(2) *Definitive drug class procedures* are qualitative or quantitative tests that identify possible use or non-use of a drug. These tests identify specific drugs and associated metabolites, if performed. (A presumptive test is not required prior to a definitive drug test.)

Qualitative assays detect whether a particular substance is present. **Quantitative assays** detect the amount of a substance in a specimen.

The material for drug class procedures may be any specimen type unless otherwise specified in the code descriptor (e.g., urine, blood, oral fluid, meconium, hair). Procedures can be qualitative, semiquantitative, or quantitative depending on the purpose of the testing. Therapeutic drug assay procedures are typically quantitative tests and the specimen type is whole blood, serum, plasma, or cerebrospinal fluid. When the same procedure(s) is performed on more than one specimen type (e.g., hair and urine), the appropriate code is reported separately for each specimen type using modifier -59.

Drugs or classes of drugs may be commonly assayed first by a presumptive screening method followed by a definitive drug identification method. Presumptive methods include immunoassays, enzymatic methods, chromatographic methods without mass spectrometry, or mass spectrometry without adequate drug resolution by chromatography.

Drugs or classes of drugs may be assayed first using a presumptive screening method followed by a definitive drug identification method. The drug class and methodology must be determined when reporting codes for presumptive procedures.

EXAMPLE 1: Patient underwent alcohol drug screen (Drug Class List A) using an instrumented test system. Report code 80305.

EXAMPLE 2: Patient underwent definitive drug testing for three or more types of anabolic steroids on the same encounter date. Report code 80328.

EXAMPLE 3: Patient underwent a total digoxin therapeutic drug assay procedure to monitor his clinical response to treatment. (The patient's blood was drawn for this laboratory procedure.) Report code 80162.

EXAMPLE 4: Patient underwent Breathalyzer testing for presence of alcohol (ethanol). Report code 82075.

Evocative/Suppression Testing

Evocative/suppression test panels include the administration of evocative or suppressive agents and the baseline and subsequent measurement of their effect on chemical constituents. These codes are reported for the laboratory component of the testing protocol. (**Evocative** means to cause a specific response; this term is used to describe various tests intended to cause production of hormones or other secretions.)

Coding Tip

Report a code from the CPT Medicine section for administration (e.g., infusion) of the evocative or suppressive agents. To locate the administration of agent code, refer to the Hydration, Therapeutic, Prophylactic, Diagnostic Injections and Infusions, and Chemotherapy and Other Highly Complex Drug or Highly Complex Biologic Agent Administration subsection of CPT Medicine.

Physician attendance and monitoring during evocative/suppression testing is reported with codes from the CPT Evaluation and Management section.

Consultations (Clinical Pathology)

The physician (e.g., the pathologist) review of laboratory test results is typically considered a non-face-to-face service, and the review of laboratory results is not a separately reportable service. However, when a patient's attending physician requests that a pathologist provide consultation services regarding pathology and/or laboratory test results, clinical pathology consultation codes are reported (80500–80502). The clinical pathology consultation requires

- Additional medical interpretative judgment

NOTE:

A physician (e.g., a pathologist) who reports test results but who does not provide medical interpretive judgment has not provided clinical pathology consultation services.

- Preparation of a written report

Clinical pathology consultation codes are differentiated according to whether a review of the patient's history and medical records was performed as part of the clinical pathology consultation service.

EXAMPLE: A surgeon orders a clinical pathology consultation to determine a patient's suitability for surgery based on the results of clinical laboratory tests. The pathologist documents a written consultation report that includes a review of patient records, including the patient's history and current laboratory results, and medical judgment about the patient's candidacy for surgery. Report code 80502.

A pathologist who provides a clinical pathology consultation service (which includes examination of the patient) reports an appropriate evaluation and management code (e.g., outpatient, inpatient, or consultation). The pathologist is responsible for ensuring that the criteria for reporting the evaluation and management code have been met and a report has been appropriately documented in the medical record.

Clinical pathology consultation services are performed

- At the request of another physician when test result(s) require additional medical interpretation
- When material (e.g., tissue slides) is referred by another pathologist or facility

Urinalysis

Most urine tests are performed to diagnose or monitor renal or urinary tract disease. Urine testing is easily performed and does not require an invasive skin puncture. Urine collection containers (Figure 18-2) used for routine urinalysis are made of material that is clear (translucent), and they contain lids that can be secured to prevent spills during transport. For example, protein in the urine may indicate glomerulonephritis, and urine cultures monitor the effectiveness of antibiotic treatment for urinary tract infections.

Urinalysis codes are reported for the analysis of one or more components of the urine. The reported code is based on method (e.g., dipstick), purpose (e.g., a pregnancy test), or element evaluated (e.g., bilirubin, bacteriuria screen).

Quantitative urine tests often require a timed collection. Timed urine collection is often performed because substances (e.g., hormones, proteins, and electrolytes) are excreted over a 24-hour period. Because exercise, hydration, and body metabolism affect excretion rates, these time periods may range anywhere from 2 to 24 hours.

A **reagent strip automated urine analyzer** (or **Chemstrip automated urine analyzer**) (Figure 18-3) is used to determine various components in the urine (including glucose, albumin, hemoglobin, and bile concentrations, as well as urinary pH, specific gravity, protein, ketone bodies, nitrites, and leukocyte esterase). A **dipstick** (Figure 18-4) is a small strip of plastic that is infused with a chemical that reacts to products in urine by changing color. It is considered preliminary and may be performed for screening purposes.

Coding Tip

Analysis of urine is also classified in other Pathology and Laboratory subsections. For example, a urine chloride test is reported with code 82436 from the Chemistry subsection.

The appropriate handling and storage of urine is necessary to prevent changes that adversely impact accurate results. Many **analytes** (substance or chemical compound undergoing analysis) require the use of preservatives so that they remain viable during the collection period. The choice of preservative depends on the type of collection. For example, sodium fluoride is used to preserve glucose in a 24-hour urine collection.

EXAMPLE: Nonautomated urinalysis by dipstick, without microscopy. Report code 81002.

FIGURE 18-2 Urine collection container

FIGURE 18-3 Chemstrip automated urine analyzer

© Suthep/Shutterstock.com

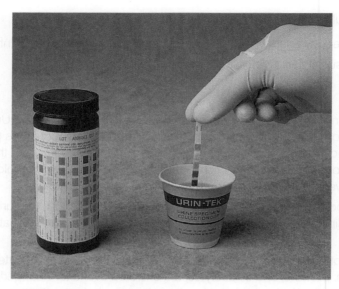

FIGURE 18-4 Dipstick used for routine urinalysis

Molecular Pathology

Molecular pathology laboratory procedures involve the analysis of nucleic acid to detect gene variants, which may be indicative of certain conditions (e.g., constitutional disorders, neoplasia, histocompatibility enzymes). Codes are organized as Tier 1 and Tier 2 molecular pathology laboratory procedures. CPT incorporates the Human Genome Organization–approved gene names in code descriptions along with proteins or diseases associated with the genes. Molecular pathology notes indicate that any procedures performed prior to cell lysis, such as microdissection, are to be reported separately, and an extensive list of definitions is also included.

- Tier 1 molecular pathology laboratory codes are assigned for gene-specific and genomic procedures according to the *analyte* (substance or chemical compound undergoing analysis) or the *allele* (genetic variants).

- Tier 2 codes are assigned for procedures not listed in Tier 1, and they are classified according to level of technical resources and interpretive professional work required. (Tier 2 procedures are performed less frequently than Tier 1 procedures.)

- If a tested analyte or allele is not represented by a Tier 1 code or the technical resources/interpretive professional work is not described in a Tier 2 code, report an appropriate methodology code.

> **EXAMPLE:** Patient underwent the *BRCA1* and *BRCA2* gene analysis laboratory procedure to determine her risk for hereditary breast and ovarian cancer. Report code 81162.

Coding Tip

When tests require that a physician or other qualified health care professional interpret the results, and the provider performs the interpretation only, add modifier -26 (Professional Component) to the code.

Genomic Sequencing Procedures and Other Molecular Multianalyte Assays

Genomic sequencing procedures (GSPs) and *other molecular multianalyte assays GSPs* are DNA or RNA sequence analysis methods that simultaneously assay multiple genes or genetic regions relevant to a clinical situation.

> **EXAMPLE:** Patient underwent genome sequence analysis for Huntington's disease. Report code 81425.

Multianalyte Assays with Algorithmic Analyses

Multianalyte Assays with Algorithmic Analyses (MAAAs) are performed to determine discrete genetic values, properties, or characteristics, and the results are potentially of independent medical significance or useful in the medical management of a patient (e.g., determine patient's risk for certain diseases).

> **EXAMPLE:** Patient underwent oncology (ovarian) biochemical assays of two proteins (CA-125 and HE4), utilizing serum, with menopausal status, with the algorithm reported as a risk score. Report code 81500.

Chemistry

Chemistry codes are reported for quantitative tests unless the code description indicates otherwise. (Presumptive and/or definitive drug testing procedures are reported with drug assay codes.) Chemical tests performed on body materials are obtained from any source (e.g., blood or urine) unless the code description specifies otherwise. Codes in the chemistry subsection are listed in an alphabetical order.

To properly assign codes from the Chemistry subsection, locate the code that describes the analyte to be tested (the specific substance to be analyzed).

When a chemistry test is performed on multiple specimens from different sources, or on specimens that are obtained at different times, the analyte is reported separately for each source and for *each* specimen.

> **EXAMPLE:** Patient underwent two lab tests to determine total bilirubin levels. A specimen was obtained during the morning and afternoon on April 5. Report codes 82247 and 82247-91.

Stool includes waste products of digested food bile, mucus, epithelial cells, and bacteria. Stool studies are performed to evaluate bowel function (e.g., for intestinal bleeding, infections, infestations, inflammation, malabsorption, and diarrhea).

> **EXAMPLE:** Patient underwent occult blood testing by peroxidase activity, qualitative, feces, single specimen. Report code 82272.

Body fluids can be tested for blood urea nitrogen (BUN) and creatinine to determine whether the fluid is urine. For example, code 84560 is reported for uric acid testing, other source, which is helpful in obstetrics to differentiate amniotic fluid from urine.

Hematology and Coagulation

Hematology is the study of the function and disorders of blood (Figure 18-5). *Coagulation* is the process of blood clotting. Hematology and coagulation codes are reported for laboratory tests performed to evaluate blood and blood clotting, such as CBC, clotting factor tests, clotting inhibitor tests, and prothrombin and thrombin time. Bone marrow, smear interpretation is also classified in the Hematology and Coagulation subsection. (Bone marrow biopsy and cell block interpretations are reported with a code from the Surgical Pathology subsection.)

Platelet count codes are integrated into the blood count series of codes. Codes for the current manual microscopic review of blood describe the microscopic examination of a blood smear with a manual differential leukocyte (WBC) count.

FIGURE 18-5 Blood components

Codes for automated CBC and automated differential WBC count are reported when blood is tested to determine the following levels:

- Hemoglobin (Hgb)
- Hematocrit (Hct)
- Red blood cell (RBC)
- White blood cell (WBC)
- Platelet

The automated differential WBC count determines the number of basophils, eosinophils, monocytes, lymphocytes, and neutrophils. (When a manual cell count of erythrocytes, leukocytes, or platelets is performed, the appropriate code is reported for *each* type.)

> **EXAMPLE 1:** Patient underwent manual CBC to determine Hct, Hgb, RBC, and WBC levels. Report codes 85014, 85018, 85032, and 85032-59. (Code 85032 is reported twice to reflect erythrocyte and leukocyte testing.)

> **EXAMPLE 2:** Patient underwent an automated CBC and an automated differential WBC count. Report code 85025 *or* codes 85027 and 85004, depending on the laboratory's processing of the WBC differential.

Specific methodologies for measuring D-dimer fibrin degradation products, based on the sensitivity of the analysis, are differentiated as

- Qualitative or semiquantitative
- Quantitative
- Ultrasensitive, qualitative or semiquantitative

> **EXAMPLE:** Patient underwent qualitative fibrin degradation products D-dimer test. Report code 85378.

FIGURE 18-6 Serological centrifuge

Immunology

Immunology is the study of the immune system. Immunology codes classify antigen and antibody laboratory studies and tissue typing. Antigen and antibody studies measure the reaction of

- **Antigens** (Ag): Foreign substances that elicit the formation of antibodies
- **Antibodies** (Ab): Proteins in the body made by the immune system that fight infection and disease

(An **adjuvant** is a substance administered with an antigen that enhances the response to the antigen.) Figure 18-6 contains a serological centrifuge, which is used to spin test tubes of blood to test for agglutination reactions (clumping of blood cells). Hemagglutination (agglutination of red blood cells) is a method used to visualize antigen–antibody reactions.

> **EXAMPLE:** Patient underwent HIV-1 antibody test to determine exposure to human immunodeficiency virus and subsequent antibody development. Report code 86701.

Immunoglobulins are proteins produced by plasma cells that help fight infection. Some immunoglobulins (e.g., gamma globulins) are involved in immune responses to bacteria or foreign substances (e.g., allergens or transplanted tissue). Immunoglobulins include IgA, IgD, IgE, IgG, and IgM. Two codes are reported for the quantitative and qualitative measurement of IgE.

- Quantitative or semiquantitative allergen-specific IgE, crude allergen extract, each (86003)
- Qualitative allergen-specific IgE multiallergen screen (using a disk, sponge, or card) (86005)

> **EXAMPLE:** Patient underwent quantitative allergen-specific IgE testing, 5 allergens. Report code 86003 five times.

Tumor antigen codes are reported to indicate the presence of a tumor marker in the patient's blood.

> **EXAMPLE:** Patient with previously treated stage II and stage III breast cancer underwent immunoassay for tumor antigen CA 125 to test for recurrence of breast cancer. Report code 86304.

Laboratory tests performed to identify specific antibodies are performed using a multistep method. Codes for tissue typing describe procedures performed to determine compatibility between a recipient and donors for organ or bone marrow transplants.

> **EXAMPLE:** Patient underwent HLA typing of single antigen A10. Report code 86812. (HLA is the abbreviation for human leukocyte antigen, which determines graft acceptance.)

Transfusion Medicine

Transfusion medicine codes are often reported by blood banks, and they describe blood preparation services for transfusion. For transfusion services, report the appropriate CPT code as well as a HCPCS level II code for the blood product transfused. (The service code is reported with the date of service for the transfusion, not the date the blood was collected.) When autologous blood is collected but not transfused, report the appropriate code with the number of units collected but not transfused.

The collection, modification, treatment, and processing of autologous blood specimens for transplantation are classified as (1) predeposited or (2) intra- or postoperative salvage. When processing and storage costs are incurred for unused blood or blood products, the provider may submit charges when patient-specific preparation was done (e.g., blood typing and cross-matching).

> **EXAMPLE:** Patient underwent transfusion of one unit of frozen blood, which included freezing (and preparation) as well as thawing. Report code 86932. (If the type of blood product had been stated in the example, such as plasma, report more specific HCPCS level II code P9017 instead.)

NOTE:

A transfusion APC (ambulatory payment classification) payment is paid just once per day regardless of the number of units or different types of products transfused when reporting codes for a health care facility (e.g., acute care hospital outpatient department).

Microbiology

Microbiology is the study of microbes (e.g., bacteria, parasites, and viruses). Microbiology codes (87003–87999) include bacteriology, mycology, parasitology, and virology, and the codes are intended to describe primary definitive (or final) bacterial cultures. To properly assign microbiology codes, determine the following:

- Source
- Handling method
- Stains performed
- Identification technique used

It is appropriate to separately report multiple procedures when various microbiology testing procedures are performed.

Microscopic examinations evaluate cytologic specimens to identify bacteria and other infecting organisms (e.g., determining hormone receptor assay results, chromatin identification, culture and sensitivity testing). Microbiology subsection notes provide instruction about the presumptive identification of microorganisms and definitive identification.

- **Presumptive identification** is the identification by colony morphology, growth on selective media, Gram stains, or up to three tests (e.g., catalase, oxidase, indole, or urease).
- **Definitive identification** of microorganisms is the identification to the genus or species level that requires additional tests (e.g., biochemical panels or slide cultures). The word "definitive" refers to the final culture that identifies the organism. Reporting these codes indicates that a specific organism genus or group (e.g., *Staphylococcus, Salmonella*, or *Streptococcus*) has been identified.

When additional studies involve molecular probes, chromatography, or immunologic techniques, report the codes separately in addition to definitive identification codes. For multiple specimens/sites, add modifier -59 to the microbiology code. For repeat laboratory tests performed on the same day, add modifier -91 to the microbiology code.

A **Gram stain** is a method of classifying all bacteria as gram positive or gram negative. The shape of the organism (e.g., spherical or rod-shaped) may also be helpful in the identification of the infecting organism. When the Gram stain indicates Gram negative rods, the infection may be caused by *Escherichia coli*. With knowledge of Gram stain results, the physician can initiate antibiotic treatment based on the organism's identity.

EXAMPLE: A fluorescent stain for bacteria, primary source smear with interpretation, was performed. Report code 87206.

Anatomic Pathology

Anatomical pathology codes are reported for physician (pathologist) services only. Physician services involved in performing **necropsy** (autopsy) are specific to the following:

- Portions of the body
- Gross examination
- Regional examination
- Forensic examination
- Infant/stillborn

EXAMPLE: The pathologist performed a gross and microscopic autopsy that included the brain of a stillborn infant. Report code 88029. (**Gross examination** involves visually evaluating a specimen with the naked eye.)

Cytopathology

Cytopathology is the study of diseased cells. Specimen cells are typically obtained using brushing, washing, needle biopsy, or fine-needle aspiration. Thus, the patient record must be reviewed to determine the collection method to correctly report cytopathology codes. Cytopathology subsection codes are reported for various cytopathology procedures, as follows:

- Cytopathology collection methods (e.g., brushings, fluids, smears, washings)
- Cervical or vaginal cytopathology physician interpretation
- Cytopathological smears and cytopathology of fluids, washings or brushing from sources other than cervical or vaginal
- Cytohistologic studies of fine-needle aspirate
- Cervical and vaginal screening for cells collected in preservative fluid using an automated thin manual layer preparation.
- Flow cytometry tests

Pap smear (Figure 18-7) screening and physician interpretation using different methods for preparation, screening, and reporting are reported with cytopathology codes.

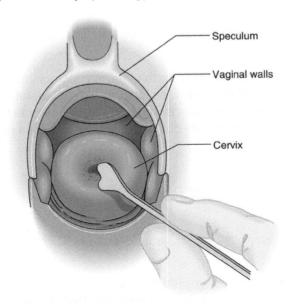

FIGURE 18-7 Performing a Pap smear

- Bethesda System of reporting
- Non-Bethesda reporting
- Thin-layer preparations
- Automated screening with any system of reporting

The **Bethesda System** is a format for reporting cervical/vaginal cytology that includes a state of specimen adequacy, the general category (e.g., if the specimen is within normal limits), and a descriptive diagnosis (e.g., benign cellular changes). (HCPCS level II codes P3000 and P3001 for screening Papanicolaou smears also classify cytopathology services.)

 Coding Tip

Cytopathology notes provide instruction to report its codes in addition to the screening code when these additional services are provided.

- Cytopathology, cervical or vaginal (any reporting system), requiring interpretation by physician (88141)

- Cytopathology, slides, cervical or vaginal, definitive hormonal evaluation (e.g., maturation index, karyopyknotic index, estrogenic index) (List separately in addition to code[s] for other technical and interpretation services.) (88155)

EXAMPLE: Cytopathology evaluation of fine-needle aspirate, interpretation, and report. Report code 88173.

Cytogenetic Studies

Cytogenetics is the study of the cell and its heredity-related components, including chromosomes. Cytogenetic studies codes are reported for tests performed to study cellular ("cyto") structure and function related to heredity ("genetics").

Cytogenetic tests are performed based on the nature of the disorder for which the patient is being tested because the cell culture and analytical standards are disease dependent, not tissue dependent.

EXAMPLE 1: Tissue culture for non-neoplastic disorders, lymphocyte. Report code 88230.

EXAMPLE 2: Tissue culture for neoplastic disorders, solid tumor. Report code 88239.

Cryopreservation services codes are reported for the freezing, storage, and subsequent thawing of cells, as well as the expansion of established cell lines for subsequent laboratory testing. For some testing procedures (e.g., tests for genetic disorders), the cell line is frozen to preserve the culture, and subsequent thawing must be done before an analysis can be completed. (An **aliquot** is a portion of a specimen used for testing.)

EXAMPLE 1: Cryopreservation, freezing and storage of cells, each cell line. Report code 88240.

EXAMPLE 2: Thawing and expansion of frozen cells, each aliquot. Report code 88241.

White blood cells (e.g., T lymphocytes) are typically used as the specimen for chromosome analysis. **Chromosomal breakage syndromes** include genetic disorders that are usually transmitted in agenetic autosomal recessive mode. The syndromes are characterized by a defect in DNA repair mechanisms and a predisposition to cancer. Codes for chromosome analysis for breakage syndromes are classified according to the

- Name of the specific syndrome being investigated (e.g., Fanconi anemia)
- Specific technique for analysis

Codes for cytogenetic studies include a combination of codes used to describe the

- Type of tissue cultured
- Special culture techniques or treatments of the culture

- Numbers of cells studied and analyzed
- Special analysis techniques used

Thus, submitting a claim for a single cytogenetic study typically requires reporting three or more codes.

> **EXAMPLE:** Cytogenetic study of a standard karyotype on peripheral blood lymphocytes is reported with a code for lymphocyte culture (88230), a code for chromosome analysis counting 15 to 20 cells, 2 karyotypes with banding (88262), and a code to describe the physician work of interpretation and report of the cytogenetic testing performed (88291).

Molecular cytogenetics includes the **fluorescence *in situ* hybridization (FISH)** method, which is performed to detect submicroscopic changes in chromosomes (e.g., genetic disorders, such as Williams syndrome) or for identification of unknown chromosomal material. Chromosomal aberrations can also be identified using FISH analyses in patients with other constitutional or acquired (e.g., neoplastic) disorders.

> **EXAMPLE:** Molecular cytogenetics test, DNA probe fluorescent *in situ* hybridization (FISH) test. Report code 88271.

Surgical Pathology

Surgical pathology codes are reported for the gross and microscopic examination of specimens submitted for pathologic evaluation (Figure 18-8). (A *specimen* is tissue submitted to the pathology department for evaluation; it is also the unit of service used to report surgical pathology codes.) Surgical pathology levels of service are determined by the following:

- Type of exam
- Type of tissue

 Coding Tip

- Code 88291 is reported in addition to the appropriate cytogenetic testing code(s) to describe the (physician) interpretation and documentation of a report of cytogenetics and molecular cytogenetics testing.
- Code 88300 is reported for specimens that require gross (macroscopic) examination only.

(A)   (B)

FIGURE 18-8 Tissue biopsy (A) A small piece of tissue is surgically removed (B) Pathologist views tissue under microscope, looking for presence of disease

When multiple individual tissue specimens are submitted from the same patient, a separate code is reported for each specimen.

> **EXAMPLE:** Two separate frozen sections of breast tissue were evaluated by the pathologist during surgery. Report codes 88331 and 88332.

Surgical pathology notes provide instruction that surgical pathology services include accession, examination, and reporting. **Accession** is the assignment of a number to record the order of tissue acquisition; an *accession number* is assigned to each pathology case (e.g., 05-00101 for the facility's 101ST case in 2005).

Notes also identify and define the *specimen* as the unit of service for reporting surgical pathology codes. These codes are reported according to the extent and complexity of the evaluation.

- Level I surgical pathology code 88300 is reported for any specimen the examining pathologist believes can be accurately diagnosed *without* microscopic examination.
- Level II surgical pathology code 88302 is reported when gross *and* microscopic examination is performed to confirm identification of a specimen or the absence of disease.
- Level III through level VI codes 88304–88309 are reported when gross and microscopic examinations are performed, and these codes describe levels of service for specimens that require increasingly complex levels of physician (pathologist) work, from lowest to highest, due to a presumed presence of disease. Code descriptions include specimen sites and specific types of disease.
  - Uncomplicated specimen (e.g., hemorrhoids)
  - Single complicated specimen (e.g., kidney resection)
  - Multiple complicated specimens (e.g., breast with regional lymph nodes)

> **EXAMPLE:** Cervical carcinoma was diagnosed upon endo cervical biopsy. Patient subsequently underwent a hysterectomy. Pathologist examined the endo cervix and uterus. Codes 88305 and 88309 are reported whether or not residual cancer is found.

Pathology consultation codes describe the opinion or advice about the presence or absence of diseased or abnormal tissue, as requested by another physician. The consulting pathologist prepares consultation reports and written interpretations about slides or other material received from another facility.

Pathology consultations performed during surgery are also interoperative pathology examinations that assist in determining an immediate surgical course (e.g., breast biopsy resulting in total mastectomy during same operative episode). Pathological consultation during surgery include macroscopic (gross) tissue review only, frozen section, or cytological examinations.

> **EXAMPLE:** A sigmoid colon biopsy is sent to the pathologist during surgery for immediate diagnosis. The pathologist examines the specimen and provides a pathological diagnosis of diverticulosis without microscopic examination of the tissue. Report code 88329.

In Vivo (e.g., Transcutaneous) Laboratory Procedures

The *in vivo* (e.g., transcutaneous) procedures subsection contains codes that classify bilirubin and hemoglobin tests.

 NOTE:

> A total transcutaneous bilirubin test is usually performed on newborns to diagnose jaundice, and testing is done four times a day or more to monitor the condition and determine the efficiency of therapy.

> **EXAMPLE:** Patient underwent total transcutaneous bilirubin test. Report code 88720.

Other Procedures

The other procedures subsection includes laboratory and pathology procedures that are not classified in other Pathology and Laboratory subsections.

EXAMPLE: Patient underwent sweat collection via iontophoresis. Report code 89230.

Reproductive Medicine Procedures

Reproductive medicine procedures codes classify new technology and evolving reproductive medical practices such as the following:

- Oocyte/embryo culture and fertilization techniques
- Oocyte/embryo biopsy techniques
- Freezing, thawing, and storage techniques

(These procedures are performed in highly specialized clinical laboratories.)

When reporting the culture and fertilization of oocytes, report the appropriate code one time for the culture and fertilization, regardless of the number of eggs fertilized.

EXAMPLE: Patient underwent culture and fertilization of six embryos in less than four days. Report code 89250. (Code 89250 is reported just once.)

Co-culture techniques performed on tissue cultures of human embryos, oviductal, uterine, granulosa, or other cells involve the isolation of the cells, culture, plating, and the co-culture of these cells with human embryos. This procedure may involve microscopic and cytochemical examination of the culture cells to determine their viability or functionality.

The preparation of embryo for transfer, using any method, includes removing the embryo(s) from culture, preparing the embryo(s) for transfer, loading the embryo(s) into a catheter, transporting the embryo(s) to the transfer room for transfer to the patient, and examining the catheter after transfer to ensure that no embryo(s) are retained.

 Coding Tip

Microtechnique is a micromanipulation technique used for preparing an embryo for transfer.

The preparation and examination of the oocyte prior to fertilization (e.g., stripping of the granulosa, cumulus oophorous, and corona radiation and verifying extrusion of the first polar body) are included in assisted oocyte fertilization procedures. Preparation and examination procedures are *not* separately coded and reported during oocyte fertilization.

Sperm identification and preparation prior to injection into the cytoplasm of the oocyte are coded and reported separately with sperm isolation and preparation codes, as appropriate.

 NOTE:

Methods of assisted oocyte fertilization include the following:
- Intracytoplasmic sperm injection (ICSI)
- Subzonal insertion (SZI)
- Partial zona dissection (PZD)

Sperm identification from aspiration other than seminal fluid (e.g., from the vas deferens or epididymis) excludes identification of sperm from seminal fluid, which is described by other codes.

The work of identifying sperm does *not* include the work of assisted oocyte fertilization by any method (e.g., microtechnique), which is reported with a separate code (e.g., 89280, Assisted oocyte fertilization, microtechnique; less than or equal to 10 oocytes).

EXAMPLE: Simple preparation sperm isolation procedure with semen analysis, in preparation for insemination. Report code 89260.

Proprietary Laboratory Analyses

The Proprietary Laboratory Analysis (PLA) subsection contains codes reported for proprietary clinical laboratory analyses conducted by a single (sole-source) laboratory *or* licensed/marketed to multiple providing laboratories that are cleared/approved by the Food and Drug Administration (FDA). These advanced diagnostic laboratory tests (ADLTs) and clinical diagnostic laboratory tests (CDLTs) are defined under the Protecting Access to Medicare Act (PAMA) of 2014. The range of medical laboratory tests include multianalyte assays with algorithmic analyses (MAAA) and genomic sequencing procedures (GSPs). Codes in the Proprietary Laboratory Analyses subsection are released on a quarterly basis to expedite reporting, and they are published electronically at the AMA website (www.amaassn.org).

EXAMPLE: Patient underwent proprietary laboratory analysis which included red blood cell antigen typing, DNA, human erythrocyte antigen gene analysis of 35 antigens from 11 blood groups, utilizing whole blood, and common RBC alleles. Report code 0001U.

Exercise 18.3 – Pathology and Laboratory Subsections

Instructions: Assign CPT code(s) and appropriate modifier(s) to each statement.

1. Physician office lab performs a nonautomated dipstick urinalysis with microscopy.

2. Routine venipuncture. Quantitative therapeutic drugs assay to determine digoxin level.

3. Laboratory panel that includes carbon dioxide, chloride, potassium, and sodium.

4. Two separately identified basal cell carcinomas are submitted for diagnosis and evaluation of adequacy of the surgical margins. The first basal cell carcinoma specimen required frozen section from one block to confirm the adequacy of excision. The second basal cell carcinoma specimen required two frozen sections on two blocks to assure adequate excision. Surgical pathology evaluation of the two separately identified basal cell carcinomas is also performed.

5. The physician's office staff performed a urine pregnancy test using dipstick reagents that chemically react with urine. A change in color indicated positive findings and the presence of hormones found in the urine of women in early pregnancy.

6. Specimen collection via arterial puncture and blood gas determination (pH only).

Exercise 18.3 – *continued*

7. Laboratory panel included the following tests: total calcium, carbon dioxide, chloride (blood), creatinine (blood), serum sodium, and quantitative urea nitrogen.

_____

8. A segment of sigmoid colon with tumor was sent to the pathologist for frozen section during surgery so that immediate diagnosis could be made. The pathologist created the frozen section, examined the specimen, and rendered an intraoperative pathological diagnosis.

_____

9. Partial thromboplastin time to measure the efficiency of plasma in forming thromboplastin. Patient has had blood clots, and this test is needed to monitor the effectiveness of anticoagulant heparin therapy. The method used was automated coagulation instrumentation.

_____

10. Glucose screening using Dextrostix reagent strip method, capillary blood, 49-year-old patient.

_____

11. Breast biopsy was sent to the pathologist during the operative procedure for immediate diagnosis. The pathologist examined the specimen and selected a portion to prepare as a block for frozen section, which was microscopically examined. Surgical pathology evaluation of the breast biopsy tissue was also performed, and it did not require microscopic evaluation of surgical margins.

_____

12. Lipid panel using automated equipment was performed and included testing of HDL, total serum cholesterol, triglycerides, and quantitative glucose.

_____

13. General health panel.

_____

14. Metabolic panel using automated equipment, which included carbon dioxide, chloride, creatinine, glucose, potassium, sodium, and BUN.

_____

15. Antibody identification test for leukocyte antibodies.

_____

16. Pinworm exam using cellophane tape prep.

_____

17. As the result of an appendectomy due to acute appendicitis, the appendix was sent to surgical pathology for gross and microscopic examination by the pathologist.

_____

18. Sensitivity study using agar diffusion methodology was performed to assess whether antibiotic treatment with methicillin would be effective for a patient diagnosed with a staphylococcal B infection.

_____

19. Collection of sweat from a patient via iontophoresis to rule out cystic fibrosis.

_____

20. Right and left obturator lymph nodes were removed during radical prostatectomy and were submitted as separate specimens for immediate diagnosis to assess metastatic disease involvement. The pathologist examined the specimens and selected two blocks from the right specimen and three blocks from the left specimen to create frozen sections. Each frozen section was examined microscopically. Pathologist also evaluated right and left obturator lymph nodes and prostate tissue for surgical pathology.

_____

Summary

CPT pathology and laboratory codes describe services performed on specimens (e.g., body fluids, tissue, or cytological specimens) to evaluate, prevent, diagnose, or treat a disease. Most clinical laboratory service codes include a technical component, and some include both a technical and a professional component. The Pathology and Laboratory section is organized according to type of procedure performed, and procedures are listed alphabetically within each subsection. Because many laboratory and pathology tests can be performed using different methods, patient record documentation must be reviewed along with code descriptions and instructional notes. Guidelines located at the beginning of the Pathology and Laboratory section provide instruction about services in pathology and laboratory, separate or multiple procedures, subsection information, unlisted services or procedures, and special reports.

Internet Links

Clinical Laboratory Improvement Amendments (CLIA): Go to *www.cdc.gov*, click on "C" in the CDC A–Z Index (at the top), and scroll down and click on the CLIA (Clinical Laboratory Improvement Amendments) link.

National Coverage Determinations for Laboratory Services: Go to *www.cms.gov*, click on the Medicare link, then scroll down to the Coverage heading, click on the Medicare Coverage-General Information link, click on the Lab NCDs – ICD-10 link, and scroll down and click on the Index of Lab NCDs link to view them.

Review

Multiple Choice

Instructions: Circle the most appropriate response.

1. Coders do not assign codes to pathology and laboratory procedures performed on an _____ basis because such services do not impact _____ assignment and facility reimbursement.
   - a. inpatient, diagnosis-related group (DRG)
   - b. inpatient, prospective payment system (PPS)
   - c. outpatient, diagnosis-related group (DRG)
   - d. outpatient, prospective payment system (PPS)

2. Laboratory codes (80047–87999) describe the _____ of lab tests.
   - a. collection
   - b. performance
   - c. performance and collection
   - d. performance, collection, and clinical consultation

3. Which modifier is added to pathology and laboratory codes when procedures or services are repeated on the same date of service to obtain multiple results?
   - a. -59
   - b. -90
   - c. -91
   - d. -QW

4. When an unlisted procedure or service code is reported on a claim, what is attached to the submitted claim to clarify the service or procedure performed?
   - a. Accession code
   - b. Entire patient record
   - c. Special report
   - d. Waiver number

5. Code(s) from the _____ subsection of Pathology and Laboratory are often reported by blood banks.
   a. drug testing and therapeutic drug assays
   b. hematology and coagulation
   c. other procedures
   d. transfusion medicine

6. Which is a substance administered with an antigen to enhance the response to the antigen?
   a. Adjuvant
   b. Aliquot
   c. Assay
   d. Specimen

7. IgA, IgD, IgE, IgG, and IgM are considered:
   a. analytes.
   b. antigens.
   c. immunoglobulins.
   d. specimens.

8. Physician attendance and monitoring during evocative or suppressive agents testing is reported with codes from the:
   a. clinical pathology consultation subsection of Pathology and Laboratory.
   b. Evaluation and Management section of CPT.
   c. Medicine section of CPT.
   d. Surgery section of CPT.

9. Which is the study of diseased cells?
   a. Cytology
   b. Cytopathology
   c. Immunology
   d. Pathology

10. Codes from the _____ subsection of Pathology and Laboratory are reported for tests performed to study cellular structure and function related to heredity.
    a. anatomical pathology
    b. cytogenetic studies
    c. cytopathology
    d. organ or disease-oriented panels

11. A patient presents with symptoms of dehydration. The physician ordered an electrolyte panel, which included carbon dioxide, chloride, potassium, and sodium. Which CPT code(s) are assigned?
    a. 80051
    b. 80051, 82374, 82435, 84132, 84295
    c. 82374, 82435, 84132, 84295
    d. 82374, 82435, 84133, 84300

12. Urinalysis. Which CPT code is assigned?
    a. 81000
    b. 81001
    c. 81002
    d. 81003

13. Qualitative fetal hemoglobin. Which CPT code is assigned?
    a. 83030   b. 83033   c. 83036   d. 83045

14. Qualitative analysis of organic acids, three specimens. Which CPT code(s) are assigned?
    a. 83918, 83918, 83918
    b. 83918, 83918-91, 83918-91
    c. 83919, 83919, 83919
    d. 83919, 83919-91, 83919-91

15. Alkaline phosphatase isoenzymes. Which CPT code is assigned?
    a. 84060
    b. 84075
    c. 84078
    d. 84080

16. CBC, automated, including Hgb, Hct, RBC, WBC, and platelet count. Which CPT code(s) are assigned?
    a. 85004, 85014
    b. 85025
    c. 85027
    d. 85032

17. ABO, Rh, and MN blood typing for paternity testing. Which CPT code is assigned?

    a. 86900

    b. 86901

    c. 86905

    d. 86910

18. Thromboplastin time, partial (PTT) in plasma. Which CPT code is assigned?

    a. 85260

    b. 85347

    c. 85705

    d. 85730

19. RBC antibody screen, two different techniques. Which CPT code(s) are assigned?

    a. 86850

    b. 86850, 86850

    c. 86850, 86850-51

    d. 86850, 86850-91

20. *Chlamydia* culture. Which CPT code is assigned?

    a. 87110

    b. 87270

    c. 87487

    d. 87810

Coding Practice

Instructions: Assign CPT code(s) and appropriate modifier(s) to each case.

1. ORGAN OR DISEASE-ORIENTED PANELS: A patient's blood is sent for the following tests: rubella antibody, Rh(D) and ABO blood typing, automated CBC and WBC, qualitative syphilis test, RBC antibody screen, and a hepatitis B surface antigen.

_____

2. ORGAN OR DISEASE-ORIENTED PANELS: A patient's blood is sent for the following tests: albumin, carbon dioxide, calcium, sodium, glucose, chloride, creatinine, urea nitrogen, potassium, phosphorus inorganic, and complete CBC (automated).

_____

3. MOLECULAR PATHOLOGY: Urinalysis, automated with identification of sediments via microscope.

_____

4. OTHER PROCEDURES: Sperm isolation procedure including sperm wash and complete semen analysis.

_____

5. EVOCATIVE/SUPPRESSION TESTING: ACTH, prolactin, HGH, cortisol, TSH, LH, and FSH done after intramuscular injection of suppressive agents.

_____

6. MICROBIOLOGY: Microorganism analysis of primary source for *Bordetella pertussis*.

_____

7. CHEMISTRY: *Helicobacter pylori* blood test.

_____

8. HEMATOLOGY AND COAGULATION: Blood analysis for hematocrit (Hct) level.

_____

9. CHEMISTRY: Direct measurement of blood O_2 saturation level.

_____

10. SURGICAL PATHOLOGY: Intraoperative consultation of breast tissue, single specimen; gross examination and frozen section.

_____

11. MICROBIOLOGY: Examination of nail for the presence of fungi using KOH method.

_____

12. CHEMISTRY: Testing of blood for level of TSH and T3 uptake.

_____

13. DRUG ASSAY: Urine sample used to perform drug screening using a chromatographic method.

_____

14. IMMUNOLOGY: Blood test for ANA antibodies to rule out SLE.

_____

15. SURGICAL PATHOLOGY: Gross and microscopic pathology examination of tissue taken from a patient during a radical TURP procedure.

_____

16. IMMUNOLOGY: _Shigella_ antibody titer testing of blood sample.

_____

17. CHEMISTRY: Testing for triglyceride level.

_____

18. IMMUNOLOGY: Blood analysis for presence of _Chlamydia_ antibody.

_____

19. SURGICAL PATHOLOGY: Gross and microscopic pathology examination of paranasal tissue taken during a biopsy.

_____

20. IMMUNOLOGY: Prick test of skin for _Candida albicans_.

_____

21. TRANSFUSION MEDICINE: Testing of blood to determine Rh negative or Rh positive.

_____

22. CHEMISTRY: Radioimmunoassay of blood for total PSA.

_____

23. IMMUNOLOGY: T-cell count, total.

_____

24. SURGICAL PATHOLOGY: Gross and microscopic examination of Morton's neuroma.

_____

25. IMMUNOLOGY: CCP antibody test to rule out rheumatoid arthritis.

_____

26. ANATOMIC PATHOLOGY: Total postmortem examination of a male stillborn infant.

_____

27. CYTOPATHOLOGY: Analysis of thin prep of cervical scraping specimen performed under pathologist supervision (manual screening).

_____

28. OTHER PROCEDURES: Specimen of knee synovial fluid for cell count.

_____

29. MOLECULAR PATHOLOGY: Gene analysis, FXN (frataxin). (Patient is being genetically tested for presence of Friedreich ataxia.)

_____

30. ANATOMIC PATHOLOGY: Autopsy of a 45-year-old male patient's heart.

_____

CPT Medicine

Chapter Outline

Overview of Medicine Section

Medicine Section Guidelines

Medicine Subsections

Chapter Objectives

At the conclusion of this chapter, the student should be able to:

1. Define key terms related to the CPT Medicine Section.
2. Summarize the organization, format, and content of the CPT Medicine section.
3. Interpret the CPT Medicine Section guidelines.
4. Assign codes from the subsections of CPT Medicine.

Key Terms

adjuvant chemotherapy

allergen

allergen immunotherapy

allergy sensitivity test

autonomic function test

biofeedback

capitated payment
method

cardiac catheterization

cardiography

central motor evoked
potential study

chemotherapy

chiropractic manipulative
treatment (CMT)

determination of
refractive state

dose

duplex scan

echocardiography

electrocardiography

electromyography

gamma globulin

hemodialysis

hyperventilation

immune globulin (Ig)

immune serum globulin

intradermal test
(intracutaneous)

intravenous push

manometry

minimally invasive
procedure

multiple sleep latency

narcosynthesis

needle
electromyography

noninvasive procedure

orbicularis oculi

oscilloscope

osteopathic manipulative
treatment (OMT)

patch test
(epicutaneous)

peritoneal dialysis

pharmacologic
management

photic stimulation

physiatrist

physical medicine and
rehabilitation

polysomnography

psychotherapy

puncture, prick,
or scratch test
(percutaneous)

renal dialysis

short-latency
somatosensory
evoked potential study

sleep laboratory

sleep staging

sleep study

Tensilon test

visual evoked potential
(VEP) test

Introduction

The CPT Medicine section is the last section of CPT, and its codes for noninvasive or minimally invasive diagnostic and therapeutic procedures and services can be reported along with those from all other sections.

Overview of Medicine Section

The Medicine section classifies procedures and services that are procedure oriented (e.g., immunizations), that apply to various medical specialties (e.g., gastroenterology, ophthalmology, otorhinolaryngology, and psychiatry), and that apply to different types of health care providers (e.g., physical therapists and occupational therapists). Medicine section procedures are *noninvasive* or *minimally invasive* diagnostic and therapeutic procedures and services. **Noninvasive procedures** require no surgical incision or excision, and they are not open procedures. **Minimally invasive procedures** include percutaneous access. Medicine is the last section of CPT, and its codes can be reported along with those from all other sections.

NOTE:

The Other Procedures code below each subheading classifies an unlisted procedure performed on the anatomical site. When reporting an unlisted procedure code, include documentation about the procedure performed with the submitted claim. (Other Procedures subheadings are not included throughout this chapter of the textbook except when codes that describe additional procedures are included.)

Exercise 19.1 – Overview of Medicine Section

Instructions: Complete each statement.

1. When no surgical incision or excision is required to perform a procedure, it is considered _____.

2. Percutaneous access procedures are considered _____.

3. Codes from the Medicine section _____ (can/cannot) be reported with codes from other CPT sections.

4. The Medicine section contains codes for _____ procedures and services.

5. The Medicine section classifies procedures and services that are _____, that apply to various medical specialties, and that apply to different types of health care providers.

Medicine Section Guidelines

Guidelines located at the beginning of the Medicine section provide instruction about the following:

- Add-on codes
- Separate procedures
- Unlisted service or procedure
- Special report
- Imaging guidance
- Supplied materials

Instructional notes appear throughout the Medicine section to provide coding clarification and direction. Almost every Medicine subsection contains notes unique to that subsection.

Add-On Codes

Add-on codes are reported for procedures and services performed in *addition* to a *primary procedure*. Modifiers -50 (bilateral procedure) and -51 (multiple procedures) are not reported with add-on codes; instead, report the add-on code twice for a bilateral procedure. They are identified in the CPT with a plus symbol (**+**). A parenthetical note located below an add-on code identifies the primary procedure to which an add-on code applies.

> **EXAMPLE:** A 6-year-old male patient underwent Hib booster immunization administration, which required a three-dose schedule of intramuscular injections. One claim was prepared to report the three injections. Report codes 90471, 90472, 90472, and 90647.

Separate Procedures

Some procedures and services classified in the Medicine section are considered an integral component of a complete procedure or service, and they are identified by the description "separate procedure." Do not report a "separate procedure" code in addition to a code for the comprehensive (or complete) procedure *unless the "separate procedure" is performed independently or is distinct from other services provided at the same time.*

When a "separate procedure" is performed independently or is distinct from other services provided at the same time, add modifier -59 (Distinct Procedural Service) to the "separate procedure" code. Modifier -59 indicates that the procedure was performed as a distinct, independent procedure.

> **EXAMPLE:** Patient underwent orthoptic training and gonioscopy. Report codes 92065 and 92020-59.

Bundled Medicine Codes

When reporting codes for outpatient hospital services and physician office services, use outpatient code editor (OCE) software or national correct coding initiative (NCCI) software to identify bundled codes for procedures and services considered necessary to accomplish the major procedure. Bundled procedure and services codes are *not* separately coded and reported with the major procedure code. Reporting the component codes in addition to the major procedure code is considered *unbundling*, which is fraud.

> **EXAMPLE:** Patient underwent a stress test. Report code 93015. (Do *not* report codes 93016, 93017, and/or 93018 with code 93015. Doing so is considered unbundling.)

Multiple Medicine Codes

When multiple procedures and/or services are performed on the same date, report a separate code for each procedure and/or service.

> **EXAMPLE:** An established patient received 60 minutes of outpatient individual psychotherapy, and after psychotherapy the psychologist prepared a mandatory progress report and submitted it to the third-party payer. Report codes 90837 and 90889.

Unlisted Service or Procedure

CPT unlisted procedure and service codes are assigned when there is no specific code that accurately describes the procedure or service performed. When reporting an unlisted procedure code to a third-party payer, submit a written report (e.g., a copy of an operative report) that describes the procedure or service performed.

Special Report

When an unlisted procedure or service code is reported to a third-party payer, a special report is submitted that describes the procedure or service performed. Special reports may also be required for procedures and services that are rarely provided or are new in order to establish that the procedure is necessary. As a minimum, documentation in a special report includes the following:

- Adequate definition or description of the nature, extent, and need for the procedure or service
- Time, effort, and equipment necessary to provide the procedure or service

The following additional items may also be documented in a special report:

- Complexity of symptoms
- Concurrent problems
- Diagnostic and therapeutic procedures
- Final diagnosis
- Follow-up care
- Pertinent physical findings

Imaging Guidance

When imaging guidance or imaging supervision and interpretation is performed as part of a Medicine procedure, the Radiology guidelines apply.

Supplied Materials

Supplies and materials provided by the physician (e.g., drugs or sterile trays) other than those typically included with a procedure or service are reported separately. Report CPT code 99070 or a specific HCPCS level II code for materials and supplies provided.

EXAMPLE: Patient underwent chemotherapy administration (intramuscular) of vincristine sulfate, 1 mg. Report CPT code 96401 and HCPCS level II code J9370. (HCPCS level II code J9370 is more specific than CPT code 99070, which is a nonspecific supplies and materials code.)

Exercise 19.2 – Medicine Section Guidelines

Instructions: Complete each statement.

1. Instructional _____ appear throughout the Medicine section to provide coding clarification and direction.
2. When multiple procedures and/or services are performed on the same date, report a(n) _____ code for each procedure and/or service.
3. Add-on codes are reported for procedures and services performed in addition to a primary procedure, and they are identified in CPT with a(n) _____ symbol.
4. Some procedures and services classified in the Medicine section are considered an integral component of a complete procedure or service, and they are identified by the description _____.
5. Supplies and materials provided by the physician, other than those typically included with a procedure or service, are reported with CPT code 99070 or a specific _____ code for materials and supplies provided.

Medicine Subsections

Medicine subsections include the following:

- Immune globulins, serum or recombinant products
- Immunization administration for vaccines/toxoids
- Vaccines, toxoids
- Psychiatry
- Biofeedback
- Dialysis
- Gastroenterology
- Ophthalmology
- Special otorhinolaryngologic services

- Cardiovascular
- Noninvasive vascular diagnostic studies
- Pulmonary
- Allergy and clinical immunology
- Endocrinology
- Neurology and neuromuscular procedures
- Medical genetics and genetic counseling services
- Adaptive Behavior Services
- Central nervous system assessments/tests (e.g., neurocognitive, mental status, speech testing)
- Health and behavior assessment/intervention
- Hydration, therapeutic, prophylactic, diagnostic injections and infusions, and chemotherapy and other highly complex drug or highly complex biologic agent administration
- Photodynamic therapy

- Special dermatological procedures
- Physical medicine and rehabilitation
- Medical nutrition therapy
- Acupuncture
- Osteopathic manipulative treatment
- Chiropractic manipulative treatment
- Education and training for patient self-management
- Non-face-to-face nonphysician services
- Special services, procedures, and reports
- Qualifying circumstances for anesthesia
- Moderate (conscious) sedation
- Other services and procedures
- Home health procedures/services
- Medication therapy management services

Immune Globulins, Serum or Recombinant Products

An **immune globulin (Ig)** (**gamma globulin** or **immune serum globulin**) is a sterilized solution obtained from pooled human blood plasma, which contains immunoglobulins (or antibodies) that protect against infectious agents that cause various diseases. (Antibodies are substances in blood plasma that fight infection.) Immune globulins are administered to patients who need to use someone else's antibodies to help fight off or prevent illnesses from occurring. Ig formulations produced from donors include high levels of antibodies against hepatitis B (hepatitis B immune globulin-HBIG), rabies (rabies immune globulin-RIG), tetanus (tetanus immune globulin-TIG), and varicella (chicken pox; varicella zoster immune globulin-VZIG).

 NOTE:

The administration of an Ig provides temporary protection and is *not* considered an immunization, which provides longer-term protection.

Immune globulin codes are reported for the *supply of the immune globulin product*, which includes broad-spectrum and anti-infective immune globulins, antitoxins, and other isoantibodies. The *administration* of an immune globulin is reported separately with a code from the Therapeutic, Prophylactic, and Diagnostic Injections and Infusions subsection of the Medicine section.

 Coding Tip

Do not add modifier -51 (Multiple Procedures) to immune globulin codes.

- Intravenous infusion
- Subcutaneous infusion
- Intramuscular or subcutaneous injection
- Intravenous push

EXAMPLE: Intramuscular injection of 250 units of human tetanus immune globulin (TIg) was administered to a patient. Report codes 90389 and 96372.

Immunization Administration for Vaccines/Toxoids

Immunization administration for vaccines/toxoids codes are reported in addition to codes from the Medicine subsection entitled *Vaccines, Toxoids*. The immunization administration for vaccines/toxoids include the following:

- Administrative staff services (e.g., appointment scheduling, preparing a patient's record, and submitting an insurance claim to a payer)
- Clinical staff services (e.g., taking vital signs, assessing past reactions and contraindications, preparing and administering the vaccine/toxoid, monitoring reactions, and documenting in the record)

The following types of immunization administration for vaccines/toxoids are reported:

- Intradermal, intramuscular, percutaneous, and subcutaneous injections
- Intranasal and oral administration

The immunization administration of *pediatric* vaccines/toxoids is reported with codes 90460–90461 to accurately describe the work involved, which includes patient/family counseling provided by the physician during the administration of a vaccine/toxoid.

> **EXAMPLE:** A 6-year-old female patient received immunization administration (intramuscular injection) of the rabies vaccine. Physician discussed the vaccine composition with the patient's mother, including risks and benefits. Report codes 90460 and 90675.

Coding Tip

- Report immunization administration for vaccines/toxoids codes in addition to vaccine/toxoid codes.
- Do not report immunization administration codes for the administration of allergy injections or testing, chemotherapy, placement of catheters, transfusions, or venipuncture. Refer to the appropriate Surgery or Medicine subsection for reporting such codes.

Vaccines, Toxoids

Vaccines/toxoids codes identify the vaccine/toxoid product only. They are reported in addition to immunization administration for vaccines/toxoids codes.

> **EXAMPLE:** An 18-year-old female patient received immunization administration (subcutaneous injection) of an MMR booster. Report codes 90471 and 90707.

Coding Tip

Do not add modifier -51 (Multiple Procedures) to vaccines/toxoids codes.

- When vaccines/toxoids codes are reported during a preventive medicine encounter, add modifier -25 to the evaluation and management code (e.g., 99392-25).
- New vaccines have been approved for use by the Food and Drug Administration (FDA) over recent years. CPT created a new symbol ($\nearrow$) to indicate that FDA approval is pending, which means it is anticipated that the vaccines will receive FDA approval, but that approval was pending at the time of publication. Once the vaccine is approved by the FDA, the symbol will be removed.

Reporting Evaluation and Management Service Codes with Vaccines/Toxoids Codes

There is considerable confusion regarding whether a provider should report an evaluation and management (E/M) service for an encounter for immunization administration of vaccines/toxoids. Correct coding depends on whether the provider performed a medically necessary E/M service *in addition to the immunization administration*. To assign an E/M code in addition to the immunization administration code, the E/M service must exceed services included with immunization administration codes.

 NOTE:

Reporting E/M service code 99211 does not require the presence of the physician or the documentation of key components.

EXAMPLE: Physician provided a level 3 E/M service to a 48-year-old male patient to medically manage his hypertension. During the same encounter, the physician administered a flu shot (influenza vaccine, inactivated [IIV], subunit, adjuvanted, intramuscular injection). Report codes 99213-25, 90471, and 90653.

Psychiatry

Psychiatrists, psychologists, and licensed clinical social workers report psychiatry codes for psychotherapy services, which include the following headings and subheadings:

- Interactive complexity
- Psychiatric diagnostic procedures

  ○ Psychotherapy
  ○ Other psychotherapy
  ○ Other psychiatric services or procedures

 Coding Tip

- Psychiatric evaluation and management (E/M) services are reported by physicians, nurse practitioners, and physician assistants. Psychologists and licensed clinical social workers do not report codes from the CPT E/M section.

- Psychiatric consultation includes examination of the patient, exchange of information with the primary care physician or other pertinent individuals (e.g., family members and caretakers), and preparation of reports. Because no psychiatric treatment is provided during a psychiatric consultation, report the appropriate evaluation and management consultation code.

Interactive Complexity

Interactive complexity refers to specific communication factors that complicate the delivery of a psychiatric procedure, such as difficult communication with verbally undeveloped patients. The interactive complexity code is reported as an add-on code in addition to codes for diagnostic psychiatric evaluation, psychotherapy, psychotherapy performed with evaluation and management, and group psychology.

Psychiatric Diagnostic Procedures

Psychiatric diagnostic evaluation services include the following:

- History
- Mental status
- Recommendations

EXAMPLE: Patient received interactive psychiatric diagnostic interview examination services as the result of her parents finding out that she was being routinely bullied at elementary school. Report code 90791.

Psychotherapy

Psychotherapy is the treatment of mental illness and behavioral disturbances in which the provider uses definitive therapeutic communication in an attempt to alleviate emotional disturbances, reverse or change maladaptive patterns of behavior, and encourage personality growth and development.

EXAMPLE: Patient underwent 30 minutes of psychotherapy. Report code 90832.

Other Psychotherapy

Psychotherapy for crisis involves an urgent assessment and history of a patient's crisis state, which is typically life threatening or complex, requiring immediate attention to a patient in high distress. A mental status exam and disposition is included, and treatment consists of psychotherapy, mobilization of resources to defuse the crisis and restore safety, and implementation of psychotherapeutic interventions to minimize the potential for psychological trauma.

Psychoanalysis attempts to gain insight into a patient's motivations and conflicts to change maladaptive behavior (e.g., an inability to cope with the challenges of everyday living). The psychoanalysis code is reported on a per-day basis. Do not confuse psychoanalysis and psychotherapy codes. The psychoanalysis code refers to the practice of psychoanalysis (e.g., patient is treated by a physician who is credentialed to practice analytic therapy, and psychoanalysis is the treatment being used).

Family psychotherapy involves the patient's family in the treatment process, and the dynamics within the family are the focus of the psychotherapeutic sessions. Family psychotherapy may be performed with or without the patient present. Codes reported are based on whether the patient is present or not and whether multiple family groups are being treated.

EXAMPLE: Psychotherapy was provided on May 5 to the families of three different patients who reside in a drug treatment center. Report code 90849 on the insurance claim for *each* patient.

Other Psychiatric Services or Procedures

Other psychiatric services or procedures include the following:

- Pharmacologic management
- Narcosynthesis
- Electroconvulsive therapy
- Individual psychophysiological therapy incorporating biofeedback training
- Hypnotherapy
- Environmental intervention for medical management
- Psychiatric evaluation of hospital records
- Interpretation or explanation of psychiatric examination/procedure results
- Preparation of report of patient's psychiatric status, history, treatment, or progress for the benefit of other physicians, agencies, or third-party payers

Pharmacologic management is the evaluation of a patient's medications for affect (such as a patient's reaction to medication), proper dosage (e.g., a therapeutic dose), and renewal of prescribed medications. Pharmacologic management is provided by a physician (such as a psychiatrist) to a patient who undergoes psychotherapy from a nonphysician colleague (e.g., a psychologist or a licensed clinical social worker) or when a patient's condition is being effectively treated by psychotropic drugs alone. Generally, the patient does not receive other services from the physician during the encounter. When an evaluation and management (E/M) service is provided by the physician, the pharmacologic management is included in the E/M service. It is not coded and reported separately. (The psychotherapy provided during pharmacologic management is minimal and is also not coded or reported separately.)

Narcosynthesis is a form of psychotherapy that is provided when the patient is under the influence of a drug, such as a sedative or narcotic (e.g., a barbiturate, benzodiazepine-type drug that is administered intravenously). The administration of a medication to release inhibitions allows a patient to discuss issues that are too difficult to verbalize otherwise.

Electroconvulsive therapy is used to treat depression or life-threatening psychosis (e.g., severe affective disorders or schizophrenia) and involves the application of electric current to the brain through scalp electrodes. The term *electroconvulsive* refers to a convulsive response to an electrical stimulus. In electroconvulsive therapy, it is necessary to monitor the patient (e.g., management of the seizure, observation, and decisions regarding further treatment). If the psychiatrist also administers anesthesia for the electroconvulsive therapy, report the appropriate anesthesia code (00104), which includes cardiac and oxygen saturation monitoring.

> **EXAMPLE:** Patient underwent narcosynthesis for psychiatric diagnostic and therapeutic purposes. Amytal (amobarbital), 125 milligrams was injected prior to therapy. Report codes 90865, 96372, and J0300.

Biofeedback

Biofeedback is a technique that trains the patient to gain some control over autonomic body functions. Biofeedback services include the following:

- Reviewing the patient's history
- Preparing the biofeedback equipment
- Placing electrodes on the patient
- Reading and interpreting responses
- Monitoring the patient
- Controlling muscle responses

 Coding Tip

During individual psychophysiological therapy that incorporates biofeedback training, a separate biofeedback code is *not* reported.

The code for biofeedback services may include different types of administration (e.g., electromyogram application), and it is intended to identify all methods of biofeedback provided, even when more than one modality is performed during the same session. Electromyogram is a nerve-conduction study that plots the electrical activity produced by muscle contractions. **Manometry** is a diagnostic test that measures muscle function using a pressure-sensitive tube.

> **EXAMPLE 1:** Patient underwent 15 minutes biofeedback of perineal muscles for bladder training to prevent urinary incontinence. Treatment included use of manometry. Report code 90912.

> **EXAMPLE 2:** Patient underwent 30 minutes of individual psychophysiological therapy that included biofeedback training and behavior-modifying psychotherapy. Report code 90875. (Do *not* report code 90901 for biofeedback in addition to 90875.)

Dialysis

The Dialysis subsection includes the following headings:

- Hemodialysis
- Miscellaneous dialysis procedures
- End-stage renal disease services
- Other dialysis procedures

FIGURE 19-1 Hemodialysis filters waste from the patient's blood. Blood leaves the body via an artery, is filtered, and then is returned into a vein.

Renal dialysis artificially removes toxic waste products from the body when the patient's kidneys are unable to perform this function because of disease or deterioration. Dialysis is used for acute, temporary kidney failure (e.g., acute renal failure) or chronic renal failure (e.g., end-stage renal disease). The following types of dialysis are used, depending on the patient's condition and whether the patient is experiencing acute or chronic renal failure:

- **Hemodialysis:** Process of removing waste products, toxins, and excess fluids from the blood; patient's blood is diverted into a dialyzer, where it is treated and returned into the patient's circulation by another tube inserted into a different blood vessel (Figure 19-1)
- **Peritoneal dialysis:** Soft catheter is inserted into abdominal cavity and dialysate fluid is infused at intermittent times

Coding Tip

All evaluation and management (E/M) services related to end-stage renal disease (ESRD) and rendered during dialysis are included in the dialysis procedure code. An E/M service related to ESRD performed on the day of dialysis is not separately coded and reported. When the patient receives E/M services for a completely different condition that is not related to ESRD, report an appropriate E/M service code and add modifier -25 (significant, separately identifiable E/M service by the same physician on the same day as the procedure or other service).

Hemodialysis

Hemodialysis service codes include all E/M services related to the patient's renal disease *on the day of the hemodialysis procedure.* These codes are reported when hemodialysis services are provided to ESRD and non-ESRD patients in an inpatient setting and to non-ESRD patients in an outpatient setting.

EXAMPLE: A 54-year-old patient was admitted as a hospital inpatient for treatment of ESRD. Admission date was August 5, and discharge date was August 10. The patient underwent hemodialysis procedures on August 5, 7, and 9, which included evaluation by his attending physician. Report codes 90935, 90935, and 90935. (Attending physician should report appropriate inpatient evaluation and management service codes with modifier -25 for provision of services unrelated to ESRD and the hemodialysis procedure on those dates. For other dates, such as August 6, 8, and 10, the attending physician should report appropriate inpatient E/M service codes for daily care and discharge services.)

Miscellaneous Dialysis Procedures

Miscellaneous dialysis procedures codes include peritoneal dialysis, hemofiltration, and other continuous renal replacement therapies (for single physician evaluation or repeated physician evaluations).

EXAMPLE: Patient underwent peritoneal dialysis, which required repeated physician evaluations on the same date of treatment. Report code 90947.

End-Stage Renal Disease (ESRD) Services

ESRD services are typically performed as outpatient procedures, and reimbursement is usually made according to a monthly capitated payment method.

NOTE:

A **capitated payment method** is the result of an agreement between a third-party payer and a health care provider in which the provider agrees to provide services to a patient in return for a fixed monthly payment.

- ESRD services codes are reported *once per month per patient* (every 30 days). The appropriate code is reported just once, at the conclusion of a full month of ESRD services.

EXAMPLE: A 48-year-old patient received ESRD-related services two times each week during the entire month of June. Report code 90960.

- ESRD service codes can also be reported when less than a *full month of services* are provided to a patient. The appropriate code is reported for each day of service (e.g., when a patient requires less than a month's ESRD services after inpatient hospitalization).

EXAMPLE: A 54-year-old patient was hospitalized for ESRD from July 5 to July 20, and upon discharge received outpatient ESRD services on July 22, 24, 26, 28, and 30. Report codes 90970, 90970, 90970, 90970, and 90970 for outpatient ESRD services.

Coding Tip

- For patients under 20 years of age, ESRD codes include monitoring of nutrition, assessment of growth and development, and parental counseling.
- ESRD codes include physician services related to establishing a dialyzing cycle, evaluation and management of the dialysis visits, and patient management during the dialysis, provided during a full month.

Other Dialysis Procedures

Other dialysis procedures include dialysis training (e.g., completed course of training, an individual training session), hemoperfusion (e.g., using activated charcoal or resin), and unlisted dialysis procedures (inpatient or outpatient).

EXAMPLE: Patient completed an entire course of outpatient dialysis training during the month of June. Report code 90989.

Gastroenterology

The Gastroenterology subsection classifies gastroenterology tests (e.g., motility, acid perfusion) and also includes the following headings:

- Gastric physiology
- Other procedures

 Coding Tip

Gastroenterology tests are frequently performed in conjunction with gastrointestinal (GI) endoscopic procedures. Do *not* report codes separately from the Gastroenterology subsection of the Medicine section with Surgery section GI endoscopic procedures.

Gastroenterology procedures (Table 19-1) are found in the Surgery section. Related diagnostic services are found in the Pathology and Laboratory and Radiology sections.

EXAMPLE: Patient underwent gastric motility (manometric) studies. Report code 91020.

TABLE 19-1 Gastroenterology Procedures and Services

Procedure	Description
Esophageal or gastric intubation and collection of washings	• Tube is inserted through nose or mouth into esophagus or stomach. • One or more washings are obtained for *cytology* (study of cells).
Esophageal, gastric, or duodenal motility	• Tube is inserted through patient's nose or mouth into the esophagus, stomach, or duodenum. • Tube is slowly withdrawn to test muscles for weakness or abnormality (manometry).
Acid perfusion test of esophagus (or Bernstein test)	• Nasogastric tube is inserted into the esophagus. • Mild hydrochloric acid is poured through the tube in an attempt to recreate and evaluate gastric reflux symptoms. • Test is done to determine whether chest pain is due to acid reflux and not a cardiac condition.
Gastroesophageal reflux test	• Electrode is inserted through nasal catheter into esophagus to determine pH levels. • Electrode remains in esophagus over a period of time to obtain multiple levels (to determine acid reflux or non-acid reflux).
Esophageal balloon distention provocation study	• Local anesthetic is administered to numb the throat. • Balloon is inserted into esophagus and is expanded in multiple sites to increasing degrees to provoke chest pain. • This is done to rule out a cardiac source of existing chest pain.
Gastric analysis test (or Hollander test)	• Nasogastric tube is inserted through patient's nose or mouth into the stomach. • Stimulant is injected into the stomach (e.g., histamine, insulin, pentagastrin, calcium, or secretin). • Gastric contents are suctioned through the tube and are analyzed.
Gastric saline load test	• Nasogastric tube is inserted through patient's nose or mouth into the stomach. • Gastric contents are suctioned, and stomach is filled with saline. • After 30 minutes, gastric contents are resuctioned and measured to determine presence of impaired gastric emptying.

TABLE 19-1 *(continued)*

Procedure	Description
Breath hydrogen test	• Patient's exhalations are tested for hydrogen to determine whether undigested food is entering the duodenum. • Test is administered over a period of 3 to 5 hours, after patient has fasted for 12 hours and has swallowed test sugars (e.g., fructose, lactose, or lactulose).
Placement of intestinal bleeding tube	• Intestinal bleeding tube is inserted through mouth into duodenum. • Tube is monitored and used to suppress bleeding, if present.
Gastric intubation for aspiration or lavage	• Nasogastric tube is inserted through patient's nose or mouth into the stomach. • Gastric contents are suctioned to remove ingested poisons or to decompress intestinal blockage.
Gastrointestinal (GI) tract imaging	• Patient swallows a capsule that provides color imaging as it passes through the GI system. • Data are transmitted from the capsule to a data recorder.
Rectal sensation, tone, and compliance test	• Balloon is inserted into the patient's rectum and gradually inflated. • Reactions to various levels of inflation are studied.
Anorectal manometry	• This measures pressure of anal sphincter to diagnose constipation or incontinence.
Pulsed irrigation of fecal impaction (or pulsed irrigation evaluation, PCE)	• Automated enema is inserted for cases of chronic constipation when the patient has no voluntary bowel control (e.g., a paraplegic patient).
Electrogastrography (EGG)	• Electrodes are attached to the patient's abdomen. • Myoelectrical activity is detected and recorded.

Ophthalmology

Ophthalmology services include the following headings:

- General ophthalmological services
- Special ophthalmological services
- Contact lens services
- Spectacle services (including prosthesis for aphakia)

General Ophthalmological Services

General ophthalmological services codes are reported for new or established patient examinations. A physician (such as an ophthalmologist) can report an appropriate evaluation and management (E/M) service code instead of a general ophthalmological service code. *Do not report a general ophthalmological services code in addition to an E/M service code.*

Ophthalmologists have a choice when assigning codes for E/M services because they provide unique and specialized services that do not match criteria associated with E/M codes. Instead of reporting codes from the E/M section, an ophthalmologist may report codes from the Medicine section. These codes describe intermediate and comprehensive levels of service, which are defined by CPT.

When services provided are less than those described by general ophthalmological services codes, the ophthalmologist should report the appropriate E/M codes.

- Intermediate ophthalmological services include history, general medical observation, external ocular and adnexal examination, and other diagnostic procedures as indicated. This may include the use of mydriasis for ophthalmoscopy.

EXAMPLE: Established patient was seen in the office by her ophthalmologist for evaluation of glaucoma. Interval history, external examination, ophthalmoscopy, biomicroscopy, and tonometry were performed to evaluate the patient's response to glaucoma treatment. Report code 92012.

- Comprehensive ophthalmological services include a general evaluation of the complete visual system (e.g., history, general medical observation, external and ophthalmoscopic examinations, gross visual fields and basic sensorimotor examination, biomicroscopy, examination with cycloplegia or mydriasis, and tonometry). In addition, diagnostic and treatment procedures are included. Comprehensive services may be performed during multiple sessions or visits.

EXAMPLE: An established patient previously diagnosed with glaucoma was seen in her ophthalmologist's office. The ophthalmic technician tested the patient's visual acuity, gross visual field by confrontation, ocular motility including primary gaze alignment, and intraocular pressures. The ophthalmologist examined the patient's ocular adnexae, including lids, lacrimal glands, lacrimal drainage, orbits, and preauricular lymph nodes. The pupils and irises were also examined. The ophthalmologist performed a slit lamp examination of the corneas, anterior chambers, and lenses. He also inspected the patient's bulbar and palpebral conjunctivae. The ophthalmologist prescribed medication and ordered lab work. Report code 92014.

Special Ophthalmological Services

Special ophthalmological services codes classify services that are not considered part of a general ophthalmological examination. They are considered significant, separately identifiable services, which means that their codes are reported in addition to codes for general ophthalmological examination services, when performed.

 Coding Tip

Routine ophthalmoscopy is included in general ophthalmological services. However, other special ophthalmological services are not included, and they should be coded and reported separately when performed (e.g., a determination of refractive state).

Determination of refractive state establishes whether a prescription is required for vision correction. It is performed using an eye chart and refractor (a device that contains a wide range of lens strengths that can be easily and quickly changed). The fitting of glasses or contact lenses is *not* included with determination of refractive state services.

EXAMPLE: Patient underwent determination of refractive state. Report code 92015.

Code 92025 is reported for computerized corneal topography (also called computer-assisted keratography or videokeratography), during which a digital camera is used to capture an image of the patient's cornea for computer analysis.

Contact Lens Services and Spectacle Services (Including Prosthesis for Aphakia)

When contact lens or spectacle services are provided, supply of the contact lenses or spectacles (glasses) is not included. Report an appropriate HCPCS level II code for the supply of materials.

EXAMPLE: Patient underwent fitting of bifocal spectacles. Ophthalmologist provided "sphere, bifocal, plano to plus or minus 4.00d, per lens" glasses to the patient. Report codes 92341 and V2200.

Special Otorhinolaryngologic Services

Special Otorhinolaryngologic services include the following headings:

- Vestibular function tests, without electrical recording
- Vestibular function tests, with recording (e.g., ENG)
- Audiologic function tests
- Evaluative and therapeutic services
- Special diagnostic procedures
- Other procedures

When otorhinolaryngologic services are performed during an evaluation and management (E/M) service, do not code and report the component procedures separately (e.g., otoscopy, tuning fork test, whispered voice test). Special otorhinolaryngologic services that are *not* typically included in a comprehensive otorhinolaryngologic evaluation are reported separately.

> **EXAMPLE:** An otorhinolaryngologist performed a level 4 E/M service in the office, during which he reviewed the established patient's history, performed an external inspection of the ears, and conducted a rhinoscopic examination of the nose. Otoscopic examination of the external auditory canals and tympanic membranes revealed negative findings. Hearing assessment was performed with tuning forks, whispered voice, and finger-rub techniques. Report code 99214 from the E/M section. Do *not* report separate codes for the hearing assessments performed.

> **NOTE:**
>
> During a level 4 E/M service, such as presented in the previous example, when the physician also performs a positional nystagmus test and nasal function studies, codes 92532 and 92512 are reported in addition to E/M code 99214.

Audiologic function tests with medical diagnostic evaluation codes include testing of both ears. Do *not* add modifier -50 (Bilateral Procedure) to these codes.

> **EXAMPLE:** Patient underwent a pure-tone screening test, air only, both ears. Report code 92551.

Codes for audiometric tests are reported separately only when calibrated electronic equipment is used. For pure-tone audiometry, earphones are used. The patient responds to different tone pitches (frequencies). Air and bone thresholds are similar to pure-tone audiometry procedures, except a bone oscillator is used instead of earphones.

> **EXAMPLE:** Patient underwent pure-tone audiometry, air and bone, left ear. Report code 92553-52.

Cardiovascular

Cardiovascular services include the following headings:

- Therapeutic services and procedures
- Cardiography
- Cardiovascular monitoring services
- Implantable, insertable, and wearable cardiac device evaluations
- Echocardiography
- Cardiac catheterization
- Intracardiac electrophysiological procedures/ studies
- Peripheral arterial disease rehabilitation
- Noninvasive physiologic studies and procedures
- Home and Outpatient International Normalized Radio (INR) Monitoring Services
- Other procedures

 Coding Tip

- Many therapeutic and diagnostic cardiovascular procedure codes include intravenous or intra-arterial access, electrocardiographic monitoring, and agents administered by injection or infusion. Therefore, do not separately report these codes for routine access, monitoring, injection, or infusion services.

- Cardiovascular code descriptions often state "with interpretation," or "tracing only," whereas others describe the total (global, technical, and professional) service. Be sure to carefully review code descriptions before reporting a code.

Therapeutic Services and Procedures

Therapeutic services performed during a heart catheterization, after the diagnostic images are obtained, are reported in addition to the heart catheterization codes (e.g., balloon angioplasty). Therapeutic procedures include the following:

- Cardiopulmonary resuscitation
- Transcutaneous pacing
- Cardioversion
- Circulatory assist procedures
- Thrombolysis
- Transcatheter placement of stents
- Percutaneous transluminal coronary balloon angioplasty
- Atherectomy

Percutaneous coronary artery interventions include stent placement (Figure 19-2), atherectomy, and balloon angioplasty (Figure 19-3). For a given coronary artery and its branches, report only the most complex intervention, regardless of the number of stent placements, atherectomies, or balloon angioplasties performed in that coronary artery and its branches. (Stent placement is considered more complex than an atherectomy. An atherectomy is considered more complex than a balloon angioplasty.) Do not add modifier -59 to codes reported for percutaneous coronary artery stent placement, atherectomy, or balloon angioplasty. These interventions are reported with an appropriate modifier to indicate in which coronary artery the procedure was performed. These modifiers are the following:

- -LC (left circumflex coronary artery)
- -RC (right coronary artery)
- -LD (left anterior descending coronary artery)

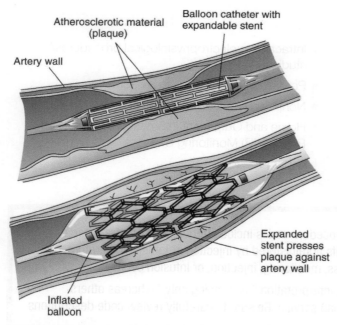

FIGURE 19-2 A stent is inserted after balloon angioplasty to prevent restenosis of the treated artery.

FIGURE 19-3 Balloon angioplasty is performed to open a blocked coronary artery.

Coding Tip

Medicare recognizes the following three coronary arteries for reimbursement purposes when considering first and additional vessel interventions:

- Left anterior descending
- Left circumflex
- Right coronary

Therefore, it is possible to report up to three percutaneous interventions if an intervention is performed in each of the three coronary arteries or their branches.

- The first procedure is reported with a primary code that describes the most complex procedure performed.
- Procedures performed in other coronary arteries are reported with the add-on codes.

When cardiopulmonary resuscitation (CPR) is performed *without* other evaluation and management services, the time required to perform CPR is not included in determining the critical care or other time-based evaluation and management services. Codes from the E/M section are reported for time-based critical care services and prolonged management services.

EXAMPLE: A "code blue" is called on a hospital inpatient. The responding physician directs cardiopulmonary resuscitation. After the patient is resuscitated, the patient's attending physician resumes patient care. Report code 92950 for CPR.

Cardiography

Cardiography, or **electrocardiography**, is a diagnostic procedure that records the heart's electronic activity with a cardiograph and produces a cardiogram (or electrocardiogram, ECG, or EKG) (Figure 19-4). Cardiography codes are reported for routine electrocardiograms and other procedures (e.g., vector cardiogram, 24-hour monitoring, and patient demand recordings when ordered by the provider). Be sure to identify the total, professional, and technical components (and appropriate modifiers) before reporting cardiography codes.

The routine monitoring of EKG rhythm and hemodynamics, including cardiac outputs, is included as part of critical care evaluation and management services. Therefore, do not separately report EKG rhythm strip and cardiac output measurement review codes with critical care services.

EXAMPLE: Patient underwent routine ECG (tracing only) in the physician's office. Report code 93005.

Cardiovascular Monitoring Services

Cardiovascular monitoring services (e.g., pacemaker programming) use in-person and remote technology to assess cardiovascular rhythm data.

EXAMPLE: Patient underwent transtelephonic rhythm strip pacemaker evaluation of her multiple lead pacemaker system for a period of 60 days, which included physician analysis, review, and documented report. Report code 93293 just once.

Implantable, Insertable, and Wearable Cardiac Device Evaluations

Cardiac device evaluation services are diagnostic medical procedures using in-person and remote technology to assess cardiac device therapy and cardiovascular physiologic data.

EXAMPLE: Patient underwent a 30-day remote interrogation device evaluation that required a subcutaneous cardiac rhythm monitor system. Analysis of recorded heart rhythm data, and physician analysis, review and report were included. Report code 93298.

FIGURE 19-4 Electrocardiogram showing disruptions of heart rhythms (A) Paroxysmal atrial tachycardia (PAT) (B) Atrial fibrillation (C) Ventricular fibrillation

Echocardiography

Echocardiography (Figure 19-5) is a diagnostic procedure that uses ultrasound to obtain two-dimensional images of the heart and great arteries (aorta, vena cavae). Echocardiography codes include the total procedure. When just the professional component is performed, add modifier -26 to the code.

> **EXAMPLE:** Patient underwent transesophageal echocardiography for congenital cardiac anomalies, which included placement of the probe, image acquisition, and interpretation and report. Report code 93315.

Cardiac Catheterization

Cardiac catheterization (Figure 19-6) is an invasive diagnostic medical procedure that includes several components. The procedure begins when the physician introduces one or more catheters into peripheral arteries

FIGURE 19-5 Echocardiography: The large area of red shows the flow of blood through an abnormal opening between the aorta and right atrium.

FIGURE 19-6 Cardiac catheterization: Once the catheter is inserted in the heart, a contrast medium is injected and an angiogram is performed to detect coronary vessel patency (openness).

and/or veins. Cardiac catheterizations include introduction, positioning (and repositioning) of catheter(s), recording of intracardiac and/or intravascular pressure(s), and final evaluation and preparation of a report.

Cardiac output measurement is routinely performed during cardiac catheterization procedures. These codes are not reported in addition to cardiac catheterization codes.

Fluoroscopic guidance procedures are integral to invasive intravascular procedures, and codes for such procedures are not reported separately.

When reporting codes for cardiac catheterization procedures, review patient-record documentation to determine the following:

- Catheter placement
- Injection procedure
- Supervision and interpretation of fluoroscopic guidance

The femoral artery is the most common access point for cardiac catheterization (such as left heart catheterization, aortography, coronary angiography, internal mammary artery injection, vein bypass graft injection, and for other left heart procedures and coronary artery interventions). Right heart catheterization and pulmonary arteriography are most often performed via the right femoral vein. Each catheter is then positioned in a branch vessel or a cardiac chamber. During the catheterization procedure, recordings are made for measurement of intracardiac and intravascular pressure, oxygen saturation or blood gases, and cardiac output.

Angiography, frequently performed during a diagnostic catheterization, may require the assignment of a separate code. Angiography involves injecting a contrast medium and imaging the vessel (e.g., in order to determine the location or severity of obstructive lesions or abnormalities). Repositioning the catheter may be necessary during the procedure to perform injection of contrast for angiography. A final evaluation of all data and a report are required.

> **EXAMPLE:** Patient underwent combined right and left heart catheterization, which included intraprocedural injection for left ventriculography with imaging supervision and interpretation. Report code 93453.

Endomyocardial biopsy provides tissue for direct pathologic evaluation of cardiac muscle using a special biopsy catheter with a bioptome tip (an open tip that closes to obtain tissue sample) to obtain myocardial tissue samples. To monitor a cardiac transplant patient for signs of rejection, the physician inserts a bioptome-tip catheter and, under fluoroscopy, advances it to the right ventricle. The instrument obtains myocardial tissue that is submitted for pathologic examination.

Insertion of a Swan-Ganz catheter is included in the cardiac catheterization codes. It is not separately reported *except when performed as a separate and distinct procedure from the heart catheterization.* A Swan-Ganz catheter is a flexible, multiple-lumen, balloon-tipped flotation catheter that is introduced through a major peripheral vein (e.g., the jugular or subclavian). It is passed under pressure waveform guidance, with or without fluoroscopy, through the right atrium, right ventricle, and pulmonary artery. Then the balloon is inflated and the tip measures pressure-transmitted retrograde from the left side of the heart (left ventricular end-diastolic pressure), as well as central venous pressure. With the balloon deflated, the catheter measures pulmonary artery systolic, diastolic, and mean pressures; it then allows infusion (and some patients are fitted with pacing electrodes).

> **EXAMPLE:** During postoperative recovery after a heart catheterization, the patient's condition became unstable, and the physician inserted a Swan-Ganz flow-directed catheter for evaluation and monitoring. Report code 93503.

Intracardiac Electrophysiological Procedures/Studies

Intracardiac electrophysiological procedures and studies describe services that record, map, or change heart conduction (e.g., recording bundle of His, mapping tachycardia during repair surgery). Many of these codes contain instructional notes that indicate their use with other codes. Intracardiac electrophysiological procedures (EP) may be diagnostic or therapeutic, and these procedures include the insertion and repositioning of catheters.

Peripheral Arterial Disease Rehabilitation

Peripheral arterial disease (PAD) is a disease in which plaque builds up in arteries that carry blood to the head, organs, and limbs; plaque consists of cholesterol, calcium, fat, fibrous tissue, and other substances in the blood. PAD rehabilitation includes physical exercise that consists of a series of sessions, each session lasting 45–60 minutes, and involves use of either a motorized treadmill or a track.

> **EXAMPLE:** During a series of three sessions, as part of PAD rehabilitation with supervision by an exercise physiologist, the patient exercised on a motorized treadmill for 45 minutes. Report codes 93668, 93668, and 93668.

Noninvasive Physiologic Studies and Procedures

Noninvasive physiologic studies and procedures include bioimpedance-derived physiologic cardiovascular analysis, electronic analysis of antitachycardia pacemaker system, temperature gradient studies, and so on.

> **EXAMPLE:** Patient underwent a procedure for determination of venous pressure. Report code 93770.

Home and Outpatient International Normalized Radio (INR) Monitoring Services

Home and Outpatient International Normalized Radio (INR) Monitoring Services describe the management of warfarin therapy, including ordering, review, and interpretation of new INR test result(s), patient instructions, and dosage adjustments as needed. When a significantly, separately identifiable evaluation and management

(E/M) service is provided on the same day as code 93792 services, the appropriate E/M service is reported using modifier -25. Code 93793 is *not* reported on the same day as an E/M service because its anticoagulant management services are part of the E/M service. Codes 93792 and 93793 are also *not* reported with E/M services for telephone or online services for home and outpatient INR monitoring, chronic care management and complex chronic care management, or transitional care management services.

EXAMPLE 1: Anticoagulant management was provided to a patient taking warfarin, which included the review and interpretation of a new home international normalized ratio (INR) test result, and patient instructions. The patient's dosage is unchanged. No additional tests are required. Report code 93793.

EXAMPLE 2: Patient received level 3 emergency department services for management of uncontrolled type 1 diabetes mellitus and face-to-face patient training for initiation of home international normalized ratio (INR) monitoring, which included use and care of the INR monitor, obtaining a blood sample, instructions for reporting home INR test results, and documentation of the patient's ability to perform testing and report results. Report codes 99283-25 and 93792.

EXAMPLE 3: Patient received level 3 established patient office encounter evaluation and management services and anticoagulant management of his warfarin. Report code 99213 only. (Do not report code 93793.)

Other Procedures

Cardiac rehabilitation is a customized program of exercise and education. Cardiac rehabilitation programs typically last about three to six months, during which the patient works with cardiologists, nurse educators, dietitians, exercise rehabilitation specialists, occupational therapists, physical therapists, psychologists, and psychiatrists. Because the cardiac rehabilitation codes describe comprehensive services provided by a physician for cardiac rehabilitation, all services related to cardiac rehabilitation are included. Thus, it would *not* be appropriate to report a separate evaluation and management service code unless it is an unrelated, separately identifiable service.

 Coding Tip

All intracardiac electrophysiological procedures/studies codes are exempt from modifier -51.

EXAMPLE: On November 15, 20, and 25, a patient received physician services for outpatient cardiac rehabilitation without continuous ECG monitoring. Report codes 93797, 93797, and 93797 for each date of service.

Noninvasive Vascular Diagnostic Studies

Noninvasive vascular diagnostic studies (e.g., a duplex scan) include ultrasound scanning to display two-dimensional structure and motion, and the codes classify arterial and venous studies. They also identify anatomical structures or areas to be evaluated. (A **duplex scan** is a noninvasive test that is performed to evaluate a vessel's blood flow.) Headings include the following:

- Cerebrovascular arterial studies
- Extremity arterial studies (including digits)
- Extremity venous studies (including digits)
- Visceral and penile vascular studies
- Extremity arterial-venous studies
- Other noninvasive vascular diagnostic studies

EXAMPLE: Patient underwent a duplex scan of lower extremity arteries, bilaterally. Report code 93925.

Pulmonary

Pulmonary codes are reported for therapeutic and diagnostic pulmonary services. When pulmonary services are provided during an evaluation and management (E/M) encounter (e.g., hospital inpatient visit, emergency department service, office visit), report a code from the Pulmonary subsection of the Medicine section in addition to the appropriate E/M code.

Pulmonary headings include

- *Ventilator management* provided to patients in hospital inpatient and observation care settings, nursing facilities, and for whom home care is provided

> **EXAMPLE:** A hospital inpatient was treated with a mechanical ventilator that was applied with a mask over his nose and mouth to assist with breathing due to emphysema. Initial ventilator management services were provided on April 5, and subsequent ventilator management services were provided on April 6 and 7. Report codes 94002, 94003, and 94003. (Do not report modifier -51 with code 94003.)

- *Pulmonary diagnostic testing and therapies* that include laboratory procedures and interpretation of test results (e.g., spirometry, vital capacity, and thoracic gas volume)

> **EXAMPLE:** During a level 3 outpatient E/M service to evaluate cystic fibrosis, the patient underwent outpatient pulmonary function testing to assess maximum breathing capacity and maximal voluntary ventilation. The physician interpreted the results of testing and adjusted the patient's medications. Report codes 99213 and 94200.

Allergy and Clinical Immunology

The Allergy and Clinical Immunology subsection includes the following headings:

- Allergy testing
- Ingestion challenge testing
- Allergen immunotherapy

Allergy Testing

Allergy sensitivity tests are performed on skin (cutaneous) and mucous membranes to identify the source of a patient's allergies (e.g., pollen as a source). Allergy skin tests include

- **Puncture, prick, or scratch test (percutaneous):** Tiny drops of purified allergen extracts are pricked or scratched into the skin's surface. The test is performed to identify allergies to pollen, mold, pet dander, dust mites, foods, insect venom, and penicillin (Figure 19-7).
- **Intradermal test (intracutaneous):** Purified allergen extracts are injected into the skin of patient's arm (Figure 19-8). The test is performed when an allergy to insect venom or penicillin is suspected.
- **Patch test (epicutaneous):** An allergen is applied to a patch, which is placed on skin. The test is performed to identify substances that cause contact dermatitis, such as latex, medications, fragrances, preservatives, hair dyes, metals, and resins.

> **EXAMPLE:** Patient underwent two patch tests. Report codes 95044 and 95044.

Ingestion Challenge Testing

Ingestion challenge testing includes the sequential and incremental ingestion of test items. Examples of test items include drugs, foods, and other substances. Patient assessment and monitoring activities (e.g., blood pressure) that are performed during ingestion challenge testing are *not* separately reported. However, intervention therapy (e.g., injection of epinephrine), when performed, is reported separately along with appropriate evaluation and management service code(s).

> **EXAMPLE:** Patient underwent 120 minutes of ingestion challenge testing (strawberries). Report code 95076.

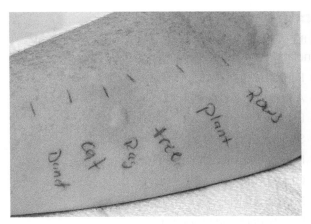

FIGURE 19-7 In scratch (percutaneous) tests, allergens are placed on the skin, the skin is scratched, and the allergen is labeled. Reactions usually occur within 20 minutes. Pictured is a reaction to ragweed.

FIGURE 19-8 Intradermal skin test

Allergen Immunotherapy

Allergen immunotherapy (also known as allergy shots, allergy vaccines, desensitization shots, or hypo-sensitization shots) contains small amounts of **allergens** (allergy-causing substances to which a patient reacts) to increase the patient's tolerance to allergens. Code descriptions indicate whether the allergenic extract is provided or not.

 NOTE:

An allergen immunotherapy **dose** is the amount of antigen administered in a single injection from a multiple-dose vial.

EXAMPLE: A primary care provider administers a single allergy injection using allergenic extract that was previously prepared by an allergist and brought to the office by the patient. Report code 95115.

Allergen immunotherapy is administered on a schedule; patients typically receive treatment once or twice a week for about three to six months, and then once a month for three to five years. There are usually two phases of treatment.

- The buildup phase, during which patients receive shots one or two times per week for about three to six months
- The maintenance phase, during which patients receive shots every two to four weeks for five months or longer

Endocrinology

Continual glucose (blood sugar) monitoring for up to 72 hours involves the subcutaneous placement of a sensor from which data are sent to a monitor. The patient calibrates the monitor on a daily basis.

EXAMPLE: Dr. Jones was provided with a printout of recorded data from a subcutaneous sensor inserted into patient Mary Smith. The sensor facilitated ambulatory continuous glucose monitoring of interstitial tissue fluid for 72 hours. Dr. Jones analyzed and interpreted the data and prepared a report. Report code 95251.

Neurology and Neuromuscular Procedures

Neurology and neuromuscular codes classify diagnostic and therapeutic services that do not require surgical procedures. The Neurology and Neuromuscular subsection includes the following headings:

- Sleep medicine testing
- Routine electroencephalography (EEG)
- Electrocortiography
- Range-of-motion testing
- Electromyography
- Ischemic muscle testing and guidance for chemodenervation
- Nerve conduction tests

- Intraoperative neurophysiology
- Autonomic function tests
- Evoked potentials and reflex tests
- Special EEG tests
- Neurostimulators, analysis-programming
- Other procedures
- Motion analysis
- Functional brain mapping

Sleep Medicine Testing

Sleep testing includes sleep studies and polysomnography, which are performed for the continuous monitoring and recording of various physiological parameters of sleep for six or more hours. Sleep testing is usually done in a health care facility's **sleep laboratory**, which is managed by a sleep technologist who explains and performs the sleep studies. (Sleep studies and polysomnographies are ordered, reviewed, and interpreted by physicians.) Sleeping rooms typically contain regular (not hospital) beds, an attached bathroom, and a television.

Sleep medicine testing codes include physician review and interpretation of data, and the preparation of a report.

- **Multiple sleep latency** is the observation of a patient during at least a six-hour period of sleep and includes assessment of sleep latency (dormancy) and/or wakefulness after the sleep period.

- **Sleep studies** evaluate adult and pediatric patients during sleep by monitoring brainwaves, heart rate, and eye movements. They are performed to diagnose sleep disorders, which include breathing, movement, and neurologic disorders that occur at night. Electrodes are applied to the patient's scalp, sides of the head, below the chin, chest, and legs. A sensor is placed next to the nose and mouth to measure airflow. A pulse oximetry clip is placed on the patient's finger to measure blood oxygen levels. Patients are also videotaped while asleep.

- **Polysomnography** is a sleep study that includes sleep staging with additional parameters of sleep (e.g., belts can be placed around the rib cage and abdomen to measure breathing movements). **Sleep staging** includes a 1-4 lead EEG, electro-oculogram (EOG), and submental electromyogram (EMG). Parameters that determine the polysomnography code to report include the following:

- Airflow
- Body positions
- Continuous blood pressure monitoring
- Electrocardiogram
- End tidal gas analysis
- Extended EEG monitoring
- Extremity muscle activity

- Gas exchange by oximetry
- Gastroesophageal reflux
- Motor activity movement
- Penile tumescence
- Snoring
- Transcutaneous monitoring
- Ventilation and respiratory effort

EXAMPLE: A patient with a history of sleep apnea undergoes a sleep study, during which he is monitored for six hours. Polysomnography includes the measurement of respiration, airflow, muscle activity, continuous monitoring of blood pressure, and sleep staging with EEG, electro-oculogram, and submental electromyogram. Report code 95808.

Routine Electroencephalography (EEG)

EEG procedures include the use of the following, when appropriate:

- **Hyperventilation:** Deep or rapid breathing
- **Photic stimulation:** Reaction to light

Extended EEG codes are reported to test various stages of activity and sleep.

> **EXAMPLE:** Patient underwent a 60-minute EEG test, which included photic (pertaining to light) stimulation. Report code 95812.

Electrocorticography

Electrocorticography (ECoG) procedures include the recording of an EEG from electrodes directly on or in the brain. An ECG code is reported when an electrocorticogram is performed during surgery or after the physician has inserted electrodes into the brain for EEG recording.

> **EXAMPLE:** Patient underwent electrocorticography during brain surgery. Report code 95829 (in additional to appropriate brain surgery codes from the Surgery section).

Range-of-Motion Testing

Range-of-motion testing codes are reported for muscle testing, range-of-motion measurements and reports, and Tensilon testing for myasthenia gravis. The **Tensilon test** involves injecting the drug Tensilon (or its generic, edrophonium chloride) into a vein to block the action of the enzyme that breaks down the neurotransmitter acetylcholinesterase. The patient is then observed for rapid improvement in strength (e.g., use of eye muscles).

> **EXAMPLE:** Patient underwent range-of-motion measurements (including physician report) of each extremity. Report code 95851.

Electromyography

Electromyography (EMG) is a test that is used to detect nerve function by measuring the electrical activity generated by muscles. **Needle electromyography** testing involves inserting needle electrodes into skeletal muscles and observing electrical activity of those muscles using an **oscilloscope** (a device that displays electrical waveforms on a monitor) and a loudspeaker.

> **EXAMPLE:** Patient underwent limited needle EMG study of the left bicep muscle. Report code 95870.

Ischemic Muscle Testing and Guidance for Chemodenervation

Ischemic muscle testing and guidance for chemodenervation services are performed to treat various neurological conditions.

> **EXAMPLE:** Patient underwent ischemic limb exercise test with collection of several specimens to determine the presence of muscle metabolites. Report code 95875.

Nerve Conduction Tests

Nerve conduction tests are performed for sensory conduction, motor conduction, or Hoffman's reflex (H-reflex) (knee jerk reflex). For sensory conduction and H-reflex testing, electrodes are placed directly over the nerve; for motor conduction testing, electrodes are placed over the motor point of a specific muscle; then, electrical stimulation is applied. Amplitude, conduction velocity, and latency of the stimulation are measured.

> **EXAMPLE:** Patient underwent three nerve conduction studies due to left leg numbness. Report code 95908.

Intraoperative Neurophysiology

Intraoperative neurophysiology testing codes are reported when performed during a surgical procedure. (The primary procedure code is reported as the first-listed procedure.)

> **EXAMPLE:** Patient underwent EEG needle electromyography of one extremity, during which 15 minutes of intraoperative neurophysiology testing was also performed. Report codes 95860 and 95940.

Autonomic Function Tests

Autonomic function tests evaluate autonomic nervous system functioning (e.g., heart or lungs).

> **EXAMPLE:** Patient underwent autonomic function testing, during which he was instructed to perform the Valsalva maneuver and then lie on a tilt table. The patient's blood pressure was monitored both during the maneuver and while on the tilt table. Report code 95922.

Evoked Potentials and Reflex Tests

A **short-latency somatosensory evoked potential study** involves electrically stimulating nerves to evaluate their responsiveness to the body's superficial surface and internal structures (e.g., the organs). (The appropriate code is reported according to testing site.) A **central motor evoked potential study** uses low-voltage electrodes, which are placed on the scalp and target sites to test the nervous system's pathway. A **visual evoked potential (VEP) test** of the central nervous system (CNS) involves stimulating the eye using the checkerboard or flash technique to monitor the patient's response. An **orbicularis oculi** (blink) test is monitored with sensors.

> **EXAMPLE 1:** Patient underwent a short-latency somatosensory evoked potential study, stimulation of any/all peripheral nerves or skin sites, recording from the central nervous system; in upper limbs. Report code 95925.

> **EXAMPLE 2:** Patient underwent VEP testing of the CNS using the flash technique. Report code 95930.

Special EEG Tests

Continuous electroencephalographic monitoring services codes are reported when a separately identifiable long-term or monitoring service is performed.

> **EXAMPLE:** Patient underwent EEG during carotid artery (nonintracranial) surgery. Report code 95955.

Neurostimulators, Analysis-Programming

Neurostimulators and analysis-programming codes are reported when a previously implanted neurostimulator pulse generator system is electronically analyzed to determine battery status, pulse amplitude and duration, rate, and so on.

> **EXAMPLE:** Patient underwent electronic analysis of implanted neurostimulator pulse generator system without reprogramming. Report code 95970.

Other Procedures

Other procedures codes are reported for the refill and maintenance of implantable infusion pumps or reservoirs for drug delivery, for canalith repositioning, per day, and for an unlisted neurological or neuromuscular diagnostic procedure.

> **EXAMPLE:** Patient with terminal cancer undergoes a procedure to have implantable pump located in his spine refilled and maintained to ensure delivery of 500 mg of morphine sulfate, which is the loading dose prescribed for palliative care. Report codes 95990 and S0093.

Motion Analysis

Motion analysis codes are reported for services performed during major diagnostic or therapeutic decision making. During human motion analysis, patient movements are recorded, digitized, copied onto a computer, and processed.

When a physician reviews and interprets the results of motion analysis and documents a written report, the appropriate code is reported just once in addition to the motion analysis tests performed. Modifier -51 is added to that review and interpretation code when the service is provided during the same encounter as motion analysis testing.

> **EXAMPLE:** In the motion analysis lab, a patient is instructed to walk along a special walkway that includes a pressure sensor platform, which is positioned on the walkway. As the patient walks, pressure data are recorded and later analyzed for areas of the foot (e.g., hallux, heel, and metatarsal heads). The peak pressure is calculated for all areas, and the highest pressure is measured. Report code 96001. (Do not report bilateral -50 or directional -LT/-RT modifiers.)
>
> Next, the patient undergoes testing for dynamic plantar pressure measurements during walking, dynamic surface electromyography during walking or other functional activities, and dynamic fine wire electromyography during walking or other functional activities. Codes 96001, 96002, and 96003 are reported. The provider then reviews and interprets all test results and prepares a written report. Code 96004 is reported.

Functional Brain Mapping

Functional brain mapping is a process by which a series of tests is administered by a physician or a psychologist to assess cognition, language, memory, movement, and sensation. The results of testing are documented in a report to identify expected versus observed locations of brain activity documented as the patient performs assigned tasks.

During functional brain mapping, the patient undergoes functional neuroimaging of the brain, which is also called functional magnetic resonance imaging (fMRI) of the brain. Report a Radiology code (e.g., Magnetic resonance imaging, brain, functional MRI) in addition to the functional brain mapping code when a physician or psychologist entirely administers the functional brain mapping.

> **EXAMPLE:** Dr. Sanders performs a functional brain mapping with fMRI on a 49-year-old patient who has been experiencing memory losses and motor problems to assess cognition, language, memory, movement, and sensation. Report codes 96020 and 70555.

Medical Genetics and Genetic Counseling Services

Medical genetics and genetic counseling services are reported when a trained genetic counselor meets with an individual, couple, or family to investigate the family's genetic history and to assess risks associated with genetic defects in offspring.

> **EXAMPLE:** A married couple, who was referred to a trained genetic counselor by their fertility doctor, received 60 minutes of medical genetic counseling. Report codes 96040, 96040. (Code 96040 is reported for *each* 30-minute session of counseling.)

Adaptive Behavior Services

Adaptive behavior services include adaptive behavior assessments and adaptive behavior treatment for deficient adaptive behaviors (e.g., impaired communication), maladaptive behaviors (e.g., repetitive behaviors), and other impaired functioning (e.g., difficulty following instructions).

> **EXAMPLE:** Patient underwent 30 minutes of behavior identification–supporting assessment. Report codes 97152, 97153.

Central Nervous System Assessments/Tests (e.g., Neuro-Cognitive, Mental Status, Speech Testing)

Central nervous system assessments/tests codes are reported when tests are performed to measure cognitive function of the central nervous system (e.g., cognitive processes, visual motor responses, and abstractive abilities). Several testing procedures are included, such as psychological testing which includes psychodiagnostic assessment of personality, psychopathology, emotionality, and intellectual abilities (e.g., WAIS-R, Rorschach, and MMPI tests).

> **EXAMPLE:** Patient underwent developmental speech and language delay screening, using a standardized instrument, with scoring and documentation. Report code 96110.

Health Behavior Assessment and Intervention

Health behavior assessment and intervention codes are reported for tests that identify the psychological, behavioral, emotional, cognitive, and social elements involved in the prevention, treatment, or management of physical health problems. The focus of the assessment is not on mental health, but on biopsychosocial factors that are considered important to physical health problems and treatments. Health and behavior intervention procedures are used to modify factors affecting the patient. The focus of the intervention is to improve the patient's health and well-being by using cognitive, behavioral, social, and/or psychophysiological procedures.

Health and behavior assessment/intervention codes describe services associated with an acute or chronic illness that does not meet the criteria for psychiatric diagnosis, prevention of a physical disability, and maintenance of health. If the patient requires psychotherapy or other psychiatric services/procedures and/or health and behavior assessment/intervention, report the primary service performed for each date of service.

> **EXAMPLE:** A psychiatrist performed a health behavior assessment of a child who was diagnosed with leukemia and who was suffering from severe distress and combativeness to chemotherapy administration. Report codes 96150, 96150, and 96150.

Hydration, Therapeutic, Prophylactic, Diagnostic Injections and Infusions, and Chemotherapy and Other Highly Complex Drug or Highly Complex Biologic Agent Administration

The hydration, therapeutic, prophylactic, diagnostic injections and infusions, and chemotherapy and other highly complex drug or highly complex biologic agent administration codes include the following headings:

- Hydration
- Therapeutic, prophylactic, and diagnostic injections and infusions (excludes chemotherapy and other highly complex drug or highly complex biologic agent administration)
- Chemotherapy and other highly complex drug or highly complex biologic agent administration

 NOTE:

> Patient record documentation should include physician verification of the patient's treatment plan and direction of staff who provide injection and infusion services.

The following services are included, which means they are not separately coded and reported:

- Administration of local anesthesia
- Intravenous (IV) insertion
- Access to indwelling IV, subcutaneous catheter, or port
- Flushing performed upon completion of infusion
- Routine syringes, tubing, and other supplies

When multiple injections or infusions or combination services are provided, report the initial code only once except *when two separate intravenous (IV) sites are required*. When the length of infusion time is included in the code description, report the code based on actual infusion time.

Hydration

Hydration codes are reported for the intravenous infusion of prepackaged fluids and electrolytes (e.g., normal saline and normal saline with potassium chloride, up to 30 mEq). When reporting these codes, review the patient record for documentation that the physician supervised

- Patient assessment (e.g., history and examination)
- Patient consent (e.g., discussion of risks and benefits)
- Patient safety (e.g., proper dose was administered; patient's response to infusion, including adverse reaction)
- Staff members who provided infusion services (e.g., the nursing staff)

EXAMPLE: Patient received initial intravenous infusion hydration of 1,000 cubic centimeters lactated Ringer's (pH–balanced electrolyte solution) for 60 minutes. Report codes 96360 and J7120.

Therapeutic, Prophylactic, and Diagnostic Injections and Infusions

Therapeutic, prophylactic, and diagnostic injections and infusions codes are reported for the administration of substances (other than hydration) and drugs. When reporting these codes, review the patient record for documentation that the physician supervised

- Patient assessment
- Patient safety
- Patient consent
- Staff members who provided injection and/or infusion services

EXAMPLE 1: Patient underwent therapeutic injection (intramuscular) of kanamycin sulfate, 500 mg. Report codes 96372 and J1840.

EXAMPLE 2: Patient underwent routine insertion of an IV catheter for one-hour IV infusion of 1,000 milliliters of potassium chloride and magnesium sulfate. Report codes 96365 and S5013.

EXAMPLE 3: Male patient, age 54, underwent nontunneled central venous access catheter (CVAC) procedure prior to one-hour intravenous infusion of 1,000 milliliters of potassium chloride and magnesium sulfate drug therapy. Report codes 36556, 96365, and S5013.

Staff members who administer therapeutic, prophylactic, and diagnostic injections (Figure 19-9) and infusions undergo special training to learn how to assess patients, provide informed consent, monitor patient safety, and administer injections and infusions. **Intravenous push** is an:

- Injection administered by a health care professional who is in constant attendance to administer the injection and observe the patient
- Infusion of 15 minutes or less

FIGURE 19-9 Angles of injection for administration of therapeutic, prophylactic, and diagnostic medications

Coding Tip

- Any fluid used to administer a drug (e.g., flushing of IV with saline solution between drug therapies) is considered incidental hydration, and a separate hydration code is not reported.
- Report HCPCS level II codes for the supply of drugs (e.g., J0280, aminophylline).
- The administration of IV fluids to maintain line patency (unblocked condition) is not separately coded and reported.

Chemotherapy and Other Highly Complex Drug or Highly Complex Biologic Agent Administration

Chemotherapy is the treatment of cancer with drugs that serve to destroy cancer cells or slow the growth of cancer cells, keep cancer from spreading to other parts of the body, and prevent recurrence of the cancer. Chemotherapy administered in addition to other cancer treatments, such as surgery and/or radiation therapy, is called **adjuvant chemotherapy**.

Codes in this subheading classify the parenteral administration of chemotherapeutic agents, which means that the chemotherapy is administered by a route *other than by mouth*, such as implantation (of a catheter or port), infusion, or injection.

Coding Tip

To report chemotherapy infusion, select the appropriate code(s) from the chemotherapy administration series of codes. These codes can be separately billed when an E/M service is rendered on the same day as the chemotherapy administration.

- The flushing of a vascular access port (e.g., saline solution) prior to the administration of chemotherapeutic agents is integral to the chemotherapy administration. It is not coded and reported separately.
- When infusion of hydrating solutions (e.g., saline solution) or drugs (e.g., heparin) other than antineoplastic drugs is a necessary and integral part of a procedure, a code for that infusion is *not* reported separately.

EXAMPLE: The infusion of a hydrating solution is started prior to the administration of chemotherapy. The infusion of the hydrating solution is included in the reported chemotherapy code, and it is not reported separately.

There are many chemotherapy drugs currently available to treat cancer, and chemotherapy is administered in a variety of ways, depending on the drugs used and the type of cancer.

Oral chemotherapy is administered by mouth in the form of a pill, capsule, or liquid, while parenteral methods of chemotherapy administration include the following:

- Implantation of a catheter or port into a central vein or body cavity
- Infusion or injection of intravenous (IV) chemotherapy into a vein
- Injection of intramuscular (IM) chemotherapy is injected into the muscle
- Injection of subcutaneous (SQ) chemotherapy under the skin

When different techniques are used to parenterally administer chemotherapy (e.g., injection, infusion, implantation) *during the same encounter*, report a separate code for each parenteral method.

EXAMPLE 1: A patient diagnosed with malignant melanoma, skin of scalp, undergoes one hour of intravenous infusion of chemotherapy and intralesional chemotherapy administration to the scalp lesion. Report codes 96405 and 96413.

EXAMPLE 2: A patient was administered three injections of antineoplastic drugs and an infusion of antineoplastic drugs for two hours during one encounter. Report codes 96401, 96401, 96401, 96413, and 96415.

When an intravenous infusion of saline (an antiemetic) or other nonchemotherapy drug is administered at the same time as the chemotherapeutic agent(s), *these infusions are not coded and reported separately.* However, the supply of the drugs *is* reported separately with HCPCS level II codes. If hydration or intravenous infusion is administered on the same day, but sequentially rather than at the same time as the chemotherapeutic agents, codes for the infusions are reported. Modifier -59 (Distinct Procedural Service) is added to these codes to indicate that the infusions were administered at different times.

Coding Tip

Report code 96365 (IV infusion, for therapy, prophylaxis, or diagnosis, initial; up to one hour) to indicate an infusion of drugs (e.g., antihypertensive medication) *other than antineoplastic drugs.* Code 96366 is reported for each additional hour of infusion, up to eight hours.

EXAMPLE: Patient receives nonchemotherapy infusions for 60 minutes. Report code 96365 along with the HCPCS level II code[s] for the drugs administered.

Chemotherapy and other highly complex drug or highly complex biologic agent administration services are independent of the patient's evaluation and management (E/M) services and may occur sequentially on the same day. If performed, the appropriate E/M code should be reported as an additional code. Preparation of chemotherapy agent(s) is included in the service for administration of the agent, and it is not coded and reported separately.

Medications (e.g., antibiotics, steroidal agents, antiemetics, narcotics, analgesics, and biological agents) administered independently or sequentially as supportive management of chemotherapy administration are separately coded and reported, as appropriate. It is appropriate to report separately the appropriate HCPCS level II code(s) for the supply of chemotherapy drugs in addition to the code(s) for chemotherapy administration.

Photodynamic Therapy

Photodynamic therapy is administered by

- External application of light to destroy premalignancies
- Endoscopic application of light that activates photosensitive drugs to ablate abnormal tissue

Coding Tip

A photodynamic therapy code is reported for each exposure session, *not* for each lesion treated.

Photodynamic therapy (PDT) is the application of a photosensitizing agent (e.g., 20 percent topical aminolevulinic acid HCl) directly onto a patient's lesions to treat premalignant cells (e.g., nonhyperkeratotic actinic keratosis) or abnormal cells. The patient returns for a scheduled encounter during which a photodynamic therapy illuminator (light) is directed on the treated lesions. A cytotoxic reaction results when the topical agent applied to the lesions is irradiated, killing premalignant or abnormal cells, preventing their spread.

NOTE:

Ocular photodynamic therapy consultation is reported with Surgery code 67221.

EXAMPLE: On May 1, single unit dosage of 20 percent topical aminolevulinic acid HCl was applied and illuminated/ activated as the photosensitive drug. The patient returned on May 2 and underwent photodynamic therapy via external application of light to destroy premalignant lesions of the skin and adjacent mucosa. Report 96567. (Do *not* report a separate CPT code for application of the drug. However, HCPCS level II code J7308 is reported for supply of the topical drug.)

Special Dermatological Procedures

Special dermatological procedures codes describe dermatology procedures that are usually (but not always) performed in addition to an appropriate evaluation and management (E/M) service code.

EXAMPLE: During a level 3 outpatient consultation encounter, the dermatologist performed a detailed history and examination; medical decision making was of low complexity. The dermatologist used ultraviolet light (actinotherapy) to treat the two areas of acne frontalis. Report codes 99243 and 96900.

Physical Medicine and Rehabilitation

Physical medicine and rehabilitation is a branch of medicine that focuses on the prevention, diagnosis, and treatment of disorders of the musculoskeletal, cardiovascular, and pulmonary systems that may produce temporary or permanent impairment. A **physiatrist** is a physician who specializes in physical medicine and rehabilitation and treats acute/chronic pain and musculoskeletal disorders. Physiatrists also treat disorders of the musculoskeletal system that result in severe functional limitations (e.g., a baby with a birth defect, the victim of a bad car accident, an elderly person with a broken hip). Physiatrists coordinate the long-term rehabilitation process for patients with spinal-cord injuries, cancer, stroke, brain injuries, amputations, and multiple sclerosis or other neurological disorders. The specialty focuses on the restoration of function to people with problems ranging from simple physical mobility issues to those with complex cognitive involvement.

Physiatrists offer a broad spectrum of medical services (e.g., the prescription of drugs or assistive devices such as a brace or artificial limb). However, they do not perform surgery. Physiatrists use diverse modalities (any physical agent applied to produce therapeutic changes) that include therapies such as heat and cold, electrotherapies, massage, biofeedback, traction, and therapeutic exercise.

EXAMPLE 1: Patient underwent diathermy. Report code 97024.

EXAMPLE 2: A diabetic patient presents for treatment of a chronic open wound on the left foot. The wound measures 4 cm × 3 cm (or 12 sq cm), and the physician treats it by using surgical scissors to perform sharp selective debridement. Report code 97597.

Medical Nutrition Therapy

Medical nutrition therapy is classified according to

- Type of assessment
- Individual or group therapy
- Length of time

> **EXAMPLE:** Patient underwent medical nutrition therapy reevaluation and assessment. The provider spent 30 minutes face-to-face with the patient. Report codes 97803 and 97803.

Acupuncture

Acupuncture treatment is classified as face-to-face patient contact for 15-minute increments of time and according to whether electrical stimulation was provided.

> **EXAMPLE:** Patient underwent acupuncture, which included five needles. The provider spent 30 minutes of one-on-one contact with the patient. Report codes 97810 and 97811.

Osteopathic Manipulative Treatment

Manipulative and body-based practices focus primarily on the structures and systems of the body, including the bones and joints, the soft tissues, and the circulatory and lymphatic systems. **Osteopathic manipulative treatment (OMT)** is a manual treatment performed by a physician, during which emphasis is placed on normal body mechanics and manipulative methods to detect and correct structure. Osteopathic practice includes diagnostic and therapeutic techniques (e.g., musculoskeletal manipulations as well as prescriptions and other therapies) and preventive measures. Combining available medical procedures with OMT provides patients the most comprehensive care. The osteopathic codes are reported according to the number of body regions treated. It is also appropriate to report codes for other restorative modalities and procedures performed on the same day when medically necessary.

 Coding Tip

- A provider who performs OMT cannot report anesthesia services separately (e.g., nerve blocks and epidural injections) for OMT.
- According to Medicare, postoperative pain management after OMT (e.g., a nerve block or an epidural injection) is not reported separately. However, epidural or nerve block injections unrelated to the OMT may be reported with an OMT code by adding modifier -59.

> **EXAMPLE:** The osteopathic physician provided osteopathic manipulative treatment to four body regions. Report code 98926.

Chiropractic Manipulative Treatment

Chiropractic manipulative treatment (CMT) is a form of manual treatment to influence joint and neurophysiological function. This treatment may be accomplished using a variety of techniques.

CMT codes include a premanipulation patient assessment. However, additional E/M services may be reported separately by adding modifier -25 if the patient's condition requires a separate E/M service beyond the usual preservice and postservice work associated with the CMT procedure.

For purposes of CMT, the five spinal regions include the following:

- Cervical region (e.g., atlanto-occipital joint)
- Thoracic region (e.g., costovertebral and costotransverse joints)
- Lumbar region
- Sacral region
- Pelvic region (e.g., sacroiliac joint)

The five extraspinal regions include the head (including temporomandibular joint, excluding atlanto-occipital), lower extremities, upper extremities, rib cage (excluding costotransverse and costovertebral joints), and abdomen.

> **EXAMPLE:** A chiropractor provided chiropractic manipulative treatment to four regions of the spine. Report code 98941.

Coding Tip

Medicare covers CMT for five spinal regions. Physical therapy services reported with codes 97112, 97124, and 97140 are not separately reportable when performed in a spinal region undergoing CMT. If physical therapy services are performed in a different region than CMT, the physical therapy codes are reported with modifier -59.

Confusion about Medicare's chiropractic coverage resulted in publication of the CMS article entitled "Addressing Misinformation Regarding Chiropractic Services and Medicare: Information for Medicare Fee-for-Service Health Care Professionals." (Go to www.cms.gov, enter "SE0749" in the "Search CMS.gov" box, click the Search button, and locate the PDF file. Or, go to www.google.com and enter SE0749.pdf to locate the document.)

Education and Training for Patient Self-Management

Education and training for patient self-management is performed by a qualified, nonphysician health care professional who uses a standardized curriculum. The codes are classified according to the length of time spent face-to-face with one or more patients.

> **EXAMPLE:** Patient underwent education and training for self-management of her recently diagnosed diabetes mellitus. The nonphysician health care professional spent 30 minutes providing face-to-face instruction. Report code 98960.

Non-Face-to-Face Nonphysician Services

Non-face-to-face nonphysician services that are provided by a qualified health care professional (nonphysician) include the following:

- Telephone services
  - Codes for telephone services are not reported when they result in a patient encounter within 24 hours or at the next available urgent visit appointment. Such telephone services are considered part of the preservice work for the subsequent face-to-face encounter.
  - Telephone service codes are also not reported when the call is related to a service performed and reported by the provider within the past seven days or within the postoperative period of a previously completed procedure.

> **EXAMPLE:** Patient was out of the country and became concerned about panic attacks she was experiencing. She reached out to her primary care provider who initiated a 25-minute telephone call, which included medical discussion evaluation and management services and instructions about proper use of prescribed medication. Report code 98968.

- Qualified nonphysician health care professional digital evaluation and management service in response to a patient's online inquiry using Internet resources
  - To report codes for online medical evaluation services, the qualified nonphysician health care professional must provide a personal, timely response to the inquiry and the encounter must be permanently stored via electronic means or hard copy.
    - Online medical evaluation codes are not reported when related to a service performed and reported by the same provider within the past seven days or within the postoperative period of a previously completed procedure. The online service is considered part of the previous service or procedure.
    - Each code is reported just once for the same episode of care during a seven-day period.

Special Services, Procedures, and Reports

Special services, procedures, and reports codes classify the completion of special reports and performance of adjunctive services. These codes describe special circumstances under which a basic procedure is performed.

EXAMPLE 1: The physician office handled and conveyed a specimen for transfer to a laboratory. Report code 99000. (If provided, report a service code for obtaining the specimen, such as venipuncture.)

EXAMPLE 2: A patient was referred to physical therapy after orthopedic surgery. The patient required a 30-day interim visit to the surgeon. Report code 99024 for the surgeon visit. (The code is reported on a claim although the payer does not reimburse for the service provided because its payment was bundled in the previously submitted surgery code. Code 99024 allows for internal tracking of postoperative care services provided by the surgeon during the global surgical period, which reduces the risk of complications of surgery, helps manage side effects of treatment, and supports recovery. Thus, code 99024 supports the quality of care provided to patients.)

Qualifying Circumstances for Anesthesia

Qualifying circumstances for anesthesia codes describe situations that complicate the administration of anesthesia services (e.g., emergencies, extreme age, hypotension, and hypothermia). Codes 99100–99140 are add-on codes, which means that they are reported in addition to the anesthesia service code reported from the Anesthesia section.

EXAMPLE: An otherwise unusually healthy 84-year-old patient underwent left hip replacement surgery, which required the administration of general anesthesia by the anesthesiologist. Report codes 01214-P1-AA (general anesthesia service) and 99100.

Moderate (Conscious) Sedation

Moderate (conscious) sedation codes classify a drug-induced depression of consciousness that requires no interventions to maintain airway patency or ventilation. CPT specifies that moderate (conscious) sedation does not include pain control, minimal sedation (e.g., anxiolysis), deep sedation, or monitored anesthesia care (MAC). Subsection notes specify services that are included in moderate (conscious) sedation codes (e.g., IV access, administration of agent, and monitoring oxygen saturation). The surgeon who performs the surgical procedure provides moderate (conscious) sedation services. An *independent trained observer* is present during surgery to monitor the patient's sedation. When another physician (e.g., an anesthesiologist) provides general anesthesia, regional anesthesia, or monitored anesthesia care, that other physician reports an appropriate anesthesia code and its modifiers.

EXAMPLE 1: A 68-year-old patient received 15 minutes of moderate (conscious) sedation services, which were provided by the same physician who removed a superficial orthopedic wire. An independent trained observer was present to monitor the patient's sedation. Report codes 20670 (removal of superficial implant) and 99156.

EXAMPLE 2: A 19-year-old male patient was prepped and draped for brain surgery, and he received moderate (conscious) sedation in the form of a narcotic called remifentanil (brand name Ultiva) administered in combination with propofol. An independent trained observer was present to monitor the patient's sedation. It was determined that the patient could feel no pain but would be able to communicate with the operating room staff and surgeon during the procedure. Trephination craniectomy and bone flap craniotomy were performed after intraoperative brain magnetic resonance imaging (MRI) confirmed the exact location of the supratentorial tumor. It was noted that the tumor was pressing on the area of the cerebrum that controls the ability to read and speak.

During the procedure, the patient remained heavily sedated but conscious so the surgeon could talk with him while mapping the brain's sensors. The patient read a book aloud during the procedure; when the surgeon pressed on a sensitive region of the brain, the patient's reading was affected, letting the surgeon know which areas to avoid. Upon completion of brain mapping, the risky areas were marked by placing lettered pieces of paper directly onto the brain to identify the areas of risk. The surgeon then opened the brain's outer membrane and, layer by layer, removed the tumor. The patient felt no pain (because the brain has no pain receptors), and the tumor was submitted to pathology for analysis. The patient tolerated the one-hour procedure well and was transported to the recovery room in stable condition. The patient will undergo repeat MRI in 30 days to verify total resection of the tumor. Report codes 61510, 70551, 99156 (first 15 minutes), and 99157, 99157, and 99157 (subsequent 45 minutes). (Code 99156 is reported once for the first 15 minutes of moderate [conscious] sedation. Then, code 99157 is assigned three times for the subsequent 45 minutes of moderate [conscious] sedation.)

Other Services and Procedures

Other services and procedures codes are reported for services and procedures that cannot be classified in another subsection of the Medicine section (e.g., anogenital examination, vision screening by nonoptical professionals, hypothermia treatment).

> **EXAMPLE:** Patient underwent therapeutic phlebotomy. Report code 99195.

Home Health Procedures/Services

Home health procedures/services codes are reported by nonphysician health care professionals who perform procedures and provide services to the patient in the patient's residence (the patient's home, assisted living facility, or group home). *Home infusion procedures/services* are reported for the provision of home infusion services, and the codes are based on length of infusion time.

> **EXAMPLE 1:** Patient received a home visit from a registered nurse for mechanical ventilation care. Report code 99504.

> **EXAMPLE 2:** Patient underwent three hours of home infusion on May 14. Report codes 99601 and 99602.

Medication Therapy Management Services

Medication therapy management services (MTMS) describe face-to-face patient assessments and interventions performed by a pharmacist to

- Optimize the patient's response to medications.
- Manage treatment-related medication interactions or complications.

Documentation of MTMS includes review of the pertinent patient history and medication profile (prescription and nonprescription) as well as recommendations for improving health outcomes and compliance with treatment.

> **EXAMPLE:** An established patient received 15 minutes of medication therapy management face-to-face services, which was provided by a pharmacist. Report code 99606.

 NOTE:

MTMS codes are not reported to describe the provision of product-specific information at the point of dispensing or any other routine dispensing-related activities.

Exercise 19.3 – Medicine Subsections

Instructions: Assign CPT code(s) and appropriate modifier(s) to each statement.

1. Oral immunization administration.

_____

2. A 60-minute individual psychotherapy session rendered during partial hospitalization, which included modifying the patient's obsessive-compulsive behavior.

_____

Exercise 19.3 – *continued*

3. A physician performed a coronary angioplasty and percutaneous transcatheter placement of intracoronary stents in the left anterior descending coronary artery and the right inferior coronary artery.

   _____

4. A 10-year-old patient received ESRD dialysis-related services daily from July 1 through July 3.

   _____

5. A patient received a Rocephin intravenous (IV) push through an existing IV line. The IV was flushed with normal saline before and after administration of the antibiotic to check for patency and to clear the IV line.

   _____

Summary

The Medicine section classifies procedures and services that are procedure-oriented, that apply to various medical specialties, and that apply to different types of health care providers. Guidelines located at the beginning of the Medicine section provide instruction about multiple procedures, add-on codes, separate procedures, subsection information, unlisted service or procedure, special reports, and materials supplied by the physician. Instructional notes appear throughout the Medicine section to provide coding clarification and direction. Almost every Medicine subsection contains notes unique to the subsection.

Internet Links

American Chiropractic Association: *www.acatoday.org*

American Physical Therapy Association (APTA): *www.apta.org*

Chemotherapy: Go to *www.cancer.gov*, scroll over About Cancer and click on the Treatment link to view types of cancer treatment, including chemotherapy.

National Center for Complementary and Integrative Medicine (at the National Institutes of Health): *www.nccam.nih.gov*

Review

Multiple Choice

Instructions: Circle the most appropriate response.

1. Which is a manual treatment performed to influence joint and neurophysiological function?
   a. Bilevel (biphasic) positive airway pressure (BiPAP)
   b. Chiropractic manipulative treatment (CMT)
   c. Intermittent positive pressure breathing (IPPB)
   d. Osteopathic manipulative treatment

2. A physician who specializes in physical medicine and rehabilitation and who treats acute/chronic pain and musculoskeletal disorders is a(n) _____.
   a. doctor of osteopathy
   b. internist
   c. psychologist
   d. physiatrist

3. Chemotherapy administered in addition to other cancer treatments, such as surgery and/or radiation therapy, is called _____ chemotherapy.
   a. adjacent
   b. adjudicate
   c. adjunct
   d. adjuvant

4. Which uses low-voltage electrodes that are placed on the scalp and target sites to test the nervous system's pathway?
   a. Central motor evoked potential study
   b. Orbicularis oculi (blink) test
   c. Short-latency somatosensory evoked potential study
   d. Visual evoked potential (VEP) test

5. Which is a biofeedback diagnostic test that measures muscle function using a pressure-sensitive tube?
   a. Electrocardiography
   b. Electromyogram
   c. Manometry
   d. Tensilon test

6. Which Medicine subsection classifies drug-induced depression of consciousness that requires no interventions to maintain airway patency or ventilation?
   a. Moderate (Conscious) Sedation
   b. Other Services and Procedures
   c. Photodynamic Therapy
   d. Noninvasive Vascular Diagnostic Studies

7. Which is considered an epicutaneous allergy sensitivity test?
   a. Intradermal test
   b. Patch test
   c. Puncture test
   d. Scratch test

8. End-stage renal disease (ESRD) codes include monitoring of nutrition, assessment of growth and development, and parental counseling for patients under the age of _____.
   a. 14   b. 18   c. 20   d. 25

9. The Medicine section classifies procedures and services that are:
   a. diagnosis-oriented and that apply to a limited number of medical specialties.
   b. diagnosis-oriented and that apply to many medical specialties.
   c. procedure-oriented and that apply to a limited number of medical specialties.
   d. procedure-oriented and that apply to many medical specialties.

10. Which of the following is identified in the CPT with a plus symbol and usually contains a parenthetical note that identifies the primary procedure to which the code applies?
    a. Add-on code
    b. Multiple or bundled code
    c. Separate procedure code
    d. Unlisted service or procedure code

11. A 42-year-old patient received a hepatitis A immunization injection. Which CPT code(s) are assigned?
    a. 90632, 90471   b. 90636, 90471   c. 90746, 90471   d. 90749, 90471

12. Binaural hearing aid check. Which CPT code is assigned?
    a. 92590   b. 92591   c. 92592   d. 92593

13. Cardiovascular stress test, bicycle with continuous electrocardiographic monitoring, interpretation and report only. Which CPT code is assigned?
    a. 93015   b. 93016   c. 93017   d. 93018

14. A 30-day, patient-initiated spirometric recording, including hook-up, reinforced education, data transmission and capture, trend analysis, and periodic recalibration as well as physician review and interpretation. Which CPT code is assigned?

    a. 94010   **b.** 94014   **c.** 94015   **d.** 94016

15. Inhalation bronchial challenge testing with histamine. Which CPT code is assigned?

    a. 95070   **b.** 95071   **c.** 95076   **d.** 95199

16. Comprehensive, computer-based motion analysis by videotaping and 3D kinematics, with dynamic plantar pressure measurements during walking. Which CPT code is assigned?

    a. 96000   **b.** 96001   **c.** 96002   **d.** 96004

17. Physical therapy reevaluation. Which CPT code is assigned?

    a. 97161   **b.** 97162   **c.** 97163   **d.** 97164

18. A patient and his wife received 30 minutes of face-to-face education and training from a qualified nurse practitioner for patient self-management of diabetic testing supplies. Which CPT code(s) are assigned?

    a. 98960   **c.** 98961
    b. 98960, 98960-59   **d.** 99078

19. During a therapeutic service, a 15-year-old patient required 15 minutes of moderate (conscious) sedation in addition to the normal anesthesia. The physician administered the sedation, and an independently trained observer monitored the patient's level of consciousness and physiological status for 30 minutes. Which CPT code is assigned?

    a. 99151   **b.** 99152   **c.** 99155   **d.** 99156

20. A psychiatrist used dolls to communicate with a 5-year-old patient during a psychiatric interview. Which CPT code is assigned?

    a. 90791   **b.** 90792   **c.** 90845   **d.** 90847

Coding Practice

Instructions: Assign CPT code(s) and appropriate modifier(s) to each case.

1. OPHTHALMOLOGY: The patient's prescription for bifocal lens was recorded, facial measurements were taken, and adjustment of eyeglasses was done.

2. CNS ASSESSMENTS/TESTS: The patient had standard cognitive performance testing for one hour done on November 15. This was done on a computer. A neuropsychologist interpreted the results and documented the report.

3. OPHTHALMOLOGY: The patient arrived at the office for an examination. The patient has never been seen in this practice. The patient complains of redness of both eyes and a decrease in visual acuity. After reviewing the patient's medical history, including medications, the patient's eyes are examined with the ophthalmoscope. Using a slit lamp exam, several small healing ulcers of the right and left cornea are seen. The patient is given instructions for eye irrigation and a prescription for steroidal eye drops.
DIAGNOSIS: Viral keratitis.

4. GASTROENTEROLOGY: Patient presented for a Bernstein test. After insertion of a nasogastric (NG) tube, a solution was passed through the tube to record any complaints of chest pain. The first solution was saline, and the patient did not report any pain. The second solution was hydrochloric acid, and this solution did elicit a pain response in the patient. The Bernstein test was positive for esophagitis.

5. NONINVASIVE VASCULAR DIAGNOSTIC STUDIES: Patient underwent a complete transcranial Doppler study of his intracranial arteries.

_____

6. SPECIAL OTORHINOLARYNGOLOGIC SERVICE: The patient, a 7-year-old female, presented for visual reinforcement audiometry (VRA) evaluation. After being placed in a sound booth, both voice and lighted toys were used for hearing assessment. An audiogram recorded the findings, which were normal.

_____

7. PULMONARY: The patient, a 14-year-old with cystic fibrosis, was seen for chest wall cupping to help clear mucous secretion. This initial demonstration was also observed by the patient's mother as a teaching opportunity for home care by the parent.

_____

8. CARDIOVASCULAR: Patient received outpatient cardiac rehabilitation during the sixth week of his post-operative period. He had previously undergone coronary artery bypass graft surgery of four vessels. This session included exercise and a review of diet restrictions with the patient.

_____

9. BIOFEEDBACK: Biofeedback for perineum and urethral muscles to assist with the patient's urine incontinence, 15 minutes. Electromyogram (EMG) was used to measure contractions and muscle pressure.

_____

10. CARDIOVASCULAR: The patient presented three years' postimplantation of a dual-chamber pacemaker device. Analysis was done while the patient was at rest and while on a treadmill. No pacemaker reprogramming was needed.

_____

11. CARDIOVASCULAR: After placing the patient in the supine position, ultrasound was used to record cardiac function. The patient's ventricular septal defect (VSD), which is a congenital heart condition, was identified. The size of the defect was 2.0 mm. The remainder of the cardiac structures appeared normal in size and function.

_____

12. CHIROPRACTIC MANIPULATIVE TREATMENT: After placing the patient on the adjustment table, chiropractic manipulation of C7, T4, and L1 were performed to reduce subluxation and increase blood flow. The patient was scheduled for another appointment in one week's time.

_____

13. VACCINES, TOXOIDS: A 40-year-old male patient presented for a hepatitis A and hepatitis B vaccine. This was administered by the nursing staff, IM in the left arm.

_____

14. PHYSICAL MEDICINE AND REHABILITATION: A primary care physician provided 30 minutes of training in using adaptive utensils for eating. During the encounter, safety procedures while cooking were also discussed with this patient, who has diagnoses of arthritis and type 2 diabetes mellitus.

_____

15. NEUROLOGY AND NEUROMUSCULAR PROCEDURES: Patient was awake when electrodes were placed on his head for recording. An electro-encephalogram (EEG) was performed during a 90-minute period. The patient was awake for the entire EEG.

_____

16. GASTROENTEROLOGY: Gastric electrical activity was measured by placing electrodes on the patient's skin over his abdominal cavity. The recording of gastric activity showed that the patient had decreased activity in the large intestine.

_____

17. SPECIAL OTORHINOLARYNGOLOGIC SERVICES: The patient presented with facial paralysis of the left side of the lower face. An electroneuronography was done to measure nerve conduction. Electrodes were placed over the site of the paralysis.
DIAGNOSIS: Bell's palsy.

_____

18. IMMUNE GLOBULINS, SERUM OR RECOMBINENT PRODUCTS: A 25-year-old patient received intramuscular hepatitis B immune globulin (HBIG) (human) injection, which was administered by the nursing staff.

_____

19. PSYCHIATRY: Patient participated in a psychotherapy session for a total of 30 minutes. This session was done at a local community hospital in the mental health inpatient unit.

_____

20. CARDIOVASCULAR: After placing electrodes on the patient's chest, the heart's activity was recorded. The 12-lead strip was reviewed and a report was written by the attending physician.

_____

21. CARDIOVASCULAR: Under adequate anesthesia, incisions were made in the left leg of the patient for access of the femoral catheter. A second site allowed for insertion of the balloon-tipped catheter. After threading the balloon catheter to the heart, the blocked coronary artery was identified. The balloon was inflated, which resulted in movement of the arthrosclerosis plaque to the sides of the artery. The balloon catheter was advanced to the second blocked artery. The same inflation method was done, with good result. The balloon catheter was withdrawn. The incision sites were closed with sutures and pressure dressings.

_____

22. CARDIOVASCULAR: While the patient was exercising on a stationary bicycle, continuous electrocardiogram (ECG) monitoring and recording was done. The patient's cardiologist was in attendance for the entire 45-minute stress test. At the conclusion of the test, the physician provided a written report on the findings and the interpreted ECG recordings.

_____

23. GASTROENTEROLOGY: Patient underwent gastroesophageal reflux test via esophagus, which included placement of nasal catheter pH electrodes, recording, analysis, and interpretation.

_____

24. HOME HEALTH PROCEDURES/SERVICES: A 15-year-old patient was recently diagnosed with asthma. A home health nurse visited on May 6 to provide training in the use of bronchodilators for both the patient and mother.

_____

25. PHYSICAL MEDICINE AND REHABILITATION: A patient is status post left side cerebrovascular accident (CVA). He presents for physical therapy evaluation to regain strength and mobility on the left side. The patient underwent moderate complexity physical therapy evaluation.

_____

26. ALLERGY AND CLINICAL IMMUNOLOGY: Using allergen vials specifically kept in the office for a certain patient, a pollen and grass mix was injected into the upper-right arm. A dust mites, cat dander, and feather mixture was injected into the patient's upper-left arm. The patient was observed in the waiting room for 30 minutes postinjection, with no reaction.

_____

27. SPECIAL DERMATOLOGICAL PROCEDURES: Using a laser, approximately 25 pulses were delivered to a patient's psoriasis lesions on the elbows and forearms. Total area of treatment measured approximately 10 sq cm.

_____

28. IMMUNE GLOBULINS, SERUM OR RECOMBINANT PRODUCTS: Rabies immune globulin was administered intramuscularly (IM) to the patient's upper-left arm.

_____

29. DIALYSIS: ESRD services for a 25-year-old male for the month of September. Number of visits to a physician for the month totaled 4.

_____

30. CHEMOTHERAPY ADMINISTRATION: Intravenous (IV) infusion of chemotherapy drugs, two hours.

_____

Insurance and Reimbursement Overview

20: Insurance and Reimbursement, 808

Insurance and Reimbursement

Chapter Outline

Third-Party Payers

Health Care Reimbursement Systems

Impact of HIPAA on Reimbursement

Chapter Objectives

At the conclusion of this chapter, the student should be able to:

1. Define key terms related to insurance and reimbursement.
2. Describe the types of third-party payers.
3. Describe the types of health care reimbursement systems, including payment systems, fee schedules, exclusions, case-mix analysis, severity of illness and intensity of services systems, physician documentation for medical necessity of Medicare Part A hospital inpatient admissions, and critical pathways.
4. Describe the impact of HIPAA on health care reimbursement related to health care access/ portability/renewability, preventing health care fraud and abuse, administrative simplification, and medical liability reform.

Key Terms

abuse

ambulance fee schedule

ambulatory payment classification (APC)

ambulatory surgical center (ASC) payment rate

ANSI ASC X12N 837

Balanced Budget Act of 1997

Balanced Budget Refinement Act of 1999 (BBRA)

BlueCross and BlueShield (BCBS)

breach of confidentiality

cafeteria plan

capitation

case mix

case-mix adjustment

charge description master (CDM)

chargemaster

chargemaster review process

check digit

Civilian Health and Medical Program of the Department of Veterans Affairs (CHAMPVA)

Civil Monetary Penalties Act

clinical laboratory fee schedule

closed-panel HMO

commercial payer

compliance guidance

confidentiality

Consolidated Omnibus Budget Reconciliation Act of 1985

consumer-directed health plan (CDHP)

conversion factor

covered benefit

covered entity

critical pathways

customized sub-capitation plan (CSCP)

decrypt

Deficit Reduction Act of 1984

Designated Standard Maintenance Organization (DSMO)

diagnosis-related groups (DRGs)

digital

direct contract model HMO

disclosed

DRG creep

durable medical equipment, prosthetics, orthotics, and supplies (DMEPOS) fee schedule

electronic data interchange (EDI)

electronic transaction standard

employer self-insurance plan

encounter form

encrypt

end-stage renal disease (ESRD) composite payment rate system

exclusion

exclusive provider organization (EPO)

explanation of benefits (EOB)

False Claims Act (FCA)

Federal Anti-kickback Statute

Federal Claims Collection Act of 1966

Federal Employee Health Benefits Program (FEHBP or FEP)

Federally Qualified Health Centers (FQHCs)

fee-for-service

fee schedule

flat file

flexible spending account (FSA)

fraud

government-sponsored programs

group model HMO

group practice without walls (GPWW)

health care reimbursement account (HCRA)

health insurance claim

health insurance policy

health maintenance organization (HMO)

health reimbursement arrangement (HRA)

health savings account (HSA)

health savings security account (HSSA)

HIPAA administrative simplification (AS)

HIPAA standards for privacy of individually identifiable health information

hold harmless clause

Home Assessment Validation and Entry (HAVEN)

home health prospective payment system (HH PPS)

hospital readmission reduction program (HRRP)

indemnification

Indian Health Service (IHS)

individual practice association (IPA) HMO

inpatient prospective payment system (IPPS)

inpatient psychiatric facility prospective payment system (IPF PPS)

inpatient rehabilitation facility prospective payment system (IRF PPS)

integrated delivery system (IDS)

integrated provider organization (IPO)

intensity of services (IS)

IPPS 3-day payment window

IPPS 72-hour rule

IPPS transfer rule

IRF PPS 1-day payment window

IRF PPS 24-hour rule

IRF PPS transfer rule

long-term (acute) care hospital prospective payment system (LTCH PPS)

LTCH PPS 1-day payment window

LTCH PPS 24-hour rule

major diagnostic category (MDC)

managed care

management service organization (MSO)

Medicaid

medical foundation

Medicare

Medicare administrative contractor (MAC)

Medicare physician fee schedule (MPFS)

Medicare Prescription Drug, Improvement, and Modernization Act of 2003 (MMA)

Medicare severity diagnosis-related groups (MS-DRGs)

Medicare severity long-term (acute) care diagnosis-related groups (MS-LTCH-DRGs)

Medicare Summary Notice (MSN)

Military Health System (MHS)

minimum data set (MDS)

national health plan identifier (HPID)

national individual identifier (patient identifier)

national limitation amount (NLA)

national provider identifier (NPI)

national standard employer identifier number (EIN)

network model HMO

network provider

noncovered benefits

nonparticipating provider (nonPAR)

Omnibus Budget Reconciliation Act of 1980

Omnibus Budget Reconciliation Act of 1987 (OBRA)

Omnibus Budget Reconciliation Act of 1989

Omnibus Consolidated and Emergency Supplemental Appropriations Act (OCESAA) of 1999

open-panel HMO

outlier

outpatient encounter

outpatient prospective payment system (OPPS)

outpatient visit

overpayment

overpayment recovery

participating provider (PAR)

patient-driven payment model (PDPM)

Payment Error and Prevention Program (PEPP)

physician-hospital organization (PHO)

Physicians at Teaching Hospitals (PATH) initiative

physician self-referral law

point-of-service plan (POS)

preauthorization

pre-existing medical condition

preferred provider organization (PPO)

present on admission (POA) indicator

privacy

privacy rule

privileged communication

Programs of All-inclusive Care for the Elderly (PACE)

prospective cost-based rate

prospective payment system (PPS)

prospective price-based rate

protected health information (PHI)

relative value unit (RVU)

remittance advice (remit)

Resident Assessment Validation and Entry (RAVEN)

resource-based relative value scale (RBRVS) system

revenue code

roster billing

safe harbor regulation

security

security rule

self-referral

severity of illness (SI)

skilled nursing facility prospective payment system (SNF PPS)

staff model HMO

Stark I

Stark II

State Children's Health Insurance Program (SCHIP)

status indicator (SI)

superbill

Tax Equity and Fiscal Responsibility Act of 1983 (TEFRA)

TRICARE

triple option plan

value-based purchasing (VBP)

wage index

workers' compensation

Introduction

This chapter includes a discussion of third-party payers, health care reimbursement methodologies, and the impact of HIPAA on health care reimbursement. Third-party payers process health insurance claims to reimburse providers (e.g., physicians, health care facilities) for services provided to patients for covered benefits. Health care reimbursement methodologies were originally developed by the Centers for Medicare & Medicaid Services (CMS) to control health care costs associated with government programs; however, most third-party payers have also adopted them. HIPAA has impacted health care reimbursement as a result of the implementation of federal regulations such as administrative simplification, privacy and security of protected health information, and more. Health reform has been impacted by implementation of the Patient Protection and Affordable Care Act (PPACA) of 2010, Health Care and Education Reconciliation Act (HCERA), and Tax Cuts and Job Acts of 2017.

Health Reform

In 2010, two significant federal laws were implemented that resulted in health reform.

- The Patient Protection and Affordable Care Act (PPACA) (also called Obamacare)
  - Allows young adults to remain on a parent's plan until the age of 26
  - Assists employers that provide retiree health benefits
  - Creates health insurance exchanges

- Ends insurance company abuses
- Establishes a competitive health insurance market
- Expands Medicaid eligibility
- Immediately establishes a plan for the uninsured
- Maintains employer-sponsored coverage for most Americans who currently have it
- Prohibits the denial of coverage/claims based on pre-existing conditions

- Provides 32 million uninsured children and families with access to coverage
- Provides incentives for businesses to provide health care benefits
- Reduces the maximum time period for submitting Medicare fee-for-service claims to one calendar year after the date of service
- Subsidizes insurance premiums
- Supports medical research

- The Health Care and Education Reconciliation Act (HCERA) amended the PPACA to

  - Close the Medicare Part D "donut hole" by 2011, and give seniors a rebate of $250.
  - Tax "Cadillac health care plans" effective 2018.
  - Eliminate several special deals given to senators.
  - Establish a Medicare tax on unearned incomes of families who earn more than $250,000 annually.
  - Extend the ban on lifetime limits and rescission of coverage to all existing health plans within six months.
  - Increase Medicaid payment rates to primary care physicians to match Medicare payment rates, and
  - Provide states that already insure childless adults under Medicaid with more federal money for covering that group through 2018.

- Increase tax credits to buy insurance.
- Offer more generous subsidies to lower income groups.
- Provide a 50 percent discount to Medicare patients on brand-name drugs effective 2011 (and by 2020, provide up to a 75 percent discount on brand-name and generic drugs, eventually closing the coverage gap).
- Require doctors who treat Medicare patients to be reimbursed at the full rate.

The costs of the above provisions are offset by a variety of taxes, fees, and cost-saving measures, such as new Medicare taxes for high-income brackets, taxes on indoor tanning, cuts to the Medicare Advantage program in favor of traditional Medicare, and fees on medical devices and pharmaceutical companies. Tax Cuts and Job Acts of 2017 legislation repealed the *health care mandate* (tax penalty for individuals who did not buy health insurance) for tax returns filed in 2019 and later.

Effective 2019, CMS improved program integrity to enhance consumer choice by removing provisions that discouraged payers from offering plans that address specific needs of Americans, increased state flexibility to help lower health insurance premiums and stabilize premium increases, and reduced regulatory burdens to mitigate any harmful impacts of the PPACA and to empower states to regulate their own health insurance market.

Third-Party Payers

A third-party payer is an insurance company or other organization (e.g., a Medicare administrative contractor) that processes health care claims for reimbursement of procedures and services. Payers serve as **Medicare administrative contractors (MACs)** by processing claims for physicians (Medicare Part B); health care facilities (Medicare Part A); suppliers of durable medical equipment, prosthetics, orthotics, and supplies (DMEPOS); and home health and hospice agencies. The CMS, an administrative agency in the Department of Health & Human Services (DHHS), selects the MACs through a competitive bidding process.

Title IX of the **Medicare Prescription Drug, Improvement, and Modernization Act of 2003 (MMA)** called for the elimination of carriers, fiscal intermediaries (FIs), and durable medical equipment regional carriers (DMERCs) and the creation of Medicare administrative contractors. The MMA limits **indemnification** (insurance against loss) for adverse judgments against MACs and associated legal costs. Providers no longer nominate carriers or FIs, and they also no longer have a right to choose who will review claims or pay benefits. MACs integrate Medicare Part A and Part B functions into one contract, and providers have a single point of contact for all claims-related activity. MACs have been established in 15 jurisdictions throughout the United States, and eight specialty MACs were also created to process durable medical equipment claims and home health care claims (four MACs for each).

NOTE:

By 2010, Medicare had eliminated the following to create 23 Medicare Administrative Contractors (MACs) that consolidated the administration of Medicare Part A and B benefits so that Medicare beneficiaries have claims processed by one contractor. (Carrier and fiscal intermediary language still appears in some Medicare literature.)

- *Carriers* (processed Medicare Part B claims)
- *Fiscal intermediaries (FIs)* (processed Medicare Part A claims)
- *Durable medical equipment carriers (DMERCs)* (processed durable medical equipment, prosthetics, orthotics, and supplies [DMEPOS])

Durable medical equipment, prosthetics, orthotics, and supplies (DMEPOS) claims are processed by DME MACs, and home health and hospice (HH&H) claims are processed by HH&H MACs.

A **health insurance policy** is an agreement between an individual and a third-party payer (or insurance company) that contains a list of reimbursable medical benefits, or **covered benefits** (which might include office visits, inpatient hospitalizations, laboratory, tests, prescription medications, treatment services, and so on). The policy also lists procedures and services that are *not* covered by the third-party payer, called **noncovered benefits**, and when an individual undergoes procedures or receives services that are not covered by the policy, the individual is responsible for reimbursing the health care provider directly (e.g., with cosmetic surgery). A health care provider is a physician or other health care practitioner (e.g., a nurse practitioner) who provides services to patients.

After patient care has been delivered, the provider submits a **health insurance claim** to an insurance plan to request reimbursement for procedures performed or services provided (e.g., CMS-1500, UB-04). The CMS-1500 (Figure 20-1) is a standard claim submitted by physician offices to third-party payers. The UB-04 (or CMS-1450) (Uniform Bill, first implemented as the UB-92 in 1992 and revised to create the UB-04 in 2004, which was implemented in 2007) (Figure 20-2) is a standard claim submitted by health care institutions to payers for inpatient and outpatient services. CMS-1500 and UB-04 claims can also be submitted as electronic data interchange (EDI) transactions using specialized software (Figure 20-3), which is discussed later in this chapter.

Effective March 1, 2007, health plans and health care clearinghouses were required to accept the new UB-04. A health care clearinghouse processes or facilitates the processing of health information (such as a claim) received from another entity (such as a provider or payer) from a nonstandard into a standard format.

Determining which claim (e.g., CMS-1500, UB-04) to submit, as well as which coding system to use to report codes on the claim, depends on the health care setting (Table 20-1). Noninstitutional providers (e.g., physician offices, independent labs, ambulance companies that are not associated with a hospital, ambulatory surgery centers, and independent diagnostic testing facilities) and suppliers (for durable medical equipment, prosthetics, orthotics, and supplies dealers) submit the CMS-1500 claim to third-party payers, and they report ICD-10-CM diagnosis and HCPCS/CPT procedure and service codes (and HCPCS/CPT modifiers). Institutional providers (e.g., hospitals, nursing facilities, comprehensive outpatient rehabilitation facilities, community mental health centers, outpatient physical therapy facilities, rehabilitation agencies, and end-stage renal facilities) submit the UB-04 (or CMS-1450) claim to payers. For inpatient claims, ICD-10-CM diagnosis and ICD-10-PCS procedure codes are reported, and for outpatient claims (e.g., emergency department and outpatient care), ICD-10-CM diagnosis and HCPCS/CPT procedure and service codes (and HCPCS/CPT modifiers) are reported.

Before delivering health care services to patients, some payers require providers to obtain **preauthorization** (prior approval) of treatment (e.g., when specialists are involved) and to submit post-treatment reports. If the provider does not meet the preauthorization requirements, the claim is denied. If the patient's insurance policy contains a **hold harmless clause** (which holds that the patient is not responsible for paying what the insurance plan denies), the health care provider is prohibited from collecting payment from the patient. Claims are also denied if the medical necessity of procedures or services is not established. This means that every procedure or service reported on the claim must be linked to a condition that justifies the necessity for performing that procedure or providing that service. If the procedures or services delivered are determined to be unreasonable or unnecessary, the claim is denied.

HEALTH INSURANCE CLAIM FORM

APPROVED BY NATIONAL UNIFORM CLAIM COMMITTEE (NUCC) 02/12

☐☐ PICA | PICA ☐☐

| 1. MEDICARE ☐ (Medicare#) | MEDICAID ☐ (Medicaid#) | TRICARE ☐ (ID#/DoD#) | CHAMPVA ☐ (Member ID#) | GROUP HEALTH PLAN ☐ (ID#) | FECA BLK LUNG ☐ (ID#) | OTHER ☒ (ID#) | 1a. INSURED'S I.D. NUMBER (For Program in Item 1) **225120661W** |

| 2. PATIENT'S NAME (Last Name, First Name, Middle Initial) **PUBLIC, JOHN, Q** | 3. PATIENT'S BIRTH DATE MM **03** DD **09** YY **1945** SEX M ☒ F ☐ | 4. INSURED'S NAME (Last Name, First Name, Middle Initial) **PUBLIC, JOHN, Q** |

| 5. PATIENT'S ADDRESS (No., Street) **10A SENATE AVENUE** | 6. PATIENT RELATIONSHIP TO INSURED Self ☒ Spouse ☐ Child ☐ Other ☐ | 7. INSURED'S ADDRESS (No., Street) |

| CITY **ANYWHERE** STATE **NY** | 8. RESERVED FOR NUCC USE | CITY STATE |

| ZIP CODE **12345-1234** TELEPHONE (Include Area Code) ( ) | | ZIP CODE TELEPHONE (Include Area Code) ( ) |

| 9. OTHER INSURED'S NAME (Last Name, First Name, Middle Initial) | 10. IS PATIENT'S CONDITION RELATED TO: | 11. INSURED'S POLICY GROUP OR FECA NUMBER |

| a. OTHER INSURED'S POLICY OR GROUP NUMBER | a. EMPLOYMENT? (Current or Previous) YES ☐ NO ☒ | a. INSURED'S DATE OF BIRTH MM **03** DD **09** YY **1945** SEX M ☒ F ☐ |

| b. RESERVED FOR NUCC USE | b. AUTO ACCIDENT? YES ☐ NO ☒ PLACE (State) | b. OTHER CLAIM ID (Designated by NUCC) |

| c. RESERVED FOR NUCC USE | c. OTHER ACCIDENT? YES ☐ NO ☒ | c. INSURANCE PLAN NAME OR PROGRAM NAME **METROPOLITAN** |

| d. INSURANCE PLAN NAME OR PROGRAM NAME | 10d. CLAIM CODES (Designated by NUCC) | d. IS THERE ANOTHER HEALTH BENEFIT PLAN? YES ☐ NO ☒ If yes, complete items 9, 9a, and 9d. |

READ BACK OF FORM BEFORE COMPLETING & SIGNING THIS FORM.

12. PATIENT'S OR AUTHORIZED PERSON'S SIGNATURE I authorize the release of any medical or other information necessary to process this claim. I also request payment of government benefits either to myself or to the party who accepts assignment below.

SIGNED **SIGNATURE ON FILE** DATE

13. INSURED'S OR AUTHORIZED PERSON'S SIGNATURE I authorize payment of medical benefits to the undersigned physician or supplier for services described below.

SIGNED **SIGNATURE ON FILE**

| 14. DATE OF CURRENT ILLNESS, INJURY, or PREGNANCY (LMP) MM **01** DD **05** YY **YYYY** QUAL. **431** | 15. OTHER DATE QUAL. MM DD YY | 16. DATES PATIENT UNABLE TO WORK IN CURRENT OCCUPATION FROM MM DD YY TO MM DD YY |

| 17. NAME OF REFERRING PROVIDER OR OTHER SOURCE **DN IVAN GOODOC MD** | 17a. 17b. NPI **3456789012** | 18. HOSPITALIZATION DATES RELATED TO CURRENT SERVICES FROM MM DD YY TO MM DD YY |

| 19. ADDITIONAL CLAIM INFORMATION (Designated by NUCC) | | 20. OUTSIDE LAB? YES ☐ NO ☒ $ CHARGES |

21. DIAGNOSIS OR NATURE OF ILLNESS OR INJURY Relate A-L to service line below (24E) ICD Ind. **0**

A. **J180** B. **R350** C. D.
E. F. G. H.
I. J. K. L.

| 22. RESUBMISSION CODE ORIGINAL REF. NO. |
| 23. PRIOR AUTHORIZATION NUMBER |

24. A. DATE(S) OF SERVICE From MM DD YY	To MM DD YY	B. PLACE OF SERVICE	C. EMG	D. PROCEDURES, SERVICES, OR SUPPLIES (Explain Unusual Circumstances) CPT/HCPCS	MODIFIER	E. DIAGNOSIS POINTER	F. $ CHARGES	G. DAYS OR UNITS	H. EPSDT Family Plan	I. ID. QUAL.	J. RENDERING PROVIDER ID. #
1	01 09 YYYY		11		99213		A	75 00	1		NPI	
2	01 09 YYYY		11		81001		B	10 00	1		NPI	
3	01 09 YYYY		11		71046		A	50 00	1		NPI	
4											NPI	
5											NPI	
6											NPI	

| 25. FEDERAL TAX I.D. NUMBER **111234523** SSN ☐ EIN ☒ | 26. PATIENT'S ACCOUNT NO. **12-1** | 27. ACCEPT ASSIGNMENT? (For govt. claims, see back) YES ☒ NO ☐ | 28. TOTAL CHARGE $ **135 00** | 29. AMOUNT PAID $ **10 00** | 30. Rsvd for NUCC Use |

| 31. SIGNATURE OF PHYSICIAN OR SUPPLIER INCLUDING DEGREES OR CREDENTIALS (I certify that the statements on the reverse apply to this bill and are made a part thereof.) SIGNED **ERIN A HELPER MD** DATE **MMDDYYYY** | 32. SERVICE FACILITY LOCATION INFORMATION a. NPI b. | 33. BILLING PROVIDER INFO & PH # (**101**) **1111234** **ERIN A HELPER MD** **101 MEDIC DRIVE** **ANYWHERE NY 12345** a. **1234567890** b. |

NUCC Instruction Manual available at: www.nucc.org PLEASE PRINT OR TYPE

FIGURE 20-1 Completed CMS-1500 claim

CARRIER

PATIENT AND INSURED INFORMATION

PHYSICIAN OR SUPPLIER INFORMATION

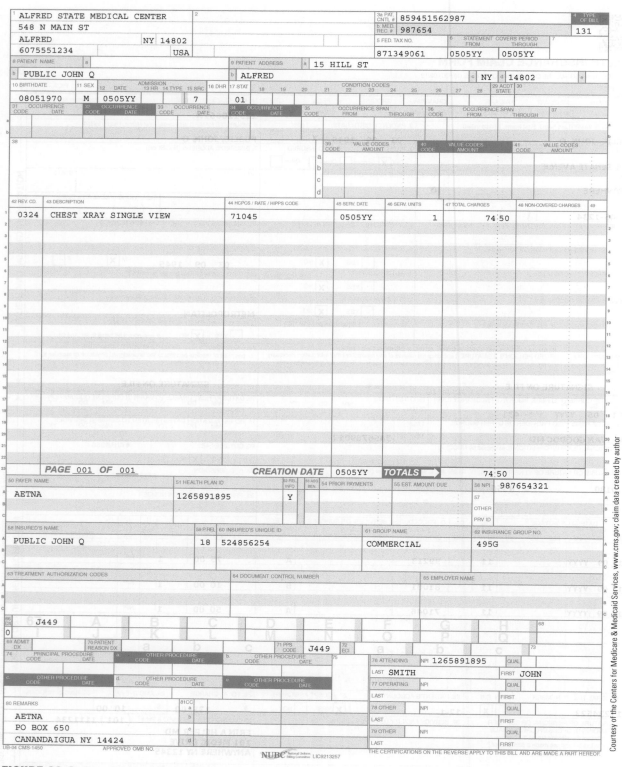

FIGURE 20-2 Completed UB-04 claim

FIGURE 20-3 Sample UB-04 software screen

Health Insurance Marketplace

The *Patient Protection and Affordable Care Act (PPACA)* was signed into federal law on March 23, 2010, and resulted in the creation of a *Health Insurance Marketplace* (or *health insurance exchange*), abbreviated as the Marketplace, effective October 1, 2013. The PPACA is abbreviated as the *Affordable Care Act (ACA)*, and it has been nicknamed *Obamacare* (because it was signed into federal law by President Obama). *The Health Insurance Marketplace does NOT replace other health insurance programs (e.g., individual and group commercial health insurance, Medicaid, Medicare, TRICARE).*

The Marketplace allows Americans to purchase health coverage that fits their budget and meets their needs. It is a resource where individuals, families, and small businesses can:

- Learn about their health coverage options
- Compare health insurance plans based on costs, benefits, and other important features
- Choose a plan
- Enroll in coverage

The Marketplace includes information about programs to help people with low to moderate income and resources pay for health coverage. Information includes ways to save on the monthly premiums and out-of-pocket costs of coverage available through the Marketplace and information about other programs, including Medicaid and the State Children's Health Insurance Program (SCHIP). The Marketplace encourages competition among private health plans, and it is accessible through websites, call centers, and in-person assistance. In some states it is run by the state, and in others it is run by the federal government.

TABLE 20-1 Claims and Coding Systems According to Type of Health Care Setting

Claim	Codes Reported	Health Care Setting
CMS-1491	ICD-10-CM diagnosis codes and HCPCS level II	Ambulance services
CMS-1500	ICD-10-CM diagnosis codes, CPT, and HCPCS level II	Noninstitutional providers and suppliers • Ambulatory surgery centers[1] • Anesthesiologists who administer hospital-based inpatient and outpatient anesthesia • Certified portable x-ray services • Home health agencies and hospices[2] • Independent clinical laboratories located at physician offices, group practices, hospitals, nursing facilities, end-stage renal disease facilities, pharmacies, home health agencies, rural health clinics, health fairs, anatomical testing laboratories, and nuclear medicine providers • Independent diagnostic testing facilities (e.g., a certified mammography center) • Physician, chiropractor, optometrist, and podiatrist offices • Privately practicing occupational therapists and physical therapists • Roster billing[3] for flu and pneumonia vaccinations
UB-04	ICD-10-CM diagnosis and ICD-10-PCS procedure codes	Institutional providers (inpatient) • Acute care hospitals • Long-term care facilities • Psychiatric hospitals • Rehabilitation facilities • Short-term hospitals • Hospices (inpatient respite care)[4]
UB-04	ICD-10-CM diagnosis codes, CPT, and HCPCS level II	Institutional providers (outpatient) • Hospital emergency departments • Hospital outpatient departments
UB-04	ICD-10-CM diagnosis codes, CPT, HCPCS level II, and HIPPS codes	Noninstitutional providers (outpatient) • Home health agencies[5] • Hospices (home care)[5]

[1]Some ambulatory surgery centers submit the UB-04 claim instead of the CMS-1500 claim.

[2]Some home health agencies and hospices submit the UB-04 claim instead of the CMS-1500 claim.

[3]**Roster billing** is a simplified process available to public health clinics and other noninstitutional entities that offer mass immunization programs. Hospices also submit claims for the administration of pneumococcal pneumonia, influenza virus, and hepatitis B vaccines.

[4]Respite care includes services that provide primary caregivers (e.g., the spouse of a terminally ill person) with temporary relief from tasks associated with caregiving (e.g., in-home assistance, short hospital or nursing facility stays, adult day care).

[5]Physicians who are not employees of the HHA and/or hospice and who provide professional home care services for home health agencies and hospices submit claims with ICD-10-CM diagnosis codes and CPT and HCPCS level II procedure/service codes.

Most individuals who do not currently have health insurance through their place of work or otherwise are eligible to use the Health Insurance Marketplace (www.healthcare.gov) to compare and choose a plan. To be eligible for health coverage through the marketplace, individuals must:

• Be a U.S. citizen or national (or be lawfully present)

• Live in the United States

• Not be incarcerated

Types of Third-Party Payers

Third-party payers include the following:

- BlueCross and BlueShield (BCBS)
- Commercial insurance companies
- Employer self-insurance plans
- Government-sponsored programs (e.g., Medicare)
- Managed care plans (e.g., HMO)
- Workers' compensation

 NOTE:

> Patient data and ICD-10-CM/PCS, CPT, and/or HCPCS level II codes that are entered in the hospital's computer system populate the UB-04 claim, and the hospital's billing department reviews the completed UB-04 claim for accuracy and submits it to third-party payers.
>
> When third-party payers deny a claim, the billing department collaborates with the health information department to re-review the submitted claim to correct data entry and coding errors. If codes submitted were correct, the billing department and health information department also collaborate when writing an appeal to the third-party payer, which may include supporting patient record documentation.

BlueCross and BlueShield (BCBS)

BlueCross and BlueShield (BCBS) payers cover the costs of hospital care and physicians, services. BlueCross initially covered just hospital care, and BlueShield covered just physicians, services; today, both offer a full range of health care coverage. While each independent BCBS plan serves its local community, its membership in the BCBS Association allows it to link with other local plans so that regional and national employers can be served (e.g., an employee can receive health care services while traveling).

 NOTE:

> In some states (e.g., California, Idaho, and Washington), BCBS payers are organized as two separate insurance companies. In other states (e.g., Missouri, New York, and Pennsylvania), BCBS payers are organized as multiple insurance companies according to region.

Commercial Payers

Commercial payers include private health insurance and employer-based group health insurance. Private health insurance usually consists of an indemnity plan, which covers individuals for certain health care expenses. The insurance company reimburses the patient or the provider, depending on the contract language. Individuals pay annual premiums (with predetermined rates).

Employer-based group health insurance is often provided as an employee benefit. The employer typically pays 80 percent of insurance premiums, and the employee pays the remaining 20 percent. The employer generally contracts with a commercial health insurance plan (e.g., Aetna).

Employer Self-Insurance Plans

For **employer self-insurance plans**, an employer accepts direct responsibility (or the risk) for paying employees' health care without purchasing health insurance and creates an employer self-insurance plan. Usually, the plan contracts with a third-party administrator (TPA), which is an organization that provides the following services to employers (and insurance companies):

- *Benefit design*: Medical services covered by the plan
- *Claims administration*: Processing claims to reimburse services
- *Utilization review or utilization management*: Reviewing medical care for appropriateness, necessity, and quality (e.g., preadmission authorization)

Government-Sponsored Programs

Government-sponsored programs include:

- CHAMPVA
- Federal Employee Health Benefits Program (FEHBP or FEP)
- Indian Health Service (IHS)
- Medicaid and SCHIP
- Medicare
- Military Health System (MHS)
- Programs of All-inclusive Care for the Elderly (PACE)
- TRICARE

The **Civilian Health and Medical Program of the Department of Veterans Affairs (CHAMPVA)** program provides health care benefits to dependents of veterans who

- Are rated as 100 percent permanently and totally disabled as a result of service-connected conditions
- Died as a result of service-connected conditions
- Died on duty with fewer than 30 days of active service

The **Federal Employee Health Benefits Program (FEHBP or FEP)** is a voluntary health care program that covers federal employees, retirees, and their dependents and survivors. The **Indian Health Service (IHS)** is a DHHS agency that provides federal health care services to American Indians and Alaska natives.

Medicaid (Title XIX of the Social Security Act Amendments of 1965) is a joint federal and state program that provides health care coverage to low-income populations and certain aged and disabled individuals. It is an entitlement program that is jointly financed by state and federal governments, with federal spending levels determined by the number of participants and services provided. The **State Children's Health Insurance Program (SCHIP)** was established to provide health assistance to uninsured, low-income children either through separate programs or through expanded eligibility under state Medicaid programs.

Medicare (Title XVIII of the Social Security Act Amendments of 1965) provides health care coverage to elderly and disabled persons; federal spending is funded by the Medicare Trust Fund (payroll tax). Medicare administrative contractors review local coverage determinations (LCDs) and national coverage determinations (NCDs) to specify under what clinical circumstances a service is covered, considered to be reasonable and necessary, and correctly coded. The **Programs of All-inclusive Care for the Elderly (PACE)** are community-based Medicare and Medicaid programs that provide integrated health care and long-term care services to elderly persons who require a nursing-facility level of care.

The **Military Health System (MHS)** provides and maintains readiness to provide health care services and support to members of the Uniformed Services during military operations. It also provides health care services and support to members of the Uniformed Services, their family members, and others entitled to Department of Defense health care.

TRICARE is the military health plan that covers active duty and retired members of the Uniformed Services and their dependents. It combines military health care resources (e.g., military treatment facilities) and networks of civilian health care professionals. TRICARE was formerly called CHAMPUS (Civilian Health and Medical Program of the United States).

NOTE:

The Recovery Audit Contractor (RAC) program was implemented nationwide in 2009 as part of the Medicare Prescription Drug, Improvement, and Modernization Act of 2003 (MMA), and four regional RACs were named. Its purpose is to safeguard the Medicare Trust Fund by having RACs evaluate individual provider compliance to (1) identify overpayments (and underpayments) made by Medicare and Medicaid and (2) recover overpayments made to durable medical equipment (DME) providers, health care facilities, and physician practices. For example, RACs use proprietary software to detect errors in codes reported on CMS-1500 claims. (Go to www.cms.gov/rac to review results of RAC activity.) RACs also monitor Medicare's post-acute care transfer (PACT) policy that can result in reduced payments for transferring hospitals, depending on the discharge status code reported (e.g., 03-Medicare SNF with Medicare certification in anticipation of skilled care).

RACs are not the same as Medicare's Comprehensive Error Rate Testing (CERT) program, which was implemented in 2003 (and currently operates parallel to the RAC program) to evaluate Medicare administrative contractors' (MAC) program performance. For example, CERT assesses the ability of an MAC to detect errors that are considered fraudulent.

The MMA also imposed Medicare fee-for-service contracting reform, directing CMS to use competitive measures to replace the Medicare fiscal intermediaries and carriers with MACs. CMS also established Zone Program Integrity Contractors (ZPICs) to perform program integrity functions in the newly established MAC jurisdictions (or zones). ZPICs are expected to perform program integrity functions for Medicare Parts A through D, DME, home health, hospice, and Medi-Medi programs.

Managed Care

Managed care combines the financing and delivery of health care services to replace conventional fee-for-service health insurance plans with more affordable care for consumers and providers who agree to certain restrictions (e.g., patients receive care from participating providers). (Managed care plans range from structured closed-panel staff model health maintenance organizations to less structured preferred provider organizations.)

A **participating provider (PAR)** is a member of a managed care plan, while a **nonparticipating provider (nonPAR)** is not a member of the plan. (PAR and nonPAR providers are also associated with traditional health insurance plans. Patients may incur higher out-of-pocket costs when receiving care from nonPARs.)

Fee-for-service plans reimburse providers for individual health care services rendered, while managed care is financed according to a method called **capitation**. *Capitation* is the term used when providers accept preestablished payments for providing health care services to enrollees over a period of time, usually one year. If the managed care physician provides services that cost less than the capitation amount, the physician keeps any profits. If services provided cost more than the capitation amount, the physician loses money. Patients who subscribe to managed care plans receive care from *their primary care provider (PCP)*, the physician responsible for supervising and coordinating health care services, for preauthorizing referrals to specialists, and for inpatient hospital admissions, except in emergencies.

Types of managed care plans include the following:

- Exclusive provider organization (EPO)
- Health maintenance organization (HMO)
- Point-of-service plan (POS)
- Preferred provider organization (PPO)
- Triple option plan (TPO) (also called cafeteria plan)

Exclusive Provider Organization

An **exclusive provider organization (EPO)** is a managed care plan that provides benefits to subscribers if they receive services from network providers. (EPOs are regulated by state insurance departments.) A **network provider** is a physician or health care facility under contract to the managed care plan. Network providers usually sign exclusive contracts with the EPO, which means they cannot contract with other managed care plans. Subscribers are generally required to coordinate health care services through their PCP.

An **integrated delivery system (IDS)** is an organization of affiliated provider sites (e.g., hospitals, ambulatory surgical centers, or physician groups) that offer joint health care services to subscribers. Integrated delivery systems are also known as

- Accountable health plans
- Delivery systems
- Health delivery networks
- Horizontally integrated systems

- Vertically integrated systems
- Vertically integrated plans (VIPs)

- Integrated service networks (ISNs)

Integrated delivery system models include the following:

- **Physician-hospital organization (PHO):** Owned by hospital(s) and physician groups that obtain managed care plan contracts; physicians maintain their own practices and provide health care services to plan members
- **Management service organization (MSO):** Usually owned by physicians or a hospital; provides practice management and administrative and support services to individual physician practices
- **Group practice without walls (GPWW):** Establishes a contract that allows physicians to maintain their own offices and share services such as appointment scheduling and billing
- **Integrated provider organization (IPO):** Manages the delivery of health care services offered by hospitals, physicians who are employees of the IPO, and other health care organizations such as ambulatory surgery clinics and nursing facilities
- **Medical foundation:** Nonprofit organization that contracts with and acquires the clinical and business assets of physician practices; the foundation is assigned a provider number and manages the practice's business

Health Maintenance Organization

A **health maintenance organization (HMO)** is an alternative to traditional group health insurance coverage that provides comprehensive health care services to voluntarily enrolled members on a prepaid basis. It provides preventive care services to promote "wellness" or good health, thus reducing the overall cost of medical care. An HMO often requires patients to pay a *copayment* (or *copay*), which is a fee paid by the patient to the provider at the time health care services are rendered.

HMOs must meet requirements of the HMO Act of 1973 as well as rules and regulations of individual states. They are organized in the following way:

- **Closed-panel HMO:** Health care is provided in an HMO-owned center or satellite clinic, or by physicians who belong to a specially formed medical group that serves the HMO.
- **Open-panel HMO:** Health care is provided by individuals who are not employees of the HMO or who do not belong to a specially formed medical group that serves the HMO.

Closed-panel HMOs include the following models:

- **Group model HMO:** Contracted health care services are delivered to subscribers by participating physicians *who are members of an independent multispecialty group practice.*
- **Staff model HMO:** Health care services are provided to subscribers by *physicians employed by the HMO.*

Open-panel HMOs include the following models:

- **Direct contract model HMO:** Contracted health care services are delivered to subscribers by *individual physicians in the community.*
- **Individual practice association (IPA) HMO:** Contracted health care services are delivered to subscribers by *physicians who remain in their independent office settings.*
- **Network model HMO:** Contracted health care services are provided to subscribers by *two or more physician multispecialty group practices.*

Point-of-Service Plan

A **point-of-service plan (POS)** offers patients the freedom to use an HMO panel of providers or to self-refer to non-HMO providers. If the enrollee chooses to receive all medical care from the HMO network of health care providers or obtains an authorization from the POS primary care physician for specialty care outside the HMO network, the enrollee pays only the regular copayment or a small charge for the visit, and no deductible or coinsurance responsibility applies. If the enrollee sees a non-HMO panel specialist without a referral from the PCP, this is called a **self-referral**, and the enrollee will have greater out-of-pocket expenses (e.g., a large deductible of about $250 plus 20 percent of coinsurance charges).

Preferred Provider Organization

A **preferred provider organization (PPO)** is a network of physicians and hospitals that join together to contract with insurance companies, employers, or other organizations. PPOs provide health care to subscribers for a discounted fee.

Triple Option Plan (or Cafeteria Plan)

A **triple option plan**, or **cafeteria plan**, is offered by either a single insurance plan or as a joint venture among two or more third-party payers. They provide a choice of HMO, PPO, or traditional health insurance plans.

Consumer-Directed Health Plan

Managed care is currently challenged by the growth of consumer-directed health plans, which define employer contributions and ask employees to be more responsible for health care decisions and cost-sharing. A **consumer-directed health plan (CDHP)** is a sort of "401(k) plan" for health care. It includes many choices that provide individuals with an incentive to control the costs of health benefits and health care. Individuals have greater freedom in spending health care dollars up to a designated amount and can receive full coverage for in-network preventive care. In return, individuals assume significantly higher cost-sharing expenses after the designated amount has been expended. (The catastrophic limit is usually higher than those common in other plans.)

The CDHP has become a popular alternative to the increased costs of traditional health insurance premiums and the limitations associated with managed care plans. They include the following tiers:

- *Tax-exempt account*, which is used to pay for health care expenses and provides more flexibility than traditional managed care plans in terms of access to providers and services
- *Out-of-pocket payments for health care expenses*, which are made after the tax-exempt account is expended and before the deductible for high-deductible insurance has been met; this tier actually represents a gap in coverage
- *High-deductible insurance policy*, which reimburses allowable health care expenses after the high deductible has been paid

The CDHPs usually provides Internet-based support so individuals can track health care expenses, improve their health by viewing useful information and learning about preventive services, obtain information about provider quality, and receive notification about provider group-rate pricing. A variety of types of consumer-directed health plans are available to individuals, all of which are subject to modification as legislation is passed and payers alter program requirements.

CDHPs include the following types:

- Customized sub-capitation plan (CSCP)
- Flexible spending account (FSA)
- Health Savings Account (HSA) or Health Savings Security Account (HSSA)
- Health reimbursement arrangement (HRA)
- Health care reimbursement account (HCRA)

Customized Sub-Capitation Plan

A **customized sub-capitation plan (CSCP)** funds health care expenses with insurance coverage, and the individual selects one of each type of provider to create a customized network and pays the resulting customized insurance premium. Each provider is paid a fixed amount per month to provide only the care that an individual needs from that provider (*a sub-capitation payment*).

Flexible Spending Account

A **flexible spending account (FSA)** is a tax-exempt account offered by employers to any number of employees, which individuals use to pay health care bills. Employees contribute funds to the FSA through a salary reduction agreement and withdraw funds to pay medical bills. Funds in an FSA are exempt from both income tax and Social Security tax. (Employers may also contribute to FSAs.) By law, employees forfeit unspent funds remaining in the FSA at the end of the year.

 NOTE:

In managed care, the primary care provider receives a *capitation payment* and is responsible for managing all of an individual's health care, which includes reimbursing health care expenses provided by other caregivers (e.g., labs and specialists).

Health Savings Account or Health Savings Security Account

A **health savings account (HSA)** or **health savings security account (HSSA)** allows participants to enroll in a relatively inexpensive, high-deductible insurance plan, and a tax-deductible savings account is opened to cover current and future medical expenses. Money deposited (and earnings) is tax-deferred, and money is withdrawn to cover qualified medical expenses tax-free. Money can be withdrawn for purposes other than health care expenses after payment of income tax, plus a 15 percent penalty. Unused balances "roll over" from year to year, and if an employee changes jobs, the HSA or HSSA can continue to be used to pay for qualified health care expenses.

Health Care Reimbursement Account

A **health care reimbursement account (HCRA)** is a tax-exempt account that is used to pay for health care expenses. The individual decides, in advance, how much money to deposit in an HCRA (and unused funds are lost).

Health Reimbursement Arrangement

A **health reimbursement arrangement (HRA)** is a tax-exempt account offered by employers with more than 50 employees, which individuals use to pay health care bills. The Internal Revenue Service (IRS) issued a tax guidance for HRAs in 2002 that stated the HRA must be used for qualified health care expenses, requires enrollment in a high-deductible insurance policy, and a provision must be in place to allow individuals to accumulate unspent money for future years. If an employee changes jobs, the HRA can continue to be used to pay for qualified health care expenses.

Workers' Compensation

Workers' compensation is a state-mandated insurance program that reimburses health care costs and lost wages if an employee suffers a work-related disease or injury. Qualified employees and their dependents are eligible for reimbursement.

Exercise 20.1 – Third-Party Payers

Instructions: Complete each statement.

1. Third-party payers that process health care claims for reimbursement of Medicare Part A, Part B, and DME procedures, services, and supplies are called MACs, which is the abbreviation for_____.

2. The administrative agency in the Department of Health & Human Services (DHHS) that selects payers to process Medicare health care claims through a competitive bidding process is called CMS, which is the abbreviation for _____.

3. The standard claim submitted by physician offices to third-party payers is called the CMS-1500, and the claim submitted by health care institutions is called the _____.

Exercise 20.1 – *continued*

4. An organization that processes or facilitates the processing of health information received from another entity from a nonstandard into a standard format is called a(n) _____.

5. If the patient's insurance policy contains a statement that the patient is not responsible for paying what the insurance plan denies, the health care provider is prohibited from collecting payment from the patient. This statement is called a(n) _____ harmless clause.

6. The government-sponsored health program that provides health care benefits to active military and their dependents is called _____.

7. The joint federal and state program that provides health care coverage to low-income populations and certain aged and disabled individuals is called _____.

8. The government-sponsored health program that provides health care coverage to elderly and disabled persons is called _____.

9. The combined financing and delivery of health care services to replace conventional fee-for-service health insurance plans with more affordable care for consumers and providers who agree to certain restrictions is called _____ care.

10. The type of plan that reimburses providers for individual health care services rendered is called _____.

Health Care Reimbursement Systems

Prior to implementation of major government-sponsored health programs (e.g., Medicare and Medicaid) in 1965, health care services were reimbursed by the following payers:

- BlueCross and BlueShield (private and group health plans)
- Commercial health insurance (private)
- Employer-based group health insurance and self-insurance plans
- Government-sponsored programs, limited to the following:
  - Indian Health Service (limited eligibility)
  - Dependents' medical care program (health care for dependents of active military personnel)
- Prepaid health plans (forerunner of managed care)
- Self-pay (patients paid cash)
- Workers' compensation (limited eligibility)

Payers (except prepaid or managed care plans) typically reimbursed physicians on a fee-for-service basis, which is a retrospective payment system that billed payers after health care services were provided to the patient. Hospital reimbursement was generated on a *per diem* basis (Latin meaning "by the day"), which meant payers used a retrospective payment system to issue payment that was based on actual daily charges.

EXAMPLE: Payers typically reimbursed providers for 80 percent of charges submitted, and patients paid the remaining 20 percent (coinsurance). Thus, a provider who submitted a charge of $120 was paid $96 by the payer and $24 by the patient. (Government programs, such as Medicare, establish a physician fee schedule for services provided. The physician is reimbursed 80 percent of the fee schedule.)

Prospective Payment Systems, Fee Schedules, and Exclusions

Health care costs increased dramatically with implementation of government-sponsored health programs in 1965. This led to the creation and implementation of prospective payment systems and fee schedules (Table 20-2) for

TABLE 20-2 Prospective Payment Systems and Fee Schedules, Year Implemented, and Prospective Rate Type

Prospective Payment System (PPS) and Fee Schedules	Year	Type
Ambulance Fee Schedule	2002	Cost-based
Ambulatory Surgical Center (ASC) Payment Rates[1]	1994	Price-based
Clinical Laboratory Fee Schedule	1985	Cost-based
Durable Medical Equipment, Prosthetics, Orthotics, and Supplies (DMEPOS) Fee Schedule	1989	Cost-based
End-Stage Renal Disease (ESRD) Composite Payment Rate System	2005	Price-based
Federally Qualified Health Center Prospective Payment System (FQHC PPS)	2014	Price-based
Home Health Prospective Payment System (HH PPS) (Home Health Resource Groups, HHRGs)	2000	Price-based
Hospice Payment System	1983	Cost-based
Hospital Inpatient Prospective Patient System (IPPS)	1983	Price-based
Hospital Outpatient Prospective Payment System (OPPS)	2001	Price-based
Inpatient Psychiatric Facility Prospective Payment System (IPF PPS)	2004	Cost-based
Inpatient Rehabilitation Facility Prospective Payment System (IRF PPS)	2002	Price-based
Long-Term (Acute) Care Hospital Prospective Payment System (LTC PPS)	2001	Price-based
Resource Based Relative Value Scale (RBRVS) System	1992	Cost-based
Skilled Nursing Facility Prospective Payment System (SNF PPS)[2]	1998	Price-based

[1]Effective January 1, 2008, the OPPS payment amount was substituted for the ASC standard overhead amount for surgical procedures performed at an ASC.

[2]The SNF PPS was originally based on resource-utilization groups (RUGs) effective from 1998-2018; in 2019 the patient-driven payment model (PDPM) was implemented.

government health programs. The purpose was to control costs by reimbursing facilities with preestablished rates for inpatient care provided. Shortly after passage of Medicare and Medicaid legislation in 1965, Congress began investigating prospective payment systems. A **prospective payment system (PPS)** is a reimbursement methodology that establishes predetermined rates based on patient category or type of facility (with annual increases based on an inflation index and a geographic wage index). The CMS manages implementation of Medicare PPS, fee schedules, and exclusions according to

- Prospective cost-based rates
- Prospective price-based rates

Prospective cost-based rates are based on reported health care costs (e.g., charges) from which a prospective *per diem* rate is determined. Annual rates are usually adjusted using actual costs from the prior year. This method may be based on the facility's case mix (patient acuity of types and categories of patients). Prospective payment systems based on this reimbursement methodology include ambulance fee schedules.

Prospective price-based rates are associated with a particular category of patient (e.g., inpatients), and rates are established by the payer (e.g., Medicare) prior to the provision of health care services. PPSs based on this reimbursement methodology include diagnosis-related groups (DRGs) for inpatient care.

Typically, third-party payers adopt PPSs, fee schedules, and exclusions after Medicare has implemented them; payers modify them to suit their needs. A **fee schedule** is cost-based, fee-for-service reimbursement methodology that includes a list of maximum fees and corresponding procedures/services, which payers use to compensate providers for health care services delivered to patients. **Exclusions** are "Medicare PPS Excluded Cancer Hospitals" (e.g., Roswell Park Memorial Institute in Buffalo, New York) that applied for and were granted waivers from mandatory participation in the hospital inpatient PPS.

EXAMPLE: Prior to 1983, acute care hospitals generated invoices based on total charges for an inpatient stay. In 1982, an eight-day inpatient hospitalization at $225 per day (including ancillary service charges) would be billed $1,800. This *per diem* reimbursement rate actually discouraged hospitals from limiting inpatient lengths of stay. In 1983, a PPS rate of $950 would be reimbursed for the same inpatient hospitalization, regardless of length of stay (unless the case qualified for additional reimbursement as an outlier). The PPS rate encourages hospitals to limit inpatient lengths of stay because any reimbursement received in excess of the actual cost of providing care can be retained by the facility. (In this example, if the $950 PPS rate had been paid in 1980, the hospital would have absorbed the $850 loss.)

Inpatient Prospective Payment System (1983)

The **Tax Equity and Fiscal Responsibility Act of 1983 (TEFRA)** legislated implementation of the hospital **inpatient prospective payment system (IPPS)**, which uses diagnosis-related groups (DRGs) to reimburse short-term hospitals a predetermined rate for Medicare inpatient services. (Other payers have adopted the IPPS.)

NOTE:

Certain cancer hospitals that applied and received waivers from CMS are considered excluded hospitals, which means that they do not participate in the IPPS.

Diagnosis-related groups (DRGs) (Figure 20-4) classify inpatient hospital cases into groups that are expected to consume similar hospital resources.

- Each DRG has a payment weight assigned to it that is based on the average resources used to treat Medicare patients in that DRG.
- DRGs are organized into **major diagnostic categories (MDCs)**, which are mutually exclusive categories that are loosely based on body systems (e.g., nervous system).
- Inpatient cases that are unusually costly are called **outliers**, and the IPPS payment is increased to protect the hospital from large financial losses due to unusually expensive cases.

To determine an IPPS (DRG or MS-DRG) payment, hospitals submit a UB-04 claim for each inpatient to a *Medicare administrative contractor (MAC)*, which is a third-party payer that contracts with Medicare to carry out the operational functions of the Medicare program.

- Based on the information provided on the UB-04, the case is categorized into a DRG, which determines the reimbursement provided to the hospital.
- DRG payments are then adjusted to accommodate the wage index applicable to the area where the hospital is located, a cost-of-living adjustment factor for hospitals located in Alaska and Hawaii, a percentage add-on payment for hospitals that serve a disproportionate share of low-income patients, and/or a percentage add-on payment if the hospital is an approved teaching hospital.
- In addition, if a case is categorized as an outlier, additional payments are added to the DRG-adjusted base payment rate.

Costs not considered when calculating the Medicare DRG-adjusted base payment rates are as follows:

- *Direct costs* of medical education for interns and residents, which are based on a per-resident payment amount
- *Reasonable costs* for (1) hospital bad debts attributable to nonpayment of the Medicare deductible and coinsurance, and (2) heart, liver, lung, and kidney acquisition costs incurred by an approved transplant facility

Medicare Severity Diagnosis-Related Groups (MS-DRGs)
MDC 02 – Diseases and Disorders of the Eye

CC = complication(s) and/or comorbidity(ies)
MCC = major complication(s) and/or cormorbidity(ies)

MS-DRG	Description
113	Orbital procedures w CC/MCC

MS-DRG: 113
Title: Orbital procedures w CC/MCC
Type: SURG
Major Diagnostic Category (MDC): 02 DISEASES & DISORDERS OF THE EYE
Relative Weight: 1.4141
Geometric Mean Length of Stay (days): 3.8
Arithmetic Mean Length of Stay (days): 5.5

Related Codes

MS-DRG	Title	Relative Weight	Length of Stay
113	Orbital procedures w CC/MCC	1.4141	3.8
114	Orbital procedures w/o CC/MCC	1.0292	2.0
115	Extraocular procedures except orbit	1.1185	3.3
116	Intraocular procedures w CC/MCC	0.8891	2.2
117	Intraocular procedures w/o CC/MCC	0.7094	1.5

Crosswalk of CMS-DRG to MS-DRG

CMS-DRG	MDC	MS-DRG
037 - ORBITAL PROCEDURES	02	113 - Orbital procedures w CC/MCC

MS-DRG	Description
114	Orbital procedures w/o CC/MCC
115	Extraocular procedures except orbit
116	Intraocular procedures w CC/MCC
117	Intraocular procedures w/o CC/MCC
121	Acute major eye infections w CC/MCC
122	Acute major eye infections w/o CC/MCC
123	Neurological eye disorders
124	Other disorders of the eye w MCC
125	Other disorders of the eye w/o MCC

FIGURE 20-4 Medicare severity diagnosis-related groups (MS-DRGs), major diagnostic category 02

The **IPPS 3-day payment window** (or **IPPS 72-hour rule**) requires outpatient preadmission services provided by a hospital on the day of or during the three days prior to a patient's inpatient admission to be covered by the IPPS DRG payment and reported on the UB-04 with ICD-10-CM and ICD-10-PCS codes for

- Diagnostic services (e.g., lab testing)
- Therapeutic (or nondiagnostic) services

Medicare also requires that physicians, services clinically related to an inpatient admission and provided within 72 hours of the admission be paid at the lower facility rate (instead of the usually greater office or nonfacility rate). CMS requires that HCPCS level II modifier -PD (diagnostic or related nondiagnostic item or service provided in a wholly owned or wholly operated entity to a patient who is admitted as an inpatient within three days) to identify claims for related services provided within 72 hours of an inpatient admission. As a result of this new requirement

- Physician office claims must be held for at least three days prior to submission, and CMS requires hospitals to notify physician offices about related inpatient admissions.
- Modifier -PD must be added to CPT and HCPCS level II codes that are reported on CMS-1500 claims for any inpatients who received physician office services within 72 hours prior to admission.

In practice, physician offices need to implement a process to ensure that claims submission is delayed by three days. Also, an office staff member needs to review daily list(s) of inpatient admissions received from local hospital(s) to identify patients whose claims need to be modified by adding -PD to CPT codes.

EXAMPLE: A 79-year-old established female Medicare patient receives physician office evaluation and management (E/M) services (99214) for complaints of chest pain and shortness of breath. Her general practitioner (GP) performs a 12-lead ECG (93000), which indicates the patient is currently experiencing a myocardial infarction (MI). The patient is immediately transported by ambulance to the local hospital and admitted to the intensive care unit. Because the patient is admitted within 72 hours of the office visit, the E/M services (99214-PD) are paid to the physician at the lesser facility rate (instead of the physician office rate), and only the professional component rate of the ECG (93010-PD) is paid to the physician (instead of the higher global procedure rate). (CPT code 93010 is reported for the professional component of the ECG, not 93000 which is reported for the global service.)

According to CMS, all nondiagnostic services (other than ambulance and maintenance renal dialysis services) furnished by a hospital on the date of admission or during the three-day payment window are deemed to be related to the admission and, therefore, must be bundled with the inpatient stay if the services were provided on the day of or during the three days prior to a patient's inpatient admission. The exception to the rule is when a hospital determines, attests, and documents that the service furnished during the three-day payment window is *clinically distinct or independent from the reason for the patient's admission*. Hospitals are required to report condition code 51 with the nondiagnostic service CPT or HCPCS level II code on the outpatient UB-04.

 NOTE:

Medicare implemented **Medicare severity diagnosis-related groups (MS-DRGs)** in 2007 to classify inpatient hospital cases into groups according to similar resource utilization. Hospitals receive a predetermined payment according to MS-DRG for treating Medicare patients. Like the original DRGs, the MS-DRGs are based on diagnoses, procedures, other demographic information, and the presence of complications or comorbidities (CCs). However, hospital inpatients are distinguished according to those with no CCs, CCs, or major CCs (MCCs). This allows Medicare to distinguish "sick patients" from "very sick patients" and to reimburse hospitals accordingly. As such, the number of MS-DRGs expands to 745 (as compared to 538 original DRGs). MS-DRGs also emphasize the importance of proper documentation of patient care, relating it to reimbursement optimization (e.g., increased diagnosis specificity to justify more severe illnesses resulting in increased reimbursement). Facilities implement clinical documentation improvement (CDI) programs to ensure thorough and accurate documentation in patient records. (*To optimize reimbursement* means to legally enhance reimbursement from payers to providers, such as assigning specific codes based on documentation in the patient record.)

Other systems developed for payment purposes (based on CMS's DRG system) include the following:

- *All Patient Refined DRGs (APR-DRGs)*, which classify the non-Medicare population, such as HIV patients, neonates, and pediatric patients
- *International Refined DRGs (IR-DRGs)*, which were created by other countries that adapted DRGs for their own use, comparing resource usage across health care facilities and regions and incorporating the concept of severity of illness adjustments using multiple levels of comorbid and complication (CC) conditions
- *New York All Patient DRGs (AP-DRGs)*, which classify the nonelderly population in New York State
- *Yale Refined Diagnosis-Related Groups (RDRGs)*, which refined the original DRGs to incorporate a measure of severity, expanding the number of DRGs to 1,263 RDRGs

An **IPPS transfer rule** states that any patient with a diagnosis associated with one to 10 CMS-determined DRGs who is discharged to a post-acute provider is treated as a transfer case. This means that hospitals are paid a graduated *per diem* rate for each day of the patient's stay, not to exceed the prospective payment DRG rate.

(Outliers are also recognized for extraordinarily high-cost cases.) CMS identified 10 high-volume DRGs that contain a disproportionate percentage of discharges to post-acute care settings (e.g., DRG 14—Specific Cerebrovascular Disorders Except Transient Ischemic Attack). CMS defines the following as post-acute care settings:

- Hospitals or distinct units excluded from the prospective payment system
- Skilled nursing facilities
- Patient's home under a written plan of care for the provision of home health services from a home health agency if the services begin within three days of discharge

 NOTE:

Services that are distinct from and unrelated to the inpatient admission are separately billed by the hospital *if documentation supports that the service is unrelated to the inpatient admission.*

The Department of Health & Human Services, Office of Inspector General (OIG) monitors hospital readmissions that seem to focus on revenue generation rather than medical necessity when determining DRGs. When a patient is readmitted to a hospital on the day of discharge, the hospital should treat the readmission as a continuous episode of care. This means that the new admission is combined with the previous admission and that the hospital receives reimbursement for just one episode of care (according to the DRG generated). If the patient is transferred to another hospital, that admission is considered a transfer (not a new admission) and the two hospitals cost-split the DRG reimbursement rate. To convince the OIG that the hospital is properly classifying readmissions and transfers, consider implementing software that flags same-day readmissions for review, ensure that hospital discharge planners accurately assess the patient's condition upon discharge, and remind providers to document the fact that patients were discharged in a timely manner.

Hospital-Acquired Conditions and Present on Admission Reporting Guidelines

The Deficit Reduction Act of 2005 resulted in implementation of a quality adjustment in Medicare diagnosis-related group (DRG) payments for certain hospital-acquired conditions. CMS calls the program *Hospital-Acquired Conditions and Present on Admission Indicator Reporting (HAC & POA).*

All claims submitted for inpatient admissions to general acute care hospitals or other health care facilities are required to report the **present on admission (POA) indicator,** which is assigned by the coder to the principal and secondary diagnoses and external cause of injury code reported on the UB-04 or 837 Institutional (837I) electronic claim.

- The coder reviews the patient record to determine whether a condition was present on admission or not.
- Issues related to inconsistent, missing, conflicting, or unclear documentation are resolved by the provider as a result of the "physical query" process.

In this context, "present on admission" is defined as "present at the time the order for inpatient admission occurs." Thus, conditions that develop during an outpatient encounter, including emergency department, observation, or outpatient surgery, are considered as present on admission upon admission of the patient as a hospital inpatient. CMS reporting options and definitions include the following, and payment is made for "Y" and "W" indicators:

- Y = Yes (diagnosis was present at the time of inpatient admission)
- N = No (diagnosis was not present at the time of inpatient admission)
- U = Unknown (documentation is insufficient to determine if the condition was present at the time of inpatient admission)
- W = Clinically undetermined (provider is unable to clinically determine whether the condition was present at the time of inpatient admission)
- Blank = Unreported/not used (exempt from POA reporting) (the field is blank for factors that do not represent a current disease or for a condition that is always present on admission)

Coding for Diagnosis-Related Groups (DRGS)

Diagnoses and procedures are assigned ICD-10-CM/PCS codes, and they are sequenced according to CMS official coding guidelines and the Uniform Hospital Discharge Data Set (UHDDS). This means that hospitals are not required to assign codes to every diagnosis and procedure documented in the patient record. However, hospitals must evaluate their institutional data needs to develop coding policies, which will determine the assignment of ICD-10-CM/PCS codes to diagnoses and procedures. When assigning codes to *comorbidities* (coexisting conditions) and *complications* (conditions that develop during inpatient admission), be sure to carefully review patient record documentation to assign the most specific code possible. Revisions to the MS-DRGs comorbidities and complications (CC) list eliminated many diagnoses that were considered CCs in the past. As a result, physicians must be educated about the importance of proper documentation practices.

EXAMPLE: Under MS-DRGs

- Chronic obstructive pulmonary disease (COPD) is not a CC. However, acute exacerbation of COPD is a CC.
- Congestive heart failure (CHF) is not a CC. However, chronic systolic heart failure is a CC and acute systolic heart failure is a major CC (MCC).

ICD-10-PCS codes are assigned for documented OR (operating room) and non-OR procedures. (Non-OR procedures are performed in the patient's room, emergency department, radiology department, and so on.) Whether ICD-10-PCS codes are assigned to other procedures, such as ancillary tests (e.g., EKG, laboratory tests, and so on), is dependent on the hospital's coding policy.

The *present on admission (POA)* indicator differentiates between patient conditions present upon inpatient admission and those that develop during the inpatient admission. Claims that do not report the POA indicator are returned to the facility for correction. *Hospital-acquired conditions* that are reported as not present at the time of admission are not considered when calculating the MS-DRG payment. This means that such conditions, even if included on the CC and MCC lists, are not considered a CC or MCC if diagnosed during the inpatient stay and the facility will not receive additional payment for such conditions.

Value-Based Purchasing

Hospital **value-based purchasing (VBP)** is part of a long-standing CMS effort to link Medicare's inpatient prospective payment system (IPPS) to a value-based system for the purpose of improving health care quality, including the quality of care provided in the inpatient hospital setting, which affects payment for inpatient stays to over 3,500 hospitals. Participating hospitals are paid for inpatient acute care services based on quality of care, not just quantity of services provided. The inpatient hospital VBP was authorized by the Patient Protection and Affordable Care Act (PPACA). A hospital quality data reporting infrastructure was developed as part of the Hospital Inpatient Quality Reporting (IQR) Program, as authorized by the Medicare Prescription Drug, Improvement, and Modernization Act of 2003 (MMA).

The *Hospital Inpatient Quality Reporting (Hospital IQR) program* was developed to equip consumers with quality of care information so they can make more informed decisions about health care options. The Hospital IQR program requires hospitals to submit specific quality measures data about health conditions common among Medicare beneficiaries and that typically result in hospitalization. Eligible hospitals that do not participate in the Hospital IQR program will receive an annual market basket update with a 2.0 percentage point reduction.

The **hospital readmission reduction program (HRRP)** requires CMS to reduce payments to IPPS hospitals with excess readmissions, and utilizes readmission measures established by CMS (e.g., hospital inpatient admission within 30 days of discharge from the same hospital). CMS also established payment adjustment policies to determine which hospitals are subject to the HRRP, the methodology to calculate the hospital readmission payment adjustment factor, the portion of the IPPS payment used to calculate readmission payment adjustment amounts, and a process for hospitals to review readmission information and submit corrections before readmission rates are publicized.

Skilled Nursing Facility Prospective Payment System (1998)

The **Balanced Budget Act of 1997** legislated implementation of the **skilled nursing facility prospective payment system (SNF PPS)**, which originally classified residents into *resource utilization groups (RUGs)* to reimburse Medicare SNF services according to a *per diem* prospective rate adjusted for case mix.

Effective 2019, the **patient-driven payment model (PDPM)** was implemented as a new case-mix reimbursement system that connects payment to patients' conditions and care needs instead of the volume of services provided. (In addition to IRFs, the PDPM applies to long-term acute care facility and skilled nursing facility payments.) The PDPM classification methodology uses a combination of six payment components to derive payment, five of which are case-mix adjusted to cover utilization of SNF resources that vary according to patient characteristics. The sixth non-case-mix adjusted component addresses utilization of resources that do not vary by patient. A resident assessment instrument (RAI) completed on each SNF patient captures the **minimum data set (MDS)** according to the following schedule: 5, 14, 30, 60, and 90 days after admission. **Resident Assessment Validation and Entry (RAVEN)** software, developed by CMS, is a data entry system that allows SNFs to capture and transmit the MDS.

 NOTE:

Medicare introduced the first prospective payment system (PPS) to pay for inpatient hospital care, and other prospective payment systems were adopted in subsequent years (e.g., SNF PPS). Under the inpatient prospective payment system (IPPS), inpatients are discharged once the acute phase of illness has passed and hospitals are reimbursed according to diagnosis-related groups. The patients are often transferred to other types of health care, such as outpatient care, skilled care facilities, rehabilitation hospitals, and home health care. The transfer facilities provide an appropriate level of health care in a safe and cost-effective manner after the patient's attending physician (with the assistance of discharge planners, case managers, social workers, nurses, and others) has determined which facility is best by evaluating the patient's medical condition, special needs, and treatment goals.

CMS adopted a *SNF all-cause all-condition hospital readmission measure* and a *SNF Value-Based Purchasing (VBP) Program* to promote higher quality and more efficient health care for Medicare beneficiaries as well as value-based incentive payments for qualified SNFs.

Each component of the *patient-driven payment model (PDPM) payment* is calculated by multiplying the case-mix index (CMI) that corresponds to the patient's case-mix group (CMG) by the wage-adjusted component base payment rate. (The specific day in the variable *per diem* adjustment schedule is also factored in, when applicable.) PDPM components are then totaled together along with the non-case-mix component payment rate to create a patient's total SNF PPS (PDPM) *per diem* rate.

Home Health Prospective Payment System (2000)

The **Omnibus Consolidated and Emergency Supplemental Appropriations Act (OCESAA) of 1999** legislated implementation of the **home health prospective payment system (HH PPS)** for Medicare home health services, which uses home health resource groups (HHRGs) to reimburse Medicare home health care services according to prospectively determined rates and requires recertification every 60 days (or more frequently when there is a beneficiary elected transfer, a significant change in condition resulting in a change in the case-mix assignment, or a discharge and return to the same home health agency during the 60-day episode) by the physician who reviews the plan of care.

 NOTE:

Medicare does not reimburse durable medical equipment (DME) during the initial 60 days that a patient receives home care services. DME is reimbursed according to a fee schedule during this period.

Home health agencies (HHAs) were reimbursed under a fee-for-service system until Medicare transitioned to the HH PPS for 60-day periods of home health care. Rates for each 60-day episode of HHA care are adjusted by case-mix methodology based on entry of data elements from the outcome and assessment information set (OASIS) into **Home Assessment Validation and Entry (HAVEN)** data entry software. The HHA clinician (such as a registered nurse) conducts a comprehensive assessment and collects OASIS data elements to capture clinical severity factors, functional

TABLE 20-3 Sample Hospice Payment System Rates

Level of Hospice Care	Hospice Payment Rate
Routine home care (Days 1–60)	$191 per day
Routine home care (Days 61+)	$150 per day
Continuous home care	$965 per day or $40 per hour
Inpatient respite care	$171 per day
General inpatient care	$734 per day
Aggregate reimbursement cap per beneficiary served	$28,500
Inpatient days cap	20% of total days of hospice service

severity factors, and service utilization factors that influence case mix. Each data element is assigned a score value, and the scores are totaled (by HAVEN software) to determine the patient's case-mix group (and the reimbursement rate).

Hospice Payment System

Medicare's hospice program was established by the *Tax Equity and Fiscal Responsibility Act (TEFRA) of 1982*, which expanded the scope of Medicare benefits by authorizing coverage for hospice care for terminally ill beneficiaries and established a fee-for-service payment rate system. The *Patient Protection and Affordable Care Act of 2010* reformed the hospice payment rate system (Table 20-3) to implement aggregate expenditures to control Medicare hospice costs.

Medicare pays a daily rate for each day a patient is enrolled in the hospice benefit, regardless of the number of services provided on a given day. Payments are made based on the *level of care* required to meet the patient's and family's needs, including:

- Routine home care
- Continuous home care
- Inpatient respite care
- General inpatient care

 NOTE:

Routine home care payments are made at a higher payment rate for the first 60 days of hospice care, and a reduced payment rate for hospice care for 61 days and over.

A service intensity add-on (SIA) payment in addition to the per diem RHC rate is made for services furnished during the last seven days of a patient's life. SIA eligibility criteria include the following:

- The day is a routine home care level of care day.
- The day occurs during the last seven days of the patient's life, and the patient is discharged expired.
- Direct patient care is furnished by a registered nurse (RN) or social worker, respectively, that day

The SIA payment is equal to the continuous home care hourly payment rate multiplied by the amount of direct patient care furnished by an RN or social worker during the seven-day period for a minimum of 15 minutes and up to four hours total per day.

Daily hospice payment rates are adjusted for differences in wage rates among markets. Each level of hospice care's base rate has a labor share (adjusted by the hospice wage index) and a nonlabor share. Base rates are updated annually, based on the hospital market basket update.

Two caps affect Medicare payments under the hospice benefit:

- *Inpatient cap* (number of days of inpatient care furnished is limited to not more than 20 percent of total patient care days)

- *Aggregate* cap (limits the amount of Medicare payments a provider may receive in an accounting year, and it is calculated by multiplying the number of hospice beneficiaries during the accounting year by a per-beneficiary *cap amount*.)

There are two methods for counting beneficiaries:

- *Patient-by-patient proportional method* (counts only that fraction which represents the portion of a patient's total days of care in all hospices and all years that was spent in that hospice in that cap year)
- *Streamlined method* (counts those beneficiaries who received care from a single hospice in the initial year of election only)

When a beneficiary receives care from more than one hospice, the patient-by-patient proportional method is used. The aggregate payment cap is then compared with actual aggregate payments made to the hospice during the cap year; any payments in excess of the cap are considered overpayments and must be refunded to Medicare by the hospice.

Outpatient Prospective Payment System (2000)

The Balanced Budget Act of 1997 legislated implementation of the hospital **outpatient prospective payment system (OPPS)**, which uses **ambulatory payment classifications (APCs)** to reimburse hospital outpatient services. Outpatient health care services are organized clinically and according to resources required.

A reimbursement rate is established for each APC (Figure 20-5) and, depending on services provided, hospitals can be paid for more than one APC per encounter, with second and subsequent APCs discounted at 50 percent (if they are designated with status indicator "T").

Each CPT and HCPCS level II code is assigned a **status indicator (SI)** as a payment indicator to identify how each code is paid (or not paid) under the OPPS. For example, status indicator "S" refers to "significant procedures for which the multiple procedure reduction does not apply." This means that the CPT and/or HCPCS level II code is paid the full APC reimbursement rate. OPPS status indicator "T" refers to "services to which the multiple procedure

---

Outpatient Prospective Payment System (OPPS) Formula

(APC Weight × Conversion Factor × Wage Index) + Add-On Payments = Payment

NOTE: When a patient undergoes multiple procedures and services on the same day, multiple APCs are generated and payments are added together. APC software automatically discounts multiple APC payments when appropriate (e.g., bilateral procedure).

EXAMPLE: Using the sample data below, the OPPS payment for a patient who underwent cataract procedure with intraocular lens implant, chest x-ray, and ureteral reflux study in Buffalo, New York is calculated as 437.02. (NOTE: Add-on payments do not apply to this example and APC payments were not discounted.)

$$(22.98 \times \$54.561 \times 0.8192) + (0.78 \times \$54.561 \times 0.8192) + (4.29 \times \$54.561 \times 0.8192)$$

$$\$1,027.12 + \$34.86 + \$191.75 = \$1,253.73$$

Conversion Factor = $54.561
Wage Index = 0.8192

HCPCS Code	Description	APC	APC Weight
66984	Cataract procedure with intraocular lens implant	246	22.98
71020	Chest x-ray	260	0.78
78740	Ureteral reflux study	292	4.29

FIGURE 20-5 Formula for determining OPPS payments

payment reduction applies." (CPT modifier -51 is not added to codes reported for OPPS payment consideration.) This means that the reported CPT and/or HCPCS level II code will be paid a discounted APC reimbursement rate when reported with other procedures on the same claim.

NOTE:

The OPPS does not cover payment of professional services, which are reported on the CMS-1500 claim and reimbursed according to a fee schedule, such as the Medicare Physician Fee Schedule (MPFS). Hospitals report outpatient encounters on the UB-04 (or CMS-1450) claim using ICD-10-CM for diagnoses and CPT and HCPCS level II for procedures and services.

The unit of payment for the OPPS is an outpatient visit or encounter. An **outpatient encounter** (or **outpatient visit**) includes all outpatient procedures and services (e.g., same-day surgery, x-rays, laboratory tests, and so on) provided during one day to the same patient. Thus, a patient who undergoes multiple outpatient procedures and receives multiple services on the same day will be assigned to one or more outpatient groups (called APCs). Each APC is weighted and has a prospective payment amount associated with it; if a patient is assigned multiple APCs, the payments are totaled to provide reimbursement to the hospital for the encounter. (APC payments may be discounted when certain procedures or services are provided, such as bilateral procedures.) A **wage index** adjusts payments to account for geographic variations in hospitals' labor costs.

APC grouper software is used to assign an APC to each CPT and/or HCPCS level II code reported on an outpatient claim, as well as to ICD-10-CM codes as appropriate. Outpatient code editor (OCE) software is used in conjunction with the APC grouper to identify Medicare claims edits and assign APC groups to reported codes.

NOTE:

Add-ons that can increase OPPS payments include pass-through payments that provide additional reimbursement to hospitals that use innovative (new and improved) biologicals, drugs, and technical devices. During committee meetings, health care personnel routinely discuss "pass-through payments" due to new technology, such as innovative medical devices (e.g., using surgical glue instead of stitches) and new drugs and vaccines (e.g., human papillomavirus [HPV] vaccine). Other add-ons include outlier payments for high-cost services, hold harmless payments for certain hospitals, and transitional payments to limit losses under the OPPS. The hospital profits if the payment rate is higher than the cost of care provided, and the hospital loses money if the payment rate is lower than the cost of care provided.

EXAMPLE: OCE software reviews "to/from" dates of service to identify and reject claims that are submitted for reimbursement as hospital-based outpatient care when, in fact, the claim should be processed as inpatient care.

NOTE:

A Medicare patient's coinsurance amount is initially calculated for each APC based on 20 percent of the national median charge for services in the APC. The coinsurance amount for an APC does not change until the amount becomes 20 percent of the total APC payment, and no coinsurance amount can be greater than the hospital inpatient deductible in a given year.

NOTE:

New York State is phasing in ambulatory patient groups (APGs) as a new payment methodology for most Medicaid outpatient services (e.g., outpatient clinic, ambulatory surgery, and emergency department services). Implementation of APGs will result in

- Higher payments for higher intensity services and lower payments for lower intensity services
- The transition of funds from inpatient to outpatient services to support quality outpatient care and to address the problem of avoidable hospitalizations

Inpatient Psychiatric Facility Prospective Payment System (2004)

The **inpatient psychiatric facility prospective payment system (IPF PPS)** was implemented as a result of Medicare, Medicaid, and SCHIP Balanced Budget Refinement Act of 1999 (BBRA) provisions that required implementation of a *per diem* patient classification system that reflects differences in patient resource use and costs. The IPF PPS replaced a reasonable cost-based payment system and affected approximately 2,000 facilities; its purpose is to promote long-term cost control and utilization management. Licensed psychiatric facilities and hospital-based psychiatric units were reimbursed according to the new PPS, which was phased in over a three-year period beginning in 2004.

Health information department coders use ICD-10-CM to assign codes to inpatient behavioral health diagnoses and ICD-10-PCS to assign codes procedures. Coders then enter data into DRG software to calculate the IPF PPS DRG. Inpatient psychiatric facilities are reimbursed according to a *per diem* payment that is calculated using DRG data, wage-adjusted rates, and facility-level adjusters. (IPPS MS-DRGs reimburse acute care hospitals a flat payment based on ICD-10-CM/PCS codes and other data.) Providers use the *Diagnostic and Statistical Manual of Mental Disorders (DSM)*, which is published by the American Psychiatric Association. Although *DSM* codes do not affect IPF PPS rates, the manual contains diagnostic assessment criteria that are used as tools to identify psychiatric disorders. The *DSM* includes psychiatric disorders and codes, provides a mechanism for communicating and recording diagnostic information, and is used in the areas of research and statistics. (Currently, *DSM-5* is in use.)

Inpatient Rehabilitation Facility Prospective Payment System (2002)

The Balanced Budget Act (BBA) of 1997 authorized implementation of the **inpatient rehabilitation facility prospective payment system (IRF PPS)**, which utilizes information from a patient assessment instrument (IRF PAI) to classify patients according to the *patient-driven payment model* (also adopted for SNFs and LTCHs).

The **IRF PPS 1-day payment window** (or **IRF PPS 24-hour rule**) requires that outpatient preadmission services provided by an IRF up to one day prior to a patient's inpatient admission be covered by the IRF PPS payment.

The **IRF PPS transfer rule** is similar to the IPPS transfer rule, except that for the IRF, the rule covers all patient diagnoses. If a patient is transferred from an IRF to another rehabilitation facility, an acute inpatient hospital, a long-term care hospital, or a nursing home that accepts payment under Medicare or Medicaid, the patient's length of stay must be reviewed. A patient who is discharged to home, outpatient therapy, home health, or a day rehabilitation program is not considered a transfer. If a patient remains in the IRF for more than three days—which is the defining length of stay for a short stay carrying its own payment classification, but fewer days than defined by the case-mix group (CMG)—the transfer payment methodology is triggered. The transfer payment methodology reimburses a *per diem*–based payment for the number of days of care in the facility prior to a transfer.

Long-Term (Acute) Care Hospital Prospective Payment System (2001)

The **Balanced Budget Refinement Act of 1999 (BBRA)** mandated implementation of the **long-term (acute) care hospital prospective payment system (LTCH PPS)**, which uses information from long-term acute care hospital patient records to classify patients into distinct **Medicare severity long-term (acute) care diagnosis-related groups (MS-LTC-DRGs)** based on the *patient-driven payment model* (also adopted for SNFs and LTCHs). The LTCH PPS replaced the reasonable cost-based payment system authorized by TEFRA, which mandated DRGs (and exempted long-term acute care hospitals from participation).

The **LTCH PPS 1-day payment window** (or **LTCH PPS 24-hour rule**) requires that outpatient preadmission services provided by a long-term acute care hospital up to one day prior to a patient's inpatient admission be covered by the MS-LTCH-DRG payment.

 NOTE:

Do not confuse the LTCH PPS with the SNF PPS, discussed previously in this chapter. Long-term acute care hospitals are categorized as short-term hospitals, while skilled nursing facilities (SNFs) are considered long-term care facilities (LTCFs) (e.g., nursing facilities). Medicare even certifies long-term acute care hospitals as "short-term acute care hospitals."

Clinical Laboratory Fee Schedule (1985)

The **Deficit Reduction Act of 1984** established the **clinical laboratory fee schedule** as a methodology for determining fees for existing tests, and one year later the **Consolidated Omnibus Budget Reconciliation Act of 1985** established a **national limitation amount (NLA)**, which serves as a payment ceiling or "cap" on the amount Medicare could pay for each test, originally set at 115 percent of the median of all carrier-set rates. It eventually dropped to 74 percent.

Durable Medical Equipment, Prosthetics, Orthotics, and Supplies Fee Schedule (1989)

The **durable medical equipment, prosthetics, orthotics, and supplies (DMEPOS) fee schedule** is a payment methodology mandated by the **Omnibus Budget Reconciliation Act of 1987 (OBRA)**. The fee schedule was implemented in 1989 (except for the surgical dressing fee schedule, which was implemented in 1994; and the parenteral and enteral nutrition [PEN] fee schedule, which was implemented in 2002). The fee schedule is released annually and updated quarterly to implement fee schedule amounts for new codes and to revise any amounts for existing codes that were calculated in error.

Resource-Based Relative Value Scale System (1992)

The **Omnibus Budget Reconciliation Act of 1989** implemented the **resource-based relative value scale (RBRVS) system**, which is used to reimburse physician services covered by Medicare Part B. The RBRVS system replaced the Medicare physician payment system of "customary, prevailing, and reasonable" (CPR) charges under which physicians were reimbursed according to the historical record of the charge for the provision of each service. This system, now called the **Medicare physician fee schedule (MPFS)**, reimburses providers according to predetermined rates assigned to services, and it is revised by CMS each year. All services are standardized to measure the value of a service as compared with other services provided. These standards, called **relative value units (RVUs)**, are payment components consisting of the following:

- *Physician work*, which reflects the physician's time and intensity in providing the service (e.g., judgment, technical skill, and physical effort)
- *Practice expense*, which reflects overhead costs involved in providing a service (e.g., rent, utilities, equipment, and staff salaries)
- *Malpractice expense*, which reflects malpractice expenses (e.g., costs of liability insurance)

 NOTE:

Most third-party payers, including state Medicaid programs, have adopted aspects of the MPFS. Thus, the MPFS contains fees for services not commonly provided to Medicare patients (e.g., obstetrical services).

Payment limits were also established by adjusting the RVUs for each locality by geographic adjustment factors (GAF), called *geographic cost practice indices (GPCIs)*, so that Medicare providers are paid differently in each state and also within each state (e.g., New York State has five separate payment localities). An annual **conversion factor** (dollar multiplier) converts RVUs into payments using a formula (Figure 20-6).

Ambulatory Surgical Centers Payments (1994)

The **Omnibus Budget Reconciliation Act of 1980** mandated that an ambulatory surgery center (ASC) could participate in Medicare if certain conditions were met (e.g., if the ASC was state-licensed) and stated that the **ambulatory surgical centers (ASCs) payment rates** are "expected to be calculated on a prospective basis … utilizing sample survey and similar techniques to establish reasonable estimated overhead allowances for each of the listed procedures which take account of volume (within reasonable limits)." Prior to 2008, procedures included on the ASC list were assigned to one of nine payment groups based on an estimate of the costs incurred by the facility to perform the procedure.

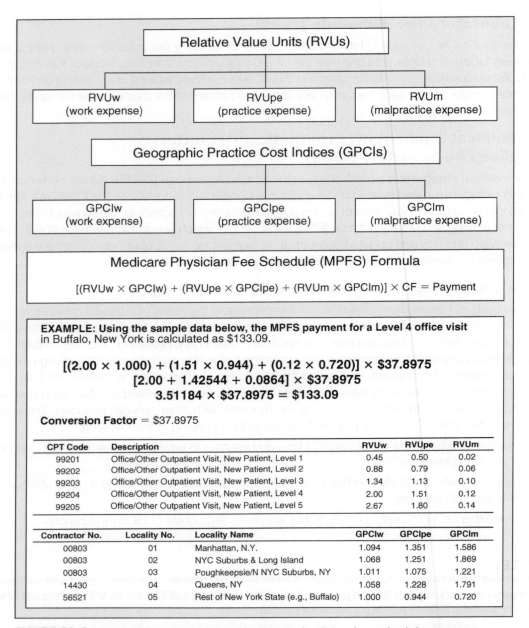

FIGURE 20-6 Formula for determining Medicare physician fee schedule payments

The Medicare Prescription Drug, Improvement, and Modernization Act of 2003 (MMA) mandated implementation of a revised payment system for ASC surgical services by no later than January 1, 2008. Under the revised payment system, implemented January 1, 2008, Medicare will use the ambulatory payment classification (APC) groups and relative payment weights to reimburse ASCs for surgical procedures performed. (The payment weights are multiplied by an ASC conversion factor to calculate ASC payment rates.)

ASC relative payment weights will be updated each year using the national OPPS relative payment weights for that calendar year and, for office-based procedures, the practice expense payments under the physician fee schedule will also be updated for that calendar year. Medicare plans to make the relative payment weights budget neutral to ensure that changes in the relative payment weights from year to year do not cause the estimated amount of expenditures to ASCs to increase or decrease as a function of those changes. Medicare will also maintain and update an "exclusionary list of procedures" for which an ASC facility fee is not paid (because those procedures are included on the OPPS inpatient list).

Ambulance Fee Schedule (2002)

The Balanced Budget Act of 1997 legislated implementation of an **ambulance fee schedule**, which reimburses ambulance service providers a preestablished fee for each service provided. Characteristics of the fee schedule consist of the following:

- Seven categories of ground ambulance services, ranging from basic life support to specialty care transport, and two categories of air ambulance services are established.

- Payment for each category is based on the relative value assigned to the service, adjusted to reflect wage differences in different parts of the country (mileage also will affect payment levels).

- Ambulance providers will not be allowed to charge beneficiaries more than their deductible and 20 percent of Medicare's fee for the service. (Under the old payment system, providers could charge beneficiaries higher rates.)

- The fee schedule allows for increased payments when an ambulance service is provided in rural areas.

End-Stage Renal Disease Composite Payment Rate System (2005)

The **end-stage renal disease (ESRD) composite payment rate system** for dialysis services is based on a case-mix adjusted composite rate. It is a single-payment fixed rate that does not vary according to the characteristics of the beneficiary treated (and includes the cost of some drugs, laboratory tests, and other items and services provided to Medicare beneficiaries receiving dialysis). The Medicare Prescription Drug, Improvement, and Modernization Act (MMA) of 2003 established the ESRD composite payment rate system.

ESRD facilities determine the best payment rate for rendered services. They can maintain their current exception rate or be paid according to the ESRD composite payment rate system, which provides greater payments to facilities that treat more complicated and resource-intensive ESRD patients.

Federally Qualified Health Centers Prospective Payment System (FQHC PPS) (2014)

Federally Qualified Health Centers (FQHCs) are safety net providers that primarily provide services typically furnished in an outpatient clinic (e.g., community health centers). The FQHC PPS for medically necessary primary health services and qualified preventive health services furnished by an FQHC practitioner is the basis for reimbursement. The FQHC PPS base payment rate has been updated annually using the FQHC *market basket*, which replaced the *Medicare Economic Index* as the index for establishing Medicare values for reimbursement.

Case-Mix Analysis, Severity of Illness (SI), and Intensity of Services (IS) Systems

Implementation of Medicare PPS resulted in health care facilities analyzing their **case mix** (patient acuity) to

- Forecast health care trends unique to their individual settings.

- Ensure that they continue to provide appropriate services to their patient populations.

- Recognize that different patients require different resources for care.

EXAMPLE: Upon review of Sunnyvale Hospital's case mix, the greatest number of patients receive cardiovascular services. Wheaton Hospital's case mix indicates that the majority of its patients receive labor and delivery services. Knowing the case mix allows the hospitals to customize services required of their respective patient populations.

In addition, Medicare and other payers are interested in reviewing case-mix data because they recognize that some facilities may serve caseloads that include disproportionate shares of patients with above-average (or below-average) care needs.

Multiple possible payment rates (e.g., RUG categories) based on patients' anticipated care needs allow payment systems to decrease the average difference between the preestablished payment and each patient's actual cost to the facility (called a **case-mix adjustment**). This also results in a reduced risk to facilities and to payers, and facilities are also willing to admit high-resource cases because higher payments can be anticipated. It creates a disincentive for facilities to admit large volumes of low-need, low-cost patients, which will result in lower payments.

Health care facilities use case-mix, intensity of service, and severity of illness software to analyze and measure standards of patient care to assess quality, including the following:

- Acute Physiological and Chronic Health Evaluation (APACHE)
- Atlas Outcomes/MediQual Systems (formerly Medical Illness Severity Grouping System, or MEDISGRPS)
- Comprehensive Severity Index (CSI)
- Patient Management Categories (PMCs)
- Severity of Illness Index (SOII)

Severity of illness (SI) is the physiologic complexity that comprises the extent and interaction of a patient's disease(s) as presented to medical personnel. Severity of illness scores are based on physiologic measures (not just ICD-10-CM codes) of the degree of abnormality of individual signs and symptoms of a patient's disease(s). The more abnormal the signs and symptoms, the higher the score.

 NOTE:

Intensity of services and severity of illness is commonly abbreviated as SI/IS or SIIS.

A health care facility's utilization management (UM) team determines whether a patient's illness is severe enough to require the current or proposed level of care by evaluating the documentation of objective clinical indicators of illness (e.g., sign, symptoms, laboratory findings). In addition, the UM team also determines **intensity of services (IS)**, which involves determining whether provided services are appropriate for the patient's current or proposed level of care (e.g., intravenous medications, heart monitoring, surgical interventions). The ultimate goal is to ensure that patients receive the appropriate level of care. If the patient's severity of illness and/or intensity of services does not meet criteria for the level of care provided, the patient is transferred to the appropriate level of care.

EXAMPLE: A patient is admitted as a hospital inpatient from the facility's emergency department after work up for severe chest pain. Upon initial review of patient record documentation, the patient's laboratory results revealed positive cardiac enzymes, positive electrocardiogram (EKG) suggestive of ischemia, and continued chest pain. Thus, *severity of illness* for inpatient hospitalization was met. Upon further review of the patient record, documentation indicated the patient received intravenous nitroglycerin for chest pain and underwent cardiac catheterization, which revealed two blocked coronary arteries. Patient underwent surgical placement of stents in the blocked arteries. Thus, *intensity of services* for inpatient hospitalization was also met.

Risk management tools that identify the risk of dying include the following:

- Acute Physiological and Chronic Health Evaluation (APACHE)
- Medicare Mortality Predictor System (MMPS)

EXAMPLE: The Health Data Institute created MMPS software to capture data on Medicare patients admitted with stroke, pneumonia, myocardial infarction, and congestive heart failure. The purpose was to predict death within 30 days of hospital admission because these conditions accounted for 13 percent of discharges and 31 percent of 30-day mortality for Medicare patients over age 64 prior to 1988. The MMPS system was "calibrated on a stratified, random sample of 5,888 discharges (about 1,470 for each condition) from seven states, with stratification by hospital type to make the sample nationally representative," and predictors were abstracted from the patient record. The organization determined that "risk-adjusted predicted group mortality rates may be useful in interpreting information on unadjusted mortality rates, and patient-specific predictions may be useful in identifying unexpected deaths for clinical review."

SOURCE: "Predicting hospital-associated mortality for Medicare patients: A method for patients with stroke, pneumonia, acute myocardial infarction, and congestive heart failure," by J. Daley, S. Jencks, D. Draper, G. Lenhart, N. Thomas, and J. Walker, Baxter Healthcare Corp., Health Data Institute, Lexington, Mass. *Journal of the American Medical Association* 260, no. 24 (December 23, 1988).

Physician Documentation for Medical Necessity of Medicare Part A Hospital Inpatient Admissions

In 2014, CMS issued a final rule (CMS-1599-F) called the *2-Midnight Rule*, which modified and clarified the policy about Medicare Administrative Contractor (MAC) review of inpatient hospital and critical access hospital (CAH) admissions for payment purposes. Under the final rule, surgical procedures, diagnostic tests, and other treatments (in addition to services designated as inpatient-only) are generally appropriate for inpatient hospital admission and payment under Medicare Part A when the physician expects the beneficiary to require a stay that crosses at least two midnights and admits the beneficiary to the hospital based upon that expectation. The rule was published as a response to facilities' and beneficiaries' concerns about increasingly long stays as outpatients (e.g., observation care) due to hospital uncertainties about payment.

Physicians are responsible for documenting the medical necessity of an inpatient admission, which CMS calls *physician certification*. Physician documentation includes authentication of the admission order, reason for inpatient services (including the data points physicians use to reach their conclusion that the patient requires inpatient admission), estimated or actual length of time the beneficiary requires inpatient status in the hospital, and plans for posthospital care. In addition, physicians must clearly document any unexpected change in patient status (e.g., improvement) specific to the clinical issues in the case. CMS recommends that such documentation be included in the discharge order.

According to CMS, the regulation specifies that the decision to admit should generally be based on the physician's reasonable expectation of a length of stay spanning two or more midnights, taking into account complex medical factors that must be documented in the medical record. Because this is based upon the physician's expectation, as opposed to a retroactive determination based on actual length of stay, unforeseen circumstances that result in a shorter stay than the physician's reasonable expectation may still result in a hospitalization that is appropriately considered inpatient. As enumerated in the final rule, CMS anticipates that most of these situations will arise in the context of beneficiary death, transfer, or departure against medical advice. However, CMS does recognize that on occasion there may be situations in which the beneficiary improves much more rapidly than the physician's reasonable expectation. Such instances must be clearly documented and the initial expectation of a hospital stay spanning two or more midnights must have been reasonable in order for this circumstance to be an acceptable inpatient admission payable under Part A.

CMS further clarifies that the more usual situation would be the one in which the physician's initial expectation of the beneficiary's length of stay is uncertain. If the physician is uncertain whether the beneficiary will be able to be discharged after one midnight in the hospital or whether the beneficiary will require a second midnight of care, the initial day should be spent in observation until it is clearly expected that a second midnight would be required, at which time the physician may order inpatient admission. If the physician believes that a rare and unusual circumstance exists in which an inpatient admission is warranted, but does not expect the beneficiary to require two or more midnights in the hospital, the physician may admit the beneficiary to inpatient status but should thoroughly document why inpatient admission and Medicare Part A payment is appropriate.

Critical Pathways

Critical pathways are interdisciplinary guidelines developed by hospitals to facilitate management and delivery of quality clinical care in a time of constrained resources. They allow for the planning of provision of clinical services that have expected time frames and resources targeted to specific diagnoses and/or procedures. The targeted clinical services are frequently those that are high in volume and resource use and, therefore, are costly. Critical pathways are usually interdisciplinary in focus, merging medical and nursing plans of care with other disciplines (e.g., physical therapy, nutrition, and mental health). Critical pathways essentially can be viewed as interdisciplinary practice guidelines with predetermined standards of care. They provide opportunities for collaborative practice and team approaches that can maximize the expertise of multiple disciplines.

 NOTE:

Originally, critical pathways began with admission and ended with discharge from the hospital. Now that they are being implemented in other health care settings, there is potential for pathways to be focused more on the full range of an episode of care.

Revenue Cycle Management

Revenue cycle management is the process by which health care facilities and providers ensure their financial viability by increasing revenue, improving cash flow, and enhancing the patient's experience. In a physician practice, revenue cycle management is also called *accounts receivable management*. Hospitals use a chargemaster to record encounter data about ambulatory care provided to patients. The **chargemaster**, or **charge description master (CDM)** (Figure 20-7), is a document that contains a computer-generated list of procedures, services, and supplies, as well as corresponding revenue codes along with charges for each. A **revenue code** is a four-digit UB-04 code that is assigned to each procedure, service, or supply to indicate the location or type of service provided to an institutional patient, such as radiology or laboratory. Physician offices and clinics use an **encounter form**, or **superbill** (Figure 20-8), to record encounter data about office procedures and services provided to patients.

Chargemaster and encounter form data are entered in a patient accounting system, and charges are automatically posted to the insurance claim (UB-04 or CMS-1500, depending on the health care setting). The claim is submitted to the third-party payer to generate payment for services provided (e.g., emergency department, laboratory, physician office, or radiology). Chargemasters and encounter forms allow for accurate and efficient billing of services rendered.

Chargemaster

A chargemaster usually contains the following:

- *Department code*: Refers to the specific ancillary department where the service is performed
- *Service code*: Internal identification of specific service rendered
- *Service description*: Narrative description of the service, procedure, or supply
- *Revenue code*: Four-digit UB-04 code assigned to each procedure, service, or supply that indicates the location or type of service provided to a patient
- *Charge amount*: Dollar amount the facility charges for each procedure, service, or supply
- *Relative value units (RVUs)*: Numeric value assigned to a procedure that is based on difficulty and time consumed

A **chargemaster review process** is routinely conducted by designated hospital personnel (e.g., coding specialists) to ensure accurate reimbursement by updating CPT and HCPCS level II codes and linking each to appropriate UB-04 revenue codes. These designated individuals must have knowledge of proper revenue and

(A)

Revenue Codes and the Chargemaster

> NOTE: Before 2002, revenue codes consisted of only three digits.

Revenue Codes are four-digit codes preprinted on a facility's chargemaster to indicate the location or type of service provided to an institutional patient. (They are also reported in FL 42 of the UB-04.)

EXAMPLE: **REVENUE CODES**

Code	Complete description	Abbreviated description
0270	Medical/surgical supplies	MED-SURG SUPPLIES
0450	Emergency department services	EMER/FACILITY CHARGE
0981	Emergency department physician fee	EMER/PHYSICIAN FEE

The *chargemaster* (or *charge description master, CDM*) is a document that contains a computer-generated list of procedures, services, and supplies with chargees for each. Chargemaster data are entered in the facility's patient accounting system, and charges are automatically posted to the patient's bill (UB-04). The bill is submitted to the payer to generate payment for ancillary and other services (e.g., emergency department, laboratory, radiology, and so on). The chargemaster allows the facility to accurately and efficiently bill for the patient services rendered, and it usually contains the following:

- Department code (refers to the specific ancillary department where the service is performed)
- Service code (internal identification of specific service rendered)
- Service description (narrative description of the service, procedure, or supply)
- Revenue code (UB-04 revenue code that is assigned to each procedure, service, or product)
- Charge amount (dollar amount facility charges for each procedure, service, or supply)
- Relative value units (RVUs) (numeric value assigned to a procedure; based on difficulty and time consumed)

(B)

EXAMPLE: **CHARGEMASTER**

GOODMEDICINE HOSPITAL   Printed on
ANYWHERE US 12345   04/15/YYYY

DEPARTMENT CODE: 01.855

DEPARTMENT: Radiology

SERVICE CODE	SERVICE DESCRIPTION	REVENUE CODE	CPT CODE	CHARGE	RVU
8550001	Chest x-ray, single view	0324	71010	74.50	0.70
8550002	Chest x-ray, two views	0324	71020	82.50	0.95
8500025	Bone scan, limited area	0350	72132	899.50	8.73
8500026	Bone scan, whole body	0350	72133	999.50	11.10

FIGURE 20-7 Revenue codes and chargemaster (A) Explanation of revenue codes (B) Sample portion of hospital chargemaster

expense matching to the Medicare cost center report (e.g., revenue codes) and must be willing to spend the time necessary on an extremely detailed and time-consuming task. Because it results in generation of gross revenue for the health care facility, all who use the chargemaster must be educated about its proper use and its impact on the facility's financial status.

 NOTE:

Chargemasters (and encounter forms) are usually developed using database software that allows for the entry of thousands of items and potential charges. Each item includes an accounting code number, a CPT/HCPCS code number, and a brief narrative description.

Commercial software (e.g., Optum360's www.ChargemasterExpert.com online product) helps health care facilities maintain an accurate and complete chargemaster for billing and compliance purposes. The result is fewer claims denials and more accurate outpatient reimbursement.

ENCOUNTER FORM

Tel: (101) 555-1111	Kim Donaldson, M.D.	EIN: 11-9876543
Fax: (101) 555-2222	INTERNAL MEDICINE	NPI: 1234567890
	101 Main Street, Suite A	
	Alfred, NY 14802	

OFFICE VISITS	NEW	EST	OFFICE PROCEDURES		INJECTIONS	
☐ Level I	99201	99211	☐ EKG with interpretation	93000	☐ Influenza virus vaccine	___
☐ Level II	99202	99212	☐ Oximetry with interpretation	94760	☐ Admin of Influenza vaccine	G0008
☐ Level III	99203	99213	**LABORATORY TESTS**		☐ Pneumococcal vaccine	90732
☐ Level IV	99204	99214	☐ Blood, occult (feces)	82270	☐ Admin of pneumococcal vaccine	G0009
☐ Level V	99205	99215	☐ Skin test, Tb, intradermal (PPD)	86580	☐ Hepatitis B vaccine	90746
					☐ Admin of Hepatitis B vaccine	G0010
					☐ Tetanus and diptheria toxoids vaccine	90714
					☐ Immunization administration	90471

DIAGNOSIS

☐ Abnormal heart sounds	R00.9	☐ Chronic ischemic heart disease	I25.9	☐ Hypertension	I10
☐ Abdominal pain	R10.8__	☐ Chronic obstructive lung disease	J44.9	☐ Hormone replacement	Z79.890
☐ Abnormal feces	R19.5	☐ Congestive heart failure	I50.9	☐ Hyperlipidemia	E78.5
☐ Allergic rhinitis	J30.9	☐ Cough	R05	☐ Hyperthyroidism	E05.9__
☐ Anemia, pernicious	D51.0	☐ Depressive disorder	F32.9	☐ Influenza	J11.1
☐ Anxiety	F41.9	☐ Diabetes mellitus, type 2	E11.____	☐ Loss of weight	R63.4
☐ Asthma	J45.909	☐ Diarrhea	R19.7	☐ Nausea	R11.0
☐ Atrophy, cerebral	G31.9	☐ Dizziness	R42	☐ Nausea with vomiting	R11.2
☐ B-12 deficiency	D51.9	☐ Emphysema	J43.__	☐ Pneumonia	J18.__
☐ Back pain	M54.9	☐ Fatigue	R53.83	☐ Sore throat	J02.9
☐ Bronchitis	J40	☐ Fever	R50.9	☐ Vaccine, hepatitis B	Z23
☐ Cardiovascular disease	I25.1__	☐ Gastritis	K29.50	☐ Vaccine, influenza	Z23
☐ Cervicalgia	M54.2	☐ Heartburn	R12	☐ Vaccine, pneumococcus	Z23
☐ Chest pain	R07.9	☐ Hematuria	R31.9	☐ Vaccine, tetanus toxoid	Z23
☐	___	☐	___	☐	___

PATIENT IDENTIFICATION		FINANCIAL TRANSACTION DATA	
PATIENT NAME:		INVOICE NO.	
PATIENT NUMBER:		ACCOUNT NO.	
DATE OF BIRTH:		TOTAL FOR SERVICE:	$
ENCOUNTER DATE		AMOUNT RECEIVED:	$
DATE OF SERVICE:	/ /	PAID BY:	☐ Cash
RETURN VISIT DATE			☐ Check
DATE OF RETURN VISIT:	/ /	CASHIER'S INITIALS:	☐ Credit Card

FIGURE 20-8 Sample encounter form (superbill)

Encounter Form

Encounter form data are entered in the office's practice management software to generate the CMS-1500 claim that is submitted to the payer. (Many physician offices still complete paper-based CMS-1500 claims, which are submitted to health care clearinghouses to be converted to a standardized format. The health care clearinghouse submits the standardized claims data to the payer, where they are processed to generate physician reimbursement.) Similar to the chargemaster review process, the encounter form should be assigned to one individual in the physician's office who will take responsibility for reviewing and updating it twice a year when codes (e.g., ICD-10-CM, ICD-10-PCS, CPT, and HCPCS level II codes) are added, deleted, and revised. (This process used to be conducted just once each year until 2004, when federal regulations required that code changes be issued twice each year.)

 NOTE:

Hospitals submit UB-04 claims to payers for inpatient and ambulatory care encounters, and physicians submit CMS-1500 claims for office encounters. Most health care settings participate in electronic data interchange (EDI) with third-party payers and health care clearinghouses.

Revenue Cycle Management

Revenue cycle management includes the following features, typically in this order:

- *Physician order* for inpatient admission or outpatient services is documented by responsible physician.

- *Patient registration*: Patient is admitted as an inpatient or scheduled for outpatient services.

  - Appropriate consents for treatment and release of information are obtained.
  - Patient demographic and insurance information is collected.
  - Patient's insurance coverage is validated and utilization management is performed (e.g., clinical reviews) to determine medical necessity.
  - Preadmission clearance (e.g., precertification, pre-authorization, screening for medical necessity).

- *Charge capture (or data capture)*: Providers use chargemasters or encounter forms to select procedures or services provided (ancillary departments, such as the laboratory, use automated systems that link to the chargemaster).

- *Diagnosis and procedure coding*: Assignment of appropriate ICD-10-CM, ICD-10-PCS, and/or CPT/HCPCS codes, typically performed by health information management personnel, to assign APCs, DRGs, and so on.

- *Patient discharge processing*: Patient information is verified, discharge instructions are provided, patient follow-up visit is scheduled, consent forms are reviewed for signatures, and patient policies are explained to the patient.

- *Billing and claims processing*: All patient information and codes are input into the billing system, and

CMS-1500 or UB-04 claims are generated and submitted to third-party payers.

- *Resubmitting claims*: Before reimbursement is received from third-party payers, late charges, lost charges, or corrections to previously processed CMS-1500 or UB-04 claims are entered, and claims are resubmitted to payers—this may result in payment delays and claims denials.

- *Third-party payer reimbursement posting*: Payment from third-party payers is posted to appropriate accounts, and rejected claims are resubmitted with appropriate documentation; this process includes electronic remittance, which involves receiving reimbursement from third-party payers electronically.

- *Appeals process*: Analysis of reimbursement received from third-party payers identifies variations in expected payments or contracted rates and may result in submission of appeal letters to payers.

- *Patient billing*: Self-pay balances are billed to the patient; these include deductibles, copayments, and non-covered charges.

- *Self-pay reimbursement posting*: Self-pay balances received from patients are posted to appropriate accounts.

- *Collections*: Payments not received from patients in a timely manner result in collections letters being mailed to patients until payment is received; if payment is still not received, the account is turned over to an outside collections agency.

- *Collections reimbursement posting*: Payments received from patients are posted to appropriate accounts.

(continues)

Revenue Cycle Management (*continued*)

- *Auditing process*:
  - *Compliance monitoring*: Level of compliance with established managed care contracts is monitored; provider performance per managed care contractual requirements is monitored; compliance risk is monitored.

  - *Denials management*: Claims denials are analyzed to prevent future denials; rejected

claims are resubmitted with appropriate documentation.

  - *Tracking of resubmitted claims and appeals for denied claims*: Resubmitted claims and appealed claims are tracked to ensure payment by payers.

  - *Posting lost charges and late charges*: Late claims are submitted.

Permission to reprint granted by MedAssets.

Exercise 20.2 – Health Care Reimbursement Systems

Completion: Complete each statement.

1. A payer reimburses a provider 80 percent of charges submitted, and the patient is responsible for paying the remaining 20 percent coinsurance amount. Mary Allen underwent an office procedure, for which the physician billed her payer $1,500. The payer reimburses the provider the amount of $1200, and the patient reimburses the provider the amount of $ _____.

2. Two patients each undergo a four-day inpatient stay at an acute care hospital for treatment of a myocardial infarction (heart attack). The patient who has Aetna commercial insurance company can expect the hospital to be reimbursed at 80 percent of the *per diem* basis. The Medicare patient can expect the Medicare administrative contractor (MAC) to reimburse the hospital on a prospective payment basis. Daily charges incurred for the four-day stay were $1,400 per day; the DRG prospective payment rate for a myocardial infarction is $4,500. Aetna will reimburse the hospital $4480. The MAC will reimburse the hospital $ _____.

(continues)

Exercise 20.2 – *continued*

3. Designated hospital personnel routinely conduct the _____ review process to ensure accurate reimbursement by updating CPT and HCPCS codes and linking each to appropriate UB-04 revenue codes.

4. The federal legislation that resulted in the implementation of the _____ hospital PPS is called TEFRA.

5. The outpatient hospital PPS establishes a payment rate for outpatient care by using APCs, which is the abbreviation for _____, to organize similar health care services clinically and according to resources required.

Matching: Match the payment system with the type of prospective rate. Answers may be used more than once.

_____ 6. Ambulance fee schedule	a. Cost-based
_____ 7. Ambulatory surgical center rates	b. Price-based
_____ 8. Home health prospective payment system	
_____ 9. Long-term (acute) care hospital prospective payment system	
_____ 10. Resource-based relative value scale system	

Matching: Match the present on admission (POA) indicator with each case scenario. Answers may be used more than once.

a. Y = Yes (diagnosis present at the time of inpatient admission)

b. N = No (diagnosis was not present at the time of inpatient admission)

c. U = Unknown (documentation is insufficient to determine if the condition was present at the time of inpatient admission)

d. W = Clinically undetermined (provider is unable to clinically determine whether the condition was present at the time of inpatient admission)

e. Blank = Unreported/not used (exempt from POA reporting) (the field is blank for factors that do not represent a current disease or for a condition that is always present on admission)

_____ 11. A patient is admitted to the hospital for open cholecystectomy due to acute cholecystitis with cholelithiasis. After 24 hours of intravenous antibiotic therapy, the surgery is successfully performed. What is the POA indicator for the acute cholecystitis with cholelithiasis?

_____ 12. A patient was admitted for inpatient hospitalization due to weakness and unsteady gait, and a diagnosis of cerebrovascular accident was established. What is the POA indicator for the cerebrovascular accident?

_____ 13. A hospital inpatient falls out of bed on day 2 of his stay and fractures his left hip. What is the POA indicator for the left hip fracture?

_____ 14. An 84-year-old patient is admitted for inpatient hospitalization due to fever with a temperature of 104 degrees, severe weakness, dehydration, and productive cough. The diagnosis is established as viral pneumonia. During admission, her condition rapidly deteriorates and she is admitted to the intensive care unit. The physician documents severe sepsis as a secondary diagnosis. When queried as to whether the sepsis was present on admission, the physician replies by stating that the patient went downhill so fast that he does not know if the sepsis was present on admission. What is the POA indicator for the severe sepsis?

_____ 15. Twin liveborn infants are delivered via cesarean section in the hospital. The physician documents that Twin A has neonatal bradycardia. What is the POA indicator for Twin A's neonatal bradycardia?

Impact of HIPAA on Reimbursement

The Health Insurance Portability and Accountability Act of 1996 (HIPAA) amended the Internal Revenue Code of 1986 to improve portability and continuity of health insurance coverage in the group and individual markets; to combat waste, fraud, and abuse in health insurance and health care delivery; to promote the use of medical savings accounts; to improve access to long-term care services and coverage; to simplify the administration of health insurance by creating unique identifiers for providers, health plans, employers, and individuals; to create standards for electronic health information transactions; and to create privacy and security standards for health information.

 NOTE:

> The Federal False Claims Act provides CMS with regulatory authority to enforce fraud and abuse statutes for the Medicare program, and HIPAA extends that authority to all federal and state health care programs.

HIPAA legislation is organized according to five titles.

- Title I—Health Care Access, Portability, and Renewability
- Title II—Preventing Health Care Fraud and Abuse, Administrative Simplification, and Medical Liability Reform
- Title III—Tax-Related Health Provisions
- Title IV—Application and Enforcement of Group Health Plan Requirements
- Title V—Revenue Offsets

Health Care Access, Portability, and Renewability

HIPAA provisions were designed to improve the portability and continuity of health coverage by limiting exclusions for **pre-existing medical conditions**, which are illnesses or injuries that required treatment during a prescribed period of time (e.g., six months) prior to the insured's effective date of coverage under a new insurance policy. HIPAA provisions require that individuals be granted credit for prior health coverage and that a process be implemented to transmit certificates and other information concerning prior coverage to a new group health plan or issuer. Individuals will also be allowed to enroll in health coverage when they lose other health coverage, change from group to individual coverage, or gain a new dependent. HIPAA prohibits discrimination practices associated with health coverage enrollment eligibility and the establishment of premiums (for employees and their dependents) based on health status. The availability of health insurance coverage is also guaranteed to employees of small companies, and both small and large group markets are guaranteed renewability of health insurance coverage. HIPAA preserves the traditional role of individual states in regulating health insurance, and states are provided with flexibility to require greater protection.

 NOTE:

> This section will cover health care access, portability and renewability, prevention of health care fraud and abuse, administrative simplification, and medical liability reform issues.

Preventing Health Care Fraud and Abuse

HIPAA defines **fraud** as "an intentional deception or misrepresentation that someone makes, knowing it is false, that could result in an unauthorized payment." The attempt itself is considered fraud, regardless of whether it is successful. Fraud is an act that represents a crime against payers or other health care programs (e.g., Medicare), or attempts or conspires to commit those crimes. **Abuse** "involves actions that are inconsistent with accepted, sound, medical, business, or fiscal practices." Abuse includes actions that result in unnecessary costs to payers and government programs (e.g., Medicare), reimbursement for services not medically necessary, or that fails to meet professionally recognized standards for health care services. The difference between fraud and abuse is the individual's intent; however, both have the same impact in that they steal valuable resources from the health care industry.

Examples of fraud include the following:

- Billing Medicare for services or supplies not provided
- Entering another person's Medicare number on a claim to obtain reimbursement for a patient not eligible for Medicare
- Unbundling codes reported on claims (reporting multiple codes to increase reimbursement, when a single combination code should be reported)
- Upcoding claims submitted to payers (reporting codes not supported by documentation in the patient record to increase reimbursement)
- Misrepresenting the diagnosis to justify payment
- Soliciting, offering, or receiving a kickback
- Falsifying certificates of medical necessity, plans of treatment, and medical records to justify payment.

 NOTE:

According to the Department of Health & Human Services, Office of Inspector General, providers are not subject to criminal, civil, or administrative penalties for innocent or negligent errors. The False Claims Act covers offenses committed with actual knowledge of the falsity of the claim, reckless disregard, or deliberate ignorance of the falsity of the claim. The False Claims Act does not cover mistakes, errors, or negligence. The Civil Monetary Penalties Law is an administrative remedy that is similar in scope and effect to the False Claims Act, and it also has exactly the same standard of proof.

EXAMPLE: The medical review of claims submitted to Medicare by a physician group practice that contains mental health providers identified a pattern of psychiatric services billed on behalf of nursing facility patients with a medical history of dementia. Review of patient record documentation at the nursing facility revealed no mental health care physician orders or plans of treatment. This is considered billing for services not furnished, and it is an example of fraud.

Examples of abuse include the following:

- Billing a Medicare patient using a higher fee schedule rate than used for non-Medicare patients
- Submitting claims to Medicare when Medicare is not the beneficiary's primary payer
- Submitting excessive charges for services or supplies
- Submitting claims for services that are not medically necessary
- Violating Medicare's participating provider agreements with payers
- Improper billing practices that result in payment by a government program when the claim is the legal responsibility of another payer.

 NOTE:

Medical necessity requires the documentation of services or supplies that are proper and are needed for the diagnosis or treatment of a medical condition; are provided for the diagnosis, direct care, and treatment of a medical condition; meet the standards of good medical practice in the local area; and are not mainly for the convenience of the physician.

EXAMPLE: During her first 30 days on the job, Sally Adams mistakenly submitted CMS-1500 claims to Medicare instead of the patients' workers' compensation payers. When she noticed the error, she informed her supervisor, who immediately contacted the Medicare administrative contractors to cancel processing of the submitted claims. Sally then correctly submitted the CMS-1500 claims to the workers' compensation payers. This is considered submitting claims to Medicare when Medicare is not the beneficiary's primary payer, and it is an example of abuse if not corrected.

DRG Creep

Health Care Fraud and Abuse: Diagnosis Related Group (DRG) Creep, by W. McKay Henderson, Partner, Price Waterhouse Coopers, Health Care Fraud and Abuse Practice. (Permission to reuse granted by W. McKay Henderson, Price Waterhouse, Inc.)

What is it? **DRG creep** focuses on the medical necessity and billing patterns of DRG coding to determine whether the claims that hospitals submit accurately reflect the care required or given to the patient. The intent is to prevent hospitals from maximizing Medicare reimbursements by choosing diagnosis codes that result in higher payments.

What separates a simple miscoding error from a false claim? The Office of Inspector General (OIG) contends that fraudulent upcoding maximized reimbursement revenue by hiring consultants or investing in sophisticated computer packages to help increase

their reimbursements. And the DOJ and OIG put a stop to it. (*To maximize revenue* means to fraudulently increase reimbursement from payers to providers, such as reporting codes not supported by documentation that increase the DRG payment rate.)

How does upcoding happen? It is speculated that the government believes the upcoding trend is due to either computer software packages that assign the link between ICD-10-CM/PCS codes and DRGs, and/ or to consultants who have trained the hospital staff who assign DRG codes. As part of its investigation, the DOJ requested hospitals to provide not only medical records and hospital documentation but also audit results, analyses of computer programs, and all consultants' reports. Those hospitals and medical centers that voluntarily disclose overpayments related to DRG miscoding may receive a reduction in fines and penalties levied against them.

Deterring Fraud and Abuse

CMS employs a four-part strategy to deter fraud and abuse, which focuses on prevention, early detection, coordination, and enforcement.

- Prevention involves paying the claim correctly the first time, and it is the most desirable approach. It is also the best way to guarantee initial accuracy of claims and payments, and it avoids the requirement to "pay and chase" providers, which is a lengthy, uncertain, and expensive process.

- Early detection identifies patterns of fraudulent activity by using data to monitor unusual billing patterns and other indicators of the integrity and financial status of providers, promptly identifying and collecting overpayments, and making appropriate referrals to law enforcement. If CMS finds errors, repayment is pursued and further action may be warranted depending on the facts and circumstances of each case.

- Coordination with partners is another important way by which CMS maximizes its success in preventing fraud; information and tactics for fighting fraud and abuse are shared with individual states, the DOJ, and the private sector.

- When fraudulent providers are discovered, enforcement action is taken against them (e.g., suspension of payment, referral to OIG for potential exclusion from Medicare program, disenrollment, collection of overpayments, and imposition of civil monetary penalties). Investing in prevention, early detection, and enforcement has a proven record of returns to the Medicare Trust Fund; the Medicare Integrity Program originally saved an estimated $7.5 billion in fiscal year 1997, mostly by preventing inappropriate payments through audits, medical reviews, and ensuring that Medicare does not pay for claims owed by private insurers. The Correct Coding Initiative (CCI) was implemented to reduce Medicare program expenditures by detecting inappropriate coding on claims and denying payment for them.

The Health Insurance Association of America (HIAA) conducts surveys that report statistics about the following health care fraud activities:

- Billing patients for services already paid for and accepting kickbacks for patient referrals
- Committing mail or wire fraud

- Falsifying patient's diagnosis to justify tests, surgeries, or other procedures
- Misrepresenting noncovered treatments as medically necessary covered treatments for the purpose of obtaining higher insurance payments
- Performing medically unnecessary services
- Performing procedures for the sole purpose of producing insurance payments
- Sales of durable medical equipment that is not needed or unnecessary

Regulating Fraudulent Practices

When a Medicare provider commits fraud, an investigation is conducted by the Department of Health & Human Services (DHHS). The Office of Inspector General (OIG) prepares the case for referral to the DOJ for criminal and/or civil prosecution. A person found guilty of Medicare fraud faces criminal, civil, and/or administrative sanction penalties, including the following:

- Civil penalties ranging from $5,000 to $10,000 per false claim *plus* triple damages
- Criminal fines and/or imprisonment for up to 10 years if convicted of health care fraud or, for violations of the Medicare/Medicaid Anti-kickback Statute, imprisonment of up to five years and/or a criminal fine of up to $25,000
- Administrative sanctions, which include up to a $10,000 civil monetary penalty per line item on a false claim, assessments of up to triple the amount falsely claimed, and/or exclusion from participation in Medicare and state health care programs.

In addition to these penalties, those who commit health care fraud can be tried for mail and wire fraud.

Medicare fraudulent practices are regulated by the following:

- Civil Monetary Penalties Act
- Compliance guidelines
- Federal Claims Collection Act of 1966
- Health Insurance Portability and Accountability Act (HIPAA)
- Correct Coding Initiative (CCI)

- False Claims Act (FCA)
- Federal Anti-kickback Statute
- Physician self-referral laws (Stark I and Stark II)
- Physicians at Teaching Hospitals (PATH) initiative
- Payment Error and Prevention Program (PEPP)

The **Civil Monetary Penalties Act** imposes a maximum penalty of up to $10,000 plus a maximum assessment of up to three times the amount claimed by providers who knew that a procedure/service was not rendered as submitted on the claim. Violators can also be excluded from participation in government programs (e.g., Medicaid or Medicare).

 NOTE:

By law, providers are not subject to civil, criminal, or administrative sanction penalties for innocent errors, or even for negligence.

EXAMPLE: A provider bills Medicare for services provided to a patient that are not documented in the patient record. The charges submitted on the claim total $95. If found guilty of fraud, the provider would be required to pay a fine in the amount of $10,285.

The DHHS Office of the Inspector General (OIG) developed a series of provider-specific **compliance guidances**, which identify risk areas and offer concrete suggestions to improve and enhance an organization's internal controls so that billing practices and other business arrangements are in compliance with Medicare's rules and regulations. Voluntary compliance guidelines have been established for the following:

- Ambulance industry
- Ambulance suppliers
- Clinical laboratories

- Durable medical equipment, prosthetics, orthotics, and supply industry
- Home health agencies

- Hospices
- Hospital industry
- Hospitals
- Individual and small-group physician practices

- Nursing facilities
- Medicare Advantage organizations
- Pharmaceutical manufacturers
- Third-party medical billing companies

A voluntary compliance program helps providers avoid generating erroneous and fraudulent claims by ensuring that submitted claims are true and accurate, expediting and optimizing proper payment of claims, minimizing billing mistakes, and preventing conflicts with self-referral and anti-kickback statutes.

EXAMPLE: If a coder determines that a physician's documentation is unclear or conflicting, the coder should ask the physician for clarification. In some facilities, the policy is to have the coder contact the physician directly. In others, the coder completes a preprinted form, entering pertinent information about the need for clarification, and this form is forwarded to the physician.

The National Correct Coding Initiative (NCCI) was developed by CMS to promote national correct coding methodologies, eliminate improper coding, and reduce Medicare program expenditures by detecting inappropriate codes on claims and denying payment for them. The principles for the CCI are to ensure that the service

- Represents the standard of care in accomplishing the overall procedure
- Is necessary to successfully accomplish the comprehensive procedure (and that failure to perform the service may compromise the success of the procedure)
- Does not represent a separately identifiable procedure unrelated to the comprehensive procedure planned

(The HCPCS level II and CPT coding systems are used by physicians and others to describe services rendered.) CCI edits are based on HCPCS level II and CPT coding principles along with current standards of medical and surgical coding practice, input from specialty societies, and analysis of current coding practice. Table 20-4 contains a list of CCI terms, definitions, and examples.

The federal **False Claims Act (FCA)** was enacted in 1863 in response to widespread abuses by government contractors during the Civil War, and it was amended in 1986 to strengthen the law and increase monetary awards (e.g., up to $10,000 per false claim, plus three times the amount of damages that the government sustains). It imposes civil liability on those who submit false/fraudulent claims to the government for payment and can exclude violators from participation in government programs (e.g., Medicaid and Medicare).

 NOTE:

Qui tam provisions of the FCA encourage and reward private individuals (sometimes called *whistle-blowers*) who are aware of fraud being committed against the government to report that information. In addition, the FCA only covers offenses that are committed with actual knowledge of the falsity of the claim, or reckless disregard or deliberate ignorance of the truth or falsity of a claim. The FSA does not penalize mistakes, errors, or negligence. The OIG has stated that it is mindful of the difference between innocent errors (e.g., erroneous claims) and reckless or intentional conduct (e.g., fraudulent claims).

The **Federal Anti-kickback Statute** prohibits the offer, payment, receipt, or solicitation of compensation for referring Medicaid/Medicare patients and imposes a $25,000 fine per violation, plus imprisonment for up to 10 years. Civil penalties may also be imposed, and violators can be excluded from participation in government programs (e.g., Medicaid and Medicare). **Safe harbor regulations** were also implemented, which specify various payment and business practices that, although potentially capable of inducing referrals of business reimbursable under federal health care programs, would not be treated as criminal offenses under the Anti-kickback Statute.

TABLE 20-4 National Correct Coding Initiative (NCCI) Terms and Definitions

Term	Definition	Example	
CCI Edits	Pairs of HCPCS level II and/or CPT codes, which are not separately payable except under certain circumstances (e.g., reporting appropriate modifier). The edits are applied to services billed by the same provider for the same beneficiary on the same date of service.	A surgeon intends to perform laparoscopic cholecystectomy; upon visualization of the gallbladder, it is determined that an open cholecystectomy is required. If the surgeon reports CPT codes for removal of an organ through an open incision, as well as with laparoscopy, the CCI edit results in claims denial.	NOTE: If a laparoscopic procedure becomes an open procedure, report only the open procedure code.
Comprehensive Code	The major procedure or service when reported with another code. The comprehensive code represents greater work, effort, and time as compared to the other code reported (also called *Column 1* codes). Higher payments are associated with comprehensive codes.	A patient undergoes deep biopsy as well as superficial biopsy of the same site. If the surgeon reports CPT codes for the deep and superficial biopsies, the CCI edit results in claims denial.	NOTE: Report only the deep biopsy when both deep and superficial biopsies are performed at the same location.
Component Code	The lesser procedure or service when reported with another code. The component code is part of a major procedure or service and is often represented by a lower work relative value unit (RVU) under the Medicare Physician Fee Schedule as compared to the other code reported (also called *Column 2* codes). Lower payments are associated with component codes.	If the surgeon determines that the superficial biopsy code should be reported in addition to the deep biopsy code, supporting documentation in the patient's record must be evident.	NOTE: To have component code(s) considered for possible reimbursement, attach a modifier to the code(s). A modifier is a two-digit code added to a code to indicate a procedure or service has been altered (e.g., bilateral procedure).
Column1/ Column 2 Edit Table	Code combinations (or edit pairs), where comprehensive code and only the comprehensive code is paid. (If clinical circumstances justify appending a CCI-associated modifier to either code of a code pair edit, payment of both codes may be allowed.)	Figure 20-9 contains a partial listing of the table of Column 1/Column 2 codes. Refer to Column 1, code 10121. If code 10121 is reported on a CMS-1500 claim, none of the codes from Column 2 can be reported on the same claim (unless a modifier is attached and supporting documentation is found in the patient's record).	NOTE: Column 2 codes are components of Column 1 codes, which means a Column 1 code includes all procedures/ services described by Column 2 codes. Thus, Column 2 codes cannot be reported with Column 1 codes because overpayments would result.
Mutually Exclusive Codes	Procedures or services that could not reasonably be performed at the same session by the same provider on the same beneficiary.	A claim that contains codes for cystourethroscopy, with internal urethrotomy of a female (CPT code 52270) with that of a male (CPT code 52275) will result in denial as a result of this CCI edit.	NOTE: To have mutually exclusive code(s) considered for possible reimbursement, attach a modifier to the code(s).
Mutually Exclusive Edit Table	Code combinations (or edit pairs), where one of the procedures/ services would not reasonably be performed with the other. (If clinical circumstances justify adding a CCI modifier to either code of a code pair edit, payment of both codes may be allowed.)	Figure 20-10 contains a partial listing of the table of mutually exclusive codes. Refer to Column 1, code 10060. If code 10060 is reported on a CMS-1500 claim, none of the codes from Column 2 can be reported on the same claim (unless a modifier is attached and supporting documentation is found in the patient's record).	NOTE: When mutually exclusive codes are reported on the same claim (for the same date of service), reimbursement is based on the lower-paying code.

NATIONAL CORRECT CODING INITIATIVE COLUMN 1/COLUMN 2 EDITS					
Column 1	Column 2	* = In existence prior to 1996	Effective Date	Deletion Date * = no data	Modifier 0 = not allowed 1 = allowed 9 = not applicable
10021	J2001		20040701	*	1
10021	36000		20021001	*	1
10021	64415		20021001	*	1
10021	64416		20030101	*	1
10021	64417		20021001	*	1

FIGURE 20-9 Sample of NCCI Column 1/Column 2 edits

NATIONAL CORRECT CODING INITIATIVE MUTUALLY EXCLUSIVE EDITS					
Column 1	Column 2	* = In existence prior to 1996	Effective Date	Deletion Date * = no data	Modifier 0 = not allowed 1 = allowed 9 = not applicable
10060	11401		19960101	*	1
10060	11402		19960101	*	1
10060	11403		19960101	*	1
10060	11404		19960101	*	1
10060	11406		19960101	*	1

FIGURE 20-10 Sample of NCCI mutually exclusive edits

EXAMPLE: The DHHS implemented a safe harbor for the waiver or reduction of coinsurance or deductible amounts (cost-sharing amounts) for inpatient hospital services reimbursed under the PPS. For full or partial waivers to be protected, three standards had to be met: (1) the hospital could not claim waived amounts as bad debt or otherwise shift the cost of the waivers; (2) the hospital could not discriminate in offering waivers or reductions based on the patient's reason for admission; and (3) the waivers or reductions could not result from an agreement between the hospital and a third-party payer. The DHHS concluded that waivers of cost-sharing amounts for inpatient hospital services that complied with these standards would not increase costs to the Medicare program, shift costs to other payers, or increase patient demand for inpatient hospital services.

Subtitle A of the Health Insurance Portability and Accountability Act of 1997 (HIPAA) authorized implementation of a fraud and abuse control program, which coordinates federal, state, and local law enforcement programs to control fraud and abuse with respect to health plans; conducts investigations, audits, evaluations, and inspections relating to delivery of and payment for health care in the United States; facilitates enforcement of health care fraud and abuse provisions; provides for modification and establishment of safe harbors; and issues advisory opinions and special fraud alerts to provide for reporting and disclosure of certain final adverse actions against health care providers, suppliers, or practitioners.

The **Federal Claims Collection Act of 1966** established uniform procedures for government agencies to follow in the collection, compromise, suspension, termination, or referral for litigation of debts owed to the government. This means that MACs (as agents of the federal government) are responsible for attempting to collect **overpayments,** which are funds that a provider or beneficiary receives in excess of amounts due and payable under Medicare and Medicare statutes and regulations. Any review conducted by the MAC for overpayment recovery must be done within three calendar years after the year in which the overpayment was made. Once a determination of overpayment has been made, the amount so determined is a debt owed to the U.S. government.

NOTE:

The Act does not apply where there is an indication of fraud, for which such cases are submitted to the OIG for review and referral to the DOJ.

Examples of overpayments include the following:

- Payment based on a charge that exceeds the reasonable charge

- Duplicate processing of charges and/or claims

- Payment made to the wrong payee (e.g., payment made to a provider on a nonassigned claim, or payment made to a beneficiary on an assigned claim)

- Payment for noncovered items and services, including medically unnecessary services

- Incorrect application of the deductible, coinsurance, or copayment

- Payment for items or services rendered during a period of nonentitlement

- Primary payment for items or services for which another entity is the primary payer

- Payment for items or services rendered after the beneficiary's date of death (postpayment reviews are conducted to identify and recover payments with a billed date of service that is after the beneficiary's date of death)

Once a Medicare administrative contractor determines that an overpayment was made, it proceeds with recovery by issuing an overpayment demand letter (Figure 20-11) to the provider. The letter contains information about the review and statistical sampling methodology used, as well as corrective actions to be taken. Corrective actions include payment suspension, imposition of civil monetary penalties, institution of prepayment or postpayment review, and additional edits.

NOTE:

A provider is not liable for overpayments received if found to be without fault as determined by the MAC, such as when reasonable care was exercised in billing and accepting payment and the provider had a reasonable basis for assuming that payment was correct. In addition, if the provider had a reason to question the payment and promptly brought the question to the attention of the MAC, the provider may be found without liability.

The **Payment Error and Prevention Program (PEPP)** identifies and reduces improper Medicare payments, resulting in a reduction in the Medicare payment error rate. It also participates in **overpayment recovery** by collecting overpayments made by Medicare, Medicaid, and other payers.

A **physician self-referral law**, **Stark I**, enacted as part of the Omnibus Budget Reconciliation Act of 1989, prohibits a physician from referring Medicare patients to clinical laboratory services where they or a member of their family have a financial interest. (The financial interest includes both ownership/investment interests and compensation arrangements.) By 1994, because some providers routinely waived coinsurance and copayments, the DHHSOIG issued the following fraud alert:

Routine waiver of deductibles and copayments by charge-based providers, practitioners or suppliers is unlawful because it results in (1) false claims, (2) violations of the anti-kickback statute, and (3) excessive utilization of items and services paid for by Medicare.

(The only exception to the alert is waiving deductibles and copayments for financial hardship cases, but this *cannot be done on a routine* basis.)

```
┌─────────────────────────────────────────────────────────────────┐
│                  EMPIRE MEDICARE ADMINISTRATIVE CONTRACTOR         │
│                P.O. Box 1000 • Albany, NY 12246 • (800) 555-1234   │
│  ───────────────────────────────────────────────────────────────  │
│                                                                     │
│   June 15, YYYY                                                     │
│                                                                     │
│                                                                     │
│   Patient Billing Department                                        │
│   Alfred State Medical Center                                       │
│   100 Main Street                                                   │
│   Alfred NY 14802                                                   │
│                                                                     │
│   RE:    PATIENT:          Mary Sue Patient                         │
│          SSN:              123-45-6789                              │
│          CLAIM #:          987654321                                │
│          DATE OF SERVICE:  April 5, YYYY                            │
│                                                                     │
│   Dear Provider,                                                    │
│                                                                     │
│   Please be advised that an overpayment of benefits has been made   │
│   for the above named patient. In order to resolve this matter, we  │
│   are asking you to make repayment. Please make your check payable  │
│   to:                                                               │
│                                                                     │
│   EMPIRE MEDICARE ADMINISTRATIVE CONTRACTOR                         │
│   in the amount of:                                                 │
│                                                                     │
│   $995.00                                                           │
│                                                                     │
│   and forward it to:                                                │
│                                                                     │
│   EMPIRE MAC                                                        │
│   P.O. Box 1000                                                     │
│   Albany, NY 12246                                                  │
│                                                                     │
│   We are requesting this refund due to the following reason:        │
│                                                                     │
│   CLAIM WAS PROCESSED IN DUPLICATE.                                 │
│                                                                     │
│   If you have any questions, please feel free to contact us.        │
│                                                                     │
│   Sincerely,                                                        │
│                                                                     │
│   Mary Louse Smith                                                  │
│   Claims Analysis (39-392)                                          │
│                                                                     │
└─────────────────────────────────────────────────────────────────┘
```

FIGURE 20-11 Sample overpayment recovery letter

In 1995, the **Stark II** physician self-referral law expanded the Stark I law by including referrals of Medicare *and* Medicaid patients for the following designated health care services (DHCS):

- Clinical laboratory services
- Durable medical equipment and supplies
- Home health services
- Inpatient and outpatient hospitalization services
- Occupational therapy services
- Outpatient prescription drugs
- Parenteral and enteral nutrients, equipment, and supplies
- Physical therapy services
- Prosthetics, orthotics, and prosthetic devices and supplies
- Radiation therapy services and supplies
- Radiology services, including MRIs, CT scans, and ultrasound services

Medicare Part A reimburses health care facilities for costs associated with training residents. The **Physicians at Teaching Hospitals (PATH) initiative** resulted from the discovery that some health care organizations were billing Medicare Part B for services that were already paid under Part A. The PATH initiative requires a national review of teaching hospitals' compliance with reimbursement rules and training of physicians who provide services at teaching facilities.

Administrative Simplification

The purpose of **HIPAA administrative simplification (AS)** provisions is to develop standards for the maintenance and transmission of health information required to identify individual patients. These standards are designed to improve efficiency and effectiveness of the health care system by standardizing the interchange of electronic data for specified administrative and financial transactions. In addition, the intent is to protect the security and confidentiality of electronic health information. HIPAA provisions require compliance by all health care organizations that maintain or transmit electronic health information. The law also establishes significant penalties for violations (e.g., $100 for each violation, a $25,000 maximum penalty for violations of an identical requirement, a $50,000 wrongful disclosure penalty and/or imprisonment of not more than one year, a $100,000 penalty for offenses under false pretenses and/or imprisonment of not more than 5 years, and a $250,000 penalty for offense with intent to sell information and/or imprisonment of not more than 10 years).

NOTE:

HIPAA established the **Designated Standard Maintenance Organization (DSMO)**, which is made up of organizations that agree to maintain the electronic transactions standards adopted by the Secretary of DHHS and to develop or modify adopted standards. Approved DSMOs include the Accredited Standards Committee X12, Dental Content Committee of the American Dental Association, Health Level Seven (HL7), National Council for Prescription Drug Programs, National Uniform Billing Committee, and National Uniform Claim Committee.

Unique Identifiers

HIPAA administrative simplification provisions require the following national identifiers to be established:

- **National standard employer identifier number (EIN).** The IRS's federal tax identification number was adopted as the national employer identifier, retaining the hyphen after the first two numbers (e.g., 12-3456789). The EIN is assigned to employers who, as sponsors of health insurance for their employers, must be identified in health care transactions.
- **National provider identifier (NPI).** HIPAA provisions require hospitals, doctors, nursing homes, and other health care providers to obtain a unique identifier consisting of 10 numeric digits (e.g., 1234567890) for filing electronic claims with public and private insurance programs. Providers apply for the NPI once and keep it if they relocate or change specialties. Currently, health care providers are assigned different ID numbers by each health plan, which results in slower payments, increased costs, and a lack of coordination.

NOTE:

A **check digit** is a one-digit character, alphabetic or numeric, that is used to verify the validity of a unique identifier.

- **National health plan identifier (HPID).** The HPID is assigned to third-party payers, and it contains 10 numeric positions including a check digit in the tenth position (e.g., 1234567890). (The HPID was formerly called the PlanID and the PAYERID.)
- **National individual identifier (patient identifier).** The HIPAA provision for a national individual identifier (or patient identifier) has been withdrawn. Although HIPAA included a requirement for the assignment of a unique personal health care identifier to each person in the United States, Congress is proposing legislation that would eliminate the requirement to establish a national individual identifier.

Electronic Health Care Transactions

HIPAA requires payers to implement **electronic transaction standards,** a uniform language for electronic data interchange. **Electronic data interchange (EDI)** is the computer-to-computer transfer of data between provider and third-party payer (or provider and health care clearinghouse) in a data format agreed upon by the sending and receiving parties. HIPAA's administrative simplification provisions directed the federal government to adopt national electronic standards for the automated transfer of certain health care data among health care payers (e.g., Medicare administrative contractors), payers (e.g., BCBS), and providers (e.g., hospitals and physicians). The provisions enable the entire health care industry to communicate electronic data using a single set of standards, eliminating all nonstandard formats currently in use. The standards allow a health care provider to submit a standard transaction for eligibility, authorization, referrals, claims, or attachments containing the same standard data content to any payer. This "simplifies" clinical, billing, and other financial applications, and it reduces costs.

Computer-generated paper claims are not considered EDI. Providers that generate paper-based claims submit them to health care clearinghouses, which convert them to a standardized electronic format for submission to payers. A health care clearinghouse performs centralized claims processing for providers and health care plans; it receives claims from providers, transmits claims to payers, receives remittance advice and payment instructions from payers, and transmits that information to providers (all in a HIPAA-compliant format). A health care clearinghouse also conducts eligibility and claim status queries in the format prescribed by HIPAA.

A **remittance advice (remit)** (Figure 20-12) is a statement sent by the payer to the provider, which details how submitted claims were processed and contains reimbursement amounts. If a claim is denied, an explanation of denial is included on the remittance advice. Providers may receive an electronic remittance advice (ERA) or a paper-based statement, called a standard paper remittance (SPR). The remittance advice includes the following information: patient name, health insurance claim number (HICN), provider's name, date(s) of service, type of service, procedure codes and modifiers, charges (both submitted and allowed), reimbursement amount including any deductions (e.g., copayments), reason and/or remark codes (e.g., explanation of denial), and an indication that the claim has been forwarded to a supplemental carrier for processing, if applicable.

EXAMPLE: Health care providers submit electronic claims data to payers on computer tape, diskette, or by computer modem or fax. The payer receives the claim, processes the data, and sends the provider the results of processing electronic claims (an electronic remittance advice).

```
ABC INSURANCE COMPANY
100 MAIN STREET
ALFRED NY 14802
1-800-555-1234                         REMITTANCE ADVICE

DAVID MILLER, M.D.                                              PROVIDER #: 123456
101 NORTH STREET                                               PAGE #: 1 OF 1
                                                               DATE: 04/05/YY
ALFRED, NY 14802                                               CHECK/EFT#: 000235698

PERF PROV  SERV DATE  POS NOS  PROC  MODS BILLED  ALLOWED DEDUCT   COINS GRP/RC AMT PROV PD

NAME BAKER, JENNY   HIC 235962541     ACNT BAKE1234567-01     ICN 1235626589651   ASG Y  MOA MA01
236592ABC  0405 0405YY 11  1 99213    75.00   50.00  0.25    0.00  CO-42 15.00    50.00
PT RESP  10.31        CLAIM TOTALS    75.00   50.00  0.25    0.00        15.00

                                                                          NET   50.00

TOTALS: # OF    BILLED    ALLOWED   DEDUCT    COINS    TOTAL    PROV PD   PROV    CHECK
        CLAIMS  AMT       AMT       AMT       RC AMT   AMT      ADJ AMT   AMT     AMT
        1       75.00     50.00     0.25      15.00    65.25    50.00     0.00    50.00
```

FIGURE 20-12 Sample remittance advice (single claim)

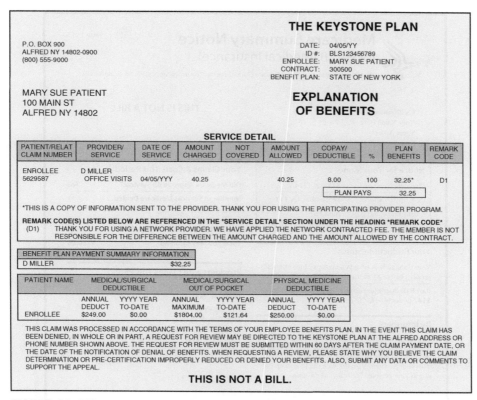

THE KEYSTONE PLAN

P.O. BOX 900
ALFRED NY 14802-0900
(800) 555-9000

DATE: 04/05/YY
ID #: BLS123456789
ENROLLEE: MARY SUE PATIENT
CONTRACT: 300500
BENEFIT PLAN: STATE OF NEW YORK

MARY SUE PATIENT
100 MAIN ST
ALFRED NY 14802

**EXPLANATION
OF BENEFITS**

SERVICE DETAIL

PATIENT/RELAT CLAIM NUMBER	PROVIDER/ SERVICE	DATE OF SERVICE	AMOUNT CHARGED	NOT COVERED	AMOUNT ALLOWED	COPAY/ DEDUCTIBLE	%	PLAN BENEFITS	REMARK CODE
ENROLLEE 5629587	D MILLER OFFICE VISITS	04/05/YYY	40.25		40.25	8.00	100	32.25*	D1
						PLAN PAYS		32.25	

*THIS IS A COPY OF INFORMATION SENT TO THE PROVIDER. THANK YOU FOR USING THE PARTICIPATING PROVIDER PROGRAM.

REMARK CODE(S) LISTED BELOW ARE REFERENCED IN THE "SERVICE DETAIL" SECTION UNDER THE HEADING "REMARK CODE"
(D1)   THANK YOU FOR USING A NETWORK PROVIDER. WE HAVE APPLIED THE NETWORK CONTRACTED FEE. THE MEMBER IS NOT RESPONSIBLE FOR THE DIFFERENCE BETWEEN THE AMOUNT CHARGED AND THE AMOUNT ALLOWED BY THE CONTRACT.

BENEFIT PLAN PAYMENT SUMMARY INFORMATION
D MILLER $32.25

PATIENT NAME	MEDICAL/SURGICAL DEDUCTIBLE		MEDICAL/SURGICAL OUT OF POCKET		PHYSICAL MEDICINE DEDUCTIBLE	
	ANNUAL DEDUCT	YYYY YEAR TO-DATE	ANNUAL MAXIMUM	YYYY YEAR TO-DATE	ANNUAL DEDUCT	YYYY YEAR TO-DATE
ENROLLEE	$249.00	$0.00	$1804.00	$121.64	$250.00	$0.00

THIS CLAIM WAS PROCESSED IN ACCORDANCE WITH THE TERMS OF YOUR EMPLOYEE BENEFITS PLAN. IN THE EVENT THIS CLAIM HAS BEEN DENIED, IN WHOLE OR IN PART, A REQUEST FOR REVIEW MAY BE DIRECTED TO THE KEYSTONE PLAN AT THE ALFRED ADDRESS OR PHONE NUMBER SHOWN ABOVE. THE REQUEST FOR REVIEW MUST BE SUBMITTED WITHIN 60 DAYS AFTER THE CLAIM PAYMENT DATE, OR THE DATE OF THE NOTIFICATION OR DENIAL OF BENEFITS. WHEN REQUESTING A REVIEW, PLEASE STATE WHY YOU BELIEVE THE CLAIM DETERMINATION OR PRE-CERTIFICATION IMPROPERLY REDUCED OR DENIED YOUR BENEFITS. ALSO, SUBMIT ANY DATA OR COMMENTS TO SUPPORT THE APPEAL.

THIS IS NOT A BILL.

FIGURE 20-13A Sample explanation of benefits (EOB)

An **explanation of benefits (EOB)** (Figure 20-13A) is sent to the patient by the payer, and it contains the same information as the remittance advice but it is in an easy-to-read format. Medicare patients receive a **Medicare Summary Notice (MSN)** (Figure 20-13B) (instead of an EOB), which is an easy-to-read monthly statement that clearly lists health insurance claims information.

 NOTE:

The MSN replaced the Explanation of Medicare Benefits (EOMB), the Medicare Benefits Notice (Part A), and benefit denial letter.

Effective 2003, electronic claims will not be processed by Medicare administrative contractors if they are not in an electronic format. Advantages of EDI include the following:

- Claim status and eligibility information in 24 hours or less
- Cost effectiveness and reduction in opportunity for error
- Electronic funds transfer of accounts receivable into the provider's bank
- Electronic remittances sent to a provider-preferred location
- Faster payment of electronic claims
- Lower administrative, postage, and handling costs
- Online receipt or acknowledgment
- Standardized electronic claims submission, coordination of benefits exchange, and remittance receipts reduce system costs.

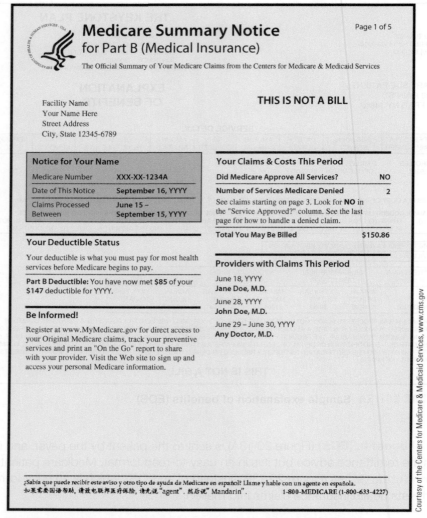

FIGURE 20-13B Sample Medicare Summary Notice (MSN)

Three electronic formats are supported for health care claims transactions, including the UB-04 flat-file format (Figure 20-14), the National Standard Format (NSF) (Figure 20-15), and the **ANSI ASC X12N 837** format (American National Standards Institute, Accredited Standards Committee, Insurance Subcommittee X12N, claims validation table 837) (Figure 20-16).

 NOTE:

A flat file consists of a series of fixed-length records (e.g., eight spaces for the patient's date of birth). The UB-04 flat file is used to bill institutional services (e.g., hospitals), and the National Standard Format (NSF) flat file is used to bill physician and noninstitutional services (e.g., the physician's office). ANSI ASC X12N 837 is a variable-length file format that is used to bill institutional, professional, dental, and drug claims. The flat-file formats were developed for use in claims processing software application programs because the ANSI ASC X12N 837 format is not suitable for use in an application program, and it must be translated into a flat-file format prior to claims processing.

Medicare administrative contractors do not accept flat-file format transactions for claims submission. Medicare administrative contractors also do not send electronic remittance advices in the flat-file format or exchange electronic eligibility queries/responses in any version not adopted as a national standard in the final rules for the HIPAA Administrative Simplification transaction standards. However, providers can use health care clearinghouses to translate outgoing and/or incoming electronic transactions, which will convert flat-file formats to the ANSI ASC X12N 837 format. Providers who do not use a health care clearinghouse must install software that can send and receive files in the ANSI ASC X12N 837 format.

```
MSG_HDR BCBS ECM_Y06 SndApp SndFac RcApp RcFac 200601052369 56941
INS_CLM 562697 20060105 20060110 ADL05691125.00
PRV_DT1M_P Smith DKSL23659
PRV_DT1M_H Jones DLEP65915
PAT_IDF DCB5432 Green 19941205
CRD_STS YYN
SRV_CMN GM 20060105 50.00
SRV_FEE CP 45.00
SRV_FEE CK 12.00
SRV_CMN GM 20060106 55.00
SRV_FEE CO 10.00
SRV_FEE RK
```

FIGURE 20-14 Sample UB-04 electronic flat-file format

```
ELECTRONIC MEDIA CLAIMS NATIONAL STANDARD FORMAT
RECORD NAME: CLAIM HEADER RECORD "PATIENT DATA"        RECORD TYPE: CA0

                                                          FIELD POSITIONS
FIELD NUMBER      FIELD NAME        FIELD LENGTH  FIELD TYPE   FROM    TO

   01.0      RECORD ID "CA0"            3             X         01      03
   02.0      RESERVED (CA0-02.0)        2             X         04      05
   03.0      PATIENT CONTROL NUMBER    17             X         06      22
   04.0      PATIENT LAST NAME         20             X         23      42
   05.0      PATIENT FIRST NAME        12             X         43      54
   06.0      PATIENT MIDDLE INITIAL     1             X         55      55
   07.0      PATIENT GENERATION         3             X         56      58
   08.0      PATIENT DATE OF BIRTH      8             X         59      66
   09.0      PATIENT GENDER             1             X         67      67
   10.0      PATIENT TYPE OF RESIDENCE  1             X         68      68
```

FIGURE 20-15 Portion of electronic medical claims National Standard Format (NSF)

UB-04 data elements in ANSI ASC X12N 837 format	Description of data elements
ST*837*123456~ BHT*0019*00*A98765*YYYY0504*0830~	Header
NM1*41*2*GOODMEDICINE HOSPITAL*****54*888229999~	Submitter name
NM1*40*2*CAPITAL BLUE CROSS*****54*16000~	Receiver name
HL*1**20*1~	Service provider hierarchical level for submitter
NM1*85*2*GOODMEDICINE HOSPITAL*****54*888229999~ REF*1J*898989~	Service provider name
HL*2*1*22*1~ SBR*P********BL~	Subscriber (patient) hierarchical level
NM1*IL*1*PUBLIC*JOHN*Q**MI*GRNESSC1234~ N3*1247 HILL STREET~ N4*ANYWHERE*US*12345~ DMG*D8*19820805*M**::RET:3::RET:2~ REF*SY*150259874~	Subscriber (patient) name
NM1*PR*2*CAPITAL BLUE CROSS*****PI*00303~	Payer name
CLM*ABH123456*5015***11:A:1~ DTP*096*TM*1200~ DTP*434*RD8*YYYY0504-YYYY0510~ DTP*435*DT*YYYY05101100~ CL1*2*1*01~ HI*BK:66411*BJ:66411~ HI*BF:66331:::::::Y*BF:66111:::::::N*BF:V270:::::::N~ HI*BR:7569:D8:YYYY0510~	Claim information
SE*91*123456~	Trailer

FIGURE 20-16 Portion of UB-04 data submitted in ANSI ASC X12N 837 electronic format

HIPAA administrative simplification provisions also require the following code sets to be used:

- *Current Dental Terminology (CDT)*: Dental services
- *International Classification of Diseases, 10th Revision, Clinical Modification (ICD-10-CM)*: All diagnoses
- *International Classification of Diseases, 10th Revision, Procedure Classification System (ICD-10-PCS)*: Hospital inpatient procedures and services only.
- *Current Procedural Terminology (CPT)*: Outpatient hospital and physician procedures and services
- *Health Care Common Procedure Coding System, Level II (National codes)*: Outpatient hospital and physician procedures and services, and institutional/professional pharmacy transactions
- *National Drug Code (NDC)*: Retail pharmacy transactions

 NOTE:

No standard code set was adopted for nonretail pharmacy drug claims.

Privacy and Security Rules

Any information communicated by a patient to a health care provider is considered **privileged communication**, which means that it is private. Patients have the right to **confidentiality**, which is the process of keeping privileged communication secret and means that information cannot be disclosed without the patient's authorization. (Exceptions include information released via *subpoena duces tecum*, court order, and according to statutory reporting requirements.) A **breach of confidentiality** occurs when patient information is **disclosed** (or released) to other(s) who do not have a right to access the information. In this situation, the disclosing provider failed to obtain patient authorization to release privileged communication; this results in violation of federal law (HIPAA). According to HIPAA privacy and security provisions, patients have the right to an expectation of **privacy** regarding their privileged communication, which means information cannot be disclosed without their authorization. **Security** safeguards also must be implemented to ensure that facilities, equipment, and patient information are safe from damage, loss, tampering, theft, or unauthorized access.

The **HIPAA standards for privacy of individually identifiable health information**, or **privacy rule**, include provisions that protect the security and confidentiality of health information. Because the use and disclosure of health information is inconsistently protected by state laws, patients' privacy and confidentiality is also inconsistently protected. The HIPAA privacy rule establishes standards to protect the confidentiality of individually identifiable health information maintained or transmitted electronically in connection with certain administrative and financial transactions (e.g., electronic transfer of health insurance claims). The rule provides new rights for individuals with respect to protected health information (PHI) and mandates compliance by **covered entities**, which are private and public sector organizations that must follow HIPAA provisions. For the privacy rule, covered entities include health care providers that conduct certain transactions in electronic forms, health plans, and health care clearinghouses.

 NOTE:

HIPAA is the first federal law that governs the privacy of health information nationwide. If security policies and procedures are not established and enforced, concerns might be raised about the security of patient information during legal proceedings. This could result in questioning the integrity of the medical record.

Protected health information (PHI) is information that is identifiable to an individual (or individual identifiers) such as name, address, telephone number, date of birth, Medicaid ID number and other medical record numbers, Social Security number (SSN), and name of employer. In most instances, covered entities are required to obtain an individual's authorization prior to disclosing the individual's health information, and HIPAA has established specific requirements for an authorization form. All medical records and other individually identifiable health information used or disclosed by a covered entity in any form, whether electronically, paper-based, or verbally, are covered by the privacy rule.

The HIPAA **security rule** contains standards and safeguards for PHI that is collected, maintained, used, or transmitted electronically. Covered entities impacted by this rule include health plans, health care clearinghouses, and certain health care providers. CMS is responsible for overseeing compliance with and complaints about security rules.

The standard for electronic signature is **digital**, which applies a mathematical function to the electronic document resulting in a unique bit string (computer code) called a message digest, which is encrypted and appended to the electronic document. (**Encrypt** means to encode a computer file, making it safe for electronic transmission so unauthorized parties cannot read it.) The recipient of the transmitted electronic document **decrypts** (decodes) the message digest and compares the decoded digest to the transmitted version. If they are identical, the message is unaltered and the identity of the signer is proven.

The DHHS Medicare Program, other federal agencies operating health plans or providing health care, state Medicaid agencies, private health plans, health care providers, and health care clearinghouses must assure their customers (e.g., patients, insured individuals, providers, and health plans) that the integrity, confidentiality, and availability of electronic PHI they collect, maintain, use, or transmit is protected. The confidentiality of health information is threatened not only by the risk of improper access to stored information, but also by the risk of interception during electronic transmission of the information. The purpose of the *security rule* is to adopt national standards for safeguards to protect the confidentiality, integrity, and availability of electronic PHI. Prior to publication of the *security rule*, no standard measures existed in the health care industry to address all aspects of the security of electronic health information while being stored or during the exchange of that information between entities. In general, security provisions should include the following procedures:

- Define authorized users of patient information to control access.
- Implement a tracking procedure to sign out records to authorized personnel.
- Limit record storage access to authorized users.
- Lock record storage areas at all times.
- Require the original medical record to remain in the facility at all times (except when a court order requires the original medical record to be submitted to the court clerk).

Although security and privacy are linked, be sure you do not confuse the purpose of each rule. The *security rule* defines administrative, physical, and technical safeguards to protect the availability, confidentiality, and integrity of PHI. The standards require covered entities to implement basic safeguards to protect electronic PHI from unauthorized access, alteration, deletion, and transmission. In contrast, the *privacy rule* establishes standards for how PHI should be controlled; it also establishes what uses (e.g., continuity of care) and disclosures (e.g., third-party reimbursement) are authorized or required, as well as what rights patients have with respect to their health information (e.g., patient access).

Medical Liability Reform

The threat of excessive awards in medical liability cases has increased providers' liability insurance premiums, which has resulted in increases in health care costs. Because of this, some providers have stopped practicing medicine in areas of the country where liability insurance costs are highest, and the direct impact on individuals and communities across the country has been reduced access to quality medical care. Although medical liability reform was included in HIPAA legislation, no final rule was published. Although individual states, such as Ohio, have passed medical liability reform, the U.S. Congress is also formulating separate federal medical liability reform legislation. The Senate introduced legislation that will implement reasonable, comprehensive, and effective health care liability reforms designed to improve the availability of health care services in cases in which health care liability actions have been shown to be a factor in the decreased availability of services; reduce the incidence of "defensive medicine" and lower the cost of health care liability insurance, all of which contribute to the escalation of health care costs; ensure that persons with meritorious health care injury claims receive fair and adequate compensation, including reasonable noneconomic damages;

improve the fairness and cost-effectiveness of our current health care liability system to resolve disputes over, and provide compensation for, health care liability by reducing uncertainty in the amount of compensation provided to injured individuals; and provide increased sharing of information in the health care system, which will reduce unintended injury and improve patient care. (Go to http://thomas.loc.gov, select All Legislation from the drop down menu (located at top left), and enter medical liability reform in the "Search Within" box to view any proposed legislation.)

Exercise 20.3 – Impact of HIPAA on Reimbursement

Matching: Match the term in Column 2 with the example in Column 1. Answers may be used more than once.

_____ 1. Submitting excessive charges for services or supplies

_____ 2. Unbundling codes reported on claims

_____ 3. Billing Medicare for services or supplies not provided

_____ 4. Submitting claims for services that aren't medically necessary

_____ 5. Violating Medicare participating provider agreements with payers

a. Abuse

b. Fraud

Completion: Complete each statement.

1. Formerly called the PlanID, the identifier assigned to third-party payers that contains 10 numeric positions including a check digit in the tenth position is called the HPID, which is the abbreviation for _____.

2. The IRS's federal tax identification number is assigned to employers who, as sponsors of health insurance for their employers, must be identified in health care transactions; it was adopted as the national standard EIN, which is the abbreviation for _____.

3. Health care providers must obtain an NPI, which is the abbreviation for _____, which consists of nine alphanumeric characters plus a check digit, and is used for filing electronic claims with public and private insurance programs.

4. The computerized exchange of health information between provider and payer in a format agreed upon by the sending and receiving parties is called EDI, which is the abbreviation for_____.

5. HIPAA requires the implementation of standards and safeguards to protect health information that is collected, maintained, used, or transmitted electronically, which is called the _____ rule.

Summary

A third-party payer is an insurance company or other organization (e.g., a Medicare administrative contractor) that processes health care claims for reimbursement of procedures and services. Third-party payers include BlueCross and BlueShield (BCBS), commercial insurance companies, employer self-insurance plans, government-sponsored programs (e.g., Medicaid, Medicare, and TRICARE), managed care plans (e.g., a health maintenance organization), and workers' compensation. A health insurance policy is an agreement between an individual and a third-party payer (or insurance company) that contains a list of reimbursable medical benefits (or covered benefits) (e.g., office visits, inpatient hospitalizations, laboratory, tests, prescription medications, and treatment services).

Government programs reimburse providers according to prospective cost-based rates and prospective payment systems. Typically, third-party payers adopt prospective payment systems, fee schedules, and exclusions after Medicare has implemented them; payers modify them to suit their needs.

The Health Insurance Portability and Accountability Act of 1996 (HIPAA) amended the Internal Revenue Code of 1986 to improve portability and continuity of health insurance coverage in the group and individual markets; combat waste, fraud, and abuse in health insurance and health care delivery; promote the use of medical savings accounts; improve access to long-term care services and coverage; simplify the administration of health insurance by creating unique identifiers for providers, health plans, employers, and individuals; create standards for electronic health information transactions; and create privacy and security standards for health information.

Health reform was implemented as a result of the Patient Protection and Affordable Care Act (PPACA), which is also called Obamacare, and the Health Care and Education Reconciliation Act (HCERA), which amended the PPACA.

Internet Links

Accredited Standards Committee X12N (ASC X12N): *www.x12.org*

Centers for Medicare & Medicaid Services: *www.cms.gov*

CMS Quarterly Provider Update: Go to *www.cms.gov*, click on the Regulations & Guidance link, and then click on the Quarterly Provider Updates link below the Regulations & Policies heading.

Health Care Compliance Association (HCCA): Go to *www.hcca-info.org*, click on Publications, click on Newsletter, scroll down to Free Newsletters, and click on Compliance Weekly News to subscribe for free.

Health Level Seven (HL7): *www.hl7.org*

Health Reform: Go to *www.healthcare.gov* to learn more about the *Health Insurance Marketplace*.

Medicare Conditions for Coverage and Conditions of Participation: Go to *www.cms.gov*, click on the Regulations & Guidance link, then click on the Conditions for Coverage (CfCs) & Conditions of Participation (CoPs) link below the Legislation heading.

Medicare Payment Systems: Go to *www.cms.gov*, click on the Medicare link, and then click on one or more of the topics below the Medicare Fee-for-Service Payment heading.

Medicare Preventive Services (coverage issues): Go to *www.cms.gov*, click on the Medicare link, then click on the Preventive Services link, which is located below the Prevention heading.

National Uniform Billing Committee: *www.nubc.org*

National Uniform Claim Committee: *www.nucc.org*

Office of Inspector General of the U.S. Department of Health & Human Services: *www.oig.hhs.gov*

Quality Improvement Organizations: Go to *www.cms.gov*, click on the Medicare link and then scroll down and click on the Quality Improvement Organizations link below the Quality Initiatives/Patient Assessment Instruments heading.

Workgroup for Electronic Data Interchange (WEDI): *www.wedi.org*

Review

Multiple Choice

Instructions: Circle the most appropriate response.

1. An insurance policy is an agreement between a third-party payer and a(n):
   a. health care facility.
   b. health care provider.
   c. individual.
   d. insurance company.

2. Which of the following prohibits the health care provider from collecting payment from the patient for claims that the insurance plan has denied?

    a. Hold harmless clause   **c.** Medical necessity

    b. Indemnification   **d.** Preauthorization

3. Under an employer self-insurance plan, who would be responsible for payment of the employees' health care?

    a. Employee   **c.** Third-party payer

    b. Employer   **d.** Workers' compensation

4. Which third-party payer is state-mandated rather than government-sponsored?

    a. Indian Health Service (IHS)

    b. Programs of All-inclusive Care for the Elderly (PACE)

    c. State Children's Health Insurance Program (SCHIP)

    d. Workers' compensation

5. A patient who has the option to be seen by a non-HMO provider without obtaining a referral from the primary care physician (PCP), thus incurring a greater out-of-pocket expense, would be using which type of managed care plan?

    a. Exclusive provider organization (EPO)   **c.** Point-of-service plan (POS)

    b. Health maintenance organization (HMO)   **d.** Preferred provider organization (PPO)

6. In the customized sub-capitation type of consumer-directed health plan, each provider is paid:

    a. a fixed amount per month to manage all of an individual's health care, which includes reimbursing for services provided by labs and specialists.

    b. a fixed amount per month to provide only the care that an individual needs from that provider.

    c. a variable amount per month to manage all of an individual's health care from a tax-exempt account established by an employee.

    d. both a fixed and a variable amount each month to manage an individual's health care when the employee uses the provider's services.

7. A cancer hospital that has been granted a waiver from mandatory participation in the hospital inpatient prospective payment system is called a(n) _____ by CMS.

    a. exception   **b.** exclusion   **c.** pardon   **d.** release

8. Which prospective payment system uses information from the patient assessment instrument to classify patients into groups based on clinical characteristics and expected resource needs?

    a. HH PPS   **b.** IRF PPS   **c.** LTC PPS   **d.** OPPS

9. The IPPS payment window for outpatient preadmission services provided by a long-term (acute) care hospital is _____ hours.

    a. 24   **b.** 36   **c.** 48   **d.** 72

10. The Health Care and Education Reconciliation Act (HCERA) _____.

    a. closed the Medicare Part D "donut hole"

    b. established the health insurance exchange

    c. implemented Obamacare

    d. resulted in national health care

11. Case-mix adjustments:

    a. allow payment systems to increase preestablished payments.

    b. create an incentive for facilities to admit large volumes of low-cost patients.

    c. result in fewer possible payment rates based on anticipated care needs.

    d. result in higher anticipated payments for high-resource cases.

12. Severity of illness (SI) scores are based on _____.
    a. DRG assignment
    b. ICD-10-CM codes
    c. physiologic measures, signs, and symptoms
    d. the admission diagnosis

13. Monitoring unusual billing patterns and other indicators is an example of which of the strategies used by CMS to deter fraud and abuse?
    a. Coordination   b. Early detection   c. Enforcement   d. Prevention

14. A person found guilty of Medicare fraud faces _____.
    a. administrative sanction penalties
    b. civil penalties
    c. criminal, civil, and administrative sanction penalties
    d. criminal penalties

15. When a modifier is added to a code to indicate that the procedure or service is part of a major procedure or service, the code is known as a _____.
    a. code combination   c. comprehensive code
    b. component code   d. mutually exclusive code

16. Under the Federal Claims Collection Act of 1966, any review conducted by a Medicare administrative contractor for recovery of overpaid funds must be done within how many calendar years after the year in which the overpayment was made?
    a. Two   b. Three   c. Five   d. Seven

17. HIPAA administrative simplification provisions require that national identifiers be established. Which identifier has been withdrawn and is awaiting legislation by Congress to eliminate the requirement?
    a. National health plan identifier (HPID)
    b. National individual identifier (patient identifier)
    c. National provider identifier (NPI)
    d. National standard employer identifier number (EIN)

18. Which was published by HIPAA to adopt standards and safeguards to protect health information that is collected, maintained, used, or transmitted electronically?
    a. Confidentiality rule   c. Privacy rule
    b. Disclosure rule   d. Security rule

19. Which is a statement sent by the payer to the provider that contains reimbursement amounts and details how submitted claims were processed?
    a. Electronic data interchange (EDI)   c. Remittance advice
    b. Explanation of benefits (EOB)   d. Transaction for eligibility

20. The threat of excessive awards in medical liability cases has resulted in:
    a. decreased health care costs.
    b. increased access to quality medical care.
    c. increased liability insurance premiums for providers.
    d. increased numbers of practicing providers.

21. The Recovery Audit Contract (RAC) program was implemented as part of _____ legislation.
    a. HIPAA   c. SSA amendments
    b. MMA   d. TEFRA

22. Medicare's Comprehensive Error Rate Testing (CERT) program was implemented to evaluate:
    a. individual provider compliance with Medicare regulations.
    b. Medicare administrative contractor (MAC) program performance.
    c. reimbursement made to hospitals serving more acutely ill patients.
    d. the transition from CMS-DRGs to MS-DRGs throughout the country.

23. Under the MS-DRG PPS, the abbreviation MCC refers to _____ comorbid and complication conditions.
    a. major   c. MedPAC
    b. Medicare   d. major diagnostic categories

24. All claims submitted for inpatient admissions to general acute care hospitals or other health care facilities are required to report the _____ indicator, which is assigned by the coder to the principal and secondary diagnoses and external cause of injury code reported on the UB-04 or 837 Institutional (electronic) claim.
    a. CMS   b. DRG   c. MDC   d. POA

25. Which did Medicare implement October 1, 2007, to classify inpatient hospital cases into groups according to similar resource utilization?
    a. AP-DRGs   b. APR-DRGs   c. MS-DRGs   d. RDRGs

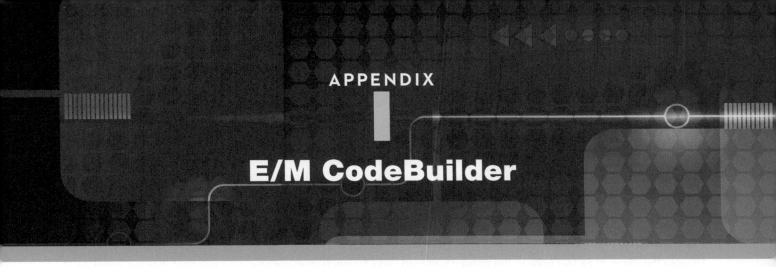

E/M CodeBuilder

For use with CMS *1994 or 1997 Documentation Guidelines for Evaluation & Management Coding,* which are located in the *Evaluation and Management Services* document on the Student Companion Site at http://login.cengage.com.

 NOTE:

Make copies of this *E/M CodeBuilder* (or print the document at the Student Companion Site at http://login.cengage.com) to use when assigning E/M codes. Use of this document will reinforce the process required to assign E/M codes.

Introduction

The evaluation and management (E/M) code reported to a third-party payer must be supported by documentation in the patient's record (e.g., SOAP or clinic note, diagnostic test results, operative findings). Although providers are responsible for selecting the E/M code from the encounter form, superbill, or chargemaster at the time patient care is rendered, insurance specialists audit records to make sure that the appropriate level of E/M code was reported to the third-party payer.

This *E/M CodeBuilder* form can be used for that purpose, and it can also be used as a tool to teach appropriate assignment of E/M level codes. To assign a code, just review the documentation in the patient's record, record your findings (based on the directions provided), and refer to the CPT coding manual to select the E/M code to be reported.

E/M code selection is based on three key components: *history, examination,* and *medical decision making.* This *E/M CodeBuilder* form emphasizes those components. It is important to be aware that contributory components (*counseling* and *coordination of care*) also play an important role in selecting the E/M code when documentation in the patient record indicates that counseling or coordination of care dominated the visit. In this situation, the contributory component of *time* can be considered a key or controlling factor in selecting a level of E/M service (code).

 NOTE:

Time and *nature of presenting problem* are listed in some E/M code descriptions to assist in determining which code number to report.

Selecting the Level of History

To select the level of history, review the following elements in the patient record. If an element is not documented, it cannot be considered when selecting the level of E/M service code.

- History of present illness (HPI)
- Review of systems (ROS)
- Past, family, and/or social history (PFSH)

History of Present Illness (HPI)

Review the clinic or SOAP note in the patient's record, and for each documented HPI element (below), enter an X in the box in front of the element on this form. Then, total the Xs and enter that number on the line in front of the Total Score (below). Finally, select the level of HPI based on the total number of elements documented, and enter an X in the appropriate box.

- ☐ **Location:** Of pain/discomfort (e.g., is pain diffused/localized or unilateral/bilateral; does it radiate or refer?).
- ☐ **Duration:** Of pain/discomfort; length of time condition has persisted (e.g., pain began three days ago).
- ☐ **Quality:** A description of the quality of the symptom (e.g., is pain described as sharp, dull, throbbing, stabbing, constant, intermittent, acute or chronic, stable, improving, or worsening?).
- ☐ **Severity:** Use of self-assessment scale to measure subjective levels (e.g., on a scale of 1–10, how severe is the pain?), or comparison of pain quantitatively with previously experienced pain.
- ☐ **Timing:** Establishing onset of pain and chronology of pain development (e.g., migraine in the morning).
- ☐ **Context:** Where was the patient and what was he or she doing when pain began (e.g., was patient at rest or involved in an activity; was pain aggravated or relieved, or does it recur, with a specific activity; did situational stress or some other factor precede or accompany the pain)?
- ☐ **Modifying factors:** What has patient attempted to do to relieve pain (e.g., heat vs. cold; does it relieve or exacerbate pain; what makes the pain worse; have over-the-counter drugs been attempted—with what results)?
- ☐ **Associated signs/symptoms:** Clinician's impressions formulated during the interview may lead to questioning about additional sensations or feelings (e.g., diaphoresis associated with indigestion or chest pain, blurred vision accompanying a headache, etc.).

_____ **Total Score:**   Enter the score for number of Xs entered above (representing number of HPI elements), and enter an X in front of the HPI type below.

- ☐ Brief HPI (1–3 elements)
- ☐ Extended HPI (4 or more elements)

Review of Systems (ROS)

Review the clinic or SOAP note in the patient's record, and for each documented ROS element, enter an X in the box in front of the element on this form. Then, total the Xs and enter that number on the line in front of the Total Score. Finally, select the level of ROS based on the total number of elements documented, and enter an X in the appropriate box.

- ☐ Constitutional symptoms
  - ☐ Allergic/Immunologic
  - ☐ Cardiovascular

☐ Ears, nose, mouth, throat

☐ Endocrine

☐ Eyes

☐ Gastrointestinal

☐ Genitourinary

☐ Hematologic/Lymphatic

☐ Integumentary (including breasts)

☐ Musculoskeletal

☐ Neurologic

☐ Psychiatric

☐ Respiratory

_____ **Total Score:** Enter the score for number of Xs entered above (representing number of ROS elements), and enter an X in front of the ROS type below.

☐ None

☐ Problem pertinent ROS (1 body system documented)

☐ Extended ROS (2–9 body systems documented)

☐ Complete ROS (all body systems documented)

Past, Family, and/or Social History (PFSH)

Review the clinic or SOAP note in the patient's record, and for each documented PFSH element, enter an X in the box in front of the element on this form. Then, total the Xs and enter that number on the line in front of the Total Score. Finally, select the level of PFSH based on the total number of elements documented, and enter an X in the appropriate box.

☐ Past history (patient's past experience with illnesses, operations, injuries, and treatments)

☐ Family history (review of medical events in the patient's family, including diseases that may be hereditary or place the patient at risk)

☐ Social history (an age-appropriate review of past and current activities, such as alcohol use, occupation, and so on)

_____ **Total Score:** Enter the score for number of Xs entered above (representing number of PFSH elements), and enter an X in front of the PFSH type below.

☐ None

☐ Pertinent PFSH (1 history area documented)

☐ Complete PFSH (2 or 3 history areas documented)

Level of History

Circle the type of HPI, ROS, and PFSH in the following table (as determined from the entries selected above); then, circle the appropriate Extent of History determined in the following table.

HPI:	Brief	Brief	Extended	Extended
ROS:	None	Problem Pertinent	Extended	Complete
PFSH:	None	None	Pertinent	Complete
EXTENT OF HISTORY:	PROBLEM FOCUSED	EXPANDED PROBLEM FOCUSED	DETAILED	COMPREHENSIVE

Selecting the Level of Examination

To select the level of examination, first determine whether a *single organ examination* (specialist exam such as ophthalmologist) or a *general multisystem examination* (e.g., family practitioner) was completed.

Single Organ System Examination

The single organ system examinations recognized by CPT are described in the *Evaluation and Management Services* document (located on the Student Companion Site at http://login.cengage.com). Single organ system examinations are usually performed by specialists (e.g., ophthalmologist, psychiatrist). You will notice variations among types of single organ examinations, which reflect differing emphases among specialties. Enter an X in front of the appropriate exam type below, after determining which content and documentation requirements of a single organ system examination have been met.

☐ PROBLEM FOCUSED EXAMINATION (1–5 elements identified by a bullet)

☐ EXPANDED PROBLEM FOCUSED EXAMINATION (at least 6 elements identified by a bullet)

☐ DETAILED EXAMINATION (at least 12 elements identified by a bullet)

☐ COMPREHENSIVE EXAMINATION (all elements identified by a bullet; document every element in each box)

- OR -

General Multisystem Exam

General multisystem examinations are described in the *Evaluation and Management Services* document (located on the Student Companion Site at http://login.cengage.com). General multisystem examinations are performed by both general practitioners and specialists. Enter an X in front of the organ system or body area when the maximum number of allowed elements has been documented. For example, when two or more Neck examinations are documented, you can enter an X in front of that body area. *If less than the number of elements located in parentheses is documented, do not enter an X in front of that organ system or body area.*

☐ Constitutional (2)
☐ Cardiovascular (7)
☐ Chest (breasts) (2)
☐ Ears, nose, mouth, throat (6)
☐ Eyes (3)
☐ Gastrointestinal (abdomen) (5)
☐ Genitourinary (male–3; female–6)
☐ Lymphatic (2)
☐ Musculoskeletal (6)
☐ Neck (2)
☐ Neurologic (3)
☐ Psychiatric (4)
☐ Respiratory (4)

☐ Skin (2)

_____ **Total Score:**   Enter the score for number of Xs entered (representing number of exam elements), and enter an X in front of the exam type below.

☐ PROBLEM FOCUSED EXAMINATION (1–5 elements identified by a bullet on *CMS Documentation Guidelines for Evaluation & Management Services*)

☐ EXPANDED PROBLEM FOCUSED EXAMINATION (at least 6 elements identified by a bullet on *CMS Documentation Guidelines for Evaluation & Management Services*)

☐ DETAILED EXAMINATION (at least 2 elements identified by a bullet from each of 6 organ systems or body areas, or at least 12 elements identified by a bullet in two or more systems or areas, on *CMS Documentation Guidelines for Evaluation & Management Services*)

☐ COMPREHENSIVE EXAMINATION (documentation of all elements identified by a bullet in at least 9 organ systems or body areas, and documentation of at least 2 elements identified by a bullet from each of 9 organ systems or body areas, on *CMS Documentation Guidelines for Evaluation & Management Services*)

Medical Decision Making

Select the appropriate level of medical decision making based upon the following criteria:

Number of Diagnoses or Management Options	Amount/Complexity of Data to Be Reviewed	Risk of Complications and/or Morbidity/Mortality	Medical Decision Making
Minimal	Minimal or none	Minimal	Straightforward
Limited	Limited	Low	Low complexity
Multiple	Moderate	Moderate	Moderate complexity
Extensive	Extensive	High	High complexity

E/M Code Selection

Select the E/M code based on selection of level of history, examination, and medical decision making:

History:	Problem focused	Expanded problem focused	Expanded problem focused	Detailed	Comprehensive
Examination:	Problem focused	Expanded problem focused	Expanded problem focused	Detailed	Comprehensive
Medical Decision Making:	Straightforward	Low complexity	Moderate complexity	Moderate complexity	High complexity

Go to the appropriate E/M category/subcategory, and select the code based upon the previously selected information.

BIBLIOGRAPHY

Books and Manuals

American Medical Association. (2019). *CPT*. Chicago, IL: Author.

Centers for Medicare & Medicaid Services. (2020). *Internet-only manuals*. Washington, DC: Department of Health and Human Services.

Ehrlich, A., Schroeder, C. L., Ehrlich, L., & Schroeder, K. (2017). *Medical terminology for health professionals*. Clifton Park, NY: Cengage Learning.

Green, M. A. (2020). *Understanding health insurance: A guide to billing and reimbursement*. Clifton Park, NY: Cengage Learning.

Green, M. A., & Bowie, M. J. (2016). *Essentials of health information management: Principles and practices*. Clifton Park, NY: Cengage Learning.

Merriam-Webster. (2006). *Merriam-Webster's medical desk dictionary*. Clifton Park, NY: Cengage Learning.

Neighbors, M., & Tannehill-Jones, R. (2019). *Human diseases*. Clifton Park, NY: Cengage Learning.

Optum360. (2020). *HCPCS level II*. Salt Lake City, UT: Author.

Optum360. (2020). *ICD-10-CM*. Salt Lake City, UT: Author.

Optum360. (2020). *ICD-10-PCS*. Salt Lake City, UT: Author.

Rizzo, D. C. (2016). *Fundamentals of anatomy and physiology*. Clifton Park, NY: Cengage Learning.

Scott, A., & Fong, E. (2019). *Body structures & functions*. Clifton Park, NY: Cengage Learning.

Woodrow, R., Colbert, B., & Smith, D. (2015). *Essentials of pharmacology for health occupations*. Clifton Park, NY: Cengage Learning.

Journals and Newsletters

Coding clinic for HCPCS. Chicago, IL: American Hospital Association.

Coding clinic for ICD-10-CM and ICD-10-PCS. Chicago, IL: American Hospital Association.

CPT assistant. Chicago, IL: American Medical Association.

For the record. Spring City, PA: Great Valley Publishing Co., Inc.

Healthcare business monthly. Salt Lake City, UT: AAPC.

Journal of the American Health Information Management Association. Chicago, IL: American Health Information Management Association.

Internet-Based Resources

AAPC ICD-10 Code Translator
http://www.aapc.com

CMS Medicare Manuals
http://www.cms.gov

Coding Institute Blog
http://blog.codinginstitute.com

Find-A-Code Medical Coding and Billing Database
https://www.findacode.com

Medical Newswire
http://medicalnewswire.com

Medline Plus Encyclopedia
https://medlineplus.gov

Optum360 Coding
https://www.optum360coding.com

World Health Organization
http://www.who.int

Software

Find-A-Code, LLC. (2020). *Code-A-Note*. Spanish Fork UT: Author.

Optum360. (2020). *Encoder Pro Expert*. Salt Lake City, UT: Author.

NOTE: The chapter in which each term appears as a key term is indicated in parentheses.

A

ablation (12) removal.

abuse (20) actions that are inconsistent with accepted, sound medical, business, or fiscal practices; includes actions that result in unnecessary costs to payers and government programs, that result in reimbursement for services not medically necessary, or that fail to meet professionally recognized standards for health care services.

accession (18) assignment of a number to record the order of tissue acquisition.

acellular dermal replacement (12) bioengineered artificial skin.

actinic keratosis (AK) (12) common sun-induced skin lesion of the epidermis that has the potential to become skin cancer.

acute care facility (ACF) (6) hospital that provides health care services to patients who have serious, sudden, or acute illnesses or injuries and/or who need certain surgeries.

acute care hospital (6) *see* short-term hospital.

add-on code (9) reported when another procedure is performed in addition to the primary procedure during the same operative session; modifiers -50 (bilateral procedure) and -51 (multiple procedures) are *not* used with add-on codes.

adenoids (14) located at the rear of the nose; contain lymphoid tissue that helps fight infections.

adjacent tissue transfer/rearrangement (12) closure of defects by relocating a flap of adjacent normal, healthy tissue to a defect.

adjuvant (18) substance administered with an antigen that enhances the response to the antigen.

adjuvant chemotherapy (19) chemotherapy administered in addition to other cancer treatments, such as surgery and/or radiation therapy.

adjuvant technique (14) additional procedure or technique that may be required during a lower extremity bypass graft procedure.

admitting diagnosis (6) provisional or tentative diagnosis entered in a field on the inpatient face sheet by admissions office staff; it is often a sign or symptom.

advance beneficiary notice (ABN) (8) waiver signed by the patient acknowledging that because medical necessity for a procedure, service, or supply cannot be established, the patient accepts responsibility for reimbursing the provider or DMEPOS dealer for costs associated with the procedure, service, or supply.

advance care planning (10) face-to-face services between physician or other qualified health care professional and patient, family member, or surrogate for the purpose of counseling and discussing advance directives, with or without completing relevant legal forms (e.g., health care proxy).

advancement flap (12) movement of tissue in a straight line from donor to defect site using a sliding process; once movement is achieved, the flap is sutured in place.

airway management (11) ensuring an open airway to the patient's lungs.

A-line (11) *see* intra-arterial line.

aliquot (18) portion of a specimen used for testing.

allergen (19) allergy-causing substances to which a patient reacts.

allergen immunotherapy (19) small amounts of allergens administered to increase a patient's tolerance to allergens.

allergy sensitivity test (19) performed on skin (cutaneous) and mucous membranes to identify the source of a patient's allergies.

allogenous (13) graft that involves tissue organ transplanted from one person to another.

allograft (12) transplantation of tissue from someone of the same species.

ambulance fee schedule (20) reimburses ambulance service providers a preestablished fee for each service provided.

ambulatory care (7) *see* outpatient care.

ambulatory patient (7) patient who is treated and released the same day and who does not stay overnight in the hospital.

ambulatory payment classification (APC) (20) hospital outpatient payment system (OPPS) that reimburses hospital outpatient services, which are organized clinically and according to resources required.

ambulatory surgery patient (7) patient who undergoes procedures that can be performed on an outpatient basis, with the patient treated and released the same day.

ambulatory surgical center (ASC) payment rate (20) reimbursement rate calculated on a prospective basis; rate is based on sample survey data and use of similar surgical techniques to establish reasonable estimated overhead allowances for each listed procedure.

A-mode (17) one-dimensional display that reflects the length of time a sound reaches a structure and is reflected back.

amplitude modulation (17) *see* A-mode.

analgesia (11) loss of pain sensation without loss of consciousness.

analgesic (11) drug that reduces pain, resulting in analgesia.

analyte (18) substance or chemical compound undergoing analysis.

ancillary service (6) diagnostic and/or therapeutic service provided to inpatients and outpatients.

anesthesia (11) process of inducing a loss of sensitivity to pain in all or part of the body, resulting from the administration of an anesthetic.

anesthesia conversion factor (11) dollar amount assigned to a geographic location.

anesthesia time unit (11) based on total anesthesia time and reported as one unit for each 15 minutes (or fraction thereof) of anesthesia time.

anesthesiologist (11) physician who, after medical school, completes a one-year internship and three-year residency in anesthesia.

anesthetic (11) drug or agent that causes a loss of feeling, awareness, and/or consciousness.

aneurysm (14) bulge in an artery that can weaken the arterial wall and eventually burst, resulting in hemorrhage.

angiogenesis (14) growth of new capillaries.

angiography (17) x-ray of a blood vessel after injection of contrast material.

angioscopy (14) microscopic visualization of substances as they pass through capillaries.

anoscopy (15) diagnostic procedure during which anal mucosa and the lower rectum are visualized using an anoscope.

ANSI ASC X12N 837 (20) variable-length file format that is used to bill institutional, professional, dental, and drug claims.

antepartum care (16) begins with conception and ends with delivery, including initial and subsequent history; physical examinations; documentation of weight, blood pressures, and fetal heart tones; routine chemical urinalysis (glucose); monthly visits up to 28 weeks' gestation; biweekly visits to 36 weeks' gestation; and weekly visits until delivery.

anterior approach (16) making an incision overlying the intervertebral disc by cutting through epidermis, dermis, subcutaneous, fascia, and muscle tissue.

anterolateral approach (16) making an incision along (and removing) the rib that corresponds to the vertebra that is located above the compressed intervertebral disk.

anteroposterior projection (17) patient is positioned with his or her back parallel to the film; the x-ray beam travels from front to back, or anterior to posterior.

antibody (18) proteins in the body made by the immune system that fight infection and disease.

antigen (18) foreign substances that elicit the formation of antibodies.

aortic anomaly (14) results from unusual patterns of aortic development and includes conditions such as tracheal decompression (or tracheomalacia), aberrant vessels (or vascular ring formation), aortopulmonary septal defect (APSD), patent ductus arteriosus, coarctation of aorta, and hypoplastic aortic arch (or interrupted aortic arch).

aortic sinus (14) *see* sinus of Valsalva.

aortography (17)   x-ray of the aorta after injection of contrast material.

Appendix A of CPT (8)   contains a list of CPT modifiers and detailed descriptions.

Appendix B of CPT (9)   contains annual CPT coding changes that include added, deleted, and revised CPT codes; it serves as the basis for updating interoffice documents and billing tools.

Appendix C of CPT (9)   contains clinical examples for codes found in the Evaluation and Management section.

Appendix D of CPT (9)   contains a list of add-on codes that are identified throughout CPT with a plus (+) symbol.

Appendix E of CPT (9)   contains a list of codes that are exempt from modifier -51 reporting rules and that are identified throughout CPT with a forbidden (⊘) symbol.

Appendix F of CPT (9)   contains a list of codes that are exempt from modifier -63.

Appendix J of CPT (9)   contains an electrodiagnostic medicine listing of sensory, motor, and mixed nerves that are reported for motor and nerve studies codes.

Appendix K of CPT (9)   contains a list of codes that are pending FDA approval but that have been assigned CPT codes; in the CPT manual, these codes are preceded by the flash (✗) symbol.

Appendix L of CPT (9)   contains a list of vascular families that is intended to assist in the selection of first-, second-, third-, and beyond third-order branch arteries.

Appendix M of CPT (9)   contains a list of deleted CPT codes and descriptions with a crosswalk to new CPT codes.

Appendix N of CPT (9)   contains a list of CPT codes that do not appear in numerical order. CPT codes are resequenced (instead of deleted and renumbered) so that existing codes can be relocated to a more appropriate location; out-of-sequence codes are preceded by the number symbol (#).

Appendix O of CPT (9)   includes administrative codes for procedures that by their nature are typically unique to a single clinical laboratory or manufacturer.

Appendix P of CPT (9)   includes codes for electronic communication using interactive telecommunications equipment (e.g., audio, video). In the CPT manual, these codes are preceded by the star (★) symbol. Modifier -95 is reported with Appendix P codes.

application service provider (ASP) (1)   third-party entity that manages and distributes software-based services and solutions to customers across a wide area network (WAN) from a central data center.

arterial puncture (18)   puncture of an artery with a needle for the purpose of drawing blood.

arteriography (11)   visualization of an artery via x-ray after injection of a radiopaque substance.

arteriovenous fistula (14)   abnormal passageway between an artery and a vein, which allows blood to flow directly into a vein.

arthrocentesis (13)   procedure done to puncture a joint for fluid removal or medication injection.

arthrodesis (13)   surgical fixation of a joint.

arthrography (17)   x-ray of a joint after injection of contrast material.

arthroscopy (13)   visual examination of the inside of a joint.

artificial ankylosis (13)   see arthrodesis.

arytenoidectomy (13)   excision of an arytenoid cartilage, which is located in the bilateral vocal fold.

arytenoidopexy (13)   surgical fixation of arytenoidal cartilage and/or surrounding muscles.

assay (18)   measurement of the amount of a constituent in a specimen, such as via laboratory test.

Assessment (A) (1)   judgment, opinion, or evaluation made by the health care provider; considered part of the problem-oriented record (POR) SOAP note.

assumption coding (1)   inappropriate assignment of codes based on assuming, from a review of clinical evidence in the patient's record, that the patient has certain diagnoses or received certain procedures/services even though the provider did not specifically document those diagnoses or procedures/services.

auditory system (16)   organized anatomically according to the external ear; middle ear; inner ear; and temporal bone, middle fossa approach.

augmentation (13)   process of enlarging or increasing.

autogenous (13)   originating in the patient's body.

autograft (12)   transplantation of tissue from the same individual.

automated case abstracting software (1)   software program that is used to collect and report inpatient and outpatient data for statistical analysis and reimbursement purposes.

automated record (1)   type of record that is created using computer technology.

autonomic function test (19)   evaluates autonomic nervous system functioning.

axial plane (17)   see transverse plane.

axis of classification (ICD-10-PCS) (6)   the sections, body parts, root operations, and so on that comprise the 7-character ICD-10-PCS code; each axis specifies information about the procedure performed, and within a defined code range, a character specifies the same type of information for that axis of classification.

B

backbench work (13)   preparing the cadaver donor heart and/or lung allograft prior to lung transplantation and dissecting allograft from surrounding soft tissues to prepare the aorta, superior vena cava, inferior vena cava, pulmonary artery, left atrium, trachea, pulmonary venous/atrial cuff, and/or bronchus for implantation.

Balanced Budget Act of 1997 (20)   legislated implementation of the skilled nursing facility prospective payment system, which uses resource utilization groups, version III (RUG-III), to reimburse Medicare SNF services according to a per diem prospective rate adjusted for case mix; also legislated implementation of an ambulance fee schedule, which reimburses ambulance service providers a preestablished fee for each service provided.

Balanced Budget Refinement Act of 1999 (BBRA) (20)   mandated implementation of the long-term (acute) care hospital prospective payment system, which uses information from long-term acute care hospital patient records to classify patients into distinct long-term (acute) care hospital diagnosis-related groups based on clinical characteristics and expected resource needs.

base unit value (11)   represents the degree of difficulty associated with providing anesthesia for a surgical procedure.

bed count (6)   see bed size.

bed size (6)   total number of inpatient beds for which a facility is licensed by the state; facility must be equipped and staffed to care for these patient admissions.

bedsore (12)   see pressure ulcer.

behavioral health care hospital (6)   health care facility that specializes in treating individuals with mental health diagnoses.

Bell's palsy (16)   unilateral paralysis of facial muscles resulting from dysfunction of the 7th cranial nerve, probably due to a viral infection.

benign (4)   not cancerous.

Bethesda system (18)   format for reporting cervical/vaginal cytology that includes a state of specimen adequacy, the general category, and a descriptive diagnosis.

Bier block (11)   see intravenous regional anesthesia.

biliary system (15)   organs and duct system that create, transport, store, and release bile into the duodenum (as part of the digestive process); includes the gallbladder, bile ducts inside the liver, bile ducts outside the liver, hepatic ducts, common bile duct, and cystic duct.

biofeedback (19)   technique that trains the patient to gain some control over autonomic body functions.

biometric A-scan (17)   diagnostic ultrasound that produces a one-dimensional view of normal and abnormal eye tissue and precise measurements of the eye's length.

biomicroscopy (17)   optical instrument that looks like a microscope with two eyepieces.

biopsy (12)   removal and examination of tissue to establish a diagnosis, confirm a diagnosis, or determine the extent of a disease.

bipolar cautery (15)   technique that uses an electric current that flows from one tip of the forceps to the other and does not require a grounding pad.

blepharoplasty (12)   any surgical repair of an eyelid.

block (radiology) (17)   device used when a radiology procedure is performed; made of lead or another heavy metal, it is placed between the radiation beam and that portion of the patient's body that requires protection from radiation.

block (tissue) (18)   portion of tissue obtained from a specimen that is placed in support medium, such as paraffin.

blocking (17)   device, such as lead, that shields or protects critical or sensitive organs during radiology treatment.

blood (14) tissue that consists of plasma, red blood cells, white blood cells, and platelets (or thrombocytes).

BlueCross and BlueShield (BCBS) (20) a health insurance organization that covers the costs of hospital care and physician services; BlueCross initially covered just hospital care and BlueShield covered just physicians' services; today each offers a full range of health care coverage.

blue reference symbol (⟳) (9) located below a code description in some CPT coding manuals to indicate that the coder should refer to the *CPT Assistant* monthly newsletter.

bone density study (17) evaluates diseases of the bone; used to assess the response of bone disease to treatment.

bone marrow (14) spongy material that fills large bones' cavities; consists of red marrow (produces red blood cells, white blood cells, and platelets) and yellow marrow (replaces red marrow with fatty tissue that does not produce blood cells).

bone marrow aspiration (14) use of a needle to remove a sample of the liquid bone marrow for examination under a microscope.

bone marrow biopsy (14) boring a small hole into a long bone and using a large, hollow needle to remove bone marrow for examination under a microscope.

breach of confidentiality (20) occurs when patient information is disclosed to other(s) who do not have a right to access the information.

brightness mode (17) *see* B-scan.

bronchoscopy (13) visual examination of the interior of the bronchus.

brushing (13) combing the mucous lining of the trachea or bronchus with a bronchial brush to collect cells.

B-scan (17) diagnostic ultrasound that produces a two-dimensional cross-sectional view of tissues that cannot be seen directly; it reflects sound waves bouncing off tissues or organs; e.g., used to locate a lesion and determine its shape; also called brightness mode (B-mod).

bullet symbol (9) symbol (•) located to the left of CPT codes that identifies new procedures and services added to CPT.

bunion (13) caused by bone inflammation and swelling and results in medial deviation and axial rotation of the first metatarsophalangeal (MTP) joint.

burr hole (16) small opening in the skull made with a surgical drill.

C

cadaver donor cardiectomy with or without pneumonectomy (14) harvesting the allograft (heart with or without lung tissue) and preserving the allograft with cold preservation solution and cold maintenance.

cadaver donor pneumonectomy (13) harvesting the allograft (lung tissue) and preserving the allograft with cold preservation solution and cold maintenance.

cafeteria plan (20) *see* triple option plan.

cancer staging (14) determination that cancer has or has not spread anatomically from its point of origin.

cannula (11) hollow needle.

capitated payment method (19) agreement between a third-party payer and a health care provider in which the provider agrees to provide services to a patient in return for a fixed monthly payment.

capitation (20) provider accepts a preestablished contracted payment for providing health care services to enrollees over a period of time, usually one year.

capnography (11) monitoring carbon dioxide levels.

carcinoma (Ca) *in situ* (4) malignant tumor that is localized, circumscribed, encapsulated, and noninvasive, but has not spread to deeper or adjacent tissues or organs.

cardiac ablation (14) stops atrial or ventricular fibrillation by using radiofrequency waves (modified electrical energy) to create small scars on the heart's surface.

cardiac blood pool imaging (17) use of a gamma camera for sampling, which is performed repetitively over several hundred heartbeats during the transition of the radionuclide through the central circulation.

cardiac catheterization (19) invasive diagnostic medical procedure that includes several components, beginning when the physician introduces one or more catheters into peripheral arteries and/or veins.

cardiac tumor (14) growth that develops in the heart's endocardium, myocardium, or pericardium.

cardiac valve (14) flap of tissue that keeps blood flowing in one direction to allow for the efficient one-way flow of blood through the heart's chambers.

cardiography (19) diagnostic procedure that records the heart's electronic activity with a cardiograph and produces a cardiogram (or electrocardiogram, ECG or EKG).

cardiopulmonary bypass (14) procedure to divert blood from the heart to the aorta, using a pump oxygenator.

care plan oversight services (10) cover the physician's time supervising a complex and multidisciplinary care treatment program for a specific patient who is under the care of a home health agency, hospice, or nursing facility.

carotid body (16) tissue that contains many capillaries; located at the point where the carotid artery branches in the neck.

carpal tunnel (16) eight bones in the wrist (carpals) that form a tunnel-like structure; the tunnel is filled with flexor tendons that control finger movement and provide a pathway for the median nerve to reach sensory cells in the hand.

carpal tunnel syndrome (16) painful progressive condition caused by compression of the median nerve at the wrist.

case management (10) process in which a physician or another qualified health care professional is responsible for direct care of a patient and for the coordination and control of access to or initiation and/or supervision of other health care services needed by the patient.

case mix (20) types and categories of patients cared for by a health care facility.

case-mix adjustment (20) decrease of average difference between preestablished payment and each patient's actual cost to a facility.

category (2) three-character ICD-10-CM disease code within a section.

Category I code (9) procedures/services identified by a five-digit CPT code and descriptor nomenclature; this type of code is traditionally associated with CPT and organized within six sections.

Category I PLA symbol (9) symbol (↑↓) identifies CPT category I PLA codes.

Category II code (9) optional CPT "performance measurements" tracking code that is assigned an alphanumerical identifier with a letter in the last field; this type of code is located after the CPT Medicine section.

Category III code (9) "emerging technology" temporary CTP code assigned for data collection purposes that is assigned an alphanumerical identifier with a letter in the last field; this type of code is located after the Medicine section, and it will be archived after five years if it is not accepted for placement within Category I sections of CPT.

caudal anesthesia (11) local anesthetic injected into the caudal canal, which is the sacral portion of the spinal canal.

cell washing (13) flushing fluid into an area and removing the fluid, using aspiration technique to collect cells.

Centers for Medicare & Medicaid Services (CMS) (1) administrative agency in the federal Department of Health & Human Services.

central motor evoked potential study (19) testing a patient's nervous system's pathway by placing low-voltage electrodes on the scalp and target sites.

central nervous system (CNS) (11) brain and spinal cord.

central venous access device (CVAD) (11) thin plastic tube that is inserted into a vein and connected to a monitor.

central venous pressure catheter (11) *see* central venous pressure (CVP) line.

central venous pressure (CVP) line (11) catheter that is inserted through a vein in the neck or a vein in the upper chest under the collar bone and then into a large central vein in the chest.

certificate of medical necessity (CMN) (8) prescription for durable medical equipment, services, and supplies.

certified registered nurse anesthetist (CRNA) (11) licensed registered nurse who has earned a bachelor's degree in science or nursing, has at least one year of acute care nursing experience, has completed a 24- to 36-month nurse anesthesia program leading to a master's degree, and has passed the national certification exam.

charge description master (CDM) (20) *see* chargemaster.

chargemaster (20) document that contains a computer-generated list of procedures, services, and supplies and corresponding revenue codes along with charges for each.

chargemaster review process (20) routinely conducted by designated hospital personnel to ensure accurate reimbursement by updating CPT and HCPCS codes and linking each to appropriate UB-04 revenue codes.

check digit (20) one-digit character, alphabetical or numerical, that is used to verify the validity of a unique identifier.

cheiloplasty (15) plastic surgery of the lips.

chemical peel (12) use of chemical agents to remove wrinkles and abnormal pigmentation.

chemosurgery (12) use of chemicals to destroy diseased tissue, such as for skin cancer.

chemotherapy (19) treatment of cancer with drugs that serve to destroy cancer cells or slow the growth of cancer cells and keep cancer from spreading to other parts of the body, preventing recurrence of the cancer.

Chemstrip automated urine analyzer (18) *see* reagent strip automated urine analyzer.

chief complaint (CC) (10) patient's description of medical condition stated in the patient's own words.

chiropractic manipulative treatment (CMT) (19) manual treatment performed to influence joint and neurophysiological function.

cholecystectomy (15) surgical removal of the gallbladder.

choroid (16) opaque layer behind the retina that contains blood vessels.

chromosomal breakage syndrome (18) genetic disorder that is usually transmitted in a genetic autosomal recessive mode.

chyle (14) digestive fluid that contains proteins and fats.

ciliary body (16) adjusts the shape of the lens and focuses light rays onto the retina.

ciliary muscle (16) *see* ciliary body.

Civilian Health and Medical Program of the Department of Veterans Affairs (CHAMPVA) (20) program that provides health care benefits to dependents of veterans rated as 100 percent permanently and totally disabled as a result of service-connected conditions, veterans who died as a result of service-connected conditions, and veterans who died on duty with less than 30 days of active service.

Civil Monetary Penalties Act (20) imposes a maximum penalty of up to $10,000 plus a maximum assessment of up to three times the amount claimed by providers who knew that a procedure/service was not rendered as submitted on the claim.

claims examiner (1) *see* health insurance specialist.

classification system (1) *see* coding system.

clearinghouse (1) public or private entity that processes or facilitates the processing of health information and claims from a nonstandard to a standard format.

cleft lip (11) congenital deformity of the upper lip that failed to close during development; types include unilateral, bilateral, and median (harelip) and may be accompanied by defects of the maxilla and hard palate.

clinical examples (10) contained in Appendix C of the CPT coding manual; assist providers in selecting the appropriate code for documented E/M services.

clinical laboratory fee schedule (20) methodology for determining fees for laboratory tests as a result of enacted legislation called the Deficit Reduction Act of 1984; the Consolidated Omnibus Budget Reconciliation Act of 1985 later established a national limitation amount (NLA) on the clinical laboratory fee schedule.

Clinical Laboratory Improvement Act of 1988 (CLIA) (18) certification that is required to perform certain pathology and laboratory tests (and to submit claims to Medicare and Medicaid).

clinic outpatient (7) patient who receives scheduled diagnostic and therapeutic care.

closed fracture (5) type of fracture that is contained beneath the skin and has intact ligaments and skin.

closed fracture treatment (13) fracture site that is not surgically opened or exposed.

closed laparoscopy (15) insufflation of the abdominal cavity using a percutaneously placed needle; performed to examine peritoneal contents using a laparoscope.

closed-panel HMO (20) HMO-owned center or satellite clinic that provides health care services.

CMS-1450 (1) *see* UB-04.

CMS-1500 (1) standard claim submitted by physicians' offices to third-party payers.

cochlear implant (16) implanted electronic device for treatment of sensory deafness.

code (1) numerical and alphanumerical characters that are reported to health plans for health care reimbursement and to external agencies (e.g., state departments of health) for data collection, in addition to being reported internally (e.g., acute care hospital) for education and research.

coder (1) acquires a working knowledge of coding systems (e.g., CPT, HCPCS level II, ICD-10-CM, and ICD-10-PCS), coding principles and rules, government regulations, and third-party payer requirements to ensure that all diagnoses (conditions), services (e.g., office visit), and procedures (e.g., surgery and x-ray) documented in patient records are coded accurately for reimbursement, research, and statistical purposes.

coding (1) assignment of codes to diagnoses, services, and procedures based on patient record documentation.

coding conventions (ICD-10-CM/PCS) (3) general rules used in the ICD-10-CM classification system that are independent of coding guidelines.

  abbreviations (3) use of NEC (not elsewhere classifiable) and NOS (not otherwise specified). (NEC and NOS abbreviations do *not* appear in ICD-10-PCS.)

    NEC (not elsewhere classifiable) (3) equivalent of "other specified"; identifies codes that are to be assigned when information needed to assign a more specific code cannot be located in the coding manual.

    NOS (not otherwise specified) (3) equivalent of "unspecified"; identifies codes that are to be assigned when information needed to assign a more specific code cannot be obtained from the provider.

  and (3) interpreted as meaning "and/or."

  boxed note (3) defines terms, provides coding instruction, and lists fifth-digit subclassifications for categories that use the same fifth digits; Index to Procedures boxed notes also provide coding instruction and list fourth-digit subclassifications for categories that use the same fourth digits. (Boxed notes do not appear in ICD-10-CM or ICD-10-PCS.)

  code also (3) ICD-10-CM note that provides instruction that two codes may be required to fully describe a condition; this note does *not* provide sequencing direction.

  cross-references (3) instruction to refer to another entry in the index (e.g., *see*, *see also*, *see* condition) or tabular list (e.g., *see* category) to assign the correct code.

    see (3) instructional term that directs the coder to refer to another term in the indexes.

    see also (3) instructional term that is located after a main term or subterm in the index and directs the coder to another main term (or subterm) that may provide additional useful index entries.

    see category (3) instructional term that directs the coder to the tabular list, where a code can be selected from the options provided there.

    see condition (3) instructional term that directs the coder to the main term in the index for a condition.

  default code (3) ICD-10-CM code listed next to a main term in the index; represents that condition that is most commonly associated with the main term, or is the unspecified code for the condition.

  due to (3) index subterm (in alphabetical order) that indicates the presence of a cause-and-effect (or causal) relationship between two conditions.

  eponym (3) disease, syndrome, or procedure named for a person.

  etiology and manifestation rules (3) include the following in the tabular list: code first underlying disease; code, if applicable, any causal condition first; in diseases classified elsewhere; and use additional code.

    code first underlying disease (3) tabular list instructional note that assists with proper sequencing of codes.

    code, if applicable, any causal condition first (3) tabular list instructional note that requires causal conditions to be sequenced first, if present.

    in diseases classified elsewhere (3) indicates that manifestation codes are a component of the etiology/manifestation coding convention.

    use additional code (3) instructional note that assists in proper sequencing of the codes.

  excludes1 note (3) appears below codes in the ICD-10-CM tabular list to direct the coder to another location in the tabular list to classify conditions that are excluded from the code—either the original code or the code to which the excludes1 note directs you.

  excludes2 note (3) appears below codes in the ICD-10-CM tabular list to direct the coder to another location in the tabular list to classify conditions that are excluded from the code; both the original code and the code to which the excludes2 note directs you can be reported if documentation supports both conditions.

  format (3) for ease of reference, index subterms are indented two spaces below a main term; second, third, and fourth qualifiers are indented two, four, and six spaces, respectively, below the subterm.

  in (3) index subterm (in alphabetical order) that indicates the presence of a cause-and-effect (or causal) relationship between two conditions.

includes note (3) appears immediately below tabular list codes to further define terms or provide examples.

inclusion term (3) listed below certain codes in the tabular lists; includes conditions or procedures for which that code number is to be assigned; can be synonyms of the code title or, for "other" codes, a list of conditions or procedures assigned to that code.

manifestation (3) condition that occurs as the result of another condition; a manifestation code is always reported as a secondary code.

modifier (3) additional term included after the colon in the ICD-10-CM tabular lists that is to be included in the statement to classify a condition or procedure.

other (3) when this word appears in an ICD-10-CM code description, the code is assigned when patient record documentation provides detail for which a specific code does not exist.

other specified (3) when this phrase appears in an ICD-10-CM code description, the code is assigned when patient record documentation provides detail for which a specific code does not exist.

punctuation (3) brackets, parentheses, and colons.

   brackets (3) used in the index to enclose manifestation codes; used in the tabular list to enclose synonyms, alternative wording, and explanatory phrases.

   colon (3) used after an incomplete term in the tabular list when one or more additional terms (called modifiers) after the colon must be documented in the diagnostic or procedural statement to classify a condition or procedure.

   parentheses (3) used in the index and tabular list to enclose non-essential modifiers, which are supplementary words that may be present in or absent from the physician's statement of a disease or procedure without affecting the code number to which it is assigned.

syndrome (3) association of clinically recognizable features such as signs, symptoms, and characteristics that often occur together, so that the presence of one or more features alerts the health care provider as to the possible presence of the others; coders should follow ICD-10-CM index guidance when assigning codes to a syndrome; in the absence of index guidance, assign codes for the documented manifestations of the syndrome.

tables (3) index feature that organizes subterms, second qualifiers, and third qualifiers and their codes in columns and rows to make it easier to select the proper code. (Tables also appear in ICD-10-PCS, which facilitate assignment of values to create the seven-character code.)

trust the index (3) concept that inclusion terms listed in the Tabular List of Diseases are not meant to be exhaustive and that additional terms found only in the Index to Diseases (but not in the Tabular List of Diseases) may also be assigned to a code.

typeface (3) for ease of reference, index main terms are boldfaced and manifestation codes are italicized.

unspecified code (3) assigned when patient record documentation is insufficient to assign a more specific code.

use (3) directs the coder to a body part or a device in the ICD-10-PCS index.

with (3) index term that is located immediately below the main term, *not in alphabetical order*.

coding system (1) organizes a medical nomenclature according to similar conditions, diseases, procedures, and services; it contains codes for each.

cold biopsy forceps (15) technique that does not use electrocoagulation; the polyp is simply pulled from the colon wall.

colectomy (15) removal of part or all of the large intestine.

colonoscopy (15) visual examination of the entire colon, from the rectum to the cecum, and may include the terminal ileum.

colostomy (15) removal of a portion of the colon or rectum; the remaining colon is brought to the abdominal wall.

column 1/column 2 edits (9) code pairs that should not be billed together because one service inherently includes the other; previously called comprehensive/component edits.

combination code (2) single code used to classify two diagnoses (or procedures), a diagnosis with an associated secondary process (manifestation), or a diagnosis with an associated complication.

commercial payer (20) private health insurance company or employer-based group health insurance company.

commissurotomy (14) narrowed valve leaflets are widened by carefully opening the fused leaflets with a scalpel.

comorbidity (6) coexisting condition (e.g., diabetes mellitus) that is treated during the same encounter as or impacts the medical management of another condition (e.g., myocardial infarction).

compensator (17) irregularly shaped beam-modifying device used to reconfigure beam intensity so it matches irregular tissue contour.

complex fistulectomy (15) excision of multiple fistulas.

compliance guidance (20) document that identifies risk areas and offers concrete suggestions to improve and enhance an organization's internal controls so that billing practices and other business arrangements are in compliance with Medicare's rules and regulations.

complication (6) condition that occurs during the course of an inpatient hospital episode.

component coding (17) reporting a radiology procedure code and a surgical procedure code to completely describe the service provided.

composite graft (14) vein and synthetic graft material or segments of veins from two or more locations.

compound fracture (5) *see* open fracture.

comprehensive examination (10) general multisystem examination or complete examination of a single organ system.

comprehensive history (10) chief complaint, extended history of present illness, review of systems directly related to the problem(s) identified in the history of present illness in addition to a review of all additional body systems, and complete past/family/social history.

computed axial tomography (CT) (CAT) (17) x-ray of horizontal and vertical cross-sectional views or "slices" of the body that are computer-processed to create three-dimensional, or 3D, images.

computed tomography angiography (CTA) (17) x-rays of different angles to create cross-sectional images of organs, bones, and tissues that visualize blood flow in arterial and venous vessels throughout the body.

computer-assisted coding (CAC) (1) uses computer software to automatically generate medical codes by "reading" transcribed clinical documentation; uses "natural language processing" theories to generate codes that are reviewed and validated by coders for reporting on third-party payer claims.

concha (13) *see* turbinates.

concurrent care (10) provision of similar services, such as hospital inpatient visits, to the same patient by more than one provider on the same day.

concurrent coding (1) review of records and/or use of encounter forms and chargemasters to assign codes during an inpatient stay or an outpatient encounter; typically performed for outpatient encounters because encounter forms and chargemasters are completed in "real time" by health care providers as part of the charge-capture process.

concurrent medically directed anesthesia procedure (11) maximum number of procedures an anesthesiologist or a CRNA medically directs within the context of a single procedure when the procedures overlap.

confidentiality (20) process of keeping privileged communication secret; means that information cannot be disclosed without the patient's authorization.

conization (16) removal of a cone-shaped piece of tissue.

conjunctiva (16) mucous membrane that lines the underside of each eyelid and forms a protective covering over the exposed surface of the eyeball.

Consolidated Omnibus Budget Reconciliation Act of 1985 (20) federal legislation that established a national limitation amount, which serves as a payment ceiling, or cap, on the amount Medicare could pay for each test.

consultation (10) examination of a patient by a health care provider, usually a specialist, for the purpose of advising the referring or attending physician in the evaluation and/or management of a specific problem with a known diagnosis.

consumer-directed health plan (CDHP) (20) a sort of "401(K)" plan for health care"; includes many choices that provide individuals with an incentive to control the costs of health benefits and health care.

contiguous sites (4) adjacent locations as in cancer of multiple sites that overlap or border each other (e.g., nasopharynx and oropharynx cancer).

continent ileostomy (15) surgical variation of an ileostomy in which a reservoir pouch is created inside the abdomen using a portion of the terminal ileum, a valve is constructed in the pouch, and a stoma is brought through the abdominal wall.

continuity of care (1) documenting patient care services so that others who treat the patient have a source of information on which to base additional care and treatment.

contrast agent (17) radiopaque substances (solid or liquid) that obstruct the passage of x-rays, making the structure containing the agent appear white on radiographic film; administered to provide better radiographic visualization of organs studied.

contrast material (17)   see contrast agent.

contrast medium (11)   see contrast agent; plural is *contrast media*.

contrast medium injection device (17)   instrument used to deliver a predetermined amount of contrast, typically for vascular imaging procedures.

contributory components (10)   include counseling, coordination of care, nature of presenting problem, and time; they are used to select the appropriate E/M service code when patient record documentation indicates that they were the focus of the visit.

conversion factor (20)   dollar multiplier that converts relative value units into payments using a formula.

cooperating parties for the ICD-10-CM/PCS (2)   AHA, AHIMA, CMS, and NCHS.

coordination of care (10)   component in which physician makes arrangements with other providers or agencies for services to be provided to a patient.

cornea (16)   transparent layer on the eye's surface; covers the iris and pupil; provides focusing power.

corneal pachymetry (17)   noninvasive ultrasound procedure that determines thickness of the cornea.

coronal plane (17)   divides the body into anterior or ventral and posterior or dorsal portions at a right angle to the sagittal plane, separating the body into front and back; also called ventral or dorsal plane.

coronary artery bypass graft (CABG) (14)   procedure performed to improve flow of blood to the heart.

coronary endarterectomy (14)   removal of the inner layer of coronary arteries that contain cholesterol plaques.

corpectomy (16)   removal of a portion of the vertebra and adjacent intervertebral disks.

costovertebral (16)   area of the thoracic spine where the rib meets the vertebra.

costovertebral approach (16)   procedure performed where the ribs articulate with thoracic vertebrae.

counseling (10)   as related to CPT E/M coding, a discussion with a patient and/or family concerning one or more of the following areas: diagnostic results, impressions, and recommended diagnostic studies; prognosis; risks and benefits of management (treatment) options; instructions for management (treatment) and follow-up; importance of compliance with chosen management (treatment) options; risk factor reduction; and patient and family education.

covered benefit (20)   reimbursable medical benefit.

covered entity (20)   private or public sector organization that must follow HIPAA provisions.

critical access hospital (CAH) (6)   located more than 35 miles from any hospital or another CAH; state certified as being a necessary provider of health care to area residents.

critical care (10)   delivery of medical care services to critically ill or injured patients who require the full, exclusive attention of the physician.

critical illness or injury (10)   one that acutely impairs one or more vital organ systems, jeopardizing the patient's survival.

critical pathways (20)   interdisciplinary guidelines developed by health care facilities to facilitate management and delivery of quality clinical care in a time of constrained resources; allow for the planning of provision of clinical services that have expected time frames and resources targeted to specific diagnoses and/or procedures.

cross-over vein graft (14)   making an incision to expose the vein's incompetent valve, dividing that section of the vein, and connecting it to a nearby vein that has functioning valves.

cryosurgery (12)   application of extreme cold, such as liquid nitrogen, to destroy abnormal tissue cells, such as warts or small skin tumors.

Current Procedural Terminology (CPT) (1)   coding system used by physicians and outpatient health care settings to assign CPT codes for reporting procedures and services on health insurance claims; considered level I of the Healthcare Common Procedure Coding System (HCPCS); published and updated by the American Medical Association (AMA) to classify procedures and services; listing of descriptive terms and identifying codes for reporting medical services and procedures; provides a uniform language that describes medical, surgical, and diagnostic services to facilitate communication among providers, patients, and third-party payers.

customized sub-capitation plan (CSCP) (20)   funds health care expenses with insurance coverage; individual selects one of each type of provider to create a customized network and pays the resulting customized insurance premium.

cutdown (14)   a procedure whereby a catheter is inserted directly into a vein through an incision.

cystography (17)   x-ray of the urinary bladder after injection of contrast material.

cystometrogram (15)   records urinary bladder pressure at various volumes; useful in diagnosing bladder outlet obstruction and other voiding dysfunctions.

cystoscopy (15)   allows for direct visual examination of urinary bladder and urethra.

cystourethroscopy (15)   see cystoscopy.

cytogenetics (18)   study of the cell and its heredity-related components, including chromosomes.

cytopathology (18)   study of diseased cells.

cytoreduction surgery (17)   see debulking.

D

database (1)   contains a minimum data set of patient information collected on each patient, including chief complaint; present conditions and diagnoses; social data; past, personal, medical, and social history; review of systems; physical examination; and baseline laboratory data; considered part of the problem-oriented record (POR).

Data Elements for Emergency Department Systems (DEEDS) (7)   collection of data reported by hospital-based emergency departments for the purpose of reducing incompatibility in emergency department records.

debulking (17)   surgical removal of part of a malignant tumor to enhance the effectiveness of radiation oncology treatment.

decrypt (20)   decode.

decubitus ulcer (12)   see pressure ulcer.

DEEDS (7)   see Data Elements for Emergency Department Systems (DEEDS)

defect (12)   wound that is the result of surgical intervention or trauma.

Deficit Reduction Act of 1984 (20)   established the clinical laboratory fee schedule as a methodology for determining fees for existing tests.

definitive identification (18)   specialized testing performed for identification at the genus or species level.

delivery/birthing room attendance and resuscitation services (10)   services provided for attendance at delivery, initial stabilization of the newborn, and delivery/birthing room resuscitation.

delivery services (16)   services from patient admission to the hospital through delivery of the placenta.

demographic data (1)   patient identification information that is collected according to facility policy (e.g., patient's name, date of birth, mother's maiden name, and Social Security number).

dermabrasion (12)   use of a rotary device to sand down raised lesions or thickened tissue, regenerating smoother skin; performed for conditions such as acne scarring, wrinkles, rhytids, and general keratosis.

descriptive qualifiers (9)   clarify assignment of a CPT code; occur in the middle of a main clause or after the semicolon; may or may not be enclosed in parentheses.

Designated Standard Maintenance Organization (DSMO) (20)   to maintain electronic transactions standards adopted by the Secretary of DHHS and develops or modifies adopted standards.

destruction (12)   ablation of benign, premalignant, or malignant tissues by any method.

detailed examination (10)   extended examination of the affected body area(s) and other symptomatic or related organ system(s).

detailed history (10)   includes chief complaint, extended history of present illness, problem pertinent system review extended to include a limited number of additional systems, and pertinent past/family/social history directly related to patient's problem.

determination of refractive state (19)   establishes whether a prescription is required for vision correction.

diagnosis-related groups (DRGs) (20)   classify inpatient hospital cases into groups that are expected to consume similar hospital resources; each DRG has a payment weight assigned to it that is based on the average resources used to treat Medicare patients in that DRG.

Diagnostic and Statistical Manual (DSM) of Mental Disorders (1)   manual published by the American Psychiatric Association that contains diagnostic assessment criteria used as tools to identify psychiatric disorders; DSM includes psychiatric disorders and codes, provides a mechanism for communicating and recording diagnostic information, and is used in the areas of research and statistics.

Diagnostic Coding and Reporting Guidelines for Outpatient Services (7)   developed by the federal government and approved for use by hospitals and providers for coding and reporting hospital-based outpatient services and provider-based office visits.

diagnostic endoscopy (15)   use of instrumentation for surgical visualization to determine extent of disease.

diagnostic mammography (17)   assessment of suspected disease of breasts.

diagnostic/management plan (1)   information about the patient's condition and the planned management of conditions; considered part of the problem-oriented record (POR).

diagnostic procedure (12)   laboratory, radiographic, and other tests performed to evaluate the patient's complaints or symptoms and to establish the diagnosis.

diaphragm (15)   thin muscle below the heart and lungs; separates the chest from the abdomen.

digestive system (15)   bodily system that begins at the mouth and extends to the anus.

digital (20)   applies a mathematical function to an electronic document, resulting in a unique bit string (computer code), called a message digest, that is encrypted and appended to the electronic document.

dipstick (18)   small strip of plastic that is infused with a chemical; reacts to products in urine by changing color.

direct contract model HMO (20)   contracted health care services delivered to subscribers by individual physicians in the community.

direct laryngoscopy (13)   insertion of a flexible (fiberoptic) or rigid laryngoscope to visualize throat structures.

discectomy (16)   removal of an intervertebral disc.

discharge note (1)   documented in the progress note section of the problem-oriented record (POR) to summarize the patient's care, treatment, response to care, and condition on discharge.

disclosed (20)   released.

dislocation (13)   total displacement of bone from its joint.

diverticula (15)   small pouches (herniations) in the colon that bulge outward through weak spots.

diverticulosis (15)   presence of diverticula in the mucosa and submucosal, through or between fibers of the colon's major muscle layer.

DME MAC medical review policies (8)   local coverage determinations and national coverage determinations.

documentation (1)   includes dictated and transcribed, typed or handwritten, and computer-generated notes and reports recorded in the patient's records by a health care professional.

Documentation Guidelines for Evaluation and Management Services **(10)**   explain how E/M codes are assigned according to elements associated with comprehensive multisystem and single-system examinations.

document imaging (1)   converting paper records to an electronic image and saved on storage media.

donor site (12)   anatomical site from which healthy skin is removed.

Doppler ultrasonography (17)   evaluates movement by measuring changes in the frequency of echoes reflected from moving structures.

dose (19)   amount of antigen administered in a single injection from a multiple-dose vial.

dosimetry (17)   measurement and calculation of radiation treatment doses.

double pedicle flap (12)   maintains blood supply from both ends of a flap incision that was made to create a curvilinear flap contiguous with the defect; flap is pivoted and sutured in place over the defect.

downcoding (1)   routinely assigning lower-level CPT codes as a convenience instead of reviewing patient record documentation and the coding manual to determine the proper code to be reported.

DRG creep (20)   federal Department of Justice (DOJ) initiative that focuses on medical necessity and billing patterns of DRG coding to determine whether claims hospitals submit accurately reflect care required or provided to the patient; DOJ investigates claims for which facilities receive higher reimbursement as a result of reporting higher paying ICD codes.

dual chamber (14)   contains two electrodes; one placed in the right atrium and the other is in the right ventricle.

dual energy x-ray absorptiometry (DEXA) (17)   bone density study that uses two x-ray beams with different levels of energy pulsing alternately to create the image.

duplex scan (19)   noninvasive test that is performed to evaluate a vessel's blood flow.

duplicate PLA symbol (9)   symbol (✳) identifies duplicate proprietary laboratory analyses (PLA) tests.

durable medical equipment, prosthetics, orthotics, and supplies (DME-POS) (8)   includes items such as artificial limbs, braces, medications, surgical dressings, and wheelchairs.

durable medical equipment, prosthetics, orthotics, and supplies (DME-POS) dealer (8)   supply patients with durable medical equipment.

durable medical equipment, prosthetics, orthotics, and supplies (DME-POS) fee schedule (20)   payment methodology mandated by the Omnibus Budget Reconciliation Act of 1987 (OBRA); the fee schedule is released annually and updated on a quarterly basis to implement fee schedule amounts for new codes and to revise any amounts for existing codes that were calculated in error.

dura mater (11)   membrane that forms the outer covering of the central nervous system.

E

echo (17)   effect of a sound that reflects off a distant surface and returns to its source.

echocardiography (19)   diagnostic procedure that uses ultrasound to obtain two-dimensional images of the heart and/or great arteries (aorta and vena cavae).

electrocardiography (19)   *see* cardiography.

electrocautery snare (15)   technique that uses a wire loop to encircle, not grasp, a polyp.

electroconvulsive therapy (ECT) (11)   briefly applying an electric current to the brain to produce a seizure; its purpose is to relieve depression, schizophrenia, and severe affective disorders.

electromyography (19)   test used to detect nerve function by measuring the electrical activity generated by muscles.

electronic data interchange (EDI) (20)   computer-to-computer transfer of data between provider and third-party payer (or provider and health care clearing house) in a data format agreed upon by the sending and receiving parties.

electronic health record (EHR) (1)   collection of patient information documented by a number of providers at one or more facilities regarding one patient; multidisciplinary and multienterprise approach to record keeping because it has the ability to link patient information created at different locations according to a unique patient identifier; provides access to complete and accurate health problems, status, and treatment data; contains alerts and reminders for health care providers.

electronic medical record (EMR) (1)   created on a computer, using a keyboard, a mouse, an optical pen device, a voice recognition system, a scanner, or a touch screen; records are created using vendor software, which also assists in provider decision making regarding patient care and treatment.

electronic transaction standard (20)   uniform language for electronic data interchange.

electrophysiology (14)   study of heart arrhythmias.

electrosurgery (12)   use of an electrical device to destroy abnormal tissue.

embolectomy (14)   surgical removal of an embolus.

embolus (14)   blood clot that circulates throughout the bloodstream.

emergency condition (11)   results when a delay in treatment of the patient would lead to a significant increase in threat to life or body part.

emergency department service (10)   provided in a hospital, and open 24 hours a day for the purpose of providing unscheduled episodic services to patients who require immediate medical attention.

emergency patient (7)   patient treated for urgent problems and either released the same day or admitted to the hospital as an inpatient.

employer self-insurance plan (20)   employer accepts direct responsibility for (or the risk of) paying employees' health care without purchasing health insurance.

en bloc **(14)**   as a whole.

encoder (2)   software that automates the coding process; software search features facilitate the location and verification of diagnosis and procedure codes.

encoding (1)   process of standardizing data by assigning numeric values (codes or numbers) to text or other information.

encounter (2)   face-to-face contact between a patient and a health care provider who assesses and treats the patient's condition; Medicare uses the term *encounter* in the guidelines for coding and reporting to indicate all health care settings, including inpatient hospital admissions.

encounter form (20)   document used to record encounter data about office procedures and services provided to patients.

encrypt (20) to encode a computer file, making it safe for electronic transmission so that unauthorized parties cannot read it.

endocardium (14) inner lining of the heart.

endocrine system (16) composed of glands including the adrenal, gonads, pancreas, parathyroid, pituitary, thymus, and thyroid.

endorectal pull-through (15) *see* ileoanal anastomosis.

endoscopic retrograde cholangiopancreatography (ERCP) (15) passing an endoscope through the esophagus, stomach, and duodenum to the ducts of the biliary tree and pancreas.

endoscopy (12) procedure performed to visualize a body cavity, using a medical instrument that consists of a long tube that can be inserted into the body, either through a small incision or a natural opening.

endotracheal tube (ET) (11) artificial airway used for short-term airway management or mechanical ventilation due to potential or actual respiratory system insufficiency.

end-stage renal disease (ESRD) composite payment rate system (20) single-payment fixed rate that does not vary according to the characteristics of the beneficiary treated (and includes the cost of some drugs, laboratory tests, and other items and services provided to Medicare beneficiaries receiving dialysis).

enterectomy (15) resection of small bowel segments.

enterolysis (15) freeing of intestinal adhesions.

enucleation of the eye (16) severing of the eyeball from extraorbital muscles and the optic nerve and its removal.

epidural anesthesia (11) local anesthetic injected into the epidural space, where it acts primarily on spinal nerve roots; anesthetized area includes the abdomen or chest to large regions of the body.

epidurography (17) performed to assess the structure of the spine's epidural space prior to percutaneous epidural adhesiolysis (to identify nerve construction or inflammation and the degree of fluid flow in the epidural space).

equivalent dose (17) radiation quantity measured by roentgen-equivalent-man (rem).

esophageal varices (15) uneven, enlarged, tortuous veins of the esophagus.

esophagogastroduodenoscopy (EGD) (15) use of a fiberoptic endoscope to visualize the esophagus, stomach, and proximal duodenum.

esophagogastroscopy (15) *see* upper GI endoscopy.

esophagoscopy (15) visualization of the esophagus, using an endoscope.

essential modifier (2) *see* subterm.

established patient (10) one who *has* received professional services within the past three years from the physician or from another physician of the same exact specialty or subspecialty who belongs to the same group practice.

etiology (2) cause of disease.

evidence-based coding (1) clicking on codes that CAC software generates to review electronic health record documentation (evidence) used to generate the code; when it is determined that documentation supports the CAC-generated code, the coding auditor clicks to accept the code; when documentation does not support the CAC-generated code, the coding auditor replaces it with an accurate code.

evidence-verification coding (1) *see* evidence-based coding.

evisceration of ocular contents (16) removal of the contents of the eyeball; the sclera remains intact.

evocative (18) causing a specific response; this term is used to describe various tests intended to cause production of hormones or other secretions.

excision (12) removal of a portion or all of an organ or another tissue, using a scalpel or another surgical instrument.

excisional biopsy (12) removal of a lump or suspicious area in its entirety.

exclusion (20) "Medicare PPS Excluded Cancer Hospital" that applies for and is granted a waiver from mandatory participation in the hospital inpatient PPS.

exclusive provider organization (EPO) (20) managed care plan that provides benefits to subscribers if they receive services from network providers.

exenteration of the orbit (16) removal of orbital contents; may also include removal of bone, muscle, and/or the myocutaneous flap.

expanded problem focused examination (10) limited examination of the affected body area or organ system and other symptomatic or related organ system(s).

expanded problem focused history (10) chief complaint, brief history of present illness, and problem pertinent system review.

explanation of benefits (EOB) (20) statement sent by the payer to the patient that contains the same information as a remittance advice but in an easy-to-read format.

extensive cellulitis (12) acute inflammation of skin's connective tissue, caused by infection with bacteria.

extensor tendons (13) tendons that serve to straighten the fingers.

extent of examination (10) categorized according to problem focused examination, expanded problem focused examination, detailed examination, and comprehensive examination.

extent of history (10) categorized according to problem focused history, expanded problem focused history, detailed history, or comprehensive history.

external catheter (11) catheter that is not implanted under the patient's skin and does not require a needle to be inserted into the skin to deliver medications.

external ear (16) auricle and external auditory meatus.

external fixation device (13) hardware inserted through bone and skin that is held rigid with cross-braces outside of the body; external fixation is always removed after the fracture has healed.

external radiation (17) radiation administered by a machine outside the body.

extracapsular cataract extraction (ECCE) (16) removal of lens and anterior portion of capsule.

extracorporeal life support (ECLS) (14) *see* extracorporeal membrane oxygenation (ECMO).

extracorporeal membrane oxygenation (ECMO) (14) provide cardiac and/or respiratory support to the heart and/or lungs, which allow them to rest and recover when patients are sick or injured.

extracorporeal shock wave lithotripsy (ESWL) (11) use of ultrasound shock waves to crush calculi (stones) located in the bladder, renal pelvis, or ureter.

extradural procedure (11) performed on the outer side of the dura mater.

eye and ocular adnexa (16) describes procedures performed on the eyeball, anterior and posterior segment, ocular adnexa, and conjunctivae.

eyeball (16) consists of the choroid, retina, and sclera.

eye socket (16) *see* orbit.

F

face-to-face time (10) amount of time the office or outpatient care provider spends with the patient and/or family.

False Claims Act (FCA) (20) law enacted in 1863 in response to widespread abuses by government contractors during the Civil War; amended in 1986 to strengthen the law and increase monetary awards.

family history (10) review of medical events in the patient's family, including diseases that may be hereditary or that may present a risk to the patient.

Federal Anti-kickback Statute (20) prohibits the offer, payment, receipt, or solicitation of compensation for referring Medicaid/Medicare patients and imposes a $25,000 fine per violation, plus imprisonment for up to 10 years.

Federal Claims Collection Act of 1966 (20) law that established uniform procedures for government agencies to follow in the collection, compromise, suspension, termination, or referral for litigation of debts owed to the government.

Federal Employee Health Benefits Program (FEHBP or FEP) (20) voluntary health care program that covers federal employees, retirees, and their dependents and survivors.

Federally Qualified Health Centers (FQHCs) (20) safety net providers that primarily provide services typically furnished in an outpatient clinic; FQHC PPS for medically necessary primary health services and qualified preventive health services furnished by an FQHC practitioner is the basis for reimbursement; and the FQHC *market basket* establishes Medicare values for reimbursement.

fee-for-service (20) method of reimbursing providers for individual health care services rendered.

fee schedule (20) cost-based fee-for-service reimbursement methodology that includes a list of maximum fees and corresponding procedures/services; payers use fee schedules to compensate providers for health care services delivered to patients.

female genital system (16) includes the vulva, perineum, and introitus; vagina; cervix uteri; and uterus, oviduct (fallopian tube), and ovary.

femur (13) long bone of the thigh; articulates with the hip bone, tibia, and patella.

field block (11) subcutaneous injection of local anesthetic in area bordering the field to be anesthetized.

fine-needle aspiration (FNA) (12) procedure in which a thin needle is inserted through a mass several times to remove fluid from a cyst or cells from a solid mass; suction is applied as the needle is withdrawn to obtain strands of single cells for cytological diagnosis.

first-listed diagnosis (7) diagnosis, condition, problem, or other reason for encounter/visit documented in the patient record to be chiefly responsible for the services provided.

first-order vessels (14) blood vessels that extend as primary arterial branches from the aorta.

flap (12) relocation of a mass of tissue (usually skin) that has been partially removed from one part of the body so it retains its own blood supply.

flash symbol (9) symbol () located to the left of CPT codes that identifies products pending FDA approval but that have been assigned a CPT code.

flat file (20) fixed-length file format that was developed for use in claims processing (because the ANSI ASC X12 837 variable-length file format is not suitable for use in an application program and must be translated into a flat file format prior to claims processing).

flexible spending account (FSA) (20) tax-advantaged account that contains automatic deposits of a portion of an employee's pretax paycheck; money in the account is used to pay for qualified medical expenses not covered by insurance (e.g., coinsurance, copayments, certain FSA-approved over-the-counter medications and supplies for chronic conditions).

flexor tendons (13) tendons that serve to bend the fingers.

fluid management (11) administering IV fluids to avoid dehydration, maintain an effective circulating volume, and prevent inadequate tissue perfusion.

fluorescence *in situ* hybridization (FISH) (18) test performed to detect submicroscopic changes in chromosomes (e.g., genetic disorders such as Williams syndrome) or to identify unknown chromosomal material.

fluoroscopy (17) procedure in which a continuous x-ray beam generates a movie-like image that is viewed on a monitor; used for invasive procedures such as intravenous/intra-arterial catheterization and extracorporeal shock wave lithotripsy.

forbidden symbol (9) symbol (⊘) located to the left of CPT codes that identifies codes exempt from modifier -51.

fraction (in radiation treatment management) (17) single session of radiation treatment delivered to a specific area of interest.

fracture (5) break in a bone resulting from injury or a disease process.

fraud (20) intentional deception or misrepresentation that someone makes, knowing it is false, that could result in an unauthorized payment.

free flap (12) flap consisting of skin and subcutaneous tissue with a pedicle composed only of nutrient vessels, which is detached from the donor site and reattached at the recipient site via microvascular anastomosis.

free skin graft (12) complete separation of skin from the donor site before being transferred to the recipient site.

frontal plane (17) *see* coronal plane.

full-thickness skin graft (12) removal (harvesting) of epidermis and dermis for grafting.

functional modifier (9) pricing modifier that a third-party payer considers when determining reimbursement.

G

gamma globulin (19) *see* immune globulin.

gastrectomy (15) removal of all or a portion of the stomach.

general anesthesia (11) administration of anesthetic agents that are inhaled or administered intravenously.

general equivalence mapping (GEM) (2) published crosswalks of codes that facilitate the location of corresponding diagnosis and procedure codes between two code sets, such as ICD-9-CM and ICD-10-CM.

general hospital (6) acute care facility that provides emergency care, general surgery, and inpatient admission services based on licensing by the state.

glabellar frown lines (12) vertical furrows located in the forehead area between the eyebrows.

global period (12) time established (0, 10, or 90 days) for each surgical procedure.

global service (17) combined technical and professional components.

global surgical package (12) ensures that payments are made consistently for the same services across all Medicare administrative contractor jurisdictions and prevents Medicare payments for services that are more or less comprehensive than intended.

globe (16) *see* eyeball.

government-sponsored programs (20) include CHAMPVA, Federal Employee Health Benefits Program, Indian Health Service, Medicaid, Medicare, Military Health System, Programs of All-inclusive Care for the Elderly, and TRICARE.

graft (12) procedures that involve moving healthy tissue from one site to another to replace diseased or defective tissue.

Gram stain (18) method of classifying all bacteria as gram positive or gram negative.

gray (gy) (17) newer radiation terminology for the amount of radiant energy absorbed in a tissue; 1 gray equals 100 rads.

gray-scale ultrasound (17) *see* B-scan.

green reference symbol (9) symbol (⊃) located below a code description to indicate that the coder should refer to the *CPT Assistant* monthly newsletter and/or the *CPT Changes: An Insider's View* annual publication that contains all coding changes for the current year.

gross examination (18) evaluating a specimen visually, with the naked eye.

group model HMO (20) contracted health care services delivered to subscribers by participating physicians who are members of an independent multispecialty group practice.

group practice without walls (GPWW) (20) contract that allows physicians to maintain their own offices and share services such as appointment scheduling and billing.

guidelines (9) define terms and explain the assignment of codes for procedures and services located in a particular section of the CPT.

H

harvesting (13) removing tissue for transplantation.

HCPCS level I (8) five-digit Current Procedural Terminology (CPT) codes developed and published by the American Medical Association (AMA).

HCPCS level II (1) coding system managed by the Centers for Medicare & Medicaid Services (CMS) that classifies medical equipment, injectable drugs, transportation services, and other services not classified in the CPT.

HCPCS level II miscellaneous codes (8) include *miscellaneous/not otherwise classified* codes that are reported when a DMEPOS dealer submits a claim for a product or service for which there is no existing HCPCS level II code.

HCPCS level II modifiers (8) two-digit alpha or alphanumeric codes added to any HCPCS level I (CPT) or II (national) code to provide additional information regarding the product or service reported.

HCPCS level II permanent national codes (8) maintained by the HCPCS National Panel, which unanimously makes decisions about additions, revisions, and deletions.

HCPCS level II temporary codes (8) maintained by the CMS and other members of the HCPCS National Panel, independent of permanent level II codes, and allow payers the flexibility to establish codes that are needed before the next January 1 annual update.

HCPCS national codes (1) *see* HCPCS level II.

health care clearinghouse (1) *see* clearinghouse.

Healthcare Common Procedure Coding System (HCPCS) (1) includes level I codes (CPT) and level II codes (HCPCS level II national codes).

health care provider (1) *see* provider.

health care reimbursement account (HCRA) (20) tax-exempt account that is used to pay for health care expenses.

health data collection (1) performed by health care facilities to do administrative planning, to submit statistics to state and federal government agencies (and other organizations), and to report health claim data to third-party payers for reimbursement purposes.

health insurance claim (20) electronic transmission or paper-based document submitted by the provider to an insurance plan to request reimbursement for procedures performed or services provided.

health insurance policy (20) agreement between an individual and a third-party payer (or insurance company) that contains a list of reimbursable medical benefits.

Health Insurance Portability and Accountability Act of 1996 (HIPAA) (1) federal legislation that amended the Internal Revenue Code of 1986 to improve portability and continuity of health insurance coverage in the group and individual markets, combat waste/fraud/abuse in health insurance and health care delivery, promote the use of medical savings accounts, improve access to long-term care services and coverage, simplify the administration of health insurance by creating unique identifiers for providers/health plans/employers, create standards for electronic health information transactions, and create privacy/security standards for health information.

health insurance specialist (1) employed by third-party payers to review health-related claims to determine whether the costs are reasonable and medically necessary based on the patient's diagnosis.

health maintenance organization (HMO) (20) alternative to traditional group health insurance coverage that provides comprehensive health care services to voluntarily enrolled members on a prepaid basis.

health plan (1) contract established by an insurance company to reimburse health care facilities and patients for procedures and services provided.

health reimbursement arrangement (HRA) (20) tax-exempt account offered by employers with more than 50 employees, which individuals use to pay health care bills.

health savings account (HSA) (20) allows participants to enroll in a relatively inexpensive, high-deductible insurance plan, and a tax-deductible savings account is opened to cover current and future medical expenses; money deposited (and earnings) is tax-deferred, and money is withdrawn to cover qualified medical expenses tax-free.

health savings security account (HSSA) (20) *see* health savings account.

heart murmur (14) extra heart sound.

hematology (18) study of the function and disorders of blood.

hemic system (14) blood-producing system.

hemodialysis (19) process of removing waste products, toxins, and excess fluids from the blood; patient's blood is diverted into a dialyzer, where it is treated and returned to the patient's circulation by another tube inserted into a different blood vessel.

heparin (11) anticoagulant that prevents blood clots from developing in a catheter.

hepatotomy (15) open drainage of abscess or cyst.

hernia (15) protrusion of internal organs through a weakening in the musculature.

HIPAA administrative simplification (AS) (20) developed standards for the maintenance and transmission of health information required to identify individual patients; designed to improve efficiency and effectiveness of the health care system by standardizing the interchange of electronic data for specified administrative and financial transactions.

HIPAA standards for privacy of individually identifiable health information (20) provisions that protect the security and confidentiality of health information.

history (10) interview of the patient that includes the following elements: history of the present illness (including the patient's chief complaint), a review of systems, and a past/family/social history.

history of present illness (HPI) (10) chronological description of patient's present condition from time of onset to present.

hold harmless clause (20) statement that the patient is not responsible for paying what the insurance plan denies.

Home Assessment Validation and Entry (HAVEN) (20) software that allows for entry of data elements from the outcome and assessment information set (OASIS), which is used to determine the reimbursement rate for home health agency care based on a case mix methodology.

home health prospective payment system (HH PPS) (20) uses home health resource groups (HHRGs) to reimburse Medicare home health care services according to prospectively determined rates.

home services (10) provided to individuals and families in their place of residence to promote, maintain, or restore health and/or to minimize the effects of disability and illness, including terminal illness.

horizontal plane (17) *see* transverse plane.

horizontal triangle symbols (9) symbols (►◄) that surround revised guidelines and notes; these symbols are *not* used for revised code descriptions.

hospital discharge service (10) includes the final examination of the patient; discussion of the hospital stay with the patient and/or caregiver; instructions for continuing care provided to the patient and/or caregiver; and preparation of discharge records, prescriptions, and referral forms.

hospital inpatient service (10) provided to hospital inpatients, including partial hospitalization services, and indicated when the patient's condition requires services and/or procedures that cannot be performed in any other place of service without putting the patient at risk.

hospitalist (1) physician who provides care for hospital inpatients.

hospital readmission reduction program (HRRP) (20) requires CMS to reduce payments to inpatient prospective payment system (IPPS) hospitals with excess readmissions, and utilizes readmission measures established by CMS.

hot biopsy forceps (15) technique that uses tweezer-like forceps connected to a monopolar electrocautery unit and a grounding pad to remove lesions or polyps.

hybrid record (1) combined paper-based and computer-generated (electronic) documents.

hyperthermia (17) use of an external heat-generating source to produce localized heating.

hyperventilation (19) deep or rapid breathing.

hypopharynx (15) organ that extends from the upper edge of the epiglottis to the larynx/esophagus juncture.

hypovolemia (11) abnormally decreased blood volume.

hysteroscopy (16) visualization of the cervical canal and uterine cavity using a hysteroscope.

I

ICD-10 Coordination and Maintenance Committee (2) NCHS and CMS Department of HHS federal agencies that are responsible for overseeing all changes and modifications to ICD-10-CM (NCHS) and ICD-10-PCS (CMS).

ileoanal anastomosis (15) common alternative to conventional ileostomy, and it is not considered an ostomy because there is no stoma.

ileostomy (15) removal of the colon and rectum with the small intestine brought to the abdominal wall.

immobilize (13) *see* stabilize.

immune globulin (Ig) (19) sterilized solution obtained from pooled human blood plasma, which contains immunoglobulins (or antibodies) that protect against infectious agents that cause various diseases.

immune serum globulin (19) *see* immune globulin.

immunoglobulin (18) protein produced by plasma cells that help fight infection; antibody that protects against infectious agents that cause various diseases.

immunology (18) study of the immune system.

implantable defibrillator (14) similar to a pacemaker in that it includes a pulse generator and electrodes, but it uses a combination of antitachycardia pacing and low-energy cardioversion or defibrillating shocks to regulate the patient's heartbeat and prevent arrhythmias.

implanted port (11) small reservoir that has a rubber plug attached to the catheter and is inserted into the patient's vein below the collar bone and threaded into the superior vena cava.

incision (12) a cut made with a knife, electrosurgical unit, or laser especially for surgical purposes (e.g., on body tissue).

incisional biopsy (12) removal of a portion of a lesion by slicing into it or incising it.

incision and drainage (I&D) (12) cutting open a lesion and draining its contents.

incomplete abortion (16) miscarriage in which part, but not all, of the uterine contents are expelled.

inconclusive diagnosis (7) *see* qualified diagnosis.

indemnification (20) insurance against loss.

Index (ICD-10-PCS) (6) organizes ICD-10-PCS main terms in alphabetical order, providing the first 3–4 characters (and sometimes all 7 characters) of a code as well as direction to a specific location in the Tables.

indexed (1) identified according to a unique identification number.

Index to Diseases and Injuries (2) alphabetical listing of ICD-10-CM main terms and their codes; subdivided into Index to Diseases and Injuries (includes a Neoplasm Table and a Table of Drugs and Chemicals) and Index to External Causes of Injury; main terms are boldfaced, and subterms and qualifiers are indented below main terms.

Indian Health Service (IHS) (20) DHHS agency that provides federal health care services to American Indians and Alaska Natives.

indirect laryngoscopy (13) insertion of a small hand mirror in the patient's mouth at the back of the throat while the physician wears headgear that contains a mirror and light source; the mirror worn by the physician reflects light into the patient's mouth, allowing the physician to visualize the patient's throat.

individual practice association (IPA) HMO (20) contracted services enables to be delivered to subscribers by physicians who remain in their independent office settings.

induced abortion (16) deliberate termination of pregnancy.

infant (10) very young child, up to one year old.

inferred words (9) used to save space in the CPT index when referencing subterms.

infiltration anesthesia (11) topical injection of local anesthetic into tissue.

informational modifiers (9) clarify aspects of the procedure or service provided for the payer.

initial plan (1) documentation of the strategy for managing patient care and actions taken to investigate the patient's condition and to treat/educate the patient; the initial plan consists of three categories: diagnostic/management plans, therapeutic plans, and patient education plans; considered part of the problem-oriented record (POR).

inner ear (16) includes the cochlea, saccule, acoustic nerve, semicircular canals, utricle, and superior and inferior vestibular nerves.

inpatient (6) patient who remains overnight in a facility for 24 or more hours and who is provided with room and board and nursing services.

inpatient neonatal and pediatric critical care and intensive service (10) provided to critically ill neonates and infants by a physician.

inpatient prospective payment system (IPPS) (20) implemented as part of the Tax Equity and Fiscal Responsibility Act of 1982 (TEFRA); uses diagnosis-related groups (DRGs) to classify inpatient hospital cases into groups that are expected to consume similar hospital resources.

inpatient psychiatric facility prospective payment system (IPF PPS) (20) *per diem* patient classification system that reflects differences in patient resource use and costs; IPF PPS replaced a reasonable cost-based payment system; promotes long-term cost control and utilization management.

inpatient rehabilitation facility prospective payment system (IRF PPS) (20) use of information from a patient assessment instrument (PAI) to classify patients into distinct groups based on clinical characteristics and expected resource needs.

integrated delivery system (IDS) (20) organization of affiliated provider sites that offer joint health care services to subscribers.

integrated provider organization (IPO) (20) manages the delivery of health care services offered by hospitals, physicians who are employees of the IPO, and other health care organizations such as ambulatory surgery clinics and nursing facilities.

integrated record (1) arranged in strict chronological date order (or in reverse date order), which allows for observation of how the patient is progressing according to test results and how the patient responds to treatment based on test results.

intensity of service (IS) (20) determining whether the provided service is appropriate for the patient's severity of illness.

intensivist (10) physician who has received extensive training and experience in critical care and who specializes in the care of critically ill patients, usually in an intensive care unit (ICU).

interfacility transport (10) transfer of a patient from one health care facility to another; usually involves use of an ambulance or a helicopter.

internal catheter (11) catheter implanted completely under the skin.

internal fixation device (13) pins, screws, and/or plates inserted through or within a fracture area to stabilize and immobilize the injury; often called open reduction with internal fixation, or ORIF.

internal radiation (17) radiation placed inside the body.

International Classification of Diseases (ICD) **(2)** published by the World Health Organization and used to classify mortality data from death certificates.

International Classification of Diseases for Oncology, Third Edition (ICD-O-3) **(1)** implemented in 2001 to classify a tumor according to primary site (topography) and morphology (histology, behavior, and aggression of tumor).

International Classification of Diseases, Ninth Revision, Clinical Modification (ICD-9-CM) **(1)** adopted in 1979 to classify diagnoses (Volumes 1 and 2) and procedures (Volume 3); all health care facilities assigned ICD-9-CM codes to report diagnoses, and hospitals reported ICD-9-CM procedure codes for inpatient procedures and services; replaced by ICD-10-CM and ICD-10-PCS in 2015.

International Classification of Diseases, Tenth Revision, Clinical Modification (ICD-10-CM) **(1)** developed by the Centers for Medicare & Medicaid Services (CMS) to classify all diseases and injuries.

International Classification of Diseases, Tenth Revision, Clinical Modification/Procedure Coding System (ICD-10-CM/PCS) **(1)** shortened name the Centers for Medicare & Medicaid Services uses to identify the classification systems.

International Classification of Diseases, Tenth Revision, Procedure Coding System (ICD-10-PCS) **(1)** developed by the National Center for Health Statistics (NCHS) to classify inpatient procedures and services.

International Classification of Functioning, Disability and Health (ICF) **(1)** classifies health and health-related domains that describe body functions and structures, activities, and participation; complements ICD-10, looking beyond mortality and disease.

internship (1) student placement in a health care facility to provide on-the-job experience prior to graduation.

internship supervisor (1) person to whom a student reports at an internship site.

intersex surgery (16) performed as a series of staged procedures to transform the normal adult genitalia of one sex to that of the other sex; also called genital reconstructive surgery or sex reassignment surgery.

interventional radiologic procedure (17) use of percutaneous or minimally invasive techniques under imaging guidance to diagnose and treat conditions.

interventional therapeutic radiological procedure (11) minimally invasive image-guided therapeutic procedure that is used to treat diseases, such as radiofrequency ablation of liver tumors.

intra-arterial cannula (11) *see* intra-arterial line.

intra-arterial catheter (11) *see* intra-arterial line.

intra-arterial line (11) thin plastic tube, cannula, or catheter that is inserted into an artery and connected to a monitor to measure immediate changes in intra-arterial blood pressure and concentrations of oxygen and carbon dioxide; also used to collect frequent blood samples for lab tests.

intracapsular cataract extraction (ICCE) (16) removal of lens and surrounding capsule.

intracranial (11) introduced into or within the skull.

intradermal test (intracutaneous) (19) injection of purified allergen extracts into skin to test for allergy to suspected insect venom or penicillin.

intraservice time (10) a variable that is predictive of the "work" of E/M services, which includes face-to-face time for office and other outpatient visits or unit/floor time for hospital and other inpatient visits.

intrathecal (17) fluid-filled space between layers of tissue that cover the brain and spinal cord.

intravenous push (19) injection administered by a health care professional who is in constant attendance to administer the injection and observe the patient.

intravenous regional anesthesia (11) insertion of IV cannula into the extremity on which the procedure is to be performed and a tourniquet applied to interrupt blood circulation; then a large volume of local anesthetic injected into a peripheral vein, anesthetizing the extremity.

introduction (12) procedures that inject, insert, puncture, or scope.

IPPS 3-day payment window (20) requires outpatient preadmission services provided by a hospital up to three days prior to a patient's inpatient admission to be covered by the IPPS DRG payment for diagnostic services or therapeutic services for which the inpatient principal diagnosis code (ICD-10-CM) exactly matches that for preadmission services.

IPPS 72-hour rule (20) *see* IPPS 3-day payment window.

IPPS transfer rule (20) states that any patient with a diagnosis from one of ten CMS-determined diagnosis-related groups who is discharged to a post acute provider is treated as a transfer case.

IRF PPS 1-day payment window (20) requires that outpatient preadmission services provided by an IRF up to one day prior to a patient's inpatient admission be covered by the IRF PPS payment.

IRF PPS 24-hour rule (20) *see* IRF PPS 1-day payment window.

IRF PPS transfer rule (20) states that any patient who is discharged to an inpatient rehabilitation facility is treated as a transfer case.

iris (16) colored tissue that surrounds the pupil of the eye.

island flap (12) flap consisting of skin and subcutaneous tissue with a pedicle comprised only of nutrient vessels; also called island pedicle flap.

island pedicle flap (12) *see* island flap.

J

jamming (1) routinely assigning an unspecified ICD-10-CM disease code instead of reviewing the coding manual to select the appropriate code number.

J-pouch (15) *see* ileoanal anastomosis.

K

key components (10) history, examination, and medical decision making; required when selecting an E/M level of service code.

kidney (15) filters and cleans blood, producing urine that carries waste.

knee (13) "hinge" joint composed of bones, cartilage, ligaments, and tendons.

Kock pouch (15) *see* continent ileostomy.

L

lacrimal apparatus (16) contains structures that produce, store, and remove tears.

lacrimal puncta (16) small openings in the inner canthus of the eyelids that channel tears.

laminectomy (16)   excision of the entire posterior arch or lamina of a vertebra.

laminotomy (16)   removal of part of the lamina from one side of the vertebra.

laparoscopy (15)   examination of the peritoneal contents using a laparoscope that is inserted through the abdominal wall.

laryngoscopy (13)   visualization of the back of the throat, including the larynx and vocal cords.

larynx (13)   voice box.

LASER (light amplification by stimulated emission of radiation) (12)   device filled with a gas, liquid, or solid substance that is stimulated to emit light to a specific wavelength for the purpose of burning, cutting, or dissolving tissue.

laser-assisted uvulopalatoplasty (15)   procedure that uses a laser technique to remove tissue from the uvula, soft palate, and pharynx.

laser technique (15)   technique that is most suitable for treatment of rectal lesions and uses a waveguide to deliver the laser beam through the endoscope to the lesion.

lateral extracavitary approach (LECA) (16)   making a midline incision in the area of the affected vertebral segment, which is inferiorly curved out to the lateral plane.

laterality (2)   in ICD-10-CM, whether the condition occurs on the left, the right, or is bilateral; in CPT, whether the procedure is performed bilaterally; in CPT, when laterality is not indicated in the procedure description for paired organs or body parts, add HCPCS level II modifier -LT or -RT to indicate the left or right side, respectively.

lateral projection (17)   positioning patient at a right angle to the film, so the x-ray beam travels through the side of the body.

LEEP electrodissection conization (16)   superficial dissection of the cervix.

LeFort I (13)   procedure that brings the lower midface forward (from the level of the upper teeth) to just above the nostrils.

LeFort II (13)   surgical fracture of the midfacial skeleton at an apex near the superior aspect of the nasal bones.

LeFort III (13)   procedure that brings the entire midface forward, from the upper teeth to just above the cheekbones.

legacy classification system (2)   *see* legacy coding system.

legacy coding system (2)   classification system that is used as archive data; it is no longer supported or updated; for example, when ICD-10-CM and ICD-10-PCS were implemented, ICD-9-CM became a legacy coding system.

lens (16)   clear, flexible, curved structure that focuses images on the retina of the eye.

lesion (11)   abnormal tissue resulting from autoimmune or metabolic disorders, infection, neoplasm, or trauma.

ligament (13)   tissue that connects bone to bone.

Limberg flap (12)   *see* rhomboid flap.

listserv (1)   *see* online discussion board.

lithotripsy (15)   *see* percutaneous lithotomy.

lithotripter (11)   device that administers a high-voltage electrical discharge through a spark gap under water, which produces a compressive force and breaks apart the stones so they can pass in urine.

local anesthesia (11)   applying a topical agent on the body's surface or injecting a local anesthetic agent for the purpose of numbing a small part of the body; appropriate for minor surgeries.

local coverage determinations (LCDs) (8)   define coverage criteria, payment rules, and documentation required as applied to DMEPOS claims processed by DME MACs for frequently ordered DMEPOS equipment, services, and supplies; formerly called local medical review policies (LMRPs).

Logical Observation Identifiers Names and Codes (LOINC) (1)   electronic database and universal standard used to identify medical laboratory observations and for the purpose of clinical care and management.

LOINC (1)   *see* Logical Observation Identifiers Names and Codes (LOINC)

long-term acute care hospital (LTACH) (6)   health care facility designed specifically for patients who need functional restoration and/or rehabilitation and medical management for an average of three to six weeks; LTAC hospitals have an average inpatient length of stay of more than 25 days and provide extended medical and rehabilitative care for patients who are clinically complex and may suffer from multiple acute or chronic conditions.

long-term (acute) care hospital prospective payment system (LTCH PPS) (20)   uses information from long-term care hospital patient records to classify patients into distinct long-term (acute) care diagnosis-related groups based on clinical characteristics and expected resource needs.

long-term hospital (6)   *see* long-term acute care (LTAC) hospital.

loop electrodissection conization (16)   deep dissection of the cervix.

low birth weight (10)   less than 1,500 grams.

LTCH PPS 1-day payment window (20)   requires that outpatient preadmission services provided by a long-term acute care hospital up to one day prior to a patient's inpatient admission be covered by the LTC PPS diagnosis-related group payment.

LTCH PPS 24-hour rule (20)   *see* LTC PPS 1-day payment window.

lumbar puncture (LP) (11)   inserting a cannula at the L3-4 or L4-5 (lumbar vertebrae) to remove cerebrospinal fluid for diagnostic or therapeutic purposes.

lumen (11)   opening.

lumpectomy (12)   partial mastectomy.

luxation (13)   *see* dislocation.

lymph (14)   clear fluid that contains chyle, some red blood cells, and lymphocytes, which help fight infection and disease.

lymphatic system (14)   consists of the spleen, thymus, tonsils, adenoids, vessels that carry lymph, and lymph nodes.

lymph nodes (14)   clusters of bean-shaped nodules that act as the body's filtration system, removing cell waste and excess fluid and helping to fight infection.

M

magnetic resonance angiography (MRA) (17)   noninvasive diagnostic study that is used to evaluate disorders of arterial and venous structures.

magnetic resonance imaging (MRI) (17)   noninvasive x-ray procedure that uses an external magnetic field to produce a two-dimensional view of an internal organ or structure such as the brain or spinal cord.

main term (2)   printed in boldfaced type and followed by the ICD-10-CM code number.

major diagnostic category (MDC) (20)   refers to mutually exclusive categories that are loosely based on body systems (e.g., nervous system); diagnosis-related groups (DRGs) are organized into MDCs.

male genital system (16)   includes the prostate, seminal vesicles, penis, testicles (testes), epididymis, tunica vaginalis, vas deferens, scrotum, spermatic cord, seminal vesicles, and prostate.

malignant (4)   cancerous.

malunion (5)   failure of the ends of a fractured bone to heal (unite).

mammography (17)   radiological examination of the soft tissue and internal structures of the breast.

managed care (20)   combines financing and delivery of health care services; replaces conventional fee-for-service health insurance plans with more affordable care for consumers and providers who agree to certain restrictions.

management service organization (MSO) (20)   physician- or hospital-owned organization that provides practice management, administrative, and support services to individual physician practices.

manipulation (13)   realignment of bones.

manometry (19)   diagnostic test that measures muscle function using a pressure-sensitive tube.

manual record (1)   paper-based record that includes handwritten progress notes and physician orders, graphic charts, and so on.

mass spectrometry (11)   monitors proper levels of the anesthetic.

maximizing reimbursement (6)   reimbursement that is *not* permitted because it involves selecting and reporting as principal diagnosis the ICD-10-CM code that results in the highest level of reimbursement for the facility whether that diagnosis meets the criteria for selection or not; it also includes assigning a higher-paying ICD-10-CM code to a diagnosis (or ICD-10-CM or CPT/HCPCS code to a procedure) even if patient record documentation does not support that code selection.

Maze procedure (14)   stops atrial fibrillation or atrial flutter by using incisions in heart tissue to stop abnormal heart rhythm.

Meckel's diverticulum (15)   common congenital abnormality of the gastrointestinal tract that results in a pouch in the wall of the small bowel that contains remnants of fetal gastrointestinal tissue.

mediastinum (15)   space in the thoracic cavity between the lungs that contains the aorta, the esophagus, the heart, and other structures.

Medicaid (20)   joint federal and state program that provides health care coverage to low-income populations and certain aged and disabled individuals.

medical assistant (1)   health care professional employed by a provider to perform administrative and clinical tasks.

medical coding process (1)   requires the review of patient record documentation to identify diagnoses, procedures, and services for the purpose of assigning ICD-10-CM/PCS, HCPCS level II, and/or CPT codes.

medical decision making (MDM) (10) refers to the complexity of establishing a diagnosis and/or selecting a management option as measured by the number of diagnoses or management options, the amount and/or complexity of data to be reviewed, and the risk of complications and/or morbidity or mortality.

medical foundation (20) nonprofit organization that contracts with and acquires the clinical and business assets of physician practices; the foundation is assigned a provider number and manages the practice's business.

medical management software (1) combination practice management and medical billing software that automates the daily workflow and procedures of a physician's office or clinic.

medical necessity (1) determination that a service or procedure rendered is reasonable and necessary for the diagnosis or treatment of an illness or injury.

medical nomenclature (1) includes clinical terminologies and clinical vocabularies that are used by health care providers to document patient care; *clinical terminologies* include designations, expressions, symbols, and terms used in the field of medicine, and *clinical vocabularies* include clinical phrases or words along with their meanings.

medical record (1) *see* patient record.

Medicare (20) provides health care coverage to elderly and disabled persons; federal spending is funded by the Medicare Trust Fund (payroll tax).

Medicare administrative contractor (MAC) (20) processes claims for physicians, health care facilities, and suppliers of durable medical equipment, prosthetics, orthotics, and supplies.

Medicare Benefit Policy Manual **(8)** provides direction about services and procedures to be reimbursed by the Medicare administrative contractor.

Medicare National Coverage Determinations Manual **(8)** indicates whether a service is covered or excluded under the Medicare program.

Medicare physician fee schedule (MPFS) (20) common name for resource-based relative value scale system, which is used to reimburse physician services covered by Medicare Part B.

Medicare Prescription Drug, Improvement, and Modernization Act (MMA) (2) federal legislation that requires all code sets to be valid at the time services are provided.

Medicare Prescription Drug, Improvement, and Modernization Act of 2003 (MMA) (20) eliminated carriers, fiscal intermediaries, and durable medical equipment regional carriers and created Medicare administrative contractors.

Medicare Pricing, Data Analysis, and Coding (PDAC) contractor (8) assists suppliers and manufacturers in determining HCPCS codes to be used; previously called the Statistical Analysis Durable Medical Equipment Regional Carrier (SADMERC).

Medicare severity diagnosis-related groups (MS-DRGs) (20) classify inpatient hospital cases into groups according to similar resource utilization, which results in hospitals receiving a predetermined payment according to MS-DRG for treating Medicare patients; like the original DRGs, MS-DRGs are based on diagnoses, procedures, other demographic information, and the presence of complications or comorbidities (CCs); however, hospital inpatients are distinguished according to those with no CCs, CCs, or major CCs (MCCs), which allows Medicare to distinguish "sick patients" from "very sick patients" and reimburse hospitals accordingly; the number of MS-DRGs expands to 745 (as compared to 538 original DRGs).

Medicare severity long-term (acute) care diagnosis-related groups (MS-LTCH-DRGs) (20) based on clinical characteristics and expected resource needs; replaced the reasonable cost-based LTCH PPS authorized by TEFRA that had mandated the implementation of DRGs (and originally exempted long-term acute care hospitals from participation).

Medicare Summary Notice (MSN) (20) an easy-to-read monthly statement sent to Medicare beneficiaries, which clearly lists health insurance claims information.

megaelectron volt (17) *see* MeV.

megavolt (17) *see* MeV.

metastatic cancer (4) *see* secondary malignancy.

MeV (17) 1 million electron volts.

microbiology (18) study of microbes.

microdermabrasion (12) skin-freshening technique used to repair facial skin that is damaged by the sun and the effects of aging.

microtechnique (18) one of three types of micromanipulation techniques that may be used for the preparation of an embryo for transfer.

middle ear (16) includes the tympanic membrane, auditory ossicles, muscles, and conduction pathways.

midsagittal plane (17) vertically divides the body through the midline into two equal left and right halves.

Military Health System (MHS) (20) provides and maintains readiness to provide health care services and support to members of the Uniformed Services during military operations; also provides health care services and support to members of the Uniformed Services, their family members, and others entitled to Department of Defense health care.

minimally invasive procedure (19) includes percutaneous access.

minimum data set (MDS) (20) standardized, primary screening and assessment tool of health status that forms the foundation of the comprehensive assessment for all residents in a Medicare or Medicaid-certified long-term care facility; contains items that measure physical, psychological and psychosocial functioning, which provide a multidimensional view of the patient's functional capacities and helps staff to identify health problems.

missed abortion (16) miscarriage in which a dead fetus and other products of conception remain in the uterus for four or more weeks.

M-mode (17) one-dimensional display that reflects the movement of structures.

moderate (conscious) sedation (12) moderate sedation or analgesia that results in a drug-induced depression of consciousness.

modified Maze procedure (14) *see* cardiac ablation.

modified radical mastectomy (12) total mastectomy that includes removal of the breast and nipple, axillary lymph nodes, and pectoralis minor muscle.

modifying unit (11) part of anesthesia formula that recognizes added complexities associated with the administration of anesthesia, including physical factors and difficult circumstances.

Mohs microsurgery (12) technique of excising skin tumors by removing tumor tissue layer by layer, examining the removed portion microscopically for malignant cells, and repeating the procedure until the entire tumor is removed.

monitored anesthesia care (MAC) (11) administration of varying amounts of local, regional, and certain mind-altering drugs by an anesthesiologist or a CRNA during a patient's diagnostic or therapeutic procedure.

morbidity (2) disease.

mortality (2) death.

motion mode (17) *see* M-mode.

mucocutaneous margin (15) consists of mucous membrane and skin.

multiaxial structure (ICD-10-PCS) (6) a value from each of seven hierarchies (positions) is assigned to construct an ICD-10-PCS code.

multihospital system (6) two or more hospitals owned, managed, or leased by a single organization; these may include acute, long-term, pediatric, rehabilitation, or psychiatric care facilities.

multiple codes (2) more than one ICD-10-CM code that is assigned to completely classify the elements of a complex diagnosis (or procedure) statement.

multiple sleep latency (19) observation of a patient during at least a six-hour period of sleep and includes assessment of sleep latency (dormancy) and/or wakefulness after the sleep period.

mutually exclusive edit (9) code pairs that, for clinical reasons, are unlikely to be performed on the same patient on the same day.

mycocutaneous flap (12) autologous graft consisting of both skin and muscle tissue from the donor site.

myocardium (14) muscle layer of the heart.

myringotomy (16) surgical incision of the tympanic membrane; usually performed to release pressure or fluid.

N

narcosynthesis (19) form of psychotherapy that is provided when the patient is under the influence of a drug, such as a sedative or narcotic.

nasal vestibule (13) entrance to the nose.

nasopharynx (15) located above the soft palate.

National Correct Coding Initiative (NCCI) (9) implemented by the Centers for Medicare & Medicaid Services (CMS) to promote national correct coding methodologies and to control the improper assignment of codes that results in inappropriate reimbursement of Medicare Part B claims.

national coverage determinations (NCDs) (8) define coverage criteria, payment rules, and documentation required as applied to DMEPOS claims processed by DME MACs for frequently ordered DMEPOS equipment, services, and supplies.

National Drug Codes (NDC) **(1)** contains prescription drugs and a few selected over-the-counter (OTC) products, which pharmacies use to report transactions and some health care professionals use for reporting on claims.

national health plan identifier (HPID) (20)   assigned to third-party payers; contains 10 numerical positions including a check digit in the tenth position (e.g., 1234567890); formerly called the PAYERID.

national individual identifier (patient identifier) (20)   HIPAA provision for a national individual identifier (or patient identifier) that has been withdrawn.

national limitation amount (NLA) (20)   serves as a payment ceiling, or cap, on the amount Medicare could pay for each test.

national provider identifier (NPI) (20)   assigned to hospitals, doctors, nursing homes, and other health care providers; contains 10 numerical digits (e.g., 1234567890).

national standard employer identifier number (EIN) (20)   IRS's federal tax identification number (EIN) adopted as the national employer identifier, retaining the hyphen after the first two numbers (e.g., 12-3456789); the EIN is assigned to employers who, as sponsors of health insurance for their employees, must be identified in health care transactions.

nature of the presenting problem (10)   disease, condition, illness, injury, symptom, sign, finding, complaint, or other reason for the encounter, with or without a diagnosis being established at the time of the encounter.

necropsy (18)   autopsy.

needle core biopsy (12)   tissue sample obtained using a hand-operated needle or stereotactic localization.

needle electromyography (19)   inserting needle electrodes into skeletal muscles and observing electrical activity of those muscles using an oscilloscope and a loudspeaker.

neonate (10)   newborn, up to 28 days old.

neoplasm (4)   new growth, or tumor, in which cell reproduction is out of control.

nephrectomy (15)   surgical removal of a kidney.

nerve plexus (11)   network of intersecting nerves.

nervous system (16)   includes the central nervous system and the peripheral nervous system.

network model HMO (20)   contracted health care services provided to subscribers by two or more physician multispecialty group practices.

network provider (20)   physician or health care facility under contract to the managed care plan.

neuroplasty (16)   freeing or decompression of an intact nerve from scar tissue.

neurorrhaphy (16)   repair of nerves.

neurostimulator (16)   electrode and pulse generator that are implanted along the spine to alleviate pain or control spasms.

newborn care services (10)   includes services provided to newborns in a variety of health care settings.

newborn patient (6)   patient who receives infant care upon birth and, if necessary, receives neonatal intensive care (either within a hospital or as the result of transfer to another hospital).

new patient (10)   one who has *not* received any professional services within the past three years from the physician or from another physician of the same exact specialty or subspecialty who belongs to the same group practice.

Nissen fundoplasty (15)   mobilizing the lower end of the esophagus by suturing the fundus of the stomach around the circumference of the lower esophagus at the esophagogastric junction.

noncovered benefits (20)   procedures and services that are not covered by the third-party payer.

nonessential modifier (2)   qualifying word contained in parentheses after the main term in the ICD-10-CM Index to Diseases and Injuries that does not have to be included in the diagnostic or procedural statement for the code number listed after the parentheses to be assigned.

noninvasive procedure (19)   requires no surgical incision or excision; not an open procedure.

nonparticipating provider (nonPAR) (20)   health care provider (e.g., physician) who is not a member of a health care plan; nonPAR providers do not receive reimbursement directly from a payer; the reimbursement is sent to the patient, and the nonPAR provider must collect payment for services rendered from the patient.

non-segmental instrumentation (13)   fixation at each end of the construct (structure) that may span several vertebral segments without attachment to the intervening segments.

nonselective vascular catheterization (14)   introduction of a catheter into a vessel without further advancement past the punctured vessel *or* introduction of a catheter into any portion of the aorta or vena cava from any approach (e.g., axillary, brachial, femoral, jugular).

nontunneled catheter (11)   *see* external catheter.

nonunion (5)   *see* malunion.

notes (9)   appear throughout CPT sections to clarify the assignment of codes.

Notice of Exclusions from Medicare Benefits (NEMB) (9)   form completed and signed by a Medicare beneficiary before items, procedures, and services excluded from Medicare benefits are provided.

nuclear imaging (17)   noninvasive x-ray procedure that creates an image by measuring radiation emission, or radiation "uptake," of body areas after the administration of a radionuclide.

nuclear medicine (17)   use of radioactive elements for diagnostic imaging and radiopharmaceutical therapy.

number symbol (9)   symbol (#) located to the left of CPT codes to indicate out-of-numerical sequence codes.

Objective (O) (1)   observations about the patient, such as physical findings or lab or x-ray results; considered part of the problem-oriented record (POR) SOAP note.

oblique projection (17)   positioning the patient with the body slanted sideways toward the film, halfway between a parallel and right-angle position; the x-ray beam travels through this angle of the body.

observation patient (7)   patient who receives services furnished on a hospital's premises that are ordered by a physician (or another authorized individual), including use of a bed and periodic monitoring by nursing or other staff, and that are reasonable and necessary to evaluate the outpatient's condition or determine the need for possible admission as an inpatient.

observation service (10)   provided in a hospital outpatient setting; the patient is considered an outpatient.

obturator (13)   object used to close a gap.

ocular adnexa (16)   includes the orbit, eye muscles, eyelids, eyelashes, conjunctiva, and lacrimal apparatus.

ocular implant (16)   inserted inside the muscular cone.

office or other outpatient services (10)   provided in a physician's office, a hospital outpatient department, or another ambulatory care facility.

***Official ICD-10-CM Guidelines for Coding and Reporting* (2)**   rules developed to accompany and complement official conventions and instructions provided in ICD-10-CM.

***Official ICD-10-PCS Guidelines for Coding and Reporting* (2)**   rules developed to accompany and complement official conventions and instructions provided in ICD-10-PCS.

omentectomy (16)   surgical removal of the omentum.

Omnibus Budget Reconciliation Act of 1980 (20)   federal legislation mandating that an ambulatory surgery center could participate in Medicare if certain conditions were met and stating that the ambulatory surgical center's payments are "expected to be calculated on a prospective basis...utilizing sample survey and similar techniques to establish reasonable estimated overhead allowances for each of the listed procedures which take account of volume (within reasonable limits)."

Omnibus Budget Reconciliation Act of 1987 (OBRA) (20)   federal legislation that mandated the payment methodology for durable medical equipment, prosthetics, orthotics, and supplies fee schedule.

Omnibus Budget Reconciliation Act of 1989 (20)   federal legislation that implemented the resource-based relative value scale (RBRVS) system, which is used to reimburse physician services covered by Medicare Part B.

Omnibus Consolidated and Emergency Supplemental Appropriations Act (OCESAA) of 1999 (20)   federal legislation that implemented the home health prospective payment system for Medicare home health services.

one-lung ventilation (OLV) (11)   isolation of the right or left lung so that one lung is ventilated and the other is allowed to collapse.

online discussion board (1)   Internet-based or e-mail discussion forum that covers a variety of topics and issues.

oocyte (16)   immature female reproductive cell, or egg.

oophorectomy (16)   surgical removal of an ovary or ovaries.

open biopsy (12)   incisional or excisional removal of a lesion.

open fracture (5)   type of fracture that has an associated open wound.

open fracture treatment (13)   surgically opening a fracture site or exposing it so treatment can be provided.

open laparoscopy (15)   insufflation of the abdomen using a trocar, which is placed under direct vision (using a laparoscope) after making a small celiotomy incision.

open-panel HMO (20) health care provided by individuals who are not employees of the HMO or who do not belong to a specially formed medical group that serves the HMO.

operating microscope (16) used during a surgical procedure to perform microsurgery techniques.

optimizing reimbursement (6) determining which of several diagnoses to report as the principal diagnosis when multiple diagnoses equally meet the criteria for selection as the principal diagnosis.

orbicularis oculi (19) blink test that is monitored with sensors.

orbit (16) bony cavity in the skull that contains and protects the eyeball and its associated blood vessels, muscles, and nerves.

orbital implant (16) inserting an implant outside the muscular cone into the eye socket, and placing an intraocular lens (IOL).

organ harvest (11) surgical removal of an organ for transplantation.

oropharynx (15) area between the soft palate and the upper portion of the epiglottis, including the tonsils.

orthotics (8) branch of medicine that deals with the design and fitting of orthopedic (relating to bone disorders) devices.

oscilloscope (19) device that displays electrical waveforms on a monitor.

osteogenesis (13) bone growth.

osteopathic manipulative treatment (OMT) (19) manual treatment performed by a physician during which emphasis is placed on normal body mechanics and manipulative methods to detect and correct structure.

osteophytectomy (16) removal of bone spurs to relieve compression of the spinal cord or nerve roots.

osteotomy (13) surgical incision into bone.

ostomy (15) surgically creating an opening in the body for the discharge of body wastes.

other (additional) diagnoses (6) any condition that coexists at the time of admission, that develops subsequently, or that affects the treatment received and/or the length of stay.

other significant procedure (6) surgical in nature, carries an operative or anesthetic risk, requires highly trained personnel, or requires special facilities or equipment; also called a secondary procedure.

Outcome and Assessment Information Set (OASIS) (7) core set of comprehensive assessments for adult home care patients used to measure patient outcomes for Outcome-Based Quality Improvement (OBQI); conduct patient assessment, patient care planning, and internal HHA performance improvements; and generate agency-level case mix reports that contain aggregate statistics about various patient characteristics such as demographic, health, or functional status at start of care; HHAs use Home Assessment and Validation and Entry (HAVEN) data entry software to report OASIS data.

outlier (20) inpatient case that is unusually costly.

outpatient (7) *see* ambulatory patient.

outpatient care (7) any health care service provided to a patient who is not admitted to a facility.

outpatient encounter (20) all outpatient procedures and services (e.g., same-day surgery, x-rays, laboratory tests, and so on) provided during one day to the same patient; also called outpatient visit.

outpatient prospective payment system (OPPS) (20) uses ambulatory payment classifications (APCs) to reimburse hospital outpatient services.

outpatient visit (20) *see* outpatient encounter.

overcoding (1) reporting codes for signs and symptoms associated, in addition to an established diagnosis code.

overlapping sites (4) *see* contiguous sites.

overpayment (20) reimbursement a provider or beneficiary receives in excess of amount due.

overpayment recovery (20) collecting excess payments made by Medicare, Medicaid, and other payers.

P

pacemaker (14) device that regulates the patient's heartbeat to prevent arrhythmias; includes a pulse generator and electrodes.

palatopharyngoplasty (15) surgical resection of excess tissue from the uvula, soft palate, and pharynx to open the airway.

panniculectomy (11) surgical removal of excess abdominal panniculus.

panniculus adiposus (11) layer of subcutaneous adipose tissue, or fat, below the dermis that contains fat deposits, blood vessels, and nerves.

pannus (11) *see* panniculus adiposus.

parenterally (17) other than by mouth or rectum, such as implantation, infusion, or injection.

paring and curettement (12) removal of growths or other material from the wall of a cavity or another surface.

partial hospitalization (10) short-term, intensive treatment program in which individuals who are experiencing an acute episode of an illness can receive medically supervised treatment during a significant number of daytime or nighttime hours.

partial mastectomy (12) involves making an incision through skin and fascia over the breast tumor and clamping lymphatic and blood vessels; the physician then excises the tumor mass along with a section of breast tissue.

participating provider (PAR) (20) health care provider (e.g., physician) who is a member of a health care plan; PAR providers receive reimbursement directly from the payer.

past medical history (10) summary of past illnesses, operations, injuries, treatments, and known allergies.

patch test (epicutaneous) (19) applying an allergen to a patch, which is placed on skin; the test is performed to identify substances that cause contact dermatitis, such as latex, medications, fragrances, preservatives, hair dyes, metals, and resins.

patency (14) open and unblocked status of a blood vessel or another tube in the body.

patient-driven payment model (20) implemented as a new case-mix reimbursement system that connects payment to patients' conditions and care needs instead of the volume of services provided; applies to IRF, LTCF, and SNF settings; replaced resource-utilization groups (RUGs).

patient education plan (1) program to educate the patient about conditions for which the patient is being treated; considered part of the problem-oriented record (POR).

patient record (1) business record for an inpatient or outpatient encounter that documents health care services provided to a patient; stores patient demographic data and documentation that supports diagnoses and justifies treatment; and contains results of treatment provided.

Payment Error and Prevention Program (PEPP) (20) identifies and reduces improper Medicare payments, resulting in a reduction in the Medicare payment error rate.

pediatric critical care patient transport (10) includes the physical attendance and direct face-to-face care provided by a physician during the interfacility transport of a critically ill or critically injured patient aged 24 months or younger.

pedicle skin graft (12) transferring a portion of skin graft to the recipient area, and attaching a remaining portion (the base) to the donor site so there is a vasculature and nerve supply for the recipient area.

percutaneous lithotomy (15) two-stage procedure that requires a percutaneous nephrostomy and dilation of the nephrostomy tract.

percutaneous needle biopsy (13) insertion of a long needle through the skin and into other tissue (e.g., chest wall, lung, or mediastinum) to obtain tissue for diagnostic evaluation.

percutaneous skeletal fixation (13) use of an external or internal fixation device to stabilize and immobilize a fracture; types include external fixation and internal fixation.

percutaneous vertebroplasty (13) process of injecting material (e.g., cement) into vertebral body to reinforce that body using image guidance.

pericardial sac (14) *see* pericardium.

pericardiectomy (14) removal of part of the pericardium (to treat chronic pericarditis).

pericardiocentesis (14) insertion of a needle to withdraw fluid from the pericardial sac.

pericardiotomy (14) requires thoracotomy as incision for pericardial drainage, fluid collection, or foreign body removal.

pericardium (14) membrane that surrounds the heart; also called pericardial sac.

perinatal period (5) interval of time occurring before, during, and up to 28 days following birth.

peripherally (14) access via a peripheral vein.

peripheral nerve block (11) injection of local anesthetic in the vicinity of a peripheral nerve to anesthetize that nerve's area of innervation.

peristalsis (15) wavelike motions that propel urine.

peritoneal dialysis (19) insertion of soft catheter into abdominal cavity and infusion of dialysate fluid at intermittent times.

peritoneoscopy (15) *see* laparoscopy.

pharmacologic management (19)   evaluation of a patient's medications for effect, proper dosage, and renewal of prescribed medications.

phlebotomy (18)   *see* venipuncture.

photic stimulation (19)   reaction to light.

photons (17)   invisible electromagnetic energy waves.

physiatrist (19)   physician who specializes in physical medicine and rehabilitation and treats acute/chronic pain and musculoskeletal disorders.

physical examination (10)   assessment of the patient's organ and body systems.

physical medicine and rehabilitation (19)   branch of medicine that focuses on the prevention, diagnosis, and treatment of disorders of the musculoskeletal, cardiovascular, and pulmonary systems that may produce temporary or permanent impairment.

physical status modifier (11)   added to each reported anesthesia code to indicate the patient's condition at the time anesthesia was administered.

physician-hospital organization (PHO) (20)   owned by hospital(s) and physician groups that obtain managed care plan contracts; physicians maintain their own practices and provide health care services to plan members.

physician query process (1)   contacting the responsible physician to request clarification about documentation and codes to be assigned; the process is activated when the coder notices a problem with documentation quality.

Physicians at Teaching Hospitals (PATH) initiative (20)   federal program that resulted from the discovery that some health care organizations were billing Medicare Part B for services that were already paid under Part A.

physician self-referral law (20)   prohibits a physician from referring Medicare patients to clinical laboratory services where they or a member of their family have a financial interest; enacted as part of the Omnibus Budget Reconciliation Act of 1989.

pilonidal cyst (12)   entrapped epithelial tissue and hair located in the sacral area at the top of the crease between the buttocks, which can become infected.

placeholder (2)   use of the letter "x" in certain ICD-10-CM codes to allow for future expansion.

place of service (POS) (10)   the physical location where health care is provided to patients.

plan (P) (1)   diagnostic, therapeutic, and education plans to resolve the problems; considered part of the problem-oriented record (POR) SOAP note.

plane of view (17)   terminology used when performing a radiology procedure.

pleura (13)   membrane that envelopes the lungs and lines the walls of the pleural cavity.

pleural effusion (13)   fluid in the pleural cavity preventing the lung from fully expanding, making it difficult for the patient to breathe.

plexus anesthesia (11)   injection of local anesthetic in the vicinity of a nerve plexus.

plus symbol (9)   symbol (+) located to the left of CPT codes that identifies add-on codes (also located in Appendix D of CPT) for procedures that are commonly, but not always, performed at the same time and by the same surgeon as the primary procedure.

pneumocentesis (13)   puncture of the pleural space with a transthoracic needle to drain fluid or to obtain material for diagnostic study.

pneumonectomy (13)   removal of the entire lung or one or more lobes of the lung.

point-of-service plan (POS) (20)   offers patients the freedom to use an HMO panel of providers or to self-refer to non-HMO providers.

polysomnography (19)   sleep study that includes sleep staging with additional parameters of sleep.

port (17)   skin site where radiation beams enter the body.

positron emission tomography (PET) (17)   producing x-ray images of the body after administering radioisotopes, which tracks metabolism or blood flow, not anatomy.

postanesthesia evaluation (11)   evaluation of the patient during recovery from anesthesia, as well as evaluation, treatment, and follow-up of possible anesthesia-related complications.

posteroanterior (PA) projection (17)   positioning the patient as facing the film and parallel to it; the x-ray beam travels from back to front, or posterior to anterior.

postoperative pain management (11)   administration of epidural or subarachnoid medications on the date(s) of service after the date of surgery.

postpartum care (16)   begins after vaginal or cesarean section delivery and includes the recovery room visit; any uncomplicated inpatient hospital and outpatient postpartum visits; episiotomy; and repair of cervical, vaginal, or perineal lacerations.

preadmission testing (PAT) (7)   occurs after a surgical patient registers with a facility's admitting department, when the patient undergoes preoperative nursing assessment and receives preanesthesia evaluation by an anesthesiologist.

preanesthesia evaluation (11)   assessing information from the patient's record, interviewing the patient, conducting a physical examination, evaluating preoperative test results, and ensuring that informed anesthetic consent has been obtained.

preauthorization (20)   prior approval.

pre-existing medical condition (20)   illness or injury that required treatment during a prescribed period of time prior to the insured's effective date of coverage under a new insurance policy.

preferred provider organization (PPO) (20)   network of physicians and hospitals that join together to contract with insurance companies, employers, or other organizations.

preoperative clearance (10)   occurs when a surgeon requests that a specialist or another physician examine a patient and indicate whether the patient can withstand the expected risks of a specific surgery.

present on admission (POA) indicator (20)   assigned to each diagnosis and external cause of injury code that is coded and reported on inpatient UB-04 or 837 Institutional (electronic) claims.

pressure ulcer (12)   ulceration of the skin and underlying tissue that occurs over a bony prominence.

presumptive identification (18)   identification by colony morphology, growth on selective media, or Gram stains.

preventive medicine services (10)   include routine examinations or risk management counseling for children and adults who exhibit no overt signs or symptoms of a disorder while presenting to the medical office for a preventive medical physical.

pricing modifier (9)   *see* functional modifier.

primary care (7)   acute care and preventive services provided as outpatient care and referred to as the *point of first contact*.

primary care provider (7)   manages and coordinates the patient's care, including referring the patient to a medical specialist for consultation and a second opinion; physician responsible for supervising and coordinating health care services and preauthorizing referrals to specialists and for overseeing inpatient hospital admissions, except in emergencies.

primary defect (12)   wound resulting from initial surgical intervention (e.g., excision of lesion) or trauma (e.g., deep abrasions).

primary malignancy (4)   original tumor site.

principal diagnosis (6)   condition established after study to be chiefly responsible for occasioning the admission of the patient to the hospital for care.

principal procedure (6)   performed for definitive treatment rather than for diagnostic or exploratory purposes, necessary to treat a complication, or is most closely related to the principal diagnosis.

privacy (20)   patient's right to prohibit disclosure of information without his or her authorization.

privacy rule (20)   *see* HIPAA standards for privacy of individually identifiable health information.

privileged communication (20)   any information communicated by a patient to a health care provider.

problem focused examination (10)   limited examination of the affected body area or organ system.

problem focused history (10)   consists of chief complaint and brief history of present illness or problem.

problem list (1)   serves as a table of contents for the patient record because it is filed at the beginning of the record and contains a numbered list of the patient's problems, which helps to index documentation throughout the record; considered part of the problem-oriented record (POR).

problem-oriented record (POR) (1)   systematic method of documentation that consists of four components: database, problem list, initial plan, and progress notes.

proctectomy (15)   surgical removal of the rectum.

proctosigmoidoscopy (15)   visual examination of the rectum and sigmoid colon.

professional component (17)   services provided by the physician, which include supervising the performance of a diagnostic imaging procedure, interpreting imaging films, and documenting the imaging report.

professional services (10)   face-to-face services provided by a physician or nonphysician practitioner (e.g., nurse practitioner, physician assistant) and reported by assigning an E/M code.

Programs of All-inclusive Care for the Elderly (PACE) (20)   community-based Medicare and Medicaid programs that provide integrated health care and long-term care services to elderly persons who require a nursing-facility level of care.

progress notes (1) narrative notes documented by the provider to demonstrate continuity of care and the patient's response to treatment; when using the SOAP format, a narrative is documented for each problem assigned to the patient according to subjective (S), objective (O), assessment (A), and plan (P).

prohibitory symbol (9) *see* forbidden symbol.

prolonged services (10) physicians' services involving patient contact that are considered beyond the usual service in either an inpatient or an outpatient setting.

prospective cost-based rate (20) based on reported health care costs from which a prospective *per diem* rate is determined; annual rate is usually adjusted using actual costs from the prior year; may be based on the facility's case mix (patient acuity of types and categories of patients).

prospective payment system (PPS) (20) reimbursement methodology that establishes predetermined rates based on patient category or type of facility, with annual increases based on an inflation index and a geographic wage index.

prospective price-based rate (20) associated with a particular category of patient; rate is established by the payer prior to the provision of health care services.

prosthetics (8) branch of medicine that deals with the design, production, and use of artificial body parts.

protected health information (PHI) (20) information that is identifiable to an individual, such as name, address, telephone numbers, date of birth, and Medicaid ID number.

provider (1) physician or other health care professional who performs procedures or provides services to patients.

psychotherapy (19) treatment of mental and emotional disorders by having patients talk about their condition(s) and related issues with a mental health physician or therapist.

pull-through (15) *see* ileoanal anastomosis.

pulmonary wedge pressure (11) indirect measurement of left atrial pressure that is useful in the diagnosis of left ventricular failure and mitral valve disease.

pulse oximetry (11) arterial oxyhemoglobin saturation.

pump oxygenator (11) device that substitutes for the heart (pump) and lungs (oxygenator) during open heart surgery.

puncture, prick, or scratch test (percutaneous) (19) procedure in which tiny drops of purified allergen extracts are pricked or scratched into the skin's surface; performed to identify allergies to pollen, mold, pet dander, dust mites, foods, insect venom, and penicillin.

pupil (16) black opening in the center of the iris that permits light to enter the eye.

pyramidal fracture (13) *see* LeFort II.

Q

qualified diagnosis (7) diagnosis documented as probable, suspected, questionable, rule out, or working diagnosis.

qualifying circumstance (11) coded when anesthesia services are provided during situations or circumstances that make anesthesia administration more difficult.

qualitative assay (18) detects whether a particular substance is present.

quantitative A-scan (17) diagnostic ultrasound that produces quantitative data about the posterior eye segment and evaluates tissue consistency, mobility, and vascularity.

quantitative assay (18) detects the amount of a substance in a specimen.

R

radiation absorbed dose (rad) (17) amount of radiant energy absorbed in a tissue.

radiation oncology (17) specialty of medicine that utilizes high-energy ionizing radiation in the treatment of malignant neoplasms and certain nonmalignant conditions.

radical mastectomy (12) total mastectomy, which includes removal of the breast and nipple, pectoralis muscles (major and/or minor), axillary lymph nodes, and internal mammary lymph nodes.

radiographic projection (17) describes the path that the x-ray beam travels through the body, from entrance to exit.

radiologic guidance (17) performed during a procedure to visualize access to an anatomical site fluoroscopic guidance to guide the placement, replacement, or removal of a catheter, central venous access device (CVAD), or needle.

radiologist (17) physician who has undergone specialized training to interpret diagnostic x-rays, perform specialized x-ray procedures, and administer radiation for the treatment of disease.

radiology (17) branch of medicine that uses imaging techniques to diagnose and treat disease.

radionuclide (17) radioactive material, such as an isotope of iodine.

radiopaque (11) cannot be penetrated by electromagnetic radiation.

radiopharmaceutical therapy (17) destroys diseased tissue, such as a malignant neoplasm.

random pattern flap (12) mycocutaneous flap with a random pattern of arteries.

range of codes (9) code numbers separated by a dash or a series of codes separated by commas in the CPT index.

reagent strip automated urine analyzer (18) instrumentation used to determine various components in the urine.

real-time scan (17) two-dimensional display of structures and movement that indicates the movement, shape, and size of the tissue or organ.

recipient heart with or without lung allotransplantation (14) removal (harvesting) of heart with or without lung tissue; includes transplantation of the allograft and care of the recipient.

recipient lung allotransplantation (13) transplantation of a single or double lung allograft and care of the recipient.

recipient site (12) anatomical site to which healthy skin is attached.

reconstruction (12) surgical rebuilding of a body part, such as the breast or the knee joint.

reconstruction of the vena cava (14) surgical procedure performed to correct a congenital defect or to repair the vena cava when the patient sustains trauma or the vena cava is damaged due to long-term drug therapy.

red reference symbol (9) symbol located below a code description to indicate that the coder should refer to the *Clinical Examples in Radiology* quarterly newsletter.

reduction (13) *see* manipulation.

referral (10) recommendation to transfer a patient's care from one provider to another.

referred outpatient (7) patient who receives diagnostic or therapeutic care because such care is unavailable in the primary care provider's office.

regional anesthesia (11) anesthesia agents injected into or near the spinal fluid and around a nerve or network of nerves to block the nerve supply to a specific part of the body.

rehabilitation hospital (6) health care facility that admits patients who are diagnosed with trauma or disease and who need to learn how to function.

relative value unit (RVU) (20) payment component that consists of physician work, practice expense, and malpractice expense.

remittance advice (remit) (20) statement sent by the payer to the provider that details how submitted claims were processed and contains reimbursement amounts.

removal (12) procedures performed to eliminate tissue (e.g., amputations) or take something out (e.g., removal of implants, such as buried wire, pins, or screws).

renal dialysis (19) artificial removal of toxic waste products from the body when the patient's kidneys are unable to perform this function due to disease or deterioration.

repair (12) procedure performed to surgically improve improperly functioning parts of the body.

replantation (13) surgical reattachment of a finger, a hand, a toe, a foot, a leg, or an arm that has been completely severed from a person's body.

Resident Assessment Validation and Entry (RAVEN) (20) data entry system that allows a skilled nursing facility (SNF) to capture and transmit the minimum data set (MDS).

resident physician (1) individual who participates in an approved graduate medical education (GME) program.

residual effect (2) condition produced (sequela) after the acute phase of an illness or injury has terminated.

resource-based relative value scale (RBRVS) system (20) used to reimburse physician services covered by Medicare Part B, and is now called the Medicare physician fee schedule (MPFS).

retina (16) part of eye that contains nerve tissue.

revenue code (20) four-digit UB-04 code that is assigned to each procedure, service, or supply to indicate the location or type of service provided to an institutional patient, such as radiology or laboratory.

review of systems (ROS) (10)   *see* system review.

revision (12)   surgical modification of a previous procedure or a device.

rhinoplasty (15)   repair of a skin defect of the nose using harvested tissue or plastic surgery to change the nose's shape or size.

rhomboid flap (12)   random pattern flap that can be raised on any or all corners of a parallelogram configuration, typically 120 and 60 degrees; also called Limberg flap.

rhytidectomy (12)   excision of a section of skin to eliminate wrinkles.

rhytides (13)   wrinkles.

roentgen (17)   international unit of exposure dose for x-rays or gamma rays.

roentgen-equivalent-man (rem) (17)   unit of measurement that includes different biological responses to different kinds of radiation.

roster billing (20)   simplified claims submission process available to public health clinics and other noninstitutional entities that offer mass immunization programs.

rotation flap (12)   incision made to create a curvilinear flap contiguous with the defect; flap is dissected, freed, and pivoted and sutured in place over the defect.

rule of nines (12)   divides total body surface area (BSA) into nine segments by percentage.

RxNorm (1)   provides normalized names for clinical drugs and links its names to many of the drug vocabularies commonly used in pharmacy management and drug interaction software, including those of First Databank, Micromedex, MediSpan, Gold Standard Drug Database, and Multum; by providing links among these vocabularies, RxNorm can mediate messages among systems that do not use the same software and vocabulary.

S

saddle block anesthesia (11)   *see* caudal anesthesia.

safe harbor regulation (20)   specifies various payment and business practices that, although potentially capable of inducing referrals of business reimbursable under the federal health care programs, would not be treated as criminal offenses under the anti-kickback statute.

sagittal plane (17)   vertically divides the body into unequal left and right portions.

salpingo-oophorectomy (16)   surgical removal of both fallopian tubes and ovaries.

saphenopopliteal vein anastomosis (14)   surgical incision to expose the saphenous vein and connect it to the popliteal vein using end-to-end anastomosis.

scanner (1)   equipment that captures paper record images onto the storage media.

sclera (16)   white of the eye that comprises the eye's outer layer; contains fibrous tissue that maintains the eye's shape and protects the eye's inner layers.

screening mammography (17)   radiographic (x-ray) of the breast that is performed when a patient presents without signs and symptoms of breast disease.

secondary defect (12)   wound resulting from removal of tissue to create flap(s) or graft(s).

secondary malignancy (4)   tumor that has metastasized, or spread, to a secondary site either adjacent to the primary site or to a remote region of the body.

secondary procedure (6)   *see* other significant procedure.

second-order vessels (14)   branch from first-order vessel.

second-stage fistulectomy/fistulotomy (15)   in treatment of anal fistulas, use of a seton to cut through the fistula; the seton is left in place until later removal.

section (18)   thin slice of tissue prepared from a block that is examined.

sectionalized record (1)   *see* source-oriented record.

security (20)   ensures that facilities, equipment, and patient information are safe from damage, loss, tampering, theft, or unauthorized access.

security rule (20)   HIPAA regulation that requires covered entities to adopt standards and safeguards to protect health information that is collected, maintained, used, or transmitted electronically.

sedation (11)   administration of medication into a vein to relieve pain and anxiety, making the patient feel calm.

segmental instrumentation (13)   fixation at each end of the construct (structure) and includes at least one additional interposed bony attachment.

selective vascular catheterization (14)   insertion and manipulation or guidance of a catheter into the branches of the arterial system (other than the aorta or the vessel punctured) for the purpose of performing diagnostic or therapeutic procedures.

self-referral (20)   an enrollee seeing a non-HMO panel specialist without a referral from the primary care physician.

semicolon (9)   symbol (;) used to save space in CPT code descriptions.

separate procedure (12)   performed as an integral component of a total service or procedure.

septal defects (14)   occurs when the tissue does not completely close between the heart's chambers.

septic abortion (16)   abortion-related pelvic and uterine infection.

septum (14)   tissue that separates the heart's left and right sides.

sequela (2)   residual (long-term condition produced) that develops after the acute phase of an illness or injury has ended. (Historically, ICD-9-CM referred to a sequela as a *late effect* of an illness or injury.)

seton (15)   large silk suture or rubber bands.

severity of illness (SI) (20)   physiological complexity that comprises the extent and interactions of a patient's disease(s) as presented to medical personnel; medically justifies intensity of service.

shaving (12)   horizontal slicing to remove epidermal and dermal lesions; removal includes scissoring or any sharp method.

shock therapy (11)   *see* electroconvulsive therapy.

short-latency somatosensory evoked potential study (19)   electrical stimulation of nerves to evaluate their responsiveness to the body's superficial surface and internal structures.

short-term hospital (6)   average length of stay (LOS) of 4–5 days and a total LOS of fewer than 25 days.

shunting procedure (14)   performed to move blood from one area to another for conditions such as atrial septal defect (ASD), coarctation of the aorta, patent ductus arteriosus (PDA), tricuspid atresia, and ventricular septal defect (VSD).

side view (17)   *see* lateral projection.

sigmoidoscopy (15)   visual examination of the entire rectum and sigmoid colon and may include a portion of the descending colon.

simple closure (12)   *see* simple repair.

simple fracture (5)   *see* closed fracture.

simple repair (12)   involves the use of staples, sutures, and/or tissue adhesives to repair superficial wounds involving epidermis, dermis, and/or subcutaneous tissues; also called one-layer closure, nonlayered closure, and single-layer closure.

single chamber (14)   contains a single electrode that is positioned in the heart's right atrium *or* right ventricle.

single code (9)   single code number listed in the CPT index.

single hospital (6)   hospital that is self-contained and not part of a larger organization.

single photon emission computerized tomography (SPECT) (17)   three-dimensional x-ray images of internal organs produced after administration of a radioactive material, which visualize anatomy and function.

sinus of Valsalva (14)   anatomical dilation of ascending aorta that occurs just above aortic valve (e.g., left anterior aortic sinus that gives rise to the left coronary artery); defects include aneurysms and fistulas for which repair and closure procedures are performed.

skeletal traction (13)   exerts a pulling force on the affected limb to realign bone or joint.

skilled nursing facility prospective payment system (SNF PPS) (20)   uses the patient-driven payment model (PDPM).

skin substitute graft (12)   include nonautologous human skin (e.g., acellular dermal), non-human skin substitute grafts (e.g., xenograft), and biological products that form a sheet scaffolding for skin growth.

sleep laboratory (19)   area in a hospital facility that is managed by a sleep technologist who explains and performs the sleep studies.

sleep staging (19)   during a sleep study (polysomnography), involves the use of a 1-4 lead electroencephalogram (EEG), electro-oculogram (EOG), and submental electromyogram (EMG).

sleep study (19)   evaluation of adult and pediatric patients during sleep by monitoring brain waves, heart rate, and eye movements; performed to diagnose sleep disorders, which include breathing, movement, and neurologic disorders that occur at night.

slit lamp exam (17)   high-intensity light source that can be focused to shine as a slit to visualize anterior structures, including the eyelid, sclera, conjunctiva, iris, natural crystalline lens, and cornea.

SNOMED CT (1)   *see Systemized Nomenclature of Medicine Clinical Terms*

social history (10)   age-appropriate review of past and current activities such as daily routine, dietary habits, exercise routine, marital status, occupation, sleeping patterns, smoking, use of alcohol and other drugs, and sexual activities.

somatic nerves (16)   control voluntary movements and conscious sensation; include voluntary motor and sensory nerves.

source-oriented record (SOR) (2)   reports organized according to documentation source, each of which is located in a labeled section of the record.

special evaluation and management services (10)   provided for establishment of baseline information prior to life or disability insurance certificates being issued and for examination of a patient with a work-related or medical disability problem.

special report (9)   document that must accompany the claim to describe the nature, extent, and need for the procedure or service when an unlisted procedure or service code is reported.

specialty coders (1)   individuals who have obtained advanced training in medical specialties (e.g., anesthesia, obstetrics) and who are skilled in that medical specialty's compliance and reimbursement areas. In addition to maintaining core credential(s), completes rigorous, in-depth exam, and earns additional continuing education units biannually. Specialty coders typically analyze provider documentation for accuracy, completeness, and timeliness; maintain and update chargemasters and/or encounter forms; meet with coding staff to educate them about revised rules and regulations; review patient charges to accuracy in reported codes and modifiers and enter billing edits; and write letters of appeals to address third-party payer reimbursement denials.

specialty hospital (6)   health care facility that delivers care to a particular population of patients or type of disease.

specimen (18)   tissue submitted for laboratory or pathological evaluation; also the unit of service used to report surgical pathology codes.

spinal anesthesia (11)   local anesthetic injected into cerebrospinal fluid at the lumbar spine, where it acts on spinal nerve roots and part of the spinal cord; anesthetized area extends from the legs to the abdomen or chest.

spinal tap (11)   *see lumbar puncture.*

spleen (14)   organ that produces mature lymphocytes, destroys worn-out red blood cells, and serves as a reservoir for blood.

splenoportography (14)   radiographic visualization of the splenic and portal veins.

split-thickness skin graft (12)   graft of entire epidermis and a portion of the dermis; typically used to repair edematous, infected, or large wounds (e.g., result of burns).

stabilize (13)   to secure bone in a fixed position.

stab phlebectomy (14)   multiple tiny incisions made over varicose vein sites; at each stab site the varicosity is extracted and then the varicose segment is removed.

staff model HMO (20)   health care services provided to subscribers by physicians employed by an HMO.

standby service (10)   physician, or other qualified health care professional, spending a prolonged period of time *without patient contact* waiting for an event to occur that will require the physician's or professional's service.

Stark I (20)   *see physician self-referral law.*

Stark II (20)   expanded the Stark I physician self-referral law by including referrals of Medicare and Medicaid patients for designated health care services.

star symbol (★) (9)   indicates that a code may be reported for synchronous telemedicine services. (CPT Appendix P contains a list of CPT codes that may be used for synchronous telemedicine services.)

State Children's Health Insurance Program (SCHIP) (20)   federal health program established to provide health assistance to uninsured, low-income children either through separate programs or through expanded eligibility under state Medicaid programs.

status indicator (SI) (20)   payment indicator that identifies how each code is paid (or not paid) under the Outpatient Prospective Payment System (OPPS).

stem cells (14)   cells contained in bone marrow.

stented valve (14)   includes framework on which the replacement heart valve is mounted to provide support for the valve's leaflets.

stentless valve (14)   an actual heart valve obtained from either a human donor (homograft) or a pig; it does not contain framework.

stereotactic localization (12)   use of specialized three-dimensional imaging to target a nonpalpable lesion.

stereotaxis (16)   use of a stereotactic guidance system to allow the physician to determine three-dimensional coordinates in order to create a lesion on the spinal cord (to alleviate chronic pain in a particular part of the body); to stimulate the spinal cord percutaneously (to create a lesion that will block pain); or to facilitate the biopsy, aspiration, or excision of a spinal cord lesion.

stoma (15)   surgically created opening between ureter, small intestine, or large intestine, through to abdominal wall.

strabismus (16)   improperly aligned eyes.

stroma (12)   supporting tissue (matrix) of an organ.

subacute care patient (6)   receives specialized services such as chemotherapy, injury rehabilitation, ventilator support, wound care, and other types of health care services provided to seriously ill patients.

subcategory (2)   ICD-10-CM codes that contain four, five, six, or seven characters; subcategory codes that require additional characters are invalid if the fifth, sixth, or seventh character(s) is absent.

subcutaneous fistulectomy (15)   removal of an anal fistula, without division of the sphincter muscle.

subglottic stenosis (13)   narrowing of the airway below the vocal cords, adjacent to the cricoid cartilage.

subjective (S) (1)   patient's statement about how he or she feels, including symptomatic information; considered part of the problem-oriented record (POR) SOAP note.

subluxation (13)   partial displacement of a bone from its joint.

submuscular fistulectomy (15)   removal of an anal fistula, including division of the sphincter muscle.

subterm (2)   qualifying word listed below the main term in the ICD-10-CM Index to Diseases and Injuries; list alternate sites, etiology, or clinical status.

superbill (20)   *see encounter form.*

supervision and interpretation (17)   term for the radiological portion of a procedure when two different physicians perform the surgical and radiological components of a procedure.

surface anesthesia (11)   topical application of local anesthetic cream, solution, or spray to skin or mucous membranes.

surgical curettement (12)   scraping tissue to remove abnormal tissue.

surgical endoscopy (15)   performed when anything in addition to visualization is done, such as the removal of a foreign body.

surgical package (12)   services performed that are integral to the standard of medical/surgical services, such as the cleansing, shaving, and prepping of skin and the insertion of intravenous access for medication.

suture (12)   surgical closure of a wound, using catgut, glue, silk thread, wire, or other materials.

Swan-Ganz catheter (11)   thin, flexible, flow-directed multilumen plastic tube (or catheter) that is advanced from a peripheral vein into the right atrium and then positioned in a branch of the pulmonary artery.

swing bed (6)   allows a rural hospital to admit a nonacute care patient.

sympathectomy (14)   excision of a segment of the sympathetic nerve.

sympathetic nerves (16)   part of the involuntary autonomic nervous system; originate in the thoracic and lumbar regions of the spinal cord; inhibit the physiological effects of the parasympathetic nervous system.

***Systematized Nomenclature of Medicine, Clinical Terms* (SNOMED CT) (1)**   comprehensive and multilingual clinical terminology of body structures, clinical findings, diagnoses, medications, outcomes, procedures, specimens, therapies, and treatments.

system review (10)   inventory by systems to document subjective symptoms stated by the patient; also provides an opportunity to gather information that the patient may have forgotten to mention or that may have seemed unimportant.

systemic radiation therapy (17)   unsealed radioactive materials that travel throughout the body.

T

Tables (ICD-10-PCS) (6)   used to construct a complete and valid ICD-10-PCS code; contain terms (and definitions) and rows that contain values (characters) needed to construct a valid code.

Tabular List of Diseases and Injuries (2)   chronological list of ICD-10-CM codes, divided into 21 chapters based on body system or condition.

Tax Equity and Fiscal Responsibility Act of 1983 (TEFRA) (20)   federal legislation that resulted in implementation of the inpatient prospective payment system, which uses diagnosis-related groups to reimburse short-term hospitals a predetermined rate for Medicare inpatient services.

teaching hospital (1)   hospital engaged in an approved graduate medical education (GME) residency program in medicine, osteopathy, dentistry, or podiatry.

teaching physician (1)   physician (other than another resident physician) who supervises residents during patient care.

tear apparatus (16)   *see* lacrimal apparatus.

technical component (17)   use of equipment and supplies as well as the employment of radiological technologists to perform diagnostic imaging examinations and administer radiation therapy treatments.

tenosynovitis (16)   swollen tendon sheaths.

Tensilon test (19)   involves injecting the drug Tensilon (or its generic form edrophonium chloride) into a vein to block the action of the enzyme that breaks down the neurotransmitter acetylcholinesterase.

tetralogy of Fallot (14)   congenital heart condition that includes a ventral septal defect, stenosis of the infundibulum, hypertrophy of the right ventricle, and an abnormally positioned aorta.

therapeutic apheresis (14)   removal of blood components, cells, or plasma solute and retransfusion of the remaining components into the patient.

therapeutic plan (1)   specific medications, goals, procedures, therapies, and treatments used to treat the patient; considered part of the problem oriented record (POR).

therapeutic port film (17)   x-rays taken during delivery of radiation treatment that utilize the treatment beam of the machine.

therapeutic surgical procedure (12)   performed to treat specific conditions or injuries; includes the procedure itself and normal, uncomplicated follow-up care.

third-order vessels (14)   blood vessels that branch from second-order vessels.

third-party administrator (TPA) (1)   entity that processes health care claims and performs related business functions for a health plan; the TPA might contract with a health care clearinghouse to standardize data for claims processing.

third-party payer (1)   *see* health plan.

thoracentesis (13)   surgical puncture of the chest wall with a needle to obtain fluid from the pleural cavity.

thoracoscopy (13)   visual examination of the pleural cavity; provides an alternative to open lung or thoracotomy procedures to treat pleural disorders surgically.

thrombectomy (14)   surgical removal of a thrombus.

thromboendarterectomy (14)   surgical excision of a thrombus and atherosclerotic inner lining from an obstructed artery.

thymus (14)   produces T lymphocytes, which are important to the body's immune function.

tibia (13)   larger of the two lower leg bones.

tibial plateau (13)   lower portion of the femur, which articulates with the tibia.

tissue approximation (12)   method of replacing sutures with material or substance (e.g., surgical glue), which facilitates enhanced cosmetic results and faster healing of defects.

tissue-cultured autograft (12)   graft material supplied by laboratories; such grafting is often performed as part of a staged procedure.

tissue rearrangement (12)   defined by anatomical site and size of defect; includes excision of the defect or lesion.

tonsils (14)   located at the back of the throat; contain lymphoid tissue that helps fight infections.

total mastectomy (12)   surgical removal of the entire breast, including the pectoral fascia and a sampling of axillary lymph nodes.

total pneumonectomy (13)   removal of the entire lung.

trachea (13)   windpipe.

tracheobronchoscopy (13)   visual examination of the interior of the trachea and bronchus.

trachoma (16)   chronic inflammation of the conjunctiva in which granulations form.

transfer note (1)   documentation when a patient is transferred to another facility; summarizes the reason for admission, current diagnoses and medical information, and reason for transfer.

transfer of care (10)   occurs when a provider who is managing some or all of a patient's problems relinquishes that responsibility to another provider who explicitly agrees to accept this responsibility and who, from the initial encounter, is *not* providing consultative services; the provider transferring care no longer manages these problems but may continue to manage other conditions.

transitional pass-through payment (8)   temporary additional payment (over and above the OPPS payment) made for certain innovative medical devices, drugs, and biologicals provided to Medicare beneficiaries.

transmyocardial revascularization (TMR) (14)   procedure that uses a high-powered laser to create small channels in the heart muscle to increase blood supply to the myocardium.

transpedicular approach (16)   performed through and inside the pedicle (segment between transverse process and vertebral body) of a thoracic vertebra to access a thoracic disk.

transposition of great vessels (14)   congenital reversal of the aorta and pulmonary artery.

transurethral resection of the prostate (TURP) (15)   resection of the prostate gland via transurethral approach using an electrosurgical device.

transurethral ureteroscopic lithotripsy (15)   procedure in which a cystoscope is inserted through the urethra into the bladder and a ureteroscope is passed into the ureters.

transverse plane (17)   horizontally divides the body into superior and inferior portions.

treatment volume determination (17)   region within the body to which radiation therapy is directed.

triage (7)   organized method of identifying and treating patients according to urgency of care required.

triangle symbol (9)   symbol (▲) located to the left of CPT codes that identifies revised code descriptions.

TRICARE (20)   military health plan that covers active duty and retired members of the uniformed services and their dependents.

triple option plan (20)   health plan that is offered as a single insurance plan or as a joint venture among two or more third-party payers.

truncus arteriosus (14)   congenital malformation in which just one artery arises from the heart to form the aorta and pulmonary artery.

tube pericardiostomy (14)   insertion of a tube for drainage or specimen collection.

tunneled (14)   implanted.

tunneled catheter (11)   *see* internal catheter.

turbinates (13)   bony plates covered by spongy mucosa with curved margins; there are three turbinates on each side of the nasal vestibule: inferior, middle, and superior.

tympanoplasty (16)   repair or reconstruction of the eardrum.

tympanostomy (16)   *see* myringotomy.

type 1 diabetes mellitus (4)   a condition in which the patient's body is unable to produce insulin.

type 2 diabetes mellitus (4)   a condition in which the patient's body is unable to properly use insulin produced.

type of service (TOS) (10)   refers to the kind of health care services provided to patients, including critical care, consultation, initial hospital care, subsequent hospital care, and confirmatory consultation.

U

UB-04 (1)   standard claim submitted by health care institutions to payers for inpatient and outpatient services.

ultrasonography (17)   *see* ultrasound.

ultrasound (17)   high-frequency sound waves that bounce off internal organs and create echoes; the echo pattern is displayed on the ultrasound machine monitor.

UMLS (1)   *see* Unified Medical Language System (UMLS)

unbundling (1)   reporting multiple codes to increase reimbursement when a single combination code should be reported.

uncertain behavior (4)   subsequent morphology or behavior that cannot be predicted based on the submitted specimen; the tissue appears to be in transition, and the pathologist cannot establish a definitive diagnosis.

undermining (12)   process of using a surgical instrument to separate skin and mucosa from its underlying stroma so that the tissue can be stretched and moved to overlay a defect.

Unified Medical Language System (UMLS) (1) set of files and software that allows many health and biomedical vocabularies and standards to enable interoperability among computer systems; used to enhance or develop applications, including electronic health records, classification tools, dictionaries and language translators; used to link health information, medical terms, drug names, and billing codes across different computer systems.

Uniform Ambulatory Care Data Set (UACDS) (7) established by the federal government as a standard data set for ambulatory care facility records.

Uniform Hospital Discharge Data Set (UHDDS) (6) established by the federal government to define data collected for inpatient hospitalizations.

unit/floor time (10) amount of time the provider spends at the patient's bedside and at management of the patient's care on the unit or floor.

unlisted procedure (9) code assigned when the provider performs a procedure or service for which there is no CPT code.

unlisted service (9) *see* unlisted procedure.

unspecified nature (4) neoplasm is identified, but the results of pathology examination are not available; thus, there is no indication as to histology or nature of the tumor.

upcoding (1) reporting codes that are not supported by documentation in the patient record for the purpose of increasing reimbursement.

upper GI endoscopy (15) direct visualization of the esophagus and the stomach.

uptake (17) absorption by a tissue of a substance, material, or mineral and its permanent or temporary retention.

ureter (15) tube that conveys urine from each kidney to the urinary bladder; there are two ureters.

ureterolithotomy (15) surgical removal of stones from the ureter.

urethra (15) muscular tube that discharges urine from the urinary bladder to the outside of the body.

urethrocystoscopy (11) visualization of urethra and urinary bladder.

urethroplasty (15) surgical repair of the urethra.

urinary bladder (15) hollow organ that serves as a reservoir for urine until it passes from the body (via urination).

urinary system (15) consists of the kidneys, ureters, urinary bladder, and urethra.

uroflowmetry (15) measures the amount of urine that flows from the urinary bladder per second.

uvea (16) eye's vascular layer, which includes the choroid, ciliary body, and iris.

V

vaginal birth after cesarean (VBAC) (16) planned vaginal birth after previous cesarean section.

value (ICD-10-PCS) (6) characters (individual letters and numbers) assigned to each of seven unique hierarchies (positions), which construct a valid ICD-10-PCS code.

value-based purchasing (VBP) (20) part of a long-standing CMS effort to link Medicare's inpatient prospective payment system (IPPS) to a value-based system for the purpose of improving health care quality, including the quality of care provided in the inpatient hospital setting, which affects payment for inpatient stays to over 3,500 hospitals; participating hospitals are paid for inpatient acute care services based on quality of care, not just quantity of services provided.

valvular atresia (14) valve failure to develop properly; completely closed at birth.

valvular heart disease (14) abnormality or dysfunction of one or more of the heart's four valves (aortic, mitral, pulmonary, and tricuspid).

valvular prolapse (14) condition in which two valvular flaps do not close properly, resulting in backflow of blood.

valvular regurgitation (14) backflow of blood because one or more cardiac valves close improperly.

valvular stenosis (14) narrowing of one or more cardiac valves.

valvuloplasty (14) open-heart surgery during which the surgeon removes the damaged valve and replaces it with a prosthetic, homograft or allograft, stented, or stentless valve.

valvulotomy (14) open-heart surgery in which an incision is made into a valve to repair valvular damage.

varicocele (16) abnormal dilation of the veins of the spermatic cord in the scrotum.

vascular family (14) group of vessels that is accessed by the same first-order vessel and is supplied by the same primary branch from the aorta.

vas deferens (16) tube that carries spermatozoa from the testis.

venipuncture (18) puncture of a vein with a needle for the purpose of drawing blood; most common method of collecting blood specimens.

venography (17) x-ray of a vein after injection of contrast material.

venous anomaly (14) associated with systemic veins and pulmonary veins, and includes conditions such as cor triatriatum, pulmonary vein stenosis, Scimitar syndrome, supravalvar mitral ring, and total anomalous pulmonary venous return (TAPVR).

venous valve transposition (14) surgical procedure performed to treat chronic deep venous insufficiency.

ventricular assist device (VAD) (14) provides temporary support for the heart by substituting for left or right heart function.

vertebral augmentation (13) process of creating a cavity in a vertebral body followed by injecting material (e.g., cement) under image guidance.

very low birth weight (10) 1,500–2,500 grams.

view (17) patient's position in relation to the camera during radiographic procedures.

visceral arteries (14) supply blood to the intestines, liver, and spleen.

visual evoked potential (VEP) test (19) stimulation of the eye using the checkerboard or flash technique to monitor the patient's response.

volvulus (15) twisting or displacement of the intestines, causing obstruction.

V-Y plasty (12) procedure whereby, after surgical creation of a V-shaped incision, the edges of the incision are drawn together and sutured, converting the incision to a Y shape.

W

wage index (20) adjusts payments to account for geographic variations in hospitals' labor costs.

wedge (17) treatment beam-modifying device that acts to change the beam intensity profile.

Whipple procedure (15) surgical removal of the pancreas, duodenum, bile duct, and stomach with reconstruction.

workers' compensation (20) state-mandated insurance program that reimburses health care costs and lost wages if an employee suffers a work-related disease or injury.

W-plasty (12) surgical trimming of both edges of a wound or defect into the shape of a W or multiple Ws.

X

xenograft (12) surgical transplantation of tissue from a different species.

x-ray (17) radiographic visualization or imaging of internal body structures using low-dose high-energy radiation.

x-ray beam (17) consists of invisible electromagnetic energy waves that are emitted from a radiation machine and used to produce images and treat disease.

Z

Z-plasty (12) making a surgical incision along with two additional incisions, one above and another below, creating a Z formation.

INDEX

A

AAPC (American Academy of Professional Coders), 5
Abbreviations, 88–89
Abdomen, 520, 619–620
Aberrant vessels, 565
Ablation, 461
Abnormal clinical and laboratory findings, 175–178
Abnormal findings, 220
Abortion, 170, 656
Abuse
  adult and child, 187
  health care, 846–854
  in pregnant patient, 170
Accession, 756
Accessory sinuses, 532–534
Acellular dermal replacement, 485
Actinic keratosis (AK), 488
Acupuncture, 797
Acute care facilities/hospitals, 210–212
Acute conditions, 66
Acute myocardial infarction (AMI), 150
Acute respiratory failure, 152
Adaptive behavior services, 791
Add-on codes, 469, 767
Adenoidectomy, 602–603
Adenoids, 582, 602–603
Adjacent tissue transfer/rearrangement, 473, 483–484
Adjuvant chemotherapy, 794
Adjuvant techniques, 573, 751
Administration (ICS-10-PCS), 245
Administrative simplification, 855–860
Admission
  from observation unit, 218
  from outpatient surgery, 218
Admission reporting guidelines, 828
Admission services, 389
Admissions/encounters for rehabilitation, 218
Admitting diagnosis, 213
Adrenal glands, 657
Adult abuse, neglect, and maltreatment, 187
Advance beneficiary notice (ABN), 313
Advance care planning, 407
Advanced diagnostic laboratory tests (ADLTs), 758
Advancement flap, 484
Adverse effects, 179–182, 185–186
Affordable Care Act (ACA), 812–813, 815–816, 831
Aftercare codes, 200–201
Aggregate cap, 832
AHA Coding Clinic for HCPCS, 11
AHA Coding Clinic for ICD-10-CM and ICD-10-PCS, 11
Airway management, 425
Alcohol use, in pregnancy, childbirth, and puerperium, 168
A-line, 429
Aliquot, 754
All Patient Refined DRGs (APR-DRGs), 827
Allergen immunotherapy, 787
Allergens, 787

Allergy and clinical immunology, 786–787
Allergy sensitivity tests, 786, 787
Allergy testing, 786
Allogenous grafts, 509
Alternative billing codes (ABC codes), 22
Ambulance fee schedule, 837
Ambulatory care, 266–271
Ambulatory patient groups (APGs), 833
Ambulatory patients, 267
Ambulatory payment classification (APCs), 832–833
Ambulatory surgery, 277
Ambulatory surgical center payments, 835–837
American Association of Medical Assistants (AAMA), 6
American Dental Association (ADA), 22
American Health Information Management Association (AHIMA), 5, 60
American Hospital Association (AHA), 11, 12, 50, 60
American Medical Association (AMA), 9, 295, 315, 325, 364
American Medical Billing Association (AMBA), 6
American Medical Technologists (AMT), 6
Amniocentesis, 653
A-mode (amplitude modulation), 713
Analgesia, 419
Analysis-programming, 790
Analytes, 747
Anatomic pathology, 753
Anatomical site is not documented, 129
Ancillary services, 210
"And," 99–100
Anemia, 136
Anesthesia, 419
  qualifying circumstances for, 799
  types of, 419–422
Anesthesia (CPT), 418–456
  burn excisions or debridement, 447
  central venous access devices, 428–429
  drug administration codes, 430
  emergency endotracheal tube intubation, 428
  forearm, wrist, and hand, 445
  guidelines, 425–438
  head, 439–440
  intra-arterial lines, 429
  intrathoracic, 441, 442
  introduction to, 419
  knee and popliteal area, 445
  lower abdomen, 443
  lower leg, 445
  modifiers, 430–432
  monitored anesthesia care, 423–434
  neck, 440
  obstetric, 447
  other procedures, 447–448
  overview of, 422–424
  pelvis, 444
  perineum, 444
  qualifying circumstances, 436
  radiological procedures, 446–447
  reporting codes, 427–428
  separate or multiple procedures, 436

  services, 435–436
  shoulder and axilla, 445
  special report, 436
  spine and spinal cord, 441, 442
  subsections, 438–448
  supplied materials, 436
  terminology, 419–422
  thorax, 440–441
  time reporting, 432–435
  unlisted service or procedure, 436
  upper abdomen, 441, 443
  upper arm and elbow, 445
  upper leg, 444
Anesthesia conversion factor, 434
Anesthesia time units, 432
Anesthesiologist, 419
Anesthetic, 419
Aneurysm, 561, 570
Aneurysm repair, 570–571
Angina, 149, 216
Angiogenesis, 555
Angiography, 696, 697, 783–784
Angioplasty, 572
Angioscopy, 572
Annuloplasty, 519
Anoscopy, 615
ANSI ASC 12N 837, 858, 859
Antepartum services, 652–653
Anterior approach, 666
Anterior segment, 673–674
Anterolateral approach, 666
Anteroposterior projection, 696
Antibiotic-resistance infections, 120
Antibodies, 751
Antigens, 751
Anus, 615–616
Aortic anomalies, 565
Aortic sinus, 564
Aortography, 696
Aortopulmonary septal defect (APSD), 565
Appendectomy, 613
Appendix, 613
Application service provider (ASP), 6
Approach, 242–243
Arrow symbol, 337
Arterial blood gases, 578
Arterial puncture, 739
Arterial transposition, 573–574
Arteries and Veins (CPT), 569–582
  adjuvant techniques, 573
  aneurysms repair, 570–571
  angioscopy, 572
  arterial puncture, 578
  arterial transposition, 573–574
  arteriovenous fistula repair, 571–572
  blood vessel repair, 572
  bypass graft, 573
  central venous access procedures, 576–578
  composite grafts, 573
  dialysis circuit, 579

embolectomy/thrombectomy, 569
endoscopy, 581
endovascular revascularization, 580
excision, exploration, repair, revision, 574
hemodialysis access, 579
intervascular cannulation, 579
intraosseous, 578
intravascular ultrasound services, 581
ligation, 581
overview of, 569
portal decompression procedures, 579
shunt insertion, 579
thromboendarterectomy, 572
transcatheter procedures, 579
vascular embolization and occlusion, 580–581
vascular injection procedures, 574–576
venous reconstruction, 569
Arteriovenous fistula, 561, 571–572
Arthrocentesis, 508
Arthrodesis, 517, 519
Arthrography, 696
Arthroscopy, 526–527
Artificial ankylosis, 519
Arytenoidectomy, 535
Arytenoidopexy, 535
Assay, 745–746
Assessment (A), 32
Assisted living facilities, 399
Assumption coding, avoiding, 13–14
Asthma, 151–152
Atherectomy, 780
Atherosclerotic coronary artery disease, 149
Atrial septal defect (ASD), 564
Audiometric tests, 779
Auditory system, 677–680
Augmentation, 509
Autogenous tissue, 509
Autograft, 484
Automated case abstracting software, 34
Automated record formats, 32–33
Automated records, 31, 32–33
Autonomic function tests, 790
Autonomic nervous system, 668–670
Axial plane, 695

B

Back, 514
Backbench work, 541, 566
Bacteria, 117
Bacterial sepsis of newborn, 173
Balanced Budget Act of 1997, 830, 832, 834
Balanced Budget Refinement Act of 1999 (BBRA),
834
Balloon angioplasty, 780
Base unit value, 432
Bed count, 211
Bed size, 211
Bedsores, 489
Behavior, 25
Behavior code, in pathology laboratories, use of, 25
Behavioral disorders, 140–141
Behavioral health care hospitals, 211
Bell's palsy, 679
Benign, 125, 126
Benign lesions, 490
Benign prostate disease, 643
Bethesda System, 754
Bier block, 421
Biliary tract, 617–618

Biofeedback, 773
Biometric A-scan, 714
Biomicroscopy, 714
Biopsy, 473
    breast, 492–494
Biopsy procedures, 234–235
Bipolar cautery, 614
Bladder, 626–630
Bleparoplasty, 488
Blindness, 145
Blocking, 721
Blom-Singer prosthesis, 537
Blood, 582
Blood and blood-forming organs diseases, 135–137
Blood vessel repair, 572
Blue reference symbol, 336
BlueCross and BlueShield (BCBS), 817
Body parts bilateral, 241
    branches of, 240
    coronary arteries, 241
    fingers and toes, 242
    general guidelines, 240
    skin, subcutaneous tissue, and fascia overlying
        joint, 241
    tendons, ligaments, bursae, and fascia near
        joint, 241
    upper and lower intestinal tract, 242
Body system, general coding guidelines, 231
Boldfaced type, 331
Bone density studies, 718
Bone marrow, 136, 584
Bone marrow aspiration, 584
Bone marrow biopsy, 584
Bone/joint studies, 718
Borderline diagnosis, 70
Boxed notes, 90–91
Brachytherapy, 247–248, 723, 725–726
Brain, 659–662
Breach of confidentiality, 860
Breast
    biopsies, 492–494
    diagnostic testing, 492–496
    mammography, 717–718
    mastectomy, 494–495
    repair and reconstruction, 495–496
Brightness mode, 713
Bronchi, 536–538
Bronchial thermoplasty, 538
Bronchoscopy, 537–538
Brushing, 537
B-scan, 713
Bullet symbol, 334
Bundled medicine codes, 767
Bunion, 524
Burns, 179, 184–185, 489–490
Burr hole, 660
Bursae, 241
Bypass graft, 573
Bypass procedures, 235

C

Cadaver donor cardiectomy, 566
Cadaver donor pneumonectomy, 541
Cafeteria plan, 821
Cancer, 24, 126
Capitation, 819
Capnography, 425
Carcinoma, 24
Carcinoma (Ca) in situ, 126

Cardiac ablation, 558
Cardiac anomalies, 563
Cardiac assist, 567
Cardiac blood pool imaging, 728
Cardiac catheterization, 782–784
Cardiac device evaluations, 781
Cardiac tumor, 554–555
Cardiac valves, 559–561
Cardiography, 781
Cardiopulmonary bypass, 550
Cardiopulmonary resuscitation (CPR), 781
Cardiovascular monitoring services, 781
Cardiovascular monitoring system, 558
Cardiovascular services, 779–785
Cardiovascular system, 728–729
Cardiovascular System (CPT), 549–582
    arteries and veins, 569–582
    heart and pericardium, 554–568
    notes, 550–554
    overview of, 549
    selective vascular catheterization, 550–554
Care management services, 406–407
Care plan oversight services, 403
Career as coder, 4–7
Carotid body, 657
Carpal tunnel, 669
Carpal tunnel release, 669–670
Carpal tunnel syndrome, 669–670
Carriers, 812
Case management services, 403
Case-mix adjustment, 838
Case-mix analysis, 837–838
Cataract removal, 674
Category, 59–60
Category I codes (CPT), 327, 328
Category II codes (CPT), 327, 329
Category III codes (CPT), 327, 329–330
Catheter implantation, 664
Caudal anesthesia, 421
Cell washing, 537
Centers for Disease Control and Prevention (CDC),
    27, 46
Centers for Medicare & Medicare Services (CMS), 9,
    352–353, 810
Central motor potential study, 790
Central nervous system assessments/tests, 791
Central venous access devices (CVADs), 428–429
Central venous access procedures, 576–578
Central venous pressure catheter, 428
Central venous pressure (CVP), 428
Cerebral infarction, 149
Cerebrospinal fluid (CSF) shunt, 662, 663
Cerebrovascular accident, 149
Cerebrovascular disease, 149
Certificate of medical necessity (CMN), 314–315
Certified Ambulatory Surgical Center Coder
    (CASCC), 5
Certified Medical Assistant (CMA), 6
Certified Medical Billing Specialist (CMBS), 6
Certified Medical Reimbursement Specialist (CMRS)
    exam, 6
Certified Professional Biller (CPB), 6
Certified registered nurse anesthetist (CRNA), 419
Cesarean delivery, 655
Charge description master (CDM), 840
Chargemaster review process, 840–841
Chargemasters, 12, 840–842
Cheiloplasty, 598
Chemical peel, 488
Chemistry, 749

Chemodenervation, 669, 789

Chemosurgery, 461

Chemotherapy, 794–795

Chemstrip automated urine analyzer, 747

Chief complaint, 370

Child abuse, neglect, and maltreatment, 187

Childbirth, 164–171

Chiropractic (ICS-10-PCS), 247

Chiropractic manipulative treatment (CMT), 797–798

Chlamydia, 117

Cholecystectomy, 618, 619

Choroid, 672

Chromosomal abnormalities, 174–175

Chromosomal breakage syndrome, 754–755

Chronic care management services, 406

Chronic conditions, 66

Chronic diseases, 275

Chronic kidney disease, 147–148, 163–164

Chronic obstructive pulmonary disease (COPD), 151–152

Chronic pain, 143

Chronic pain syndrome, 144

Chyle, 583

Ciliary body, 672

Ciliary muscle, 672

Circulatory system diseases, 147–151

Civil Monetary Penalties Act, 849

Civilian Health and Medical Program of the Department of Veterans Affairs (CHAMPVA), 818

Claims examiner, 6

Classification system, 8, 21–22

Clearinghouses, 10

Cleft palate, 601

Clinical and laboratory findings, abnormal, 175–178

Clinical brachytherapy, 725–726

Clinical Care Classification (CCC) System, 22

Clinical criteria, 104–105

Clinical documentation improvement (CDI) program, 18

Clinical examples, 367

Clinical intracavitary hyperthermia, 725

Clinical laboratory fee schedule, 835

Clinical Laboratory Improvement Act of 1988 (CLIA), 741

Clinical pathology, 746–747

Clinical terminologies, 8

Clinical treatment planning, 720–722

Cloning, documentation, 33

Closed fracture treatment, 504

Closed fractures, 178–179, 503, 504, 505, 506

Closed laparoscopy, 606

Closed-panel HMO, 820

CMS-1450 claim, 34

CMS-1500 claim, 34, 39, 812, 813, 840

Coagulation, 749–750

Coagulation defect, 136

Coarctation of the aorta, 564, 565

Cochlear implant, 679

Code, 8

    locating in ICD-10-CM, 62–63

"Code, if applicable, any causal condition first" rule, 98

"Code, if applicable" notes, 66

Code 99211, 384

Code assignment, 104–105

"Code first" notes, 66

Code first underlying disease, 98

Code for histologic grading and differentiation, 26

Code of ethics, 12

Code sets, 9–10

Coder

    career as, 4–7

    knowledge needed by, 4

    training, 4–5

Coding, 8

    avoiding assumption, 13–14

    computer-assisted, 19–21

    concurrent, 12, 13

    documentation as basis for, 30–33

    evidence-based, 20

    level of detail in, 64, 273–274

    professions related to, 6–7

    quality, 12–13

    retrospective, 12

    steps to accurate, 12

Coding compliance program, 18–19

Coding conventions

    defined, 85

    ICD-10-CM and ICD-10-PCS, 84–112

    ICD-10-PCS, 230–231

Coding credentials, 5–6

Coding guidelines

    diagnosis, 62–71

    ICD-10-CM, 113–208

Coding internship, 5

Coding manuals, 47

    ICD-10-PCS, 74

Coding process, 11–19

Coding references, 10–11

Coding systems, 8–11

Cognitive assessment and care plan services, 406

Cold biopsy forceps, 614

Colectomy, 610

Colon, 613–615

Colonoscopy, 613–614

Colostomy, 610, 610–611

Colpocleisis, 512

Coma scale, 177

Combination codes, 66

Commercial payers, 817

Commissurotomy, 560

Communicable disease, 195

Comorbidities, 829

Comorbidities and/or complications (CCs), 219

Compensators, 722

Complete procedure, 700–701

Complex chronic care managment services, 406

Complex fistulectomy, 616

Complex repair/closure, 481–482

Complexity of medical decision making, 374–376

Compliance guidelines, 849–850

Complicated fractures, 178–179

Complications, 829

Complications of care, 69, 187–188

Complications of surgery and medical care, 217

Composite grafts, 573

Comprehensive Error Rate testing (CERT) program, 819

Comprehensive examination, 371

Comprehensive history, 370

Computed axial tomography (CAT), 696

Computed tomography angiography (CTA), 696, 708–709

Computed tomography (CT), 706, 708–709

Computer-assisted coding (CAC), 19–21, 48–49, 50

Computer-based patient record (CPR), 31

Conchae, 530

Concurrent care, 366–367

Concurrent coding, 12, 13

Concurrent medically directed anesthesia procedures, 435

Conditions

    acute, 66

    chronic, 66

    ill-defined, 214–215

    impending or threatened, 67

    integral to disease process, 65

    multiple coding for single, 65–66

    not integral to disease process, 65

    previous, stated as diagnosis, 220

    two or more comparative or contrasting, 216–217

    two or more interrelated, 215

    two or more that equally meet definition for principal diagnosis, 215–216

Conditions for Coverage (CfC), 11

Conditions of Participation (CoP), 11

Confidentiality, 860–861

Congenital heart defects, 563–565

Congenital malformations, deformation, and chromosomal abnormalities, 174–175

Conization, 648

Conjunctiva, 675–676

Conjunctivoplasty, 676

Conmponent coding, 702–703

Connective tissue diseases, 161–163

Consolidated Omnibus Budget Reconciliation Act of 1985, 835

Consultations, 390–393, 746–747

Consumer-directed health plan (CDHP), 821

Contact lens services, 778

Continent ileostomy, 611

Continuity of care, 30

Contraception, 203

Contrast agents, 703–704

Contrast medium injection device, 703

Contributory components, 369, 377–380

Cooperating Parties for the ICD-10-CM/PCS, 60

Coordination of care, 378–379

Cor triatriatum, 564

Cornea, 672

Corneal pachymetry, 714

Corneal transplant, 673

Coronal plane, 695

Coronary arteries, 241

Coronary artery bypass graft (CABG), 562–563

Coronary bypass procedures, 235–236

Coronary endarterectomy, 563

Corpectomy, 665

Correct Coding Initiative (CCI), 352–353

Corrosions, 184–185

Costovertebral approach, 665

Counseling, 202, 378

Counseling risk factor reduction and behavior change intervention, 404

Covered benefits, 812

Covered entities, 860

CPT. see Current Procedural Terminology (CPT) coding system

CPT Assistant, 11, 338

Credentials, 5–6

Critical access hospitals (CAHs), 211

Critical care, 395–397

Critical illness or injury, 395

Critical pathways, 840

Cross-over vein graft, 569

Cross-references, 103–104, 332

Cryosurgery, 461

Current Dental Terminology (CDT), 22

Current Procedural Terminology (CPT) coding system, 9. *see also* Anesthesia; Evaluation and Management; Medicine; Pathology and Laboratory; Surgery
  appendices, 333–334
  code categories, 327, 328–330
  descriptive qualifiers, 340
  guidelines, 339–340
  history of, 325–326
  index, 330–332
  introduction to, 324–359
  modifiers, 341–350, 431–432
  NCCI and, 351–354
  number format, 330
  organization of, 328–330
  overview of, 326–328
  sections, subsections, categories, and subcategories, 337–341
  symbols, 334–337
  unbundling codes, 353–354
Customized sub-capitation plan (CSCP), 821
Cutdown, 578
Cystography, 696
Cystometrogram, 628
Cystoscopy, 628
Cystourethroscopy, 628, 628–629
Cytogenetic studies, 754–755
Cytopathology, 753–754
Cytoreduction surgery, 720

D

Data
  hospital, 34
  physician office, 34
Data Elements for Emergency Department Systems (DEEDS), 266
Database, 32
Death NOS, 177
Debulking, 720
Decortication, 539–540
Decubitus ulcers, 489
Default code, 54
Default codes, 85
Deficit Reduction Act, 828
Deficit Reduction Act of 1984, 835
Definitive identification, 752
Delivery after previous cesarean delivery, 655
Delivery services, 653–655
Delivery/birth room attendance and resuscitation services, 405
Demographic data, 30
Denotoalveolar structures, 600
Dental caries, 158
Department of Health & Human Services (DHHS), 9
Dermabrasion, 487
Dermatological procedures, 796
Descriptive qualifiers, 340
Designated Standard Maintenance Organization (DSMO), 855
Destruction, 490–491
Detailed examination, 371
Detailed history, 370
Determination of refractive state, 778
Device, 243–244
Diabetes mellitus, 138–139
  gestational, 168
Diagnosis
  admitting, 213
  borderline, 70
  first-listed, 115, 272–273
  other/additional, 219, 221
  previous conditions stated at, 220
  principal, 115, 215–216
  principle, 213–214
  qualified, 217–218
  secondary, 115
  uncertain, 217–218, 221, 274–275
Diagnosis code, reporting same, more than once, 68
Diagnosis-related groups (DRGs), 825–826, 828, 829
Diagnostic and Statistical Manual of Mental Disorders (DSM), 23, 834
Diagnostic Coding and Reporting Guidelines for Outpatient Services, 272–278
Diagnostic endoscopy, 604
Diagnostic mammography, 717
Diagnostic procedures, 462
  follow-up care for, 467
Diagnostic Radiology (Diagnostic Imaging) (CPT), 705–713
Diagnostic services, 276
Diagnostic ultrasound, 713–716
Diagnostic/management plans, 32
Dialysis, 773–776
Dialysis circuit, 579
Diaphragm, 594–595
Digestive System (CPT), 596–621
  abdomen, peritoneum, and omentum, 619–620
  anus, 615–616
  appendix, 613
  biliary tract, 617–618
  colon and rectum, 613–615
  dentoalveolar structures, 600
  esophagus, 603–607
  intestines, 609–612
  lips, 598–599
  liver, 617
  Meckel's diverticulum and mesentery, 612
  oral cavity, 598–603
  overview of, 596–598
  palate and uvula, 600–601
  pancreas, 618–619
  pharynx, adenoids, and tonsils, 602–603
  salivary gland and ducts, 601–602
  stomach, 607–608
  tongue and floor of mouth, 600
  vestibule of mouth, 600
Digestive system diseases, 157–158
Digital signature, 861
Dilation and curettage, 649
Dipstick, 747
Direct contract model HMO, 820
Direct laryngoscopy, 535
Discectomy, 665
Discharge notes, 32
Discharge services, 389–390
Disclosure, 860
Dislocation, 504, 505, 512
Diverticula, 612
Diverticulosis, 612
DME MAC medical review policies, 314–315
DMEPOS claims, 314–315
Document imaging, 33
Documentation
  as basis for coding, 30–33
  by clinicians other than patient's provider, 68–69
  cloning, 33
  of complications of care, 69
  defined, 30
  patient record, 313–315
Documentation cloning, 33
Documentation Guidelines for Evaluation and Management Services, 364–365
Domiciliary, rest home, or custodial care services, 399
Donors, 202
Doppler ultrasound, 715
Dosimetry, 723
Double pedicle flap, 484
Downcoding, 11
Drainage device, 244
DRG creep, 848
Drug assay, 745–746
Dual energy x-ray absorptiometry (DEXA), 718
Due to, 100–101
Duodenal ulcer, 608
Duplex scan, 785
Durable medical equipment carriers (DMERCs), 812
Durable medical equipment (DME), 295
Durable medical equipment, prosthetics, orthotics, and supplies (DMEPOS), 296
Durable medical equipment, prosthetics, orthotics, and supplies (DMEPOS) dealers, 296
Durable medical equipment, prosthetics, orthotics, and supplies (DMEPOS) fee schedule, 835

E

Ear, 678–680
Ear and mastoid process diseases, 146
Echocardiography, 782, 783
Education and training for patient self-management, 798
Elbow, 521
Electrocardiography, 781
Electrocautery snare, 614
Electroconvulsive therapy, 773
Electrocorticography (ECoG), 789
Electroencephalography (EEG), 789, 790
Electromyography (EMG), 789
Electronic data interchange (EDI), 856–860
Electronic health care transactions, 856–860
Electronic health records (EHRs), 31, 32
  automated physician query process and, 14
  concurrent coding and, 13
Electronic medical records (EMRs), 33
Electronic transaction standards, 856
Electrophysiology, 558
Electrosurgery, 461
E/M CodeBuilder, 867–871
Embolectomy, 569
Embolization procedures, 238
E-Medsys, 36, 38
Emergency condition, 437
Emergency department CPT E/M codes, 369
Emergency department services, 393–394
Emergency patients, 267
Employer identifier number (EIN), 855
Employer self-insurance plans, 817–818
Employment opportunities, 6
Empyema, 540
Empyemectomy, 540
Encoders, 47
Encoding, 9
Encounter, 51
Encounter forms, 12, 840, 842–843
Encryption, 861
Endocardium, 554
Endocrine diseases, 137–139
Endocrine system, 640, 656–658, 727
Endocrinology, 787
Endomyocardial biopsy, 784

Endorectal pull-through, 615
Endoscopic decompression of neural elements, 664–668
Endoscopic retrograde cholangiopancreatography (ERCP), 604, 606
Endoscopy, 526–527, 532–533, 537–538
Endotracheal tune (ET), 428
Endovascular repair of descending thoracic aorta, 566
Endovascular revascularization, 580
End-stage renal disease (ESRD) composite payment rate system, 837
End-stage renal disease (ESRD) services, 775
Enterectomy, 610
Enteroenterostomy, 610
Enterolysis, 609
Enterostomy, 610–611
Enucleation of the eye, 672
Epidural anesthesia, 421
Epidurography, 710
Epiglottidectomy, 535
Eponyms, 87
Equivalent dose, 697
Esophageal varices, 605
Esophagogastroduodenoscopy (EGD), 604
Esophagogastroscopy, 604
Esophagoscopy, 604
Esophagus, 603–607
Essential modifiers, 55
Established patient, 365
Ethics, code of, 12
Etiology, 58
Etiology and manifestation rules, 97–99
Evaluation and Management (CPT), 360–417
    advance care planning, 407
    care management services, 406–407
    care plan oversight services, 403
    case management services, 403
    categories and subcategories, 382–409
    classification of E/M services, 364–365
    code assignment, 376–377
    cognitive assessment and care plan services, 406
    consultations, 390–393
    contributory components, 369, 377–380
    critical care services, 395–397
    delivery/birth room attendance and resuscitation services, 405
    domiciliary, rest home, or custodial care or home care plan oversight services, 399
    emergency department services, 393–394
    general behavioral health integration care management, 408
    guidelines, 364–368
    home services, 399–400
    hospital inpatient services, 387–390
    hospital observation services, 384–386
    inpatient neonatal and pediatric critical care and intensive services, 405–406
    introduction to, 361
    key components, 369–377
    levels of service, 368–381
    newborn care services, 405
    non-face-to-face services, 404
    nursing facility services, 397–398
    office and other outpatient services, 382–384
    overview of, 361–364
    place of service, 362
    preventive medicine services, 403–404
    prolonged services, 400–402
    psychiatric collaborative care management services, 407

    radiology, 701
    special evaluation and management services, 405
    transitional care management services, 407
    type of service, 362–363
Evidence-based coding, 20
Evidence-verification coding, 20
Evisceration of ocular contents, 672
Evocative/suppression testing, 746
Evoked potentials, 790
Excision, 236, 508
Excision for graft, 236
Excisional biopsy, 493
Excludes1 notes, 94–95
Excludes2 notes, 95
Exclusions, 823–825
Exclusive provider organization (EPO), 819–820
Exenteration of the orbit, 673
Expanded problem focused examination, 371
Expanded problem focused history, 370
Explanation of benefits (EOB), 857
Extensor tendons, 521
Extent of examination, 371, 373–374
Extent of history, 370–372, 372
External catheter, 429
External cause of morbidity codes, 70–71
External causes
    injury, poisoning, and consequences of, 178–188
    of morbidity, 189–193
External ear, 678
External fixation device, 504, 506, 508
External radiation, 720
Extracapsular cataract extraction (ECCE), 674
Extracorporeal life support services (ECLS), 567
Extracorporeal membrane oxygenation (ECMO), 567
Extracorporeal or Systemic Assistance and Performance (ICS-10-PCS), 246
Extracorporeal or Systemic Therapies (ICS-10-PCS), 246
Extracorporeal shock wave lithotripsy (ESWL), 624
Extracranial nerves, 668–670
Extradural exploration/decompression, 665–666
Eye and adnexa diseases, 144–146
Eye and ocular adnexa, 671–677
Eye socket, 675
Eyeball, 672–673

F

Face-to-face time, 379–380
Factitious disorder, 141
Fallopian tubes, 650–651
False Claims Act (FCA), 850
Family history, 371
Family planning, 203
Family psychotherapy, 772
Fascia, 241
Federal Anti-kickback Statute, 850
Federal Claims Collection Act of 1966, 852
Federal Employee Health Benefits Program (FEHBP or FEP), 818
Federally Qualified Health Centers (FQHCs), 837
Federally Qualified Health Centers (FQHCs) prospective payment system, 837
Fee schedules, 823–825
Fee-for-service plans, 819
Female genital system, 646–651
Femoral angiogram, 580
Femur, 522–523
Fetal growth retardation, 173
Fibrinolytic agents, 541

Fibula, 524
Field block, 420
Fine-needle aspiration (FNA), 492
Fingers, 521
First-listed diagnosis, 115, 272–273
First-order vessels, 552–553
Fiscal intermediaries, 812
Fistulectomy, 616
Fistulotomy, 616
Flank, 514
Flap, 473, 487
Flash symbol, 336
Flat file, 858
Flexible spending account (FSA), 822
Flexor tendons, 521
Fluid management, 425
Fluorescence in situ hybridization (FISH), 755
Fluoroscopy, 697, 707–708
Follow-up care
    for diagnostic procedures, 467
    for therapeutic surgical procedures, 468
Follow-up codes, 201–202
Food and Drug Administration (FDA), 27
Foot, 524
Forbidden symbol, 335
Forearm, 521
Format, 85–87
Fraction, 724
Fractures, 162, 178–179, 183–184, 239, 503–506, 512, 518
Fraud and abuse, 846–854
Free flap, 484
Free skin grafts, 485
Frontal plane, 695
Full-thickness skin grafts, 485–486
Functional brain mapping, 791
Functional modifiers, 341
Functional quadriplegia, 177
Fungi, 117
Fusion procedures of spine, 237

G

Gamma globulin, 769
Ganglion cyst, 508
Gastrectomy, 607
Gastric ulcer, 608
Gastroenterology, 776–777
Gastroesophageal reflux disease (GERD), 606
Gastrointestinal system, 728
Gastrostomy, 598
General anesthesia, 420
General behavioral health integration care management, 408
General equivalence mappings (GEMs), 77–78
General hospitals, 211
General medical examinations, 277
General multisystem examination, 870–871
Genetic counseling services, 791
Genitourinary system, 730
Genitourinary system diseases, 163–164
Genomic sequencing procedures (GSP), 747, 758
Gestational diabetes, 168
Glabellar frown lines, 488
Glaucoma, 145
Global service, 699
Global surgical package, 464–467
Globe, 672
Government-sponsored programs, 818–819
Grafts, 461, 473, 509

Gram stain, 752
Gray (gy), 697
Gray-scale ultrasound, 713
Great vessels, 559
Green reference symbol, 336
Group model HMO, 820
Group practice without walls (GPWW), 820
Guidelines, 339

H

Hand, 521
Harvesting, 509
HCPCS level I, 295
HCPCS level II, 9
HCPCS level II coding system, 294–322
    Administrative, Miscellaneous, and Investigational, 308
    assigning codes, 305–312
    Behavioral Health and/or Substance Abuse Treatment Services, 309
    Chemotherapy Drugs, 309
    code sections, 307–312
    determining payer responsibility, 312–315
    Diagnostic Radiology Services, 311
    Drugs Other Than Chemotherapy Drugs, 309
    Durable Medical Equipment, 309
    Enteral and Parenteral Therapy, 308
    Hearing Services, 312
    Hospital Outpatient Payment System, 308–309
    index, 306–307
    Laboratory Services, 311
    Medical Services, 310
    Medical Surgical Supplies, 308
    miscellaneous codes, 298
    modifiers, 298–304, 430–431
    national codes, 9
    Orthotics, 310
    Outpatient PPS, 308
    overview of, 295–296
    permanent national codes, 298
    Prosthetics, 310
    Q Codes, 311
    responsibility for, 297
    temporary codes, 298, 299
    Temporary Codes Assigned by CMS, 311
    Temporary Codes Assigned to DME Regional Carriers (MACs), 310
    Temporary Codes Established by Medicaid, 311
    Temporary National Codes, 311
    Temporary Procedures/Professional Services, 309
    Transportation Services including Ambulance, 308
    types of codes, 297–298
    Vision Services, 312
HCPCS level III coding system, 296
Head prosthesis, 511
Health and behavior assessment/intervention, 792
Health care access, 846
Health Care and Education Reconciliation Act (HCERA), 810, 811
Health care clearinghouses, 10
Health care fraud and abuse, 846–854
Health care portability, 846
Health care providers, 10
Health care reimbursement account (HCRA), 822
Health care reimbursement systems, 823–845
Health care renewability, 846
Health data collection, 33–39
Health insurance claim, 812–814
Health Insurance Marketplace, 815–816

Health insurance policy, 812
Health Insurance Portability and Accountability Act of 1996 (HIPAA), 9–10, 51, 325, 810
    access, portability, and renewability, 846
    administrative simplification, 855–860
    CPT coding and, 338
    impact on reimbursement, 846–862
    medical liability reform, 861–862
    Official Guidelines for Coding and Reporting and, 61
    preventing health care fraud and abuse, 846–854
    privacy and security rules, 860–861
Health Insurance Prospective Payment System (HIPPS) rate codes, 23–24
Health insurance specialist, 6–7
Health maintenance organization (HMO), 820
Health plans, 10
Health reform, 810–811
Health reimbursement arrangement (HRA), 822
Health savings account (HSA), 822
Health savings security account (HSSA), 822
Health screenings, 277–278
Health status and contact with health services, 194–206
Healthcare Common Procedure Coding System (HCPCS), 9, 325
Heart and Pericardium (CPT), 554–568
    cardiac anomalies, 563
    cardiac assist, 567
    cardiac tumor, 554–555
    cardiac valves, 559–561
    congenital heart defects, 563–565
    coronary artery anomalies, 561
    coronary artery bypass graft, 562–563
    coronary endarterectomy, 563
    electrophysiologic operative procedures, 558
    endovascular repair of descending thoracic aorta, 566
    extracorporeal membrane oxygenation or life support services, 567
    heart and great vessels, 559
    heart/lung transplantation, 566
    implantable hemodynamic monitors, 559
    other valvular procedures, 561
    pacemaker or implantable defibrillator, 555–557
    patient-activated event recorder, 558
    pericardium, 554
    pulmonary artery, 566
    subcutaneous cardiac rhythm monitor, 558–559
    thoracic aortic aneurysm, 566
    transmyocardial revascularization, 555
Heart disease, hypertension with, 147, 148
Heart murmur, 563
Heart/lung transplantation, 566
Helminths, 117
Hematology, 749–750
Hematoma, 530
Hematopoietic cell transplantation (HCT), 585
Hematopoietic progenitor cells (HPCs), 585
Hematopoietic system, 728
Hemic and Lymphatic Systems (CPT), 582–586
    general, 584–585
    lymph nodes and lymphatic channels, 585
    overview of, 582–583
    spleen, 583–584
    transplantation and post-transplantation cellular infusions, 585
Hemodialysis, 774–775
Hemodialysis access, 579
Hemorrhoidectomy, 616
Hepatotomy, 617

Hernia, 620
Herniated intervertebral discs, excision of, 664–668
Hip joint, 522
Histologic grading and differentiation, code for, 26
History of present illness (HPI), 370, 868
History Z codes, 198–199
Hold harmless clause, 812
Home Assessment and Validation Entry (HAVEN), 266, 830
Home health agencies, 400
Home Health Care Classification (HHCC) System, 22
Home health procedures/services, 800
Home health prospective payment system (HH PPS), 830–831
Home services, 399–400
Horizontal plane, 695
Horizontal triangle symbols, 334
Hospice payment system, 831–832
Hospital data, reporting, 34, 35
Hospital discharge services, 389–390
Hospital inpatient coding, 209–264
    acute care facilities/hospitals, 210–212
    administration, 245
    chiropractic, 247
    diagnoses, 213–221, 251–253
    diagnostic audiology, 248
    extracorporeal therapies, 246
    ICD-10-PCS coding conventions, 230–231
    ICD-10-PCS procedures, 224–251
    imaging, 247
    measurement and monitoring, 246
    medical and surgical, 231–244
    mental health, 249
    nuclear medicine, 247
    obstetrics, 244–245
    osteopathic, 246
    physical rehabilitation, 248
    placement, 245
    procedures, 222–224, 251–253
    radiation therapy, 247
    Section X, 250
    substance abuse treatment, 249
    systemic therapies, 246
Hospital Inpatient Quality Reporting program, 829
Hospital inpatient services, 387–390
Hospital Observation Services (CPT), 384–386
Hospital outpatient services, 267
Hospital readmission reduction program (HRRP), 829
Hospital readmissions, 829
Hospital-acquired conditions, 828, 829
Hospital-Acquired Conditions and Present on Admission Reporting Guidelines, 828
Hospitalist services, 387
Hospitalists, 30
Hospitals, 30, 210–212
Hot biopsy forceps, 614
Human immunodeficiency virus (HIV), 117–120
Humerus, 521
Hybrid records, 31
Hydration, 792–793
Hypertension, 147–149, 158
Hypertensive cerebrovascular disease, 148
Hypertensive chronic kidney disease, 147–148
Hypertensive crisis, 148
Hyperthermia, 725
Hyperventilation, 789
Hypopharynx, 602
Hypoplastic aortic arch, 565
Hypovolemia, 428

Hysterectomy, 649–650
Hysteroscopy, 650

I

ICD-10 Coordination and Maintenance Committee, 48–49
ICD-10-CM coding guidelines
  blood and blood-forming organ diseases, 135–137
  chapter-specific diagnosis, 115–206
  circulatory system diseases, 147–151
  congenital malformations, deformations, and chromosomal abnormalities, 174–175
  digestive system diseases, 157–158
  ear and mastoid process diseases, 146
  endocrine, nutritional, and metabolic diseases, 137–139
  external causes of morbidity, 189–193
  eye and adnexa diseases, 144–146
  general, 62–71
  genitourinary system diseases, 163–164
  health status and contact with health services, 194–206
  infectious and parasitic diseases, 116–124
  injury, poisoning, and consequences of external causes, 178–188
  mental, behavioral, and neurodevelopmental disorders, 140–141
  musculoskeletal and connective tissue diseases, 161–163
  neoplasms, 125–135
  nervous system diseases, 142–144
  Official Guidelines for Coding and Reporting, 60–62
  perinatal period conditions, 171–174
  pregnancy, childbirth, and puerperium, 164–171
  respiratory system diseases, 151–153
  skin and subcutaneous tissue diseases, 158–160
  symptoms, signs, and abnormal clinical and laboratory findings, not otherwise classified, 175–178
ICD-10-CM Official Guidelines for Coding and Reporting, 11
ICD-10-PCS codes, 36
ICD-10-PCS Index, 224–226
  coding conventions, 225–226
  main terms, 224–225
  purpose of, 224
  root operation and procedure type main terms, 225
ICD-10-PCS Official Guidelines for Coding and Reporting, 11
ICD-10-PCS tables, 226–229
ICD-O morphology codes, 24–25
Ileonal anastomosis, 615
Ileostomy, 610–611
Ill-defined conditions, 214–215
Imaging (ICS-10-PCS), 247
Imaging guidance, 470, 702, 768
Immune globulins, 769
Immune mechanism disorders, 135–137
Immune serum globulin, 769
Immunization administration, 770
Immunoglobulins, 751
Immunology, 751
Impending or threatened condition, 67
Implantable defibrillator, 555–557
Implantable hemodynamic monitors, 559
Implanted port, 429
Implants, 509
"In," 101
In diseases classified elsewhere, 98
In vitro fertilization (IVF), 651

In vivo (transcutaneous) laboratory procedures, 756
Incision and drainage (I&D), 473–474
Incisional biopsy, 493
Includes notes, 93–94
Inclusion terms, 95–96
Incomplete abortion, 656
Inconclusive diagnoses, 274–275
Indemnification, 811
Index to Diseases and Injuries, 45, 53–57
  basic steps for using, 56–57
  locating code in, 62–63
Index to External Causes of Injuries, 54
Indexed, 33
Indian Health Service (IHS), 818
Indirect laryngoscopy, 535
Individual practice association (IPA) HMO, 820
Induced abortion, 656
Infants, 203, 405
Infectious and parasitic diseases, 116–124
Inferred words, 332
Infiltration anesthesia, 420
Influenza, 152
Informational modifiers, 341
Ingestion challenge testing, 786
Inguinal hernia, 620
Initial hospital care, 388
Initial observation care, 386
Initial plan, 32
Injury, poisoning, and consequences of external causes, 178–188
Inner ear, 679
Inoculations and vaccinations, 195–196
Inoperable primary site with metastasis, 129
Inpatient cap, 831
Inpatient consultations, 392–393
Inpatient diagnosis coding guidelines, 213–221
Inpatient neonatal and pediatric critical care, 406
Inpatient neonatal intensive care services, 405–406
Inpatient procedure coding guidelines, 222–224
Inpatient prospective payment systems, 825–828, 830
Inpatient psychiatric facility prospective payment system (IPF PPS), 834
Inpatient rehabilitation facility prospective payment system (IRF PPS), 834
Inpatients, 211
Insertable loop recorder, 558
Inspection procedures, 237–238
Insurance and reimbursement, 808–866
  health care reimbursement systems, 823–845
  HIPPA and, 846–862
  introduction to, 812–813
  third-party payers, 811–823
Integrated delivery system (IDS), 819–820
Integrated provider organization (IPO), 820
Integrated records, 31, 32
Integumentary System (CPT), 472–496
  breast, 492–496
  burns, 489–490
  destruction, 490–491
  introduction, 480
  nails, 478–479
  other procedures, 486–488
  pilonidal cyst, 479
  pressure ulcer, 489
  repair (closure), 481–490
  skin, subcutaneous and accessory structures, 473–478
Intensity modulated radiation therapy (IMRT), 723
Intensity of services (IS), 838

Intensivist, 397
Interactive complexity, 771
Intermediate repair/closure, 481–482
Internal catheter, 429
Internal fixation device, 504, 506
Internal radiation, 720
International Classification of Diseases for Oncology, Third Edition (ICD-O-s), 24–25, 130
International Classification of Diseases (ICD), 62
  history of, 50–51
International Classification of Diseases, Ninth Revision, Clinical Modification (ICD-9-CM), 9
  as legacy coding system, 77–78
International Classification of Diseases, Tenth Revision, Clinical Modification (ICD-10-CM), 9
  coding conventions, 84–112
  coding guidelines, 113–208
  format and structure of, 48
  general diagnosis coding guidelines, 62–71
  Index to Diseases and Injuries, 53–57
  main terms, subterms, and qualifiers, 55–56
  mandatory reporting of codes, 51–52
  outpatient and physician office coding, 265–292
  overview of, 45–53
  Tabular List of Diseases and Injuries, 58–60
  updating, 48–50
International Classification of Diseases, Tenth Revision, Clinical Modification/Procedure Coding System (ICD-10-CM/PCS), 9
International Classification of Diseases, Tenth Revision, Procedure Coding System (ICD-10-PCS), 9
  build-a-code using, 75–76
  code structure of, 73–74, 229
  coding conventions, 84–112, 230–231
  coding manual format, 74
  development of, 72–73
  Index, 224–226
  index and tables, 72–77
  overview of, 45–53
  procedure coding, 224–251
  tables, 226–229
  updating, 48–50
  values, 229–230
International Classification of Functioning, Disability and Health (ICF), 27
International normalized radio (INR) monitoring services, 784–785
International Refined DRGs (APR-DRGs), 827
Internship, 5
Internship supervisor, 5
Intersex surgery, 645–646
Interventional radiological procedures, 708
Intestines, 609–612
Intoxication, 181
Intra-arterial cannula, 429
Intra-arterial catheter, 429
Intra-arterial lines, 429
Intracapsular cataract extraction (ICCE), 674
Intracardiac electrophysiological procedures/studies, 784
Intradermal test, 786, 787
Intraoperative neurophysiology, 790
Intraosseous, 578
Intraservice time, 379–380
Intraspinal lesion, 667
Intravascular cannulation for extracorporeal circulation, 579
Intravascular ultrasound services, 581
Intravenous push, 793
Intravenous regional anesthesia, 421

Introduction, 480
Introduction or removal, 508
IPPS 3-day payment window, 826–827
IPPS 72-hour rule, 826–827
IPPS transfer rule, 827
IRF PPS 1-day payment window, 834
IRF PPS 24-hour rule, 834
Iris, 672
Ischemic muscle testing, 789
Island flap, 484
Italicized type, 331

J

Jamming, 11
J-pouch, 615

K

Key components, 369–377
Kidney disease, 147–148, 163–164
Kidney transplant complications, 187–188
Kidney transplantation, 624, 624–625
Kidneys, 623–625
Knee, 522–524, 524
Kock pouch, 611
Kyphosis, 517

L

Labor, stages of, 654
Laboratory findings, abnormal, 175–178
Lacrimal apparatus, 675
Lacrimal puncta, 676
Laminectomy, 666–667
Laminotomy, 664
Laparoscopy, 606
Large intestine, 597
Laryngectomy, 535
Laryngoscopy, 535
Laryngotomy, 535
Larynx, 534–536
LASER (light amplification by stimulated emission of radiation), 461
Laser technique, 614–615
Late effects, 67
Lateral extracavitary approach (LECA), 666
Lateral projection, 696
Laterality, 68
Le Fort I, 512
Le Fort II, 512
LEEP electrodissection, 649
LeFort III, 512
Legacy classification system, 77–78
Legacy coding system, 77–78
Lens, 672
Lesion removal, 474–478
Level of detail, in coding, 64, 273–274
Level of examination, 870
Level of history, 869
Liability reform, 861–862
Ligaments, 241, 523, 524
Lips, 598–599
Listserv, 7, 8
Lithotripsy, 624
Liver, 617
Local anesthesia, 420
Local coverage determinations (LCDs), 314–315
Local infiltration, 467

Local Medicare carriers (LMCs), 296
Logical Observation Identifiers Names and Codes (LOINC), 27, 28
Long-term (acute) care hospital prospective payment system (LTCH PPS), 834
Long-term acute care hospitals (LTACH), 211
Long-term hospitals, 211
Loop conization, 649
Loop electrodissection conization, 649
Lordosis, 517
Low birth weight, 173, 406
Lower intestinal tract, 242
LTCH PPS 1-day payment window, 834
LTCH PPS 24-hour rule, 834
Lumpectomy, 493–494
Lung transplantation, 541
Lungs, 539–542
Luxation, 504
Lymph, 583
Lymph nodes, 582–583, 585
Lymphatic channels, 585
Lymphatic system, 582–583, 728

M

Magnetic resonance angiography (MRA), 710
Magnetic resonance imaging (MRI), 697, 710, 711
Main terms, 55–56
Major comorbidities and/or complications (MCCs), 219
Major diagnostic categories (MDCs), 825
Male genital system, 640, 841–844
Malignancies, 127–129
Malignant, 125
Malignant lesions, 490
Mammography, 717–718
Managed care, 819
Management service organization (MSO), 820
Manipulation of spine, 518
Manometry, 773
Manual record formats, 31–32
Manual records, 31
Mass spectrometry, 425
Mastectomy, 494–495
Mastoid process diseases, 146
Maternity Care and Delivery (CPT), 652–656
Maximizing reimbursement, 216
Maze procedure, 558
Measurement and Monitoring (ICS-10-PCS), 246
Meckel's diverticulum, 612
Mediastinum, 594–595
Mediastinum and Diaphragm (CPT), 594–595
Medicaid, 818
Medical and Surgical (ICD-10-PCS), 231–244
Medical assistant, 6, 7
Medical Association Biller (MAB), 6
Medical coding process, 11–19
Medical decision making (DMM), 374–376, 871
Medical examinations, 277
Medical foundation, 820
Medical genetics, 791
Medical liability reform, 861–862
Medical management software, 34, 35–39
Medical necessity, 31, 52
Medical necessity of Medicare Part A hospital inpatient admissions, 839–840
Medical nomenclature, 8
Medical nutrition therapy, 796–797
Medical radiation physics, 723
Medical record, 30

Medical specialties, 268–271
Medicare, 818
Medicare administrative contractors (MACs), 811–812, 825
Medicare administrator contractors (MACs), 296, 825
Medicare Benefit Policy Manual, 297
Medicare Catastrophic Coverage Act, 51
Medicare National Coverage Determinations Manual, 297
Medicare Part A hospital inpatient order and physician certification, 212
Medicare physician fee schedule (MPFS), 835, 837
Medicare Prescription Drug, Improvement, and Modernization Act (MMA), 50, 325, 811, 819, 836, 837
Medicare Pricing, Data Analysis, and Coding (PDAC) contractor, 296
Medicare severity diagnosis-related groups (MS-DRGs), 219, 826, 827
Medicare severity long-term (acute) care diagnosis-related groups (MS-LTC-DRGs), 834
Medicare Summary Notice (MSN), 857, 858
Medication administration record (MAR), 4
Medication therapy management services (MTMS), 800
Medicine (CPT), 765–806
    acupuncture, 797
    allergy and clinical immunology, 786–787
    biofeedback, 773
    cardiovascular, 779–785
    central nervous system assessments/tests, 791
    chemotherapy, 794–795
    chiropractic manipulative treatment, 797–798
    dialysis, 773–776
    education and training for patient self-management, 798
    endocrinology, 787
    gastroenterology, 776–777
    guidelines, 766–768
    health and behavior assessment/intervention, 792
    home health procedures/services, 800
    hydration, 792–793
    immune globulins, serum or recombinant products, 769
    immunization administration for vaccines/toxoids, 770
    ischemic muscle testing and guidance for chemodenervation, 789
    medical genetics and genetic counseling services, 791
    medical nutrition therapy, 796–797
    medication therapy management services, 800
    moderate (conscious) sedation, 799
    neurology and neuromuscular procedures, 788–789
    non-face-to-face nonphysician services, 798
    noninvasive vascular diagnostic studies, 785
    ophthalmology, 777–778
    osteopathic manipulative treatment, 797
    other services and procedures, 800
    overview of, 766
    photodynamic therapy, 795–796
    physical medicine and rehabilitation, 796
    psychiatry, 771–773
    pulmonary, 786
    qualifying circumstances for anesthesia, 799
    special dermatological procedures, 796
    special otorhinolaryngologic services, 778–779
    special services, procedures, and reports, 798–799
    subsections, 768–801
    therapeutic, prophylactic, and diagnostic injections and infusions, 793–794
    vaccines/toxoids, 770–772

Megaelectron volts, 724
Megavolts, 724
Meninges, 659–662
Mental disorders, 140–141
Mental Health (ICS-10-PCS), 249
Mental status exam, 791
Mesentery, 612
Metabolic diseases, 137–139
Metacarpal/metatarsal/digital block, 467
Metastasis, 129
Metastatic cancer, 126
Methicillin-resistant Staphylococcus aureus (MRSA), 123–124
MeV (megaelectron volts, megavolts), 724
Microbiology, 752
Microdermabrasion, 487
Microtechnique, 757
Middle ear, 679
Middle fossa approach, 679
Midsagittal plane, 695
Military Health System (MHS), 818
Minimum data set (MDS), 830
Missed abortion, 656
M-mode, 713
Moderate (conscious) sedation, 467, 799
Modified Maze procedure, 558
Modified radical mastectomy, 494–495
Modifiers
    anesthesia, 430–432
    CPT, 341–350, 431–432
    HCPCS level II, 298–304, 430–431
    physical status, 431
    radiology codes, 699–700
Modifying units, 434
Mohs micrographic surgery, 491
Mohs microsurgery, 473
Molecular multianalyte assays, 748–749
Molecular pathology, 748
Monitored anesthesia care (MAC), 423–434
Morbidity, 45
Morbidity, external causes of, 189–193
Morphology, of neoplasms, 130
Mortality, 45
Motion analysis, 790–792
Motion mode, 713
Mouth
    tongue and floor of, 600
    vestibule of, 600
Mucocutaneous margin, 596
Multianalyte assays with algorithmic analyses (MAAAs), 748, 758
Multiaxial, 45
Multihospital systems, 211
Multiple births, 655
Multiple codes, 66
    medicine, 767
    for single condition, 65–66
Multiple sleep latency, 788
Muscle testing, 789
Musculoskeletal system, 728
Musculoskeletal System (CPT), 502–528
    abdomen, 520
    application of casts and strapping, 525–526
    back and flank, 514
    endoscopy/arthroscopy, 526–527
    femur (thigh region) and knee joint, 522–524
    foot and toe, 524
    forearm and wrist, 521
    general, 507–511

hand and fingers, 521
head, 511–513
humerous (upper arm) and elbow, 521
leg (tibia and fibula) and ankle joint, 524
neck (soft tissue) and thorax, 513–514
notes, 503–507
pelvis and hip joint, 522
shoulder, 520–521
spine (vertebral column), 515–520
Musculoskeletal system diseases, 161–163
Mycocutaneous flap, 484
Mycoplasmas, 117
Myocardial perfusion, 729
Myocardium, 554

N

Nails, 478–479
Narcosynthesis, 773
Nasal vestibule, 530
Nasopharynx, 602
National Center for Health Statistics (NCHS), 48–49, 60
National Correct Coding Initiative (NCCI), 11, 351–354, 850, 851–852
National coverage determinations (NCDs), 314–315, 741
National Drug Codes (NDC), 27
National Drug File—Reference Terminology (NDF-RT), 28
National health plan identifier (HPID), 855
National Health Service's Clinical Terms Version 3, 28
National individual identifier, 855
National Library of Medicine (NLM), 28
National limitation amount (NLA), 835
National provider identifier (NPI), 855
National standard employer identifier number, 855
National Standard Format (NSF), 858, 859
Nature of the presenting problem, 379
NEC (not elsewhere classifiable), 88
Neck, 513–514
Necropsy, 753
Needle core biopsy, 493
Needle electromyography, 789
Neglect, 187
Neonates, 405
Neoplasms, 125–135
    morphology of, 130
    pain related to, 143–144
Nephrectomy, 624
Nerve block, 668
Nerve conduction tests, 789
Nerve plexus, 420
Nervous system
    diseases, 142–144
    extracranial and peripheral nerves, and autonomic nervous system, 668–670
    overview of, 658–659
    radiology codes, 729
    skull, meninges, and brain, 659–662
    spine and spinal cord, 662–668
Network model HMO, 820
Network provider, 819
Neuro-cognitive testing, 791
Neurodevelopmental disorders, 140–141
Neurology, 788–789
Neurolytic agents, 669
Neuromuscular procedures, 788–789
Neuroplasty, 669–670
Neurorrhaphy, 670

Neurostimulators, 662, 667, 669, 790
Neutron beam radiation therapy, 724
New patient, 365
New Technology (ICS-10-PCS), 250
New York All Patient DRGs (AP-DRGs), 827
Newborn care services, 405
Newborn patients, 211
Newborn sepsis, 123
Newborns and infants, 203
NIH stroke scale (NIHSS), 177
Nissen fundoplasty, 606
Noncovered benefits, 812
Nonessential modifiers, 55
Non-face-to-face nonphysician services, 798
Non-face-to-face services, 404
Noninvasive vascular diagnostic studies, 785
Nonparticipating providers (nonPARs), 819
Non-segmental instrumentation, 519
Nonselective vascular catheterization, 551, 711
Nontunneled catheter, 429
NOS (not otherwise specified), 88
Nose, 529–532
Notes, 339
Notice of Exclusion from Medicare Benefits (NEMB), 352
Nuclear imaging, 697
Nuclear medicine, 247, 727–730
Number symbol, 336
Nursing facility services, 397–398
Nutritional deficiencies, 137–139

O

Objective (O), 32
Oblique projection, 696
Observation care discharge services, 386
Observation codes, 200
Observation or inpatient care services, 389
Observation patients, 267
Observation services, 384–386
Obstetrical discharges, 164–171
Obstetrical ultrasound procedures, 715–716
Obstetrics (ICS-10-PCS), 244–245
Obturator, 511
Ocular adnexa, 675
Ocular implant, 673
Office or Other Outpatient Services (CPT), 382–384, 391–392
Official ICD-10-CM Guidelines for Coding and Reporting, 60–62, 114–115, 115. see also ICD-10-CM coding guidelines
Official ICD-10-PCS Guidelines for Coding and Reporting, 60, 114–115
Omentectomy, 651
Omentum, 619–620
Omnibus Budget Reconciliation Act of 1980, 835
Omnibus Budget Reconciliation Act of 1987, 835
Omnibus Budget Reconciliation Act of 1989, 835, 853
Omnibus Consolidated and Emergency Supplemental Appropriations Act (OCESAA), 830
Online discussion boards, 7, 8
Oocyte, 651
Oophorectomy, 651
Open biopsy, 493
Open fractures, 178–179, 503, 504, 505
Open laparoscopy, 606
Open-panel HMO, 820
Operating microscope, 641, 680–682
Ophthalmology, 777–778

Optimizing reimbursement, 216
Oral cavity, 598–602
Orbicularis oculi, 790
Orbit, 675
Orbital implant, 673
Organ or disease-oriented panels, 744–745
Oropharynx, 602
Orthotics, 310
Oscilloscope, 789
Osteogenesis, 509
Osteopathic (ICS-10-PCS), 246
Osteopathic manipulative treatment (OMT), 797
Osteoporosis, 162
Osteotomy, 516–517
Ostomy, 610–611
Other, 97
Other (additional) diagnoses, 219–220, 221
Other emergency services, 394
Other Procedures (ICS-10-PCS), 246
Other specified, 97
Otorhinolaryngologic services, 778–779
Outcome and Assessment Information Set (OASIS), 24, 266
Outcome-Based Quality Improvement (OBQI), 266
Outliers, 825
Outpatient and physician office coding, diagnoses, 265–292
Outpatient care, 266–271
Outpatient Code Editor with Ambulatory Payment Classification (OCE/APC), 11
Outpatient encounter, 833
Outpatient prospective payment system (OPPS), 369, 832–833
Outpatient surgery, 277
Outpatient visit, 833
Outpatients, 267
Ovaries, 650–651
Overcoding, 11
Overpayment recovery, 853–854
Overpayments, 852–853

P

Pacemaker, 555–557
Pain, 142–144
    due to medical devices, 187
Palate, 600–601
Palatopharyngoplasty, 601
Pancreas, 618–619, 657
Parasitic diseases, 116–124
Parathyroid, 657
Parenterally, 708
Paring and curettement, 473
Partial hospitalization, 387
Participating providers (PARs), 819
Past, family, and/or social history (PFSH), 869
Past medical history, 371
Patch test, 786
Patency, 573
Patent ductus arteriosus (PDA), 564, 565
Pathologic fractures, 162
Pathology and Laboratory (CPT), 737–764
    anatomic pathology, 753
    chemistry, 749
    consultations (clinical pathology), 746–747
    cytogenetic studies, 754–755
    cytopathology, 753–754
    drug assay and therapeutic drug assays, 745–746
    evocative/suppression testing, 746
    genomic sequencing procedures, 748

    guidelines, 742–744
    hematology and coagulation, 749–750
    immunology, 751
    microbiology, 752
    modifier-51 and-91, 743
    molecular multianalyte assays, 748–749
    molecular pathology, 748
    organ or disease-oriented panels, 744–745
    other procedures, 757
    overview of, 738–742
    professional and technical components, 739–741
    proprietary laboratory analysis, 758
    reproductive medicine procedures, 757–758
    section tables, 741
    services, 742
    special report, 743
    specimen collection, 739
    subsections, 744–759
    surgical pathology, 755–756
    transfusion medicine, 752
    urinalysis, 747–748
    in vivo (transcutaneous) laboratory procedures, 756
Patient education plans, 32
Patient identifier, 855
Patient Protection and Affordable Care Act (PPACA), 812–813, 815–816, 831
Patient record, 30
Patient record documentation, 313–315
Patient record formats, 31–33
Patient self-management, 798
Patient-activated event recorder, 558
Patient-driven payment model (PDPM), 830
Payer responsibility, determining, 312–315
Payment Error and Prevention Program (PEPP), 853
Pediatric and neonatal critical care services, 405–406
Pediatric critical care patient transport, 406
Pedicle skin grafts, 485
Pelvis, 522
Percutaneous augmentation, 519
Percutaneous lithotomy, 624
Percutaneous needle biopsy, 540
Percutaneous pleural biopsy, 540
Percutaneous skeletal fixation, 503, 504
Percutaneous vertebroplasty, 518
Pericardial sac, 554
Pericardiectomy, 554
Pericardiocentesis, 554
Pericardiotomy, 554
Pericardium, 554
Perinatal period, 171–174
Peripheral arterial disease (PAD), 784
Peripheral catheter, 578
Peripheral nerve block, 420
Peripheral nerves, 668–670
Peristalsis, 625
Peritoneal dialysis, 774
Peritoneoscopy, 606
Peritoneum, 619–620
Pharmacologic management, 772–773
Pharmacology, 4
Pharyngolaryngectomy, 535
Pharynx, 602–604
Phlebotomy, 739
Photic stimulation, 789
Photodynamic therapy, 795–796
Photons, 696
Physiatrists, 796
Physical examination, 371, 373–374

Physical medicine and rehabilitation, 796
Physical Rehabilitation and Diagnostic Audiology (ICS-10-PCS), 248
Physical status modifiers, 431
Physician certification, 212
Physician office coding, 265–292
Physician office data, reporting, 34
Physician query process, 14–18
Physician self-referral law, 853–854
Physician-hospital organization (PHO), 820
Physicians
    resident, 30, 383–384
    teaching, 30, 383–384
Physicians at Teaching Hospitals (PATH) initiative, 854
Pilonidal cyst, 479
PLA symbol, 337
Place of service (POS), 362
Placeholder, 59–60
Placement (ICS-10-PCS), 245
Plan (P), 32
Planes of view, 695
Pleura, 539–542
Pleural effusion, 540
Pleural scarification, 539
Pleurectomy, 539
Pleurodesis agents, 541
Plexus anesthesia, 420
Plus symbol, 335
Pneumocentesis, 540
Pneumonia, ventilator associated, 152–153
Pneumonoectomy, 540
Point-of-service plans (POS), 820–821
Poisoning, 179–182, 185–186
Polyps, 614
Polysomnography, 788
Portal decompression procedures, 579
Portal hypertension, 158
Positron emission tomography (PET), 697, 728
Post-acute care transfer (PACT), 819
Postanesthesia evaluation, 425
Posterior segment, 674
Posteroanterior (PA) projection, 696
Postoperative pain, 143
Postoperative pain management, 429
Postpartum care, 655
Postprocedural infection, sepsis due to, 120–123
Postprocedural septic shock, 120–123
Practitioner order, 212
Preanesthesia evaluation, 425
Pre-existing medical conditions, 846
Preferred provider organization (PPO), 821
Pregnancy, childbirth, and puerperium, 164–171, 202–203
Premalignant lesions, 490
Prematurity, 173
Prenatal visits, 277
Preoperative clearance, 392
Preoperative evaluations, 276
Present on admission (POA) indicator, 828, 829
Pressure ulcer, 159–160, 489
Presumptive identification, 752
Preventive medicine services, 403–404
Previous conditions, stated as diagnosis, 220
Pricing modifiers, 341
Primary care, 267
Primary care providers, 267
Primary malignancy, 127–129
Principal diagnosis, 115, 215–216

Principal procedure, 222–224
Principle diagnosis, 213–214
Privacy and security rules, 860–861
Privacy rule, 860
Privileged communication, 860
Problem focused examination, 371
Problem focused history, 370
Problem list, 32
Problem-oriented record (POR), 31, 32
Procedure data report, 36
Procedures
   ICD-10-PCS procedure coding, 224–251
   principal, 222–224
   significant other, 222–224
Proctectomy, 615
Proctosigmoidoscopy, 613
Products of conception, 245
Professional associations, 7–8
Professional component, 699, 739–741
Professional services, 366
Programs of All-inclusive Care for the Elderly
   (PACE), 818
Progress notes, 32
Prohibitory symbol, 335
Prolonged services, 400–402
Prophylactic organ removal, 204
Proprietary laboratory analysis (PLA), 738, 758
Prospective cost-based rates, 824
Prospective payment systems (PPS), 823–832,
   829, 830
Prospective price-based rates, 824
Prostate cancer, 643–644
Prostatectomy, 630
Prosthetics, 310, 511
Protected health information (PHI), 860–861
Protecting Access to Medicare Act (PAMA), 758
Proton beam treatment delivery, 725
Protozoans, 117
Providers, 10
Psychiatric collaborative care management
   services, 407
Psychiatry, 771–773
Psychoactive substance use, abuse, and
   dependence, 140–141
Psychoanalysis, 772
Psychotherapy, 772
Puerperal sepsis, 168
Puerperium, 164–171
Pull-through, 615
Pulmonary artery, 566
Pulmonary emboli, 729
Pulmonary hypertension, 149
Pulmonary services, 786
Pulmonary vein stenosis, 564
Pulmonary wedge pressure, 429
Pulse oximetry, 425
Punctuation, 89–90
Puncture, prick, or scratch test, 786, 787
Pupil, 672
Purpura, 136
Pyramidal fracture, 512

Q

Qualified diagnosis, 217–218
Qualifiers, 55–56
Qualifying circumstances, 436
Qualitative assays, 745
Quality, coding, 12–13
Quantitative A-scan, 714
Quantitative assays, 745

R

Radial keratotomy, 673
Radiation absorbed dose (rad), 697
Radiation oncology, 719–727
Radiation Therapy (ICS-10-PCS), 247–248
Radiation treatment delivery, 724
Radiation treatment management, 724–725
Radical mastectomy, 494–495
Radiographic projection, 696
Radiologic guidance, 716–717
Radiologist, 694
Radiology, 694
Radiology (CPT), 693–736
   administration of contrast materials, 703–704
   bone/joint studies, 718
   breast mammography, 717–718
   code modifiers, 699–700
   diagnostic radiology, 705–713
   diagnostic ultrasound, 713–716
   guidelines, 702–705
   nuclear medicine, 727–730
   overview of, 694, 698–701
   professional and technical components, 698–700
   radiation oncology, 719–727
   radiologic guidance, 716–717
   subsections, 705–730
   terminology, 694–698
Radiology procedures, 696–697
Radiology services
   anesthesia for, 446–447
   modifiers added to, 303
Radiopharmaceutical therapy, 727
Radium implant devices, 721
Random pattern flap, 484
Range of codes, 332
Range-of-motion testing, 789
Reagent strip automated urine analyzer, 747
Real-time scan, 713
Recipient heart with or without lung
   allotransplantation, 566
Recipient lung allotransplantation, 541
Reconstruction of the vena cava, 569
Recovery Audit Contractor (RAC) program, 819
Rectum, 613–615
Red blood cells, 136
Red marrow, 584
Red reference symbol, 336
Reexcision of tumors, 129
Referrals, 391
Reflex tests, 790
Regional anesthesia, 421
Registered Medical Assistant (RMA), 6
Rehabilitation hospitals, 211
Reimbursement. see Insurance and reimbursement
Relative value units (RVUs), 835
Release procedures, 238–239
Remittance advice, 856
Renal dialysis, 774
Renal transplantation, 624–625, 625
Repair (closure), 481–490
Repeated falls, 177
Replantation, 509
Reportable Condition Mapping Tool (RCMT), 27
Reproductive medicine procedures, 757–758
Reproductive system, 645
Resection, 236
Resident Assessment Validation and Entry (RAVEN),
   830
Resident physician, 30, 383–384

Residual effect, 67
Resource utilization groups (RUGs), 830
Resource-based relative value scale (RBRVS)
   system, 835
Respiratory system, 729
Respiratory System (CPT), 528–542
   accessory sinuses, 532–534
   larynx, 534–536
   lungs and pleura, 539–542
   nose, 529–532
   overview of, 528–529
   trachea and bronchi, 536–538
Respiratory system diseases, 151–153
Reticuloendothelial system, 728
Retina, 672
Retinopathy, 148
Retrospective coding, 12
Revenue code, 840
Revenue cycle management, 840–844
Review of systems (ROS), 868–869
Rhinoplasty, 599
Rhomboid flap, 484
Rhytidectomy, 488
Rhytides, 509
Rickettsias, 117
Roentgen, 697
Roentgen-equivalent-man (rem), 697
Root operation
   biopsy followed by definitive treatment, 235
   biopsy procedure, 234
   bypass procedures, 235
   control vs. more definitive operations, 236
   coronary bypass procedures, 235–236
   discontinued or incomplete procedure, 234
   excision for graft, 236–237
   excision vs. resection, 236
   fusion procedures of spine, 237
   general coding guidelines, 231–233
   inspection procedures, 237–238
   multiple procedures, 233–234
   occlusion vs. restriction for vessel embolization
      procedures, 238
   overlapping body layers, 235
   release procedures, 238–239
   release vs. division, 239
   reposition for fracture treatment, 239
   transfer procedure using multiple tissue layers, 240
   transplantation vs. administration, 239
Rotation flap, 484
Routine examinations, 203–204, 277–278
Rule of nines, 180, 489
RxNorm, 27–28
   purpose of, 28
   scope of, 28

S

Saddle block anesthesia, 421
Safe harbor regulations, 850
Sagittal plane, 695
Salivary gland and ducts, 601–602
Salpingo-oophorectomy, 651
Saphenopopliteal vein anastomosis, 569
Scanners, 33
Sclera, 672
Scoliosis, 517
Screening codes, 199–200
Screening mammography, 717
Scrimitar syndrome, 564
Secondary diabetes mellitus, 139

Secondary diagnosis, 115
Secondary hypertension, 148
Secondary malignancy, 126, 127–129
Second-order vessels, 552–553
Second-stage fistulectomy, 616
Section X (ICS-10-PCS), 250
Security rules, 860–861
Sedation, 421
See, 103
See also, 103
See category, 103
See condition, 103
Segmental instrumentation, 519
Selective vascular catheterization, 550–554, 711
Self-referral, 821
Semicolons, 334
Separate procedure, 469, 767
Sepsis and severe sepsis, 120–123, 168
    bacterial sepsis of newborn, 173
    puerperal, 168
Septal defects, 563–564
Septic abortion, 656
Septic shock, 120–123, 168
Septum, 563
Sequelae (late effects), 67, 192–193
Sequelae of cerebrovascular disease, 149
Service intensity add-on (SIA) payment, 831
Seton, 616
7th character requirement, 182–183
Severity of illness (SI), 838
Sex reassignment surgery, 645–646
Sharps containers, 739
Shaving, 473
Short-latency somatosensory evoked potential study, 790
Short-term hospital, 211
Shoulder, 520–521
Shunt, spinal CSF, 668
Shunt insertion, 579
Shunting procedures, 564
Side view, 696
Sigmoidoscopy, 613
Signs and symptoms, 64, 70, 175–178, 214–215, 273
Simple closure, 477
Simple mastectomy, 494–495
Simple repair, 477
Simple repair/closure, 481–482
Single codes, 332
Single hospitals, 211
Single organ system examination, 870
Single-photon emission computed tomography (SPECT), 697, 728
Sinus of Valsalva, 564
Sinusotomy, 535
Skilled nursing facility prospective payment system (SNF PPS), 830
Skin and subcutaneous tissue diseases, 158–160
Skin grafts, 484–486, 487
Skin lesions, 474–478
Skin replacement surgery flaps, 484–486
Skin substitute grafts, 484
Skull, 659–662
Sleep laboratory, 788
Sleep medicine testing, 788
Sleep staging, 788
Sleep studies, 788
Small intestine, 596
Social history, 371
Somatic nerves, 668
Source-oriented record (SOR), 31

Special dermatological procedures, 796
Special evaluation and management services, 405
Special otorhinolaryngologic services, 778–779
Special report, 367, 470, 767–768, 798–799
Specialty hospitals, 211
Specimen coding, 25
Specimens, 738, 739
Spectacle services, 778
Speech testing, 791
Spinal anesthesia, 421
Spinal cord, 662–668
Spinal instrumentation, 519
Spinal shunt, 668
Spine (vertebral column), 515–520, 662–668
Spine, fusion procedures of, 237
Spleen, 582, 583–584
Splenoportography, 584
Split-thickness skin grafts, 485–486
Spontaneous abortion, 170
Stab phlebectomy, 581
Staff model HMO, 820
Standard paper remittance (SPR), 856
Standby services, 402
Star symbol, 336
Stark I, 853
Stark II, 854
State Children's Health Insurance Program (SCHIP), 818
Status codes, 196–198
Status indicator (SI), 832
Stem cells, 584
Stent placement, 780
Stented valve, 561
Stentless valve, 561
Stereotactic body radiation therapy (SBRT), 541, 724
Stereotactic radiation therapy, 541
Stereotactic radiation treatment delivery, 724
Stereotactic radiosurgery (SRS), 724
Stereotaxis, 667
Stillbirth, 173
Stomach, 607–608
Strabismus, 675
Subacute care patients, 211
Subcategory, 59–60
Subcutaneous cardiac rhythm monitor, 558–559
Subcutaneous fistulectomy, 616
Subcutaneous tissue diseases, 158–160
Subglottic stenosis, 509
Subjective (S), 32
Submuscular fistulectomy, 616
Subsequent hospital care, 388–390
Subsequent observation care, 386
Substance Abuse Treatment (ICS-10-PCS), 249
Substance use, abuse, and dependence, 140–141
    in pregnancy, childbirth, and puerperium, 168
Subterms, 55–56
Superbill, 840
Supervision and interpretation, 703
Supplied materials, 468, 768
Supravalvar mitral ring, 564
Supravalvular mitral ring, 564
Surface anesthesia, 420
Surgery (CPT)
    auditory system, 677–680
    cardiovascular system, 549–582
    digestive system, 596–621
    endocrine system, 640, 656–658
    eye and ocular adnexa, 671–677
    female genital system, 646–651

general subsection, 472
guidelines, 463–471
hemic and lymphatic systems, 582–586
integumentary system, 472–496
intersex, 645–646
introduction to, 458
male genital system, 640, 641–644
maternity care and delivery, 652–656
mediastinum and diaphragm, 594–595
musculoskeletal system, 502–528
nervous system, 658–671
operating microscope, 641, 680–681
organization of, 460–463
overview of, 458–460
reporting multiple procedures/services, 468–469
reproductive system, 645
respiratory system, 528–542
services, 463
supplied materials, 468
urinary system, 621–632
Surgery, ambulatory (outpatient), 277
Surgical collapse therapy, 542
Surgical complications, 217
Surgical curettement, 461
Surgical destruction, 470
Surgical endoscopy, 604
Surgical package, 464–467
Surgical pathology, 755–756
Surgical procedures, modifiers added to, 302–303
Sutures, 461
Swan-Ganz catherization, 429, 784
Sympathetic nerves, 668
Syndromes, 69, 85
System review (ROS), 371
Systematized Nomenclature of Medicine Clinical Terms (SNOMED CT), 28–29
Systemic inflammatory response syndrome (SIRS), 177
Systemic radiation therapy, 720

T

Table of Drugs and Chemicals, 54, 92, 93, 181
Table of Neoplasms, 54, 92, 126, 126–127
Tables, 91–93
    ICD-10-PCS, 226–229
Tabular List of Diseases and Injuries, 45, 46, 54, 58–60
    locating code in, 62–63
Tax Cuts and Job Acts, 810
Tax Equity and Fiscal Responsibility Act (TEFRA), 825, 831
Teaching hospitals, 30
Teaching physician, 30, 383–384
Tear apparatus, 675
Technical component, 699, 739–741
Temporal bone, 679
Tendons, 241
Tenosynovitis, 669
Tensilon test, 789
Terrorism, 193
Tetralogy of Fallot, 563
Therapeutic, prophylactic, and diagnostic injections and infusions, 793–794
Therapeutic apheresis, 576
Therapeutic drug assays, 745–746
Therapeutic plans, 32
Therapeutic port films, 724
Therapeutic services, 276
Therapeutic surgical procedures, 462
    follow-up care for, 468

Third-order vessels, 552–553
Third-party administrators (TPAs), 10
Third-party payers, 10, 811–812
Thoracentesis, 540
Thoracic aortic aneurysm, 565–566
Thoracoplasty, 542
Thoracoscopy, 541
Thoracotomy, 540
Thorax, 513–514
Threatened condition, 67
Thrombectomy, 569
Thromboendarterectomy, 572
Thymus, 582, 657
Thyroid gland, 657, 727
Tibia, 523, 524
Tibial plateau, 523
Time reporting, 432–435
Tissue rearrangement, 484, 487
Tissue-cultured autografts, 484
Tobacco use, in pregnancy, childbirth, and
    puerperium, 168
Toes, 524
Tonsillectomy, 602–603
Tonsils, 582, 602–603
Tooth decay, 158
Topical anesthesia, 467
Total anomalous pulmonary venous return
    (TAPVR), 564
Total mastectomy, 494–495
Toxic effects, 179–182, 185–186
Trachea, 536–538
Tracheal decompression, 565
Tracheal puncture, 537
Tracheostoma revision, 537
Tracheostomy, 537
Trachoma, 675
Training, for coding career, 4–5
Transcatheter procedures, 579, 712
Transfer note, 32
Transfer of care, 367
Transfer procedure, 240
Transfusion medicine, 752
Transient hypertension, 148
Transient ischemic attack (TIA), 149
Transitional care management services, 407
Transitional pass-through payments, 308
Transmyocardial revascularization (TMR), 555
Transpedicular approach, 665
Transplant complications, 187–188
Transplantations, 239
Transposition of great vessels, 564–565
Transurethral resection of the prostate (TURP),
    629, 644
Transurethral ureteroscopic lithotripsy, 629
Transverse plane, 695
Treatment devices, 723
Treatment plan, 217
Treatment volume determination, 720
Triangle symbol, 334
TRICARE, 818
Tricuspid atresia, 564
Triple option plan, 821
Truncus arteriosus, 565
Trust the index, 96

Tubal ligation, 650–651
Tube pericardiostomy, 554
Tumors, reexicision of, 129
Tunneled catheter, 429, 576
Turbinates, 530–531
2-Midnight Rule, 212, 839–840
Tympanoplasty, 679
Tympanostomy, 679
Type of service (TOS), 362–363
Typeface, 85–87

U

UB-04 claim, 34, 35, 39, 812, 814, 815, 840, 859
Ulcer
    non-pressure chronic, 160
    pressure, 159–160
Ultrasonic guidance procedures, 716
Ultrasound/ultrasonography, 697
Umbilical hernia, 620
Unbundling, 11
Uncertain behavior, 126
Uncertain diagnosis, 217–218, 221, 274–275
Underdosings, 179–182, 185–186
Unified Medical Language System (UMLS), 29
Uniform Ambulatory Care Data Set (UACDS), 266
Uniform Hospital Discharge Data Set (UHDDS),
    213, 829
Unit/floor time, 379–380
Unlisted procedures, 339, 470, 743, 767
Unlisted services, 339, 367, 470, 743, 767
Unspecified codes, 70, 97
Unspecified nature, 126
Upcoding, 11
Upper arm, 521
Upper GI endoscopy, 604
Upper intestinal tract, 242
Upper respiratory system, 530
Uptake, 727
Ureter, 625–626
Ureterolithotomy, 625
Urethra, 630–631
Urethroplasty, 631
Urinalysis, 747–748
Urinary System (CPT), 621–632
    bladder, 626–630
    female, 622
    kidney, 623–625
    male, 622
    overview of, 621–622
    ureter, 625–626
    urethra, 630–631
Urinary tract infection, 622
Uroflowmetry, 628
Use, 103
"Use additional code" notes, 65, 98
Uvula, 600–601

V

Vaccinations, 195–196
Vaccines/toxoids, 770–772
Vaginal birth after cesarean (VBAC), 655
Value-based purchasing, 829

Valvular atresia, 559
Valvular prolapse, 559
Valvular regurgitation, 559
Valvular stenosis, 559
Valvuloplasty, 559–560
Valvulotomy, 560
Varicocele, 642
Vas deferens, 642
Vascular embolization and occlusion, 580–581
Vascular family, 552
Vascular injection procedures, 574–576
Vascular procedures, 711–712
Vascular ring formation, 565
Venipuncture, 739
Venography, 697
Venous anomalies, 564
Venous reconstruction, 569
Venous valve transposition, 569
Ventilator associated pneumonia, 152–153
Ventricular assist device (VAD), 567
Ventricular septal defect (VSD), 564
Vertebral augmentation, 518
Vertebral interspace, 519
Vertebral segment, 519
Very low birth weight, 406
Vestibule of mouth, 600
Video-assisted thoracic surgery (VATS), 541
View, 696
Viruses, 117
Visual evoked potential (VEP) test, 790
Voice button, 537
Volvulus, 609
Vulvectomy, 647–648
V-Y-plasty, 484

W

Wage index, 833
Wagstaff-LeFort fracture, 512
Wedges, 722
Whipple procedure, 618
White blood cells, 136
"With," 102–103
Workers' compensation, 822
Wound exploration—trauma, 507
Wound repair (closure), 482–483
W-plasty, 484
Wrist, 521

X

Xenograft, 485
X-ray beam, 696, 697

Y

Yale Refined Diagnosis-Related Groups (RDRGs),
    827
Yellow marrow, 584

Z

Z codes, 71, 182, 194–206
Zika virus, 124
Z-plasty, 484